The Beckett Mar...

Your one-stop shop for all your collecting needs!

Shop over **26 million** sports, non-sports, and gaming cards.

or Scan Me

STAR WARS

COLLECTIBLES PRICE GUIDE-2022

FOUNDER: DR. JAMES BECKETT III

EDITED BY MATT BIBLE WITH THE BECKETT PRICE GUIDE STAFF

BECKETT is a registered trademark of BECKETT COLLECTIBLES LLC, DALLAS, TEXAS

Manufactured in the United States of America | Published by Beckett Collectibles LLC

Beckett Collectibles LLC
4635 McEwen Dr., Dallas, TX 75244
(972) 991-6657 • beckett.com

First Printing
ISBN: 978-1-953801-11-1

TOP 10

VINTAGE STAR WARS ACTION FIGURES

1977-78 STAR WARS BOBA FETT (ROCKET FIRING PROTOTYPE)

1977-78 STAR WARS 12-BACKS A JAWA (VINYL CAPE)

1980-82 STAR WARS EMPIRE STRIKES BACK FX-7 (MEDICAL DROID) PALITOY

1985 STAR WARS POWER OF THE FORCE YAK FACE

1983 STAR WARS RETURN OF THE JEDI LUKE SKYWALKER (JEDI KNIGHT) LILY LEDY

1977-78 STAR WARS 12-BACKS A DARTH VADER (DOUBLE TELESCOPING LIGHTSABER)

1977-78 STAR WARS 12-BACKS A BEN (OBI-WAN) KENOBI (DOUBLE TELESCOPING LIGHTSABER)

1977-78 STAR WARS 12-BACKS A LUKE SKYWALKER (DOUBLE TELESCOPING LIGHTSABER)

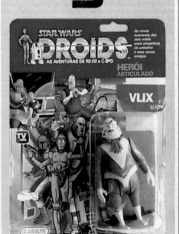

1985 STAR WARS DROIDS VLIX GLASSLITE

1977-78 STAR WARS 21-BACKS B BOBA FETT

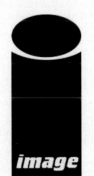

TOP 10

VINTAGE STAR WARS VEHICLES & PLAYSETS

1

1977-78 STAR WARS VEHICLES
MILLENNIUM FALCON

2

1978 STAR WARS PLAYSETS DEATH STAR
SPACE STATION (KENNER)

3

1978 STAR WARS VEHICLES X-WING
FIGHTER

4

1978 STAR WARS PLAYSETS CANTINA
ADVENTURE SET (SEARS)

5

1983 STAR WARS RETURN OF THE JEDI
VEHICLES TIE INTERCEPTOR

6

1980-82 STAR WARS EMPIRE STRIKES
BACK VEHICLES SNOWSPEEDER

7

1983 STAR WARS RETURN OF THE JEDI
VEHICLES IMPERIAL SHUTTLE

8

1980-82 STAR WARS EMPIRE STRIKES
BACK VEHICLES AT-AT

9

1978 STAR WARS VEHICLES
LAND SPEEDER

10

1983 STAR WARS RETURN OF THE JEDI
VEHICLES Y-WING FIGHTER

TOP 10

STAR WARS BLACK SERIES

BY KYLE DOBBINS

1

BOBA FETT AND HAN SOLO IN CARBONITE
(2013 SDCC EXCLUSIVE)

2

BOBA FETT
(SDCC KENNER TRIBUTE EXCLUSIVE)

3

GRAND ADMIRAL THRAWN
(2017 SDCC EXCLUSIVE)

4

JABBA'S RANCOR PIT
(TOYS R US EXCLUSIVE)

5

SPECIAL FORCES TIE FIGHTER
AND PILOT ELITE

6

JABBA'S THRONE ROOM
(2014 SDCC EXCLUSIVE)

7

LUKE SKYWALKER X-WING PILOT
(CELEBRATION ORLANDO EXCLUSIVE)

8

REY VS. KYLO REN
(2018 SDCC EXCLUSIVE)

9

ANAKIN SKYWALKER
(EPISODE III

10

CAPTAIN REX
(2017 HASCON EXCLUSIVE)

TOP 20

STAR WARS TRADING CARD SETS

1

2017 STAR WARS STELLAR SIGNATURES

2

2007 STAR WARS 30TH ANNIVERSARY

3

1977 STAR WARS

4

2015 STAR WARS MASTERWORK

5

1993-95 STAR WARS GALAXY

6

2001 STAR WARS EVOLUTION

7

1995 STAR WARS WIDEVISION

8

2004 STAR WARS HERITAGE

9

1980 STAR WARS EMPIRE STRIKES BACK

10

2020 WOMEN OF STAR WARS

TOP 20

STAR WARS TRADING CARD SETS

11

2016 STAR WARS MASTERWORK

12

1996 STAR WARS 3-DI WIDEVISION

13

2015 STAR WARS HIGH TEK

14

2013 STAR WARS JEDI LEGACY

15

2017 STAR WARS 40TH ANNIVERSARY

16

2002 STAR WARS ATTACK OF THE CLONES WIDEVISION

17

2019-PRESENT STAR WARS LIVING SET

18

1996 STAR WARS FINEST

19

2014 STAR WARS RETURN OF THE JEDI 3-D WIDEVISION

20

1977 STAR WARS WONDER BREAD

TOP 10

STAR WARS RELIC CARD SETS

1

2019 STAR WARS THE RISE OF SKYWALKER SERIES ONE MILLENNIUM FALCON RELICS

2

2020 STAR WARS THE RISE OF SKYWALKER SERIES TWO MILLENNIUM FALCON RELICS

3

2013 STAR WARS JEDI LEGACY CHEWBACCA FUR RELICS

4

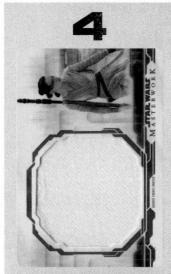

2017 STAR WARS MASTERWORK SOURCE MATERIAL JUMBO SWATCH RELICS

5

2013 STAR WARS JEDI LEGACY JABBA'S SAIL BARGE RELICS

6

2015 STAR WARS THE FORCE AWAKENS SERIES ONE FIRST ORDER STORMTROOPER COSTUME RELICS

7

2018 STAR WARS FINEST LIGHTSABER HILT MEDALLIONS

8

2015 STAR WARS MASTERWORK RETURN OF THE JEDI BUNKER RELICS

9

2013 STAR WARS JEDI LEGACY EWOK FUR RELICS

10

2017 STAR WARS THE LAST JEDI SERIES ONE SOURCE MATERIAL FABRIC RELICS

TOP 20

CERTIFIED AUTOGRAPHED CARDS

1

2016 STAR WARS MASTERWORK
AUTOGRAPHS DAISY RIDLEY

2

2001 STAR WARS EVOLUTION
AUTOGRAPHS CARRIE FISHER

3

2007 STAR WARS 30TH ANNIVERSARY
AUTOGRAPHS HARRISON FORD

4

2004 STAR WARS HERITAGE
AUTOGRAPHS MARK HAMILL

5

2002 STAR WARS ATTACK OF THE CLONES
WIDEVISION AUTOGRAPHS FRANK OZ

6

2004 STAR WARS HERITAGE AUTOGRAPHS
JAMES EARL JONES

7

2001 STAR WARS EVOLUTION
AUTOGRAPHS IAN MCDIARMID

8

2019 STAR WARS CHROME LEGACY
PREQUEL TRILOGY AUTOGRAPHS
EWAN MCGREGOR

9

2016 STAR WARS MASTERWORK
AUTOGRAPHS ADAM DRIVER

10

2016 STAR WARS ROGUE ONE SERIES ONE
AUTOGRAPHS FELICITY JONES

TOP 20

CERTIFIED AUTOGRAPHED CARDS

11

2007 STAR WARS 30TH ANNIVERSARY
AUTOGRAPHS JOHN WILLIAMS

12

2001 STAR WARS EVOLUTION
AUTOGRAPHS BILLY DEE WILLIAMS

13

2001 STAR WARS EVOLUTION
AUTOGRAPHS KENNY BAKER

14

2001 STAR WARS EVOLUTION
AUTOGRAPHS PETER MAYHEW

15

2001 STAR WARS EVOLUTION
AUTOGRAPHS ANTHONY DANIELS

16

2005 STAR WARS REVENGE OF THE SITH
AUTOGRAPHS SAMUEL L. JACKSON

17

2006 STAR WARS EVOLUTION UPDATE
AUTOGRAPHS HAYDEN CHRISTENSEN

18

2010 STAR WARS EMPIRE STRIKES BACK
3-D WIDEVISION AUTOGRAPHS
IRVIN KERSHNER

19

2001 STAR WARS EVOLUTION
AUTOGRAPHS JEREMY BULLOCH

20

2010 STAR WARS EMPIRE STRIKES BACK
3-D WIDEVISION AUTOGRAPHS
RALPH MCQUARRIE

TOP 20

STAR WARS FUNKO POP VINYL

1

#23 DARTH MAUL (HOLOGRAPHIC)/480*
(2012 SDCC EXCLUSIVE)

2

#26 6B LUKE SKYWALKER (GOLD)/80*
(2019 FUNKO FUNDAYS EXCLUSIVE)

3

#14 SHADOW TROOPER/480*
(2011 SDCC EXCLUSIVE)

4

#25 501ST CLONE TROOPER/480*
(2012 SDCC EXCLUSIVE)

5

#32 BOBA FETT DROIDS/480*
(2013 SDCC EXCLUSIVE)

6

#24 BIGGS DARKLIGHTER/480*
(2012 SDCC EXCLUSIVE)

7

#6B CHEWBACCA (FLOCKED)/480*
(2011 SDCC EXCLUSIVE)

8

#128A QUI GON JINN/2000*
(2016 NYCC EXCLUSIVE)

9

#306A SITH TROOPER
(2019 SDCC EXCLUSIVE)

10

#15 HAN SOLO STORMTROOPER/1000*
(2011 ECCC EXCLUSIVE)

TOP 20

STAR WARS FUNKO POP VINYL

11

#16 LUKE SKYWALKER
STORMTROOPER/1000*
(2011 ECCC EXCLUSIVE)

12

#33B DARTH VADER (HOLOGRAPHIC
GLOW-IN-THE-DARK)
(2014 PARIS EXPO EXCLUSIVE)

13

Boba Fett

#297K BOBA FETT (CAMO)/1000*
(2020 NYCC EXCLUSIVE)

14

OBI-WAN KENOBI

#392 OBI-WAN KENOBI (GLOW-IN-
THE-DARK)/3000* (2021 STAR WARS
CELEBRATION EXCLUSIVE)

15

GREEDO
VINYL BOBBLE-HEAD

#7A GREEDO V
(2011)

16

HOLOGRAPHIC DARTH VADER

33A DARTH VADER (HOLOGRAPHIC
GLOW-IN-THE-DARK)
(2014 DALLAS COMIC CON EXCLUSIVE)

17

THE MANDALORIAN

#326B THE MANDALORIAN
(2019 D23 EXCLUSIVE)

18

SHOCK TROOPER

#42B SHOCK TROOPER
(2015 STAR WARS
CELEBRATION EXCLUSIVE)

19

PRINCESS LEIA

#54A PRINCESS LEIA (BOUSSH
UNMASKED)/1008*
(2015 SDCC EXCLUSIVE)

20

CAPTAIN REX

#274A CAPTAIN REX
(2018 NYCC EXCLUSIVE)

TOP 10

LEGO STAR WARS SETS

BY KYLE DOBBINS

1

10179
ULTIMATE COLLECTOR'S
MILLENNIUM FALCON

2

10019
REBEL BLOCKADE RUNNER

3

10143
DEATH STAR II

4

YODACHRON
YODA CHRONICLES PROMOTIONAL SET

5

10195
REPUBLIC DROPSHIP WITH AT-OT WALKER

6

10221
SUPER STAR DESTROYER

7

75192
MILLENNIUM FALCON

8

10030
IMPERIAL STAR DESTROYER

9

10123
CLOUD CITY

10

10018
DARTH MAUL

TOP 30

BEST-SELLING STAR WARS CHARACTERS

1

DARTH VADER

2

THE MANDALORIAN/DIN DJARIN

3

LUKE SKYWALKER

4

BOBA FETT

5

THE CHILD (BABY YODA)/GROGU

6

R2-D2

7

HAN SOLO

8

CHEWBACCA

9

PRINCESS LEIA

10

OBI-WAN KENOBI

TOP 30

BEST-SELLING STAR WARS CHARACTERS

11

YODA

12

C-3PO

13

KYLO REN

14

REY

15

DARTH MAUL

16

BB-8 (SKETCH ART BY KRIS PENIX)

17

POE DAMERON

18

JABBA THE HUTT

19

FINN

20

AHSOKA TANO

TOP 30

BEST-SELLING STAR WARS CHARACTERS

21

DARTH SIDIOUS/EMPEROR PALPATINE

22

LANDO CALRISSIAN

23

MAZ KANATA

24

MACE WINDU

25

JANGO FETT

26

ANAKIN SKYWALKER

27

CAPTAIN REX

28

PADME AMIDALA (SKETCH ART BY ANDREW FRY)

29

QUI-GON JINN

30

JAWAS

BOUNTY HUNTER
STRIKES BACK

BOBA FETT, THE GALAXY'S MOST DANGEROUS BOUNTY HUNTER, HAS NEVER BEEN MORE POPULAR.

BY DAVID LEE

Two minutes, 45 seconds.

That's Boba Fett's total screen time in the original Star Wars trilogy. We also see him as a boy—the son of bounty hunter Jango Fett—in "Attack of the Clones" and "Revenge of the Sith." Add those appearances, and total screen time ticks up to just 5 minutes. That's less time than Darth Maul and General Grievous got.

Still, Boba Fett quickly became, and remains, one of the most iconic characters in the entire Star Wars universe. Sparse appearances can make a big impact and generate intrigue. Heck, even Darth Vader appeared for just 34 total minutes in the original trilogy. When these characters are on screen, you notice and you remember. Today, BobaFettFanClub.com, the largest online Fett fan community, has more than 13,500 registered members.

Fett is a quiet and menacing mystery. He's dangerous, a bit creepy, even. He's not for the Dark Side or the Light Side. He's for himself, and the one who's paying him. He speaks just four lines of dialog in the original trilogy and carries himself with complete confidence, void of emotion.

Jeremy Bulloch and Peter Mayhew (Chewbacca) together in 2012.

GETTY IMAGES

"PUT CAPTAIN SOLO
IN THE CARGO HOLD."

"YOU NEVER SEE HIS FACE. BOBA FETT WAS THE HELMET, ARMOR AND JETPACK."

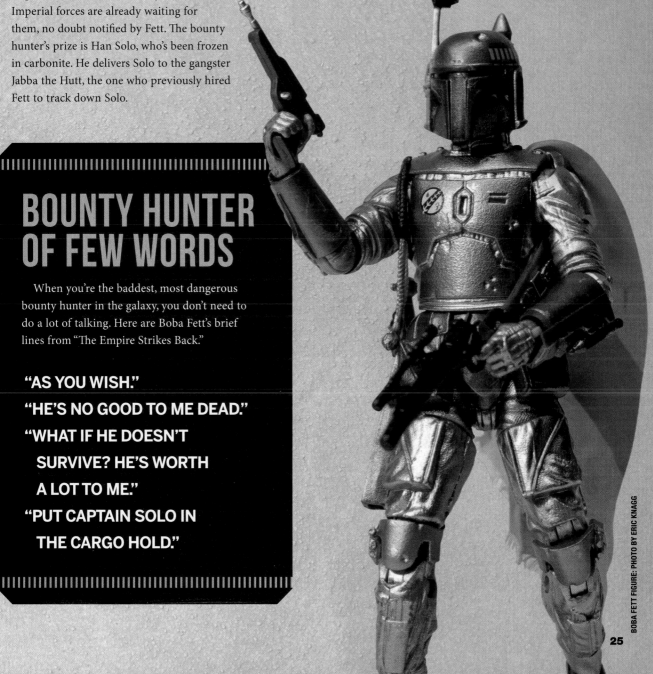

A cross between a Wild West gunslinger and space pirate, Fett just looks cool. In one short scene, you can hear the sound of spurs clanking as he walks. His Spartan-like helmet and armor have seen plenty of violence, with battle-scarred scuffs, chips and dents. He wears a cape and a jetpack with a missile, and he's armed with an arsenal of hidden weaponry. You never see his face. Boba Fett was the helmet, armor and jetpack.

The character appeared in a cartoon Christmas special and had his first action figure released before he made his film debut in "The Empire Strikes Back" as a bounty hunter hired to track down Millennium Falcon. He follows the rebel heroes in his own ship, Slave 1, to the Cloud City where Vader's Imperial forces are already waiting for them, no doubt notified by Fett. The bounty hunter's prize is Han Solo, who's been frozen in carbonite. He delivers Solo to the gangster Jabba the Hutt, the one who previously hired Fett to track down Solo.

BOUNTY HUNTER OF FEW WORDS

When you're the baddest, most dangerous bounty hunter in the galaxy, you don't need to do a lot of talking. Here are Boba Fett's brief lines from "The Empire Strikes Back."

"AS YOU WISH."

"HE'S NO GOOD TO ME DEAD."

"WHAT IF HE DOESN'T SURVIVE? HE'S WORTH A LOT TO ME."

"PUT CAPTAIN SOLO IN THE CARGO HOLD."

Fett's fate (or so it seemed) in "Return of the Jedi" is rather humiliating and pitiful for such an iconic character. During Luke Skywalker's attempt to rescue Han Solo, Solo accidently ignites Fett's jetpack. Fett slams into the side of a ship and helplessly falls into the Sarlacc pit. Certainly not a fitting end for the galaxy's coolest bounty hunter. More than 40 years later, we discovered that wasn't the end of Boba Fett. His character was the inspiration behind Disney's hit series, "The Mandalorian." Set several years after the events of "Return of the Jedi," it explores the legend of the elite warriors from Mandalore.

Fett makes a surprise reappearance in season two, on a mission to retrieve his original armor, which also survived the Sarlacc pit. He joins forces with Din Djarin, the main character. The end of season two teased an upcoming Disney+ spinoff series, "The Book of Boba Fett," which will follow him as he attempts to take over Jabba's crime empire. There's no denying the show has evolved Fett's character and revitalized his popularity for a new generation of fans.

THE MAN UNDER THE HELMET: JEREMY BULLOCH (1945-2020)

Actor Jeremy Bulloch was 34 when he put on the Boba Fett suit for "The Empire Strikes Back." The English actor died in December 2020 at the age of 75, less than two months after his beloved character was revived in "The Mandalorian." Even though his character only appeared fewer than 3 minutes, Bulloch drew inspiration for Fett from Clint Eastwood's character in the Man with No Name trilogy with his slow walk, poncho and pistol. "I thought of Boba Fett as Clint Eastwood in a suit of armor," Bulloch once said in an interview. "You put on that outfit, you put on that helmet, and you become quite a badass."

Bulloch did appear in "The Empire Strikes Back" out of the helmet and armor, but as another character. He was called to portray Imperial officer Lieutenant Sheckil, the one escorting Princess Leia away and holding her back as she tries to warn Luke Skywalker of Darth Vader's trap.

Jeremy Bulloch was a popular signer at Star Wars conventions.

GETTY IMAGES

Jeremy Bulloch
"Boba Fett"

© LUCASFILM, LTD. (LFL) 1980. All Rights Reserved

30
**

1980 Topps Star
Wars Empire Strikes
Back Sticker #30
Boba Fett RC

"IN 1979 I WAS CALLED ONTO THE SET OF 'EMPIRE STRIKES BACK' TO PLAY BOBA FETT, AND SINCE THAT DAY IT HAS CHANGED THE ENTIRE DIRECTION OF MY LIFE IN SUCH A WONDERFUL WAY."

THE BOUNTY HUNTER STRIKES BACK

More than 20 years later, he made a cameo appearance in "Revenge of the Sith" as Captain Jeremoch Colton, piloting General Kenobi, Bail Organa and Yoda to Coruscant.

Bulloch's acting career spanned more than 50 years. He regularly attended conventions around the world, signing autographs and taking pictures with fans until he retired from touring in 2018. In a letter to his fans, Bulloch wrote:

"It is with a heavy heart that I have decided to stop attending conventions and hang up the Fett helmet. It has not been an easy decision to make. In 1979 I was called onto the set of 'Empire Strikes Back' to play Boba Fett, and since that day it has changed the entire direction of my life in such a wonderful way. It has been a privilege to have had the opportunity to inspire so many generations of Star Wars fans."

JEREMY BULLOCH
AS **BOBA FETT**

Boba Fett threw out the ceremonial first pitch before Star Wars night in Oakland in 2013.

ESTIMATED BOBA

BORN	10 YEARS OLD	13 YEARS OLD	32 YEARS OLD
"STAR WARS EPISODE I: THE PHANTOM MENACE"	"STAR WARS EPISODE II: ATTACK OF THE CLONES"	"STAR WARS EPISODE III: REVENGE OF THE SITH"	"STAR WARS EPISODE IV: A NEW HOPE"

GETTY IMAGES

FETT TIMELINE

35 YEARS OLD
"STAR WARS EPISODE V:
THE EMPIRE STRIKES BACK"

36 YEARS OLD
"STAR WARS EPISODE VI:
RETURN OF THE JEDI"

41 OR SO YEARS OLD
"THE MANDALORIAN"

(SOURCE: BOBAFETTFANCLUB.COM)

MODERN BOBA FETT MUST-HAVE

The very face of scum and villainy has returned to the Star Wars live-action universe. After a 37 year absence, Boba Fett is back and his return has created quite the buzz in the collectibles community. With his own limited TV series in the works, collectibles of the galaxy's most-renowned bounty hunter may soon skyrocket even higher in popularity. Here is just a small sample of modern-day Boba Fett collectibles to watch.

01 2011-21 FUNKO POP VINYL STAR WARS #32 BOBA FETT DROIDS/480*

Boba Fett has the most variants in the Star Wars Funko Pop line but this one is a cut above the others. It was offered as a 2013 SDCC exclusive limited to 480 pieces and features his variant colored armor from the animated series, Star Wars Droids.

02 2010-21 STAR WARS VINTAGE COLLECTION BOBA FETT FOIL CARD BACK

This was produced as a throwback to Boba's original 1980 Empire Strikes Back figure by Kenner. However, the foil versions were scarcely produced and have increased in popularity and value over time.

03 2006 STAR WARS COMICS BOBA FETT: OVERKILL(ADAM HUGHES COVER)

Very few Star Wars characters could lead their own stand-alone comic but Boba Fett is one of those exceptions. With a story by Thomas Andrews and artwork by Francisco Ruiz Velasco, this issue solidifies Boba Fett into Star Wars mythos even more. Plus, highly graded versions of this comic can fetch big bucks.

18+ | 75277 | 625 pcs/pzs

04 2019-21 STAR WARS LIVING SET #234 BOBA FETT/3,700*

This trading card was the first collectible to offer Boba's new look to collectors. It features the art of Kris Penix and sold a total print run of 3,700 cards.

05 2020 LEGO STAR WARS HELMET COLLECTION #75277 BOBA FETT BUILDING KIT

The LEGO Star Wars Helmet Collection is an overall hit with builders but Boba stands out because it's quite a simple build. When built, this 625 brick piece stands 18 inches tall on a black base. It even has a moveable rangefinder that you can adjust as you see fit.

Beckett Star Wars Collectibles Price Guide – 2022

WHAT'S LISTED?

Products in the price guide typically:

- Are produced by licensed manufacturers
- Are widely available
- Have market activity on single items

WHAT THE COLUMNS MEAN

The LO and HI columns reflect current retail selling ranges. The HI column on the right generally represents the full retail selling price. The LO column on the left generally represents the lowest price one would expect to find with extensive shopping.

CONDITION

Prices in this issue reflect the highest raw condition (i.e. not professionally graded by a third party) of the card commonly found at shows, shops, online, and right out of the pack for brand new releases. This generally means NrMint to Mint condition. Action figure prices are based on Mint condition. Action figures that are loose (out-of-package) are generally sold for 50 percent of the listed price, but may list for less/more depending on popularity, condition, completeness, and market sales.

CURRENCY

This price guide is intended to reflect the entire North American market. While not all the cards/figures are produced in the United States, they will reflect the market value in U.S. dollars.

GLOSSARY/LEGEND

Our glossary defines terms most frequently used in the action figure/non-sports card collecting hobby. Some of these terms are common to other types of collecting. Some terms may have several meanings depending on the use and context.

ALB	Album exclusive card. This indicates that a card was only available in a collector album or binder that was devoted to a certain product.
AU	Certified autograph
BB	Box bottom - A card or panel of cards on the bottom of a trading card box.
BI	Box incentive
BN	Barnes & Noble exclusive
BT	Box topper - A card, either regulation or jumbo-sized, that is inserted in the top of a box of trading cards.
C	Common card
CI	Case-Incentive or Case Insert - A unique card that is offered as an incentive to purchase a case (or cases) of trading cards.
COA	Certificate of Authenticity - A certificate issued by the manufacturer to insure a product's authenticity.
COR	Corrected version of an error (ERR) card
CT	Case-topper exclusive card
D23	Disney D23 Convention
ECCC	Emerald City Comic Con
EE	Entertainment Earth exclusive - An exclusive that was offered for sale on Entertainment Earth's website.
EL	Extremely limited
ERR	Error card - A card with erroneous information, spelling, or depiction on either side of the card, most of which are not corrected by the manufacturer.
EXCH	Exchange card
FACT	Factory set exclusive
FLK	Flocked variant - This description applies exclusively to Funko products.
FOIL	holofoil
GCE	Galactic Convention Exclusive - This description applies specifically to Funko products.
GEN	General distribution - This term most usually applies to promotional cards.
GITD	Glow-in-the-Dark variant - This description usually applies to Funko products.
GS	GameStop exclusive
HOLO	hologram

HT	Hot Topic exclusive
L	Limited
LE	Limited Edition
LS	Limited Series
MEM	Memorabilia card
MET	Metallic variant - This describes a metallic version of a Funko product.
NNO	Unnumbered card
NSU	Non-Sports Update exclusive card
NYCC	New York Comic Con
OPC	O-Pee-Chee (a Canadian subsidiary of Topps)
R	Rare card
RED	Redemption card
SDCC	San Diego Comic Con
SI	Set-Incentive
SP	Single or Short Print - A short print is a card that was printed in less quantity compared to the other cards in the same series.
SR	Super Rare card
SWC	Star Wars Celebration
TW	Toy Wars exclusive
U	Uncommon card
UER	Uncorrected error
UNC	Uncut sheet or panel
UR	Ultra Rare card
VAR	Variation card - One of two or more cards from the same series, with the same card number, that differ from one another in some way. This sometimes occurs when the manufacturer notices an error in one or more of the cards, corrects the mistake, and then resumes the printing process. In some cases, one of the variations may be relatively scarce.
VAULT	This description applies specifically to Funko products and indicates a figurine that has been re-released by the company.
VL	Very Limited
VR	Very Rare card
WG	Walgreen's exclusive
WM	Walmart exclusive

As with any publication, we appreciate reader feedback. While there are many listings, not all collectibles may be priced due to market constraints. If you have any questions, concerns, or suggestions, please contact us at: **nonsports@beckett.com**

Action Figures and Figurines

PRICE GUIDE

VINTAGE

1977-78 Star Wars 12-Backs A

NNO Ben Kenobi grey hair	600.00	1200.00
NNO Ben Kenobi white hair	500.00	1000.00
NNO Ben Kenobi (w/double telescoping lightsaber)	4000.00	8000.00
NNO C-3PO	500.00	1000.00
NNO Chewbacca	500.00	1000.00
NNO Darth Vader	1000.00	2000.00
NNO Darth Vader (w/double telescoping lightsaber)	5000.00	10000.00
NNO Death Squad Commander	400.00	800.00
NNO Han Solo (small head)	1000.00	2000.00
NNO Jawa (plastic cape)	6000.00	12000.00
NNO Luke Skywalker (blond hair)	1250.00	2500.00
NNO Luke Skywalker/telescoping lightsaber	10000.00	20000.00
NNO Princess Leia	1000.00	2000.00
NNO R2-D2	500.00	1000.00
NNO Stormtrooper	400.00	800.00

1977-78 Star Wars 12-Backs B

NNO Ben Kenobi (grey hair)	500.00	1000.00
NNO Ben Kenobi (white hair)	750.00	1500.00
NNO C-3PO	400.00	800.00
NNO Chewbacca	400.00	800.00
NNO Darth Vader	1000.00	2000.00
NNO Death Squad Commander	300.00	600.00
NNO Han Solo (small head)	750.00	1500.00
NNO Jawa	450.00	900.00
NNO Luke Skywalker (w/blond hair)	750.00	1500.00
NNO R2-D2	500.00	1000.00
NNO Stormtrooper	350.00	700.00
NNO Tusken Raider	300.00	600.00

1977-78 Star Wars 12-Backs C

NNO C-3PO	300.00	600.00
NNO Chewbacca	400.00	800.00
NNO Darth Vader	750.00	1500.00
NNO Death Squad Commander	450.00	850.00
NNO Han Solo (large head)	600.00	1200.00
NNO Jawa	400.00	800.00

NNO Luke Skywalker (blond hair)	750.00	1500.00
NNO Luke Skywalker (w/double telescoping lightsaber)	4000.00	8000.00
NNO Princess Leia	400.00	800.00
NNO R2-D2	400.00	800.00
NNO Stormtrooper	350.00	700.00
NNO Tusken Raider	300.00	600.00

1977-78 Star Wars 12-Backs D

NNO C-3PO	400.00	750.00
NNO Chewbacca	400.00	800.00
NNO Luke Skywalker (blond hair)	500.00	1000.00
NNO Princess Leia	350.00	700.00
NNO R2-D2	300.00	600.00
NNO Death Squad Commander	400.00	800.00

1977-78 Star Wars 12-Backs E

NNO R2-D2	1000.00	2000.00

1977-78 Star Wars 20-Backs A

NNO Ben Kenobi (white hair)	250.00	500.00
NNO C-3PO	200.00	400.00
NNO Chewbacca	200.00	400.00
NNO Death Squad Commander	150.00	300.00
NNO Han Solo (large head)	350.00	700.00
NNO Jawa	200.00	400.00
NNO Princess Leia	250.00	500.00
NNO Stormtrooper	200.00	350.00
NNO Tusken Raider	150.00	300.00

1977-78 Star Wars 20-Backs B

NNO Chewbacca	150.00	300.00
NNO Death Squad Commander	200.00	400.00
NNO Death Star Droid	200.00	400.00
NNO Greedo	600.00	1200.00
NNO Hammerhead	750.00	1500.00
NNO Luke X-Wing Pilot	300.00	600.00
NNO Power Droid	750.00	1500.00
NNO R5-D4	750.00	1500.00
NNO Snaggletooth (red)	1000.00	1500.00
NNO Stormtrooper	125.00	250.00
NNO Walrus Man	300.00	600.00

1977-78 Star Wars 20-Backs C

NNO Chewbacca	200.00	400.00
NNO Death Squad Commander	150.00	300.00
NNO Jawa	200.00	400.00
NNO Stormtrooper	150.00	300.00
NNO Hammerhead	200.00	400.00
NNO Luke X-Wing Pilot	150.00	300.00

1977-78 Star Wars 20-Backs D

NNO Jawa	225.00	450.00
NNO Death Star Droid	200.00	400.00
NNO Luke X-Wing Pilot	200.00	350.00
NNO R5-D4	200.00	350.00

Top of middle column (continuation of 12-Backs A list):

NNO Luke Skywalker (blond hair)	750.00	1500.00
NNO Luke Skywalker (w/double telescoping lightsaber)	4000.00	8000.00
NNO Princess Leia	400.00	800.00
NNO R2-D2	400.00	800.00
NNO Stormtrooper	350.00	700.00
NNO Tusken Raider	300.00	600.00

1977-78 Star Wars 20-Backs E

NNO	Ben Kenobi (white hair)	200.00	400.00
NNO	Chewbacca	300.00	600.00
NNO	Darth Vader	350.00	700.00
NNO	Death Squad Commander	150.00	300.00
NNO	Jawa	225.00	450.00
NNO	Luke Skywalker (blond hair)	400.00	800.00
NNO	Princess Leia	300.00	600.00
NNO	Stormtrooper	200.00	400.00
NNO	Tusken Raider	200.00	350.00
NNO	Greedo	300.00	600.00
NNO	Hammerhead	200.00	400.00
NNO	Luke X-Wing Pilot	300.00	600.00
NNO	Power Droid	300.00	600.00
NNO	R5-D4	250.00	500.00
NNO	Snaggletooth (red)	250.00	500.00
NNO	Walrus Man	200.00	400.00

1977-78 Star Wars 20-Backs F

NNO	Darth Vader	250.00	500.00
NNO	Princess Leia	200.00	400.00

1977-78 Star Wars 20-Backs G

NNO	Death Squad Commander	200.00	400.00
NNO	Han Solo (large head)	200.00	350.00
NNO	Jawa	125.00	250.00
NNO	Luke Skywalker (blond hair)	600.00	1200.00
NNO	Tusken Raider	200.00	400.00

1977-78 Star Wars 20-Backs H

NNO	Tusken Raider	150.00	300.00

1977-78 Star Wars 20-Backs I

NNO	Jawa	150.00	300.00

1977-78 Star Wars 20-Backs J

NNO	Jawa	150.00	300.00
NNO	Stormtrooper	250.00	500.00
NNO	Walrus Man	200.00	400.00

1977-78 Star Wars 20-Backs K

NNO	Jawa	150.00	300.00
NNO	Stormtrooper	200.00	400.00
NNO	Tusken Raider	150.00	300.00

1977-78 Star Wars 21-Backs A1

NNO	Ben Kenobi (white hair)	200.00	350.00
NNO	Darth Vader	300.00	600.00
NNO	Han Solo (large head)	300.00	600.00
NNO	Jawa	150.00	300.00

1977-78 Star Wars 21-Backs A2

NNO	Luke Skywalker (blond hair)	300.00	600.00
NNO	R2-D2	250.00	500.00
NNO	Greedo	225.00	450.00
NNO	Hammerhead	150.00	300.00
NNO	Luke X-Wing Pilot	250.00	500.00
NNO	Power Droid	200.00	350.00
NNO	R5-D4	200.00	400.00
NNO	Snaggletooth (red)	200.00	400.00
NNO	Walrus Man	200.00	350.00

1977-78 Star Wars 21-Backs B

NNO	Boba Fett	4000.00	8000.00
NNO	C-3PO	225.00	450.00
NNO	Darth Vader	300.00	600.00
NNO	Death Squad Commander	250.00	500.00
NNO	Greedo	250.00	500.00
NNO	Hammerhead	150.00	300.00
NNO	Han Solo (large head)	300.00	600.00
NNO	Luke Skywalker (blond hair)	350.00	700.00
NNO	Luke X-Wing Pilot	250.00	500.00
NNO	Power Droid	200.00	400.00
NNO	Princess Leia	300.00	600.00
NNO	R2-D2	150.00	300.00
NNO	R5-D4	250.00	500.00
NNO	Snaggletooth (red)	225.00	450.00

NNO	Tusken Raider	150.00	300.00
NNO	Walrus Man	150.00	300.00

1977-78 Star Wars 21-Backs C

NNO	Ben Kenobi (white hair)	125.00	250.00
NNO	C-3PO	150.00	300.00
NNO	Chewbacca	225.00	450.00
NNO	Darth Vader	300.00	600.00
NNO	Death Squad Commander	125.00	250.00
NNO	Han Solo (large head)	200.00	350.00
NNO	Luke Skywalker (blond hair)	300.00	600.00
NNO	Princess Leia	250.00	500.00
NNO	R2-D2	200.00	400.00
NNO	Greedo	200.00	400.00
NNO	Luke X-Wing Pilot	200.00	400.00
NNO	Power Droid	500.00	1000.00
NNO	Snaggletooth (red)	150.00	300.00
NNO	Walrus Man	200.00	400.00

1977-78 Star Wars 21-Backs D

NNO	Luke Skywalker (blond hair)	300.00	600.00

1977-78 Star Wars 21-Backs E4

NNO	Walrus Man	150.00	300.00

1977-78 Star Wars 21-Backs E5

NNO	Walrus Man	150.00	300.00

1977-78 Star Wars 21-Backs F

NNO	Walrus Man	150.00	300.00

1977-78 Star Wars (loose)

NNO	Ben Kenobi (grey hair)	30.00	60.00
NNO	Ben Kenobi (white hair)	30.00	60.00
NNO	Boba Fett	30.00	75.00
NNO	C-3PO	20.00	40.00
NNO	Chewbacca	20.00	40.00
NNO	Darth Vader	30.00	60.00
NNO	Death Squad Commander	20.00	40.00
NNO	Death Star Droid	15.00	30.00
NNO	Greedo	17.50	35.00
NNO	Hammerhead	15.00	30.00
NNO	Han Solo (large head)	30.00	60.00
NNO	Han Solo (small head)	30.00	60.00
NNO	Jawa	30.00	75.00
NNO	Luke Skywalker (blond hair)	40.00	80.00
NNO	Luke Skywalker (brown hair)	75.00	150.00
NNO	Luke Skywalker X-wing	25.00	50.00
NNO	Power Droid	17.50	35.00
NNO	Princess Leia	50.00	100.00

Also at the top of the right column:

NNO	Tusken Raider	150.00	300.00
NNO	Walrus Man	150.00	300.00

NNO	R2-D2	20.00	40.00
NNO	R5-D4	15.00	30.00
NNO	Snaggletooth blue	150.00	300.00
NNO	Snaggletooth (red)	20.00	40.00
NNO	Stormtrooper	17.50	35.00
NNO	Tusken Raider	20.00	40.00
NNO	Walrus Man	17.50	35.00

1978 Star Wars Accessories

NNO	1977 Early Bird Package w/figures Chewbacca, Leia, Luke, R2-D2	3500.00	6000.00
NNO	Mini Collector's Case	200.00	400.00

1978 Star Wars Accessories (loose)

NNO	Mini Collector's Case	25.00	50.00

1978 Star Wars Playsets

NNO	Cantina Adventure Set/Greedo	500.00	1000.00
NNO	Creature Cantina Action	300.00	600.00
NNO	Death Star Space Station	250.00	500.00
NNO	Droid Factory	200.00	400.00
NNO	Jawa Sandcrawler (radio controlled)	750.00	1500.00
NNO	Land of the Jawas	125.00	250.00

1978 Star Wars Playsets (loose)

NNO	Cantina Adventure Set/Greedo	100.00	200.00
NNO	Creature Cantina Action	100.00	200.00
NNO	Death Star Space Station	150.00	300.00
NNO	Droid Factory	75.00	150.00
NNO	Jawa Sandcrawler (radio controlled)	300.00	600.00
NNO	Land of the Jawas	75.00	150.00

1978 Star Wars Vehicles

NNO	Imperial Troop Transporter	150.00	300.00
NNO	Land Speeder	125.00	250.00
NNO	Millenium Falcon	400.00	800.00
NNO	Patrol Dewback	100.00	200.00
NNO	Sonic Controlled Land Speeder	250.00	500.00
NNO	TIE Fighter	250.00	500.00
NNO	TIE Fighter Darth Vader	150.00	300.00
NNO	X-Wing Fighter	150.00	300.00

1978 Star Wars Vehicles (loose)

NNO	Imperial Troop Transporter	50.00	100.00
NNO	Land Speeder	30.00	60.00
NNO	Millenium Falcon	75.00	150.00
NNO	Patrol Dewback	30.00	60.00
NNO	Sonic Controlled Land Speeder	100.00	200.00
NNO	TIE Fighter	25.00	50.00

NNO	TIE Fighter Darth Vader	30.00	60.00
NNO	X-Wing Fighter	30.00	60.00

1979-80 Star Wars 12-Inch

NNO	Ben Kenobi	125.00	250.00
NNO	Boba Fett	400.00	800.00
NNO	C-3PO	100.00	200.00
NNO	Chewbacca	200.00	350.00
NNO	Darth Vader	200.00	400.00
NNO	Han Solo	250.00	500.00
NNO	IG-88	500.00	1000.00
NNO	Jawa	125.00	250.00
NNO	Luke Skywalker	225.00	450.00
NNO	Princess Leia	200.00	400.00
NNO	R2-D2	250.00	500.00
NNO	Stormtrooper	100.00	200.00

1979-80 Star Wars 12-Inch (loose)

NNO	Ben Kenobi	30.00	75.00
NNO	Boba Fett	150.00	300.00
NNO	C-3PO	25.00	50.00
NNO	Chewbacca	30.00	60.00
NNO	Darth Vader	30.00	60.00
NNO	Han Solo	100.00	200.00
NNO	IG-88	150.00	300.00
NNO	Jawa	50.00	100.00
NNO	Luke Skywalker	30.00	60.00
NNO	Princess Leia	30.00	60.00
NNO	R2-D2	30.00	75.00
NNO	Stormtrooper	25.00	50.00

1980-82 Star Wars Empire Strikes Back 21-Backs G

NNO	Ben Kenobi	150.00	300.00
NNO	Boba Fett	750.00	1500.00
NNO	C-3PO	150.00	300.00
NNO	Chewbacca	125.00	250.00
NNO	Darth Vader	350.00	700.00
NNO	Death Squad Commander	300.00	600.00
NNO	Death Star Droid	125.00	250.00
NNO	Greedo	150.00	300.00
NNO	Hammerhead	150.00	300.00
NNO	Han Solo (Large Head)	150.00	300.00
NNO	Jawa	200.00	400.00
NNO	Luke Skywalker (Blond Hair)	500.00	1000.00
NNO	Luke X-Wing Pilot	150.00	300.00
NNO	Power Droid	200.00	350.00
NNO	Princess Leia	300.00	600.00
NNO	R2-D2	225.00	450.00
NNO	R5-D4	200.00	400.00
NNO	Sand People	150.00	300.00

NNO	Snaggletooth (Red)	150.00	300.00
NNO	Stormtrooper	1200.00	2000.00
NNO	Walrus Man	125.00	250.00

1980-82 Star Wars Empire Strikes Back 21-Backs H1

NNO	Ben Kenobi	125.00	250.00
NNO	Luke X-Wing Pilot		

1980-82 Star Wars Empire Strikes Back 21-Backs H2

NNO	Walrus Man	200.00	400.00

1980-82 Star Wars Empire Strikes Back 21-Backs I

NNO	Boba Fett	1250.00	2500.00
NNO	Greedo	150.00	300.00
NNO	Hammerhead	200.00	400.00

1980-82 Star Wars Empire Strikes Back 31-Backs A

NNO	Ben Kenobi	125.00	200.00
NNO	Bespin Security Guard (White)	75.00	150.00
NNO	Boba Fett	1500.00	3000.00
NNO	Bossk	250.00	500.00
NNO	Chewbacca	150.00	300.00
NNO	FX-7	200.00	350.00
NNO	Greedo	125.00	250.00
NNO	Han Solo (Large Head)	150.00	300.00
NNO	Han Solo (Small Head)	125.00	250.00
NNO	Han Solo Hoth	125.00	250.00
NNO	IG-88	200.00	400.00
NNO	Imperial Stormtrooper Hoth	150.00	300.00
NNO	Jawa	125.00	250.00
NNO	Luke X-Wing Pilot	150.00	300.00
NNO	Power Droid	150.00	300.00
NNO	R2-D2		
NNO	R5-D4	250.00	500.00
NNO	Snaggletooth (Red)	100.00	200.00
NNO	Star Destroyer Commander	200.00	350.00
NNO	Stormtrooper	125.00	250.00

1980-82 Star Wars Empire Strikes Back 31-Backs B

NNO	C-3PO	150.00	300.00
NNO	Darth Vader	125.00	250.00
NNO	Death Star Droid	200.00	400.00
NNO	Hammerhead	125.00	250.00
NNO	Lando Calrissian (Without Teeth)	125.00	250.00
NNO	Luke Bespin (Blond Hair/Walking)	300.00	600.00

NNO	Luke Skywalker (Blond Hair)	350.00	700.00
NNO	Princess Leia	300.00	600.00
NNO	Princess Leia Bespin (Flesh Neck)	200.00	400.00
NNO	Rebel Soldier Hoth	100.00	200.00
NNO	Sand People	125.00	250.00
NNO	Star Destroyer Commander	150.00	300.00
NNO	Stormtrooper	150.00	300.00
NNO	Walrus Man	100.00	200.00

1980-82 Star Wars Empire Strikes Back 31-Backs C

NNO R5-D4

1980-82 Star Wars Empire Strikes Back 32-Backs A

NNO	Bespin Security Guard (White)	75.00	150.00
NNO	Boba Fett	1000.00	2000.00
NNO	C-3PO	100.00	200.00
NNO	Chewbacca	75.00	150.00
NNO	FX-7	100.00	200.00
NNO	Han Solo Hoth	100.00	200.00
NNO	IG-88	200.00	350.00
NNO	Luke Skywalker (Blond Hair)	275.00	550.00
NNO	Princess Leia	300.00	600.00
NNO	Rebel Soldier Hoth	75.00	150.00
NNO	Stormtrooper	150.00	300.00
NNO	Walrus Man	100.00	200.00

1980-82 Star Wars Empire Strikes Back 32-Backs B

NNO	Ben Kenobi	100.00	200.00
NNO	Bossk	100.00	200.00
NNO	Darth Vader	100.00	200.00
NNO	Greedo		
NNO	Han Solo (Large Head)	225.00	450.00
NNO	Imperial Stormtrooper Hoth	125.00	250.00
NNO	Lando Calrissian (Without Teeth)		
NNO	Luke Bespin (Blond Hair/Gun Drawn)	225.00	450.00
NNO	Luke X-Wing Pilot	125.00	250.00
NNO	Princess Leia Bespin (Flesh Neck)	125.00	250.00
NNO	R2-D2	600.00	1200.00
NNO	Star Destroyer Commander	100.00	200.00
NNO	Yoda (Orange Snake)	125.00	250.00

1980-82 Star Wars Empire Strikes Back 32-Backs C

NNO	Bespin Security Guard (White)	75.00	150.00
NNO	Imperial Stormtrooper Hoth		

1980-82 Star Wars Empire Strikes Back 41-Backs A

NNO	2-1B	150.00	300.00
NNO	4-LOM		
NNO	AT-AT Commander		
NNO	AT-AT Driver	125.00	250.00
NNO	Ben Kenobi	200.00	350.00
NNO	Bespin Security Guard (Black)		
NNO	Bespin Security Guard (White)	100.00	200.00
NNO	Boba Fett	400.00	800.00
NNO	Bossk	75.00	150.00
NNO	C-3PO	125.00	250.00
NNO	C-3PO (Removable Limbs)		
NNO	Chewbacca	100.00	200.00
NNO	Cloud Car Pilot		
NNO	Darth Vader	250.00	500.00
NNO	Death Star Droid	150.00	300.00
NNO	Dengar	100.00	200.00
NNO	FX-7	150.00	300.00
NNO	Greedo	125.00	250.00
NNO	Hammerhead	75.00	150.00
NNO	Han Solo (Large Head)	250.00	500.00
NNO	Han Solo Bespin	200.00	350.00
NNO	Han Solo Hoth	100.00	200.00
NNO	IG-88	75.00	150.00
NNO	Imperial Commander	75.00	150.00
NNO	Imperial Stormtrooper Hoth	60.00	120.00
NNO	Imperial TIE Fighter Pilot		
NNO	Jawa	100.00	200.00
NNO	Lando Calrissian (With Teeth)		
NNO	Lando Calrissian (Without Teeth)		
NNO	Lobot	100.00	200.00
NNO	Luke Bespin (Blond Hair/Gun Drawn)	225.00	450.00
NNO	Luke Bespin (Brown Hair/Gun Drawn)	300.00	600.00
NNO	Luke Hoth		
NNO	Luke Skywalker (Blond Hair)	225.00	450.00
NNO	Luke X-Wing Pilot	200.00	400.00
NNO	Power Droid	100.00	200.00
NNO	Princess Leia	200.00	400.00
NNO	Princess Leia Hoth	225.00	450.00
NNO	R2-D2	200.00	350.00
NNO	R2-D2 (Sensorscope)		
NNO	R5-D4	150.00	300.00
NNO	Rebel Commander	125.00	250.00
NNO	Rebel Soldier Hoth	100.00	200.00
NNO	Sand People	125.00	250.00
NNO	Snaggletooth (Red)	150.00	300.00
NNO	Star Destroyer Commander	100.00	200.00
NNO	Stormtrooper	250.00	500.00
NNO	Walrus Man	125.00	250.00
NNO	Yoda (Orange Snake)	125.00	250.00
NNO	Zuckuss	125.00	250.00

1980-82 Star Wars Empire Strikes Back 41-Backs B

NNO	2-1B	125.00	250.00
NNO	Boba Fett	500.00	1000.00
NNO	Bossk	100.00	200.00
NNO	C-3PO	100.00	200.00
NNO	FX-7	125.00	250.00
NNO	Han Solo (Large Head)	250.00	500.00
NNO	Lobot	60.00	120.00
NNO	Luke Bespin (Blond Hair/Gun Drawn)	250.00	500.00
NNO	Luke X-Wing Pilot	100.00	200.00
NNO	Rebel Soldier Hoth	75.00	150.00
NNO	Stormtrooper	200.00	400.00
NNO	Yoda (Brown Snake)		
NNO	Yoda (Orange Snake)	150.00	300.00

1980-82 Star Wars Empire Strikes Back 41-Backs C

NNO	AT-AT Driver	150.00	300.00
NNO	Bespin Security Guard (White)	50.00	100.00
NNO	Chewbacca	200.00	350.00
NNO	Han Solo Hoth	75.00	150.00
NNO	IG-88	125.00	250.00
NNO	Imperial Commander	60.00	120.00
NNO	Jawa	100.00	200.00
NNO	Luke Skywalker (Blond Hair)		
NNO	Princess Leia	300.00	600.00
NNO	Rebel Commander	50.00	100.00
NNO	Star Destroyer Commander	100.00	200.00
NNO	Ugnaught	75.00	150.00
NNO	Walrus Man	125.00	250.00

1980-82 Star Wars Empire Strikes Back 41-Backs D

NNO 2-1B	100.00	200.00
NNO Boba Fett	1000.00	2000.00
NNO FX-7	60.00	120.00
NNO Han Solo (Large Head)	200.00	350.00
NNO Han Solo Bespin	150.00	300.00
NNO Imperial Stormtrooper Hoth	100.00	200.00
NNO Lando Calrissian (With Teeth)	100.00	200.00
NNO Lobot	75.00	150.00
NNO Luke Bespin (Brown Hair/Gun Drawn)	225.00	450.00
NNO Luke X-Wing Pilot	200.00	400.00
NNO Princess Leia Bespin (Neck Painted/Front)	100.00	200.00
NNO Princess Leia Hoth	200.00	400.00
NNO Rebel Soldier Hoth	75.00	150.00
NNO Stormtrooper	125.00	250.00
NNO Yoda (Brown Snake)	200.00	400.00
NNO Yoda (Orange Snake)	125.00	250.00

1980-82 Star Wars Empire Strikes Back 41-Backs E

NNO AT-AT Driver	100.00	200.00
NNO Bespin Security Guard (White)	60.00	120.00
NNO C-3PO	200.00	350.00
NNO Chewbacca	200.00	350.00
NNO Dengar	75.00	150.00
NNO Greedo	100.00	200.00
NNO Han Solo Hoth	100.00	200.00
NNO IG-88	100.00	200.00
NNO Imperial Commander	75.00	150.00
NNO Imperial Stormtrooper Hoth	100.00	200.00
NNO Jawa	125.00	250.00
NNO Luke Skywalker (Blond Hair)		
NNO Luke Skywalker (Brown Hair)		
NNO Princess Leia	300.00	600.00
NNO Rebel Commander	75.00	150.00
NNO Rebel Soldier Hoth		
NNO Sand People	75.00	150.00
NNO Snaggletooth (Red)	100.00	200.00
NNO Star Destroyer Commander	150.00	300.00
NNO Ugnaught	60.00	120.00
NNO Walrus Man	125.00	250.00

1980-82 Star Wars Empire Strikes Back 45-Backs A

NNO 2-1B	75.00	150.00
NNO 4-LOM		
NNO AT-AT Commander	60.00	120.00
NNO Ben Kenobi	125.00	250.00
NNO Bespin Security Guard (Black)	50.00	100.00
NNO Bespin Security Guard (White)	50.00	100.00
NNO Bossk	125.00	250.00
NNO C-3PO		
NNO Chewbacca	125.00	250.00
NNO Cloud Car Pilot	75.00	150.00

NNO Darth Vader	200.00	400.00
NNO Death Star Droid	125.00	250.00
NNO Greedo	125.00	250.00
NNO Hammerhead	100.00	200.00
NNO Han Solo (Large Head)	200.00	350.00
NNO Han Solo Bespin	150.00	300.00
NNO Han Solo Hoth	100.00	200.00
NNO Imperial Commander	60.00	120.00
NNO Imperial Stormtrooper Hoth	125.00	250.00
NNO Imperial TIE Fighter Pilot		
NNO Jawa	150.00	300.00
NNO Lando Calrissian (With Teeth)	75.00	150.00
NNO Lobot	50.00	100.00
NNO Luke Bespin (Blond Hair/Walking)		
NNO Luke Bespin (Brown Hair/Gun Drawn)	225.00	450.00
NNO Luke Hoth	125.00	250.00
NNO Luke Skywalker (Brown Hair)		
NNO Luke X-Wing Pilot	200.00	400.00
NNO Princess Leia	250.00	500.00
NNO Princess Leia Bespin (Flesh Neck)		
NNO Princess Leia Bespin (Neck Painted/Front)	125.00	250.00
NNO Princess Leia Hoth	100.00	200.00
NNO R2-D2		
NNO R2-D2 (Sensorscope)	200.00	400.00
NNO R5-D4	100.00	200.00
NNO Rebel Commander	50.00	100.00
NNO Rebel Soldier Hoth	75.00	150.00
NNO Sand People	100.00	200.00
NNO Snaggletooth (Red)	100.00	200.00
NNO Star Destroyer Commander	125.00	250.00
NNO Stormtrooper	75.00	150.00
NNO Ugnaught	75.00	150.00
NNO Walrus Man	100.00	200.00
NNO Yoda (Brown Snake)	100.00	200.00
NNO Zuckuss		

1980-82 Star Wars Empire Strikes Back 45-Backs B

NNO AT-AT Commander		
NNO Bespin Security Guard (Black)	75.00	150.00
NNO Darth Vader		
NNO Imperial Stormtrooper Hoth		
NNO Rebel Soldier Hoth		

1980-82 Star Wars Empire Strikes Back 47-Backs A

NNO 2-1B	75.00	150.00
NNO 4-LOM		
NNO AT-AT Commander	60.00	120.00
NNO AT-AT Driver	75.00	150.00
NNO Ben Kenobi	125.00	250.00
NNO Bespin Security Guard (Black)	50.00	100.00
NNO Bespin Security Guard (White)	60.00	120.00
NNO Boba Fett	1000.00	2000.00
NNO Bossk	75.00	150.00

NNO C-3PO (Removable Limbs)	125.00	250.00
NNO Chewbacca	100.00	200.00
NNO Cloud Car Pilot	75.00	150.00
NNO Darth Vader	150.00	300.00
NNO Death Star Droid	100.00	200.00
NNO Dengar	75.00	150.00
NNO FX-7	100.00	200.00
NNO Greedo	150.00	300.00
NNO Hammerhead	125.00	250.00
NNO Han Solo (Large Head)	225.00	450.00
NNO Han Solo Bespin	200.00	400.00
NNO Han Solo Hoth	125.00	250.00
NNO IG-88	100.00	200.00
NNO Imperial Commander	50.00	100.00
NNO Imperial Stormtrooper Hoth	100.00	200.00
NNO Imperial TIE Fighter Pilot	100.00	200.00
NNO Jawa	75.00	150.00
NNO Lando Calrissian (With Teeth)	75.00	150.00
NNO Lobot	50.00	100.00
NNO Luke Bespin (Brown Hair/Gun Drawn)	225.00	450.00
NNO Luke Hoth	125.00	250.00
NNO Luke Skywalker (Blond Hair)		
NNO Luke Skywalker (Brown Hair)		
NNO Luke X-Wing Pilot	125.00	250.00
NNO Power Droid	75.00	150.00
NNO Princess Leia	250.00	500.00
NNO Princess Leia Bespin (Neck Painted/Front)	150.00	300.00
NNO Princess Leia Hoth	200.00	350.00
NNO R2-D2 (Sensorscope)	150.00	300.00
NNO R5-D4	125.00	250.00
NNO Rebel Commander	60.00	120.00
NNO Rebel Soldier Hoth	60.00	120.00
NNO Sand People	125.00	250.00
NNO Snaggletooth (Red)	125.00	250.00
NNO Star Destroyer Commander	150.00	300.00
NNO Stormtrooper	100.00	200.00
NNO Ugnaught	60.00	120.00
NNO Walrus Man	125.00	250.00
NNO Yoda (Brown Snake)	200.00	350.00
NNO Yoda (Orange Snake)	75.00	150.00

1980-82 Star Wars Empire Strikes Back 48-Backs A

NNO 2-1B	100.00	200.00
NNO AT-AT Commander	45.00	90.00
NNO Ben Kenobi	75.00	150.00
NNO Bespin Security Guard (Black)	45.00	90.00
NNO Bespin Security Guard (White)		
NNO C-3PO (Removable Limbs)	225.00	450.00
NNO Chewbacca	125.00	250.00
NNO Cloud Car Pilot	75.00	150.00
NNO Han Solo Hoth	100.00	200.00
NNO Imperial Commander	75.00	150.00
NNO Imperial Stormtrooper Hoth	200.00	350.00
NNO Imperial TIE Fighter Pilot	125.00	250.00
NNO Luke Hoth	200.00	350.00
NNO Luke X-Wing Pilot	150.00	300.00
NNO Princess Leia Hoth	125.00	250.00
NNO R2-D2 (Sensorscope)	200.00	350.00
NNO Rebel Commander	75.00	150.00
NNO Sand People	200.00	400.00
NNO Snaggletooth (Red)	100.00	200.00
NNO Stormtrooper	150.00	300.00
NNO Zuckuss	150.00	300.00

1980-82 Star Wars Empire Strikes Back 48-Backs B

NNO 4-LOM		
NNO Ben Kenobi	125.00	250.00
NNO Bespin Security Guard (Black)	50.00	100.00
NNO Bespin Security Guard (White)	75.00	150.00
NNO Bossk	125.00	250.00
NNO C-3PO (Removable Limbs)	150.00	300.00
NNO Darth Vader	200.00	400.00
NNO Dengar	75.00	150.00

NNO	FX-7	75.00	150.00
NNO	Imperial Commander	60.00	120.00
NNO	Imperial Stormtrooper Hoth	100.00	200.00
NNO	Imperial TIE Fighter Pilot	75.00	150.00
NNO	Lando Calrissian (With Teeth)		
NNO	Luke Bespin (Blond Hair/Gun Drawn)		
NNO	Luke Bespin (Brown Hair/Gun Drawn)		
NNO	Luke X-Wing Pilot	125.00	250.00
NNO	Rebel Commander	50.00	100.00
NNO	Rebel Soldier Hoth	60.00	120.00
NNO	Star Destroyer Commander	100.00	200.00
NNO	Stormtrooper	125.00	250.00
NNO	Ugnaught	75.00	150.00
NNO	Yoda (Brown Snake)	200.00	400.00
NNO	Zuckuss	100.00	200.00

1980-82 Star Wars Empire Strikes Back 48-Backs C

NNO	2-1B	125.00	250.00
NNO	4-LOM	125.00	250.00
NNO	AT-AT Commander	60.00	120.00
NNO	AT-AT Driver	125.00	250.00
NNO	Ben Kenobi (grey hair)	150.00	300.00
NNO	Bespin Security Guard (Black)	50.00	100.00
NNO	Boba Fett	1250.00	2500.00
NNO	Bossk	100.00	200.00
NNO	C-3PO (Removable Limbs)	200.00	400.00
NNO	Chewbacca	150.00	300.00
NNO	Cloud Car Pilot	100.00	200.00
NNO	Darth Vader	125.00	250.00
NNO	FX-7	75.00	150.00
NNO	Han Solo Bespin	125.00	250.00
NNO	Han Solo Hoth	100.00	200.00
NNO	IG-88	150.00	300.00
NNO	Imperial Commander	60.00	120.00
NNO	Imperial TIE Fighter Pilot	125.00	250.00
NNO	Jawa	100.00	200.00
NNO	Lando Calrissian (With Teeth)	75.00	150.00
NNO	Lobot	60.00	120.00
NNO	Luke Bespin (Brown Hair/Gun Drawn)	250.00	500.00
NNO	Luke Hoth	150.00	300.00
NNO	Luke X-Wing Pilot	150.00	300.00
NNO	Rebel Commander	60.00	120.00
NNO	Rebel Soldier Hoth	75.00	150.00
NNO	Sand People	125.00	250.00
NNO	Snaggletooth (Red)	125.00	250.00
NNO	Star Destroyer Commander	150.00	300.00
NNO	Stormtrooper	150.00	300.00
NNO	Ugnaught	75.00	150.00
NNO	Yoda (Brown Snake)	300.00	600.00
NNO	Zuckuss	150.00	300.00

1980-82 Star Wars Empire Strikes Back (loose)

NNO	2-1B	15.00	30.00
NNO	4-LOM	15.00	30.00
NNO	AT-AT Commander	12.50	25.00
NNO	AT-AT Driver	12.50	25.00
NNO	Bespin guard (black)	15.00	30.00
NNO	Bespin guard (white)	12.50	25.00
NNO	Bossk	15.00	30.00
NNO	C-3PO (removable limbs)	15.00	30.00
NNO	Cloud Car Pilot	30.00	75.00
NNO	Dengar	10.00	20.00
NNO	FX-7	10.00	20.00
NNO	Han Solo (Bespin)	15.00	30.00
NNO	Han Solo (Hoth gear)	12.50	25.00
NNO	IG-88	20.00	40.00
NNO	Imperial Commander	12.50	25.00
NNO	Imperial Stormtrooper (Hoth)	20.00	40.00
NNO	Lando Calrissian	15.00	30.00
NNO	Lando Calrrissian (no teeth)	12.50	25.00
NNO	Lobot	10.00	20.00
NNO	Luke Skywalker	25.00	50.00
NNO	Luke Skywalker	25.00	50.00

	(Bespin yellow hair brown legs)		
NNO	Luke Skywalker	30.00	75.00
NNO	Luke Skywalker	25.00	50.00
NNO	Luke Skywalker	30.00	75.00
NNO	Luke Skywalker (Hoth gear)	12.50	25.00
NNO	Princess Leia Organa	30.00	60.00
NNO	Princess Leia Organa	30.00	60.00
NNO	Princess Leia Organa	45.00	90.00
	(Bespin gold/green neck)		
NNO	Leia Organa (Hoth gear)	30.00	60.00
NNO	R2-D2 (sensorscope)	17.50	35.00
NNO	Rebel Commander	10.00	20.00
NNO	Rebel Soldier (Hoth gear)	10.00	20.00
NNO	TIE Fighter Pilot	15.00	30.00
NNO	Ugnaught	15.00	30.00
NNO	Yoda (brown snake)	50.00	100.00
NNO	Yoda (orange snake)	40.00	80.00
NNO	Zuckuss	12.50	25.00

1980-82 Star Wars Empire Strikes Back Accessories

NNO	Darth Vader Case	100.00	200.00
NNO	Darth Vader Case/Boba Fett/IG88		
NNO	Mini Collector's Case	125.00	250.00

1980-82 Star Wars Empire Strikes Back Accessories (loose)

NNO	Darth Vader Case		
NNO	Mini Collector's Case		

1980-82 Star Wars Empire Strikes Back Playsets

NNO	Cloud City	400.00	800.00
NNO	Dagobah	100.00	200.00
NNO	Darth Vader/ Star Destroyer	250.00	500.00
NNO	Droid Factory	150.00	300.00
NNO	Hoth Ice Planet	100.00	200.00
NNO	Imperial Attack Base	300.00	600.00
NNO	Land of the Jawas	125.00	250.00
NNO	Rebel Command Center	350.00	700.00
NNO	Turret and Probot	100.00	200.00

1980-82 Star Wars Empire Strikes Back Playsets (loose)

NNO	Cloud City	75.00	150.00
NNO	Dagobah	30.00	60.00
NNO	Darth Vader/ Star Destroyer	60.00	120.00
NNO	Droid Factory	50.00	100.00
NNO	Hoth Ice Planet	30.00	75.00
NNO	Imperial Attack Base	30.00	60.00
NNO	Land of the Jawas	50.00	100.00
NNO	Rebel Command Center	40.00	80.00
NNO	Turret and Probot	30.00	60.00

1980-82 Star Wars Empire Strikes Back Vehicles

NNO	AT-AT	225.00	450.00
NNO	Imperial Cruiser	125.00	250.00
NNO	Imperial Transport	50.00	100.00
NNO	Millennium Falcon	125.00	250.00
NNO	Rebel Transport	100.00	200.00
NNO	Scout Walker	75.00	150.00
NNO	Slave 1	125.00	250.00
NNO	Snowspeeder (blue box)	75.00	150.00
NNO	Snowspeeder (pink box)	75.00	150.00
NNO	Tauntaun	40.00	80.00
NNO	Tauntaun (split belly)	75.00	150.00
NNO	TIE Fighter	150.00	300.00
NNO	Twin Pod Cloud Car	50.00	100.00
NNO	Wampa	50.00	100.00
NNO	X-Wing Fighter (battle damage red photo background box)	100.00	200.00
NNO	X-Wing Fighter (battle damage landscape photo background box)	100.00	200.00

1980-82 Star Wars Empire Strikes Back Vehicles (loose)

NNO	AT-AT	60.00	120.00
NNO	Imperial Cruiser	30.00	75.00
NNO	Rebel Transport	30.00	60.00
NNO	Scout Walker	25.00	50.00
NNO	Slave 1	40.00	80.00
NNO	Snowspeeder	30.00	60.00
NNO	Tauntaun	15.00	30.00
NNO	Tauntaun split belly	20.00	40.00
NNO	Twin Pod Cloud Car	20.00	40.00
NNO	Wampa	15.00	30.00
NNO	X-Wing Fighter	30.00	75.00

1980 Star Wars Empire Strikes Back Micro Set

NNO	Bespin Control Room	25.00	50.00

NNO	Bespin Freeze Chamber	100.00	200.00
NNO	Bespin Gantry	30.00	75.00
NNO	Bespin World	150.00	300.00
NNO	Death Star Compactor	100.00	200.00
NNO	Death Star Escape	50.00	100.00
NNO	Death Star World	150.00	300.00
NNO	Hoth Generator Attack	40.00	80.00
NNO	Hoth Ion Cannon	125.00	250.00
NNO	Hoth Turret Defense	75.00	150.00
NNO	Hoth Wampa Cave	30.00	75.00
NNO	Hoth World	150.00	300.00
NNO	Imperial TIE Fighter	75.00	150.00
NNO	Millenium Falcon	350.00	700.00
NNO	Snowspeeder	200.00	400.00
NNO	X-Wing	100.00	200.00

1980 Star Wars Empire Strikes Back Micro Set (loose)

NNO	Bespin Control Room	7.50	15.00
NNO	Bespin Freeze Chamber	12.50	25.00
NNO	Bespin Gantry	7.50	15.00
NNO	Bespin World	12.50	25.00
NNO	Death Star Compactor	12.50	25.00
NNO	Death Star Escape	7.50	15.00
NNO	Death Star World	12.50	25.00
NNO	Hoth Generator Attack	7.50	15.00
NNO	Hoth Ion Cannon	10.00	20.00
NNO	Hoth Turret Defense	6.00	12.00
NNO	Hoth Wampa Cave	7.50	15.00
NNO	Hoth World	12.50	25.00
NNO	Imperial Tie Fighter	6.00	12.00
NNO	Millenium Falcon	12.50	25.00
NNO	Snowspeeder	6.00	12.00
NNO	X-Wing	7.50	15.00
NNO	AT-AT	6.00	12.00
NNO	AT-AT Operator	.75	2.00
NNO	Ben Kenobi	1.50	4.00
NNO	Boba Fett	.75	2.00
NNO	C-3PO	.75	2.00
NNO	Chewbacca	.75	2.00
NNO	Chewbacca (with wrench)	.75	2.00
NNO	Darth Vader	1.25	3.00
NNO	Darth Vader (lightsaber)	1.25	3.00
NNO	Darth Vader (unpainted)	1.25	3.00
NNO	Han Solo	1.25	3.00
NNO	Han Solo (carbonite)	1.25	3.00
NNO	Han Solo (in cuffs)	1.25	3.00
NNO	Han Solo (stormtrooper)	1.25	3.00
NNO	Lando Calrissian	.75	2.00
NNO	Lobot	.75	2.00
NNO	Luke Skywalker	1.25	3.00
NNO	Luke Skywalker (hanging)	1.25	3.00
NNO	Luke Skywalker (lightsaber)	1.25	3.00
NNO	Luke Skywalker (stormtrooper)	1.25	3.00
NNO	Princess Leia	1.25	3.00
NNO	Princess Leia (holding gun)	1.25	3.00
NNO	Probot	.75	2.00
NNO	Rebel (crouching)	.75	2.00
NNO	Rebel (gun at side/unpainted)	.75	2.00
NNO	Rebel (gun on hip/unpainted)	.75	2.00
NNO	Rebel (gun on sholder/unpainted)	.75	2.00
NNO	Rebel (gun on shoulder)	.75	2.00
NNO	Rebel (laying)	.75	2.00
NNO	Rebel (laying unpainted)	.75	2.00
NNO	Rebel (on Tauntaun)	.75	2.00
NNO	Rebel (on Tauntaun w/blaster)	.75	2.00
NNO	Rebel (w/blaster at side)	.75	2.00
NNO	Rebel (w/blaster brown)	.75	2.00
NNO	Rebel (w/blaster white)	.75	2.00
NNO	Stormtrooper	.75	2.00
NNO	Stormtrooper (firing)	.75	2.00
NNO	Stormtrooper (kneeling)	.75	2.00
NNO	Stormtrooper (on gun)	.75	2.00
NNO	Stormtrooper (walking)	.75	2.00
NNO	TIE Fighter Pilot	.75	2.00
NNO	Turret Operator	.75	2.00
NNO	Wampa	1.00	2.50

NNO	X-Wing Pilot	.75	2.00
NNO	X-Wing Pilot (crouching)	.75	2.00
NNO	X-Wing Pilot (sitting)	.75	2.00

1980 Star Wars Empire Strikes Back Mini Rigs

NNO	CAP-2	30.00	60.00
NNO	INT-4	30.00	60.00
NNO	MLC-3	30.00	75.00
NNO	MTV-7	25.00	50.00
NNO	PDT-8	50.00	100.00
NNO	Tripod Laser Canon	20.00	40.00

1980 Star Wars Empire Strikes Back Mini Rigs (loose)

NNO	CAP-2	7.50	15.00
NNO	INT-4	10.00	20.00
NNO	MLC-3	7.50	15.00
NNO	MTV-7	7.50	15.00
NNO	PDT-8	10.00	20.00
NNO	Tripod Laser Canon	10.00	20.00

1983 Star Wars Return of the Jedi 48-Backs D

NNO	2-1B	100.00	200.00
NNO	4-LOM	75.00	150.00
NNO	AT-AT Commander	50.00	100.00
NNO	AT-AT Driver	125.00	250.00
NNO	Ben Kenobi	60.00	120.00
NNO	Bespin Security Guard (black)	75.00	150.00
NNO	Bespin Security Guard (white)		
NNO	Boba Fett	1250.00	2500.00
NNO	Bossk	125.00	250.00
NNO	C-3PO (removable limbs)	60.00	120.00
NNO	Chewbacca	100.00	200.00
NNO	Cloud Car Pilot	100.00	200.00
NNO	Darth Vader	150.00	300.00
NNO	Death Star Droid	100.00	200.00
NNO	Dengar	30.00	80.00
NNO	FX-7	75.00	150.00
NNO	Greedo	125.00	250.00
NNO	Hammerhead	100.00	200.00
NNO	Han Solo (large head)		
NNO	Han Solo (Bespin)	150.00	300.00
NNO	Han Solo (Hoth gear)	150.00	300.00
NNO	IG-88	125.00	250.00
NNO	Imperial Commander	75.00	150.00
NNO	Imperial Stormtrooper Hoth	150.00	300.00
NNO	Imperial TIE Fighter Pilot	60.00	120.00
NNO	Jawa	100.00	200.00
NNO	Lando Calrissian (with teeth)	60.00	120.00
NNO	Lobot	50.00	100.00
NNO	Luke Bespin (brown hair gun drawn)	200.00	350.00
NNO	Luke Hoth	200.00	400.00
NNO	Luke Skywalker (brown hair)	250.00	500.00
NNO	Luke X-Wing Pilot		
NNO	Power Droid	225.00	450.00
NNO	Princess Leia	600.00	1200.00
NNO	Princess Leia (Bespin neck painted front)	125.00	250.00
NNO	Princess Leia (Hoth)	400.00	800.00
NNO	R2-D2 (sensorscope)		
NNO	R5-D4	125.00	250.00
NNO	Rebel Commander	75.00	150.00
NNO	Sand People	75.00	150.00
NNO	Snaggletooth (red)	75.00	150.00
NNO	Stormtrooper	60.00	120.00
NNO	Ugnaught	75.00	150.00
NNO	Walrus Man	100.00	200.00
NNO	Yoda (brown snake)	300.00	600.00
NNO	Zuckuss	60.00	120.00

NNO	4-LOM	75.00	150.00
NNO	Admiral Ackbar	50.00	100.00
NNO	AT-AT Driver	125.00	250.00
NNO	Ben Kenobi	100.00	200.00
NNO	Bespin Security Guard (black)	50.00	100.00
NNO	Bib Fortuna	75.00	150.00
NNO	Biker Scout	100.00	200.00
NNO	Boba Fett	1500.00	3000.00
NNO	C-3PO (removable limbs)	75.00	150.00
NNO	Chewbacca	100.00	200.00
NNO	Chief Chirpa	50.00	100.00
NNO	Cloud Car Pilot	75.00	150.00
NNO	Darth Vader	125.00	250.00
NNO	Death Star Droid		
NNO	Dengar		
NNO	Emperor's Royal Guard	60.00	120.00
NNO	Gamorrean Guard	30.00	75.00
NNO	General Madine	30.00	60.00
NNO	Han Solo (large head)	225.00	450.00
NNO	Imperial TIE Fighter Pilot		
NNO	Jawa	100.00	200.00
NNO	Klaatu	40.00	80.00
NNO	Lando Calrisian (skiff)	50.00	100.00
NNO	Logray	35.00	70.00
NNO	Luke Hoth	100.00	200.00
NNO	Luke Jedi Knight (blue lightsaber)	500.00	1000.00
NNO	Luke Jedi Knight (green lightsaber)	150.00	300.00
NNO	Luke X-Wing Pilot	125.00	250.00
NNO	Nien Nunb	50.00	100.00
NNO	Princess Leia (Boushh)	100.00	200.00
NNO	R2-D2 (sensorscope)	100.00	200.00
NNO	Rebel Commando	50.00	100.00
NNO	Ree-Yees	45.00	90.00
NNO	Squid Head	50.00	100.00
NNO	Stormtrooper	100.00	200.00
NNO	Weequay	30.00	60.00
NNO	Yoda (brown snake)	150.00	300.00
NNO	Yoda (brown snake/new image)	75.00	150.00
NNO	Zuckuss	20.00	40.00

1983 Star Wars Return of the Jedi 65-Backs B

NNO	2-1B	75.00	150.00
NNO	4-LOM	50.00	100.00
NNO	Admiral Ackbar	50.00	100.00
NNO	AT-AT Commander	30.00	75.00
NNO	AT-AT Driver	75.00	150.00
NNO	Ben Kenobi	100.00	200.00
NNO	Bespin Security Guard (black)	50.00	100.00
NNO	Bib Fortuna	30.00	60.00
NNO	Biker Scout	75.00	150.00
NNO	Bossk	100.00	200.00
NNO	C-3PO (removable limbs)	75.00	150.00
NNO	Chewbacca	75.00	150.00
NNO	Chief Chirpa	30.00	75.00
NNO	Cloud Car Pilot	40.00	80.00

NNO	Darth Vader (new image)	150.00	300.00
NNO	Death Star Droid	125.00	250.00
NNO	Emperor's Royal Guard	60.00	120.00
NNO	Gamorrean Guard	30.00	75.00
NNO	General Madine	30.00	75.00
NNO	Han Solo (large head)	200.00	350.00
NNO	Han Solo (Bespin)	100.00	200.00
NNO	Han Solo (Hoth gear)	125.00	250.00
NNO	IG-88	100.00	200.00
NNO	Imperial Commander	30.00	75.00
NNO	Imperial Stormtrooper Hoth	100.00	200.00
NNO	Imperial TIE Fighter Pilot	60.00	120.00
NNO	Jawa	75.00	150.00
NNO	Klaatu	30.00	60.00
NNO	Lando Calrisian (skiff)	50.00	100.00
NNO	Lando Calrissian (with teeth)	60.00	120.00
NNO	Logray	30.00	75.00
NNO	Luke Jedi Knight (blue lightsaber)	350.00	700.00
NNO	Luke Skywalker (blond hair)	300.00	600.00
NNO	Luke X-Wing Pilot	100.00	200.00
NNO	Nien Nunb	50.00	100.00
NNO	Power Droid	75.00	150.00
NNO	Princess Leia (Bespin neck painted/front picture)	125.00	250.00
NNO	Princess Leia (Boushh)	75.00	150.00
NNO	Princess Leia (Hoth gear)	125.00	250.00
NNO	R2-D2 (sensorscope)	100.00	200.00
NNO	R5-D4	100.00	200.00
NNO	Rebel Commander	30.00	75.00
NNO	Rebel Commando	40.00	90.00
NNO	Rebel Soldier Hoth		
NNO	Ree-Yees	30.00	75.00
NNO	Sand People	100.00	200.00
NNO	Squid Head	30.00	60.00
NNO	Star Destroyer Commander	100.00	200.00
NNO	Stormtrooper	100.00	200.00
NNO	Ugnaught	50.00	100.00
NNO	Weequay	30.00	60.00
NNO	Yoda (brown snake)	125.00	250.00
NNO	Zuckuss	60.00	120.00

1983 Star Wars Return of the Jedi 65-Backs C

NNO	4-LOM	60.00	120.00
NNO	Admiral Ackbar	30.00	75.00
NNO	Ben Kenobi (new image)	100.00	200.00
NNO	Bib Fortuna	40.00	80.00
NNO	Biker Scout	100.00	200.00
NNO	Boba Fett (new image)	1000.00	2000.00
NNO	C-3PO (removable limbs)	100.00	200.00
NNO	Chewbacca (new image)	100.00	200.00
NNO	Chief Chirpa	50.00	100.00
NNO	Darth Vader (new image)	100.00	200.00
NNO	Emperor's Royal Guard	75.00	150.00
NNO	Gamorrean Guard	30.00	75.00
NNO	General Madine	40.00	80.00
NNO	Han Solo (large head/new image)	200.00	400.00
NNO	Imperial TIE Fighter Pilot	75.00	150.00
NNO	Jawa	100.00	200.00

NNO	Klaatu	40.00	80.00
NNO	Klaatu (skiff)		
NNO	Lando Calrisian (skiff)	60.00	120.00
NNO	Logray	40.00	80.00
NNO	Luke Jedi Knight (blue lightsaber)	250.00	500.00
NNO	Luke Jedi Knight (green lightsaber)	125.00	250.00
NNO	Nien Nunb	60.00	120.00
NNO	Princess Leia (Boushh)	75.00	150.00
NNO	R2-D2 (sensorscope)	75.00	150.00
NNO	Rebel Commando	30.00	75.00
NNO	Ree-Yees	35.00	70.00
NNO	Squid Head	40.00	80.00
NNO	Stormtrooper	75.00	150.00
NNO	Weequay	30.00	60.00
NNO	Yoda (brown snake/new image)	200.00	350.00
NNO	Zuckuss	100.00	200.00

1983 Star Wars Return of the Jedi 65-Backs D

NNO	2-1B	60.00	120.00
NNO	Admiral Ackbar	40.00	80.00
NNO	Biker Scout	100.00	200.00
NNO	Chewbacca	120.00	200.00
NNO	Chief Chirpa	30.00	75.00
NNO	Darth Vader (new image)	125.00	250.00
NNO	Gamorrean Guard	30.00	60.00

1983 Star Wars Return of the Jedi 65-Backs E

NNO	General Madine	30.00	60.00

1983 Star Wars Return of the Jedi 77-Backs A

NNO	2-1B	75.00	150.00
NNO	4-LOM	50.00	100.00
NNO	8D8	30.00	60.00
NNO	Admiral Ackbar	30.00	75.00
NNO	AT-AT Commander	50.00	100.00
NNO	AT-AT Driver	100.00	200.00
NNO	AT-ST Driver	30.00	75.00
NNO	Ben Kenobi (new image)	100.00	200.00
NNO	Bespin Security Guard (black)	50.00	100.00
NNO	Bespin Security Guard (white)	60.00	120.00
NNO	Bib Fortuna	40.00	80.00
NNO	Biker Scout	75.00	150.00
NNO	Boba Fett (new image)	1000.00	2000.00
NNO	Bossk	100.00	200.00
NNO	B-Wing Pilot	30.00	60.00
NNO	C-3PO (removable limbs)	75.00	150.00
NNO	Chewbacca (new image)	125.00	250.00
NNO	Chief Chirpa	35.00	70.00
NNO	Cloud Car Pilot	30.00	60.00
NNO	Darth Vader (new image)	60.00	120.00
NNO	Death Star Droid	30.00	60.00
NNO	Dengar	30.00	60.00
NNO	Emperor's Royal Guard	40.00	80.00
NNO	FX-7	30.00	60.00
NNO	Gamorrean Guard	25.00	50.00

NNO	General Madine	20.00	40.00
NNO	Greedo	40.00	80.00
NNO	Hammerhead	25.00	50.00
NNO	Han Solo (large head/new image)	100.00	200.00
NNO	Han Solo (Bespin)	60.00	120.00
NNO	Han Solo (Hoth gear)	60.00	120.00
NNO	Han Solo (trench coat)	30.00	60.00
NNO	IG-88	20.00	40.00
NNO	Imperial Commander	40.00	80.00
NNO	Imperial Stormtrooper Hoth	40.00	80.00
NNO	Imperial TIE Fighter Pilot	50.00	100.00
NNO	Jawa	50.00	100.00
NNO	Klaatu	20.00	40.00
NNO	Klaatu (skiff)	20.00	40.00
NNO	Lando Calrisian (skiff)	25.00	50.00
NNO	Lando Calrissian (with teeth)	30.00	60.00
NNO	Lobot	30.00	60.00
NNO	Logray	20.00	40.00
NNO	Luke Bespin (brown hair gun drawn)	150.00	300.00
NNO	Luke Hoth	60.00	120.00
NNO	Luke Jedi Knight (green lightsaber)	75.00	150.00
NNO	Luke Skywalker (blond hair gunner	350.00	600.00
NNO	Luke X-Wing Pilot	100.00	200.00
NNO	Nien Nunb	25.00	50.00
NNO	Nikto	20.00	40.00
NNO	Power Droid	50.00	100.00
NNO	Princess Leia	450.00	800.00
NNO	Princess Leia (Bespin neck painted/front picture)		
NNO	Princess Leia (Boushh)	40.00	80.00
NNO	Princess Leia (poncho)	40.00	80.00
NNO	Princess Leia (Hoth gear)	125.00	250.00
NNO	Prune Face	20.00	40.00
NNO	R2-D2 (sensorscope)	40.00	80.00
NNO	R5-D4	50.00	100.00
NNO	Rancor Keeper	20.00	40.00
NNO	Rebel Commander	30.00	60.00
NNO	Rebel Commando	20.00	40.00
NNO	Rebel Soldier Hoth	50.00	100.00
NNO	Ree-Yees	20.00	40.00
NNO	Sand People	40.00	80.00
NNO	Snaggletooth (red)	50.00	100.00
NNO	Squid Head	20.00	40.00
NNO	Star Destroyer Commander	100.00	200.00
NNO	Stormtrooper	50.00	100.00
NNO	Teebo	20.00	40.00
NNO	The Emperor	40.00	80.00
NNO	Ugnaught	40.00	80.00
NNO	Walrus Man	30.00	60.00
NNO	Weequay	20.00	40.00
NNO	Wicket	40.00	80.00
NNO	Yoda (brown snake/new image)	60.00	120.00
NNO	Zuckuss	20.00	40.00

1983 Star Wars Return of the Jedi 77-Backs B

NNO	2-1B		
NNO	AT-AT Commander	75.00	150.00
NNO	AT-ST Driver	40.00	80.00
NNO	Bespin Security Guard (black)	30.00	60.00
NNO	Bespin Security Guard (white)	60.00	120.00
NNO	Biker Scout	75.00	150.00
NNO	Chief Chirpa	30.00	75.00
NNO	Darth Vader (new image)	125.00	250.00
NNO	Dengar	100.00	200.00
NNO	FX-7		
NNO	Gamorrean Guard	40.00	80.00
NNO	General Madine	30.00	75.00
NNO	Hammerhead	75.00	150.00
NNO	Han Solo (large head/new image)	300.00	600.00
NNO	Han Solo (trench coat)	75.00	150.00
NNO	Imperial TIE Fighter Pilot		
NNO	Klaatu	30.00	60.00
NNO	Luke Bespin (brown hair/gun drawn)	200.00	400.00
NNO	Luke X-Wing Pilot	125.00	250.00
NNO	Nikto	30.00	60.00
NNO	Power Droid	100.00	200.00
NNO	Princess Leia (poncho)	75.00	150.00
NNO	Princess Leia (Hoth gear)	200.00	400.00

NNO	Prune Face	30.00	75.00
NNO	Rancor Keeper	30.00	75.00
NNO	Rebel Soldier Hoth	60.00	120.00
NNO	Ree-Yees	30.00	60.00
NNO	Snaggletooth (red)	100.00	200.00
NNO	Squid Head	40.00	80.00
NNO	Stormtrooper	125.00	250.00
NNO	Teebo	40.00	80.00
NNO	Ugnaught	50.00	100.00
NNO	Weequay	25.00	50.00

1983 Star Wars Return of the Jedi 79-Backs A

NNO	8D8	40.00	80.00
NNO	AT-AT Driver	100.00	200.00
NNO	AT-ST Driver	50.00	100.00
NNO	Ben Kenobi (new image)	100.00	200.00
NNO	Boba Fett (new image)	400.00	800.00
NNO	B-Wing Pilot	50.00	100.00
NNO	C-3PO (removable limbs)	75.00	150.00
NNO	Darth Vader (new image)	125.00	250.00
NNO	Emperor's Royal Guard	75.00	150.00
NNO	Gamorrean Guard	50.00	100.00
NNO	Greedo	75.00	150.00
NNO	Han Solo Trench Coat	100.00	200.00
NNO	Imperial TIE Fighter Pilot	100.00	200.00
NNO	Jawa	125.00	250.00
NNO	Klaatu	45.00	90.00
NNO	Klaatu (skiff)	50.00	100.00
NNO	Lando Calrisian (skiff)	60.00	120.00
NNO	Lando Calrissian (with teeth)	60.00	120.00
NNO	Luke Jedi Knight (green lightsaber)	150.00	300.00
NNO	Nikto	40.00	80.00
NNO	Princess Leia (Boushh)	60.00	120.00
NNO	Princess Leia (poncho)	75.00	150.00
NNO	Prune Face	50.00	100.00
NNO	Rancor Keeper	25.00	50.00
NNO	Ree-Yees	20.00	40.00
NNO	Snaggletooth (red)	30.00	75.00
NNO	Stormtrooper	75.00	150.00
NNO	Teebo	50.00	100.00
NNO	The Emperor	100.00	200.00
NNO	Ugnaught	60.00	120.00
NNO	Walrus Man		
NNO	Wicket	100.00	200.00
NNO	Yoda (brown snake/new image)	150.00	300.00
NNO	Zuckuss	60.00	120.00

1983 Star Wars Return of the Jedi 79-Backs B

NNO	8D8	50.00	100.00
NNO	AT-ST Driver	40.00	80.00
NNO	Bib Fortuna	25.00	50.00
NNO	B-Wing Pilot	40.00	80.00
NNO	Chewbacca (new image)	125.00	250.00

NNO	Chief Chirpa	30.00	60.00
NNO	Darth Vader (new image)	125.00	250.00
NNO	Emperor's Royal Guard	60.00	120.00
NNO	Gamorrean Guard	50.00	100.00
NNO	Han Solo Bespin		
NNO	Klaatu	25.00	50.00
NNO	Klaatu (skiff)	40.00	80.00
NNO	Lando Calrisian (skiff)	60.00	120.00
NNO	Logray	30.00	60.00
NNO	Luke Jedi Knight (green lightsaber)	125.00	250.00
NNO	Luke X-Wing Pilot	125.00	250.00
NNO	Princess Leia (Boushh)	75.00	150.00
NNO	Princess Leia (poncho)		
NNO	R5-D4		
NNO	Rancor Keeper	30.00	60.00
NNO	Rebel Commando	45.00	90.00
NNO	Ree-Yees	50.00	100.00
NNO	Teebo	30.00	75.00
NNO	The Emperor	125.00	250.00
NNO	Weequay	25.00	50.00
NNO	Wicket	60.00	120.00

1983 Star Wars Return of the Jedi 79-Backs C

NNO	Lumat	100.00	200.00
NNO	Paploo	75.00	150.00

1983 Star Wars Return of the Jedi (loose)

NNO	8D8	10.00	20.00
NNO	Admiral Ackbar	12.50	25.00
NNO	Amanaman	125.00	250.00
NNO	Barada	75.00	150.00
NNO	Ben Kenobi (blue saber)		
NNO	Bib Fortuna	12.50	25.00
NNO	Biker Scout (long mask)	25.00	50.00
NNO	Biker Scout (short mask)	50.00	100.00
NNO	B-Wing Pilot	25.00	50.00
NNO	Chief Chirpa	10.00	20.00
NNO	Dengar (white face)		
NNO	Emperor	10.00	20.00
NNO	Emperors Royal Guard	15.00	30.00
NNO	Gamorrean Guard	10.00	20.00
NNO	General Madine	12.50	25.00
NNO	Han Solo (carbonite)	100.00	200.00
NNO	Han Solo (trench coat)	20.00	40.00
NNO	Imperial Dignitary	60.00	120.00
NNO	Imperial Gunner	150.00	300.00
NNO	Klaatu	10.00	20.00
NNO	Klaatu (skiff)	12.50	25.00
NNO	Lando Calrissian (skiff)	10.00	20.00
NNO	Logray	10.00	20.00
NNO	Luke Skywalker	150.00	300.00
NNO	Luke Skywalker (stormtrooper)	60.00	120.00
NNO	Luke Skywalker Jedi Knight (blue lightsaber)	40.00	80.00
NNO	Luke Skywalker Jedi Knight(green lightsaber)	45.00	90.00
NNO	Lumat	10.00	20.00
NNO	Nien Nunb	12.50	25.00
NNO	Nikto	45.00	90.00
NNO	Paploo	20.00	40.00
NNO	Princess Leia Organa (Boushh)	30.00	75.00
NNO	Princess Leia Organa (poncho)	20.00	40.00
NNO	Prune Face	20.00	40.00
NNO	Rancor Keeper	10.00	20.00
NNO	Rebel Commando	10.00	20.00
NNO	Ree-Yees	75.00	150.00
NNO	Romba	20.00	40.00
NNO	Squid Head	12.50	25.00
NNO	Teebo		
NNO	Weequay		
NNO	Wicket		

1983 Star Wars Return of the Jedi Accessories

NNO	C-3PO Case	125.00	250.00
NNO	Chewy Strap	30.00	75.00
NNO	Darth Vader Case	125.00	250.00
NNO	Jedi Vinyl Case	200.00	350.00
NNO	Laser Rifle Case	125.00	250.00

1983 Star Wars Return of the Jedi Accessories (loose)

NNO	C-3PO Case	25.00	50.00
NNO	Chewy Strap	15.00	30.00
NNO	Darth Vader Case	25.00	50.00
NNO	Jedi Vinyl Case	50.00	100.00
NNO	Laser Rifle Case	50.00	100.00

1983 Star Wars Return of the Jedi Playsets

NNO	Ewok Village	150.00	300.00
NNO	Jabba The Hutt	150.00	300.00
NNO	Jabba The Hutt Dungeon	125.00	250.00
NNO	Jabba The Hutt Dungeon	400.00	800.00

1983 Star Wars Return of the Jedi Playsets (loose)

NNO	Ewok Village	50.00	100.00
NNO	Jabba The Hutt	50.00	100.00
NNO	Jabba The Hutt Dungeon	30.00	60.00

1983 Star Wars Return of the Jedi Vehicles

NNO	AT-AT	400.00	800.00
NNO	B-Wing Fighter	200.00	400.00
NNO	Ewok Assault Catapult	50.00	100.00
NNO	Ewok Glider	30.00	60.00
NNO	Imperial Shuttle	300.00	600.00
NNO	Millenium Falcon	150.00	300.00
NNO	Rancor	100.00	200.00

NNO Scout Walker	100.00	200.00
NNO Speeder Bike	30.00	75.00
NNO Sy Snootles and the Rebo Band	125.00	250.00
(w/Sy Snootles/Droopy McCool/Max Rebo)		
NNO TIE Fighter (battle damage)	125.00	250.00
NNO TIE Interceptor	150.00	300.00
NNO X-Wing (battle damage)	125.00	250.00
NNO Y-Wing	125.00	250.00

1983 Star Wars Return of the Jedi Vehicles
(loose)

NNO AT-AT	75.00	150.00
NNO B-Wing Fighter	60.00	120.00
NNO Droopy McCool	30.00	60.00
NNO Ewok Assault Catapult	15.00	30.00
NNO Ewok Glider	15.00	30.00
NNO Imperial Shuttle	125.00	250.00
NNO Max Rebo	25.00	50.00
NNO Millenium Falcon	75.00	150.00
NNO Rancor	50.00	100.00
NNO Scout Walker	30.00	60.00
NNO Speeder Bike	20.00	40.00
NNO Sy Snootles	30.00	75.00
NNO TIE Fighter (battle damage)	20.00	40.00
NNO TIE Interceptor	50.00	100.00
NNO X-Wing (battle damage)	30.00	75.00
NNO Y-Wing	50.00	100.00

1983 Star Wars Return of the Jedi Tri-Logo

NNO 2-1B	30.00	60.00
NNO 8D8	30.00	60.00
NNO A-Wing Pilot	40.00	80.00
NNO Admiral Ackbar	20.00	40.00
NNO Amanaman	100.00	200.00
NNO Anakin Skywalker	25.00	50.00
NNO AT-AT Commander	20.00	40.00
NNO AT-ST Driver	30.00	60.00
NNO B-Wing Pilot	20.00	40.00
NNO Barada	40.00	80.00
NNO Ben Kenobi (blue lightsaber)	60.00	120.00
NNO Bespin Guard (black/ tri-logo back only)	150.00	300.00
NNO Bespin Guard (white/ tri-logo back only)	250.00	500.00
NNO Bib Fortuna	15.00	30.00
NNO Biker Scout (long mask)	30.00	60.00
NNO Boba Fett	350.00	700.00
NNO Bossk	40.00	80.00
NNO C-3PO (removable limbs)	40.00	80.00
NNO Chewbacca	40.00	80.00
NNO Darth Vader	75.00	150.00
NNO Death Star Droid	40.00	80.00
NNO Dengar	25.00	50.00
NNO Emperor	30.00	60.00
NNO Emperors Royal Guard	150.00	300.00
NNO FX-7	30.00	60.00
NNO Gamorrean Guard	30.00	60.00

NNO General Madine	60.00	120.00
NNO Greedo (tri-logo back only)	60.00	120.00
NNO Hammerhead (tri-logo back only)	40.00	80.00
NNO Han Solo	75.00	150.00
NNO Han Solo (carbonite)	250.00	500.00
NNO IG-88	100.00	200.00
NNO Imperial Commander	50.00	100.00
NNO Imperial Dignitary	125.00	250.00
NNO Imperial Gunner	125.00	250.00
NNO Jawa	500.00	1000.00
NNO Klaatu	15.00	30.00
NNO Klaatu (skiff)	25.00	50.00
NNO Lando Calrissian	40.00	80.00
NNO Lando Calrissian (skiff)	30.00	60.00
NNO Lobot	30.00	60.00
NNO Luke Skywalker (Bespin)	200.00	400.00
NNO Luke Skywalker (gunner card)	125.00	250.00
NNO Luke Skywalker (Hoth gear)	200.00	400.00
NNO Luke Skywalker Jedi Knight	40.00	80.00
NNO Luke Skywalker (stormtrooper)	150.00	300.00
NNO Luke Skywalker (poncho)	30.00	60.00
NNO Luke Skywalker X-wing	100.00	200.00
NNO Lumat	30.00	60.00
NNO Nien Nunb	50.00	100.00
NNO Nikto	15.00	30.00
NNO Paploo	15.00	30.00
NNO Princess Leia Organa	60.00	120.00
NNO Princess Leia Organa (Bespin turtle neck)	60.00	120.00
NNO Princess Leia Organa (Boushh)	75.00	150.00
NNO Princess Leia Organa (poncho)	50.00	100.00
NNO Prune Face	25.00	50.00
NNO R2-D2 (sensorscope/blue background card)	20.00	40.00
NNO R2-D2 (sensorscope/sparks card)	75.00	120.00
NNO R5-D4	30.00	60.00
NNO Rancor	20.00	40.00
NNO Rebel Soldier (Hoth gear)	40.00	80.00
NNO Ree-Yees	20.00	40.00
NNO Romba	30.00	60.00
NNO Snowtrooper	30.00	60.00
NNO Squid Head	25.00	50.00
NNO Stormtrooper	100.00	200.00
NNO TIE Fighter Pilot	30.00	60.00
NNO Ugnaught	30.00	60.00
NNO Warok	50.00	100.00
NNO Wicket	40.00	80.00
NNO Yak Face	1200.00	2500.00
NNO Yoda (brown snake)	50.00	100.00
NNO Yoda (orange snake)	500.00	900.00

1985 Star Wars Droids Cartoon

NNO A-Wing Pilot	500.00	750.00
NNO Boba Fett	4000.00	8000.00
NNO C-3PO	750.00	1500.00
NNO Jann Tosh	125.00	250.00
NNO Jord Dusat	150.00	300.00
NNO Kea Moll	100.00	200.00
NNO Kez-Iban	200.00	400.00
NNO R2-D2	750.00	1500.00
NNO Sise Fromm	600.00	1200.00
NNO Thall Joben	150.00	300.00
NNO Tig Fromm	325.00	650.00
NNO Uncle Gundy	150.00	300.00

1985 Star Wars Droids Cartoon (loose)

NNO A-Wing Pilot	125.00	250.00
NNO Boba Fett	250.00	500.00
NNO C-3PO	250.00	500.00
NNO Jann Tosh	75.00	150.00
NNO Jord Dusat	60.00	120.00
NNO Kea Moll	60.00	120.00
NNO Kez-Iban	75.00	150.00
NNO R2-D2	300.00	600.00
NNO Sise Fromm	400.00	800.00
NNO Thall Joben	75.00	150.00
NNO Tig Fromm	150.00	300.00
NNO Uncle Gundy	75.00	150.00

1985 Star Wars Droids Cartoon Coins (loose)

NNO A-Wing Pilot	100.00	200.00
NNO Boba Fett	250.00	500.00
NNO C-3PO	75.00	150.00
NNO Jann Tosh	25.00	60.00
NNO Jord Dusat	20.00	50.00
NNO Kea Moll	20.00	50.00
NNO Kez-Iban	25.00	60.00
NNO R2-D2	75.00	150.00
NNO Sise Fromm	75.00	150.00
NNO Thall Joben	20.00	50.00
NNO Tig Fromm	60.00	120.00
NNO Uncle Gundy	20.00	50.00

1985 Star Wars Droids Cartoon Vehicles

NNO A-Wing Fighter	600.00	1200.00
NNO ATL Interceptor	300.00	600.00
NNO Sidegunner	200.00	400.00

1985 Star Wars Droids Cartoon Vehicles (loose)

NNO A-Wing Fighter	300.00	600.00
NNO ATL Interceptor	150.00	300.00
NNO Sidegunner	75.00	150.00

1988 Star Wars Droids Cartoon Glasslite

NNO C-3PO	
NNO Jord Dusat	
NNO Kea Moll	
NNO Kez Iban	
NNO R2-D2	
NNO Thall Joben	
NNO Vlix	

1988 Star Wars Droids Cartoon Glasslite Vehicles

NNO Interceptor	
NNO Side Gunner	

1985 Star Wars Ewoks Cartoons

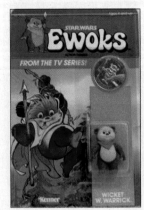

NNO Dulok Scout	100.00	200.00
NNO Dulok Shaman	125.00	250.00
NNO King Gorneesh	75.00	150.00
NNO Lady Gorneesh	100.00	200.00

NNO	Logray	200.00	350.00
NNO	Wicket	300.00	500.00

1985 Star Wars Ewoks Cartoons (loose)

NNO	Dulok Scout	30.00	75.00
NNO	Dulok Shaman	60.00	120.00
NNO	King Gorneesh	30.00	75.00
NNO	Lady Gorneesh	50.00	100.00
NNO	Logray	75.00	150.00
NNO	Wicket	100.00	200.00

1985 Star Wars Ewoks Cartoons Coins (loose)

NNO	Dulok Scout	10.00	25.00
NNO	Dulok Shaman	12.00	30.00
NNO	King Gorneesh	10.00	25.00
NNO	Lady Gorneesh	10.00	25.00
NNO	Logray	12.00	30.00
NNO	Wicket	15.00	40.00

1985 Star Wars Power of the Force

NNO	A-Wing Pilot	300.00	600.00
NNO	Amanaman	250.00	500.00
NNO	Anakin Skywalker	2500.00	5000.00
NNO	AT-AT Driver	600.00	1200.00
NNO	AT-ST Driver	100.00	200.00
NNO	B-Wing Pilot	100.00	200.00
NNO	Barada	125.00	250.00
NNO	Ben Kenobi (blue saber)	150.00	300.00
NNO	Biker Scout	200.00	400.00
NNO	C-3PO (removable limbs)	125.00	250.00
NNO	Chewbacca	200.00	400.00
NNO	Darth Vader	300.00	600.00
NNO	Emperor	150.00	300.00
NNO	EV-9D9	225.00	450.00
NNO	Gamorrean Guard	200.00	400.00
NNO	Han Solo (carbonite)	350.00	700.00
NNO	Han Solo (trench coat)	300.00	500.00
NNO	Imperial Dignitary	125.00	250.00
NNO	Imperial Gunner	200.00	400.00
NNO	Jawa	125.00	250.00
NNO	Lando Calrissian (general)	150.00	300.00
NNO	Luke Skywalker (Hoth gear)		
NNO	Luke Skywalker (Jedi)	300.00	500.00
NNO	Luke Skywalker (poncho)	300.00	500.00
NNO	Luke Skywalker (stormtrooper)	750.00	1500.00
NNO	Luke Skywalker X-wing	225.00	450.00
NNO	Lumat	125.00	250.00
NNO	Nikto	1500.00	3000.00
NNO	Paploo	150.00	300.00
NNO	Princess Leia (poncho)	125.00	250.00
NNO	R2-D2 (lightsaber)	750.00	1500.00
NNO	Romba	125.00	250.00
NNO	Stormtrooper	125.00	250.00
NNO	Teebo	200.00	400.00
NNO	TIE Fighter Pilot		

NNO	Ugnaught		
NNO	Warok	200.00	400.00
NNO	Wicket	150.00	300.00
NNO	Yak Face	3000.00	6000.00
NNO	Yoda (brown snake)	1500.00	3000.00

1985 Star Wars Power of the Force (loose)

NNO	A-Wing Pilot	100.00	200.00
NNO	Amanaman	150.00	300.00
NNO	Anakin Skywalker	30.00	60.00
NNO	AT-AT Driver	15.00	30.00
NNO	AT-ST Driver	30.00	60.00
NNO	B-Wing Pilot	25.00	50.00
NNO	Barada	75.00	150.00
NNO	Ben Kenobi (blue saber)	20.00	40.00
NNO	Biker Scout	15.00	30.00
NNO	C-3PO (removable limbs)	25.00	50.00
NNO	Chewbacca	15.00	30.00
NNO	Darth Vader	25.00	50.00
NNO	Emperor	20.00	40.00
NNO	EV-9D9	125.00	250.00
NNO	Gamorrean Guard	15.00	30.00
NNO	Han Solo (carbonite)	150.00	300.00
NNO	Han Solo (trench coat)	30.00	60.00
NNO	Imperial Dignitary	75.00	150.00
NNO	Imperial Gunner	125.00	250.00
NNO	Jawa	20.00	40.00
NNO	Lando Calrissian (general)	100.00	200.00
NNO	Luke Skywalker (Hoth gear)	15.00	30.00
NNO	Luke Skywalker (Jedi)	50.00	100.00
NNO	Luke Skywalker (poncho)	150.00	300.00
NNO	Luke Skywalker (stormtrooper)	250.00	500.00
NNO	Luke Skywalker X-wing	20.00	40.00
NNO	Lumat	60.00	120.00
NNO	Nikto	20.00	40.00
NNO	Paploo	60.00	120.00
NNO	Princess Leia (poncho)	30.00	75.00
NNO	R2-D2 (lightsaber)	300.00	600.00
NNO	Romba	100.00	200.00
NNO	Stormtrooper	25.00	50.00
NNO	Teebo	20.00	40.00
NNO	TIE Fighter Pilot	15.00	30.00
NNO	Ugnaught	15.00	30.00
NNO	Warok	100.00	200.00
NNO	Wicket	25.00	50.00
NNO	Yak Face	300.00	600.00
NNO	Yoda (brown snake)	75.00	150.00

1985 Star Wars Power of the Force Coins (loose)

NNO	A-Wing Pilot	12.00	30.00
NNO	Amanaman	15.00	40.00
NNO	Anakin Skywalker	200.00	400.00
NNO	AT-AT Driver	150.00	300.00
NNO	AT-ST Driver	20.00	50.00
NNO	B-Wing Pilot	30.00	75.00
NNO	Barada	15.00	40.00
NNO	Ben Kenobi (blue saber)	75.00	150.00
NNO	Biker Scout	30.00	75.00
NNO	C-3PO (removable limbs)	25.00	60.00
NNO	Chewbacca	30.00	75.00
NNO	Darth Vader	50.00	100.00
NNO	Emperor	60.00	120.00
NNO	EV-9D9	15.00	40.00
NNO	Gamorrean Guard	100.00	200.00
NNO	Han Solo (carbonite)	30.00	75.00
NNO	Han Solo (trench coat)	50.00	100.00
NNO	Imperial Dignitary	15.00	40.00
NNO	Imperial Gunner	20.00	50.00
NNO	Jawa	75.00	150.00

NNO	Lando Calrissian (general)	12.00	30.00
NNO	Luke Skywalker (Hoth gear)	10.00	20.00
NNO	Luke Skywalker (Jedi)	125.00	250.00
NNO	Luke Skywalker (poncho)	12.00	30.00
NNO	Luke Skywalker (stormtrooper)	15.00	40.00
NNO	Luke Skywalker X-wing	100.00	200.00
NNO	Lumat	30.00	75.00
NNO	Nikto		
NNO	Paploo	20.00	50.00
NNO	Princess Leia (poncho)	25.00	60.00
NNO	R2-D2 (lightsaber)	20.00	50.00
NNO	Romba	10.00	25.00
NNO	Stormtrooper	50.00	100.00
NNO	Teebo	50.00	100.00
NNO	TIE Fighter Pilot	50.00	100.00
NNO	Ugnaught		
NNO	Warok	12.00	30.00
NNO	Wicket	25.00	60.00
NNO	Yak Face	200.00	400.00
NNO	Yoda (brown snake)	75.00	150.00

1985 Star Wars Power of the Force Vehicles

NNO	Ewok Battle Wagon	300.00	600.00
NNO	Imperial Sniper Vehicle	200.00	400.00
NNO	Sand Skimmer	200.00	350.00
NNO	Security Scout	250.00	500.00
NNO	Tattoine Skiff	600.00	1200.00

1985 Star Wars Power of the Force Vehicles (loose)

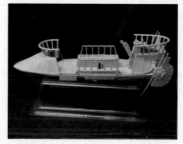

NNO	Ewok Battle Wagon	150.00	300.00
NNO	Imperial Sniper Vehicle	125.00	200.00
NNO	Sand Skimmer	50.00	100.00
NNO	Security Scout	100.00	200.00
NNO	Tattoine Skiff	250.00	500.00

1988 Star Wars Power of the Force Glasslite

NNO	C-3PO
NNO	Chewbacca
NNO	Darth Vader
NNO	Han Solo
NNO	Luke Skywalker
NNO	Princess Leia
NNO	R2-D2
NNO	Snowtrooper
NNO	Stormtrooper

1988 Star Wars Power of the Force Glasslite Vehicles

NNO	TIE Fighter
NNO	X-Wing Fighter

1988 Star Wars Uzay Savascilari Turkish Bootlegs

NNO	Stormtroper (Asker)(single arm band)
NNO	Stormtroper (Asker)(double arm band)
NNO	Imperial Stormtroper (Imperatorlugun Askeri)
NNO	AT-Driver (Surucu)(gold rocks on card)

NNO AT-Driver (Surucu)(silver rocks on card)
NNO Darth Vader (Kara Lider)(no dot on chest)
NNO Darth Vader (Kara Lider)(dot on chest)
NNO Chewbacca (Aslan Adam)(space background)
NNO Chewbacca (Aslan Adam)(profile shot)
NNO T E Fighter Pilot (Savas Polotu)(black boots)
NNO T E Fighter Pilot (Savas Polotu)(unpainted boots)
NNO See Threep (CPO)(no text on front)
NNO See Threep (CPO)(text on front)

NNO Death Star Droid
NNO Blue Stars
NNO Emperor's Royal Guard (dark red cape)
NNO Emperor's Royal Guard (light red cape)
NNO Emperor's Royal Guard (no cape)
NNO Imperial Gunner (tan background)
NNO Imperial Gunner (green background)
NNO Arfive Defour (R2-D4)
NNO Arfive Defour (R2-D4)(printing error)

NNO Head Man
NNO Artoo Detoo (R2-D2)(white scope)
NNO Artoo Detoo (R2-D2)(gray scope)

1988 Star Wars Uzay Savascilari Turkish Bootlegs Vehicles

NNO MTV-7
NNO MLC-3

MODERN

ACTION FIGURES AND FIGURINES

2018 Solo A Star Wars Story Force Link 2.0

NNO	Chewbacca	6.00	12.00
NNO	Darth Vader	10.00	20.00
NNO	Emperor's Royal Guard		
NNO	Han Solo		
NNO	K-2SO		
NNO	Kylo Ren		
NNO	L3-37		
NNO	Luke Skywalker Jedi Knight		
NNO	Luke Skywalker Jedi Master		
NNO	Maz Kanata		
NNO	Moloch		
NNO	Princess Leia Organa		
NNO	Qi'Ra		
NNO	Quay Tolsite		
NNO	Range Trooper		
NNO	Rey		
NNO	Rio Durant		
NNO	Stormtrooper		
NNO	Stormtrooper Officer		
NNO	Supreme Leader Snoke		
NNO	Tobias Beckett		
NNO	Val		

2018 Solo A Star Wars Story Force Link 2.0 2-Packs

NNO	C-3PO & R2-D2		
NNO	Han Solo/Chewbacca	15.00	30.00
NNO	Lando Calrissian/Kessel Guard	10.00	20.00
NNO	Qui-Gon Jinn/Darth Maul (w/probe droid)	7.50	15.00
NNO	Rebolt/Corellian Hound	20.00	40.00
NNO	Rose Tico (w/BB-8)/BB-9E	7.50	15.00

2018 Solo A Star Wars Story Force Link 2.0 Creatures

NNO	Rathtar (w/Bala-Tik)	10.00	20.00
NNO	Wampa (w/Luke Skywalker)	15.00	30.00

2018 Solo A Star Wars Story Force Link 2.0 Multi-Packs

NNO	Han Solo/Qi'Ra/Range Trooper/Weazel	30.00	60.00
	(Mission on Vandor 4-Pack)		
NNO	Kylo Ren/Maz Kanata/Poe Dameron/Rey/Snowtrooper		
	(Last Jedi 5-Pack Entertainment Earth Exclusive)		
NNO	Starter Set (w/Han Solo)	12.50	25.00
NNO	Trooper 6-Pack		
	(2018 Targe Exclusive)		

2018 Solo A Star Wars Story Force Link 2.0 Playsets

NNO	Kessel Mine Escape (w/Han Solo)		
NNO	Vandor-1 Heist (w/Chewbacca)		

2018 Solo A Star Wars Story Force Link 2.0 Vehicles

NNO	A-Wing Fighter (w/Tallie)		
NNO	Imperial AT-DT Walker (w/Stormtrooper)	40.00	80.00
NNO	Kessel Run Millennium Falcon (w/Han Solo)	50.00	100.00
NNO	M-68 Landspeeder (w/Han Solo)	15.00	30.00
NNO	Swoop Bike (w/Enfys Nest)	25.00	50.00
NNO	TIE Fighter (w/TIE Fighter Pilot)	30.00	60.00

2007-08 Star Wars 30th Anniversary Collection

1	Darth Vader (w/30th Anniversary coin album)	10.00	25.00
2	Galactic Marine	4.00	8.00
3	Mustafar Lava Miner	4.00	8.00
4	R2-D2	4.00	8.00
5	Obi-Wan Kenobi	4.00	8.00
6	Mace Windu	6.00	12.00
7	Airborne Trooper	4.00	8.00
8	Super Battle Droid	4.00	8.00
9	Concept Stormtrooper (McQuarrie Signature Series)	4.00	8.00
10	Rebel Honor Guard (Yavin)	4.00	8.00
11	Han Solo (smuggler)	4.00	8.00
12	Luke Skywalker (Yavin ceremony)	4.00	8.00
13	Death Star Trooper	5.00	10.00
14	Biggs Darklighter (Rebel pilot)	4.00	8.00
15	Concept Boba Fett (McQuarrie Signature Series)	12.00	25.00
16	Darth Vader (removable helmet)	4.00	8.00
17	Biggs Darklighter (academy gear)	4.00	8.00
18	Luke Skywalker (moisture farmer)	8.00	15.00
19	Jawa & LIN Droid (Tatooine scavenger)	4.00	8.00
20	Imperial Stormtrooper (Galactic Empire)	4.00	8.00
21	Concept Chewbacca (McQuarrie Signature Series)	6.00	12.00
22	M'liyoom Onith (Hementhe)	5.00	10.00
23	Elis Helrot (Givin)	5.00	10.00
24	Boba Fett (animated debut)	6.00	12.00
25	Luke Skywalker (Jedi Knight)	4.00	8.00
26	CZ-4 (CZ-Series droid)	4.00	8.00
27	Umpass-Stay (Klatooinian)	4.00	8.00
28	Concept Darth Vader (McQuarrie Signature Series)	8.00	15.00
29	Hermi Odle (Baragwin)	12.00	25.00
30	C-3PO & Salacious Crumb (Jabba's Servants)	10.00	20.00
31	Roron Corobb (Jedi Knight)	6.00	12.00
32	Yoda & Kybuck (Jedi Master)	4.00	8.00
33	Anakin Skywalker (Jedi Knight)	4.00	8.00
34	Darth Revan (Sith Lord)	30.00	60.00
35	Darth Malak (Sith Lord)	15.00	30.00
36	Pre-Cyborg Grievous	20.00	40.00
	(Kaleesh warlord Qymaen jai Sheelal)		
37	Concept Starkiller Hero (McQuarrie Signature Series)	4.00	8.00
38	Han Solo (w/torture rack)	10.00	20.00
39	Lando Calrissian (smuggler)	4.00	8.00
40	General McQuarrie (Rebel officer)	4.00	8.00
41	4-LOM (bounty hunter)	4.00	8.00
42	Concept Snowtrooper (McQuarrie Signature Series)	4.00	8.00
43	Romba & Graak (Ewok warriors)	12.00	25.00
44	Tycho Celchu (A-Wing pilot)	4.00	8.00
45	Anakin Skywalker (Jedi Spirit)	10.00	20.00
46	R2-D2 (w/cargo net)	4.00	8.00
47	Concept Han Solo (McQuarrie Signature Series)	12.00	25.00
48	Darth Vader (hologram)	4.00	8.00
49a	Clone Trooper (7th Legion Trooper)	4.00	8.00
49b	Clone Trooper (Revenge of the Sith stand/no coin)	4.00	8.00
50a	Clone Trooper (Hawkbat Batallion)	8.00	15.00
50b	Clone Trooper (Hawkbat Batallion	4.00	8.00
	Revenge of the Sith stand/no coin)		
51a	R2-B1 (astromech droid)	4.00	8.00
51b	R2-B1 (Revenge of the Sith stand/no coin)	4.00	8.00
52	Naboo Soldier (Royal Naboo Army)	6.00	12.00
53a	Rebel Vanguard Trooper (Star Wars: Battlefront)	4.00	8.00
53b	Rebel Vanguard Trooper (Expanded Universe stand/no coin)	4.00	8.00
54	Pax Bonkik (Rodian podracer mechanic)	4.00	8.00
55	Clone Trooper (training fatigues)	8.00	15.00
56a	Padme Amidala (Naboo Senator)	4.00	8.00
56b	Padme Amidala (Attack of the Clones stand/no coin)	4.00	8.00
57a	Jango Fett (bounty hunter)	4.00	8.00
57b	Jango Fett (Attack of the Clones stand/no coin)	10.00	20.00
58a	Voolvif Monn (Jedi Master)	4.00	8.00
58b	Voolvif Monn (Expanded Universe stand/no coin)	4.00	8.00
59	Destroyer Droid (droideka)	4.00	8.00
60	Concept Rebel Trooper (McQuarrie Signature Series)	4.00	8.00

2007-08 Star Wars 30th Anniversary Collection
Battle Packs

1 Battle of Geonosis (Jango Fett/Obi-Wan	20.00	40.00
Kenobi/Count Dooku/Aayla Secura)		
2 Battle on Mygeeto (Galactic Marine/Ki-Adi Mundi	30.00	60.00
Clone Commander Bacara/Super Battle Droid/Tri-Droid)		
3 Betrayal at Bespin (Boba Fett/Chewbacca	20.00	40.00
Darth Vader/Han Solo/Princess Leia)		
4 Capture of Tantive IV (Darth Vader	20.00	40.00
2 Rebel Troopers/2 Stormtroopers)		
5 Clone Attack on Coruscant	25.00	50.00
(Clone Trooper Commander/4 Clone Troopers)		
6 Droid Factory Capture (C-3PO with droid head	20.00	40.00
R2-D2/Jango Fett/Anakin/Destroyer Droid)		
7 Hoth Patrol (Luke Skywalker/Tauntaun/Wampa)	20.00	40.00
8 Jedi vs Sith (Yoda/Anakin Skywalker	10.00	20.00
Asajj Ventress/General Grievous/Obi-Wan)		
9 Jedi vs. Sidious (Darth Sidious/Kit Fisto	10.00	20.00
Mace Windu/Saesee-Tiin/Agen Kolar)		
10 Jedi Training on Dagobah (Yoda/R2-D2	10.00	20.00
Luke Skywalker/Spirit of Obi-Wan/Darth Vader)		
11 The Hunt for Grievous (Captain Fordo	30.00	60.00
Clone Trooper Gunner/3 Clone Troopers)		

2007-08 Star Wars 30th Anniversary Collection
Battle Packs Exclusives

1 Ambush on Ilum	30.00	60.00
(R2-D2/C-3PO/Padme/Chameleon Droids)		
(2007 Target Exclusive)		
2 ARC-170 Elite Squad	50.00	100.00
(Astromech Droid/2 Clone pilots/2 Clone Troopers)		
(2007 Target Exclusive)		
3 Arena Encounter	100.00	200.00
(Anakin Skywalker/Padme Amidala/Obi-Wan/Creatures)		
(2007 Toys R Us Exclusive)		
4 AT-RT Assault Squad	25.00	50.00
(2 AT-RT's/2 AT-RT Drivers/Clone Commander)		
(2007 Target Exclusive)		
5 Attack on Kashyyyk	20.00	40.00
(Darth Vader/2 Stormtroopers/2 Wookiee warriors)		
(2008 Target Exclusive)		
6 Bantha with Tusken Raiders	30.00	60.00
(brown - Bantha/2 Tusken Raiders/Tusken female)		
(2007 Toys R Us Exclusive)		
7 Bantha with Tusken Raiders	50.00	100.00
(tan - Bantha/2 Tusken Raiders/Tusken female)		
(2007 Toys R Us Exclusive)		
8 Battle Rancor	60.00	120.00
(w/Felucian warrior)		
(2008 Target Exclusive)		
9 Betrayal on Felucia	20.00	40.00
(Aayla Secura/4 Clone Troopers yellow)		
(2007 Target Exclusive)		
10 STAP Attack	25.00	50.00
(2 Battle Droids/Super Battle Droid/2 STAP's)		
(2008 Toys R Us Exclusive)		
11 Treachery on Saleucami	30.00	60.00
(Commander Neyo/Clone Trooper red/2 BARC Speeder Bikes)		
(2007 Walmart Exclusive)		

2007-08 Star Wars 30th Anniversary Collection
Comic Packs

1 Carnor Jax & Kir Kanos		
(2006 Internet Exclusive)		
2 Darth Vader & Rebel Officer		
3 Governor Tarkin & Stormtrooper		
4 Chewbacca & Han Solo		
5 Quinlan Vos & Vilmarh Grahrk		
6 Luke Skywalker & R2-D2		
7 Obi-Wan Kenobi & ARC Trooper		
8 A'sharad Hett & The Dark Woman	20.00	40.00
9 Leia Organa & Darth Vader		
10 Mara Jade & Luke Skywalker	20.00	40.00
11 Anakin Skywalker & Assassin Droid		
12 Baron Soontir Fel & Derek Hobbie Klivian		
13 Koffi Arana & Bultar Swan		
14 Lt. Jundland & Deena Shan		
15 Mouse & Basso		
16 Clone Commando & Super Battle Droid	30.00	60.00
NNO Obi-Wan Kenobi & Bail Organa		
(2007 Walmart Exclusive)		
NNO Boba Fett & RA-7 Droid (Wal-Mart Exclusive)	12.00	25.00
NNO Commander Keller & Galactic Marine		
(2007 Walmart Exclusive)		
NNO Count Dooku & Anakin Skywalker		
NNO Kashyyyk Trooper & Wookiee Warrior		
NNO Lando Calrissian & Stormtrooper		

2007-08 Star Wars 30th Anniversary Collection
Commemorative Tins

1 Episode I (Darth Maul/Anakin Skywalker	50.00	100.00
Qui-Gon Ginn/R2-D9)		
2 Episode II (Clone Trooper blue	20.00	40.00
Anakin Skywalker/Count Dooku/Boba Fett)		
3 Episode III (Yoda/Mace Windu		
Anakin Skywalker/Clone Trooper yellow shins)		
4 Episode IV (Stormtrooper black shoulders	20.00	40.00
Princess Leia/Darth Vader/C-3PO)		
5 Episode V (Snowtrooper/Luke Skywalker hoth		
Han Solo hoth/Chewbacca hoth)		
6 Episode VI (Bike Trooper/Darth Vader	20.00	40.00
Princess Leia endor/Rebel Trooper)		
7 The Modal Nodes Cantina Band	30.00	60.00

8 Episode II		
(Mace Windu/Sora Bulq/Oppo Rancisis/Zam Wesell)		
(2007 K-Mart Exclusive)		
9 Episode III		
(Commander Cody/Anakin/General Grievous/Clone Pilot)		
(2007 K-Mart Exclusive)		
10 Episode VI		
(Darth Vader/R5-J2/Biker Scout/Death Star Gunner)		
(2007 K-Mart Exclusive)		

2007-08 Star Wars 30th Anniversary Collection
Evolutions

1 Anakin Skywalker to Darth Vader	20.00	40.00
2 Clone Trooper to Stormtrooper	20.00	40.00
3 The Sith		
4 The Fett Legacy	25.00	50.00
5 The Jedi Legacy	20.00	40.00
6 The Sith Legacy		
7 Vader's Secret Apprentice/Secret Apprentice/Sith Lord/Jedi Knight	30.00	75.00

2007-08 Star Wars 30th Anniversary Collection
Exclusives

1 Cantina Band Member	20.00	40.00
(2007 Disney Weekends Exclusive)		
2 Concept General Grievous	15.00	30.00
(2007 SWS Exclusive)		
3 Concept Luke Skywalker (McQuarrie Signature Series)	15.00	30.00
(2007 C4 & CE Exclusive)		
4 Concept Obi-Wan & Yoda (McQuarrie Signature Series)	20.00	40.00
(2007 SDCC Exclusive)		
5 Concept R2-D2 & C-3PO (McQuarrie Signature Series)	12.00	25.00
(2007 C4 & CE Exclusive)		
6 Darth Vader & Incinerator Troopers (The Force Unleashed)	25.00	50.00
(2008 Walmart Exclusive)		
7 Emperor Palpatine & Shadow Stormtroopers (The Force Unleashed)		
(2008 Walmart Exclusive)		
8 R2-KT	30.00	60.00
(2007 Shared Exclusive)		
9 Shadow Scout Trooper & Speeder Bike	15.00	30.00
(2007 SDCC Exclusive)		
10 Shadow Troopers 2-Pack		
(2008 Jedi-Con Exclusive)		
11 Star Wars Collector Coin		
(2007 Toy Fair Exclusive)		
12 Stormtrooper Commander	25.00	50.00
(2008 GameStop Exclusive)		

2007-08 Star Wars 30th Anniversary Collection
Force Unleashed

9	Imperial EVO Trooper	8.00	15.00
10	Imperial Jumptrooper	10.00	20.00
11a	Maris Brood (flesh)	15.00	30.00
11b	Maris Brood (white)	10.00	20.00
12	Darth Vader (battle-damaged)	10.00	20.00
13	Rahm Kota	20.00	40.00
14	Emperor's Shadow Guard	20.00	40.00
15	Juno Eclipse	10.00	20.00

2007-08 Star Wars 30th Anniversary Collection
Multi-Packs

1	Clone Pack (Battlefront II)		
	(2007 Shared Exclusive)		
2	Droid Pack (Battlefront II)	25.00	50.00
	(2007 Shared Exclusive)		
3	Clones & Commanders Gift Pack	20.00	40.00
	(Toys R Us Exclusive)		
4	I Am Your Father's Day Gift Pack (2007 Walmart Exclusive)		
5	The Max Rebo Band Jabba's Palace Entertainers	30.00	60.00
	(2007 Walmart Exclusive)		
6	The Max Rebo Band Jabba's Palace Musicians	40.00	80.00
	(2007 Walmart Exclusive)		
7	Republic Elite Forces Mandalorians & Clone Troopers		
	(2007 Entertainment Earth Exclusive)		
8	Republic Elite Forces Mandalorians & Omega Squad	75.00	150.00
	(2007 Entertainment Earth Exclusive)		

2007-08 Star Wars 30th Anniversary Collection
Revenge of the Sith

1	Obi-Wan Kenobi	6.00	12.00
2	Darth Vader	10.00	20.00
3	Clone Commander (green)	5.00	10.00
4	Kashyyyk Trooper	8.00	15.00
5	Tri-Droid	8.00	15.00
6	2-1B Surgical Droid	6.00	12.00
7	Po Nudo	8.00	15.00
8	Mustafar Panning Droid	6.00	12.00

2007-08 Star Wars 30th Anniversary Collection
Saga Legends

1	501st Legion Trooper	8.00	15.00
2	Boba Fett	15.00	30.00
3	C-3PO (w/battle droid head)	6.00	12.00
4	Chewbacca	6.00	12.00
5	Clone Trooper (AOTC)	8.00	15.00
6	Clone Trooper (ROTS)	6.00	12.00
7	Darth Maul	8.00	15.00
8	Darth Vader	8.00	15.00
9	Darth Vader (as Anakin Skywalker)	8.00	15.00
10	Destroyer Droid	6.00	12.00
11	General Grievous	12.00	25.00

12	Obi-Wan Kenobi	6.00	12.00
13	Princess Leia (Boushh disguise)	8.00	15.00
14	R2-D2 (electronic)	10.00	20.00
15	Saesee Tiin	8.00	15.00
16	Shock Trooper	10.00	20.00
17	Yoda	8.00	15.00

2007-08 Star Wars 30th Anniversary Collection
Saga Legends Battle Droid 2-Packs

1	Battle Droids 2-Pack I (tan infantry & commander)	8.00	15.00
2	Battle Droids 2-Pack II (maroon blaster and lightsaber damage)	8.00	15.00
3	Battle Droids 2-Pack III (tan blaster and lightsaber damage)	8.00	15.00
4	Battle Droids 2-Pack IV (tan dirty & clean)	8.00	15.00

2007-08 Star Wars 30th Anniversary Collection
Saga Legends Fan's Choice (2007)

1	Biker Scout	8.00	15.00
2	Biker Scout (w/Clone Wars sticker)		
3	Clone Commander (Coruscant)	12.00	25.00
4	Clone Trooper Officer (red)	8.00	15.00
5	Clone Trooper Officer (yellow)	8.00	15.00
6	Clone Trooper Officer (green)	10.00	20.00
7	Clone Trooper Officer (blue)	6.00	12.00
8	Dark Trooper (Fan's Choice Figure #1)	12.00	25.00
9	Imperial Officer (brown hair)	6.00	12.00
10	Imperial Officer (blonde hair)	8.00	15.00
11	Imperial Officer (red hair)		
12	Pit Droids 2-Pack (white)		
13	Pit Droids 2-Pack (brown)		
14	Pit Droids 2-Pack (orange)	12.00	25.00
15	R4-I9	10.00	20.00
16	RA-7	6.00	12.00
17	Sandtrooper (dirty; tan shoulder)	8.00	15.00
18	Sandtrooper (dirty; orange shoulder)	10.00	20.00
19	Sandtrooper (clean; black shoulder)	25.00	50.00
20	Sandtrooper (clean; white shoulder)	12.00	25.00
21	Sandtrooper (dirty; red shoulder)		
22	TC-14	10.00	20.00

2007-08 Star Wars 30th Anniversary Collection
Saga Legends Fan's Choice (2008)

1	501st Legion Trooper		
2	Commander Neyo	10.00	20.00
3	Covert Ops Clone Trooper (gold coin)	10.00	20.00
4	Pit Droids 2-Pack (white)	8.00	15.00
5	Pit Droids 2-Pack (maroon)	8.00	15.00
6	Pit Droids 2-Pack (orange)	8.00	15.00
7	Shadow Stormtrooper	12.00	25.00
8	Utapau Shadow Trooper	12.00	25.00
9	Zev Senesca	8.00	15.00

2007-08 Star Wars 30th Anniversary Collection
Silver Coins

1a	Darth Vader
1b	30th Anniversary Coin Album
2	Galactic Marine
3	Mustafar Lava Miner
4	R2-D2
5	Obi-Wan Kenobi
6	Mace Windu
7	Airborne Trooper
8	Super Battle Droid
9	Concept Stormtrooper (McQuarrie Signature Series)
10	Rebel Honor Guard
11	Han Solo
12	Luke Skywalker ceremony
13	Death Star Trooper
14	Biggs Darklighter
15	Concept Boba Fett (McQuarrie Signature Series)
16	Darth Vader
17	Biggs Darklighter
18	Luke Skywalker tatooine
19	Jawa & Lin Droid
20	Imperial Stormtrooper
21	Concept Chewbacca (McQuarrie Signature Series)
22	M'liyoom Onith
23	Elis Helrot
24	Boba Fett
25	Luke Skywalker
26	CZ-4
27	Umpass-Stay
28	Concept Darth Vader (McQuarrie Signature Series)
29	Hermi Odle
30	C-3PO & Salacious Crumb
31	Roron Corobb
32	Yoda & Kybuck
33	Anakin Skywalker
34	Darth Revan
35	Darth Malak
36	Pre-Cyborg Grievous
37	Concept Starkiller Hero
38	Han Solo
39	Lando Calrissian
40	General McQuarrie
41	4-LOM
42	Concept Snowtrooper (McQuarrie Signature Series)
43	Romba & Graak
44	Tycho Celchu
45	Anakin Skywalker (Jedi Spirit)
46	R2-D2
47	Concept Han Solo (McQuarrie Signature Series)
48	Darth Vader (hologram)
49	Clone Trooper (7th Legion Trooper)
50	Clone Trooper (Hawkbat Batallion)
51	R2-B1
52	Naboo Soldier
53	Rebel Vanguard Trooper
54	Pax Bonkin
55	Clone Trooper (training fatigues)
56	Padme Amidala
57	Jango Fett
58	Voolvif Monn
59	Destroyer Droid
60	Concept Rebel Trooper (McQuarrie Signature Series)

2007-08 Star Wars 30th Anniversary Collection Ultimate Galactic Hunt

1	Airborne Trooper	12.00	25.00
2	Biggs Darklighter (Rebel pilot)	7.50	15.00
3	Boba Fett (animated debut)	12.00	25.00
4	Concept Boba Fett (McQuarrie Signature Series)	20.00	40.00
5	Concept Chewbacca (McQuarrie Signature Series)	15.00	30.00
6	Concept Stormtrooper (McQuarrie Signature Series)	12.00	25.00
7	Darth Vader (Sith Lord)	10.00	20.00
8	Galactic Marine	10.00	20.00
9	Han Solo (smuggler)	7.50	15.00
10	Luke Skywalker (Yavin ceremony)	6.00	12.00
11	Mace Windu	7.50	15.00
12	R2-D2	6.00	12.00

2007-08 Star Wars 30th Anniversary Collection Ultimate Galactic Hunt Gold Coins

1	Airborne Trooper	6.00	12.00
2	Biggs Darklighter	4.00	8.00
3	Boba Fett	6.00	12.00
4	Concept Boba Fett (McQuarrie Signature Series)	10.00	20.00
5	Concept Chewbacca (McQuarrie Signature Series)	7.50	15.00
6	Concept Stormtrooper (McQuarrie Signature Series)	6.00	12.00
7	Darth Vader	5.00	10.00
8	Galactic Marine	5.00	10.00
9	Han Solo	4.00	8.00
10	Luke Skywalker	3.00	6.00
11	Mace Windu	4.00	8.00
12	R2-D2	3.00	6.00

2007-08 Star Wars 30th Anniversary Collection Vehicles

1	Aayla Secura's Jedi Starfighter	20.00	40.00
2	ARC-170 Fighter (Clone Wars)	50.00	100.00
3	AT-AP Walker	20.00	40.00
4	Anakin Skywalker's Jedi Starfighter (Coruscant)	20.00	40.00
5	Anakin Skywalker's Jedi Starfighter (Mustafar)	20.00	40.00
6	Darth Vader's Sith Starfighter	40.00	80.00
7	Darth Vader's TIE Advanced Starfighter	30.00	60.00
8	General Grievous' Starfighter	25.00	50.00
9	Hailfire Droid	25.00	50.00
10	Mace Windu's Jedi Starfighter	15.00	30.00
11	Obi-Wan's Jedi Starfighter (Coruscant)	25.00	50.00
12	Obi-Wan's Jedi Starfighter (Utapau)	25.00	50.00
13	Saesee Tiin's Jedi Starfighter	20.00	40.00
14	Sith Infiltrator	25.00	50.00
15	TIE Fighter	15.00	30.00
16	Trade Federation Armored Assault Tank (AAT)	20.00	40.00
17	V-Wing Starfighter/ spring-open wings	50.00	100.00

2007-08 Star Wars 30th Anniversary Collection Vehicles Exclusives

1	Elite TIE Inteceptor/181st Squadron TIE Pilot	75.00	150.00
	(Toys R Us exclusive)		
2	Obi-Wan's Jedi Starfighter (w/hyperspace ring)	25.00	50.00
	(2007 Toys R Us Exclusive)		
3	TIE Bomber (w/TIE Bomber Pilot)	30.00	75.00
	(2007 Target Exclusive)		
4	TIE Fighter (w/TIE Pilot/opening cockpit and ejecting wing panels)	25.00	50.00
	(2007 Toys R Us Exclusive)		
5	Y-Wing Fighter (w/Lt. Lepira & R5-F7)	75.00	150.00
	(2007 Toys R Us Exclusive)		

1998-99 Star Wars Action Collection

1	AT-AT Driver	15.00	30.00
2	Barquin D'an	10.00	20.00

3	Chewbacca in Chains	15.00	30.00
4	Emperor Palpatine	12.00	25.00
5	Grand Moff Tarkin	12.00	25.00
6	Greedo	15.00	30.00
7	Han Solo (carbonite)	15.00	30.00
	(Target Exclusive)		
8	Han Solo (Hoth)	15.00	30.00
9	Jawa	10.00	20.00
10	Luke Skywalker (ceremonial dress)		
11	Luke Skywalker (Hoth)	15.00	30.00
12	Luke Skywalker (Jedi Knight)	12.00	25.00
13	Princess Leia (Hoth)	12.00	25.00
	(Service Merchandise Exclusive)		
14	R2-D2	20.00	40.00
15	R2-D2 (detachable utility arms)	20.00	40.00
16	R5-D4	15.00	30.00
	(Walmart Exclusive)		
17	Sandtrooper (w/droid)	8.00	15.00
18	Snowtrooper	12.00	25.00
19	Snowtrooper (blue variant)		
20	Wicket	20.00	40.00
	(Walmart Exclusive)		
21	Yoda	20.00	40.00

1998-99 Star Wars Action Collection Electronic

1	Boba Fett	25.00	50.00
	(KB Toys Exclusive)		
2	Darth Vader	20.00	40.00

1998-99 Star Wars Action Collection Multi-Packs

1	C-3PO and R2-D2 2-Pack	40.00	80.00
2	Emperor Palpatine and Royal Guard 2-Pack	20.00	40.00
3	Wedge Antilles and Biggs Darklighter 2-Pack	25.00	50.00
	(FAO Schwarz Exclusive)		
4	Luke (Tatooine)/Leia (Boushh)/Han (Bespin) 3-Pack	40.00	80.00
	(KB Toys Exclusive)		
5	Luke/Han/Snowtrooper/AT-AT Driver Hoth 4-Pack	60.00	120.00
	(JC Penney Exclusive)		

2020 Star Wars Battle Bobblers

NNO C-3PO vs. Trooper
NNO R2-D2 vs. Yoda
NNO Vader vs. Luke
NNO Boba Fett vs. Han Solo
NNO Porgs vs. Chewie
NNO Stormtrooper vs. BB-8

1993 Star Wars Bend Ems

1 Admiral Ackbar	7.50	15.00
2 Ben Kenobi	10.00	20.00
3 Bib Fortuna	7.50	15.00
4 Boba Fett	15.00	30.00
5 C-3PO	10.00	20.00
6 Chewbacca	7.50	15.00
7 Darth Vader	12.50	25.00
8 Emperor	10.00	20.00
9 Emperor's Royal Guard	7.50	15.00
10 Gamorrean Guard	7.50	15.00
11 Han Solo	10.00	20.00
12 Lando Calrissian	7.50	15.00
13 Leia Organa	10.00	20.00
14 Luke Skywalker	10.00	20.00
15 Luke Skywalker X-wing	10.00	20.00
16 R2-D2	7.50	15.00
17 Stormtrooper	7.50	15.00
18 Tusken Raider	7.50	15.00
19 Wicket	7.50	15.00
20 Yoda	7.50	15.00
21 4-Piece A New Hope	20.00	40.00
(Chewbacca/Luke Skywalker/R2-D2/Tusken Raider)		
22 4-Piece Empire Strikes Back	20.00	40.00
(Han Solo/Darth Vader/Yoda/Lando Calrissian)		
23 4-Piece Return of the Jedi	25.00	50.00
(Admiral Ackbar/Boba Fett/Wicket/Bib Fortuna)		
24 4-Piece Gift Set 1	20.00	40.00
(Ben Kenobi/Leia Organa/Han Solo/C-3PO)		
25 4-Piece Gift Set 2	20.00	40.00
(Storm Trooper/Wicket/Yoda/Chewbacca)		
26 4-Piece Gift Set 3	20.00	40.00
(Storm Trooper/R2-D2/C-3PO/Darth Vader)		
27 4-Piece Gift Set 4	20.00	40.00
(Emperor/C-3PO/Luke Skywalker/Darth Vader)		
28 6-Piece Gift Set 1	25.00	50.00

(Darth Vader/Stormtrooper/Luke Skywalker/R2-D2/C-3PO)		
29 6-Piece Gift Set 2	25.00	50.00
(Stormtrooper/Darth Vader/Emperor's Royal Guard		
Admiral Ackbar/Lando Calrissian/Chewbacca)		
30 8-Piece Gift Set	25.00	50.00
(Darth Vader/Luke Skywalker/C-3PO/Emperor		
Stormtrooper/R2-D2/Princess Leia/Ewok)		
31 10-Piece Gift Set	30.00	60.00
(R2-D2/Stormtrooper/Darth Vader/Admiral Ackbar		
Chewbacca/Han Solo/Princess Leia/Luke Skywalker		
Bib Fortuna/Emperor's Royal Guard)		

2014-15 Star Wars Black Series 3.75-Inch Blue

1 R5-G19	12.50	25.00
2A Luke Skywalker Hoth	7.50	15.00
(incorrect elbow pegs)		
2B Luke Skywalker Hoth	8.00	20.00
3 Darth Vader	30.00	75.00
4 Darth Malgus	30.00	60.00
5 Starkiller	50.00	100.00
6 Yoda	12.50	25.00
(pack forward)		
7 Darth Vader	12.50	25.00
(Dagobah Test)		
8 Stormtrooper	15.00	30.00
9 Captain Rex	25.00	50.00
10 Jon Dutch Vander	10.00	20.00
11 Chewbacca	10.00	20.00
12 Clone Commander Wolffe	20.00	40.00
13 Clone Commander Doom	25.00	50.00
14 Imperial Navy Commander	15.00	30.00
15 Commander Thorn	40.00	80.00
16 C-3PO	15.00	30.00
17 Princess Leia Organa	15.00	30.00
18 Mosep Binneed	20.00	40.00
19 Han Solo	15.00	30.00
20 Jawas	25.00	50.00

2014-15 Star Wars Black Series 3.75-Inch Blue Exclusives

1 Battle on Endor 8-Pack	80.00	150.00
(Toys R Us Exclusive)		
2 Jabba's Rancor Pit	250.00	500.00

2013-14 Star Wars Black Series 3.75-Inch Orange

1 Padme Amidala	40.00	80.00
2 Clone Trooper Sergeant	20.00	40.00
3A Anakin Skywalker	15.00	30.00
3B Anakin Skywalker	20.00	40.00
4 Biggs Darklighter	15.00	30.00
5A Luke Skywalker	10.00	20.00
5B Luke Skywalker	10.00	20.00
6 Darth Vader	20.00	40.00
7 Biker Scout	12.50	25.00
8 Clone Pilot	15.00	30.00
9 R2-D2	30.00	60.00
10 Pablo-Jill	40.00	80.00
11 Luminara Unduli	20.00	40.00
12A 41st Elite Corps Clone Trooper	20.00	40.00
(incorrect markings)		
12B 41st Elite Corps Clone Trooper	12.50	25.00
(correct markings)		
13 Stormtrooper	12.50	25.00
14 Mara Jade	40.00	80.00
15 Merumeru	15.00	30.00
16 Clone Commander Neyo	20.00	40.00
17 Vizam	10.00	20.00
18 Darth Plageuis	60.00	120.00
19 Mace Windu	25.00	50.00

20 Bastila Shan	50.00	100.00
21 Luke Skywalker	12.50	25.00
22 Yoda	30.00	75.00
23 Toryn Farr	15.00	30.00
24 Snowtrooper Commander	25.00	50.00
25 Dak Ralter	30.00	60.00
26 Darth Vader	25.00	50.00
27 Jabba's Skiff Guard	15.00	30.00
28 Ree-Yees	15.00	30.00
29 Wedge Antilles	20.00	40.00
31 Republic Trooper	75.00	150.00

2013-14 Star Wars Black Series 3.75-Inch Orange Exclusives

1 Luke Skywalker Hoth Battle Gear	6.00	12.00
2 R5-D4		

2015-18 Star Wars Black Series 3.75-Inch Red

NNO Admiral Ackbar	7.50	15.00
NNO Ahsoka Tano	30.00	60.00
NNO AT-ST Driver	40.00	80.00
NNO Boba Fett (prototype fatigues)	30.00	60.00
NNO Captain Cassian Andor	8.00	20.00
NNO Captain Phasma	12.50	25.00
NNO Chewbacca	10.00	20.00
NNO Darth Vader	12.50	25.00
NNO Elite Praetorian Guard	15.00	30.00
NNO Emperor's Royal Guard	12.50	25.00
NNO Finn (Jakku)	7.50	15.00
NNO First Order Stormtrooper	7.50	15.00
NNO First Order Stormtrooper Executioner	10.00	20.00
NNO Han Solo	7.50	15.00
NNO Han Solo (Starkiller Base)	7.50	15.00
NNO Imperial Death Trooper	12.50	25.00
NNO Kylo Ren	12.50	25.00
NNO Lando Calrissian	7.50	15.00
NNO Luke Skywalker	7.50	15.00
NNO Luke Skywalker (Jedi Master)	12.50	25.00
NNO Poe Dameron	7.50	15.00
NNO Ponda Baba	7.50	15.00
NNO Princess Leia Organa	8.00	15.00
NNO Princess Leia Organa (D'Qar Gown)	15.00	30.00
NNO Rey (Jakku)	12.50	25.00
NNO Rose Tico	6.00	12.00
NNO Sandtrooper	7.50	15.00
NNO Scarif Stormtrooper Squad Leader	12.50	25.00
NNO Sentry Droid Mark IV		
NNO Sergeant Jyn Erso	6.00	12.00
NNO Tusken Raider	7.50	15.00

2015-19 Star Wars Black Series Red Vehicles

1 Special Forces TIE Fighter and Pilot Elite	125.00	250.00
2 X-34 Landspeeder (w/Luke Skywalker)	50.00	100.00
3 Rey's Speeder (Jakku)	30.00	75.00
4 Dewback & Sandtrooper	60.00	120.00
5 Enfys Nest's Swoop Bike	30.00	60.00
6 Snowspeeder (w/Dak Ralter)	100.00	200.00

2014-15 Star Wars Black Series 6-Inch Blue

1 Sandtrooper	30.00	75.00
2 Darth Vader	20.00	40.00
3 Luke Skywalker	30.00	75.00
4 Chewbacca	30.00	60.00
5 TIE Pilot	15.00	30.00
6 Yoda	15.00	30.00
7 Clone Trooper Sergeant	50.00	100.00
8 Obi-Wan Kenobi	20.00	40.00
9 Han Solo Stormtrooper	20.00	40.00
10 Bossk	50.00	100.00

ACTION FIGURES AND FIGURINES

11 Luke Skywalker	30.00	60.00
12 Emperor Palpatine	50.00	100.00
13 Clone Trooper Captain	40.00	80.00
14 IG-88	25.00	50.00
15 Princess Leia	50.00	100.00
16 Clone Commander Cody	60.00	120.00

2014-15 Star Wars Black Series 6-Inch Blue Deluxe

1 Han Solo (w/Tauntaun)	75.00	150.00
2 Jabba the Hutt	60.00	120.00
3 Luke Skywalker (w/Wampa)	75.00	150.00
4 Scout Trooper (w/Speeder Bike)	60.00	120.00

2013-20 Star Wars Black Series 6-Inch Exclusives

NNO Admiral Ackbar & First Order Officer 2-Pack	20.00	40.00
NNO Admiral Ackbar	15.00	30.00
(2017 Toys R Us Exclusive)		
NNO Admiral Piett	12.50	25.00
(2019 Walgreens Exclusive)		
NNO Astromech 3-Pack	100.00	200.00
NNO Boba Fett (carbonized)	30.00	60.00
(2020 Fan Channel Exclusive)		
NNO Boba Fett (Prototype Armor)	25.00	50.00
(2014 Walgreens Exclusive)		
NNO Boba Fett and Han Solo in Carbonite	150.00	300.00
NNO C-3PO & Babu Frik	30.00	60.00
(2019 Target Exclusive)		
NNO C-3PO	20.00	40.00
NNO Cantina Showdown	75.00	150.00
NNO Captain Cardinal	50.00	100.00
(2020 Target Exclusive)		
NNO Captain Phasma (Quicksilver Baton)	15.00	30.00
NNO Captain Rex	125.00	250.00
NNO Chewbacca & C-3PO	40.00	80.00
(2019 Amazon Exclusive)		
NNO Chewbacca	20.00	40.00
(2018 Target Exclusive)		
NNO Clone Commander Obi-Wan Kenobi	60.00	120.00
(2019 Walgreens Exclusive)		
NNO Commander Fox	75.00	150.00
(2019 GameStop Exclusive)		
NNO Commander Gree	30.00	60.00
NNO Commander Wolffe	20.00	40.00
(2017 Disney Store Exclusive)		
NNO Darth Maul (Jedi Duel)	100.00	200.00
NNO Darth Vader (carbonized)	20.00	40.00
(2020 Amazon Exclusive)		
NNO Darth Vader Emperor's Wrath	15.00	30.00
(2015 Walgreen's Exclusive)		
NNO DJ R-3X	25.00	50.00
(2020 Target Exclusive)		
NNO Elite Praetorian Guard (w/heavy blade)	30.00	60.00
NNO Elite Snowtrooper (Collector Mystery Box)	30.00	75.00
(2019 Target Exclusive)		
NNO Emperor Palpatine and Throne	150.00	300.00
NNO First Order Jet Trooper (carbonized)	15.00	30.00
(2019 Walmart Exclusive)		
NNO First Order Officer	10.00	20.00
(2017 Toys R Us Exclusive)		
NNO First Order Snowtrooper Officer	20.00	40.00
NNO First Order Stormtrooper (w/extra gear)	25.00	50.00
NNO First Order Stormtrooper Executioner	10.00	20.00
(2017 Target Exclusive)		
NNO First Order Stormtrooper Officer	25.00	50.00
NNO Gamorrean Guard	30.00	60.00
NNO General Veers	25.00	50.00
NNO Grand Admiral Thrawn	150.00	300.00
NNO Guards 4-Pack	75.00	150.00

NNO Han Solo & Princess Leia Organa	50.00	100.00
NNO Han Solo (Exogorth Escape)	50.00	100.00
NNO Heavy Battle Droid	15.00	30.00
(2020 GameStop Exclusive)		
NNO Hondo Ohnaka	25.00	50.00
(2020 Target Exclusive)		
NNO IG-11	25.00	50.00
(2019 Best Buy Exclusive)		
NNO Imperial AT-ACT Driver	30.00	75.00
NNO Imperial Forces 4-Pack	75.00	150.00
NNO Imperial Hovertank Pilot	20.00	40.00
NNO Imperial Jumptrooper	30.00	60.00
NNO Imperial Shadow Squadron	125.00	250.00
NNO Imperial Shock Trooper	30.00	60.00
NNO Inferno Squad Agent	15.00	30.00
NNO Jabba's Throne Room	200.00	400.00
NNO Jango Fett (Gaming Greats)	25.00	50.00
(2020 GameStop Exclusive)		
NNO Jedi Knight Revan	30.00	75.00
(2020 GameStop Exclusive)		
NNO Kylo Ren (throne room)	25.00	50.00
NNO Kylo Ren (unmasked)	75.00	150.00
NNO Kylo Ren	15.00	30.00
(2015 K-Mart Exclusive)		
NNO Luke Skywalker (Ceremonial Outfit)	15.00	30.00
(2019 Convention Exclusive)		
NNO Luke Skywalker (Death Star Escape)	20.00	40.00
NNO Luke Skywalker (Jedi Knight)	50.00	100.00
(2019 Walmart Exclusive)		
NNO Luke Skywalker (Skywalker Strikes)	20.00	40.00
(2019 Fan Channel Exclusive)		
NNO Luke Skywalker (w/Ach-to base)	15.00	30.00
(2017 Target Exclusive)		
NNO Luke Skywalker X-Wing Pilot	125.00	250.00
NNO Mandalorian (carbonized)	25.00	50.00
(2020 Target Exclusive)		
NNO Moloch	25.00	50.00
NNO Mountain Trooper	15.00	30.00
(2020 Target Exclusive)		
NNO Obi-Wan Kenobi (Jedi Duel)	75.00	150.00
NNO Obi-Wan Kenobi	75.00	150.00
NNO Obi-Wan Kenobi (Force spirit)	20.00	40.00
NNO Phase II Clone Trooper 4-Pack	40.00	80.00
NNO Poe Dameron and Riot Control Stormtrooper	20.00	40.00
(2015 Target Exclusive)		
NNO Princess Leia (Bespin Escape)	25.00	50.00
NNO Purge Stormtrooper	20.00	40.00
(2019 GameStop Exclusive)		
NNO Red Squadron 3-Pack	60.00	120.00
(2018 Amazon Exclusive)		
NNO Resistance Tech Rose	15.00	30.00
NNO Rey (Jedi Training) & Luke Skywalker (Jedi Master) 2-Pack	35.00	70.00
NNO Rey (Starkiller Base)	15.00	30.00
NNO Rey (w/Crait base)#[(2017 Toys R Us Exclusive)	15.00	30.00
NNO Rogue One 3-Pack	30.00	60.00
NNO Scarif Stormtrooper	15.00	30.00
(2016 Walmart Exclusive)		
NNO Second Sister Inquisitor (carbonized)	25.00	50.00
(2019 GameStop Exclusive)		
NNO Sergeant Jyn Erso (Eadu)	12.50	25.00
NNO Sergeant Jyn Erso	40.00	80.00
NNO Shadow Stormtrooper	15.00	30.00
(2020 GameStop Exclusive)		
NNO Sith Trooper (carbonized)	50.00	100.00
(2019 Amazon Exclusive)		
NNO Sith Trooper (multiple weapons)	40.00	80.00
NNO Stormtrooper (carbonized)	20.00	40.00
(2020 Fan Channel Exclusive)		
NNO Stormtrooper (Mimban)	25.00	50.00
NNO Stormtrooper (w/blast accessories)	50.00	100.00
(2018 Toys R Us International Exclusive)		

NNO Stormtrooper Commander	20.00	40.00
(2020 GameStop Exclusive)		
NNO Stormtrooper Evolution 4-Pack	50.00	100.00
(2015 Amazon Exclusive)		
NNO Supreme Leader Snoke (Throne Room)	30.00	60.00
NNO X-34 Landspeeder (w/Luke Skywalker)	60.00	120.00
NNO Yoda (Force spirit)	25.00	50.00
(2019 Walmart Exclusive)		
NNO Zuckuss	15.00	30.00

2018-20 Star Wars Black Series 6-Inch Multi-Packs

NNO The Child (w/frog and bowl)		
NNO Porgs 2-Pack	10.00	20.00

2019 Star Wars Black Series 6-Inch Multipacks

NNO Droid Depot 4-Pack	50.00	100.00
NNO First Order 4-Pack	60.00	120.00
NNO Smuggler's Run 5-Pack	50.00	100.00

2013-14 Star Wars Black Series 6-Inch Orange

1 Luke Skywalker X-Wing Pilot	25.00	50.00
2 Darth Maul	40.00	80.00
3 Sandtrooper	30.00	75.00
4 R2-D2	50.00	100.00
5 Princess Leia Organa (Slave attire)	75.00	150.00
6 Boba Fett	40.00	80.00
7 Greedo	50.00	100.00
8 Han Solo	20.00	40.00
9 Stormtrooper	30.00	60.00
10 Obi-Wan Kenobi	25.00	50.00
11 Luke Skywalker Bespin Gear	20.00	40.00
12 Anakin Skywalker	60.00	120.00
13 Clone Trooper	25.00	50.00

2015-20 Star Wars Black Series 6-Inch Red

1A Finn Jakku	12.00	25.00
(Glossy Head)		
1B Finn Jakku	12.00	25.00
(Matte Head)		
2A Rey and BB-8	12.00	25.00
(Clean)		
2B Rey and BB-8	12.00	25.00
(Dirty)		
3 Kylo Ren	10.00	20.00
4 First Order Stormtrooper	10.00	20.00
5 Chewbacca	10.00	20.00
6 Captain Phasma	20.00	40.00
7 Poe Dameron	10.00	20.00
8 Guavian Enforcer	12.00	25.00
9A Constable Zuvio	10.00	20.00
(green helmet)		
9B Constable Zuvio	10.00	20.00
(brown helmet)		
10A Resistance Soldier	20.00	40.00
(green helmet)		
10B Resistance Soldier	10.00	20.00
(brown helmet)		
11 First Order TIE Fighter Pilot	15.00	30.00
12 First Order Snowtrooper	12.00	25.00
13 First Order General Hux	15.00	30.00
14 X-Wing Pilot Asty	15.00	30.00
15 Jango Fett	10.00	20.00
16 First Order Flametrooper	10.00	20.00
17 Finn (FN-2187)	20.00	40.00
18 Han Solo	12.00	25.00
19 Kanan Jarrus	15.00	30.00
20 Ahsoka Tano	20.00	40.00
21 Luke Skywalker	10.00	20.00

22 Sergeant Jyn Erso (Jedha)	15.00	30.00
23 Captain Cassian Andor (Eadu)	10.00	20.00
24 K-2SO	12.50	25.00
25 Imperial Death Trooper	12.50	25.00
26 Kylo Ren (unmasked)	12.50	25.00
27 Director Krennic	10.00	20.00
28 Scarif Stormtrooper Squad Leader	20.00	40.00
29 C-3PO (Resistance Base)	10.00	20.00
30 Princess Leia Organa	12.50	25.00
31 AT-AT Pilot/AT-AT Driver	20.00	40.00
32 Obi-Wan Kenobi	15.00	30.00
33 Sabine Wren	25.00	50.00
34 Darth Revan	20.00	40.00
35 Snowtrooper	10.00	20.00
36 Chirrut Imwe	20.00	40.00
37 Baze Malbus	15.00	30.00
38 Imperial Royal Guard	10.00	20.00
39 Lando Calrissian	12.50	25.00
40 Qui-Gon Jinn	15.00	30.00
41 Tusken Raider	15.00	30.00
42 Hera Syndulla	20.00	40.00
43 Darth Vader	12.50	25.00
44 Rey (Jedi Training)	12.50	25.00
45 Kylo Ren	12.50	25.00
46 Luke Skywalker (Jedi Master)	12.50	25.00
47 Grand Admiral Thrawn	25.00	50.00
48 Stormtrooper	15.00	30.00
49 Maz Kanata	10.00	20.00
50 Elite Praetorian Guard	15.00	30.00
51 Finn (First Order Disguise)	10.00	20.00
52 General Leia Organa	12.50	25.00
53 Poe Dameron	10.00	20.00
54 Supreme Leader Snoke	12.50	25.00
55 Rose Tico	10.00	20.00
56 Jaina Solo	20.00	40.00
57 DJ	10.00	20.00
58 Rey	10.00	20.00
59 Captain Rex	30.00	75.00
60 Death Squad Commander	15.00	30.00
61 Jawa	10.00	20.00
62 Han Solo	12.50	25.00
63 Grand Moff Tark (w/IT-O Droid)	20.00	40.00
64 Range Trooper	10.00	20.00
65 Lando Calrissian	12.50	25.00
66 Qi'Ra	12.50	25.00
67 4-LOM	25.00	50.00
68 Tobias Beckett	20.00	40.00
69 Rebel Fleet Trooper	20.00	40.00
70 Han Solo (Bespin)	12.50	25.00
71 Val (Vandor-1)	10.00	20.00
72 Imperial Patrol Trooper	12.50	25.00
73 L3-37	12.50	25.00
74 Dengar	30.00	60.00
75 Princess Leia Organa (Hoth)	10.00	20.00
76 Lando Calrissian (Skiff)	12.50	25.00
77 Rio Durant	10.00	20.00
78 Han Solo (Mimban)	25.00	50.00
79 Dryden Vos	15.00	30.00
80 Vice Admiral Holdo	10.00	20.00
81 Padme Amidala	10.00	20.00
82 Mace Windu	12.50	25.00
83 Battle Droid	25.00	50.00
84 Chopper (C1-10P)	25.00	50.00
85 Obi-Wan Kenobi (Padawan)	30.00	75.00
86 Ezra Bridger	50.00	100.00
87 Doctor Aphra	75.00	150.00
88 BT-1 (Beetee)	25.00	50.00

89 0-0-0 (Triple Zero)	60.00	120.00
90A Supreme Leader Kylo Ren	25.00	50.00
90B Supreme Leader Kylo Ren	25.00	50.00
(Triple Force Friday First Edition)		
91A Rey & D-0	12.50	25.00
91B Rey & D-0	25.00	50.00
(Triple Force Friday First Edition)		
92A Sith Trooper	12.50	25.00
92B Sith Trooper	25.00	50.00
(Triple Force Friday First Edition)		
93A Cal Kestis (w/BD-1)	40.00	80.00
93B Cal Kestis (w/BD-1)	60.00	120.00
(Triple Force Friday First Edition)		
94A The Mandalorian	25.00	50.00
94B The Mandalorian	100.00	200.00
(Triple Force Friday First Edition)		
95A Second Sister Inquisitor	40.00	80.00
95B Second Sister Inquisitor	50.00	100.00
(Triple Force Friday First Edition)		
96A Offworld Jawa	15.00	30.00
96B Offworld Jawa	25.00	50.00
(Triple Force Friday First Edition)		
97A First Order Stormtrooper (w/riot gear)	17.50	35.00
97B First Order Stormtrooper (w/riot gear)	20.00	40.00
(Triple Force Friday First Edition)		
98 Jannah	8.00	20.00
99 First Order Jet Trooper	12.50	25.00
100A Luke Skywalkwer (Yavin Ceremony)	12.50	25.00
ERR (misspelled last name)		
100B Luke Skywalker (Yavin Ceremony)	12.50	25.00
COR		
101 Cara Dune	60.00	120.00
102 Wedge Antilles	15.00	30.00
103 Zorii Bliss	12.50	25.00
104 Commander Bly	20.00	40.00
105 Knight of Ren	20.00	40.00
106 Sith Jet Trooper	15.00	30.00
107 Count Dooku (AOTC)	25.00	50.00
108 Battle Droid (Geonosis)	20.00	40.00
109 Plo Koon	25.00	50.00
110 Anakin Skywalker (Padawan)	15.00	30.00
111 Obi-Wan Kenobi (Jedi Knight)	20.00	40.00
112 Kit Fisto	20.00	40.00

2017 Star Wars Black Series 40th Anniversary 6-Inch

NNO Artoo Detoo	30.00	60.00
NNO Ben (Obi-Wan) Kenobi	25.00	50.00
NNO Chewbacca	30.00	60.00
NNO Darth Vader Legacy Pack	20.00	40.00
NNO Death Squad Commander	15.00	30.00
NNO Han Solo	25.00	50.00
NNO Jawa	20.00	40.00
NNO Luke Skywalker	20.00	40.00
NNO Luke Skywalker X-Wing Pilot	100.00	200.00
NNO Princess Leia Organa	15.00	30.00
NNO R5-D4	25.00	50.00
NNO Sand People	30.00	60.00
NNO See Threepio	25.00	50.00
NNO Stormtrooper	30.00	60.00

2017 Star Wars Black Series 40th Anniversary Titanium Series 3.75-Inch

1 Darth Vader	15.00	30.00
2 Obi-Wan Kenobi	12.00	25.00
3 Luke Skywalker	12.00	25.00
4 Princess Leia Organa	12.00	25.00
5 Han Solo	15.00	30.00

2019-21 Star Wars Black Series Archive

NNO 501st Legion Clone Trooper	45.00	90.00
NNO Anakin Skywalker	75.00	150.00
NNO Boba Fett	50.00	100.00
NNO Bossk	40.00	80.00
NNO Clone Commander Cody	30.00	60.00
NNO Darth Maul	30.00	75.00
NNO Darth Revan	40.00	80.00
NNO Grand Admiral Thrawn	20.00	40.00
NNO Han Solo (Hoth)	15.00	30.00
NNO IG-88	25.00	50.00
NNO Imperial Death Trooper	20.00	40.00
NNO Imperial Hovertank Driver	15.00	30.00
NNO Luke Skywalker (Hoth)	12.50	25.00
NNO Luke Skywalker (X-Wing)	10.00	25.00
NNO Obi-Wan Kenobi	20.00	40.00
NNO Princess Leia Organa	30.00	60.00
NNO Scout Trooper	25.00	50.00
NNO Shoretrooper	20.00	40.00
NNO Tusken Raider	15.00	30.00
NNO Yoda	15.00	30.00

2020 Star Wars Black Series Attack of the Clones 6-Inch

1 Clone Trooper (blue)	30.00	60.00
(Walgreens Exclusive)		
2 Clone Trooper	25.00	50.00

2020 Star Wars Black Series The Bad Batch 6-Inch

1 Hunter	20.00	40.00
2 Crosshair	25.00	50.00
3 Elite Squad Trooper	15.00	30.00
5 Wrecker	40.00	80.00

2017-18 Star Wars Black Series Centerpieces

NNO Rey vs. Kylo Ren	100.00	200.00
1 Darth Vader	30.00	60.00
2 Luke Skywalker	20.00	40.00
3 Kylo Ren	20.00	40.00
4 Rey	30.00	60.00

2020-21 Star Wars Black Series The Clone Wars 6-Inch

1 Clone Trooper	25.00	50.00
2 Ahsoka Tano	40.00	80.00
3 332nd Ahsoka's Clone Trooper	30.00	60.00
4 Mandalorian Loyalist	25.00	50.00
5 Mandalorian Super Commando	30.00	75.00
6 Cad Bane	30.00	60.00
7 Asajj Ventress	20.00	40.00
8 Aurra Sing	25.00	50.00
9 212th Battalion Clone Trooper		

2019-20 Star Wars Black Series Deluxe

D1 General Grievous	40.00	80.00
D2 Heavy Infantry Mandalorian	20.00	40.00
D3 Imperial Probe Droid	25.00	50.00
D4 Luke Skywalker & Yoda (Jedi Training)	20.00	40.00

2020-21 Star Wars Black Series Empire Strikes Back 6-Inch

1 Darth Vader	30.00	60.00
2 Luke Skywalker	20.00	40.00
3 Hoth Rebel Trooper	15.00	30.00

2020 Star Wars Black Series Empire Strikes Back 40th Anniversary 6-Inch

NNO 4-LOM	20.00	40.00
NNO Artoo-Detoo (R2-D2) (Dagobah)	25.00	50.00
NNO AT-AT Driver	15.00	30.00
NNO Boba Fett	30.00	60.00
NNO Boba Fett	150.00	300.00
(SDCC Kenner Tribute Exclusive)		
NNO Chewbacca	25.00	50.00
NNO Darth Vader	20.00	40.00
NNO Han Solo (Bespin)	15.00	30.00
NNO Han Solo (Carbonite)	30.00	60.00
NNO Imperial Snowtrooper (Hoth)	20.00	40.00
NNO Imperial TIE Fighter Pilot	12.50	25.00
NNO Lando Calrissian	12.50	25.00
NNO Luke Skywalker (Bespin)	12.50	25.00
NNO Luke Skywalker (Dagobah)	15.00	30.00
NNO Luke Skywalker (Snowspeeder)	15.00	30.00
NNO Princess Leia Organa (Hoth)	15.00	30.00
NNO Rebel Soldier (Hoth)	12.50	25.00
NNO Yoda	15.00	30.00
NNO Zuckuss	15.00	30.00

2020-22 Star Wars Black Series Exclusives 6-Inch

NNO Anakin Skywalker	25.00	50.00
(Target Exclusive)		
NNO ARC Trooper Captain		
(Walmart Exclusive)		
NNO Armorer	50.00	100.00
(Hasbro Pulse Exclusive)		
NNO Battle Droid	15.00	30.00
(Best Buy Exclusive)		
NNO Boba Fett (Droids)		
(Target Exclusive)		
NNO Cad Bane (w/Todo 360)	75.00	150.00
(Hasbro Pulse Exclusive)		
NNO Clone Pilot Hawk	20.00	40.00
(Target Exclusive)		
NNO Clone Trooper Echo	20.00	40.00
(Target Exclusive)		
NNO General Grievous		
(Walmart Exclusive)		
NNO George Lucas (in stormtrooper disguise)		
(Fan Channel Exclusive)		
NNO Greedo (classic)		
(Amazon Exclusive)		
NNO Greedo		

(Hasbro Pulse Exclusive)		
NNO Han Solo		
(Hasbro Pulse Exclusive)		
NNO Jar Jar Binks		
(Best Buy Exclusive)		
NNO Jawa		
(Amazon Exclusive)		
NNO Luke Skywalker		
(Hasbro Pulse Exclusive)		
NNO Mace Windu		
(Best Buy Exclusive)		
NNO Mace Windu		
(Walmart Exclusive)		
NNO Obi-Wan Kenobi	20.00	40.00
(Amazon Exclusive)		
NNO Obi-Wan Kenobi	30.00	75.00
(Target Exclusive)		
NNO Princess Leia Organa		
(Hasbro Pulse Exclusive)		
NNO Qui-Gon Jinn		
(Best Buy Exclusive)		
NNO Trapper Wolf		
(Hasbro Pulse Exclusive)		

2020 Star Wars Black Series Holiday Edition 6-Inch

NNO Clone Trooper w/Porg GS	25.00	50.00
NNO Imperial Stormtrooper w/Porg AMZ	30.00	60.00
NNO Range Trooper w/D-0 TAR	20.00	40.00
NNO Sith Trooper w/Babu-Frik BB	25.00	50.00
NNO Snowtrooper w/Porg WM	25.00	50.00

2020-21 Star Wars Black Series The Mandalorian 6-Inch

1 The Mandalorian	25.00	50.00
2 Stormtrooper	20.00	40.00
3 Incinerator Stormtrooper	30.00	60.00
4 The Armorer	15.00	30.00
5 Din Djarin w/Grogu	40.00	80.00
(Target Exclusive)		
6 Greef Karga	15.00	30.00
7 Kuiil	15.00	30.00
8 Moff Gideon	15.00	30.00
9 Stormtrooper	30.00	60.00
(Target Exclusive)		
10 Bo-Katan Kryze	20.00	40.00
11 Q9-0	20.00	40.00

2020-21 Star Wars Black Series The Mandalorian 6-Inch Vehicles

NNO Speeder Bike Scout Trooper & The Child	60.00	120.00

2020-21 Star Wars Black Series The Mandalorian Credit Collection 6-Inch

NNO Armorer		
(GameStop Exclusive)		
NNO Cara Dune	30.00	60.00
(Target Exclusive)		
NNO Din Djarin		
(Amazon Exclusive)		
NNO Greef Karga		
(Fan Channel Exclusive)		
NNO Heavy Infantry Mandalorian	30.00	60.00
(Best Buy Exclusive)		
NNO IG-11	15.00	30.00
(GameStop Exclusive)		
NNO Imperial Death Trooper	15.00	30.00
(Amazon Exclusive)		
NNO Kuiil		
(Amazon Exclusive)		
NNO The Mandalorian (Din Djarin)	20.00	40.00

(Amazon Exclusive)		
NNO Moff Gideon		
(Best Buy Exclusive)		

2020 Star Wars Black Series The Phantom Menace 6-Inch

1 Jar Jar Binks	12.50	25.00

2020 Star Wars Black Series Rebels 6-Inch

1 Garazeb "Zeb" Orrelios	25.00	50.00
2 C1-10P "Chopper"	30.00	75.00
3 Ezra Bridger	30.00	60.00
4 Kanan Jarrus	20.00	40.00
5 Hera Syndulla	25.00	50.00
6 Sabine Wren	25.00	50.00
7 Ahsoka Tano	30.00	60.00

2020-21 Star Wars Black Series Return of the Jedi 6-Inch

1 Admiral Ackbar	15.00	30.00
2 Teebo	20.00	40.00
3 Princess Leia Organa (Endor)	20.00	40.00
4 Luke Skywalker (Endor)	20.00	40.00
5 Han Solo (Endor)	17.50	35.00
6 Boba Fett	20.00	40.00
7 Lando Calrissian		
8 Bib Fortuna		

2020 Star Wars Black Series The Rise of Skywalker 6-Inch

1 Dark Rey	20.00	40.00

2013-16 Star Wars Black Series Titanium Series

1 Millennium Falcon	10.00	20.00
2 Resistance X-Wing	8.00	15.00
3A Kylo Ren's Command Shuttle	6.00	12.00
3B Kylo Ren Command Shuttle (black)	6.00	12.00
4 First Order Special Forces Tie Fighter	6.00	12.00
5 Rey's Speeder (Jakku)	10.00	20.00
6 First Order Star Destroyer	8.00	15.00
7 X-Wing	12.00	25.00
8 Y-Wing	15.00	30.00
9 Luke Skywalker Landspeeder	10.00	20.00
10 Slave I	12.00	25.00
11 First Order Snowspeeder	5.00	10.00
12 Poe's X-Wing Fighter	5.00	10.00
13 First Order Tie Fighter	4.00	8.00
14 First Order Transporter	4.00	8.00
15 Tie Advanced	5.00	10.00
16 B-Wing	12.00	25.00
17 Snowspeeder	8.00	15.00
18 AT-AT	30.00	60.00
19 Jakku Landspeeder	8.00	15.00
20 A-Wing	15.00	30.00
21 Sith Infiltrator	8.00	15.00
22 Anakin Skywalker's Jedi Starfighter	12.00	30.00
23 Republic Gunship	12.00	25.00
24 Star Destroyer	6.00	12.00
25 Imperial Shuttle	30.00	60.00
26 The Ghost	6.00	12.00
27 Jango Fett's Slave I	8.00	15.00
28 Inquisitor's Tie Advanced Prototype	6.00	12.00
29 Rebel U-Wing Fighter	8.00	15.00
30 TIE Striker	8.00	15.00
31 Imperial Cargo Shuttle SW-0608	8.00	15.00

2003-05 Star Wars Clone Wars

NNO	Anakin Skywalker	6.00	12.00
NNO	ARC Trooper (blue)	5.00	10.00
NNO	ARC Trooper (blue w/gray shoulder pad and thick blue chin paint)	5.00	10.00
NNO	ARC Trooper (red)	5.00	10.00
NNO	Yoda	5.00	10.00
NNO	Obi-Wan Kenobi (General of The Republic Army)	4.00	8.00
NNO	Durge Commander of the Seperatist Forces	10.00	20.00
NNO	Asajj Ventress (Sith Apprentice)	5.00	10.00
NNO	Mace Windu (General of the Republic Army)	5.00	10.00
NNO	Kit Fisto	8.00	15.00
NNO	Clone Trooper (facing left)	8.00	15.00
NNO	Clone Trooper (facing right)	30.00	60.00
NNO	Saesee Tiin	8.00	15.00

2003-05 Star Wars Clone Wars Deluxe

1	Clone Trooper (w/speeder bike)	8.00	15.00
2	Spider Droid	6.00	12.00
3	Durge (w/swoop bike)	15.00	30.00

2003-05 Star Wars Clone Wars Multipacks

NNO	Clone Trooper Army	8.00	15.00
NNO	Clone Trooper Army (w/blue lieutenant)	10.00	20.00
NNO	Clone Trooper Army (w/green sergeant)	8.00	15.00
NNO	Clone Trooper Army (w/red captain)	8.00	15.00
NNO	Clone Trooper Army (w/yellow commander)	8.00	15.00
NNO	Droid Army	6.00	12.00
NNO	Jedi Knight Army	6.00	12.00

2003-05 Star Wars Clone Wars Value Packs

NNO	Anakin Skywalker/Clone Trooper (blue)	5.00	10.00
NNO	ARC Trooper/Clone Trooper	10.00	20.00
NNO	Yoda/Clone Trooper (yellow)	5.00	10.00

2003-05 Star Wars Clone Wars Vehicles

NNO	Anakin Skywalker's Jedi Starfighter	25.00	50.00
NNO	Armored Assault/ Tank (AAT)	50.00	100.00
NNO	Command Gunship	30.00	75.00
NNO	Geonosian Starfighter	15.00	30.00
NNO	Hailfire Droid	12.00	25.00
NNO	Jedi Starfighter	15.00	30.00

2003-05 Star Wars Clone Wars Animated Series

NNO	Anakin Skywalker	12.50	25.00
NNO	Anakin Skywalker (no sleeves torn pants)	5.00	12.00
NNO	ARC Trooper		
NNO	Asajj Ventress	12.50	25.00
NNO	Clone Trooper	5.00	10.00
NNO	Clone Trooper (blue)	12.00	30.00
NNO	Clone Trooper (red)		
NNO	Clone Trooper (yellow)	6.00	12.00
NNO	Count Dooku	5.00	10.00
NNO	Durge	5.00	10.00
NNO	General Grievous		
NNO	Mace Windu	5.00	10.00
NNO	Obi-Wan Kenobi		
NNO	Yoda		

2003-05 Star Wars Clone Wars Animated Series Commemorative DVD Collection

NNO	Volume 1 Jedi Force (Anakin Skywalker/ARC Trooper/Obi-Wan Kenobi)	15.00	30.00
NNO	Volume 1 Sith Attack (Asojj Ventress/Durge/General Grievous)	12.00	25.00
NNO	Volume 2 (Anakin Skywalker tattoo Clone Trooper/Saesee Tiin)		
NNO	Volume 2 (Clone Commander Cody General Grievous/Obi-Wan Kenobi)		

2003-05 Star Wars Clone Wars Animated Series Maquettes

NNO	ARC Trooper Captain	
NNO	Anakin Skywalker	
NNO	Asajj Ventress	
NNO	Bariss Offee & Luminara Unduli	
NNO	General Grievous	
NNO	Obi-Wan Kenobi	
NNO	Padme Amidala	
NNO	Yoda	

2008-13 Star Wars The Clone Wars Battle Packs

NNO	Ambush at Abregado	30.00	75.00
NNO	Ambush on the Vulture's Claw	30.00	75.00
NNO	Anti-Hailfire Droid Squad	30.00	75.00
NNO	ARC Troopers	120.00	250.00
NNO	Army of the Republic		
NNO	Assault on Ryloth	30.00	60.00
NNO	Assault on Geonosis	15.00	30.00
NNO	AT-TE Assault Squad	20.00	40.00
NNO	Battle of Orto Plutonia	15.00	30.00
NNO	B'omarr Monastery Assault	30.00	60.00
NNO	Cad Bane's Escape	30.00	60.00
NNO	Capture of the Droids	12.50	25.00
NNO	Clone Troopers & Droids	25.00	50.00
NNO	Defend Kamino	75.00	150.00
NNO	Holocron Heist	20.00	40.00
NNO	Hunt for Grievous	25.00	50.00
NNO	Jabba's Palace	15.00	30.00
NNO	Jedi Showdown	20.00	40.00
NNO	Mandalorian Warriors	75.00	150.00
NNO	Republic Troopers	30.00	75.00
NNO	Rishi Moon Outpost Attack	50.00	100.00
NNO	Speeder Bike Recon	15.00	30.00
NNO	Stop the Zillo Beast	20.00	40.00

2008-13 Star Wars The Clone Wars Battle Packs Exclusives

1	Assassin Spider Droid & Clones (Toys R Us Exclusive)		
2	Battle of Christophsis (ultimate) (2008 Target Exclusive)	90.00	175.00
3	Darth Maul Returns (2012 Target Exclusive)	25.00	50.00
4	Hidden Enemy (w/DVD) (2010 Target Exclusive)	30.00	75.00
5	Hostage Crisis (w/DVD) (Target Exclusive)	15.00	30.00
6	Obi-Wan & 212th Attack Battalion (2008 Target Exclusive)	50.00	100.00
7	Rise of Boba Fett (ultimate) (2010 Toys R Us Exclusive)	120.00	250.00
8	Yoda & Coruscant Guard (2008 Target Exclusive)	30.00	60.00

2008-13 Star Wars The Clone Wars Blue and Black

CW1	Captain Rex	12.50	25.00
CW2	Obi-Wan Kenobi	10.00	20.00
CW3	Clone Commander Cody	7.50	15.00
CW4	Destroyer Droid	7.50	15.00
CW5	Yoda	7.50	15.00
CW6	Count Dooku	10.00	20.00
CW7	Anakin Skywalker	10.00	20.00
CW8	Pre Vizsla	15.00	30.00
CW9	Mandalorian Police Officer	6.00	12.00
CW10	General Grievous	15.00	30.00
CW11	Aurra Sing	12.50	25.00
CW12	Captain Rex (cold weather gear)	12.50	25.00
CW13	Cad Bane	10.00	20.00
CW14	Clone Pilot Odd Ball	12.50	25.00
CW15	Asajj Ventress	20.00	40.00
CW16	Super Battle Droid	10.00	20.00
CW17	Ahsoka Tano	20.00	40.00
CW18	ARF Trooper	12.50	25.00
CW19	Battle Droid	10.00	20.00
CW20	Mace Windu	10.00	20.00
CW21	Commander Gree	15.00	30.00
CW22	Battle Droid Commander	15.00	30.00
CW23	Kit Fisto	10.00	20.00
CW24	ARF Trooper (jungle deco)	12.50	25.00
CW25	Ki-Adi-Mundi	12.50	25.00
CW26	Clone Trooper (flamethrower)	15.00	30.00
CW27	R2-D2	8.00	15.00
CW28	Clone Pilot Goji	15.00	30.00
CW29	Mandalorian Warrior	25.00	50.00
CW30	R4-P17	10.00	20.00
CW31	Shaak Ti	20.00	40.00
CW32	Boba Fett	10.00	20.00
CW33	Embo	15.00	30.00
CW34	Undead Geonosian	7.50	15.00
CW35	Clone Trooper Draa	20.00	40.00
CW36	Quinlan Vos	15.00	30.00
CW37	Cato Parasiti	10.00	20.00
CW38	Clone Commander Jet	25.00	50.00
CW39	Hondo Ohnaka	20.00	40.00
CW40	Obi-Wan Kenobi (new outfit)	10.00	20.00
CW41	Clone Trooper Hevy (training armor)	12.50	25.00
CW42	Cad Bane (w/TODO-360)	15.00	30.00
CW43	R7-A7	12.50	25.00
CW44	Ahsoka (new outfit)	60.00	120.00
CW45	Anakin Skywalker (new outfit)	12.50	25.00
CW46	Aqua Battle Droid	7.50	15.00
CW47	El-Les	12.50	25.00

CW48	Clone Commander Wolffe	30.00	75.00
CW49	Riot Control Clone Trooper	25.00	50.00
CW50	Barriss Offee	20.00	40.00
CW51	Eeth Koth	20.00	40.00
CW52	Clone Commander Colt	60.00	120.00
CW53	Plo Koon (cold weather gear)	7.50	15.00
CW54	Saesee Tin	25.00	50.00
CW55	Savage Opress (shirtless)	12.50	25.00
CW56	ARF Trooper (Kamino)	20.00	40.00
CW57	Stealth Ops Clone Trooper	15.00	30.00
CW58	Even Piell	25.00	50.00
CW59	Savage Opress (armored apprentice)	30.00	60.00
CW60	Kit Fisto (cold weather gear)	12.50	25.00
CW61	Seripas	30.00	60.00
CW62	Captain Rex (jet propulsion pack)	30.00	75.00
CW63	Chewbacca	10.00	20.00
CW64	R7-D4 (Plo Koon's astromech droid)	7.50	15.00
CW65	Jar Jar Binks	10.00	20.00

2008-13 Star Wars The Clone Wars Blue and White

1	Anakin Skywalker		
2	Obi-Wan Kenobi		
3	Yoda		
4	Captain Rex		
5	Clone Trooper		
6	General Grievous		
7	Battle Droid		
8	R2-D2		
9	Ahsoka Tano		
10	Clone Commander Cody		
11	Clone Pilot Odd Ball		
12	Super Battle Droid	15.00	30.00
13	Count Dooku		
14	Plo Koon	10.00	20.00
15	Asajj Ventress		
16	C-3PO	6.00	12.00
17	Destroyer Droid	7.50	15.00
18	IG-86 Assassin Droid		
19	Clone Trooper (212th Attack Battalion)		
20	Padme Amidala (diplomat)		
21	Clone Trooper (space gear)		
22	Magnaguard	10.00	20.00
23	R3-S6 (Goldie)		
24	Jar Jar Binks		
25	Rocket Battle Droid		
26	Clone Trooper (41st Elite Corps)	10.00	20.00
27	Kit Fisto		

2008-13 Star Wars The Clone Wars Darth Maul Pack

CW1	Anakin Skywalker (new sculpt)	7.50	15.00
CW2	Clone Trooper (Phase II armor)	15.00	30.00
CW3	Savage Opress (shirtless)	12.50	25.00
CW4	Cad Bane	12.50	25.00
CW5	Yoda	6.00	12.00
CW6	Plo Koon (cold weather gear)	10.00	20.00
CW7	Clone Commander Cody (jet propulsion pack)	15.00	30.00
CW8	Mace Windu	6.00	12.00
CW9	Chewbacca	7.50	15.00
CW10	Aqua Battle Droid	7.50	15.00
CW11	Republic Commando Boss	12.50	25.00
CW12	Obi-Wan Kenobi	12.50	25.00
CW13	Captain Rex (Phase II)	15.00	30.00
CW14	Aayla Secura	15.00	30.00
CW15	Ahsoka Tano (scuba gear)	30.00	75.00
CW16	Training Super Battle Droid	10.00	20.00
CW17	Clone Commander Wolffe (Phase II)	25.00	50.00
CW18	Clone Commander Fox (Phase II)	20.00	40.00

2008-13 Star Wars The Clone Wars Deluxe Figures and Vehicles

NNO	212th Battalion Clone Troopers & Jet Backpacks	25.00	50.00
NNO	Armored Scout Tank (w/Battle Droid)	12.50	25.00
NNO	Armored Scout Tank (w/Tactical Droid)	15.00	30.00
NNO	AT-RT (w/ARF Trooper Boil)	20.00	40.00
NNO	Attack Cycle (w/General Grievous)	15.00	30.00
NNO	Attack Recon Fighter (w/Anakin Skywalker)	20.00	40.00
NNO	BARC Speeder (w/Commander Cody)	15.00	30.00
NNO	BARC Speeder (w/Clone Trooper)	15.00	30.00
NNO	BARC Speeder Bike (w/Clone Trooper Jesse)	25.00	50.00
NNO	BARC Speeder Bike (w/Obi-Wan Kenobi)	15.00	30.00
NNO	Can-Cell (w/Anakin Skywalker)	15.00	30.00
NNO	Crab Droid	20.00	40.00
NNO	Desert Skiff (w/Anakin Skywalker)	12.50	25.00
NNO	Freeco Speeder (w/Clone Trooper)	10.00	20.00
NNO	Freeco Speeder (w/Obi-Wan Kenobi)	15.00	30.00
NNO	Mandalorian Speeder (w/Mandalorian Warrior)	30.00	60.00
NNO	Naboo Star Skiff (w/Anakin Skywalker)	15.00	30.00
NNO	Pirate Speeder Bike (w/Cad Bane)	12.50	25.00

NNO Republic Assault Submarine with Scuba Clone Trooper	25.00	50.00
NNO Republic Attack Dropship with Clone Pilot		
NNO Republic Scout Speeder with ARF Trooper	15.00	30.00
NNO Separatist Droid Speeder with Battle Droid	15.00	30.00
NNO Speeder Bike with Castas	10.00	20.00
NNO Speeder Bike with Count Dooku	20.00	40.00
NNO Speeder Bike with Plo Koon		
NNO Turbo Tank Support Squad	25.00	50.00
NNO Y-Wing Scout Bomber with Clone Trooper Pilot	20.00	40.00

2008-13 Star Wars The Clone Wars Deluxe Figures and Vehicles Exclusives

1 AT-RT with ARF Trooper	25.00	50.00
(Walmart Exclusive)		
2 BARC Speeder with Clone Trooper Buzz	30.00	60.00
(Walmart Exclusive)		
3 Separatist Speeder with Geonosian Warrior	15.00	30.00
(2011 Toys R Us Exclusive)		
4 STAP with Battle Droid		
(2010 Toys R Us Exclusive)		

2008-13 Star Wars The Clone Wars Exclusives

1 Captain Rex	12.50	25.00
(2008 Sneak Preview Mailaway Exclusive)		
2 Clone Captain Lock	12.50	25.00
(2011 K-Mart Exclusive)		
3 Clone Trooper: 501st Legion	15.00	30.00
(2008 Wal-Mart Exclusive)		
4 Clone Trooper: Senate Security	15.00	30.00
(2008 SDCC Exclusive)		
5 Commander Fox	20.00	40.00
(2008 Target Exclusive)		
6 Commander Ponds	25.00	50.00
(2009 Toys R Us Exclusive)		
7 General Grievous: Holographic	10.00	20.00
(2008 Toys R Us Exclusive)		
8 Kul Teska	15.00	30.00
(2010 Toys R Us Exclusive)		
9 Nahdar Vebb	15.00	30.00
(2009 Mailaway Exclusive)		
10 Nikto Skiff Guard Puko Naga	10.00	20.00
(2010 Toys R Us Exclusive)		
11 Sgt. Bric & Galactic Battle Mat	20.00	40.00
(2010 Mailaway Exclusive)		
12 Stealth Operation Clone Trooper: Commander Blackout	15.00	30.00
(2011 Toys R Us Exclusive)		

2008-13 Star Wars The Clone Wars Red and White

KIT FISTO

CW1 General Grievous	10.00	20.00
CW2 Clone Trooper (space gear)	15.00	30.00
CW3 Rocket Battle Droid	10.00	20.00
CW4 Clone Trooper (41st Elite Corps)	15.00	30.00
CW5 Kit Fisto	10.00	20.00
CW6 Mace Windu	10.00	20.00
CW7 Admiral Yularen	15.00	30.00
CW8 Jawas	10.00	20.00
CW9 Commander Gree	20.00	40.00
CW10 ARF Trooper	12.50	25.00
CW11 Heavy Assault Super Battle Droid	7.50	15.00
CW12 Obi-Wan Kenobi (space suit)	7.50	15.00
CW13 4A-7	10.00	20.00
CW14 Yoda	10.00	20.00
CW15 Whorm Loathsom	10.00	20.00
CW16 Commando Droid	15.00	30.00
CW17 Clone Trooper Echo	20.00	40.00
CW18 Anakin Skywalker	7.50	15.00
CW19 Obi-Wan Kenobi	10.00	20.00
CW20 Clone Trooper Denal	20.00	40.00
CW21 Anakin Skywalker (space suit)	7.50	15.00
CW22 Cad Bane	10.00	20.00
CW23 Ahsoka Tano (space suit)	15.00	30.00
CW24 Captain Rex	12.50	25.00
CW25 R2-D2	7.50	15.00
CW26 Ahsoka Tano	15.00	30.00
CW27 Count Dooku	10.00	20.00
CW28 Commander Cody	12.50	25.00
CW29 Destroyer Droid	7.50	15.00
CW30 Luminara Unduli	12.50	25.00
CW31 Captain Argyus	15.00	30.00
CW32 Clone Commander Thire	20.00	40.00
CW33 Battle Droid (AAT Driver)	15.00	30.00
CW34 Matchstick	15.00	30.00
CW35 Padme Amidala (adventurer suit)	15.00	30.00
CW36 Clone Tank Gunner	20.00	40.00
CW37 Ziro's Assassin Droid	10.00	20.00
CW38 Clone Trooper Jek	30.00	60.00
CW39 Commander Bly	30.00	75.00
CW40 Aayla Secura	10.00	20.00
CW41 Hondo Ohnaka	30.00	75.00
CW42 Anakin Skywalker (cold weather gear)	7.50	15.00
CW43 Thi-Sen	15.00	30.00
CW44 Clone Commander Stone	25.00	50.00
CW45 Darth Sidious	75.00	150.00
CW46 Commander TX-20	20.00	40.00
CW47 Firefighter Droid	25.00	50.00
CW48 Obi-Wan Kenobi (cold weather gear)	10.00	20.00
CW49 Magnaguard (w/cape)	20.00	40.00
CW50 Captain Rex (cold assault gear)	12.50	25.00

2008-13 Star Wars The Clone Wars Vehicles

JEDI STARFIGHTER

NNO Ahsoka Tano's Delta Starfighter		
NNO Anakin's Delta Starfighter	8.00	15.00
NNO Anakin's Modified Jedi Starfighter	15.00	40.00
NNO ARC-170 Starfighter (Imperial Shadow Squadron)		
NNO AT-AP Walker		
NNO AT-TE (All Terrain Tactical Enforcer)		
NNO Clone Turbo Tank	150.00	300.00
NNO Corporate Alliance Tank Droid	30.00	60.00
NNO Droid Tri-Fighter		
NNO General Grievous' Starfighter	20.00	40.00
NNO Hailfire Droid (Remote Control)	20.00	40.00
NNO Homing Spider Droid	25.00	50.00
NNO Hyena Bomber	25.00	50.00
NNO Jedi Turbo Speeder	30.00	60.00
NNO MagnaGuard Fighter	12.50	25.00
NNO Mandalorian Assault Gunship	50.00	100.00
NNO Obi-Wan Kenobi's Delta Starfighter		
NNO Obi-Wan's Jedi Starfighter (Utapau)		
NNO Plo Koon's Delta Starfighter	15.00	30.00
NNO Republic Attack Shuttle	75.00	150.00
NNO Republic AV-7 Mobile Cannon	30.00	75.00
NNO Republic Fighter Tank		
NNO Republic Fighter Tank (blue deco)		
NNO Republic Fighter Tank (green deco)		
NNO Republic Fighter Tank (Remote Control)	25.00	50.00
NNO Republic Swamp Speeder	30.00	60.00
NNO Separatist Droid Gunship	30.00	75.00
NNO Trade Federation Armored Assault Tank (AAT - brown/blue)	20.00	40.00
NNO Trade Federation Armored Assault Tank (AAT)	30.00	60.00
NNO V-19 Torrent Starfighter		
NNO Vulture Droid	20.00	40.00
NNO V-Wing Starfighter	20.00	40.00
NNO Xanadu Blood	30.00	75.00
NNO Y-Wing Bomber	75.00	150.00

2008-13 Star Wars The Clone Wars Vehicles Exclusives

NNO ARC-170 Starfighter (flaming wampa)		
(Toys R Us Exclusive)		
NNO Hailfire Droid & General Grievous		
(Toys R Us Exclusive)		
NNO Kit Fisto's Delta Starfighter		
(Walmart Exclusive)		
NNO Octuptarra Droid	30.00	75.00
(Walmart Exclusive)		
NNO Republic Gunship (crumb bomber)		
(Toys R Us Exclusive)		
NNO Republic Gunship (Lucky Lekku)	125.00	250.00
(Walmart Exclusive)		
NNO V-Wing Starfighter & V-Wing Pilot		
(Toys R Us Exclusive)		
NNO V-Wing Starfighter (Imperial)	30.00	75.00
(Toys R Us Exclusive)		

2008-13 Star Wars The Clone Wars Yoda Pack

CW1 Obi-Wan Kenobi
CW2 Savage Opress (armoured apprentice)
CW3 Anakin Skywalker
CW4 Captain Rex   15.00   30.00
CW5 R2-D2
CW6 501st Legion Clone Trooper   60.00   120.00
CW7 Clone Commander Cody (jet propulsion pack)
CW8 Darth Maul   30.00   60.00
CW9 Battle Droid   15.00   30.00

1996-99 Star Wars Collector Series

1 Admiral Ackbar		20.00	40.00
2 AT-AT Driver		15.00	30.00
3 Boba Fett		25.00	50.00
4 C-3PO		20.00	40.00
5 Cantina Band - Doikk Na'ts (w/Fizzz)		12.00	25.00
(Walmart Exclusive)			
6 Cantina Band - Figrin D'an (w/Kloo Horn)		10.00	20.00
(Walmart Exclusive)			
7 Cantina Band - Ickabel (w/fanfar)		12.00	25.00
(Walmart Exclusive)			
8 Cantina Band - Nalan (w/Bandfill)		10.00	20.00
(Walmart Exclusive)			
9 Cantina Band - Tech (w/Omni Box)		12.00	25.00
(Walmart Exclusive)			
10 Cantina Band - Tedn (w/fanfar)		10.00	20.00
(Walmart Exclusive)			
11 Chewbacca		20.00	40.00
12 Darth Vader		15.00	30.00
13 Greedo		15.00	30.00
(JC Penney Exclusive)			
14 Han Solo		15.00	30.00
15 Lando Calrissian		12.00	25.00
16 Luke Skywalker		15.00	30.00

17 Luke Skywalker (Bespin)		12.00	25.00
18 Luke Skywalker (X-Wing Pilot)		20.00	40.00
19 Obi-Wan Kenobi		15.00	30.00
20 Princess Leia		15.00	30.00
21 Sandtrooper		15.00	30.00
22 Stormtrooper		15.00	30.00
23 TIE Fighter Pilot		20.00	40.00
24 Tusken Raider (blaster and binoculars)		12.00	25.00
25 Tusken Raider (gaderffi stick)		12.00	25.00

1996-99 Star Wars Collector Series 2-Packs

1 Grand Moff Tarkin and Imperial Gunner		25.00	50.00
(FAO Schwarz Exclusive)			
2 Han Solo and Luke Skywalker (stormtrooper gear)		30.00	60.00
(KB Toys Exclusive)			
3 Han Solo and Tauntaun		30.00	60.00
4 Luke Hoth and Wampa		25.00	50.00
5 Luke Jedi and Bib Fortuna		25.00	50.00
(FAO Schwarz Exclusive)			
6 Obi-Wan Kenobi vs. Darth Vader (electronic)		25.00	50.00
(JC Penney/KB Toys Exclusive)			
7 Princess Leia and R2-D2 (Jabba's prisoners)			
(FAO Schwarz/KB Toys Exclusive)			

1996-99 Star Wars Collector Series European Exclusives

1 Han Solo (drawing action)		12.00	25.00
2 Luke Skywalker (drawing action)			

1996-99 Star Wars Collector Series Masterpiece Edition

1 Anakin Skywalker/Story of Darth Vader		10.00	20.00
2 Aurra Sing/Dawn of the Bounty Hunters		12.00	25.00
3 C-3PO/Tales of the Golden Droid		20.00	40.00

2006 Star Wars Customs

NNO Boba Fett's/ Outlaw Chopper
NNO Darth Vader's/ Imperial Chopper
NNO Luke Skywalker's/ Rebel Chopper

2006 Star Wars Customs International

NNO Boba Fett's/ Outlaw Chopper
NNO Darth Vader's/ Imperial Chopper
NNO Luke Skywalker's/ Rebel Chopper

2008-10 Star Wars Diamond Select

1 Anakin Skywalker		25.00	50.00
2 Darth Maul		30.00	75.00
3 Emperor Palpatine		25.00	50.00
4 Luke Skywalker Jedi Knight		60.00	120.00
5 Mace Windu		30.00	60.00
6 Obi-Wan Kenobi (ROTS)		30.00	60.00

2012-13 Star Wars Discover the Force

NNO Aurra Sing		12.50	25.00
NNO Darth Maul		8.00	15.00
NNO Destroyer Droid		6.00	12.00
NNO G8-R3		12.00	25.00
NNO Gungan Warrior		8.00	15.00
NNO Mawhonic		6.00	12.00
NNO Obi-Wan Kenobi		8.00	15.00
NNO Qui-Gon Jinn		6.00	12.00
NNO Ric Olie		6.00	12.00
NNO Naboo Pilot		5.00	10.00
NNO Tusken Raider		5.00	10.00
NNO Yoda		8.00	15.00

2012-13 Star Wars Discover the Force Battle Packs

NNO Mos Espa Arena		20.00	40.00
(C-3PO/Anakin/Sebulba/2 Pit Droids)			
NNO Royal Starship Droids			
(R2-B1/R2-R9/R2-D2/R2-N3)			

2012-13 Star Wars Discover the Force Vehicles-Creatures

NNO Dewback		20.00	40.00
NNO Vulture Droid			

2010-15 Star Wars Disney Characters Exclusives

NNO Bad Pete as Jango Fett		20.00	40.00
(2015 Star Wars Weekends Exclusive)/2002			
NNO Donald Duck as Darth Maul		25.00	50.00
(2012 Star Wars Weekends Exclusive)			
NNO Donald Duck as Savage Opress		25.00	50.00
(2012 Star Wars Weekends Exclusive)/2012			
NNO Donald Duck as Shadow Trooper		30.00	60.00
(2010 Star Wars Celebration Exclusive)/5000			
NNO Mickey Mouse and Donald Duck as X-Wing Luke and Han Solo		15.00	30.00
(2014 Star Wars Weekends Exclusive)/1980			
NNO Mickey Mouse/Chip & Dale as Luke Skywalker and Ewoks		20.00	40.00
(2013 Star Wars Weekends Exclusive)/1983			
NNO Pluto and Minnie Mouse as R2-D2 and Princess Leia		30.00	60.00
(2015 Star Wars Weekends Exclusive)/1977			
NNO Stitch as Emperor Palpatine		15.00	30.00
(2010 Star Wars Weekends Exclusive)/1980			
NNO Stitch as Hologram Yoda		15.00	30.00
(2011 Star Tours Opening Exclusive)/2011			

2007 Star Wars Disney Characters Series 1

NNO Donald Duck as Han Solo		12.50	25.00
NNO Goofy as Darth Vader		10.00	20.00
NNO Mickey Mouse as Luke Skywalker		12.50	25.00
NNO Minnie Mouse as Princess Leia		7.50	15.00
NNO Stitch as Emperor Palpatine		12.50	25.00

2008 Star Wars Disney Characters Series 2

NNO Donald Duck as Darth Maul
NNO Goofy as Jar Jar Binks
NNO Mickey Mouse as Anakin Skywalker
NNO Minnie Mouse as Padme Amidala
NNO Stitch as Yoda

2009 Star Wars Disney Characters Series 3

NNO Chip & Dale as Ewoks	20.00	40.00
NNO Donald Duck as Stormtrooper	12.50	25.00
NNO Goofy as Chewbacca	15.00	30.00
NNO Mickey Mouse as Luke Skywalker (X-Wing Pilot)	12.50	25.00
NNO Minnie Mouse as Slave Leia		

2010 Star Wars Disney Characters Series 4

NNO Bad Pete as Boba Fett	20.00	40.00
NNO Donald Duck as Han in Carbonite	10.00	20.00
NNO Goofy as C-3PO	20.00	40.00
NNO Mickey Mouse as Jedi Knight Luke Skywalker		
NNO Minnie Mouse as Princess Leia Boushh	15.00	30.00

2011 Star Wars Disney Characters Series 5

NNO Daisy Duck as Aurra Sing	15.00	30.00
NNO Donald Duck as Commander Cody		
NNO Goofy as Cad Bane		
NNO Dewey/Huey/Louie as Jawas	20.00	40.00
NNO Stitch as General Grievous	25.00	50.00

2012 Star Wars Disney Characters Series 6

NNO Donald Duck as Darth Maul	20.00	40.00
NNO Goofy as TC-14	12.50	25.00
NNO Mickey Mouse as Anakin Skywalker	25.00	50.00
NNO Minnie Mouse as Queen Amidala	12.50	25.00
NNO Pluto as R2-D2	20.00	40.00
NNO Stitch as Yoda		

2015-21 Star Wars Disney Parks Droid Factory

NNO 4-LOM		
(2020)		
NNO BB-19H		
(2019 Holiday Exclusive)		
NNO BB-8	7.50	15.00
(2017)		
NNO BB-BOO20		
(2020 Halloween Exclusive)		
NNO BB-H20		
(2020 Holiday Exclusive)		
NNO C1-10P Chopper	15.00	30.00
(Disney Exclusive)		
NNO CB-23		
(SW Resistance Disney Exclusive)		
NNO Holographic R2-D2		
(Disney Exclusive)		
NNO R2-BOO	20.00	40.00
(2016 Halloween Exclusive)		
NNO R2-D60	25.00	50.00
(2015 Disneyland 60th Anniversary Exclusive)		
NNO R2-H15	30.00	75.00
(2015 Holiday Exclusive)		
NNO R2-H16	15.00	30.00
(2016 Holiday Exclusive)		
NNO R2-RN8W		
(2021 Disney Pride Month Exclusive)		
NNO R3-BOO17 (glow-in-the-dark)	60.00	120.00
(2017 Halloween Exclusive)		

NNO R-3D0	10.00	20.00
(Disney Exclusive)		
NNO R3-H17	20.00	40.00
(2017 Holiday Exclusive)		
NNO R4-BOO18	12.50	25.00
(2018 Halloween Exclusive)		
NNO R4-D23		
(2015 D23 Expo Exclusive)		
NNO R4-H18	25.00	50.00
(2018 Holiday Exclusive)		
NNO R5-BOO19	17.50	35.00
(2019 Halloween Exclusive)		
NNO R5-D23	20.00	40.00
(2017 D23 Expo Exclusive)		
NNO R5-M4	12.50	25.00
(2016 May 4th Exclusive)		
NNO R6-W1CH		
(2021 Halloween Exclusive)		

2015-21 Star Wars Disney Parks Droid Factory Multipacks

NNO 3PO Droid/BB Unit/R4 Unit/CZ Droid		
NNO Artoo Detoo (R2-D2)/See-Threepio (C-3PO)	30.00	75.00
(2017 40th Anniversary Exclusive)		
NNO BB-8/2BB-2/BB-4/BB-9E	25.00	50.00
NNO C2-B5/R2-BHD/R3-M2/R5-SK1	30.00	75.00
NNO D-0/R5-2JE/R6-LE5/R2-SHP		
NNO R0-4L0/R2-Q2/R4-M9/R5-X3		
NNO R1-J1/B-R72/L4-R6/C2-B9/EG-01		
NNO R4-X2/Y5-X2	20.00	40.00
NNO R5-013/R2-C2/R5-S9/R5-P8	25.00	50.00
NNO RA-7/BB Unit/R2 Unit/C1 Droid		
NNO RS-F1P/R5-232/R2-S8/R5-PHT		

2017-21 Star Wars Disney Store Toybox

1 Kylo Ren	10.00	20.00
2 Rey	10.00	20.00
3 Stormtrooper	7.50	15.00
4 Darth Vader	7.50	15.00
5 Luke Skywalker	12.50	25.00
6 Boba Fett	10.00	20.00
7 Princess Leia Organa	7.50	15.00
8 Han Solo	10.00	20.00
9 Chewbacca		
10 Yoda/Force Ghost Yoda 2-Pack		
11 Poe Dameron (w/BB-8)		
12 C-3PO (w/R2-D2)		
13 Kylo Ren		
14 Rey		
15 Sith Trooper		
16 Darth Maul		
17 Jango Fett		
18 Din Djarin (w/Grogu)		
19 Darth Vader		
20 Stormtrooper		
21 General Grievous		
22 Ahsoka Tano (w/Captain Red)		
23 Wrecker		

2017-21 Star Wars Disney Store Toybox Vehicles

NNO Millennium Falcon (w/Han Solo & Chewbacca)
NNO Millennium Falcon (w/Rey/BB-8/D-0)
NNO Slave 1 (w/Boba Fett)
NNO TIE Fighter (w/Kylo Ren)
NNO TIE Fighter (w/TIE Fighter Pilot)

2015 Star Wars Elite Series

NNO Anakin Skywalker	25.00	50.00
NNO Boba Fett (w/cape)	20.00	40.00
NNO Boba Fett (w/o cape)	30.00	75.00
NNO Darth Maul	30.00	60.00
NNO Darth Vader	20.00	40.00
NNO General Grievous	50.00	100.00
NNO Prototype Boba Fett	30.00	75.00
NNO Stormtrooper	15.00	30.00

2015-16 Star Wars Elite Series

NNO C-3PO	20.00	40.00
NNO Captain Phasma	10.00	20.00
NNO Finn	10.00	20.00
NNO Finn (w/lightsaber)	10.00	20.00
NNO Flametrooper	15.00	30.00
NNO FN-2187 (Finn)	12.50	25.00
NNO Han Solo	15.00	30.00
NNO Kylo Ren	10.00	20.00
NNO Kylo Ren (unmasked)	12.00	25.00
NNO Poe Dameron	10.00	20.00
NNO R2-D2	20.00	40.00
NNO Rey and BB-8	12.00	25.00
NNO Rey and BB-8 (w/lightsaber)	15.00	30.00
NNO Stormtrooper	10.00	20.00
NNO Stormtrooper (squad leader)	12.50	25.00
NNO Stormtrooper (w/riot gear)	12.50	25.00
NNO Stormtrooper Officer	15.00	30.00
NNO TIE Fighter Pilot	12.50	25.00

2016-17 Star Wars Elite Series

NNO Baze Malbus	10.00	20.00
NNO Bodhi Rook	10.00	20.00
NNO C2-B5	12.00	25.00
NNO Captain Cassian Andor	8.00	15.00
NNO Chirrut Imwe	10.00	20.00
NNO Imperial Death Trooper	15.00	30.00
NNO K-2SO	10.00	20.00
NNO Sergeant Jyn Erso	10.00	20.00
NNO Stormtrooper	10.00	20.00

2017-18 Star Wars Elite Series

NNO Elite Praetorian Guard	15.00	30.00
NNO First Order Judicial	30.00	60.00
NNO Kylo Ren	15.00	30.00
NNO Luke Skywalker	15.00	30.00
NNO R2-D2	20.00	40.00
NNO Rey	20.00	40.00

2018-19 Star Wars Elite Series

NNO Gonk Droid	15.00	30.00
NNO R2-D2	25.00	50.00
NNO R4-G9	20.00	40.00
NNO R5-D4	20.00	40.00
NNO TC-14	25.00	50.00

2016-17 Star Wars Elite Series 11-Inch

NNO Darth Vader	20.00	40.00
NNO Death Trooper	15.00	30.00
NNO Director Orson Krennic	20.00	40.00
NNO Jyn Erso	20.00	40.00
NNO Kylo Ren	15.00	30.00
NNO Princess Leia Organa	25.00	50.00
NNO Rey	15.00	30.00

2015-17 Star Wars Elite Series Multipacks and Exclusives

NNO	8-Piece Gift Set	500.00	750.00
	Darth Maul/Anakin/Grievous/Stormtrooper		
	Vader/C-3PO/R2-D2/Boba Fett)		
	(2016 D23 Exclusive)		
NNO	Deluxe Gift Set	60.00	120.00
	Stormtrooper/Phasma/Kylo Ren/Finn/Flametrooper		
NNO	Droid Gift Pack	25.00	50.00
	BB-8, C-3PO, R2-D2		
NNO	Han Solo & Luke Skywalker w/blond hair (Stormtrooper Disguise)50.00	100.00	
NNO	Han Solo & Luke Skywalker w/brown hair (Stormtrooper Disguise)25.00	50.00	
NNO	Princess Leia & Darth Vader/1000*	75.00	150.00
	(2017 D23 Exclusive)		

1999-00 Star Wars Episode I 2-Packs

1	Darth Maul and Sith Infiltrator	8.00	15.00
2	Final Jedi Duel (Qui-Gon Jinn/Darth Maul break apart)	20.00	50.00

1999-00 Star Wars Episode I Accessory Sets

1	Flash Cannon	8.00	15.00
2	Gungan Catapult	10.00	20.00
3	Hyperdrive Repair Kit	25.00	50.00
4	Naboo Accessory Set	8.00	15.00
5	Pod Race Fuel Station	8.00	15.00
6	Rappel Line Attach	12.00	25.00
7	Sith Accessory Set	8.00	15.00
8	Tatooine Accessory Set	8.00	15.00
9	Tatooine Disguise Set	12.00	25.00
10	Underwater Accessory Set	8.00	15.00

1999-00 Star Wars Episode I Action Collection 12-Inch

1	Anakin Skywalker (fully poseable)	10.00	20.00
2	Anakin Skywalker (w/Theed Hangar Droid)	20.00	40.00
3	Battle Droid (w/blaster rifle)	15.00	30.00
4	Battle Droid Commander(#(w/electrobinoculars)	10.00	20.00
5	Boss Nass	15.00	30.00
6	Chancellor Valorum & Coruscant Guard	20.00	40.00
7	Darth Maul (w/lightsaber)	12.00	25.00
8	Darth Maul & Sith Speeder	20.00	40.00
	(Walmart Exclusive)		
9	Jar Jar Binks (fully poseable)	12.00	25.00
10	Mace Windu (w/lightsaber)	15.00	30.00
11	Obi-Wan Kenobi (w/lightsaber)	12.00	25.00
12	Pit Droids (fully poseable)	12.00	20.00
13	Qui-Gon Jinn (w/lightsaber)	15.00	30.00
14	Qui-Gon Jinn (Tatooine)	10.00	20.00
15	R2-A6 (metalized dome)	20.00	40.00
16	Sebulba (w/Chubas)	12.00	25.00
17	Watto (w/data pad)	10.00	20.00

1999-00 Star Wars Episode I Battle Bags

1	Sea Creatures I	6.00	12.00
2	Sea Creatures II	6.00	12.00
3	Swamp Creatures I	6.00	12.00
4	Swamp Creatures II	6.00	12.00

1999-00 Star Wars Episode I Bonus Battle Droid 2-Packs

NNO	Anakin Skywalker (Naboo)/Battle Droid (tan clean)		
NNO	Anakin Skywalker (Tatooine)/Battle Droid (tan clean)	10.00	20.00
NNO	Battle Droid (tan clean)/Battle Droid (tan clean)		
NNO	Battle Droid (tan clean)/Battle Droid (gold/dirty)		
NNO	Battle Droid (tan clean)/Battle Droid (tan/blast on chest)		
NNO	Battle Droid (tan clean)/Battle Droid (tan/slash on chest/burn marks)		
NNO	C-3PO/Battle Droid (tan clean)	15.00	30.00
NNO	Captain Panaka/Battle Droid (tan clean)		
NNO	Darth Maul (Jedi duel)/Battle Droid (tan clean)	7.50	15.00
NNO	Darth Maul (Tatooine)/Battle Droid (tan clean)	7.50	15.00
NNO	Darth Sidious/Battle Droid (tan clean)		
NNO	Destroyer Droid/Battle Droid (tan clean)	12.50	25.00
NNO	Jar Jar Binks/Battle Droid (tan clean)	12.50	25.00
NNO	Naboo Royal Security/Battle Droid (tan clean)		
NNO	Nute Gunray/Battle Droid (tan clean)	15.00	30.00
NNO	Obi-Wan Kenobi (Jedi duel)/Battle Droid (tan clean)	6.00	12.00
NNO	Obi-Wan Kenobi (Jedi Knight)/Battle Droid (tan clean)	6.00	12.00
NNO	Padme Naberrie/Battle Droid (tan clean)		
NNO	Queen Amidala (Naboo)/Battle Droid (tan clean)	6.00	12.00
NNO	Queen Amidala (red senate gown)/Battle Droid (tan clean)		
NNO	Qui-Gon Jinn/Battle Droid (tan clean)		
NNO	Qui-Gon Jinn (Jedi Master)/Battle Droid (tan clean)	12.50	25.00
NNO	R2-D2/Battle Droid (tan clean)	15.00	30.00
NNO	Ric Olie/Battle Droid (tan clean)		
NNO	Rune Haako/Battle Droid (tan clean)		
NNO	Senator Palpatine/Battle Droid (tan clean)		
NNO	Watto/Battle Droid (tan clean)	20.00	40.00
NNO	Yoda/Battle Droid (tan clean)	6.00	12.00

1999-00 Star Wars Episode I Bonus Pit Droid 2-Packs

NNO	Anakin Skywalker (Tatooine)/Pit Droid (maroon)		
NNO	Anakin Skywalker (Tatooine)/Pit Droid (orange)		
NNO	Anakin Skywalker (Tatooine)/Pit Droid (white)		
NNO	Darth Maul (Jedi duel)/Pit Droid (maroon)	25.00	50.00
NNO	Darth Maul (Jedi duel)/Pit Droid (orange)		
NNO	Darth Maul (Jedi duel)/Pit Droid (white)		
NNO	Darth Sidius (hologram)/Pit Droid (maroon)		
NNO	Darth Sidius (hologram)/Pit Droid (orange)		
NNO	Darth Sidius (hologram)/Pit Droid (white)		
NNO	Naboo Royal Guard/Pit Droid (maroon)	10.00	20.00
NNO	Naboo Royal Guard/Pit Droid (orange)	20.00	40.00
NNO	Naboo Royal Guard/Pit Droid (white)	15.00	30.00
NNO	Obi-Wan Kenobi (Jedi Knight)/Pit Droid (maroon)		
NNO	Obi-Wan Kenobi (Jedi Knight)/Pit Droid (orange)		
NNO	Obi-Wan Kenobi (Jedi Knight)/Pit Droid (white)		

1999-00 Star Wars Episode I CommTech Cinema Scenes

1 Mos Espa Encounter (Sebulba/Jar Jar Binks/Anakin Skywalker)	12.00	25.00
2 Tatooine Showdown (Darth Maul/Qui-Gon Jinn Tatooine		
Anakin Skywalker Tatooine)	8.00	20.00
3 Watto's Box (Watto/Graxol Kelvyyn/Shakka)	25.00	50.00

1999-00 Star Wars Episode I CommTech Collection 1

1a Anakin Skywalker Naboo (new sticker)	6.00	12.00
1b Anakin Skywalker Naboo (no new sticker)	12.00	25.00
2a Anakin Skywalker Naboo pilot (new sticker)	6.00	12.00
2b Anakin Skywalker Naboo pilot (no new sticker)	3.00	6.00
3a Anakin Skywalker Tatooine (.00)	10.00	20.00
3b Anakin Skywalker Tatooine (.0100)	3.00	6.00
3c Anakin Skywalker Tatooine (.01 innovision back)	3.00	6.00
4a Battle Droid (tan clean .00)	5.00	10.00
4b Battle Droid (tan clean .01)	5.00	10.00
4c Battle Droid (tan clean .02 innovision back)	5.00	10.00
5a Battle Droid (tan slash on chest w/burn marks .00)	8.00	15.00
5b Battle Droid (tan slash on chest w/burn marks .01)	4.00	8.00
5c Battle Droid (tan slash on chest		
w/burn marks .02 innovision back)	3.00	6.00
6a Battle Droid (tan blast on chest .00)	4.00	8.00
6b Battle Droid (tan blast on chest .01)	3.00	6.00
6c Battle Droid (tan blast on chest .02 innovision back)	6.00	12.00
7a Battle Droid (gold/dirty .00)	3.00	6.00
7b Battle Droid (gold/dirty .01)	3.00	6.00
7c Battle Droid (gold/dirty .02 innovision back)	3.00	6.00
8a Darth Maul Jedi duel (.00)	8.00	15.00
8b Darth Maul Jedi duel (.01/ innovision back)	3.00	6.00
8c Darth Maul Jedi duel (.02)	5.00	10.00
8d Darth Maul Jedi duel (.0000 large eyes different		
face more red paint on)	4.00	8.00
8e Darth Maul Jedi duel (white strip on package		
card instead of yellow)	3.00	6.00
9a Darth Maul Sith Lord (new sticker)	5.00	10.00
9b Darth Maul Sith Lord (no new sticker)	5.00	10.00
10a Darth Maul Tatooine (new sticker)	4.00	8.00

10b Darth Maul Tatooine (new sticker/hologram chip sticker)	3.00	6.00
10c Darth Maul Tatooine (no new sticker)	3.00	6.00
10d Darth Maul Tatooine (no new sticker/hologram chip sticker)	3.00	6.00
10e Darth Maul Sith Lord (new sticker/white strip on package card)	3.00	6.00
11a Destroyer Droid battle damaged (new sticker)	5.00	10.00
11b Destroyer Droid battle damaged (no new sticker)	3.00	6.00
12a Jar Jar Binks (.00 large package photo)	12.00	25.00
12b Jar Jar Binks (.0100 small package photo)	3.00	6.00
12c Jar Jar Binks (.0200/ innovision back)	3.00	6.00
13 Jar Jar Binks (Naboo swamp)	4.00	8.00
14a Obi-Wan Kenobi Jedi duel (.00)	4.00	8.00
14b Obi-Wan Kenobi Jedi duel (.0100)	3.00	6.00
15a Obi-Wan Kenobi Jedi Knight (new sticker)	4.00	8.00
15b Obi-Wan Kenobi Jedi Knight (no new sticker)	3.00	6.00
16a Obi-Wan Kenobi Naboo (new sticker)	6.00	12.00
16b Obi-Wan Kenobi Naboo (no new sticker)	3.00	6.00
17a Padme Naberrie (.00)	10.00	20.00
17b Padme Naberrie (.0100 innovision back)	3.00	6.00
18a Queen Amidala Coruscant (new sticker)	4.00	8.00
18b Queen Amidala Coruscant (no new sticker)	4.00	8.00
19a Queen Amidala Naboo (.00)	3.00	6.00
19b Queen Amidala Naboo (.0100 innovision back)	6.00	12.00
20a Qui-Gon Jinn (.00)	6.00	12.00
20b Qui-Gon Jinn (.0100 innovision back)	4.00	8.00
21a Qui-Gon Jinn Jedi Master (new sticker)	3.00	6.00
21b Qui-Gon Jinn Jedi Master (no new sticker)	3.00	6.00
22a Qui-Gon Jinn Naboo (new sticker)	5.00	10.00
22b Qui-Gon Jinn Naboo (no new sticker)	3.00	6.00

1999-00 Star Wars Episode I CommTech Collection 2

1a C-3PO (.00)	5.00	10.00
1b C-3PO (.01 innovision back)	20.00	40.00
2a Captain Panaka (wrong chip line on back	5.00	10.00
they need her to sign a treaty)		
2b Captain Panaka (correct chip line on back	5.00	10.00
this battle I do not think)		
3a Darth Sidious (.00)	5.00	10.00
3b Darth Sidious (.01/innovision back)	3.00	6.00
4 Darth Sidious (holograph)	15.00	30.00
5a Destroyer Droid (new sticker)	6.00	12.00
5b Destroyer Droid (no new sticker)	4.00	8.00
6a Naboo Royal Guard	8.00	15.00
6b Naboo Royal Security	3.00	6.00
7a Nute Gunray (new sticker)	5.00	10.00
7b Nute Gunray (no new sticker)	8.00	15.00
8a R2-B1 (.0000/Astromech back/no space)	8.00	15.00
8b R2-B1 (.0100/Astromech back/space)	8.00	15.00
9a R2-D2 (large packing bubble/new sticker)	6.00	12.00
9b R2-D2 (small packing bubble)	6.00	12.00
10 Pit Droids	5.00	10.00
11 Queen Amidala (battle)	6.00	12.00
12a Ric Olie (.00)	3.00	6.00
12b Ric Olie (.0100/innovision back)	3.00	6.00
13a Rune Haako (new sticker)	4.00	8.00
13b Rune Haako (no new sticker)	3.00	6.00
14a Senator Palpatine (.00)	3.00	6.00
14b Senator Palpatine (.0100/innovision back)	3.00	6.00
15 Sio Bibble	10.00	20.00
16a Watto (.00)	3.00	6.00
16b Watto (.0100 innovision back)	3.00	6.00
17a Yoda (episode 1 on front)	3.00	6.00
17b Yoda (no episode 1 on front)	5.00	10.00

1999-00 Star Wars Episode I CommTech Collection 3

1 Adi Gallia	4.00	8.00
2a Boss Nass (.00)	3.00	6.00
2b Boss Nass (.01/innovision back)	3.00	6.00
3a Captain Tarpals (.00)	5.00	10.00
3b Captain Tarpals (.01)	3.00	6.00
4a Chancellor Valorum (.00/warning)	3.00	6.00
4b Chancellor Valorum (.00/no warning)	3.00	6.00
4c Chancellor Valorum (.01/no warning)	3.00	6.00
4d Chancellor Valorum (.02/no warning)	3.00	6.00
5a Gasgano with Pit Droid (.0100)	5.00	10.00
5b Gasgano with Pit Droid (.0200)	3.00	6.00
6a Ki-Adi-Mundi (.0000)	3.00	6.00
6b Ki-Adi-Mundi (.0100/innovision back)	3.00	6.00
7a Mace Windu (.0000)	3.00	6.00
7b Mace Windu (.0100/innovision back)	3.00	6.00
8a Ody Mandrell and Otoga (222 Pit Droid)	3.00	6.00
8b Ody Mandrell and Otoga (222 Pit Droid/hologram chip sticker)	3.00	6.00
9a OOM-9 (binoculars in package)	3.00	6.00
9b OOM-9 (binoculars in package/hologram chip sticker)	3.00	6.00
9c OOM-9 (binoculars in right hand)	3.00	6.00
9d OOM-9 (binoculars in left hand/hologram chip sticker)	5.00	10.00
10 TC-14 Protocol Droid	8.00	15.00

1999-00 Star Wars Episode I CommTech Figure Collector 2-Packs

1 Anakin Skywalker naboo/Obi-Wan Kenobi naboo	12.00	25.00
2 Battle Droid (tan blast on chest)/Darth Maul Tatooine		
3 Battle Droid (tan slash on chest w/burn marks)/Darth Maul Tatooine		
4 Darth Maul Jedi duel/Anakin Skywalker Tatooine	10.00	20.00
5 Jar Jar Binks/Qui-Gon Jinn	6.00	12.00
6 Padme Naberrie/Obi-Wan Kenobi Jedi Knight		
7 Queen Amidala Naboo/Qui-Gon Jinn Jedi Knight		

1999-00 Star Wars Episode I Creature 2-Packs

1 Ammo Wagon and Falumpaset	20.00	40.00
2 Eopie (w/Qui-Gon Jinn)		

3 Fambaa (w/Gungan warrior)		50.00	100.00
4 Jabba the Hut (w/two-headed announcer)		10.00	20.00
5 Kaadu and Jar Jar Binks		10.00	20.00
6 Opee and Qui-Gon Jinn		10.00	20.00

1999-00 Star Wars Episode I Deluxe

1 Darth Maul		3.00	6.00
2 Obi-Wan Kenobi		3.00	6.00
3 Qui-Gon Jinn		5.00	10.00

1999-00 Star Wars Episode I Electronic Talking 12-Inch

1 C-3PO		15.00	30.00
2 Darth Maul		10.00	20.00
3 Jar Jar Binks		15.00	30.00
4 Qui-Gon Jinn		12.00	25.00
5 TC-14		20.00	40.00

1999-00 Star Wars Episode I Epic Force

1 Darth Maul		8.00	15.00
2 Obi-Wan Kenobi		10.00	20.00
3 Qui-Gon Jinn		8.00	15.00

1999-00 Star Wars Episode I Invasion Force

1 Armored Scout Tank (w/Battle Droid tan clean)		6.00	12.00
2 Gungan Assault Cannon (w/Jar Jar Binks)		6.00	12.00
3 Gungan Scout Sub (w/Obi-Wan Kenobi Naboo water)		8.00	15.00
4 Sith Attack Speeder (w/Darth Maul Tatooine)		10.00	20.00

1999-00 Star Wars Episode I Jabba Glob

1 Jabba the Hutt		10.00	20.00

1999-00 Star Wars Episode I Light-Up

1 Darth Maul hologram/ Wal-Mart exclusive			
2 Qui-Gon Jinn Hologram		10.00	20.00
(Walmart Exclusive)			

1999-00 Star Wars Episode I Playsets

1 R2-D2 Carryall		12.00	25.00
2 Theed Generator Complex (w/Battle Droid)		12.00	25.00
3 Theed Hangar Power Spin Qui-Gon Jinn/Battle Droid break up		25.00	50.00

1999-00 Star Wars Episode I Portrait Edition 12-Inch

1 Princess Leia (ceremonial dress)		20.00	40.00
2 Queen Amidala (black travel gown)		12.00	25.00
3 Queen Amidala (return to Naboo)		15.00	30.00
4 Queen Amidala (Senate gown)		15.00	30.00
5 Return to Naboo 2-Pack/Padme/Qui Gon Ginn			

1999-00 Star Wars Episode I Vehicles

1 Anakin's Podracer		20.00	40.00
2 Flash Speeder		15.00	30.00
3 Naboo Fighter		15.00	30.00
4 Naboo Royal Starship		100.00	200.00
5 Sith Speeder (w/Darth Maul Jedi duel)		8.00	15.00
6 Stap and Battle Droid (burn marks on arms and legs)		8.00	15.00
7 Sebulba's Podracer (w/Sebulba podrace gear)		15.00	30.00
8 Trade Federation Droid Fighters		15.00	30.00
9 Trade Federation Tank		20.00	40.00

2015-16 Star Wars The Force Awakens 12-Inch

1 BB-8		10.00	20.00
2 Chewbacca		20.00	40.00
3 Darth Vader		12.00	25.00
4 Fifth Brother Inquisitor		7.50	15.00
5 Finn (Jakku)		10.00	20.00
6 First Order Flametrooper		10.00	20.00
7 First Order Stormtrooper		8.00	15.00
8 First Order TIE Fighter Pilot		7.50	15.00
9 Kylo Ren		7.50	15.00
10 R2-D2		10.00	20.00
11 Rey (Jakku)		10.00	20.00

2015-16 Star Wars The Force Awakens 12-Inch Vehicles

NNO Assault Walker (w/Riot Control Stormtrooper)		12.00	25.00
NNO Speeder Bike (w/Poe Dameron)		12.00	25.00

2015-16 Star Wars The Force Awakens Armor Up 1

NNO Boba Fett		7.50	15.00
NNO Captain Phasma (Epic Battles)		10.00	20.00
(Toys R Us Exclusive)			
NNO Chewbacca		7.50	15.00
NNO Finn (Jakku)		7.50	15.00
NNO Finn (Starkiller Base)		6.00	12.00
NNO First Order Flametrooper		6.00	12.00
NNO First Order Stormtrooper		10.00	20.00
NNO First Order TIE Fighter Pilot		10.00	20.00
NNO Kylo Ren		7.50	15.00
NNO Luke Skywalker		7.50	15.00
NNO Poe Dameron		7.50	15.00
NNO Poe Dameron (Epic Battles)		6.00	12.00
(Toys R Us Exclusive)			

2015-16 Star Wars The Force Awakens Build-a-Weapon Collection

NNO Admiral Ackbar		6.00	12.00
NNO Captain Phasma		7.50	15.00
NNO Captain Rex		10.00	20.00
NNO Constable Zuvio		6.00	12.00
NNO Darth Maul			
NNO Darth Vader		6.00	12.00
NNO Ezra Bridger		6.00	12.00
NNO Fifth Brother		7.50	15.00
NNO Finn (FN-2187)		7.50	15.00
NNO Finn (Jakku)		7.50	15.00
NNO First Order Flametrooper		6.00	12.00
NNO First Order Snowtrooper		5.00	10.00
NNO First Order Stormtrooper (running image)		6.00	12.00
NNO First Order Stormtrooper (shooting blaster image)		6.00	12.00
NNO First Order Stormtrooper Squad Leader		10.00	20.00
NNO First Order TIE Fighter Pilot		5.00	10.00
NNO General Hux		5.00	10.00
NNO Goss Toowers		5.00	10.00
NNO Guavian Enforcer		6.00	12.00
NNO Han Solo		7.50	15.00
NNO Hassk Thug		5.00	10.00
NNO Inquisitor		10.00	20.00
NNO Kanan Jarrus		5.00	10.00
NNO Kanan Jarrus (stormtrooper disguise)		6.00	12.00
NNO Kylo Ren (Force grip image)		7.50	15.00
NNO Kylo Ren (lightsaber image)		6.00	12.00
NNO Kylo Ren Unmasked		7.50	15.00
NNO Luke Skywalker (Episode V)		6.00	12.00
NNO Nien Nunb		6.00	12.00
NNO Poe Dameron		6.00	12.00
NNO Princess Leia			
NNO PZ-4CO		5.00	10.00
NNO Resistance Trooper		6.00	12.00
NNO Rey (Resistance fatigues)		7.50	15.00
NNO Rey (Starkiller Base)		7.50	15.00
NNO Sabine Wren		6.00	12.00
NNO Sarco Plank		6.00	12.00
NNO Seventh Sister			
NNO Tasu Leech		6.00	12.00
NNO Unkar Plutt		6.00	12.00
NNO X-Wing Pilot Asty		3.00	6.00

2015-16 Star Wars The Force Awakens Multi-Packs

1 BB-8, Unkar's Thug, Jakku Scavenger 3-Pack	8.00	15.00
2 Forest Mission 5-Pack	20.00	40.00
BB-8, Kylo Ren, Chewbacca, Stormtrooper, Resistance Trooper		
(Amazon Exclusive)		
3 Takodana Encounter 4-Pack	12.00	25.00
Maz Kanata, Rey, Finn, BB-8		
4 Troop Builder 7-Pack	30.00	60.00
(Kohl's Exclusive)		

2015-16 Star Wars The Force Awakens 2-Packs

NNO Anakin Skywalker & Yoda	12.00	25.00
NNO Clone Commander Cody & Obi-Wan Kenobi	8.00	15.00
NNO Darth Vader & Ahsoka Tano	12.00	25.00
NNO First Order Snowtrooper Officer & Snap Wexley	8.00	15.00
NNO Garazeb Orrelios & C1-10P Chopper	8.00	20.00
NNO Han Solo & Princess Leia	8.00	15.00
NNO R2-D2 & C-3PO	10.00	20.00
NNO Sidon Ithano & First Mate Quiggold	6.00	12.00

2015-16 Star Wars The Force Awakens Vehicles

1 Assault Walker (w/Stormtrooper Sergeant)	12.50	25.00
2 Battle Action Millennium Falcon (w/Finn, BB-8, Chewbacca)	60.00	120.00
3 Desert Assault Walker (w/Stormtrooper Officer)	12.50	25.00
(2015 Entertainment Earth Exclusive)		
4 Desert Landspeeder (w/Jakku Finn)	15.00	30.00
5 Elite Speeder Bike (w/Special Edition Stormtrooper)	10.00	20.00
6 First Order Snowspeeder (w/Snowspeeder Officer)	15.00	30.00
7 First Order Special Forces TIE Fighter (w/TIE Fighter Pilot)	12.50	25.00
8 Poe Dameron's Black Squadron X-Wing (w/Poe Dameron)	30.00	75.00
9 Rey's Speeder (w/Special Edition Rey)	10.00	20.00
10 Slave I (w/Boba Fett)	25.00	50.00
11 Y-Wing Scout Bomber (w/Kanan Jarrus)	12.50	25.00

2005 Star Wars Force Battlers

1 Anakin Skywalker	
2 Chewbacca	
3 Clone Trooper	

---

4 Darth Vader/ slashing attack		
5 Darth Vader/ missle-launching/ glider cape		
6 Emperor Palpatine		
7 General Grievous		
8 Han Solo		
9 Luke Skywalker	12.00	25.00
10 Mace Windu	8.00	15.00
11 Obi-Wan Kenobi		
12 Yoda		

2006 Star Wars Force Battlers

NNO Chewbacca	
NNO General Grievous	
NNO Jango Fett	
NNO Obi-Wan Kenobi	

2006 Star Wars Force Battlers International

NNO Darth Vader/ with missle-launching/ glider cape	
NNO Emperor Palpatine	

2017 Star Wars Forces of Destiny

NNO Ahsoka Tano	
NNO Endor Adventure (Princess Leia Organa & Wicket)	
NNO Jyn Erso	
NNO Luke Skywalker & Yoda	
NNO Padme Amidala	
NNO Princess Leia & R2-D2	
NNO Princess Leia & R2-D2 (Platinum Edition)	
NNO Rey of Jakku	
NNO Rey of Jakku & BB-8	
NNO Rey of Jakku & Kylo Ren	
NNO Roaring Chewbacca	
NNO Sabine Wren	

2004-10 Star Wars Galactic Heroes

1 4-LOM/Bossk	8.00	15.00
2 Ahsoka Tano/Captain Rex	15.00	30.00
3 Ahsoka Tano/R3-S6 Goldie	8.00	15.00
4 Anakin Skywalker/Clone Trooper (white)	6.00	12.00
5 Anakin Skywalker/Clone Trooper (blue)	6.00	12.00
6 Anakin Skywalker/Count Dooku	6.00	12.00
7 Anakin Skywalker/STAP		
8 Asajj Ventress/Count Dooku	12.00	25.00
9 AT-AT Commander/AT-AT Driver	8.00	15.00
10 Battle Droid/Clone Trooper	6.00	12.00
11 C-3PO/Chewbacca	8.00	15.00
12 Chewbacca/Clone Trooper	6.00	12.00
13 Chewbacca/Death Star Droid/Mouse Droid	8.00	15.00
14 Chewbacca/Disassembled C-3PO	10.00	20.00
15 Clone Trooper/Dwarf Spider Droid	8.00	15.00
16 Clone Trooper/Mace Windu	8.00	15.00
17 Commander Bly/Aayla Secura	12.00	25.00
18 Dark Side Anakin/Clone Trooper	8.00	12.00
19 Darth Maul/Sith Speeder	8.00	15.00
20 Darth Vader/Holographic Emperor Palpatine		
21 Death Star Trooper/Imperial Officer	6.00	12.00
22 Dengar/Boba Fett	12.00	25.00
23 Duros/Garindan		
24 Emperor Palpatine/Shock Trooper		
25 Emperor Palpatine/Yoda	6.00	15.00
26 Figrin D'an/Hammerhead	6.00	12.00
27 Grand Moff Tarkin/Imperial Officer	5.00	10.00
28 Greedo/Han Solo	15.00	30.00
29 Han Solo/Logray	8.00	15.00
30 IG-86/Clone Commander Thire		

---

31 IG-88/Zuckuss	6.00	12.00
32 Jango Fett/Obi-Wan Kenobi	8.00	15.00
33 Jar Jar Binks/Destroyer Droid		
34 Jawa/Tusken Raider	6.00	12.00
35 Ki-Adi-Mundi/Commander Bacara		
36 Kit Fisto/General Grievous	8.00	15.00
37 Kit Fisto/Mace Windu	10.00	20.00
38 Luke Skywalker (w/Yoda)/Spirit of Obi-Wan	6.00	12.00
39 Luke Skywalker Stormtrooper/Han Solo Stormtrooper	10.00	20.00
40 Luke Skywalker/Darth Vader	8.00	15.00
41 Luke Skywalker/Gamorrean Guard	6.00	12.00
42 Luke Skywalker/Han Solo		
43 Luke Skywalker/Lando Calrissian	6.00	12.00
44 Luke Skywalker/R2-D2	6.00	12.00
45 Luke Skywalker/Speeder	15.00	30.00
46 Nien Nunb/Admiral Ackbar	10.00	20.00
47 Obi-Wan Kenobi/Clone Commander Cody		
48 Obi-Wan Kenobi/Clone Trooper (blue Star Wars logo)		
49 Obi-Wan Kenobi/Clone Trooper (red Star Wars logo)		
50 Obi-Wan Kenobi/Darth Maul	8.00	15.00
51 Obi-Wan Kenobi/Darth Vader	6.00	12.00
52 Obi-Wan Kenobi/Durge	6.00	12.00
53 Obi-Wan Kenobi/General Grievous		
54 Padme Amidala/Anakin Skywalker	12.00	25.00
55 Padme Amidala/Clone Trooper		
56 Padme Amidala/Jar Jar Binks		
57 Plo Koon/Captain Jag		
58 Ponda Baba/Snaggletooth		
59 Princess Leia (Endor general)/Rebel Commando (Battle of Endor)		
60 Princess Leia Boushh/Han Solo		
61 Princess Leia/Darth Vader		
62 Princess Leia/Han Solo	12.00	25.00
63 R2-D2 (serving tray)/Princess Leia (slave)		
64 R2-D2/Jawas		
65 Royal Guard/Imperial Gunner		
66 Saesee Tiin/Agen Kolar		
67 Sandtrooper/Obi-Wan Kenobi		
68 Scout Trooper/Speeder Bike	6.00	12.00
69 Shaak Ti/Magna Guard		
70 Skiff Guard/Lando Calrissian	8.00	15.00
71 Snowtrooper/Rebel Trooper		
72 Stormtrooper/Rebel Trooper		
73 Super Battle Droid/Luminara Unduli		
74 Super Battle Droid/R2-D2		
75 Tarfful/Commander Gree		
76 Wedge/TIE Pilot		
77 Weequay/Barada		
78 Yoda/Clone Trooper		
79 Yoda/Kashyyyk Trooper		

2004-10 Star Wars Galactic Heroes Backpack Heroes

1 Boba Fett	
2 Darth Tater	

3 Darth Vader
4 Han Solo
5 Luke Skywalker
6 Yoda

2004-10 Star Wars Galactic Heroes Cinema Scenes

1 Assault on Ryloth
2 Assault on the Death Star
3 Assault on the Death Star 2
4 Battle of Geonosis
5 Battle of Hoth
6 Battle of Naboo
7 Battle of Kashyyyk
8 Battle of Mustafar
9 Cantina Band
10 Cantina Encounter
11 Death Star Escape
12 Endor Attack
13 Endor Celebration
14 Escape from Mos Eisley
15 Geonosis Battle Arena
16 Hoth Snowspeeder Assault
17 Jabba's Palace
18 Jabba's Sail Barge
19 Jabba's Skiff The Pit of Carkoon
20 Jedi Starfighter
21 Jedi vs. Sith
22 Kamino Showdown
23 Millennium Falcon
24 Purchase of the Droids
25 Rancor Pit
26 Shadow Squadron Y-Wing
27 Slave I and Boba Fett
28 Speeder Bike Chase
29 Vader's Bounty Hunters
30 Vader's TIE Fighter (w/Darth Vader)
31 X-Wing Dagobah Landing

2004-10 Star Wars Galactic Heroes Exclusives

1 Scout Trooper
(2004 SDCC Exclusive)
2 Yoda/R2-D2
(2004 Burger King Exclusive)

2004-10 Star Wars Galactic Heroes Singles

1 Anakin Skywalker
2 Battle Droid
3 Boba Fett
4 Bossk
5 C-3PO
6 Chewbacca
7 Clone Trooper
8 Darth Maul
9 Darth Vader
10 Han Solo
11 Luke Skywalker
12 Obi-Wan Kenobi
13 R2-D2

2004-10 Star Wars Galactic Heroes Stocking Stuffers

1 Darth Vader/Boba Fett/Stormtrooper
2 Han Solo/Chewbacca/C-3PO
3 Luke Skywalker/Yoda/R2-D2
4 Obi-Wan Kenobi/Anakin Skywalker/Shock Trooper

2004-10 Star Wars Galactic Heroes Vehicles

1 Anakin's Delta Starfighter
2 Landspeeder
3 Millennium Falcon
4 Obi-Wan's Starfighter
5 Snowspeeder
6 X-Wing Fighter
7 X-Wing Racer

2019 Star Wars Galaxy of Adventures 3.75-Inch

NNO	Boba Fett	10.00	20.00
NNO	Chewbacca	6.00	12.00
NNO	Darth Maul	7.50	15.00
NNO	Darth Vader	10.00	20.00
NNO	General Grievous	7.50	15.00
NNO	Han Solo	7.50	15.00
NNO	Kylo Ren	7.50	15.00
NNO	Luke Skywalker	7.50	15.00
NNO	Obi-Wan Kenobi	6.00	12.00
NNO	Princess Leia Organa	7.50	15.00
NNO	R2-D2	6.00	12.00
NNO	Rey	10.00	20.00
NNO	Stormtrooper	7.50	15.00
NNO	Yoda	7.50	15.00

2019 Star Wars Galaxy of Adventures 5-Inch

NNO	Darth Vader	12.50	25.00
NNO	C-3PO		
NNO	Han Solo		
NNO	Chewbacca	7.50	15.00
NNO	Kylo Ren	10.00	20.00
NNO	Rey	12.50	25.00
NNO	Jet Trooper	7.50	15.00
NNO	Finn	7.50	15.00

2019 Star Wars Galaxy of Adventures 5-Inch Multipacks

NNO D-0/BB-8/R2-D2 3-Pack
NNO Kylo Ren/Rey 2-Pack

2019 Star Wars Galaxy of Adventures 5-Inch Vehicle

NNO	Treadspeeder (w/First Order Driver)	20.00	40.00

2015 Star Wars Hero Mashers

NNO	Boba Fett	5.00	10.00
NNO	Bossk	5.00	10.00
NNO	Darth Vader	6.00	12.00
NNO	General Grievous	7.50	15.00
NNO	Jar Jar Binks	5.00	10.00
NNO	Kanan Jarrus	7.50	15.00
NNO	Zeb Orrelios		

2015 Star Wars Hero Mashers Deluxe

NNO	Anakin Skywalker with Speeder Bike	12.50	25.00
NNO	Darth Maul with Sith Speeder Bike	10.00	20.00
NNO	Han Solo vs. Boba Fett	10.00	20.00
NNO	Luke Skywalker vs. Darth Vader	15.00	30.00
NNO	Yoda vs. Emperor Palpatine	15.00	30.00

2019-20 Star Wars HyperReal

NNO Darth Vader
NNO Luke Skywalker

2004-05 Star Wars Jedi Force Blue

ACTION FIGURES AND FIGURINES

NNO Anakin Skywalker (w/Jedi Pod)		
NNO Anakin Skywalker (w/rescue glider)		
NNO C-3PO/R2-D2		
NNO Chewbacca (w/Wookiee Action Tool)		
NNO Chewbacca (w/Wookiee Scout Flyer)		
NNO Darth Vader (w/Imperial Claw Droid)		
NNO Han Solo (w/Jet Bike)		
NNO Luke Skywalker (w/Jedi Jet Pack)		
NNO Luke Skywalker (w/Speeder Bike)		
NNO Luke Skywalker (w/Speeder Board)		
NNO Luke's X-Wing		
NNO Mace Windu (w/Jedi Grappling Hook)		
NNO Obi-Wan Kenobi (w/Boga)		
NNO Yoda (w/Swamp Stomper)		

2004-05 Star Wars Jedi Force White

NNO Anakin Skywalker/Jar Jar Binks		
NNO Anakin Skywalker's Jedi Starfighter (w/R2-D2)		
NNO BARC Speeder Bike (w/Anakin Skywalker)	10.00	20.00
NNO C-3PO/R2-D2		
NNO Darth Vader/Stormtrooper		
NNO Freeco Bike (w/Obi-Wan Kenobi)		
NNO Han Solo/Chewbacca		
NNO Landspeeder (w/Luke Skywalker)		
NNO Millennium Falcon (w/Han Solo/Chewbacca)		
NNO Obi-Wan Kenobi/Commander Cody		
NNO Snowspeeder (w/Luke Skywalker/Han Solo)		
NNO Yoda/Luke Skywalker		

2017 Star Wars The Last Jedi Big Figs

NNO Captain Phasma	15.00	30.00
NNO Elite Praetorian Guard	12.50	25.00
NNO First Order Executioner	25.00	50.00
NNO First Order Stormtrooper	10.00	20.00
NNO Kylo Ren	12.50	25.00
NNO Poe Dameron	10.00	20.00
NNO Rey	12.50	25.00

2017 Star Wars The Last Jedi Force Link

1 C-3PO	6.00	12.00
2 C'Ai Threnalli	6.00	12.00
(Entertainment Earth Exclusive)		
3 Chewbacca (w/porg)	7.50	15.00
4 DJ (Canto Bight)	5.00	10.00
5 Emperor Palpatine		
6 Finn (Resistance Fighter)	6.00	12.00
7 First Order Flametrooper	7.50	15.00
(Entertainment Earth Exclusive)		
8 First Order Stormtrooper	7.50	15.00
9 General Hux (w/mouse droid)	5.00	10.00
10 General Leia Organa	7.50	15.00
11 Jyn Erso (Jedha)	6.00	12.00
12 Kylo Ren	7.50	15.00
13 Luke Skywalker (Jedi Exile)	7.50	15.00
14 Luke Skywalker (Jedi Master)	7.50	15.00
15 Obi-Wan Kenobi	7.50	15.00
16 Poe Dameron (Resistance Pilot)	5.00	10.00
17 R2-D2	6.00	12.00
18 Resistance Gunner Paige	6.00	12.00
19 Resistance Gunner Rose	6.00	12.00
20 Rey (Island Journey)	6.00	12.00
21 Rey (Jedi Training)	10.00	20.00
22 Yoda	10.00	20.00

2017 Star Wars The Last Jedi Force Link 2-Packs

NNO Bala-Tik (w/Rathtar)	7.50	15.00
NNO Chirrut Imwe & Baze Malbus	12.50	25.00
NNO Darth Vader (w/Imperial probe droid)		

NNO Finn & Captain Phasma	15.00	30.00
(Entertainment Earth Exclusive)		
NNO Han Solo & Boba Fett	10.00	20.00
NNO Rey (Jedi Training) & Elite Praetorian Guard	7.50	15.00
NNO Rose Tico (w/BB-8 & BB-9E)	7.50	15.00

2017 Star Wars The Last Jedi Force Link Multipacks

NNO Battle on Crait 4-Pack	15.00	30.00
Rey/First Order Walker Driver		
First Order Gunner/Rose		
NNO Emperor Palpatine/Luke Skywalker/Emperor's Royal Guard 3-Pack	10.00	20.00
(Target Exclusive)		
NNO Era of the Force 8-Pack		
Yoda/Luke/Kylo Ren/Rey		
Darth Maul/Mace Windu		
Obi-Wan Kenobi/Darth Vader		
(Target Exclusive)		
NNO Luke Skywalker/Resistance Tech Rose	20.00	40.00
Rey (Jedi Training)/First Order Stormtrooper 4-Pack		

2017 Star Wars The Last Jedi Force Link Sets

NNO BB-8 2-in-1 Mega Playset	20.00	40.00
NNO Starter Set (w/Elite Praetorian Guard)		
(Toys R Us Exclusive)		
NNO Starter Set (w/Kylo Ren)	7.50	15.00
NNO Starter Set (w/Stormtrooper Executioner)	15.00	30.00
(Toys R Us Exclusive)		

2017 Star Wars The Last Jedi Force Link Vehicles

1 Canto Bight Police Speeder (w/Canto Bight Police)	10.00	20.00
2 Kylo Ren's TIE Silencer (w/Kylo Ren)	20.00	40.00
3 Resistance A-Wing Fighter (w/Resistance Pilot Tallie)	12.50	25.00
4 Ski Speeder (w/Poe Dameron)		
5 TIE Fighter (w/TIE Fighter Pilot)	15.00	30.00
(Walmart Exclusive)		
6 X-Wing Fighter (w/Poe Dameron)	30.00	75.00
(Toys R Us Exclusive)		

2017 Star Wars The Last Jedi S.H. Figuarts

NNO Captain Phasma	30.00	60.00
NNO Elite Praetorian Guard (w/dual blades)	20.00	40.00
NNO Elite Praetorian Guard (w/single blade)	20.00	40.00
NNO Elite Praetorian Guard (w/whip staff)	25.00	50.00
NNO First Order Executioner	25.00	50.00
NNO First Order Stormtrooper	30.00	75.00
NNO Kylo Ren	50.00	100.00
NNO Rey	50.00	100.00

2008-10 Star Wars The Legacy Collection Battle Packs

NNO Battle at the Sarlaac Pit (ultimate)	50.00	100.00
(2008 Target Exclusive)		
NNO Battle of Endor		
NNO Birth of Darth Vader	20.00	40.00
NNO Clone Attack on Coruscant	20.00	40.00
NNO Disturbance at Lars Homestead	75.00	150.00
(2008 Toys R Us Exclusive)		
NNO Duel on Mustafar		
NNO Gelagrub Patrol	20.00	50.00

NNO Geonosis Assault	50.00	100.00
NNO Hoth Recon Patrol	30.00	60.00
NNO Hoth Speeder Bike Patrol	25.00	50.00
NNO Jedi Training on Dagobah		
NNO Jedi vs. Darth Sidious	15.00	30.00
NNO Kamino Conflict		
NNO Resurgence of the Jedi	20.00	40.00
NNO Scramble on Yavin	100.00	175.00
NNO Shield Generator Assault	25.00	50.00
NNO Tatooine Desert Ambush		
NNO Training on the Falcon	30.00	75.00

2008-10 Star Wars The Legacy Collection Build-A-Droid Wave 1

BD1a Han Solo/ with R4-D6 left leg	6.00	12.00
BD1b Han Solo/ with R4-D6 left leg/ first day of issue sticker		
BD2a Luke Skywalker/ with R4-D6 right leg		
BD2b Luke Skywalker/ with R5-A2 head/ and center leg		
BD2c Luke Skywalker/ with R4-D6 right leg/ first day of issue sticker		
BD3a Chewbacca/ with R4-D6 head/ and center leg		
BD3b Chewbacca/ with R4-D6 head/ and center leg/ first day of issue sticker		
BD4a Leektar/Nippet/ with R4-D6 torso		
BD4b Leektar/Nippet/ with R4-D6 torso/ first day of issue sticker		
BD5a Ak-Rev/ with R7-Z0 left leg		
BD5b Ak-Rev/ with R7-Z0 left leg/ first day of issue sticker	6.00	12.00
BD6a Yarna D'Al'Gargan/ with R7-Z0 right leg	8.00	15.00
BD6b Yarna D'Al'Gargan/ with R7-Z0 right leg/ first day of issue sticker	6.00	12.00
BD7a Bane Malar/ with R7-Z0 torso		
BD7b Bane Malar/ with R7-Z0 torso/ first day of issue sticker		
BD8a Darth Vader/ multi-piece helmet/ with R7-Z0 head		
BD8b Darth Vader/ multi-piece helmet/ with R7-Z0 head/ first day of issue sti		
BD8c Darth Vader/ multi-piece helmet/ with MB-RA-7 head		

2008-10 Star Wars The Legacy Collection Build-A-Droid Wave 2

BD9 Obi-Wan Kenobi general/ with R4-J1 left leg	10.00	20.00
BD10 Clone Scuba Trooper/ with R4-J1 head/ and center leg	6.00	12.00
BD11 Saesee Tiin general/ with R7-T1 right leg		
BD12 Padme Amidala snow/ with R7-T1 left leg		
BD13 IG Lancer Droid/ with R4-J1 torso		
BD14 Mon Calimari Warrior/ with R7-T1 Torso	8.00	15.00
BD15 Quarren Soldier/ with R7-T1 head/ and center leg		
BD16 Clone Trooper blue/ with cannon/with R4-J1 right leg		

2008-10 Star Wars The Legacy Collection Build-A-Droid Wave 3

BD17a Clone Trooper coruscant/ landing platform/ with RD6-RA7 torso	10.00	20.00
BD17b Clone Trooper coruscant/ landing platform/ with MB-RA-7 right arm		
BD18a Jodo Kast/ with RD6-RA7 head	10.00	20.00
BD18b Jodo Kast/ with MB-RA-7 left leg		
BD19 Yaddle/Evan Piell/ with RD6-RA7 right leg	15.00	30.00
BD20a Saleucami Trooper/ with 5D6-RA7 left leg		
BD20b Saleucami Trooper/ with MB-RA-7 right leg		
BD21 Count Dooku/ holographic transmission/ with RD6-RA7 right arm		
BD22 Imperial Engineer/ with RD6-RA7 left arm		

2008-10 Star Wars The Legacy Collection Build-A-Droid Wave 4

BD23 Stass Allie/ with MB-RA-7 left arm	12.00	25.00
BD24a Commander Faie/ with MB-RA-7 torso	10.00	20.00
BD24b Commander Faie/ with R5-A2 left leg	10.00	20.00
BD25a General Grievous/ with MB-RA-7 head	12.00	25.00
BD25b General Grievous/ with R5-A2 right leg		
BD26a Bail Organa/ light skin/ with MB-RA-7 left arm		
BD26b Bail Organa/ dark skin/ with MB-RA-7 left arm		
BD27a Breha Organa/ light skin/ with MB-RA-7 left leg		
BD27b Breha Organa/ dark skin/ with MB-RA-7 left leg		
BD28 FX-6/ with MB-RA-7 right leg	10.00	20.00
BD29 Clone Trooper 327th Star/ Corps yellow shoulder/ with MB-RA-7 torso		

BD29a Clone Trooper 327th Star/ Corps yellow shoulder/ with R5-A2 torso
BD29b Clone Trooper 327th Star/ Corps yellow shoulder/ with MB-RA-7 torso
BD29c Clone Trooper 327th Star/ Corps yellow shoulder/ with R5-A2 torso

2008-10 Star Wars The Legacy Collection Comic Packs Blue and White

1 Asajj Ventress and Tol Skorr
2 Anakin Skywalker and Durge
3 Anakin Skywalker and Assassin Droid
4 Darth Talon and Cade Skywalker
5 Antares Draco and Ganner Krieg
6 Fenn Shysa and Dengar
7 Princess Leia and Tobbi Dala
8 Leia Organa and Prince Xizor
9 Grand Admiral Thrawn and Talon Karrde
10 Darth Vader and Grand Moff Trachta
11 Darth Vader and Princess Leia
12 Clone Emperor and Luke Skywalker
13 Quinlan Vos and Commander Faie
14 Wedge Antilles and Borsk Fey'lya
15 Luke Skywalker and Deena Shan
16 Ki-Adi-Mundi and Sharad Hett

2008-10 Star Wars The Legacy Collection Comic Packs Blue and White Exclusives

NNO Ibtisam and Nrin Vakil   25.00   50.00
(2008 Walmart Exclusive)
NNO Janek Sunber and Amanin   15.00   30.00
(2008 Walmart Exclusive)
NNO Machook/Keoulkeech/Kettch   30.00   60.00
(2008 Walmart Exclusive)

2008-10 Star Wars The Legacy Collection Comic Packs Red and White

1 Darth Vader and Rebel Officer
2 Chewbacca and Han Solo
3 Yuuzhan Vong and Kyle Katarn

---

4 Wedge Antilles and Borsk Fey'lya
5 Luke Skywalker and Deena Shan
6 Ki-Adi-Mundi and Sharad Hett
7 Lumiya and Luke Skywalker
8 Darth Krayt and Sigel Dare
9 Clone Trooper and Clone Commander
10 Clone Trooper Lieutenant and Clone Trooper
11 Ulic Qel-Droma and Exar Kun
12 T'ra Saa and Tholme
13 Stormtrooper and Blackhole Hologram

2008-10 Star Wars The Legacy Collection Comic Packs Red and White Exclusives

NNO Baron Soontir Fel and Ysanne Isard (X-Wing Rogue Squadron)
(2010 Entertainment Earth Exclusive)
NNO Deliah Blue and Darth Nihl (Legacy)
(2010 Entertainment Earth Exclusive)
NNO IG-97 and Rom Mohc
(2009 Walmart Exclusive)
NNO Jaraal and Rohlan Dyre (Knights of the Old Republic)
(2010 Entertainment Earth Exclusive)
NNO Montross and Jaster Mareel (Jango Fett Open Seasons)
(2010 Entertainment Earth Exclusive)
NNO Plourr Ilo and Dllr Nep
(2009 Online Exclusive)
NNO Storm Commando and General Weir
(2009 Walmart Exclusive)

2008-10 Star Wars The Legacy Collection Creatures

1 Dewback (w/Imperial sandtrooper)   25.00   50.00
(2009 Walmart Exclusive)
2 Jabba's Rancor (w/Luke Skywalker)   60.00   120.00
(2008 Target Exclusive)

2008-10 Star Wars The Legacy Collection Evolutions

1 Clone Commandos   50.00   100.00
(2009 Walmart Exclusive)
2 Imperial Pilot Legacy I   15.00   30.00
3 Imperial Pilot Legacy II   15.00   30.00
(2009 Walmart Exclusive)
4 Rebel Pilot Legacy I   15.00   40.00
5 Rebel Pilot Legacy II   25.00   50.00
6 Rebel Pilot Legacy III   30.00   75.00
(2009 Walmart Exclusive)
7 The Fett Legacy   15.00   40.00
8 The Jedi Legacy
9 The Padme Amidala Legacy   12.00   25.00
10 The Sith Legacy   60.00   120.00
11 Vader's Secret Apprentice   30.00   60.00

2008-10 Star Wars The Legacy Collection Geonosis Battle Arena 2009 Edition

---

1 Coleman Trebor Vs. Jango Fett
2 Kit Fisto Vs. Geonosis Warrior
3 Mace Windu Vs. Battle Droid Commander
4 Joclad Danva Vs. Battle Droid
5 Roth Del Masona Vs. Super Battle Droid
6 Yoda Vs. Destroyer Droid

2008-10 Star Wars The Legacy Collection Geonosis Battle Arena 2010 Edition

1 Obi-Wan Kenobi & Super Battle Droid
2 Rodian Jedi & Battle Droid
3 Anakin Skywalker & Droideka
4 Shaak Ti & Geonosian Warrior
5 Nicanas Tassu & Count Dooku
6 C-3PO & R2-D2

2008-10 Star Wars The Legacy Collection Greatest Hits 2008

GH1	Commander Gree	6.00	12.00
GH2	Kashyyyk Trooper	6.00	12.00
GH3	Darth Vader (Battle Damage)	10.00	20.00
GH4	Imperial EVO Trooper	6.00	12.00

2008-10 Star Wars The Legacy Collection Saga Legends Blue and White

SL1 R2-D2 (electronic)
SL2 Yoda and Kybuck
SL3 Darth Vader (Anakin Skywalker)
SL4 Obi-Wan Kenobi
SL5 Clone Trooper (AOTC)
SL6 C-3PO
SL7 General Grievous
SL8 Mace Windu
SL9 Plo Koon
SL10 Super Battle Droid
SL11 Destroyer Droid
SL13 Darth Vader
SL14 Darth Maul
SL15 Jango Fett
SL16 501st Legion Trooper
SL17 Shock Trooper
SL18 BARC Trooper
SL19 ARC Trooper
SL21 Sandtrooper
SL22 Luke Skywalker (X-Wing pilot)
SL23 ARC trooper Commander (red)
SL24 Tri-Droid
SL25 Snowtrooper
SL26 Saesee Tiin
SL27 Clone Trooper (ROTS)
SL12a Clone Trooper Officer (red)
SL12b Clone Trooper Officer (yellow)
SL12c Clone Trooper Officer (blue)
SL12d Clone Trooper Officer (green)
SL20a Battle Droids (tan)
SL20b Battle Droids (brown)

ACTION FIGURES AND FIGURINES

2008-10 Star Wars The Legacy Collection Saga Legends Red and White

SL1	R2-D2 (electronic)
SL2	Darth Vader (Anakin Skywalker)
SL3	Obi-Wan Kenobi
SL4	Clone Trooper (Episode II)
SL5	Super Battle Droid
SL6	Darth Vader
SL7	Darth Maul
SL8	501st Legion Trooper
SL9	Yoda
SL10	Sandtrooper
SL11	Saesee Tiin
SL12	Clone Trooper (Episode III)
SL13	Plo Koon
SL14	Shocktrooper
SL15a	Chewbacca I
SL15b	Chewbacca II
SL16	Han Solo
SL17	Luke Skywalker

2008-10 Star Wars The Legacy Collection Vehicles

1	AT-ST	30.00	75.00
	(2009 Walmart Exclusive)		
2	Dagger Squadron B-Wing Fighter	50.00	100.00
	(2008 Toys R Us Exclusive)		
3	Darth Vader's TIE Advanced x1 Starfighter	15.00	30.00
4	Green Leader's A-Wing Fighter	50.00	100.00
	(2008 Walmart Exclusive)		
5	Millennium Falcon	300.00	600.00
6	Speeder Bike (w/biker scout)	25.00	50.00
	(Toys R Us Exclusive)		
7	TIE Fighter		
8	TIE Fighter Pirate		
	(PX Previews Exclusive)		
9	TIE Fighter Shadows of the Empire	150.00	300.00
	(2009 Target Exclusive)		
10	TIE Interceptor	30.00	60.00
	(2009 Toys R Us Exclusive)		
11	Wedge Antilles' X-Wing Starfighter	120.00	200.00
	(2009 Target Exclusive)		

2020 Star Wars The Mandalorian Bounty Collection Series 1

NNO	The Child (eating frog)
NNO	The Child (Force push)
NNO	The Child (in blanket)
NNO	The Child (sad face)
NNO	The Child (w/ball)
NNO	The Child (w/bowl)

2020 Star Wars The Mandalorian Talking Plush

NNO The Child

2008-09 Star Wars Mighty Muggs

NNO	Anakin Skywalker		
NNO	Asajj Ventress		
NNO	Boba Fett	8.00	15.00
NNO	C-3PO	8.00	15.00
NNO	Captain Rex	6.00	12.00
NNO	Chewbacca	8.00	15.00
NNO	Commander Cody	12.00	25.00
NNO	Count Dooku	6.00	12.00
NNO	Darth Maul	6.00	12.00
NNO	Darth Maul (shirtless)	6.00	12.00
NNO	Darth Revan	10.00	20.00
NNO	Darth Vader	8.00	15.00
NNO	Darth Vader (unmasked)		
NNO	Emperor	5.00	10.00
NNO	Gamorrean Guard	5.00	10.00
NNO	General Grievous	12.00	25.00
NNO	Grand Moff Tarkin		
NNO	Han Solo	8.00	15.00
NNO	Han Solo (Hoth)	10.00	20.00
NNO	Jango Fett	6.00	12.00
NNO	Lando Calrissian	8.00	15.00
NNO	Luke (Bespin)	8.00	15.00
NNO	Luke Skywalker	8.00	15.00
NNO	Luke Skywalker (Hoth)	8.00	15.00
NNO	Mace Windu		
NNO	Obi-Wan Kenobi (old)	6.00	12.00
NNO	Obi-Wan Kenobi (young)		
NNO	Plo Koon		
NNO	Princess Leia		
NNO	Qui-Gon Jinn	8.00	15.00
NNO	Royal Guard		
NNO	Stormtrooper	6.00	12.00
NNO	Wampa	5.00	10.00
NNO	Wicket	5.00	10.00
NNO	Yoda	8.00	15.00

2008-09 Star Wars Mighty Muggs Exclusives

1	Admiral Ackbar		
	(2008 PX Previews Exclusive)		
2	Biggs Darklighter		
	(2009 Target Exclusive)		
3	Bossk		
	(2009 Target Exclusive)		
4	Commander Gree		
	(2008 SDCC Exclusive)		
5	Shadow Trooper		
	(2008 PX Previews Exclusive)		
6	Shock Trooper	8.00	15.00
	(2009 Target Exclusive)		
7	Snowtrooper	8.00	15.00
	(2009 Target Exclusive)		
8	Teebo		
	(2009 Target Exclusive)		

2020-21 Star Wars Mission Fleet

NNO	Ahsoka Tano
NNO	Blurrg (w/Kuiil)
NNO	Boba Fett
NNO	Chewbacca
NNO	Clone Trooper
NNO	Darth Maul
NNO	Shock Trooper

2020-21 Star Wars Mission Fleet Vehicles

NNO AT-RT (w/Captain Rex)

NNO	Barc Speeder (w/Obi-Wan Kenobi)
NNO	Jedi Starfighter (w/Anakin Skywalker)
NNO	Jedi Starfighter (w/Obi-Wan Kenobi)
NNO	Millennium Falcon (w/Han Solo)
NNO	Razor Crest (w/Mandalorian)
NNO	Speeder Bike (w/IG-11 and Child)
NNO	Speeder Bike (w/Mandalorian and Child)
NNO	Speeder Bike (w/Scout Trooper)
NNO	TIE Advanced (w/Darth Vader)
NNO	TIE Whisper (w/Kylo Ren)
NNO	X-Wing Fighter (w/Luke Skywalker)

2012 Star Wars Movie Heroes

MH1	Shock Trooper	10.00	20.00
MH2	Super Battle Droid	7.50	15.00
MH3	R2-D2	10.00	20.00
MH4	Battle Droid (repaint)	6.00	12.00
MH4	Battle Droid (variant)	6.00	12.00
MH5	Darth Maul (repaint)		
MH6	Darth Vader	7.50	15.00
MH7	General Grievous	15.00	30.00
MH8	Obi-Wan Kenobi	5.00	10.00
MH9	Yoda	6.00	12.00
MH10	Qui-Gon Jinn	5.00	10.00
MH11	Clone Trooper (with Jetpack)	6.00	12.00
MH12	Destroyer Droid	5.00	10.00
MH13	Jar Jar Binks	5.00	10.00
MH14	Anakin Skywalker	5.00	10.00
MH15	Darth Maul (Spinning Action)		
MH16	Obi-Wan Kenobi (Light-Up Lightsaber)		
MH17	Padme Amidala	6.00	12.00
MH18	Qui-Gon Jinn (Light-Up Lightsaber)	5.00	10.00
MH19	Anakin Skywalker (Light-Up Lightsaber)		
MH20	Darth Vader (Light-Up Lightsaber)	12.50	25.00
MH21	Luke Skywalker (zipline backpack)	7.50	15.00
MH22	Battle Droid (The Phantom Menace)(exploding action)		
MH23	Sandtrooper (Light-Up Weapon)		
MH24	Boba Fett (zipline jetpack)		

2012 Star Wars Movie Heroes Battle Packs

NNO	Bespin Battle	20.00	40.00
NNO	Duel on Naboo	15.00	30.00
NNO	Ewok Pack		
NNO	Geonosis Arena Battle		
NNO	Rebel Heroes		
NNO	Rebel Pilots		
NNO	Republic Troopers		

2012 Star Wars Movie Heroes Exclusives

NNO	Darth Maul Returns
NNO	Podracer Pilots
	(Toys R Us Exclusive)

2012 Star Wars Movie Heroes Vehicles

NNO Anakin Skywalker's Jedi Starfighter (The Clone Wars)		
NNO Anakin Skywalker's Podracer	20.00	40.00
NNO Attack Recon Fighter with Anakin Skywalker		
NNO BARC Speeder with Clone Trooper		
NNO Naboo Royal Fighter with Obi-Wan Skywalker		
NNO Naboo Starfighter	60.00	120.00
NNO Republic Assault Submarine with Scuba Clone Trooper		
NNO Republic Attack Dropship with Clone Pilot		
NNO Sebulba's Podracer		
NNO Sith Infiltrator		
NNO Sith Speeder with Darth Maul		
NNO Speeder Bike with Scout and Cannon		
(Toys R Us Exclusive)		
NNO STAP with Battle Droid		
NNO Trade Federation AAT (Armored Assault Tank)		

2005 Star Wars M&M's Chocolate Mpire

1	Chewbacca/Mace Windu	6.00	12.00
2	Clone Trooper/Darth Vader	6.00	12.00
3	Count Dooku/Darth Maul	12.00	25.00
4	Emperor Palpatine/Anakin Skywalker	12.00	25.00
5	General Grievous/Obi-Wan Kenobi	8.00	15.00
6	Han Solo/Boba Fett	10.00	20.00
7	Luke Skywalker/Princess Leia	8.00	15.00
8	Queen Amidala/R2-D2/C-3PO	8.00	15.00

2007 Star Wars Order 66 Target Exclusives

1	Emperor Palpatine/Commander Thire	12.00	25.00
2	Mace Windu/Galactic Marine	10.00	20.00
3	Darth Vader/Commander Bow	12.00	25.00
4	Obi-Wan Kenobi/AT-RT Driver	10.00	20.00
5	Anakin Skywalker/Airborne Trooper	12.00	25.00
6	Yoda/Kashyyyk Trooper	10.00	20.00

2008 Star Wars Order 66 Target Exclusives

1	Obi-Wan Kenobi/ARC Trooper Commander	12.00	25.00
2	Anakin Skywalker/ARC Trooper	10.00	20.00
3	Tsui Choi/BARC Trooper	15.00	30.00
4	Emperor Palpatine/Commander Vill	12.00	25.00
5	Luminara Unduli/AT-RT Driver	10.00	20.00
6	Master Sev/ARC Trooper	15.00	30.00

2004-05 Star Wars The Original Trilogy Collection

1	Luke Skywalker (Dagobah training)	6.00	12.00
2	Yoda (Dagobah training)	3.00	6.00
3	Spirit Obi-Wan Kenobi	8.00	15.00
4	R2-D2 (Dagobah training)	6.00	12.00
5	Luke Skywalker (X-Wing pilot)	8.00	15.00
6	Luke Skywalker (Jedi Knight)	8.00	15.00
7	Han Solo (Mos Eisley escape)	3.00	6.00
8	Chewbacca (Hoth escape)	6.00	12.00
9	Princess Leia	10.00	20.00
10	Darth Vader (throne room)	8.00	15.00
11	Scout Trooper	6.00	12.00
12	R2-D2	8.00	15.00
13	C-3PO	8.00	15.00

14	Boba Fett	12.00	25.00
15	Obi-Wan Kenobi	12.00	25.00
16	Stormtrooper (Death Star attack)	8.00	15.00
17	Wicket	3.00	6.00
18	Princess Leia (Cloud City)	8.00	15.00
19	Cloud Car Pilot	3.00	6.00
20	Lobot	3.00	6.00
21	TIE Fighter Pilot	8.00	15.00
22	Greedo	6.00	12.00
23	Tusken Raider	10.00	20.00
24	Jawas	3.00	6.00
25	Snowtrooper	6.00	12.00
26	Luke Skywalker (Bespin)	8.00	15.00
27	IG-88	12.00	25.00
28	Bossk	6.00	12.00
29	Darth Vader (Hoth)	10.00	20.00
30	Gamorrean Guard	10.00	20.00
31	Bib Fortuna	3.00	6.00
32	Darth Vader	3.00	6.00
33	Lando Calrissian (skiff guard)	6.00	12.00
34	Princess Leia (sail barge)	15.00	30.00
35	Han Solo (AT-ST driver uniform)	3.00	6.00
36	General Madine	3.00	6.00
37	Lando Calrissian (General)	8.00	15.00
38a	Imperial Trooper (white)	3.00	6.00
38b	Imperial Trooper (gray)	3.00	6.00

2004-05 Star Wars The Original Trilogy Collection 12-Inch

1	Boba Fett	30.00	60.00
2	Chewbacca	20.00	40.00
3	Luke Skywalker	20.00	40.00
4	Stormtrooper	15.00	30.00

2004-05 Star Wars The Original Trilogy Collection Cards

1	Pablo-Jill/ genosis arena
2	Yarua (Coruscant Senate)
3	Sly Moore (Coruscant Senate)
4	Queen Amidala (celebration ceremony)
5	Rabe (Queen's chambers)
6	Feltipern Trevagg (cantina encounter)
7	Myo (cantina encounter)
8	Dannik Jerrico (cantina encounter)
9	Luke Skywalker (Dagobah training)
10	Darth Vader (Death Star hangar)
11	Stormtrooper (Death Star attack)
12	Sandtrooper (Tatooine search)
13	Scout Trooper (Endor raid)
14	Han Solo (Mos Eisley escape)
15	Chewbacca (Hoth escape)
16	Yoda (Dagobah training)

2004-05 Star Wars The Original Trilogy Collection DVD Collection

1	A New Hope	6.00	12.00
2	Empire Strikes Back	10.00	20.00
3	Return of the Jedi	8.00	15.00

2004-05 Star Wars The Original Trilogy Collection Exclusives

1	Darth Vader (silver)	10.00	20.00
	(2004 Toys R Us Exclusive)		
2	Emperor Palpatine (executor transmission)		
	(2004 StarWarsShop.com Exclusive)		
3	Holiday Darth Vader	30.00	60.00
	(2005 StarWarsShop.com Exclusive)		
4	Holographic Princess Leia	12.00	25.00
	(2005 SDCC Exclusive)		

5	Holiday Edition Jawas	15.00	30.00
	(2004 Entertainment Earth Exclusive)		
6	Luke Skywalker's Encounter with Yoda		
	(2004 Encuentros Mexico Exclusive)		
7	Wedge Antilles		
	(2005 Internet Exclusive)		

2004-05 Star Wars The Original Trilogy Collection Multipacks

1	Clone Trooper/Troop Builder 4-Pack	25.00	50.00
	Clone Trooper/Clone Trooper/Clone Tr		
2	Clone Trooper Builder 4-Pack (white w/battle damage)	30.00	60.00
3	Clone Trooper Builder 4-Pack (colored)		
4	Clone Trooper Builder 4-Pack (colored w/battle damage)	20.00	40.00
5	Endor Ambush (Han Solo/Logray/Rebel Trooper/Wicket/Speeder)	12.00	25.00
6	Naboo Final Combat (Battle Droid tan	20.00	40.00
	Gungan Soldier/Captain Tarpals/Kaad)		

2004-05 Star Wars The Original Trilogy Collection Screen Scenes

1	Mos Eisley Cantina I/Dr. Evanzan/Wuher/Kitik Keed'kak	30.00	60.00
2	Mos Eisley Cantina II (Obi-Wan Kenobi/Ponda Baba/Zutton)	30.00	60.00
3	Jedi High Council I (Qui-Gon Jinn/Ki-Adi Mundi/Yoda)		
4	Jedi High Council II (Plo Koon/Obi-Wan Kenobi/Eeth Koth)		
5	Jedi High Council III (Anakin Skywalker/Saesee Tiin/Adi Gallia)		
6	Jedi High Council IV (Shaak Ti/Agen Kolar/Stass Allie)		

2004-05 Star Wars The Original Trilogy Collection Transitional

1	Pablo-Jill (Geonosis Arena)	6.00	12.00
2	Yarua (Wookiee Senator)	10.00	20.00
3	Sly Moore	5.00	10.00
4	Queen Amidala (Naboo Celebration)	5.00	10.00
5	Rabe (Royal Handmaiden)	4.00	10.00
6	Feltipern Trevagg (Cantina)	8.00	15.00
7	Myo (Cantina)	8.00	15.00
8	Dannik Jerriko (Cantina Encounter)	8.00	15.00
9	Luke Skywalker (Dagobah Training)		
10	Darth Vader (Death Star Hangar)	15.00	30.00
11	Stormtrooper (Death Star Attack)		
12	Sandtrooper (Tatooine Search)		
13	Scout Trooper (Endor Raid)		
14	Han Solo (Mos Eisley Escape)		
15	Chewbacca (Hoth Escape)	12.00	25.00
16	Yoda (Dagobah Training)		

2004-05 Star Wars The Original Trilogy Collection Vehicles

1	Darth Vader's TIE Fighter	30.00	75.00
2	Millennium Falcon		
3	Millennium Falcon (w/Chewbacca/Han/Luke/Obi-Wan/C-3PO/R2-D2)		
	(2004 Sam's Club Exclusive)		
4	Sandcrawler (w/RA-7 and Jawas)	100.00	200.00
5	Slave I (w/Boba Fett in tan cape)	75.00	150.00
6	TIE Fighter	30.00	75.00
7	TIE Fighter & X-Wing Fighter	30.00	75.00
8	X-Wing Fighter		
9	Y-Wing Fighter (w/pilot)		

2004-05 Star Wars The Original Trilogy 1Collection Vintage

1 Boba Fett (ROTJ)	15.00	30.00
2 C-3PO (ESB)	6.00	12.00
3 Chewbacca (ROTJ)	12.00	25.00
4 Darth Vader (ESB)	8.00	15.00
5 Han Solo (SW)	6.00	12.00
6 Lando Calrissian (ESB)	12.00	25.00
7 Luke Skywalker (SW)	6.00	12.00
8 Obi-Wan Kenobi (SW)	5.00	10.00
9 Princess Leia Organa (SW)	5.00	10.00
10 R2-D2 (ROTJ)	15.00	30.00
11 Stormtrooper (ROTJ)	8.00	15.00
12 Yoda ESB	6.00	12.00

2000-02 Star Wars Power of the Jedi Action Collection 12-Inch

1 4-LOM	12.00	25.00
2 Bossk	15.00	30.00
3 Captain Tarpals (w/Kaadu)	20.00	40.00
4 Death Star Droid	15.00	30.00
5 Death Star Trooper	20.00	40.00
6 Han Solo Stormtrooper	15.00	30.00
7 IG-88	8.00	15.00
8 Luke Skywalker & Yoda	20.00	40.00
9 Luke Skywalker (100th figure)	30.00	60.00
10 Luke Skywalker (w/speeder bike)	40.00	80.00

2000-02 Star Wars Power of the Jedi Attack of the Clones Sneak Preview

1 Clone Trooper	4.00	8.00
2 Jango Fett	5.00	10.00
3 R3-T7	6.00	12.00
4 Zam Wesell	4.00	8.00

2000-02 Star Wars Power of the Jedi Collection 1

1 Anakin Skywalker (mechanic)	8.00	15.00
2 Aurra Sing (bounty hunter)	6.00	12.00
3 Battle Droid (boomer damage)	4.00	8.00
4 Ben Obi Wan Kenobi (Jedi Knight)	5.00	10.00
5 Chewbacca (Millennium Falcon mechanic)	10.00	20.00
6 Darth Maul (final duel)	6.00	12.00
7 Darth Maul (Sith Apprentice)	5.00	10.00
8 Darth Vader (Dagobah)	8.00	15.00
9 Darth Vader (Emperor's wrath)	5.00	10.00
10 Han Solo (Bespin capture)	4.00	8.00
11 Han Solo (Death Star escape)	6.00	12.00
12 Leia Organa (general)	5.00	10.00
13 Luke Skywalker (X-Wing Pilot)	4.00	8.00
14 Obi-Wan Kenobi (cold weather gear)	4.00	8.00
15 Obi-Wan Kenobi (Jedi)	4.00	8.00
16 Qui-Gon Jinn (Jedi training gear)	8.00	15.00
17 Qui-Gon Jinn (Mos Espa disguise)	4.00	8.00
18 R2-D2 (Naboo escape)	5.00	10.00
19 Sandtrooper (Tatooine patrol)	6.00	12.00

2000-02 Star Wars Power of the Jedi Collection 2

1 Battle Droid (security)	4.00	8.00
2 Bespin Guard (cloud city security)	4.00	8.00

3 BoShek	8.00	15.00
4 Boss Nass (Gungan sacred place)	4.00	8.00
5 Chewbacca (Dejarik Champion)	10.00	20.00
6 Coruscant Guard	5.00	10.00
7 Eeth Koth (Jedi Master)	6.00	12.00
8 Ellorrs Madak (Fan's Choice Figure #1)	5.00	10.00
9 Fode and Beed (pod race announcers)	5.00	10.00
10 FX-7 (medical droid)	10.00	20.00
11 Gungan Warrior	4.00	8.00
12 IG-88 (bounty hunter)	12.00	25.00
13 Imperial Officer	4.00	8.00
14 Jar Jar Binks (Tatooine)	4.00	8.00
15 Jek Porkins (X-Wing pilot)	10.00	20.00
16 K-3PO (Echo Base protocol droid)	6.00	12.00
17 Ketwol	4.00	8.00
18 Lando Calrissian (Bespin escape)	6.00	12.00
19 Leia Organa (Bespin escape)	8.00	15.00
20 Mas Amedda	5.00	10.00
21 Mon Calamari (officer)	8.00	15.00
22 Obi-Wan Kenobi (Jedi training gear)	4.00	8.00
23 Plo Koon (Jedi Master)	4.00	8.00
24 Queen Amidala (royal decoy)	6.00	12.00
25 Queen Amidala (Theed invasion)	6.00	12.00
26 R4-M9	8.00	15.00
27 R2-Q5 (Imperial astromech droid)	8.00	15.00
28 Rebel Trooper (Tantive IV defender)	4.00	8.00
29 Sabe (Queen's decoy)	5.00	10.00
30 Saesee Tiin (Jedi Master)	4.00	8.00
31 Scout Trooper (Imperial patrol)	6.00	12.00
32 Sebulba (Boonta Eve Challenge)	5.00	10.00
33 Shmi Skywalker	5.00	10.00
34 Teebo	6.00	12.00
35 Tessek	5.00	10.00
36 Tusken Raider (desert sniper)	6.00	12.00
37 Zutton (Snaggletooth)	5.00	10.00

2000-02 Star Wars Power of the Jedi Deluxe

1 Amanaman (w/Salacious Crumb)	10.00	20.00
(Fan's Choice Figure #2)		
2 Darth Maul (w/Sith Attack Droid)	8.00	15.00
3 Luke Skywalker (in Echo Base Bacta Tank)	10.00	20.00
4 Princess Leia (Jabba's prisoner w/sail barge cannon)	8.00	15.00

2000-02 Star Wars Power of the Jedi Masters of the Darkside

1 Darth Vader and Darth Maul	6.00	30.00

2000-02 Star Wars Power of the Jedi Mega Action

1 Darth Maul	12.00	25.00
2 Destroyer Droid	20.00	40.00
3 Obi-Wan Kenobi	12.00	25.00

2000-02 Star Wars Power of the Jedi Playsets

1 Carbon Freezing Chamber (w/Bespin guard)	40.00	80.00

2000-02 Star Wars Power of the Jedi Special Edition

1 Boba Fett (300th figure)	15.00	30.00
2 Rorworr (Wookiee scout)	5.00	10.00

2000-02 Star Wars Power of the Jedi Vehicles

1 B-Wing Fighter (w/Sullustan pilot)	40.00	80.00
2 Imperial AT-ST & Speeder Bike (w/Paploo)	25.00	50.00
3 Luke Skywalker's Snowspeeder (w/Dack Ralter)	40.00	80.00
4 TIE Bomber	25.00	50.00
5 TIE Interceptor (w/Imperial pilot)	30.00	60.00

1995-00 Star Wars Power of the Force 3-Packs

NNO Lando/Chewbacca/Han Solo	10.00	20.00
NNO Lando/Luke Dagobah/TIE Fighter Pilot	10.00	20.00
NNO Luke Jedi/AT-ST Driver/Leia Boushh	20.00	40.00
NNO Luke Stormtrooper/Tusken Raider/Ben Kenobi	12.50	25.00
NNO Luke/Ben Kenobi/Darth Vader	10.00	20.00
NNO Stormtrooper/R2-D2/C-3PO	10.00	20.00

1995-00 Star Wars Power of the Force Accessories

1 Escape the Death Star Action Figure Game	20.00	40.00
2 Millennium Falcon Carrying Case (w/Imperial Scanning Trooper)	20.00	40.00
3 Millennium Falcon Carrying Case (w/Wedge)	15.00	30.00
4 Power of the Force Carrying Case	6.00	12.00
5 Talking C-3PO Carrying Case	25.00	50.00

1995-00 Star Wars Power of the Force Cinema Scenes

1 Cantina Aliens	10.00	20.00
2a Cantina Showdown (.00)	6.00	12.00
2b Cantina Showdown (.01)	6.00	12.00
3a Death Star Escape (.00)	12.00	25.00
3b Death Star Escape (.01)	12.00	25.00
4a Final Jedi Duel (.00)	10.00	20.00
4b Final Jedi Duel (.01)	12.50	25.00
5 Jabba the Hutt's Dancers	15.00	30.00
6 Jabba's Skiff Guards	12.50	25.00
7 Jedi Spirits	10.00	20.00
8 Mynock Hunt	12.50	25.00
9 Purchase of the Droids	10.00	20.00
10 Rebel Pilots	10.00	20.00

1995-00 Star Wars Power of the Force Comm-Tech

1 Admiral Motti	20.00	40.00
2a Darth Vader (holographic chip)	8.00	15.00
2b Darth Vader (white chip)	8.00	15.00
3 Greedo	7.50	15.00
4 Han Solo	6.00	12.00
5a Jawa (w/Gonk Droid holographic chip)	8.00	15.00
5b Jawa (w/Gonk Droid white chip)	8.00	15.00
6 Luke Skywalker (w/T16 Skyhopper)	6.00	12.00
7 Princess Leia	8.00	15.00
8 R2-D2 (w/Princess Leia)	10.00	20.00
9 Stormtrooper	10.00	20.00
10a Wuher (no sticker)	8.00	15.00
(2000 Fan Club Exclusive)		
10b Wuher (sticker)	6.00	12.00
(2000 Fan Club Exclusive)		

1995-00 Star Wars Power of the Force Complete Galaxy

1 Dagobah (w/Yoda)	8.00	15.00
2 Death Star (w/Darth Vader)	12.00	25.00
3a Endor (w/Ewok) (.00)	15.00	30.00
3b Endor (w/Ewok) (.01)	15.00	30.00
4 Tatooine (w/Luke)	10.00	20.00

1995-00 Star Wars Power of the Force Creatures

1 Bantha & Tusken Raider	50.00	100.00
2 Dewback & Sandtrooper	30.00	75.00
3a Jabba the Hutt & Han Solo (Han on left)		
3b Jabba the Hutt & Han Solo (Han on right)	15.00	30.00
4 Rancor & Luke Skywalker	30.00	60.00
5 Ronto & Jawa	20.00	40.00
6 Tauntaun & Han Solo	25.00	50.00
7 Tauntaun & Luke Skywalker	25.00	50.00
8 Wampa & Luke Skywalker	20.00	40.00

1995-00 Star Wars Power of the Force Deluxe

NNO Boba Fett (photon torpedo)	12.50	25.00
NNO Boba Fett (proton torpedo)	10.00	20.00
NNO Han Solo (Smuggler's Flight)	7.50	15.00
NNO Hoth Rebel Soldier	7.50	15.00
NNO Luke Skywalker (Desert Sport Skiff)	25.00	50.00
NNO Probe Droid (printed warning/green cardback)	12.50	25.00
NNO Probe Droid (printed warning/red cardback)	7.50	15.00
NNO Probe Droid (warning sticker/red cardback)	10.00	20.00
NNO Snowtrooper (Tripod Cannon)	12.50	25.00
NNO Stormtrooper (Crowd Control)(no sticker)	7.50	15.00
NNO Stormtrooper (Crowd Control)(warning sticker)	7.50	15.00

1995-00 Star Wars Power of the Force Epic Force

1 Bespin Luke Skywalker	5.00	12.00
2 Boba Fett	20.00	40.00
3 C-3PO	8.00	15.00
4 Chewbacca	5.00	12.00
5 Darth Vader	15.00	30.00
6 Han Solo	5.00	12.00
7 Obi-Wan Kenobi	7.50	15.00
8 Princess Leia	4.00	8.00
9 Stormtrooper	6.00	12.00

1995-00 Star Wars Power of the Force Exclusives

1a B-Omarr Monk (.00)	12.50	25.00
(1997 Online Exclusive)		
1b B-Omarr Monk (.01)	12.50	25.00
(1997 Online Exclusive)		
2 C-3PO (greenish tint)	15.00	30.00
(Japanese Exclusive)		
3 Cantina Band Member	6.00	15.00
(1997 Fan Club Exclusive)		
4 Han Solo (w/Tauntaun)	15.00	30.00
(1997 Toys R Us Exclusive)		
5 Han Solo Stormtrooper	8.00	15.00
(Kellogg's Mail Order Exclusive)		
6 Kabe and Muftak	15.00	30.00
7 Luke Skywalker Jedi Knight	10.00	20.00
(Theater Edition Exclusive)		
8 Oola & Salacious Crumb	20.00	40.00
9 Spirit of Obi-Wan Kenobi	8.00	15.00
(Frito-Lay Mail Order Exclusive)		
10 Spirit of Obi-Wan Kenobi		
(UK Special Edition Exclusive)		

1995-00 Star Wars Power of the Force Expanded Universe Vehicles

1 Airspeeder (w/pilot)	20.00	40.00
2 Cloud Car (w/pilot)	10.00	20.00
3 Rebel Speeder Bike (w/pilot)	12.00	25.00

1995-00 Star Wars Power of the Force Flashback

1 Anakin Skywalker	5.00	10.00
2 Aunt Beru	7.50	15.00
3 C-3PO (removable arm)	10.00	20.00
4 Darth Vader	10.00	20.00
5 Emperor Palpatine	8.00	15.00
6 Hoth Chewbacca	6.00	12.00
7 Luke Skywalker	7.50	15.00
8 Obi-Wan Kenobi	6.00	12.00
9 Princess Leia (ceremonial dress)	7.50	15.00
10a R2-D2 (pop-up lightsaber)(forward position)	7.50	15.00
10b R2-D2 (pop-up lightsaber)(slanted)	7.50	15.00
11 Yoda	6.00	12.00

1995-00 Star Wars Power of the Force Freeze Frame Collection 1

1 C-3PO (removable limbs)	7.50	15.00
2a Endor Rebel Commando (.00)	5.00	10.00
2b Endor Rebel Commando (.01)	5.00	10.00
3 Garindan (long snoot)	10.00	20.00
4 Han Solo	6.00	12.00
5 Han Solo (Bespin)	6.00	12.00
6a Han Solo (carbonite)(.04)	7.50	15.00
6b Han Solo (carbonite)(.05)	7.50	15.00
7a Han Solo (Endor)(.01)	5.00	10.00
7b Han Solo (Endor)(.02)	5.00	10.00
8a Hoth Rebel Soldier (.02)	5.00	10.00
8b Hoth Rebel Soldier (.03)	5.00	10.00
9a Lando Calrissian (General)(.00)	5.00	10.00
9b Lando Calrissian (General)(.01)	5.00	10.00
10a Lando Calrissian (Skiff guard)(.01)	5.00	10.00
10b Lando Calrissian (Skiff guard)(.02)	5.00	10.00
11 Lobot	5.00	10.00
12a Luke Skywalker (Bespin)(w/gold buckle)(.00)	6.00	12.00
12b Luke Skywalker (Bespin)(w/gold buckle)(.01)	6.00	12.00
12c Luke Skywalker (Bespin)(w/silver buckle)(.00)	6.00	12.00
12d Luke Skywalker (Bespin)(w/silver buckle)(.01)	6.00	12.00
13 Luke Skywalker (blast shield helmet)	7.50	15.00
14 Luke Skywalker (ceremonial)	5.00	10.00
15a Luke Skywalker (stormtrooper disguise)(.03)	7.50	15.00
15b Luke Skywalker (stormtrooper disguise)(.04)	5.00	10.00
16 Mon Mothma	6.00	12.00
17a Obi-Wan Kenobi (.03)	7.50	15.00
17b Obi-Wan Kenobi (.04)	7.50	15.00
18 Orrimaarko (Prune Face)	10.00	20.00
19 Princess Leia Organa (Ewok celebration)	5.00	10.00
20a Princess Leia Organa (Jabba's prisoner)(.01)	7.50	15.00
20b Princess Leia Organa (Jabba's prisoner)(.02)	7.50	15.00
21 Princess Leia Organa (new likeness)	5.00	10.00
22a R2-D2 (Death Star slide)	6.00	12.00
22b R2-D2 (Imperial slide)	6.00	12.00
23a Rebel Fleet Trooper (.01)	6.00	12.00
23b Rebel Fleet Trooper (.02)	6.00	12.00
23c Rebel Fleet Trooper (w/sticker)(.01)	5.00	10.00

1995-00 Star Wars Power of the Force Freeze Frame Collection 2

1 8D8	7.50	15.00
2a Admiral Ackbar (comlink wrist blaster)	6.00	12.00
2b Admiral Ackbar (wrist blaster)	6.00	12.00
3 Biggs Darklighter	4.00	8.00
4 EV-9D9	5.00	10.00
5 Ewoks Wicket & Logray	12.50	25.00
6 Gamorrean Guard	6.00	12.00
7a Han Solo (Bespin)(.02)	7.50	15.00
7b Han Solo (Bespin)(.03)	7.50	15.00
8 Lak Sivrak	6.00	12.00
9 Malakili (Rancor Keeper)	5.00	10.00

10 Nien Nunb	5.00	10.00
11 Saelt-Marae (Yak Face)	5.00	10.00
12 Ugnaughts	7.50	15.00

1995-00 Star Wars Power of the Force Freeze Frame Collection 3

1 AT-AT Driver	10.00	20.00
(1998 Fan Club Exclusive)		
2 Boba Fett	6.00	15.00
3a Captain Piett (baton sticker)	5.00	10.00
3b Captain Piett (pistol sticker)	5.00	10.00
4 Darth Vader	6.00	12.00
5 Darth Vader (removable helmet)	8.00	15.00
6 Death Star Droid (w/mouse droid)	8.00	15.00
7 Death Star Trooper	12.00	25.00
8 Emperor Palpatine	8.00	15.00
9 Emperor's Royal Guard	8.00	15.00
10 Grand Moff Tarkin	6.00	12.00
11a Ishi Tib (brown pouch)	5.00	10.00
11b Ishi Tib (gray pouch)	5.00	10.00
12 Pote Snitkin	12.00	25.00
(1999 Internet Exclusive)		
13 Princess Leia Organa (Hoth)	8.00	15.00
(1999 Fan Club Exclusive)		
14 Ree-Yees	6.00	12.00
15 Sandtrooper	25.00	50.00
16 Snowtrooper	5.00	10.00
17 Stormtrooper	5.00	10.00
18 TIE Fighter Pilot	5.00	10.00
19 Weequay	90.00	175.00
20 Zuckuss	4.00	8.00

1995-00 Star Wars Power of the Force Green Collection 1

1a Bib Fortuna (hologram)	6.00	12.00
1b Bib Fortuna (photo)	6.00	12.00
2 Boba Fett (hologram)	15.00	30.00
3 C-3PO (hologram)	8.00	15.00
4a Chewbacca	10.00	20.00
4b Chewbacca (hologram)	4.00	8.00
5a Darth Vader	6.00	12.00
5b Darth Vader (hologram)	8.00	15.00
6a Death Star Gunner	6.00	12.00
6b Death Star Gunner (hologram)	6.00	12.00
7a Emperor Palpatine	6.00	12.00
7b Emperor Palpatine (hologram)	6.00	12.00
8 Garindan (long snoot)	4.00	8.00
9a Greedo	6.00	12.00
9b Greedo (hologram)	6.00	12.00
10a Han Solo	5.00	10.00
10b Han Solo (hologram)	6.00	12.00
11a Han Solo (Bespin)	6.00	12.00
11b Han Solo (Bespin)(hologram)	6.00	12.00
12a Han Solo (carbonite stand-up bubble)	8.00	15.00
12b Han Solo (carbonite stand-up bubble)(hologram)	8.00	15.00
13a Han Solo (Endor blue pants)	8.00	15.00
13b Han Solo (Endor blue pants)(hologram)	8.00	15.00
13c Han Solo (Endor brown pants)	10.00	20.00
14 Hoth Rebel Soldier (hologram)	5.00	10.00
15 Lando Calrissian	20.00	40.00
16 Lando Calrissian (Skiff guard)(hologram)	6.00	12.00
17a Luke Skywalker (ceremonial)	5.00	10.00
17b Luke Skywalker (ceremonial)(hologram)	5.00	10.00
18 Luke Skywalker (Hoth)(hologram)	5.00	10.00
19a Luke Skywalker (Jedi Knight)	6.00	12.00
19b Luke Skywalker (Jedi Knight)(hologram)	6.00	12.00
20 Luke Skywalker (stormtrooper disguise)(hologram)	6.00	12.00

21 Luke Skywalker (X-Wing pilot)(hologram)	8.00	15.00
22a Obi-Wan Kenobi (hologram)	5.00	10.00
22b Obi-Wan Kenobi (photo)	5.00	10.00
23a Princess Leia Organa (Jabba's prisoner)	5.00	10.00
23b Princess Leia Organa (Jabba's prisoner) (hologram)	5.00	10.00
24a Princess Leia Organa (photo)		
24b Princess Leia Organa (three-ring belt)	10.00	20.00
24c Princess Leia Organa (two-ring belt)(hologram)	8.00	15.00
25 R2-D2	10.00	20.00
26 Rebel Fleet Trooper (hologram)	5.00	10.00
27a Sandtrooper	8.00	15.00
27b Sandtrooper (hologram)	8.00	15.00
28a Yoda	6.00	12.00
28b Yoda (hologram)	6.00	12.00

1995-00 Star Wars Power of the Force Green Collection 2

1a 2-1B (.00)	5.00	10.00
1b 2-1B (.00)(hologram)	6.00	12.00
1c 2-1B (.01)	4.00	8.00
1d 2-1B (.01)(hologram)	6.00	12.00
2a 4-LOM	6.00	12.00
2b 4-LOM (hologram)	6.00	12.00
3 Admiral Ackbar	4.00	8.00
4a ASP-7 (hologram)	5.00	10.00
4b ASP-7 (photo)	5.00	10.00
5a AT-ST Driver	7.50	15.00
5b AT-ST Driver (hologram)	5.00	10.00
6a Bib Fortuna (hologram/stand-up bubble)	4.00	8.00
6b Bib Fortuna (hologram/straight bubble)	5.00	10.00
7a Bossk (.00)(hologram)	4.00	8.00
7b Bossk (.00)(photo)	4.00	8.00
7c Bossk (.01)(photo)	6.00	12.00
8 Clone Emperor Palpatine (Expanded Universe)	8.00	15.00
9 Darktrooper (Expanded Universe)	10.00	20.00
10a Dengar (hologram)	7.50	15.00
10b Dengar (photo)	6.00	12.00
11a EV-9D9 (hologram)	6.00	12.00
11b EV-9D9 (photo)	6.00	12.00
12 Gamorrean Guard (hologram)	5.00	10.00
13 Grand Admiral Thrawn (Expanded Universe)	20.00	40.00
14a Grand Moff Tarkin	5.00	10.00
14b Grand Moff Tarkin (hologram)	5.00	10.00
15a Han Solo (carbonite)	6.00	12.00
15b Han Solo (carbonite)(hologram)	7.50	15.00
16a Hoth Rebel Soldier	5.00	10.00
16b Hoth Rebel Soldier (hologram)	5.00	10.00
17 Imperial Sentinel (Expanded Universe)	10.00	20.00
18a Jawas	5.00	10.00
18b Jawas (hologram)	5.00	10.00
18c Jawas (new bubble)	6.00	12.00
18d Jawas (new bubble)(hologram)	6.00	12.00
19 Kyle Katarn (Expanded Universe)	10.00	20.00
20a Luke Skywalker (ceremonial)(hologram)	5.00	10.00
20b Luke Skywalker (ceremonial/different head)		
21 Luke Skywalker (Expanded Universe)	10.00	20.00
22a Luke Skywalker (Hoth)	5.00	10.00
22b Luke Skywalker (Hoth)(hologram)	5.00	10.00
23a Luke Skywalker (Jedi Knight)	6.00	12.00
23b Luke Skywalker (Jedi Knight)(hologram)	7.50	15.00
24a Luke Skywalker (stormtrooper disguise)	7.50	15.00
24b Luke Skywalker (stormtrooper disguise)(hologram)	6.00	12.00
25 Malakili (Rancor Keeper)(hologram)	4.00	8.00
26 Mara Jade (Expanded Universe)	15.00	30.00
27a Momaw Nadon (Hammerhead)	3.00	8.00
27b Momaw Nadon (Hammerhead)(hologram)	4.00	8.00
28 Nien Nunb (hologram)	4.00	8.00
29a Ponda Baba (black bear) (hologram)	5.00	10.00

29b Ponda Baba (gray beard) (hologram)	5.00	10.00
30 Princess Leia (Expanded Universe)	8.00	15.00
31a R5-D4 (no warning sticker/L-latch)	5.00	10.00
31b R5-D4 (no warning sticker/L-latch)(hologram)	5.00	10.00
31c R5-D4 (no warning sticker/straight latch)	5.00	10.00
31d R5-D4 (no warning sticker/straight latch)(hologram)	5.00	10.00
31e R5-D4 (warning sticker/L-latch)		
31f R5-D4 (warning sticker/L-latch)(hologram)	5.00	10.00
31g R5-D4 (warning sticker/straight latch)	5.00	10.00
31h R5-D4 (warning sticker/straight latch)(hologram)	5.00	10.00
32a Rebel Fleet Trooper		
32b Rebel Fleet Trooper (hologram)		
33 Saelt-Marae (Yak Face)(hologram)		
34 Spacetrooper (Expanded Universe)	8.00	15.00
35 TIE Fighter Pilot (hologram)		
36 Tusken Raider (hologram)	4.00	8.00
37 Weequay		
38a Yoda		
38b Yoda (hologram)		

1995-00 Star Wars Power of the Force Green Collection 3

1 AT-ST Driver	5.00	10.00
2 AT-ST Driver (hologram)	5.00	10.00
3 Boba Fett (hologram)	12.00	25.00
4 Darth Vader (hologram)	4.00	8.00
5a Death Star Gunner	5.00	10.00
5b Death Star Gunner (hologram)	5.00	10.00
6 Emperor Palpatine (hologram)	4.00	8.00
7a Emperor's Royal Guard	6.00	12.00
7b Emperor's Royal Guard (hologram)	6.00	12.00
8a Garindan (long snoot)(hologram)	4.00	8.00
8b Garindan (long snoot)(photo)	4.00	8.00
9 Grand Moff Tarkin	4.00	8.00
10a Ponda Baba (black beard)	5.00	10.00
10b Ponda Baba (gray beard)	50.00	100.00
11a Sandtrooper	5.00	10.00
11b Sandtrooper (hologram)	5.00	10.00
12a Snowtrooper		
12b Snowtrooper (hologram)		
13a Stormtrooper	5.00	10.00
13b Stormtrooper (holosticker)	5.00	10.00
14 TIE Fighter Pilot (hologram)	6.00	12.00
15 Weequay (hologram)	4.00	8.00

1995-00 Star Wars Power of the Force Gunner Stations

1a Gunner Station (Millennium Falcon w/Han Solo)(.00)	6.00	12.00
1b Gunner Station (Millennium Falcon w/Han Solo)(.01)	6.00	12.00
2a Gunner Station (Millennium Falcon w/Luke Skywalker)(.00)	6.00	12.00
2b Gunner Station (Millennium Falcon w/Luke Skywalker)(.01)	6.00	12.00
3 Gunner Station (TIE Fighter w/Darth Vader)	8.00	15.00

1995-00 Star Wars Power of the Force Max Rebo Band Pairs

1a Droopy McCool & Barquin D'an (CGI Sy Snootles on back)	12.00	25.00
(1998 Walmart Exclusive)		
1b Droopy McCool & Barquin D'an (puppet Sy Snootles on back)	8.00	15.00
(1998 Walmart Exclusive)		
2 Max Rebo & Doda Bodonawieedo	15.00	30.00
3a Sy Snootles & Joh Yowza (CGI Sy Snootles on back)	12.00	25.00
(1998 Walmart Exclusive)		
3b Sy Snootles & Joh Yowza (puppet Sy Snootles on back)	8.00	15.00
(1998 Walmart Exclusive)		

1995-00 Star Wars Power of the Force Millennium Mint

1 C-3PO	5.00	12.00
2a Chewbacca (.00)	6.00	12.00
(1998 Toys R Us Exclusive)		
2b Chewbacca (.01/new insert)	6.00	12.00
(1998 Toys R Us Exclusive)		
3 Emperor Palpatine	5.00	12.00
(1998 Toys R Us Exclusive)		
4a Han Solo (Bespin)(.00)	6.00	12.00
(1998 Toys R Us Exclusive)		
4b Han Solo (Bespin)(.01/new insert)	12.00	25.00
(1998 Toys R Us Exclusive)		
5a Luke Skywalker (Endor gear)(.00)	10.00	20.00
(1998 Toys R Us Exclusive)		
5b Luke Skywalker (Endor gear)(.01)	8.00	15.00
(1998 Toys R Us Exclusive)		
6a Princess Leia (Endor gear)(.00)	12.00	25.00
(1998 Toys R Us Exclusive)		

6b Princess Leia (Endor gear)(.01)	10.00	20.00
(1998 Toys R Us Exclusive)		
7a Snowtrooper (.00)	6.00	12.00
(1998 Toys R Us Exclusive)		
7b Snowtrooper (.01)	8.00	15.00
(1998 Toys R Us Exclusive)		

1995-00 Star Wars Power of the Force Orange

1 Chewbacca	6.00	12.00
2a Darth Vader (long saber)	8.00	15.00
2b Darth Vader (short saber/long tray)	10.00	20.00
2c Darth Vader (short saber/short tray)	6.00	12.00
3 Han Solo	6.00	12.00
4a Stormtrooper	6.00	12.00
4b Stormtrooper (holosticker)	6.00	12.00

1995-00 Star Wars Power of the Force Playsets

1a Cantina Pop-Up Diorama (w/sandtrooper)	12.00	25.00
(Retail Store Version - 25" sticker correction)		
1b Cantina Pop-Up Diorama (w/sandtrooper)	15.00	30.00
(Retail Store Version - 25" wide description)		
1c Cantina Pop-Up Diorama (w/sandtrooper)		
(Retail Store Version - 26" wide description)		
2 Cantina Pop-Up Diorama		
(1997 Mail Order Exclusive)		
3 Death Star Escape	12.50	25.00
4 Detention Block Rescue	15.00	30.00
5a Endor Attack (no warning sticker)		
5b Endor Attack (warning sticker)	30.00	60.00
6a Hoth Battle (no warning sticker)	25.00	50.00
6b Hoth Battle (warning sticker)	20.00	40.00
7a Jabba's Palace (w/Han Solo)(podrace arena bio card)		
7b Jabba's Palace (w/Han Solo)(podracer bio card)	15.00	30.00
8 Millennium Falcon Cockpit	20.00	40.00
(PC Explorer Game)		

1995-00 Star Wars Power of the Force Power F/X

1 Ben (Obi-Wan) Kenobi	5.00	10.00
2 Darth Vader	5.00	10.00
3a Emperor Palpatine (.00)	6.00	12.00
3b Emperor Palpatine (.01)	4.00	8.00
4 Luke Skywalker	6.00	12.00
5a R2-D2 (.00)	4.00	8.00
5b R2-D2 (.01)	4.00	8.00
5c R2-D2 (.02)	4.00	8.00
5d R2-D2 (.103)	4.00	8.00

1995-00 Star Wars Power of the Force Princess Leia Collection

1a Princess Leia & Han Solo (gold border)	4.00	8.00
1b Princess Leia & Han Solo (gray border)	10.00	20.00
2a Princess Leia & Luke Skywalker (gold border)	8.00	15.00
2b Princess Leia & Luke Skywalker (gray border)	10.00	20.00
3a Princess Leia & R2-D2 (gold border)	25.00	50.00
3b Princess Leia & R2-D2 (gray border)	10.00	20.00
4a Princess Leia & Wicket (gold border)	4.00	8.00
4b Princess Leia & Wicket (gray border)	10.00	20.00

1995-00 Star Wars Power of the Force Red

1a Boba Fett (full circle)	7.50	15.00
1b Boba Fett (half circle)	20.00	40.00
1c Boba Fett (no circle)	12.00	25.00
2 C-3PO (.00)	6.00	12.00
3 Death Star Gunner	7.50	15.00
4 Greedo	5.00	10.00
5a Han Solo (carbonite block)	7.50	15.00
5b Han Solo (carbonite freezing chamber)	6.00	12.00
6a Han Solo (Hoth - closed hand)	6.00	12.00
6b Han Solo (Hoth - open hand)	6.00	12.00
7 Jawas	6.00	12.00
8 Lando Calrissian	3.00	6.00
9a Luke Skywalker (Dagobah - long saber)	6.00	12.00
9b Luke Skywalker (Dagobah - short saber/long tray)	10.00	20.00
9c Luke Skywalker (Dagobah - short saber/short tray)		
10a Luke Skywalker (Jedi Knight - black vest)	6.00	12.00
10b Luke Skywalker (Jedi Knight - brown vest)	10.00	20.00
11a Luke Skywalker (long saber)	8.00	15.00
11b Luke Skywalker (short saber/long tray)	6.00	12.00
11c Luke Skywalker (short saber/short tray)	6.00	12.00
12a Luke Skywalker (stormtrooper disguise)	8.00	15.00
12b Luke Skywalker (stormtrooper disguise)(hologram)	7.50	15.00
13a Luke Skywalker (X-Wing pilot - long saber)	10.00	20.00
13b Luke Skywalker (X-Wing pilot - short saber/long tray)	5.00	10.00
13c Luke Skywalker (X-Wing pilot - short saber/short tray)		
14 Momaw Nadon (Hammerhead) (warning sticker)	4.00	8.00
15a Obi-Wan Kenobi (hologram)	5.00	10.00
15b Obi-Wan Kenobi (short saber/long tray)	5.00	10.00
15c Obi-Wan Kenobi (short saber/short tray)	5.00	10.00
15d Obi-Wan Kenobi (long saber)	15.00	30.00
15e Obi-Wan Kenobi (photo)		
16a Princess Leia Organa (2-band belt)	6.00	12.00
16b Princess Leia Organa (3-band belt)	6.00	12.00
16c Princess Leia Organa (hologram)		
17a R2-D2	12.50	25.00
17b R2-D2 (hologram)		
18a R5-D4 (no warning sticker/straight latch)	6.00	12.00
18b R5-D4 (warning sticker/straight latch)		
19 Sandtrooper		
20a TIE Fighter Pilot (printed warning)	4.00	8.00
20b TIE Fighter Pilot (SOTE)		
20c TIE Fighter Pilot (warning sticker)		
21a Tusken Raider (closed left hand)	6.00	12.00
21b Tusken Raider (open left hand)		
22a Yoda (.00)	6.00	12.00
22b Yoda (.00)(hologram)		
22c Yoda (.01)		

1995-00 Star Wars Power of the Force Vehicles

NNO	AT-AT Walker (electronic)(no sticker)	60.00	120.00
NNO	AT-AT Walker (electronic)(sticker of figure's legs)		
NNO	AT-ST Scout Walker	30.00	60.00
NNO	A-Wing Fighter	25.00	50.00
NNO	Cruisemissile Trooper (.00)		
NNO	Cruisemissile Trooper (.01)		
NNO	Darth Vader's TIE Fighter	25.00	50.00
NNO	Landspeeder	12.00	25.00
NNO	Luke Skywalker's Red Five X-Wing Fighter	50.00	100.00
NNO	Millennium Falcon (electronic)	60.00	120.00
NNO	Power Racing Speeder Bike (w/scout)		
NNO	Rebel Snowspeeder (electronic)	30.00	75.00
NNO	Speeder Bike (w/Leia in Endor fatigues)(grassy background)		
NNO	Speeder Bike (w/Leia in Endor fatigues)(rocky background)	15.00	30.00
NNO	Speeder Bike (w/Luke in Endor fatigues glove)	30.00	60.00
NNO	Speeder Bike (w/Luke in Endor fatigues no glove)	12.50	25.00
NNO	Speeder Bike (w/scout)(aggressiveness removed)		
NNO	Speeder Bike (w/scout)(aggressiveness)		
NNO	Speeder Bike (w/scout)(Canadian windowless package)		
NNO	Speeder Bike (w/scout)(Topps Widevision card)	10.00	20.00
NNO	STAP and Battle Droid Sneak Preview (beige rod)	10.00	20.00
NNO	STAP and Battle Droid Sneak Preview (brown rod)	12.00	25.00
NNO	T-16 Skyhopper		
NNO	Tatooine Skiff	60.00	120.00
NNO	TIE Fighter	25.00	50.00
NNO	X-Wing Fighter (electronic green box)	15.00	30.00
NNO	X-Wing Fighter (electronic red box)	30.00	60.00
NNO	Y-Wing Fighter	40.00	80.00

2014-15 Star Wars Rebels Hero Series

1	Agent Kallus	12.00	25.00
2	Clone Trooper	6.00	12.00
3	Darth Vader	7.50	15.00
4	Ezra Bridger	10.00	20.00
5	Garazeb Orrelios	15.00	30.00
6	Heroes and Villains	20.00	50.00
	(2014 Target Exclusive)		
7	Kanan Jarrus	12.00	25.00
8	Luke Skywalker	12.00	25.00
9	Stormtrooper	10.00	20.00
10	The Inquisitor	8.00	15.00

2014-15 Star Wars Rebels Mission Series

MS1	Garazeb Orrelios/Stormtrooper	8.00	15.00
MS2	R2-D2/C-3PO	15.00	30.00
MS3	Luke Skywalker/Darth Vader	10.00	20.00
MS4	Darth Sidious/Yoda	12.00	25.00
MS5	Boba Fett/Stormtrooper	12.00	25.00
MS7	Wullffwarro/Wookiee Warrior	8.00	15.00
MS8	Sabine Wren/Stormtrooper	20.00	40.00
MS9	Cikatro Vizago/IG-RM	10.00	20.00
MS10	Wicket/Biker Scout	8.00	15.00
MS11	Bossk/IG-88	10.00	20.00
MS15	Luke Skywalker/Han Solo	12.00	25.00
MS16	R2-D2/Yoda	15.00	30.00
MS17	TIE Pilot/Stormtrooper	8.00	15.00
MS18	Ezra Bridger/Kanan Jarrus	8.00	15.00
MS19	Stormtrooper Commander/Hera Syndulla	12.00	25.00
MS20	Princess Leia/Luke Skywalker Stormtrooper	10.00	20.00

2014-15 Star Wars Rebels Saga Legends

SL1	Stormtrooper	6.00	12.00
SL2	Ezra Bridger	8.00	15.00
SL3	The Inquisitor	7.50	15.00
SL4	Kanan Jarrus	6.00	12.00
SL5	Agent Kallus	12.00	30.00
SL6	C1-10P (Chopper)	12.00	30.00
SL7	Jango Fett	6.00	12.00
SL8	Clone Trooper	6.00	12.00
SL9	Darth Vader	10.00	20.00
SL10	Luke Skywalker (Jedi Knight)	7.50	15.00
SL11	Obi-Wan Kenobi	7.50	15.00
SL12	Snowtrooper	10.00	20.00
SL13	TIE Pilot	5.00	10.00
SL14	AT-DP Driver	20.00	40.00
SL15	Clone Commander Gree	6.00	12.00
SL16	Plo Koon	5.00	10.00
SL17	Jedi Temple Guard	30.00	75.00
SL18	AT-AT Driver	6.00	12.00
SL22	Luke Skywalker (X-Wing Pilot)	7.50	15.00
SL23	Lando Calrissian	7.50	15.00
SL24	Han Solo	8.00	15.00
SL25	Luke Skywalker (Endor)	7.50	15.00
SL26	Commander Bly	6.00	12.00
SL27	Han Solo (Endor)	8.00	15.00
SL28	Princess Leia (Endor)	6.00	12.00

2018 Star Wars Resistance Collection

NNO	Commander Pyre		
NNO	First Order Stormtrooper		
NNO	Kaz Xiono		
NNO	Major Vonreg		
NNO	Synara San		
NNO	Torra Doza		

2018 Star Wars Resistance Collection 1 2-Packs

NNO	Jarek Yeager & Bucket	
NNO	Poe Dameron & BB-8	

2019 Star Wars Resistance

NNO	Commander Pyre	
NNO	First Order Stormtrooper	
NNO	Jarek Yeager & Bucket (R1-J5)	
NNO	Kaz Xiono	
NNO	Major Vonreg	
NNO	Poe Dameron & BB-8	
NNO	Synara San	
NNO	Torra Doza	

2019 Star Wars Retro Collection

NNO	Chewbacca	25.00	50.00
NNO	Darth Vader	40.00	80.00
NNO	Darth Vader (prototype edition)	75.00	150.00
	(Target Exclusive)		
NNO	Grand Moff Tarkin	30.00	60.00
	(Escape from Death Star Game Exclusive)		
NNO	Han Solo	20.00	40.00
NNO	Luke Skywalker		
NNO	Princess Leia Organa		
NNO	Stormtrooper		

2019 Star Wars Retro Collection Multipacks

NNO	Escape from Death Star Board Game (w/Grand Moff Tarkin)	
NNO	Promotional Early Bird Certificate/Figure Six-Pack	

2020 Star Wars Retro Collection

NNO	Boba Fett	20.00	40.00
NNO	Han Solo (Hoth)		
NNO	Lando Calrissian		
NNO	Luke Skywalker (Bespin)		
NNO	Luke Skywalker (snowspeeder gear)		
	(Hoth Ice Planet Adventure Exclusive)		

NNO Princess Leia Organa (Hoth)
NNO Remnant Stormtrooper
(The Mandalorian Monopoly Exclusive)
NNO Yoda

2020 Star Wars Retro Collection Multipacks

NNO Hoth Ice Planet Adventure Game (w/Luke Skywalker snowspeeder gear)
NNO The Mandalorian Monopoly (w/Remnant Stormtrooper)

2021 Star Wars Retro Collection

NNO Boba Fett (prototype edition)	25.00	50.00
(Target Exclusive)		
NNO Cara Dune	15.00	30.00
NNO Din Djarin	12.50	25.00
NNO Greef Karga		
NNO Grogu		
NNO IG-11		
NNO Kuiil		
NNO Moff Gideon		
NNO Stormtrooper (prototype edition)		
(Target Exclusive)		

2022 Star Wars Retro Collection

NNO Death Trooper
NNO Din Djarin
NNO Bo-Katan Kryze
NNO Boba Fett
NNO Armorer
NNO Ahsoka Tano

2005 Star Wars Revenge of the Sith

III1 Obi-Wan Kenobi (slashing attack)	8.00	15.00
III2 Anakin Skywalker (slashing attack straight saber red)	6.00	12.00
III2a Anakin Skywalker (slashing attack bent saber red)	4.00	8.00
III2b Anakin Skywalker (slashing attack bent saber pink)	4.00	8.00
III3 Yoda (firing cannon)	4.00	8.00
III4 Super Battle Droid (firing arm blaster)	10.00	20.00
III5 Chewbacca (Wookiee rage)	8.00	15.00
III6a Clone Trooper (white - quick draw attack)	6.00	12.00
III6b Clone Trooper (red - quick draw attack)	6.00	12.00
III7 R2-D2 (droid attack)	5.00	10.00
III8 Grievous's Bodyguard (battle attack)	4.00	8.00
III9 General Grievous (four lightsaber attack)	4.00	8.00
III10 Mace Windu (Force combat)	6.00	12.00
III11 Darth Vader (lightsaber attack)	4.00	8.00
III12 Emperor Palpatine (firing Force lightning)	5.00	10.00
III13 Count Dooku (Sith Lord)	5.00	10.00
III14 Chancellor Palpatine (supreme chancellor)	4.00	8.00
III15 Bail Organa (Republic Senator)	5.00	10.00
III16 Plo Koon (Jedi Master)	4.00	8.00
III17 Battle Droid (separatist army)	5.00	10.00
III18 C-3PO (protocal droid)	4.00	8.00
III19 Padme republic senator	10.00	20.00
III20 Agen Kolar (Jedi Master)	6.00	12.00
III21 Shaak Ti (Jedi Master)	10.00	20.00
III22 Kit Fisto (Jedi Master)	6.00	12.00
III23a Royal Guard (blue - senate security)	6.00	12.00
III23b Royal Guard (red - senate security)	8.00	15.00
III24 Mon Mothma (Republic Senator)	6.00	12.00
III25 Tarfful (firing bowcaster)	4.00	8.00
III26 Yoda (spinning attack)	6.00	12.00
III27 Obi-Wan Kenobi (Jedi kick)	4.00	8.00
III28 Anakin Skywalker (slashing attack)	8.00	15.00
III29 Ki-Adi-Mundi (Jedi Master)	5.00	10.00
III30 Saesee Tiin (Jedi Master)	5.00	10.00
III31 Luminara Unduli (Jedi Master)	6.00	12.00
III32 Aayla Secura (Jedi Knight)	8.00	15.00
III33a Clone Commander (red - battle gear)	8.00	15.00
III33b Clone Commander (green - battle gear)	8.00	15.00

III34a Clone Pilot (firing cannon)	5.00	10.00
III34b Clone Pilot (black - firing cannon)	5.00	10.00
III35a Palpatine (red lightsaber - lightsaber attack)	6.00	12.00
III35b Palpatine (blue lightsaber - lightsaber attack)	6.00	12.00
III36 General Grievous (exploding body)	10.00	20.00
III37 Vader's Medical Droid (chopper droid)	4.00	8.00
III38 AT-TE Tank Gunner (clone army)	6.00	12.00
III39 Polis Massan (medic droid)	4.00	8.00
III40 Mas Amedda (Republic Senator)	5.00	10.00
III41 Clone Trooper (white - super articulation)	5.00	10.00
III42 Neimoidian Warrior (Neimoidian weapon attack)	4.00	8.00
III43a Warrior Wookie (dark - wookie battle bash)	4.00	8.00
III43b Warrior Wookie (light - wookie battle bash)	12.00	25.00
III44 Destroyer Droid (firing arm blaster)	8.00	15.00
III45 Tarkin (Governor)	4.00	8.00
III46 Ask Aak (Senator)	6.00	12.00
III47 Meena Tills (Senator)	4.00	8.00
III48 R2-D2 (try me electronic)	6.00	12.00
III49 Commander Bacara (quick-draw attack)	5.00	10.00
III50 Anakin Skywalker (battle damaged)	8.00	15.00
III51 Captain Antilles (Senate security)	4.00	8.00
III52 Jett Jukassa (Jedi Padawan)	4.00	8.00
III53 Utapaun Warrior (Utapaun security)	5.00	10.00
III54 AT-RT Driver (missile-firing blaster)	12.00	25.00
III55 Obi-Wan Kenobi (w/pilot gear)	8.00	15.00
III56 Mustafar Sentury (spinning energy bolt)	5.00	10.00
III57 Commander Bly (battle gear)	8.00	15.00
III58 Wookie Commando (Kashyyyk battle gear)	6.00	12.00
III59 Commander Gree (battle gear)	10.00	20.00
III60 Grievous's Bodyguard (battle attack)	6.00	12.00
III61 Passel Argente (separatist leader)	6.00	12.00
III62 Cat Miin (separatist)	4.00	8.00
III63 Neimoidian Commander (separatist bodyguard)	4.00	8.00
III64 R4-P17 (rolling action)	8.00	15.00
III65 Tactical Ops Trooper (Vader's legion)	6.00	12.00
III66 Plo Koon (Jedi hologram transmission)	8.00	15.00
III67 Aayla Secura (Jedi hologram transmission)	5.00	10.00
III68 Wookiee Heavy Gunner (blast attack)	5.00	10.00

2005 Star Wars Revenge of the Sith 12-Inch

1 Anakin Skywalker/Darth Vader (ultimate villain)	30.00	60.00
2 Barriss Offee	15.00	30.00
3 Chewbacca	20.00	40.00
(2005 KB Toys Exclusive)		
4 Clone Trooper	12.00	25.00
5 Darth Sidious		
6 General Grievous	30.00	60.00
7 Shaak Ti	15.00	30.00

2005 Star Wars Revenge of the Sith Accessories

10 Darth Vader Carrying Case (w/Clone Trooper & Anakin Skywalker)		
20 Darth Vader Carrying Case (w/Darth Vader & Obi-Wan Kenobi)		

2005 Star Wars Revenge of the Sith Battle Arena

1 Bodyguard vs. Obi-Wan (Utapau landing platform)	8.00	15.00
2 Dooku vs Anakin (Trade Federation cruiser)	8.00	15.00
3 Sidius vs. Mace (Chancellor's office)	8.00	15.00

2005 Star Wars Revenge of the Sith Battle Packs

NNO Assault on Hoth (General Veers/Probot/3 Snowtroopers)		
NNO Attack on Coruscant (5 Clone Troopers)	30.00	60.00
NNO Imperial Throne Room (Emperor Palpatine		
Imperial Dignitary/2 Royal Guards/Stormtrooper)		
NNO Jedi Temple Assault (Anakin/Clone Pilot/3 Special Ops Troopers)		
NNO Jedi vs. Sith (Anakin/Asajj Ventress	20.00	40.00
General Grievous/Obi-Wan/Yoda)		
NNO Jedi vs. Separatists (Anakin/Darth Maul	15.00	30.00
Jango Fett/Obi-Wan/Mace Windu)		
NNO Rebel vs. Empire (Chewbacca/Vader/Han/Luke/Stormtrooper)	20.00	40.00

2005 Star Wars Revenge of the Sith Collectible Cup Figures

1 Boba Fett	12.00	25.00
2 Clone Trooper		
3 Darth Vader	10.00	20.00
4 General Grievous		
5 Han Solo	10.00	20.00
6 Obi-Wan Kenobi	10.00	20.00
7 Princess Leia		
8 Stormtrooper	8.00	15.00
9 Yoda	8.00	15.00

2005 Star Wars Revenge of the Sith Commemorative Episode III DVD Collection

1 Jedi Knights (Anakin Skywalker/Mace Windu/Obi-Wan Kenobi)	10.00	20.00
2 Sith Lords (Emperor Palpatine/Darth Vader/Count Dooku)	10.00	20.00
3 Clone Troopers (3 Clone Troopers)	12.00	25.00

2005 Star Wars Revenge of the Sith Creatures

10 Boga (w/Obi-Wan Kenobi)	20.00	40.00

2005 Star Wars Revenge of the Sith Deluxe

1 Anakin Skywalker (changes to Darth Vader)	15.00	30.00
2 Clone Trooper (firing jet pack)	5.00	10.00
3 Clone Troopers (Build Your Army - 3 white)	8.00	15.00
4 Clone Troopers (Build Your Army - 2 white and 1 red)	10.00	20.00
5 Clone Troopers (Build Your Army - 2 white and 1 green)	8.00	15.00
6 Clone Troopers (Build Your Army - 2 white and 1 blue)	12.00	25.00
7 Crab Droid (moving legs/missile launcher)	12.00	25.00
8 Darth Vader (rebuild Darth Vader)	10.00	20.00
9 Emperor Palpatine (changes to Darth Sidious)	8.00	15.00
10 General Grievous (secret lightsaber attack)	15.00	30.00
11 Obi-Wan Kenobi (Force jump attack - w/super battle droid)	5.00	10.00
12 Spider Droid (firing laser action)	5.00	10.00
13 Stass Allie (exploding action - w/BARC speeder)	5.00	10.00
14 Vulture Droid (blue - firing missile launcher)	6.00	12.00

15 Vulture Droid (brown - firing missile launcher) 10.00 20.00
16 Yoda (fly into battle - w/can-cell) 8.00 15.00

2005 Star Wars Revenge of the Sith Evolutions

1 Anakin Skywalker to Darth Vader 12.00 25.00
2 Clone Trooper (Attack of the Clones
Revenge of the Sith/A New Hope) 15.00 30.00
3 Clone Trooper (Attack of the Clones
Revenge of the Sith - gray/A New Hope - gray) 15.00 30.00
4 Sith Lords (Darth Maul/Darth Tyranus/Darth Sidious) 15.00 30.00

2005 Star Wars Revenge of the Sith Exclusives

1 Anakin Skywalker Paris-Mai
(2005 Star Wars Reunion Convention Exclusive)
2 Clone Trooper (Neyo logo)
(2005 Target Exclusive)
3 Clone Trooper (Sith logo)
(2005 Target Exclusive) 12.00 25.00
4 Covert Ops Clone Trooper
(2005 StarWarsShop.com Exclusive)
5 Darth Vader (Duel at Mustafar) 8.00 15.00
(2005 Target Exclusive)
6 Darth Vader (lava reflection) 8.00 15.00
(2005 Target Exclusive)
7 Darth Vader 12.00 25.00
(2005 Celebration III Exclusive)
8 Holographic Emperor 6.00 12.00
(2005 Toys R Us Exclusive)
9 Holographic Yoda (Kashyyyk transmission) 6.00 12.00
(2005 Toys R Us Exclusive)
10 Obi-Wan Kenobi (Duel at Mustafar) 12.00 25.00
(2005 Target Exclusive)
11 R2-D2 (remote control)
(2005 Japanese Exclusive)
12 Utapau Shadow Trooper (super articulation) 10.00 20.00
(2005 Target Exclusive)

2005 Star Wars Revenge of the Sith Kay Bee Toys Collector Packs

1 Luminara Unduli/Count Dooku/Royal Guard/Kit Fisto 20.00 40.00
Darth Vader/Bail Organa/C-3PO/Ki-Adi-Mundi/Chancellor Palpatine

2005 Star Wars Revenge of the Sith Playsets

1 Mustafar Final Duel/Anakin
Skywalker/Obi-Wan Kenobi
2 Mustafar Final Duel (w/Obi-Wan 40.00 80.00
Darth Vader/4 Clone Troopers)

2005 Star Wars Revenge of the Sith Promos

1 Anakin Skywalker
2 Darth Vader

2005 Star Wars Revenge of the Sith Sneak Preview

1 General Grievous 8.00 15.00
2 Tion Medon 4.00 8.00
3 Wookie Warrior 4.00 8.00
4 R4-G9 4.00 8.00
NNO Anakin's Jedi Starfighter (vehicle) 15.00 30.00

2005 Star Wars Revenge of the Sith Super Deformed

1 Boba Fett 6.00 12.00
2 C-3PO 6.00 12.00
3 Chewbacca 6.00 12.00
4 Darth Maul 6.00 12.00
5 Darth Vader 6.00 12.00
6 R2-D2 6.00 12.00
7 Stormtrooper 6.00 12.00
8 Yoda 6.00 12.00

2005 Star Wars Revenge of the Sith Vehicles

1 Anakin's Jedi Starfighter (w/Anakin) 20.00 40.00
(2005 Toys R Us Exclusive)
2 ARC-170 Fighter 50.00 100.00
3 ARC-170 Fighter (w/4 Troopers) 75.00 150.00
4 AR-RT/AR-RT Driver
5 AR-RT/AR-RT Driver (w/Clone Trooper white)
6 Barc Speeder (w/Barc Trooper & Wookiee warrior)
7 Barc Speeder (w/Barc Trooper)
8 Droid Tri-Fighter
9 Grievous's Wheel Bike (w/General Grievous) 25.00 50.00
10 Millennium Falcon
11 Obi-Wan's Jedi Starfighter 20.00 40.00
12 Obi-Wan's Jedi Starfighter (w/Obi-Wan) 12.00 25.00
(2005 Toys R Us Exclusive)
13 Plo Koon's Jedi Starfighter 15.00 30.00
(2005 Target Exclusive)
14 Republic Gunship 100.00 200.00
15 Wookiee Flyer (w/Wookiee warrior)

2016 Star Wars Rogue One 2-Packs

NNO Baze Malbus vs. Imperial Stormtrooper 7.50 15.00
NNO Captain Cassian Andor vs. Imperial Stormtrooper 12.50 25.00
NNO First Order Snowtrooper Officer vs. Poe Dameron 8.00 15.00
NNO Moroff vs. Scariff Stormtrooper Squad Leader 7.50 15.00
NNO Rebel Commander Pao vs. Imperial Death Trooper 10.00 20.00
NNO Seventh Sister Inquisitor vs. Darth Maul 15.00 30.00
NNO Captain Phasma vs. Finn 10.00 20.00

2016 Star Wars Rogue One Big Figs

NNO Imperial Death Trooper 15.00 30.00
NNO Imperial Stormtrooper 15.00 30.00
NNO K-2SO 15.00 30.00
NNO Sergeant Jyn Erso 12.00 25.00

2016 Star Wars Rogue One Build-A-Weapon

1 Admiral Raddus 10.00 20.00
2 Bodhi Rook 12.00 25.00

3 Captain Cassian Andor (Eadu) 8.00 15.00
4 Chirrut Imwe 8.00 15.00
5 Darth Vader 8.00 15.00
6 Director Krennic 6.00 12.00
7 Fenn Rau 60.00 120.00
8 Galen Erso 12.00 25.00
9 Grand Admiral Thrawn (admiral rank) 15.00 30.00
10 Grand Admiral Thrawn (director rank) 30.00 60.00
11 Imperial Death Trooper (Specialist Gear) 10.00 20.00
12 Imperial Ground Crew 6.00 12.00
13 Imperial Stormtrooper 6.00 12.00
14 K-2SO 6.00 12.00
15 Kanan Jarrus (stormtrooper disguise)(Star Wars Rebels) 10.00 20.00
16 Kylo Ren (The Force Awakens) 8.00 15.00
17 Lieutenant Sefla 6.00 12.00
18 Princess Leia Organa (Star Wars Rebels) 6.00 12.00
19 Rey (Jakku)(The Force Awakens) 6.00 12.00
20 Sabine Wren (Star Wars Rebels) 6.00 12.00
21 Sergeant Jyn Erso (Eadu) 6.00 12.00
22 Sergeant Jyn Erso (Imperial Ground Crew Disguise) 8.00 15.00
23 Sergeant Jyn Erso (Jedha) 6.00 12.00
24 Shoretrooper 8.00 15.00

2016 Star Wars Rogue One Hero Series

NNO Captain Cassian Andor 8.00 15.00
NNO First Order Stormtrooper
NNO Imperial Death Trooper 8.00 15.00
NNO Sergeant Jyn Erso 8.00 15.00
NNO Shoretrooper

2016 Star Wars Rogue One Multipacks

NNO Eadu 3-Pack 12.00 25.00
Sergeant Jyn Erso/Captain Cassian Andor/K-2SO
(Walmart Exclusive)
NNO Jedha Revolt 4-Pack 15.00 30.00
Edrio Two Tubes/Saw Gerrera/Sergeant Jyn Erso/Imperial Hovertank Pilot
NNO Rey vs. Kylo Ren
Poe Dameron vs. First Order TIE Fighter Pilot
Finn vs. FN-2199
NNO Scarif 4-Pack 12.00 25.00
Rebel Commando Pao/Moroff/Imperial Death Trooper/Imperial Stormtrooper
(Kohl's Exclusive)
NNO Star Wars 8-Pack 15.00 30.00
Darth Maul/Jango Fett/Obi-Wan/Chewbacca
Darth Vader/Luke/Rey/BB-8
(Target Exclusive)

2016 Star Wars Rogue One Vehicles

NNO Assault Walker (w/stormtrooper sergeant)(The Force Awakens) 20.00 40.00
NNO A-Wing (w/Hera Syndulla)(Star Wars Rebels) 20.00 40.00
NNO Ezra Bridger's Speeder (w/Ezra Bridger)(Star Wars Rebels) 12.00 25.00
NNO First Order Snowspeeder (w/stormtrooper)(The Force Awakens) 15.00 30.00
NNO Imperial AT-ACT Playset (w/Jyn Erso/astromech droid/driver) 75.00 150.00
NNO Imperial Speeder (w/AT-DP pilot)(Star Wars Rebels) 12.00 25.00
NNO Imperial TIE Striker (w/pilot) 20.00 40.00
NNO Imperial TIE Striker (w/pilot) 10.00 20.00
(Toys R Us Exclusive)
NNO Rebel U-Wing Fighter (w/Cassian Andor) 20.00 40.00
NNO Y-Wing Scout Bomber (w/Kanan Jarrus) 20.00 40.00

2015-16 Star Wars S.H. Figuarts

NNO	Battle Droid	30.00	60.00
NNO	Captain Phasma	30.00	60.00
NNO	Clone Trooper (Phase 1)	25.00	50.00
NNO	Darth Maul	50.00	100.00
NNO	Darth Vader (w/display stand)	80.00	150.00
NNO	First Order Riot Control Stormtrooper	30.00	60.00
NNO	First Order Stormtrooper	30.00	60.00
NNO	First Order Stormtrooper Heavy Gunner	40.00	80.00
NNO	Jango Fett	40.00	80.00
NNO	Kylo Ren		
NNO	Luke Skywalker (Episode IV)	40.00	80.00
NNO	Luke Skywalker (Episode VI)	60.00	120.00
NNO	Mace Windu	40.00	80.00
NNO	Obi-Wan Kenobi (Episode I)	30.00	60.00
NNO	Scout Trooper and Speeder Bike	120.00	200.00
NNO	Shadow Trooper	40.00	80.00
NNO	Stormtrooper	50.00	100.00

2002-04 Star Wars Saga 12-Inch

NNO	Anakin Skywalker	12.50	25.00
NNO	Anakin Skywalker (w/slashing lightsaber)	15.00	30.00
NNO	AT-ST Driver	15.00	30.00
NNO	Biker Scout	30.00	75.00
NNO	Clone Commander	8.00	15.00
NNO	Clone Trooper (black-and-white)	12.50	25.00
NNO	Clone Trooper (red-and-white)	12.50	25.00
NNO	Count Dooku	25.00	50.00
NNO	Dengar	12.50	25.00
NNO	Ewok 2-Pack (Logray & Keoulkeech)	20.00	40.00
NNO	Gamorrean Guard	25.00	50.00
NNO	Garindan	20.00	40.00
NNO	Geonosian Warrior	12.50	25.00
NNO	Han Solo		
NNO	Imperial Officer	10.00	20.00
NNO	Jango Fett	30.00	75.00
NNO	Jango Fett (electronic battling)	20.00	40.00
NNO	Jawas	25.00	50.00
NNO	Ki-Adi-Mundi	20.00	40.00
NNO	Lando Calrissian (Skiff disguise)	12.00	25.00
NNO	Luke Skywalker & Tauntaun	50.00	100.00
NNO	Luke Skywalker (w/slashing lightsaber)	25.00	50.00
NNO	Mace Windu	15.00	30.00
NNO	Obi-Wan Kenobi	12.00	25.00
NNO	Obi-Wan Kenobi (electronic battling)	10.00	20.00
NNO	Obi-Wan Kenobi (Tatooine encounter)	20.00	40.00
NNO	Padme Amidala	15.00	30.00
NNO	Plo Koon		
NNO	Princess Leia (Boushh) & Han Solo (carbonite)	30.00	60.00
NNO	Princess Leia (w/speeder bike)	30.00	75.00
NNO	Super Battle Droid	12.00	25.00
NNO	Yoda (w/hoverchair)	20.00	40.00
NNO	Zam Wesell	12.00	25.00
NNO	Zuckuss	20.00	40.00

2002-04 Star Wars Saga 12-Inch Character Collectibles

NNO	Anakin Skywalker		
NNO	Darth Vader		
NNO	Jango Fett	30.00	60.00
NNO	Mace Windu	10.00	20.00

2002-04 Star Wars Saga Accessory Sets

NNO	Arena Conflict with/Battle Droid brown	12.00	25.00
NNO	Death Star (w/Death Star trooper and droids)	10.00	20.00
NNO	Endor Victory (w/scout trooper)	10.00	20.00
NNO	Hoth Survival (w/Hoth Rebel soldier)	7.50	15.00

2002-04 Star Wars Saga Arena Battle Beasts

NNO	Acklay	25.00	50.00
NNO	Reek	15.00	30.00

2002-04 Star Wars Saga Cinema Scenes

NNO	Death Star Trash Compactor (Chewbacca & Princess Leia)	20.00	40.00
NNO	Death Star Trash Compactor (Luke Skywalker & Han Solo)	25.00	50.00
NNO	Geonosian War Chamber (Nute Gunray/Passel Argente/Shu Mai)	12.00	25.00
NNO	Geonosian War Chamber (Poggle the Lesser/Count Dooku/San Hill)	12.00	25.00
NNO	Jedi High Council (Mace Windu Oppo Rancisis/Even Piell)	20.00	40.00
NNO	Jedi High Council (Yareal Poof Depa Billaba/Yaddle)	10.00	20.00

2002-04 Star Wars Saga Collectible Cup Figures

NNO	Episode I/Darth Maul	10.00	20.00
NNO	Episode II Anakin Skywalker	10.00	20.00
NNO	Episode IV Obi-Wan Kenobi	10.00	20.00
NNO	Episode V Luke Skywalker	10.00	20.00
NNO	Episode VI Princess Leia Organa	12.00	25.00

2002-04 Star Wars Saga Collection 1 (2002)

1	Anakin Skywalker (outland peasant disguise)	6.00	12.00
2	Padme Amidala (arena escape)	6.00	12.00
3	Obi-Wan Kenobi (Coruscant chase)	6.00	12.00
4	C-3PO (protocol droid)	5.00	10.00
5	Kit Fisto (Jedi Master)	5.00	10.00
6	Super Battle Droid	5.00	10.00
17	Clone Trooper	6.00	12.00
18	Zam Wesell (bounty hunter)	6.00	12.00
22	Anakin Skywalker (hangar duel)	12.00	25.00
23	Yoda (Jedi Master)		
27	Count Dooku (Dark Lord)	6.00	12.00
28	Mace Windu (Geonosian rescue)	8.00	15.00
29	Luke Skywalker (Bespin duel)	8.00	15.00
30	Darth Vader (Bespin duel)	6.00	12.00
31	Jango Fett (final battle)	5.00	10.00
36	Obi-Wan Kenobi (Jedi starfighter)	12.00	25.00
37	Han Solo (Endor bunker)		

38	Chewbacca (Cloud City capture w/C-3PO)	6.00	12.00
40	Djas Puhr (bounty hunter)	6.00	12.00
41	Padme Amidala (Coruscant attack)	6.00	12.00
43	Anakin Skywalker (Tatooine attack)	6.00	12.00
47	Jango Fett (Slave-1 pilot)	5.00	10.00
48	Destroyer Droid (Geonosis battle)		
49	Clone Trooper (Republic gunship pilot)	8.00	15.00
53	Yoda (Jedi High Council)		

2002-04 Star Wars Saga Collection 1 (2003)

1	Obi-Wan Kenobi (acklay battle)	5.00	10.00
2	Mace Windu (arena confrontation)	5.00	10.00
3	Darth Tyranus (Geonosian escape)	8.00	15.00
7	Anakin Skywalker (secret ceremony)	8.00	15.00
8	Boba Fett (The Pit of Carkoon)	8.00	15.00
9	R2-D2 (droid factory)	6.00	12.00
13	Han Solo (Hoth rescue)		
14	Chewbacca (mynock hunt)	5.00	10.00
17	Luke Skywalker (throne room duel)	5.00	10.00
18	Darth Vader (throne room duel)	6.00	12.00
19	Snowtrooper (The Battle of Hoth)	8.00	15.00
20	Jango Fett (Kamino duel)		
21	C-3PO (Tatooine attack)		

2002-04 Star Wars Saga Collection 2 (2002)

7	Boba Fett (Kamino escape)	8.00	15.00
8	Tusken Raider Female (w/Tusken child)	6.00	12.00
9	Captain Typho (Padme's head of security)	5.00	10.00
10	Shaak Ti (Jedi Master)	5.00	10.00
11a	Battle Droid (arena battle tan)	5.00	10.00
11b	Battle Droid (arena battle brown)	12.00	25.00
12	Plo Koon (arena battle)		
13	Jango Fett (Kamino escape)	8.00	15.00
14	R2-D2 (Coruscant sentry)	8.00	15.00
15	Geonosian Warrior	5.00	10.00
16	Dexter Jettster (Coruscant informant)	5.00	10.00
19	Royal Guard (Coruscant security)	6.00	12.00
20	Saesee Tin (Jedi Master)	5.00	10.00
21	Nikto (Jedi Knight)	6.00	12.00
24	Jar Jar Binks (Gungan Senator)	5.00	10.00
25	Taun We (Kamino cloner)	6.00	12.00
26	Luminara Unduli	5.00	10.00
32	Qui-Gon Jinn (Jedi Master)	6.00	12.00
33a	Endor Rebel Soldier (facial hair)		
33a	Endor Rebel Soldier (no facial hair)		
34	Massiff (w/Geonosian handler)	8.00	15.00
35	Orn Free Taa (senator)		
39	Supreme Chancellor Palpatine		
42	Darth Maul (Sith training)	5.00	10.00
44	Ki-Adi-Mundi (Jedi Master)	5.00	10.00
45	Ephant Man (Jabba's head of security)		
46	Teemto Pagalies (pod racer)		
50	Watto (Mos Espa junk dealer)	5.00	10.00
51	Lott Dod (Neimoidian Senator)		
52	Tusken Raider (w/massiff)	6.00	12.00
54	Rebel Trooper (Tantive IV defender)		
55	Imperial Officer		
56	Eeth Koth (Jedi Master)		
57	Teebo		

2002-04 Star Wars Saga Collection 2 (2003)

4 Padme Amidala (droid factory chase)		
5 SP-4 & JN-66 (research droids)	6.00	12.00
6 Tusken Raider (Tatooine camp ambush)	5.00	10.00
10 Lama Su (w/clone child)	10.00	20.00
11 Aayla Secura (Battle of Geonosis)	8.00	15.00
12 Barriss Offee (Luminara Unduli's Padawan)	6.00	12.00
15 Yoda and Chian (Padawan lightsaber training)		
16 Ashla & Jemba (Jedi Padawans)	8.00	15.00
22 Padme Amidala (secret ceremony)	10.00	20.00
23 Wat Tambor (Geonosis war room)	10.00	20.00
24 Coleman Trebor (Battle of Geonosis)		
25 Darth Maul (Theed hangar duel)	8.00	15.00
26 Princess Leia Organa (Imperial captive)	5.00	10.00
27 Han Solo (fight to Alderaan)		
28 WA-7 (Dexter's diner)	8.00	15.00
29 Lt. Dannl Faytonni (Coruscant Outlander club)		
30 The Emperor (throne room)		
31 Luke Skywalker (Tatooine encounter)	5.00	10.00
32 Darth Vader (Death Star clash)	8.00	15.00
33 Bail Organa (Alderaan Senator)	6.00	12.00
34 Stormtrooper (McQuarrie concept)	8.00	15.00
35 Imperial Dignitary Janus Greejatus		
(Death Star procession)		
36 Padme Amidala (Lars' homestead)	15.00	30.00
37 Achk Med-Beq (Coruscant Outlander club)	6.00	12.00
38 Ayy Vida (Outlander nightclub patron)	10.00	20.00
39 Obi-Wan Kenobi (Outlander nightclub patron)	6.00	12.00
40 Elan Sleazebaggano (Outlander nightclub encounter)	8.00	15.00
41 Imperial Dignitary Kren Blista-Vanee		
(Death Star procession)		

2002-04 Star Wars Saga Deluxe

NNO Anakin Skywalker (w/Force flipping attack)	4.00	8.00
NNO Anakin Skywalker (w/lightsaber slashing action)	6.00	12.00
NNO C-3PO (w/droid factory assembly line)	4.00	8.00

NNO Clone Trooper (w/speeder bike)	6.00	12.00
NNO Darth Tyranus (w/Force flipping attack)	4.00	8.00
NNO Flying Geonosian (w/sonic blaster and attack pod)	4.00	8.00
NNO Jango Fett (Kamino showdown)	4.00	8.00
NNO Jango Fett (w/electronic backpack and snap-on armor)	4.00	8.00
NNO Mace Windu (w/blast apart droid tan)	4.00	8.00
NNO Mace Windu (w/blast apart droid brown)	4.00	8.00
NNO Nexu (w/snapping jaw and attack roar)	12.00	25.00
NNO Obi-Wan Kenobi (Kamino showdown)	4.00	8.00
NNO Obi-Wan Kenobi (w/Force flipping attack)	4.00	8.00
NNO Spider Droid (w/rotating turret and firing cannon)	4.00	8.00
NNO Super Battle Droid Builder (w/droid factory assembly mold)	4.00	8.00
NNO Yoda (w/Force powers)	10.00	20.00

2002-04 Star Wars Saga Exclusives

NNO Boba Fett (silver)	15.00	30.00
(2003 Convention Exclusive)		
NNO C-3PO (Santa) & R2-D2 (reindeer)	12.00	25.00
(2002 Holiday Edition Exclusive)		
NNO Clone Trooper (silver)	6.00	12.00
(2003 Toys R Us Exclusive)		
NNO Clone Trooper/Super Battle Droid	12.00	25.00
(2004 Jedi Con Exclusive)		
NNO Commander Jorg Sacul	20.00	40.00
(2002 Celebration 2 Exclusive)		
NNO Darth Vader (silver)	30.00	60.00
(2002 New York Toy Fair Exclusive)		
NNO R2-D2 (silver)	15.00	30.00
(2002 Toys R Us Silver Anniversary Exclusive)		
NNO Sandtrooper (silver)		
(2004 SDCC Exclusive)		
NNO Yoda (Santa)		
(2003 Holiday Edition Exclusive)		

2002-04 Star Wars Saga Mos Eisley Cantina Bar

NNO Dr. Evezan		
NNO Greedo	8.00	15.00
NNO Kitik Keed'kak		
NNO Momaw Nadon		
NNO Ponda Baba		
NNO Wuher		

2002-04 Star Wars Saga Multipacks

NNO Endor Soldiers (w/four soldiers paint may vary slightly)		
NNO Imperial Forces (Darth Vader	15.00	30.00
Stormtrooper/AT-ST Driver/R4-I9)		
NNO Jedi Warriors (Obi-Wan Kenobi	10.00	20.00
Saesee Tiin/Plo Koon/Fi-Ek Sirch)		
NNO Light Saber Action Pack		
(Anakin Skywalker/Count Dooku/Yoda)		
NNO Rebel Troopers Builder Set		
NNO Sandtroopers Builder Set		
(orange, black, gray, & white shoulder pad)		
NNO Skirmish at Karkoon	10.00	20.00
(Han Solo/Klaatu/Nikto/Barada)		
NNO Stormtroopers Builder Set		
NNO The Battle of Hoth (Luke	20.00	40.00
Leia/Chewbacca/R3-A2/Tauntaun)		
NNO Ultimate Bounty (Boba Fett	12.00	25.00
Bossk/IG-88/Aurra Sing w/swoop vehicle)		
NNO Value 4-Pack (Zam Wesell		
Battle Droid/Kit Fisto/Super Battle Droid)		

2002-04 Star Wars Saga Playsets

NNO Geonosian Battle Arena	60.00	120.00

2002-04 Star Wars Saga Playskool

NNO Arena Adventure	12.00	25.00
NNO Duel with Darth Maul	25.00	50.00
NNO Fast through the Forest	8.00	15.00
NNO Millennium Falcon Adventure	20.00	40.00
NNO The Stompin' Wampa		
NNO X-Wing Adventure	25.00	50.00

2002-04 Star Wars Saga Re-Issues

NNO Anakin Skywalker (hangar duel)	8.00	15.00
2002 Star Wars Saga Collection 1		
NNO C-3PO (Death Star escape)		
1997-98 Star Wars Power of the Force Green		
NNO Chewbacca (escape from Hoth)		
2000-01 Star Wars Power of the Jedi		
NNO Darth Maul (Theed hangar duel)		
2003 Star Wars Saga Collection 2		
NNO Darth Vader (Death Star clash)		
2003 Star Wars Saga Collection 2		
NNO Han Solo (flight to Alderaan)		
2003 Star Wars Saga Collection 2		
NNO Luke Skywalker (Tatooine encounter)		
2003 Star Wars Saga Collection 2		
NNO Obi-Wan Kenobi (Coruscant chase)		
2002 Star Wars Saga Collection 1		
NNO Princess Leia Organa (Death Star captive)	10.00	20.00
2003 Star Wars Saga Collection 2		
NNO R2-D2 (Tatooine mission)		
2000-01 Star Wars Power of the Jedi		
NNO Stormtrooper (Death Star chase)	8.00	15.00
1998-99 Star Wars Power of the Force		
NNO Yoda (Battle of Geonosis)		
2002 Star Wars Saga Collection 1		

2002-04 Star Wars Saga Ultra With Accessories

NNO C-3PO with Escape Pod	12.00	25.00
NNO Ewok (w/attack glider)		
NNO General Rieekan (w/Hoth tactical screen)	20.00	40.00
NNO Jabba's Palace Court Denizens		
NNO Jabba the Hutt (w/pipe stand)		
NNO Jango Fett (Kamino confrontation)		
NNO Obi-Wan Kenobi (Kamino confrontation)	15.00	30.00
NNO Wampa (w/Hoth cave)		

2002-04 Star Wars Saga Vehicles

NNO	Anakin Skywalker's Speeder	10.00	20.00
NNO	Anakin Skywalker's Swoop Bike (w/Anakin)	20.00	40.00
NNO	A-Wing Fighter	20.00	40.00
NNO	Darth Tyranus's Speeder Bike (w/Darth Tyranus)	15.00	30.00
NNO	Imperial Dogfight TIE Fighter	20.00	40.00
NNO	Imperial Shuttle	120.00	200.00
NNO	Jango Fett's Slave 1	25.00	50.00
NNO	Jedi Starfighter	15.00	30.00
NNO	Jedi Starfighter (w/Obi-Wan Kenobi)	20.00	40.00
NNO	Landspeeder (w/Luke Skywalker)	20.00	40.00
NNO	Luke Skywalker's X-Wing Fighter (w/R2-D2)	60.00	120.00
NNO	Red Leader's X-Wing Fighter (w/Red Leader)	30.00	60.00
NNO	Republic Gunship	75.00	150.00
NNO	TIE Bomber	30.00	75.00
NNO	Zam Wesell's Speeder	10.00	20.00

2002-04 Star Wars Saga Wave 1 Hoth

1	Hoth Trooper (Hoth evacuation)	8.00	15.00
2	R-3PM (Hoth evacuation)		
3	Luke Skywalker (Hoth attack)		

2002-04 Star Wars Saga Wave 2 Tatooine

4	Luke Skywalker (Jabba's Palace)	6.00	12.00
5	R2-D2 (Jabba's sail barge)	8.00	15.00
6	R1-G4 (Tatooine transaction)		

2002-04 Star Wars Saga Wave 3 Jabba's Palace

7	Lando Calrissian (Jabba's sail barge)	5.00	10.00
8	Rappertunie (Jabba's Palace)		
9	J'Quille (Jabba's sail barge)	12.00	25.00
10	Tanus Spojek		
11	TIE Fighter Pildof		

2002-04 Star Wars Saga Wave 4 Battle of Yavin

12	General Jan Dodonna (Battle of Yavin)		
13	Dutch Vander Gold Leader (Battle of Yavin)		
14	TIE Fighter Pilot (Battle of Yavin)	6.00	12.00
15	Captain Antilles		

2002-04 Star Wars Saga Wave 5 Star Destroyer

16	Admiral Ozzel		
17	Dengar (executor meeting)		
18	Bossk (executor meeting)		

2002-04 Star Wars Saga Wave 6 Battle of Endor

19	Han Solo (Endor strike)		
20	General Madine (Imperial shuttle capture)		
21	Lando Calrissian (Death Star attack)	6.00	12.00

2006-07 Star Wars The Saga Collection

SAGA1	Princess Leia boushh	7.50	15.00
SAGA2	Han Solo carbonite	7.50	15.00
SAGA3	Bib Fortuna	12.50	25.00
SAGA4	Barada skiff	4.00	8.00
SAGA5	Chewbacca/ boushh prisoner	6.00	12.00
SAGA6	Boba Fett	7.50	15.00
SAGA7	General Veers	12.50	25.00
SAGA8	Major Bren Derlin	6.00	12.00
SAGA9	AT-AT Driver	4.00	8.00

SAGA10	R2-D2	6.00	12.00
SAGA11	Snowtrooper	5.00	10.00
SAGA12	General Rieeken	4.00	8.00
SAGA13	Darth Vader	7.50	15.00
SAGA14	Power Droid	10.00	20.00
SAGA15	Sora Bulq	6.00	12.00
SAGA16	Sun Fac	10.00	20.00
SAGA17	C-3PO with/ battle droid head/ droid head on	4.00	8.00
SAGA18	Poggle the Lesser	4.00	8.00
SAGA19	Yoda	7.50	15.00
SAGA20	Jango Fett	5.00	10.00
SAGA21	Scorch	15.00	30.00
SAGA22	Firespeeder Pilot	4.00	8.00
SAGA23	Lushros Dofine	6.00	12.00
SAGA24	Clone Commander Cody/ orange highlights	7.50	15.00
SAGA25	Anakin Skywalker	5.00	10.00
SAGA26	Utapau Clone Trooper	7.50	15.00
SAGA27	Holographic Ki-Adi-Mundi	5.00	10.00
SAGA28	Obi-Wan Kenobi beard	4.00	8.00
SAGA29	Faul Maudama	6.00	12.00
SAGA30	General Grievous	7.50	15.00
SAGA31	Momaw Nadon/ clear cup	5.00	10.00
SAGA32	R5-D4	4.00	8.00
SAGA33	Hem Dazon blue cup	4.00	8.00
SAGA34	Garindan	10.00	20.00
SAGA35	Han Solo	6.00	12.00
SAGA36	Luke Skywalker	4.00	8.00
SAGA37	Sandtrooper	6.00	12.00
SAGA38	Darth Vader bespin/ saber fight	7.50	15.00
SAGA39	Chief Chirpa	10.00	20.00
SAGA40	Moff Jerjerrod	6.00	12.00
SAGA41	Death Star Gunner	7.50	15.00
SAGA42	C-3PO (with/ ewok throne/ unpainted knees)	10.00	20.00
SAGA43	Emperor Palpatine	6.00	12.00
SAGA44	Luke Skywalker	4.00	8.00
SAGA45	Darth Vader/ shocked by emperor	6.00	12.00
SAGA46	Rebel Trooper/ endor black	4.00	8.00
SAGA47	Obi-Wan Kenobi/ no beard	5.00	10.00
SAGA48	Holographic Darth Maul	4.00	8.00
SAGA49	Rep Been	5.00	10.00
SAGA50	Naboo Soldier yellow	6.00	12.00
SAGA51	Dud Bolt & Mars Guo	5.00	10.00
SAGA52	Gragra	7.50	15.00
SAGA53	Sith Training Darth Maul	7.50	15.00
SAGA54	Chewbacca with/ electronic C-3PO	10.00	20.00
SAGA55	Kit Fisto	4.00	8.00
SAGA56	Holographic Clone Commander Cody	5.00	10.00
SAGA57	Clone Trooper 442nd Siege Batallion (green highlights)	15.00	30.00
SAGA58	R5-J2	12.50	25.00
SAGA59	Clone Trooper Fifth Fleet Security/ (blue stripes on head/shoulder)	10.00	20.00
SAGA60	Clone Trooper Sergeant	7.50	15.00
SAGA61	Super Battle Droid	6.00	12.00
SAGA62	Battle Droids (green and yellow)	4.00	8.00
SAGA63	Holographic Obi-Wan Kenobi	7.50	15.00
SAGA64	Commander Oppo (blue highlights/ blue shoulder)	5.00	10.00
SAGA65	Elite Corps Clone Commander	4.00	8.00
SAGA66	R4-K5 Darth Vader's Astromech Droid	4.00	8.00
SAGA67	Padme Amidala	4.00	8.00
SAGA68	Combat Engineer Clone Trooper (brown highlights)	4.00	8.00
SAGA69	Yareal Poof	4.00	8.00
SAGA70	Aurra Sing	4.00	8.00
SAGA71	Kitik Keed'Kak	4.00	8.00
SAGA72	Nabrun Leids & Kabe	4.00	8.00
SAGA73	Labria	4.00	8.00
SAGA74	R4-M6 Mace Windu's Astromech Droid	4.00	8.00
SAGA17a	C-3PO with/ battle droid head/ C-3PO head on	4.00	8.00
SAGA31a	Momaw Nadon/ blue cup	5.00	10.00
SAGA33a	Hem Dazon white cup	4.00	8.00
SAGA42a	C-3PO (with/ ewok throne/ painted knees)	10.00	20.00
SAGA46a	Rebel Trooper/ endor white	4.00	8.00

2006-07 Star Wars The Saga Collection Battle Packs

1	Battle Above the Sarlacc (Boba Fett Lando Calrissian skiff/Han Solo carbonite)	25.00	50.00
2	Jedi vs. Darth Sidious (Darth Sidious Kit Fisto/Mace Windu/Saesee Tiin)	25.00	50.00
3	Sith Lord Attack (Obi-Wan Kenobi Qui-Gon Jinn/Darth Maul/Battle Droid tan)	20.00	40.00

2006-07 Star Wars The Saga Collection Battle Packs Exclusives

1	Mace Windu's Attack Batallion (Mace Windu Clone Trooper purple/ with sk)	50.00	100.00
2	Skirmish in the Senate (Emperor Palpatine Yoda/Clone Trooper red/Clone)	20.00	40.00
3	The Hunt for Grievous (Clone Trooper red Clone Trooper blue/Clone Trooper	30.00	75.00

2006-07 Star Wars The Saga Collection Commemorative DVD Collection

1	Luke Skywalker/Darth Vader/Obi-Wan Kenobi	10.00	20.00
2	Han Solo/Chewbacca/Stormtrooper	10.00	20.00
3	Luke Skywalker/Emperor Palpatine/R2-D2/C-3PO	15.00	30.00

2006-07 Star Wars The Saga Collection Episode III Greatest Battles Collection

1	501st Legion Trooper (blue with orange feet)	6.00	12.00
2	AT-TE Tank Gunner (gold helmet highlights)	6.00	12.00
3	C-3PO	4.00	8.00
4	Count Dooku	10.00	20.00
5	Royal Guard Blue	5.00	10.00
6	Padme	5.00	10.00
7	R4-G9	4.00	8.00
8	Kit Fisto	6.00	12.00
9	Wookiee Warrior	4.00	8.00
10	R2-D2	6.00	12.00
11	Shock Trooper	4.00	8.00
12	Obi-Wan Kenobi (flight helmet)	4.00	8.00
13	Emperor Palpatine	4.00	8.00
14a	Clone Commander (green with skirt sash)	7.50	15.00
14b	Clone Commander (red with skirt sash)	10.00	20.00

2006-07 Star Wars The Saga Collection Episode III Heroes & Villains Collection

1	Darth Vader	4.00	8.00
2	Anakin Skywalker	4.00	8.00
3	Yoda	4.00	8.00
4	Commander Bacara	4.00	8.00

5 Clone Trooper	4.00	8.00
6 Clone Pilot black	4.00	8.00
7 Chewbacca	4.00	8.00
8 Obi-Wan Kenobi	4.00	8.00
9 General Grievous cape	4.00	8.00
10 Mace Windu	4.00	8.00
11 R2-D2	4.00	8.00
12 Destroyer Droid	4.00	8.00
9a General Grievous/ no cape	4.00	8.00

2006-07 Star Wars The Saga Collection Exclusives

1 501st Stormtrooper	15.00	30.00
(2006 SDCC Exclusive)		
2 Clone Trooper (Saleucami)		
(2006 Toys R Us French Exclusive)		
3 Darth Vader	30.00	75.00
(2006 UK Woolworth's Exclusive)		
4 Demise of General Grievous	6.00	12.00
(2006 Target Exclusive)		
5 Early Bird Certificate Package		
(2005 Walmart Exclusive)		
6 Early Bird Kit (Luke Skywalker, Princess Leia, Chewbacca, and R2-D2)	30.00	75.00
(2005 Mailaway Exclusive)		
7 George Lucas Stormtrooper	30.00	75.00
(2006 Mailaway Exclusive)		
8 Separation of the Twins Leia Organa (w/Bail Organa)	15.00	30.00
(2005 Walmart Exclusive)		
9 Separation of the Twins Luke Skywalker (w/Obi-Wan Kenobi)	12.00	25.00
(2005 Walmart Exclusive)		
10 Shadow Stormtrooper	12.00	25.00
(2006 Starwarsshop.com Exclusive)		

2006-07 Star Wars The Saga Collection International

SAGA1 Princess Leia Boushh	
SAGA2 Han Solo (in carbonite)	
SAGA3 Bib Fortuna	
SAGA4 Barada Skiff Guard	
SAGA5 Chewbacca (Boushh Prisoner)	
SAGA6 Boba Fett	

2006-07 Star Wars The Saga Collection Multipacks

NNO Droid Pack I/R4-A22/R2-C4/R3-T2/R2-Q2/R3-T6	30.00	60.00
(2006 Entertainment Earth Exclusive)		
NNO Droid Pack II/R4-E1/R2-X2/R2-M5/R2-A6/R3-Y2	30.00	60.00
(2006 Entertainment Earth Exclusive)		
NNO Episode III Gift Pack/Darth Vader	20.00	40.00
General Grievous/Obi-Wan Kenobi/R2-D2		
(2006 UK Woolworth's Exclusive)		
NNO Jedi Knights/Anakin Skywalker		
Mace Windu/Obi-Wan Kenobi		
(2005 UK Argos Exclusive)		
NNO Lucas Collector's Set/Zett Jukassa	12.50	25.00

Baron Papanoida/Terr Taneel/Chi Eekway		
(2006 Starwarsshop.com Exclusive)		
NNO Revenge of the Sith Collector's Set		
(UK Exclusive)		

2006-07 Star Wars The Saga Collection Previews Exclusives

NNO Death Star Briefing (Darth Vader	60.00	120.00
Grand Moff Tarkin/Admiral Motti/General)		
NNO The Hunt For the Millenium Falcon	30.00	60.00
(Darth Vader/Dengar/IG-88/Boba Fett)		
NNO Republic Commando Delta Squad		
(Delta Three-Eight orange/Scoarch blue)		

2006-07 Star Wars The Saga Collection Ultimate Galactic Hunt

NNO AT-AT Driver (ESB Stand)	6.00	12.00
NNO Anakin Skywalker (ROTS Stand)	4.00	8.00
NNO Boba Fett (ROTJ Stand)	30.00	60.00
NNO Commander Cody (ROTS Stand)	4.00	8.00
NNO Darth Vader (ESB Stand)	4.00	8.00
NNO General Grievous (ROTS Stand)	6.00	12.00
NNO Han Solo Carbonite (ROTJ Stand)	6.00	12.00
NNO Obi-Wan Kenobi (ROTS Stand)	4.00	8.00
NNO Scorch Republic Commando (SW Stand)	8.00	15.00
NNO Snowtrooper (ESB Stand)	8.00	15.00

2006-07 Star Wars The Saga Collection Ultimate Galactic Hunt Vehicles

NNO Republic Gunship	150.00	300.00
(Toys R Us Exclusive)		

2006-07 Star Wars The Saga Collection Ultimate Galactic Hunt Vintage

NNO Bossk	10.00	20.00
NNO IG-88	12.50	25.00
NNO Han Solo Hoth	15.00	30.00
NNO Luke Skywalker Bespin	15.00	30.00
NNO Princess Leia Organa (Endor combat poncho)	10.00	20.00
NNO Imperial Stormtrooper Hoth	12.50	25.00

2006-07 Star Wars The Saga Collection Vehicles

NNO Anakin's Jedi Starfighter	20.00	40.00
NNO Darth Vader's TIE Advanced X1 Starfighter		
NNO Droid Tri-Fighter		
NNO General Grievous's Wheel Bike		
NNO Obi-Wan's Jedi Starfighter		
NNO Mace Windu's Jedi Starfighter		

2006-07 Star Wars The Saga Collection Vehicles Exclusives

NNO Luke Skywalker's X-Wing (w/Luke Skywalker Dagobah)	75.00	150.00
(Toys R Us Exclusive)		
NNO TIE Fighter (w/Tie Fighter Pilot)		
(Toys R Us Exclusive		
NNO Imperial Shuttle (Royal Guard red/Darth Vader)	250.00	400.00
(Target Exclusive)		
NNO Kit Fisto's Jedi Starfighter	20.00	40.00
(Target Exclusive		
NNO Rogue Two Snowspeeder (w/Zev Senesca)	50.00	100.00

2006-07 Star Wars The Saga Collection Vintage

NNO Biker Scout	8.00	15.00
NNO Greedo	6.00	12.00
NNO Han Solo (w/cape)	6.00	12.00
NNO Luke Skywalker X-Wing Pilot	10.00	20.00
NNO Sand People	6.00	12.00

2010 Star Wars Saga Legends

SL1 Bossk	12.00	25.00
SL2 IG-88	10.00	20.00
SL3 Zuckuss	8.00	15.00
SL4 Greedo	8.00	15.00
SL5 Jango Fett	6.00	12.00
SL6a Darth Vader	6.00	12.00
SL6b Darth Vader (unmasked)	8.00	15.00
SL7 Princess Leia Boushh	10.00	20.00
SL8 Darth Maul	6.00	12.00
SL9 General Grievous	10.00	20.00
SL10 Clone Trooper	8.00	15.00
SL11 Darth Vader (Anakin Skywalker)	8.00	15.00
SL12 Obi-Wan Kenobi	6.00	12.00
SL13 Yoda	8.00	15.00
SL14 R2-D2	8.00	15.00
SL15 Shocktrooper	15.00	30.00
SL16 Clone Trooper (Revenge of the Sith)	8.00	15.00
SL17 C-3PO	8.00	15.00
SL18 Chewbacca	8.00	15.00
SL19 501st Legion Trooper	12.00	25.00
SL20 Battle Droid 2-Pack	6.00	12.00
SL21 Luke Skywalker	8.00	15.00
SL22 Han Solo (Hoth)	8.00	15.00
SL23 Snowtrooper	10.00	20.00

2013 Star Wars Saga Legends

SL1 Mace Windu	6.00	12.00
SL2 Clone Trooper		
SL3 Anakin Skywalker	6.00	12.00
SL4 Obi-Wan Kenobi (ROTS)	8.00	15.00
SL5 Super Battle Droid	8.00	15.00
SL6 R4-P17		
SL7 Yoda		
SL8 Shock Trooper		
SL9 Boba Fett		
SL10 Captain Rex		
SL11 Stormtrooper		
SL12 Clone Commander Cody		
SL13 Obi-Wan Kenobi (Clone Wars)		
SL14 Luke Skywalker		
SL15 Darth Maul		
SL16 Snowtrooper		

2013 Star Wars Saga Legends Mission Series

MS1 Darth Vader/Seeker Droid (Star Destroyer)	7.50	15.00
MS2 Anakin/501st Legion Trooper (Coruscant)	6.00	12.00
MS3 Battle Droid/Jango Fett (Geonosis)	10.00	20.00
MS4 Battle Droid/212th Battalion Clone Trooper (Utapau)	15.00	30.00
MS5 R2-D2/C-3PO (Tantive IV)	12.50	25.00
MS6 Obi-Wan Kenobi/Darth Maul (Mandalore)	15.00	30.00
MS7 Han Solo/Chewbacca (Death Star)	10.00	20.00
MS8 Obi-Wan Kenobi/General Grievous (Utapau)	7.50	15.00
MS9 Luke Skywalker/Darth Vader (Bespin)	15.00	30.00
MS10 Darth Sidious/Yoda (Senate Duel)	12.50	25.00

2013 Star Wars Saga Legends Multi-Packs

NNO Battle of Geonosis I (Jedi Knights)
(2013 Toys R Us Exclusive)
NNO Battle of Geonosis II (Jedi Knights)
(2013 Toys R Us Exclusive)
NNO The Evolution of Darth Vader
NNO The Rise of Darth Vader
(2013 Target Exclusive)

2013 Star Wars Saga Legends Vehicles

NNO Obi-Wan's Jedi Starfighter (red)
NNO Obi-Wan's Jedi Starfighter (blue)

1996 Star Wars Shadows of the Empire

1	Boba Fett vs IG-88/ with comic book	12.00	25.00
2	Chewbacca/ bounty hunter disguise	8.00	15.00
3	Darth Vader vs Prince Xizor with comic book	12.00	25.00
4	Dash Rendar	10.00	20.00
5	Luke Skywalker/ imperial guard	10.00	20.00
6	Prince Xizor	6.00	12.00
7	Princess Leia/ boushh disguise	10.00	20.00

1996 Star Wars Shadows of the Empire European

1	Chewbacca bounty/ hunter disguise	12.50	25.00
2	Dash Rendar	10.00	20.00
3	Luke Skywalker/ imperial guard	15.00	30.00
4	Princess Leia/ boushh disguise	10.00	20.00
5	Prince Xizor	15.00	30.00

1996 Star Wars Shadows of the Empire Vehicles

1	Boba Fett's Slave I	40.00	80.00
2	Dash Rendar's Outrider	25.00	50.00
3	Swoop with Swoop Trooper	12.00	25.00
4	Speeder Bike/ with Endor Trooper	12.00	25.00

2010-12 Star Wars Sideshow

NNO	Commander Bacara Base Art	100.00	200.00
NNO	Tusken Raider		
NNO	Tusken Raider (Gaffi weapon)	120.00	250.00

2010-12 Star Wars Sideshow 12-Inch

NNO	Commander Praji	100.00	200.00
NNO	Grand Admiral Thrawn		
NNO	Grand Admiral Thrawn (command chair)/750*	800.00	1200.00
NNO	General Obi-Wan Kenobi Clone Wars	60.00	120.00
NNO	General Obi-Wan Kenobi Clone Wars (w/Captain Rex hologram)/1500*	75.00	150.00

2010-12 Star Wars Sideshow 12-Inch Environments

NNO	Han Solo in Carbonite/2000*	250.00	400.00
NNO	Imperial Throne	175.00	350.00
NNO	Jabba's Throne	500.00	700.00

2010-12 Star Wars Sideshow Action Heroes

NNO	C-3PO	200.00	350.00
NNO	R2-D2	100.00	200.00
NNO	TC-14		

2010-12 Star Wars Sideshow Heroes of the Rebellion

NNO	Anakin Skywalker Clone Wars		
NNO	Anakin Skywalker Clone Wars w/Rotta the Hutt)/750*		
NNO	Han Solo & Luke Skywalker Stormtroopers (SDCC Exclusive)	120.00	250.00
NNO	Han Solo Bespin	60.00	120.00
NNO	Han Solo Bespin (w/Mynock)/2000*	50.00	100.00
NNO	Han Solo Smuggler	75.00	150.00
NNO	Han Solo Smuggler Cantina Blaster Pistol/1977*		
NNO	Lando Calrissian		
NNO	Lando Calrissian (w/Bespin communicator)/750*		
NNO	Luke Skywalker Episode IV		
NNO	Luke Skywalker Episode IV (hat and googles)/1977*		
NNO	Luke Skywalker Rebel Commander	200.00	400.00
NNO	Luke Skywalker Rebel Commander (missing hand)/1980*	120.00	250.00
NNO	Luke Skywalker Rebel Hero/600* (30th Anniversary Exclusive)	30.00	75.00
NNO	Padme Amidala Ilum Mission	30.00	75.00
NNO	Princess Leia Boushh	75.00	120.00
NNO	Princess Leia Boushh (Ubese blaster pistol)/2500*	60.00	120.00
NNO	Princess Leia	50.00	100.00
NNO	Princess Leia (wrist binders)/1977*		

2010-12 Star Wars Sideshow Jedi Order

NNO	Aayla Secura (SDCC Exclusive)	120.00	200.00
NNO	Anakin Skywalker	50.00	100.00
NNO	Anakin Skywalker (w/holographic Sidious)/1750*	60.00	120.00
NNO	Ki-Adi-Mundi	50.00	100.00
NNO	Kit Fisto	50.00	100.00
NNO	Kit Fisto (w/Battle Droid head)/1250*	60.00	120.00
NNO	Luke Skywalker Jedi Knight	50.00	100.00
NNO	Luke Skywalker Jedi Knight (blaster)/1250*	60.00	120.00
NNO	Mace Windu	50.00	100.00
NNO	Mace Windu (w/Jango Fett's helmet)/1750*	60.00	120.00
NNO	Obi-Wan Kenobi	50.00	100.00
NNO	Obi-Wan Kenobi (blaster)/1750*	60.00	120.00
NNO	Obi-Wan Kenobi Episode IV	50.00	100.00
NNO	Obi-Wan Kenobi Episode IV (holographic Leia)/1977*	75.00	150.00
NNO	Obi-Wan Kenobi Jedi Knight	30.00	75.00
NNO	Obi-Wan Kenobi Jedi Knight (Kamino dart)/1000*	50.00	100.00
NNO	Plo Koon		
NNO	Plo Koon (twin-bladed lightsaber gauntlet)/1500*	60.00	120.00
NNO	Qui-Gon Jinn	30.00	75.00
NNO	Qui-Gon Jinn (poncho)/2000*	50.00	100.00

2010-12 Star Wars Sideshow Legendary 40-Inch

NNO Darth Maul

2010-12 Star Wars Sideshow Lords of the Sith

NNO	Asajj Ventress	120.00	200.00
NNO	Asajj Ventress (eye paint)/2000*	75.00	150.00
NNO	Darth Maul	75.00	150.00
NNO	Darth Maul (damage saber hilt)/LE	500.00	800.00
NNO	Darth Vader Episode IV		
NNO	Darth Vader Episode IV (Force choke)/1977*		
NNO	Darth Vader Sith Apprentice (SDCC Exclusive)		
NNO	Emperor Palpatine		
NNO	Emperor Palpatine (angry head)/1000*		
NNO	Darth Sidious (hologram and mechno-chair)/5000* (SDCC Exclusive)	50.00	100.00
NNO	Palpatine and Sidious	120.00	250.00
NNO	Palpatine and Sidious (statue)/2000*	100.00	200.00

2010-12 Star Wars Sideshow Militaries

NNO	Admiral Piett	120.00	250.00
NNO	Captain Antilles	100.00	200.00
NNO	Clone Trooper Episode II Phase 1	100.00	200.00
NNO	Coruscant Clone Trooper		
NNO	Coruscant Clone Trooper (41st Elite Corps display base)	100.00	175.00
NNO	Endor Rebel Commando Sergeant	50.00	100.00
NNO	Endor Rebel Infantry	50.00	100.00
NNO	Endor Striker Force Bundle		
NNO	Imperial Shock Trooper	100.00	200.00
NNO	Imperial Shock Trooper (display base)/750*	100.00	200.00
NNO	Nik Sant Endor Rebel Commando Pathfinder	50.00	100.00
NNO	Rebel Fleet Trooper	120.00	200.00
NNO	Sandtrooper		
NNO	Sandtrooper (holding droid piece)/1000*		
NNO	Sandtrooper Corporal	100.00	175.00
NNO	Sandtrooper Squad Leader		
NNO	Stormtrooper	120.00	200.00
NNO	Stormtrooper (stand)/1500*	100.00	200.00
NNO	Stormtrooper Commander	100.00	200.00
NNO	Stormtrooper Commander (base)/1000*	150.00	300.00
NNO	Utapau Clone Trooper	75.00	150.00
NNO	Utapau Clone Trooper (Utapau base)/1500*	100.00	175.00

2010-12 Star Wars Sideshow Premium Format

NNO Han Solo Carbonite

2010-12 Star Wars Sideshow Scum and Villainy

NNO	Bib Fortuna	50.00	100.00
NNO	Bib Fortuna (ceremonial staff)/2500*	60.00	120.00
NNO	Boba Fett	150.00	300.00
NNO	Buboicullaar Creature Pack		
NNO	Buboicullaar Creature Pack (scratching womp rat)/1500*		
NNO	Jabba the Hutt	200.00	350.00
NNO	Jabba the Hutt (ctup)	250.00	400.00
NNO	Salacious Crumb Creature Pack		
NNO	Salacious Crumb Creature Pack (w/dwarf varactyl)		

2019 Star Wars Skywalker Saga Commemorative Edition 2-Packs

NNO C-3PO/BB-8/R2-D2
NNO Darth Maul/Yoda
NNO Darth Vader/Stormtrooper
NNO Finn/Poe Dameron
NNO Han Solo/Princess Leia
NNO Kylo Ren/Rey
NNO Luke Skywalker/Chewbacca
NNO Mace Windu/Jango Fett
NNO Obi-Wan Kenobi/Anakin Skywalker

2005 Star Wars Special Edition 500th Figure

1 Darth Vader/ meditation chamber

2013 Star Wars Titan Heroes 12-Inch

NNO	Anakin Skywalker	12.50	25.00
NNO	Clone Trooper		
NNO	Darth Vader	12.50	25.00
NNO	Luke Skywalker	7.50	15.00
NNO	Obi-Wan Kenobi		

2005-10 Star Wars Transformers

NNO	Anakin Skywalker/Jedi Starfighter	12.00	25.00
NNO	Boba Fett/Slave One	15.00	30.00
NNO	Clone Pilot/ARC-170 Fighter	15.00	30.00
NNO	Clone Pilot/ARC-170 Fighter (repaint)	12.00	25.00
NNO	Darth Maul/Sith Infiltrator	10.00	20.00
NNO	Darth Vader/Death Star	30.00	60.00
NNO	Darth Vader/Sith Starfighter	15.00	30.00
NNO	Darth Vader/TIE Advanced	12.00	25.00
NNO	Emperor Palpatine/Imperial Shuttle	10.00	20.00
NNO	General Grievous/Wheel Bike	12.00	30.00
NNO	Jango Fett/Slave One	12.00	25.00
NNO	Luke Skywalker/Snowspeeder	15.00	30.00
NNO	Luke Skywalker/X-Wing Fighter	25.00	50.00
NNO	Obi-Wan Kenobi/Jedi Starfighter	12.00	25.00

2005-10 Star Wars Transformers Crossovers

NNO	Anakin Skywalker to Jedi Starfighter	8.00	15.00
NNO	Anakin Skywalker to Y-Wing Bomber	10.00	20.00
NNO	Captain Rex to AT-TE	12.00	25.00
NNO	Darth Vader to TIE Advanced X1 Starfighter	12.00	25.00
NNO	Obi-Wan Kenobi to Jedi Starfighter	10.00	20.00
NNO	Yoda to Republic Attack Shuttle	12.00	25.00

2005-10 Star Wars Transformers Deluxe

NNO	Han Solo and Chewbacca/Millennium Falcon	30.00	75.00

2002-07 Star Wars Unleashed

NNO	Aayla Secura	15.00	30.00
NNO	Anakin Skywalker (2005)	15.00	30.00
NNO	Anakin Skywalker (rage)	12.00	25.00
NNO	Asajj Ventress	15.00	30.00
NNO	Aurra Sing	15.00	30.00

NNO	Boba Fett	25.00	50.00
NNO	Bossk	15.00	30.00
NNO	Chewbacca (2004)	10.00	20.00
NNO	Chewbacca (2006)	15.00	30.00
NNO	Clone Trooper (red)	15.00	30.00
NNO	Clone Trooper (white)	12.00	25.00
NNO	Count Dooku	15.00	30.00
NNO	Darth Maul (fury)	15.00	30.00
NNO	Darth Sidious	25.00	50.00
NNO	Darth Tyranus (dissension)	6.00	12.00
NNO	Darth Vader (2005)	15.00	30.00
NNO	Darth Vader (power)	12.00	25.00
NNO	Darth Vader (redemption)	30.00	75.00
NNO	General Grievous	15.00	30.00
NNO	General Grievous	20.00	40.00
	(2006 Target Exclusive)		
NNO	Han Solo	20.00	40.00
NNO	Han Solo Stormtrooper	15.00	30.00
NNO	IG-88	15.00	30.00
NNO	Jango and Boba Fett (intensity)	15.00	30.00
NNO	Luke Skywalker	20.00	40.00
NNO	Luke Skywalker (snowspeeder pilot)	15.00	30.00
NNO	Mace Windu (honor)	12.00	25.00
NNO	Obi-Wan Kenobi (2003)	15.00	30.00
NNO	Obi-Wan Kenobi (2005)	15.00	30.00
NNO	Padme Amidala (courage)	30.00	60.00
NNO	Palpatine vs. Yoda	20.00	40.00
NNO	Princess Leia	30.00	75.00
NNO	Shock Trooper	15.00	30.00
NNO	Stormtrooper	20.00	40.00
NNO	Tusken Raider	10.00	20.00
NNO	Yoda	15.00	30.00

2006-08 Star Wars Unleashed Battle Packs

NNO	Attack on Tantive IV Commanders		
NNO	Attack on Tantive IV Rebel Blockade Troopers		
NNO	Attack on Tantive IV Stormtrooper Boarding Party		
NNO	Battle of Felucia Aayla Secura's 327th Star Corps		
NNO	Battle of Geonosis The Clone Wars		
NNO	Battle of Hoth Evacuation at Echo Base		
NNO	Battle of Hoth Imperial Encounter		
NNO	Battle of Hoth Imperial Invasion		
NNO	Battle of Hoth Imperial Stormtroopers		
NNO	Battle of Hoth Rebel Alliance Troopers		
NNO	Battle of Hoth Snowspeeder Assault		
NNO	Battle of Hoth Snowtrooper Battalion		
NNO	Battle of Hoth Wampa Assault		
NNO	Battle of Kashyyyk Droid Invasion		
NNO	Battle of Kashyyyk and Felucia Heroes	30.00	60.00
NNO	Battle of Kashyyyk Wookiee Warriors	15.00	30.00
NNO	Battle of Kashyyyk Yoda's Elite Clone Troopers		
NNO	Battle of Utapau Battle Droids		
NNO	Battle of Utapau Clone Trooper Attack Battalion	12.50	25.00
NNO	Battle of Utapau Commanders	12.00	25.00
NNO	Battle of Utapau Utapaun Warriors	10.00	20.00
NNO	Clone Wars 501st Legion		
NNO	Clone Wars ARC Troopers		
NNO	Clone Wars Battle of Mon Calamari		
NNO	Clone Wars Clone Pilots and AT-TE Gunners		
NNO	Clone Wars Clone Troopers		
NNO	Clone Wars Jedi Generals		
NNO	Clone Wars Jedi Heroes		
NNO	Clone Wars Jedi vs. Sith	15.00	30.00
NNO	Clone Wars Theed Battle Heroes		
NNO	Clone Wars Vader's Bounty Hunters		
NNO	Death Star Encounters Imperial and Rebel Commanders		
NNO	Death Star Encounters Imperial and Rebel Pilots		
NNO	Death Star Encounters Imperial Troops		
NNO	Order 66 A New Empire		
NNO	Order 66 Jedi Masters	7.50	15.00
NNO	Order 66 Shock Trooper Battalion		
NNO	Order 66 Vader's 501st Legion		
NNO	The Force Unleashed Empire		
NNO	The Force Unleashed Imperial Troopers		
NNO	The Force Unleashed Unleashed Warriors		
NNO	Trouble on Tatooine Cantina Encounter		
NNO	Trouble on Tatooine Jawas and Droids		

NNO	Trouble on Tatooine Sandtrooper Search		
NNO	Trouble on Tatooine The Streets of Mos Eisley		
NNO	Trouble on Tatooine Tusken Raiders		
NNO	Ultimate Battles 187th Legion Troopers		
NNO	Ultimate Battles Battle Droid Factory		
NNO	Ultimate Battles Mygeeto Clone Battalion		

2007 Star Wars Unleashed Battle Packs Singles

1	Commander Bly
2	Darth Vader
3	Darth Vader (Anakin Skywalker)
4	Han Solo
5	Luke Skywalker
6	Mace Windu
7	Obi-Wan Kenobi
8	Shock Trooper
9	Stormtrooper

2005-07 Star Wars Unleashed Tubed Packs

NNO	Anakin Skywalker	25.00	50.00
NNO	ARC Heavy Gunner		
NNO	Boba Fett	25.00	50.00
	(2006 Target Exclusive)		
NNO	Darth Vader	12.00	25.00
	(2005 Best Buy Exclusive)		
NNO	Darth Vader		
	(2006 KB Toys Exclusive)		
NNO	Darth Vader	10.00	20.00
	(2006 Walmart Exclusive)		
NNO	Luke Skywalker		
	(2006 Walmart Exclusive)		
NNO	Obi-Wan Kenobi	15.00	30.00
NNO	Shadow Stormtrooper	8.00	15.00

2010-21 Star Wars The Vintage Collection

VC1a	Dengar (age warning on left back)	50.00	100.00
VC1b	Dengar (age warning on bottom back)	100.00	200.00
VC2a	Leia (Hoth)(age warning on left back)	50.00	100.00
VC2b	Leia (Hoth)(age warning on bottom back)	20.00	40.00
VC3a	Han Solo (Echo Base)(age warning on left back)	15.00	30.00
VC3b	Han Solo (Echo Base)(age warning on bottom back)	12.50	25.00
VC3c	Han Solo (Echo Base)(FOIL card)	50.00	100.00
VC4a	Luke Skywalker (Bespin)(age warning on left back)	75.00	150.00
VC4b	Luke Skywalker (Bespin)(age warning on bottom back)	50.00	100.00
VC4c	Luke Skywalker (Bespin)(FOIL card)	50.00	100.00
VC5a	AT-AT Commander (age warning on left back)	125.00	250.00
VC5b	AT-AT Commander (age warning on bottom back)	75.00	150.00
VC6a	See-Threepio (C-3PO)(age warning on left back)	15.00	30.00
VC6b	See-Threepio (C-3PO)(age warning on bottom back)	20.00	40.00
VC7	Dack Ralter	40.00	80.00
VC8a	Darth Vader (age warning on left back)	15.00	30.00
VC8b	Darth Vader (age warning on bottom back)	25.00	50.00
VC8c	Darth Vader (Boba Fett sticker/plus shipping and handling)	20.00	40.00
VC8d	Darth Vader (barcode #54674 sticker)	20.00	40.00
VC8e	Darth Vader (barcode #54674 printed)	20.00	40.00
VC8f	Darth Vader (Revenge of the Jedi)	75.00	150.00
VC8g	Darth Vader (Return of the Jedi)	25.00	50.00
VC8h	Darth Vader (Wave 1 ESB figure back)	15.00	30.00
VC8i	Darth Vader (FOIL card)	100.00	200.00
VC9aa	Boba Fett (age warning on left back)	75.00	150.00
VC9ab	Boba Fett (age warning on bottom back)	20.00	40.00
VC9ac	Boba Fett (black gun barrel)	25.00	50.00
VC9ad	Boba Fett (no warning on card back)	60.00	120.00
VC9ae	Boba Fett (FOIL card)	200.00	400.00
VC9ba	Boba Fett (Revenge of the Jedi)	30.00	75.00
VC9bb	Boba Fett (Return of the Jedi)	25.00	50.00
VC10a	4-LOM (age warning on left back)	25.00	60.00
VC10b	4-LOM (age warning on bottom back)	25.00	60.00
VC11a	(Twin-Pod) Cloud Car Pilot (age warning on left back)	30.00	60.00
VC11b	(Twin-Pod) Cloud Car Pilot (age warning on bottom back)	25.00	50.00
VC12a	Darth Sidious	50.00	100.00
VC12b	Darth Sidious (FOIL card)	100.00	200.00
VC13a	Anakin Skywalker (Darth Vader)	30.00	60.00
	(Boba Fett mailway sticker front)		
VC13b	Anakin Skywalker (Darth Vader)	60.00	120.00
VC13c	Anakin Skywalker (Darth Vader)	60.00	120.00

(Boba Fett sticker/shipping and handling)		
VC13d Anakin Skywalker (Darth Vader)(barcode #54885)		
VC13e Anakin Skywalker (Darth Vader)(FOIL card)	125.00	250.00
VC14a Sandtrooper (dim photo front)	10.00	20.00
VC14b Sandtrooper (bright photo front)	10.00	20.00
VC14c Sandtrooper (Boba Fett sticker/shipping and handling)	17.50	35.00
VC14d Sandtrooper (barcode #54573 sticker)	12.50	25.00
VC14e Sandtrooper (barcode #54573 printed)	25.00	50.00
VC14e Sandtrooper (FOIL card)	75.00	150.00
VC15a Clone Trooper (dim photo front)	30.00	75.00
VC15b Clone Trooper (bright photo front)	60.00	120.00
VC15c Clone Trooper (Boba Fett sticker/shipping and handling)	12.50	25.00
VC15d Clone Trooper (barcode #54888 sticker)	15.00	30.00
VC15e Clone Trooper (barcode #54888 printed)	12.50	25.00
VC15f Clone Trooper (FOIL card)	50.00	100.00
VC16a Obi-Wan Kenobi	20.00	40.00
VC16b Obi-Wan Kenobi (FOIL card)	150.00	300.00
VC17a General Grievous (Boba Fett sticker on front)	30.00	75.00
VC17b General Grievous (barcode #54572 sticker)	30.00	60.00
VC17c General Grievous (barcode #54572 printed)	30.00	75.00
VC17d General Grievous (FOIL card)	125.00	250.00
VC18a MagnaGuard	25.00	50.00
VC18b MagnaGuard (FOIL card)	100.00	200.00
VC19a Clone Commander Cody (dim photo front)	50.00	100.00
VC19b Clone Commander Cody (bright photo front)	75.00	150.00
VC19c Clone Commander Cody (FOIL card)	125.00	250.00
VC20a Yoda	100.00	200.00
VC20b Yoda (Boba Fett sticker front)	60.00	120.00
VC20c Yoda (Canadian art variant)	625.00	1250.00
VC21a Gamorrean Guard (1st Boba Fett rocket sticker)	25.00	50.00
VC21b Gamorrean Guard (2nd Boba Fett rocket sticker)	30.00	60.00
VC21c Gamorrean Guard (barcode #54898 sticker)	30.00	60.00
VC21d Gamorrean Guard (barcode #54898 printed)	20.00	40.00
VC21e Gamorrean Guard (Darth Maul sticker front)	50.00	100.00
VC22a Admiral Ackbar (1st Boba Fett rocket sticker)	25.00	50.00
VC22b Admiral Ackbar (2nd Boba Fett rocket sticker)	25.00	50.00
VC22c Admiral Ackbar (barcode #54900)	15.00	30.00
VC22d Admiral Ackbar (barcode #52864)	15.00	30.00
VC23a Luke Skywalker (Jedi Knight Outfit / Endor Captive)	30.00	75.00
VC23b Luke Skywalker (Jedi Knight Outfit / Endor Captive)	15.00	30.00
(2nd Boba Fett rocket sticker)		
VC23c Luke Skywalker (Jedi Knight Outfit / Endor Captive)	25.00	50.00
VC23d Luke Skywalker (Jedi Knight Outfit / Endor Captive)	20.00	40.00
(barcode #54902)		
VC23e Luke Skywalker (Jedi Knight Outfit / Endor Captive)		
(portrait back)		
VC23f Luke Skywalker (Jedi Knight Outfit / Endor Captive)		
(no warning on back)		
VC23g Luke Skywalker (Jedi Knight Outfit / Endor Captive)	50.00	100.00
(Revenge of the Jedi)		
VC23h Luke Skywalker (Jedi Knight Outfit / Endor Captive)	20.00	40.00
(barcode #52867)		
VC24a Wooof (Klaatu)(1st Boba Fett rocket sticker)	50.00	100.00
VC24b Wooof (Klaatu)(2nd Boba Fett rocket sticker)	30.00	75.00
VC24c Wooof (Klaatu)(barcode #54905)	20.00	40.00
VC24d Wooof (Klaatu)(figures left off backs)		
VC25a R2-D2 (w/Pop-Up Lightsaber)	50.00	100.00
VC25b R2-D2 (w/Pop-Up Lightsaber)	17.50	35.00
(2nd Boba Fett rocket sticker)		
VC25c R2-D2 (w/Pop-Up Lightsaber)	20.00	40.00
(R2-D2 back)		
VC25d R2-D2 (w/Pop-Up Lightsaber)	75.00	150.00
VC25e R2-D2 (w/Pop-Up Lightsaber)		
(no warning on back)		
VC26aa Rebel Commando (1st Boba Fett rocket sticker)	30.00	75.00
VC26ab Rebel Commando (2nd Boba Fett rocket sticker)	20.00	40.00
VC26ac Rebel Commando (barcode #54907)	15.00	30.00
VC26ba Rebel Commando (Version II)(Return of the Jedi logo)	30.00	75.00
VC26bb Rebel Commando (Version II)(Revenge of the Jedi logo)	75.00	150.00
VC27a Wicket (1st Boba Fett rocket sticker)	20.00	40.00
VC27b Wicket (2nd Boba Fett rocket sticker)	25.00	50.00
VC27c Wicket (barcode #54908)	20.00	40.00
VC27d Wicket (barcode #52900)	20.00	40.00
VC27e Wicket (no warning on back)		
VC28a Wedge Antilles (card image on back)	30.00	60.00
VC28b Wedge Antilles (film image on back)		
VC28ca Wedge Antilles (light violet background)	30.00	60.00
VC28cb Wedge Antilles (dark blue to violet background)	30.00	75.00
VC29 Kit Fisto	75.00	150.00
VC30 Zam Wesell	50.00	100.00
VC31a Obi-Wan Kenobi (figures left of cardbacks)	30.00	60.00
VC31b Obi-Wan Kenobi (Prototype Boba Fett sticker)	60.00	120.00
VC32a Anakin Skywalker (Peasant Disguise)	30.00	60.00
VC32b Anakin Skywalker (Peasant Disguise)(Boba Fett sticker front)	12.50	25.00
VC33 Padme Amidala (Peasant Disguise)	75.00	150.00
VC34a Jango Fett (figures left of cardbacks)	125.00	250.00
VC34b Jango Fett (no warning on back)	20.00	40.00
VC34c Jango Fett (Prototype Boba Fett sticker)	100.00	200.00
VC35 Mace Windu	75.00	150.00
VC36a Senate Guard (close-up photo front)	20.00	40.00
VC36b Senate Guard (wide photo front)	30.00	60.00
VC37 Super Battle Droid	60.00	120.00
VC38 Clone Trooper (212th Battalion)	100.00	200.00
VC39 Luke Skywalker (Death Star Escape)	40.00	80.00
VC40 R5-D4	50.00	100.00
VC41a Stormtrooper (barcode #62162 sticker)	20.00	40.00
VC41b Stormtrooper (barcode #62162 printed)	20.00	40.00
VC41c Stormtrooper (warning sticker on front)		
VC41d Stormtrooper (Revenge of the Jedi)	60.00	120.00
VC41e Stormtrooper (Return of the Jedi)	50.00	100.00
VC42 Han Solo (Yavin Ceremony)	40.00	80.00
VC43 Commander Gree (Greatest Hits)	100.00	200.00
VC44 Luke Skywalker (Dagobah Landing)	125.00	250.00
VC45 Clone Trooper (Phase I)	30.00	60.00
VC46 AT-RT Driver	65.00	130.00
VC47 General Lando Calrissian	30.00	60.00
VC48 Weequay (Skiff Master)	30.00	75.00
VC49 Fi-Ek Sirch (Jedi Knight)	20.00	40.00
VC50 Han Solo (Bespin Outfit)	25.00	50.00
VC51 Barriss Offee (Jedi Padawan)	50.00	100.00
VC52 Rebel Fleet Trooper	30.00	60.00
VC53 Bom Vimdin (Cantina Patron)	25.00	50.00
VC54 ARC Trooper Commander (Captain Fordo)	125.00	250.00
VC55 Logray (Ewok Medicine Man)	30.00	60.00
VC56a Kithaba (Skiff Guard)(black headband)	40.00	80.00
VC56b Kithaba (Skiff Guard)(red headband)	50.00	100.00
VC57a Dr. Cornelius Evazan (pink scar)	30.00	75.00
VC57b Dr. Cornelius Evazan (no pink scar)	50.00	100.00
VC58 Aayla Secura	75.00	150.00
VC59 Nom Anor	30.00	75.00
VC60 Clone Trooper (501st Legion)	125.00	250.00
VC61 Prototype Armour Boba Fett	75.00	150.00
VC62 Han Solo (In Trench Coat)	20.00	40.00
VC63 B-Wing Pilot (Keyan Farlander)	12.50	25.00
VC64 Princess Leia (Slave Outfit)	200.00	400.00
VC65 TIE Fighter Pilot	25.00	50.00
VC66 Salacious Crumb	350.00	700.00
VC67 Mouse Droid	300.00	600.00
(2011 SDCC Exclusive)		
VC68 Rebel Soldier (Echo Base Battle Gear)	50.00	100.00
VC69 Bastila Shan	100.00	200.00
VC70 Ponda Baba (Walrus Man)	60.00	120.00
VC71 Mawhonic	30.00	75.00
VC72 Naboo Pilot	30.00	60.00
VC73 Aurra Sing	75.00	150.00
VC74 Gungan Warrior	40.00	80.00
VC75 Qui-Gon Jinn	30.00	60.00
VC76 Obi-Wan Kenobi (Jedi Padawan)	50.00	100.00
VC77 Ratts Tyerell & Pit Droid	30.00	60.00
VC78 Battle Droid	20.00	40.00
VC79 Darth Sidious	50.00	100.00
VC80 Anakin Skywalker (Jedi Padawan)	30.00	60.00
VC81 Ben Quadinaros & Pit Droid	20.00	40.00
VC82 Daultay Dofine	30.00	60.00
VC83 Naboo Royal Guard	20.00	40.00
VC84 Queen Amidala (Post-Senate)	25.00	50.00
VC85 Quinlan Vos (Mos Espa)	40.00	80.00
VC86 Darth Maul	25.00	50.00
VC87 Luke Skywalker (Lightsaber Construction)	30.00	60.00
VC88 Princess Leia (Sandstorm Outfit)	50.00	100.00
VC89 Lando Calrissian (Sandstorm Outfit)	25.00	50.00
VC90 Colonel Cracken (Millennium Falcon Crew)	25.00	50.00
VC91 Rebel Pilot (Mon Calamari)	40.00	80.00
VC92 Anakin Skywalker (The Clone Wars)	25.00	50.00
VC93 Darth Vader (A New Hope)	40.00	80.00
VC94 Imperial Navy Commander	30.00	75.00
VC95 Luke Skywalker (Hoth Outfit)	20.00	40.00
VC96 Darth Malgus (The Old Republic)	60.00	120.00
VC97 Clone Pilot Davijaan (Oddball)	50.00	100.00
VC98 Grand Moff Tarkin	100.00	200.00
VC99 Nikto (Vintage)	75.00	150.00
VC100 Galen Marek (The Force Unleashed II)	125.00	250.00
VC101 Shae Vizsla	200.00	400.00
VC102 Ahsoka Tano (The Clone Wars)	400.00	800.00
VC103 Obi-Wan Kenobi (The Clone Wars)	30.00	60.00
VC104 Lumat	100.00	200.00
VC105 Emperor's Royal Guard	25.00	50.00
VC106 Nien Nunb	60.00	120.00
VC107 Weequay (Hunter)	100.00	200.00
VC108a Jar Jar Binks	60.00	120.00
VC108b Jar Jar Binks (lost line)		
VC109a Clone Trooper Lieutenant	100.00	200.00
VC109b Clone Trooper Lieutenant (lost line)		
VC110a Shock Trooper	60.00	120.00
VC110b Shock Trooper (lost line)		
VC111a Leia Organa (Bespin)	50.00	100.00
VC111b Leia Organa (Bespin) (lost line)		
VC112a Sandtrooper (with Patrol Droid)	100.00	200.00
VC112b Sandtrooper (with Patrol Droid) (lost line)		
VC113 Republic Trooper	150.00	300.00
VC114 Orrimarko	60.00	120.00
VC115a Darth Vader (Emperor's Wrath)	125.00	250.00
VC115b Darth Vader (Emperor's Wrath) (lost line)		
VC116 Rey (Jakku)	15.00	30.00
VC117 Kylo Ren	15.00	30.00
VC118 First Order Stormtrooper	12.50	25.00
VC119 Jyn Erso	12.50	25.00
VC120 Rebel Soldier (Hoth)	15.00	30.00
VC121 Supreme Leader Snoke	10.00	20.00
VC122 Rey (Island Journey)	20.00	40.00
VC123 Stormtrooper (Mimban)	20.00	40.00
VC124 Han Solo	12.50	25.00
VC125 Enfys Nest	15.00	30.00
VC126 Imperial Assault Tank Driver	40.00	80.00
VC127 Imperial Death Trooper	12.50	25.00
VC128 Range Trooper	15.00	30.00
VC129 Doctor Aphra	20.00	40.00
VC130 Captain Cassian Andor	12.50	25.00
VC131 Luke Skywalker	12.50	25.00
VC132 Saelt-Marae	12.50	25.00
VC133 Scarif Stormtrooper	25.00	50.00
VC134 Princess Leia Organa (Boushh)	20.00	40.00
VC135 Klaatu (Skiff Guard)	15.00	30.00
VC136 Han Solo (Carbonite)	25.00	50.00
VC137 Ree Yees	15.00	30.00
VC138 Elite Praetorian Guard	15.00	30.00
VC139 Lando Calrissian	10.00	20.00
VC140 Imperial Stormtrooper	20.00	40.00
VC141 Chewbacca	15.00	30.00
VC142 Captain Phasma	20.00	40.00
VC143 Han Solo (Stormtrooper)	25.00	50.00
VC144 Lando Calrissian (Skiff Guard)	10.00	20.00
VC145 41st Elite Corps Clone Trooper	25.00	50.00
VC146 Luke Skywalker (Crait)	60.00	120.00
VC147 Death Star Gunner	30.00	60.00
VC148 Imperial Assault Tank Commander	60.00	120.00
VC149 Artoo-Detoo (R2-D2)	25.00	50.00
VC150 Princess Leia Organa (Yavin)	20.00	40.00
VC151 Luke Skywalker (Yavin)	15.00	30.00
(Walmart Exclusive)		
VC152 Vedain	12.50	25.00
(Skiff Guard 3-Pack)		
VC153 Vizam	12.50	25.00
(Skiff Guard 3-Pack)		
VC154 Brock Starsher	12.50	25.00
(Skiff Guard 3-Pack)		
VC155 Knight of Ren	20.00	40.00
VC156 Rey	50.00	100.00
VC157 Zorii Bliss	25.00	50.00
VC158 Luke Skywalker (X-Wing Pilot)	25.00	50.00
VC159 Sith Jet Trooper	20.00	40.00
VC160 Poe Dameron	15.00	30.00
VC161 Jawa	12.50	25.00
VC162A Sith Trooper (w/armory pack)	20.00	40.00

(2019 Amazon Exclusive)

VC163	Shadow Trooper	20.00	40.00
VC164	Cara Dune	15.00	30.00
VC165	Remnant Stormtrooper	15.00	30.00
VC166	The Mandalorian	20.00	40.00
VC167	Power Droid	15.00	30.00
VC168	Clone Commander Wolffe	12.50	25.00
VC169	Luke Skywalker (Stormtrooper)	20.00	40.00
VC170	K-2SO	10.00	20.00
VC171	Stormtrooper	25.00	50.00
VC172	Clone Trooper Fives	30.00	60.00
VC173	Hondo Ohnaka	20.00	40.00
VC174	Chirrut Imwe	15.00	30.00
VC175	Luke Skywalker	20.00	40.00
VC176	Clone Trooper Echo	15.00	30.00
VC177A	Incinerator Stormtrooper	20.00	40.00
VC177B	Din Djarin (w/Grogu)	25.00	50.00
VC178	Darth Vader	12.50	25.00
VC179	Armorer	15.00	30.00
VC180	Moff Gideon	12.50	25.00
VC181	Din Djarin	15.00	30.00
VC182	Captain Rex	12.50	25.00
VC183	Rebel Fleet Trooper	25.00	50.00
VC184	Grogu (w/Pram)	15.00	30.00
VC185	Greef Karga	10.00	20.00
VC186	Boba Fett	20.00	40.00
VC187	Princess Leia Organa	15.00	30.00
VC189	Zutton (Snaggletooth)	12.50	25.00
VC190	Paploo	15.00	30.00
(2021 Walmart Exclusive)			
VC191	Princess Leia Organa (Endor)	15.00	30.00
(2021 Walmart Exclusive)			
VC192	AT-ST Driver	10.00	20.00
(2021 Walmart Exclusive)			
VC193	Battle Droid	10.00	20.00
VC194	Shadow Stormtrooper	15.00	30.00
VC195	Purge Stormtrooper	20.00	40.00
(2021 Entertainment Earth Exclusive)			
VC196	Biker Scout	20.00	40.00
(2021 Fan Channel Exclusive)			
VC197	Death Star Droid	12.50	25.00
(2021 Walmart Exclusive)			
VC198	Luke Skywalker (Endor)	25.00	50.00
(2021 Walmart Exclusive)			
VC199	Tusken Raider	20.00	40.00
(2021 Walmart Exclusive)			
VC201	Darth Maul		

VC202	Ahsoka Tano		
VC203	Jawa		
VC205	Lando Calrissian		

2010-21 Star Wars The Vintage Collection Creatures

NNO	Luke Skywalker's Tauntaun	100.00	200.00

2010-21 Star Wars The Vintage Collection Exclusives

NNO	Jocasta Nu	200.00	400.00
NNO	Stewart Storm Trooper/1		
(2010 Jon Stewart One-of-a-Kind Exclusive)			
VCP3	Boba Fett (rocket-firing)	125.00	250.00
VCP12	4-LOM/Zuckuss 2-Pack	125.00	250.00

2010-21 Star Wars The Vintage Collection Multipacks

NNO	501st Legion Arc Troopers (Echo/Fives/Jesse)	150.00	300.00
(Hasbro Pulse Exclusive)			
NNO	Android 3-Pack	125.00	250.00
NNO	Death Star Scanning Crew	75.00	150.00
NNO	Doctor Aphra Comic Set	50.00	100.00
(2018 SDCC Exclusive)			
NNO	Droid 3-Pack	60.00	120.00
NNO	Endor AT-ST Crew 2-Pack	40.00	80.00
NNO	Ewok Assault Catapult	75.00	150.00
NNO	Ewok Scouts 2-Pack	60.00	120.00
NNO	Hero 3-Pack	50.00	100.00
NNO	Imperial 3-Pack	75.00	150.00
NNO	Imperial Forces 3-Pack	125.00	250.00
NNO	Imperial Scanning Crew	75.00	150.00
NNO	Lost Line Carbon Freeze Chamber 7-Figure Set	100.00	200.00
(2012 SDCC Exclusive)			
NNO	Rebel 3-Pack	60.00	120.00
NNO	Revenge of the Jedi 14-Figure Death Star Set	750.00	1500.00
(2011 SDCC Exclusive)			
NNO	Skiff Guard 3-Pack (Special)	25.00	50.00
(Fan Channels Exclusive)			
NNO	Special Action Figure Set	75.00	150.00
NNO	Special Action Figure Set	30.00	60.00
Jedi Luke, X-Wing Luke, Stormtrooper Luke			

NNO	Villain 3-Pack 2012	15.00	30.00
Sand People, Boba Fett, Snaggletooth			
(Target Exclusive)			
NNO	Villain 3-Pack	20.00	40.00
Stormtrooper, Darth Vader, Death Star Trooper			
(Target Exclusive)			

2010-21 Star Wars The Vintage Collection Playsets

NNO	Carbon-Freezing Chamber	60.00	120.00
NNO	Jabba's Palace Adventure Set	40.00	80.00
(Walmart Exclusive)			
NNO	Tantive IV	75.00	150.00

2010-21 Star Wars The Vintage Collection Vehicles

NNO	AT-AP	100.00	200.00
NNO	Biggs' Red 3 X-Wing Fighter	75.00	150.00
NNO	B-Wing Starfighter	125.00	250.00
NNO	Imperial AT-AT (ESB)	250.00	400.00
(Toys R Us Exclusive)			
NNO	Imperial AT-AT (ROTJ)	200.00	350.00
(Toys R Us Exclusive)			
NNO	Imperial Combat Assault Tank (Rogue One)	60.00	120.00
NNO	Imperial Combat Assault Tank	75.00	150.00
(2018)			
NNO	Imperial TIE Fighter	75.00	150.00
(2018 Walmart Exclusive)			
NNO	Imperial TIE Fighter	125.00	250.00
NNO	Imperial Troop Transport (The Mandalorian)	50.00	100.00
NNO	Jabba's Sail Barge	1500.00	3000.00
(HasLab Exclusive)			
NNO	Landspeeder	125.00	250.00
NNO	Luke Skywalker's X-Wing Fighter	100.00	200.00
NNO	Millennium Falcon	600.00	1200.00
NNO	Obi-Wan Kenobi's Jedi Starfighter	100.00	200.00
NNO	Rebel Armored Snowspeeder	125.00	250.00
NNO	Republic Gunship	600.00	1200.00
NNO	Scout Walker AT-ST	100.00	200.00
NNO	Slave I	125.00	250.00
NNO	Tatooine Skiff	60.00	120.00
NNO	TIE Interceptor	200.00	400.00
NNO	V-19 Torrent Starfighter	75.00	150.00
NNO	Y-Wing Starfighter	100.00	200.00

FIGURINES

2011-12 Funko Blox

23	Darth Vader	10.00	20.00
24	Boba Fett	8.00	15.00
25	Stormtrooper	8.00	12.00

2017-19 Funko Dorbz Star Wars

1	Luke Skywalker	7.50	15.00
2	Princess Leia	7.50	15.00
3A	Darth Vader	10.00	20.00
(2017)			
3B	Darth Vader HOLO CH	10.00	20.00
4	Han Solo	6.00	12.00
5A	Chewbacca	10.00	20.00
5B	Chewbacca FLK CH	15.00	30.00
6	C-3PO	7.50	15.00

7	Stormtrooper	10.00	20.00
8	Jawa	7.50	15.00
9	Luke Skywalker w/Speeder	20.00	40.00
10	Tusken Raider w/Bantha	20.00	40.00
11	Han Solo	10.00	20.00
(2018)			
12A	Chewbacca	7.50	15.00
(2018)			
12B	Chewbacca FLK CH	15.00	30.00
13	Qi'Ra	6.00	12.00
(2018)			
14A	Lando Calrissian		
(2018)			
14B	Lando Calrissian White Cape CH	20.00	40.00

2017-19 Funko Dorbz Star Wars Multi-Pack

COMMON DORBZ			
NNO	Greedo/Walrus Man/Snaggletooth D23	20.00	40.00

2014-16 Funko Fabrikations

2	Yoda	8.00	15.00
3	Boba Fett	6.00	12.00
4	Greedo	6.00	12.00
12	Darth Vader	6.00	12.00
13	Chewbacca	6.00	12.00
26	Wicket Warrick	10.00	20.00
27	Princess Leia	12.00	25.00
29	Stormtrooper	6.00	12.00

2009 Funko Force Star Wars

NNO	501st Clone Trooper/1008* SDCC	30.00	60.00
NNO	Boba Fett	7.50	15.00
NNO	Chewbacca	6.00	12.00
NNO	Darth Maul	15.00	30.00
NNO	Darth Vader	7.50	15.00
NNO	Emperor Palpatine	12.50	25.00
NNO	Shadow Trooper	12.50	25.00
NNO	Shocktrooper	20.00	40.00
NNO	Stormtrooper	12.50	25.00
NNO	Yoda	7.50	15.00

2015-18 Funko Hikari Star Wars

NNO	Boba Fett Clear Glitter/750* NYCC	25.00	50.00
NNO	Boba Fett Glitter/1200*	20.00	40.00
NNO	Boba Fett Infrared/1000* SDCC	25.00	50.00
NNO	Boba Fett Infrared/1000* SCE	25.00	50.00
NNO	Boba Fett Midnight/1000* SWC	60.00	120.00
NNO	Boba Fett Prism/750*	30.00	60.00
NNO	Boba Fett Proto/250* FS	30.00	75.00
NNO	Boba Fett/1500*	20.00	40.00
NNO	Bossk MET/1000*	25.00	50.00
NNO	Bossk Planet X/600*	20.00	40.00
NNO	Bossk Prism/500* EE	25.00	50.00
NNO	Bossk Rainbow/550* SLCC	30.00	75.00
NNO	Bossk Starfield/500* NYCC	30.00	75.00
NNO	Bossk/1000*	25.00	50.00
NNO	C-3PO Clear Glitter/750* SLCC	30.00	60.00
NNO	C-3PO Dirty Penny/500* TT	30.00	75.00
NNO	C-3PO Red/750* SLCC	25.00	50.00
NNO	C-3PO Rusty/500* Gemini	25.00	50.00
NNO	C-3PO/1500*	20.00	40.00
NNO	Captain Phasma Alloy/250*	30.00	60.00
NNO	Captain Phasma Blue Steel/400*	30.00	75.00
NNO	Captain Phasma Classic/500*	25.00	50.00
NNO	Captain Phasma Cold Steel/250*	30.00	60.00
NNO	Captain Phasma Meltdown/100* HT	100.00	175.00
NNO	Clone Trooper Dirty Penny/250* EE	25.00	50.00
NNO	Clone Trooper Rusty White/250* GS	20.00	40.00
NNO	Clone Trooper 442 Siege Glitter/100*	60.00	120.00
NNO	Clone Trooper 442 Siege/900*	20.00	40.00
NNO	Clone Trooper 501st Glitter/250*	30.00	75.00
NNO	Clone Trooper 501st/1500* SDCC	20.00	40.00
NNO	Clone Trooper Starfield/1000* SWC	25.00	50.00
NNO	Clone Trooper Utapau Glitter/100* EE	50.00	100.00
NNO	Clone Trooper Utapau/600* EE	25.00	50.00
NNO	Clone Trooper/1500*	15.00	30.00
NNO	Darth Vader Holographic GITD/300* Gemini	30.00	75.00
NNO	Darth Vader Holographic/750*	25.00	50.00
NNO	Darth Vader Infrared/500* EE	30.00	60.00
NNO	Darth Vader Lightning/1500*	20.00	40.00
NNO	Darth Vader Matte Back/1200* SDCC	25.00	50.00
NNO	Darth Vader Starfield/750*Gemini	30.00	75.00
NNO	Darth Vader/1500*	20.00	40.00
NNO	E-3PO/500*	20.00	40.00
NNO	FO Snowtrooper Ice Storm/500*	20.00	40.00
NNO	FO Snowtrooper Iron Age/250*	25.00	50.00
NNO	Stormtrooper Inferno/250*	30.00	75.00
NNO	FO Stormtrooper Kiln/400*	30.00	75.00
NNO	FO Stormtrooper Nocturne/400*	30.00	60.00
NNO	FO Stormtrooper Phantasm/250*	30.00	60.00
NNO	FO Stormtrooper/500*	15.00	30.00
NNO	Greedo Mystic Powers/750*	30.00	75.00
NNO	Greedo Platinum/600* NYCC	25.00	50.00
NNO	Greedo Sublime/750*	15.00	30.00
NNO	Greedo Verdigris/500* SWC	30.00	60.00
NNO	Greedo Original/2000*	20.00	40.00
NNO	K-3PO/750*	20.00	40.00
NNO	Kylo Ren Alchemy/300*	25.00	50.00
NNO	Kylo Ren Dark Side/500*	20.00	40.00
NNO	Kylo Ren Live Wire/250*	60.00	120.00
NNO	Kylo Ren Onyx/150* HT	75.00	150.00
NNO	Kylo Ren Rage/250* HT	60.00	120.00
NNO	Shadow Trooper/1000*	20.00	40.00
NNO	Snowtrooper Celsius/400*	30.00	60.00
NNO	Snowtrooper Galaxy/250*	20.00	40.00
NNO	Stormtrooper Blue MET/1000*	20.00	40.00
NNO	Stormtrooper Cosmic/2000* SDCC LC	15.00	30.00
NNO	Stormtrooper Green/100* ECCC	75.00	150.00
NNO	Stormtrooper Ice/750* SWC	60.00	120.00
NNO	Stormtrooper Prism/750* TT	30.00	75.00
NNO	Stormtrooper Relic/500*	20.00	40.00
NNO	Stormtrooper Rusty Silver/750*	25.00	50.00
NNO	Stormtrooper Starfield/750*	20.00	40.00
NNO	Stormtrooper/1500*	30.00	60.00
NNO	Wampa Bloody/750*	20.00	40.00
NNO	Wampa Glitter/750*	20.00	40.00
NNO	Wampa Grey Skull/250* EE	20.00	40.00
NNO	Wampa Ice/500* Gemini	30.00	60.00

2017-18 Funko Hikari XS Star Wars

NNO	Chopper (black)	7.50	15.00
(2017 Smuggler's Bounty Exclusive)			
NNO	Chopper (clear)	4.00	8.00
(2017 Smuggler's Bounty Exclusive)			
NNO	Chopper (gold)	5.00	10.00
(2017 Smuggler's Bounty Exclusive)			
NNO	Chopper (orange)	4.00	8.00
(2017 Smuggler's Bounty Exclusive)			
NNO	Chopper (red)	4.00	8.00
(2017 Smuggler's Bounty Exclusive)			
NNO	Darth Vader (black)	6.00	12.00
(2017 Smuggler's Bounty Exclusive)			
NNO	Darth Vader (blue)	4.00	8.00
(2017 Smuggler's Bounty Exclusive)			
NNO	Darth Vader (gold)	15.00	30.00
(2017 Smuggler's Bounty Exclusive)			
NNO	Darth Vader (red)	5.00	10.00
(2017 Smuggler's Bounty Exclusive)			
NNO	Darth Vader (silver)	4.00	8.00
(2017 Smuggler's Bounty Exclusive)			
NNO	Greedo 2-Pack (blue & clear)	10.00	20.00
(2017 Galactic Convention Exclusive)			
NNO	Greedo 2-Pack (blue & clear)	10.00	20.00
(2017 Star Wars Celebration Exclusive)			
NNO	Greedo 2-Pack (green & gold)	6.00	12.00
(2017 Galactic Convention Exclusive)			
NNO	Greedo 2-Pack (green & gold)	12.50	25.00
(2017 Star Wars Celebration Exclusive)			

2005-18 Funko Mini Wacky Wobblers Star Wars

NNO	C-3PO	12.50	25.00
NNO	C-3PO/R2-D2 Ulta Mini	7.50	15.00
NNO	Chewbacca	20.00	40.00
NNO	Darth Vader	10.00	20.00
NNO	Darth Vader/Stormtrooper	7.50	15.00
NNO	Darth Vader Holiday	7.50	15.00
NNO	Jawa Holiday	12.50	25.00
NNO	R2-D2	7.50	15.00
NNO	R2-D2 Holiday	7.50	15.00
NNO	Star Wars 5Pk	15.00	30.00
NNO	Stormtrooper	7.50	15.00
NNO	Yoda	5.00	10.00
NNO	Yoda & Chewbacca (ultra mini)	7.50	15.00
NNO	Yoda (holiday)	6.00	12.00

2012 Funko Mini Wacky Wobblers Star Wars Monster Mash-Ups

NNO	Chewbacca	7.50	15.00
NNO	Darth Vader	7.50	15.00
NNO	Jawa	12.50	25.00
NNO	Stormtrooper	10.00	20.00
NNO	Tusken Raider	7.50	15.00
NNO	Yoda	7.50	15.00

2017 Funko MyMoji Star Wars

COMMON MYMOJI		2.50	5.00
NNO	Chewbacca (laughing)	4.00	8.00
NNO	Chewbacca (smiling)	4.00	8.00
NNO	Chewbacca (surprised)	2.50	5.00
NNO	Darth Vader (angry)	4.00	8.00
NNO	Darth Vader (sad)	2.50	5.00
NNO	Darth Vader (staring)	2.50	5.00
NNO	Jabba (bored)	2.50	5.00
NNO	Jabba (closed eyes)	4.00	8.00
NNO	Jabba (sad)	4.00	8.00
NNO	Luke Skywalker (big smile)	2.50	5.00
NNO	Luke Skywalker (closed eyes)	2.50	5.00
NNO	Luke Skywalker (sad)	2.50	5.00
NNO	Princess Leia (big smile)	3.00	6.00
NNO	Princess Leia (closed eyes)	2.50	5.00
NNO	Princess Leia (sad)	2.50	5.00
NNO	Wampa (angry)	2.50	5.00
NNO	Wampa (bored)	2.50	5.00
NNO	Wampa (sad)	2.50	5.00
NNO	Wicket (laughing)	2.50	5.00
NNO	Wicket (sad)	2.50	5.00
NNO	Wicket (smiling)	2.50	5.00
NNO	Yoda (closed eyes)	2.50	5.00
NNO	Yoda (curious)	2.50	5.00
NNO	Yoda (smiling)	4.00	8.00

2018 Funko Mystery Minis Solo A Star Wars Story

COMMON MYSTERY MINI		3.00	6.00
NNO	Chewbacca	4.00	8.00
NNO	Chewbacca (prisoner)	4.00	8.00
(Target Exclusive)			
NNO	Dryden Voss	7.50	15.00
NNO	Enfys Nest	3.00	6.00
NNO	Han Solo	4.00	8.00
NNO	Han Solo (pilot)	125.00	250.00
(Target Exclusive)			
NNO	Han Solo (prisoner)	7.50	15.00
(Target Exclusive)			
NNO	L3-37	15.00	30.00
NNO	Lando Calrissian	4.00	8.00
NNO	Patrol Trooper	6.00	12.00
NNO	Qi'Ra	3.00	6.00
NNO	Qi'Ra (dress)	7.50	15.00
(Target Exclusive)			
NNO	Range Trooper	10.00	20.00
(Target Exclusive)			
NNO	Rio Durant	5.00	10.00
NNO	Tobias Beckett	4.00	8.00
NNO	Tobias Beckett (w/rifle)	15.00	30.00
(Target Exclusive)			
NNO	Val	15.00	30.00
NNO	Weazel	5.00	10.00

2017 Funko Mystery Minis Star Wars

NNO	C-3PO	3.00	6.00
NNO	Chewbacca	4.00	8.00
NNO	Chewbacca (w/bowcaster)	10.00	20.00
(Walmart Exclusive)			
NNO	Darth Vader (Force Choke)	75.00	150.00
(Hot Topic Exclusive)			
NNO	Darth Vader (Force Lift)	15.00	30.00
NNO	Darth Vader (lightsaber)	25.00	50.00
(GameStop Exclusive)			
NNO	Grand Moff Tarkin	4.00	8.00
NNO	Greedo	4.00	8.00
NNO	Greedo (pistol up)	20.00	40.00
(Hot Topic Exclusive)			

NNO	Hammerhead	4.00	8.00
NNO	Han Solo	6.00	12.00
NNO	Han Solo (stormtrooper)	12.00	25.00
(GameStop Exclusive)			
NNO	Jawa	6.00	12.00
NNO	Luke Skywalker	10.00	20.00
NNO	Luke Skywalker (stormtrooper)	15.00	30.00
(GameStop Exclusive)			
NNO	Obi Wan Kenobi	4.00	8.00
NNO	Obi Wan Kenobi (Force Ghost)	30.00	75.00
(Walmart Exclusive)			
NNO	Ponda Baba	3.00	6.00
NNO	Princess Leia	2.50	5.00
NNO	Shadow Trooper	5.00	10.00
NNO	Snaggletooth	2.50	5.00
NNO	Stormtrooper	4.00	8.00
NNO	TIE Pilot	30.00	75.00
(Hot Topic Exclusive)			
NNO	Tusken Raider	20.00	40.00
(Walmart Exclusive)			

2018 Funko Mystery Minis Star Wars Empire Strikes Back

COMMON MYSTERY MINI		3.00	6.00
NNO	4-LOM	25.00	50.00
(GameStop Exclusive)			
NNO	Boba Fett	30.00	60.00
NNO	Bossk	75.00	150.00
(Hot Topic Exclusive)			
NNO	Chewbacca	3.00	6.00
NNO	Darth Vader	3.00	6.00
NNO	Dengar	30.00	75.00
NNO	Han Solo (Bespin)	3.00	6.00
NNO	Han Solo (Hoth)	12.50	25.00
(Hot Topic Exclusive)			
NNO	IG-88	12.50	25.00
NNO	Imperial AT-AT Driver	15.00	30.00
(GameStop Exclusive)			
NNO	Lando Calrissian	6.00	12.00
NNO	Lobot	25.00	50.00
(Target Exclusive)			
NNO	Luke Skywalker (Bespin)	12.50	25.00
(Target Exclusive)			
NNO	Luke Skywalker (Hoth)	15.00	30.00
NNO	Princess Leia (Bespin)	7.50	15.00
(GameStop Exclusive)			
NNO	Princess Leia (Hoth)	7.50	15.00
NNO	R2-D2	3.00	6.00
NNO	Snowtrooper	20.00	40.00
(Hot Topic Exclusive)			
NNO	Wampa	7.50	15.00
NNO	Yoda	4.00	8.00
NNO	Zuckuss	60.00	120.00
(Target Exclusive)			

2017 Funko Mystery Minis Star Wars The Last Jedi

COMPLETE SET (24)

NNO	BB-8	2.50	5.00
NNO	BB-9E	6.00	12.00
NNO	C'ai Threnalli	50.00	100.00
(Walgreens Exclusive)			
NNO	Captain Phasma	4.00	8.00
NNO	Chewbacca (w/porg)	4.00	8.00
NNO	DJ	4.00	8.00
NNO	Finn	7.50	15.00
NNO	Finn (First Order uniform)	3.00	6.00
NNO	First Order Executioner	7.50	15.00
(GameStop Exclusive)			
NNO	Kylo Ren	25.00	50.00
NNO	Kylo Ren (unmasked)	60.00	120.00
(Walmart Exclusive)			
NNO	Poe Dameron	3.00	6.00
NNO	Porg	12.00	25.00
NNO	Porg (wings open)	15.00	30.00
(GameStop Exclusive)			
NNO	Praetorian Guard	5.00	10.00
NNO	Praetorian Guard (w/staff)	6.00	12.00
(Walgreens Exclusive)			
NNO	Praetorian Guard (w/whip)	12.50	25.00
(Walmart Exclusive)			
NNO	Princess Leia	6.00	12.00
NNO	Resistance BB Unit	6.00	12.00
NNO	Rey	4.00	8.00
NNO	Rey (cloaked)	8.00	15.00
(GameStop Exclusive)			
NNO	Rose	3.00	6.00
NNO	Supreme Leader Snoke	3.00	6.00
NNO	Supreme Leader Snoke (holographic)	10.00	20.00
(Walgreens Exclusive)			

2017-19 Funko Mystery Minis Star Wars Smuggler's Bounty

NNO	Darth Maul	6.00	12.00
NNO	Darth Vader (hands on hips)		
(2019)			
NNO	Emperor Palpatine	10.00	20.00
NNO	Lando Calrissian	7.50	15.00
NNO	Luke Skywalker TFA	7.50	15.00
NNO	Luke Skywalker TLJ	10.00	20.00

2018-21 Funko Pop PEZ Star Wars

NNO	Boba Fett Prototype	7.50	15.00
NNO	Boba Fett	7.50	15.00
NNO	Bossk	6.00	12.00
NNO	Gamorrean Guard GCE	6.00	12.00
NNO	Gamorrean Guard SWC	5.00	10.00
NNO	Greedo	4.00	8.00
NNO	Jabba the Hutt GCE	6.00	12.00
NNO	Jabba the Hutt SWC	10.00	20.00
NNO	Jawa	6.00	12.00
NNO	Lando Calrissian Skiff	5.00	10.00
NNO	Logray	5.00	10.00
NNO	The Mandalorian/The Child	15.00	30.00
NNO	Ponda Boba Blue Stem CH	15.00	30.00
NNO	Ponda Boba	4.00	8.00
NNO	Salacious Crumb GCE	6.00	12.00
NNO	Salacious Crumb SWC	10.00	20.00
NNO	Snaggletooth Blue Stem CH	15.00	30.00
NNO	Snaggletooth	4.00	8.00
NNO	Tusken Raider	5.00	10.00

2015-21 Funko Pop Vinyl Conan O'Brien

6	Stormtrooper Conan COCO SDCC	60.00	120.00
10	Jedi Conan COCO SDCC	60.00	120.00
14	Rebel Pilot Conan COCO SDCC	30.00	60.00

2011-20 Funko Pop Vinyl Freddy Funko

A9A	Clone Trooper/48* SDCC	750.00	1500.00
A9B	Cl.Trooper Blue Hair/12* SDCC	1500.00	3000.00
28A	Boba Fett/196* SDCC	2000.00	4000.00
28B	B.Fett Red Hair/24* SDCC	5000.00	10000.00
46	Kylo Ren/400* FD	500.00	1000.00
SE	Poe Dameron/200* FD	400.00	800.00
SE	Yoda/450* FD	600.00	1200.00
SE	C-3PO/520* FD	750.00	1500.00

2017-21 Funko Pop Vinyl MLB

SE	Kevin Kiermaier Han Solo RAYS	12.50	25.00

2011-21 Funko Pop Vinyl Star Wars

1A	Darth Vader	7.50	15.00
1B	Darth Vader MET HT	20.00	40.00
2A	Yoda	7.50	15.00
2B	Yoda Spirit WG ERR	15.00	30.00
2C	Yoda Spirit WG COR Sticker	15.00	30.00
2C	Yoda Spirit WG COR	15.00	30.00
3A	Han Solo V	225.00	450.00
3B	Han Solo VAULT	30.00	60.00
4	Princess Leia	10.00	20.00
5A	Stormtrooper	15.00	30.00
5B	Stormtrooper Red TAR	7.50	15.00
6A	Chewbacca	10.00	20.00
6B	Chewbacca FLK/480* SDCC	1000.00	1500.00
6C	Chewbacca Hoth GS	10.00	20.00
6D	Chewbacca Hoth EB	20.00	40.00
6E	Chewbacca Hoth UT	30.00	60.00
7A	Greedo V	500.00	1000.00
7B	Greedo VAULT	12.50	25.00
8A	Boba Fett	12.50	25.00
8B	Boba Fett Prototype WG ERR	17.50	35.00
8C	Boba Fett Prototype WG COR	17.50	35.00
8D	Boba Fett Prototype WG COR Sticker	17.50	35.00
9A	Darth Maul	7.50	15.00
9B	Darth Maul Gold MET WM	10.00	20.00
10A	Obi-Wan Kenobi V	200.00	400.00
10B	Obi-Wan VAULT	25.00	50.00
10C	Obi-Wan Kenobi Tatooine AMZ	20.00	40.00
11A	Luke Skywalker Jedi Knight V	100.00	200.00
11B	Jedi Luke Skywalker VAULT	50.00	100.00
12A	Gamorrean Guard V	100.00	200.00
12B	Gamorrean Guard VAULT	7.50	15.00
13A	C-3PO	10.00	20.00
13B	C-3PO Gold Chrome SDCC	50.00	100.00
13C	C-3PO Gold Chrome SCE	25.00	50.00
14	Shadow Trooper/480* SDCC	1500.00	2500.00
15	H.Solo Stormtrooper/1000* ECCC	600.00	1200.00
16	L.Skywalker Stormtrooper/1000* ECCC	600.00	1200.00
17	Luke Skywalker X-Wing	15.00	30.00
18A	Slave Leia V	100.00	200.00
18B	Slave Leia VAULT	50.00	100.00
19A	Tusken Raider V	50.00	100.00
19B	Tusken Raider VAULT	10.00	20.00
20A	Jawa V	50.00	100.00
20B	Jawa VAULT	10.00	20.00
21A	Clone Trooper V	125.00	250.00
21B	Clone Trooper VAULT	30.00	75.00
22	Jabba the Hutt	15.00	30.00
23	Darth Maul HOLO/480* SDCC	3500.00	7000.00
24	Biggs Darklighter/480* SDCC	750.00	1500.00
25	501st Clone Trooper/480* SDCC	1000.00	2000.00

26A Wicket the Ewok	15.00	30.00
26B Wicket the Ewok FLK FT	125.00	250.00
27 Jar Jar Binks V	125.00	250.00
28 Admiral Ackbar V	30.00	60.00
29 Queen Amidala V	175.00	350.00
30 Lando Calrissian V	60.00	120.00
31A R2-D2	10.00	20.00
31B R2-D2 Futura TAR	15.00	30.00
31C R2-D2 Dagobah TAR	12.50	25.00
32 Boba Fett Droids/480* SDCC	1000.00	2000.00
33A Darth Vader HOLO GITD DCC	500.00	1000.00
33B Darth Vader HOLO GITD PE	600.00	1200.00
34A Luke Skywalker Hoth V	7.50	15.00
34B Luke Skywalker Hoth w/Pin AMZ	12.50	25.00
35 Bossk V	30.00	75.00
36 The Emperor V	30.00	60.00
37 Hammerhead V	15.00	30.00
38 Biker Scout V	15.00	30.00
39A 6" Wampa V	7.50	15.00
39B Wampa 6" FLK HT	12.50	25.00
40 Holographic Emperor TW	25.00	100.00
41A R2-Q5 GCE	20.00	40.00
41B R2-Q5 SWC	50.00	100.00
42A Shock Trooper GCE	100.00	200.00
42B Shock Trooper SWC	250.00	500.00
43A Unmasked Vader GCE	12.50	25.00
43B Unmasked Vader SWC	75.00	150.00
44A R2-R9 GCE	25.00	50.00
44B R2-R9 SWC	75.00	150.00
45 R2-B1 GS	7.50	15.00
46A E-3PO GCE	12.50	25.00
46B E-3PO SWC	40.00	80.00
47A Han Solo Hoth GS	10.00	20.00
47B Han Solo Hoth EB	10.00	20.00
48A Figrin D'an GS	10.00	20.00
48B Figrin D'an EB	10.00	20.00
49 Luke Skywalker Tatooine	25.00	50.00
50 Princess Leia Boussh	10.00	20.00
51A TIE Fighter Pilot	6.00	12.00
51B TIE Pilot MET	15.00	30.00
52 Nalan Cheel	6.00	12.00
53 Bib Fortuna	6.00	12.00
54A Leia Boussh Unmasked SDCC	300.00	600.00
54B Leia Boussh Unmasked SCE	250.00	500.00
55 K-3PO B&N	7.50	15.00
56A Snowtrooper WG ERR	10.00	20.00
56B Snowtrooper WG COR	10.00	20.00
56C Snowtrooper WG COR Sticker	10.00	20.00
57A Imperial Guard WG ERR	7.50	15.00
57B Imperial Guard WG COR	7.50	15.00
57C Imperial Guard WG COR Sticker	7.50	15.00
58A Rey	6.00	12.00
59 Finn	5.00	10.00
60 Kylo Ren	6.00	12.00
61A BB-8	6.00	12.00
61B BB-8 Rainbow FS	15.00	30.00
62 Poe Dameron V	5.00	10.00
63A Chewbacca	7.50	15.00
63B Chewbacca FLK SB	12.50	25.00
63C Chewbacca Blue Chrome SWC	40.00	80.00
63D Chewbacca Gold Chrome GCE	6.00	12.00
63E Chewbacca Gold MET WM	7.50	15.00
64A C-3PO	6.00	12.00
64B C-3PO MET B&N	10.00	20.00
64C C-3PO Futura TAR	20.00	40.00
65A Captain Phasma	5.00	10.00
65B Captain Phasma Last Jedi Box	7.50	15.00
66 First Order Stormtrooper	10.00	20.00
67A First Order Snowtrooper	5.00	10.00
67B First Order Snowtrooper Last Jedi Box	5.00	10.00
68A First Order Flametrooper	6.00	12.00
68B First Order Flametrooper Last Jedi Box	7.50	15.00
69 Blue Snaggletooth CH SB	20.00	40.00
70 Red Snaggletooth SB	10.00	20.00
71 Shadow Guard WG	7.50	15.00
72 Poe Dameron No Helmet WM	6.00	12.00
73 Rey w/Goggles HT	7.50	15.00
74 FO Stormtrooper w/Rifle AMZ	10.00	20.00
75 FO Stormtrooper w/Shield WG	10.00	20.00
76 Finn Stormtrooper GS	7.50	15.00
77 Kylo Ren Unhooded TAR	7.50	15.00
78 R2-L3 Dorkside Toys	25.00	50.00
79 Han Solo	6.00	12.00
80 Princess Leia	7.50	15.00
81 Admiral Ackbar	6.00	12.00
82 Nien Nunb	6.00	12.00
83 Sidon Ithano	5.00	10.00
84 Varmik	5.00	10.00
85 Finn w/Lightsaber B&N	7.50	15.00
86 Han Solo Snow Gear LC	5.00	10.00
87 Kylo Ren Unmasked WM	10.00	20.00
88 Nien Nunb w/Helmet GS	7.50	15.00
89 TIE Fighter Pilot SB	6.00	12.00
A90 TIE Fighter Pilot Red Stripe SB CH	12.50	25.00
B90A Luke Ceremony SWC	50.00	100.00
B90B Luke Ceremony GCE	10.00	20.00
A91 Captain Phasma MET SB	12.50	25.00
B91A Han Ceremony SWC	10.00	20.00
B91B Han Ceremony GCE	10.00	20.00
92 AT-AT Driver WG	7.50	15.00
93A Luke Skywalker Bespin	7.50	15.00
93B Luke Skywalker Bespin Gold WM	10.00	20.00
94A Luke Skywalker Bespin SWC	50.00	100.00
94B Luke Skywalker Bespin GCE	12.50	25.00
95 Ree Yees WG	7.50	15.00
96 Kit Fisto WG	25.00	50.00
97 Plo Koon WG	20.00	40.00
98 Blue Senate Guard SWC	25.00	50.00
99 Old Ben Kenobi SB	12.50	25.00
100 FN-2187 TAR	20.00	40.00

101A 4-LOM SWC	30.00	75.00
101B 4-LOM GCE	20.00	40.00
102 Bobe Fett Action SB	40.00	80.00
103 IG-88 SB	7.50	15.00
104 Rey w/Lightsaber	7.50	15.00
105 Kylo Ren Unmasked Action	10.00	20.00
106 Luke Skywalker Force Awakens	5.00	10.00
107 General Leia	6.00	12.00
108 Maz Kanata	6.00	12.00
109 General Hux	6.00	12.00
110 Snap Wexley	6.00	12.00
111 FN-2199 V	7.50	15.00
112 Guavian	5.00	10.00
113 ME-809	6.00	12.00
114A Rey Jedi Temple WG	7.50	15.00
114B Rey Jedi Temple Gold MET WM	7.50	15.00
115A Han Solo w/Bowcaster SDCC	20.00	40.00
115B Han Solo w/Bowcaster SCE	10.00	20.00
116A BB-8 w/Lighter SDCC	30.00	75.00
116B BB-8 w/Lighter SCE	10.00	20.00
117 Poe Dameron Jacket/Blaster HT	6.00	12.00
118 Maz Kanata Goggles Up TAR	6.00	12.00
119 Rey X-Wing Helmet GS	10.00	20.00
120 Poe Dameron X-Wing Jumpsuit FYE	7.50	15.00
121 R2-D2 Jabba's Sail Barge SB	10.00	20.00
122 Zuckuss TW	7.50	15.00
123 Luke Skywalker (Endor)	10.00	20.00
124A Dagobah Yoda	7.50	15.00
124B Yoda Blue Chrome SWC	75.00	150.00
124C Yoda Gold Chrome GCE	10.00	20.00
124D Yoda Green Chrome SDCC	25.00	50.00
124E Yoda Green Chrome SCE	10.00	20.00
124F Yoda Gold MET WM	7.50	15.00
124G Yoda Green ECCC	25.00	50.00
124H Yoda Green SCE	20.00	40.00
A125 Hoth Han Solo w/Tauntaun SB	30.00	60.00
B125A Princess Leia Hoth SWC	30.00	75.00
B125B Princess Leia Hoth GCE	30.00	60.00
126A Luke Skywalker Hood SWC	75.00	150.00
126B Luke Skywalker Hood GCE	60.00	120.00
127A Garindan SWC	25.00	50.00
127B Garindan GCE	12.50	25.00
128A Qui Gon Jinn NYCC	750.00	1500.00
128B Qui Gon Jinn HOLO SWC	75.00	150.00
128C Qui Gon Jinn HOLO GCE	60.00	120.00
129 General Grievous WG	40.00	80.00
130A Ahsoka HT	50.00	100.00
130B Ahsoka GITD Comikaze	50.00	100.00
131 Sabine Masked WG	25.00	50.00
132 Kanan	25.00	50.00
133A Chopper	25.00	50.00
133B Chopper Imperial SWC	25.00	50.00
133C Chopper Imperial GCE	20.00	40.00
134 Ezra	25.00	50.00
135 Sabine	25.00	50.00
136 Hera	25.00	50.00
137 Zeb	25.00	50.00
138 Jyn Erso	6.00	12.00
139 Captain Cassian Andor	5.00	10.00
140 Chirrut Imwe	5.00	10.00
141 Baze Malbus	7.50	15.00
142 Director Orson Krennic	5.00	10.00
143 Darth Vader	10.00	20.00
144 Imperial Death Trooper	7.50	15.00
145 Scarif Stormtrooper	6.00	12.00
146 K-2SO	7.50	15.00
147 C2-B5	5.00	10.00
148 Jyn Erso Mountain Gear SB	6.00	12.00
149 Death Trooper Sniper SB	7.50	15.00
150 Jyn Erso Hooded HT	5.00	10.00
151 Capt. C.Andor Brown Jacket TAR	5.00	10.00
152 Jyn Erso Imperial Disguise TAR	7.50	15.00
153 Saw Gerrera WM	5.00	10.00
154 Imp. Death Trooper Black MET WM	12.50	25.00
155 Bistan NYCC	5.00	10.00
156 Scarif Stormtrooper Striped WG	10.00	20.00
157A Vader Force Choke GS	20.00	40.00
157B D.Vader Force Choke Blue Chr. SWC	150.00	300.00
157C D.Vader Force Choke Gold Chr. GCE	12.50	25.00
157D Darth Vader Red Chrome TAR RC	7.50	15.00
157E Darth Vader Gold Chrome MCM	12.50	25.00
157F Darth Vader Black Chrome SB	15.00	30.00
157G Darth Vader Gold MET WM	6.00	12.00
157H Darth Vader Futura NYCC/TAR	40.00	80.00
157I Darth Vader Futura TAR	30.00	60.00
158 Darth Vader Bespin SB	12.50	25.00
159 Grand Moff Tarkin SB	20.00	40.00
160 Max Rebo SS	20.00	40.00
161 Rey w/Jacket TAR	6.00	12.00
162 Young Anakin	12.50	25.00
164 Captain Rex SB	20.00	40.00
165 Darth Maul Rebels SB	30.00	75.00
166 The Inquisitor	25.00	50.00
167 Seventh Sister	12.50	25.00
168 Fifth Brother	12.50	25.00
169A Han Solo SWC	40.00	80.00
169B Han Solo GCE	15.00	30.00
170A Grand Admiral Thrawn SWC	250.00	500.00
170B Grand Admiral Thrawn GCE	125.00	250.00
171A 442nd Clone Trooper SWC	75.00	150.00
171B 442nd Clone Trooper GCW	40.00	80.00
172 Mace Windu WG	25.00	50.00
173A Muftak ECCC	25.00	50.00
173B Muftak SPCE	10.00	20.00
174A Rey w/Speeder SWC	30.00	60.00
174B Rey w/Speeder GCE	25.00	50.00

No.	Item		
175	Luke w/Speeder SB	15.00	30.00
A176	Darth Vader w/TIE Fighter TAR	25.00	50.00
B176	Commander Cody WG	50.00	100.00
177A	Saw Gerrera w/Hair NYCC	15.00	30.00
177B	Saw Gerrera w/Hair FCE	12.50	25.00
178A	Jyn Erso w/Helmet NYCC	15.00	30.00
178B	Jyn Erso w/Helmet FCE	10.00	20.00
179A	K-2SO Action Pose NYCC	15.00	30.00
179B	K-2SO Action Pose FCE	15.00	30.00
180	R5-D4 SB	7.50	15.00
181	C-3PO Unfinished SB	15.00	30.00
182A	Snoke GITD SDCC	30.00	75.00
182B	Supreme Leader Snoke GITD SCE	20.00	40.00
183A	Bodhi Rook SDCC	20.00	40.00
183B	Bodhi Rook SCE	7.50	15.00
184A	Tank Trooper SDCC	12.50	25.00
184C	Combat Assault Tank Trooper SCE	6.00	12.00
185	Young Jyn Erso	12.50	25.00
186	Galen Erso	5.00	10.00
187	Weeteef Cyubee	7.50	15.00
188A	Death Star Droid Rogue One NYCC	10.00	20.00
188B	Death Star Droid Rogue One FCE	7.50	15.00
189	Death Star Droid Black	6.00	12.00
190A	Rey	7.50	15.00
190B	Rey GITD COST	10.00	20.00
191	Finn	5.00	10.00
192	Poe Dameron	6.00	12.00
193	Luke Skywalker	6.00	12.00
194A	Kylo Ren	6.00	12.00
194B	Kylo Ren GITD COST	15.00	30.00
194C	Kylo Ren HOLO TAR OL	30.00	75.00
194D	Kylo Ren Gold MET WM	7.50	15.00
195A	Chewbacca w/Porg	10.00	20.00
195B	Chewbacca w/Porg FLK FYE	12.50	25.00
196	BB-8	6.00	12.00
197	Rose	6.00	12.00
198A	Porg	6.00	12.00
198B	Porg Open Mouth CH	12.50	25.00
198C	Porg FLK HT	5.00	10.00
198D	Porg Open Mouth FLK HT	30.00	60.00
198E	Porg Wings Open TAR	5.00	10.00
198F	Porg 10" TAR	12.50	25.00
199	Supreme Leader Snoke	5.00	10.00
200	Praetorian Guard	7.50	15.00
201	First Order Executioner	6.00	12.00
202A	BB-9E	7.50	15.00
202B	BB-9E Chrome BL	5.00	10.00
203	Kylo Ren w/Helmet TRU	7.50	15.00
205	Rose SS	5.00	10.00
207	DJ GS	5.00	10.00
208	Praetorian Guard w/Swords WG	7.50	15.00
209	Praetorian Guard w/Whip WG	7.50	15.00
210	Resistance BB-Unit Orange NBC	7.50	15.00
211	Resistance BB Unit WM	5.00	10.00
212	Medical Droid WG	6.00	12.00
213A	Boba Fett w/Slave I NYCC	75.00	150.00
213B	Boba Fett w/Slave I FCE	75.00	150.00
214	Obi-Wan Kenobi ROTS SB	45.00	90.00
215	Kylo Ren w/TIE Fighter	12.50	25.00
217	Aayla Secura SB	25.00	50.00
218	Princess Leia WM	6.00	12.00
219	Wedge Antilles w/Snow Speeder WG	10.00	20.00
220	BB-8 Baseball and Bat Giants	20.00	40.00
221	TIE Fighter Pilot w/TIE Fighter	10.00	20.00
A222	Escape Pod Landing WM	15.00	30.00
222B	Duel on Mustafar SB	75.00	150.00
223	Cantina Faceoff WM	15.00	30.00
224	Trash Compactor Escape WM	10.00	20.00
225	Death Star Duel WM	15.00	30.00
226	Cloud City Duel WG	30.00	60.00
227	Poe Dameron w/X-Wing SB	15.00	30.00
228	Princess Leia w/Speeder Bike	7.50	15.00

No.	Item		
229	Luke Skywalker w/Speeder Bike CH	12.50	25.00
230A	Dengar NYCC	20.00	40.00
230B	Dengar FCE	10.00	20.00

No.	Item		
231	Young Anakin Podracing WG	12.50	25.00
232	Luke Skywalker w/X-Wing 40th Anniv.	50.00	100.00
233	Count Dooku SB	30.00	75.00
234	Scout Trooper w/Speeder SB	20.00	40.00
235	Vice Admiral Holdo	7.50	15.00
236	Chewbacca w/AT-ST	30.00	60.00
237A	Padme Amidala ECCC	100.00	200.00
237B	Padme Amidala SCE	30.00	75.00
238	Han Solo	7.50	15.00
239A	Chewbacca	7.50	15.00
239B	Chewbacca FLK BL	10.00	20.00
239C	Chewbacca FLK MCM	12.50	25.00
240	Lando Calrissian	6.00	12.00
241	Qi'Ra	7.50	15.00
242	Tobias Beckett	6.00	12.00
243	Val	7.50	15.00
244	Rio Durant	6.00	12.00
245	L3-37	6.00	12.00
246	Range Trooper	7.50	15.00
247	Enfys Nest	6.00	12.00
248A	Han Solo Goggles TAR	6.00	12.00
248B	Mudtrooper FS	50.00	100.00
250	Tobias Beckett w/Pistols WM	5.00	10.00
251	Lando Calrissian White Cape HT	6.00	12.00
252A	Stormtrooper SDCC	75.00	150.00
252B	Stormtrooper SCE	20.00	40.00
252C	Stormtrooper PX	25.00	50.00
253	Dryden Voss FYE	7.50	15.00
254A	Dryden Gangster TAR	6.00	12.00
254B	Dryden Gangster TRU	7.50	15.00
255	Han Solo Vest WG	5.00	10.00
256	Vulptex Crystal Fox	7.50	15.00
257	Rematch on the Supremacy	7.50	15.00
258	Ewok w/Speeder Bike FS	30.00	75.00
260	C'ai Threnalli	6.00	12.00
261	Porg Frowning	6.00	12.00
262A	Cad Bane SDCC	75.00	150.00
262B	Cad Bane SCE	30.00	75.00
263	Caretaker	6.00	12.00
264	Clash on the Supremacy Rey	15.00	30.00
265	Clash on the Supremacy Kylo	30.00	60.00
266A	Luke Skywalker	12.50	25.00
266B	Luke Skywalker Gold/80* FD	2000.00	3000.00
267	Paige	5.00	10.00
268	Ahsoka	12.50	25.00
269	Yoda	10.00	20.00
270	Obi-Wan Kenobi	12.50	25.00
271	Anakin Skywalker	40.00	80.00
272	Ahsoka Force Push HT	17.50	35.00
273	Obi-Wan Kenobi Hooded WG	20.00	40.00
274A	Captain Rex NYCC	300.00	600.00
274B	Captain Rex FCE	250.00	400.00
275	R2-D2 w/Antlers	7.50	15.00
276	C-3PO w/Santa Hat	10.00	20.00
277A	Yoda Santa Eyes Half Open	7.50	15.00
277B	Yoda Sant Eyes Fully Open	6.00	12.00
278	Chewbacca Christmas Lights	12.50	25.00
279A	Darth Vader Candy Cane Lightsaber	7.50	15.00
279B	Darth Vader GITD Candy Cane Lightsaber CH	15.00	30.00

No.	Item		
280	Boba Gets His Bounty SB	40.00	80.00
281	Anakin Skywalker Dark Side Eyes WG	40.00	80.00
282	Lando Calrissian Skiff SB	7.50	15.00
283	Klaatu SB	7.50	15.00
284	Dagobah Face-Off SB	15.00	30.00
285A	Jango Fett Jet Pack WG	30.00	75.00
285B	Jango Fett Jet Pack Gold MET WM	12.50	25.00
286	Han Solo	7.50	15.00
287A	Princess Leia	7.50	15.00
287B	Princess Leia Gold MET WM	7.50	15.00
288A	Darth Vader	6.00	12.00
288B	Darth Vader GITD CH	12.50	25.00
289	Emperor Palpatine Force Lightning	12.50	25.00
290A	Wicket	10.00	20.00
290B	Wicket Endor AMZ		
291	Lando Calrissian	6.00	12.00
292	Baby Nippet FLK TAR	7.50	15.00
293	Wicket 10" TAR	30.00	60.00
294	Encounter on Endor	7.50	15.00
295A	Princess Leia Blue Chrome SWC	60.00	120.00
295B	Princess Leia Gold Chrome GCE	6.00	12.00
296A	Stormtrooper Blue Chrome SWC	50.00	100.00
296B	Stormtrooper Gold Chrome GCE	10.00	20.00
296C	Stormtrooper Futura TAR	20.00	40.00
296D	Stormtrooper Rainbow	5.00	12.00
296E	Stormtrooper Empire Logo WC	50.00	100.00
296F	Stormtrooper Empire Logo WCE	30.00	60.00
297A	Boba Fett Blue Chrome SWC	150.00	300.00
297B	Boba Fett Gold Chrome GCE	20.00	40.00
297C	Boba Fett Green Chrome SDCC	30.00	75.00
297D	Boba Fett Green Chrome SCE	20.00	40.00
297E	Boba Fett Futura TAR	50.00	100.00
297F	Boba Fett Futura Black TAR		
297G	Boba Fett Futura Red TAR	60.00	120.00
297H	Boba Fett Futura Black ECCC	125.00	250.00
297I	Boba Fett Futura Black SCE	30.00	60.00
297J	Boba Fett Futura Red WC	25.00	50.00
297K	Boba Fett Futura Red WCE	25.00	50.00
297K	Boba Fett Camo/1000* NYCC	600.00	1200.00
297L	Boba Fett Camo/1000* FCE	400.00	800.00
297M	Boba Fett Retro BAIT	25.00	50.00
297N	Boba Fett Retro/6* May 4th		
298A	Watto SWC	20.00	40.00
298B	Watto GCE	12.50	25.00
299A	Darth Maul SWC	100.00	200.00
299B	Darth Maul GCE	30.00	75.00
300	Chewbacca Oxygen Mask SB	20.00	40.00
301	DJ R3X GE	17.50	35.00
302	Hondo Ohnaka GE	17.50	35.00
303	Aurra Sing SB	15.00	30.00
304	Sebulba SB	7.50	15.00
305	Boba Fett Animated GSFIC	12.50	25.00
306A	Sith Trooper SDCC	1000.00	1500.00
306B	Sith Trooper		
307	Rey	7.50	15.00
308A	Kylo Ren	7.50	15.00
308B	Kylo Ren Lights/Sound	20.00	40.00
308C	Kylo Ren GITD TAR	10.00	20.00
309	Finn	10.00	20.00
310	Poe Dameron	6.00	12.00
311	Zorii Bliss	6.00	12.00
312	D-O	5.00	10.00
313	Lando Calrissian	6.00	12.00
314	BB-8	7.50	15.00
315	Jannah	7.50	15.00
316	Rose	6.00	12.00
317	First Order Jet Trooper	10.00	20.00
318	Sith Jet Trooper	6.00	12.00
319	Lieutenant Connix	6.00	12.00
320	First Order Tread Speeder	15.00	30.00
A321	Han Solo/M.Falcon AMZ	50.00	100.00
B321	Supreme Leader Kylo Ren/TIE Whisper	10.00	20.00
322A	Sandtrooper NYCC	50.00	100.00
322B	Sandtrooper FCE	25.00	50.00

324	Kylo Ren Supreme Leader Hooded SB	12.50	25.00
325A	Knight of Ren w/Long Axe SB	7.50	15.00
325B	Knight of Ren w/Long Axe Hematite AMZ	15.00	30.00
326A	The Mandalorian	7.50	15.00
326B	The Mandalorian D23	500.00	1000.00
327	Cara Dune	20.00	40.00
328	IG-11	10.00	20.00
329	Kuiil	7.50	15.00
330A	The Mandalorian Pistol NYCC	300.00	500.00
330B	The Mandalorian Pistol FCE	150.00	300.00
331A	Knight of Ren w/Blaster GS	7.50	15.00
331B	Knight of Ren w/Blaster Hematite	6.00	12.00
332A	Knight of Ren w/Club HT	10.00	20.00
332B	Knight of Ren w/Club Hematite	10.00	20.00
333A	Knight of Ren w/Scythe FS	12.50	25.00
333B	Knight of Ren w/Scythe Hematite	6.00	12.00
334A	Knight of Ren w/Cannon WM	6.00	12.00
334B	Knight of Ren w/Cannon Hematite	7.50	15.00
335A	Knight of Ren w/Heavy Blade FYE	7.50	15.00
335B	Knight of Ren w/Heavy Blade Hematite	6.00	12.00
336	D-O 10" TAR	15.00	30.00
337	Cal Kestis with BD-1	25.00	50.00
338	Second Sister	7.50	15.00
339A	Purge Trooper GS	30.00	60.00
339B	Purge Trooper EB	12.50	25.00
340	Babu Frik SB	30.00	60.00
341	C-3PO w/Bowcaster SB	7.50	15.00
342	Jawa Futura TAR	15.00	30.00
343	Darth Vader Electrical	15.00	30.00
344	Kylo Ren 10" GITD	25.00	50.00
345A	Mandalorian	12.50	25.00
345B	Mandalorian Chrome Beskar Armor AMZ	15.00	30.00
345C	Mandalorian Red Chrome Beskar Armor TAR	20.00	40.00
346	The Client	7.50	15.00
347	Greef Karga	7.50	15.00
348	Heavy Infantryman Mandalorian	7.50	15.00
349	Q9-0	6.00	12.00
350	Incinerator Stormtrooper	10.00	20.00
351	Offworld Jawa	7.50	15.00
352	Covert Mandalorian	7.50	15.00
353	The Armorer	10.00	20.00
354A	Death Watch Mandalorian GS	20.00	40.00
354B	Death Watch Mandalorian EB	12.50	25.00
355	The Mandalorian Flame Gauntlet TAR	15.00	30.00
356	Cara Dune FYE	30.00	60.00
357	Trandoshan Thug WG	10.00	20.00
358	The Mandalorian on Blurrg	20.00	40.00
359	Dark Side Rey	10.00	20.00
360	C-3PO Red Eyes	7.50	15.00
361	Death Watch Mandalorian No Stripes GS	50.00	100.00
362	Princess Leia	7.50	15.00
363	Luke Skywalker/Yoda	10.00	20.00
364	Han Solo Carbonite	7.50	15.00
365	Darth Vader/Meditation	20.00	40.00
366	Luke w/Tauntaun	15.00	30.00
367	Boba Fett 10" TAR	30.00	75.00
368	The Child	7.50	15.00
369	The Child 10"	30.00	60.00
370	The Child w/Control Knob GS	15.00	30.00
371	Jawa Classic	6.00	12.00
372	Echo Base Wampa AMZ	20.00	40.00
373	Echo Base Han w/Tauntaun AMZ	20.00	40.00
374	Echo Base Chewbacca FLK AMZ	12.50	25.00
375	Echo Base Probe Droid AMZ	15.00	30.00
376	Echo Base Princess Leia AMZ	20.00	40.00
377	Echo Base Vader/Snowtrooper AMZ	25.00	50.00
378	The Child w/Cup	10.00	20.00
379	The Child w/Frog	7.50	15.00
A380A	Moff Gideon	6.00	12.00
B380	Mandalorian w/Child 10" Chrome	30.00	75.00
A380B	Moff Gideon GITD TAR	15.00	30.00
382A	Lesson in the Force SWC	40.00	80.00
382B	Lesson in the Force GCE	30.00	60.00
383A	Sith Jet Trooper Flying SDCCD	30.00	60.00

383B	Sith Jet Trooper Flying SCE	10.00	20.00
384	The Child Concerned TAR	12.50	25.00
385	The Child Force Push WM	12.50	25.00
386A	Concept Starkiller SWC	15.00	30.00
386B	Concept Starkiller GCE	10.00	20.00
387A	Concept Chewbacca SWC	20.00	40.00
387B	Concept Chewbacca GCE	20.00	40.00
388A	Concept Boba Fett SWC	75.00	150.00
388B	Concept Boba Fett GCE	100.00	200.00
389A	Concept Darth Vader SWC	25.00	50.00
389B	Concept Darth Vader GCE	25.00	50.00
390	Mandalorian and Child	25.00	50.00
391A	Stormtrooper 10" SWC	50.00	100.00
391B	Stormtrooper 10" GCE	30.00	75.00
391C	Stormtrooper 10" Art TARC	30.00	60.00
392	Obi-Wan Kenobi GITD SWC	600.00	1200.00
393	Yoda Hooded GS	10.00	20.00
394A	Shadow Stormtrooper GS	25.00	50.00
394B	Shadow Stormtrooper EB	10.00	20.00
395A	Darth Malak GS	20.00	40.00
395B	Darth Malak EB	12.50	25.00
396A	Darth Revan GS	30.00	75.00
396B	Darth Revan EB	20.00	40.00
397	CB-6B TAR	12.50	25.00
398A	The Child w/Pendant NYCC	30.00	60.00
398B	The Child w/Pendant FCE	20.00	40.00
399A	Luke Skywalker Jedi Training NYCC	30.00	60.00
399B	Luke Skywalker Jedi Training FCE	20.00	40.00
400A	Princess Leia Jedi Training NYCC	25.00	50.00
400B	Princess Leia Jedi Training FCE	20.00	40.00
401	M5-R3 TAR	7.50	15.00
402	The Mandalorian with the Child	15.00	30.00
403	Cara Dune	20.00	40.00
404	The Mythrol	7.50	15.00
405	The Child	10.00	20.00
406	Gamorrean Fighter	10.00	20.00
407	The Child with Egg Canister	20.00	40.00
408A	The Mandalorian Flying w/Blaster GS	10.00	20.00
408B	The Mandalorian Flying w/Blaster GITD GS	20.00	40.00
409	Ahsoka	12.50	25.00
410	Darth Maul	17.50	35.00
411	Gar Saxon	10.00	20.00
412	Bo-Katan Kryze	12.50	25.00
413	Wrecker	12.50	25.00
414	Ahsoka Mechanic	12.50	25.00
415	Mandalorian Super Commando FS	30.00	60.00
416	The Mandalorian & Child on Bantha	30.00	75.00
417	Darth Vader Pink	12.50	25.00
418	Stormtrooper Pink	10.00	20.00
419	Chewbacca Pink	10.00	20.00
420	R2-D2 Pink	30.00	60.00
421	Yoda Pink	12.50	25.00
422	Qui-Gon Jinn Tatooine AMZ	12.50	25.00
423	Concept C-3PO	7.50	15.00
424	Concept R2-D2	7.50	15.00
425	Concept Yoda	12.50	25.00
426	Concept Darth Vader	7.50	15.00
427	IG-11 w/Child GS	30.00	60.00
428	Darth Vader Fist FS	20.00	40.00
429A	Bastilla Shan GS	15.00	30.00
429B	Bastilla Shan EB	12.50	25.00
430A	Jedi Revan GS	25.00	50.00
430B	Jedi Revan EB	20.00	40.00
431	Ben Solo	10.00	20.00
432	Rey Yellow Lightsaber	12.50	25.00
433	Emperor Palpatine	7.50	15.00
434	Rey Two Lightsabers	7.50	15.00
435	Babu Frik 10"	12.50	25.00
436	BHC Boba Fett GS	30.00	60.00
437	BHC Bossk GS	20.00	40.00
438	BHC IG-88 GS	25.00	50.00
439	BHC 4-LOM GS		
440	BHC Dengar GS		
441	BHC Zuckuss GS		

443	Wrecker	10.00	20.00
444A	Crosshair	12.50	25.00
444B	Crosshair Kamino with Pin AMZ	20.00	40.00
445	Tech	7.50	15.00
446A	Hunter	12.50	25.00
446B	Hunter Kamino AMZ	20.00	40.00
447	Echo	20.00	40.00
448	Omega TAR	15.00	30.00
449	General Grievous 4 Lightsabers HT	20.00	40.00
450	Darth Maul w/Dark & Lightsaber CC	20.00	40.00
451A	Rey Jakku VF	30.00	75.00
451B	Rey Jakku SCE	10.00	20.00
452A	Imperial Super Commando VF	30.00	75.00
452B	Imperial Super Commando SCE	20.00	40.00
453	Luke Skywalker Retro TAR	15.00	30.00
454	C-3PO Retro TAR	20.00	40.00
455	Stormtrooper Retro TAR	20.00	40.00
456	Darth Vader Retro TAR	17.50	35.00
457	Nightbrother GS	7.50	15.00
459	Princess Leia Yavin AMZ	7.50	15.00
460A	Iden Versio GS	7.50	15.00
460B	Iden Versio Armor GS CH	40.00	80.00
461	Mandalorian & Grogu w/o Helmet	10.00	20.00
462	Boba Fett	10.00	20.00
463A	Bo-Katan Kryze	7.50	15.00
463B	Bo-Katan Kryze w/o Helmet CH	30.00	60.00
464	Ahsoka	7.50	15.00
465	Grogu w/Cookies	15.00	30.00
466	Dark Trooper	10.00	20.00
467	Ahsoka AMZ	17.50	35.00
468	Grogu w/Butterfly GS	15.00	30.00
469	Grogu w/Chowder Squid TAR	12.50	25.00
470	CS Stormtrooper w/Lightsaber	7.50	15.00
471	CS Snowtrooper	7.50	15.00
472	CS Han Solo w/Lightsaber	7.50	15.00
473	CS Stormtrooper w/Saber & Shield FS	10.00	20.00
474	Grogu Macy's		
475	Grogu 10" Macy's		
478A	Boba Fett Desert Gear NYCC	100.00	200.00
478B	Boba Fett Desert Gear FCE		

2011-21 Funko Pop Vinyl Star Wars Multi-Packs

NNO	Anakin/Yoda/Obi-Wan GITD AMZ	30.00	75.00
NNO	BB-8/BB-9E BB	7.50	15.00
NNO	BB-8 Gold Dome HT BF	10.00	20.00
NNO	Biggs/Wedge/Porkins WM	12.50	25.00
NNO	CS Yoda/Vader/R2/C-3PO AMZ	25.00	50.00
NNO	D-O/BB-8 BAM!	12.50	25.00
NNO	Fighting Droids GS	7.50	15.00
NNO	First Order Kylo Ren/Snoke/BB-9E COSTCO	15.00	30.00
NNO	First Order Kylo Ren/Snoke/Executioner/BB-9E COSTCO	20.00	40.00
NNO	Greedo/Hammerhead/Walrus Man WM	7.50	15.00
NNO	Gunner/Officer/Trooper WM	20.00	40.00
NNO	Han Solo/Chewbacca SB	20.00	40.00
NNO	Han Solo/Princess Leia	20.00	40.00
NNO	Jabba/Slave Leia/Salacious Crumb WM	30.00	75.00
NNO	Jango Fett GITD/LEGO Star Wars III Bundle	30.00	75.00
NNO	Kylo Ren/Rey B&N	20.00	40.00
NNO	Lobot/Ugnaught/Bespin Guard WM	7.50	15.00
NNO	Luke Skywalker & Wampa SDCC	150.00	300.00
NNO	Mandalorian/IG-11 B&N	50.00	100.00
NNO	Praetorian Guards POPCULTCHA	25.00	50.00
NNO	Princess Leia/R2-D2 SDCC	12.50	25.00
NNO	Princess Leia/R2-D2 SCE	7.50	15.00
NNO	R2-D2 Gold Dome HT BF	10.00	20.00
NNO	Rancor/Luke/Slave Oola PX	30.00	60.00
NNO	Rebel Rey/Chewbacca/BB-8 COSTCO	7.50	15.00
NNO	Rebel Rey/Luke/Chewbacca/BB-8 COSTCO	30.00	60.00

NNO	Rogue One Jyn/Cassian/K-2SO/C2-B5/Krennic	125.00	250.00
NNO	Sandtrooper/Dewback WM	15.00	30.00
NNO	Tarfful/Unhooded Emperor/Clone Trooper WM	25.00	50.00
NNO	Teebo/Chirpa/Logray WM	25.00	50.00

2021 Funko Pop Vinyl Pocket Pop Keychains Star Wars

NNO	Boba Fett	7.50	15.00
NNO	C-3PO	6.00	12.00
NNO	Chewbacca	7.50	15.00
NNO	The Child	7.50	15.00
NNO	The Child Using Force	7.50	15.00
NNO	The Child with Cup	6.00	12.00
NNO	Darth Vader	6.00	12.00
NNO	Grogu Macy's		
NNO	Han Solo	7.50	15.00
NNO	IG-11	7.50	15.00
NNO	Luke Skywalker	7.50	15.00
NNO	Mandalorian	6.00	12.00
NNO	Mandalorian Flying	7.50	15.00
NNO	Moff Gideon	6.00	12.00
NNO	Princess Leia	7.50	15.00
NNO	R2-D2	7.50	15.00
NNO	Stormtrooper	7.50	15.00
NNO	Yoda	6.00	12.00

2015-16 Funko Super Shogun

2	Shadowtrooper SWC	120.00	200.00
3	Boba Fett ROTJ SWC	120.00	200.00
4	Boba Fett ESB	60.00	120.00
5	Boba Fett Proto/400* FS	150.00	250.00

2017-18 Funko Vynl Star Wars

NNO	Chewbacca + C-3PO	7.50	15.00
NNO	Darth Vader + Stormtrooper	7.50	15.00
NNO	Han Solo + Greedo	6.00	12.00
NNO	Han Solo + Lando Calrissian	6.00	12.00
NNO	Luke Skywalker + Darth Vader	7.50	15.00
NNO	Luke Skywalker + Princess Leia	10.00	20.00
NNO	Obi-Wan Kenobi + Darth Maul	5.00	10.00

2007-16 Funko Wacky Wobblers Star Wars

NNO	4-LOM	6.00	12.00
NNO	501st Clone Trooper	15.00	30.00
NNO	Admiral Ackbar	25.00	50.00
NNO	Ahsoka Tano	25.00	50.00
NNO	Anakin Skywalker Clone Wars	7.50	15.00
NNO	Battle Droid	10.00	20.00
NNO	Boba Fett	7.50	15.00
NNO	Boba Fett Chrome Base	15.00	30.00
NNO	Bossk	7.50	15.00
NNO	C-3PO	7.50	15.00
NNO	C-3PO TFA	7.50	15.00
NNO	Cantina Band	10.00	20.00
NNO	Captain Phasma	6.00	12.00

NNO	Captain Rex	10.00	20.00
NNO	Captain Red Chrome Base	12.50	25.00
NNO	Chewbacca	7.50	15.00
NNO	Chewbacca Chrome Base	25.00	50.00
NNO	Chewbacca TFA	5.00	10.00
NNO	Clone Trooper	25.00	50.00
NNO	Clone Trooper Utapau AFE	10.00	20.00
NNO	Clone Trooper (yellow)	15.00	30.00
(2008)			
NNO	Clone Trooper Denal Chrome Base WM	12.50	25.00
NNO	Clone Trooper Sinker	75.00	150.00
NNO	Clone Troooper Denal WM	7.50	15.00
NNO	Commander Gree/1500* DIAMOND	7.50	15.00
NNO	Darth Maul	15.00	30.00
NNO	Darth Maul HOLO Chrome Base/12* SDCC	90.00	175.00
NNO	Darth Maul HOLO/480* SDCC	60.00	120.00
NNO	Darth Vader	7.50	15.00
NNO	Darth Vader (chrome base)	25.00	50.00
NNO	Darth Vader Holiday EE	7.50	15.00
NNO	Darth Vader HOLO SDCC/WWC	20.00	40.00
NNO	Darth Vader HOLO Chrome Base SDCC/WWC	25.00	50.00
NNO	Emperor Palpatine	25.00	50.00
NNO	Emperor Palpatine (chrome base)	25.00	50.00
NNO	Finn	6.00	12.00
NNO	Finn/Kylo Ren HMV	15.00	30.00
NNO	Finn Stormtrooper	5.00	10.00
NNO	First Order Flametrooper	6.00	12.00
NNO	First Order Snowtrooper	5.00	10.00
NNO	First Order Stormtrooper	6.00	12.00
NNO	Gamorrean Guard	12.50	25.00
NNO	General Grievous	10.00	20.00
NNO	Greedo	7.50	15.00
NNO	Greedo Chrome Base	25.00	50.00
NNO	Han Solo	12.50	25.00
NNO	Han Solo Stormtrooper/1008* SDCC	20.00	40.00
NNO	Holiday C-3PO	7.50	15.00
NNO	Holiday Special Boba Fett	10.00	20.00
NNO	Holiday Yoda	7.50	15.00
NNO	Jango Fett	7.50	15.00
NNO	Jawa	10.00	20.00
NNO	K-3PO/1500*	6.00	12.00
NNO	Kylo Ren	5.00	10.00
NNO	Kylor Ren No Hood	6.00	12.00
NNO	Luke Skywalker	20.00	40.00
NNO	Luke Skywalker (stormtrooper)	25.00	50.00
(2008 Entertainment Earth Exclusive)			
NNO	Luke Skywalker X-Wing Pilot	20.00	40.00
NNO	Obi-Wan Kenobi	25.00	50.00
NNO	Obi-Wan Kenobi (Clone Wars)	12.50	25.00
NNO	Obi-Wan Kenobi Force Ghost NYCC	15.00	30.00
NNO	Obi-Wan Kenobi Force Ghost Chrome Base	25.00	50.00
NNO	Princess Leia	7.50	15.00
NNO	R2-D2	7.50	15.00
NNO	R2-Q2/756* EE		
NNO	R2-R9/756* EE	7.50	15.00
NNO	R2-X2/756* EE	20.00	40.00
NNO	Rey	6.00	12.00
NNO	Shadow Stormtrooper SDCC	12.50	25.00
NNO	Shock Trooper/1008* SDCC	30.00	75.00
NNO	Slave Leia	10.00	20.00
NNO	Stormtrooper	7.50	15.00
NNO	TC-14/480* SDCC	25.00	50.00
NNO	TIE Fighter Pilot	12.50	25.00
NNO	Tusken Raider	7.50	15.00
NNO	Wicket	7.50	15.00
NNO	Wicket Chrome Base	30.00	60.00
NNO	Yoda	6.00	12.00
NNO	Yoda Chrome Base	15.00	30.00
NNO	Yoda Force Ghost	6.00	12.00
NNO	Yoda Force Ghost/1500* DIAMOND SDCC	25.00	50.00
NNO	Yoda (holiday)	6.00	12.00

2010 Funko Wacky Wobblers Star Wars Monster Mash-Ups

NNO	Chewbacca	6.00	12.00
NNO	Darth Vader	6.00	12.00
NNO	Stormtrooper	7.50	15.00
NNO	Yoda	5.00	10.00

2016-18 Funko Wobblers Star Wars

COMMON FIGURINE			
NNO	Boba Fett (prototype)	15.00	30.00
(2017 Galactic Convention Exclusive)			
NNO	Boba Fett Proto SWC	15.00	30.00
NNO	Boba Fett	6.00	12.00
NNO	Captain Cassian Andor	4.00	8.00
NNO	Chewbacca	6.00	12.00
NNO	Darth Vader	7.50	15.00
NNO	First Order Executioner	6.00	12.00
NNO	Han Solo (Solo film)	7.50	15.00
(2018)			
NNO	Imperial Death Trooper	6.00	12.00
NNO	Jyn Erso	5.00	10.00
NNO	Lando Calrissian	6.00	12.00
(2018)			
NNO	Princess Leia	7.50	15.00
NNO	Rey	7.50	15.00
NNO	Scarif Stormtrooper	6.00	12.00

2017 Vinylmation Eachez Star Wars The Last Jedi

NNO	Praetorian Guard Single Blade	30.00	75.00
NNO	Praetorian Guard Double Blade (chaser)	50.00	100.00
NNO	Praetorian Guard Whip	12.00	25.00

2012-13 Vinylmation Star Wars Disney Characters

NNO	Boba Fett Pete	6.00	12.00
NNO	Chewbacca Goofy	20.00	40.00
(LE 1500)			
NNO	Darth Vader Goofy	8.00	15.00
NNO	Emperor Stitch	25.00	50.00
(LE 2000)			
NNO	Ewok Chip	20.00	40.00
(LE 1500)			
NNO	Ewok Dale	20.00	40.00
(LE 1500)			
NNO	Han Solo Donald	30.00	60.00
(LE 1500)			
NNO	Jedi Mickey	20.00	40.00
(LE 2000)			
NNO	Princess Leia Minnie	10.00	20.00
NNO	Stormtrooper Donald	6.00	12.00
NNO	X-Wing Pilot Luke Mickey	12.00	25.00
NNO	Yoda Stitch	20.00	40.00

2015 Vinylmation Star Wars The Force Awakens Series 1

NNO	BB-8	10.00	20.00
NNO	C-3PO	4.00	8.00
NNO	Finn (leather jacket)	5.00	10.00
NNO	Finn (stormtrooper)		
NNO	First Order Stormtrooper	12.00	25.00
NNO	Han Solo (chaser)	15.00	30.00
NNO	Kylo Ren	10.00	20.00
NNO	Poe Dameron	4.00	8.00
NNO	Rey		
NNO	Rey (desert wear)	30.00	75.00

2016 Vinylmation Star Wars The Force Awakens Series 2

NNO	Admiral Ackbar	5.00	10.00
NNO	Captain Phasma		
NNO	Ello Asty (w/ helmet)	6.00	12.00
NNO	Ello Asty (helmetless)		
NNO	First Mate Guiggold	4.00	8.00
NNO	First Order Snowtrooper	6.00	12.00
NNO	First Order TIE Fighter Pilot	8.00	15.00
NNO	First Order TIE Fighter Pilot (red mark)		
NNO	Princess Leia	12.00	25.00
NNO	Sidon Ithano	5.00	10.00

2017 Vinylmation Star Wars The Last Jedi

NNO	BB-9E
NNO	DJ
NNO	Finn
NNO	General Hux
NNO	General Leia Organa
NNO	Kylo Ren
NNO	Luke Skywalker
NNO	Luke Skywalker Island (variant)
NNO	Poe Dameron
NNO	Rey
NNO	Rey Island (variant)
NNO	Rose
NNO	Snoke (chaser)
NNO	Stormtrooper Executioner

2015 Vinylmation Star Wars Rebels

NNO	Chopper
	(LE 2500)
NNO	Inquisitor
NNO	Zeb
	(LE 2500)

2016 Vinylmation Star Wars Rogue One

NNO	Admiral Raddus	8.00	15.00
NNO	Baze Malbus	6.00	12.00
NNO	Bistan	4.00	8.00
NNO	C2-B5	6.00	12.00
NNO	Cassian Andor	8.00	15.00
NNO	Chirrut Imwe	8.00	15.00
NNO	Director Orson Krennic	6.00	12.00
NNO	Imperial Death Trooper (w/o shoulder pad)	8.00	15.00
NNO	Imperial Death Trooper (w/ shoulder pad)	30.00	75.00
NNO	Jyn Erso (w/o helm)	8.00	15.00
NNO	Jyn Erso (w/ helm)	60.00	120.00
NNO	K-2SO	10.00	20.00
NNO	Rebel Commando Pao	8.00	15.00
NNO	Saw Gererra	12.00	25.00

2011 Vinylmation Star Wars Series 1

NNO	Boba Fett	12.00	25.00
NNO	C-3PO	8.00	15.00
NNO	Chewbacca	6.00	12.00
NNO	Darth Vader	10.00	20.00
NNO	Han Solo	12.00	25.00
NNO	Lando	10.00	20.00
NNO	Leia	6.00	12.00
NNO	Luke	6.00	12.00
NNO	Obi-Wan Kenobi Ghost	30.00	60.00
	(super chaser)		
NNO	Obi-Wan Kenobi	8.00	15.00
	(chaser)		
NNO	R2-D2	6.00	12.00
NNO	Stormtrooper	8.00	15.00
NNO	Yoda	8.00	15.00

2012 Vinylmation Star Wars Series 2

NNO	Darth Vader	20.00	40.00
NNO	Garindan	25.00	50.00
	(chaser)		
NNO	Grand Moff Tarkin	6.00	12.00
NNO	Greedo	6.00	12.00
NNO	Han Solo	6.00	12.00
NNO	Hologram Princess Leia	30.00	60.00
	(LE 2500) Celebration VI Exclusive		
NNO	Jawa	15.00	30.00
	(LE 2000)		
NNO	Luke Skywalker	8.00	15.00
NNO	Muftak	6.00	12.00
NNO	Obi-Wan Kenobi	8.00	15.00
NNO	Ponda Baba	6.00	12.00
NNO	Princess Leia	8.00	15.00
NNO	R5-D4		
	(LE 2000)		
NNO	Tusken Raider	8.00	15.00
NNO	Wedge Antilles	6.00	12.00

2013 Vinylmation Star Wars Series 3

NNO	Admiral Ackbar	10.00	20.00
NNO	Bib Fortuna	6.00	12.00
NNO	Biker Scout	8.00	15.00
NNO	Emperor Palpatine	30.00	60.00
	(chaser)		
NNO	Emperor's Royal Guard	10.00	20.00
NNO	Gamorrean Guard	6.00	12.00
NNO	Helmetless Princess Leia in Boushh Disguise		
	(variant)		
NNO	Lando Calrissian Skiff Guard Disguise	8.00	15.00
NNO	Logray	10.00	20.00
NNO	Luke Skywalker Jedi	8.00	15.00
NNO	Nien Nunb	6.00	12.00
NNO	Princess Leia in Boushh Disguise	15.00	30.00
NNO	Wicket	10.00	20.00

2014 Vinylmation Star Wars Series 4

NNO	4-LOM	6.00	12.00
NNO	Bespin Princess Leia	6.00	12.00
NNO	Boba Fett Concept	20.00	40.00
	(combo topper)		
NNO	Boba Fett Holiday Special		
	(LE 1500)		
NNO	Boba Fett	15.00	30.00
	(combo topper)		
NNO	Bossk	6.00	12.00
NNO	Dagobah Luke Skywalker 9-Inch	30.00	60.00
	(LE 2000)		
NNO	Dengar	6.00	12.00
NNO	Han Solo Carbonite	50.00	100.00
	(LE 2000)		
NNO	Han Solo Hoth	6.00	12.00
NNO	Holographic Emperor	12.00	25.00
	(LE 2000)		

NNO	Jabba the Hutt and Salacious Crumb 9-Inch	30.00	60.00
	(LE 2000)		
NNO	Luke Skywalker Hoth	6.00	12.00
NNO	R2-D2 Dagobah	12.00	25.00
NNO	R2-D2	15.00	30.00
	(variant)		
NNO	R2-MK	8.00	15.00
NNO	Rancor and Malakili 9-and-3-Inch Combo	40.00	80.00
NNO	Snowtrooper	10.00	20.00
NNO	Tauntaun	6.00	12.00
NNO	Ugnaught	6.00	12.00
NNO	Wampa Attacked Luke		
	(variant)		
NNO	Wampa	15.00	30.00
	(chaser)		
NNO	Yoda 9-Inch		
	(LE 2000)		
NNO	Zuckuss	6.00	12.00

2015 Vinylmation Star Wars Series 5

NNO	Death Star and Trooper 9-and-3-Inch Combo	40.00	80.00
	(LE 1000)		
NNO	Death Star Droid	8.00	15.00
NNO	Dr. Evazan	6.00	12.00
NNO	Duros		
NNO	Figrin D'an	15.00	30.00
	(instrument 1)		
NNO	Figrin D'an	20.00	40.00
	(instrument 2)		
NNO	Figrin D'an	20.00	40.00
	(instrument 3)		
NNO	Figrin D'an	15.00	30.00
	(instrument 4)		
NNO	Figrin D'an	20.00	40.00
	(instrument 5)		
NNO	Han Solo Stormtrooper	12.00	25.00
NNO	Heroes of Yavin Han		
	(LE 2500)		
NNO	Heroes of Yavin Luke	12.00	25.00
	(LE 2500)		
NNO	Jabba the Hutt	6.00	12.00
NNO	Jawa	20.00	40.00
	(LE 2500)		
NNO	Labria	6.00	12.00
NNO	Luke Skywalker Stormtrooper	50.00	100.00
	(variant)		
NNO	Luke Skywalker X-Wing Pilot	10.00	20.00
	(combo topper)		
NNO	Momaw Nadon	6.00	12.00
NNO	Power Droid	10.00	25.00
	(LE 2500)		
NNO	Princess Leia	6.00	12.00
NNO	Sandtrooper	8.00	15.00
NNO	Snaggletooth	10.00	20.00
	(chaser)		
NNO	Tie Fighter Pilot	10.00	20.00

2016 Vinylmation Star Wars Series 6

NNO	Anakin/Yoda/Obi-Wan Spirits
	(LE 2500)
NNO	Han Solo
NNO	Klaatu
NNO	Luke Skywalker
NNO	Luke Skywalker (w/o helmet)
NNO	Max Rebo
NNO	Oola
NNO	Princess Leia
NNO	Princess Leia (chaser)
NNO	Stormtrooper
NNO	Stormtrooper Battle Damaged (variant)
NNO	Teebo
NNO	Wicket 9"
	(LE 1000)

Trading Cards

PRICE GUIDE

STAR WARS FILMS

A NEW HOPE

1977 Star Wars

Han Solo and Chewbacca

COMPLETE SET W/STICKERS (330)	500.00	1000.00
COMP.SER.1 SET W/STICKERS (66)	300.00	600.00
COMP.SER.2 SET W/STICKERS (66)	150.00	300.00
COMP.SER.3 SET W/STICKERS (66)	125.00	250.00
COMP.SER.4 SET W/STICKERS (66)	125.00	250.00
COMP.SER.5 SET W/STICKERS (66)	100.00	200.00
UNOPENED SER.1 BOX (36 PACKS)	5000.00	10000.00
UNOPENED SER.1 PACK (7 CARDS+1 STICKER)	150.00	300.00
UNOPENED SER.2 BOX (36 PACKS)	2000.00	4000.00
UNOPENED SER.2 PACK (7 CARDS+1 STICKER)	75.00	150.00
UNOPENED SER.3 BOX (36 PACKS)	1500.00	3000.00
UNOPENED SER.3 PACK (7 CARDS+1 STICKER)	50.00	100.00
UNOPENED SER.4 BOX (36 PACKS)	1500.00	3000.00
UNOPENED SER.4 PACK (7 CARDS+1 STICKER)	50.00	100.00
UNOPENED SER.5 BOX (36 PACKS)	1250.00	2500.00
UNOPENED SER.5 PACK (7 CARDS+1 STICKER)	30.00	80.00
COMMON BLUE (1-66)	1.00	2.50
COMMON RED (67-132)	.40	1.00
COMMON YELLOW (133-198)	.40	1.00
COMMON GREEN (199-264)	.40	1.00
COMMON ORANGE (265-330)	.40	1.00
1 Luke Skywalker	25.00	60.00
2 C-3PO and R2-D2	2.50	6.00
3 The Little Droid R2-D2	6.00	15.00
4 Space pirate Han Solo	10.00	25.00
5 Princess Leia Organa	12.00	30.00
6 Ben Kenobi	4.00	10.00
7 The villainous Darth Vader	12.00	30.00
8 Grand Moff Tarkin	2.50	6.00
10 Princess Leia captured!	1.00	5.00
207A C-3PO A.Daniels ERR Obscene	60.00	120.00
207B C-3PO A.Daniels COR Airbrushed	10.00	25.00

1977 Star Wars Stickers

COMPLETE SET (55)	100.00	200.00
COMPLETE SERIES 1 (11)	50.00	100.00
COMPLETE SERIES 2 (11)	15.00	40.00
COMPLETE SERIES 3 (11)	15.00	40.00

COMPLETE SERIES 4 (11)	12.00	30.00
COMPLETE SERIES 5 (11)	12.00	30.00
COMMON STICKER (1-11)	3.00	8.00
COMMON STICKER (12-22)	2.00	5.00
COMMON STICKER (23-33)	1.50	4.00
COMMON STICKER (34-44)	1.25	3.00
COMMON STICKER (45-55)	1.25	3.00
1 Luke Skywalker	12.00	30.00
2 Princess Leia Organa	6.00	15.00
3 Han Solo	6.00	15.00
4 Chewbacca the Wookiee	5.00	12.00
5 See-Threepio	4.00	10.00
6 Artoo-Detoo	8.00	20.00
7 Lord Darth Vader	20.00	50.00
8 Grand Moff Tarkin	4.00	10.00
9 Ben (Obi-Wan) Kenobi	4.00	10.00
12 Han and Chewbacca	5.00	12.00
13 Alec Guinness as Ben	3.00	8.00
14 The Tusken Raider	2.50	6.00
15 See-Threepio	3.00	8.00
16 Chewbacca	3.00	8.00
18 The Rebel Fleet	2.50	6.00
19 The Wookiee Chewbacca	4.00	10.00
20 R2-D2 and C-3PO	2.50	6.00
23 Dave Prowse as Darth Vader	5.00	12.00
28 Peter Cushing as Grand Moff Tarkin	2.50	6.00
29 Han Solo Hero Or Mercenary?	4.00	10.00
30 Stormtroopers	3.00	8.00
31 Princess Leia Comforts Luke	3.00	8.00
32 Preparing for the Raid	2.00	5.00
34 The Star Warriors Aim for Action!	1.50	4.00
35 Han Solo (Harrison Ford)	5.00	12.00
36 Star Pilot Luke Skywalker	2.50	6.00
37 The Marvelous Droid See-Threepio!	2.00	5.00
38 R2-D2 (Kenny Baker)	2.50	6.00
40 Darth Vader (David Prowse)	12.00	30.00
42 Luke Poses with His Weapon	4.00	10.00
45 A Crucial Moment for Luke Skywalker	2.50	6.00
46 Chewie Aims for Danger!	1.50	4.00
48 Inside the Sandcrawler	1.50	4.00
50 George Lucas and Greedo	1.50	4.00
51 Technicians Ready C-3PO for the Cameras	1.50	4.00

1977 Star Wars Mexican

COMPLETE SET (66)	30.00	600.00
UNOPENED PACK (2 CARDS)	35.00	40.00
COMMON CARD (1-66)	5.00	12.00

1977 Star Wars OPC

COMPLETE SET (264)	200.00	400.00
COMPLETE SERIES 1 SET (66)	100.00	200.00
COMPLETE SERIES 2 SET (66)	60.00	120.00
COMPLETE SERIES 3 SET (132)	50.00	100.00
UNOPENED SERIES 1 BOX (36 PACKS)		
UNOPENED SERIES 1 PACK (7 CARDS+1 STICKER)		
UNOPENED SERIES 2 BOX (36 PACKS)		
UNOPENED SERIES 2 PACK (7 CARDS+1 STICKER)		
UNOPENED SERIES 3 BOX (36 PACKS)		
UNOPENED SERIES 3 PACK (7 CARDS+1 STICKER)		

COMMON BLUE (1-66)	2.50	5.00
COMMON RED (67-132)	1.25	3.00
COMMON ORANGE (133-264)	.50	1.25

1978 Star Wars General Mills

COMPLETE SET (18)	12.00	30.00
COMMON CARD (1-18)	1.00	2.50

1977 Star Wars Tip Top Ice Cream

COMPLETE SET (15)	150.00	300.00
COMMON CARD	15.00	40.00
UNNUMBERED SET LISTED ALPHABETICALLY		
ALSO KNOWN AS R2-D2 SPACE ICE		

1977 Star Wars Wonder Bread

COMPLETE SET (16)	100.00	200.00
COMMON CARD (1-16)	5.00	12.00
1 Luke Skywalker	10.00	25.00
3 Princess Leia Organa	8.00	20.00
4 Han Solo	10.00	25.00
5 Darth Vader	20.00	50.00
9 Chewbacca	6.00	15.00
10 Jawas	6.00	15.00
11 Tusken Raiders	6.00	15.00
13 Millenium Falcon	8.00	20.00
15 X-Wing	6.00	15.00
16 Tie-Vader's Ship	6.00	15.00

1995 Star Wars Widevision

COMPLETE SET (120)	15.00	40.00
UNOPENED BOX (36 PACKS)	80.00	100.00
UNOPENED PACK (10 CARDS)	2.50	3.00
COMMON CARD (1-120)	.20	.50

1995 Star Wars Widevision Finest

COMPLETE SET (10)	40.00	100.00
COMMON CARD (1-10)	5.00	12.00
STATED ODDS 1:11		

2007 Star Wars 30th Anniversary

COMPLETE SET (120)	5.00	12.00
UNOPENED HOBBY BOX (24 PACKS)	200.00	225.00
UNOPENED HOBBY PACK (7 CARDS)	10.00	12.00
UNOPENED RETAIL BOX (24 PACKS)		
UNOPENED RETAIL PACK (7 CARDS)		
COMMON CARD (1-120)	.15	.40
*BLUE: 4X TO 10X BASIC CARDS		
*RED: 8X TO 20X BASIC CARDS		
*GOLD/30: 80X TO 150X BASIC CARDS		

2007 Star Wars 30th Anniversary Animation Cels

COMPLETE SET (9)	6.00	15.00
COMMON CARD (1-9)	1.50	4.00
STATED ODDS 1:6 RETAIL		

2007 Star Wars 30th Anniversary Autographs

COMMON AUTO (UNNUMBERED)	10.00	20.00
STATED ODDS 1:43 HOBBY		
NNO Anthony Daniels	400.00	600.00
NNO Carrie Fisher	400.00	800.00
NNO Christine Hewett	12.00	30.00
NNO Colin Higgins	15.00	40.00
NNO David Prowse	200.00	400.00
NNO Gary Kurtz	30.00	75.00
NNO George Roubichek	12.00	30.00
NNO Harrison Ford	3000.00	5000.00
NNO Joe Viskocil	15.00	40.00
NNO John Dykstra	20.00	50.00
NNO John Williams	1000.00	2000.00
NNO Jon Berg	12.00	30.00
NNO Ken Ralston	15.00	40.00
NNO Kenny Baker	150.00	300.00
NNO Lorne Peterson	12.00	30.00
NNO Maria De Aragon	15.00	40.00
NNO Norman Reynolds	25.00	60.00
NNO Peter Mayhew	150.00	300.00
NNO Phil Tippet	30.00	75.00
NNO Richard Edlund	15.00	40.00
NNO Richard LeParmentier	8.00	20.00
NNO Rusty Goffe	20.00	50.00

2007 Star Wars 30th Anniversary Blister Bonus

COMPLETE SET (3)	3.00	8.00
COMMON CARD (1-3)	1.25	3.00
STATED ODDS 1:BLISTER PACK		

2007 Star Wars 30th Anniversary Magnets

COMPLETE SET (9)	12.00	30.00
COMMON CARD (UNNUMBERED)	1.50	4.00
STATED ODDS 1:8 RETAIL		

2007 Star Wars 30th Anniversary Original Series Box-Toppers

SERIES 1 (1-66) BLUE	12.00	30.00
SERIES 2 (67-132) RED	12.00	30.00
SERIES 3 (133-198) YELLOW	12.00	30.00
SERIES 4 (199-264) GREEN	12.00	30.00
SERIES 5 (265-330) ORANGE SP	30.00	80.00
STATED ODDS 1:BOX		

2007 Star Wars 30th Anniversary Sketches

STATED ODDS 1:50 HOBBY
UNPRICED DUE TO SCARCITY

NNO Adam Hughes
NNO Alexander Buechel
NNO Allison Sohn
NNO Amy Pronovost
NNO Brandon McKinney
NNO Brian Ashmore
NNO Brian Denham
NNO Brian Rood
NNO Cat Staggs
NNO Chris Eliopoulous
NNO Christian Dalla Vecchia
NNO Craig Rousseau
NNO Cynthis Cummens
NNO Dave Dorman
NNO David Rabbitte
NNO Davide Fabbri
NNO Doug Cowan
NNO Gabe Hernandez
NNO Grant Gould
NNO Ingrid Hardy
NNO Jan Duursema
NNO Jeff Chandler
NNO Jessica Hickman
NNO Joe Corroney
NNO John Watkins-Chow
NNO Joseph Booth
NNO Josh Fargher
NNO Josh Howard
NNO Juan Carlos Ramos
NNO Justin Chung
NNO Katie Cook
NNO Kevin Graham
NNO Leah Mangue
NNO Len Bellinger
NNO Mark Brooks
NNO Matt Busch
NNO Otis Frampton
NNO Paul Gutierrez
NNO Phil Noto

NNO Rafael Kayanen
NNO Robert Teranishi
NNO Russell Walks
NNO Ryan Waterhouse
NNO Sarah Wilkinson
NNO Sean Pence
NNO Stephane Roux
NNO Tom Hodges

2007 Star Wars 30th Anniversary Triptych Puzzle

COMPLETE SET (27)	12.00	25.00
COMMON CARD (1-27)	.75	2.00
STATED ODDS 1:3		

2017 Star Wars 40th Anniversary

COMPLETE SET (200)	10.00	25.00
UNOPENED BOX (24 PACKS)	120.00	150.00
UNOPENED PACK (8 CARDS)	5.00	6.50
COMMON CARD (1-200)	.20	.50
*GREEN: .5X TO 1.2X BASIC CARDS	.40	1.00
*BLUE: .6X TO 1.5X BASIC CARDS	.50	1.25
*PURPLE/100: 3X TO 8X BASIC CARDS	2.50	6.00
*GOLD/40: 6X TO 15X BASIC CARDS	5.00	12.00
*RED/1: UNPRICED DUE TO SCARCITY		
*P.P.BLACK/1: UNPRICED DUE TO SCARCITY		
*P.P.CYAN/1: UNPRICED DUE TO SCARCITY		
*P.P.MAGENTA/1: UNPRICED DUE TO SCARCITY		
*P.P.YELLOW/1: UNPRICED DUE TO SCARCITY		

2017 Star Wars 40th Anniversary Autographed Medallions

STATED PRINT RUN 10 SER.#'d SETS
UNPRICED DUE TO SCARCITY

AD Anthony Daniels
CF Carrie Fisher
HF Harrison Ford
KB Kenny Baker
MH Mark Hamill

2017 Star Wars 40th Anniversary Autographs

COMMON AUTO	6.00	15.00
*PURPLE/40: .6X TO 1.5X BASIC AUTOS		
*GOLD/10: 1X TO 2.5X BASIC AUTOS		
*RED/1: UNPRICED DUE TO SCARCITY		
*P.P.BLACK/1: UNPRICED DUE TO SCARCITY		
*P.P.CYAN/1: UNPRICED DUE TO SCARCITY		
*P.P.MAGENTA/1: UNPRICED DUE TO SCARCITY		
*P.P.YELLOW/1: UNPRICED DUE TO SCARCITY		
RANDOMLY INSERTED INTO PACKS		
AAAH Alan Harris	6.00	15.00
AAAL Al Lampert	10.00	20.00
AABF Barbara Frankland	10.00	25.00
AABL Bai Ling	8.00	20.00
AACR Clive Revill	10.00	25.00
AADL Denis Lawson	10.00	25.00
AADR Deep Roy	10.00	25.00
AAFF Femi Taylor	8.00	20.00
AAGB Glyn Baker	8.00	20.00
AAGH Garrick Hagon	8.00	20.00
AAGR George Roubicek	10.00	25.00
AAHQ Hugh Quarshie	10.00	25.00
AAIL Ian Liston	10.00	25.00
AAJB Jeremy Bulloch	15.00	40.00
AAJK Jack Klaff	10.00	25.00
AAKC Kenneth Colley	8.00	20.00
AAKR Kipsang Rotich	10.00	25.00
AAMC Michael Carter	12.00	30.00
AAMW Matthew Wood	10.00	25.00
AAPS Paul Springer	8.00	20.00
AARO Richard Oldfield	10.00	25.00
AASC Stephen Costantino	8.00	20.00
AATR Tim Rose	8.00	20.00
AACDW Corey Dee Williams	8.00	20.00
AAPBL Paul Blake	10.00	25.00
AAPBR Paul Brooke	8.00	20.00

2017 Star Wars 40th Anniversary Celebration Orlando Promos

Luke Skywalker

COMPLETE SET (4)	225.00	450.00
COMMON CARD (C1-C4)	50.00	100.00
C1 Luke Skywalker	80.00	150.00
C2 Princess Leia	80.00	150.00
C3 Han Solo	60.00	120.00

2017 Star Wars 40th Anniversary Classic Stickers

COMMON CARD	12.00	30.00

STATED PRINT RUN 100 SER.#'d SETS

2017 Star Wars 40th Anniversary Dual Autographs

STATED PRINT RUN 3 SER.#'d SETS
UNPRICED DUE TO SCARCITY

NNO Daniels/Baker
NNO Daniels/Mayhew
NNO Fisher/Davis
NNO Barclay/Carter
NNO Hamill/Baker

2017 Star Wars 40th Anniversary Medallions

COMMON MEDALLION	6.00	15.00
MILLENNIUM FALCON (1-12)		
DEATH STAR (13-23)		
*BLUE/40: .5X TO 1.2X BASIC MEDALLIONS	8.00	20.00
*PURPLE/25: .6X TO 1.5X BASIC MEDALLIONS	10.00	25.00
*GOLD/10: 1.2X TO 3X BASIC MEDALLIONS	20.00	50.00
*RED/1: UNPRICED DUE TO SCARCITY		

2017 Star Wars 40th Anniversary Patches

COMMON CARD (1-20)	5.00	12.00
*BLUE/40: 6X TO 1.5X BASIC CARDS	8.00	20.00
*PURPLE/25: 1X TO 2.5X BASIC CARDS	12.00	30.00
*GOLD/10: 1.5X TO 4X BASIC CARDS	20.00	50.00

RANDOMLY INSERTED INTO PACKS
TARGET EXCLUSIVE

2017 Star Wars 40th Anniversary Quad Autographed Booklet

STATED PRINT RUN 2 SER.#'d SETS
UNPRICED DUE TO SCARCITY

NNO Hamill/Fisher/Daniels/Baker

2017 Star Wars 40th Anniversary Six-Person Autographed Booklet

STATED PRINT RUN 2 SER.#'d SETS
UNPRICED DUE TO SCARCITY

NNO Ford/Hamill/Fisher
Daniels/Baker/Mayhew

2017 Star Wars 40th Anniversary Sketches

UNPRICED DUE TO SCARCITY

NNO Adam Worton
NNO Alex Iniguez
NNO Andrew Lopez
NNO Angelina Benedetti
NNO Anil Sharma
NNO Anthony Skubis
NNO Ashleigh Popplewell
NNO Ben Abu Saada
NNO Bob Hepner
NNO Brad Hudson
NNO Brad Utterstrom
NNO Brandon Pyle
NNO Brendan Purchase
NNO Brent Ragland
NNO Can Baran
NNO Carlos Cabaleiro
NNO Cathy Razim
NNO Chad LaForce
NNO Chad Scheres
NNO Charlie Cody
NNO Chris West
NNO Clinton Yeager
NNO Corey Galal
NNO Dan Bergren
NNO Dan Burn Webster
NNO Dan Curto
NNO Daniel Cooney
NNO Danny Kidwell
NNO Darrin Pepe
NNO Dave Dabila
NNO David Rabbitte
NNO Dylan Riley
NNO Elfie Lebouleux
NNO Eric Lehtonen
NNO Eric Muller
NNO Frank Kadar
NNO Freddy Lopez
NNO George Joseph
NNO Ingrid Hardy
NNO Jamie Cosley
NNO Jamie Richards
NNO Jamie Thomas
NNO Jason Brower
NNO Jason Durden
NNO Jason Sobol
NNO Jay Machand
NNO Jeff Mallinson
NNO Jessica Hickman
NNO Jim Mehsling
NNO JM Smith
NNO John Sloboda
NNO Jon Gregory
NNO Kaela Croft
NNO Kallan Archer
NNO Kate Carleton
NNO Kelly Greider
NNO Kevin Graham
NNO Kevin P. West
NNO Kris Penix
NNO Kyle Babbitt
NNO Kyle Hickman
NNO Luke Preece
NNO Marcia Dye
NNO Mark Mangum
NNO Mark Stroud
NNO Marsha Parkins
NNO Matt Langford
NNO Matt Maldonado
NNO Matt Soffe

NNO Matt Steffens
NNO Matt Stewart
NNO Michael Mastermaker
NNO Michelle Rayner
NNO Mike Barnard
NNO Mike James
NNO Mohammad Jilani
NNO Neil Camera
NNO Norvierto P. Basio
NNO Phil Hassewer
NNO Rey Paez
NNO Rich Molinelli
NNO Robert Hendrickson
NNO Roy Cover
NNO Sarah Wilkinson
NNO Shane McCormack
NNO Solly Mohamed
NNO Stephanie Swanger
NNO Ted Dastick Jr.
NNO Tiffany Groves
NNO Tim Dowler
NNO Tim Proctor
NNO Tina Berardi
NNO Todd Aaron Smith
NNO Tom Carlton
NNO Ward Silverman

2017 Star Wars 40th Anniversary Triple Autographs

STATED PRINT RUN 3 SER.#'d SETS
UNPRICED DUE TO SCARCITY

TABDM Baker/Daniels/Mayhew
TAHBB Hamill/Barclay/Bauersfeld
TAHHK Hamill/Hagon/Klaff
TAPMW Park/McDiarmid/Wood

2017 Star Wars 1978 Sugar Free Wrappers Set

COMPLETE SET (49)	10.00	25.00
COMPLETE FACTORY SET (51)		
COMMON CARD (1-49)	.30	.75
*BLUE/75: 2X TO 5X BASIC CARDS	1.50	4.00
*GREEN/40: 4X TO 10X BASIC CARDS	3.00	8.00
*GOLD/10: 6X TO 15X BASIC CARDS	5.00	12.00
*RED/1: UNPRICED DUE TO SCARCITY		

2017 Star Wars 1978 Sugar Free Wrappers Set Autographs

*BLUE/25: UNPRICED DUE TO SCARCITY
*GREEN/10: UNPRICED DUE TO SCARCITY
*GOLD/5: UNPRICED DUE TO SCARCITY
*RED/1: UNPRICED DUE TO SCARCITY
STATED ODDS 2:SET

NNO Alan Harris	10.00	25.00
NNO Angus MacInnes	10.00	25.00
NNO Anthony Daniels		
NNO Anthony Forrest		
NNO Barbara Frankland	15.00	40.00
NNO Billy Dee Williams	100.00	200.00
NNO Caroline Blakiston	20.00	50.00
NNO Carrie Fisher		
NNO Clive Revill	15.00	40.00
NNO Corey Dee Williams	10.00	25.00
NNO David Ankrum	25.00	60.00
NNO Deep Roy	12.00	30.00
NNO Denis Lawson	15.00	40.00
NNO Dermot Crowley	12.00	30.00
NNO Dickey Beer	12.00	30.00
Barada		
NNO Dickey Beer	15.00	40.00
Boba Fett		
NNO Dickey Beer	10.00	25.00
Scout Trooper		
NNO Erik Bauersfeld		
NNO Femi Taylor	10.00	25.00
NNO Garrick Hagon	10.00	25.00
NNO Harrison Ford		
NNO Ian McDiarmid		
NNO Jeremy Bulloch	20.00	50.00
NNO John Morton	10.00	25.00

NNO John Ratzenberger	10.00	25.00
NNO Julian Glover	12.00	30.00
NNO Kenneth Colley	8.00	20.00
NNO Kenny Baker		
NNO Mark Capri	8.00	20.00
NNO Mark Dodson	12.00	30.00
NNO Mark Hamill		
NNO Michael Carter	10.00	25.00
NNO Mike Quinn	12.00	30.00
Nien Nunb		
NNO Mike Quinn	15.00	40.00
Sy Snootles		
NNO Pam Rose	6.00	20.00
NNO Paul Blake	10.00	25.00
NNO Peter Mayhew		
NNO Rusty Goffe	8.00	20.00
NNO Sean Crawford	8.00	20.00
NNO Tim Dry	8.00	20.00
NNO Tim Rose	12.00	30.00
NNO Toby Philpott	10.00	25.00
NNO Warwick Davis	15.00	40.00

2013 Star Wars Illustrated A New Hope

COMPLETE SET (100)	8.00	20.00
COMMON CARD (1-100)	.20	.50

*PURPLE: 2.5X TO 6X BASIC CARDS
*BRONZE: 5X TO 12X BASIC CARDS
*GOLD/10: 50X TO 120X BASIC CARDS
*P.P.BLACK/1: UNPRICED DUE TO SCARCITY
*P.P.CYAN/1: UNPRICED DUE TO SCARCITY
*P.P.MAGENTA/1: UNPRICED DUE TO SCARCITY
*P.P.YELLOW/1: UNPRICED DUE TO SCARCITY

2013 Star Wars Illustrated A New Hope Sketchagraphs

1 Anthony Daniels
Aston Roy Cover/20
2 Anthony Daniels
Chad "CWM" McCown
3 Anthony Daniels
Chris Meeks
4 Anthony Daniels
Darrin Pepe
5 Anthony Daniels
Denae Frazier
6 Anthony Daniels
Grant Gould/48
7 Anthony Daniels
Jason Chalker
8 Anthony Daniels
Kris Penix
9 Anthony Daniels
Kyle Babbitt
10 Anthony Daniels
Robert Jimenez/45
11 Anthony Daniels
Robert Teranishi
12 Anthony Daniels
Scott Rorie
13 Anthony Daniels
Val Hochberg
14 Anthony Daniels
Paul "Gutz" Gutierrez
15 David Ackroyd
Aston Roy Cover
16 David Ackroyd
Darrin Pepe
17 David Ackroyd
Denae Frazier
18 David Ackroyd
Grant Gould
19 David Ackroyd
Jason Chalker
20 David Ackroyd
Kris Penix
21 David Ackroyd
Kyle Babbitt
22 David Ackroyd
Paul "Gutz" Gutierrez

23 David Ackroyd
Scott Rorie
24 David Ackroyd
Val Hochberg
25 David Paymer
Chad "CWM" McCown
26 David Paymer
Darrin Pepe
27 David Paymer
Denae Frazier
28 David Paymer
Grant Gould
29 David Paymer
Kris Penix
30 David Paymer
Kyle Babbitt
31 David Paymer
Mikey Babinski
32 David Paymer
Paul "Gutz" Gutierrez
33 David Paymer
Robert Teranishi
34 David Paymer
Scott Rorie
35 David Paymer
Val Hochberg
36 David Paymer
Wilson Ramos Jr.
37 Garrick Hagon
Aston Roy Cover
38 Garrick Hagon
Chad "CWM" McCown
39 Garrick Hagon
Chris Meeks
40 Garrick Hagon
Darrin Pepe
41 Garrick Hagon
Denae Frazier
42 Garrick Hagon
Grant Gould
43 Garrick Hagon
Jason Chalker
44 Garrick Hagon
Kris Penix
45 Garrick Hagon
Kyle Babbitt
46 Garrick Hagon
Mikey Babinski
47 Garrick Hagon
Paul "Gutz" Gutierrez
48 Garrick Hagon
Robert Jimenez
49 Garrick Hagon
Robert Teranishi
50 Garrick Hagon
Scott Rorie
51 Garrick Hagon
Val Hochberg
52 Kale Browne
Aston Roy Cover
53 Kale Browne
Chad "CWM" McCown
54 Kale Browne
Denae Frazier
55 Kale Browne
Grant Gould
56 Kale Browne
Jason Crosby
57 Kale Browne
Mikey Babinski
58 Kale Browne
Paul "Gutz" Gutierrez
59 Kale Browne
Robert Jimenez
60 Kale Browne
Robert Teranishi
61 Kale Browne
Scott Rorie
62 Kale Browne
Val Hochberg
63 Kale Browne
Wilson Ramos Jr.

64 Mark Hamill
Aston Roy Cover
65 Mark Hamill
Chad "CWM" McCown
66 Mark Hamill
Chris Meeks
67 Mark Hamill
Darrin Pepe
68 Mark Hamill
Denae Frazier
69 Mark Hamill
Grant Gould
70 Mark Hamill
Jason Chalker
71 Mark Hamill
Kyle Babbitt
72 Mark Hamill
Mikey Babinski
73 Mark Hamill
Robert Teranishi
74 Mark Hamill
Scott Rorie
75 Mark Hamill
Val Hochberg
76 Pam Rose
Aston Roy Cover
77 Pam Rose
Chad "CWM" McCown
78 Pam Rose
Chris Meeks
79 Pam Rose
Darrin Pepe
80 Pam Rose
Denae Frazier
81 Pam Rose
Grant Gould
82 Pam Rose
Jason Chalker
83 Pam Rose
Kris Penix
84 Pam Rose
Mikey Babinski
85 Pam Rose
Robert Teranishi
86 Pam Rose
Scott Rorie
87 Pam Rose
Val Hochberg
88 Pam Rose
Aston Roy Cover
89 Peter Mayhew
Aston Roy Cover
90 Peter Mayhew
Chad "CWM" McCown
91 Peter Mayhew
Chris Meeks
92 Peter Mayhew
Darrin Pepe
93 Peter Mayhew
Denae Frazier
94 Peter Mayhew
Grant Gould
95 Peter Mayhew
Jason Chalker
96 Peter Mayhew
Kris Penix
97 Peter Mayhew
Kyle Babbitt
98 Peter Mayhew
Mikey Babinski
99 Peter Mayhew
Paul "Gutz" Gutierrez
100 Peter Mayhew
Robert Jimenez
101 Peter Mayhew
Robert Teranishi
102 Peter Mayhew
Scott Rorie
103 Peter Mayhew
Val Hochberg

2013 Star Wars Illustrated A New Hope Film Cels

COMPLETE SET (20)	250.00	500.00
COMMON CARD (FR1-FR20)	12.00	30.00
FR8 Greedo's Bounty	15.00	40.00
FR14 The Final Encounter	60.00	120.00

2013 Star Wars Illustrated A New Hope Movie Poster Reinterpretations

COMPLETE SET (9)	5.00	12.00
COMMON CARD (MP1-MP9)	1.25	3.00
*P.P.BLACK/1: UNPRICED DUE TO SCARCITY		
*P.P.CYAN/1: UNPRICED DUE TO SCARCITY		
*P.P.MAGENTA/1: UNPRICED DUE TO SCARCITY		
*P.P.YELLOW/1: UNPRICED DUE TO SCARCITY		
STATED ODDS 1:3		

2013 Star Wars Illustrated A New Hope One Year Earlier

COMPLETE SET (18)	5.00	12.00
COMMON CARD (OY1-OY18)	.60	1.50
*P.P.BLACK/1: UNPRICED DUE TO SCARCITY		
*P.P.CYAN/1: UNPRICED DUE TO SCARCITY		
*P.P.MAGENTA/1: UNPRICED DUE TO SCARCITY		
*P.P.YELLOW/1: UNPRICED DUE TO SCARCITY		
STATED ODDS 1:2		

2013 Star Wars Illustrated A New Hope Panorama Sketches

NNO Adrianna Vanderstelt
NNO Brandon Gallo
NNO Brian Deguire
NNO Choot McCan
NNO Chris Hamer
NNO Chris West
NNO Christian Slade
NNO Darrin Pepe
NNO Dave Strong
NNO David Green
NNO David Rabbitte

NNO GeckoArt/50*
NNO Ingrid Hardy/15*
NNO Irma Ahmed
NNO Jake Myler/50*
NNO Jason Chalker
NNO Jason Crosby/50*
NNO Jason Flowers
NNO Jerry Vanderstelt
NNO Joanne Ellen Patak
NNO Joe Hogan
NNO John Haun/50*
NNO John Soukup/50*
NNO Josh Howard
NNO Justice41/25*
NNO Kevin Graham
NNO Kimberly Dunaway
NNO Kris Penix
NNO Lawrence Reynolds
NNO Linzy Zorn
NNO Marck Labas
NNO Matt Busch
NNO Matt Hebb/50*
NNO Matte Chero/50*
NNO McHero
NNO Michael Locoduck Duron
NNO Mikey Babinski
NNO Pablo Diaz/50*
NNO Patrick Richardson/50*
NNO Rachel Kaiser/50*
NNO Robert Hendrickson
NNO Roberto Jimenez/50*
NNO Scott Zambelli/50*
NNO Shea Standefer
NNO Stephanie Swanger
NNO Steve Oatney
NNO Tim Proctor
NNO Todd Smith
NNO Val Hochberg
NNO Vanessa Banky
NNO William O'Neill
NNO Wilson Ramos Jr.

2013 Star Wars Illustrated A New Hope Radio Drama Puzzle

COMPLETE SET (6)	5.00	12.00
COMMON CARD (1-6)	1.50	4.00
*P.P.BLACK/1: UNPRICED DUE TO SCARCITY		
*P.P.CYAN/1: UNPRICED DUE TO SCARCITY		
*P.P.MAGENTA/1: UNPRICED DUE TO SCARCITY		
*P.P.YELLOW/1: UNPRICED DUE TO SCARCITY		
STATED ODDS 1:8		

2013 Star Wars Illustrated A New Hope The Mission Destroy the Death Star

COMPLETE SET (12)	30.00	60.00
COMMON CARD (1-12)	3.00	8.00
*P.P.BLACK/1: UNPRICED DUE TO SCARCITY		
*P.P.CYAN/1: UNPRICED DUE TO SCARCITY		
*P.P.MAGENTA/1: UNPRICED DUE TO SCARCITY		
*P.P.YELLOW/1: UNPRICED DUE TO SCARCITY		
STATED ODDS 1:12		

2013 Star Wars Illustrated A New Hope Promos

COMPLETE SET (4)	5.00	12.00

2018 Star Wars A New Hope Black and White

COMPLETE SET (140)	15.00	40.00
UNOPENED BOX (7 PACKS)		
UNOPENED PACK (8 CARDS)		
COMMON CARD (1-140)	.25	.60
*SEPIA: .75X TO 2X BASIC CARDS	.50	1.25
*BLUE: 1X TO 2.5X BASIC CARDS	.60	1.50

*GREEN/99: 3X TO 8X BASIC CARDS	2.00	5.00
*PURPLE/25: 8X TO 20X BASIC CARDS	5.00	12.00
*RED/10: UNPRICED DUE TO SCARCITY		
*METAL/1: UNPRICED DUE TO SCARCITY		

2018 Star Wars A New Hope Black and White Autographs

COMMON AUTO	6.00	15.00
*BLUE/99: .5X TO 1.2X BASIC AUTOS		
*GREEN/25: .6X TO 1.5X BASIC AUTOS		
*PURPLE/10: UNPRICED DUE TO SCARCITY		
*RED/1: UNPRICED DUE TO SCARCITY		
STATED ODDS 1:18		
NNO Al Lampert	8.00	20.00
NNO Annette Jones	8.00	20.00
NNO Barbara Frankland	8.00	20.00
NNO Denis Lawson	12.00	30.00
NNO Garrick Hagon	8.00	20.00
NNO Paul Blake	10.00	25.00

2018 Star Wars A New Hope Black and White Autographs Blue

*BLUE: .5X TO 1.2X BASIC AUTOS
STATED ODDS 1:62
STATED PRINT RUN 99 SER.#'d SETS

NNO Peter Mayhew	30.00	75.00

2018 Star Wars A New Hope Black and White Autographs Green

*GREEN: .6X TO 1.5X BASIC AUTOS
STATED ODDS 1:202
STATED PRINT RUN 25 SER.#'d SETS

NNO Anthony Daniels	75.00	150.00
NNO Kenny Baker	60.00	120.00

2018 Star Wars A New Hope Black and White Behind-the-Scenes

COMPLETE SET (41)	20.00	50.00
COMMON CARD (BTS1-BTS41)	2.00	5.00
STATED ODDS 1:2		

2018 Star Wars A New Hope Black and White Concept Art

COMPLETE SET (12)	10.00	25.00
COMMON CARD (CA1-CA12)	1.50	4.00
STATED ODDS 1:4		

2018 Star Wars A New Hope Black and White Dual Autographs

STATED ODDS 1:1,677
UNPRICED DUE TO SCARCITY

NNO A.Lampert/G.Roubicek
NNO A.MacInnes/G.Hagon
NNO D.Lawson/D.Ankrum
NNO H.Ford/P.Mayhew
NNO J.Klaff/A.MacInnes
NNO K.Baker/A.Daniels

2018 Star Wars A New Hope Black and White Iconic Characters

COMPLETE SET (12)	15.00	40.00
COMMON CARD (IC1-IC12)	2.00	5.00
STATED ODDS 1:12		
IC1 Luke Skywalker	4.00	10.00
IC2 Han Solo	5.00	12.00
IC3 Princess Leia Organa	4.00	10.00
IC4 Chewbacca	2.50	6.00
IC5 Ben (Obi-Wan) Kenobi	4.00	10.00
IC7 R2-D2	2.50	6.00
IC8 Darth Vader	5.00	12.00

2018 Star Wars A New Hope Black and White Posters

COMPLETE SET (12)	12.00	30.00
COMMON CARD (PO1-PO12)	1.50	4.00
STATED ODDS 1:6		

2018 Star Wars A New Hope Black and White Shaped Sketches

STATED ODDS 1:182
UNPRICED DUE TO SCARCITY

NNO Adam Talley
NNO Andrew Lopez
NNO Andy Bohn
NNO Chris Quinn

NNO Chris Willdig
NNO Dan Curto
NNO Dan Gorman
NNO Darren Coburn-James
NNO Dylan Riley
NNO Eli Hyder
NNO Huy Truong
NNO James O'Riley
NNO Jeff Abar
NNO John DiBiase
NNO John Pleak
NNO Juan Rosales
NNO Kris Penix
NNO Mark Mangum
NNO Mark Stroud
NNO Matt Stewart
NNO Mike Mastermaker
NNO Nathan Kennett
NNO Nathan Ohlendorf
NNO Patrick Giles
NNO Ray Richardson
NNO K. Grimm

2018 Star Wars A New Hope Black and White Six-Person Autograph

STATED ODDS 1:88,844
STATED PRINT RUN 1 SER.#'d SET
UNPRICED DUE TO SCARCITY

NNO Ford/Hamill/Fisher/Mayhew/Baker/Daniels

2018 Star Wars A New Hope Black and White Sketches

STATED ODDS 1:17
UNPRICED DUE TO SCARCITY

NNO Adam Harris
NNO Adam Talley
NNO Adrian Ropp
NNO Alex Inguez
NNO Alex Mines
NNO Allen Grimes
NNO Allycat
NNO Andrew Lopez
NNO Andy Bohn
NNO Angelina Benedetti
NNO Anil Sharma
NNO Anthony Skubis
NNO Basak Cetinkaya
NNO Ben AbuSaada
NNO Ben Goddard
NNO Bianca Thompson
NNO Bob Stevlic
NNO Brad Utterstrom
NNO Brandon Bracamonte
NNO Brandon Pyle
NNO Brendan Purchase
NNO Brendan Shaw
NNO Brett Farr
NNO Bryce King
NNO Carlos Cabaleiro
NNO Carolyn Craggs
NNO Chad Scheres
NNO Chris Henderson
NNO Chris Quinn
NNO Chris Thorne
NNO Clinton Yeager
NNO Colin Arthurs
NNO Corey Galal
NNO D.J. Coffman
NNO Dan Bergren
NNO Dan Curto
NNO Daniel Reneau
NNO Darren Coburn-James
NNO Darrin Pepe
NNO Dave Fowler
NNO David Day
NNO David Roman
NNO Dean Drummond
NNO Dennis Gortakowski
NNO Don Pedicini Jr.
NNO Doug Snodgrass
NNO DuMarquez Advosze
NNO Dylan Riley
NNO Eli Hyder

NNO Eric Lehtonen
NNO Eric White
NNO Erin Lefler
NNO Frank Kadar
NNO Garrett Dix
NNO Gerard Garcia Jr.
NNO Humberto Fuentes
NNO Huy Truong
NNO Ian MacDougall
NNO Ibrahim Ozkan
NNO J. Hammond
NNO J.L. Martin
NNO James Dickson
NNO James O'Riley
NNO Jamie Cosley
NNO Jamie Richards
NNO Jason Adams
NNO Jason Davies
NNO Jason Kimble
NNO Jeff Abar
NNO Jeff Carlisle
NNO Jeff Mallinson
NNO Jerry Bennett
NNO Jessica Hickman
NNO Jim Sabo
NNO John DiBiase
NNO John Pleak
NNO John Still
NNO Jon Arton
NNO Jose Ventura
NNO Joshua Bommer
NNO Juan Rosales
NNO Jude Gallagher
NNO Kaela Croft
NNO Keith Carter
NNO Kevin Cleveland
NNO Kris Penix
NNO Kurt Ruskin
NNO Lak Lim
NNO Lawrence Reynolds
NNO Lee Brown
NNO Louise Draper
NNO Marcia Dye
NNO Marcus Rocco
NNO Mark Mangum
NNO Marlo Agunos
NNO Marsha Parkins
NNO Matt Langford
NNO Matt Maldonado
NNO Matt Steffens
NNO Matthew Skip Charron
NNO Mayumi Seto
NNO Michelle Rayner
NNO Mike James
NNO Mike Spivey
NNO Mohamed Jilani
NNO Nathan Kennett
NNO Nathan Ohlendorf
NNO Neil Camera
NNO Nicholas Baltra
NNO Nick Justus
NNO Omar Salinas
NNO Pablo Diaz
NNO Patricio Carrasco
NNO Patrick Davis
NNO Patrick Giles
NNO Phil Hassewer
NNO Phillip Trujillo
NNO Quentin Aldredge
NNO Rey Paez
NNO Richard Serrao
NNO Robert Teranishi
NNO Rodney Roberts
NNO Ronnie Crowther
NNO Roy Cover
NNO Ryan Santos
NNO Sammy Gomez
NNO Scott Houseman
NNO Shane Molina
NNO Solly Mohamed
NNO Stephanie Rosales
NNO Stephanie Swanger

NNO Ted Dastick Jr.
NNO Tom Ameci
NNO Trent Westbrook
NNO Ward Silverman

2018 Star Wars A New Hope Black and White Triple Autographs

STATED ODDS 1:2,693
UNPRICED DUE TO SCARCITY

NNO Lampert/Forest/Roubicek
NNO Hagon/Klaff/MacInnes
NNO Baker/Goffe/Daniels
NNO Mayhew/Baker/Daniels

EMPIRE STRIKES BACK

1980 Star Wars Empire Strikes Back

"WELCOME, YOUNG LUKE!"

COMPLETE SET W/STICKERS (440)	125.00	250.00
COMPLETE SET (352)	100.00	200.00
COMPLETE SERIES 1 SET W/STICKERS (165)	75.00	150.00
COMPLETE SERIES 1 SET (132)	50.00	100.00
COMPLETE SERIES 2 SET W/STICKERS (165)	50.00	100.00
COMPLETE SERIES 2 SET (132)	30.00	75.00
COMPLETE SERIES 3 SET W/STICKERS (110)	30.00	75.00
COMPLETE SERIES 3 SET (88)	25.00	60.00
UNOPENED SERIES 1 BOX (36 PACKS)	750.00	1500.00
UNOPENED SERIES 1 PACK (12 CARDS+1 STICKER)	25.00	50.00
UNOPENED SERIES 1 COL.BOX (80 CARDS+COL.BOX)	100.00	200.00
UNOPENED SERIES 1 RACK BOX (24 PACKS)		
UNOPENED SERIES 1 RACK PACK (51 CARDS)	75.00	150.00
UNOPENED SERIES 2 BOX (36 PACKS)	300.00	600.00
UNOPENED SERIES 2 PACK (12 CARDS+1 STICKER)	10.00	20.00
UNOPENED SERIES 3 BOX (36 PACKS)	250.00	500.00
UNOPENED SERIES 3 PACK (12 CARDS+1 STICKER)	8.00	15.00
COMMON SERIES 1 CARD (1-132)	.60	1.50
COMMON SERIES 2 CARD (133-264)	.50	1.25
COMMON SERIES 3 CARD (265-352)	.60	1.50

1980 Star Wars Empire Strikes Back Stickers

COMPLETE SET (88)	15.00	40.00
COMPLETE SERIES 1 SET (33)	50.00	100.00
COMPLETE SERIES 2 SET (33)	15.00	40.00
COMPLETE SERIES 3 SET (22)	12.00	30.00
COMMON CARD (1-33)	2.50	6.00
COMMON CARD (34-66)	1.00	2.50
COMMON CARD (67-88)	1.25	3.00

1980 Star Wars Empire Strikes Back 5X7 Photos

COMPLETE SET (30)	25.00	50.00
UNOPENED BOX (36 PACKS)		
UNOPENED PACK (1 CARD)		
COMMON CARD (1-30)	1.50	4.00

1980 Star Wars Empire Strikes Back 5X7 Photos Test Issue

COMPLETE SET (30)	100.00	200.00
COMMON CARD (1-30)	3.00	8.00

1980 Star Wars Empire Strikes Back Hershey's

COMPLETE SET (5)	12.00	30.00
COMMON CARD	4.00	10.00
UNNUMBERED SET		
1 Boba Fett	5.00	12.00

1980 Star Wars Empire Strikes Back Twinkies New Zealand

COMPLETE SET (6)	15.00	40.00
COMMON CARD (UNNUMBERED)	4.00	10.00

1980 Star Wars Empire Strikes Back York Peanut Butter Discs

COMPLETE SET (6)	12.00	30.00
COMMON CARD (1-6)	3.00	8.00

1995 Star Wars Empire Strikes Back Widevision

COMPLETE SET (144)	12.00	30.00
UNOPENED BOX (36 PACKS)	30.00	40.00
UNOPENED PACK (9 CARDS)	1.00	1.25
COMMON CARD (1-144)	.25	.60

1995 Star Wars Empire Strikes Back Widevision Finest

COMPLETE SET (10)	40.00	100.00
COMMON CARD (C1-C10)	4.00	10.00
STATED ODDS 1:12		

1995 Star Wars Empire Strikes Back Widevision Mini Posters

COMPLETE SET (6)	40.00	80.00
COMMON CARD (1-6)	6.00	15.00
STATED ODDS 1:BOX		

1995 Star Wars Empire Strikes Back Widevision Promos

COMMON CARD	2.00	5.00
NNO 3-Card Sheet	5.00	12.00
P1-P3		

2010 Star Wars Empire Strikes Back 3-D Widevision

COMPLETE SET (48)	10.00	25.00
COMMON CARD (1-48)	.40	1.00
P1 Luke Skywalker PROMO	8.00	20.00

2010 Star Wars Empire Strikes Back 3-D Widevision Autographs

COMMON AUTO	125.00	250.00
STATED ODDS 1:1,055		
1 Irvin Kershner	500.00	1000.00
2 Ralph McQuarrie	300.00	500.00
4 David Prowse	250.00	400.00
6 Carrie Fisher	500.00	800.00
8 Mark Hamill	400.00	600.00

2010 Star Wars Empire Strikes Back 3-D Widevision Sketches

STATED ODDS 1:24 H, 1:72 R
UNPRICED DUE TO SCARCITY

NNO Adrian Rivera
NNO Alex Alderete
NNO Alex Buechel
NNO Beck Kramer
NNO Ben Curtis Jones
NNO Bill Pulkovski
NNO Braden Lamb
NNO Brandon Kenney
NNO Brent Engstrom
NNO Brian Ashmore
NNO Brian Rood
NNO Bruce Gerlach
NNO Bryan Morton
NNO Cal Slayton
NNO Carolyn Edwards
NNO Cassandra Siemon
NNO Cat Staggs
NNO Chris Eliopoulos
NNO Chris Henderson
NNO Chris Houghton
NNO Chris Uminga
NNO Clay McCormack
NNO Cynthia Cummens Narcisi
NNO Dan Bergren
NNO Dan Curto
NNO Dan Masso
NNO Darrin Radimaker
NNO David Day
NNO David Rabbitte
NNO Denise Vasquez
NNO Dennis Budd
NNO Erik Maell
NNO Gabe Farber
NNO Geoff Munn
NNO Hayden Davis
NNO Howard Shum
NNO Ingrid Hardy
NNO Irma Ahmed
NNO Jake Minor
NNO James Bukauskas
NNO Jamie Snell
NNO Jan Duursema
NNO Jason Davies
NNO Jason Hughes
NNO Jason Keith Phillips
NNO Jason Sobol
NNO Jeff Confer
NNO Jen Mercer
NNO Jeremy Treece
NNO Jerry Vanderstelt
NNO Jessica Hickman
NNO Jim Kyle
NNO Joe Corroney
NNO John Beatty
NNO John Haun
NNO John McCrea
NNO John P. Wales
NNO John Soukup

NNO Rich Molinelli
NNO Jon Morris
NNO Juan Carlos Ramos
NNO Karen Krajenbrink
NNO Katie Cook
NNO Katie McDee
NNO Kevin Doyle
NNO Kevin Graham
NNO Kevin Liell
NNO Lance Sawyer
NNO Lauren Perry
NNO Lawrence Snelly
NNO Leah Mangue
NNO Lee Kohse
NNO Lin Workman
NNO Lord Mesa
NNO Mark Dos Santos
NNO Mark McHaley
NNO Mark Raats
NNO Martheus Wade
NNO Matt Minor
NNO Matt Olson
NNO Michael Duron
NNO Monte Moore
NNO Nolan Woodard
NNO Randy Martinez
NNO Rhiannon Owens
NNO Rich Woodall
NNO Robert Hendrickson
NNO Robert Teranishi
NNO Ryan Hungerford
NNO Sarah Wilkinson
NNO Scott Daly
NNO Scott DM Simmons
NNO Scott Rorie
NNO Scott Zirkel
NNO Sean Pence
NNO Shea Standefer
NNO Shelli Paroline
NNO Soni Alcorn-Hender
NNO Spencer Brinkerhoff III
NNO Stephanie Yue
NNO Steve Oatney
NNO Steve Stanley
NNO Steven Miller
NNO Ted Dastick
NNO Tim Proctor
NNO Tod Allen Smith
NNO Tom Hodges
NNO Tomoko Taniguchi
NNO Zack Giallongo

1996 Star Wars Empire Strikes Back 3-Di

P1 AT-ATs	2.00	5.00

2019 Star Wars Empire Strikes Back Black and White

COMPLETE SET (150)	20.00	50.00
UNOPENED BOX (7 PACKS)	55.00	70.00
UNOPENED PACK (8 CARDS)	8.00	10.00
COMMON CARD (1-150)	.30	.75
*SEPIA: 1X TO 2.5X BASIC CARDS		
*BLUE HUE: 2.5X TO 6X BASIC CARDS		
*GREEN HUE/99: 4X TO 10X BASIC CARDS		
*PURPLE HUE/25: 6X TO 15X BASIC CARDS		
*RED HUE/10: UNPRICED DUE TO SCARCITY		
*ORANGE HUE/5: UNPRICED DUE TO SCARCITY		
*METAL/1: UNPRICED DUE TO SCARCITY		

2019 Star Wars Empire Strikes Back Black and White Autographs

*BLUE HUE/99: .5X TO 1.2X BASIC AUTOS
*GREEN HUE/25: .6X TO 1.5X BASIC AUTOS
*PURPLE HUE/10: UNPRICED DUE TO SCARCITY
*ORANGE HUE/5: UNPRICED DUE TO SCARCITY
*RED HUE/1: UNPRICED DUE TO SCARCITY
STATED ODDS 1:22

AAH Alan Harris	10.00	25.00
ACM Cathy Munro	8.00	20.00
ACP Chris Parsons	8.00	20.00
ACR Clive Revill	6.00	15.00
AHW Howie Weed	8.00	20.00
AJB Jeremy Bulloch	20.00	50.00

AJM	John Morton/Dak'	8.00	20.00
AJR	John Ratzenberger	15.00	40.00
AKC	Kenneth Colley	8.00	20.00
AMC	Mark Capri	6.00	15.00
AMJ	Milton Johns	10.00	25.00
ARO	Richard Oldfield	8.00	20.00
AJMB	John Morton/Boba Fett's Double	10.00	25.00

2019 Star Wars Empire Strikes Back Black and White Behind-the-Scenes

COMPLETE SET (40)	25.00	60.00
COMMON CARD (BTS1-BTS40)	1.25	3.00
STATED ODDS 1:2		

2019 Star Wars Empire Strikes Back Black and White Color Short-Printed Autographs

STATED ODDS 1:3,947

ACAD Anthony Daniels
ACCF Carrie Fisher
ACHF Harrison Ford
ACKB Kenny Baker
ACPM Peter Mayhew

2019 Star Wars Empire Strikes Back Black and White Concept Art

COMPLETE SET (10)	12.00	30.00
COMMON CARD (CA1-CA10)	2.00	5.00
STATED ODDS 1:4		

2019 Star Wars Empire Strikes Back Black and White Dual Autographs

STATED ODDS 1:525
UNPRICED DUE TO SCARCITY

DABD K.Baker/A.Daniels
DABH J.Bulloch/A.Harris
DAWM B.Williams/P.Mayhew
DAFF H.Ford/C.Fisher
DAHM A.Harris/C.Munroe
DALM D.Lawson/J.Morton
DALO D.Lawson/R.Oldfield
DAPM C.Parsons/C.Munroe

2019 Star Wars Empire Strikes Back Black and White Iconic Characters

| COMMON CARD (IC1-IC20) | 5.00 | 12.00 |
| STATED ODDS 1:12 | | |

2019 Star Wars Empire Strikes Back Black and White Posters

COMPLETE SET (10)	12.00	30.00
COMMON CARD (PO1-PO10)	2.00	5.00
STATED ODDS 1:6		

2019 Star Wars Empire Strikes Back Black and White Six-Person Autograph

STATED ODDS 1:74,984
STATED PRINT RUN 1 SER.#'d SET
UNPRICED DUE TO SCARCITY

NNO H.Ford/C.Fisher/B.Williams
A.Daniels/K.Baker/P.Mayhew

2019 Star Wars Empire Strikes Back Black and White Sketches

UNPRICED DUE TO SCARCITY

NNO Alex Mines
NNO Andrew Arensberg
NNO Andrew Fry
NNO Andrew Joynes
NNO Andrew Sanchez
NNO Andy Bohn
NNO Andy Duggan
NNO Angel Aviles
NNO Anil Sharma
NNO Anthony Figaro
NNO Anthony Skubis
NNO Ari Arnaldsson
NNO Ashlee Brienzo
NNO Ashley Marsh
NNO Atni Ellison
NNO Barry Renshaw
NNO Basak Cetinkaya
NNO Ben AbuSaada
NNO Bill Pulkovski
NNO Brad Hudson
NNO Brad Utterstrom
NNO Brendan Purchase
NNO Brent Ragland
NNO Brent Scotchmer
NNO Brian Axtell
NNO Brian Kong
NNO Bruce Gerlach
NNO Caleb Hildenbrandt
NNO Caleb King
NNO Can Baran
NNO Candice Dailey
NNO Carlos Cabaleiro
NNO Carolyn Craggs
NNO Chris Kay
NNO Chris Quinn
NNO Chris Thorne
NNO Colin Arthurs
NNO Cyrus Sherkat
NNO Dan Gorman
NNO Dan Tearle
NNO Darrin Pepe
NNO David Jackowski
NNO Dean Drummond
NNO Dylan Riley
NNO Eli Hyder
NNO Eric Lehtonen
NNO Eric Muller
NNO Francisco Rivera
NNO Frank Kadar
NNO Frank Sansone
NNO Fredd Gorham
NNO Gabe Farber
NNO Garrett Dix
NNO Gorkem Demir
NNO Huy Truong
NNO Ian MacDougall
NNO Ingrid Hardy
NNO Ivan Rodriguez
NNO James Henry Smith
NNO Jamie Cosley
NNO Jamie Richards
NNO Jason Miller
NNO Jason Queen
NNO Jay Manchand
NNO Jessica Hickman
NNO Jim Mehsling
NNO John Bruce
NNO John DiBiase
NNO John Pleak
NNO Jon McKenzie
NNO Jonathan Beistline
NNO Jose Ventura
NNO Josh Church
NNO Jude Gallagher
NNO Justin Castaneda
NNO Keith Farnum
NNO Kelly Baber
NNO Kevin Cleveland
NNO Kevin Liell

NNO Kevin P. West
NNO Laura Atkinson
NNO Laura Martin
NNO Lee Lightfoot
NNO Lindsey Greyling
NNO Lloyd Mills
NNO Logan Monette
NNO Louise Draper
NNO Madison Emerick
NNO Maggie Ransom
NNO Mai Irving
NNO Marcia Dye
NNO Marlo Agunos
NNO Marsha Parkins
NNO Matt Applegate
NNO Matt Maldonado
NNO Matt Stewart
NNO Matthew Hirons
NNO Matthew Lopez
NNO Matthew Sutton
NNO Michael Mastermaker
NNO Michael Sealie
NNO Michelle Rayner
NNO Mick and Matt Glebe
NNO Mohammad Jilani
NNO Nathan Ohlendorf
NNO Neil Camera
NNO Nicholas Baltra
NNO Nick Allsopp
NNO Nick Gribbon
NNO Nick Justus
NNO Omar Salinas
NNO Oscar Chavez
NNO Patricio Carrasco
NNO Paul Schiers
NNO Phil Hassewer
NNO Phillip Trujillo
NNO Rachel Brady
NNO Rebecca Sharp
NNO Rees Finlay
NNO Rich Henneman
NNO Richard Serrao
NNO Rob Teranishi
NNO Robert Hendrickson
NNO Rodney Roberts
NNO Ronnie Crowther
NNO Ryan Crosby
NNO Ryan Finley
NNO Ryan Olsen
NNO Ryan Santos
NNO Sammy Gomez
NNO Scott Harrell
NNO Seth Groves
NNO Shaow Siong
NNO Solly Mohamed
NNO Stephanie Swanger
NNO Steve Fuchs
NNO Thomas Amici
NNO Tim Proctor
NNO Tim Shinn
NNO Tony Poulson
NNO Travis Kinnison
NNO Trent Westbrook
NNO Veronica Smith
NNO Vincent D'Ippolito
NNO Ward Silverman
NNO Zach Woolsey

2019 Star Wars Empire Strikes Back Black and White Triple Autographs

STATED ODDS 1:728
UNPRICED DUE TO SCARCITY

TABMP J.Bulloch/C.Munroe/C.Parsons
TAFFW H.Ford/C.Fisher/B.Williams
TALMO D.Lawson/J.Morton/R.Oldfield
TAMBD P.Mayhew/K.Baker/A.Daniels
TAMPH C.Munroe/C.Parsons/A.Harris

2015 Star Wars Illustrated Empire Strikes Back

COMPLETE SET (100)	10.00	25.00
COMMON CARD (1-100)	.20	.50
*PURPLE: 5X TO 12X BASIC CARDS	2.50	6.00
*BRONZE: 8X TO 20X BASIC CARDS	4.00	10.00
*GOLD/10: 20X TO 50X BASIC CARDS	10.00	25.00
*P.P.BLACK/1: UNPRICED DUE TO SCARCITY		
*P.P.CYAN/1: UNPRICED DUE TO SCARCITY		
*P.P.MAGENTA/1: UNPRICED DUE TO SCARCITY		
*P.P.YELLOW/1: UNPRICED DUE TO SCARCITY		

2015 Star Wars Illustrated Empire Strikes Back
Celebration VII Promos

COMPLETE SET (10)	10.00	25.00
COMMON CARD (1-10)	1.50	4.00

2015 Star Wars Illustrated Empire Strikes Back
Artist Autographs

COMMON BUSCH (EVEN #'s)	5.00	12.00
COMMON MARTINEZ (ODD #'s)	5.00	12.00

2015 Star Wars Illustrated Empire Strikes Back
Film Cel Relics

COMPLETE SET (25)	100.00	200.00
COMMON CARD (SKIP #'d)	6.00	15.00
FR2 Back at Echo Base	8.00	20.00
FR3 Monster in the Snow	8.00	20.00
FR6 The Imperial Walkers	10.00	25.00
FR7 Luke Vs. the AT-AT	8.00	20.00
FR8 Imperial Pursuit	10.00	25.00
FR9 Asteroid Field	8.00	20.00
FR10 Dagobah Landing	8.00	20.00
FR13 Message From the Emperor	12.00	30.00
FR15 Bounty Hunters Assemble	8.00	20.00
FR16 Failure at the Cave	10.00	25.00
FR20 A Most Gracious Host	10.00	25.00
FR25 You Are not a Jedi Yet	10.00	25.00
FR26 Lando's Redemption	8.00	20.00
FR27 Battle in the Gantry	10.00	25.00
FR28 The Truth Revealed	8.00	20.00
FR29 Rescuing Luke	15.00	40.00
FR30 Saying Farewell	8.00	20.00

2015 Star Wars Illustrated Empire Strikes Back
Movie Poster Reinterpretations

COMPLETE SET (10)	8.00	20.00
COMMON CARD (MP1-MP10)	1.50	4.00
*P.P.BLACK/1: UNPRICED DUE TO SCARCITY		
*P.P.CYAN/1: UNPRICED DUE TO SCARCITY		
*P.P.MAGENTA/1: UNPRICED DUE TO SCARCITY		
*P.P.YELLOW/1: UNPRICED DUE TO SCARCITY		
STATED ODDS 1:3		

2015 Star Wars Illustrated Empire Strikes Back
One Year Earlier

COMPLETE SET (18)	15.00	40.00
COMMON CARD (OY1-OY18)	1.50	4.00
*P.P.BLACK/1: UNPRICED DUE TO SCARCITY		
*P.P.CYAN/1: UNPRICED DUE TO SCARCITY		
*P.P.MAGENTA/1: UNPRICED DUE TO SCARCITY		
*P.P.YELLOW/1: UNPRICED DUE TO SCARCITY		
STATED ODDS 1:2		

2015 Star Wars Illustrated Empire Strikes Back
Panorama Sketches

UNPRICED DUE TO SCARCITY

NNO Adrianna Vanderstelt
NNO Adrian Rivera
NNO Andrew "Drone" Cosson
NNO Andrew Jones
NNO Angelina Benedetti
NNO Art O'Callaghan
NNO Barush Merling
NNO Ben Dunn
NNO Bill Pulkovski
NNO Brandon Gallo
NNO Brent Raglund
NNO Brian K. O'Connell
NNO Bruce Gerlach
NNO Carla Rodriguez
NNO Carlos Cabaleiro
NNO Charles Hall
NNO Chris Eliopoulos
NNO Chris Henderson
NNO Chris West
NNO Dan Bergren
NNO Dan Curto
NNO Dan Gorman
NNO Dan Nokes
NNO Dan Smith
NNO Daniel Benitez, Arturo "JAR" Ramìrez
NNO Danny Haas
NNO Darrin Pepe
NNO David J. Williams
NNO David Rabbitte
NNO Denae Frazier
NNO Elfie Lebouleux
NNO Eric Bell
NNO Eric Lehtonen
NNO Eric McConnell
NNO Erik Hodson
NNO Erik Maell
NNO FLOSI
NNO Francois Chartier
NNO Ingrid Hardy
NNO Jared Hickman
NNO Jason Adams
NNO Jason Chalker
NNO Jason Crosby
NNO Jason Sobol
NNO Jeff Zapata
NNO Jeffrey "JSB" Benitez
NNO Jenn DePaola

NNO Jessica Hickman
NNO Joanne Ellen Patak
NNO Joe Corroney
NNO Joe Hogan
NNO Joel Carroll
NNO John Soukup
NNO Josh Bodwell
NNO Kaela Croft
NNO Kate Carleton
NNO Kevin Doyle
NNO Kimberly Dunaway
NNO Kris Penix
NNO Lak Lim
NNO Lee Kohse
NNO Lee Lightfoot
NNO Marck Labas
NNO Matt Busch
NNO Matt Hebb
NNO Michael "Locoduck" Duron
NNO Michael Leavitt
NNO Mick and Matt Glebe
NNO Mikey Babinsky
NNO Norvien Basio
NNO Pablo Diaz
NNO Pat Barrett
NNO Patrick Richardson
NNO Paul "Gutz" Gutierrez
NNO Peejay Catacutan
NNO Rhiannon Owens
NNO Rich Kunz
NNO Rich Molinelli
NNO Robert Jimenez
NNO Robert Teranishi
NNO Ron Conley
NNO Roy Cover
NNO Russ Maheras
NNO Sarah Wilkinson
NNO Scott Zambelli
NNO Sean Pence
NNO Sol Mohamed
NNO Stephanie Swanger
NNO Steve Black
NNO Steven Burch
NNO Tanner Padlo
NNO Thom "TG" Glinski
NNO Thom Zahler
NNO Tim Proctor
NNO Tom Kelly
NNO Tony Miello
NNO Veronica O'Connell

2015 Star Wars Illustrated Empire Strikes Back
Sketchagraphs

NNO Anthony Daniels
Adam Talley
NNO Anthony Daniels
Carlos Cabaleiro
NNO Anthony Daniels
Kevin Graham
NNO Anthony Daniels
Kris Penix
NNO Anthony Daniels
Mikey Babinski
NNO Billy Dee Williams
Andrew "Drone" Cosson
NNO Billy Dee Williams
Bill Pulkovski
NNO Billy Dee Williams
Carlos Cabaleiro
NNO Billy Dee Williams
Darrin Pepe
NNO Billy Dee Williams
Jason Crosby
NNO Billy Dee Williams
Jason Sobol
NNO Billy Dee Williams
Kevin Graham
NNO Billy Dee Williams
Kimberly Dunaway
NNO Billy Dee Williams
Kyle Babbitt
NNO Billy Dee Williams
Mikey Babinski

NNO Billy Dee Williams
Rich Molinelli
NNO Billy Dee Williams
Roy Cover
NNO David Ackroyd
Erik Maell
NNO David Ackroyd
Jason Crosby
NNO David Ackroyd
Wilson Ramos Jr.
NNO David Paymer
Erik Maell
NNO Jay O. Sanders
Bruce Gerlach
NNO Jay O. Sanders
Cal Sparrow
NNO Jay O. Sanders
Carlos Cabaleiro
NNO Jay O. Sanders
Dan Curto
NNO Jay O. Sanders
Eric Lehtonen
NNO Jay O. Sanders
Jason Crosby
NNO Jay O. Sanders
Jason Sobol
NNO Jay O. Sanders
Joe Hogan
NNO Jay O. Sanders
John Soukup
NNO Jay O. Sanders
Josh Bodwell
NNO Jay O. Sanders
Kevin Graham
NNO Jay O. Sanders
Kyle Babbitt
NNO Jay O. Sanders
Mikey Babinski
NNO Jay O. Sanders
Pat Barrett
NNO Jay O. Sanders
Roy Cover
NNO Jeremy Bulloch
Ben Dunn
NNO Jeremy Bulloch
Bill Pulkovski
NNO Jeremy Bulloch
Brandon Gallo
NNO Jeremy Bulloch
Carlos Cabaleiro
NNO Jeremy Bulloch
Dan Curto
NNO Jeremy Bulloch
Danny Haas
NNO Jeremy Bulloch
Eric Lehtonen
NNO Jeremy Bulloch
Jason Crosby
NNO Jeremy Bulloch
Jason Sobol
NNO Jeremy Bulloch
Joe Hogan
NNO Jeremy Bulloch
John Soukup
NNO Jeremy Bulloch
Kyle Babbitt
NNO Jeremy Bulloch
Mikey Babinski
NNO Jeremy Bulloch
Rich Molinelli
NNO Jeremy Bulloch
Roy Cover
NNO Paul Hecht
Andrew "Drone" Cosson
NNO Paul Hecht
Ashleigh Popplewell
NNO Paul Hecht
Bill Pulkovski
NNO Paul Hecht
Brandon Gallo
NNO Paul Hecht
Bruce Gerlach

NNO Paul Hecht
Carlos Cabaleiro
NNO Paul Hecht
Dan Curto
NNO Paul Hecht
Danny Haas
NNO Paul Hecht
Eric Lehtonen
NNO Paul Hecht
Jason Crosby
NNO Paul Hecht
John Soukup
NNO Paul Hecht
Josh Bodwell
NNO Paul Hecht
Kate Carleton
NNO Paul Hecht
Kevin Graham
NNO Paul Hecht
Kimberly Dunaway
NNO Paul Hecht
Kyle Babbitt
NNO Paul Hecht
Mikey Babinski
NNO Paul Hecht
Rich Molinelli
NNO Paul Hecht
Roy Cover
NNO Peter Friedman
Andrew "Drone" Cosson
NNO Peter Friedman
Ben Dunn
NNO Peter Friedman
Brandon Gallo
NNO Peter Friedman
Bruce Gerlach
NNO Peter Friedman
Cal Sparrow
NNO Peter Friedman
Carlos Cabaleiro
NNO Peter Friedman
Dan Curto
NNO Peter Friedman
Eric Lehtonen
NNO Peter Friedman
Jason Sobol
NNO Peter Friedman
Joe Hogan
NNO Peter Friedman
Kevin Graham
NNO Peter Friedman
Kimberly Dunaway
NNO Peter Friedman
Kyle Babbitt
NNO Peter Friedman
Mikey Babinski
NNO Peter Friedman
Pat Barrett
NNO Peter Friedman
Roy Cover
NNO Peter Mayhew
Adam Talley
NNO Peter Mayhew
Andrew "Drone" Cosson
NNO Peter Mayhew
Ben Dunn
NNO Peter Mayhew
Bill Pulkovski
NNO Peter Mayhew
Bruce Gerlach
NNO Peter Mayhew
Carlos Cabaleiro
NNO Peter Mayhew
Dan Gorman
NNO Peter Mayhew
Eric Lehtonen
NNO Peter Mayhew
Jason Crosby
NNO Peter Mayhew
Jason Sobol
NNO Peter Mayhew
John Soukup

NNO Peter Mayhew
Josh Bodwell
NNO Peter Mayhew
Kimberly Dunaway
NNO Peter Mayhew
Mikey Babinski
NNO Peter Michael Goetz
Andrew "Drone" Cosson
NNO Peter Michael Goetz
Ashleigh Popplewell
NNO Peter Michael Goetz
Ben Dunn
NNO Peter Michael Goetz
Bruce Gerlach
NNO Peter Michael Goetz
Cal Sparrow
NNO Peter Michael Goetz
Carlos Cabaleiro
NNO Peter Michael Goetz
Dan Curto
NNO Peter Michael Goetz
Darrin Pepe
NNO Peter Michael Goetz
Eric Lehtonen
NNO Peter Michael Goetz
Jason Sobol
NNO Peter Michael Goetz
Joe Hogan
NNO Peter Michael Goetz
John Soukup
NNO Peter Michael Goetz
Kate Carleton
NNO Peter Michael Goetz
Kevin Graham
NNO Peter Michael Goetz
Kimberly Dunaway
NNO Peter Michael Goetz
Mikey Babinski
NNO Peter Michael Goetz
Pat Barrett
NNO Peter Michael Goetz
Rich Molinelli
NNO Peter Michael Goetz
Roy Cover
NNO Sketchagraph Redemption Card

2015 Star Wars Illustrated Empire Strikes Back Sketches

UNPRICED DUE TO SCARCITY

NNO Adam Talley
NNO Adrianna Vanderstelt
NNO Adrian Rivera
NNO Andrew "Drone" Cosson
NNO Andrew Jones
NNO Angelina Benedetti
NNO Art O'Callaghan
NNO Ashleigh Popplewell
NNO Barush Merling
NNO Ben Dunn
NNO Bill Pulkovski
NNO Brandon Baselice
NNO Brandon Gallo
NNO Brent Raglund
NNO Brian DeGuire
NNO Brian K. O'Connell
NNO Bruce Gerlach
NNO Carla Rodriguez
NNO Carlos Cabaleiro
NNO Charles Hall
NNO Chris Eliopoulos
NNO Chris Henderson
NNO Chris West
NNO Dan Bergren
NNO Dan Curto
NNO Dan Gorman
NNO Dan Nokes
NNO Dan Smith
NNO Daniel Benitez, Arturo "JAR" Ramìrez
NNO Danny Haas
NNO Darrin Pepe
NNO David J. Williams
NNO David Rabbitte

NNO Denae Frazier
NNO Elfie Lebouleux
NNO Eric Bell
NNO Eric Lehtonen
NNO Eric McConnell
NNO Erik Hodson
NNO Erik Maell
NNO FLOSI
NNO Francois Chartier
NNO Ingrid Hardy
NNO Jared Hickman
NNO Jason Adams
NNO Jason Chalker
NNO Jason Crosby
NNO Jason Flowers
NNO Jason Sobol
NNO Jeff Zapata
NNO Jeffrey "JSB" Benitez
NNO Jenn DePaola
NNO Jessica Hickman
NNO Joanne Ellen Patak
NNO Joe Corroney
NNO Joe Hogan
NNO Joel Biske
NNO Joel Carroll
NNO John Soukup
NNO Josh Bodwell
NNO Kaela Croft
NNO Karen Hinson
NNO Kate Carleton
NNO Kevin Doyle
NNO Kevin Graham
NNO Kimberly Dunaway
NNO Kris Penix
NNO Lak Lim
NNO Lee Kohse
NNO Lee Lightfoot
NNO Marck Labas
NNO Matt Busch
NNO Matt Hebb
NNO Michael "Locoduck" Duron
NNO Michael Leavitt
NNO Mick and Matt Glebe
NNO Mikey Babinsky
NNO Norvien Basio
NNO Pablo Diaz
NNO Pat Barrett
NNO Patrick Giles
NNO Patrick Richardson
NNO Paul "Gutz" Gutierrez
NNO Peejay Catacutan
NNO Rhiannon Owens
NNO Rich Kunz
NNO Rich Molinelli
NNO Robert Jimenez
NNO Robert Teranishi
NNO Ron Conley
NNO Roy Cover
NNO Russ Maheras
NNO Sarah Wilkinson
NNO Scott Zambelli
NNO Sean Pence
NNO Sol Mohamed
NNO Stephanie Swanger
NNO Steve Black
NNO Steven Burch
NNO Tanner Padlo
NNO Thom "TG" Glinski
NNO Thom Zahler
NNO Tim Proctor
NNO Tod Allen Smith
NNO Tom Kelly
NNO Tony Miello
NNO Veronica O'Connell

2015 Star Wars Illustrated Empire Strikes Back The Force Awakens Inserts

COMPLETE SET (4)	20.00	50.00
COMMON CARD (SKIP #'d)	8.00	20.00

2015 Star Wars Illustrated Empire Strikes Back The Mission Capture Skywalker

COMPLETE SET (10)	12.00	30.00

COMMON CARD (1-10)	2.50	6.00
*P.P.BLACK/1: UNPRICED DUE TO SCARCITY		
*P.P.CYAN/1: UNPRICED DUE TO SCARCITY		
*P.P.MAGENTA/1: UNPRICED DUE TO SCARCITY		
*P.P.YELLOW/1: UNPRICED DUE TO SCARCITY		
STATED ODDS 1:8		
3 Han Solo	3.00	8.00
9 Boba Fett	4.00	10.00

2016 Star Wars Empire Strikes Back Bonus Abrams

1 Display Box, Series 1, 1980
2 Sticker No. 29, Series 1, 1980
3 Sticker No. 57, Series 2, 1980
4 Card No. 347, Series 3, 1980
NNO Darth Vader
(Star Wars Card Trader Promo)

RETURN OF THE JEDI

1983 Star Wars Return of the Jedi

A TOPPS PICTURE CARD SERIES

STAR WARS
RETURN OF THE JEDI
132 CARDS • 33 STICKERS
TM & © Lucasfilm Ltd. (LFL) 1983. All rights reserved. Topps Chewing Gum, Inc. Authorized User

COMPLETE SET W/STICKERS (275)	75.00	150.00
COMPLETE SET (220)	60.00	120.00
COMPLETE SERIES 1 SET W/STICKERS (165)		
COMPLETE SERIES 1 SET (132)	30.00	75.00
COMPLETE SERIES 2 SET W/STICKERS (110)		
COMPLETE SERIES 2 SET (88)	20.00	50.00
UNOPENED SERIES 1 BOX (36 PACKS)	200.00	400.00
UNOPENED SERIES 1 PACK (12 CARDS+1 STICKER)	8.00	12.00
UNOPENED SERIES 2 BOX (36 PACKS)	150.00	300.00
UNOPENED SERIES 2 PACK (12 CARDS+1 STICKER)	6.00	10.00
COMMON SERIES 1 CARD (1-132)	.50	1.25
COMMON SERIES 2 CARD (133-264)	.50	1.25

1983 Star Wars Return of the Jedi Stickers

COMPLETE SET W/VARIANTS (88)	50.00	100.00
COMPLETE SET W/O VARIANTS (55)	30.00	75.00
COMPLETE S1 SET A&B (66)	25.00	60.00
COMPLETE S1 SET (33)	8.00	20.00
COMPLETE S2 SET (22)	25.00	60.00
COMMON S1 PURPLE (1-11)	.40	1.00
COMMON S1 YELLOW (1-11)	.60	1.50
COMMON S1 RED (12-22)	.75	2.00
COMMON S1 TURQUOISE (12-22)	.40	1.00
COMMON S1 GREEN (23-33)	.60	1.50
COMMON S1 ORANGE (23-33)	.40	1.00
COMMON S2 (34-55)	1.50	4.00
STATED ODDS 1:1		

2014 Star Wars Return of the Jedi 3-D Widevision

COMPLETE SET (44)	12.00	30.00
COMMON CARD (1-44)	.50	1.25
TOPPS WEBSITE EXCLUSIVE SET		

2014 Star Wars Return of the Jedi 3-D Widevision Autographs

COMMON AUTO (UNNUMBERED)	10.00	25.00
STATED ODDS 1:SET		
NNO Carrie Fisher	600.00	1000.00
NNO Femi Taylor	15.00	40.00
NNO Jeremy Bulloch	50.00	100.00
NNO Kenneth Colley	15.00	40.00

NNO Mark Hamill	500.00	800.00
NNO Mike Quinn	20.00	50.00
NNO Peter Mayhew	75.00	150.00
NNO Tim Rose	20.00	50.00

2014 Star Wars Return of the Jedi 3-D Widevision Manufactured Patches

COMPLETE SET (4)	50.00	100.00
COMMON CARD	10.00	25.00
STATED ODDS ONE PATCH/SKETCH PER SET		

2014 Star Wars Return of the Jedi 3-D Widevision Sketch Card Relics

1 Ewok
2 Jabba's Sail Barge
3 Logray
4 Teebo
5 Wicket W. Warrick

2020 Star Wars Return of the Jedi Black and White

COMPLETE SET (133)	12.00	30.00
COMMON CARD (1-133)	.25	.60
*SEPIA: .5X TO 1.2X BASIC CARDS		
*BLUE: .75X TO 2X BASIC CARDS		
*GREEN/99: 2X TO 5X BASIC CARDS		
*PURPLE/25: 3X TO 8X BASIC CARDS		
*RED/10: UNPRICED DUE TO SCARCITY		
*ORANGE/5: UNPRICED DUE TO SCARCITY		
*METAL/1: UNPRICED DUE TO SCARCITY		

2020 Star Wars Return of the Jedi Black and White Autographs

COMMON AUTO	5.00	12.00
*GREEN/25: UNPRICED DUE TO SCARCITY		
*PURPLE/10: UNPRICED DUE TO SCARCITY		
*ORANGE/5: UNPRICED DUE TO SCARCITY		
*RED/1: UNPRICED DUE TO SCARCITY		
RANDOMLY INSERTED INTO PACKS		
ACB Caroline Blakiston	6.00	15.00
ADR Deep Roy	8.00	20.00
AFT Femi Taylor	6.00	15.00
AJB Jeremy Bulloch	15.00	40.00
AMC Michael Carter	6.00	15.00
APB Paul Brooke	6.00	15.00
ATR Tim Rose	6.00	15.00
ADBB Dickey Beer	10.00	25.00
AMQS Mike Quinn	6.00	15.00

2020 Star Wars Return of the Jedi Black and White Behind-the-Scenes

COMPLETE SET (24)	12.00	30.00
COMMON CARD (BTS1-BTS24)	1.00	2.50
RANDOMLY INSERTED INTO PACKS		

2020 Star Wars Return of the Jedi Black and White Concept Art

COMPLETE SET (19)	15.00	40.00
COMMON CARD (CA1-CA19)	1.25	3.00
RANDOMLY INSERTED INTO PACKS		

2020 Star Wars Return of the Jedi Black and White Dual Autographs

UNPRICED DUE TO SCARCITY
DABC C.Blakiston/D.Crowley
DACC K.Colley/D.Crowley
DADE W.Davis/M.Edmonds
DADP M.Dodson/T.Philpott
DAFF H.Ford/C.Fisher
DAMP I.McDiarmid/M.Pennington
DARB T.Rose/C.Blakiston
DAWM B.Williams/P.Mayhew
DAWR S.Williamson/D.Roy

2020 Star Wars Return of the Jedi Black and White Iconic Characters

COMPLETE SET (15)	12.00	30.00
COMMON CARD (IC1-IC15)	1.50	4.00
RANDOMLY INSERTED INTO PACKS		

2020 Star Wars Return of the Jedi Black and White Panoramic Sketches

UNPRICED DUE TO SCARCITY
NNO Adam Everett Beck
NNO Alex Iniguez

NNO Andy Bohn
NNO Andy Duggan
NNO Angel Aviles
NNO Anil Sharma
NNO Anthony Skubis
NNO Anthony Ellison
NNO Ashlee Brienzo
NNO Ashley Marsh
NNO Barry Renshaw
NNO Basak Cetinkaya
NNO Ben AbuSaada
NNO Brad Hudson
NNO Brent Scotchmer
NNO Brett Farr
NNO Bruce Gerlach
NNO Caleb Hildenbrandt
NNO Caleb King
NNO Carlos Cabaleiro
NNO Carolyn Craggs
NNO Chris Kay
NNO Chris Quinn
NNO Cisco Rivera
NNO Colin Arthurs
NNO Corey Galal
NNO Dan Tearle
NNO Darrin Pepe
NNO David Jackowski
NNO Dean Drummond
NNO Dylan Riley
NNO Eric Lehtonen
NNO Frank Kadar
NNO Frank Sansone
NNO Gabe Farber
NNO Garrett Dix
NNO George Joseph
NNO Huy Truong
NNO Ian MacDougall
NNO Ingrid Hardy
NNO Jamie Cosley
NNO Jamie Richards
NNO Jason Davies
NNO Jason Queen
NNO Jason Sobol
NNO Jessica Hickman
NNO Jim Mehsling
NNO John Bruce
NNO John DiBiase
NNO John Pleak
NNO Jonathan Beistline
NNO Jose Ventura
NNO Josh Church
NNO Jude Gallagher
NNO Justin Castaneda
NNO Kaela Croft
NNO Keith Farnum
NNO Kelly Baber
NNO Kevin Cleveland
NNO Laura Atkinson
NNO Lindsey Greyling
NNO Logan Monette
NNO Louise Draper
NNO Mai Irving
NNO Marcia Dye
NNO Marsha Parkins
NNO Matt Langford
NNO Matt Stewart
NNO Matthew Hirons
NNO Michael Mastermaker
NNO Michael Sealie
NNO Michelle Rayner
NNO Mick and Matt Glebe
NNO Mohammad Jilani
NNO Neil Camera
NNO Nicholas Baltra
NNO Nick Allsopp
NNO Nick Gribbon
NNO Omar Salinas
NNO Patricio Carrasco
NNO Rebecca Sharp
NNO Rees Finlay
NNO Rey Paez
NNO Rich Hennemann

NNO Rich Molinelli
NNO Richard Serrao
NNO Rob Teranishi
NNO Robert Hendrickson
NNO Rodney Roberts
NNO Ryan Crosby
NNO Ryan Finley
NNO Ryan Olsen
NNO Ryan Santos
NNO Sammy Gomez
NNO Shaow Siong
NNO Solly Mohamed
NNO Steve Fuchs
NNO Ted Dastick Jr.
NNO Thomas Amici
NNO Tim Dowler
NNO Tim Shinn
NNO Trent Westbrook
NNO Veronica Smith
NNO Vincenzo D'Ippolito
NNO Ward Silverman
NNO Zach Woolsey

2020 Star Wars Return of the Jedi Black and White Posters

COMPLETE SET (6)	5.00	12.00
COMMON CARD (P1-P6)	1.00	2.50
RANDOMLY INSERTED INTO PACKS		

2020 Star Wars Return of the Jedi Black and White Shaped Sketches

UNPRICED DUE TO SCARCITY

NNO Adam Everett Beck
NNO Alex Iniguez
NNO Andy Bohn
NNO Andy Duggan
NNO Angel Aviles
NNO Anil Sharma
NNO Anthony Skubis
NNO Anthony Ellison
NNO Ashlee Brienzo
NNO Ashley Marsh
NNO Barry Renshaw
NNO Basak Cetinkaya
NNO Ben AbuSaada
NNO Brad Hudson
NNO Brent Scotchmer
NNO Brett Farr
NNO Bruce Gerlach
NNO Caleb Hildenbrandt
NNO Caleb King
NNO Carlos Cabaleiro
NNO Carolyn Craggs
NNO Chris Kay
NNO Chris Quinn
NNO Cisco Rivera
NNO Colin Arthurs
NNO Corey Galal
NNO Dan Tearle
NNO Darrin Pepe
NNO David Jackowski
NNO Dean Drummond
NNO Dylan Riley
NNO Eric Lehtonen
NNO Frank Kadar
NNO Frank Sansone
NNO Gabe Farber
NNO Garrett Dix
NNO George Joseph
NNO Huy Truong
NNO Ian MacDougall
NNO Ingrid Hardy
NNO Jamie Cosley
NNO Jamie Richards
NNO Jason Davies
NNO Jason Queen
NNO Jason Sobol
NNO Jessica Hickman
NNO Jim Mehsling
NNO John Bruce
NNO John DiBiase
NNO John Pleak
NNO Jonathan Beistline

NNO Jose Ventura
NNO Josh Church
NNO Jude Gallagher
NNO Justin Castaneda
NNO Kaela Croft
NNO Keith Farnum
NNO Kelly Baber
NNO Kevin Cleveland
NNO Laura Atkinson
NNO Lindsey Greyling
NNO Logan Monette
NNO Louise Draper
NNO Mai Irving
NNO Marcia Dye
NNO Marsha Parkins
NNO Matt Langford
NNO Matt Stewart
NNO Matthew Hirons
NNO Michael Mastermaker
NNO Michael Sealie
NNO Michelle Rayner
NNO Mick and Matt Glebe
NNO Mohammad Jilani
NNO Neil Camera
NNO Nicholas Baltra
NNO Nick Allsopp
NNO Nick Gribbon
NNO Omar Salinas
NNO Patricio Carrasco
NNO Rebecca Sharp
NNO Rees Finlay
NNO Rey Paez
NNO Rich Hennemann
NNO Rich Molinelli
NNO Richard Serrao
NNO Rob Teranishi
NNO Robert Hendrickson
NNO Rodney Roberts
NNO Ryan Crosby
NNO Ryan Finley
NNO Ryan Olsen
NNO Ryan Santos
NNO Sammy Gomez
NNO Shaow Siong
NNO Solly Mohamed
NNO Steve Fuchs
NNO Ted Dastick Jr.
NNO Thomas Amici
NNO Tim Dowler
NNO Tim Shinn
NNO Trent Westbrook
NNO Veronica Smith
NNO Vincenzo D'Ippolito
NNO Ward Silverman
NNO Zach Woolsey

2020 Star Wars Return of the Jedi Black and White Six-Person Autograph

NNO Ford/Fisher/Williams/Daniels/Baker/Mayhew

2020 Star Wars Return of the Jedi Black and White Sketches

UNPRICED DUE TO SCARCITY

NNO Adam Everett Beck
NNO Alex Iniguez
NNO Andy Bohn
NNO Andy Duggan
NNO Angel Aviles
NNO Anil Sharma
NNO Anthony Skubis
NNO Anthony Ellison
NNO Ashlee Brienzo
NNO Ashley Marsh
NNO Barry Renshaw
NNO Basak Cetinkaya
NNO Ben AbuSaada
NNO Brad Hudson
NNO Brent Scotchmer
NNO Brett Farr
NNO Bruce Gerlach
NNO Caleb Hildenbrandt
NNO Caleb King
NNO Carlos Cabaleiro

NNO Carolyn Craggs
NNO Chris Kay
NNO Chris Quinn
NNO Cisco Rivera
NNO Colin Arthurs
NNO Corey Galal
NNO Dan Tearle
NNO Darrin Pepe
NNO David Jackowski
NNO Dean Drummond
NNO Dylan Riley
NNO Eric Lehtonen
NNO Frank Kadar
NNO Frank Sansone
NNO Gabe Farber
NNO Garrett Dix
NNO George Joseph
NNO Huy Truong
NNO Ian MacDougall
NNO Ingrid Hardy
NNO Jamie Cosley
NNO Jamie Richards
NNO Jason Davies
NNO Jason Queen
NNO Jason Sobol
NNO Jessica Hickman
NNO Jim Mehsling
NNO John Bruce
NNO John DiBiase
NNO John Pleak
NNO Jonathan Beistline
NNO Jose Ventura
NNO Josh Church
NNO Jude Gallagher
NNO Justin Castaneda
NNO Kaela Croft
NNO Keith Farnum
NNO Kelly Baber
NNO Kevin Cleveland
NNO Laura Atkinson
NNO Lindsey Greyling
NNO Logan Monette
NNO Louise Draper
NNO Mai Irving
NNO Marcia Dye
NNO Marsha Parkins
NNO Matt Langford
NNO Matt Stewart
NNO Matthew Hirons
NNO Michael Mastermaker
NNO Michael Sealie
NNO Michelle Rayner
NNO Mick and Matt Glebe
NNO Mohammad Jilani
NNO Neil Camera
NNO Nicholas Baltra
NNO Nick Allsopp
NNO Nick Gribbon
NNO Omar Salinas
NNO Patricio Carrasco
NNO Rebecca Sharp
NNO Rees Finlay
NNO Rey Paez
NNO Rich Hennemann
NNO Rich Molinelli
NNO Richard Serrao
NNO Rob Teranishi
NNO Robert Hendrickson
NNO Rodney Roberts
NNO Ryan Crosby
NNO Ryan Finley
NNO Ryan Olsen
NNO Ryan Santos
NNO Sammy Gomez
NNO Shaow Siong
NNO Solly Mohamed
NNO Steve Fuchs
NNO Ted Dastick Jr.
NNO Thomas Amici
NNO Tim Dowler
NNO Tim Shinn
NNO Trent Westbrook

NNO Veronica Smith
NNO Vincenzo D'Ippolito
NNO Ward Silverman
NNO Zach Woolsey

2020 Star Wars Return of the Jedi Black and White Triple Autographs

UNPRICED DUE TO SCARCITY

NNO Williams/Rotich/Lawson
NNO Blakiston/Crowley/Rose
NNO Ford/Fishe /Williams
NNO Mayhew/Baker/Daniels
NNO Philpott/Carter/Taylor

2020 Star Wars Return of the Jedi Black and White Triptych Sketches

UNPRICED DUE TO SCARCITY

NNO Adam Everett Beck
NNO Alex Iniguez
NNO Andy Bohn
NNO Andy Duggan
NNO Angel Aviles
NNO Anil Sharma
NNO Anthony Skubis
NNO Anthony Ellison
NNO Ashlee Brienzo
NNO Ashley Marsh
NNO Barry Renshaw
NNO Basak Cetinkaya
NNO Ben AbuSaada
NNO Brad Hudson
NNO Brent Scotchmer
NNO Brett Farr
NNO Bruce Gerlach
NNO Caleb Hildenbrandt
NNO Caleb King
NNO Carlos Cabaleiro
NNO Carolyn Craggs
NNO Chris Kay
NNO Chris Quinn
NNO Cisco Rivera
NNO Colin Arthurs
NNO Corey Galal
NNO Dan Tearle
NNO Darrin Pepe
NNO David Jackowski
NNO Dean Drummond
NNO Dylan Riley
NNO Eric Lehtonen
NNO Frank Kadar
NNO Frank Sansone
NNO Gabe Farber
NNO Garrett Dix
NNO George Joseph
NNO Huy Truong
NNO Ian MacDougall
NNO Ingrid Hardy
NNO Jamie Cosley
NNO Jamie Richards
NNO Jason Davies
NNO Jason Queen
NNO Jason Sobol
NNO Jessica Hickman
NNO Jim Mehsling
NNO John Bruce
NNO John DiBiase
NNO John Pleak
NNO Jonathan Beistline
NNO Jose Ventura
NNO Josh Church
NNO Jude Gallagher
NNO Justin Castaneda
NNO Kaela Croft
NNO Keith Farnum
NNO Kelly Baber
NNO Kevin Cleveland
NNO Laura Atkinson
NNO Lindsey Greyling
NNO Logan Monette
NNO Louise Draper
NNO Mai Irving
NNO Marcia Dye
NNO Marsha Parkins

NNO Matt Langford
NNO Matt Stewart
NNO Matthew Hirons
NNO Michael Mastermaker
NNO Michael Sealie
NNO Michelle Rayner
NNO Mick and Matt Glebe
NNO Mohammad Jilani
NNO Neil Camera
NNO Nicholas Baltra
NNO Nick Allsopp
NNO Nick Gribbon
NNO Omar Salinas
NNO Patricio Carrasco
NNO Rebecca Sharp
NNO Rees Finlay
NNO Rey Paez
NNO Rich Hennemann
NNO Rich Molinelli
NNO Richard Serrao
NNO Rob Teranishi
NNO Robert Hendrickson
NNO Rodney Roberts
NNO Ryan Crosby
NNO Ryan Finley
NNO Ryan Olsen
NNO Ryan Santos
NNO Sammy Gomez
NNO Shaow Siong
NNO Solly Mohamed
NNO Steve Fuchs
NNO Ted Dastick Jr.
NNO Thomas Amici
NNO Tim Dowler
NNO Tim Shinn
NNO Trent Westbrook
NNO Veronica Smith
NNO Vincenzo D'Ippolito
NNO Ward Silverman
NNO Zach Woolsey

2016 Star Wars Return of the Jedi Bonus Abrams

1 Display Box, Series 1, 1983
2 Card No. 1, Series 1, 1983
Art By Drew Struzan
3 Card No. 133, Series 2, 1983
Art By Tim Reamer
4 Sticker No. 49, Series 2, 1983

1983 Star Wars Return of the Jedi Kellogg's Stick'R Series

COMPLETE SET (10)	12.00	30.00
COMMON CARD (1-10)	2.00	5.00

1983 Star Wars Return of the Jedi OPC

COMPLETE SET (132)	25.00	60.00
UNOPENED BOX (36 PACKS)	125.00	150.00
UNOPENED PACK	4.00	5.00
COMMON CARD (1-132)	.30	.75

1997 Star Wars Return of the Jedi Special Edition

NNO Crescent City Con XII

1996 Star Wars Return of the Jedi Widevision

INT. COCKPIT — MILLENNIUM FALCON

COMPLETE SET (144)	10.00	25.00
UNOPENED BOX (24 PACKS)	50.00	60.00
UNOPENED PACK (9 CARDS)	1.50	2.00
COMMON CARD (1-144)	.20	.50

DIII Admiral Akbar

1996 Star Wars Return of the Jedi Widevision Finest

COMPLETE SET (10)	40.00	80.00
COMMON CARD (C1-C10)	4.00	10.00
STATED ODDS 1:12		

1996 Star Wars Return of the Jedi Widevision Mini Posters

COMPLETE SET (6)	40.00	80.00
COMMON CARD (1-6)	6.00	15.00
STATED ODDS 1:BOX		

1996 Star Wars Return of the Jedi Widevision Promos

COMMON CARD	2.00	5.00
P6 Luke, Han, & Chewbacca in Jabba's Palace	25.00	60.00
NNO 1-Card Sheet		
Complete the Trilogy		

THE PHANTOM MENACE

1999 Star Wars Episode One Widevision Series One

COMPLETE SET (80)	8.00	20.00
UNOPENED HOBBY BOX (36 PACKS)	45.00	60.00
UNOPENED HOBBY PACK (8 CARDS)	1.50	2.00
UNOPENED RETAIL BOX (11 PACKS)	30.00	45.00
UNOPENED RETAIL PACK (8 CARDS)	2.75	4.00
COMMON CARD (1-80)	.25	.60

1999 Star Wars Episode One Widevision Series One Chrome

COMPLETE SET (8)	30.00	60.00
COMMON CARD (C1-C8)	4.00	10.00
STATED ODDS 1:12		

1999 Star Wars Episode One Widevision Series One Expansion

COMPLETE SET (40)	30.00	60.00
COMMON CARD (X1-X40)	1.00	2.50
STATED ODDS 1:2		

1999 Star Wars Episode One Widevision Series One Foil

COMPLETE SET (10)	30.00	60.00
COMMON CARD (F1-F10)	3.00	8.00

1999 Star Wars Episode One Widevision Series One Stickers

COMPLETE SET (16)	8.00	20.00
COMMON CARD (S1-S16)	.60	1.50

1999 Star Wars Episode One Widevision Series One Tin Inserts

COMPLETE SET (5)	12.00	30.00
COMMON CARD (1-5)	4.00	10.00
STATED ODDS ONE PER RETAIL TIN		
2 Darth Maul	5.00	12.00

1999 Star Wars Episode One Widevision Series Two

COMPLETE SET (80)	8.00	20.00
UNOPENED HOBBY BOX (36 PACKS)	40.00	50.00
UNOPENED HOBBY PACK (8 CARDS)	1.25	1.50
UNOPENED RETAIL BOX (24 PACKS)	35.00	45.00
UNOPENED RETAIL PACK (8 CARDS)	1.50	1.75
COMMON CARD (1-80)	.25	.60

1999 Star Wars Episode One Widevision Series Two Box-Toppers

COMPLETE SET (3)	10.00	20.00
COMMON CARD (1-3)	4.00	10.00
STATED ODDS 1:HOBBY BOX		

1999 Star Wars Episode One Widevision Series Two Chrome Hobby

COMPLETE SET (4)	12.00	25.00
COMMON CARD (HC1-HC4)	4.00	10.00
STATED ODDS 1:18 HOBBY		

1999 Star Wars Episode One Widevision Series Two Chrome Retail

COMPLETE SET (4)	20.00	40.00
COMMON CARD (C1-C4)	6.00	15.00
STATED ODDS 1:18 RETAIL		

1999 Star Wars Episode One Widevision Series Two Embossed Hobby

COMPLETE SET (6)	8.00	20.00
COMMON CARD (HE1-HE6)	2.50	6.00
STATED ODDS 1:12 HOBBY		

1999 Star Wars Episode One Widevision Series Two Embossed Retail

COMPLETE SET (6)	20.00	40.00
COMMON CARD (E1-E6)	4.00	10.00
STATED ODDS 1:12 RETAIL		

1999 Star Wars Episode One Widevision Series Two Promos

COMPLETE SET (2)	3.00	8.00
COMMON CARD (P1-P2)	2.00	5.00

2000 Star Wars Episode One 3-D

COMPLETE SET (46)	20.00	40.00
UNOPENED BOX (36 PACKS)	45.00	60.00
UNOPENED PACK (2 CARDS)	1.50	2.00
COMMON CARD (1-46)	.50	1.25

2000 Star Wars Episode One 3-D Multi-Motion

COMPLETE SET (2)	10.00	25.00
COMMON CARD (1-2)	6.00	15.00

1999 Star Wars Episode I Bluebird Potato Chips New Zealand

COMPLETE SET (30)	10.00	25.00
COMMON CARD (1-30)	.60	1.50

1999 Star Wars Episode I Family Toy

COMPLETE SET (3)	8.00	20.00
COMMON CARD	4.00	10.00

1999 Star Wars Episode I Flip Images

COMPLETE SET (6)	5.00	12.00
COMMON CARD	1.25	3.00
UNNUMBERED SET		

1999 Star Wars Episode I Hallmark

H1 Anakin Skywalker and Obi-Wan Kenobi	2.00	5.00
H2 Obi-Wan Kenobi and Yoda	2.00	5.00
H3 Qui-Gon Jinn and Obi-Wan Kenobi	2.00	5.00

1999 Star Wars Episode I iKon

01. Padmé

COMPLETE SET (60)	6.00	15.00
UNOPENED BOX (36 PACKS)		
UNOPENED PACK (6 CARDS)		
COMMON CARD (1-60)	.20	.50
*SILVER: 1.5X TO 4X BASIC CARDS		
*GOLD: 2.5X TO 6X BASIC CARDS		

1999 Star Wars Episode I KFC Australia

COMPLETE SET (10)	3.00	8.00
COMMON CARD (1-10)	.50	1.25

1999 Star Wars Episode I KFC UK

COMPLETE SET (20)	8.00	20.00
COMMON CARD (1-20)	.60	1.50
STATED ODDS 1:		

1999 Star Wars Episode I Lay's Minis

COMPLETE SET (12)	6.00	15.00
COMMON CARD (1-12)	.75	2.00

1999 Star Wars Episode I Pepsi Collector Can Contest Cards

1 Anakin Skywalker
2 Sebulba
3 Qui-Gon Jinn
4 Watto
5 Jabba the Hutt
6 Senator Palpatine
7 R2-D2
8 Darth Sidious
9 Darth Maul
10 Jar Jar Binks
11 Mace Windu
12 Obi-Wan Kenobi
13 Captain Panaka
14 Rune Haako
15 Ric Olie
16 Destroyer Droid
17 Queen Amidala
18 Padme
19 Shmi Skywalker
20 Battle Droid
21 Chancellor Valorum
22 C-3PO
23 Nute Gunray
24 Boss Nass

1999 Star Wars Episode I The Phantom Menace Harmony Foods

COMPLETE SET (24)	50.00	100.00
COMMON CARD (1-24)	2.00	5.00

1999 Star Wars Episode I The Phantom Menace Kentucky Fried Chicken Employee Stickers

COMPLETE SET (5)	6.00	15.00
COMMON CARD (UNNUMBERED)	2.00	5.00

1999 Star Wars Episode I The Phantom Menace Show Promo

NNO DLP Exclusive Presentation	5.00	12.00

2001 Star Wars Episode I The Phantom Menace Walmart DVD Promos

COMPLETE SET (4)	3.00	8.00
COMMON CARD	1.25	3.00

1999 Star Wars Episode I Star Mart

NNO Anakin Skywalker	2.00	5.00
NNO C-3PO	2.00	5.00
NNO Darth Maul	2.00	5.00
NNO R2-D2	2.00	5.00

2019 Star Wars On-Demand Phantom Menace 20th Anniversary

COMPLETE SET (25)	8.00	20.00
COMMON CARD (1-25	.60	1.50
*SILVER: 1.2X TO 3X BASIC CARDS		
*BLUE/10: UNPRICED DUE TO SCARCITY		
*PURPLE/5: UNPRICED DUE TO SCARCITY		
*GOLD/1: UNPRICED DUE TO SCARCITY		

2019 Star Wars On-Demand Phantom Menace 20th Anniversary Autographs

COMMON AUTO	6.00	15.00
*BLUE/10: UNPRICED DUE TO SCARCITY		
*PURPLE/5: UNPRICED DUE TO SCARCITY		
*GOLD/1: UNPRICED DUE TO SCARCITY		
STATED OVERALL ODDS 1:SET		
1 Ian McDiarmid		
2 Samuel L. Jackson		
3 Ray Park	30.00	75.00
5 Anthony Daniels		
6 Kenny Baker	75.00	150.00

2019 Star Wars On-Demand Phantom Menace 20th Anniversary Dual Autographs

UNPRICED DUE TO SCARCITY

1 Ian McDiarmid/Samuel L. Jackson
2 Ian McDiarmid/Ray Park
3 Anthony Daniels/Kenny Baker
4 Silas Carson/Jerome Blake

2019 Star Wars On-Demand Phantom Menace 20th Anniversary Jedi Council

COMPLETE SET (12)	150.00	300.00
COMMON CARD (1-12)	10.00	25.00
STATED ODDS 1:2		

ATTACK OF THE CLONES

2002 Star Wars Attack of the Clones

ANAKIN SKYWALKER

COMPLETE SET (100)	5.00	12.00
UNOPENED BOX (36 PACKS)	45.00	60.00
UNOPENED PACK (7 CARDS)	1.50	2.00
COMMON CARD (1-100)	.15	.40

2002 Star Wars Attack of the Clones Foil

COMPLETE SET (10)	6.00	15.00
COMMON CARD (1-10)	.75	2.00

2002 Star Wars Attack of the Clones Panoramic Fold-Outs

COMPLETE SET (5)	12.00	30.00
COMMON CARD (1-5)	3.00	8.00
STATED ODDS 1:12		

2002 Star Wars Attack of the Clones Prisms

COMPLETE SET (8)	8.00	20.00
COMMON CARD (1-8)	1.25	3.00

2002 Star Wars Attack of the Clones Promos

COMMON CARD	1.25	3.00
B1 UK Distribution	2.50	6.00
(Album Exclusive)		

P4 Star Wars Insider/Star Wars Gamer Exclusive	3.00	8.00
P6 Star Wars Celebration II Exclusive	3.00	8.00
NNO Best Buy Soundtrack Exclusive	3.00	8.00

2002 Star Wars Attack of the Clones Widevision

COMPLETE SET (80)	5.00	12.00
COMMON CARD (1-80)	.15	.40

2002 Star Wars Attack of the Clones Widevision Autographs

COMPLETE SET (24)		
COMMON AUTO (UNNUMBERED)	10.00	25.00
STATED ODDS 1:24		
NNO Ahmed Best	50.00	100.00
NNO Alethea McGrath	20.00	50.00
NNO Amy Allen	15.00	40.00
NNO Andrew Secombe	15.00	40.00
NNO Ayesha Dharker	20.00	50.00
NNO Bodie Taylor	15.00	40.00
NNO Bonnie Piesse	60.00	120.00
NNO Daniel Logan	25.00	60.00
NNO David Bowers	15.00	40.00
NNO Frank Oz	800.00	1500.00
NNO Jay Laga'aia	25.00	60.00
NNO Joel Edgerton	60.00	120.00
NNO Kenny Baker	150.00	300.00
NNO Leeanna Walsman	15.00	40.00
NNO Mary Oyaya	20.00	50.00
NNO Matt Doran	15.00	40.00
NNO Nalini Krishan	15.00	40.00
NNO Rena Owen	15.00	40.00
NNO Ronald Falk	50.00	100.00
NNO Silas Carson/Ki-Adi-Mundi	60.00	120.00
NNO Silas Carson/Nute Gunray	60.00	120.00

2002 Star Wars Attack of the Clones Widevision Promos

P1 Spider Droid	.60	1.50
(Non-Sport Update Exclusive)		
S1 Spider Droid		
(UK Exclusive)		

2002 Star Wars Attack of the Clones Widevision DVD Promos

COMPLETE SET (5)	3.00	8.00
COMMON CARD (W1-W5)	1.00	2.50

2016 Star Wars Attack of the Clones 3-D Widevision

MEETING WITH THE CHANCELLOR

COMPLETE SET (44)	12.00	30.00
COMMON CARD (1-44)	.50	1.25

2016 Star Wars Attack of the Clones 3-D Widevision Autographs

COMMON AUTO	12.00	30.00
*SILVER/25: UNPRICED DUE TO SCARCITY		
*GOLD/10: UNPRICED DUE TO SCARCITY		
*RED/1: UNPRICED DUE TO SCARCITY		
STATED ODDS 1:SET		
NNO Alan Ruscoe	15.00	40.00
NNO Amy Allen	12.00	30.00
NNO Daniel Logan	15.00	40.00
NNO Jesse Jensen	15.00	40.00
NNO Jett Lucas	15.00	40.00
NNO Kenny Baker	80.00	150.00

NNO Matthew Wood	25.00	60.00
Magaloof		
NNO Oliver Ford	15.00	40.00

2016 Star Wars Attack of the Clones 3-D Widevision Dual Autographs

1 Allen/Krishan
2 Jensen/Shapi
3 Carson/Jensen

2016 Star Wars Attack of the Clones 3-D Widevision Medallions

COMPLETE SET (10)	175.00	350.00
COMMON CARD (MC1-MC10)	15.00	40.00
*SILVER/25: X TO X BASIC CARDS		
*GOLD/10: X TO X BASIC CARDS		
*RED/1: UNPRICED DUE TO SCARCITY		
STATED ODDS PATCH OR MEDALLION 1:1		

2016 Star Wars Attack of the Clones 3-D Widevision Patches

COMPLETE SET (12)	200.00	350.00
COMMON CARD (MP1-MP12)	15.00	40.00
*SILVER/25: X TO X BASIC CARDS		
*GOLD/10: X TO X BASIC CARDS		
*RED/1: UNPRICED DUE TO SCARCITY		
STATED ODDS PATCH OR MEDALLION 1:1		

2002 Star Wars Episode II Instant Win

COMPLETE SET (5)	5.00	12.00
COMMON CARD (UNNUMBERED)	1.50	4.00

2002 Star Wars Episode II Jedi Fruit Rolls

COMPLETE SET (6)	5.00	12.00
UNNUMBERED SET		
1 Luke vs. Darth Vader	3.00	8.00
2 Luke vs. Darth Vader	3.00	8.00
3 Obi-Wan vs. Count Dooku	.75	2.00
4 Obi-Wan vs. Darth Vader	2.00	5.00
5 Obi-Wan vs. Jango Fett	.75	2.00
6 Qui-Gon Jinn vs. Darth Maul	1.25	3.00

REVENGE OF THE SITH

2005 Star Wars Revenge of the Sith

MACE VS. PALPATINE

COMPLETE SET (90)	5.00	12.00
UNOPENED HOBBY BOX (36 PACKS)	65.00	80.00
UNOPENED HOBBY PACK (7 CARDS)	2.00	2.50
UNOPENED RETAIL BOX (24 PACKS)	30.00	40.00
UNOPENED RETAIL PACK (7 CARDS)	1.50	1.75
COMMON CARD (1-90)	.15	.40

2005 Star Wars Revenge of the Sith Blister Bonus

COMPLETE SET (3)	6.00	15.00
COMMON CARD (B1-B3)	2.50	6.00
STATED ODDS ONE PER BLISTER PACK		

2005 Star Wars Revenge of the Sith Embossed Foil

COMPLETE SET (10)	20.00	50.00
COMMON CARD (1-10)	2.50	6.00
STATED ODDS 1:6 RETAIL		

2005 Star Wars Revenge of the Sith Etched Foil Puzzle

COMPLETE SET (6)	12.00	30.00
COMMON CARD (1-6)	2.50	6.00
STATED ODDS 1:6		

2005 Star Wars Revenge of the Sith Flix-Pix

COMPLETE SET (68)	50.00	100.00
UNOPENED BOX (36 PACKS)	100.00	150.00
UNOPENED PACK	3.00	5.00

COMMON CARD (1-68)	1.00	2.50
CL (TRI-FOLD INSERT)	.40	1.00

2005 Star Wars Revenge of the Sith Holograms
COMPLETE SET (3)	5.00	12.00
COMMON CARD (1-3)	2.00	5.00
STATED ODDS 1:14 RETAIL		

2005 Star Wars Revenge of the Sith Lenticular Morph Hobby
COMPLETE SET (2)	5.00	12.00
COMMON CARD (1-2)	3.00	8.00
STATED ODDS 1:24 HOBBY		

2005 Star Wars Revenge of the Sith Lenticular Morph Retail
COMPLETE SET (2)	5.00	12.00
COMMON CARD (1-2)	3.00	8.00
STATED ODDS 1:24 RETAIL		

2005 Star Wars Revenge of the Sith Sketches
COMPLETE ARTIST LIST (41)
STATED ODDS 1:36
GROUP A ODDS 1:777
GROUP B ODDS 1:357
GROUP C ODDS 1:493
GROUP D ODDS 1:863
GROUP E ODDS 1:194
GROUP F ODDS 1:1,131
GROUP G ODDS 1:134
GROUP H ODDS 1:333
GROUP I ODDS 1:221
UNPRICED DUE TO SCARCITY

NNO Amy Pronovost B
NNO Brandon McKinney B
NNO Brent Woodside B
NNO Brian Rood C
NNO Cat Staggs A
NNO Chris Eliopoulos A
NNO Chris Trevas B
NNO Christian Dalla Vecchia G
NNO Cynthia Cummens B
NNO Dan Norton E
NNO Dan Parsons E
NNO Dave Dorman B
NNO Dave Fox A
NNO David Rabbitte B
NNO Davide Fabbri G
NNO Grant Gould G
NNO Howard Shum G
NNO James Hodgkins F
NNO Jeff Carlisle A
NNO Jeff Chandler A
NNO Joe Corroney C
NNO John McCrea G
NNO Joseph Booth C
NNO Juan Carlos Ramos A
NNO Justin Chung A
NNO Kieron Dwyer B
NNO Kilian Plunkett A
NNO Matt Busch E
NNO Matt Haley C
NNO Mike Lilly C
NNO Monte Moore A
NNO Otis Frampton D
NNO Paul Gutierrez E
NNO Randy Martinez I
NNO Robert Teranishi E
NNO Russ Walks B
NNO Ryan Benjamin E
NNO Sarah Wilkinson E
NNO Scott Erwert B
NNO Thomas Hodges H
NNO William O'Neill D

2005 Star Wars Revenge of the Sith Stickers
COMPLETE SET (10)	2.50	6.00
COMMON CARD (1-10)	.40	1.00
STATED ODDS 1:3 RETAIL		

2005 Star Wars Revenge of the Sith Tattoos
COMPLETE SET (10)	4.00	10.00
COMMON CARD (1-10)	1.00	2.50
STATED ODDS 1:3 RETAIL		

2005 Star Wars Revenge of the Sith Tin Gold
COMPLETE SET (6)	5.00	12.00
COMMON CARD (A-F)	1.00	2.50
STATED ODDS ONE PER TIN		

2005 Star Wars Revenge of the Sith Tin Story
COMPLETE SET (6)	5.00	12.00
COMMON CARD (1-6)	1.00	2.50
STATED ODDS ONE PER TIN		

2005 Star Wars Revenge of the Sith Promos
COMMON CARD (P1-P5)	1.00	2.50
P3 The Circle is Complete	15.00	40.00
(Star Wars Shop)		

2005 Star Wars Revenge of the Sith Medalionz
COMPLETE SET (24)	15.00	40.00
COMMON CARD (1-24)	1.00	2.50
*GOLD: .8X TO 2X BASIC MED.		
CL Checklist	.20	.50

2005 Star Wars Revenge of the Sith Widevision

COMPLETE SET (80)	5.00	12.00
UNOPENED HOBBY BOX (24 PACKS)	25.00	40.00
UNOPENED HOBBY PACK (6 CARDS)	1.50	2.00
UNOPENED RETAIL BOX (24 PACKS)	25.00	40.00
UNOPENED RETAIL PACK (6 CARDS)	1.50	2.00
COMMON CARD (1-80)	.15	.40

2005 Star Wars Revenge of the Sith Widevision Autographs
COMMON CARD (UNNUMBERED)	12.00	30.00
STATED ODDS 1:48 HOBBY		
NNO Matthew Wood	75.00	150.00
NNO Peter Mayhew	100.00	200.00
NNO Samuel L. Jackson	750.00	1500.00

2005 Star Wars Revenge of the Sith Widevision Chrome Hobby
COMPLETE SET (10)	12.50	30.00
COMMON CARD (H1-H10)	1.50	4.00
STATED ODDS 1:6 HOBBY		

2005 Star Wars Revenge of the Sith Widevision Chrome Retail
COMPLETE SET (10)	15.00	40.00
COMMON CARD (R1-R10)	2.00	5.00
STATED ODDS 1:60 RETAIL		

2005 Star Wars Revenge of the Sith Widevision Flix-Pix
COMPLETE SET (10)	15.00	40.00
COMMON CARD (1-10)	2.00	5.00
STATED ODDS 1:6		

2015 Star Wars Revenge of the Sith 3-D Widevision
COMPLETE SET (44)	10.00	25.00
COMPLETE FACTORY SET (46)	60.00	120.00
COMMON CARD (1-44)	.40	1.00

2015 Star Wars Revenge of the Sith 3-D Widevision Autographs
COMMON AUTO	15.00	40.00
*SILVER/15: UNPRICED DUE TO SCARCITY		
*GOLD/1: UNPRICED DUE TO SCARCITY		
NNO Peter Mayhew	60.00	120.00
NNO Jeremy Bulloch	25.00	60.00
NNO Bai Ling	30.00	80.00

2015 Star Wars Revenge of the Sith 3-D Widevision Medallions
COMPLETE SET (8)	100.00	200.00
COMMON MEM	15.00	40.00
*SILVER/30: .6X TO 1.5X BASIC MEM		
*GOLD/1: UNPRICED DUE TO SCARCITY		
STATED PRINT RUN 60 SER.#'d SETS		

2015 Star Wars Revenge of the Sith 3-D Widevision Patches

AUTHENTIC PATCH CARD
COMPLETE SET (4)	50.00	100.00
COMMON MEM	15.00	40.00
*SILVER/30: .6X TO 1.5X BASIC MEM		
*GOLD/1: UNPRICED DUE TO SCARCITY		
STATED PRINT RUN 60 SER.#'d SETS		

2015 Star Wars Revenge of the Sith 3-D Widevision Sketch Medallions
COMMON CARD	50.00	100.00
1 Anakin Skywalker	60.00	120.00
2 Darth Vader	50.00	100.00
3 Chewbacca	100.00	200.00
4 Clone Trooper	50.00	100.00
5 General Grievous	50.00	100.00
6 R2-D2	50.00	100.00
7 C-3PO	80.00	150.00
8 Yoda		

THE FORCE AWAKENS

2017 Star Wars The Force Awakens 3-D Widevision
COMPLETE SET (44)	12.00	30.00
COMPLETE BOXED SET (46)		
COMMON CARD (1-44)	.40	1.00

2017 Star Wars The Force Awakens 3-D Widevision Autographs
COMMON AUTO	6.00	15.00
*BLUE/50: UNPRICED DUE TO SCARCITY		
*BLACK/25: UNPRICED DUE TO SCARCITY		
*ORANGE/10: UNPRICED DUE TO SCARCITY		
*GOLD/5: UNPRICED DUE TO SCARCITY		
*RED/1: UNPRICED DUE TO SCARCITY		
STATED ODDS 2:SET		
WVAAJ Andrew Jack	6.00	15.00
WVAASH Arti Shah	8.00	20.00
WVABH Brian Herring	10.00	25.00
WVABV Brian Vernel	6.00	15.00
WVACC Crystal Clarke	8.00	20.00
WVAEE Emun Elliott	6.00	15.00
WVAHW Harriet Walter	6.00	15.00
WVAIU Iko Uwais	10.00	25.00
WVAJH Jessica Henwick	10.00	25.00
WVAKF Kate Fleetwood	6.00	15.00
WVAPW Paul Warren	6.00	15.00
WVATC Tosin Cole	6.00	15.00
WVAYR Yayan Ruhian	6.00	15.00

TRADING CARDS

2017 Star Wars The Force Awakens 3-D Widevision Dual Autographs

UNPRICED DUE TO SCARCITY

WVDAFG Fisher/Grunberg
WVDARB Ridley/Boyega
WVDARH Ridley/Hamill
WVDABM Boyega/Mayhew
WVDAAS Hamill/Serkis

2016 Star Wars The Force Awakens Chrome

COMPLETE SET (100)	8.00	20.00
UNOPENED BOX (24 PACKS)	50.00	70.00
UNOPENED PACK (6 CARDS)	3.00	3.50
COMMON CARD (1-100)	.25	.60
*REFRACTOR: 1.2X TO 3X BASIC CARDS	.60	1.50
*PRISM REF./99: 5X TO 12X BASIC CARDS	3.00	8.00
*SHIMMER REF./50: 10X TO 25X BASIC CARDS	6.00	15.00
*PULSAR REF./10: 15X TO 40X BASIC CARDS	10.00	25.00
*SUPERFRACTOR/1: UNPRICED DUE TO SCARCITY		
*P.P.BLACK/1: UNPRICED DUE TO SCARCITY		
*P.P.CYAN/1: UNPRICED DUE TO SCARCITY		
*P.P.MAGENTA/1: UNPRICED DUE TO SCARCITY		
*P.P.YELLOW/1: UNPRICED DUE TO SCARCITY		

2016 Star Wars The Force Awakens Chrome Autographs

COMMON CARD	5.00	12.00
*ATOMIC/99: .5X TO 1.2X BASIC CARDS		
*PRISM/50: .6X TO 1.5X BASIC CARDS		
*X-FRACTOR/25: .75X TO 2X BASIC CARDS		
*SHIMMER/10: UNPRICED DUE TO SCARCITY		
*PULSAR/5: UNPRICED DUE TO SCARCITY		
*SUPERFRACTOR/1: UNPRICED DUE TO SCARCITY		
*P.P.BLACK/1: UNPRICED DUE TO SCARCITY		
*P.P.CYAN/1: UNPRICED DUE TO SCARCITY		
*P.P.MAGENTA/1: UNPRICED DUE TO SCARCITY		
*P.P.YELLOW/1: UNPRICED DUE TO SCARCITY		
OVERALL AUTO ODDS 1:24		

CAAB Anna Brewster	8.00	20.00
CABV Brian Vernel	10.00	25.00
CAGG Greg Grunberg	10.00	25.00
CAJS Joonas Suotamo	10.00	25.00
CAKS Kipsang Rotich	8.00	20.00
CAMD Mark Dodson	10.00	25.00
CAMQ Mike Quinn	8.00	20.00
CAPM Peter Mayhew	20.00	50.00
CASA Sebastian Armesto	8.00	20.00
CAYR Yayan Ruhian	10.00	25.00
CAMWG Matthew Wood	8.00	20.00

2016 Star Wars The Force Awakens Chrome Autographs Atomic Refractors

*ATOMIC/99: .5X TO 1.2X BASIC CARDS		
CAJB John Boyega	120.00	200.00
CAWD Warwick Davis	12.00	30.00

2016 Star Wars The Force Awakens Chrome Autographs Prism Refractors

*PRISM/50: .6X TO 1.5X BASIC CARDS		
CAAD Anthony Daniels		
CAAS Andy Serkis	120.00	200.00

2016 Star Wars The Force Awakens Chrome Autographs X-fractors

*X-FRACTORS: .75X TO 2X BASIC CARDS		
CACF Carrie Fisher	120.00	250.00
CADR Daisy Ridley	600.00	1200.00
CAEB Erik Bauersfeld		
CAKB Kenny Baker	150.00	300.00
CAMWU Matthew Wood		

2016 Star Wars The Force Awakens Chrome Behind-the-Scenes

COMPLETE SET (12)	10.00	25.00
COMMON CARD (1-12)	1.25	3.00
*SHIMMER REF./50: 1X TO 2.5X BASIC CARDS	3.00	8.00
*PULSAR REF./10: UNPRICED DUE TO SCARCITY		
*SUPERFRACTOR/1: UNPRICED DUE TO SCARCITY		
*P.P.BLACK/1: UNPRICED DUE TO SCARCITY		
*P.P.CYAN/1: UNPRICED DUE TO SCARCITY		
*P.P.MAGENTA/1: UNPRICED DUE TO SCARCITY		
*P.P.YELLOW/1: UNPRICED DUE TO SCARCITY		
STATED ODDS 1:4		

2016 Star Wars The Force Awakens Chrome Dual Autographs

STATED PRINT RUN 3 SER.#'d SETS
UNPRICED DUE TO SCARCITY

CDABF Fisher/Boyega
CDAHF Hamill/Fisher
CDAMA Marshall/Armesto
CDAMS Suotamo/Mayhew
CDAWB Mayhew/Walker

2016 Star Wars The Force Awakens Chrome Heroes of the Resistance

COMPLETE SET (18)	10.00	25.00
COMMON CARD (1-18)	.75	2.00
*SHIMMER REF./50:1 X TO 2.5X BASIC CARDS	2.00	5.00

*PULSAR REF./10: UNPRICED DUE TO SCARCITY		
*SUPERFRACTOR/1: UNPRICED DUE TO SCARCITY		
*P.P.BLACK/1: UNPRICED DUE TO SCARCITY		
*P.P.CYAN/1: UNPRICED DUE TO SCARCITY		
*P.P.MAGENTA/1: UNPRICED DUE TO SCARCITY		
*P.P.YELLOW/1: UNPRICED DUE TO SCARCITY		
STATED ODDS 1:2		
1 Finn	1.25	3.00
2 Rey	1.25	3.00
3 Poe Dameron	1.00	2.50
9 BB-8	1.50	4.00
10 C-3PO	1.00	2.50
11 R2-D2	1.00	2.50
13 Han Solo	1.50	4.00
14 Chewbacca	1.00	2.50
18 General Leia Organa	1.00	2.50

2016 Star Wars The Force Awakens Chrome Medallions

COMPLETE SET (25)	200.00	400.00
COMMON CARD	3.00	8.00
*SILVER/25: .5X TO 1.2X BASIC CARDS		
*GOLD/10: UNPRICED DUE TO SCARCITY		
*PLATINUM/1: UNPRICED DUE TO SCARCITY		
M1 Han Solo	12.00	30.00
M2 General Leia Organa	12.00	30.00
M3 Admiral Ackbar	5.00	12.00
M4 Chewbacca	6.00	15.00
M5 Admiral Statura	5.00	12.00
M6 Snap Wexley	8.00	20.00
M7 Jess Testor Pava	8.00	20.00
M10 Poe Dameron	8.00	20.00
M11 Rey	20.00	50.00
M12 Finn	10.00	25.00
M13 BB-8	10.00	25.00
M14 Riot Control Stormtrooper	8.00	20.00
M16 Colonel Datoo	6.00	15.00
M17 Supreme Leader Snoke	6.00	15.00
M18 Flametrooper	5.00	12.00
M19 Kylo Ren	8.00	20.00
M20 Kylo Ren	8.00	20.00
M21 General Hux	5.00	12.00
M22 Captain Phasma	8.00	20.00
M23 FN-2187	10.00	25.00

2016 Star Wars The Force Awakens Chrome Patches

COMPLETE SET (27)	175.00	350.00
COMMON CARD (P1-P27)	5.00	12.00
*SHIMMER/199: .5X TO 1.2X BASIC CARDS		
*PULSAR/99: .6X TO 1.5X BASIC CARDS		
*SUPERFRACTOR/5: UNPRICED DUE TO SCARCITY		
P1 Rey/686	15.00	40.00
P2 Han Solo/299	8.00	20.00
P4 Finn/686	8.00	20.00
P7 Kylo Ren/401	6.00	15.00
P11 General Leia Organa/755	8.00	20.00
P15 BB-8/686	6.00	15.00
P16 Poe Dameron & BB-8/686	6.00	15.00
P17 Rey & BB-8/686	12.00	30.00
P18 R2-D2/686	6.00	15.00
P19 Rey/299	10.00	25.00
P20 Rey/686	10.00	25.00
P23 Han Solo & Chewbacca/737	10.00	25.00

2016 Star Wars The Force Awakens Chrome Power of the First Order

COLONEL DATOO
POWER OF THE FIRST ORDER

COMPLETE SET (9)	6.00	15.00
COMMON CARD (1-9)	.75	2.00

*SHIMMER REF./50: 1X TO 2.5X BASIC CARDS
*PULSAR REF./10: UNPRICED DUE TO SCARCITY
*SUPERFRACTOR/1: UNPRICED DUE TO SCARCITY
*P.P.BLACK/1: UNPRICED DUE TO SCARCITY
*P.P.CYAN/1: UNPRICED DUE TO SCARCITY
*P.P.MAGENTA/1: UNPRICED DUE TO SCARCITY
*P.P.YELLOW/1: UNPRICED DUE TO SCARCITY
STATED ODDS 1:12

1	Supreme Leader Snoke	1.50	4.00
2	Kylo Ren	1.50	4.00
3	General Hux	1.25	3.00
4	Captain Phasma	1.25	3.00

2016 Star Wars The Force Awakens Chrome Ships and Vehicles

COMPLETE SET (11)	6.00	15.00
COMMON CARD (1-11)	1.00	2.50
*SHIMMER REF./50: 1X TO 2.5X BASIC CARDS	2.50	6.00

*PULSAR REF./10: UNPRICED DUE TO SCARCITY
*SUPERFRACTOR/1: UNPRICED DUE TO SCARCITY
*P.P.BLACK/1: UNPRICED DUE TO SCARCITY
*P.P.CYAN/1: UNPRICED DUE TO SCARCITY
*P.P.MAGENTA/1: UNPRICED DUE TO SCARCITY
*P.P.YELLOW/1: UNPRICED DUE TO SCARCITY
STATED ODDS 1:8

2016 Star Wars The Force Awakens Chrome Sketches

UNPRICED DUE TO SCARCITY

NNO Alex Iniguez
NNO Angelina Benedetti
NNO Bob Stevlic
NNO Brad Hudson
NNO Brent Ragland
NNO Carlos Cabaleiro
NNO Daniel Parsons
NNO Darrin Pepe
NNO Eric Lehtonen
NNO Jason Sobol
NNO Jonathan Caustrita
NNO Kevin Graham
NNO Kevin P. West
NNO Kris Penix
NNO Marcia Dye
NNO Matt Stewart
NNO Rich Molinelli
NNO Rob Teranishi
NNO Robert Hendrickson
NNO Sarah Wilkinson
NNO Solly Mohamed
NNO Stephanie Swanger
NNO Tim Proctor
NNO Tina Berardi

2016 Star Wars The Force Awakens Chrome Triple Autographs

STATED PRINT RUN 3 SER.#'d SETS
UNPRICED DUE TO SCARCITY

CTAFBR Boyega/Fisher/Rose
CTAFGQ Fisher/Grunberg/Quinn
CTAHFB Hamill/Fisher/Boyega
CTASMA Serkis/Marshall/Armesto

2015 Star Wars The Force Awakens Dog Tags

COMPLETE SET (16)	15.00	40.00
COMMON CARD (1-16)	1.25	3.00

*GOLD: 1X TO 2.5X BASIC TAGS

1	Kylo Ren	2.00	5.00
2	Rey	2.00	5.00
3	Finn	1.50	4.00
5	Captain Phasma	1.50	4.00
10	BB-8	2.50	6.00
11	Rey	2.00	5.00
12	Finn	1.50	4.00
13	Kylo Ren	2.00	5.00

2015 Star Wars The Force Awakens Dog Tags Target Exclusives

COMPLETE SET (2)	10.00	25.00
COMMON CARD (T1-T2)	5.00	12.00

*GOLD: .75X TO 2X BASIC TAGS
EXCLUSIVE TO TARGET

T2	BB-8	8.00	20.00

2015 Star Wars The Force Awakens Dog Tags Toys 'R' Us Exclusives

COMPLETE SET (2)	10.00	25.00
COMMON CARD (TR1-TR2)	6.00	15.00

*GOLD: 1X TO 2.5X BASIC TAGS
EXCLUSIVE TO TOYS 'R' US

2015 Star Wars The Force Awakens Dog Tags Walmart Exclusives

COMPLETE SET (2)	6.00	15.00
COMMON CARD (W1-W2)	4.00	10.00

*GOLD: 1X TO 2.5X BASIC TAGS
EXCLUSIVE TO WALMART

2016 Star Wars The Force Awakens Factory Set

COMPLETE FACTORY SET (310)	40.00	80.00
COMMON CARD	.15	.40
JOURNEY TO TFA (1-110)		
TFA SERIES ONE (1-100)		
TFA SERIES TWO (1-100)		
*LIM.ED./100: 6X TO 15X BASIC CARDS	2.50	6.00

2015 Star Wars The Force Awakens Glow-in-the-Dark Decals

COMPLETE SET (7)	10.00	25.00
COMMON CARD	1.25	3.00

STATED ODDS 1:CEREAL BOX
INSERTED IN BOXES OF GENERAL MILLS CEREAL
MILLENNIUM FALCON IS KROGER EXCLUSIVE

1	BB-8	2.50	6.00
2	C-3PO and R2-D2	1.50	4.00
3	Captain Phasma	2.00	5.00
5	Kylo Ren	2.00	5.00
6	Millennium Falcon SP	5.00	12.00

Kroger Exclusive

2015 Star Wars The Force Awakens Series One

COMPLETE SET w/o SP (100)	10.00	25.00
COMMON CARD (1-100)	.20	.50

---

*LTSBR GREEN: .5X TO 1.2X BASIC CARDS
*LTSBR BLUE: .6X TO 1.5X BASIC CARDS
*LTSBR PURPLE: .75X TO 2X BASIC CARDS
*FOIL/250: 4X TO 10X BASIC CARDS
*GOLD/100: 6X TO 15X BASIC CARDS
*PLATINUM/1: UNPRICED DUE TO SCARCITY
*P.P.BLACK/1: UNPRICED DUE TO SCARCITY
*P.P.CYAN/1: UNPRICED DUE TO SCARCITY
*P.P.MAGENTA/1: UNPRICED DUE TO SCARCITY
*P.P.YELLOW/1: UNPRICED DUE TO SCARCITY
TARGET EXCLUSIVES SP 101-103

100	Han Solo & Chewbacca return home	.75	2.00
101	Maz Kanata SP	3.00	8.00
102	Wollivan SP	3.00	8.00
103	Grummgar SP	3.00	8.00

2015 Star Wars The Force Awakens Series One Autographs

ANTHONY DANIELS as
C-3PO
AUTHENTIC AUTOGRAPH

COMMON AUTO	15.00	40.00

*LTSBR PURPLE/25: UNPRICED DUE TO SCARCITY
*GOLD/10: UNPRICED DUE TO SCARCITY
*IMP. RED/1: UNPRICED DUE TO SCARCITY
*P.P.BLACK/1: UNPRICED DUE TO SCARCITY
*P.P.CYAN/1: UNPRICED DUE TO SCARCITY
*P.P.MAGENTA/1: UNPRICED DUE TO SCARCITY
*P.P.YELLOW/1: UNPRICED DUE TO SCARCITY
STATED ODDS 1:106 H; 1:12,334 R

NNO	Anthony Daniels	100.00	200.00
NNO	Carrie Fisher	200.00	350.00
NNO	Daisy Ridley	750.00	1500.00
NNO	John Boyega	100.00	200.00
NNO	Peter Mayhew	50.00	100.00

2015 Star Wars The Force Awakens Series One Behind-the-Scenes

FINN'S AWAKENING
BEHIND THE SCENES

COMPLETE SET (7)	5.00	12.00
COMMON CARD (1-7)	1.00	2.50

*LTSBR GREEN: .5X TO 1.2X BASIC CARDS
*LTSBR BLUE: .6X TO 1.5X BASIC CARDS
*LTSBR PURPLE: .75X TO 2X BASIC CARDS
*FOIL/250: 4X TO 10X BASIC CARDS
*GOLD/100: 6X TO 15X BASIC CARDS
*PLATINUM/1: UNPRICED DUE TO SCARCITY
*P.P.BLACK/1: UNPRICED DUE TO SCARCITY
*P.P.CYAN/1: UNPRICED DUE TO SCARCITY
*P.P.MAGENTA/1: UNPRICED DUE TO SCARCITY
*P.P.YELLOW/1: UNPRICED DUE TO SCARCITY
STATED ODDS 1:8 H; 1:5 R

2015 Star Wars The Force Awakens Series One
Character Montages

COMPLETE SET (8)	4.00	10.00
COMMON CARD (1-8)	.75	2.00

*LTSBR GREEN: .5X TO 1.2X BASIC CARDS
*LTSBR BLUE: .6X TO 1.5X BASIC CARDS
*LTSBR PURPLE: .75X TO 2X BASIC CARDS
*FOIL/250: 4X TO 10X BASIC CARDS
*GOLD/100: 6X TO 15X BASIC CARDS
*PLATINUM/1: UNPRICED DUE TO SCARCITY
*P.P.BLACK/1: UNPRICED DUE TO SCARCITY
*P.P.CYAN/1: UNPRICED DUE TO SCARCITY
*P.P.MAGENTA/1: UNPRICED DUE TO SCARCITY
*P.P.YELLOW/1: UNPRICED DUE TO SCARCITY
STATED ODDS 1:7 H; 1:4 R

1 Rey	1.50	4.00
5 Captain Phasma	1.25	3.00
7 BB-8	1.50	4.00

2015 Star Wars The Force Awakens Series One
Character Stickers

COMPLETE SET (18)	6.00	15.00
COMMON CARD (1-18)	.60	1.50

*LTSBR GREEN: .5X TO 1.2X BASIC CARDS
*LTSBR BLUE: .6X TO 1.5X BASIC CARDS
*LTSBR PURPLE: .75X TO 2X BASIC CARDS
*FOIL/250: 4X TO 10X BASIC CARDS
*GOLD/100: 6X TO 15X BASIC CARDS
*PLATINUM/1: UNPRICED DUE TO SCARCITY
*P.P.BLACK/1: UNPRICED DUE TO SCARCITY
*P.P.CYAN/1: UNPRICED DUE TO SCARCITY
*P.P.MAGENTA/1: UNPRICED DUE TO SCARCITY
*P.P.YELLOW/1: UNPRICED DUE TO SCARCITY
STATED ODDS 1:3 H; 1:2 R

1 Rey	1.25	3.00
5 Captain Phasma	1.00	2.50
8 BB-8	1.25	3.00
12 Rey	1.25	3.00

2015 Star Wars The Force Awakens Series One
Concept Art

COMPLETE SET (20)	8.00	20.00
COMMON CARD (1-20)	.75	2.00

*LTSBR GREEN: .5X TO 1.2X BASIC CARDS
*LTSBR BLUE: .6X TO 1.5X BASIC CARDS
*LTSBR PURPLE: .75X TO 2X BASIC CARDS
*FOIL/250: 4X TO 10X BASIC CARDS
*GOLD/100: 6X TO 15X BASIC CARDS
*PLATINUM/1: UNPRICED DUE TO SCARCITY
*P.P.BLACK/1: UNPRICED DUE TO SCARCITY
*P.P.CYAN/1: UNPRICED DUE TO SCARCITY
*P.P.MAGENTA/1: UNPRICED DUE TO SCARCITY
*P.P.YELLOW/1: UNPRICED DUE TO SCARCITY
STATED ODDS 1:3 H; 1:2 R

2015 Star Wars The Force Awakens Series One
Dual Autographs

UNPRICED DUE TO SCARCITY

1 Anthony Daniels and Kenny Baker
2 Anthony Daniels and Peter Mayhew
3 Carrie Fisher and Anthony Daniels
4 Mike Quinn and Tim Rose

2015 Star Wars The Force Awakens Series One
First Order Rises

COMPLETE SET (9)	6.00	15.00
COMMON CARD (1-9)	1.25	3.00

*LTSBR GREEN: .5X TO 1.2X BASIC CARDS
*LTSBR BLUE: .6X TO 1.5X BASIC CARDS
*LTSBR PURPLE: .75X TO 2X BASIC CARDS
*FOIL/250: 4X TO 10X BASIC CARDS
*GOLD/100: 6X TO 15X BASIC CARDS
*PLATINUM/1: UNPRICED DUE TO SCARCITY
*P.P.BLACK/1: UNPRICED DUE TO SCARCITY
*P.P.CYAN/1: UNPRICED DUE TO SCARCITY
*P.P.MAGENTA/1: UNPRICED DUE TO SCARCITY
*P.P.YELLOW/1: UNPRICED DUE TO SCARCITY
STATED ODDS 1:6 H; 1:4 R

2 Captain Phasma	1.50	4.00

2015 Star Wars The Force Awakens Series One
First Order Stormtrooper Costume Relics

COMMON CARD	12.00	30.00

*BRONZE/99: .75X TO 2X BASIC CARDS
*SILVER/50: 1.2X TO 3X BASIC CARDS
*GOLD/10: 2X TO 5X BASIC CARDS
*PLATINUM/1: UNPRICED DUE TO SCARCITY

2015 Star Wars The Force Awakens Series One
Locations

COMPLETE SET (9)	3.00	8.00
COMMON CARD (1-9)	.60	1.50

*LTSBR GREEN: .5X TO 1.2X BASIC CARDS
*LTSBR BLUE: .6X TO 1.5X BASIC CARDS
*LTSBR PURPLE: .75X TO 2X BASIC CARDS
*FOIL/250: 4X TO 10X BASIC CARDS
*GOLD/100: 6X TO 15X BASIC CARDS
*PLATINUM/1: UNPRICED DUE TO SCARCITY
*P.P.BLACK/1: UNPRICED DUE TO SCARCITY
*P.P.CYAN/1: UNPRICED DUE TO SCARCITY
*P.P.MAGENTA/1: UNPRICED DUE TO SCARCITY
*P.P.YELLOW/1: UNPRICED DUE TO SCARCITY
STATED ODDS 1:6 H; 1:4 R

2015 Star Wars The Force Awakens Series One
Medallions

COMMON CARD (M1-M66)	8.00	20.00
STATED ODDS 1:BOX		

2015 Star Wars The Force Awakens Series One
Movie Scenes

COMPLETE SET (20)	5.00	12.00
COMMON CARD (1-20)	.50	1.25

*LTSBR GREEN: .5X TO 1.2X BASIC CARDS

*LTSBR BLUE: .60X TO 1.5X BASIC CARDS
*LTSBR PURPLE: .75X TO 2X BASIC CARDS
*FOIL/250: 4X TO 10X BASIC CARDS
*GOLD/100: 6X TO 15X BASIC CARDS
*PLATINUM/1: UNPRICED DUE TO SCARCITY
*P.P.BLACK/1: UNPRICED DUE TO SCARCITY
*P.P.CYAN/1: UNPRICED DUE TO SCARCITY
*P.P.MAGENTA/1: UNPRICED DUE TO SCARCITY
*P.P.YELLOW/1: UNPRICED DUE TO SCARCITY
STATED ODDS 1:3 H; 1:2 R

2015 Star Wars The Force Awakens Series One
Sketches

NNO Alejandro Iniguez
NNO Bob Stevlic
NNO Brent Ragland
NNO Carlos Cabaleiro
NNO Dan Parsons
NNO Dan Bergren
NNO Doug Cowan
NNO Francois Chartier
NNO Gabe Farber
NNO Ingrid Hardy
NNO Jeff Mallinson
NNO Justin Mauk
NNO Kris Penix
NNO Kyle Babbitt
NNO Rob Teranishi
NNO Robert Hendrickson
NNO Sarah Wilkinson
NNO Sean Pence
NNO Stephanie Swanger
NNO Lord Mesa

2015 Star Wars The Force Awakens Series One
Triple Autographs

UNPRICED DUE TO SCARCITY

1 Carrie Fisher
Peter Mayhew/Anthony Daniels

2015 Star Wars The Force Awakens Series One
Weapons

COMPLETE SET (10)	4.00	10.00
COMMON CARD (1-10)	.60	1.50

*LTSBR GREEN: .5X TO 1.2X BASIC CARDS
*LTSBR BLUE: .6X TO 1.5X BASIC CARDS
*LTSBR PURPLE: .75X TO 2X BASIC CARDS
*FOIL/250: 4X TO 10X BASIC CARDS
*GOLD/100: 6X TO 15X BASIC CARDS
*PLATINUM/1: UNPRICED DUE TO SCARCITY
*P.P.BLACK/1: UNPRICED DUE TO SCARCITY
*P.P.CYAN/1: UNPRICED DUE TO SCARCITY
*P.P.MAGENTA/1: UNPRICED DUE TO SCARCITY
*P.P.YELLOW/1: UNPRICED DUE TO SCARCITY
STATED ODDS 1:6 H; 1:3 R

1 Kylo Ren's lightsaber	1.25	3.00
9 Han Solo's Blaster	.75	2.00

2016 Star Wars The Force Awakens Series Two

COMPLETE SET W/O SP (100)	10.00	25.00
COMPLETE SET W/SP (102)	20.00	50.00
UNOPENED HOBBY BOX (24 PACKS)	60.00	100.00
UNOPENED HOBBY PACK (8 CARDS)	2.50	4.00
COMMON CARD (1-100)	.20	.50

*LTSBR GREEN: .5X TO 1.2X BASIC CARDS
*LTSBR BLUE: .6X TO 1.5X BASIC CARDS
*LTSBR PURPLE: .75X TO 2X BASIC CARDS
*FOIL: 4X TO 10X BASIC CARDS
*GOLD/100: 6X TO 15X BASIC CARDS
*PLATINUM/1: UNPRICED DUE TO SCARCITY

*P.P.BLACK/1: UNPRICED DUE TO SCARCITY
*P.P.CYAN/1: UNPRICED DUE TO SCARCITY
*P.P.MAGENTA/1: UNPRICED DUE TO SCARCITY
*P.P.YELLOW/1: UNPRICED DUE TO SCARCITY

101 Finding Luke Skywalker SP	6.00	15.00
102 The Lightsaber Returned SP	10.00	25.00

2016 Star Wars The Force Awakens Series Two Autographs

COMMON CARD	8.00	20.00
*LTSBR PURPLE/50: .5X TO 1.2X BASIC AUTOS		
*FOIL/25: .75X TO 2X BASIC AUTOS		
*GOLD/10: UNPRICED DUE TO SCARCITY		
*IMP. RED/1: UNPRICED DUE TO SCARCITY		
*P.P.BLACK/1: UNPRICED DUE TO SCARCITY		
*P.P.CYAN/1: UNPRICED DUE TO SCARCITY		
*P.P.MAGENTA/1: UNPRICED DUE TO SCARCITY		
*P.P.YELLOW/1: UNPRICED DUE TO SCARCITY		
1 David Acord/FN-2199	20.00	50.00
2 David Acord/Teedo	15.00	40.00
4 Kenny Baker	50.00	100.00
6 John Boyega	150.00	300.00
7 Anna Brewster	12.00	30.00
8 Dante Briggins	12.00	30.00
9 Thomas Brodie-Sangster	10.00	25.00
10 Aidan Cook	12.00	30.00
11 Anthony Daniels	50.00	100.00
12 Warrick Davis	10.00	25.00
13 Harrison Ford		
14 Greg Grunberg	15.00	40.00
17 Jessica Henwick	15.00	40.00
18 Brian Herring	60.00	120.00
19 Andrew Jack	10.00	25.00
20 Billie Lourd	15.00	40.00
21 Rocky Marshall	10.00	25.00
22 Peter Mayhew	25.00	60.00
25 Arti Shah	12.00	30.00
26 Kiran Shah	10.00	25.00
27 Joonas Suotamo	15.00	40.00
28 Brian Vernel	10.00	25.00
29 Dame Harriet Walter	12.00	30.00
30 Paul Warren	10.00	25.00

2016 Star Wars The Force Awakens Series Two Card Trader Characters

COMMON CARD (1-9)	50.00	100.00
STATED PRINT RUN 100 SER.#'d SETS		
1 BB-8	60.00	120.00
3 Finn	60.00	120.00
5 Kylo Ren	80.00	150.00
6 Captain Phasma	80.00	150.00
7 Poe Dameron	60.00	120.00
8 Rey	120.00	200.00

2016 Star Wars The Force Awakens Series Two Character Poster Inserts

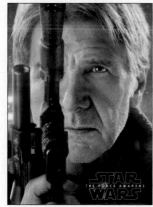

COMPLETE SET (5)	5.00	12.00
COMMON CARD (1-5)	1.50	4.00
*P.P.BLACK/1: UNPRICED DUE TO SCARCITY		
*P.P.CYAN/1: UNPRICED DUE TO SCARCITY		
*P.P.MAGENTA/1: UNPRICED DUE TO SCARCITY		

---

*P.P.YELLOW/1: UNPRICED DUE TO SCARCITY
STATED ODDS 1:24

1 Rey	2.50	6.00
2 Finn	2.50	6.00
5 Han Solo	2.00	5.00

2016 Star Wars The Force Awakens Series Two Character Stickers

LEIA ORGANA
THE RESISTANCE

COMPLETE SET (18)	6.00	15.00
COMMON CARD (1-18)	.50	1.25
*P.P.BLACK/1: UNPRICED DUE TO SCARCITY		
*P.P.CYAN/1: UNPRICED DUE TO SCARCITY		
*P.P.MAGENTA/1: UNPRICED DUE TO SCARCITY		
*P.P.YELLOW/1: UNPRICED DUE TO SCARCITY		
1 Finn	.75	2.00
2 Rey	1.00	2.50
5 Han Solo	1.00	2.50
6 Leia Organa	.75	2.00
8 Poe Dameron	1.25	3.00
11 BB-8	1.25	3.00
12 Unkar Plutt	.60	1.50
13 General Hux	.75	2.00
15 Admiral Ackbar	.60	1.50
16 Stormtrooper	.75	2.00
18 Maz Kanata	.60	1.50

2016 Star Wars The Force Awakens Series Two Concept Art

COMPLETE SET (9)	5.00	12.00
COMMON CARD (1-9)	1.00	2.50
*P.P.BLACK/1: UNPRICED DUE TO SCARCITY		
*P.P.CYAN/1: UNPRICED DUE TO SCARCITY		
*P.P.MAGENTA/1: UNPRICED DUE TO SCARCITY		
*P.P.YELLOW/1: UNPRICED DUE TO SCARCITY		

2016 Star Wars The Force Awakens Series Two Dual Autographs

STATED PRINT RUN 3 SER.#'d SETS
UNPRICED DUE TO SCARCITY

1 John Boyega/Carrie Fisher
2 Carrie Fisher/Tim Rose
3 Anthony Daniels/Peter Mayhew

2016 Star Wars The Force Awakens Series Two Dual Medallion Autographs

STATED PRINT RUN 5 SER.#'d SETS
UNPRICED DUE TO SCARCITY

1 John Boyega/Carrie Fisher

---

2 Carrie Fisher/Mike Quinn
3 Mike Quinn/Tim Rose
4 Carrie Fisher/Anthony Daniels
5 Anthony Daniels/Peter Mayhew

2016 Star Wars The Force Awakens Series Two Dual Medallions

STATED PRINT RUN 5 SER.#'d SETS
UNPRICED DUE TO SCARCITY

1 Kylo Ren/Captain Phasma
2 Rey/Finn
3 Stormtrooper/TIE Fighter Pilot
4 Finn/Poe Dameron
5 Han Solo/Rey

2016 Star Wars The Force Awakens Series Two Galactic Connexions

COMPLETE SET (5)	120.00	250.00
COMMON CARD (1-5)	30.00	80.00
STATED PRINT RUN 100 ANNCD SETS		
WAL-MART EXCLUSIVE		
3 BB-8	50.00	100.00

2016 Star Wars The Force Awakens Series Two Heroes of the Resistance

COMPLETE SET (16)	8.00	20.00
COMMON CARD (1-16)	.75	2.00
*P.P.BLACK/1: UNPRICED DUE TO SCARCITY		
*P.P.CYAN/1: UNPRICED DUE TO SCARCITY		
*P.P.MAGENTA/1: UNPRICED DUE TO SCARCITY		
*P.P.YELLOW/1: UNPRICED DUE TO SCARCITY		
2 Poe Dameron	1.00	2.50
3 Finn	1.00	2.50
4 Rey	1.25	3.00
5 Han Solo	1.50	4.00
16 BB-8	1.50	4.00

2016 Star Wars The Force Awakens Series Two Maz's Castle

COMPLETE SET (9)	5.00	12.00
COMMON CARD (1-9)	.75	2.00
*P.P.BLACK/1: UNPRICED DUE TO SCARCITY		
*P.P.CYAN/1: UNPRICED DUE TO SCARCITY		
*P.P.MAGENTA/1: UNPRICED DUE TO SCARCITY		
*P.P.YELLOW/1: UNPRICED DUE TO SCARCITY		

2016 Star Wars The Force Awakens Series Two Medallions

POE DAMERON

COMMON CARD	4.00	10.00
*SILVER p/r 244-399: .5X TO 1.2X BASIC CARDS		
*SILVER p/r 120-199: .6X TO 1.5X BASIC CARDS		
*SILVER p/r 50-99: 1X TO 2.5X BASIC CARDS		
*GOLD p/r 120-199: .6X TO 1.5X BASIC CARDS		
*GOLD p/r 74-100: .75X TO 2X BASIC CARDS		
*GOLD p/r 25-50: 1.2X TO 3X BASIC CARDS		
*PLATINUM p/r 16-25: X TO X BASIC CARDS		
*PLATINUM p/r 5-15: UNPRICED DUE TO SCARCITY		
*PLATINUM/1: UNPRICED DUE TO SCARCITY		
1 Kylo Ren	6.00	15.00
2 General Hux	5.00	12.00
3 Captain Phasma	5.00	12.00
4 FN-2187	5.00	12.00
6 Kylo Ren	6.00	15.00
12 Kylo Ren	6.00	15.00
13 Maz Kanata	5.00	12.00
14 Rey	6.00	15.00
15 BB-8	5.00	12.00
16 Han Solo	8.00	20.00
17 Chewbacca	5.00	12.00
18 Finn	6.00	15.00

19	Rey	6.00	15.00
22	Colonel Datoo	6.00	15.00
23	Captain Phasma	5.00	12.00
24	Finn	5.00	12.00
27	BB-8	5.00	12.00
28	Resistance X-Wing Fighter	5.00	12.00
29	Nien Nunb	6.00	15.00
30	C-3PO	6.00	15.00
31	R2-D2	8.00	20.00
32	Jess Testor Pava	10.00	25.00
33	Snap Wexley	6.00	15.00
34	Admiral Statura	6.00	15.00
35	Admiral Ackbar	6.00	15.00
36	Major Brance	5.00	12.00

2016 Star Wars The Force Awakens Series Two Power of the First Order

| COMPLETE SET (11) | 5.00 | 12.00 |
| COMMON CARD (1-11) | .40 | 1.00 |
*P.P.BLACK/1: UNPRICED DUE TO SCARCITY
*P.P.CYAN/1: UNPRICED DUE TO SCARCITY
*P.P.MAGENTA/1: UNPRICED DUE TO SCARCITY
*P.P.YELLOW/1: UNPRICED DUE TO SCARCITY

1	Kylo Ren	1.25	3.00
2	General Hux	1.00	2.50
3	Captain Phasma	1.25	3.00
11	Supreme Leader Snoke	1.00	2.50

2016 Star Wars The Force Awakens Series Two Quad Autographed Booklet

STATED PRINT RUN 1 SER.#'d SET
UNPRICED DUE TO SCARCITY

1 Boyega/Fisher/Rose/Quinn

2016 Star Wars The Force Awakens Series Two Sketches

NNO Bob Stevlic
NNO Brent Ragland
NNO Brian Kong
NNO Carlos Cabaleiro
NNO Dan Parsons
NNO Dan Bergren
NNO Doug Cowan
NNO Eric Lehtonen
NNO Francois Chartier
NNO Gabe Farber
NNO Ingrid Hardy
NNO Jeff Mallinson
NNO Kris Penix
NNO Kyle Babbit
NNO Rob Teranishi
NNO Robert Hendrickson
NNO Stephanie Swanger

2016 Star Wars The Force Awakens Series Two Triple Autographs

STATED PRINT RUN 3 SER.#'d SETS
UNPRICED DUE TO SCARCITY

1 Boyega/Fisher/Mayhew
2 Fisher/Rose/Quinn

ROGUE ONE

2016 Star Wars Rogue One Series One

COMPLETE SET (90)	8.00	20.00
UNOPENED BOX (24 PACKS)	80.00	100.00
UNOPENED PACK (8 CARDS)	3.00	4.00
COMMON CARD (1-90)	.25	.60
*DEATH STAR BL.: .6X TO 1.5X BASIC CARDS
*GREEN SQ.: .75X TO 2X BASIC CARDS
*BLUE SQ.: 1X TO 2.5X BASIC CARDS
*GRAY SQ./100: 4X TO 10X BASIC CARDS
*GOLD SQ./50: 6X TO 15X BASIC CARDS
*ORANGE SQ./1: UNPRICED DUE TO SCARCITY
*P.P.BLACK/1: UNPRICED DUE TO SCARCITY
*P.P.CYAN/1: UNPRICED DUE TO SCARCITY
*P.P.MAGENTA1/1: UNPRICED DUE TO SCARCITY
*P.P.YELLOW/1: UNPRICED DUE TO SCARCITY

2016 Star Wars Rogue One Series One Autographs

| COMMON CARD | 10.00 | 25.00 |
*BLACK/50: .6X TO 1.5X BASIC CARDS
*GOLD/10: UNPRICED DUE TO SCARCITY
*P.P.BLACK/1: UNPRICED DUE TO SCARCITY
*P.P.CYAN/1: UNPRICED DUE TO SCARCITY
*P.P.MAGENTA/1: UNPRICED DUE TO SCARCITY
*P.P.YELLOW/1: UNPRICED DUE TO SCARCITY
RANDOMLY INSERTED INTO PACKS

1	Donnie Yen	100.00	200.00
2	Felicity Jones	300.00	600.00
3	Forest Whitaker	100.00	200.00
4	Genevieve O'Reilly	15.00	40.00

2016 Star Wars Rogue One Series One Blueprints of Ships and Vehicles

| COMPLETE SET (8) | 5.00 | 12.00 |
| COMMON CARD (BP1-BP8) | 1.00 | 2.50 |
*P.P.BLACK/1: UNPRICED DUE TO SCARCITY
*P.P.CYAN/1: UNPRICED DUE TO SCARCITY
*P.P.MAGENTA/1: UNPRICED DUE TO SCARCITY
*P.P.YELLOW/1: UNPRICED DUE TO SCARCITY
RANDOMLY INSERTED INTO PACKS

2016 Star Wars Rogue One Series One Character Icons

| COMPLETE SET (11) | 8.00 | 20.00 |
| COMMON CARD (CI1-CI11) | 1.25 | 3.00 |
*P.P.BLACK/1: UNPRICED DUE TO SCARCITY
*P.P.CYAN/1: UNPRICED DUE TO SCARCITY
*P.P.MAGENTA/1: UNPRICED DUE TO SCARCITY
*P.P.YELLOW/1: UNPRICED DUE TO SCARCITY
RANDOMLY INSERTED INTO PACKS

2016 Star Wars Rogue One Series One Character Stickers

| COMPLETE SET (18) | 10.00 | 25.00 |
| COMMON CARD (CS1-CS18) | .75 | 2.00 |
*P.P.BLACK/1: UNPRICED DUE TO SCARCITY
*P.P.CYAN/1: UNPRICED DUE TO SCARCITY
*P.P.MAGENTA/1: UNPRICED DUE TO SCARCITY
*P.P.YELLOW/1: UNPRICED DUE TO SCARCITY
RANDOMLY INSERTED INTO PACKS

2016 Star Wars Rogue One Series One Dual Autographs

UNPRICED DUE TO SCARCITY

1 Forest Whitaker/Donnie Yen
2 Genevieve O'Reilly/Forest Whitaker
3 Paul Kasey/Nick Kellington

2016 Star Wars Rogue One Series One Gallery

| COMPLETE SET (10) | 4.00 | 10.00 |
| COMMON CARD (G1-G10) | .50 | 1.25 |
*P.P.BLACK/1: UNPRICED DUE TO SCARCITY
*P.P.CYAN/1: UNPRICED DUE TO SCARCITY
*P.P.MAGENTA/1: UNPRICED DUE TO SCARCITY
*P.P.YELLOW/1: UNPRICED DUE TO SCARCITY
RANDOMLY INSERTED INTO PACKS

G1	Jyn Erso	.75	2.00
G2	Jyn Erso	.75	2.00
G3	Jyn Erso	.75	2.00
G4	Jyn Erso	.75	2.00
G5	Jyn Erso	.75	2.00
G6	Jyn Erso	.75	2.00
G7	Jyn Erso	.75	2.00

2016 Star Wars Rogue One Series One Heroes of the Rebel Alliance

| COMPLETE SET (14) | 8.00 | 20.00 |
| COMMON CARD (HR1-HR14) | 1.00 | 2.50 |
*P.P.BLACK/1: UNPRICED DUE TO SCARCITY
*P.P.CYAN/1: UNPRICED DUE TO SCARCITY
*P.P.MAGENTA/1: UNPRICED DUE TO SCARCITY
*P.P.YELLOW/1: UNPRICED DUE TO SCARCITY
RANDOMLY INSERTED INTO PACKS

| HR1 | Jyn Erso | 1.50 | 4.00 |
| HR4 | Chirrut Imwe | 1.25 | 3.00 |

2016 Star Wars Rogue One Series One Medallions

| COMMON CARD | 4.00 | 10.00 |
*BRONZE: SAME VALUE AS BASIC
*SILVER/99: .5X TO 1.2X BASIC CARDS
*GOLD/50: .6X TO 1.5X BASIC CARDS
*PLATINUM/1: UNPRICED DUE TO SCARCITY
RANDOMLY INSERTED INTO PACKS

5	Cassian Andor/X-Wing	6.00	15.00
6	Cassian Andor/U-Wing	6.00	15.00
7	Chirrut Imwe/Y-Wing	6.00	15.00
8	Darth Vader/Death Star	6.00	15.00
9	Darth Vader/Star Destroyer	6.00	15.00
10	Death Trooper/Star Destroyer	6.00	15.00
14	Edrio Two Tubes/U-Wing	6.00	15.00
15	Jyn Erso/X-Wing	8.00	20.00
16	Jyn Erso/U-Wing	8.00	20.00
17	Jyn Erso/Death Star	8.00	20.00
18	K-2SO/X-Wing	5.00	12.00
20	Moroff/U-Wing	5.00	12.00
24	Shoretrooper/AT-ACT	5.00	12.00
25	Stormtrooper/AT-ST	5.00	12.00
27	TIE Fighter Pilot	5.00	12.00

2016 Star Wars Rogue One Series One Montages

COMPLETE SET (9)	5.00	12.00
COMMON CARD (M1-M9)	1.00	2.50

*P.P.BLACK/1: UNPRICED DUE TO SCARCITY
*P.P.CYAN/1: UNPRICED DUE TO SCARCITY
*P.P.MAGENTA/1: UNPRICED DUE TO SCARCITY
*P.P.YELLOW/1: UNPRICED DUE TO SCARCITY

2016 Star Wars Rogue One Series One Sketches

UNPRICED DUE TO SCARCITY

NNO Achilleas Kokkinakis
NNO Alex Iniguez
NNO Anil Sharma
NNO Anthony Skubis
NNO Ben AbuSaada
NNO Bill Pulkovski
NNO Bob Hepner
NNO Bob Stevlic
NNO Brad Hudson
NNO Brad Tabar
NNO Brad Utterstrom
NNO Brendan Purchase
NNO Brent Ragland
NNO Brett Farr
NNO Brian Kong
NNO Carlos Cabaleiro
NNO Cathy Razim
NNO Chad LaForce
NNO Charlie Cody
NNO Chris Meeks
NNO D.J. Coffman
NNO Dan Bergren
NNO Dan Burn Webster
NNO Dan Curto
NNO Daniel Cooney
NNO Darrin Pepe
NNO David Rabbitte
NNO Elfie Lebouleux
NNO Eric Lehtonen
NNO Eric Muller
NNO Freddy Lopez
NNO Gabe Farber
NNO George Joseph
NNO Ingrid Hardy
NNO Jamie Cosley
NNO Jason Davies
NNO Jason Durden
NNO Jeff Mallinson
NNO Jennifer Allyn
NNO Jessica Hickman
NNO Jim Mehsling
NNO John Sloboda
NNO Jon Gregory
NNO Jordan Maison
NNO Kaela Croft
NNO Kate Carleton
NNO Kevin Graham
NNO Kevin Liell
NNO Kevin P. West
NNO Kris Penix
NNO Ksenia Zelentsova
NNO Kyle Babbitt
NNO Kyle Hickman

NNO Lawrence Reynolds
NNO Lee Lightfoot
NNO Marcia Dye
NNO Mark Mangum
NNO Marsha Parkins
NNO Matt Steffens
NNO Matt Stewart
NNO Melike Acar
NNO Pablo Diaz
NNO Patrick Giles
NNO Patrick Richardson
NNO Phil Hassewer
NNO Ray Paez
NNO Rich Molinelli
NNO Robert Hendrickson
NNO Roy Cover
NNO Scott Houseman
NNO Scott Jones
NNO Shaow Siong
NNO Solly Mohamed
NNO Stephanie Swanger
NNO Steve Potter
NNO Tim Dowler
NNO Tim Proctor
NNO Tina Berardi

2016 Star Wars Rogue One Series One Triple Autographs

UNPRICED DUE TO SCARCITY

NNO Yen/Kellington/Kasey
NNO O'Reilly/Whitaker/Kasey

2016 Star Wars Rogue One Series One Villains of the Galactic Empire

COMPLETE SET (8)	6.00	15.00
COMMON CARD (VE1-VE8)	1.00	2.50

*P.P.BLACK/1: UNPRICED DUE TO SCARCITY
*P.P.CYAN/1: UNPRICED DUE TO SCARCITY
*P.P.MAGENTA/1: UNPRICED DUE TO SCARCITY
*P.P.YELLOW/1: UNPRICED DUE TO SCARCITY

2017 Star Wars Rogue One Series Two

KRENNIC AND TARKIN CONFER

COMPLETE SET (100)	6.00	15.00
UNOPENED BOX (24 PACKS)	110.00	120.00
UNOPENED PACK (8 CARDS)	5.00	6.00
COMMON CARD (1-100)	.20	.50

*DTHSTR BLACK: .6X TO 1.5X BASIC CARDS
*GREEN SQ: .75X TO 2X BASIC CARDS
*BLUE SQ: 1X TO 2.5X BASIC CARDS
*GRAY SQ/100: 5X TO 12X BASIC CARDS
*GOLD SQ/50: 10X TO 25X BASIC CARDS
*ORANGE/1: UNPRICED DUE TO SCARCITY
*RED/1: UNPRICED DUE TO SCARCITY
*P.P.BLACK/1: UNPRICED DUE TO SCARCITY
*P.P.CYAN/1: UNPRICED DUE TO SCARCITY
*P.P.MAGENTA/1: UNPRICED DUE TO SCARCITY
*P.P.YELLOW/1: UNPRICED DUE TO SCARCITY

2017 Star Wars Rogue One Series Two Autographs

FELICITY JONES AS
JYN ERSO

COMMON AUTO	10.00	25.00

*BLACK/50: .6X TO 1.5X BASIC AUTOS
*GOLD/10: 1.2X TO 3X BASIC AUTOS
*ORANGE/1: UNPRICED DUE TO SCARCITY
*P.P.BLACK/1: UNPRICED DUE TO SCARCITY
*P.P.CYAN/1: UNPRICED DUE TO SCARCITY
*P.P.MAGENTA/1: UNPRICED DUE TO SCARCITY
*P.P.YELLOW/1: UNPRICED DUE TO SCARCITY
STATED ODDS 1:36
JONES, WHITAKER, AND KELLINGTON
DO NOT HAVE BASE AUTOGRAPHS

DA Derek Arnold	12.00	30.00
DY Donnie Yen	80.00	150.00
GO Genevieve O'Reilly	8.00	20.00
RA Riz Ahmed	120.00	200.00
WD Warwick Davis	12.00	30.00
AC1 Aidan Cook	10.00	25.00
Benthic Two Tubes		
AC2 Aidan Cook	10.00	25.00
Caitken		

2017 Star Wars Rogue One Series Two Autographs Black

*BLACK/50: .6X TO 1.5X BASIC AUTOS
STATED ODDS 1:163
STATED PRINT RUN 50 SER.#'d SETS

FJ Felicity Jones	300.00	600.00
FW Forest Whitaker	100.00	200.00
NK Nick Kellington	20.00	50.00

2017 Star Wars Rogue One Series Two Character Stickers

COMPLETE SET (18)	30.00	80.00
COMMON CARD (CS1-CS18)	2.50	6.00
STATED ODDS 1:12		

CS1 Jyn Erso	5.00	12.00
CS8 Director Krennic	3.00	8.00
CS9 Darth Vader	4.00	10.00
CS10 K-2SO	3.00	8.00
CS14 Chirrut Imwe	4.00	10.00
CS18 Admiral Raddus	3.00	8.00

2017 Star Wars Rogue One Series Two Dual Autographs

UNPRICED DUE TO SCARCITY

FJFW Jones/Whitaker
FJGO Jones/O'Reilly
GOAP O'Reilly/Petrie

2017 Star Wars Rogue One Series Two Heroes of the Rebel Alliance

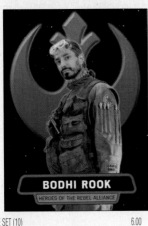

BODHI ROOK
HEROES OF THE REBEL ALLIANCE

COMPLETE SET (10)	6.00	15.00
COMMON CARD (HR1-HR10)	1.00	2.50
*P.P.BLACK/1: UNPRICED DUE TO SCARCITY		
*P.P.CYAN/1: UNPRICED DUE TO SCARCITY		
*P.P.MAGENTA/1: UNPRICED DUE TO SCARCITY		
*P.P.YELLOW/1: UNPRICED DUE TO SCARCITY		
STATED ODDS 1:7		

2017 Star Wars Rogue One Series Two Movie Posters

COMPLETE SET (10)	30.00	80.00
COMMON CARD (1-10)	3.00	8.00
*P.P.BLACK/1: UNPRICED DUE TO SCARCITY		
*P.P.CYAN/1: UNPRICED DUE TO SCARCITY		
*P.P.MAGENTA/1: UNPRICED DUE TO SCARCITY		
*P.P.YELLOW/1: UNPRICED DUE TO SCARCITY		
STATED ODDS 1:24		
1 United States Theatrical Poster	6.00	15.00
5 Cassian Andor Character Poster	4.00	10.00
6 Bodhi Rook Character Poster	5.00	12.00
7 Chirrut Imwe Character Poster	6.00	15.00
9 K-2SO Character Poster	6.00	15.00

2017 Star Wars Rogue One Series Two Patches

LT. ZAL DINNES (RED EIGHT)

COMMON CARD	5.00	12.00
*SILVER/100: .5X TO 1.2X BASIC CARDS		
*GOLD/50: .6X TO 1.5X BASIC CARDS		
*RED/10: 1.2X TO 3X BASIC CARDS		
*ORANGE/1: UNPRICED DUE TO SCARCITY		

2017 Star Wars Rogue One Series Two Prime Forces

COMPLETE SET (10)	8.00	20.00
COMMON CARD (PF1-PF10)	1.50	4.00
*P.P.BLACK/1: UNPRICED DUE TO SCARCITY		
*P.P.CYAN/1: UNPRICED DUE TO SCARCITY		
*P.P.MAGENTA/1: UNPRICED DUE TO SCARCITY		
*P.P.YELLOW/1: UNPRICED DUE TO SCARCITY		
STATED ODDS 1:2		

2017 Star Wars Rogue One Series Two Sketches

STATED ODDS 1:32
UNPRICED DUE TO SCARCITY

NNO Achilleas Kokkinakis
NNO Andrew Lopez
NNO Angelina Benedetti
NNO Anil Sharma
NNO Anthony Skubis
NNO Ben AbuSaada

NNO Bill Pulkovski
NNO Bob Hepner
NNO Brad Hudson
NNO Brendan Purchase
NNO Brent Engstrom
NNO Brent Ragland
NNO Brett Farr
NNO Bruce Gerlach
NNO Can Baran
NNO Carlos Cabaleiro
NNO Cathy Razim
NNO Chad LaForce
NNO Charlie Cody
NNO Cliff Thomas
NNO Clinton Yeager
NNO Corey Galal
NNO Dan Curto
NNO Daniel Cooney
NNO Danny Kidwell
NNO Darrin Pepe
NNO Dennis Gortakowski
NNO Elfie Lebouleux
NNO Eric Lehtonen
NNO Erik Maell
NNO Freddy Lopez
NNO George Joseph
NNO Ingrid Hardy
NNO Jamie Cosley
NNO Jason Davies
NNO Jason Durden
NNO Jason Sobol
NNO Jay Manchand
NNO Jim Mehsling
NNO JM Smith
NNO Jonathan Caustrita
NNO Jordan Maison
NNO Joshua Bommer
NNO Kallan Archer
NNO Kate Carleton
NNO Kevin Graham
NNO Kevin Liell
NNO Kevin P. West
NNO Kris Penix
NNO Kyle Hickman
NNO Lee Lightfoot
NNO Luke Preece
NNO Marcia Dye
NNO Mark Mangum
NNO Marsha Parkins
NNO Matt Langford
NNO Matt Soffe
NNO Matt Steffens
NNO Matt Stewart
NNO Melike Acar
NNO Mick and Matt Glebe
NNO Mike Barnard
NNO Mohammad Jilani
NNO Neil Camera
NNO Patrick Giles
NNO Phil Hassewer
NNO Randy Siplon
NNO Rich Molinelli
NNO Robert Hendrickson
NNO Roy Cover
NNO Ryan Moffett
NNO Shaow Siong
NNO Solly Mohamed
NNO Steve Potter
NNO Ted Dastick Jr.
NNO Tim Proctor
NNO Tina Berardi
NNO Todd Aaron Smith

2017 Star Wars Rogue One Series Two Triple Autographs

STATED ODDS 1:11,771
UNPRICED DUE TO SCARCITY

FJDYFW Jones/Yen/Whitaker
FJGOAP Jones/O'Reilly/Petrie
FWPKAC Whitaker/Kasey/Cook

2017 Star Wars Rogue One Series Two Troopers

COMPLETE SET (10)	8.00	20.00
COMMON CARD (TR1-TR10)	1.50	4.00
*P.P.BLACK/1: UNPRICED DUE TO SCARCITY		
*P.P.CYAN/1: UNPRICED DUE TO SCARCITY		
*P.P.MAGENTA/1: UNPRICED DUE TO SCARCITY		
*P.P.YELLOW/1: UNPRICED DUE TO SCARCITY		
STATED ODDS 1:2		

2017 Star Wars Rogue One Series Two Villains of the Galactic Empire

COMPLETE SET (10)	12.00	30.00
COMMON CARD (VG1-VG10)	2.50	6.00
*P.P.BLACK/1: UNPRICED DUE TO SCARCITY		
*P.P.CYAN/1: UNPRICED DUE TO SCARCITY		
*P.P.MAGENTA/1: UNPRICED DUE TO SCARCITY		
*P.P.YELLOW/1: UNPRICED DUE TO SCARCITY		
STATED ODDS 1:7		

2016-17 Star Wars Rogue One Darth Vader Continuity

COMPLETE SET (15)	20.00	50.00
COMMON CARD (1-15)	2.50	6.00
MISSION BRIEFING (1-5)		
SERIES ONE (6-10)		
SERIES TWO (11-15)		
*P.P.BLACK/1: UNPRICED DUE TO SCARCITY		
*P.P.CYAN/1: UNPRICED DUE TO SCARCITY		
*P.P.MAGENTA/1: UNPRICED DUE TO SCARCITY		
*P.P.YELLOW/1: UNPRICED DUE TO SCARCITY		
STATED ODDS 1:12		

THE LAST JEDI

2017 Star Wars The Last Jedi Disney Movie Reward Oversized Theater Promos

COMPLETE SET (9)	15.00	40.00
COMMON CARD (UNNUMBERED)	2.00	5.00
THEATER PROMOTION EXCLUSIVE		

2017 Star Wars The Last Jedi Series One

FINN

COMPLETE SET (100)	6.00	15.00
UNOPENED BOX (24 PACKS)	75.00	100.00
UNOPENED PACK (8 CARDS)	4.00	5.00
COMMON CARD (1-100)	.12	.30
*BLUE: 2X TO 5X BASIC CARDS		
*GREEN: 2.5X TO 6X BASIC CARDS		
*PURPLE: 3X TO 8X BASIC CARDS		
*RED: 4X TO 10X BASIC CARDS		
*SILVER/99: 10X TO 25X BASIC CARDS		
*GOLD/25: 20X TO 50X BASIC CARDS		
*BLACK/1: UNPRICED DUE TO SCARCITY		
*P.P.BLACK/1: UNPRICED DUE TO SCARCITY		
*P.P.CYAN/1: UNPRICED DUE TO SCARCITY		
*P.P.MAGENTA/1: UNPRICED DUE TO SCARCITY		
*P.P.YELLOW/1: UNPRICED DUE TO SCARCITY		

2017 Star Wars The Last Jedi Series One Autographs

COMMON AUTO	6.00	15.00
*RED/99: .5X TO 1.2X BASIC AUTOS		
*SILVER/25: .6X TO 1.5X BASIC AUTOS		
*GOLD/10: UNPRICED DUE TO SCARCITY		
*BLACK/1: UNPRICED DUE TO SCARCITY		
*P.P.BLACK/1: UNPRICED DUE TO SCARCITY		

*P.P.CYAN/1: UNPRICED DUE TO SCARCITY
*P.P.MAGENTA/1: UNPRICED DUE TO SCARCITY
*P.P.YELLOW/1: UNPRICED DUE TO SCARCITY

NNO Aidan Cook	8.00	20.00
NNO Andy Serkis	60.00	120.00
NNO Billie Lourd	60.00	120.00
NNO Brian Herring	12.00	30.00
NNO Crystal Clarke	10.00	25.00
NNO Dave Chapman	12.00	30.00
NNO Ian Whyte	8.00	20.00
NNO Jimmy Vee	15.00	40.00
NNO Mike Quinn	8.00	20.00
NNO Paul Kasey	10.00	25.00
NNO Tom Kane	8.00	20.00
NNO Veronica Ngo	15.00	40.00

2017 Star Wars The Last Jedi Series One Autographs Red

*RED: .5X TO 1.2X BASIC AUTOS
STATED PRINT RUN 99 SER.#'d SETS

NNO John Boyega		120.00
NNO Joonas Suotamo		75.00

2017 Star Wars The Last Jedi Series One Autographs Silver

*SILVER: X TO X BASIC AUTOS
STATED PRINT RUN 25 SER.#'d SETS

NNO Gwendoline Christie	100.00	200.00

2017 Star Wars The Last Jedi Series One Blueprints and Schematics

COMPLETE SET (8)	6.00	15.00
COMMON CARD (BP1-BP8)	1.25	3.00
*PURPLE/250: .6X TO 1.5X BASIC CARDS	2.00	5.00
*RED/199: .75X TO 2X BASIC CARDS	2.50	6.00
*SILVER/99: 1X TO 2.5X BASIC CARDS	3.00	8.00
*GOLD/25: UNPRICED DUE TO SCARCITY		
*BLACK/1: UNPRICED DUE TO SCARCITY		
*P.P.BLACK/1: UNPRICED DUE TO SCARCITY		
*P.P.CYAN/1: UNPRICED DUE TO SCARCITY		
*P.P.MAGENTA/1: UNPRICED DUE TO SCARCITY		
*P.P.YELLOW/1: UNPRICED DUE TO SCARCITY		

2017 Star Wars The Last Jedi Series One Character Portraits

COMPLETE SET (16)	12.00	30.00
COMMON CARD (CP1-CP16)	1.50	4.00
*PURPLE/250: .6X TO 1.5X BASIC CARDS	2.50	6.00
*RED/199: .75X TO 2X BASIC CARDS	3.00	8.00
*SILVER/99: 1X TO 2.5X BASIC CARDS	4.00	10.00
*GOLD/25: UNPRICED DUE TO SCARCITY		
*BLACK/1: UNPRICED DUE TO SCARCITY		
*P.P.BLACK/1: UNPRICED DUE TO SCARCITY		
*P.P.CYAN/1: UNPRICED DUE TO SCARCITY		
*P.P.MAGENTA/1: UNPRICED DUE TO SCARCITY		
*P.P.YELLOW/1: UNPRICED DUE TO SCARCITY		
RANDOMLY INSERTED INTO PACKS		

2017 Star Wars The Last Jedi Series One Character Stickers

COMPLETE SET (6)	8.00	20.00
COMMON CARD (DS1-DS6)	1.25	3.00
RANDOMLY INSERTED INTO PACKS		
DS1 Kylo Ren	1.50	4.00
DS4 Rey	3.00	8.00
DS5 Finn	2.50	6.00
DS6 Poe Dameron	2.00	5.00

2017 Star Wars The Last Jedi Series One Dual Autographs

STATED PRINT RUN 5 SER.#'d SETS
UNPRICED DUE TO SCARCITY

NNO Driver/Serkis
NNO Driver/Christie
NNO Boyega/Christie
NNO Hamill/Ridley
NNO Hamill/Vee

2017 Star Wars The Last Jedi Series One Illustrated

COMPLETE SET (11)	8.00	20.00
COMMON CARD (SWI1-SWI11)	1.25	3.00
*PURPLE/250: .6X TO 1.5X BASIC CARDS	2.00	5.00
*RED/199: .75X TO 2X BASIC CARDS	2.50	6.00
*SILVER/99: 1X TO 2.5X BASIC CARDS	3.00	8.00
*GOLD/25: UNPRICED DUE TO SCARCITY		
*BLACK/1: UNPRICED DUE TO SCARCITY		
*P.P.BLACK/1: UNPRICED DUE TO SCARCITY		
*P.P.CYAN/1: UNPRICED DUE TO SCARCITY		
*P.P.MAGENTA/1: UNPRICED DUE TO SCARCITY		
*P.P.YELLOW/1: UNPRICED DUE TO SCARCITY		
RANDOMLY INSERTED INTO PACKS		

2017 Star Wars The Last Jedi Series One Medallions

COMMON MEDALLION	4.00	10.00
*PURPLE/99: .5X TO 1.2X BASIC MEDALLIONS	5.00	12.00
*RED/25: 1.2X TO 3X BASIC MEDALLIONS	12.00	30.00
*ORANGE/1: UNPRICED DUE TO SCARCITY		
RANDOMLY INSERTED INTO PACKS		
NNO BB-8/BB-8	5.00	12.00
NNO BB-8/Resistance	6.00	15.00
NNO C-3PO/R2-D2	5.00	12.00
NNO Chewbacca/R2-D2	8.00	20.00
NNO Executioner Stormtrooper/First Order	5.00	12.00
NNO Finn/BB-8	5.00	12.00
NNO Finn/Resistance	6.00	15.00
NNO General Hux/First Order	5.00	12.00
NNO General Leia Organa/Resistance	6.00	15.00
NNO Kylo Ren/First Order	6.00	15.00
NNO Luke Skywalker/Millennium Falcon	10.00	25.00
NNO Poe Dameron/BB-8	5.00	12.00
NNO Poe Dameron/Resistance	6.00	15.00
NNO Porg/Millennium Falcon	6.00	15.00
NNO Porg/R2-D2	6.00	15.00
NNO Praetorian Guard/First Order	5.00	12.00
NNO R2-D2/Resistance	5.00	12.00
NNO Rey/BB-8	8.00	20.00
NNO Rey/Millennium Falcon	8.00	20.00
NNO Rey/Resistance	8.00	20.00
NNO Rose/Resistance	5.00	12.00

2017 Star Wars The Last Jedi Series One Red Character Illustrations

COMPLETE SET (8)	8.00	20.00
COMMON CARD (RL1-RL8)	1.50	4.00
*PURPLE/250: .6X TO 1.5X BASIC CARDS	2.50	6.00
*RED/199: .75X TO 2X BASIC CARDS	3.00	8.00
*SILVER/99: 1X TO 2.5X BASIC CARDS	4.00	10.00
*GOLD/25: UNPRICED DUE TO SCARCITY		
*BLACK/1: UNPRICED DUE TO SCARCITY		
*P.P.BLACK/1: UNPRICED DUE TO SCARCITY		
*P.P.CYAN/1: UNPRICED DUE TO SCARCITY		
*P.P.MAGENTA/1: UNPRICED DUE TO SCARCITY		
*P.P.YELLOW/1: UNPRICED DUE TO SCARCITY		
RANDOMLY INSERTED INTO PACKS		

2017 Star Wars The Last Jedi Series One Resist!

COMPLETE SET (8)	5.00	12.00
COMMON CARD (R1-R8)	1.00	2.50
*PURPLE/250: .6X TO 1.5X BASIC CARDS	1.50	4.00
*RED/199: .75X TO 2X BASIC CARDS	2.00	5.00
*SILVER/99: 1X TO 2.5X BASIC CARDS	2.50	6.00
*GOLD/25: UNPRICED DUE TO SCARCITY		
*BLACK/1: UNPRICED DUE TO SCARCITY		
*P.P.BLACK/1: UNPRICED DUE TO SCARCITY		
*P.P.CYAN/1: UNPRICED DUE TO SCARCITY		
*P.P.MAGENTA/1: UNPRICED DUE TO SCARCITY		
*P.P.YELLOW/1: UNPRICED DUE TO SCARCITY		
RANDOMLY INSERTED INTO PACKS		

2017 Star Wars The Last Jedi Series One Shaped Sketches

UNPRICED DUE TO SCARCITY

NNO Adam Worton
NNO Aleksander Gigov
NNO Alex Mines
NNO Andrew Fry
NNO Ben Goddard
NNO Brandon Pyle
NNO Brendan Purchase
NNO Brent Ragland
NNO Brent Scotchmer
NNO Bryan Silverbax
NNO Carlos Cabaleiro
NNO Carolyn Craggs
NNO Cathy Razim
NNO Chad Scheres
NNO Chris Clark
NNO Chris Quinn
NNO Chris Thorne
NNO Colin Arthurs
NNO Dan Curto
NNO Dan Gorman
NNO Danny Hayman
NNO Dave Fowler
NNO Dave Holtz
NNO Dean Drummond
NNO Doug Snodgrass
NNO Eli Hyder
NNO Erik Maell
NNO Gavin Williams
NNO Harold George
NNO Huy Truong
NNO Ingrid Hardy
NNO James O'Riley

NNO Jason Adams
NNO Jason Davies
NNO Jay Manchand
NNO Jeff Abar
NNO Jennifer Allyn
NNO Jerry Bennett
NNO Jim Mehsling
NNO JM Smith
NNO Jordan Maison
NNO Kaela Croft
NNO Kiley Beecher
NNO Kris Penix
NNO Kurt Ruskin
NNO Laura Atkinson
NNO Logan Monette
NNO Marlo Agunos
NNO Matt Buttich
NNO Matt Langford
NNO Matt Maldonado
NNO Matt Stewart
NNO Mike James
NNO Mike Spivey
NNO Nathan Ohlendorf
NNO Neil Camera
NNO Nick Justus
NNO Nicolas Baltra
NNO Pablo Diaz
NNO Patricio Carrasco
NNO Patrick Richardson
NNO Phil Hassewer
NNO Quentin Aldredge
NNO Rich Molinelli
NNO Richard Serrao
NNO Robert Hendrickson
NNO Rodney Roberts
NNO Ruvel Abril
NNO Ryan Finley
NNO Ryan Moffett
NNO Shane McCormack
NNO Shaow Siong
NNO Solly Mohamed
NNO Tim Dowler
NNO Todd Aaron Smith
NNO Trent Westbrook
NNO Ward Silverman

2017 Star Wars The Last Jedi Series One Six-Person Autograph

NNO Hamill/Ridley/Boyega/Serkis/Driver/Christie

2017 Star Wars The Last Jedi Series One Sketches

UNPRICED DUE TO SCARCITY

NNO Adam Worton
NNO Aleksander Gigov
NNO Alex Mines
NNO Andrew Fry
NNO Ben Goddard
NNO Brandon Pyle
NNO Brendan Purchase
NNO Brent Ragland
NNO Brent Scotchmer
NNO Bryan Silverbax
NNO Carlos Cabaleiro
NNO Carolyn Craggs
NNO Cathy Razim
NNO Chad Scheres
NNO Chris Clark
NNO Chris Quinn
NNO Chris Thorne
NNO Colin Arthurs
NNO Dan Curto
NNO Dan Gorman
NNO Danny Hayman
NNO Dave Fowler
NNO Dave Holtz
NNO Dean Drummond
NNO Doug Snodgrass
NNO Eli Hyder
NNO Erik Maell
NNO Gavin Williams

NNO Harold George
NNO Huy Truong
NNO Ingrid Hardy
NNO James O'Riley
NNO Jason Adams
NNO Jason Davies
NNO Jay Manchand
NNO Jeff Abar
NNO Jennifer Allyn
NNO Jerry Bennett
NNO Jim Mehsling
NNO JM Smith
NNO Jordan Maison
NNO Kaela Croft
NNO Kiley Beecher
NNO Kris Penix
NNO Kurt Ruskin
NNO Laura Atkinson
NNO Logan Monette
NNO Marlo Agunos
NNO Matt Buttich
NNO Matt Langford
NNO Matt Maldonado
NNO Matt Stewart
NNO Mike James
NNO Mike Spivey
NNO Nathan Ohlendorf
NNO Neil Camera
NNO Nick Justus
NNO Nicolas Baltra
NNO Pablo Diaz
NNO Patricio Carrasco
NNO Patrick Richardson
NNO Phil Hassewer
NNO Quentin Aldredge
NNO Rich Molinelli
NNO Richard Serrao
NNO Robert Hendrickson
NNO Rodney Roberts
NNO Ruvel Abril
NNO Ryan Finley
NNO Ryan Moffett
NNO Shane McCormack
NNO Shaow Siong
NNO Solly Mohamed
NNO Tim Dowler
NNO Todd Aaron Smith
NNO Trent Westbrook
NNO Ward Silverman

2017 Star Wars The Last Jedi Series One Source Material Fabric Relics

SOSEAR LATTA

COMMON RELIC	12.00	30.00
*SILVER/99: .5X TO 1.2X BASIC RELICS	15.00	40.00
*GOLD/25: UNPRICED DUE TO SCARCITY		
*BLACK/1: UNPRICED DUE TO SCARCITY		
RANDOMLY INSERTED INTO PACKS		

2017 Star Wars The Last Jedi Series One Triple Autographs

STATED PRINT RUN 3 SER.#'d SETS
UNPRICED DUE TO SCARCITY

NNO Driver/Serkis/Christie
NNO Herring/Daniels/Vee
NNO Hamill/Ridley/Vee

2018 Star Wars The Last Jedi Series Two

COMPLETE SET (100)	6.00	15.00
UNOPENED BOX (24 PACKS)		
UNOPENED PACK (8 CARDS)		
COMMON CARD (1-100)	.12	.30
*BLUE: 2X TO 5X BASIC CARDS	.60	1.50
*PURPLE: 3X TO 8X BASIC CARDS	1.00	2.50
*RED/199: 4X TO 10X BASIC CARDS	1.25	3.00
*BRONZE/99: 10X TO 25X BASIC CARDS	3.00	8.00
*SILVER/25: 20X TO 50X BASIC CARDS	6.00	15.00
*GOLD/10: UNPRICED DUE TO SCARCITY		
*BLACK/1: UNPRICED DUE TO SCARCITY		
*P.P.BLACK/1: UNPRICED DUE TO SCARCITY		
*P.P.CYAN/1: UNPRICED DUE TO SCARCITY		
*P.P.MAGENTA/1: UNPRICED DUE TO SCARCITY		
*P.P.YELLOW/1: UNPRICED DUE TO SCARCITY		

2018 Star Wars The Last Jedi Series Two Autographs

KIRAN SHAH AS
NEEBA'S PATROK

COMMON AUTO	6.00	15.00
*GOLD/10: UNPRICED DUE TO SCARCITY		
*BLACK/1: UNPRICED DUE TO SCARCITY		
*P.P.BLACK/1: UNPRICED DUE TO SCARCITY		
*P.P.CYAN/1: UNPRICED DUE TO SCARCITY		
*P.P.MAGENTA/1: UNPRICED DUE TO SCARCITY		
*P.P.YELLOW/1: UNPRICED DUE TO SCARCITY		
STATED ODDS 1:36		
AAD Adam Driver		
AAE Adrian Edmondson	10.00	25.00
AAL Amanda Lawrence	12.00	30.00
AAS Andy Serkis		
AADC Anthony Daniels		
ABL Billie Lourd		
ABH Brian Herring	8.00	20.00
ACC Crystal Clarke	8.00	20.00
ADR Daisy Ridley		
AGC Gwendoline Christie		
AHC Hermione Corfield	20.00	50.00
AJV Jimmy Vee	10.00	25.00
AJB John Boyega	50.00	100.00
AJS Joonas Suotamo		
AKS Kiran Shah	8.00	20.00
ALD Laura Dern		
AMQ Mike Quinn		
ATK Tom Kane		
AVN Veronica Ngo	15.00	40.00

2018 Star Wars The Last Jedi Series Two Autographs Red

*RED: .5X TO 1.2X BASIC AUTOS
STATED ODDS 1:127
STATED PRINT RUN 99 SER.#'d SETS

ALD Laura Dern	75.00	150.00

2018 Star Wars The Last Jedi Series Two Autographs Silver

STATED ODDS 1:350
STATED PRINT RUN 25 SER.#'d SETS

NNO Adam Driver	300.00	500.00
AAS Andy Serkis	60.00	120.00
AADC Anthony Daniels	100.00	200.00
AJS Joonas Suotamo	50.00	100.00

2018 Star Wars The Last Jedi Series Two Character Stickers

COMPLETE SET (10)	15.00	40.00
COMMON STICKER (CS1-CS10)	1.25	3.00
STATED ODDS 1:16		
CS1 Rey	3.00	8.00
CS2 Kylo Ren	1.50	4.00
CS3 Finn	2.00	5.00
CS4 Poe Dameron	5.00	12.00
CS5 Supreme Leader Snoke	1.50	4.00
CS6 Captain Phasma	2.00	5.00
CS8 General Leia Organa	2.00	5.00
CS10 Luke Skywalker	2.50	6.00

2018 Star Wars The Last Jedi Series Two Commemorative Patches

COMMON PATCH	3.00	8.00
*GOLD/25: UNPRICED DUE TO SCARCITY		
*BLACK/1: UNPRICED DUE TO SCARCITY		
STATED ODDS 1:67		
MEC Chewbacca	4.00	10.00
MEAH Vice Admiral Holdo	5.00	12.00
MEBB BB-8	5.00	12.00
MECB Chewbacca	4.00	10.00
MECP Captain Phasma	6.00	15.00
MECT C'ai Threnalli	5.00	12.00
MEDR Rey	6.00	15.00
MEFA Finn	6.00	15.00
MEFB Finn	6.00	15.00
MEGE General Ematt	5.00	12.00
MEJB Finn	6.00	15.00
MEKR Kylo Ren	6.00	15.00
MELO General Leia Organa	8.00	20.00
MELS Luke Skywalker	8.00	20.00
MENG Ensign Pamich Nerro Goode	5.00	12.00
MEPD Poe Dameron	5.00	12.00
MEPG Praetorian Guard	6.00	15.00
MEPT Resistance Gunner Paige Tico	5.00	12.00
MER2 R2-D2	5.00	12.00
MERA Rey	6.00	15.00
MERB Rey	6.00	15.00
MERT Rose Tico	5.00	12.00
MESE Stormtrooper Executioner	4.00	10.00
MEBB8 BB-8	5.00	12.00
MEBBR BB-8	5.00	12.00
MEC3B C-3PO	4.00	10.00
MEC3P C-3PO	4.00	10.00
MECPB Captain Phasma	6.00	15.00
MEGEA General Ematt	5.00	12.00

MEKCA Kaydel Ko Connix	6.00	15.00
MEKKC Kaydel Ko Connix	6.00	15.00
MEKRB Kylo Ren	6.00	15.00
MELOR General Leia Organa	8.00	20.00
MELSB Luke Skywalker	8.00	20.00
MENGA Ensign Pamich Nerro Goode	5.00	12.00
MEPDA Poe Dameron	5.00	12.00
MEPDB Poe Dameron	5.00	12.00
MEPDP Poe Dameron	5.00	12.00
MEPGB Praetorian Guard	6.00	15.00
MER2B R2-D2	5.00	12.00
MER2R R2-D2	5.00	12.00
MESLB Supreme Leader Snoke	5.00	12.00
MESLS Supreme Leader Snoke	5.00	12.00

2018 Star Wars The Last Jedi Series Two Dual Autographs

STATED ODDS 1:7,116
STATED PRINT RUN 5 SER.#'d SETS
UNPRICED DUE TO SCARCITY

DARD Ridley/Driver
DARS Ridley/Serkis
DASV Suotamo/Vee
DAQK Quinn/Nunb
DARK Rose/Kane

2018 Star Wars The Last Jedi Series Two Items and Artifacts

COMPLETE SET (20)	10.00	25.00
COMMON CARD (IA1-IA20)	.75	2.00
*RED/99: .5X TO 1.2X BASIC CARDS		
*BRONZE/50: .75X TO 2X BASIC CARDS		
*SILVER/25: UNPRICED DUE TO SCARCITY		
*GOLD/10: UNPRICED DUE TO SCARCITY		
*BLACK/1: UNPRICED DUE TO SCARCITY		
*P.P.BLACK/1: UNPRICED DUE TO SCARCITY		
*P.P.CYAN/1: UNPRICED DUE TO SCARCITY		
*P.P.MAGENTA/1: UNPRICED DUE TO SCARCITY		
*P.P.YELLOW/1: UNPRICED DUE TO SCARCITY		
STATED ODDS 1:1		
IA1 Skywalker's Lightsaber	2.00	5.00
IA2 Luke Skywalker's Compass	2.00	5.00
IA4 Proton Bomb	1.25	3.00
IA14 Kylo Ren's Lightsaber	3.00	8.00

2018 Star Wars The Last Jedi Series Two Leaders of the Resistance

COMPLETE SET (10)	5.00	12.00
COMMON CARD (RS1-RS10)	.75	2.00
*RED/99: .5X TO 1.2X BASIC CARDS		
*BRONZE/50: .75X TO 2X BASIC CARDS		
*SILVER/25: UNPRICED DUE TO SCARCITY		
*GOLD/10: UNPRICED DUE TO SCARCITY		
*BLACK/1: UNPRICED DUE TO SCARCITY		
*P.P.BLACK/1: UNPRICED DUE TO SCARCITY		
*P.P.CYAN/1: UNPRICED DUE TO SCARCITY		
*P.P.MAGENTA/1: UNPRICED DUE TO SCARCITY		
*P.P.YELLOW/1: UNPRICED DUE TO SCARCITY		
STATED ODDS 1:2		

2018 Star Wars The Last Jedi Series Two Leaders of the Resistance Autographs

COMPLETE SET (7)
STATED ODDS 1:5,024

UNPRICED DUE TO SCARCITY
RS3 Laura Dern
RS4 Andrew Jack
RS5 Tim Rose
RS7 Mike Quinn
RS8 Paul Kasey
RS9 Anthony Daniels
RS10 Crystal Clarke

2018 Star Wars The Last Jedi Series Two Patrons of Canto Bight

COMPLETE SET (10)	6.00	15.00
COMMON CARD (CB1-CB10)	1.25	3.00
*RED/99: .5X TO 1.2X BASIC CARDS	1.50	4.00
*BRONZE/50: .75X TO 2X BASIC CARDS	2.50	6.00
*SILVER/25: UNPRICED DUE TO SCARCITY		
*GOLD/10: UNPRICED DUE TO SCARCITY		
*BLACK/1: UNPRICED DUE TO SCARCITY		
*P.P.BLACK/1: UNPRICED DUE TO SCARCITY		
*P.P.CYAN/1: UNPRICED DUE TO SCARCITY		
*P.P.MAGENTA/1: UNPRICED DUE TO SCARCITY		
*P.P.YELLOW/1: UNPRICED DUE TO SCARCITY		
STATED ODDS 1:6		

2018 Star Wars The Last Jedi Series Two Patrons of Canto Bight Autographs

STATED ODDS 1:11,386
CB2 Kiran Shah
CB5 Warwick Davis

2018 Star Wars The Last Jedi Series Two Shaped Sketches

STATED ODDS 1:581
UNPRICED DUE TO SCARCITY

NNO Adam Talley
NNO Alex Mines
NNO Allen Grimes
NNO Andy Fry
NNO Angelina Benedetti
NNO Ashleigh Popplewell
NNO Ben Abu Saada
NNO Ben Goddard
NNO Brad Hudson
NNO Brandon Blevins
NNO Brendan Purchase
NNO Brent Ragland
NNO Brent Scotchmer
NNO Bruce Gerlach
NNO Caleb King
NNO Carlos Cabaleiro
NNO Carolyn Craggs
NNO Chad Scheres
NNO Christian Parker
NNO Colin Arthurs
NNO Dan Bergren
NNO Dan Curto
NNO Darren Coburn-James
NNO Darrin Pepe
NNO Dave Fowler
NNO David Rabbitte
NNO Eli Hyder
NNO Eric Lehtonen
NNO Gavin Williams

NNO Gorkem Demir
NNO Huy Truong
NNO Ian MacDougall
NNO Jamie Cosley
NNO Jason Adams
NNO Jason Keith Phillips
NNO Jason Sobol
NNO Jeff Abar
NNO Jeff Meuth
NNO Jim Mehsling
NNO John Bilage
NNO John Bruce
NNO Jon Arton
NNO Jose Ventura
NNO Juan Rosales
NNO Keith Carter
NNO Kevin Cleveland
NNO Kevin Graham
NNO Kevin Hawkins
NNO Kris Penix
NNO Kurt Ruskin
NNO Laura Martin
NNO Lee Lightfoot
NNO Logan Monette
NNO Louise Draper
NNO Louise Draper
NNO Mark Stroud
NNO Marlo Agunas
NNO Marsha Parkins
NNO Matt Langford
NNO Matthew Hirons
NNO Matthew Sutton
NNO Michael Bernard
NNO Mick and Matt Glebe
NNO Mike Mastermaker
NNO Mohammad Jilani
NNO Nathan Kennett
NNO Neil Camera
NNO Nicholas Baltra
NNO Nick Allsopp
NNO Nick Justus
NNO Patricio Carrasco
NNO Patrick Davis
NNO Patrick Giles
NNO Phil Hassewer
NNO Rebecca Sharp
NNO Rich Molinelli
NNO Richard Serrao
NNO Robert Teranishi
NNO Ryan Finley
NNO Ryan Santos
NNO Sebastian Cortez
NNO Shaow Siong
NNO Steve Alce
NNO Tiffany Groves
NNO Tom Amici
NNO Trent Westbrook
NNO Trevor Anderson
NNO Ward Silverman

2018 Star Wars The Last Jedi Series Two Ships and Vehicles

COMPLETE SET (10)	8.00	20.00
COMMON CARD (SV1-SV10)	1.50	4.00
*RED/99: .5X TO 1.2X BASIC CARDS	2.00	5.00
*BRONZE/50: .75X TO 2X BASIC CARDS	3.00	8.00
*SILVER/25: UNPRICED DUE TO SCARCITY		
*GOLD/10: UNPRICED DUE TO SCARCITY		
*BLACK/1: UNPRICED DUE TO SCARCITY		
*P.P.BLACK/1: UNPRICED DUE TO SCARCITY		
*P.P.CYAN/1: UNPRICED DUE TO SCARCITY		
*P.P.MAGENTA/1: UNPRICED DUE TO SCARCITY		
*P.P.YELLOW/1: UNPRICED DUE TO SCARCITY		
STATED ODDS 1:8		

2018 Star Wars The Last Jedi Series Two Six-Person Autograph

STATED ODDS 1:85,344
STATED PRINT RUN 3 SER.#'d SETS
UNPRICED DUE TO SCARCITY

NNO Ridley/Boyega/Rose/Daniels/Vee/Suotamo

2018 Star Wars The Last Jedi Series Two Sketches

STATED ODDS 1:70
UNPRICED DUE TO SCARCITY

NNO Adam Talley
NNO Alex Mines
NNO Allen Grimes
NNO Andy Fry
NNO Angelina Benedetti
NNO Ashleigh Popplewell
NNO Ben Abu Saada
NNO Ben Goddard
NNO Brad Hudson
NNO Brandon Blevins
NNO Brendan Purchase
NNO Brent Ragland
NNO Brent Scotchmer
NNO Bruce Gerlach
NNO Caleb King
NNO Carlos Cabaleiro
NNO Carolyn Craggs
NNO Chad Scheres
NNO Christian Parker
NNO Colin Arthurs
NNO Dan Bergren
NNO Dan Curto
NNO Darren Coburn-James
NNO Darrin Pepe
NNO Dave Fowler
NNO David Rabbitte
NNO Eli Hyder
NNO Eric Lehtonen
NNO Gavin Williams
NNO Gorkem Demir
NNO Huy Truong
NNO Ian MacDougall
NNO Jamie Cosley
NNO Jason Adams
NNO Jason Keith Phillips
NNO Jason Sobol
NNO Jeff Abar
NNO Jeff Meuth
NNO Jim Mehsling
NNO John Bilage
NNO John Bruce
NNO Jon Arton
NNO Jose Ventura
NNO Juan Rosales
NNO Keith Carter
NNO Kevin Cleveland
NNO Kevin Graham
NNO Kevin Hawkins
NNO Kris Penix
NNO Kurt Ruskin
NNO Laura Martin
NNO Lee Lightfoot
NNO Logan Monette
NNO Louise Draper
NNO Louise Draper
NNO Mark Stroud
NNO Marlo Agunas
NNO Marsha Parkins
NNO Matt Langford
NNO Matthew Hirons
NNO Matthew Sutton
NNO Michael Bernard
NNO Mick and Matt Glebe
NNO Mike Mastermaker
NNO Mohammad Jilani
NNO Nathan Kennett
NNO Neil Camera
NNO Nicholas Baltra
NNO Nick Allsopp
NNO Nick Justus
NNO Patricio Carrasco
NNO Patrick Davis
NNO Patrick Giles
NNO Phil Hassewer
NNO Rebecca Sharp
NNO Rich Molinelli
NNO Richard Serrao
NNO Robert Teranishi
NNO Ryan Finley

NNO Ryan Santos
NNO Sebastian Cortez
NNO Shaow Siong
NNO Steve Alce
NNO Tiffany Groves
NNO Tom Amici
NNO Trent Westbrook
NNO Trevor Anderson
NNO Ward Silverman

2018 Star Wars The Last Jedi Series Two Soldiers of the First Order

COMPLETE SET (10)	6.00	15.00
COMMON CARD (FO1-FO10)	1.25	3.00
*RED/99: .5X TO 1.2X BASIC CARDS	1.50	4.00
*BRONZE/50: .75X TO 2X BASIC CARDS	2.50	6.00
*SILVER/25: UNPRICED DUE TO SCARCITY		
*GOLD/10: UNPRICED DUE TO SCARCITY		
*BLACK/1: UNPRICED DUE TO SCARCITY		
*P.P.BLACK/1: UNPRICED DUE TO SCARCITY		
*P.P.CYAN/1: UNPRICED DUE TO SCARCITY		
*P.P.MAGENTA/1: UNPRICED DUE TO SCARCITY		
*P.P.YELLOW/1: UNPRICED DUE TO SCARCITY		
STATED ODDS 1:4		

2018 Star Wars The Last Jedi Series Two Soldiers of the First Order Autographs

FO1 Adam Driver
FO2 Gwendoline Christie
FO9 Adrian Edmondson
FO10 Andy Serkis

2018 Star Wars The Last Jedi Series Two Source Material Fabric Swatches

COMMON MEM	20.00	50.00
*GOLD/10: UNPRICED DUE TO SCARCITY		
STATED ODDS 1:360		
STATED PRINT RUN 99 SER.#'d SETS		
MR1 Caretaker's Smock	60.00	120.00
MR3 Praetorian Guard's Ceremonial Battle Skirt	50.00	100.00
MR4 Captain Peavy's First Order Uniform	25.00	60.00

2018 Star Wars The Last Jedi Series Two Teaser Posters

COMPLETE SET (6)	8.00	20.00
COMMON CARD (TP1-TP6)	2.00	5.00
STATED ODDS 1:24		
TP1 Rey	2.50	6.00
TP5 General Leia Organa	2.50	6.00

2018 Star Wars The Last Jedi Series Two Triple Autographs

STATED ODDS 1:14,232
STATED PRINT RUN SER.#'d SETS
UNPRICED DUE TO SCARCITY

TADRV Daniels/Rose/Vee
TAKKQ Kasey/Kane/Quinn
TALCN Lourd/Clarke/Ngo
TARDB Ridley/Driver/Boyega

2018 Star Wars On-Demand The Last Jedi

COMPLETE SET (20)	15.00	40.00
COMMON CARD (1-20)	1.25	3.00
*PURPLE: .75X TO 2X BASIC CARDS	2.50	6.00

2018 Star Wars On-Demand The Last Jedi Autographs

STATED OVERALL ODDS 1:SET

1A Daisy Ridley		
4A John Boyega	50.00	100.00
5A Adam Driver		

9A Gwendoline Christie		
11A Billie Lourd		
14AA Dave Chapman	8.00	20.00
14BA Brian Herring	8.00	20.00
15AA Tim Rose	15.00	40.00
15BA Tom Kane	8.00	20.00
16A Jimmy Vee	10.00	25.00
17A Anthony Daniels		
19A Andy Serkis		
21A Andrew Jack	10.00	25.00
22A Paul Kasey	8.00	20.00
23A Mike Quinn	15.00	40.00

SOLO

2018 Countdown to Solo A Star Wars Story

COMPLETE SET (25)	60.00	120.00
COMMON CARD (1-25)	4.00	10.00

2018 Solo A Star Wars Story

COMPLETE SET (100)	8.00	20.00
UNOPENED BOX (24 PACKS)	50.00	60.00
UNOPENED PACK (8 CARDS)	2.50	3.00
COMMON CARD (1-100)	.15	.40
*YELLOW: .6X TO 1.5X BASIC CARDS	.25	.60
*BLACK: .75X TO 2X BASIC CARDS	.30	.75
*SILVER: 1.5X TO 4X BASIC CARDS	.60	1.50
*PINK/99: 6X TO 15X BASIC CARDS	2.50	6.00
*ORANGE/25: 15X TO 40X BASIC CARDS	6.00	15.00
*GOLD/10: UNPRICED DUE TO SCARCITY		
*IMPERIAL RED/1: UNPRICED DUE TO SCARCITY		
*P.P.BLACK/1: UNPRICED DUE TO SCARCITY		
*P.P.CYAN/1: UNPRICED DUE TO SCARCITY		
*P.P.MAGENTA/1: UNPRICED DUE TO SCARCITY		
*P.P.YELLOW/1: UNPRICED DUE TO SCARCITY		

2018 Solo A Star Wars Story Autographs

COMMON AUTO	8.00	20.00
*PINK/99: .5X TO 1.2X BASIC AUTOS		
*ORANGE/25: .6X TO 1.5X BASIC AUTOS		
*GOLD/10: UNPRICED DUE TO SCARCITY		
*IMPERIAL RED/1: UNPRICED DUE TO SCARCITY		
*P.P.BLACK/1: UNPRICED DUE TO SCARCITY		
*P.P.CYAN/1: UNPRICED DUE TO SCARCITY		
*P.P.MAGENTA/1: UNPRICED DUE TO SCARCITY		
*P.P.YELLOW/1: UNPRICED DUE TO SCARCITY		
STATED ODDS 1:33		
AAF Anna Francolini	12.00	30.00
AAJ Andrew Jack	10.00	25.00
AAW Andrew Woodall	12.00	30.00
ADA Derek Arnold	12.00	30.00
ADT Dee Tails	10.00	25.00
AIK Ian Kenny	10.00	25.00

2018 Solo A Star Wars Story Autographs Pink

STATED ODDS 1:231		
STATED PRINT RUN 99 SER.#'d SETS		
AJS Joonas Suotamo	50.00	100.00
AWD Warwick Davis	20.00	50.00
AJSC Joonas Suotamo	50.00	100.00

2018 Solo A Star Wars Story Character Stickers

COMPLETE SET (7)	8.00	20.00
COMMON CARD (CS1-CS7)	2.00	5.00
STATED ODDS 1:12		

2018 Solo A Star Wars Story Dual Autographs

STATED PRINT RUN 10 SER.#'d SETS
UNPRICED DUE TO SCARCITY

DAJA Jack/Arnold
DAJS Jack/Suotamo
DASA Suotamo/Arnold
DASD Suotamo/Davis

2018 Solo A Star Wars Story Icons

COMPLETE SET (7)	5.00	12.00
COMMON CARD (I1-I7)	1.00	2.50
*P.P.BLACK/1: UNPRICED DUE TO SCARCITY		
*P.P.CYAN/1: UNPRICED DUE TO SCARCITY		
*P.P.MAGENTA/1: UNPRICED DUE TO SCARCITY		
*P.P.YELLOW/1: UNPRICED DUE TO SCARCITY		
STATED ODDS 1:8		

2018 Solo A Star Wars Story Manufactured Patches

COMMON PATCH	3.00	8.00
*PINK/99: .5X TO 1.2X BASIC PATCHES		
*ORANGE/25: .6X TO 1.5X BASIC PATCHES		
*GOLD/10: UNPRICED DUE TO SCARCITY		
*IMPERIAL RED/1: UNPRICED DUE TO SCARCITY		
STATED ODDS 1:32		
MPCC Chewbacca	5.00	12.00
MPCH Chewbacca	5.00	12.00
MPHM Han Solo	6.00	15.00
MPIS Imperial Fleet Trooper	4.00	10.00
MPLH L3-37	5.00	12.00
MPLM Lando Calrissian	6.00	15.00
MPME Enfys Nest	5.00	12.00
MPMS Mimban Stormtrooper	6.00	15.00
MPQC Qi'ra	8.00	20.00
MPQH Qi'ra	8.00	20.00
MPRS R5-PHT	4.00	10.00
MPSS Stormtrooper	4.00	10.00
MPTS TIE Fighter Pilot	6.00	15.00
MPENH Enfys Nest	5.00	12.00
MPHSC Han Solo	6.00	15.00
MPHSH Han Solo	6.00	15.00
MPLCH Lando Calrissian	6.00	15.00

2018 Solo A Star Wars Story Millennium Falcon Shaped Sketches

NNO Aleksandar Gigov
NNO Andy Duggan
NNO Ben AbuSaada
NNO Bill Pulkovski
NNO Brad Hudson
NNO Brandon Blevins
NNO Brent Scotchmer
NNO Chad Scheres
NNO Charlie Cody
NNO Eric White
NNO Gary Rudisill
NNO Jamie Cosley
NNO Jason Miller
NNO Jerry Bennett
NNO John DiBiase
NNO John Pleak
NNO Jordan Maison
NNO Joshua Bommer
NNO Kurt Ruskin
NNO Laura Atkinson
NNO Laura Martin
NNO Mike Mastermaker
NNO Nicholas Dertinger
NNO Nick Justus
NNO Rey Paez
NNO Rich Molinelli
NNO Ryan Crosby
NNO Ryan Olsen
NNO Sebastian Cortez
NNO Steve Fuchs
NNO Trent Westbrook
NNO Ward Silverman

2018 Solo A Star Wars Story Ships and Vehicles

COMPLETE SET (9)	4.00	10.00
COMMON CARD (SV1-SV9)	.60	1.50
*P.P.BLACK/1: UNPRICED DUE TO SCARCITY		
*P.P.CYAN/1: UNPRICED DUE TO SCARCITY		
*P.P.MAGENTA/1: UNPRICED DUE TO SCARCITY		
*P.P.YELLOW/1: UNPRICED DUE TO SCARCITY		
STATED ODDS 1:4		

2018 Solo A Star Wars Story Silhouettes

COMPLETE SET (11)	6.00	15.00
COMMON CARD (SL1-SL11)	1.00	2.50
*P.P.BLACK/1: UNPRICED DUE TO SCARCITY		
*P.P.CYAN/1: UNPRICED DUE TO SCARCITY		
*P.P.MAGENTA/1: UNPRICED DUE TO SCARCITY		
*P.P.YELLOW/1: UNPRICED DUE TO SCARCITY		
STATED ODDS 1:2		

2018 Solo A Star Wars Story Sketches

COMPLETE ARTIST LIST (133)
STATED ODDS 1:225
UNPRICED DUE TO SCARCITY

NNO Adam Harris
NNO Adam Worton
NNO Aleksandar Gigov
NNO Alex Mines
NNO Allen Grimes
NNO Allysa Pirone
NNO Andrew Fry
NNO Andrew Lopez
NNO Andy Duggan
NNO Anil Sharma
NNO Ashleigh Popplewell
NNO Basak Cetinkaya
NNO Ben AbuSaada
NNO Ben Goddard
NNO Bill Pulkovski
NNO Brad Hudson
NNO Brad Utterstrom
NNO Brandon Blevins
NNO Brandon Pyle
NNO Brendan Purchase
NNO Brent Ragland
NNO Brent Scotchmer
NNO Brett Farr
NNO Caleb King
NNO Carlos Cabaleiro
NNO Carolyn Craggs
NNO Chad Scheres
NNO Charlie Cody
NNO Chris O'Riley
NNO Chris Thorne
NNO Chris Willdig
NNO Clinton Yeager
NNO Dan Curto
NNO Dan Gorman
NNO Darren James
NNO Darrin Pepe
NNO Dave Fowler
NNO David Rabbitte
NNO Dean Drummond
NNO Dennis Gortakowski
NNO Dylan Riley
NNO Eli Hyder
NNO Eric Lehtonen
NNO Eric White
NNO Erik Maell
NNO Erin Lefler
NNO Frank Kadar
NNO Fredd Gorham
NNO Garrett Dix
NNO Gary Rudisill
NNO George Joseph
NNO Gerard Garcia Jr.
NNO Humberto Fuentes Navarro
NNO Huy Truong
NNO Ian MacDougall
NNO Ingrid Hardy
NNO Jamie Cosley
NNO Jamie Richards
NNO Jason Adams
NNO Jason Miller
NNO Jason Sobol
NNO Jay Manchand
NNO Jeff Abar
NNO Jennifer Allyn
NNO Jerry Bennett
NNO Jessica Hickman
NNO Jim O'Riley
NNO John Bruce
NNO John DiBiase
NNO John Pleak
NNO John Still
NNO Jon McKenzie
NNO Jordan Maison
NNO Joshua Bommer
NNO Jude Gallagher
NNO Kaela Croft
NNO Keith Carter
NNO Kevin Cleveland
NNO Kevin Graham
NNO Kevin Hawkins
NNO Kevin Liell
NNO Kris Penix

NNO Kurt Ruskin
NNO Kyle Hickman
NNO Laura Atkinson
NNO Laura Martin
NNO Lee Brown
NNO Lee Hunt
NNO Logan Monette
NNO Louise Draper
NNO Marcia Dye
NNO Mark Stroud
NNO Marsha Parkins
NNO Matt Langford
NNO Matthew Stewart
NNO Mayumi Seto
NNO Michael Mastermaker
NNO Michelle Rayner
NNO Mick and Matt Glebe
NNO Nathan Kennett
NNO Nathan Ohlendorf
NNO Neil Camera
NNO Nicholas Dertinger
NNO Nick Justus
NNO Nolan Dykstra
NNO Norvierto Basio
NNO Omar Salinas
NNO Patricio Carrasco
NNO Phil Hassewer
NNO Phillip Trujillo
NNO Rees Finlay
NNO Rey Paez
NNO Rich Molinelli
NNO Richard Serrao
NNO Robert Hendrickson
NNO Rodney Roberts
NNO Ryan Crosby
NNO Ryan Finley
NNO Ryan Olsen
NNO Ryan Santos
NNO Sammy Gomez
NNO Sebastian Cortez
NNO Shane Garvey
NNO Solly Mohamed
NNO Stephanie Swanger
NNO Steve Fuchs
NNO Thomas Amici
NNO Tina Berardi
NNO Tod Smith
NNO Travis Kinnison
NNO Trent Westbrook
NNO Ward Silverman
NNO Wayne Tully

2018 Solo A Star Wars Story Smooth Sayings

COMPLETE SET (8)	8.00	20.00
COMMON CARD (SS1-SS8)	1.50	4.00
*P.P.BLACK/1: UNPRICED DUE TO SCARCITY		
*P.P.CYAN/1: UNPRICED DUE TO SCARCITY		
*P.P.MAGENTA/1: UNPRICED DUE TO SCARCITY		
*P.P.YELLOW/1: UNPRICED DUE TO SCARCITY		
STATED ODDS 1:6		

2018 Solo A Star Wars Story Target Exclusive Manufactured Patches

COMMON PATCH	5.00	12.00
*PINK/99: .5X TO 1.2X BASIC PATCHES	6.00	15.00
*ORANGE/25: .6X TO 1.5X BASIC PATCHES	8.00	20.00
*GOLD/10: UNPRICED DUE TO SCARCITY		
*IMPERIAL RED/1: UNPRICED DUE TO SCARCITY		
STATED ODDS 1:TARGET BLASTER BOX		

2018 Solo A Star Wars Story Triple Autographs

STATED PRINT RUN 5 SER.#'d SETS
UNPRICED DUE TO SCARCITY

TASDA Suotamo/Davis/Arnold
TASJA Suotamo/Jack/Arnold

2018 Solo A Star Wars Story Promo

P1 Han Solo	4.00	10.00

2018 Solo A Star Wars Story Denny's

COMPLETE SET (12)	20.00	50.00
UNOPENED PACK (2 CARDS+1 COUPON)	3.00	8.00

COMMON CARD (UNNUMBERED)	2.00	5.00
*FOIL: 6X TO 15X BASIC CARDS	30.00	75.00

2018 Solo A Star Wars Story Odeon Cinemas

COMPLETE SET (4)	3.00	8.00
COMMON CARD (UNNUMBERED)	1.00	2.50

THE RISE OF SKYWALKER

2019 Star Wars The Rise of Skywalker General Mills Interactive Tattoos

NNO BB-8
NNO D-0
NNO Kylo Ren
NNO R2-D2
NNO Rey
NNO Stormtrooper

2019 Star Wars The Rise of Skywalker Series One

COMPLETE SET (99)	10.00	25.00
UNOPENED BOX (24 PACKS)		
UNOPENED PACK (8 CARDS)		
COMMON CARD (1-99)	.20	.50
*RED: .75X TO 2X BASIC CARDS		
*BLUE: 1X TO 2.5X BASIC CARDS		
GREEN: 1.2X TO 3X BASIC CARDS		
*PURPLE: 1.5X TO 4X BASIC CARDS		
*ORANGE/99: 4X TO 10X BASIC CARDS		
*GOLD/25: 6X TO 15X BASIC CARDS		
*BLACK/1: UNPRICED DUE TO SCARCITY		
*P.P.BLACK/1: UNPRICED DUE TO SCARCITY		
*P.P.CYAN/1: UNPRICED DUE TO SCARCITY		
*P.P.MAGENTA/1: UNPRICED DUE TO SCARCITY		
*P.P.YELLOW/1: UNPRICED DUE TO SCARCITY		

2019 Star Wars The Rise of Skywalker Series One Autographed Commemorative Medallions

STATED PRINT RUN 10 SER.#'d SETS
UNPRICED DUE TO SCARCITY

MCAD Adam Driver
MCBF John Boyega
MCBH Brian Herring
MCDB Dave Chapman
MCDG Domhnall Gleeson
MCDR Daisy Ridley
MCJS Joonas Suotamo
MCBDW Billy Dee Williams
MCKMT Kelly Marie Tran
MCRC3 Anthony Daniels

2019 Star Wars The Rise of Skywalker Series One Autographs

COMMON AUTO	6.00	15.00
*ORANGE/10: UNPRICED DUE TO SCARCITY		
*GOLD/5: UNPRICED DUE TO SCARCITY		
*BLACK/1: UNPRICED DUE TO SCARCITY		
*P.P.BLACK/1: UNPRICED DUE TO SCARCITY		
*P.P.CYAN/1: UNPRICED DUE TO SCARCITY		
*P.P.MAGENTA/1: UNPRICED DUE TO SCARCITY		
*P.P.YELLOW/1: UNPRICED DUE TO SCARCITY		
RANDOMLY INSERTED INTO PACKS		
AAH Amanda Hale	10.00	25.00
AAL Amanda Lawrence	8.00	20.00
ABB Brian Herring	6.00	15.00
ADB Dave Chapman	6.00	15.00
ADM Dominic Monaghan	50.00	100.00
AGF Geff Francis	10.00	25.00
AGG Greg Grunberg	12.00	30.00
AJA Josef Altin	10.00	25.00
AVR Vinette Robinson	12.00	30.00
ASPD Simon Paisley	10.00	25.00

2019 Star Wars The Rise of Skywalker Series One Autographs Blue

STATED PRINT RUN 99 SER.#'d SETS

AJB John Boyega	25.00	60.00
ANA Naomi Ackie	25.00	60.00

2019 Star Wars The Rise of Skywalker Series One Character Stickers

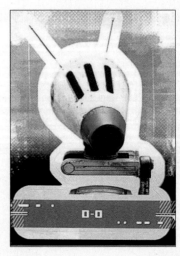

COMPLETE SET (19)	15.00	40.00
COMMON CARD (CS1-CS19)	1.25	3.00
RANDOMLY INSERTED INTO PACKS		
CS1 Rey	3.00	8.00
CS2 Kylo Ren	2.00	5.00

2019 Star Wars The Rise of Skywalker Series One
Commemorative Medallions

KYLO REN

COMMON MEM	4.00	10.00
*PURPLE/99: .5X TO 1.2X BASIC MEM		
*ORANGE/50: .6X TO 1.5X BASIC MEM		
*GOLD/25: .75X TO 2X BASIC MEM		
*BLACK/1: UNPRICED DUE TO SCARCITY		
RANDOMLY INSERTED INTO PACKS		
MCBD D-O	6.00	15.00
MCBF Finn	6.00	15.00
MCBP Poe Dameron	6.00	15.00
MCC3 C-3PO	5.00	12.00
MCCC Chewbacca	6.00	15.00
MCCL Lando Calrissian	6.00	15.00
MCCR R2-D2	5.00	12.00
MCDO D-O	8.00	20.00
MCDB BB-8	5.00	12.00
MCDR R2-D2	5.00	12.00
MCKY Kylo Ren	8.00	20.00
MCR2 R2-D2	6.00	15.00
MCRP Poe Dameron	5.00	12.00
MCRR Rey	10.00	25.00
MCTK Kylo Ren	6.00	15.00
MCBB8 BB-8	6.00	15.00
MCDC3 C-3PO	6.00	15.00
MCRC3 C-3PO	5.00	12.00

2019 Star Wars The Rise of Skywalker Series One
Costume Relics

CRF Finn
CRJ Jannah/62
CRR Rey/99
CRGP Allegiant General Pryde
CRKR Kylo Ren/99
CRLC Lando Calrissian
CRPD Poe Dameron
CRZB Zorii Bliss

2019 Star Wars The Rise of Skywalker Series One
Crush the Resistance

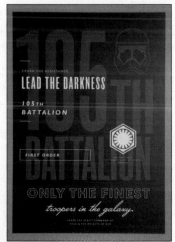

COMPLETE SET (8)	5.00	12.00
COMMON CARD (CR1-CR8)	1.00	2.50
*GREEN/299: .6X TO 1.5X BASIC CARDS		
*PURPLE/199: 1X TO 2.5X BASIC CARDS		
*RED/149: 1.2X TO 3X BASIC CARDS		
*ORANGE/99: 1.5X TO 4X BASIC CARDS		
*GOLD/25: 2.5X TO 6X BASIC CARDS		
*BLACK/1: UNPRICED DUE TO SCARCITY		
*P.P.BLACK/1: UNPRICED DUE TO SCARCITY		

*P.P.CYAN/1: UNPRICED DUE TO SCARCITY
*P.P.MAGENTA/1: UNPRICED DUE TO SCARCITY
*P.P.YELLOW/1: UNPRICED DUE TO SCARCITY
RANDOMLY INSERTED INTO PACKS

2019 Star Wars The Rise of Skywalker Series One
Dual Autographs

UNPRICED DUE TO SCARCITY

NNO A.Driver/D.Gleeson
NNO B.Lourd/G.Grunberg
NNO B.Williams/A.Daniels
NNO B.Williams/N.Ackie
NNO D.Ridley/A.Driver
NNO D.Ridley/J.Boyega
NNO D.Ridley/J.Suotamo
NNO J.Boyega/A.Daniels
NNO J.Boyega/K.Tran
NNO J.Boyega/N.Ackie
NNO J.Suotamo/B.Herring

2019 Star Wars The Rise of Skywalker Series One
Illustrated Characters

COMMON CARD (IC1-IC19)	2.00	5.00
*GREEN/299: SAME VALUE AS BASIC CARDS		
*PURPLE/199: .5X TO 1.25X BASIC CARDS		
*RED/149: .6X TO 1.5X BASIC CARDS		
*ORANGE/99: 1X TO 2.5X BASIC CARDS		
*GOLD/25: 1.2X TO 3X BASIC CARDS		
*BLACK/1: UNPRICED DUE TO SCARCITY		
*P.P.BLACK/1: UNPRICED DUE TO SCARCITY		
*P.P.CYAN/1: UNPRICED DUE TO SCARCITY		
*P.P.MAGENTA/1: UNPRICED DUE TO SCARCITY		
*P.P.YELLOW/1: UNPRICED DUE TO SCARCITY		
RANDOMLY INSERTED INTO PACKS		

2019 Star Wars The Rise of Skywalker Series One
Long Live the Resistance

COMPLETE SET (8)	4.00	10.00
COMMON CARD (RB1-RB8)	.75	2.00
*GREEN/299: .75X TO 2X BASIC CARDS		
*PURPLE/199: 1X TO 2.5X BASIC CARDS		
*RED/149: 1.2X TO 3X BASIC CARDS		
*ORANGE/99: 2X TO 5X BASIC CARDS		
*GOLD/25: 3X TO 8X BASIC CARDS		
*BLACK/1: UNPRICED DUE TO SCARCITY		
*P.P.BLACK/1: UNPRICED DUE TO SCARCITY		
*P.P.CYAN/1: UNPRICED DUE TO SCARCITY		
*P.P.MAGENTA/1: UNPRICED DUE TO SCARCITY		
*P.P.YELLOW/1: UNPRICED DUE TO SCARCITY		
RANDOMLY INSERTED INTO PACKS		

2019 Star Wars The Rise of Skywalker Series One
May the Force Be with You

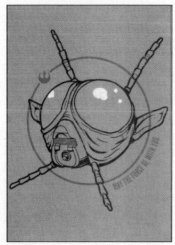

COMPLETE SET (5)	5.00	12.00
COMMON CARD (FWY1-FWY5)	1.50	4.00
*GREEN/299: SAME VALUE AS BASIC CARDS		
*PURPLE/199: .6X TO 1.5X BASIC CARDS		
*RED/149: .75X TO 2X BASIC CARDS		
*ORANGE/99: 1X TO 2.5X BASIC CARDS		
*GOLD/25: 1.5X TO 4X BASIC CARDS		
*BLACK/1: UNPRICED DUE TO SCARCITY		
*P.P.BLACK/1: UNPRICED DUE TO SCARCITY		

*P.P.CYAN/1: UNPRICED DUE TO SCARCITY
*P.P.MAGENTA/1: UNPRICED DUE TO SCARCITY
*P.P.YELLOW/1: UNPRICED DUE TO SCARCITY
RANDOMLY INSERTED INTO PACKS

2019 Star Wars The Rise of Skywalker Series One
Millennium Falcon Relics

*GOLD/4: UNPRICED DUE TO SCARCITY
*BLACK/1: UNPRICED DUE TO SCARCITY
STATED PRINT RUN 15 SER.#'d SETS

MFCS Chewbacca
MFFS Finn
MFJS Jannah
MFLS Lando Calrissian
MF3FA C-3PO
MF3NH C-3PO
MFBFA BB-8
MFCHS Chewbacca
MFCNH Chewbacca
MFFFA Finn
MFHFA Han Solo
MFHHS Han Solo
MFLHS L3-37
MFLRJ Lando Calrissian
MFQHS Qi'Ra
MFRFA R2-D2
MFRFA Rey
MFRNH R2-D2
MFTHS Tobias Beckett
MFUFA Unkar Plutt

2019 Star Wars The Rise of Skywalker Series One
Shaped Sketches

UNPRICED DUE TO SCARCITY

NNO Adam Everett Beck
NNO Adam Schickling
NNO Alex Mines
NNO Allen Grimes
NNO Andy Bohn
NNO Anil Sharma
NNO Anthony Skubis
NNO Ashlee Brienzo
NNO Ashley Marsh
NNO Basak Cetinkaya
NNO Bobby Blakey
NNO Brad Hudson
NNO Brett Farr
NNO Bruce Gerlach
NNO Candice Dailey
NNO Carlos Cabaleiro
NNO Carolyn Craggs
NNO Chris Thorne
NNO Chris Willdig
NNO Clara Bujtor
NNO Clinton Yeager
NNO Colin Arthurs
NNO Dan Gorman
NNO Dan Tearle
NNO Daniel Riveron
NNO Darrin Pepe
NNO David Storey
NNO Dean Drummond
NNO Eric Lehtonen
NNO Erik Maell
NNO Gavins Williams
NNO Gorkem Demir
NNO Ingrid Hardy
NNO Jamie Cosley
NNO Jamie Richards
NNO Jason Miller
NNO Jason Montoya
NNO Jason Sobol
NNO Jay Manchand
NNO Jeffrey Cox
NNO Jennifer Allyn
NNO Jim Mehsling
NNO John Bruce
NNO John Pleak
NNO Keith Farnum
NNO Kevin Cleveland
NNO Kevin Graham
NNO Lee Lightfoot
NNO Marcia Dye

NNO Mark Stroud
NNO Marsha Parkins
NNO Matt Langford
NNO Matt Stewart
NNO Matthew Hirons
NNO Matthew Lopez
NNO Michael Mastermaker
NNO Michelle Rayner
NNO Mohammad Jilani
NNO Neil Camera
NNO Nick Gribbon
NNO Norviento Basio
NNO Patricio Carrasco
NNO Patrick Richardson
NNO Phillip Trujillo
NNO Rees Finlay
NNO Rey Paez
NNO Rich Molinelli
NNO Richard Serrao
NNO Rob Teranishi
NNO Robert Hendrickson
NNO Ryan Finley
NNO Scott West
NNO Seth Groves
NNO Shaow Siong
NNO Solly Mohamed
NNO Thomas Amici
NNO Tim Shinn
NNO Travis Kinnison
NNO Trent Westbrook
NNO Ward Silverman
NNO Wayne Tully
NNO Zach Woolsey

2019 Star Wars The Rise of Skywalker Series One
Ships and Vehicles

COMPLETE SET (7)	4.00	10.00
COMMON CARD (SV1-SV7)	1.00	2.50

*GREEN/299: .6X TO 1.5X BASIC CARDS
*PURPLE/199: .75X TO 2X BASIC CARDS
*RED/149: X1 TO 2.5X BASIC CARDS
*ORANGE/99: 1.2X TO 3X BASIC CARDS
*BLACK/1: UNPRICED DUE TO SCARCITY
*P.P.BLACK/1: UNPRICED DUE TO SCARCITY
*P.P.CYAN/1: UNPRICED DUE TO SCARCITY
*P.P.MAGENTA/1: UNPRICED DUE TO SCARCITY
*P.P.YELLOW/1: UNPRICED DUE TO SCARCITY
RANDOMLY INSERTED INTO PACKS

2019 Star Wars The Rise of Skywalker Series One
Six-Person Autographs

NNO Ridley/Boyega/Tran/Williams/Daniels/Lourd
NNO Ridley/Boyega/Tran/Williams/Daniels/Suotamo

2019 Star Wars The Rise of Skywalker Series One
Sketches

UNPRICED DUE TO SCARCITY
NNO Adam Everett Beck
NNO Adam Schickling
NNO Alex Mines
NNO Allen Grimes

NNO Andy Bohn
NNO Anil Sharma
NNO Anthony Skubis
NNO Ashlee Brienzo
NNO Ashley Marsh
NNO Basak Cetinkaya
NNO Bobby Blakey
NNO Brad Hudson
NNO Brett Farr
NNO Bruce Gerlach
NNO Candice Dailey
NNO Carlos Cabaleiro
NNO Carolyn Craggs
NNO Chris Thorne
NNO Chris Willdig
NNO Clara Bujtor
NNO Clinton Yeager
NNO Colin Arthurs
NNO Dan Gorman
NNO Dan Tearle
NNO Daniel Riveron
NNO Darrin Pepe
NNO David Storey
NNO Dean Drummond
NNO Eric Lehtonen
NNO Erik Maell
NNO Gavins Williams
NNO Gorkem Demir
NNO Ingrid Hardy
NNO Jamie Cosley
NNO Jamie Richards
NNO Jason Miller
NNO Jason Montoya
NNO Jason Sobol
NNO Jay Manchand
NNO Jeffrey Cox
NNO Jennifer Allyn
NNO Jim Mehsling
NNO John Bruce
NNO John Pleak
NNO Keith Farnum
NNO Kevin Cleveland
NNO Kevin Graham
NNO Lee Lightfoot
NNO Marcia Dye
NNO Mark Stroud
NNO Marsha Parkins
NNO Matt Langford
NNO Matt Stewart
NNO Matthew Hirons
NNO Matthew Lopez
NNO Michael Mastermaker
NNO Michelle Rayner
NNO Mohammad Jilani
NNO Neil Camera
NNO Nick Gribbon
NNO Norviento Basio
NNO Patricio Carrasco
NNO Patrick Richardson
NNO Phillip Trujillo
NNO Rees Finlay
NNO Rey Paez
NNO Rich Molinelli
NNO Richard Serrao
NNO Rob Teranishi
NNO Robert Hendrickson
NNO Ryan Finley
NNO Scott West
NNO Seth Groves
NNO Shaow Siong
NNO Solly Mohamed
NNO Thomas Amici
NNO Tim Shinn
NNO Travis Kinnison
NNO Trent Westbrook
NNO Ward Silverman
NNO Wayne Tully
NNO Zach Woolsey

2019 Star Wars The Rise of Skywalker Series One
Triple Autographs

UNPRICED DUE TO SCARCITY

NNO Daniels/Suotamo/Herring
NNO Ridley/Driver/Boyega
NNO Ridley/Williams/Boyega
NNO Ridley/Boyega/Tran
NNO Ridley/Tran/Lourd
NNO Boyega/Grunberg/Chapman
NNO Boyega/Tran/Lourd
NNO Tran/Lourd/Grunberg

2019 Star Wars The Rise of Skywalker Series One
CineWorld UK Promos

COMPLETE SET (2)	2.00	5.00
COMMON CARD	1.25	3.00
CWD Be a Hero (Droids)	1.25	3.00
CWK Darkness Rises (Kylo Ren)	1.25	3.00

2020 Star Wars The Rise of Skywalker Series Two

COMPLETE SET (100)	6.00	15.00
UNOPENED BOX (24 PACKS)	60.00	80.00
UNOPENED PACK (8 CARDS)	2.50	4.00
COMMON CARD (1-100)	.12	.30

*BLUE: 1X TO 2.5X BASIC CARDS
*PURPLE: 2X TO 5X BASIC CARDS
*RED/199: 10X TO 25X BASIC CARDS
*BRONZE/99: 12X TO 30X BASIC CARDS
*SILVER/25: 20X TO 50X BASIC CARDS
*GOLD/10: UNPRICED DUE TO SCARCITY
*BLACK/1: UNPRICED DUE TO SCARCITY
*P.P.BLACK/1: UNPRICED DUE TO SCARCITY
*P.P.CYAN/1: UNPRICED DUE TO SCARCITY
*P.P.MAGENTA/1: UNPRICED DUE TO SCARCITY
*P.P.YELLOW/1: UNPRICED DUE TO SCARCITY

2020 Star Wars The Rise of Skywalker Series Two
Autographed Commemorative Vehicle Medallions

*BLACK/1: UNPRICED DUE TO SCARCITY
RANDOMLY INSERTED INTO PACKS

MVMABF Brian Herring
MVMAFF John Boyega
MVMAJF Naomi Ackie
MVMAKF Billie Lourd
MVMAKT Adam Driver
MVMALF Billy Dee Williams
MVMARF Daisy Ridley
MVMASX Greg Grunberg
MVMABKF Dominic Monaghan

2020 Star Wars The Rise of Skywalker Series Two Autographs

MIKE QUINN
A5

*RED/99: .5X TO 1.2X BASIC AUTOS
*SILVER/25: UNPRICED DUE TO SCARCITY
*GOLD/10: UNPRICED DUE TO SCARCITY
*BLACK/1: UNPRICED DUE TO SCARCITY
*P.P.BLACK/1: UNPRICED DUE TO SCARCITY
*P.P.CYAN/1: UNPRICED DUE TO SCARCITY
*P.P.MAGENTA/1: UNPRICED DUE TO SCARCITY
*P.P.YELLOW/1: UNPRICED DUE TO SCARCITY
RANDOMLY INSERTED INTO PACKS

AAC Aidan Cook	6.00	15.00
AAD Adam Driver		
AAL Amanda Lawrence	5.00	12.00
ABH Brian Herring	10.00	25.00
ABL Billie Lourd		
ADB Dave Chapman	10.00	25.00
ADG Domhnall Gleeson		
ADM Dominic Monaghan		
ADR Daisy Ridley		
ADW Debra Wilson	6.00	15.00
AGF Geff Francis	6.00	15.00
AGG Greg Grunberg		
AJB John Boyega		
AJS Joonas Suotamo		
AKS Kiran Shah	10.00	25.00
AMQ Mike Quinn	8.00	20.00
AMW Matthew Wood	6.00	15.00
ANA Naomi Ackie		
ANK Nick Kellington	8.00	20.00
APK Paul Kasey	6.00	15.00
ATW Tom Wilton	5.00	12.00
AWD Warwick Davis		
ABDW Billy Dee Williams		
AKMT Kelly Marie Tran		
AKRN Kipsang Rotich	8.00	20.00
ASPD Simon Paisley Day	5.00	12.00

2020 Star Wars The Rise of Skywalker Series Two Character Posters

COMPLETE SET (6)	12.00	30.00
COMMON CARD (TP1-TP6)	2.50	6.00
RANDOMLY INSERTED INTO PACKS		
TP1 Rey	4.00	10.00
TP2 Finn	2.50	6.00
TP3 Poe Dameron	2.50	6.00
TP4 Lando Calrissian	2.50	6.00
TP5 Chewbacca	2.50	6.00
TP6 Kylo Ren	3.00	8.00

2020 Star Wars The Rise of Skywalker Series Two Commemorative Vehicle Medallions

*SILVER/50: .6X TO 1.5X BASIC MEM
*GOLD/25: UNPRICED DUE TO SCARCITY
*BLACK/1: UNPRICED DUE TO SCARCITY
RANDOMLY INSERTED INTO PACKS

MVMCF C-3PO	6.00	15.00
MVMCX C'ai Threnalli	6.00	15.00
MVMFF Finn	5.00	12.00
MVMJF Jannah	8.00	20.00
MVMKF Kaydel Ko Connix		20.00
MVMKT Kylo Ren	6.00	15.00

MVMLF Lando Calrissian	5.00	12.00
MVMPF Poe Dameron	6.00	15.00
MVMPX Poe Dameron	6.00	15.00
MVMRF Rey	15.00	40.00
MVMRX R2-D2	5.00	12.00
MVMWX Wedge Antilles	6.00	15.00
MVMBKF Beaumont Kin	5.00	12.00
MVMRDF R2-D2	6.00	15.00

2020 Star Wars The Rise of Skywalker Series Two Costume Relics

ALLEGIANT GENERAL PRYDE

*SILVER/25: UNPRICED DUE TO SCARCITY
*GOLD/10: UNPRICED DUE TO SCARCITY
*BLACK/1: UNPRICED DUE TO SCARCITY
RANDOMLY INSERTED INTO PACKS

CRAT Allegiant General Pryde/Tunic	30.00	75.00
CRFT Finn/Trousers	25.00	60.00
CRFW Finn/Waistcoat Lining	25.00	60.00
CRKC Kylo Ren/Cloak Hood Lining		
CRKU Kylo Ren/Undershirt		
CRLC Lando Calrissian/Cloak Lining	60.00	120.00
CRLS Lando Calrissian/Shirt	25.00	60.00
CRPT Poe Dameron/Trousers		
CRRH Rey/Hood		
CRRT Rey/Trousers		
CRZJ Zorii Bliss/Jumpsuit Sleeve		

2020 Star Wars The Rise of Skywalker Series Two Dual Autographs

*BLACK/1: UNPRICED DUE TO SCARCITY
RANDOMLY INSERTED INTO PACKS

DAAD A.Driver/D.Gleeson
DAAJ A.Driver/J.Boyega
DAAV A.Lawrence/V.Robinson
DABG B.Lourd/G.Grunberg
DABN B.Williams/N.Ackie
DADA D.Ridley/A.Driver
DADJ D.Ridley/J.Boyega
DADK D.Ridley/K.Tran
DAGA G.Francis/A.Hale
DAGN G.Grunberg/N.Kellington
DAGS G.Francis/S.Day
DAJB J.Suotamo/B.Herring
DAJK J.Boyega/K.Tran
DAJN J.Boyega/N.Ackie
DAMP M.Quinn/P.Kasey
DASA S.Day/A.Hale
DAVJ V.Robinson/J.Altin

2020 Star Wars The Rise of Skywalker Series Two Foil Puzzle

COMPLETE SET (9)	30.00	75.00
COMMON CARD (1-9)	5.00	12.00
RANDOMLY INSERTED INTO PACKS		

2020 Star Wars The Rise of Skywalker Series Two Heroes of the Resistance

CHEWBACCA

COMPLETE SET (11)	6.00	15.00
COMMON CARD (HR1-HR11)	1.00	2.50
*RED/99: .75X TO 2X BASIC CARDS		
*BRONZE/50: 1.2X TO 3X BASIC CARDS		
*SILVER/25: UNPRICED DUE TO SCARCITY		
*GOLD/10: UNPRICED DUE TO SCARCITY		
*BLACK/1: UNPRICED DUE TO SCARCITY		
*P.P.BLACK/1: UNPRICED DUE TO SCARCITY		
*P.P.CYAN/1: UNPRICED DUE TO SCARCITY		
*P.P.MAGENTA/1: UNPRICED DUE TO SCARCITY		
*P.P.YELLOW/1: UNPRICED DUE TO SCARCITY		
RANDOMLY INSERTED INTO PACKS		
HR1 Rey	4.00	10.00

2020 Star Wars The Rise of Skywalker Series Two Heroes of the Resistance Autographs

*BLACK/1: UNPRICED DUE TO SCARCITY
RANDOMLY INSERTED INTO PACKS

HR1 Daisy Ridley
HR2 John Boyega
HR5 Naomi Ackie
HR8 Joonas Suotamo
HR10 Kelly Marie Tran

2020 Star Wars The Rise of Skywalker Series Two Image Variation Autographs

RANDOMLY INSERTED INTO PACKS

AAD2 Adam Driver		
ADG2 Domhnall Gleeson		
ADR2 Daisy Ridley		
AJB2 John Boyega		
ANA2 Naomi Ackie	25.00	60.00
ABDW2 Billy Dee Williams		

2020 Star Wars The Rise of Skywalker Series Two Millennium Falcon Relics

LUKE SKYWALKER

*GOLD/10: UNPRICED DUE TO SCARCITY
*BLACK/1: UNPRICED DUE TO SCARCITY
STATED PRINT RUN 15 SER.#'d SETS

MFE Chewbacca
MF2E R2-D2
MF2J R2-D2
MF2L R2-D2
MF2R R2-D2
MF3E C-3PO
MF3J C-3PO

MF3R C-3PO
MFCJ Chewbacca
MFCL Chewbacca
MFDL Poe Dameron
MFFL Finn
MFHE Han Solo
MFHJ Han Solo
MFLE Lando Calrissian
MFLJ Lando Calrissian
MFNJ Nien Nunb
MFPE Princess Leia Organa
MFPJ Princess Leia Organa
MFPL Porg
MFRJ Rey
MFRR Rey
MFSE Luke Skywalker
MFSJ Luke Skywalker
MFSL Luke Skywalker

2020 Star Wars The Rise of Skywalker Series Two Six-Person Autograph

SAAG Ridley/Boyega/Tran/Williams/Lourd/Monaghan

2020 Star Wars The Rise of Skywalker Series Two Sketches

RANDOMLY INSERTED INTO PACKS
UNPRICED DUE TO SCARCITY

NNO Adam Everett Beck
NNO Andrew Joynes
NNO Andrew Lopez
NNO Anil Sharma
NNO Anthony Ellison
NNO Ashlee Brienzo
NNO Ashley Marsh
NNO Barry Renshaw
NNO Brad Hudson
NNO Brendan Purchase
NNO Brent Scotchmer
NNO Brett Farr
NNO Caleb Hildenbrandt
NNO Caleb King
NNO Cameron Tobias
NNO Candice Dailey
NNO Carlos Cabaleiro
NNO Chris Kay
NNO Chris Quinn
NNO Clara Bujtor
NNO Craig Halums
NNO Cyrus Sherkat
NNO Dan Tearle
NNO Darrin Pepe
NNO David Rabbitte
NNO Dawn Murphy
NNO Eric Lehtonen
NNO Eric Muller
NNO Frank Sansone
NNO Gerry Garcia
NNO Gorkem Demir
NNO Huy Truong
NNO Ingrid Hardy
NNO Jake Minor

NNO Jason Davies
NNO Jason Queen
NNO Jay Manchand
NNO Jessica Hickman
NNO Jim Mehsling
NNO John Bruce
NNO John DiBiase
NNO Josh Church
NNO Kaela Croft
NNO Kayla Wright
NNO Kelly Baber
NNO Kevin Cleveland
NNO Laura Atkinson
NNO Lee Lightfoot
NNO Lindsey Greyling
NNO Louise Draper
NNO Marcia Dye
NNO Mark Stroud
NNO Marsha Parkins
NNO Matt Stewart
NNO Michael Mastermaker
NNO Mick and Matt Glebe
NNO Neil Camera
NNO Nick Allsopp
NNO Nick Gribbon
NNO Patricio Carrasco
NNO Rachel Brady
NNO Rebecca Sharp
NNO Rich Molinelli
NNO Rob Teranishi
NNO Robert Hendrickson
NNO Rodney Roberts
NNO Ronnie Crowther
NNO Ryan Finley
NNO Ryan Santos
NNO Scott West
NNO Sheikh Islam
NNO Solly Mohamed
NNO Steve Alce
NNO Ted Dastick Jr.
NNO Thomas Amici
NNO Tim Shinn
NNO Tod Smith
NNO Travis Kinnison
NNO Trent Westbrook
NNO Vincenzo D'Ippolito
NNO Ward Silverman
NNO Zach Woolsey

2020 Star Wars The Rise of Skywalker Series Two The Knights of Ren

COMPLETE SET (10)	5.00	12.00
COMMON CARD (KR1-KR10)	.75	2.00

*RED/99: .75X TO 2X BASIC CARDS
*BRONZE/50: 1.2X TO 3X BASIC CARDS
*SILVER/25: UNPRICED DUE TO SCARCITY
*GOLD/10: UNPRICED DUE TO SCARCITY
*BLACK/1: UNPRICED DUE TO SCARCITY
*P.P.BLACK/1: UNPRICED DUE TO SCARCITY
*P.P.CYAN/1: UNPRICED DUE TO SCARCITY
*P.P.MAGENTA/1: UNPRICED DUE TO SCARCITY
*P.P.YELLOW/1: UNPRICED DUE TO SCARCITY
RANDOMLY INSERTED INTO PACKS

2020 Star Wars The Rise of Skywalker Series Two Triple Autographs

*BLACK/1: UNPRICED DUE TO SCARCITY
RANDOMLY INSERTED INTO PACKS

TADAJ Ridley/Driver/Boyega
TADBJ Ridley/Williams/Boyega
TADJJ Ridley/Suotamo/Boyega
TADJK Ridley/Boyega/Tran
TADKB Ridley/Tran/Lourd
TAGPV Grunberg/Kasey/Robinson
TAKBG Tran/Lourd/Grunberg

2020 Star Wars The Rise of Skywalker Series Two Villains of the First Order

COMPLETE SET (9)		
COMMON CARD (VF1-VF9)	1.00	2.50

*RED/99: .6X TO 1.5X BASIC CARDS
*BRONZE/50: 1X TO 2.5X BASIC CARDS
*SILVER/25: UNPRICED DUE TO SCARCITY
*GOLD/10: UNPRICED DUE TO SCARCITY
*BLACK/1: UNPRICED DUE TO SCARCITY
*P.P.BLACK/1: UNPRICED DUE TO SCARCITY
*P.P.CYAN/1: UNPRICED DUE TO SCARCITY
*P.P.MAGENTA/1: UNPRICED DUE TO SCARCITY
*P.P.YELLOW/1: UNPRICED DUE TO SCARCITY

VF1 Kylo Ren	1.50	4.00

2020 Star Wars The Rise of Skywalker Series Two Villains of the First Order Autographs

*BLACK/1: UNPRICED DUE TO SCARCITY
RANDOMLY INSERTED INTO PACKS

VF1 Adam Driver
VF2 Domhnall Gleeson
VF6 Simon Paisley Day
VF7 Geff Francis
VF8 Amanda Hale

2020 Star Wars The Rise of Skywalker Series Two Weapons

COMPLETE SET (10)	5.00	12.00
COMMON CARD (W1-W10)	.75	2.00

*RED/99: .75X TO 2X BASIC CARDS
*BRONZE/50: 1X TO 2.5X BASIC CARDS
*SILVER/25: UNPRICED DUE TO SCARCITY
*GOLD/10: UNPRICED DUE TO SCARCITY
*BLACK/1: UNPRICED DUE TO SCARCITY
*P.P.BLACK/1: UNPRICED DUE TO SCARCITY
*P.P.CYAN/1: UNPRICED DUE TO SCARCITY
*P.P.MAGENTA/1: UNPRICED DUE TO SCARCITY
*P.P.YELLOW/1: UNPRICED DUE TO SCARCITY
RANDOMLY INSERTED INTO PACKS

W1 Skywalker Lightsaber	2.00	5.00

2019 Star Wars The Rise of Skywalker Trailer

COMPLETE SET (20)		
COMPLETE SET 1 (1-10)	10.00	25.00
COMPLETE SET 2 (11-20)		
COMMON CARD (1-10)	1.50	4.00
COMMON CARD (11-20)		

TOPPS ONLINE EXCLUSIVE

2009 Art of Star Wars Comics Postcards

COMPLETE SET (100)	12.00	30.00
COMMON CARD (1-100)	.25	.60

2014 Disney Store Star Wars North America

COMPLETE SET (9)	10.00	25.00
COMMON CARD (1-10)	.75	2.00

US/CANADA EXCLUSIVE

1 Luke Skywalker	2.00	5.00
4 Darth Vader	2.00	5.00
7 Princess Leia	2.00	5.00
9 Han Solo	2.00	5.00

2014 Disney Store Star Wars United Kingdom

COMPLETE SET (12)	15.00	40.00
COMMON CARD (1-12)	1.00	2.50

UK EXCLUSIVE

1 Chewbacca	1.25	3.00
2 Darth Vader	4.00	10.00
4 Han Solo	4.00	10.00
6 Luke Skywalker	3.00	8.00
8 Obi-Wan Kenobi	1.25	3.00
9 Princess Leia Organa	3.00	8.00
10 R2-D2 and C-3PO	1.25	3.00
11 Stormtrooper	1.25	3.00

2008 Family Guy Episode IV A New Hope

COMPLETE SET (50)	5.00	12.00
COMMON CARD (1-50)	.15	.40

CL1 ISSUED AS CASE EXCLUSIVE

CL1 Evil Empire CI	12.00	25.00

2008 Family Guy Episode IV A New Hope Droid Chat

COMPLETE SET (3)	5.00	12.00
COMMON CARD (DC1-DC3)	2.00	5.00

STATED ODDS 1:23

2008 Family Guy Episode IV A New Hope Promos

P1 Left half w/Han	1.00	2.50
Pi Right half w/Leia	1.00	2.50

2008 Family Guy Episode IV A New Hope Puzzle

COMPLETE SET (9)	4.00	10.00
COMMON CARD (NH1-NH9)	.75	2.00

STATED ODDS 1:7

2008 Family Guy Episode IV A New Hope Scenes from Space

COMPLETE SET (6)	4.00	10.00
COMMON CARD (S1-S6)	1.25	3.00

STATED ODDS 1:11

2008 Family Guy Episode IV A New Hope Spaceships and Transports

COMPLETE SET (9)	4.00	10.00
COMMON CARD (ST1-ST9)	1.00	2.50

STATED ODDS 1:9

2008 Family Guy Episode IV A New Hope What Happens Next?

COMPLETE SET (6)	4.00	10.00

COMMON CARD (WN1-WN6)	1.25	3.00

STATED ODDS 1:11

2017 Funko Pop Buttons Star Wars

NNO Boba Fett	2.00	5.00
NNO C-3PO	2.00	5.00
NNO Chewbacca	2.00	5.00
NNO Darth Maul	2.00	5.00
NNO Darth Vader	4.00	10.00
NNO Ewok (Wicket)	2.00	5.00
NNO Greedo	2.00	5.00
NNO Han Solo HT		
NNO Jabba	2.00	5.00
NNO Jabba (vaping)		
(Hot Topic Exclusive)		
NNO Luke Skywalker		
(Hot Topic Exclusive)		
NNO Luke/Han/Leia	2.00	5.00
NNO Princess Leia	6.00	15.00
NNO R2-D2	2.00	5.00
NNO Stormtroopers	2.00	5.00

2017 Funko Pop Flair Star Wars

NNO Chewbacca	1.50	4.00
NNO Darth Vader	2.50	6.00
NNO Greedo	1.25	3.00
NNO Han Solo	2.50	6.00
NNO Princess Leia	1.50	4.00
NNO Stormtrooper	1.25	3.00
NNO Yoda	1.50	4.00

2015-17 Funko Star Wars Smuggler's Bounty Patches

COMMON PATCH	2.00	5.00

SMUGGLER'S BOUNTY EXCLUSIVE

NNO BB-8	2.50	6.00
NNO Boba Fett	2.00	5.00
NNO Boushh	2.00	5.00
NNO Cassian Andor	2.00	5.00
NNO Darth Vader	2.50	6.00
NNO Greedo	2.00	5.00
NNO TIE Fighter Pilot	2.00	5.00
NNO X-Wing Pilot	2.00	5.00
NNO Yoda	2.00	5.00
NNO Zeb	2.00	5.00

2015 Star Wars Original Trilogy Series Bikkuriman Stickers

COMPLETE SET (24)	30.00	80.00
COMMON CARD	2.00	5.00

2015 Star Wars Prequel Trilogy Series Bikkuriman Stickers

COMPLETE SET (24)	25.00	60.00
COMMON CARD	1.25	3.00

1996 Star Wars 3-Di Widevision

COMPLETE SET (63)	30.00	60.00
COMMON CARD (1-63)	.60	1.50

1M STATED ODDS 1:24

1M Death Star Explosion	6.00	15.00

1996 Star Wars 3-Di Widevision Promos

3Di1 Darth Vader	2.50	6.00
3Di2 Luke Skywalker	12.00	30.00
Darth Vader/1000*		

2015 Star Wars Abrams Promos

COMPLETE SET (4)	10.00	25.00
COMMON CARD (1-4)	3.00	8.00

STATED ODDS 1:SET PER BOOK

1997 Star Wars Adventure Journal

NNO One of a Kind by Doug Shuler
NNO To Fight Another Day by Mike Vilardi
NNO Mist Encounter by Doug Shuler

2018 Star Wars Archives Signature Series Adam Driver

61 Adam Driver 2016 TFA Chrome/2	
62 Adam Driver 2016 TFA Chrome/2	
65 Adam Driver 2016 TFA Chrome/2	
66 Adam Driver 2016 TFA Chrome/1	

---

92 Adam Driver 2016 Evolution/4	
P1 Adam Driver 2015 Journey TFA Patches/1	

2018 Star Wars Archives Signature Series Adrian Edmonson

52 Adrian Edmonson 2017 TLJ S1/86	
52 Adrian Edmonson 2017 TLJ S1 Red/1	
52 Adrian Edmonson 2017 TLJ S1 Purple/35	
52 Adrian Edmonson 2017 TLJ S1 Green/50	
52 Adrian Edmonson 2017 TLJ S1 Blue/65	

2018 Star Wars Archives Signature Series Aidan Cook

16 Aidan Cook 2015 TFA S1/9	
44 Aidan Cook 2015 TFA S1/9	
44 Aidan Cook 2015 TFA S1 Green/2	
64 Aidan Cook 2016 Rogue One S1 Blue/4	
64 Aidan Cook 2016 Rogue One S1/28	

2018 Star Wars Archives Signature Series Al Lampert

10 Al Lampert 1977 SW/4	
468 Al Lampert 2013 GF2 Blue/56	

2018 Star Wars Archives Signature Series Alan Harris

13 Alan Harris 2001 Evolution/31	
31 Alan Harris 2016 Card Trader/28	
31 Alan Harris 2016 Card Trader Blue/7	
53 Alan Harris 2015 Journey TFA/51	
53 Alan Harris 2015 Journey TFA Green/7	
73 Alan Harris 1980 ESB/8	
74 Alan Harris 1980 ESB/18	
B2 Alan Harris 2016 Card Trader Bounty/6	
TC6 Alan Harris 2016 Card Trader Choice/17	
ESB4 Alan Harris 2017 GF Reborn/35	

2018 Star Wars Archives Signature Series Alan Ruscoe

60 Alan Ruscoe 2001 Evolution/35	
82 Alan Ruscoe 2012 Galactic Files/35	
8J Alan Ruscoe 2015 Chrome JvS/40	
8S Alan Ruscoe 2015 Chrome JvS Refractors/13	
8S Alan Ruscoe 2015 Chrome JvS/54	
426 Alan Ruscoe 2013 GF2/42	
TPM21 Alan Ruscoe 2017 GF Reborn/27	

2018 Star Wars Archives Signature Series Alan Tudyk

18 Alan Tudyk 2017 Rogue One S2 Black/2	
19 Alan Tudyk 2017 Rogue One S2/21	
29 Alan Tudyk 2017 Rogue One S2/20	
51 Alan Tudyk 2017 Rogue One S2/16	
56 Alan Tudyk 2017 Rogue One S2/20	
57 Alan Tudyk 2017 Rogue One S2/10	
71 Alan Tudyk 2017 Rogue One S2/20	
76 Alan Tudyk 2017 Rogue One S2/20	
C18 Alan Tudyk 2016 Rogue One S1 Icons/13	
HR3 Alan Tudyk 2016 Rogue One S1 Heroes/5	
HR4 Alan Tudyk 2017 Rogue One S2 Heroes/4	
MP2 Alan Tudyk 2016 Rogue One MB Patches/7	
PF7 Alan Tudyk 2017 Rogue One S2 PF/15	

2018 Star Wars Archives Signature Series Alistaire Petrie

10 Alistaire Petrie 2016 Rogue One S1/77
10 Alistaire Petrie 2016 Rogue One S1 Green/16
10 Alistaire Petrie 2016 Rogue One S1 Black/19

2018 Star Wars Archives Signature Series Amanda Lawrence

47 Amanda Lawrence 2017 TLJ S1 Green/50
47 Amanda Lawrence 2017 TLJ S1 Blue/65
47 Amanda Lawrence 2017 TLJ S1/85
47 Amanda Lawrence 2017 TLJ S1 Purple/35

2018 Star Wars Archives Signature Series Amy Allen

81 Amy Allen 2012 Galactic Files/14
424 Amy Allen 2013 GF2/22
AOTC18 Amy Allen 2017 GF Reborn Orange/2
AOTC18 Amy Allen 2017 GF Reborn/37

2018 Star Wars Archives Signature Series Andrew Jack

12 Andrew Jack 2016 TFA S2 Heroes/2
17 Andrew Jack 2015 TFA S1 Blue/1
31 Andrew Jack 2017 TLJ S1 Purple/35
31 Andrew Jack 2017 TLJ S1 Green/50
31 Andrew Jack 2017 TLJ S1 Blue/66
31 Andrew Jack 2017 TLJ S1/85
49 Andrew Jack 2016 Card Trader Blue/8
49 Andrew Jack 2016 Card Trader/22
TFA21 Andrew Jack 2017 GF Reborn/22

2018 Star Wars Archives Signature Series Andy Secombe

NNO Andy Secombe

2018 Star Wars Archives Signature Series Andy Serkis

1 Andy Serkis 2016 TFA Chrome Power of FO/11
10 Andy Serkis 2017 Journey TLJ/1
14 Andy Serkis 2017 Journey TLJ Characters/4
25 Andy Serkis 2017 TLJ S1/5
26 Andy Serkis 2016 Card Trader/26
30 Andy Serkis 2017 GF Reborn TFA10/30
60 Andy Serkis 2016 Card Trader Red/2
60 Andy Serkis 2016 Card Trader Blue/5
75 Andy Serkis 2016 TFA S2 Blue/4
75 Andy Serkis 2016 TFA S2 Green/5
75 Andy Serkis 2016 TFA Chrome Refractors/15
75 Andy Serkis 2016 TFA S2/16

2018 Star Wars Archives Signature Series Angus MacInnes

92 Angus MacInnes 2016 Rogue One MB Blue/1
92 Angus MacInnes 2016 Rogue One MB/47
476 Angus MacInnes 2013 GF 2/33
ANH28 Angus MacInnes 2017 GF Reborn/24

2018 Star Wars Archives Signature Series Anthony Forest

31 Anthony Forest 2016 Rogue One MB/36
94 Anthony Forest 1977 Star Wars/7
138 Anthony Forest 1977 Star Wars/9
223 Anthony Forest 2012 Galactic Files/45
WM1 Anthony Forest 2013 GF 2/17

2018 Star Wars Archives Signature Series Ashley Eckstein

AHSOKA TANO
STAR WARS REBELS

7 Ashley Eckstein 2010 CW ROTBH/3
8 Ashley Eckstein 2017 Journey TLJ Red/1
8 Ashley Eckstein 2017 Journey TLJ Green/1
8 Ashley Eckstein 2017 Journey TLJ/6
10 Ashley Eckstein 2016 Evolution/59
11 Ashley Eckstein 2016 Evolution/39
12 Ashley Eckstein 2016 Evolution/36
36 Ashley Eckstein 2008 CW/9
42 Ashley Eckstein 2010 CW ROTBH/5
44 Ashley Eckstein 2010 CW ROTBH/5
62 Ashley Eckstein 2017 Journey TLJ/9
70 Ashley Eckstein 2008 CW/6
82 Ashley Eckstein 2008 CW/15
88 Ashley Eckstein 2010 CW ROTBH/5
98 Ashley Eckstein 2016 Card Trader/30
I4 Ashley Eckstein 2013 Jedi Legacy Influencers/24
13J Ashley Eckstein 2015 Chrome JvS Refractors/16
13J Ashley Eckstein 2015 Chrome JvS/55
13S Ashley Eckstein 2015 Chrome JvS/56
231 Ashley Eckstein 2012 Galactic Files/12
ACW1 Ashley Eckstein 2017 GF Reborn/34

2018 Star Wars Archives Signature Series Ben Daniels

9 Ben Daniels 2016 Rogue One S1 Black/18
9 Ben Daniels 2016 Rogue One S1/72
9 Ben Daniels 2016 Rogue One S1 Green/15
49 Ben Daniels 2016 Rogue One S1 Blue/8
49 Ben Daniels 2016 Rogue One S1 Green/9
49 Ben Daniels 2016 Rogue One S1/37
63 Ben Daniels 2017 Rogue One S2/10

2018 Star Wars Archives Signature Series Ben Mendelsohn

5 Ben Mendelsohn 2016 Rogue One MB Patches/6
13 Ben Mendelsohn 2016 Rogue One S1 Blue/8
13 Ben Mendelsohn 2016 Rogue One S1 Black/9
13 Ben Mendelsohn 2016 Rogue One S1/38
37 Ben Mendelsohn 2017 Rogue One S2 Blue/1
37 Ben Mendelsohn 2017 Rogue One S2/11
52 Ben Mendelsohn 2016 Rogue One S1 Blue/7
52 Ben Mendelsohn 2016 Rogue One S1 Black/10
52 Ben Mendelsohn 2016 Rogue One S1/36
66 Ben Mendelsohn 2016 Rogue One S1 Green/8
66 Ben Mendelsohn 2016 Rogue One S1 Gray/8
66 Ben Mendelsohn 2016 Rogue One S1/37
83 Ben Mendelsohn 2016 Rogue One S1 Black/7
83 Ben Mendelsohn 2016 Rogue One S1 Green/8
83 Ben Mendelsohn 2016 Rogue One S1 Blue/8
83 Ben Mendelsohn 2016 Rogue One S1/39
CI2 Ben Mendelsohn 2016 Rogue One S1 Characters/14
RO6 Ben Mendelsohn 2017 GF Reborn/23
VE3 Ben Mendelsohn 2016 Rogue One S1 Villains/6

2018 Star Wars Archives Signature Series Billy Dee Williams

8 Billy Dee Williams 1980 ESB/9
64 Billy Dee Williams 2016 Evolution/1
189 Billy Dee Williams 1980 ESB/2
198 Billy Dee Williams 1980 ESB/2
IL4 Billy Dee Williams 2013 Jedi Legacy Influencers I14/7
ESB3 Billy Dee Williams 2017 GF Reborn/1

2018 Star Wars Archives Signature Series Brian Herring

6 Brian Herring 2015 TFA S1/3
6 Brian Herring 2015 TFA S1 Blue/3
7 Brian Herring 2017 40th Ann./3
10 Brian Herring 2016 TFA Chrome Refractors/1
16 Brian Herring 2016 TFA S2 Heroes/6
26 Brian Herring 2016 TFA S2/8
27 Brian Herring 2016 TFA Chrome Refractors/1
27 Brian Herring 2016 TFA S2 Green/1
28 Brian Herring 2016 TFA S2/1
28 Brian Herring 2016 TFA S2 Green/2
30 Brian Herring 2016 TFA Chrome Wave Ref./1
48 Brian Herring 2016 Card Trader/8
78 Brian Herring 2015 TFA S1 Green/1
78 Brian Herring 2015 TFA S1 Blue/1
78 Brian Herring 2015 TFA S1/3
81 Brian Herring 2015 TFA S1 Purple/1
81 Brian Herring 2015 TFA S1/11
82 Brian Herring 2015 TFA S1/5
82 Brian Herring 2015 Journey TFA Green/10
82 Brian Herring 2015 Journey TFA/19
97 Brian Herring 2016 Journey TLJ Green/1
104 Brian Herring 2015 Journey TFA Pink/1
104 Brian Herring 2015 Journey TFA Green/7
104 Brian Herring 2015 Journey TFA/20
TFA4 Brian Herring 2017 GF Reborn/10

2018 Star Wars Archives Signature Series Caroline Blakiston

9 Caroline Blakiston 2016 Rogue One MB Heroes/6
30 Caroline Blakiston 2016 Card Trader Red/2
30 Caroline Blakiston 2016 Card Trader Blue/4
30 Caroline Blakiston 2016 Card Trader/25
63 Caroline Blakiston 1983 ROTJ/11
64 Caroline Blakiston 1983 ROTJ/38
85 Caroline Blakiston 2016 Evolution/47
174 Caroline Blakiston 2012 Galactic Files/14
B15 Caroline Blakiston 2016 Card Trader Bounty/5
ROTJ8 Caroline Blakiston 2017 GF Reborn/25

2018 Star Wars Archives Signature Series Cathy Munroe

37 Cathy Munroe 2016 Card Trader/29
37 Cathy Munroe 2016 Card Trader Blue/3
89 Cathy Munroe 2001 Evolution/33
B8 Cathy Munroe 2016 Card Trader Bounty/5
ESB6 Cathy Munroe 2017 GF Reborn Orange/3
ESB6 Cathy Munroe 2017 GF Reborn/25

2018 Star Wars Archives Signature Series Chris Parsons

1 Chris Parsons 2001 Evolution/34
38 Chris Parsons 2016 Card Trader Blue/8
38 Chris Parsons 2016 Card Trader/28
53 Chris Parsons 2015 Journey TLA/13
B7 Chris Parsons 2016 Card Trader Bounty/6
136 Chris Parsons 2012 Galactic Files/38
ESB5 Chris Parsons 2017 GF Reborn/24

2018 Star Wars Archives Signature Series Corey Dee Williams

40 Corey Dee Williams 2001 Star Wars Evolution/34

2018 Star Wars Archives Signature Series Daisy Ridley

23 Daisy Ridley 2016 TFA S2/1
P6 Daisy Ridley 2015 Journey TFA Patches/1
R1 Daisy Ridley 2015 Journey TFA Heroes/1
P15 Daisy Ridley 2015 Journey TFA Patches/1

2018 Star Wars Archives Signature Series Daniel Logan

41 Daniel Logan 2012 Galactic Files/21
51 Daniel Logan 2016 Evolution Blue/4
51 Daniel Logan 2016 Evolution/48
78 Daniel Logan 2010 CW ROTBH/3
83 Daniel Logan 2010 CW ROTBH/4
408 Daniel Logan 2013 GF2/38
ACW7 Daniel Logan 2017 GF Reborn/24
AOTC5 Daniel Logan 2017 GF Reborn/28

2018 Star Wars Archives Signature Series Dave Chapman

6 Dave Chapman 2015 TFA S1/20
6 Dave Chapman 2015 TFA S1 Blue/3
9 Dave Chapman 2016 TFA Chrome Heroes/10
16 Dave Chapman 2016 TFA S2 Heroes/4
19 Dave Chapman 2015 TFA S1 Movie Scenes/6

26 Dave Chapman 2016 TFA Chrome Refractors/3
26 Dave Chapman 2016 TFA S2/16
27 Dave Chapman 2016 TFA S2 Blue/1
28 Dave Chapman 2016 TFA Chrome Refractors/1
28 Dave Chapman 2016 TFA S2/5
30 Dave Chapman 2016 TFA S2/4
30 Dave Chapman 2016 TFA Chrome/7
39 Dave Chapman 2016 TFA Chrome/9
39 Dave Chapman 2016 TFA S2/14
40 Dave Chapman 2016 TFA Chrome/3
48 Dave Chapman 2016 Card Trader Blue/4
48 Dave Chapman 2016 Card Trader/16
49 Dave Chapman 2016 TFA S2/3
49 Dave Chapman 2016 TFA Chrome/5
63 Dave Chapman 2016 TFA S2 Green/3
63 Dave Chapman 2016 TFA S2 Blue/3
63 Dave Chapman 2016 TFA S2/7
63 Dave Chapman 2016 TFA Chrome/23
73 Dave Chapman 2016 TFA S2 Blue/3
73 Dave Chapman 2016 TFA Chrome/7
73 Dave Chapman 2016 TFA S2/14
76 Dave Chapman 2015 TFA S1/25
77 Dave Chapman 2015 TFA S1/12
78 Dave Chapman 2015 TFA S1/6
79 Dave Chapman 2015 TFA S1/7
80 Dave Chapman 2015 TFA S1/6
81 Dave Chapman 2015 TFA S1 Green/3
81 Dave Chapman 2015 TFA S1/23
82 Dave Chapman 2015 Journey TFA Black/3
82 Dave Chapman 2015 Journey TFA/48
83 Dave Chapman 2015 TFA S1/5
97 Dave Chapman 2017 Journey TLJ/1
R4 Dave Chapman 2015 Journey TFA Heroes/7
104 Dave Chapman 2015 Journey TFA Black/3
104 Dave Chapman 2015 Journey to TFA Green/20
104 Dave Chapman 2015 Journey TFA/48
P18 Dave Chapman 2015 Journey TFA Patches/3
TFA4 Dave Chapman 2017 GF Reborn/16

2018 Star Wars Archives Signature Series David Acord

7 David Acord 2016 TFA S2 Maz's Castle/2
8 David Acord 2015 TFA S1/13
11 David Acord 2015 TFA S1/10
20 David Acord 2015 TFA S1 Blue/11
20 David Acord 2015 TFA S1 Green/11
20 David Acord 2015 TFA S1/28
25 David Acord 2016 TFA Chrome/4
29 David Acord 2015 TFA S1/26
43 David Acord 2016 TFA Chrome/4
52 David Acord 2016 TFA Chrome Refractors/2
52 David Acord 2015 TFA S1/6
58 David Acord 2016 Card Trader/23
61 David Acord 2016 Card Trader/23
68 David Acord 2016 TFA S2 Blue/5
68 David Acord 2016 TFA S2 Green/10
68 David Acord 2016 TFA S2/25
68 David Acord 2016 TFA Chrome Refractors/30
68 David Acord 2016 TFA Chrome/38
75 David Acord 2015 TFA S1/11
TFA29 David Acord 2017 GF Reborn/22

2018 Star Wars Archives Signature Series David Ankrum

19 David Ankrum 2016 Card Trader/13
88 David Ankrum 2016 Rogue One MB/16
88 David Ankrum 2016 Rogue One MB Black/1
9R David Ankrum 2014 Chrome 9R/11
118 David Ankrum 2012 Galactic Files/14
145 David Ankrum 2012 Galactic Files/13
175 David Ankrum 2012 Galactic Files/15
I12 David Ankrum 2013 Jedi Legacy Influencers/19
ANH23 David Ankrum 2017 GF Reborn/21

2018 Star Wars Archives Signature Series David Barclay

3 David Barclay 2017 40th Ann. Green/1
9 David Barclay 1980 ESB/10
9 David Barclay 2016 Card Trader/10
10 David Barclay 2016 Card Trader Blue/5
10 David Barclay 2016 Card Trader/19
13 David Barclay 1983 ROTJ/5
14 David Barclay 1983 ROTJ/18
15 David Barclay 1983 ROTJ/7
21 David Barclay 2012 Galactic Files/1
28 David Barclay 2017 40th Ann. Green/1
36 David Barclay 2001 Evolution/11
41 David Barclay 1999 Chrome Archives/1
46 David Barclay 1983 ROTJ/8
49 David Barclay 2015 Journey TFA Green/2
49 David Barclay 2015 Journey TFA/2
58 David Barclay 1980 ESB/7
63 David Barclay 1980 ESB/5
63 David Barclay Journey TFA/22
80 David Barclay 2015 Journey TFA Green/1
82 David Barclay 2016 Evolution/20
83 David Barclay 2016 Evolution Blue/19
83 David Barclay 2016 Evolution/19
163 David Barclay 2012 Galactic Files/11
172 David Barclay 1983 ROTJ/20
34L David Barclay Jedi Legacy/30
35J David Barclay 2015 Chrome JvS/19
35S David Barclay Chrome JvS/31
490 David Barclay 2013 GF2/1
50E David Barclay 2014 Chrome 50E/5
50R David Barclay 2014 Chrome 50R/5
519 David Barclay 2013 GF2/15
C15 David Barclay 2013 Jedi Legacy Connections/10
ESB2 David Barclay 2017 GF Reborn/22

2018 Star Wars Archives Signature Series Dee Bradley Baker

6 Dee Baker 2008 CW/6
8 Dee Baker 2010 CW ROTBH/5
94 Dee Baker 2016 Card Trader Blue/7
94 Dee Baker 2016 Card Trader/26
233 Dee Baker 2012 Galactic Files/19
475 Dee Baker 2015 Chrome JvS/8
ACW9 Dee Baker 2017 GF Reborn/1
ACW9 Dee Baker 2017 GF Reborn/27

2018 Star Wars Archives Signature Series Deep Roy

21 Deep Roy 1983 ROTJ/14
183 Deep Roy 2012 Galactic Files/32
ROTJ16 Deep Roy 2017 GF Reborn/42

2018 Star Wars Archives Signature Series Denis Lawson

19 Denis Lawson 2016 Card Trader Red/1
19 Denis Lawson 2016 Card Trader Blue/4
19 Denis Lawson 2016 Card Trader/11
83 Denis Lawson 2001 Evolution/16
88 Denis Lawson 2016 Rogue One MB/27
9R Denis Lawson 2014 Chrome Refractors/2
9R Denis Lawson 2014 Chrome 9R/12
127 Denis Lawson 1983 ROTJ/9
145 Denis Lawson 2012 Galactic Files/16
175 Denis Lawson 2012 Galactic Files/16
I12 Denis Lawson 2013 Jedi Legacy Influencers/16
ANH23 Denis Lawson 2017 GF Reborn/13
ESB13 Denis Lawson 2017 GF Reborn/15

2018 Star Wars Archives Signature Series Derek Arnold

19 Derek Arnold 2016 Rogue One S1 Blue/7
19 Derek Arnold 2016 Rogue One S1/38
34 Derek Arnold 2017 Rogue One S2 Blue/2
34 Derek Arnold 2016 Rogue One S1 Green/8
34 Derek Arnold 2016 Rogue One S1/34
58 Derek Arnold 2017 Rogue One S2 Black/2
58 Derek Arnold 2017 Rogue One S2/10
87 Derek Arnold 2016 Rogue One S1 Green/8
87 Derek Arnold 2016 Rogue One S1/39
HR10 Derek Arnold 2016 Rogue One S1 Heroes/2

2018 Star Wars Archives Signature Series Dermot Crowley

39 Dermot Crowley 2016 Card Trader Blue/6
39 Dermot Crowley 2016 Card Trader/24
ROTJ9 Dermot Crowley 2017 GF Reborn/24

2018 Star Wars Archives Signature Series Dickey Beer

47 Dickey Beer 1983 ROTJ/7
25L Dickey Beer 2013 Jedi Legacy/14
32L Dickey Beer 2013 Jedi Legacy/20
379 Dickey Beer GF2/44

2018 Star Wars Archives Signature Series Dual Autographs

18 Taylor Gray/Tiya Sircar 40th Ann./4
64 Tim Rose/Aidan Cook Rogue One S1/9
71 Tiya Sircar/Vanessa Marshall Rebels Foil/7
78 Tiya Sircar/Vanessa Marshall Rebels Foil/14
92 Tom Kane/James Taylor 40th Ann. Green/1
M5 Nick Kellington/Derek Arnold Rogue One S1 Montages/3
GM3 Taylor Gray/Tiya Sircar Card Trader GM/3
PF6 Nick Kellington/Derek Arnold Rogue One S2 PF/11
GM17 Kane/Taylor Card Trader GM/5

2018 Star Wars Archives Signature Series Felicity Jones

1 Felicity Jones 2016 Rogue One S1/6
21 Felicity Jones 2016 Rogue One S1/1
21 Felicity Jones 2016 Rogue One S1/4
24 Felicity Jones 2016 Rogue One S1/1
24 Felicity Jones 2016 Rogue One S1/6
46 Felicity Jones 2016 Rogue One S1/11
51 Felicity Jones 2016 Rogue One S1 Black/2
70 Felicity Jones 2016 Rogue One S1/1
70 Felicity Jones 2016 Rogue One S1/11
79 Felicity Jones 2016 Rogue One S1 Blue/1
79 Felicity Jones 2016 Rogue One S1/21
80 Felicity Jones 2016 Rogue One S1/11
84 Felicity Jones 2016 Rogue One S1/6
G1 Felicity Jones 2016 Rogue One S1 Gallery/1
RO1 Felicity Jones 2017 GF Reborn Blue/2

2018 Star Wars Archives Signature Series Femi Taylor

55 Femi Taylor 2001 Evolution/30
177 Femi Taylor 2012 Galactic Files/23
ROTJ5 Femi Taylor 2017 GF Reborn Blue/1
ROTJ5 Femi Taylor GF Reborn/30

2018 Star Wars Archives Signature Series Forest Whitaker

6 Forest Whitaker 2016 Rogue One S1 Green/16
6 Forest Whitaker 2016 Rogue One S1 Black/20
6 Forest Whitaker 2016 Rogue One S1/92
8 Forest Whitaker 2017 Rogue One S2 Posters/1
27 Forest Whitaker 2017 Rogue One S2/14
HR8 Forest Whitaker 2016 Rogue One S1 Heroes/4
RO7 Forest Whitaker 2017 GF Reborn/25

2018 Star Wars Archives Signature Series Garrick Hagon

10 Garrick Hagon 2001 Evolution/33
36 Garrick Hagon 2016 Card Trader Blue/4
36 Garrick Hagon 2016 Card Trader/25
89 Garrick Hagon 2016 Rogue One MB/32
111 Garrick Hagon 2007 30th Ann./10
119 Garrick Hagon 2012 Galactic Files/32
16E Garrick Hagon 2014 Chrome/5
16R Garrick Hagon 2014 Chrome/8
243 Garrick Hagon 1977 Star Wars/12
I10 Garrick Hagon 2013 Jedi Legacy Influencers I10/37
ANH25 Garrick Hagon 2017 GF Reborn/39

2018 Star Wars Archives Signature Series Genevieve O'Reilly

8 Genevieve O'Reilly 2016 Rogue One S1 Blue/15
8 Genevieve O'Reilly 2016 Rogue One S1 Black/19
8 Genevieve O'Reilly 2016 Rogue One S1/99
9 Genevieve O'Reilly 2016 Rogue One MB Heroes/4
10 Genevieve O'Reilly 2017 Rogue One S2 Black/3
10 Genevieve O'Reilly 2017 Rogue One S2/15
41 Genevieve O'Reilly 2017 Rogue One S2/16
60 Genevieve O'Reilly 2017 40th Ann./3
73 Genevieve O'Reilly 2016 Rogue One S1 Green/8
73 Genevieve O'Reilly 2016 Rogue One S1/57

84 Genevieve O'Reilly 2016 Evolution/37
91 Genevieve O'Reilly 2012 Galactic Files/15
102 Genevieve O'Reilly 2016 Rogue One MB/1
102 Genevieve O'Reilly 2016 Rogue One MB/19

2018 Star Wars Archives Signature Series Gerald Home

ROTJ15 Gerald Home 2017 GF Reborn/23

2018 Star Wars Archives Signature Series Harrison Ford

NNO Harrison Ford

2018 Star Wars Archives Signature Series Hayden Christensen

2 Hayden Christensen 2016 Evolution/8
3 Hayden Christensen 2017 Journey TLJ Red/1
3 Hayden Christensen 2016 Evolution/6
3 Hayden Christensen 2017 Journey TLJ/6
4 Hayden Christensen 2017 Journey TLJ/1
6 Hayden Christensen 2017 40th Ann./1
6 Hayden Christensen 2017 Journey TLJ/5
9 Hayden Christensen 2015 Journey TFA Black/1
9 Hayden Christensen 2015 Journey TFA Pink/1
9 Hayden Christensen 2017 Journey TLJ/4
12 Hayden Christensen 2017 Journey TLJ/3
13 Hayden Christensen 2010 CW ROTBH/8
14 Hayden Christensen 2016 Rogue One MB/4
15 Hayden Christensen 2016 Rogue One MB Black/1
17 Hayden Christensen 2015 Journey TFA Black/1
2J Hayden Christensen 2015 Chrome JvS Refractors/5
2J Hayden Christensen 2015 Chrome JvS/8
2S Hayden Christensen 2015 Chrome JvS/6
49 Hayden Christensen 2017 40th Ann. Blue/2
49 Hayden Christensen 2017 40th Ann./5
51 Hayden Christensen 2017 40th Ann./4
52 Hayden Christensen 2017 40th Ann./3
53 Hayden Christensen 2017 40th Ann./5
57 Hayden Christensen 2017 Journey TLJ Red/1
57 Hayden Christensen 2017 Journey TLJ/3
66 Hayden Christensen 2012 Galactic Files/10
71 Hayden Christensen 2016 Card Trader Blue/7
71 Hayden Christensen 2016 Card Trader/24
80 Hayden Christensen 2015 Journey TFA/6
89 Hayden Christensen 2017 40th Ann./1
93 Hayden Christensen 2004 Heritage/2
100 Hayden Christensen 2004 Heritage/1
17A Hayden Christensen 2013 Jedi Legacy/6
19A Hayden Christensen 2013 Jedi Legacy/8
21A Hayden Christensen 2013 Jedi Legacy/4
24A Hayden Christensen 2013 Jedi Legacy/6
27A Hayden Christensen 2013 Jedi Legacy/8
33A Hayden Christensen 2013 Jedi Legacy Blue/1
36A Hayden Christensen 2013 Jedi Legacy/6
38A Hayden Christensen 2013 Jedi Legacy/7
401 Hayden Christensen 2013 GF2/8
45A Hayden Christensen 2013 Jedi Legacy/5
CL7 Hayden Christensen 2012 Galactic Files Classic Lines/3
CL8 Hayden Christensen 2013 GF2/2
ROTS1 Hayden Christensen 2017 GF Reborn/24

2018 Star Wars Archives Signature Series Hermione Corfield

49 Hermione Corfield 2017 TLJ S1 Purple/36
49 Hermione Corfield 2017 TLJ S1 Green/50
49 Hermione Corfield 2017 TLJ S1 Blue/65
49 Hermione Corfield 2017 TLJ S1/85

2018 Star Wars Archives Signature Series Howie Weed

ESB15 Howie Weed 2017 GF Reborn/22

2018 Star Wars Archives Signature Series Ian McDiarmid

NNO Ian McDiarmid

2018 Star Wars Archives Signature Series Ian McElhinney

17 Ian McElhinney 2016 Rogue One S1 Green/6
17 Ian McElhinney 2016 Rogue One S1 Black/9
17 Ian McElhinney 2016 Rogue One S1/39

2018 Star Wars Archives Signature Series Jack Klaff

90 Jack Klaff 2016 Rogue One MB/48
122 Jack Klaff 2012 Galactic Files/21

2018 Star Wars Archives Signature Series James Arnold Taylor

3 James Arnold Taylor CW ROTBH/1
19 James Arnold Taylor CW ROTBH/3
26 James Arnold Taylor CW ROTBH/4
40 James Arnold Taylor CW ROTBH/3

2018 Star Wars Archives Signature Series Jason Isaacs

NNO Jason Isaacs

2018 Star Wars Archives Signature Series Jason Spisak

ACW15 Jason Spisak 2017 GF Reborn/24

2018 Star Wars Archives Signature Series Jeremy Bulloch

11 Jeremy Bulloch 2001 Evolution/19
12 Jeremy Bulloch 2016 Card Trader Blue/4
23 Jeremy Bulloch 1983 ROTJ/38
53 Jeremy Bulloch 2016 Evolution/14
53 Jeremy Bulloch 2016 Evolution/52
54 Jeremy Bulloch 2016 Evolution/48
73 Jeremy Bulloch 1980 ESB/13
75 Jeremy Bulloch 1980 ESB/22
162 Jeremy Bulloch 2012 Galactic Files/10
34J Jeremy Bulloch 2015 Chrome JvS/54
34S Jeremy Bulloch 2015 Chrome JvS/45
474 Jeremy Bulloch 2013 GF2/44
518 Jeremy Bulloch 2013 GF2/21
ESB1 Jeremy Bulloch GF Reborn/23

2018 Star Wars Archives Signature Series Jerome Blake

30 Jerome Blake 2012 Galactic Files/37
40 Jerome Blake 2006 Evolution Update/1
57 Jerome Blake 2001 Evolution/36
84 Jerome Blake 2016 Card Trader Blue/8
84 Jerome Blake 2016 Card Trader/25
382 Jerome Blake 2013 GF2/2
41J Jerome Blake 2015 Chrome JvS Refractors/6
41J Jerome Blake 2015 Chrome JvS/66
TPM15 Jerome Blake 2017 GF Reborn/23

2018 Star Wars Archives Signature Series Jesse Jensen

NNO Jesse Jensen

2018 Star Wars Archives Signature Series Jimmy Vee

13 Jimmy Vee 2017 TLJ S1 Red/1
13 Jimmy Vee 2017 TLJ S1 Purple/35
13 Jimmy Vee 2017 TLJ S1 Green/50
13 Jimmy Vee 2017 TLJ S1 Blue/66
13 Jimmy Vee 2017 TLJ S1/85

2018 Star Wars Archives Signature Series John Boyega

2 John Boyega 2015 TFA S1 Montages/1
2 John Boyega 2015 TFA S1 Green/2
4 John Boyega 2015 Journey TFA Silhouette/3
9 John Boyega 2017 Journey TLJ Green/1
9 John Boyega 2016 TFA S2/1
13 John Boyega 2016 Evolution Stained/1
21 John Boyega 2016 TFA S2/1
29 John Boyega 2016 TFA S2/1
29 John Boyega 2016 TFA S2 Blue/2
32 John Boyega 2016 TFA S2/3
38 John Boyega 2016 TFA S2/5
39 John Boyega 2016 TFA S2 Purple/1
40 John Boyega 2015 TFA S1/1
45 John Boyega 2016 TFA S2/1
67 John Boyega 2016 TFA S2/1
70 John Boyega 2016 TFA S2 Blue/1
73 John Boyega 2017 Journey TLJ/28
75 John Boyega 2017 Journey TLJ/29
82 John Boyega 2017 Journey TLJ/26
85 John Boyega 2016 TFA S2/1
89 John Boyega 2016 Evolution/1
90 John Boyega 2016 TFA S1/1
90 John Boyega 2016 TFA S2 Green/3
96 John Boyega 2017 Journey TLJ/25
97 John Boyega 2015 TFA S1/1
99 John Boyega 2015 TFA S1/1
R9 John Boyega 2015 Journey TFA Heroes/1

2018 Star Wars Archives Signature Series John Morton

11 John Morton 1980 ESB/12
20 John Morton 2016 Card Trader Blue/6
20 John Morton 2016 Card Trader/33
37 John Morton 2004 Heritage/2
38 John Morton 1980 ESB/14
50 John Morton 1999 Chrome Archives/1
91 John Morton 1980 ESB/23
98 John Morton 1980 ESB/7
C8 John Morton 2013 Jedi Legacy Connections/29
131 John Morton 2012 Galactic Files /11
146 John Morton 2012 Galactic Files/31
210 John Morton 1980 ESB/8
220 John Morton 1980 ESB/38
489 John Morton 2013 GF2/23
FQ3 John Morton 2016 Card Trader Film Quotes/8
CL10 John Morton 2012 Galactic Files Classic Lines/1
ESB14 John Morton 2017 GF Reborn Blue/1
ESB14 John Morton 2017 GF Reborn/25

2018 Star Wars Archives Signature Series Joonas Suotamo

10 Joonas Suotamo 2015 TFA S1 Movie Scenes/3
25 Joonas Suotamo 2015 TFA S1/20
41 Joonas Suotamo 2016 TFA Chrome/3
44 Joonas Suotamo 2016 TFA Chrome/1
44 Joonas Suotamo 2016 TFA Chrome/3
59 Joonas Suotamo 2016 Evolution/20
70 Joonas Suotamo 2016 TFA S2 Green/3
70 Joonas Suotamo 2016 TFA Chrome Ref./8
70 Joonas Suotamo 2016 TFA S2/9
70 Joonas Suotamo 2016 TFA S1/11
76 Joonas Suotamo 2016 TFA Chrome Ref./3

76 Joonas Suotamo 2016 TFA S2/5
76 Joonas Suotamo 2016 TFA Chrome/7
P5 Joonas Suotamo 2015 Journey TFA Patches/5
100 Joonas Suotamo 2016 TFA Factory/1
100 Joonas Suotamo 2015 TFA S1/7
109 Joonas Suotamo 2015 Journey TFA Black/2
P13 Joonas Suotamo 2015 Journey TFA Patches/4
TFA11 Joonas Suotamo 2017 GF Reborn/24

2018 Star Wars Archives Signature Series Julian Glover

29 Julian Glover 2016 Card Trader/31
31 Julian Glover 2001 Evolution/31
140 Julian Glover 2012 Galactic Files/23
30R Julian Glover 2014 Chrome/7
ESB11 Julian Glover 2017 GF Reborn/36

2018 Star Wars Archives Signature Series Ken Leung

5 Ken Leung 2016 TFA Chrome Heroes/2
15 Ken Leung 2015 TFA S1 Movie Scenes/2
27 Ken Leung 2015 TFA S1/8
51 Ken Leung 2016 Card Trader Blue/7
51 Ken Leung 2016 Card Trader/22
TFA22 Ken Leung 2017 GF Reborn/24

2018 Star Wars Archives Signature Series Kenneth Colley

4 Ken Colley 2001 Evolution/38
16 Ken Colley 2016 Card Trader Blue/8
16 Ken Colley 2016 Card Trader/28
141 Ken Colley 2012 Galactic Files/24
29E Ken Colley 2014 Chrome/1
ESB9 Ken Colley 2017 GF Reborn/26
ROTJ7 Ken Colley 2017 GF Reborn/38

2018 Star Wars Archives Signature Series Kiran Shah

35 Kiran Shah 2017 TLJ S1 Purple/35
35 Kiran Shah 2017 TLJ S1 Green/50
35 Kiran Shah 2017 TLJ S1 Blue/65
35 Kiran Shah 2017 TLJ S1/85

2018 Star Wars Archives Signature Series Lily Cole

34 Lily Cole 2017 TLJ S1 Red/1
34 Lily Cole 2017 TLJ S1 Purple/34
34 Lily Cole 2017 TLJ S1 Green/50
34 Lily Cole 2017 TLJ S1 Blue/65
34 Lily Cole 2017 TLJ S1/85

2018 Star Wars Archives Signature Series Mads Mikkelsen

2 Mads Mikkelsen Rogue One S2 Green/1
2 Mads Mikkelsen Rogue One S2/8
38 Mads Mikkelsen Rogue One S1 Blue/7
38 Mads Mikkelsen Rogue One Black/9
38 Mads Mikkelsen Rogue One S1/33
RO8 Mads Mikkelsen GF Reborn/23

2018 Star Wars Archives Signature Series Mark Dodson

16 Mark Dodson 1983 ROTJ/40
34 Mark Dodson 2016 Card Trader Red/1
34 Mark Dodson 2016 Card Trader Blue/7
34 Mark Dodson 2016 Card Trader/29
71 Mark Dodson 2001 Evolution/34
181 Mark Dodson 2012 GF Reborn/28
ROTJ14 Mark Dodson 2017 GF Reborn/42

2018 Star Wars Archives Signature Series Matt Lanter

2 Matt Lanter 2008 CW/13
9 Matt Lanter 2016 Rogue One MB/33
10 Matt Lanter 2017 40th Ann./2
10 Matt Lanter 2017 40th Ann./4
10 Matt Lanter 2016 Rogue One MB/5
23 Matt Lanter 2010 CW ROTBH/3
36 Matt Lanter 2010 CW ROTBH/3
71 Matt Lanter 2010 CW ROTBH/4
84 Matt Lanter 2008 CW/5
22A Matt Lanter 2013 Jedi Legacy/2

2018 Star Wars Archives Signature Series Matthew Wood

NNO Matthew Wood

2018 Star Wars Archives Signature Series Michaela Cottrell

25 Michaela Cottrell 2001 Evolution/39
28 Michaela Cottrell 2012 Galactic Files/29
17J Michaela Cottrell 2015 Chrome JvS Ref./24
17J Michaela Cottrell 2015 Chrome JvS/58
TPM22 Michaela Cottrell 2017 GF Reborn/31

2018 Star Wars Archives Signature Series Mike Edmonds

44 Mike Edmonds 2001 Evolution/34
82 Mike Edmonds 1983 ROTJ/8
84 Mike Edmonds 1983 ROTJ/16
85 Mike Edmonds 1983 ROTJ/33
92 Mike Edmonds 1983 ROTJ/14
103 Mike Edmonds 1983 ROTJ/4
171 Mike Edmonds 2012 Galactic Files/24

2018 Star Wars Archives Signature Series Mike Quinn

15 Mike Quinn 2016 Card Trader/29
16 Mike Quinn 2016 TFA Chrome Heroes/14
20 Mike Quinn 1983 ROTJ/41
22 Mike Quinn 1983 ROTJ/41
33 Mike Quinn 2016 Card Trader/25
39 Mike Quinn 2016 TFA Chrome Ref./4
39 Mike Quinn 2016 TFA Chrome/7
48 Mike Quinn 2016 TFA Factory/2
48 Mike Quinn 2016 TFA S1 Blue/4
48 Mike Quinn 2015 TFA S1 Green/7
48 Mike Quinn 2015 TFA S1/35
52 Mike Quinn 2001 Evolution/39
96 Mike Quinn 2016 TFA Green/4
96 Mike Quinn 2016 TFA Chrome/5
123 Mike Quinn 1983 ROTJ/28
182 Mike Quinn 2012 Galactic Files/12
184 Mike Quinn 1983 ROTJ/25
25R Mike Quinn 2014 Chrome Ref./1
25R Mike Quinn 2014 Chrome 25R/2
ROTJ12 Mike Quinn 2017 GF Reborn/25
ROTJ13 Mike Quinn 2017 GF Reborn/37

2018 Star Wars Archives Signature Series Nick Kellington

7 Nick Kellington 2016 Rogue One S1 Blue/15
7 Nick Kellington 2016 Rogue One S1 Black/17
7 Nick Kellington 2016 Rogue One S1/76
88 Nick Kellington 2016 Rogue One S1 Green/7
88 Nick Kellington 2016 Rogue One S1 Blue/8
88 Nick Kellington 2016 Rogue One S1/38
HR9 Nick Kellington 2016 Rogue One S1 Heroes/6

2018 Star Wars Archives Signature Series Nika Futterman

93 Nika Futterman 2016 Card Trader Blue/4
93 Nika Futterman 2016 Card Trader/21
30J Nika Futterman 2015 Chrome JvS/5
30S Nika Futterman 2015 Chrome JvS/4
ACW6 Nika Futterman 2017 GF Reborn/24

2018 Star Wars Archives Signature Series Oliver Ford Davies

AOTC8 Oliver Ford Davies 2017 GF Reborn/24
TPM10 Oliver Ford Davies 2017 GF Reborn/23

2018 Star Wars Archives Signature Series Orli Shoshan

65 Orli Shoshan 2012 Galactic Files/31
6J Orli Shoshan 2015 Chrome JvS/59
6S Orli Shoshan 2015 Chrome JvS/61

2018 Star Wars Archives Signature Series Paul Blake

21 Paul Blake 2016 Card Trader Blue/8
21 Paul Blake 2016 Card Trader/26
33 Paul Blake 2001 Evolution/30
73 Paul Blake 2007 30th Ann./11
B1 Paul Blake 2016 Card Trader Bounty/9
104 Paul Blake 2012 Galactic Files/28
ANH19 Paul Blake 2017 GF Reborn Orange/1
ANH19 Paul Blake 2017 GF Reborn/36

2018 Star Wars Archives Signature Series Paul Brooke

371 Paul Brooke 2013 GF2/41
ROTJ11 Paul Brooke 2013 GF Reborn Orange/1
ROTJ11 Paul Brooke 2013 GF Reborn/24

2018 Star Wars Archives Signature Series Paul Kasey

20 Paul Kasey 2017 TLJ S1 Red/1
20 Paul Kasey 2017 TLJ S1 Purple/40
20 Paul Kasey 2017 TLJ S1 Green/50
20 Paul Kasey 2017 TLJ S1 Blue/67
20 Paul Kasey 2017 TLJ S1/85

2018 Star Wars Archives Signature Series Peter Mayhew

7 Peter Mayhew 1983 ROTJ/1
8 Peter Mayhew 2016 Card Trader Blue/7
8 Peter Mayhew 2016 Card Trader/22
33 Peter Mayhew 2015 Journey TFA Black/2
33 Peter Mayhew 2015 Journey TFA/3
40 Peter Mayhew Journey TFA/1
55 Peter Mayhew 2016 Evolution/25
56 Peter Mayhew 2016 Evolution/5
57 Peter Mayhew 2016 Evolution/4
58 Peter Mayhew 2016 Evolution/3
84 Peter Mayhew 1980 ESB/8
89 Peter Mayhew 1980 ESB/5
121 Peter Mayhew 1977 Star Wars/5
128 Peter Mayhew 1977 Star Wars/5
157 Peter Mayhew 2012 Galactic Files/3
217 Peter Mayhew 1980 ESB/2
24S Peter Mayhew 2015 Chrome JvS/8
24S Peter Mayhew 2015 Chrome JvS Ref./10
306 Peter Mayhew 1980 ESB/2
513 Peter Mayhew 2013 Galactic Files/2
FQ12 Peter Mayhew 2016 Card Trader Film Quotes/3
ROTS13 Peter Mayhew 2017 GF Reborn/24

2018 Star Wars Archives Signature Series Phil Eason

86 Phil Eason 2001 Evolution/35
393 Phil Eason 2013 GF2/48

2018 Star Wars Archives Signature Series Philip Anthony-Rodriguez

96 Philip Anthony-Rodriguez 2016 Card Trader Blue/4
96 Philip Anthony-Rodriguez 2016 Card Trader/22

2018 Star Wars Archives Signature Series Ralph Brown

TPM24 Ralph Brown 2017 GF Reborn/23

2018 Star Wars Archives Signature Series Ray Park

2 Ray Park 2016 Rogue One MB/6
4 Ray Park 2017 40th Ann./5
6 Ray Park 2012 Galactic Files/3
79 Ray Park 2004 Heritage/2
79 Ray Park 2016 Card Trader/22
94 Ray Park 2016 Evolution/30
B3 Ray Park 2016 Card Trader Bounty/5
285 Ray Park 2015 Chrome JvS/13
28J Ray Park 2015 Chrome JvS/4
FQ10 Ray Park 2016 Card Trader Film Quotes/7
TPM4 Ray Park 2017 GF Reborn/23

2018 Star Wars Archives Signature Series Riz Ahmed

NNO Riz Ahmed

2018 Star Wars Archives Signature Series Robin Atkin Downes

ACW17 Robin Atkin Downes 2017 GF Reborn/24

2018 Star Wars Archives Signature Series Rusty Goffe

11 Rusty Goffe 1977 Star Wars/9
13 Rusty Goffe 1977 Star Wars/16
19 Rusty Goffe 1983 ROTJ/23
24 Rusty Goffe 2015 Journey TFA Green/15
24 Rusty Goffe 2015 Journey TFA/38
27 Rusty Goffe 2016 Card Trader Red/2
27 Rusty Goffe 2016 Card Trader Blue/7
27 Rusty Goffe 2016 Card Trader/25
38 Rusty Goffe 2001 Evolution/36
186 Rusty Goffe 1977 Star Wars/12
203 Rusty Goffe 1977 Star Wars/6
257 Rusty Goffe 1977 Star Wars/12
304 Rusty Goffe 1977 Star Wars/1
314 Rusty Goffe 1977 Star Wars/1
ANH8 Rusty Goffe 2017 GF Reborn Orange/2
ANH8 Rusty Goffe 2017 GF Reborn/25

2018 Star Wars Archives Signature Series Sam Witwer

TPM4 Sam Witwer 2017 GF Reborn/23
ACW13 Sam Witwer 2017 GF Reborn/23

2018 Star Wars Archives Signature Series Silas Carson

82 Silas Carson 2016 Card Trader Red/1
82 Silas Carson 2016 Card Trader Blue/8
82 Silas Carson 2016 Card Trader/24
14J Silas Carson 2015 Chrome JvS Ref./7
14S Silas Carson 2015 Chrome JvS/7
TPM14 Silas Carson 2017 GF Reborn Orange/2
TPM14 Silas Carson 2017 GF Reborn/25
TPM19 Silas Carson 2017 GF Reborn/24

2018 Star Wars Archives Signature Series Simon Williamson

40 Simon Williamson 2016 Card Trader Blue/7
40 Simon Williamson 2016 Card Trader/23

2018 Star Wars Archives Signature Series Stephen Stanton

WHEN TARKIN MET ANAKIN

10 Stephen Stanton 2016 Rogue One MB/1
10 Stephen Stanton 2016 Rogue One MB/28
55 Stephen Stanton 2017 Journey TLJ Green/2
55 Stephen Stanton 2017 Journey TLJ/12
60 Stephen Stanton 2016 Evolution/34
42S Stephen Stanton 2015 Chrome JvS Ref./11
42S Stephen Stanton 2015 Chrome JvS/62
HR7 Stephen Stanton 2016 Rogue One S1 Heroes/8
MP4 Stephen Stanton 2016 Rogue One MB Patches/5

2018 Star Wars Archives Signature Series Steve Blum

4 Steve Blum 2015 Rebels Foil/7
57 Steve Blum 2015 Rebels/57
74 Steve Blum 2015 Rebels Foil/5
81 Steve Blum 2015 Rebels Foil/7
85 Steve Blum 2015 Rebels/5
90 Steve Blum 2016 Card Trader Red/1
90 Steve Blum 2016 Card Trader Blue/8
90 Steve Blum 2016 Card Trader/26
REB4 Steve Blum 2017 GF Reborn/38

2018 Star Wars Archives Signature Series Taylor Gray

1 Taylor Gray 2015 Rebels/5
1 Taylor Gray 2015 Rebels Foil/6
15 Taylor Gray 2017 Journey TLJ Red/1
15 Taylor Gray 2017 Journey TLJ/6
16 Taylor Gray 2017 40th Ann./2
39 Taylor Gray 2015 Rebels/3
50 Taylor Gray 2015 Rebels Foil/5
50 Taylor Gray 2015 Rebels/6
54 Taylor Gray 2015 Rebels/6
61 Taylor Gray 2017 Journey TLJ Green/1
61 Taylor Gray 2015 Rebels/5
61 Taylor Gray 2015 Rebels Foil/7
62 Taylor Gray 2015 Rebels Foil/4
66 Taylor Gray 2015 Rebels/6
67 Taylor Gray 2015 Rebels/5
67 Taylor Gray 2015 Rebels/6
69 Taylor Gray 2015 Rebels Foil/7
69 Taylor Gray 2015 Rebels/8
73 Taylor Gray 2015 Rebels Foil/3
82 Taylor Gray 2015 Rebels Foil/6
86 Taylor Gray 2018 Card Trader Blue/6
86 Taylor Gray 2016 Card Trader/28
96 Taylor Gray 2015 Rebels Foil/6
96 Taylor Gray 2015 Rebels/6
98 Taylor Gray 2017 40th Ann./17
99 Taylor Gray 2015 Rebels/5
EL7 Taylor Gray 2016 Evolution EOTL/8
REB6 Taylor Gray 2017 GF Reborn/37

2018 Star Wars Archives Signature Series Temuera Morrison

95 Temuera Morrison 2004 Heritage/4
25A Temuera Morrison 2013 Jedi Legacy/1
25A Temuera Morrison 2013 Jedi Legacy/12
33J Temuera Morrison 2015 Chrome JvS Ref./12
33J Temuera Morrison 2015 Chrome JvS/42
33S Temuera Morrison 2015 Chrome JvS/49
AOTC4 Temuera Morrison 2017 GF Reborn/23

2018 Star Wars Archives Signature Series Tim Dry

164 Tim Dry 1983 ROTJ/43

2018 Star Wars Archives Signature Series Tim Rose

2 Tim Rose 2016 TFA Chrome BTS/5
3 Tim Rose 2001 Evolution/37
7 Tim Rose 2016 TFA S2 Heroes/7
12 Tim Rose 2017 TLJ S1/35
14 Tim Rose 2016 Card Trader Blue/8
14 Tim Rose 2016 Card Trader/22
15 Tim Rose 2016 TFA Chrome Heroes/14
28 Tim Rose 2015 TFA S1 Blue/6
28 Tim Rose 2015 TFA S1 Green/12
28 Tim Rose 2015 TFA S1/28
35 Tim Rose 2017 Journey TLJ/6
37 Tim Rose 2017 Journey TLJ/7
10E Tim Rose 2015 Chrome/16
10R Tim Rose 2014 Chrome/24
124 Tim Rose 1983 ROTJ/33
167 Tim Rose 2012 Galactic Files/27
FQ16 Tim Rose 2016 Card Trader Film Quotes/8
ROTJ17 Tim Rose 2017 GF Reborn/24

2018 Star Wars Archives Signature Series Tiya Sircar

3 Tiya Sircar 2015 Rebels Foil/6		
3 Tiya Sircar 2015 Rebels/7		
56 Tiya Sircar 2015 Rebels/6		
88 Tiya Sircar 2016 Card Trader/25		
REB3 Tiya Sircar 2017 GF Reborn/34		

2018 Star Wars Archives Signature Series Toby Philpott

3 Toby Philpott 2017 40th Ann. Green/2		
3 Toby Philpott 2017 40th Ann./5		
9 Toby Philpott 2016 Card Trader Blue/4		
9 Toby Philpott 2016 Card Trader/18		
14 Toby Philpott 1983 ROTJ/20		
15 Toby Philpott 1983 ROTJ/6		
36 Toby Philpott 2001 Evolution/20		
46 Toby Philpott 1983 ROTJ/15		
62 Toby Philpott 1999 Chrome Archives/2		
63 Toby Philpott 2015 Journey TFA Green/2		
63 Toby Philpott 2015 Journey TFA/25		
82 Toby Philpott 2016 Evolution/26		
83 Toby Philpott 2016 Evolution/36		
83 Toby Philpott 2016 EvolutionBlue /36		
86 Toby Philpott 2007 30th Ann./3		
163 Toby Philpott Galactic Files/17		
172 Toby Philpott 1983 ROTJ/19		
34L Toby Philpott 2013 Jedi Legacy/44		
35J Toby Philpott 2015 Chrome JvS/29		
35S Toby Philpott 2015 Chrome JvS/32		
50R Toby Philpott 2014 Chrome/6		
519 Toby Philpott 2013 GF2/25		
C15 Toby Philpott 2013 Jedi Legacy Connections/26		

2018 Star Wars Archives Signature Series Tom Kane

9 Tom Kane 2017 40th Ann./6		
12 Tom Kane 2017 TLJ S1 Purple/15		
12 Tom Kane 2017 TLJ S1 Green/25		
12 Tom Kane 2017 TLJ S1 Blue/35		
12 Tom Kane 2017 TLJ S1/49		
15 Tom Kane 2017 40th Ann. Green/2		
15 Tom Kane 2017 40th Ann./10		
35 Tom Kane 2010 CW ROTBH/3		
61 Tom Kane 2010 CW ROTBH/10		
76 Tom Kane 2017 TLJ S1 Red/1		
76 Tom Kane 2017 TLJ S1 Purple/15		
76 Tom Kane 2017 TLJ S1 Green/25		
76 Tom Kane 2017 TLJ S1 Blue/35		
76 Tom Kane 2017 TLJ S1/49		
92 Tom Kane 2017 40th Ann./2		
92 Tom Kane 2017 40th Ann. Green/3		

2018 Star Wars Archives Signature Series Tom Wilton

14 Tom Wilton 2015 TFA S1 Purple/5		
14 Tom Wilton 2015 TFA S1 Blue/12		
14 Tom Wilton 2015 TFA S1 Green/13		
14 Tom Wilton 2015 TFA S1/36		

2018 Star Wars Archives Signature Series Vanessa Marshall

6 Vanessa Marshall 2015 Rebels/5		
6 Vanessa Marshall 2015 Rebels Foil/6		
17 Vanessa Marshall 2016 Rogue One MB Black/1		
17 Vanessa Marshall 2016 Rogue One MB/29		
53 Vanessa Marshall 2015 Rebels Foil/6		
59 Vanessa Marshall 2015 Rebels Foil/5		
80 Vanessa Marshall 2015 Rebels/6		
84 Vanessa Marshall 2015 Rebels Foil/6		
89 Vanessa Marshall 2016 Card Trader Red/2		
89 Vanessa Marshall 2016 Card Trader Blue/6		
89 Vanessa Marshall 2016 Card Trader/27		
97 Vanessa Marshall 2015 Rebels Foil/6		
REB2 Vanessa Marshall 2017 GF Reborn Orange/4		
REB2 Vanessa Marshall 2017 GF Reborn/39		

2018 Star Wars Archives Signature Series Warwick Davis

2 Warwick Davis 2016 TFA S2 Maz's Castle/9		
24 Warwick Davis 2016 Card Trader Red/2		
24 Warwick Davis 2016 Card Trader Blue/5		
24 Warwick Davis 2016 Card Trader/24		
84 Warwick Davis 2001 Evolution/34		
138 Warwick Davis 1983 ROTJ/40		
142 Warwick Davis 1983 ROTJ/17		
169 Warwick Davis 2012 Galactic Files/12		
190 Warwick Davis 1983 ROTJ/22		
ROTJ3 Warwick Davis 2017 GF Reborn/24		

2018 Star Wars Archives Signature Series Zac Jensen

6 Zac Jensen 2015 Chrome JvS/11		
58 Zac Jensen 2012 Galactic Files/25		
59 Zac Jensen 2017 Journey TLJ/4		
78 Zac Jensen 2012 Galactic Files/23		
11J Zac Jensen 2015 Chrome JvS/53		
11S Zac Jensen 2015 Chrome JvS Ref./12		
11S Zac Jensen 2015 Chrome JvS/53		
AOTC17 Zac Jensen 2017 GF Reborn/24		

2019 Star Wars Authentics

COMPLETE SET (25)	150.00	300.00
UNOPENED BOX (1 CARD+1 AUTO'd 8X10)		
COMMON CARD (1-25)	4.00	10.00
*BLUE/25: .6X TO 1.5X BASIC CARDS		
*PURPLE/10: UNPRICED DUE TO SCARCITY		
*ORANGE/5: UNPRICED DUE TO SCARCITY		
*RED/1: UNPRICED DUE TO SCARCITY		
STATED PRINT RUN 75 SER.#'d SETS		
1 Ahsoka Tano	10.00	25.00
2 Anakin Skywalker	8.00	20.00
3 BB-8	12.00	30.00
5 Captain Tarkin	6.00	15.00
6 Chancellor Palpatine	10.00	25.00
7 Chirrut Œmwe	5.00	12.00
8 Darth Maul	10.00	25.00
9 Director Krennic	6.00	15.00
10 Dryden Vos	6.00	15.00
11 Finn	6.00	15.00
12 Han Solo	8.00	20.00
13 Jango Fett	5.00	12.00
14 Jyn Erso	6.00	15.00
15 K-2SO	5.00	12.00
16 Kanan Jarrus	6.00	15.00
17 Kylo Ren	10.00	25.00
18 Lando Calrissian	10.00	25.00
19 Maul (Sam Witwer)	8.00	20.00
20 Obi-Wan Kenobi	5.00	12.00
21 Rey	15.00	40.00
23 Seventh Sister	5.00	12.00
24 Vice Admiral Holdo	15.00	40.00

2019 Star Wars Authentics Series Two

COMPLETE SET (29)	100.00	200.00
UNOPENED BOX (1 CARD+1 AUTO'd 8X10)		
COMMON CARD (1-29)	3.00	8.00
*BLUE/25: .5X TO 1.2X BASIC CARDS		
*PURPLE/10: UNPRICED DUE TO SCARCITY		
*ORANGE/5: UNPRICED DUE TO SCARCITY		
*RED/1: UNPRICED DUE TO SCARCITY		
STATED PRINT RUN 99 SER.#'d SETS		
1 Boba Fett	4.00	10.00
2 Bo-Katan Kryze	3.00	8.00
3 C'ai Threnalli	10.00	25.00
4 Captain Needa	3.00	8.00
5 Chewbacca	3.00	8.00
6 Ezra Bridger	3.00	8.00
7 Fode	3.00	8.00
8 General Hux	3.00	8.00
9 Han Solo	6.00	15.00
10 Hera Syndulla	6.00	15.00
11 Hype Fazon	3.00	8.00
12 Iden Versio	3.00	8.00
13 Jan Dodonna	3.00	8.00
14 Jar Jar Binks	3.00	8.00

15 Jarek Yeager	3.00	8.00
16 Kazuda Xiono	10.00	25.00
17 Major Bren Derlin	3.00	8.00
18 Moff Jerjerrod	3.00	8.00
19 Obi-Wan Kenobi	6.00	15.00
20 Orka	3.00	8.00
21 PadmÈ Amidala	5.00	12.00
22 Rose Tico	3.00	8.00
23 Sabine Wren	5.00	12.00
24 Snap Wexley	3.00	8.00
25 Tallie Lintra	10.00	25.00
26 Tam Ryvora	3.00	8.00
27 The Grand Inquisitor	5.00	12.00
28 Torra Doza	3.00	8.00
29 Wicket	4.00	10.00

2020 Star Wars Authentics 8x10

UNOPENED BOX (1 AUTO+1 CARD)		
COMMON CARD	6.00	15.00
*BLUE/25: SAME VALUE AS BASIC CARDS		
*PURPLE/10: UNPRICED DUE TO SCARCITY		
*ORANGE/5: UNPRICED DUE TO SCARCITY		
*RED/1: UNPRICED DUE TO SCARCITY		
ADRR Rey	10.00	25.00
AGCC Cara Dune	8.00	20.00
AHFH Han Solo	10.00	25.00

2020 Star Wars Authentics 11x14

UNOPENED BOX (1 AUTO+1 CARD)		
COMMON CARD	6.00	15.00
*BLUE/25: SAME VALUE AS BASIC CARDS		
*PURPLE/10: UNPRICED DUE TO SCARCITY		
*ORANGE/5: UNPRICED DUE TO SCARCITY		
*RED/1: UNPRICED DUE TO SCARCITY		
AGC Cara Dune	8.00	20.00
ADRRS Rey	10.00	25.00
AHCRS Darth Vader	10.00	25.00

2021 Star Wars The Bad Batch Exclusive Set

COMPLETE SET (10)	12.00	30.00
COMMON CARD (1-10)	2.00	5.00
STATED PRINT RUN 2,504 SETS		
EXCLUSIVE TO EBAY		
9 Omega	4.00	10.00

2021 Star Wars Battle Plans

REY USES THE FORCE TO DEFEAT KYLO REN

COMPLETE SET (100)	10.00	25.00
COMMON CARD (1-100)	.20	.50
*FOILBOARD: .75X TO 2X BASIC CARDS		
*BLUE: 1.5X TO 4X BASIC CARDS		

*GREEN/99: 5X TO 12X BASIC CARDS
*ORANGE/50: 6X TO 15X BASIC CARDS
*PURPLE/25: 12X TO 30X BASIC CARDS
*BLACK/5: UNPRICED DUE TO SCARCITY
*RED/1: UNPRICED DUE TO SCARCITY
*P.P.BLACK/1: UNPRICED DUE TO SCARCITY
*P.P.CYAN/1: UNPRICED DUE TO SCARCITY
*P.P.MAGENTA/1: UNPRICED DUE TO SCARCITY
*P.P.YELLOW/1: UNPRICED DUE TO SCARCITY

2021 Star Wars Battle Plans Autographs

*BLUE/149: .5X TO 1.2X BASIC AUTOS
*GREEN/99: .6X TO 1.5X BASIC AUTOS
*ORANGE/50: .75X TO 2X BASIC AUTOS
*PURPLE/25: 1X TO 2.5X BASIC AUTOS
*BLACK/5: UNPRICED DUE TO SCARCITY
*RED/1: UNPRICED DUE TO SCARCITY
*P.P.BLACK/1: UNPRICED DUE TO SCARCITY
*P.P.CYAN/1: UNPRICED DUE TO SCARCITY
*P.P.MAGENTA/1: UNPRICED DUE TO SCARCITY
*P.P.YELLOW/1: UNPRICED DUE TO SCARCITY
STATED ODDS 1:45

AAE	Ashley Eckstein	75.00	150.00
AAH	Alan Harris	20.00	50.00
AAM	Angus MacInnes	8.00	20.00
ACE	Chris Edgerly	6.00	15.00
ACL	Charlotte Louise	10.00	25.00
ACO	Candice Orwell	20.00	50.00
ADA	David Ankrum	6.00	15.00
ADB	Dee Bradley Baker	25.00	60.00
ADC	Dermot Crowley	6.00	15.00
ADM	Dominic Monaghan	12.00	30.00
ADY	Donnie Yen		300.00
AGH	Gerald Home	15.00	40.00
AJA	Jeremy Bulloch	60.00	120.00
AJK	Jaime King	8.00	20.00
AJM	John Morton	10.00	25.00
ALL	Lex Lang	10.00	25.00
AMJ	Mark Lewis Jones	8.00	20.00
AML	Matt Lanter	25.00	60.00
AMM	Mary Elizabeth McGlynn	10.00	25.00
ANA	Naomi Ackie	10.00	25.00
ANF	Nika Futterman	30.00	75.00
AOD	Oliver Ford Davies	8.00	20.00
ARA	Riz Ahmed	25.00	60.00
ARO	Rena Owen	8.00	20.00
ARP	Ray Park	60.00	120.00
ATG	Taylor Gray	12.00	30.00
ATR	Tim Rose	10.00	25.00

2021 Star Wars Battle Plans Autographs Blue

STATED PRINT RUN 149 SER.#'d SETS

AED	Adrian Edmondson	8.00	20.00

2021 Star Wars Battle Plans Dual Autographs

*BLACK/5: UNPRICED DUE TO SCARCITY
*RED/1: UNPRICED DUE TO SCARCITY
STATED ODDS 1:1,568

DABH J.Boyega/B.Herring
DACB J.Boyega/G.Christie
DAEL M.Lanter/A.Eckstein
DAGP T.Gray/F.Prinze Jr.
DAJM T.Morrison/S.L.Jackson
DAMA D.Monaghan/N.Ackie
DAMC H.Christensen/E.McGregor
DAMP I.McDiarmid/R.Park
DATL M.Lanter/J.A.Taylor
DAWJ F.Jones/F.Whitaker

2021 Star Wars Battle Plans Galactic Adversaries

COMMON CARD (GA1-GA30)		.75	2.00

*GREEN/99: .5X TO 1.2X BASIC CARDS
*ORANGE/50: .75X TO 2X BASIC CARDS
*PURPLE/25: 1.5X TO 4X BASIC CARDS
*BLACK/5: UNPRICED DUE TO SCARCITY
*RED/1: UNPRICED DUE TO SCARCITY
STATED ODDS 1:2

GA1	Princess Leia Organa	1.50	4.00
GA2	Luke Skywalker	1.50	4.00
GA3	Han Solo	1.50	4.00
GA4	Chewbacca	1.00	2.50
GA5	R2-D2	1.00	2.50
GA6	C-3PO	1.00	2.50
GA7	Jyn Erso	1.25	3.00
GA9	Yoda	1.50	4.00
GA10	Mace Windu	1.00	2.50
GA12	Obi-Wan Kenobi	1.00	3.00
GA13	Rey	2.50	6.00
GA14	Poe Dameron	1.00	2.50
GA15	Finn	1.00	2.50
GA16	Darth Vader	2.00	5.00
GA17	Kylo Ren	1.50	4.00
GA18	Emperor Palpatine	1.00	2.50
GA20	Boba Fett	2.00	5.00
GA26	Captain Phasma	1.00	2.50
GA29	Asajj Ventress	1.25	3.00
GA30	Aurra Sing	1.00	2.50

2021 Star Wars Battle Plans Manufactured Helmet Medallion Relics

DARTH VADER

COMMON MEM		4.00	10.00

*BLUE/149: .6X TO 1.2X BASIC MEM
*GREEN/99: .75X TO 2X BASIC MEM
*ORANGE/50: 1.2X TO 3X BASIC MEM
*PURPLE/25: 2X TO 5X BASIC MEM
*BLACK/5: UNPRICED DUE TO SCARCITY
*RED/1: UNPRICED DUE TO SCARCITY

HMAV	Anakin Skywalker	6.00	15.00
HMCS	Chewbacca	5.00	12.00
HMHS	Han Solo	15.00	40.00
HMKV	Kylo Ren	8.00	20.00
HMLS	Luke Skywalker	10.00	25.00
HMLV	Luke Skywalker	10.00	25.00
HMOV	Obi-Wan Kenobi	5.00	12.00
HMPV	Padmè Amidala	12.00	30.00
HMVS	Darth Vader	10.00	25.00
HMVT	Darth Vader	10.00	25.00
HMVV	Darth Vader	10.00	25.00
HMC3S	C-3PO	6.00	15.00
HMCST	Chewbacca	5.00	12.00
HMHST	Han Solo	15.00	40.00
HMLAT	Luke Skywalker	10.00	25.00
HMLST	Princess Leia Organa	8.00	20.00
HMMST	Luke Skywalker	10.00	25.00
HMOAT	Princess Leia Organa	8.00	20.00
HMPLS	Princess Leia Organa	8.00	20.00
HMPLV	Princess Leia Organa	8.00	20.00
HMWST	Wicket W. Warrick	5.00	12.00

2021 Star Wars Battle Plans Panoramic Sketches

NNO Adam Everett Beck
NNO Carlos Cabaleiro
NNO Dawn Murphy
NNO Eric Lehtonen
NNO Gavin Williams
NNO Logan Monette
NNO Maggie Ransom
NNO Mike Mastermaker
NNO Rees Finlay

2021 Star Wars Battle Plans Sketches

UNPRICED DUE TO SCARCITY

NNO Adam Everett Beck
NNO Andrew Fry
NNO Antni Ellison
NNO Ashlee Brienzo
NNO Candice Dailey
NNO Cisco Rivera
NNO Dan Gorman
NNO Dan Riveron
NNO Frank Kadar
NNO Frank Sansone
NNO Garrett Dix
NNO Ingrid Hardy
NNO James Dickson
NNO Jamie Richards
NNO Jason Sobol
NNO John Bruce
NNO John Pleak
NNO Jonathan Beistline
NNO Jonty Gates
NNO Karl Jones
NNO Kursat Cetiner
NNO Lindsey Greyling
NNO Lucas Peverill
NNO Marcia Dye.
NNO Marlo Agunos
NNO Marsha Parkin
NNO Michael Munshaw
NNO Mike Mastermaker
NNO Nick Allsopp
NNO Nick Gribbon
NNO Quinton Baker
NNO Robert Garcia
NNO Rooney Roberts
NNO Ryan Finley
NNO Semra Bulut
NNO Shaow Siong
NNO Tim Shinn
NNO Tom Amici

2021 Star Wars Battle Plans Sourced Fabric Relics

LANDO CALRISSIAN

COMMON MEM		15.00	40.00

*GREEN/99: SAME VALUE AS BASIC
*ORANGE/50: .5X TO 1.2X BASIC MEM
*PURPLE/25: .6X TO 1.5X BASIC MEM
*BLACK/5: UNPRICED DUE TO SCARCITY
*RED/1: UNPRICED DUE TO SCARCITY
STATED ODDS 1:87
STATED PRINT RUN 149 SER.#'d SETS

FRF	Finn/149	20.00	50.00
FRL	Luke Skywalker/149	75.00	150.00
FRP	Poe Dameron/149	25.00	60.00
FRQ	Qi'ra/149	75.00	150.00
FRR	Rey/149	75.00	150.00
FRDV	Dryden Vos/149	25.00	60.00
FREN	Enfys Nest/135	30.00	75.00
FRGE	Galen Erso/149	25.00	60.00
FRJE	Jyn Erso/149	50.00	100.00
FRLC	Lando Calrissian/85	50.00	100.00
FRLS	Luke Skywalker/149	50.00	100.00

FRPD Poe Dameron/149	25.00	60.00
FRRT Rose Tico/149	50.00	100.00
FRRY Rey/149	100.00	200.00

2021 Star Wars Battle Plans Tools of Warfare

COMPLETE SET (10)	6.00	15.00
COMMON CARD (TW1-TW10)	1.00	2.50
*GREEN/99: .6X TO 1.5X BASIC CARDS		
*ORANGE/50: .75X TO 2X BASIC CARDS		
*PURPLE/25: 1.5X TO 4X BASIC CARDS		
*BLACK/5: UNPRICED DUE TO SCARCITY		
*RED/1: UNPRICED DUE TO SCARCITY		
STATED ODDS 1:4		

2021 Star Wars Battle Plans Triple Autographs

STATED PRINT RUN 10 SER.#'d SETS
UNPRICED DUE TO SCARCITY

TAFDT Dern/Fisher/Lourd
TALER Taylor/Lanter/Eckstein
TAMBB Logan/Morrison/McGregor
TARDS Ridley/Serkis/Driver
TATYA Yen/Tudyk/Ahmed

2021 Star Wars Battle Plans Ultimate Showdowns

COMPLETE SET (10)	8.00	20.00
COMMON CARD (US1-US10)	1.25	3.00
*GREEN/99: .6X TO 1.5X BASIC CARDS		
*ORANGE/50: .75X TO 2X BASIC CARDS		
*PURPLE/25: 1.5X TO 4X BASIC CARDS		
*BLACK/5: UNPRICED DUE TO SCARCITY		
*RED/1: UNPRICED DUE TO SCARCITY		
STATED ODDS 1:4		
US1 Luke Skywalker vs. Darth Vader	2.50	6.00
US2 Qui-Gon & Obi-Wan vs. Darth Maul	2.00	5.00
US3 Anakin vs. Obi-Wan	1.25	3.00
US4 Luke Skywalker vs. Darth Vader	2.50	6.00
US5 Darth Vader vs. Obi-Wan	1.25	3.00
US6 Rey vs. Kylo Ren	3.00	8.00
US7 Mace Windu vs. Palpatine	1.25	3.00
US8 Yoda vs. Palpatine	1.50	4.00
US9 Obi-Wan vs. General Grievous	1.25	3.00
US10 Kylo Ren & Rey vs. Praetorian Guards	2.50	6.00

1984 Star Wars C-3PO's Cereal Masks

COMPLETE SET (6)	150.00	300.00
COMMON CARD	12.00	30.00
STATED ODDS 1:CEREAL BOX		
1 C-3PO	60.00	120.00
2 Chewbacca	25.00	60.00
5 Stormtrooper	15.00	40.00
6 Yoda	15.00	40.00

2016 Star Wars Card Trader

COMPLETE SET (100)	6.00	15.00
UNOPENED BOX (24 PACKS)	35.00	50.00
UNOPENED PACK (6 CARDS)	2.00	3.00
COMMON CARD (1-100)	.12	.30
*BLUE: .6X TO 1.5X BASIC CARDS	.20	.50
*RED: 1.2X TO 3X BASIC CARDS	.40	1.00
*GREEN/99: 6X TO 15X BASIC CARDS	2.00	5.00
*ORANGE/50: 12X TO 30X BASIC CARDS	4.00	10.00
*BAT.DAM./10: 30X TO 80X BASIC CARDS	10.00	25.00
*SLAVE I/5: UNPRICED DUE TO SCARCITY		

2016 Star Wars Card Trader Actor Digital Autographs

COMPLETE SET (20)	150.00	300.00
COMMON CARD (DA1-DA20)	8.00	20.00
*RED/10: UNPRICED DUE TO SCARCITY		
*GOLD/5: UNPRICED DUE TO SCARCITY		
STATED ODDS 1:788		
STATED PRINT RUN 25 SER.#'d SETS		

2016 Star Wars Card Trader Bounty

COMPLETE SET (20)	15.00	40.00
COMMON CARD (B1-B20)	1.25	3.00
STATED ODDS 1:5		

2016 Star Wars Card Trader Classic Artwork

COMPLETE SET (20)	15.00	40.00
COMMON CARD (CA1-CA20))	1.25	3.00
STATED ODDS 1:5		

2016 Star Wars Card Trader Film Quotes

COMPLETE SET (20)	10.00	25.00
COMMON CARD (FQ1-FQ20)	1.00	2.50
STATED ODDS 1:4		

2016 Star Wars Card Trader Galactic Moments

COMPLETE SET (20)	15.00	40.00
COMMON CARD (GM1-GM20)	1.25	3.00
STATED ODDS 1:5		

2016 Star Wars Card Trader Reflections

COMPLETE SET (7)	12.00	30.00
COMMON CARD (R1-R7)	2.50	6.00
STATED ODDS 1:8		

2016 Star Wars Card Trader Topps Choice

COMPLETE SET (13)	15.00	40.00
COMMON CARD (TC1-TC13)	2.00	5.00
STATED ODDS 1:16		
TC4 Kabe	8.00	20.00
TC7 Lak Sivrak	3.00	8.00
TC10 Bo-Katan Kryze	3.00	8.00
TC13 Todo 360	2.50	6.00

2015 Star Wars Celebration VII Oversized Vintage Wrappers

COMPLETE SET (16)	50.00	100.00
COMMON CARD	3.00	8.00

1999 Star Wars Chrome Archives

COMPLETE SET (90)	10.00	25.00
UNOPENED BOX (36 PACKS)	65.00	80.00
UNOPENED PACK (5 CARDS)	2.00	2.50
COMMON CARD (1-90)	.20	.50

1999 Star Wars Chrome Archives Clearzone

COMPLETE SET (4)	7.50	20.00
COMMON CARD (C1-C4)	2.50	6.00

1999 Star Wars Chrome Archives Double Sided

COMPLETE SET (9)	40.00	100.00
COMMON CARD (C1-C9)	6.00	15.00

1999 Star Wars Chrome Archives Promos

P1 Hate me, Luke! Destroy me!	1.00	2.50
P2 Welcome, young Luke	1.00	2.50

2019 Star Wars Chrome Legacy

COMPLETE SET (200)	75.00	150.00
COMMON CARD (1-200)	.60	1.50
*REFRACTOR: .75X TO 2X BASIC CARDS		
*BLUE/99: 1.2X TO 3X BASIC CARDS		
*GREEN/50: 1.5X TO 4X BASIC CARDS		
*ORANGE/25: 2X TO 5X BASIC CARDS		
*BLACK/10: 4X TO 10X BASIC CARDS		
*RED/5: UNPRICED DUE TO SCARCITY		
*SUPER/1: UNPRICED DUE TO SCARCITY		

2019 Star Wars Chrome Legacy Classic Trilogy Autographs

*ORANGE/25: UNPRICED DUE TO SCARCITY		
*BLACK/10: UNPRICED DUE TO SCARCITY		
*RED/5: UNPRICED DUE TO SCARCITY		
*SUPER/1: UNPRICED DUE TO SCARCITY		
STATED ODDS 1:113		
CAAD Anthony Daniels		
CACB Caroline Blakiston	6.00	15.00
CACF Carrie Fisher		
CACR Clive Revill	6.00	15.00
CADB David Barclay	8.00	20.00
CAHF Harrison Ford		
CAJB Jeremy Bulloch		
CAKB Kenny Baker		
CAMQ Mike Quinn	5.00	12.00
CARG Rusty Goffe	5.00	12.00
CAWD Warwick Davis		
CABDW Billy Dee Williams		
CAIME Ian McDiarmid		

2019 Star Wars Chrome Legacy Concept Art

COMPLETE SET (20)	12.00	30.00
COMMON CARD (CA1-CA20)	1.00	2.50
*GREEN/50: .5X TO 1.2X BASIC CARDS		
*ORANGE/25: .6X TO 1.5X BASIC CARDS		
*BLACK/10: UNPRICED DUE TO SCARCITY		
*RED/5: UNPRICED DUE TO SCARCITY		
*SUPER/1: UNPRICED DUE TO SCARCITY		
STATED ODDS 1:3		

2019 Star Wars Chrome Legacy Droid Medallions

COMMON MEM	5.00	12.00
*GREEN/50: .6X TO 1.5X BASIC MEM		
*ORANGE/25: .75X TO 2X BASIC MEM		
*BLACK/10: UNPRICED DUE TO SCARCITY		
*RED/5: UNPRICED DUE TO SCARCITY		
*SUPER/1: UNPRICED DUE TO SCARCITY		
STATED ODDS 1:23		

2019 Star Wars Chrome Legacy Dual Autographs

*BLACK/10: UNPRICED DUE TO SCARCITY		
*RED/5: UNPRICED DUE TO SCARCITY		
*SUPER/1: UNPRICED DUE TO SCARCITY		
STATED ODDS 1:3,502		
NNO A.Driver/D.Gleeson		
NNO A.Daniels/D.Barclay		
NNO A.Daniels/K.Baker		

NNO D.Ridley/J.Boyega
NNO S.Jackson/H.Christensen

2019 Star Wars Chrome Legacy Marvel Comic Book Covers

COMPLETE SET (25)	15.00	40.00
COMMON CARD (MC1-MC25)	1.25	3.00

*GREEN/50: .6X TO 1.5X BASIC CARDS
*ORANGE/25: .75X TO 2X BASIC CARDS
*BLACK/10: UNPRICED DUE TO SCARCITY
*RED/5: UNPRICED DUE TO SCARCITY
*SUPER/1: UNPRICED DUE TO SCARCITY
STATED ODDS 1:3

2019 Star Wars Chrome Legacy New Trilogy Autographs

*ORANGE/25: UNPRICED DUE TO SCARCITY
*BLACK/10: UNPRICED DUE TO SCARCITY
*RED/5: UNPRICED DUE TO SCARCITY
*SUPER/1: UNPRICED DUE TO SCARCITY
STATED ODDS 1:225

NAAD Adam Driver		
NAAL Amanda Lawrence	5.00	12.00
NAAS Andy Serkis		
NABH Brian Herring	6.00	15.00
NABL Billie Lourd		
NADG Domhnall Gleeson		
NADR Daisy Ridley		
NAJS Joonas Suotamo		
NALD Laura Dern		
NAJBF John Boyega		
NAKMT Kelly Marie Tran		

2019 Star Wars Chrome Legacy Porg-Shaped Sketches

STATED ODDS 1:256
UNPRICED DUE TO SCARCITY

NNO Adam Beck
NNO Andrew Joynes
NNO Angel Aviles
NNO Anil Sharma
NNO Anthony Figaro
NNO Anthony Skubis
NNO Ashlee Brienzo
NNO Barry Renshaw
NNO Basak Cetinkaya
NNO Ben AbuSaada
NNO Bill Pulkovski
NNO Bobby Blakey
NNO Brad Hudson
NNO Brandon Blevins
NNO Brent Scotchmer
NNO Brett Farr
NNO Can Baran
NNO Candice Dailey
NNO Carlos Cabaleiro
NNO Carolyn Craggs
NNO Cathy Razim
NNO Clint Yeager
NNO Colin Arthurs

NNO Craig Ludwick
NNO Dan Tearle
NNO Darrin Pepe
NNO Dave Gaskin
NNO David Jones
NNO Dean Drummond
NNO Eric Lehtonen
NNO Floyd Sumner
NNO Fredd Gorham
NNO Gary Rudisill
NNO Gavin Williams
NNO Greg Tilson
NNO Huy Truong
NNO Ingrid Hardy
NNO Jamie Richards
NNO Jason Davies
NNO Jason Montoya
NNO Jason Queen
NNO Jay Manchand
NNO Jim Mehsling
NNO Joey Fitchett
NNO John Bruce
NNO John Pleak
NNO Joseph Dobbins
NNO Kaela Croft
NNO Keith Farnum
NNO Kelly Baber
NNO Kevin Cleveland
NNO Laura Atkinson
NNO Lee Hunt
NNO Lily Mercado
NNO Logan Monette
NNO Madison Emerick
NNO Marcia Dye
NNO Marsha Parkins
NNO Matt Applegate
NNO Matt Steffens
NNO Matt Stewart
NNO Matthew Hirons
NNO Matthew Lopez
NNO Michael Mastermaker
NNO Michelle Rayner
NNO Mohammad Jilani
NNO Neil Camera
NNO Nicholas Baltra
NNO Omar Salinas
NNO Patrick Davis
NNO Phil Hassewer
NNO Phillip Trujillo
NNO Quinton Baker
NNO Rebecca Sharp
NNO Rees Finlay
NNO Rich Hennemann
NNO Rich Molinelli
NNO Richard Serrao
NNO Rob Teranishi
NNO Robert Garcia
NNO Robert Hendrickson
NNO Ryan Crosby
NNO Ryan Finley
NNO Ryan Moffett
NNO Ryan Olsen
NNO Sammy Gomez
NNO Seth Groves
NNO Shaow Siong
NNO Shawn Cruz
NNO Sheikh Islam
NNO Solly Mohamed
NNO Stephanie Swanger
NNO Thomas Amici
NNO Tim Shinn
NNO Tina Berardi
NNO Tod Smith
NNO Todd Rayner
NNO Trent Westbrook
NNO Veronica Smith
NNO Victor Moreno
NNO Ward Silverman
NNO Zach Woolsey

2019 Star Wars Chrome Legacy Posters

COMPLETE SET (25)	15.00	40.00
COMMON CARD (PC1-PC25)	1.25	3.00

*GREEN/50: .6X TO 1.5X BASIC CARDS
*ORANGE/25: .75X TO 2X BASIC CARDS
*BLACK/10: UNPRICED DUE TO SCARCITY
*RED/5: UNPRICED DUE TO SCARCITY
*SUPER/1: UNPRICED DUE TO SCARCITY
STATED ODDS 1:6

2019 Star Wars Chrome Legacy Prequel Trilogy Autographs

*ORANGE/25: UNPRICED DUE TO SCARCITY
*BLACK/10: UNPRICED DUE TO SCARCITY
*RED/5: UNPRICED DUE TO SCARCITY
*SUPER/1: UNPRICED DUE TO SCARCITY
STATED ODDS 1:229

PAEM Ewan McGregor		
PAGP Greg Proops		
PAHC Hayden Christensen		
PAHQ Hugh Quarshie		
PAJB Jerome Blake	5.00	12.00
PALM Lewis MacLeod		
PAMW Matthew Wood	6.00	15.00
PARP Ray Park		
PATM Temuera Morrison		
PASLJ Samuel L. Jackson		

2019 Star Wars Chrome Legacy Sketches

STATED ODDS 1:29
UNPRICED DUE TO SCARCITY

NNO Adam Beck
NNO Andrew Joynes
NNO Angel Aviles
NNO Anil Sharma
NNO Anthony Figaro
NNO Anthony Skubis
NNO Ashlee Brienzo
NNO Barry Renshaw
NNO Basak Cetinkaya
NNO Ben AbuSaada
NNO Bill Pulkovski
NNO Bobby Blakey
NNO Brad Hudson
NNO Brandon Blevins
NNO Brent Scotchmer
NNO Brett Farr
NNO Can Baran
NNO Candice Dailey
NNO Carlos Cabaleiro
NNO Carolyn Craggs
NNO Cathy Razim
NNO Clint Yeager
NNO Colin Arthurs
NNO Craig Ludwick
NNO Dan Tearle
NNO Darrin Pepe
NNO Dave Gaskin

NNO	David Jones
NNO	Dean Drummond
NNO	Eric Lehtonen
NNO	Floyd Sumner
NNO	Fredd Gorham
NNO	Gary Rudisill
NNO	Gavin Williams
NNO	Greg Tilson
NNO	Huy Truong
NNO	Ingrid Hardy
NNO	Jamie Richards
NNO	Jason Davies
NNO	Jason Montoya
NNO	Jason Queen
NNO	Jay Manchand
NNO	Jim Mehsling
NNO	Joey Fitchett
NNO	John Bruce
NNO	John Pleak
NNO	Joseph Dobbins
NNO	Kaela Croft
NNO	Keith Farnum
NNO	Kelly Baber
NNO	Kevin Cleveland
NNO	Laura Atkinson
NNO	Lee Hunt
NNO	Lily Mercado
NNO	Logan Monette
NNO	Madison Emerick
NNO	Marcia Dye
NNO	Marsha Parkins
NNO	Matt Applegate
NNO	Matt Steffens
NNO	Matt Stewart
NNO	Matthew Hirons
NNO	Matthew Lopez
NNO	Michael Mastermaker
NNO	Michelle Rayner
NNO	Mohammad Jilani
NNO	Neil Camera
NNO	Nicholas Baltra
NNO	Omar Salinas
NNO	Patrick Davis
NNO	Phil Hassewer
NNO	Phillip Trujillo
NNO	Quinton Baker
NNO	Rebecca Sharp
NNO	Rees Finlay
NNO	Rich Hennemann
NNO	Rich Molinelli
NNO	Richard Serrao
NNO	Rob Teranishi
NNO	Robert Garcia
NNO	Robert Hendrickson
NNO	Ryan Crosby
NNO	Ryan Finley
NNO	Ryan Moffett
NNO	Ryan Olsen
NNO	Sammy Gomez
NNO	Seth Groves
NNO	Shaow Siong
NNO	Shawn Cruz
NNO	Sheikh Islam
NNO	Solly Mohamed
NNO	Stephanie Swanger
NNO	Thomas Amici
NNO	Tim Shinn
NNO	Tina Berardi
NNO	Tod Smith
NNO	Todd Rayner
NNO	Trent Westbrook
NNO	Veronica Smith
NNO	Victor Moreno
NNO	Ward Silverman
NNO	Zach Woolsey

2014 Star Wars Chrome Perspectives

COMPLETE SET (100)	30.00	60.00
UNOPENED BOX (24 PACKS)	175.00	200.00
UNOPENED PACK (6 CARDS)	8.00	10.00
COMMON CARD (1E-50E)	.40	1.00
COMMON CARD (1R-50R)	.40	1.00

*REFRACTOR: 1.2X TO 3X BASIC CARDS
*PRISM: 1.5X TO 4X BASIC CARDS
*X-FRACTOR/99: 3X TO 8X BASIC CARDS
*GOLD REF./50: 6X TO 15X BASIC CARDS

2014 Star Wars Chrome Perspectives Autograph Sketches

NNO	Anthony Wheeler
NNO	Ashleigh Popplewell
NNO	Bob Stevlic
NNO	Brandon Gallo
NNO	Brian DeGuire
NNO	Charles Hall
NNO	Chris Ring
NNO	Chris West
NNO	Dan Curto
NNO	Dan Gorman
NNO	Darrin Pepe
NNO	Eric Lehtonen
NNO	Flosi
NNO	Hayden Davis
NNO	Irma Ahmed
NNO	Jason Chalker
NNO	Jason Crosby
NNO	JD
NNO	Jeff Chandler
NNO	Jeff Zapata
NNO	Jimenez
NNO	Joe Hogan
NNO	John Soukup
NNO	Jon Rademacher
NNO	Jorge Baeza
NNO	Justin Schillerberg
NNO	Kevin Doyle
NNO	Kris Penix
NNO	Lin Workman
NNO	Melike Acar
NNO	Michael Duron
NNO	Mikey Babinski
NNO	Otto
NNO	Patricia Ross
NNO	Patrick Hamill
NNO	Richard Molinelli
NNO	Robert Hendrickson
NNO	Robert Teranishi
NNO	Roy Cover
NNO	Tina Berardi
NNO	Tom Kelly
NNO	Val Hochberg

2014 Star Wars Chrome Perspectives Autographs

COMMON AUTO	6.00	15.00
STATED ODDS 1 PER BOX W/SKETCHES		
NNO Angus MacInnes	12.00	30.00
NNO Anthony Daniels	125.00	250.00
NNO Billy Dee Williams	60.00	120.00
NNO Carrie Fisher	400.00	800.00
NNO Harrison Ford	1500.00	3000.00
NNO James Earl Jones	200.00	400.00
NNO Jeremy Bulloch	30.00	75.00
NNO John Ratzenberger	10.00	20.00
NNO Kenneth Colley	12.00	25.00
NNO Mark Capri	12.00	25.00
NNO Mark Hamill	800.00	1500.00
NNO Paul Blake	12.00	30.00

2014 Star Wars Chrome Perspectives Empire Priority Targets

COMPLETE SET (10)	8.00	20.00
COMMON CARD (1-10)	1.25	3.00
STATED ODDS 1:4		

2014 Star Wars Chrome Perspectives Empire Propaganda

COMPLETE SET (10)	15.00	40.00
COMMON CARD (1-10)	3.00	8.00
STATED ODDS 1:24		

2014 Star Wars Chrome Perspectives Helmet Medallions

COMPLETE SET (30)	75.00	200.00
COMMON CARD (1-30)	5.00	12.00
*GOLD/50: 1.2X TO 3X BASIC MEDALLIONS		
STATED ODDS 1:24		

2014 Star Wars Chrome Perspectives Rebel Propaganda

COMPLETE SET (10)	12.00	30.00
COMMON CARD (1-10)	2.00	5.00
STATED ODDS 1:12		

2014 Star Wars Chrome Perspectives Rebel Training

COMPLETE SET (10)	6.00	15.00
COMMON CARD (1-10)	1.25	3.00
STATED ODDS 1:8		

2014 Star Wars Chrome Perspectives Sketches

NNO	Angelina Benedetti
NNO	Anthony Wheeler

NNO Ashleigh Popplewell
NNO Bill Pulkovski
NNO Bob Stevlic
NNO Brandon Gallo
NNO Brian DeGuire
NNO Charles Hall
NNO Chris "Urbnpop" Hamer
NNO Chris Ring
NNO Chris West
NNO Christian N. (CNS) St. Pierre
NNO Dan Curto
NNO Dan Gorman
NNO Darrin Pepe
NNO Denae Frazier
NNO Dennis Budd
NNO Eric Lehtonen
NNO Erik Maell
NNO FLOSI
NNO Hayden Davis
NNO Irma "Aimo" Ahmed
NNO j(ay)
NNO Jan Duursema
NNO Jason Adams
NNO Jason Chalker
NNO Jason Crosby
NNO Jason Flowers
NNO Jeff Chandler
NNO Jeff Zapata
NNO Joann Ellen Patak
NNO Joe Corroney
NNO Joe Hogan
NNO John Sloboda
NNO John Soukup
NNO Jon Rademacher
NNO Jorge Baeza
NNO Josh R.
NNO Justin Chung
NNO Justin Schillerberg
NNO Karen Hinson
NNO Ken Branch
NNO Kevin Doyle
NNO Kevin Graham
NNO Kimberly Dunaway
NNO Kris Penix
NNO Krist West
NNO Kyle Babbitt
NNO Louis (LDM) De Martinis
NNO Lin Workman
NNO Lord Mesa
NNO Lynne Anderson
NNO Mark Labas
NNO Melike Acar
NNO Michael "Locoduck" Duron
NNO Mikey Babinski
NNO Otto Dieffenbach
NNO Patricia Ross
NNO Patrick (PG) Giles
NNO Patrick Hamill
NNO Randy Martinez
NNO Rich "RAM" Molinelli
NNO Robert Hendrickson
NNO Robert Jimenez
NNO Robert Teranishi
NNO Roy Cover
NNO Scott Zambelli
NNO Sean Pence
NNO Sian Mandrake
NNO Solly Mohamed
NNO Stephanie Swanger
NNO Tim Proctor
NNO Tina Berardi
NNO Tod Allen Smith
NNO Tom Kelly
NNO Tom Krohne
NNO Val Hochberg
NNO Veronica O'Connell
NNO William O'Neill

2014 Star Wars Chrome Perspectives Triple Autograph

1 H. Ford/M. Hamill/C. Fisher EXCH

2014 Star Wars Chrome Perspectives Wanted Posters Rebellion

COMPLETE SET (10)	5.00	12.00
COMMON CARD (1-10)	.75	2.00
STATED ODDS 1:2		

2015 Star Wars Chrome Perspectives Jedi vs. Sith

COMPLETE SET (100)	25.00	60.00
UNOPENED BOX (24 PACKS)	60.00.	70.00
UNOPENED PACK (6 CARDS)	3.00	4.00
COMMON CARD	.40	1.00
*REFRACTOR: 1.2X TO 3X BASIC CARDS		
*PRISM REF./199: 1.5X TO 4X BASIC CARDS		
*X-FRACTOR/99: 3X TO 8X BASIC CARDS		
*GOLD REF/50: 6X TO 15X BASIC CARDS		
*P.P.BLACK/1: UNPRICED DUE TO SCARCITY		
*P.P.CYAN/1: UNPRICED DUE TO SCARCITY		
*P.P.MAGENTA/1: UNPRICED DUE TO SCARCITY		
*P.P.YELLOW/1: UNPRICED DUE TO SCARCITY		

2015 Star Wars Chrome Perspectives Jedi vs. Sith Autographs

COMMON AUTO	6.00	15.00
*PRISM REF./50: .5X TO 1.2X BASIC AUTOS		
* X-FRACTORS/25: .6X TO 1.5X BASIC AUTOS		
*GOLD REF./10: UNPRICED DUE TO SCARCITY		
*SUPERFRACTOR/1: UNPRICED DUE TO SCARCITY		
*P.P.BLACK/1: UNPRICED DUE TO SCARCITY		
*P.P.CYAN/1: UNPRICED DUE TO SCARCITY		
*P.P.MAGENTA/1: UNPRICED DUE TO SCARCITY		
*P.P.YELLOW/1: UNPRICED DUE TO SCARCITY		
NNO Ashley Eckstein	10.00	25.00
NNO Barbara Goodson	10.00	25.00
NNO Carrie Fisher	400.00	600.00
NNO David Prowse	50.00	100.00
NNO Jerome Blake	10.00	25.00
NNO Matthew Wood	10.00	25.00
NNO Michaela Cottrell	10.00	25.00
NNO Nalini Krishan	12.00	30.00
NNO Olivia D'Abo	10.00	25.00
NNO Peter Mayhew	25.00	60.00
NNO Ray Park	20.00	50.00
NNO Sam Witwer	10.00	25.00

2015 Star Wars Chrome Perspectives Jedi vs. Sith Jedi Hunt

COMPLETE SET (10)	10.00	25.00
COMMON CARD (1-10)	2.00	5.00
*P.P.BLACK/1: UNPRICED DUE TO SCARCITY		
*P.P.CYAN/1: UNPRICED DUE TO SCARCITY		
*P.P.MAGENTA/1: UNPRICED DUE TO SCARCITY		
*P.P.YELLOW/1: UNPRICED DUE TO SCARCITY		
STATED ODDS 1:4		

2015 Star Wars Chrome Perspectives Jedi vs. Sith Jedi Information Guide

COMPLETE SET (10)	20.00	50.00
COMMON CARD (1-10)	4.00	10.00
*P.P.BLACK/1: UNPRICED DUE TO SCARCITY		
*P.P.CYAN/1: UNPRICED DUE TO SCARCITY		
*P.P.MAGENTA/1: UNPRICED DUE TO SCARCITY		
*P.P.YELLOW/1: UNPRICED DUE TO SCARCITY		
STATED ODDS 1:12		

2015 Star Wars Chrome Perspectives Jedi vs. Sith Jedi Training

COMPLETE SET (10)	12.00	30.00
COMMON CARD (1-10)	2.50	6.00
*P.P.BLACK/1: UNPRICED DUE TO SCARCITY		
*P.P.CYAN/1: UNPRICED DUE TO SCARCITY		
*P.P.MAGENTA/1: UNPRICED DUE TO SCARCITY		
*P.P.YELLOW/1: UNPRICED DUE TO SCARCITY		
STATED ODDS 1:24		

2015 Star Wars Chrome Perspectives Jedi vs. Sith Medallions

COMPLETE SET (36)	120.00	250.00
COMMON MEDALLION (1-36)	5.00	10.00
*SILVER/150: .6X TO 1.5X BASIC MEDALLIONS	6.00	15.00
*GOLD/50: .75X TO 2X BASIC MEDALLIONS	8.00	20.00
OVERALL MEDALLION ODDS 1:BOX		

2015 Star Wars Chrome Perspectives Jedi vs. Sith Rare Dual Autographs

COMMON AUTO	25.00	60.00
*P.P.BLACK/1: UNPRICED DUE TO SCARCITY		
*P.P.CYAN/1: UNPRICED DUE TO SCARCITY		
*P.P.MAGENTA/1: UNPRICED DUE TO SCARCITY		
*P.P.YELLOW/1: UNPRICED DUE TO SCARCITY		
STATED PRINT RUN 200 SER.#'d SETS		
NNO A.Allen/O.Shoshan	50.00	100.00
NNO A.Eckstein/N.Futterman	30.00	75.00
NNO A.Eckstein/O.D'Abo	50.00	100.00
NNO M.Cottrell/Z.Jensen	50.00	100.00

2015 Star Wars Chrome Perspectives Jedi vs. Sith Sith Fugitives

COMPLETE SET (10)	8.00	20.00
COMMON CARD (1-10)	1.50	4.00
*P.P.BLACK/1: UNPRICED DUE TO SCARCITY		
*P.P.CYAN/1: UNPRICED DUE TO SCARCITY		
*P.P.MAGENTA/1: UNPRICED DUE TO SCARCITY		
*P.P.YELLOW/1: UNPRICED DUE TO SCARCITY		
STATED ODDS 1:2		

2015 Star Wars Chrome Perspectives Jedi vs. Sith Sith Propaganda

COMPLETE SET (10)	12.00	30.00
COMMON CARD (1-10)	2.50	6.00

*P.P.BLACK/1: UNPRICED DUE TO SCARCITY
*P.P.CYAN/1: UNPRICED DUE TO SCARCITY
*P.P.MAGENTA/1: UNPRICED DUE TO SCARCITY
*P.P.YELLOW/1: UNPRICED DUE TO SCARCITY
STATED ODDS 1:8

2015 Star Wars Chrome Perspectives Jedi vs. Sith Sketches

NNO Aaron Lambert
NNO Achilleas Kokkinakis
NNO Adam Talley
NNO Adrian Rivera
NNO Alex Ironhed Sanchez
NNO Andrew Drone Cosson
NNO Bill Pulkovski
NNO Brad Hudson
NNO Brad Utterstrom
NNO Brent Ragland
NNO Carla Rodriguez
NNO Carlos Cabaleiro
NNO Chad McCown
NNO Charles Dowd
NNO Charles Hall
NNO Chris Ehnot
NNO Chris Henderson
NNO Chris West
NNO Crystal Bamboota Fontan
NNO Dan Bergren
NNO Dan Nokes
NNO Dan Parsons
NNO Dan Smif Smith
NNO Danny Haas
NNO Darrin Pepe
NNO David Valentine
NNO Denae Frazier
NNO Eric Kowalick
NNO Eric Lehtonen
NNO Erik Maell
NNO Francois Chartier
NNO Gavin Hunt
NNO Howard Russell
NNO Ingrid Hardy
NNO Irma Aimo Ahmed
NNO Jamie Cosley
NNO Jared Hickman
NNO Jason Adams
NNO Jason Brower
NNO Jason Chalker
NNO Jason Flowers
NNO Jeffrey Benitez
NNO Jessica Hickman
NNO Joe Hogan
NNO John Soukup
NNO Jordan Maison
NNO Josh Bodwell
NNO Josh Lyman
NNO Kaela Croft
NNO Karen Hinson
NNO Kate Carleton
NNO Kevin Graham
NNO Kevin West
NNO Kimberly Dunaway
NNO Kris Penix
NNO Kyle Babbitt
NNO Lak Lim
NNO Laura Guzzo
NNO Lee Lightfoot
NNO Lord Mesa
NNO Marcia Dye
NNO Marck Labas
NNO Mark Hammermeister
NNO Mark Picirilli
NNO Matt Stewart
NNO Matthew Sutton
NNO Melike Acar

NNO Michael Leavitt
NNO Michael Locoduck Duron
NNO Mick/Matt Glebe
NNO Norvien Basio
NNO Omar Maya Velazquez
NNO Pablo Diaz
NNO Patricia Ross
NNO Patrick Giles
NNO Paul Gutz Guttierez
NNO Peter Zuno Chan
NNO Rich Kunz
NNO Rich Molinelli
NNO Robert Hendrickson
NNO Robert Teranishi
NNO Roy Cover
NNO Ryan van der Draaij
NNO Sarah Wilkinson
NNO Scott Houseman
NNO Scott Zambelli
NNO Sean Pence
NNO Sol Mohamed
NNO Stephanie Swanger
NNO Steven Burch
NNO Sue Thomas
NNO Tanner Padlo
NNO Ted Dastick Jr.
NNO Tim Dowler
NNO Tim Shay
NNO Tina Berardi
NNO Tom Carlton
NNO Tomoko Taniguchi
NNO Tressina Bowling
NNO Ward Silverman
NNO Wilson Ramos Jr.

2015 Star Wars Chrome Perspectives Jedi vs. Sith The Force Awakens

Poe Dameron in his X-Wing

COMPLETE SET (8)	20.00	50.00
COMMON CARD	4.00	10.00

*MATTE BACK: .6X TO1.5X BASIC CARDS
STATED ODDS 1:24

2015 Star Wars Chrome Perspectives Jedi vs. Sith Ultra Rare Dual Autographs

*P.P.BLACK/1: UNPRICED DUE TO SCARCITY
*P.P.CYAN/1: UNPRICED DUE TO SCARCITY
*P.P.MAGENTA/1: UNPRICED DUE TO SCARCITY
*P.P.YELLOW/1: UNPRICED DUE TO SCARCITY
STATED PRINT RUN 3 SER.#'d SETS
UNPRICED DUE TO SCARCITY

1 I.McDiarmid/D.Prowse
2 I.McDiarmid/R.Park
3 M.Hamill/C.Fisher

2015 Star Wars Chrome Perspectives Jedi vs. Sith Ultra Rare Triple Autographs

*P.P.BLACK/1: UNPRICED DUE TO SCARCITY
*P.P.CYAN/1: UNPRICED DUE TO SCARCITY
*P.P.MAGENTA/1: UNPRICED DUE TO SCARCITY
*P.P.YELLOW/1: UNPRICED DUE TO SCARCITY
UNPRICED DUE TO SCARCITY

1 M.Hamill/D.Prowse/I.McDiarmid
2 M.Hamill/D.Prowse/R.Park

2020 Star Wars Chrome Perspectives Resistance vs. First Order

VICE ADMIRAL HOLDO

COMPLETE SET (100)	15.00	40.00
COMMON CARD	.40	1.00

*REFRACTOR: .75X TO 2X BASIC CARDS
*PRISM REF/299: 1.2X TO 3X BASIC CARDS
*BLUE REF/150: 2X TO 5X BASIC CARDS
*XFRAC/99: 3X TO 8X BASIC CARDS
*GOLD REF/50: 4X TO 10X BASIC CARDS
*ORANGE REF/25: UNPRICED DUE TO SCARCITY
*RED REF/5: UNPRICED DUE TO SCARCITY
*SUPERFR/1: UNPRICED DUE TO SCARCITY

2020 Star Wars Chrome Perspectives Resistance vs. First Order Choose Your Allegiance First Order

COMPLETE SET (15)	8.00	20.00
COMMON CARD (CF1-CF15)	1.00	2.50

*P.P.BLACK/1: UNPRICED DUE TO SCARCITY
*P.P.CYAN/1: UNPRICED DUE TO SCARCITY
*P.P.MAGENTA/1: UNPRICED DUE TO SCARCITY
*P.P.YELLOW/1: UNPRICED DUE TO SCARCITY
RANDOMLY INSERTED INTO PACKS

2020 Star Wars Chrome Perspectives Resistance vs. First Order Choose Your Allegiance Resistance

COMPLETE SET (15)	8.00	20.00
COMMON CARD (CR1-CR15)	1.00	2.50

*P.P.BLACK/1: UNPRICED DUE TO SCARCITY
*P.P.CYAN/1: UNPRICED DUE TO SCARCITY
*P.P.MAGENTA/1: UNPRICED DUE TO SCARCITY
*P.P.YELLOW/1: UNPRICED DUE TO SCARCITY
RANDOMLY INSERTED INTO PACKS

2020 Star Wars Chrome Perspectives Resistance vs. First Order Dual Autographs

*SUPERFR/1: UNPRICED DUE TO SCARCITY
STATED PRINT RUN 5 SER.#'d SETS
UNPRICED DUE TO SCARCITY

DABF T.Brodie-Sangster/K.Fleetwood
DABT J.Boyega/K.Tran
DAKH P.Kasey/J.Henwick
DALC A.Lawrence/C.Clarke
DALR K.Leung/T.Rose
DAQK M.Quinn/P.Kasey
DAWA B.Williams/N.Ackie

2020 Star Wars Chrome Perspectives Resistance vs. First Order Duel Dual Autographs

*SUPERFR/1: UNPRICED DUE TO SCARCITY
STATED PRINT RUN 5 SER.#'d SETS

UNPRICED DUE TO SCARCITY
DDABA J.Boyega/D.Accord
DDABH A.Brewster/B.Herring
DDACB G.Christie/J.Boyega
DDADB A.Driver/J.Boyega
DDAFD H.Ford/A.Driver
DDAHS B.Herring/K.Shah
DDARD D.Ridley/A.Driver
DDASD A.Serkis/A.Driver

2020 Star Wars Chrome Perspectives Resistance vs. First Order Empire at War

COMPLETE SET (20)   10.00   25.00
COMMON CARD (EW1-EW20)   1.25   3.00
*P.P.BLACK/1: UNPRICED DUE TO SCARCITY
*P.P.CYAN/1: UNPRICED DUE TO SCARCITY
*P.P.MAGENTA/1: UNPRICED DUE TO SCARCITY
*P.P.YELLOW/1: UNPRICED DUE TO SCARCITY
RANDOMLY INSERTED INTO PACKS

2020 Star Wars Chrome Perspectives Resistance vs. First Order First Order Autographs

COMMON AUTO   8.00   12.00
*ORANGE REF/25: UNPRICED DUE TO SCARCITY
*RED REF/5: UNPRICED DUE TO SCARCITY
*SUPERFR/1: UNPRICED DUE TO SCARCITY
RANDOMLY INSERTED INTO PACKS

AAE Adrian Edmondson   6.00   15.00
AMJ Michael Jibson   6.00   15.00
AMLJ Mark Lewis Jones   8.00   20.00

2020 Star Wars Chrome Perspectives Resistance vs. First Order Resistance Autographs

COMMON AUTO   5.00   12.00
*ORANGE REF/25: UNPRICED DUE TO SCARCITY
*RED REF/5: UNPRICED DUE TO SCARCITY
*SUPERFR/1: UNPRICED DUE TO SCARCITY
RANDOMLY INSERTED INTO PACKS

ABH Brian Herring   10.00   25.00
ACC Crystal Clarke   6.00   15.00
ADB Dave Chapman   6.00   15.00
AIW Ian Whyte   8.00   20.00
ANC Nathalie Cuzner   8.00   20.00
ATK Tom Kane   6.00   15.00

2020 Star Wars Chrome Perspectives Resistance vs. First Order Sketches

RANDOMLY INSERTED INTO PACKS
UNPRICED DUE TO SCARCITY

NNO Adam Everett Beck
NNO Allen Grimes
NNO Andrew Fry
NNO Andrew Joynes
NNO Angel Aviles
NNO Anthony Skubis
NNO Barry Renshaw
NNO Basak Cetinkaya
NNO Bobby Blakey
NNO Brad Hudson
NNO Brandon Blevins
NNO Brent Scotchmer
NNO Brett Farr

NNO Caleb Hildenbrandt
NNO Chris Kay
NNO Chris Thorne
NNO Colin Arthurs
NNO Craig Hallums
NNO Dan Gorman
NNO Dan Tearle
NNO Danny Kidwell
NNO Darrin Pepe
NNO Dave Gaskin
NNO Dean Drummond
NNO Eric Lehtonen
NNO Gavin Williams
NNO Gorkem Demir
NNO Guilherme Rocha
NNO Huy Truong
NNO J. David Acevedo
NNO Jamie Richards
NNO Jason Montoya
NNO Jason Queen
NNO Jay Manchand
NNO Jessica Hickman
NNO Jim Mehsling
NNO John Bruce
NNO Jose Ventura
NNO Kaela Croft
NNO Karl Jones
NNO Kayla Wright
NNO Keith Farnum
NNO Kevin Cleveland
NNO Kevin P. West
NNO Lindsey Greyling
NNO Lloyd Mills
NNO Logan Monette
NNO Marcia Dye
NNO Mark Necchi
NNO Marsha Parkins
NNO Matt Stewart
NNO Matthew Hirons
NNO Neil Camera
NNO Nicholas Baltra
NNO Nick Gribbon
NNO Patricio Carrasco
NNO Patrick Davis
NNO Quinton Baker
NNO Rees Finlay
NNO Rich Hennemann
NNO Rich Molinelli
NNO Rob Teranishi
NNO Rutvig Vaid
NNO Ryan Finley
NNO Ryan Olsen
NNO Ryan Santos
NNO Sammy Gomez
NNO Scott West
NNO Seth Groves
NNO Sheikh Islam
NNO Solly Mohamed
NNO Thomas Amici
NNO Tim Shinn
NNO Trent Westbrook
NNO Ward Silverman
NNO Zach Woolsey

2020 Star Wars Chrome Perspectives Resistance vs. First Order Triple Autographs

*SUPERFR/1: UNPRICED DUE TO SCARCITY
STATED PRINT RUN 5 SER.#'d SETS
UNPRICED DUE TO SCARCITY

TARAL Ridley/Ackie/Lourd
TARBH Ridley/Boyega/Herring
TARDS Ridley/Driver/Serkis

2004 Star Wars Clone Wars Cartoon

COMPLETE SET (90)   5.00   12.00
UNOPENED HOBBY BOX (36 PACKS)   50.00   60.00
UNOPENED HOBBY PACK (7 CARDS)   1.50   2.00
UNOPENED RETAIL BOX (36 PACKS)   55.00   65.00
UNOPENED RETAIL PACK (7 CARDS)   1.75   2.25
COMMON CARD (1-90)   .15   .40

2004 Star Wars Clone Wars Cartoon Autographs

COMMON AUTO   12.00   30.00

2004 Star Wars Clone Wars Cartoon Battle Motion

COMPLETE SET (10)   15.00   40.00
COMMON CARD (B1-B10)   2.00   5.00

2004 Star Wars Clone Wars Cartoon Sketches

RANDOMLY INSERTED INTO PACKS
UNPRICED DUE TO SCARCITY

NNO Joe Corroney
NNO Dave Dorman
NNO Davide Fabbri
NNO Tomas Giorello
NNO Rafael Kayanan
NNO John McCrea
NNO Pop Mhan
NNO Rodolfo Migliari
NNO Kilian Plunkett
NNO Paul Ruddish
NNO Genndy Tartakovsky
NNO Robert Teranishi
NNO Doug Wheatley

2004 Star Wars Clone Wars Cartoon Stickers

COMPLETE SET (10)   3.00   8.00
COMMON CARD (1-10)   .40   1.00

2008 Star Wars Clone Wars

COMPLETE SET (90)   5.00   12.00
UNOPENED BOX (36 PACKS)   40.00   50.00
UNOPENED PACK (7 CARDS)   1.50   2.00
COMMON CARD (1-90)   .15   .40
*GOLD: 8X TO 20X BASIC CARD

2008 Star Wars Clone Wars Foil

COMPLETE SET (10)   12.00   25.00
COMMON CARD (1-10)   2.00   5.00
STATED ODDS 1:3 RETAIL

2008 Star Wars Clone Wars Animation Cels

COMPLETE SET (10)   7.50   15.00
COMMON CARD (1-10)   1.25   3.00
STATED ODDS 1:6
ALSO KNOWN AS THE WHITE CELS

2008 Star Wars Clone Wars Blue Animation Cels

COMPLETE SET (5)   15.00   40.00
COMMON CARD   4.00   10.00
STATED ODDS 1:6 WALMART PACKS

2008 Star Wars Clone Wars Red Animation Cels

COMPLETE SET (5)   20.00   50.00
COMMON CARD   5.00   12.00
STATED ODDS 1:6 TARGET PACKS

2008 Star Wars Clone Wars Coins Purple

COMPLETE SET (12)   15.00   40.00
COMMON CARD (1-12)   2.50   6.00
*RED: SAME VALUE
*YELLOW: SAME VALUE
PURPLE ODDS 2:WALMART/MEIER BONUS BOX
RED ODDS 2:TARGET BONUS BOX
YELLOW ODDS 2:TRU BONUS BOX

2008 Star Wars Clone Wars Motion

COMPLETE SET (5)   4.00   8.00
COMMON CARD (1-5)   1.25   3.00
STATED ODDS 1:8 RETAIL

2008 Star Wars Clone Wars Sketches

STATED ODDS 1:24 HOBBY
UNPRICED DUE TO SCARCITY

NNO Amy Pronovost
NNO Anthony Ermio
NNO Ben Curtis Jones
NNO Bosco Ng

NNO Brent Engstrom
NNO Brian Ashmore
NNO Brian Denham
NNO Brian Kalin O'Connell
NNO Brian Kong
NNO Brian Miller
NNO Bryan Morton
NNO Cat Staggs
NNO Chelsea Brown
NNO Chris Henderson
NNO Chris Trevas
NNO Christian Dalla Vecchia
NNO Clay McCormack
NNO Cynthia Cummens
NNO Dan Parsons
NNO Daniel Cooney
NNO Danny Keller
NNO Dave Filoni
NNO Dave Fox
NNO David Le Merrer
NNO David Rabbitte
NNO Davide Fabbri
NNO Dennis Budd
NNO Don Pedicini Jr.
NNO Doug Cowan
NNO Dwayne Clare
NNO Edward Pun
NNO Erik Maell
NNO Francis Hsu
NNO Gabe Hernandez
NNO Giancarlo Volpe
NNO Grant Gould
NNO Hamilton Cline
NNO Howard Shum
NNO Ingrid Hardy
NNO Irma Ahmed (Aimo)
NNO Jackson Sze
NNO Jake Minor
NNO Jake Myler
NNO James Bukauskas (Bukshot)
NNO James Hodgkins
NNO Jamie Snell
NNO Jan Duursema
NNO Jason Hughes
NNO Jason Potratz
NNO Jason Potratz/Jack Hai
NNO Jason Sobol
NNO Jeff Carlisle
NNO Jeff Chandler
NNO Jessica Hickman
NNO Jim Kyle
NNO Joanne Ellen Mutch
NNO Joe Corroney
NNO Joel Carroll
NNO John McCrea
NNO John Watkins-Chow
NNO Jon Morris
NNO Josh Fargher
NNO Josh Howard
NNO Juan Carlos Ramos
NNO Justin Chung
NNO Karen Krajenbrink
NNO Kate Bradley
NNO Kate Glasheen
NNO Katie Cook-Wilcox
NNO Keith Phillips
NNO Kelsey Mann
NNO Kevin Doyle
NNO Kevin Graham
NNO Kilian Plunkett
NNO Kyle Babbitt
NNO Lance Sawyer
NNO Le Tang
NNO Leah Mangue
NNO Lee Kohse
NNO Len Bellinger
NNO Lord Mesa
NNO Mark McHaley
NNO Mark Walters
NNO Matt Gaser
NNO Matt Olsen
NNO Matthew Goodmanson
NNO Michael Duron
NNO Nicole Falk
NNO Noah Albrecht
NNO Pat Presley
NNO Patrick Hamill

NNO Paul Alan Ballard
NNO Paul Gutierrez
NNO Randy Bantog
NNO Rich Molinelli
NNO Rich Woodall
NNO Rob Teranishi
NNO Russel G. Chong
NNO Sergio Paez
NNO Shelli Paroline
NNO Spencer Brinkerhoff
NNO Stephanie Yue
NNO Steven Oatney
NNO Steward Lee
NNO Thang Le
NNO Tod Smith
NNO Tom Hodges
NNO Wayne Lo
NNO William O'Neill
NNO Zack Giallongo

2008 Star Wars Clone Wars Promos

COMPLETE SET (2)	2.50	6.00
COMMON CARD (P1-P2)	1.50	4.00

2008 Star Wars Clone Wars Stickers

COMPLETE SET (90)	15.00	40.00
COMMON CARD (1-90)	.40	1.00

2008 Star Wars Clone Wars Stickers Die-Cut Magnets

COMPLETE SET (9)	10.00	25.00
COMMON CARD (1-9)	2.00	5.00
STATED ODDS 1:12		

2008 Star Wars Clone Wars Stickers Die-Cut Pop-Ups

COMPLETE SET (10)	3.00	8.00
COMMON CARD (1-10)	.60	1.50
STATED ODDS 1:3		

2008 Star Wars Clone Wars Stickers Foil

COMPLETE SET (10)	5.00	12.00
COMMON CARD (1-10)	.75	2.00
STATED ODDS 1:3		

2008 Star Wars Clone Wars Stickers Temporary Tattoos

COMPLETE SET (10)	6.00	15.00
COMMON CARD (1-10)	1.00	2.50
STATED ODDS 1:4		

2008 Star Wars Clone Wars Stickers Tin Lid Stickers

COMPLETE SET (6)	12.00	30.00
STATED ODDS 1 PER TIN		
1 Anakin	3.00	8.00
2 Obi-Wan	3.00	8.00
3 Anakin and Obi-Wan	3.00	8.00
4 Clone Troopers	3.00	8.00
5 Yoda	3.00	8.00
6 Anakin and Ahsoka	3.00	8.00

2010 Star Wars Clone Wars Rise of the Bounty Hunters

COMPLETE SET (90)	4.00	10.00
UNOPENED BOX (24 PACKS)	15.00	20.00
UNOPENED PACK (7 CARDS)	.75	1.00
COMMON CARD (1-90)	.10	.30
*SILVER/100: 20X TO 50X BASIC CARDS		
*GOLD/1: UNPRICED DUE TO SCARCITY		

2010 Star Wars Clone Wars Rise of the Bounty Hunters Animator Sketches

COMPLETE ARTIST LIST (6)
STATED ODDS 1:335
UNPRICED DUE TO SCARCITY

NNO Animator Sketch Redemption
NNO A. Kirk
NNO Brian Kalin O'Connell
NNO Carlo Sansonetti
NNO Chris Glenn
NNO Juan Hernandez
NNO Ken Min
NNO Killian Plunkett
NNO Polina Hristova
NNO Vince Lee
NNO Will Nichols

2010 Star Wars Clone Wars Rise of the Bounty Hunters Cels Red

COMPLETE SET (5)	8.00	20.00
COMMON CARD (1-5)	3.00	8.00

2010 Star Wars Clone Wars Rise of the Bounty Hunters Cels Yellow

COMPLETE SET (5)	6.00	15.00
COMMON CARD (1-5)	2.50	6.00

2010 Star Wars Clone Wars Rise of the Bounty Hunters Foil

COMPLETE SET (20)	8.00	20.00
COMMON CARD (1-20)	.60	1.50
STATED ODDS 1:3		

2010 Star Wars Clone Wars Rise of the Bounty Hunters Motion

COMPLETE SET (5)	6.00	15.00
COMMON CARD (1-5)	1.50	4.00
STATED ODDS 1:6		

2010 Star Wars Clone Wars Rise of the Bounty Hunters Sketches

NNO Adrien Rivera
NNO Alex Buechel
NNO Amy Pronovost
NNO Beck Kramer
NNO Bill Pulkovski
NNO Bob Stevlic
NNO Braden Lamb
NNO Brent Engstrom
NNO Brian Miller
NNO Brian Rood
NNO Bruce Gerlach
NNO Cal Slayton
NNO Cat Staggs
NNO Dan Bergren
NNO Dan Masso
NNO David Day
NNO David Rabbitte
NNO Denise Vasquez
NNO Don Pedicini Jr
NNO Doug Cowan
NNO Gabe Farber
NNO Gary Kezele
NNO Geoff Munn
NNO George Davis
NNO Grant Gould
NNO Hayden Davis
NNO Howard Shum
NNO Ingrid Hardy
NNO Irma Ahmed
NNO Jamie Snell
NNO Jason Hughes
NNO Jason Keith Philips
NNO Jason Sobol
NNO Jeff Confer
NNO Jeremy Treece
NNO Jerry Gaylord
NNO Jessica Hickman
NNO Jim Kyle
NNO John Beatty
NNO John P. Wales
NNO John Soukup
NNO Jon Morris
NNO Juan Carlos Ramos
NNO Katie Cook
NNO Kevin Doyle
NNO Kevin Graham
NNO Kevin Liell
NNO Lance Sawyer
NNO Lawrence Snelly
NNO Lee Kohse

NNO M. Jason Reed
NNO Mark Slater
NNO Martheus Wade
NNO Matt Minor
NNO Michael Duron
NNO Nolan Woodard
NNO Otis Frampton
NNO Patrick Richardson
NNO Randy Martinez
NNO Rhiannon Owens
NNO Rich Molinelli
NNO Robert Teranishi
NNO Ryan Hungerford
NNO Sarah Wilkinson
NNO Scott Zambelli
NNO Shea Standefer
NNO Shelli Paroline
NNO Spencer Brinkerhoff
NNO Stephanie Yue
NNO Steve Oatney
NNO Tim Proctor
NNO Tod Allen Smith
NNO Tom Hodges
NNO Zack Giallongo

2010 Star Wars Clone Wars Rise of the Bounty Hunters Promos

P1 Cad Bane and Others 1.25 3.00
P3 Pre Vizsla and Mandalorian Death Watch 1.25 3.00

2018 Star Wars Clone Wars 10th Anniversary

COMPLETE SET (25) 15.00 40.00
COMMON CARD (1-25) 1.00 2.50
*PURPLE: .75X TO 2X BASIC CARDS
*BLUE/10: UNPRICED DUE TO SCARCITY
*RED/5: UNPRICED DUE TO SCARCITY
*GOLD/1: UNPRICED DUE TO SCARCITY

2018 Star Wars Clone Wars 10th Anniversary Autographs

*BLUE/10: UNPRICED DUE TO SCARCITY
*RED/5: UNPRICED DUE TO SCARCITY
*GOLD/1: UNPRICED DUE TO SCARCITY
STATED OVERALL ODDS 1:SET

1A Matt Lanter
2A Ashley Eckstein
3A James Arnold Taylor 8.00 20.00
4A Tom Kane
6A Tim Curry
7A Catherine Taber
8A Phil Lamarr
9A Nika Futterman
10A Meredith Salenger
12A Stephen Stanton
13A Daniel Logan
14A Sam Witwer
15A Anna Graves
16A Anthony Daniels
18A Dee Bradley Baker
20A Matthew Wood
21A David Tennant
22A Blair Bess
23A Cas Anvar
24A Kathleen Gati
25A George Takei

2018 Star Wars Clone Wars 10th Anniversary Dual Autographs

STATED PRINT RUN SER.#'d SETS
UNPRICED DUE TO SCARCITY

NNO J.A.Taylor/M.Lanter
NNO J.A.Taylor/S.Witwer
NNO J.A.Taylor/T.Kane
NNO M.Lanter/A.Eckstein
NNO S.Stanton/A.Eckstein

2009 Star Wars Clone Wars Widevision

COMPLETE SET (80) 5.00 12.00
UNOPENED BOX (24 PACKS) 60.00 70.00
UNOPENED PACK (7 CARDS) 2.50 3.00
COMMON CARD (1-80) ..... .15 .40
*SILVER: 5X TO 12X BASIC CARDS

2009 Star Wars Clone Wars Widevision Animation Cels

THREEPIO AND JAR JAR

COMPLETE SET (10) 6.00 15.00
COMMON CARD (1-10) ..... .75 2.00
STATED ODDS 1:4

2009 Star Wars Clone Wars Widevision Animator Sketches

COMPLETE ARTIST LIST (23)
STATED ODDS 1:223
OVERALL ODDS WITH ARTIST SKETCHES 1:24
UNPRICED DUE TO SCARCITY

NNO Thang Le
NNO Wayne Lo
NNO Bosco Ng
NNO Don Ta
NNO Ken Min
NNO Jackson Sze
NNO Chris Voy
NNO Randy Bantog
NNO Tim Brock
NNO Russell Chong
NNO Anthony Ermio
NNO Dave Filoni
NNO Davide Le Merrer
NNO Darren Marshall
NNO Brian Kalin O'Connell
NNO Sergio Paez
NNO Kilian Plunkett
NNO Pat Presley
NNO Stew Lee
NNO Jacob Stephens
NNO Le Tang
NNO Vince Lee
NNO Giancarlo Volpe

2009 Star Wars Clone Wars Widevision Artist Sketches

STATED ODDS 1:27 HOBBY PACKS
STATED ODDS 1:48 RETAIL PACKS
OVERALL ODDS WITH ANIMATOR SKETCHES 1:24
UNPRICED DUE TO SCARCITY

NNO David Day
NNO Stephanie Yue
NNO Irma Ahmed
NNO Soni Alcorn-Hender
NNO Brian Ashmore
NNO Kyle Babbitt
NNO Dan Bergren
NNO Brian Miller
NNO Spencer Brinkerhoff III
NNO Dennis Budd
NNO Alex Buechel
NNO James Bukauskas
NNO Bernard Chang
NNO Chris Henderson
NNO Matte Chero
NNO Justin Chung
NNO Hamilton Cline
NNO Katie Cook
NNO Joe Corroney
NNO Jerome Dabos
NNO Ted Dastick Jr.
NNO Hayden Davis
NNO Brian Denham
NNO Colleen Doran
NNO Kevin Doyle
NNO Michael Duron (Locoduck)
NNO Darla Ecklund
NNO Nina Edlund

NNO Carolyn Edwards
NNO Brent Engstrom
NNO Nicole Falk
NNO Gabe Farber
NNO Josh Fargher
NNO Agnieszka Garbowska
NNO Bruce Gerlach
NNO Zack Giallongo
NNO Kate Glasheen
NNO Grant Gould
NNO Kevin Graham
NNO Ingrid Hardy
NNO Jess Hickman
NNO Tom Hodges
NNO Jason Hughes
NNO Jake Minor
NNO Ben Curtis Jones
NNO Jamie Snell
NNO Danny Kelly
NNO Lee Kohse
NNO Karen Krajenbrink
NNO Jim Kyle
NNO Braden Lamb
NNO Kevin Liell
NNO Laura Martin
NNO Lawrence Snelly
NNO Erik Maell
NNO Leah Mangue
NNO Mark McHaley
NNO Lord Mesa
NNO Matt Minor
NNO Rich Molinelli
NNO Monte Moore
NNO Jon Morris
NNO Bryan Morton
NNO Cynthia (Cummens) Narcisi
NNO Nolan Woodward
NNO Steve Oatney
NNO Rhiannon Owens
NNO Shelli Paroline
NNO Don Pedicini Jr.
NNO Sean Pence
NNO Jason Keith Phillips
NNO Tim Proctor
NNO Amy Pronovost
NNO Bill Pulkovski
NNO David Rabbitte
NNO Darin Radimaker
NNO Juan Carlos Ramos
NNO Robert Hendrickson
NNO Adrian Rivera
NNO Randy Martinez
NNO Brian Rood
NNO Craig Rousseau
NNO Stephane Roux
NNO Rich Woodall
NNO Lance Sawyer
NNO Neil Segura
NNO Howard Shum
NNO Scott D. M. Simmons
NNO Steven Miller
NNO Jason Sobol
NNO Carlo Sinfuego Soriano
NNO John Soukup
NNO Cat Staggs
NNO Dave Pops Tata
NNO Rob Teranishi
NNO Jeremy Treece
NNO Francis Tsai
NNO Tod Allen Smith
NNO Uko Smith
NNO Denise Vasquez
NNO Frank Villarreal
NNO John P. Wales
NNO Russ Walks
NNO Sarah Wilkinson
NNO David Green

2009 Star Wars Clone Wars Widevision Autographs

COMMON AUTO	8.00	20.00
STATED ODDS 1:67 HOBBY; 1:174 RETAIL		
NNO James Arnold Taylor	15.00	40.00
NNO Matt Lanter	15.00	40.00
NNO Matthew Wood/Droids	15.00	40.00
NNO Matthew Wood/Grievous	15.00	40.00
NNO Nika Futterman	12.00	30.00
NNO Tom Kane	12.00	30.00

2009 Star Wars Clone Wars Widevision Foil Characters

COMPLETE SET (20)	15.00	40.00
COMMON CARD (1-20)	1.00	2.50
STATED ODDS 1:3		

2009 Star Wars Clone Wars Widevision Motion

COMPLETE SET (5)	6.00	15.00
COMMON CARD (1-5)	1.50	4.00
STATED ODDS 1:8		

2009 Star Wars Clone Wars Widevision Season Two Previews

COMPLETE SET (8)	3.00	8.00
COMMON CARD (PV1-PV8)	.50	1.25
STATED ODDS 1:2		

2019 Star Wars Comic Convention Exclusives

1 Darth Vader SWC	75.00	150.00
2 Luke Skywalker SWC		
3 Princess Leia Organa SWC	25.00	60.00
4 Han Solo SWC	30.00	75.00
5 Chewbacca SWC	30.00	75.00
6 Anakin Skywalker SDCC	12.00	30.00
7 Obi-Wan Kenobi SDCC	12.00	30.00
8 Padme Amidala SDCC	10.00	25.00
9 Qui-Gon Jinn SDCC	10.00	25.00
10 Darth Maul SDCC	20.00	50.00
11 Rey NYCC	60.00	120.00
12 Kylo Ren NYCC	20.00	50.00
13 Finn NYCC	15.00	40.00
14 Poe Dameron NYCC	25.00	60.00
15 General Hux NYCC	20.00	50.00

2017 Star Wars Countdown to The Last Jedi

COMPLETE SET (20)	75.00	150.00
COMMON CARD (1-20)	5.00	12.00
1 Rey Encounters Luke Skywalker/775*	8.00	20.00

1994 Star Wars Day

COMPLETE SET (2)	6.00	15.00
COMMON CARD (SD1-SD2)	4.00	10.00

1995 Star Wars Day

NNO Millennium Falcon w/X-Wings and TIE Fighters	5.00	12.00

1999 Star Wars Defeat the Dark Side and Win Medallions

COMPLETE SET W/O SP (16)	12.00	30.00
COMMON MEDALLION	1.00	2.50
2 Daultay Dofine/50*		
4 Yoda/1500*		
10 Shmi Skywalker/1*		
13 Battle Droid/1*		
20 Chancellor Valorum/1*		

2015 Star Wars Disney Pixar Cars Promos

COMPLETE SET (5)	30.00	80.00
COMMON CARD	10.00	25.00

2015 Star Wars Disney Store The Force Awakens Promos

Finn on the run!

COMPLETE SET (8)	20.00	50.00
COMMON CARD (SKIP #'d)	4.00	10.00
11 BB-8 on the move!	6.00	15.00
67 Kylo Ren ignites his Lightsaber!	5.00	12.00
96 The Millennium Falcon	5.00	12.00

2011 Star Wars Dog Tags

COMPLETE SET (24)	25.00	60.00
UNOPENED BOX (PACKS)		
UNOPENED PACK (1 TAG+1 CARD)		
COMMON TAG (1-24)	2.00	5.00
*SILVER: .5X TO 1.2X BASIC TAGS	2.50	6.00
*RAINBOW: 1.2X TO 3X BASIC TAGS	6.00	15.00

2001 Star Wars Evolution

COMPLETE SET (93)	5.00	12.00
UNOPENED BOX (36 PACKS)	45.00	60.00
UNOPENED PACK (8 CARDS)	1.50	2.00
COMMON CARD (1-93)	.15	.40

2001 Star Wars Evolution Autographs

COMMON AUTO	15.00	40.00
GROUP A/1000* STATED ODDS 1:37		
GROUP B/400* STATED ODDS 1:919		
GROUP C/300* STATED ODDS 1:2450		
GROUP D/100* STATED ODDS 1:3677		
NNO Anthony Daniels/100*	1000.00	1500.00
NNO Billy Dee Williams/300*	150.00	300.00
NNO Carrie Fisher/100*	1000.00	1500.00
NNO Dalyn Chew/1000*	50.00	100.00
NNO Dermot Crowley/1000*	20.00	50.00
NNO Ian McDiarmid/400*	200.00	400.00
NNO James Earl Jones/1000*	200.00	400.00
NNO Jeremy Bulloch/1000*	125.00	250.00
NNO Kenneth Colley/1000*	30.00	75.00
NNO Kenny Baker/1000*	150.00	300.00
NNO Lewis MacLeod	25.00	60.00
NNO Michael Culver/1000*	50.00	100.00
NNO Michael Pennington/1000*	25.00	60.00
NNO Michael Sheard/1000*	20.00	50.00
NNO Michonne Bourriague/1000*	20.00	50.00
NNO Peter Mayhew/400*	125.00	250.00
NNO Phil Brown/1000*	50.00	100.00

NNO Tim Rose/1000*	25.00	60.00
NNO Warwick Davis/1000*	30.00	75.00

2001 Star Wars Evolution Insert A

COMPLETE SET (12)	15.00	30.00
COMMON CARD (1A-12A)	1.50	4.00
STATED ODDS 1:6		

2001 Star Wars Evolution Insert B

COMPLETE SET (8)	20.00	40.00
COMMON CARD (1B-8B)	2.50	6.00
STATED ODDS 1:12		

2001 Star Wars Evolution Promos

COMMON CARD	1.00	2.50
P3 Nien Nunb ALPHA CON	3.00	8.00
P4 Anakin Skywalker SDCC	2.00	5.00

2006 Star Wars Evolution Update

COMPLETE SET (90)	5.00	12.00
UNOPENED BOX (24 PACKS)	40.00	50.00
UNOPENED PACK (6 CARDS)	2.00	2.25
COMMON CARD (1-90)	.15	.40
1D ISSUED AS DAMAGED AUTO REPLACEMENT		
CL1 Luke Connections CL	.40	1.00
CL2 Leia Connections CL	.40	1.00
1D Luke Skywalker SP	2.00	5.00
P1 Obi-Wan Kenobi PROMO	1.00	2.50
P2 Darth Vader PROMO	1.00	2.50

2006 Star Wars Evolution Update Autographs

COMMON AUTO (UNNUMBERED)	6.00	15.00
STATED ODDS 1:24 HOBBY		
GROUP A ODDS 1:2,005		
GROUP B ODDS 1:231		
GROUP C ODDS 1:81		
GROUP D ODDS 1:259		
GROUP E ODDS 1:48		
NNO Alec Guinness		
NNO Bob Keen B	20.00	50.00
NNO David Barclay B	20.00	50.00
NNO Garrick Hagon E	10.00	25.00
NNO George Lucas		
NNO Hayden Christensen A	800.00	1200.00
NNO James Earl Jones A	200.00	400.00
NNO John Coppinger B	15.00	40.00
NNO Maria De Aragon C	10.00	25.00
NNO Matt Sloan E	8.00	20.00
NNO Michonne Bourriague C	10.00	25.00
NNO Mike Edmonds B	15.00	40.00
NNO Mike Quinn B	20.00	50.00
NNO Nalini Krishan D	8.00	20.00
NNO Peter Cushing		
NNO Richard LeParmentier C	10.00	25.00
NNO Sandi Finlay C	8.00	20.00
NNO Toby Philpott B	20.00	50.00
NNO Wayne Pygram B	50.00	100.00

2006 Star Wars Evolution Update Etched Foil Puzzle

COMPLETE SET (6)	6.00	15.00
COMMON CARD (1-6)	1.25	3.00
STATED ODDS 1:6		

2006 Star Wars Evolution Update Galaxy Crystals

COMPLETE SET (10)	12.50	30.00
COMMON CARD (G1-G10)	1.50	4.00
STATED ODDS 1:4 RETAIL		

2006 Star Wars Evolution Update Insert A

COMPLETE SET (20)	20.00	40.00
COMMON CARD (1A-20A)	1.50	4.00
STATED ODDS 1:6		

2006 Star Wars Evolution Update Insert B

COMPLETE SET (15)	20.00	40.00
COMMON CARD (1B-15B)	2.00	5.00
STATED ODDS 1:12		

2006 Star Wars Evolution Update Luke and Leia

COMPLETE SET (2)	1000.00	2000.00
COMMON CARD (1-2)	600.00	1200.00
STATED ODDS 1:1975 HOBBY		
STATED PRINT RUN 100 SER. #'d SETS		

2016 Star Wars Evolution

COMPLETE SET (100)	8.00	20.00
UNOPENED BOX (24 PACKS)	60.00	75.00
UNOPENED PACK (8 CARDS)	2.50	3.00
COMMON CARD (1-100)	.15	.40
*LTSBR BLUE: 4X TO 10X BASIC CARDS		
*LTSBR PURPLE: 8X TO 20X BASIC CARDS		
*GOLD/50: 15X TO 40X BASIC CARDS		
*IMP.RED/1: UNPRICED DUE TO SCARCITY		
*P.P.BLACK/1: UNPRICED DUE TO SCARCITY		
*P.P.CYAN/1: UNPRICED DUE TO SCARCITY		
*P.P.MAGENTA/1: UNPRICED DUE TO SCARCITY		
*P.P.YELLOW/1: UNPRICED DUE TO SCARCITY		

2016 Star Wars Evolution Autographs

COMMON AUTO	6.00	15.00
*PURPLE/25: .6X TO 1.5X BASIC AUTOS		
*GOLD/10: UNPRICED DUE TO SCARCITY		
*IMP.RED/1: UNPRICED DUE TO SCARCITY		
*P.P.BLACK/1: UNPRICED DUE TO SCARCITY		
*P.P.CYAN/1: UNPRICED DUE TO SCARCITY		
*P.P.MAGENTA/1: UNPRICED DUE TO SCARCITY		
*P.P.YELLOW/1: UNPRICED DUE TO SCARCITY		
RANDOMLY INSERTED INTO PACKS		
NNO Alan Harris	8.00	20.00
NNO Amy Allen	10.00	25.00
NNO Andy Serkis	100.00	200.00
NNO Angus MacInnes	12.00	30.00
NNO Ashley Eckstein	20.00	50.00
NNO Clive Revill	25.00	60.00
NNO Dee Bradley Baker	8.00	20.00
NNO Deep Roy	10.00	25.00
NNO Denis Lawson	15.00	40.00
NNO Dickey Beer	12.00	30.00
NNO Freddie Prinze Jr.	60.00	120.00
NNO George Takei	15.00	40.00
NNO Greg Grunberg	15.00	40.00
NNO Harriet Walter	12.00	30.00
NNO Hugh Quarshie	20.00	50.00
NNO Jeremy Bulloch	15.00	40.00
NNO Jerome Blake	10.00	25.00
NNO John Boyega	75.00	150.00
NNO John Ratzenberger	8.00	20.00
NNO Keisha Castle-Hughes	10.00	25.00
NNO Kenneth Colley	12.00	30.00
NNO Matthew Wood	12.00	30.00
NNO Mercedes Ngoh	20.00	50.00
NNO Michael Carter	20.00	50.00
NNO Mike Quinn	8.00	20.00
NNO Orli Shoshan	8.00	20.00
NNO Paul Blake	8.00	20.00
NNO Phil Lamarr	15.00	40.00
NNO Ray Park	25.00	60.00
NNO Sam Witwer	8.00	20.00
NNO Stephen Stanton	10.00	25.00
NNO Taylor Gray	10.00	25.00
NNO Tim Dry	12.00	30.00
NNO Tiya Sircar	8.00	20.00
NNO Tom Kane	10.00	25.00
NNO Vanessa Marshall	8.00	20.00
NNO Warwick Davis	12.00	30.00

2016 Star Wars Evolution Dual Autographs

STATED PRINT RUN 3 SER.#'d SETS
UNPRICED DUE TO SCARCITY

NNO Eckstein/Baker
NNO McDiarmid/Revill
NNO McDiarmid/Wood
NNO Bulloch/Logan
NNO Hamill/Roy
NNO Carter/Wood
NNO Park/Witwer

2016 Star Wars Evolution Dual Patch Banner Books

STATED PRINT RUN 5 SER.#'d SETS
UNPRICED DUE TO SCARCITY

NNO Bail Organa/Padme Amidala
NNO Count Dooku/General Grievous
NNO Emperor Palpatine/Darth Vader
NNO Finn/Rey
NNO Kanan Jarrus/Ezra Bridger
NNO Kylo Ren/Captain Phasma
NNO Luke Skywalker/Princess Leia
NNO Yoda/Mace Windu

2016 Star Wars Evolution Evolution of the Lightsaber

COMPLETE SET (9)	12.00	30.00
COMMON CARD (EL1-EL9)	2.00	5.00
*P.P.BLACK/1: UNPRICED DUE TO SCARCITY		
*P.P.CYAN/1: UNPRICED DUE TO SCARCITY		
*P.P.MAGENTA/1: UNPRICED DUE TO SCARCITY		
*P.P.YELLOW/1: UNPRICED DUE TO SCARCITY		
STATED ODDS 1:8		

2016 Star Wars Evolution Evolution of Vehicles and Ships

COMPLETE SET (18)	8.00	20.00
COMMON CARD (EV1-EV18)	.75	2.00
*P.P.BLACK/1: UNPRICED DUE TO SCARCITY		
*P.P.CYAN/1: UNPRICED DUE TO SCARCITY		
*P.P.MAGENTA/1: UNPRICED DUE TO SCARCITY		
*P.P.YELLOW/1: UNPRICED DUE TO SCARCITY		
STATED ODDS 1:2		

2016 Star Wars Evolution Lenticular Morph

COMPLETE SET (9)	60.00	120.00
COMMON CARD (1-9)	6.00	15.00
STATED ODDS 1:72		
1 Darth Vader	10.00	25.00
2 Luke Skywalker	10.00	25.00
3 Leia Organa	8.00	20.00
4 Han Solo	10.00	25.00
9 Chewbacca	8.00	20.00

2016 Star Wars Evolution Marvel Star Wars Comics

COMPLETE SET (17)	12.00	30.00
COMMON CARD (EC1-EC17)	1.50	4.00
*P.P.BLACK/1: UNPRICED DUE TO SCARCITY		
*P.P.CYAN/1: UNPRICED DUE TO SCARCITY		
*P.P.MAGENTA/1: UNPRICED DUE TO SCARCITY		
*P.P.YELLOW/1: UNPRICED DUE TO SCARCITY		
STATED ODDS 1:4		

2016 Star Wars Evolution Patches

COMMON CARD	5.00	12.00
*SILVER/50: 5X TO 1.2X BASIC CARDS		
*GOLD/25: .6X TO 1.5X BASIC CARDS		
*IMP.RED/1: UNPRICED DUE TO SCARCITY		
*PLATINUM/10: UNPRICED DUE TO SCARCITY		
NNO Admiral Ackbar	6.00	15.00
NNO Ahsoka Tano	6.00	15.00
NNO BB-8	8.00	20.00
NNO Chancellor Palpatine	6.00	15.00
NNO Clone Trooper	6.00	15.00
NNO Darth Vader	6.00	15.00
NNO Ezra Bridger	6.00	15.00
NNO General Hux	6.00	15.00
NNO Grand Moff Tarkin	8.00	20.00
NNO Han Solo	8.00	20.00
NNO Kylo Ren	8.00	20.00
NNO Luke Skywalker	6.00	15.00
NNO Mon Mothma	6.00	15.00
NNO Poe Dameron	6.00	15.00
NNO Princess Leia Organa	6.00	15.00
NNO Qui-Gon Jinn	6.00	15.00
NNO Rey	10.00	25.00
NNO Senator Amidala	6.00	15.00
NNO Supreme Leader Snoke	6.00	15.00

2016 Star Wars Evolution Quad Autograph

STATED PRINT RUN 1 SER.#'d SET
UNPRICED DUE TO SCARCITY

1 Bulloch/Morton/Beers/Logan

2016 Star Wars Evolution Sketches

NNO Alex Buechel
NNO Angelina Benedetti
NNO Brad Hudson
NNO Brent Ragland
NNO Brian Kong
NNO Carlos Cabaleiro
NNO Christopher West
NNO Dan Bergren
NNO Dan Parsons
NNO Darrin Pepe
NNO David Rabbitte
NNO Elfie Lebouleux
NNO Eli Rutten
NNO Eric Lehtonen
NNO Francois Chartier
NNO Jason Brower
NNO Jason Crosby
NNO Jason Flowers
NNO Jason Sobol
NNO Jeff West
NNO Jeffrey Benitez

NNO Jennifer Allyn
NNO Jonathan Caustrita
NNO Keith Carter
NNO Kevin West
NNO Kris Penix
NNO Kyle Babbit
NNO Lin Workman
NNO Marcia Dye
NNO Matthew Fletcher
NNO Patrick Richardson
NNO Rich Molinelli
NNO Roy Cover
NNO Scott Jones
NNO Scott Rorie
NNO Seth Ismart
NNO Solly Mohamed
NNO Stephanie Swanger
NNO Strephon Taylor
NNO Tim Proctor
NNO Tim Shay
NNO Tina Berardi

2016 Star Wars Evolution SP Inserts

COMPLETE SET (9)	250.00	500.00
COMMON CARD (1-9)	25.00	60.00
STATED PRINT RUN 100 SER.#'d SETS		
1 Luke	30.00	80.00
Stormtrooper Disguise		
2 Leia	30.00	80.00
Boussh Disguise		
5 Vader	50.00	100.00
Birth of the Dark Lord		
6 Boba Fett	30.00	80.00
Skiff Battle		

2016 Star Wars Evolution Stained Glass Pairings

COMPLETE SET (9)	20.00	50.00
COMMON CARD (1-9)	2.50	6.00
STATED ODDS 1:24		
1 Luke Skywalker	5.00	12.00
Princess Leia		
2 Han Solo	4.00	10.00
Lando Calrissian		
4 Darth Sidious	4.00	10.00
Darth Maul		
5 Darth Vader	3.00	8.00
Grand Moff Tarkin		
6 Kylo Ren	3.00	8.00
Captain Phasma		
7 Chewbacca	3.00	8.00
C-3PO		
9 Rey	6.00	15.00
Finn		

2016 Star Wars Evolution Triple Autographs

COMPLETE SET (4)
STATED PRINT RUN 3 SER.#'d SETS
UNPRICED DUE TO SCARCITY

1 Blakinston/Crowley/Rose
2 McDiarmid/Wood/Blake
3 Bulloch/Morton/Beer
4 Gray/Eckstein/Baker

2007 Star Wars Family Guy Blue Harvest DVD Promos

COMPLETE SET (12)	3.00	8.00
COMMON CARD	.60	1.50
*GERMAN: SAME VALUE AS ENGLISH		
*ITALIAN: SAME VALUE AS ENGLISH		
*SPANISH: SAME VALUE AS ENGLISH		

1996 Star Wars Finest

COMPLETE SET (90)	10.00	25.00
UNOPENED BOX (36 PACKS)	45.00	60.00
UNOPENED PACK (5 CARDS)	1.50	2.00
COMMON CARD (1-90)	.20	.50
*REF.: 5X TO 12X BASIC CARDS		

1996 Star Wars Finest Embossed

COMPLETE SET (6)	10.00	25.00
COMMON CARD (F1-F6)	2.00	5.00

1996 Star Wars Finest Matrix

COMPLETE SET (4)	6.00	15.00
COMMON CARD (M1-M4)	2.00	5.00
NNO Exchange Card		

1996 Star Wars Finest Promos

COMPLETE SET (3)	2.50	6.00
COMMON CARD (SWF1-SWF3)	1.00	2.50
B1 Han Solo & Chewbacca ALB	3.00	8.00
NNO 1-Card Sheet		
NNO 1-Card Sheet Refractor		
NNO Star Wars Goes Split Level	200.00	400.00

2018 Star Wars Finest

COMPLETE SET W/SP (120)	75.00	150.00
COMPLETE SET W/O SP (100)	20.00	50.00
COMMON CARD (1-100)	.40	1.00
COMMON SP (101-120)	3.00	8.00
*REF.: 1.25X TO 3X BASIC CARDS		
*BLUE/150: 2X TO 5X BASIC CARDS		
*GREEN/99: 3X TO 8X BASIC CARDS		
*GOLD/50: 4X TO 10X BASIC CARDS		
*GOLD SP/50: .5X TO 1.2X BASIC CARDS		
*ORANGE/25: UNPRICED DUE TO SCARCITY		
*BLACK/10: UNPRICED DUE TO SCARCITY		
*RED/5: UNPRICED DUE TO SCARCITY		
*SUPER/1: UNPRICED DUE TO SCARCITY		

2018 Star Wars Finest Autographs

*ORANGE/25: UNPRICED DUE TO SCARCITY
*BLACK/10: UNPRICED DUE TO SCARCITY
*RED/5: UNPRICED DUE TO SCARCITY
*SUPER/1: UNPRICED DUE TO SCARCITY

FAAL Amanda Lawrence		
FADBB Dee Bradley Baker	8.00	20.00
FAHCT Hermione Corfield	10.00	25.00
FAJAT James Arnold Taylor		
FAJBM Jerome Blake	5.00	12.00
FAMEM Mary Elizabeth McGlynn	6.00	15.00
FAJZ Zac Jensen		

2018 Star Wars Finest Droids and Vehicles

COMPLETE SET (20)	12.00	30.00
COMMON CARD (DV1-DV20)	1.50	4.00
*GOLD/50: .75X TO 2X BASIC CARDS		
*RED/5: UNPRICED DUE TO SCARCITY		
*SUPER/1: UNPRICED DUE TO SCARCITY		

2018 Star Wars Finest Lightsaber Hilt Medallions

COMMON MEM	5.00	12.00
*GOLD/50: .5X TO 1.2X BASIC MEM		
*ORANGE/25: UNPRICED DUE TO SCARCITY		
*BLACK/10: UNPRICED DUE TO SCARCITY		
*RED/5: UNPRICED DUE TO SCARCITY		
*SUPER/1: UNPRICED DUE TO SCARCITY		
LMAV Asajj Ventress	6.00	15.00
LMBO Barriss Offee	6.00	15.00
LMSF Finn	6.00	15.00
LMSR Rey	15.00	40.00
LMST Shaak Ti	6.00	15.00
LMY2 Yoda	8.00	20.00
LMYC Yoda	6.00	15.00
LMA22 Anakin Skywalker	12.00	30.00
LMAS1 Anakin Skywalker	6.00	15.00
LMAS2 Ahsoka Tano	6.00	15.00
LMAS3 Ahsoka Tano	6.00	15.00
LMASC Ahsoka Tano	6.00	15.00
LMDM1 Darth Maul	10.00	25.00
LMDS3 Darth Sidious	6.00	15.00
LMDV4 Darth Vader	8.00	20.00
LMDV5 Darth Vader	10.00	25.00
LMDVR Darth Vader	10.00	25.00
LMGIR The Grand Inquisitor	8.00	20.00
LMKR7 Kylo Ren	12.00	30.00
LMKR8 Kylo Ren	12.00	30.00
LML24 Luke Skywalker	10.00	25.00
LML25 Luke Skywalker	8.00	20.00
LML28 Luke Skywalker	10.00	25.00
LMLS6 Luke Skywalker	10.00	25.00
LMLS8 Luke Skywalker	10.00	25.00
LMMW2 Mace Windu	8.00	20.00
LMO22 Obi-Wan Kenobi	6.00	15.00
LMR27 Rey	15.00	40.00
LMSAS Anakin Skywalker	10.00	25.00
LMSLS Luke Skywalker	10.00	25.00

2018 Star Wars Finest Prime Autographs

STATED PRINT RUN 10 SER.#'d SETS
UNPRICED DUE TO SCARCITY

PAAD Adam Driver
PAAS Andy Serkis
PAADC Anthony Daniels
PACF Carrie Fisher
PADR Daisy Ridley
PAHF Harrison Ford
PAKB Kenny Baker
PAPM Peter Mayhew

2018 Star Wars Finest Rogue One

COMPLETE SET (20)	20.00	50.00
COMMON CARD (RO1-RO20)	2.00	5.00
*GOLD/50: 6X TO 1.5X BASIC CARDS		
*RED/5: UNPRICED DUE TO SCARCITY		
*SUPER/1: UNPRICED DUE TO SCARCITY		

2018 Star Wars Finest Rogue One Autographs

*ORANGE/25: UNPRICED DUE TO SCARCITY
*BLACK/10: UNPRICED DUE TO SCARCITY
*RED/5: UNPRICED DUE TO SCARCITY
*SUPER/1: UNPRICED DUE TO SCARCITY

RAAP Alistair Petrie		
RAAT Alan Tudyk		
RABD Ben Daniels		
RABM Ben Mendelsohn		
RADA Derek Arnold		
RADY Donnie Yen		
RAFJ Felicity Jones		
RAFW Forest Whitaker		
RAGO Genevieve O'Reilly		
RAIM Ian McElhinney	6.00	15.00
RAMM Mads Mikkelsen		
RARA Riz Ahmed		

2018 Star Wars Finest Sketches

UNPRICED DUE TO SCARCITY

NNO Adam Beck
NNO Adam Harris
NNO Adam Talley
NNO Adam Worton
NNO Adrian Ropp
NNO Aleksandar Gigov

NNO Allen Grimes
NNO Andrew Sanchez
NNO Anil Sharma
NNO Aston Cover
NNO Barry Renshaw
NNO Basak Cetinkaya
NNO Ben AbuSaada
NNO Brad Hudson
NNO Brandon Blevins
NNO Brendan Purchase
NNO Brent Ragland
NNO Brent Scotchmer
NNO Bryce King II
NNO Caleb King
NNO Carlos Cabaleiro
NNO Carolyn Craggs
NNO Chris Thorne
NNO Colin Arthurs
NNO Cyrus Sherkat
NNO Dan Bergren
NNO Dan Curto
NNO Dan Gorman
NNO Dan Tearle
NNO Darren James
NNO Darrin Pepe
NNO Dave Strong
NNO Dean Drummond
NNO Eric Lehtonen
NNO Eric White
NNO Erin Lefler
NNO Fredd Gorham
NNO Gavin Williams
NNO Gerard Garcia Jr.
NNO Glen Kertes
NNO Gorkem Demir
NNO Greg Mitchell
NNO Huy Truong
NNO Ibrahim Ozkan
NNO Ingrid Hardy
NNO Jaime Lopez
NNO Jamie Richards
NNO Jason Adams
NNO Jay Manchand
NNO Jeff Mallinson
NNO Jeff West
NNO Jessica Hickman
NNO Jim O'Riley
NNO John Bruce
NNO Jose Ruiz
NNO Kaela Croft
NNO Keith Farnum
NNO Kelly Baber
NNO Kevin Cleveland
NNO Kevin Graham
NNO Kevin Liell
NNO Kris Penix
NNO Kurt Ruskin
NNO Laura Atkinson
NNO Logan Monette
NNO Madison Emerick
NNO Mark Picirilli
NNO Marsha Parkins
NNO Matt Soffe
NNO Matt Stewart
NNO Matthew Hirons
NNO Matthew Lopez
NNO Michael Mastermaker
NNO Michelle Rayner
NNO Mick and Matt Glebe
NNO Mohammad Jilani
NNO Nathan Kennett
NNO Neil Camera
NNO Nicholas Dertinger
NNO Nick Justus
NNO Oscar Chavez
NNO Patricio Carrasco
NNO Phil Hassewer
NNO Phillip Trujillo
NNO Rees Finlay
NNO Rich Henneman
NNO Richard Serrao
NNO Rob Teranishi

NNO Robert Hendrickson
NNO Rodney Roberts
NNO Ryan Crosby
NNO Ryan Finley
NNO Ryan Olsen
NNO Sebastian Cortez
NNO Shaow Siong
NNO Solly Mohamed
NNO Thomas Amici
NNO Tim Shinn
NNO Tod Smith
NNO Travis Kinnison
NNO Trent Westbrook
NNO Vincenzo D'Ippolito
NNO Wayne Tully
NNO Zach Woolsey

2018 Star Wars Finest Solo A Star Wars Story

COMPLETE SET (20)	15.00	40.00
COMMON CARD (S01-SO20)	1.25	3.00
*GOLD/50: .75X TO 2X BASIC CARDS		
*RED/5: UNPRICED DUE TO SCARCITY		
*SUPER/1: UNPRICED DUE TO SCARCITY		

2015 Star Wars Galactic Connexions

COMPLETE SET (75)	8.00	20.00
COMMON DISC	.20	.50
*FOIL: .6X TO 1.5X BASIC DISCS		
*BLK: .75X TO 2X BASIC DISCS		
*HOLOFOIL: .75X TO 2X BASIC DISCS		
*BLK FOIL: 1.5X TO 4X BASIC DISCS		
*CLR: 1.5X TO 4X BASIC DISCS		
*PATTERN FOIL: 2X TO 5X BASIC DISCS		
*BLK PATTERN FOIL: 2.5X TO 6X BASIC DISCS		
*JABBA SLIME GREEN: 3X TO 8X BASIC DISCS		
*CLR FOIL: 4X TO 10X BASIC DISCS		
*LTSABER RED: 4X TO 10X BASIC DISCS		
*CLR PATTERN FOIL: 8X TO 20X BASIC DISCS		
*C-3PO GOLD: 10X TO 25X BASIC DISCS		
*DEATH STAR SILVER: 12X TO 30X BASIC DISCS		
*SOLID GOLD: 20X TO 50X BASIC DISCS		

2015 Star Wars Galactic Connexions Battle Damaged Border

1 Darth Vader	250.00	500.00
Red		
2 Han Solo	150.00	300.00
Red		
3 Luke Skywalker	120.00	250.00
Red		
4 Obi-Wan Kenobi		
Red		
5 Princess Leia Organa		
Red		

2015 Star Wars Galactic Connexions Blue Starfield Exclusives

COMPLETE SET (10)	10.00	25.00
COMMON DISC	1.50	4.00

2015 Star Wars Galactic Connexions SDCC Promos

COMPLETE SET (6)	100.00	200.00
COMMON DISC	12.00	30.00
4 Stormtrooper	30.00	80.00
Red		
5 Stormtrooper	20.00	50.00
Gold		

2015 Star Wars Galactic Connexions Series 2

COMPLETE SET (75)	8.00	20.00
COMMON DISC	.20	.50
*GRAY FOIL: .6X TO 1.5X BASIC DISCS		
*BLK: .75X TO 2X BASIC DISCS		
*GRAY: .75X TO 2X BASIC DISCS		
*BLK FOIL: 1.5X TO 4X BASIC DISCS		
*CLR: 1.5X TO 4X BASIC DISCS		
*GRAY PATTERN FOIL: 2X TO 5X BASIC DISCS		
*BLK PATTERN FOIL: 2.5X TO 6X BASIC DISCS		
*JABBA SLIME GREEN: 3X TO 8X BASIC DISCS		
*CLR FOIL: 4X TO 10X BASIC DISCS		
*LTSABER PURPLE: 4X TO 10X BASIC DISCS		
*LTSABER RED: 4X TO 10X BASIC DISCS		
*CLR PATTERN FOIL: 8X TO 20X BASIC DISCS		
*C-3PO GOLD: 10X TO 25X BASIC DISCS		
*DEATH STAR SILVER: 12X TO 30X BASIC DISCS		
*SOLID GOLD: 20X TO 50X BASIC DISCS		

2012 Star Wars Galactic Files

COMPLETE SET (350)	25.00	50.00
UNOPENED BOX (24 PACKS)	80.00	100.00
UNOPENED PACK (12 CARDS)	4.00	5.00
COMMON CARD (1-350)	.15	.40
*BLUE: 8X TO 20X BASIC CARDS	3.00	8.00
*RED: 20X TO 50X BASIC CARDS	8.00	20.00
*GOLD/1: UNPRICED DUE TO SCARCITY		
*P.P.BLACK/1: UNPRICED DUE TO SCARCITY		
*P.P.CYAN/1: UNPRICED DUE TO SCARCITY		
*P.P.MAGENTA/1: UNPRICED DUE TO SCARCITY		
*P.P.YELLOW/1: UNPRICED DUE TO SCARCITY		
76 Darth Vader (Jedi Purge) SP	12.00	30.00
96 Luke Skywalker (Stormtrooper) SP	12.00	30.00
125B Princess Leia (Despair) SP	12.00	30.00

2012 Star Wars Galactic Files Autographs

COMMON AUTO	8.00	20.00
STATED ODDS ONE AUTO OR PATCH PER HOBBY BOX		
NNO Amy Allen	12.00	30.00
NNO Carrie Fisher	500.00	1000.00
NNO Felix Silla	25.00	60.00
NNO Harrison Ford	2000.00	3000.00
NNO Irvin Kershner	600.00	1000.00
NNO Jake Lloyd	100.00	200.00
NNO James Earl Jones	200.00	400.00
NNO Jeremy Bulloch	20.00	50.00
NNO Mark Hamill	500.00	1000.00
NNO Matthew Wood	15.00	40.00
NNO Peter Mayhew	125.00	250.00
NNO Ray Park	30.00	75.00
NNO Richard LeParmentier	15.00	40.00

2012 Star Wars Galactic Files Classic Lines

COMPLETE SET (10)	3.00	8.00
COMMON CARD (CL1-CL10)	.75	2.00
STATED ODDS 1:4		

2012 Star Wars Galactic Files Duels of Fate

COMPLETE SET (10)	4.00	10.00
COMMON CARD (DF1-DF10)	1.00	2.50
STATED ODDS 1:6		

2012 Star Wars Galactic Files Galactic Moments

COMPLETE SET (20)	20.00	40.00
COMMON CARD (GM1-GM20)	1.50	4.00
STATED ODDS 1:6		

2012 Star Wars Galactic Files Heroes on Both Sides

COMPLETE SET (10)	4.00	10.00
COMMON CARD (HB1-HB10)	1.00	2.50
STATED ODDS 1:6		

2012 Star Wars Galactic Files I Have a Bad Feeling About This

COMPLETE SET (8)	3.00	8.00
COMMON CARD (BF1-BF8)	.75	2.00
STATED ODDS 1:4		

2012 Star Wars Galactic Files Patches

COMMON CARD	8.00	20.00
STATED ODDS ONE AUTO OR PATCH PER HOBBY BOX		
PR1 Garven Dreis	50.00	100.00
PR2 Wedge Antilles	50.00	100.00
PR3 Biggs Darklighter	50.00	100.00
PR4 John D. Branon	50.00	100.00
PR5 Luke Skywalker	100.00	200.00
PR6 Jek Porkins	50.00	100.00
PR12 Obi-Wan Kenobi	12.00	30.00
PR13 Anakin Skywalker	15.00	40.00
PR14 Plo Koon	12.00	30.00
PR17 Luke Skywalker	75.00	150.00
PR18 Zev Senesca	40.00	80.00
PR19 Wedge Antilles	40.00	80.00
PR20 Derek Hobbie Kuvian	30.00	60.00
PR21 (Gunner) Dak Ralter	30.00	60.00
PR23 Grand Moff Tarkin	15.00	40.00
PR24 Darth Vader	15.00	40.00
PR25 Han Solo	35.00	70.00
PR26 Chewbacca	15.00	40.00
PR27 Lando Calrissian	25.00	50.00
PR28 Nien Numb	15.00	40.00

2012 Star Wars Galactic Files Sketches

NNO Adam Talley/200*
NNO Alex Buechel/50*
NNO Amy Pronovost/50*
NNO Angelina Benedetti/100*
NNO Ashleigh Popplewell/100*
NNO Bill Pulkovski
NNO Bob Stevlic/100*
NNO Brent Engstrom
NNO Brian DeGuire/100*
NNO Chris Raimo/100*
NNO Clay Rodery/100*
NNO Dan Bergren/50*
NNO Darla Ecklund
NNO Dave Strong/100*
NNO David Green
NNO David Rabbitte/130*
NNO Denae Frazier/50*
NNO Denise Vasquez/100*
NNO Diego Jourdan
NNO Eli Rutten/50*
NNO Gary Kezele/50*
NNO Howard Shum
NNO Ian Roberts/101*
NNO Ingrid Hardy/50*
NNO Irma Ahmed/100*
NNO Jamie Snell/100*
NNO Jason Durden
NNO Jason Goad
NNO Jason Sobol
NNO Jay Shimko
NNO Jennifer Mercer
NNO Jeremy Scott
NNO Joe Hogan
NNO John Ottinger
NNO Justin Chung
NNO Kate Glasheen
NNO Katie Cook
NNO Kevin Bloomfield
NNO Kevin Reinke
NNO Kimberly Dunaway
NNO Lak Lim
NNO Lance Sawyer
NNO Lark Sudol

NNO Leah Mangue
NNO Lee Kohse
NNO Lee Lightfoot
NNO Lin Workman
NNO Lord Mesa
NNO M. Jason Reed
NNO Mario Rojas
NNO Matte Chero
NNO Mike Hampton
NNO Mike Vasquez
NNO Mikey Babinski
NNO Nina Edlund
NNO Pablo Diaz
NNO Puis Calzada
NNO Rachel Kaiser
NNO Randy Martinez
NNO Rhiannon Owens
NNO Rich Molinelli
NNO Robert Teranishi
NNO Russ Maheras
NNO Scott Rorie
NNO Scott Zambelli
NNO Stephanie Swanger
NNO Ted Dastick
NNO Tim Proctor
NNO Trev Murphy
NNO Tyler Scarlet
NNO Val Hochberg
NNO Van Davis
NNO Vanessa Banky Farano
NNO Wilson Ramos Jr.
NNO Adrian Rivera
NNO Tony Miello

2013 Star Wars Galactic Files 2

DARTH ZANNAH
SITH APPRENTICE

COMPLETE SET (353)	20.00	50.00
UNOPENED BOX (24 PACKS)	70.00	80.00
COMP.SET W/O SP (350)	12.00	30.00
UNOPENED PACK (12 CARDS)	3.00	4.00
COMMON CARD (351-699)	.15	.40
COMMON SP	4.00	10.00
*BLUE/350: 2X TO 5X BASIC CARDS		
*RED/35: 15X TO 40X BASIC CARDS		
*GOLD/10: 50X TO 120X BASIC CARDS		
*P.P.BLACK/1: UNPRICED DUE TO SCARCITY		
*P.P.CYAN/1: UNPRICED DUE TO SCARCITY		
*P.P.MAGENTA/1: UNPRICED DUE TO SCARCITY		
*P.P.YELLOW/1: UNPRICED DUE TO SCARCITY		
463b Han Solo Stormtrooper SP	4.00	10.00
481b Luke Skywalker Bacta Tank SP	4.00	10.00
510b Princess Leia Slave Girl SP	4.00	10.00

2013 Star Wars Galactic Files 2 Autographs

COMMON AUTO	12.00	30.00
STATED ODDS 1:55		
NNO Billy Dee Williams	50.00	100.00
NNO Carrie Fisher	200.00	350.00
NNO Ian McDiarmid	400.00	600.00
NNO James Earl Jones	200.00	350.00
NNO Jeremy Bulloch	15.00	40.00
NNO Mark Hamill	350.00	500.00
NNO Peter Mayhew	30.00	75.00

2013 Star Wars Galactic Files 2 Dual Autographs

ANNOUNCED COMBINED PRINT RUN 200		
NNO A.Eckstein/T.Kane	100.00	200.00
NNO J.Bulloch/A.Harris	100.00	200.00
NNO J.Jones/I.McDiarmid		
NNO C.Fisher/M.Hamill		
NNO H.Ford/P.Mayhew		

2013 Star Wars Galactic Files 2 Classic Lines

COMPLETE SET (10)	3.00	8.00
COMMON CARD (CL1-CL10)	.60	1.50
*P.P.BLACK/1: UNPRICED DUE TO SCARCITY		
*P.P.CYAN/1: UNPRICED DUE TO SCARCITY		
*P.P.MAGENTA/1: UNPRICED DUE TO SCARCITY		
*P.P.YELLOW/1: UNPRICED DUE TO SCARCITY		
STATED ODDS 1:4		

2013 Star Wars Galactic Files 2 Galactic Moments

COMPLETE SET (20)	30.00	60.00
COMMON CARD (GM1-GM20)	2.00	5.00
*P.P.BLACK/1: UNPRICED DUE TO SCARCITY		
*P.P.CYAN/1: UNPRICED DUE TO SCARCITY		
*P.P.MAGENTA/1: UNPRICED DUE TO SCARCITY		
*P.P.YELLOW/1: UNPRICED DUE TO SCARCITY		
STATED ODDS 1:12		

2013 Star Wars Galactic Files 2 Honor the Fallen

COMPLETE SET (10)	4.00	10.00
COMMON CARD (HF1-HF10)	.75	2.00
*P.P.BLACK/1: UNPRICED DUE TO SCARCITY		
*P.P.CYAN/1: UNPRICED DUE TO SCARCITY		
*P.P.MAGENTA/1: UNPRICED DUE TO SCARCITY		
*P.P.YELLOW/1: UNPRICED DUE TO SCARCITY		
STATED ODDS 1:6		

2013 Star Wars Galactic Files 2 Medallions

COMMON MEDALLION (MD1-MD30)	8.00	20.00
STATED ODDS 1:55		
MD1 Luke Skywalker	12.00	30.00
MD3 Han Solo	20.00	50.00
MD5 Lando Calrissian	12.00	30.00
MD6 Han Solo	150.00	250.00
MD7 Boba Fett	30.00	75.00
MD9 Princess Leia Organa	15.00	40.00
MD10 Bail Organa	10.00	25.00
MD12 General Veers	20.00	50.00
MD13 Jawa	20.00	50.00
MD14 C-3PO	30.00	75.00
MD15 R2-D2	15.00	40.00
MD16 R5-D4	12.00	30.00
MD19 Luke Skywalker	30.00	75.00
MD20 Obi-Wan Kenobi	12.00	30.00
MD21 C-3PO & R2-D2	30.00	75.00
MD22 TIE Fighter Pilot	10.00	25.00
MD23 Darth Vader	15.00	40.00
MD24 Stormtrooper	12.00	30.00
MD25 Obi-Wan Kenobi	12.00	30.00
MD26 Plo Koon	12.00	30.00
MD27 Captain Panaka	12.00	30.00
MD28 Qui-Gon Jinn	12.00	30.00
MD29 Obi-Wan Kenobi	15.00	40.00
MD30 Queen Amidala	50.00	100.00

2013 Star Wars Galactic Files 2 Ripples in the Galaxy

COMPLETE SET (10)	4.00	10.00
COMMON CARD (RG1-RG10)	.75	2.00
*P.P.BLACK/1: UNPRICED DUE TO SCARCITY		
*P.P.CYAN/1: UNPRICED DUE TO SCARCITY		
*P.P.MAGENTA/1: UNPRICED DUE TO SCARCITY		
*P.P.YELLOW/1: UNPRICED DUE TO SCARCITY		
STATED ODDS 1:6		

TRADING CARDS

2013 Star Wars Galactic Files 2 Sketches

NNO Adam Talley/200*
NNO Adrian Rivera
NNO Angelina Benedetti
NNO Beck Seashols
NNO Bill Gallo
NNO Bill Pulkovski
NNO Bob Stevlic
NNO Brett Farr
NNO Brian DeGuire/50*
NNO Bruce Gerlach
NNO Chad McCown
NNO Chris Dee/100*
NNO Chris Henderson/100*
NNO Chris Ramiro
NNO Chris West
NNO Christian Slade
NNO Christopher West/200*
NNO Coleen Doran
NNO Dan Curto
NNO Dan Gorman
NNO Dave Strong
NNO David Day
NNO David Green
NNO David Strong/106*
NNO Denae Frazier
NNO Denise Vasquez
NNO Dennis Budd
NNO Dennis Salvatier
NNO Doran Leia
NNO Elfie Lebouleux
NNO Eric Kanalish
NNO Eric Lehtonen
NNO Erik Hodson
NNO Erik Maell
NNO Gary Kezele/100*
NNO Gavin Hunt
NNO George Deep
NNO Hayden Davis
NNO Ian Yoshio Roberts
NNO Ingrid Hardy/25*
NNO Irma Ahmed (Aimo)/100*
NNO Jason Adams
NNO Jason Davies
NNO Jason Durden/100*
NNO Jason Hughes
NNO Jason Sobol
NNO Jeff Carlisle
NNO Jenn DePaola
NNO Jennifer Mercer
NNO Jeremy Scott
NNO Jerry Fleming
NNO Jessica Hickman
NNO Joe Corroney
NNO Joe Hogan/200*
NNO John Ottinger
NNO John Soukup/100*
NNO JP Wales
NNO Kate Glasheen/100*
NNO Kevin Bloomfield/100*
NNO Kevin Doyle/100*
NNO Kimberly Dunaway
NNO Kris Penix
NNO Lak Lim
NNO Lance Sawyer
NNO Lark Sudol
NNO Lee Bradley/100*
NNO Lee Lightfoot/100*
NNO Lord Mesa/100*
NNO Mark Evans
NNO Mary Zorilita Bellamy/100*
NNO Matt Hebb
NNO Matte Chero/100*
NNO Michael Banks
NNO Michael Duron
NNO Mike Babinski
NNO Mike Hampton
NNO Mike Vasquez
NNO Monte Moore
NNO Pablo Diaz
NNO Patricia Ross/100*
NNO Peter Chan
NNO Robert Hendrickson/50*
NNO Robert Teranishi
NNO Roy Aston Cover/100*
NNO Russ Maheras
NNO Sarah Wilkinson

NNO Scott Houseman/100*
NNO Scott Zambelli/100*
NNO Sean Pence/25*
NNO Sian Mandrake
NNO Stephanie Swanger/100*
NNO Strephon Taylor
NNO Steve Lydic
NNO Steve Oatney
NNO Tim Proctor
NNO Tod Allen Smith/200*
NNO Tomoko Taniguchi
NNO Val Hochberg
NNO Vanessa Banky Farano
NNO Wayne Barnes
NNO Wilson Ramos
NNO Zach Giallongo

2013 Star Wars Galactic Files 2 The Weak Minded

COMPLETE SET (7)	2.50	6.00
COMMON CARD (WM1-WM7)	.60	1.50
*P.P.BLACK/1: UNPRICED DUE TO SCARCITY		
*P.P.CYAN/1: UNPRICED DUE TO SCARCITY		
*P.P.MAGENTA/1: UNPRICED DUE TO SCARCITY		
*P.P.YELLOW/1: UNPRICED DUE TO SCARCITY		
STATED ODDS 1:3		

2017 Star Wars Galactic Files Reborn

KANAN JARRUS

COMPLETE SET (200)	10.00	25.00
UNOPENED BOX (24 PACKS)	80.00	100.00
UNOPENED PACK (6 CARDS)	4.00	5.00
COMMON CARD	.15	.40
*ORANGE: .75X TO 2X BASIC CARDS		
*BLUE: 1.2X TO 3X BASIC CARDS		
*GREEN/199: 4X TO 10X BASIC CARDS		
*PURPLE/99: 8X TO 20X BASIC CARDS		
*GOLD/10: 20X TO 50X BASIC CARDS		
*RED/1: UNPRICED DUE TO SCARCITY		
*P.P.BLACK/1: UNPRICED DUE TO SCARCITY		
*P.P.CYAN/1: UNPRICED DUE TO SCARCITY		
*P.P.MAGENTA/1: UNPRICED DUE TO SCARCITY		
*P.P.YELLOW/1: UNPRICED DUE TO SCARCITY		

2017 Star Wars Galactic Files Reborn Autographs

COMMON AUTO	5.00	12.00
*GOLD/5-25: UNPRICED DUE TO SCARCITY		
*RED/1: UNPRICED DUE TO SCARCITY		
*P.P.BLACK/1: UNPRICED DUE TO SCARCITY		
*P.P.CYAN/1: UNPRICED DUE TO SCARCITY		
*P.P.MAGENTA/1: UNPRICED DUE TO SCARCITY		
*P.P.YELLOW/1: UNPRICED DUE TO SCARCITY		
NNO Adrienne Wilkinson	6.00	15.00
NNO Alan Tudyk	100.00	200.00
NNO Anna Graves	8.00	20.00
NNO Ashley Eckstein	12.00	30.00
NNO Bruce Spence	5.00	12.00
NNO Catherine Taber	15.00	40.00
NNO Dave Barclay	10.00	25.00
NNO David Bowers	6.00	15.00
NNO Dee Bradley	12.00	30.00
NNO Denis Lawson	10.00	25.00
NNO Freddie Prinze		
NNO George Takei	12.00	30.00
NNO Hassani Shapi	8.00	20.00

NNO Jeremy Bulloch	20.00	50.00
NNO Jerome Blake	6.00	15.00
NNO Jesse Jensen	6.00	15.00
NNO Jim Cummings	6.00	15.00
NNO Julian Glover	6.00	15.00
NNO Kath Soucie	8.00	20.00
NNO Keone Young	20.00	50.00
NNO Lewis MacLeod	5.00	12.00
NNO Mary Oyaya	12.00	30.00
NNO Megan Udall	6.00	15.00
NNO Michael Carter	8.00	20.00
NNO Michonne Bourriague	6.00	15.00
NNO Nika Futterman	12.00	30.00
NNO Oliver Ford	8.00	20.00
NNO Oliver Walpole	10.00	25.00
NNO Olivia D'Abo	8.00	20.00
NNO Phil Eason	6.00	15.00
NNO Phil LaMarr	10.00	25.00
NNO Rajia Baroudi	8.00	20.00
NNO Rena Owen	6.00	15.00
NNO Rohan Nichol	10.00	25.00
NNO Sam Witwer	15.00	40.00
NNO Stephen Stanton	25.00	60.00
NNO Tom Kenny	6.00	15.00
NNO Wayne Pygram	8.00	20.00
NNO Zac Jensen	8.00	20.00

2017 Star Wars Galactic Files Reborn Dual Autographs

COMMON CARD	15.00	40.00
STATED PRINT RUN 5-50 SER.#'d SETS		
NNO Blakiston/Rose/50	20.00	50.00
NNO Fisher/Blakiston/5		
NNO McDiarmid/Carson/5		

2017 Star Wars Galactic Files Reborn Famous Quotes

COMPLETE SET (15)	8.00	20.00
COMMON CARD (MQ1-MQ15)	1.00	2.50
*PURPLE/99: X TO X BASIC CARDS		
*GOLD/10: UNPRICED DUE TO SCARCITY		
*RED/1: UNPRICED DUE TO SCARCITY		
*P.P.BLACK/1: UNPRICED DUE TO SCARCITY		
*P.P.CYAN/1: UNPRICED DUE TO SCARCITY		
*P.P.MAGENTA/1: UNPRICED DUE TO SCARCITY		
*P.P.YELLOW/1: UNPRICED DUE TO SCARCITY		

2017 Star Wars Galactic Files Reborn Galactic Moments

VADER STRIKES DOWN KENOBI

COMPLETE SET (9)	8.00	20.00
COMMON CARD (GM1-GM9)	1.25	3.00
*PURPLE/99: X TO X BASIC CARDS		
*GOLD/10: UNPRICED DUE TO SCARCITY		
*RED/1: UNPRICED DUE TO SCARCITY		
*P.P.BLACK/1: UNPRICED DUE TO SCARCITY		
*P.P.CYAN/1: UNPRICED DUE TO SCARCITY		
*P.P.MAGENTA/1: UNPRICED DUE TO SCARCITY		
*P.P.YELLOW/1: UNPRICED DUE TO SCARCITY		

2017 Star Wars Galactic Files Reborn Locations

COMPLETE SET (10)	6.00	15.00
COMMON CARD (L1-L10)	1.00	2.50

*PURPLE/99: X TO X BASIC CARDS
*GOLD/10: UNPRICED DUE TO SCARCITY
*RED/1: UNPRICED DUE TO SCARCITY
*P.P.BLACK/1: UNPRICED DUE TO SCARCITY
*P.P.CYAN/1: UNPRICED DUE TO SCARCITY
*P.P.MAGENTA/1: UNPRICED DUE TO SCARCITY
*P.P.YELLOW/1: UNPRICED DUE TO SCARCITY

2017 Star Wars Galactic Files Reborn Six-Person Autograph

UNPRICED DUE TO SCARCITY

NNO McDiarmid/Wood/Carson/Pygram/Colley/Glover

2017 Star Wars Galactic Files Reborn Sketches

UNPRICED DUE TO SCARCITY

NNO Adam Schickling
NNO Alex Iniguez
NNO Andrew Fry
NNO Andrew Lopez
NNO Anil Sharma
NNO Anthony Skubis
NNO Ben AbuSaada
NNO Brad Hudson
NNO Brandon Blevins
NNO Brendan Purchase
NNO Brendan Shaw
NNO Brett Farr
NNO Brian Jackson
NNO Brian Kong
NNO Bruce Gerlach
NNO Carlos Cabaleiro
NNO Cathy Razim
NNO Chris Clark
NNO Chris Henderson
NNO Chris Meeks
NNO Clinton Yeager
NNO Dan Bergren
NNO Daniel Cooney
NNO Darrin Pepe
NNO Dean Drummond
NNO Don Pedicini Jr.
NNO Eddie Price
NNO Eric Lehtonen
NNO Eric White
NNO Humberto Fuentes
NNO Ibrahim Ozkan
NNO J. P. Perez
NNO Jamie Thomas
NNO Jason Sobol
NNO Jay Manchand
NNO Jeff Meuth
NNO Jennifer Allyn
NNO Jessica Hickman
NNO Jim Mehsling
NNO Jonathan Caustrita
NNO Jordan Maison
NNO Joshua Bommer
NNO Juan Rosales
NNO Kaela Croft
NNO Kallan Archer
NNO Kate Carleton
NNO Kelly Greider
NNO Kevin Liell
NNO Kris Penix
NNO Kyle Babbitt
NNO Kyle Hickman
NNO Lak Lim
NNO Louise Draper
NNO Marcia Dye
NNO Mark Mangum
NNO Marsha Parkins
NNO Matthew Pruno
NNO Matthew Sutton
NNO Matt Maldonado
NNO Matt Steffens
NNO Matt Stewart
NNO Michael Duron
NNO Michelle Rayner
NNO Mike Barnard
NNO Mike James
NNO Norvierto P. Basio
NNO Pablo Diaz
NNO Patrick Giles
NNO Paul Andrews
NNO Phil Hassewe
NNO Roy Cover
NNO Scott Houseman
NNO Shane McCormack
NNO Shaow Siong
NNO Solly Mohamed
NNO Stephanie Rosales
NNO Tiffany Groves
NNO Tim Smith
NNO Tod Smith
NNO Veronica O'Connell

2017 Star Wars Galactic Files Reborn Triple Autographs

UNPRICED DUE TO SCARCITY

NNO Fisher/Barclay/Carter
NNO Revill/Colley/Glover
NNO Prinze Jr./Gray/Eckstein
NNO Grunberg/Rotich/Rose
NNO McDiarmid/Park/Blake
NNO Hamill/Baker/Daniels
NNO Wood/Carson/Blake
NNO Witwer/Goodson/Futterman

2017 Star Wars Galactic Files Reborn Vehicle Medallions

COMMON MEM	5.00	12.00

*SILVER/99: .6X TO 1.5X BASIC MEM
*GOLD/25: 1.2X TO 3X BASIC MEM
*RED/1: UNPRICED DUE TO SCARCITY

2017 Star Wars Galactic Files Reborn Vehicles

COMPLETE SET (20)	10.00	25.00
COMMON CARD (V1-V20)	.75	2.00

*PURPLE/99: 1.5X TO 4X BASIC CARDS
*GOLD/10: UNPRICED DUE TO SCARCITY
*RED/1: UNPRICED DUE TO SCARCITY
*P.P.BLACK/1: UNPRICED DUE TO SCARCITY
*P.P.CYAN/1: UNPRICED DUE TO SCARCITY
*P.P.MAGENTA/1: UNPRICED DUE TO SCARCITY
*P.P.YELLOW/1: UNPRICED DUE TO SCARCITY

2017 Star Wars Galactic Files Reborn Weapons

CHEWBACCA'S BOWCASTER

COMPLETE SET (10)	6.00	15.00
COMMON CARD (W1-W10)	1.00	2.50

*PURPLE/99: 1.2X TO 3X BASIC CARDS
*GOLD/10: UNPRICED DUE TO SCARCITY
*RED/1: UNPRICED DUE TO SCARCITY
*P.P.BLACK/1: UNPRICED DUE TO SCARCITY
*P.P.CYAN/1: UNPRICED DUE TO SCARCITY
*P.P.MAGENTA/1: UNPRICED DUE TO SCARCITY
*P.P.YELLOW/1: UNPRICED DUE TO SCARCITY

2018 Star Wars Galactic Files

COMPLETE SET (200)	12.00	30.00
UNOPENED BOX (24 PACKS)	60.00	90.00
UNOPENED PACK (8 CARDS)	3.00	4.00
COMMON CARD (RO9-ROTS23)	.20	.50

*ORANGE: .6X TO 1.5X BASIC CARDS
*BLUE: .75X TO 2X BASIC CARDS
*GREEN/199: 4X TO 10X BASIC CARDS
*PURPLE/99: 6X TO 15X BASIC CARDS
*GOLD/10: UNPRICED DUE TO SCARCITY
*WHITE/5: UNPRICED DUE TO SCARCITY
*RED/1: UNPRICED DUE TO SCARCITY
*P.P.BLACK/1: UNPRICED DUE TO SCARCITY
*P.P.CYAN/1: UNPRICED DUE TO SCARCITY
*P.P.MAGENTA/1: UNPRICED DUE TO SCARCITY
*P.P.YELLOW/1: UNPRICED DUE TO SCARCITY

2018 Star Wars Galactic Files Autographs

*GOLD/10: UNPRICED DUE TO SCARCITY
*WHITE/5: UNPRICED DUE TO SCARCITY
*RED/1: UNPRICED DUE TO SCARCITY
*P.P.BLACK/1: UNPRICED DUE TO SCARCITY
*P.P.CYAN/1: UNPRICED DUE TO SCARCITY
*P.P.MAGENTA/1: UNPRICED DUE TO SCARCITY
*P.P.YELLOW/1: UNPRICED DUE TO SCARCITY

AAB	Ariyon Bakare	6.00	15.00
AAD	Adam Driver		
AAG	Anna Graves	5.00	12.00
AAP	Alistair Petrie		
AAT	Alan Tudyk		
ABG	Barbara Goodson		
ABP	Bonnie Piesse	5.00	12.00
ACA	Cas Anvar	10.00	25.00
ACF	Carrie Fisher		
ACR	Clive Revill		
ADM	Daniel Mays	6.00	15.00
ADR	Daisy Ridley		
ADT	David Tennant		
ADY	Donnie Yen		
AFJ	Felicity Jones		
AFW	Forest Whitaker		
AGC	Gwendoline Christie		
AGG	Greg Grunberg		
AGT	George Takei		
AHC	Hayden Christensen		
AHF	Harrison Ford		
AHS	Hugh Skinner	8.00	20.00
AIM	Ian McDiarmid		
AJB	John Boyega		
AJL	Jett Lucas	6.00	15.00
AKB	Kenny Baker		
AKF	Kate Fleetwood	5.00	12.00
AKR	Kipsang Rotich	5.00	12.00
ALD	Laura Dern		
AMS	Meredith Salenger	6.00	15.00
ARA	Riz Ahmed		
ARD	Robbie Daymond	5.00	12.00
ARN	Robert Nairne	10.00	25.00
ARP	Ray Park		
ATM	Temuera Morrison		
AVK	Valene Kane	6.00	15.00
AADT	Andy De La Tour	12.00	30.00
AAEK	Ashley Eckstein		
AAND	Anthony Daniels		
ABDW	Billy Dee Williams		
AFPJ	Freddie Prinze Jr.		
AJSC	Jordan Stephens	5.00	12.00
AMSA	Marc Silk	5.00	12.00
ASMG	Sarah Michelle Gellar		

2018 Star Wars Galactic Files Band of Heroes

THE RESISTANCE

COMPLETE SET (7)	5.00	12.00
COMMON CARD (BH1-BH7)	1.25	3.00

*PURPLE/99: X TO 1.5X BASIC CARDS
*GOLD/10: UNPRICED DUE TO SCARCITY
*WHITE/5: UNPRICED DUE TO SCARCITY
*P.P.BLACK/1: UNPRICED DUE TO SCARCITY
*P.P.CYAN/1: UNPRICED DUE TO SCARCITY
*P.P.MAGENTA/1: UNPRICED DUE TO SCARCITY
*P.P.YELLOW/1: UNPRICED DUE TO SCARCITY

2018 Star Wars Galactic Files Dual Autographs

UNPRICED DUE TO SCARCITY

DAAT R.Ahmed/A.Tudyk
DAFF H.Ford/C.Fisher
DAGB T.Gray/S.Blum
DAJW F.Jones/F.Whitaker
DAKL T.Kenny/P.LaMarr

DARB D.Ridley/J.Boyega
DARQ T.Rose/M.Quinn
DATB G.Takei/D.Baker
DATL J.A.Taylor/M.Lanter

2018 Star Wars Galactic Files Galactic Moments

COMPLETE SET (10)	6.00	15.00
COMMON CARD (GM1-GM10)	1.00	2.50

*PURPLE/99: .75X TO 2X BASIC CARDS
*GOLD/10: UNPRICED DUE TO SCARCITY
*WHITE/5: UNPRICED DUE TO SCARCITY
*P.P.BLACK/1: UNPRICED DUE TO SCARCITY
*P.P.CYAN/1: UNPRICED DUE TO SCARCITY
*P.P.MAGENTA/1: UNPRICED DUE TO SCARCITY
*P.P.YELLOW/1: UNPRICED DUE TO SCARCITY

2018 Star Wars Galactic Files Locations

COMPLETE SET (10)	8.00	20.00
COMMON CARD (L1-L10)	1.25	3.00

*PURPLE/99: .75X TO 2X BASIC CARDS
*GOLD/10: UNPRICED DUE TO SCARCITY
*WHITE/5: UNPRICED DUE TO SCARCITY
*P.P.BLACK/1: UNPRICED DUE TO SCARCITY
*P.P.CYAN/1: UNPRICED DUE TO SCARCITY
*P.P.MAGENTA/1: UNPRICED DUE TO SCARCITY
*P.P.YELLOW/1: UNPRICED DUE TO SCARCITY

2018 Star Wars Galactic Files Manufactured Movie Poster Patches

COMMON PATCH	6.00	15.00

*BLUE/99: .5X TO 1.2X BASIC PATCHES
*GREEN/50: .6X TO 1.5X BASIC PATCHES
*PURPLE/25: .75X TO 2X BASIC PATCHES
*GOLD/10: UNPRICED DUE TO SCARCITY
*WHITE/5: UNPRICED DUE TO SCARCITY
*RED/1: UNPRICED DUE TO SCARCITY

MAF Finn		
MAR Rey	10.00	25.00
MAY Yoda		
MAAA Admiral Ackbar		
MAAS Anakin Skywalker	8.00	20.00
MABF Boba Fett	10.00	25.00
MABM Baze Malbus		
MABR Bodhi Rook	15.00	40.00
MACA Cassian Andor		
MACD Count Dooku		
MACI Chirrut Imwe	10.00	25.00
MACP Captain Phasma		
MADK Director Krennic	8.00	20.00
MADM Darth Maul	10.00	25.00
MADS Darth Sidious		
MADV Darth Vader		
MAFJ Finn		
MAGH General Hux	6.00	15.00
MAHS Han Solo	12.00	30.00
MAJE Jyn Erso		
MAJF Jango Fett	6.00	15.00
MAKR Kylo Ren		
MALC Lando Calrissian	8.00	20.00
MALO Princess Leia Organa	10.00	25.00
MALS Luke Skywalker	10.00	25.00
MAPA Queen Amidala	12.00	30.00
MAPD Poe Dameron		
MARD R2-D2	8.00	20.00
MARJ Rey	15.00	40.00
MASG Saw Gerrera	15.00	40.00
MATE The Emperor	15.00	40.00
MAASM Anakin Skywalker	8.00	20.00
MAASR Anakin Skywalker	8.00	20.00
MACPO C-3PO	10.00	25.00
MADVS Darth Vader		
MAGGS General Grievous	6.00	15.00
MAGMT Grand Moff Tarkin	8.00	20.00
MAHSE Han Solo	12.00	30.00
MAHSF Han Solo	12.00	30.00
MAHSH Han Solo	12.00	30.00
MAJTH Jabba The Hutt	6.00	15.00
MAKRF Kylo Ren		
MALOF General Leia Organa	12.00	30.00
MALOJ Princess Leia Organa	10.00	25.00
MALSH Luke Skywalker	10.00	25.00
MALSJ Luke Skywalker	10.00	25.00
MALSR Luke Skywalker	10.00	25.00
MAOKC Obi-Wan Kenobi	6.00	15.00
MAOKH Obi-Wan Kenobi	6.00	15.00
MAOKS Obi-Wan Kenobi	12.00	30.00
MAOWK Obi-Wan Kenobi	6.00	15.00
MAPAC Padme Amidala	12.00	30.00
MAPDJ Poe Dameron		
MAPLO Princess Leia Organa	15.00	40.00
MAQGJ Qui-Gon Jinn	15.00	40.00
MASLS Supreme Leader Snoke		

2018 Star Wars Galactic Files Memorable Quotes

COMPLETE SET (10)	6.00	15.00
COMMON CARD (MQ1-MQ10)	1.00	2.50

*PURPLE/99: .75X TO 2X BASIC CARDS
*GOLD/10: UNPRICED DUE TO SCARCITY
*WHITE/5: UNPRICED DUE TO SCARCITY
*P.P.BLACK/1: UNPRICED DUE TO SCARCITY
*P.P.CYAN/1: UNPRICED DUE TO SCARCITY
*P.P.MAGENTA/1: UNPRICED DUE TO SCARCITY
*P.P.YELLOW/1: UNPRICED DUE TO SCARCITY

2018 Star Wars Galactic Files Sinister Syndicates

COMPLETE SET (15)	10.00	25.00
COMMON CARD (SS1-SS15)	1.25	3.00

*PURPLE/99: .75X TO 2X BASIC CARDS
*GOLD/10: UNPRICED DUE TO SCARCITY
*WHITE/5: UNPRICED DUE TO SCARCITY
*P.P.BLACK/1: UNPRICED DUE TO SCARCITY
*P.P.CYAN/1: UNPRICED DUE TO SCARCITY
*P.P.MAGENTA/1: UNPRICED DUE TO SCARCITY
*P.P.YELLOW/1: UNPRICED DUE TO SCARCITY

2018 Star Wars Galactic Files Six-Person Autograph

UNPRICED DUE TO SCARCITY

NNO Jones/Whitaker/Ahmed/Yen/Tudyk/O'Reilly

2018 Star Wars Galactic Files Sketches

UNPRICED DUE TO SCARCITY

NNO Aaron Laurich
NNO Adam Harris
NNO Adam Worton
NNO Adrian Ropp
NNO Albert Nguyen
NNO Aleksandar Gigov
NNO Alex Mines
NNO Allen Grimes
NNO Allysa Pirone
NNO Andrew Arensberg
NNO Andrew Fry
NNO Andrew Lopez
NNO Andy Bohn
NNO Angelina Benedetti
NNO Anil Sharma
NNO Ashleigh Popplewell
NNO Barry Renshaw
NNO Basak Cetinkaya
NNO Ben AbuSaada
NNO Bill Pulkovski
NNO Bobby Blakey
NNO Brad Hudson
NNO Brandon Blevins
NNO Brendan Purchase
NNO Brendan Shaw
NNO Brent Ragland
NNO Brent Scotchmer
NNO Brett Farr
NNO Bruce Gerlach
NNO Bryce King II
NNO Caleb King
NNO Carlos Cabaleiro
NNO Carolyn Craggs
NNO Chad LaForce
NNO Chad Scheres
NNO Chris Thorne
NNO Chris Willdig
NNO Christian Parker
NNO Clinton Yeager
NNO Colin Arthurs
NNO Corey Galal
NNO Dan Bergren
NNO Dan Curto
NNO Dan Gorman
NNO Dan Tearle
NNO Darren James
NNO Darrin Pepe
NNO Dave Fowler
NNO Dave Holtz
NNO Dave Strong
NNO David Angelo Roman
NNO Dean Drummond
NNO Desiree Portner
NNO Dylan Riley
NNO Edward Santia
NNO Elfie Lebouleux
NNO Eric Lehtonen
NNO Eric White
NNO Fredd Gorham
NNO Garrett Dix
NNO Gavin Williams
NNO Gerard Garcia Jr.
NNO Glenn Porzig
NNO Glenn Savage
NNO Gorkem Demir
NNO Greg Mitchell
NNO Huy Truong
NNO Ian MacDougal
NNO Ibrahim Ozkan
NNO Ingrid Hardy
NNO Jaime Lopez
NNO James Henry Smith
NNO Jamie Cosley
NNO Jamie Richards
NNO Jason Adams
NNO Jason Brower
NNO Jason Miller
NNO Jason Queen
NNO Jason Sobol
NNO Jay Manchand
NNO Jeff Abar
NNO Jessica Hickman
NNO Jim Mehsling
NNO Jim O'Riley
NNO John Bruce
NNO John DiBiase
NNO John Pleak
NNO John Still
NNO Jon McKenzie
NNO Jordan Maison
NNO Jose Ruiz
NNO Jose Ventura
NNO Joshua Bommer

NNO Jude Gallagher
NNO Kaela Croft
NNO Kallan Archer
NNO Kevin Cleveland
NNO Kevin Graham
NNO Kevin Liell
NNO Kevin West
NNO Kurt Ruskin
NNO Laura Atkinson
NNO Laura Martin
NNO Lee Hunt
NNO Lee Lightfoot
NNO Logan Monette
NNO Louise Draper
NNO Madison Emerick
NNO Maggie Ransom
NNO Marcia Dye
NNO Mark Finneral
NNO Mark Mangum
NNO Mark Stroud
NNO Marlo Agunos
NNO Marsha Parkins
NNO Matt Kilness
NNO Matt Langford
NNO Matt Maldonado
NNO Matt Stewart
NNO Matthew Hirons
NNO Matthew Lopez
NNO Michael Mastermaker
NNO Michael Mettlen
NNO Michelle Rayner
NNO Mike Barnard
NNO Mike Stephens
NNO Mohammad Jilani
NNO Nathan Kennett
NNO Neil Camera
NNO Nicholas Baltra
NNO Nicholas Dertinger
NNO Nick Allsopp
NNO Nick Justus
NNO Nolan Dykstra
NNO Omar Salinas
NNO Pablo Diaz
NNO Patricio Carrasco
NNO Phil Hassewer
NNO Phillip Trujillo
NNO Rebecca Sharp
NNO Rees Finlay
NNO Rey Paez
NNO Rich Henneman
NNO Rich Molinelli
NNO Richard Serrao
NNO Rob Teranishi
NNO Robert Hendrickson
NNO Robert Stewart IV
NNO Rodney Roberts
NNO Ronnie Crowther
NNO Ryan Crosby
NNO Ryan Finley
NNO Ryan Moffett
NNO Ryan Olsen
NNO Ryan Santos
NNO Sammy Gomez
NNO Sebastian Cortez
NNO Shane Molina
NNO Shaow Siong
NNO Sheikh Islam
NNO Solly Mohamed
NNO Steve Alce
NNO Steve Fuchs
NNO Ted Dastick Jr.
NNO Thomas Amici
NNO Tiffany Groves
NNO Tim Dowler
NNO Tim Proctor
NNO Tim Smith
NNO Tina Berardi
NNO Todd Rayner
NNO Travis Kinnison
NNO Trent Westbrook
NNO Victor Moreno
NNO Vincenzo D'Ippolito

NNO Ward Silverman
NNO Wayne Tully

2018 Star Wars Galactic Files Source Material Fabric Swatches

COMMON MEM	20.00	50.00
*PURPLE/25: UNPRICED DUE TO SCARCITY		
*GOLD/10: UNPRICED DUE TO SCARCITY		
*WHITE/5: UNPRICED DUE TO SCARCITY		
*RED/1: UNPRICED DUE TO SCARCITY		
CRGE Galen Erso's Jacket	25.00	60.00
CRJE Jyn Erso's Poncho	50.00	100.00
CRPD Poe Dameron's Shirt	25.00	60.00
CRPG Praetorian Guard's Uniform	30.00	75.00
CRRH Rey's Head Wrap	60.00	120.00
CRRJ Rey's Jacket	100.00	200.00

2018 Star Wars Galactic Files Triple Autographs

STATED PRINT RUN 5 SER.#'d SETS
UNPRICED DUE TO SCARCITY

NNO Williams/Quinn/Mayhew
NNO Mikkelsen/McGlynn/Baker

2018 Star Wars Galactic Files Vehicles

COMPLETE SET (10)	6.00	15.00
COMMON CARD (V1-V10)	1.00	2.50
*NO FOIL: .5X TO 1.2X BASIC CARDS		
*PURPLE/99: .75X TO 2X BASIC CARDS		
*GOLD/10: UNPRICED DUE TO SCARCITY		
*WHITE/5: UNPRICED DUE TO SCARCITY		
*P.P.BLACK/1: UNPRICED DUE TO SCARCITY		
*P.P.CYAN/1: UNPRICED DUE TO SCARCITY		
*P.P.MAGENTA/1: UNPRICED DUE TO SCARCITY		
*P.P.YELLOW/1: UNPRICED DUE TO SCARCITY		

2018 Star Wars Galactic Files Weapons

CHIRRUT ÎMWE'S STAFF

COMPLETE SET (10)	6.00	15.00
COMMON CARD (W1-W10)	1.00	2.50
*PURPLE/99: .75X TO 2X BASIC CARDS		
*GOLD/10: UNPRICED DUE TO SCARCITY		
*WHITE/5: UNPRICED DUE TO SCARCITY		
*P.P.BLACK/1: UNPRICED DUE TO SCARCITY		
*P.P.CYAN/1: UNPRICED DUE TO SCARCITY		
*P.P.MAGENTA/1: UNPRICED DUE TO SCARCITY		
*P.P.YELLOW/1: UNPRICED DUE TO SCARCITY		

2018-19 Star Wars Galactic Moments Countdown to Episode 9

DARTH VADER

STAR WARS: A NEW HOPE

COMMON CARD	5.00	12.00

1993-95 Star Wars Galaxy

COMPLETE SET (365)	15.00	40.00
COMP.SER 1 SET (140)	6.00	15.00
COMP.SER 2 SET (135)	6.00	15.00
COMP.SER 3 SET (90)	6.00	15.00
UNOPENED SER.1 BOX (36 PACKS)	30.00	40.00
UNOPENED SER.1 PACK (8 CARDS)	1.00	1.25
UNOPENED SER.2 BOX (36 PACKS)	20.00	30.00
UNOPENED SER.2 PACK (8 CARDS)	.75	1.00
UNOPENED SER.3 BOX (36 PACKS)	20.00	30.00
UNOPENED SER.3 PACK (7 CARDS)	.75	1.00
COMMON CARD (1-365)	.15	.40
*MIL.FALCON FOIL: .8X TO 2X BASIC CARDS		
*FIRST DAY: 1X TO 2.5X BASIC CARDS		
DARTH VADER FOIL UNNUMBERED	4.00	10.00

1993-95 Star Wars Galaxy Clearzone

COMPLETE SET (6)	15.00	40.00
COMMON CARD (E1-E6)	3.00	8.00

1993-95 Star Wars Galaxy Etched Foil

COMPLETE SET (18)	60.00	120.00
COMMON CARD (1-18)	3.00	8.00

1993-95 Star Wars Galaxy LucasArts

COMPLETE SET (12)	6.00	15.00
COMMON CARD (L1-L12)	.60	1.50

1993-95 Star Wars Galaxy Promos

0 Ralph McQuarrie (Darth Vader)	2.50	6.00
0 Drew Sturzan artwork (SW Galaxy Magazine)	1.25	3.00
0 Ken Steacy Art		
P1 Jae Lee/Rancor Monster(dealer cello pack)	1.25	4.00
P1 Jae Lee/Rancor Monster/AT-AT		
P1 Rancor Card		
AT-AT/Yoda 5X7		
P2 Chris Sprouse/Luke building lightsaber (NSU)	2.00	5.00
P2 Snowtrooper (Convention exclusive)	1.50	4.00
P3 Yoda Shrine SP	250.00	400.00
P3 Darth Vader on Hoth (NSU)	1.25	3.00
P4 Dave Gibbons/C-3PO and Jawas (SW Galaxy 1 Tin Set)		
P4 Luke on Dagobah/Art Suydam	.60	1.50
P5 Joe Phillips/Han and Chewbacca (Cards Illustrated)	2.00	5.00
P5 AT-AT	.75	2.00
P6 Tom Taggart/Boba Fett (Hero)	2.50	6.00
P6 Luke with lightsaber (SW Galaxy Magazine)		
P7 Leia with Jacen and Jania (Wizard Magazine)	2.00	5.00
P8 Boba Fett and Darth Vader (Cards Illustrated)	4.00	10.00
140 Look for Series Two (Bend Ems Toys)		
DH2 Cam Kennedy artwork/BobaFett	2.00	5.00
DH3 Cam Kennedy artwork/Millennium Falcon	2.00	5.00
NNO Jim Starlin/Stormtrooper and Ewoks (Triton #3)	1.50	4.00
NNO Tim Truman/Tuskan Raiders	3.00	8.00
NNO Boba Fett	3.00	8.00
NNO AT-AT 5 x 7 (Previews)		
NNO Boba Fett/Dengar (Classic Star Wars)	2.00	5.00
NNO Jabba the Hutt (NSU/Starlog/Wizard)	1.25	3.00
NNO Princess Leia (NSU)	1.50	4.00
NNO Sandtrooper (Wizard Magazine)	1.50	4.00
NNO Truce at Bakura (Bantam exclusive)	4.00	10.00
NNO Princess Leia/Sandtrooper 2-Card Panel (Advance exclusive)		
NNO Jabba the Hutt, Obi-Wan/Darth Vader 5X7 (Previews exclusive)		
DH1A Cam Kennedy artwork Battling Robots (Dark Lords of the Sith comic)	2.00	5.00
Series at line 8		
DH1B Cam Kennedy artwork Battling Robots (Dark Lords of the Sith comic)	2.00	5.00
Series at line 9		
SWB1 Grand Moff Tarkin (album exclusive)	4.00	10.00

2016 Star Wars Galaxy Bonus Abrams

COMPLETE SET (4)
COMMON CARD (1-4)

1 Display Box, Series 1, 1993
Art By Ken Steacy
2 A Tribute to George Lucas, Card No. 2, Series 1, 1993
Art By Drew Struzan
3 New Visions, Card No. 110, Series 1, 1993
Art By Mike Mignola
4 Levitating Yoda, Original Art for Topps Galaxy Series 2 Promo Card, 1994
Art By John Rheume

2021 Star Wars Galaxy Chrome

COMPLETE SET (100)	20.00	50.00
COMMON CARD (1-100)	.40	1.00
*REF: .75X TO 2X BASIC CARDS		
*ATOMIC/150: 3X TO 8X BASIC CARDS		

*WAVE/99: 4X TO 10X BASIC CARDS
*PRISM/75: 5X TO 12X BASIC CARDS
*MOJO/50: 6X TO 15X BASIC CARDS
*PURPLE/25: 8X TO 20X BASIC CARDS
*X-FRAC./10: UNPRICED DUE TO SCARCITY
*RED/5: UNPRICED DUE TO SCARCITY
*SUPER/1: UNPRICED DUE TO SCARCITY

2021 Star Wars Galaxy Chrome Autographs

CHANCELLOR VALORUM
AUTHENTIC AUTOGRAPH

*RED/5: UNPRICED DUE TO SCARCITY
*SUPER/1: UNPRICED DUE TO SCARCITY
STATED ODDS 1:35

GAAB Anna Brewster
GAAD Adam Driver
GAAG Anna Graves   5.00   12.00
GAAS Andy Serkis
GAAT Alan Tudyk
GABB Blair Bess
GABL Billie Lourd
GACE Chris Edgerly
GACF Carrie Fisher
GACW Carl Weathers
GADC Dermot Crowley
GADR Daisy Ridley
GADT Dee Tails
GADY Donnie Yen
GAEK Erin Kellyman
GAES Emily Swallow
GAEW Ewan McGregor
GAFJ Felicity Jones
GAFW Forest Whitaker
GAGE Giancarlo Esposito
GAGG Greg Grunberg
GAHC Hayden Christensen
GAHD Harley Durst
GAHF Harrison Ford
GAIK Ian Kenny
GAIR Ian Ruskin
GAJH Jessica Henwick
GAJK Jaime King
GAJR John Ratzenberger
GAJS Jason Spisak
GAJT John Tui
GAKB Kenny Baker
GALD Laura Dern
GAMM Mads Mikkelsen
GANA Naomi Ackie
GANF Nika Futterman
GANN Nick Nolte,
GAOA Omid Abtahi
GAPM Peter Mayhew
GAPP Pedro Pascal
GARA Riz Ahmed
GARP Ray Park
GATD Tim Dry
GATM Temuera Morrison
GATW Taika Waititi
GAVK Valene Kane
GAWD Warwick Davis
GAWH Werner Herzog
GAAND Annabelle Davis

GAASG Arti Shah
GABDW Billy Dee Williams
GACDW Corey Dee Williams
GADMB Dominic Monaghan
GAGCP Gwendoline Christie
GAHCT Hermione Corfield
GAKMT Kelly Marie Tran
GAPAR Philip Anthony-Rodriguez
GARAD Robin Atkin Downes
GASLJ Samuel L. Jackson

2021 Star Wars Galaxy Chrome Dual Autographs

*RED/5: UNPRICED DUE TO SCARCITY
*SUPER/1: UNPRICED DUE TO SCARCITY
STATED PRINT RUN SER.#'d SETS
UNPRICED DUE TO SCARCITY

DACB J.Boyega/G.Christie
DACC H.Corfield/C.Clarke
DAEB P.Bettany/A.Ehrenreich
DAFB B.Blessed/O.Ford Davies
DAFM P.Mayhew/H.Ford
DAJM M.Mikkelsen/F.Jones
DAKE Ashley Eckstein/Jaime King
DAMB E.McGregor/A.Best
DAML T.Morrison/D.Logan
DANE G.Esposito/W.Herzog
DARS J.Suotamo/D.Ridley
DASL C.Louise/S.Smart
DATE G.Takei/A.Eckstein

2021 Star Wars Galaxy Chrome Mandalorian Visions

COMPLETE SET (10)   20.00   50.00
COMMON CARD (MN1-MN10)   3.00   8.00
*GREEN/99: .6X TO 1.5X BASIC CARDS
*PURPLE/50: .75X TO 2X BASIC CARDS
*ORANGE/25: 2X TO 5X BASIC CARDS
*RED/5: UNPRICED DUE TO SCARCITY
*SUPER/1: UNPRICED DUE TO SCARCITY
STATED ODDS 1:9

2021 Star Wars Galaxy Chrome Star Wars Global Posters

COMPLETE SET (20)   15.00   40.00
COMMON CARD (GP1-GP20)   2.00   5.00
*GREEN/99: .5X TO 1.2X BASIC CARDS
*PURPLE/50: .6X TO 1.5X BASIC CARDS
*ORANGE/25: .75X TO 2X BASIC CARDS
*RED/5: UNPRICED DUE TO SCARCITY
*SUPER/1: UNPRICED DUE TO SCARCITY
STATED ODDS 1:9

2021 Star Wars Galaxy Chrome Triple Autographs

COMPLETE SET (10)
*SUPER/1: UNPRICED DUE TO SCARCITY
STATED PRINT RUN SER.#'d SETS
UNPRICED DUE TO SCARCITY

TADSC Driver/Serkis/Christie
TAEKD Ehrenreich/Davis/Kellyman
TAFET Bulloch/Morrison/Logan
TAFWM Ford/Mayhew/Williams
TAHFP Hale/Paisley Day/Francis

TALHK Lawson/Klaff/Hagon
TAMAC Rose/Blakiston/Crowley
TARBT Ridley/Boyega/Tran
TAWRQ Williamson/Quinn/Roy
TAYKK Kasey/Kellington/Yen

2021 Star Wars Galaxy Chrome Vintage Star Wars Posters

COMPLETE SET (15)   15.00   40.00
COMMON CARD (V1-V15)   2.50   6.00
*GREEN/99: .5X TO 1.2X BASIC CARDS
*PURPLE/50: .6X TO 1.5X BASIC CARDS
*ORANGE/25: .75X TO 2X BASIC CARDS
*RED/5: UNPRICED DUE TO SCARCITY
*SUPER/1: UNPRICED DUE TO SCARCITY
STATED ODDS 1:9

1999 Star Wars Galaxy Collector

COMPLETE SET W/O SP (9)   6.00   15.00
COMMON CARD (SW0-SW9)   1.25   3.00
SW0 Episode I   30.00   75.00
(Non-Sport Update Gummie Award Exclusive)

1996 Star Wars Galaxy Magazine Cover Gallery

COMPLETE SET (4)   3.00   8.00
COMMON CARD (C1-C4)   1.00   2.50

1995 Star Wars Galaxy Magazine Finest Promos

COMPLETE SET (4)   3.00   8.00
COMMON CARD (SWGM1-SWGM4)   1.50   4.00

2009 Star Wars Galaxy Series 4

COMPLETE SET (120)   5.00   12.00
UNOPENED BOX (24 PACKS)   70.00   80.00
UNOPENED PACK (7 CARDS)   3.00   4.00
UNOPENED BOX (24 PACKS)   100.00   120.00
UNOPENED PACK (7 CARDS)   5.00   6.00
COMMON CARD (1-120)   .15   .40
*P.P.BLACK/1: UNPRICED DUE TO SCARCITY
*P.P.CYAN/1: UNPRICED DUE TO SCARCITY
*P.P.MAGENTA/1: UNPRICED DUE TO SCARCITY
*P.P.YELLOW/1: UNPRICED DUE TO SCARCITY

2009 Star Wars Galaxy Series 4 Silver Foil

COMPLETE SET (15)   5.00   12.00
COMMON CARD (1-15)   .60   1.50
*BRONZE: 2X TO 5X BASIC CARDS
*GOLD: .8X TO 2X BASIC CARDS
*SILVER REF./1: UNPRICED DUE TO SCARCITY
STATED ODDS 1:3

2009 Star Wars Galaxy Series 4 Die-Cut Sketches

STATED ODDS 1:191 HOBBY
UNPRICED DUE TO SCARCITY

NNO Amy Vutiya/100*
NNO Andy Heng/100*
NNO Art Denka
NNO Artbot 138/100*
NNO Ayleen Gaspar/100*
NNO Brian Kong
NNO Brian Slivka
NNO Bryce Ward/100*
NNO Chanmen/100*
NNO Daniel Cantrell
NNO Datadub

NNO Fetts/75*
NNO Gargamel Katope/100*
NNO George Gaspar/100*
NNO Ghanmenu
NNO Gio Chiappetta/100*
NNO Goccodo
NNO Hans Yim/100*
NNO iguodo
NNO Jaguar Nono/100*
NNO Jason Atomic/100*
NNO Jeff McMillan
NNO Jeremy Madl/100*
NNO Jesse Moore/50*
NNO JK5
NNO Justin Rudy
NNO Kemilyn
NNO Kerry Lee/100*
NNO L'amour Supreme/100*
NNO Luc Hudson/100*
NNO Mad Barbarian
NNO Matt Doughty/50*
NNO MCA/100*
NNO McEavill
NNO Michael Leavitt/100*
NNO Mishka NYC/100*
NNO Neil Winn/100*
NNO Natalie To/100*
NNO Nick the Ring/172*
NNO Nix Toxic/100*
NNO Patrick Francisco/67*
NNO Phetus/100*
NNO Rob Ames/100*
NNO Russell Walks/10*
NNO RYCA/100*
NNO Sara! Antoinette Martin/100*
NNO Simeon Lipman/100*
NNO Sket One/100*
NNO $uckadelic/100*
NNO Tulip
NNO Urban Medium/100*

2009 Star Wars Galaxy Series 4 Etched Foil

COMPLETE SET (6)	6.00	12.00
COMMON CARD (1-6)	1.50	4.00
STATED ODDS 1:6		

2009 Star Wars Galaxy Series 4 Galaxy Evolutions

COMPLETE SET (6)	30.00	80.00
COMMON CARD (1-6)	8.00	20.00
STATED ODDS 1:24 RETAIL		

2009 Star Wars Galaxy Series 4 Lost Galaxy

COMPLETE SET (5)	12.00	25.00
COMMON CARD (1-5)	3.00	8.00
STATED ODDS 1:24		
YODA'S WORLD/999 STATED ODDS 1:277		
JOHN RHEAUME AUTO STATED ODDS 1:2,789		
NNO Yoda's World/999	15.00	30.00
NNOAU Yoda's World/Rheaume AU		

2009 Star Wars Galaxy Series 4 Sketches

STATED ODDS 1:24 HOBBY
UNPRICED DUE TO SCARCITY

NNO Allison Sohn
NNO Amy Pronovost
NNO Art Grafunkel
NNO Brent Engstrom
NNO Brent Schoonover
NNO Brian Kong
NNO Brian Miller
NNO Brian Rood
NNO Bruce Gerlach
NNO Bryan Morton
NNO Carolyn Edwards
NNO Cat Staggs
NNO Chris Henderson
NNO Cynthia Cummens
NNO Dan Cooney
NNO Daniel Bergren
NNO David Rabbitte
NNO Denise Vasquez
NNO Dennis Budd
NNO Don Pedicini Jr.
NNO Doug Cowan
NNO Edward Pun
NNO Erik Maell

NNO Gabe Hernandez
NNO Grant Gould
NNO Howard Shum
NNO Ingrid Hardy
NNO Irma Aimo Ahmed
NNO Jake Minor
NNO Jamie Snell
NNO Jason Davies
NNO Jason Hughes
NNO Jason Keith Phillips
NNO Jason Sobol
NNO Javier Guzman
NNO Jeff Carlisle
NNO Jerry Vanderstelt
NNO Jessica Hickman
NNO Jim Kyle
NNO Joanne Ellen Mutch
NNO Joe Corroney
NNO Joel Carroll
NNO John McCrea
NNO John Soukup
NNO John Watkins-Chow
NNO Jon Morris
NNO Jon Ocampo
NNO Joseph Booth
NNO Josh Fargher
NNO Josh Howard
NNO Justin Chung
NNO Justin Jusscope Orr
NNO Karen Krajenbrink
NNO Kate Glasheen
NNO Kate Red Bradley
NNO Katie Cook
NNO Katie McDee
NNO Ken Branch
NNO Kevin Caron
NNO Kevin Doyle
NNO Kevin Graham
NNO Kyle Babbitt
NNO Lance Sawyer
NNO Leah Mangue
NNO Lee Kohse
NNO Len Bellinger
NNO Lord Mesa
NNO Mark McHaley
NNO Mark Walters
NNO Matt Minor
NNO Micheal Locoduck Duron
NNO Monte Moore
NNO Nate Lovett
NNO Nathan E. Hamill
NNO Nicole Falk
NNO Nik Neocleous
NNO Nina Edlund
NNO Noah Albrecht
NNO Otto Dieffenbach
NNO Patrick Hamill
NNO Patrick Richardson
NNO Paul Allan Ballard
NNO Paul Gutierrez
NNO Pete Pachoumis
NNO Randy Martinez
NNO Randy Siplon
NNO Rich Molinelli
NNO Rich Woodall
NNO Russell Walks
NNO Sarah Wilkinson
NNO Scott Zirkel
NNO Sean Pence
NNO Spencer Brinkerhoff
NNO Stephanie Yue
NNO Ted Dastick Jr.
NNO Tod Allen Smith
NNO Tom Hodges
NNO Zack Giallongo

2009 Star Wars Galaxy Series 4 Sketches Retail Red

NNO Brent Engstrom
NNO Brent Schoonover
NNO Brian Kong
NNO Brian Miller
NNO Brian Rood

NNO Bryan Morton
NNO Cat Staggs
NNO Chris Henderson
NNO Dan Cooney
NNO David Rabbitte
NNO Don Pedicini Jr.
NNO Gabe Hernandez
NNO Grant Gould
NNO Howard Shum
NNO Ingrid Hardy
NNO Jamie Snell
NNO Jason Davies
NNO Jason Keith Phillips
NNO Jason Sobol
NNO Javier Guzman
NNO Jessica Hickman
NNO Jim Kyle
NNO John McCrea
NNO Jon Morris
NNO Karen Krajenbrink
NNO Kate Glasheen
NNO Katie McDee
NNO Kevin Doyle
NNO Kevin Graham
NNO Leah Mangue
NNO Lee Kohse
NNO Matt Minor
NNO Nicole Falk
NNO Paul Allan Ballard
NNO Paul Gutierrez
NNO Randy Martinez
NNO Rich Molinelli
NNO Rich Woodall
NNO Russell Walks
NNO Sarah Wilkinson
NNO Sean Pence
NNO Ted Dastick Jr.
NNO Tom Hodges

2009 Star Wars Galaxy Series 4 Promos

COMPLETE SET (4)	8.00	20.00
COMMON CARD (P1A-P3)	.75	2.00
P1A Ventress	1.50	4.00
Dooku GEN		
P1B Starcruiser crash/ (Fan Club Excl.)	6.00	15.00
P3 Group shot WW	2.00	5.00

2010 Star Wars Galaxy Series 5

COMPLETE SET (120)	8.00	20.00
COMMON CARD (1-120)	.15	.40
*P.P.BLACK/1: UNPRICED DUE TO SCARCITY		
*P.P.CYAN/1: UNPRICED DUE TO SCARCITY		
*P.P.MAGENTA/1: UNPRICED DUE TO SCARCITY		
*P.P.YELLOW/1: UNPRICED DUE TO SCARCITY		

2010 Star Wars Galaxy Series 5 Etched Foil

COMPLETE SET (6)	4.00	10.00
COMMON CARD (1-6)	1.25	3.00
STATED ODDS 1:6 H/R		

2010 Star Wars Galaxy Series 5 Silver Foil

COMPLETE SET (15)	6.00	15.00
COMMON CARD (1-15)	.60	1.50

*BRONZE FOIL: 1.2X TO 3X BASIC CARDS
*GOLD FOIL/770: 6X TO 15X BASIC CARDS
*SILVER REFR./1: UNPRICED DUE TO SCARCITY
STATED ODDS 1:3 H/R

2010 Star Wars Galaxy Series 5 Artist Sketches

STATED ODDS 1:24 HOBBY, 1:72 RETAIL
UNPRICED DUE TO SCARCITY

NNO Adrien Rivera
NNO Alex Buechel
NNO Amy Pronovost
NNO Art Grafunkel
NNO Ben Curtis Jones
NNO Bill Pulkovski
NNO Braden D. Lamb
NNO Brandon Kenney
NNO Brent Engstrom
NNO Brian Kong
NNO Brian Miller
NNO Brian Rood
NNO Bruce Gerlach
NNO Bryan Morton
NNO Cat Staggs
NNO Chris Henderson
NNO Chris Uminga
NNO Chrissie Zullo
NNO Craig Rousseau
NNO Cynthia Narcisi
NNO Dan Bergren
NNO Dan Masso
NNO Darla Ecklund
NNO Darrin Radimaker
NNO Dave Tata
NNO David Day
NNO David Rabbitte
NNO Denise Vasquez
NNO Dennis Budd
NNO Dustin Foust
NNO Erik Maell
NNO Frank Villarreal
NNO Gabe Farber
NNO Grant Gould
NNO Hayden Davis
NNO Howard Shum
NNO Ingrid Hardy
NNO Irma Ahmed
NNO Jake Minor
NNO James Bukauskas
NNO Jamie Snell
NNO Jason Davies
NNO Jason Keith Phillips
NNO Jason Sobol
NNO Jay Fosgitt
NNO Jennifer Mercer
NNO Jeremy Treece
NNO Jerry Vanderstelt
NNO Jessica Hickman
NNO Jim Kyle
NNO Joe Corroney
NNO John Beatty
NNO John Haun
NNO John P. Wales
NNO John Soukup
NNO John Watkins-Chow
NNO Jon Morris
NNO Justin Chung
NNO Karen Krajenbrink
NNO Kate Bradley
NNO Kate Glasheen
NNO Katie Cook
NNO Kevin Doyle
NNO Kevin Graham
NNO Kevin Liell
NNO Kyle Babbitt
NNO Lance Sawyer
NNO Lawrence Snelly
NNO Leah Mangue
NNO Lee Kohse
NNO Len Bellinger
NNO Lord Mesa
NNO Mark McHaley
NNO Mark Walters
NNO Martheus Wade

NNO Matt Busch
NNO Matt Minor
NNO Matte Chero
NNO Michael Duron
NNO Monte Moore
NNO Nicole Falk
NNO Nina Edlund
NNO Nolan Woodard
NNO Otto Dieffenbach
NNO Patrick Schoenmaker
NNO Paul Allan Ballard
NNO Randy Martinez
NNO Randy Siplon
NNO Rhiannon Owens
NNO Rich Molinelli
NNO Rich Woodall
NNO Robert Hendrickson
NNO Robert Teranishi
NNO Russ Walks
NNO Ryan Hungerford
NNO Sarah Wilkinson
NNO Scott DM Simmons
NNO Scott Rorie
NNO Sean Pence
NNO Shea Standefer
NNO Shelli Paroline
NNO Soni Alcorn-Hender
NNO Spencer Brinkerhoff III
NNO Stephanie Yue
NNO Steve Oatney
NNO Steve Stanley
NNO Steven Miller
NNO Ted Dastick Jr.
NNO Tim Proctor
NNO Tod Allen Smith
NNO Tom Hodges
NNO Wilson Ramos Jr.
NNO Zack Giallongo

2010 Star Wars Galaxy Series 5 Autographs

COMMON AUTO	75.00	150.00

STATED ODDS 1:274 HOBBY

DP	David Prowse	100.00	200.00
JJ	James Earl Jones	150.00	300.00
MH	Mark Hamill	600.00	1200.00
PM	Peter Mayhew	100.00	200.00

2010 Star Wars Galaxy Series 5 Die-Cut Sketches

STATED ODDS 1:192 HOBBY
UNPRICED DUE TO SCARCITY

NNO Adriean Koleric
NNO Angie Dutchess
NNO Anthony Ausgang
NNO Appro Nation
NNO Auxpeer
NNO Bill McMullen
NNO Billy Roids
NNO Brian Flynn
NNO Buff Monster
NNO Burt Banger
NNO Colin Walton
NNO Collin David
NNO Dangeruss
NNO Devil Robots
NNO Gothic Hangman
NNO Hariken
NNO Hiroshi Namiki
NNO Ilanena
NNO Jared Deal
NNO Jason Adams
NNO Jason Atomic
NNO Jesse Hernandez
NNO Kano
NNO King
NNO Kosbe
NNO Len Bellinger
NNO Michael Leavitt
NNO Mike Kelly
NNO Mio Murakami
NNO Mr. Den
NNO Plasticgod
NNO Rolo Ledesma
NNO Russell Walks

NNO Skull Toys
NNO $uckadelic
NNO Touma
NNO Tulip
NNO Uamou

2010 Star Wars Galaxy Series 5 Lost Galaxy

COMPLETE SET (5)		10.00	25.00
COMMON CARD (1-5)		3.00	8.00

STATED ODDS 1:24 HOBBY

2010 Star Wars Galaxy Series 5 Manga Sketches

STATED ODDS 1:274 HOBBY

NNO Axer
NNO Dax Gordine
NNO Eric Vedder
NNO Jennyson Allan Borlongan Rosero/(2NGAW)
NNO Tim Smith
NNO Tomoko Taniguchi
NNO Vanessa Duran
NNO Wilson Ramos Jr.

2011 Star Wars Galaxy Series 6

COMPLETE SET (120)	8.00	20.00
COMMON CARD (1-120)	.15	.40

*P.P.BLACK/1: UNPRICED DUE TO SCARCITY
*P.P.CYAN/1: UNPRICED DUE TO SCARCITY
*P.P.MAGENTA/1: UNPRICED DUE TO SCARCITY
*P.P.YELLOW/1: UNPRICED DUE TO SCARCITY

2011 Star Wars Galaxy Series 6 Silver Foil

COMPLETE SET (10)	6.00	15.00
COMMON CARD (1-10)	1.00	2.50

*BRONZE: 1.2X TO 3X BASIC CARDS
*GOLD/600: 4X TO 10X BASIC CARDS
STATED PRINT RUN 1 SER.#'d SET
STATED ODDS 1:3

2011 Star Wars Galaxy Series 6 Animation Cels

COMPLETE SET (9)	20.00	40.00
COMMON CARD (1-9)	3.00	8.00

STATED ODDS 1:4 RETAIL

2011 Star Wars Galaxy Series 6 Etched Foil

COMPLETE SET (6)	5.00	12.00
COMMON CARD (1-6)	1.25	3.00

STATED ODDS 1:6

2011 Star Wars Galaxy Series 6 Sketchagraphs

1 Amy Allen
Adam Hughes
2 Amy Allen
Alex Buechel
3 Amy Allen
Allison Sohn
4 Amy Allen
Brian Rood
5 Amy Allen
Cat Staggs
6 Amy Allen
Doug Cowan
7 Amy Allen
Grant Gould
8 Amy Allen

Jamie Snell
9 Amy Allen
Jim Kyle
10 Amy Allen
John Haun
11 Amy Allen
Kevin Doyle
12 Amy Allen
Kevin Graham
13 Amy Allen
Lin Workman
14 Amy Allen
Kyle Babbitt
15 Amy Allen
Otis Frampton
16 Amy Allen
Randy Martinez
17 Amy Allen
Rich Molinelli
18 Amy Allen
Sarah Wilkinson
19 Amy Allen
Sean Pence
20 Amy Allen
Steve Stanley
21 Amy Allen
Tim Proctor
22 Amy Allen
Tom Hodges
23 Carrie Fisher
Adam Hughes
24 Carrie Fisher
Alex Buechel
25 Carrie Fisher
Allison Sohn
26 Carrie Fisher
Brian Rood
27 Carrie Fisher
Cat Staggs
28 Carrie Fisher
Doug Cowan
29 Carrie Fisher
Grant Gould
30 Carrie Fisher
Jamie Snell
31 Carrie Fisher
Jim Kyle
32 Carrie Fisher
John Haun
33 Carrie Fisher
Kevin Doyle
34 Carrie Fisher
Kevin Graham
35 Carrie Fisher
Lin Workman
36 Carrie Fisher
Kyle Babbitt
37 Carrie Fisher
Otis Frampton
38 Carrie Fisher
Randy Martinez
39 Carrie Fisher
Rich Molinelli
40 Carrie Fisher
Sarah Wilkinson
41 Carrie Fisher
Sean Pence
42 Carrie Fisher
Steve Stanley
43 Carrie Fisher
Tim Proctor
44 Carrie Fisher
Tom Hodges
45 Jake Lloyd
Adam Hughes
46 Jake Lloyd
Alex Buechel
47 Jake Lloyd
Allison Sohn
48 Jake Lloyd
Brian Rood
49 Jake Lloyd

Cat Staggs
50 Jake Lloyd
Doug Cowan
51 Jake Lloyd
Grant Gould
52 Jake Lloyd
Jamie Snell
53 Jake Lloyd
Jim Kyle
54 Jake Lloyd
John Haun
55 Jake Lloyd
Kevin Doyle
56 Jake Lloyd
Kevin Graham
57 Jake Lloyd
Lin Workman
58 Jake Lloyd
Kyle Babbitt
59 Jake Lloyd
Otis Frampton
60 Jake Lloyd
Randy Martinez
61 Jake Lloyd
Rich Molinelli
62 Jake Lloyd
Sarah Wilkinson
63 Jake Lloyd
Sean Pence
64 Jake Lloyd
Steve Stanley
65 Jake Lloyd
Tim Proctor
66 Jake Lloyd
Tom Hodges
67 John Morton
Adam Hughes
68 John Morton
Alex Buechel
69 John Morton
Allison Sohn
70 John Morton
Brian Rood
71 John Morton
Cat Staggs
72 John Morton
Doug Cowan
73 John Morton
Grant Gould
74 John Morton
Jamie Snell
75 John Morton
Jim Kyle
76 John Morton
John Haun
77 John Morton
Kevin Doyle
78 John Morton
Kevin Graham
79 John Morton
Lin Workman
80 John Morton
Kyle Babbitt
81 John Morton
Otis Frampton
82 John Morton
Randy Martinez
83 John Morton
Rich Molinelli
84 John Morton
Sarah Wilkinson
85 John Morton
Sean Pence
86 John Morton
Steve Stanley
87 John Morton
Tim Proctor
88 John Morton
Tom Hodges
89 Jon Berg
Adam Hughes
90 Jon Berg

Alex Buechel
91 Jon Berg
Allison Sohn
92 Jon Berg
Brian Rood
93 Jon Berg
Cat Staggs
94 Jon Berg
Doug Cowan
95 Jon Berg
Grant Gould
96 Jon Berg
Jamie Snell
97 Jon Berg
Jim Kyle
98 Jon Berg
John Haun
99 Jon Berg
Kevin Doyle
100 Jon Berg
Kevin Graham
101 Jon Berg
Lin Workman
102 Jon Berg
Kyle Babbitt
103 Jon Berg
Otis Frampton
104 Jon Berg
Randy Martinez
105 Jon Berg
Rich Molinelli
106 Jon Berg
Sarah Wilkinson
107 Jon Berg
Sean Pence
108 Jon Berg
Steve Stanley
109 Jon Berg
Tim Proctor
110 Jon Berg
Tom Hodges
111 Mark Hamill
Adam Hughes
112 Mark Hamill
Alex Buechel
113 Mark Hamill
Allison Sohn
114 Mark Hamill
Brian Rood
115 Mark Hamill
Cat Staggs
116 Mark Hamill
Doug Cowan
117 Mark Hamill
Grant Gould
118 Mark Hamill
Jamie Snell
119 Mark Hamill
Jim Kyle
120 Mark Hamill
John Haun
121 Mark Hamill
Kevin Doyle
122 Mark Hamill
Kevin Graham
123 Mark Hamill
Lin Workman
124 Mark Hamill
Kyle Babbitt
125 Mark Hamill
Otis Frampton
126 Mark Hamill
Randy Martinez
127 Mark Hamill
Rich Molinelli
128 Mark Hamill
Sarah Wilkinson
129 Mark Hamill
Sean Pence
130 Mark Hamill
Steve Stanley
131 Mark Hamill

Tim Proctor
132 Mark Hamill
Tom Hodges
133 Mike Quinn
Adam Hughes
134 Mike Quinn
Alex Buechel
135 Mike Quinn
Allison Sohn
136 Mike Quinn
Brian Rood
137 Mike Quinn
Cat Staggs
138 Mike Quinn
Doug Cowan
139 Mike Quinn
Grant Gould
140 Mike Quinn
Jamie Snell
141 Mike Quinn
Jim Kyle
142 Mike Quinn
John Haun
143 Mike Quinn
Kevin Doyle
144 Mike Quinn
Kevin Graham
145 Mike Quinn
Lin Workman
146 Mike Quinn
Kyle Babbitt
147 Mike Quinn
Otis Frampton
148 Mike Quinn
Randy Martinez
149 Mike Quinn
Rich Molinelli
150 Mike Quinn
Sarah Wilkinson
151 Mike Quinn
Sean Pence
152 Mike Quinn
Steve Stanley
153 Mike Quinn
Tim Proctor
154 Mike Quinn
Tom Hodges
155 Orli Shoshan
Adam Hughes
156 Orli Shoshan
Alex Buechel
157 Orli Shoshan
Allison Sohn
158 Orli Shoshan
Brian Rood
159 Orli Shoshan
Cat Staggs
160 Orli Shoshan
Doug Cowan
161 Orli Shoshan
Grant Gould
162 Orli Shoshan
Jamie Snell
163 Orli Shoshan
Jim Kyle
164 Orli Shoshan
John Haun
165 Orli Shoshan
Kevin Doyle
166 Orli Shoshan
Kevin Graham
167 Orli Shoshan
Lin Workman
168 Orli Shoshan
Kyle Babbitt
169 Orli Shoshan
Otis Frampton
170 Orli Shoshan
Randy Martinez
171 Orli Shoshan
Rich Molinelli
172 Orli Shoshan

Sarah Wilkinson
173 Orli Shoshan
Sean Pence
174 Orli Shoshan
Steve Stanley
175 Orli Shoshan
Tim Proctor
176 Orli Shoshan
Tom Hodges
177 Ray Park
Adam Hughes
178 Ray Park
Alex Buechel
179 Ray Park
Allison Sohn
180 Ray Park
Brian Rood
181 Ray Park
Cat Staggs
182 Ray Park
Doug Cowan
183 Ray Park
Grant Gould
184 Ray Park
Jamie Snell
185 Ray Park
Jim Kyle
186 Ray Park
John Haun
187 Ray Park
Kevin Doyle
188 Ray Park
Kevin Graham
189 Ray Park
Lin Workman
190 Ray Park
Kyle Babbitt
191 Ray Park
Otis Frampton
192 Ray Park
Randy Martinez
193 Ray Park
Rich Molinelli
194 Ray Park
Sarah Wilkinson
195 Ray Park
Sean Pence
196 Ray Park
Steve Stanley
197 Ray Park
Tim Proctor
198 Ray Park
Tom Hodges

2011 Star Wars Galaxy Series 6 Sketches

NNO Adrian Rivera
NNO Agnes Garbowska
NNO Alex Buechel
NNO Amy Pronovost
NNO Art O'Callaghan
NNO Beck Seashols
NNO Bill Pulkovski
NNO Bob Stevlic
NNO Braden D. Lamb
NNO Brent Engstrom
NNO Brian Kong
NNO Bruce Gerlach
NNO Bryan Morton
NNO Cat Staggs
NNO Charles Hall
NNO Chris Henderson
NNO Cynthia Narcisi
NNO D Douglas
NNO Dan Bergren
NNO David Day
NNO David Green
NNO David Rabbitte
NNO Denae Frazier
NNO Dennis Budd
NNO Dennis Hart
NNO Don Pedicini Jr.
NNO Doug Cowan
NNO Eli Rutten

NNO Erik Maell
NNO Gabe Farber
NNO Gary Kezele
NNO Geoff Munn
NNO Hayden Davis
NNO Ingrid Hardy
NNO Irma Ahmed
NNO Jamie Snell
NNO Jason Adams
NNO Jason Durden
NNO Jason Keith Phillips
NNO Jason Sobol
NNO Jason Williams
NNO Jay Shimko
NNO Jerry The Franchize Gaylord
NNO Jessica Hickman
NNO Jim Kyle
NNO Joe Corroney
NNO Joe Hogan
NNO John Haun
NNO Jonathan D. Gordon
NNO Juan Carlos Ramos
NNO Kate Bradley
NNO Katie Cook
NNO Kevin Doyle
NNO Kevin Graham
NNO Kevin Liell
NNO Kyle Babbitt
NNO Lawrence Reynolds
NNO Leah Mangue
NNO Lee Kohse
NNO Len Bellinger
NNO Lin Workman
NNO Linzy Zorn
NNO Lord Mesa
NNO M. Jason Reed
NNO Manny Mederos
NNO Martheus Wade
NNO Matt Busch
NNO Matthew Minor
NNO Michael Locoduck Duron
NNO Mick and Matt Glebe
NNO Monte Moore
NNO Nina Edlund
NNO Nolan Woodard
NNO Otis Frampton
NNO Rachel Kaiser
NNO Randy Martinez
NNO Rhiannon Owens
NNO Rich Woodall
NNO Robert Hendrickson
NNO Robert Teranishi
NNO Russell Walks
NNO Ryan Hungerford
NNO Sanna U
NNO Sarah Wilkinson
NNO Scott Rorie
NNO Scott Zambelli
NNO Sean Pence
NNO Shea Standefer
NNO Shelli Paroline
NNO Soni Alcorn-Hender
NNO Stephanie Swanger
NNO Steve Miller
NNO Steve Oatney
NNO Steve Stanley
NNO Ted Dastick Jr.
NNO Tim Proctor
NNO Tim Smith
NNO Tod Smith
NNO Tom Hodges
NNO Tomoko Taniguchi
NNO Vanessa Banky Farano
NNO Wilson Ramos Jr.
NNO Zack Giallongo

2011 Star Wars Galaxy Series 6 Sketches Die-Cuts

NNO Abe Lincoln Jr.
NNO Arbito
NNO Aya Kakeda
NNO Billy Roids
NNO Brian Mead
NNO Burt Banger

NNO Chris Ryniak
NNO Dan Bina
NNO Dan Goodsell
NNO Dave Savage
NNO Doktor A
NNO Free Humanity
NNO Gothic Hangman
NNO JRYU
NNO Jason Atomic
NNO Jermaine Rogers
NNO John Spanky Stokes
NNO Jon-Paul Kaiser
NNO Jordana Lake
NNO Julie West
NNO Larz
NNO Len Bellinger
NNO Lorne Colon
NNO Lou Pimentel
NNO Luke Gibbons-Reich
NNO Martin Hsu
NNO Martina Secondo Russo
Frank Russo
NNO Marty Hansen THEGODBEAST
NNO Mike Egan
NNO Mike Mendez NEMO
NNO Mio Murakami
NNO Nathan Hamill
NNO olive47
NNO Omen
NNO Ritzy Periwinkle
NNO Sarah Jo Marks
NNO Scott Tolleson
NNO Sergey Safonov
NNO SHAWNIMALS
NNO Stella Bouzakis
NNO Steve Talkowski
NNO Steven Daily
NNO The Sucklord
NNO Tyson Bodnarchuk
NNO VISE ONE
NNO Wade Lageose

2011 Star Wars Galaxy Series 6 Sketches Retail Red

NNO Alex Buechel
NNO Bill Pulkovski
NNO Chris Henderson
NNO David Day
NNO David Rabbitte
NNO Erik Maell
NNO Howard Shum
NNO Jerry The Franchize Gaylord
NNO John P. Wales
NNO Justin Chung
NNO Mark Slater
NNO Michael Locoduck Duron
NNO Mick and Matt Glebe
NNO Rhiannon Owens
NNO Scott Zambelli
NNO Shea Standefer
NNO Shelli Paroline
NNO Stephanie Swanger
NNO Wilson Ramos Jr.
NNO Zack Giallongo
NNO Stephanie Yue
NNO Lee Bradley
NNO Don Pedicini Jr.
NNO Ted Dastick Jr.
NNO Tim Proctor
NNO Tim Smith 3
NNO Tod Smith
NNO Beck Seashols
NNO Juan Carlos Ramos

2012 Star Wars Galaxy Series 7

COMPLETE SET (110)	8.00	20.00
UNOPENED BOX (24 PACKS)	60.00	70.00
UNOPENED PACK (7 CARDS)	2.50	3.00
COMMON CARD (1-110)	.15	.40

*P.P.BLACK/1: UNPRICED DUE TO SCARCITY
*P.P.CYAN/1: UNPRICED DUE TO SCARCITY
*P.P.MAGENTA/1: UNPRICED DUE TO SCARCITY
*P.P.YELLOW/1: UNPRICED DUE TO SCARCITY

2012 Star Wars Galaxy Series 7 Silver Foil

COMPLETE SET (15)	6.00	15.00
COMMON CARD (1-15)	.75	2.00

*BRONZE: 1.5X TO 4X SILVER
*GOLD: 3X TO 8X SILVER
*SILVER REF/1: UNPRICED DUE TO SCARCITY
STATED ODDS 1:3

2012 Star Wars Galaxy Series 7 Cels

COMPLETE SET (9)	35.00	70.00
COMMON CARD (1-9)	4.00	10.00

2012 Star Wars Galaxy Series 7 Etched Foil

COMPLETE SET (6)	5.00	12.00
COMMON CARD (1-6)	1.50	4.00

*ORIG.ART/1: UNPRICED DUE TO SCARCITY
STATED ODDS 1:6

2012 Star Wars Galaxy Series 7 Sketchagraphs

1 Alan Flyng
Kevin Doyle
2 Alan Flyng
Brian Rood
3 Alan Flyng
Steve Oatney
4 Alan Flyng
Dan Bergren
5 Alan Flyng
Bruce Gerlach
6 Alan Flyng
Gabe Farber
7 Alan Flyng
Kyle Babbitt
8 Alan Flyng
Hayden Davis
9 Alan Flyng
David Day
10 Alan Flyng
Jamie Snell
11 Alan Flyng
Sarah Wilkinson
12 Alan Flyng
John Haun
13 Alan Flyng
Gary Kezele
14 Alan Flyng
Kevin Graham
15 Alan Flyng
Matthew Minor
16 Alan Flyng
Leah Mangue
17 Alan Flyng
Jake Minor
18 Alan Flyng
Rich Molinelli
19 Alan Flyng
Tom Hodges
20 Alan Flyng
Robert Teranishi
21 Alan Flyng
Jim Kyle
22 Alan Flyng
Sean Pence
23 Alan Flyng
Robert Hendrickson
24 Alan Flyng
Tim Proctor
25 Alan Flyng
Allison Sohn
26 Ashley Eckstein
Allison Sohn
27 Ashley Eckstein
Brian Rood
28 Ashley Eckstein
Bruce Gerlach
29 Ashley Eckstein
Dan Bergren
30 Ashley Eckstein
David Day
31 Ashley Eckstein
Gabe Farber
32 Ashley Eckstein
Gary Kezele

33 Ashley Eckstein
Hayden Davis
34 Ashley Eckstein
Jake Minor
35 Ashley Eckstein
Jamie Snell
36 Ashley Eckstein
Jim Kyle
37 Ashley Eckstein
John Haun
38 Ashley Eckstein
Kevin Doyle
39 Ashley Eckstein
Kevin Graham
40 Ashley Eckstein
Kyle Babbitt
41 Ashley Eckstein
Leah Mangue
42 Ashley Eckstein
Matthew Minor
43 Ashley Eckstein
Rich Molinelli
44 Ashley Eckstein
Robert Hendrickson
45 Ashley Eckstein
Robert Teranishi
46 Ashley Eckstein
Sarah Wilkinson
47 Ashley Eckstein
Sean Pence
48 Ashley Eckstein
Steve Oatney
49 Ashley Eckstein
Tim Proctor
50 Ashley Eckstein
Tom Hodges
51 Ben Burtt
Allison Sohn
52 Ben Burtt
Brian Rood
53 Ben Burtt
Bruce Gerlach
54 Ben Burtt
Dan Bergren
55 Ben Burtt
David Day
56 Ben Burtt
Gabe Farber
57 Ben Burtt
Gary Kezele
58 Ben Burtt
Hayden Davis
59 Ben Burtt
Jake Minor
60 Ben Burtt
Jamie Snell
61 Ben Burtt
Jim Kyle
62 Ben Burtt
John Haun
63 Ben Burtt
Kevin Doyle
64 Ben Burtt
Kevin Graham
65 Ben Burtt
Kyle Babbitt
66 Ben Burtt
Leah Mangue
67 Ben Burtt
Matthew Minor
68 Ben Burtt
Rich Molinelli
69 Ben Burtt
Robert Hendrickson
70 Ben Burtt
Robert Teranishi
71 Ben Burtt
Sarah Wilkinson
72 Ben Burtt
Sean Pence
73 Ben Burtt
Steve Oatney

74 Ben Burtt
Tim Proctor
75 Ben Burtt
Tom Hodges
76 Carrie Fisher
Allison Sohn
77 Carrie Fisher
Brian Rood
78 Carrie Fisher
Bruce Gerlach
79 Carrie Fisher
Dan Bergren
80 Carrie Fisher
David Day
81 Carrie Fisher
Gabe Farber
82 Carrie Fisher
Gary Kezele
83 Carrie Fisher
Hayden Davis
84 Carrie Fisher
Jake Minor
85 Carrie Fisher
Jamie Snell
86 Carrie Fisher
Jim Kyle
87 Carrie Fisher
John Haun
88 Carrie Fisher
Kevin Doyle
89 Carrie Fisher
Kevin Graham
90 Carrie Fisher
Kyle Babbitt
91 Carrie Fisher
Leah Mangue
92 Carrie Fisher
Matthew Minor
93 Carrie Fisher
Rich Molinelli
94 Carrie Fisher
Robert Hendrickson
95 Carrie Fisher
Robert Teranishi
96 Carrie Fisher
Sarah Wilkinson
97 Carrie Fisher
Sean Pence
98 Carrie Fisher
Steve Oatney
99 Carrie Fisher
Tim Proctor
100 Carrie Fisher
Tom Hodges
101 Catherine Taber
Allison Sohn
102 Catherine Taber
Brian Rood
103 Catherine Taber
Bruce Gerlach
104 Catherine Taber
Dan Bergren
105 Catherine Taber
David Day
106 Catherine Taber
Gabe Farber
107 Catherine Taber
Gary Kezele
108 Catherine Taber
Hayden Davis
109 Catherine Taber
Jake Minor
110 Catherine Taber
Jamie Snell
111 Catherine Taber
Jim Kyle
112 Catherine Taber
John Haun
113 Catherine Taber
Kevin Doyle
114 Catherine Taber
Kevin Graham

115 Catherine Taber
Kyle Babbitt
116 Catherine Taber
Leah Mangue
117 Catherine Taber
Matthew Minor
118 Catherine Taber
Rich Molinelli
119 Catherine Taber
Robert Hendrickson
120 Catherine Taber
Robert Teranishi
121 Catherine Taber
Sarah Wilkinson
122 Catherine Taber
Sean Pence
123 Catherine Taber
Steve Oatney
124 Catherine Taber
Tim Proctor
125 Catherine Taber
Tom Hodges
126 Dickey Beer
Allison Sohn
127 Dickey Beer
Brian Rood
128 Dickey Beer
Bruce Gerlach
129 Dickey Beer
Dan Bergren
130 Dickey Beer
David Day
131 Dickey Beer
Gabe Farber
132 Dickey Beer
Gary Kezele
133 Dickey Beer
Hayden Davis
134 Dickey Beer
Jake Minor
135 Dickey Beer
Jamie Snell
136 Dickey Beer
Jim Kyle
137 Dickey Beer
John Haun
138 Dickey Beer
Kevin Doyle
139 Dickey Beer
Kevin Graham
140 Dickey Beer
Kyle Babbitt
141 Dickey Beer
Leah Mangue
142 Dickey Beer
Matthew Minor
143 Dickey Beer
Rich Molinelli
144 Dickey Beer
Robert Hendrickson
145 Dickey Beer
Robert Teranishi
146 Dickey Beer
Sarah Wilkinson
147 Dickey Beer
Sean Pence
148 Dickey Beer
Steve Oatney
149 Dickey Beer
Tim Proctor
150 Dickey Beer
Tom Hodges
151 James Arnold Taylor
Allison Sohn
152 James Arnold Taylor
Brian Rood
153 James Arnold Taylor
Bruce Gerlach
154 James Arnold Taylor
Dan Bergren
155 James Arnold Taylor
David Day

156 James Arnold Taylor
Gabe Farber
157 James Arnold Taylor
Gary Kezele
158 James Arnold Taylor
Hayden Davis
159 James Arnold Taylor
Jake Minor
160 James Arnold Taylor
Jamie Snell
161 James Arnold Taylor
Jim Kyle
162 James Arnold Taylor
John Haun
163 James Arnold Taylor
Kevin Doyle
164 James Arnold Taylor
Kevin Graham
165 James Arnold Taylor
Kyle Babbitt
166 James Arnold Taylor
Leah Mangue
167 James Arnold Taylor
Matthew Minor
168 James Arnold Taylor
Rich Molinelli
169 James Arnold Taylor
Robert Hendrickson
170 James Arnold Taylor
Robert Teranishi
171 James Arnold Taylor
Sarah Wilkinson
172 James Arnold Taylor
Sean Pence
173 James Arnold Taylor
Steve Oatney
174 James Arnold Taylor
Tim Proctor
175 James Arnold Taylor
Tom Hodges
176 Mark Hamill
Allison Sohn
177 Mark Hamill
Brian Rood
178 Mark Hamill
Bruce Gerlach
179 Mark Hamill
Dan Bergren
180 Mark Hamill
David Day
181 Mark Hamill
Gabe Farber
182 Mark Hamill
Gary Kezele
183 Mark Hamill
Hayden Davis
184 Mark Hamill
Jake Minor
185 Mark Hamill
Jamie Snell
186 Mark Hamill
Jim Kyle
187 Mark Hamill
John Haun
188 Mark Hamill
Kevin Doyle
189 Mark Hamill
Kevin Graham
190 Mark Hamill
Kyle Babbitt
191 Mark Hamill
Leah Mangue
192 Mark Hamill
Matthew Minor
193 Mark Hamill
Rich Molinelli
194 Mark Hamill
Robert Hendrickson
195 Mark Hamill
Robert Teranishi
196 Mark Hamill
Sarah Wilkinson

197 Mark Hamill
Sean Pence
198 Mark Hamill
Steve Oatney
199 Mark Hamill
Tim Proctor
200 Mark Hamill
Tom Hodges
201 Matt Wood
Allison Sohn
202 Matt Wood
Brian Rood
203 Matt Wood
Bruce Gerlach
204 Matt Wood
Dan Bergren
205 Matt Wood
David Day
206 Matt Wood
Gabe Farber
207 Matt Wood
Gary Kezele
208 Matt Wood
Hayden Davis
209 Matt Wood
Jake Minor
210 Matt Wood
Jamie Snell
211 Matt Wood
Jim Kyle
212 Matt Wood
John Haun
213 Matt Wood
Kevin Doyle
214 Matt Wood
Kevin Graham
215 Matt Wood
Kyle Babbitt
216 Matt Wood
Leah Mangue
217 Matt Wood
Matthew Minor
218 Matt Wood
Rich Molinelli
219 Matt Wood
Robert Hendrickson
220 Matt Wood
Robert Teranishi
221 Matt Wood
Sarah Wilkinson
222 Matt Wood
Sean Pence
223 Matt Wood
Steve Oatney
224 Matt Wood
Tim Proctor
225 Matt Wood
Tom Hodges
226 Peter Mayhew
Allison Sohn
227 Peter Mayhew
Brian Rood
228 Peter Mayhew
Bruce Gerlach
229 Peter Mayhew
Dan Bergren
230 Peter Mayhew
David Day
231 Peter Mayhew
Gabe Farber
232 Peter Mayhew
Gary Kezele
233 Peter Mayhew
Hayden Davis
234 Peter Mayhew
Jake Minor
235 Peter Mayhew
Jamie Snell
236 Peter Mayhew
Jim Kyle
237 Peter Mayhew
John Haun

238 Peter Mayhew
Kevin Doyle
239 Peter Mayhew
Kevin Graham
240 Peter Mayhew
Kyle Babbitt
241 Peter Mayhew
Leah Mangue
242 Peter Mayhew
Matthew Minor
243 Peter Mayhew
Rich Molinelli
244 Peter Mayhew
Robert Hendrickson
245 Peter Mayhew
Robert Teranishi
246 Peter Mayhew
Sarah Wilkinson
247 Peter Mayhew
Sean Pence
248 Peter Mayhew
Steve Oatney
249 Peter Mayhew
Tim Proctor
250 Peter Mayhew
Tom Hodges
251 Timothy Zahn
Allison Sohn
252 Timothy Zahn
Brian Rood
253 Timothy Zahn
Bruce Gerlach
254 Timothy Zahn
Dan Bergren
255 Timothy Zahn
David Day
256 Timothy Zahn
Gabe Farber
257 Timothy Zahn
Gary Kezele
258 Timothy Zahn
Hayden Davis
259 Timothy Zahn
Jake Minor
260 Timothy Zahn
Jamie Snell
261 Timothy Zahn
Jim Kyle
262 Timothy Zahn
John Haun
263 Timothy Zahn
Kevin Doyle
264 Timothy Zahn
Kevin Graham
265 Timothy Zahn
Kyle Babbitt
266 Timothy Zahn
Leah Mangue
267 Timothy Zahn
Matthew Minor
268 Timothy Zahn
Rich Molinelli
269 Timothy Zahn
Robert Hendrickson
270 Timothy Zahn
Robert Teranishi
271 Timothy Zahn
Sarah Wilkinson
272 Timothy Zahn
Sean Pence
273 Timothy Zahn
Steve Oatney
274 Timothy Zahn
Tim Proctor
275 Timothy Zahn
Tom Hodges
276 Tom Kane
Allison Sohn
277 Tom Kane
Brian Rood
278 Tom Kane
Bruce Gerlach

279 Tom Kane
Dan Bergren
280 Tom Kane
David Day
281 Tom Kane
Gabe Farber
282 Tom Kane
Gary Kezele
283 Tom Kane
Hayden Davis
284 Tom Kane
Jake Minor
285 Tom Kane
Jamie Snell
286 Tom Kane
Jim Kyle
287 Tom Kane
John Haun
288 Tom Kane
Kevin Doyle
289 Tom Kane
Kevin Graham
290 Tom Kane
Kyle Babbitt
291 Tom Kane
Leah Mangue
292 Tom Kane
Matthew Minor
293 Tom Kane
Rich Molinelli
294 Tom Kane
Robert Hendrickson
295 Tom Kane
Robert Teranishi
296 Tom Kane
Sarah Wilkinson
297 Tom Kane
Sean Pence
298 Tom Kane
Steve Oatney
299 Tom Kane
Tim Proctor
300 Tom Kane
Tom Hodges

2012 Star Wars Galaxy Series 7 Sketches

NNO Adrian Rivera
NNO Agnes Garbowska
NNO Alex Buechel
NNO Amy Beth Christenson
NNO Ashleigh Popplewell
NNO Beck Seashols
NNO Ben Dale
NNO Bill Pulkovski
NNO Bob Stevlic
NNO Brandon Kenney
NNO Brent Engstrom
NNO Brian DeGuire
NNO Brian Miller
NNO Brian Rood
NNO Bruce Gerlach
NNO Cal Slayton
NNO Charles Hall
NNO Chris Henderson
NNO Colin Walton
NNO Cory Hamscher
NNO Cynthia Narcisi
NNO D Douglas
NNO Dan Bergren
NNO Dan Curto
NNO Darla Ecklund
NNO David Day
NNO David Rabbitte
NNO Denae Frazier
NNO Denis Medri
NNO Dennis Budd
NNO Don Pedicini Jr.
NNO Eli Rutten
NNO Erik Maell
NNO Gabe Farber
NNO Gary Kezele
NNO Hayden Davis
NNO Ingrid Hardy

NNO Irma Ahmed
NNO Jamie Snell
NNO Jason Atomic
NNO Jason Davies
NNO Jason Durden
NNO Jason Hughes
NNO Jason Sobol
NNO Jason Keith Phillips
NNO Jay Shimko
NNO Jerry Ma
NNO Jim Kyle
NNO Joe Corroney
NNO Joe Hogan
NNO John Beatty
NNO John Soukup
NNO John P Wales
NNO Jonathan D. Gordon
NNO Kate Glasheen
NNO Katie Cook
NNO Keven Reinke
NNO Kevin Doyle
NNO Kevin Graham
NNO Kevin Liell
NNO Killian Plunkett
NNO Kyle Babbitt
NNO Lak Lim
NNO Lance Sawyer
NNO Lawrence Reynolds
NNO Lee Bradley
NNO Lee Kohse
NNO Lin Workman
NNO Lord Mesa
NNO Mark McHaley
NNO Mark Slater
NNO Mike Duron
NNO Nathan Hamill
NNO Nathen Reinke
NNO Nicole Falk
NNO Nigel Sade
NNO Nina Edlund
NNO Pat Presley
NNO Patrick Richardson
NNO Patrick Schoenmaker
NNO Randy Martinez
NNO Randy Siplon
NNO Rhiannon Owens
NNO Rich Molinelli
NNO Rob Liefeld
NNO Robert Hendrickson
NNO Russell Walks
NNO Scott Rorie
NNO Scott Zambelli
NNO Shea Standefer
NNO Shelli Paroline
NNO Sian Mandrake
NNO Steph Swanger
NNO Ted Dastick Jr.
NNO Tim Proctor
NNO Tod Allen Smith
NNO Tom Hodges
NNO Trev Murphy
NNO Vanessa Banky Farano
NNO Veronica O'Connell
NNO Zack Giallongo
NNO Brian Kong
NNO Cat Staggs
NNO Chris Glenn
NNO Cole Higgins
NNO David Green
NNO Eric Komalieh
NNO Jenn DePaola
NNO Jessica Hickman
NNO Linzy Zorn
NNO Marat Mychaels
NNO Matt Busch
NNO Mikey Babinski
NNO Nicole Goff
NNO Sarah Wilkinson

NNO Sean Pence
NNO Vince Lee
NNO Will Nichols
NNO Lizzie Carr

2012 Star Wars Galaxy Series 7 Sketches Retail Red

NNO Adrian Rivera
NNO Agnes Garbowska
NNO Beck Seashols
NNO Bruce Gerlach
NNO David Rabbitte
NNO Denae Frazier
NNO Denis Medri
NNO Erik Maell
NNO Howard Shum
NNO Jason Davies
NNO Jason Durden
NNO Jay Shimko
NNO Jessica Hickman
NNO Joe Hogan
NNO John P Wales
NNO Jonathan D. Gordon
NNO Kate Glasheen
NNO Kevin Doyle
NNO Lee Bradley
NNO Lee Kohse
NNO Lord Mesa
NNO Mark Slater
NNO Rich Molinelli
NNO Scott Zambelli
NNO Shelli Paroline
NNO Sian Mandrake
NNO Steph Swanger
NNO Tod Allen Smith
NNO Trev Murphy
NNO Veronica O'Connell
NNO Wilson Ramos Jr.

2018 Star Wars Galaxy

COMPLETE SET (100)	15.00	40.00
UNOPENED BOX (24 PACKS)	65.00	80.00
UNOPENED PACK (8 CARDS)	3.00	4.00
COMMON CARD (1-100)	.40	1.00
*BLUE: .6X TO 1.5X BASIC CARDS		
*GREEN: 1.2X TO 3X BASIC CARDS		
*PURPLE/99: 2.5X TO 6X BASIC CARDS		
*ORANGE/25: 6X TO 15X BASIC CARDS		
*RED/1: UNPRICED DUE TO SCARCITY		
*P.P.BLACK/1: UNPRICED DUE TO SCARCITY		
*P.P.CYAN/1: UNPRICED DUE TO SCARCITY		
*P.P.MAGENTA/1: UNPRICED DUE TO SCARCITY		
*P.P.YELLOW/1: UNPRICED DUE TO SCARCITY		

2018 Star Wars Galaxy Art Patches

*BLUE/199: SAME VALUE AS BASIC		
*GREEN/150: .5X TO 1.2X BASIC MEM		
*PURPLE/99: .6X TO 1.5X BASIC MEM		
*ORANGE/25: .75X TO 2X BASIC MEM		
*GOLD/5: UNPRICED DUE TO SCARCITY		
*RED/1: UNPRICED DUE TO SCARCITY		
MD Droids	8.00	20.00
MDV Darth Vader	8.00	20.00
MHL Han and Leia	10.00	25.00
MJW Jawas	6.00	15.00
MLL Luke and Leia	10.00	25.00
MLS Luke Skywalker	8.00	20.00
MPL Princess Leia	8.00	20.00
MSC Salacious B. Crumb	6.00	15.00
MTR Tusken Raider	8.00	20.00
MWT Wilhuff Tarkin	6.00	15.00
MWW Wicket W. Warrick	6.00	15.00
MXW X-Wings	8.00	20.00

2018 Star Wars Galaxy Autographs

ANAKIN SKYWALKER
AUTHENTIC AUTOGRAPH

*PURPLE/10: UNPRICED DUE TO SCARCITY		
*ORANGE/5: UNPRICED DUE TO SCARCITY		
*RED/1: UNPRICED DUE TO SCARCITY		
*P.P.BLACK/1: UNPRICED DUE TO SCARCITY		
*P.P.CYAN/1: UNPRICED DUE TO SCARCITY		
*P.P.MAGENTA/1: UNPRICED DUE TO SCARCITY		
*P.P.YELLOW/1: UNPRICED DUE TO SCARCITY		
RANDOMLY INSERTED INTO PACKS		
GAAA Amy Allen	8.00	20.00
GAAD Anthony Daniels		
GAAE Ashley Eckstein		
GAAS Andrew Secombe		
GAAT Alan Tudyk		
GABL Bai Ling	6.00	15.00
GACF Carrie Fisher		
GACR Clive Revill		
GADL Daniel Logan	12.00	30.00
GADR Daisy Ridley		
GADT David Tennant		
GADY Donnie Yen		
GAEL Eric Lopez	6.00	15.00
GAFJ Felicity Jones		
GAFP Freddie Prinze Jr.		
GAFW Forest Whitaker		
GAGC Gwendoline Christie		
GAGT George Takei		
GAHC Hayden Christensen		
GAHF Harrison Ford		
GAHQ Hugh Quarshie		
GAIM Ian McDiarmid		
GAJB John Boyega		
GAJC Jim Cummings	6.00	15.00
GAJI Jason Isaacs		
GAKB Kenny Baker		
GALS Lloyd Sherr		
GAMC Michaela Cottrell	6.00	15.00
GAMK Michael Kingma		
GAMO Mary Oyaya	5.00	12.00
GANF Nika Futterman		
GANK Nalini Krishan	6.00	15.00
GAOD Olivia d'Abo		
GAPM Peter Mayhew		
GAPW Paul Warren	5.00	12.00
GARA Riz Ahmed		
GARB Raija Baroudi	6.00	15.00
GARN Rohan Nichol	5.00	12.00
GARP Ray Park		
GASB Steven Blum	5.00	12.00
GASS Stephen Stanton		
GASW Sam Witwer		
GATB Tom Baker		
GATK Tom Kenny		
GAADK Adam Driver		
GABDW Billy Dee Williams		
GADRY Deep Roy		
GAGAT James Arnold Taylor		
GAJCW John Coppinger	8.00	20.00
GAKCH Keisha Castle-Hughes		
GAPAR Philip Anthony-Rodriguez	5.00	12.00

GARWB Ralph Brown	8.00	20.00
GASMG Sarah Michelle Gellar		
GATCB Tosin Cole	5.00	12.00

2018 Star Wars Galaxy Dual Autographs

*ORANGE/5: UNPRICED DUE TO SCARCITY
*RED/1: UNPRICED DUE TO SCARCITY
STATED PRINT RUN 25 SER.#'d SETS

DABD J.Boyega/A.Driver		
DABH D.Barclay/G.Home	15.00	40.00
DABW J.Boyega/M.Wood		
DADS A.Driver/A.Serkis		
DAFD N.Futterman/A.Ventress		
DAGR G.Grunberg/K.Rotich		
DAJA F.Jones/R.Ahmed		
DATE G.Takei/A.Eckstein		
DAVR B.Vernel/Y.Ruhian	15.00	40.00
DAWU O.Walpole/M.Udall	12.00	30.00

2018 Star Wars Galaxy Etched Foil Galaxy Puzzle

COMPLETE SET (6)	15.00	40.00
COMMON CARD (GP1-GP6)	4.00	10.00
RANDOMLY INSERTED INTO PACKS

2018 Star Wars Galaxy Ghost Crew Wanted Posters

COMPLETE SET (6)	5.00	12.00
COMMON CARD (P1-P6)	1.25	3.00
*P.P.BLACK/1: UNPRICED DUE TO SCARCITY
*P.P.CYAN/1: UNPRICED DUE TO SCARCITY
*P.P.MAGENTA/1: UNPRICED DUE TO SCARCITY
*P.P.YELLOW/1: UNPRICED DUE TO SCARCITY
RANDOMLY INSERTED INTO PACKS

2018 Star Wars Galaxy Journey of Ahsoka

COMPLETE SET (10)	6.00	15.00
COMMON CARD (1-10)	1.00	2.50
*PURPLE/99: .6X TO 1.5X BASIC CARDS
*ORANGE/25: 1.2X TO 3X BASIC CARDS
*RED/1: UNPRICED DUE TO SCARCITY
*P.P.BLACK/1: UNPRICED DUE TO SCARCITY
*P.P.CYAN/1: UNPRICED DUE TO SCARCITY
*P.P.MAGENTA/1: UNPRICED DUE TO SCARCITY
*P.P.YELLOW/1: UNPRICED DUE TO SCARCITY
RANDOMLY INSERTED INTO PACKS

2018 Star Wars Galaxy Legends

COMPLETE SET (5)	10.00	25.00
COMMON CARD (C1-C5)	3.00	8.00
*PURPLE/99: .6X TO 1.5X BASIC CARDS
*RED/1: UNPRICED DUE TO SCARCITY
*P.P.BLACK/1: UNPRICED DUE TO SCARCITY
*P.P.CYAN/1: UNPRICED DUE TO SCARCITY
*P.P.MAGENTA/1: UNPRICED DUE TO SCARCITY
*P.P.YELLOW/1: UNPRICED DUE TO SCARCITY
RANDOMLY INSERTED INTO PACKS

2018 Star Wars Galaxy New Trilogy Propaganda

COMPLETE SET (6)	5.00	10.00
COMMON CARD (TP1-TP6)	1.00	2.50
*P.P.BLACK/1: UNPRICED DUE TO SCARCITY
*P.P.CYAN/1: UNPRICED DUE TO SCARCITY
*P.P.MAGENTA/1: UNPRICED DUE TO SCARCITY
*P.P.YELLOW/1: UNPRICED DUE TO SCARCITY
RANDOMLY INSERTED INTO PACKS

2018 Star Wars Galaxy Panoramic Sketches

UNPRICED DUE TO SCARCITY

NNO Adam Beck
NNO Adam Schickling
NNO Alex Iniguez
NNO Alex Mines
NNO Andrew Fernandes
NNO Andrew Fry
NNO Andrew Joynes
NNO Andrew Sanchez
NNO Andy Bohn
NNO Angel Aviles
NNO Angelina Benedetti
NNO Anil Sharma
NNO Anthony Figaro
NNO Anthony Skubis
NNO Barry Renshaw
NNO Basak Cetinkaya
NNO Ben AbuSaada
NNO Bill Pulkovski
NNO Brad Hudson
NNO Brad Utterstrom
NNO Brandon Blevins
NNO Brendan Purchase
NNO Brent Scotchmer
NNO Brett Farr
NNO Caleb King
NNO Carlos Cabaleiro
NNO Carolyn Craggs
NNO Chris Meeks
NNO Colin Arthurs
NNO Craig Ludwick
NNO Dan Bergren
NNO Dan Curto
NNO Dan Gorman
NNO Dan Tearle
NNO Darrin Pepe
NNO Dave Gaskin
NNO David Rabbitte
NNO Dean Drummond
NNO Doug Snodgrass
NNO Eli Hyder
NNO Eric Lehtonen
NNO Frank Kadar
NNO Fredd Gorham
NNO Garrett Dix
NNO George Joseph
NNO Gerard Garcia Jr.
NNO Gorkem Demir
NNO Huy Truong
NNO Ingrid Hardy
NNO James Henry Smith
NNO Jamie Cosley
NNO Jamie Richards
NNO Jason Miller
NNO Jason Queen
NNO Jason Sobol
NNO Jay Manchand
NNO Jeff Abar
NNO Jeff West

NNO Jerry Bennett
NNO Jessica Hickman
NNO Jim Mehsling
NNO Jim O'Riley
NNO Joe Corroney
NNO John Bruce
NNO John Pleak
NNO Jon McKenzie
NNO Juan Rosales
NNO Kaela Croft
NNO Keith Farnum
NNO Kelly Baber
NNO Kevin Cleveland
NNO Kevin Cogan
NNO Kevin Graham
NNO Kevin Liell
NNO Kevin P. West
NNO Kris Penix
NNO Laura Atkinson
NNO Laura Martin
NNO Lee Hunt
NNO Lee Lightfoot
NNO Logan Monette
NNO Louise Draper
NNO Madison Emerick
NNO Maggie Ransom
NNO Marcia Dye
NNO Mark Mangum
NNO Marlo Agunos
NNO Marsha Parkins
NNO Matt Applegate
NNO Matt Langford
NNO Matt Maldonado
NNO Matt Stewart
NNO Matthew Hirons
NNO Matthew Lopez
NNO Michael Mastermaker
NNO Michelle Rayner
NNO Mick and Matt Glebe
NNO Mike James
NNO Mohammad Jilani
NNO Neil Camera
NNO Nicholas Baltra
NNO Nick Allsopp
NNO Nick Justus
NNO Omar Salinas
NNO Oscar Chavez
NNO Pablo Diaz
NNO Patricio Carrasco
NNO Patrick Davis
NNO Phil Hassewer
NNO Phillip Trujillo
NNO Rebecca Sharp
NNO Rees Finlay
NNO Rich Henneman
NNO Rich Molinelli
NNO Richard Sensale
NNO Richard Serrao
NNO Rob Teranishi
NNO Robert Hendrickson
NNO Ronnie Crowther
NNO Ryan Crosby
NNO Ryan Finley
NNO Ryan Olsen
NNO Sammy Gomez
NNO Scott Harrell
NNO Shaow Siong
NNO Sheikh Islam
NNO Solly Mohamed
NNO Stephanie Rosales
NNO Stephanie Swanger
NNO Thomas Amici
NNO Tiffany Groves
NNO Tim Dowler
NNO Tim Shinn
NNO Tim Smith
NNO Tina Berardi
NNO Tod Smith
NNO Todd Aaron Smith
NNO Travis Kinnison
NNO Trent Westbrook
NNO Veronica Smith

NNO Vincenzo Dilppolito
NNO Ward Silverman
NNO Zach Woolsey

2018 Star Wars Galaxy Rogue One Propaganda

COMPLETE SET (9)	6.00	15.00
COMMON CARD (RP1-RP9)	1.25	3.00

*P.P.BLACK/1: UNPRICED DUE TO SCARCITY
*P.P.CYAN/1: UNPRICED DUE TO SCARCITY
*P.P.MAGENTA/1: UNPRICED DUE TO SCARCITY
*P.P.YELLOW/1: UNPRICED DUE TO SCARCITY
RANDOMLY INSERTED INTO PACKS

2018 Star Wars Galaxy Shaped Sketches

UNPRICED DUE TO SCARCITY

NNO Adam Beck
NNO Adam Schickling
NNO Alex Iniguez
NNO Alex Mines
NNO Andrew Fernandes
NNO Andrew Fry
NNO Andrew Joynes
NNO Andrew Sanchez
NNO Andy Bohn
NNO Angel Aviles
NNO Angelina Benedetti
NNO Anil Sharma
NNO Anthony Figaro
NNO Anthony Skubis
NNO Barry Renshaw
NNO Basak Cetinkaya
NNO Ben AbuSaada
NNO Bill Pulkovski
NNO Brad Hudson
NNO Brad Utterstrom
NNO Brandon Blevins
NNO Brendan Purchase
NNO Brent Scotchmer
NNO Brett Farr
NNO Caleb King
NNO Carlos Cabaleiro
NNO Carolyn Craggs
NNO Chris Meeks
NNO Colin Arthurs
NNO Craig Ludwick
NNO Dan Bergren
NNO Dan Curto
NNO Dan Gorman
NNO Dan Tearle
NNO Darrin Pepe
NNO Dave Gaskin
NNO David Rabbitte
NNO Dean Drummond
NNO Doug Snodgrass
NNO Eli Hyder
NNO Eric Lehtonen
NNO Frank Kadar
NNO Fredd Gorham
NNO Garrett Dix
NNO George Joseph
NNO Gerard Garcia Jr.
NNO Gorkem Demir
NNO Huy Truong
NNO Ingrid Hardy
NNO James Henry Smith
NNO Jamie Cosley
NNO Jamie Richards
NNO Jason Miller
NNO Jason Queen
NNO Jason Sobol
NNO Jay Manchand
NNO Jeff Abar
NNO Jeff West
NNO Jerry Bennett
NNO Jessica Hickman
NNO Jim Mehsling
NNO Jim OlRiley
NNO Joe Corroney
NNO John Bruce
NNO John Pleak
NNO Jon McKenzie
NNO Juan Rosales
NNO Kaela Croft

NNO Keith Farnum
NNO Kelly Baber
NNO Kevin Cleveland
NNO Kevin Cogan
NNO Kevin Graham
NNO Kevin Liell
NNO Kevin P. West
NNO Kris Penix
NNO Laura Atkinson
NNO Laura Martin
NNO Lee Hunt
NNO Lee Lightfoot
NNO Logan Monette
NNO Louise Draper
NNO Madison Emerick
NNO Maggie Ransom
NNO Marcia Dye
NNO Mark Mangum
NNO Marlo Agunos
NNO Marsha Parkins
NNO Matt Applegate
NNO Matt Langford
NNO Matt Maldonado
NNO Matt Stewart
NNO Matthew Hirons
NNO Matthew Lopez
NNO Michael Mastermaker
NNO Michelle Rayner
NNO Mick and Matt Glebe
NNO Mike James
NNO Mohammad Jilani
NNO Neil Camera
NNO Nicholas Baltra
NNO Nick Allsopp
NNO Nick Justus
NNO Omar Salinas
NNO Oscar Chavez
NNO Pablo Díaz
NNO Patricio Carrasco
NNO Patrick Davis
NNO Phil Hassewer
NNO Phillip Trujillo
NNO Rebecca Sharp
NNO Rees Finlay
NNO Rich Henneman
NNO Rich Molinelli
NNO Richard Sensale
NNO Richard Serrao
NNO Rob Teranishi
NNO Robert Hendrickson
NNO Ronnie Crowther
NNO Ryan Crosby
NNO Ryan Finley
NNO Ryan Olsen
NNO Sammy Gomez
NNO Scott Harrell
NNO Shaow Siong
NNO Sheikh Islam
NNO Solly Mohamed
NNO Stephanie Rosales
NNO Stephanie Swanger
NNO Thomas Amici
NNO Tiffany Groves
NNO Tim Dowler
NNO Tim Shinn
NNO Tim Smith
NNO Tina Berardi
NNO Tod Smith
NNO Todd Aaron Smith
NNO Travis Kinnison
NNO Trent Westbrook
NNO Veronica Smith
NNO Vincenzo Dilppolito
NNO Ward Silverman
NNO Zach Woolsey

2018 Star Wars Galaxy Six-Person Autograph

STATED PRINT RUN 1 SER.#'d SET
UNPRICED DUE TO SCARCITY

NNO Ridley/Boyega/Dern/Serkis/Driver/Christie

2018 Star Wars Galaxy Sketches

UNPRICED DUE TO SCARCITY

NNO Adam Beck
NNO Adam Schickling
NNO Alex Iniguez
NNO Alex Mines
NNO Andrew Fernandes
NNO Andrew Fry
NNO Andrew Joynes
NNO Andrew Sanchez
NNO Andy Bohn
NNO Angel Aviles
NNO Angelina Benedetti
NNO Anil Sharma
NNO Anthony Figaro
NNO Anthony Skubis
NNO Barry Renshaw
NNO Basak Cetinkaya
NNO Ben AbuSaada
NNO Bill Pulkovski
NNO Brad Hudson
NNO Brad Utterstrom
NNO Brandon Blevins
NNO Brendan Purchase
NNO Brent Scotchmer
NNO Brett Farr
NNO Caleb King
NNO Carlos Cabaleiro
NNO Carolyn Craggs
NNO Chris Meeks
NNO Colin Arthurs
NNO Craig Ludwick
NNO Dan Bergren
NNO Dan Curto
NNO Dan Gorman
NNO Dan Tearle
NNO Darrin Pepe
NNO Dave Gaskin
NNO David Rabbitte
NNO Dean Drummond
NNO Doug Snodgrass
NNO Eli Hyder
NNO Eric Lehtonen
NNO Frank Kadar
NNO Fredd Gorham
NNO Garrett Dix
NNO George Joseph
NNO Gerard Garcia Jr.
NNO Gorkem Demir
NNO Huy Truong
NNO Ingrid Hardy
NNO James Henry Smith
NNO Jamie Cosley
NNO Jamie Richards
NNO Jason Miller
NNO Jason Queen
NNO Jason Sobol
NNO Jay Manchand
NNO Jeff Abar
NNO Jeff West
NNO Jerry Bennett
NNO Jessica Hickman
NNO Jim Mehsling
NNO Jim OlRiley
NNO Joe Corroney
NNO John Bruce
NNO John Pleak
NNO Jon McKenzie
NNO Juan Rosales
NNO Kaela Croft
NNO Keith Farnum
NNO Kelly Baber
NNO Kevin Cleveland
NNO Kevin Cogan
NNO Kevin Graham
NNO Kevin Liell
NNO Kevin P. West
NNO Kris Penix
NNO Laura Atkinson
NNO Laura Martin
NNO Lee Hunt
NNO Lee Lightfoot

NNO Logan Monette
NNO Louise Draper
NNO Madison Emerick
NNO Maggie Ransom
NNO Marcia Dye
NNO Mark Mangum
NNO Marlo Agunos
NNO Marsha Parkins
NNO Matt Applegate
NNO Matt Langford
NNO Matt Maldonado
NNO Matt Stewart
NNO Matthew Hirons
NNO Matthew Lopez
NNO Michael Mastermaker
NNO Michelle Rayner
NNO Mick and Matt Glebe
NNO Mike James
NNO Mohammad Jilani
NNO Neil Camera
NNO Nicholas Baltra
NNO Nick Allsopp
NNO Nick Justus
NNO Omar Salinas
NNO Oscar Chavez
NNO Pablo Diaz
NNO Patricio Carrasco
NNO Patrick Davis
NNO Phil Hassewer
NNO Phillip Trujillo
NNO Rebecca Sharp
NNO Rees Finlay
NNO Rich Henneman
NNO Rich Molinelli
NNO Richard Sensale
NNO Richard Serrao
NNO Rob Teranishi
NNO Robert Hendrickson
NNO Ronnie Crowther
NNO Ryan Crosby
NNO Ryan Finley
NNO Ryan Olsen
NNO Sammy Gomez
NNO Scott Harrell
NNO Shaow Siong
NNO Sheikh Islam
NNO Solly Mohamed
NNO Stephanie Rosales
NNO Stephanie Swanger
NNO Thomas Amici
NNO Tiffany Groves
NNO Tim Dowler
NNO Tim Shinn
NNO Tim Smith
NNO Tina Berardi
NNO Tod Smith
NNO Todd Aaron Smith
NNO Travis Kinnison
NNO Trent Westbrook
NNO Veronica Smith
NNO Vincenzo DiIppolito
NNO Ward Silverman
NNO Zach Woolsey

2018 Star Wars Galaxy Triple Autographs
STATED PRINT RUN 5 SER.#'d SETS
UNPRICED DUE TO SCARCITY

TACMW Christensen/McDiarmid/Wood
TAESF Eckstein/Salenger/Futterman
TAFFD Ford/Fisher/Daniels
TAYKK Yen/Kellington/Kasey

2017-18 Star Wars Galaxy's Edge
NNO Blue Milk Delivered Fresh from the Farm
NNO Dok-Ondar Acquires a New Treasure
NNO Hondo and Chewie Make a Deal
NNO New Recruits Rendezvous at the Ancient Ruins
NNO The Rescue Doesn't Go as Planned
NNO Resistance Recruits Face Kylo Ren's Interrogation
NNO Rex Entertains the Crowd
NNO Trouble Is Brewing in the Cantina
NNO Vi Puts Herself in Danger
NNO Star Wars Galaxy's Edge Translator Edge

2004 Star Wars Heritage

BLESSINGS FROM BEYOND

COMPLETE SET (120)	8.00	20.00
UNOPENED BOX (36 PACKS)	65.00	70.00
UNOPENED PACK (5 CARDS)	2.00	2.50
COMMON CARD (1-120)	.15	.40

2004 Star Wars Heritage Alphabet Stickers
COMPLETE SET (30)	12.00	30.00
STATED ODDS 1:3 RETAIL

2004 Star Wars Heritage Autographs
STATED ODDS 1:578

NNO Carrie Fisher		1000.00	2000.00
NNO James Earl Jones		600.00	1200.00
NNO Mark Hamill		1000.00	2000.00

2004 Star Wars Heritage Etched Wave One

COMPLETE SET (6)	6.00	15.00
COMMON CARD (1-6)	1.25	3.00
STATED ODDS 1:9

2004 Star Wars Heritage Etched Wave Two
COMPLETE SET (6)	6.00	15.00
COMMON CARD (1-6)	1.25	3.00
STATED ODDS 1:9

2004 Star Wars Heritage Sketches
UNPRICED DUE TO SCARCITY

NNO Ray Lago
NNO Ryan Benjamin
NNO Matt Busch
NNO Jeff Carlisle
NNO Brian Ching
NNO Cynthia Cummens
NNO Dave Dorman
NNO Jan Duursema
NNO Tommy Edwards
NNO Chris Eliopoulos
NNO Davide Fabbri
NNO Tom Hodges
NNO James Hodgkins
NNO Jeff Johnson
NNO Rafael Kayanan
NNO Mike Lemos
NNO Mike Lilly
NNO Randy Martinez
NNO John McCrea
NNO Brandon McKinney
NNO Mary Mitchell

NNO Jake Myler
NNO William O'Neil
NNO Dan Parsons
NNO Dimitri Patelis
NNO Sean Phillips
NNO Kilian Plunkett
NNO David Rabitte
NNO Ron Randall
NNO Robert Teranishi
NNO Chris Trevas
NNO Russell Walks

2004 Star Wars Heritage Promos
COMMON CARD (P1-P6, S1)		.75	2.00
P1 The Phantom Menace		2.00	5.00
P2 Attack of the Clones		6.00	15.00
P6 Return of the Jedi		2.00	5.00
S1 Empire Strikes Back CT UK		2.50	6.00

2015 Star Wars High Tek

COMPLETE SET w/o SP (112)	60.00	120.00
COMPLETE SET w/SP (127)	250.00	500.00
UNOPENED BOX (8 CARDS)	100.00	120.00
COMMON CARD (1-112)	.40	1.00

*DS CORE: .5X TO 1.2X BASIC CARDS
*HOTH TAC.: .5X TO 1.2X BASIC CARDS
*TIE FRONT: .6X TO 1.5X BASIC CARDS
*VADER TIE: .6X TO 1.5X BASIC CARDS
*MIL.FALCON: .75X TO 2X BASIC CARDS
*STAR DEST.: .75X TO 2X BASIC CARDS
*CARBON: 1X TO 2.5X BASIC CARDS
*EMP.THRONE: 1X TO 2.5X BASIC CARDS
*DS EXT.: 2X TO 5X BASIC CARDS
*TIE WING: 2X TO 5X BASIC CARDS
TIDAL/99: 1.2X TO 3X BASIC CARDS
GOLD RAINBOW/50: 1.5X TO 4X BASIC CARDS
CLOUDS/25: 2X TO 5X BASIC CARDS
RED ORBIT/5: UNPRICED DUE TO SCARCITY
BLACK GALACTIC/1: UNPRICED DUE TO SCARCITY
*P.P.BLACK/1: UNPRICED DUE TO SCARCITY
*P.P.CYAN/1: UNPRICED DUE TO SCARCITY
*P.P.MAGENTA/1: UNPRICED DUE TO SCARCITY
*P.P.YELLOW/1: UNPRICED DUE TO SCARCITY

1A Luke lightsaber		3.00	8.00
1B Luke blaster SP		10.00	25.00
1C Luke Jedi Knight SP		12.00	30.00
2A Leia A New Hope		3.00	8.00
2B Leia Bespin uniform SP		15.00	40.00
2C Leia Slave SP		120.00	200.00
3A Han Solo blaster		4.00	10.00
3B Han Solo Bespin SP		20.00	50.00
3C Han Solo		12.00	30.00

Endor SP

4 Darth Vader	5.00	12.00
5A The Emperor	2.00	5.00
5B Sheev Palpatine SP	4.00	10.00
5C Darth Sidious SP	12.00	30.00
6 Yoda	1.25	3.00
7A C-3PO	4.00	10.00

shiny chrome

7B C-3PO	8.00	20.00

dirty chrome SP

8 R2-D2	1.25	3.00
9 Chewbacca	1.25	3.00
10A Lando	2.00	5.00

cape

10B Lando	8.00	20.00

blaster SP

11 Boba Fett	2.00	5.00
36A Anakin Skywalker	1.25	3.00
36B Anakin	6.00	15.00

two lightsabers SP

37A Obi-Wan Kenobi	1.25	3.00
37B Obi-Wan	12.00	30.00

young SP

37C Obi-Wan	8.00	20.00

old SP

40A Padme	1.25	3.00

dark dress

40B Padme Amidala	10.00	25.00

white outfit SP

42 Darth Maul	1.25	3.00
44B Boba Fett	25.00	60.00

armor SP

88 Anakin Skywalker	1.25	3.00
94 The Inquisitor	.75	2.00
106 Finn	3.00	8.00
107 Kylo Ren	3.00	8.00
108 Rey	5.00	12.00
109 Poe Dameron	3.00	8.00
110 BB-8	4.00	10.00
111 Captain Phasma	3.00	8.00
112 Flametrooper	2.00	5.00

2015 Star Wars High Tek Armor Tek

COMPLETE SET (10)	120.00	250.00
COMMON CARD (AT1-AT10)	8.00	20.00
STATED PRINT RUN 50 SER.#'d SETS		
AT1 Boba Fett	15.00	40.00
AT3 Commander Cody	15.00	40.00
AT4 Darth Vader	20.00	50.00
AT5 Jango Fett	12.00	30.00
AT7 Luke Skywalker	12.00	30.00
AT8 Sabine Wren	10.00	25.00
AT9 Poe Dameron	15.00	40.00
AT10 Kylo Ren	15.00	40.00

2015 Star Wars High Tek Autographs

COMMON AUTO	6.00	15.00
*TIDAL/75: .5X TO 1.2X BASIC AUTOS		
*GOLD RAINBOW/50: .6X TO 1.5X BASIC AUTOS		
*CLOUDS/25: .75X TO 2X BASIC AUTOS		
*RED ORBIT/5: UNPRICED DUE TO SCARCITY		
*P.P.BLACK/1: UNPRICED DUE TO SCARCITY		
*P.P.CYAN/1: UNPRICED DUE TO SCARCITY		
*P.P.MAGENTA/1: UNPRICED DUE TO SCARCITY		
*P.P.YELLOW/1: UNPRICED DUE TO SCARCITY		
2 Carrie Fisher	200.00	400.00
4 David Prowse	120.00	250.00
6 Deep Roy	20.00	50.00
7 Anthony Daniels	80.00	150.00
9 Peter Mayhew	25.00	60.00
11 Jeremy Bulloch	15.00	40.00
12 Paul Blake	10.00	25.00
14 Alan Harris	8.00	20.00
16 Tim Rose	10.00	25.00
20 Warwick Davis	12.00	30.00
23 Dickey Beer	10.00	25.00
27 John Ratzenberger	10.00	25.00
28 Pam Rose	30.00	80.00
29 Dickey Beer	15.00	40.00
30 Paul Brooke	10.00	25.00
42 Ray Park	20.00	50.00
49 Bai Ling	8.00	20.00
57 Amy Allen	10.00	25.00
61 Silas Carson	10.00	25.00

78 Bruce Spence	8.00	20.00
79 Wayne Pygram	10.00	25.00
80 Silas Carson	10.00	25.00
90 Andy Secombe	8.00	20.00
96 Taylor Gray	10.00	25.00
97 Vanessa Marshall	8.00	20.00
100 Tiya Sircar	12.00	30.00
102 Ashley Eckstein	10.00	25.00
104 George Takei	20.00	50.00
105 Dee Bradley Baker	12.00	30.00

2015 Star Wars High Tek Moments of Power

COMPLETE SET (15)	175.00	350.00
COMMON CARD (MP1-MP15)	8.00	20.00
STATED PRINT RUN 50 SER.#'d SETS		
MP1 Anakin Skywalker	10.00	25.00
MP2 Darth Maul	12.00	30.00
MP3 Obi-Wan Kenobi	15.00	40.00
MP4 Padme Amidala	12.00	30.00
MP6 Yoda	12.00	30.00
MP7 The Emperor	10.00	25.00
MP8 Han Solo	20.00	50.00
MP9 Luke Skywalker	15.00	40.00
MP10 Boba Fett	15.00	40.00
MP11 Chewbacca	10.00	25.00
MP13 Princess Leia Organa	15.00	40.00
MP15 Darth Vader	20.00	50.00

2015 Star Wars High Tek Sketches

NNO Achilleas Kokkinakis
NNO Adam Talley
NNO Adrian Rivera
NNO Alejandro Iniquez
NNO Andrew Cosson
NNO Bob Stevlic
NNO Brad Hudson
NNO Brent Ragland
NNO Brian Reedy
NNO Brian Kong
NNO Bruce Gerlach
NNO Carlos Cabaleiro
NNO Christopher West
NNO Crystal Bam Fontan
NNO Dan Curto
NNO Dan Bergren
NNO Darrin Pepe
NNO Dave Strong
NNO Eli Rutten
NNO Eric Lehtonen
NNO Francois Chartier
NNO Irma Ahmed
NNO Jeffrey Benitez
NNO Jessica Hickman
NNO Joe Hogan
NNO John Haun
NNO Jonathan Caustrita
NNO Kate Carleton
NNO Kevin West
NNO Kevin Graham
NNO Kevin Doyle
NNO Kevin Liell
NNO Kyle Babbitt
NNO Kyle Hickman
NNO Lawrence Reynolds
NNO Lee Lightfoot
NNO Marcia Dye
NNO Matt Hebb
NNO Matthew Stewart
NNO Matthew Sutton
NNO Michael Cohen
NNO Mike Hampton
NNO Norvien Basio
NNO Patrick Giles
NNO Rich Molinelli
NNO Ron Conley
NNO Russ Maheras
NNO Solly Mohamed
NNO Stephanie Swanger
NNO Ted Dastick
NNO Tim Dowler
NNO Tim Proctor
NNO Tom Carlton
NNO Tom Zahler
NNO Jeremy M. Jack
NNO Veronica O'Connell

2015 Star Wars High Tek Tek Heads

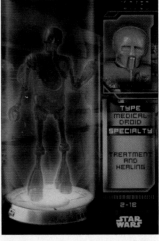

COMPLETE SET (15)	150.00	275.00
COMMON CARD (TH1-TH15)	6.00	15.00
STATED PRINT RUN 50 SER.#'d SETS		
TH1 Darth Vader	20.00	50.00
TH2 C-3PO	10.00	25.00
TH3 Luke Skywalker	10.00	25.00
TH4 R2-D2	8.00	20.00
TH5 IG-88	8.00	20.00
TH7 BB-8	12.00	30.00
TH8 FX-7	8.00	20.00
TH10 2-1B	10.00	25.00
TH12 R7-A7	10.00	25.00
TH13 General Grievous	8.00	20.00
TH14 Chopper	10.00	25.00

2016 Star Wars High Tek

COMPLETE SET W/O SP (112)	100.00	200.00
COMPLETE SET W/SP (127)	300.00	600.00
UNOPENED BOX (1 PACK/8 CARDS)	50.00	60.00
COMMON CARD (SW1-SW112)	1.25	3.00
*F1P1: SAME VALUE AS BASIC		
*F1P2: SAME VALUE AS BASIC		
*F1P3: .75X TO 2X BASIC CARDS		
*F1P4: .75X TO 2X BASIC CARDS		
*F1P5: 1.5X TO 4X BASIC CARDS		
*F2P1: SAME VALUE AS BASIC		
*F2P2: SAME VALUE AS BASIC		
*F2P3: .75X TO 2X BASIC CARDS		
*F2P4: 1X TO 2.5X BASIC CARDS		
*F2P5: 1.50X TO 4X BASIC CARDS		
*BLUE RAIN/99: .75X TO 2X BASIC CARDS		
*GOLD RAIN/50: 1.5X TO 4X BASIC CARDS		
*ORANGE MAGMA/25: 3X TO 6X BASIC CARDS		
*GREEN CUBE/10: 4X TO 10X BASIC CARDS		
*RED ORBIT/5: 6X TO 15X BASIC CARDS		
*BLACK GALACTIC/1: UNPRICED DUE TO SCARCITY		
*P.P.BLACK/1: UNPRICED DUE TO SCARCITY		
*P.P.CYAN/1: UNPRICED DUE TO SCARCITY		

*P.P.MAGENTA/1: UNPRICED DUE TO SCARCITY		
*P.P.YELLOW/1: UNPRICED DUE TO SCARCITY		
SW60A Kylo Ren	15.00	40.00
Dark Side Disciple SP		
SW72A General Leia Organa	25.00	60.00
Resistance Leader SP		
SW75A Rey	15.00	40.00
Jakku Scavenger SP		
SW75B Rey	80.00	150.00
Force Sensitive SP		
SW75C Rey	60.00	120.00
Starkiller Base Duel SP		
SW76A FN-2187	30.00	80.00
First Order Stormtrooper SP		
SW76B Flametrooper	12.00	30.00
First Order Infantry SP		
SW76C Snowtrooper	12.00	30.00
First Order Infantry SP		
SW76D TIE Pilot	12.00	30.00
First Order Pilot SP		
SW84A Han Solo	50.00	100.00
Smuggler SP		
SW87A Finn	30.00	80.00
Resistance Warrior SP		
SW87B Finn	20.00	50.00
Resistance Fighter SP		
SW88A Chewbacca	30.00	80.00
Millennium Falcon Co-Pilot SP		
SW100A Poe Dameron	25.00	60.00
Resistance Messenger SP		
SW100B Poe Dameron	15.00	40.00
Resistance Pilot SP		

2016 Star Wars High Tek Armor Tek

COMMON CARD (AT1-AT11)	8.00	20.00
STATED PRINT RUN 50 SER.#'d SETS		
AT1 Kylo Ren	15.00	40.00
AT2 Captain Phasma	12.00	30.00
AT3 Poe Dameron	10.00	25.00
AT6 First Order Tie Fighter Pilot	12.00	30.00
AT7 First Order Stormtrooper	12.00	30.00
AT8 Rey	20.00	50.00
AT9 Stormtrooper (Heavy Gunner)	10.00	25.00
AT11 Sidon Ithano	12.00	30.00

2016 Star Wars High Tek Autographs

COMMON CARD	5.00	12.00
*BLUE RAIN/75: .5X TO 1.2X BASIC CARDS		
*GOLD RAIN/50: .6X TO 1.5X BASIC CARDS		
*ORANGE MAGMA/25: .75X TO 2X BASIC CARDS		
*GREEN CUBE/10: UNPRICED DUE TO SCARCITY		
*RED ORBIT/5: UNPRICED DUE TO SCARCITY		
*BLACK GALACTIC: UNPRICED DUE TO SCARCITY		
*P.P.BLACK/1: UNPRICED DUE TO SCARCITY		
*P.P.CYAN/1: UNPRICED DUE TO SCARCITY		
*P.P.MAGENTA/1: UNPRICED DUE TO SCARCITY		
*P.P.YELLOW/1: UNPRICED DUE TO SCARCITY		
STATED ODDS 1:		
3 Aidan Cook/Cookie Tuggs	8.00	20.00
4 Alan Ruscoe/Bib Fortuna	6.00	15.00
6 Amy Allen	8.00	20.00

8 Anna Brewster	8.00	20.00
10 Ashley Eckstein	10.00	25.00
13 Brian Vernel	6.00	15.00
15 Catherine Taber	6.00	15.00
17 Cristina da Silva	8.00	20.00
20 Dave Barclay	8.00	20.00
21 David Acord/Med.Droid	6.00	15.00
22 David Acord/Voiceover	6.00	15.00
23 David Bowers	6.00	15.00
24 Dee Bradley Baker	6.00	15.00
26 Dickey Beer		
30 Harriet Walter	6.00	15.00
33 Jeremy Bulloch	12.00	30.00
38 Julie Dolan	8.00	20.00
39 Kiran Shah	6.00	15.00
40 Marc Silk	6.00	15.00
42 Mark Dodson/S.Crumb	6.00	15.00
45 Michael Kingma	6.00	15.00
47 Mike Edmonds	6.00	15.00
48 Mike Quinn	8.00	20.00
50 Paul Blake	6.00	15.00
51 Paul Springer	6.00	15.00
57 Sam Witwer	8.00	20.00
59 Sebastian Armesto	6.00	15.00
60 Silas Carson	8.00	20.00
62 Taylor Gray	6.00	15.00
63 Tim Rose	6.00	15.00
64 Tiya Sircar	6.00	15.00
66 Tosin Cole	10.00	25.00

2016 Star Wars High Tek Autographs Gold Rainbow

*GOLD RAINBOW/50: .6X TO 1.5X BASIC CARDS		
STATED ODDS 1:		
12 Brian Herring	25.00	60.00
25 Denis Lawson	15.00	40.00
67 Warwick Davis	12.00	30.00

2016 Star Wars High Tek Autographs Orange Magma Diffractor

*ORANGE MAGMA/25: .75X TO 2X BASIC CARDS		
14 Carrie Fisher	250.00	500.00
28 Freddie Prinze Jr.	30.00	80.00
37 John Boyega	120.00	250.00

2016 Star Wars High Tek Living Tek

COMMON CARD (LT1-LT13)	6.00	15.00
STATED PRINT RUN 50 SER.#'d SETS		
LT1 Crusher Roodown	10.00	25.00
LT2 Luke Skywalker	15.00	40.00
LT3 C-3PO	8.00	20.00
LT4 BB-8	12.00	30.00
LT5 GA-97	8.00	20.00
LT6 Luggabeast	8.00	20.00
LT7 PZ-4CO	8.00	20.00
LT9 B-U4D	12.00	30.00
LT11 Sidon Ithano	12.00	30.00
LT12 HURID-327	8.00	20.00
LT13 R2-D2	8.00	20.00

2017 Star Wars High Tek

UNOPENED BOX (1 PACK OF 8 CARDS)	50.00	80.00
COMMON FORM 1 (1-56)	1.00	2.50
COMMON FORM 2 (57-112)	1.50	4.00
*F1P1: .75X TO 2X BASIC CARDS	2.00	5.00
*F1P2: .75X TO 2X BASIC CARDS	2.00	5.00
*F1P3: 1X TO 2.5X BASIC CARDS	2.50	6.00
*F2P1: .6X TO 1.5X BASIC CARDS	2.50	6.00
*F2P3: .6X TO 1.5X BASIC CARDS	2.50	6.00
*TIDAL DIFF./99: 1X TO 2.5X BASIC CARDS	2.50	6.00
*F2P2: .75X TO 2X BASIC CARDS	3.00	8.00
*GOLD R.F./50: 1.2X TO 3X BASIC CARDS	3.00	8.00
*F1P4: 2X TO 5X BASIC CARDS	5.00	12.00
*F2P4: 1.2X TO 3X BASIC CARDS	5.00	12.00
*F1P5: 3X TO 8X BASIC CARDS	8.00	20.00
*F2P5: UNPRICED DUE TO SCARCITY		
*ORANGE DIFF./25: UNPRICED DUE TO SCARCITY		
*GREEN DIFF./10: UNPRICED DUE TO SCARCITY		
*RED DIFF./5: UNPRICED DUE TO SCARCITY		
*BLACK DIFF./1: UNPRICED DUE TO SCARCITY		
*P.P.BLACK/1: UNPRICED DUE TO SCARCITY		
*P.P.CYAN/1: UNPRICED DUE TO SCARCITY		
*P.P.MAGENTA/1: UNPRICED DUE TO SCARCITY		

*P.P.YELLOW/1: UNPRICED DUE TO SCARCITY		
7 Rey	2.50	6.00
14 Han Solo	1.50	4.00
15 Luke Skywalker	1.50	4.00
16 Princess Leia Organa	3.00	8.00
20 Jango Fett	2.00	5.00
36 Boba Fett	1.50	4.00
53 Kylo Ren	1.25	3.00
56 Yoda	1.25	3.00
57 Jyn Erso	4.00	10.00
62 Chirrut Imwe	2.00	5.00
68 Darth Vader	2.00	5.00

2017 Star Wars High Tek Autographs

*GREEN DIFF./10: UNPRICED DUE TO SCARCITY		
*RED DIFF./5: UNPRICED DUE TO SCARCITY		
*BLACK DIFF./1: UNPRICED DUE TO SCARCITY		
*P.P.BLACK/1: UNPRICED DUE TO SCARCITY		
*P.P.CYAN/1: UNPRICED DUE TO SCARCITY		
*P.P.MAGENTA/1: UNPRICED DUE TO SCARCITY		
*P.P.YELLOW/1: UNPRICED DUE TO SCARCITY		
RANDOMLY INSERTED INTO PACKS		
NNO Adrienne Wilkinson	6.00	15.00
NNO Alistair Petrie	6.00	15.00
NNO Angus MacInnes	6.00	15.00
NNO Anthony Forest	6.00	15.00
NNO Ariyon Bakare	10.00	25.00
NNO Ashley Eckstein	10.00	25.00
NNO Ben Daniels	6.00	15.00
NNO Brian Herring	15.00	40.00
NNO Cathy Munroe	12.00	30.00
NNO Chris Parsons	8.00	20.00
NNO Daniel Mays	15.00	40.00
NNO David Acord	6.00	15.00
NNO Derek Arnold	6.00	15.00
NNO Duncan Pow	6.00	15.00
NNO Guy Henry	20.00	50.00
NNO Ian McElhinney	6.00	15.00
NNO Ian Whyte	6.00	15.00
NNO Jeremy Bulloch	15.00	40.00
NNO Jordan Stephens	10.00	25.00
NNO Lars Mikkelsen	10.00	25.00
NNO Lloyd Sherr	6.00	15.00
NNO Matthew Wood	6.00	15.00
NNO Olivia d'Abo	6.00	15.00
NNO Stephen Stanton		
NNO Valene Kane	10.00	25.00
NNO Zarene Dallas	6.00	15.00

2017 Star Wars High Tek Dual Autographs

*GREEN DIFF./10: UNPRICED DUE TO SCARCITY		
*RED DIFF./5: UNPRICED DUE TO SCARCITY		
*BLACK DIFF./1: UNPRICED DUE TO SCARCITY		
NNO A.Graves/P.LaMarr		
NNO B.Lourd/C.Clarke		
NNO G.Takei/A.Eckstein/25		
NNO H.Quarshie/R.Brown		
NNO I.Uwais/Y.Ruhian		
NNO J.Isaacs/K.Soucie		
NNO J.Cummings/T.Gray		
NNO J.Coppinger/M.Kingma		

NNO J.Morton/A.Harris		
NNO J.Ratzenberger/A.MacInnes		
NNO M.Wood/J.Henwick		
NNO S.Witwer/A.Wilkinson		
NNO T.Rose/K.Rotich		
NNO T.Kane/C.Taber		
NNO T.Cole/M.Quinn		

2017 Star Wars High Tek Heroes and Villains of The Force Awakens

COMPLETE SET (20)	150.00	300.00
COMMON CARD (HV1-HV20)	6.00	15.00
STATED PRINT RUN 50 SER.#'d SETS		
HV1 Han Solo	10.00	25.00
HV2 Luke Skywalker	10.00	25.00
HV4 Kylo Ren	8.00	20.00
HV5 Rey	20.00	50.00
HV6 Finn	12.00	30.00
HV8 Supreme Leader Snoke	8.00	20.00
HV9 R2-D2	10.00	25.00
HV12 Snap Wexley	10.00	25.00
HV13 Captain Phasma	8.00	20.00
HV14 General Hux	8.00	20.00
HV17 Ello Asty	8.00	20.00
HV18 Unkar Plutt	8.00	20.00
HV19 Chewbacca	10.00	25.00
HV20 Riot Control Stormtrooper	12.00	30.00

2017 Star Wars High Tek A More Elegant Weapon

COMMON CARD (MW1-MW10)	10.00	25.00
STATED PRINT RUN 50 SER.#'d SETS		
MW1 Yoda	15.00	40.00
MW2 Ahsoka Tano	12.00	30.00
MW3 Anakin Skywalker	12.00	30.00
MW5 Rey	30.00	75.00
MW6 Luke Skywalker	15.00	40.00
MW7 Darth Vader	15.00	40.00
MW8 Obi-Wan Kenobi	12.00	30.00
MW10 Mace Windu	12.00	30.00

2017 Star Wars High Tek Rogue One Vehicles

STATED PRINT RUN 50 SER.#'d SETS		
RV1 Jyn Erso/U-wing	10.00	25.00
RV2 Gunner/Death Star	6.00	15.00
RV3 Krennic/Krennic's Shuttle	12.00	30.00
RV4 Tank Commander/Combat Assault Tank	6.00	15.00
RV5 Tarkin/Imperial Star Destroyer	8.00	20.00
RV6 Merrick/X-wing	12.00	30.00
RV7 TIE Striker Pilot/TIE Striker		
RV8 Cassian Andor/U-wing		
RV9 K-2SO/U-wing		
RV10 Bohdi Rook/Imperial Zeta-Class Transport	6.00	15.00

2017 Star Wars High Tek Troopers

COMMON CARD (TR1-TR16)	6.00	15.00
STATED PRINT RUN 50 SER.#'d SETS		
TR1 First Order TIE Fighter Pilot	10.00	25.00
TR2 First Order Stormtrooper	8.00	20.00
TR3 First Order Riot Control Stormtrooper	10.00	25.00
TR9 Imperial Death Trooper	15.00	40.00
TR12 Imperial Sandtrooper	10.00	25.00
TR14 Imperial TIE Fighter Pilot	8.00	20.00
TR15 Galactic Republic Clone Trooper	8.00	20.00
TR16 Galactic Marine	10.00	25.00

2020 Star Wars Holocron

IG-88

COMPLETE SET W/SP (225)	200.00	400.00
COMPLETE SET W/O SP (200)	15.00	40.00
COMMON CARD	.20	.50
COMMON SP	10.00	25.00
*FOILBOARD: .75X TO 2X BASIC CARDS		
*GREEN: 1.5X TO 4X BASIC CARDS		
*ORANGE/99: 3X TO 8X BASIC CARDS		
*PURPLE/10: UNPRICED DUE TO SCARCITY		
*BLACK/5: UNPRICED DUE TO SCARCITY		
*RED/1: UNPRICED DUE TO SCARCITY		
*P.P.BLACK/1: UNPRICED DUE TO SCARCITY		
*P.P.CYAN/1: UNPRICED DUE TO SCARCITY		
*P.P.MAGENTA/1: UNPRICED DUE TO SCARCITY		
*P.P.YELLOW/1: UNPRICED DUE TO SCARCITY		
N21 The Child	4.00	10.00
PX7 Ahsoka Tano	2.00	5.00
BH14 Boba Fett	1.25	3.00
BH15 The Mandalorian	2.00	5.00
BH2S Boba Fett SP	20.00	50.00
CD1S Qi'Ra SP	25.00	60.00
FO1S Kylo Ren SP	15.00	40.00
N21S The Child SP	50.00	100.00
BH15S The Mandalorian SP	15.00	40.00
EMP1S Darth Vader SP	15.00	40.00
REB1S Luke Skywalker SP	12.00	30.00
REB2S Princess Leia Organa SP	12.00	30.00
REB33 Cara Dune	6.00	15.00
REB3S Han Solo SP	12.00	30.00
REP6S Padme Amidala SP	20.00	50.00
REP8S C-3PO SP	12.00	30.00
REP9S R2-D2 SP	12.00	30.00
RES1S Rey SP	15.00	40.00
JEDI15 Ahsoka Tano	2.00	5.00
JEDI1S Obi-Wan Kenobi SP	12.00	30.00
JEDI3S Yoda SP	15.00	40.00
REB23S Jyn Erso SP	15.00	40.00
SITH1S Darth Maul SP	12.00	30.00
JEDI15S Ahsoka Tano SP	20.00	50.00

2020 Star Wars Holocron The Adventures of Han Solo

COMPLETE SET (20)	10.00	25.00
COMMON CARD (AH1-AH20)	1.25	3.00
*ORANGE/99: .6X TO 1.5X BASIC CARDS		
*PURPLE/10: UNPRICED DUE TO SCARCITY		
*BLACK/5: UNPRICED DUE TO SCARCITY		
*RED/1: UNPRICED DUE TO SCARCITY		
*P.P.BLACK/1: UNPRICED DUE TO SCARCITY		
*P.P.CYAN/1: UNPRICED DUE TO SCARCITY		
*P.P.MAGENTA/1: UNPRICED DUE TO SCARCITY		
*P.P.YELLOW/1: UNPRICED DUE TO SCARCITY		
STATED ODDS 1:3		

2020 Star Wars Holocron Autographs

KANAN JARRUS
AUTHENTIC AUTOGRAPH

COMMON AUTO	6.00	15.00
*GREEN/99: .5X TO 1.2X BASIC AUTOS		
*BLUE/50: .6X TO 1.5X BASIC AUTOS		
*ORANGE/25: UNPRICED DUE TO SCARCITY		
*PURPLE/10: UNPRICED DUE TO SCARCITY		
*BLACK/5: UNPRICED DUE TO SCARCITY		
*RED/1: UNPRICED DUE TO SCARCITY		
*P.P.BLACK/1: UNPRICED DUE TO SCARCITY		
*P.P.CYAN/1: UNPRICED DUE TO SCARCITY		
*P.P.MAGENTA/1: UNPRICED DUE TO SCARCITY		
*P.P.YELLOW/1: UNPRICED DUE TO SCARCITY		
STATED ODDS 1:859		
MANY OF THE KEY SIGNERS		
DO NOT HAVE BASE AUTOGRAPHS		
AAV Attila Vajda	8.00	20.00
ADA David Ankrum	8.00	20.00
AHD Harley Durst	8.00	20.00

2020 Star Wars Holocron Autographs Green

STATED ODDS 1:3,258		
STATED PRINT RUN 99 SER.#'d SETS		
ACR Clive Revill	12.00	30.00

2020 Star Wars Holocron Charting the Galaxy

COMPLETE SET (20)	12.00	30.00
COMMON CARD (CG1-CG20)	1.00	2.50
*ORANGE/99: .5X TO 1.2X BASIC CARDS		
*PURPLE/10: UNPRICED DUE TO SCARCITY		
*BLACK/5: UNPRICED DUE TO SCARCITY		
*RED/1: UNPRICED DUE TO SCARCITY		
*P.P.BLACK/1: UNPRICED DUE TO SCARCITY		
*P.P.CYAN/1: UNPRICED DUE TO SCARCITY		
*P.P.MAGENTA/1: UNPRICED DUE TO SCARCITY		
*P.P.YELLOW/1: UNPRICED DUE TO SCARCITY		
STATED ODDS 1:3		

2020 Star Wars Holocron Commemorative Creature Patches

EWOK

STAR WARS

COMMON MEM	3.00	8.00

*GREEN/99: .5X TO 1.2X BASIC MEM
*ORANGE/25: UNPRICED DUE TO SCARCITY
*PURPLE/10: UNPRICED DUE TO SCARCITY
*BLACK/5: UNPRICED DUE TO SCARCITY
*RED/1: UNPRICED DUE TO SCARCITY
STATED ODDS 1:RETAIL BOX

PCB	The Child	10.00	25.00
PCE	Chewbacca	5.00	12.00
PCJ	The Child	10.00	25.00
PCP	Chewbacca	5.00	12.00
PHE	Han Solo	8.00	20.00
PHT	Han Solo	8.00	20.00
PKB	Kuiil	4.00	10.00
PKJ	Kuiil	4.00	10.00
PLJ	Luke Skywalker	6.00	15.00
PLP	Luke Skywalker	6.00	15.00
PLT	Luke Skywalker	6.00	15.00
PMJ	Mudhorn	4.00	10.00
PPP	Paploo	5.00	12.00
PRP	Rey	8.00	20.00
PSJ	Stormtrooper	4.00	10.00
PTE	Teebo	4.00	10.00
PTT	Tauntaun	5.00	12.00
PLOE	Princess Leia Organa	6.00	15.00
POWJ	Obi-Wan Kenobi	4.00	10.00
PPGP	Porg	4.00	10.00
PTKE	Tokkat	5.00	12.00
PTMB	The Mandalorian	6.00	15.00
PTMJ	The Mandalorian	6.00	15.00

2020 Star Wars Holocron Dual Autographs

*PURPLE/10: UNPRICED DUE TO SCARCITY
*BLACK/5: UNPRICED DUE TO SCARCITY
*RED/1: UNPRICED DUE TO SCARCITY
STATED ODDS 1:43,158
STATED PRINT RUN 25 SER.#'d SETS
UNPRICED DUE TO SCARCITY

DACM H.Christensen/E.McGregor
DAES A.Ehrenreich/J.Suotamo
DAET A.Eckstein/J.Taylor
DAFS F.Prinze Jr./S.Blum
DAJT F.Jones/A.Tudyk
DAKD I.Kenny/H.Durst
DAMB P.Mayhew/K.Baker
DAPB F.Prinze Jr./T.Baker
DAPJ P.Anthony-Rodriguez/J.Isaacs
DARD D.Ridley/A.Driver

2020 Star Wars Holocron Lightsabers of the Jedi

COMPLETE SET (10)	6.00	15.00
COMMON CARD (LJ1-LJ10)	1.00	2.50

*ORANGE/99: 1.5X TO 4X BASIC CARDS
*PURPLE/10: UNPRICED DUE TO SCARCITY
*BLACK/5: UNPRICED DUE TO SCARCITY
*RED/1: UNPRICED DUE TO SCARCITY
*P.P.BLACK/1: UNPRICED DUE TO SCARCITY
*P.P.CYAN/1: UNPRICED DUE TO SCARCITY
*P.P.MAGENTA/1: UNPRICED DUE TO SCARCITY
*P.P.YELLOW/1: UNPRICED DUE TO SCARCITY
STATED ODDS 1:3

2020 Star Wars Holocron Six-Person Autographs

STATED ODDS 1:172,080
STATED PRINT RUN 1 SER.#'d SET
UNPRICED DUE TO SCARCITY

NNO Ridley/Boyega/Tran/Williams/Lourd/Ackie
NNO McGregor/Jackson/Christensen/Morrison/McDiarmid/Park
NNO Jones/Whitaker/Ahmed/Yen/Mendelsohn/Mikkelsen
NNO Prinze Jr./Anthony-Rodriguez/Gellar/Gray/Witwer/Eckstein
NNO Ford/Fisher/Mayhew/Baker/Williams/Revill

2020 Star Wars Holocron Sketches

STATED ODDS 1:258
UNPRICED DUE TO SCARCITY

NNO Adam Beck
NNO Alex Iniguez
NNO Alex Mines
NNO Allen Grimes
NNO Andrew Fernandes
NNO Andrew Fry
NNO Andrew Joynes
NNO Andy Bohn

NNO Angel Aviles
NNO Anil Sharma
NNO Anthony Ellison
NNO Anthony Skubis
NNO Ashlee Brienzo
NNO Ashley Marsh
NNO Ashley Villers
NNO Barry Renshaw
NNO Basak Cetinkaya
NNO Benjamin Lombart
NNO Bobby Blakey
NNO Brad Hudson
NNO Brendan Purchase
NNO Brent Ragland
NNO Brent Scotchmer
NNO Brett Farr
NNO Bruce Gerlach
NNO Caleb Hildenbrandt
NNO Can Baran
NNO Candice Dailey
NNO Carlos Cabaleiro
NNO Chris Colyer
NNO Chris Jenkins
NNO Chris Kay
NNO Chris Quinn
NNO Chris Thorne
NNO Cisco Rivera
NNO Clara Bujtor
NNO Colin Arthurs
NNO Cyrus Sherkat
NNO Dan Gorman
NNO Dan Tearle
NNO Daniel Riveron
NNO Darrin Pepe
NNO Dave Gaskin
NNO David Jackowski
NNO David Storey
NNO Dawn Murphy
NNO Doug Snodgrass
NNO Dylan Riley
NNO Eric Lehtonen
NNO Frank Kadar
NNO Frank Sansone
NNO Fredd Gorham
NNO Garrett Dix
NNO Gavin Williams
NNO George Joseph
NNO Gerard Garcia Jr.
NNO Guilherme Rocha
NNO Ian MacDougall
NNO Ingrid Hardy
NNO Jamie Cosley
NNO Jamie Richards
NNO Jason Adams
NNO Jason Davies
NNO Jason Miller
NNO Jason Montoya
NNO Jason Queen
NNO Jay Manchand
NNO Jeff Abar
NNO Jeff Mallinson
NNO Jeffrey Cox
NNO Jessica Hickman
NNO Jim Mehsling
NNO Jim O'Riley
NNO John Bruce
NNO John DiBiase
NNO Jon McKenzie
NNO Jonathan Beistline
NNO Jose Ventura
NNO Josh Church
NNO Jude Gallagher
NNO Justin Castaneda
NNO Kaela Croft
NNO Kallan Archer
NNO Karl Jones
NNO Keith Farnum
NNO Kevin Cleveland
NNO Kevin Graham
NNO Kursat Cetiner
NNO Kyle Hickman
NNO Lee Lightfoot

NNO Lindsey Greyling
NNO Logan Monette
NNO Louise Draper
NNO Madison Emerick
NNO Maggie Ransom
NNO Mai Irving
NNO Marcia Dye
NNO Mark Necchi
NNO Marlo Agunos
NNO Marsha Parkins
NNO Matt Stewart
NNO Matthew Hirons
NNO Matthew Lopez
NNO Mayumi Seto
NNO Michael Mastermaker
NNO Michael Sealie
NNO Michelle Rayner
NNO Mick and Matt Glebe
NNO Mike Stephens
NNO Mohammad Jilani
NNO Nathan Ohlendorf
NNO Neil Camera
NNO Nick Allsopp
NNO Nick Gribbon
NNO Norviento Basio
NNO Omar Salinas
NNO Patricio Carrasco
NNO Patrick Davis
NNO Phil Hassewer
NNO Phillip Trujillo
NNO Quinton Baker
NNO Rebecca Sharp
NNO Rees Finlay
NNO Rich Hennemann
NNO Rich Molinelli
NNO Richard Serrao
NNO Rob Teranishi
NNO Robert Hendrickson
NNO Rodney Roberts
NNO Ronnie Crowther
NNO Ryan Finley
NNO Ryan Olsen
NNO Sammy Gomez
NNO Scott Harrell
NNO Seth Groves
NNO Shane McCormack
NNO Shaow Siong
NNO Solly Mohamed
NNO Stephanie Swanger
NNO Steve Fuchs
NNO Thomas Amici
NNO Tim Dowler
NNO Tim Shinn
NNO Travis Kinnison
NNO Trent Westbrook
NNO Veronica Smith
NNO Vincenzo D'Ippolito
NNO Ward Silverman
NNO Wayne Tully
NNO Zach Woolsey

2020 Star Wars Holocron Triple Autographs

*BLACK/5: UNPRICED DUE TO SCARCITY
*RED/1: UNPRICED DUE TO SCARCITY
STATED ODDS 1:86,315

TAEBW Ehrenreich/Bettany/Sam Witwer
TARBT Ridley/Boyega/Tran
TAMJC McGregor/Jackson/Christensen
TAJAT Jones/Ahmed/Tudyk
TATPB Prinze Jr./Blum/Reubens

2015 Star Wars Honey Maid

COMPLETE SET (12)	3.00	8.00
COMMON CARD	.40	1.00
PAN1 Obi-Wan Kenobi	2.00	5.00
Darth Vader/Han Solo/Chewbacca/Storm Trooper/C-3PO		
PAN2 R2-D2	2.00	5.00
The Emperor/Yoda/Luke Skywalker/Boba Fett/Princess Leia Organa		

2020 Star Wars I Am Your Father's Day

COMPLETE SET (10)	12.00	30.00
COMMON CARD (1-10)	2.50	6.00
STATED PRINT RUN 896 SETS		

2021 Star Wars I Am Your Father's Day

COMPLETE SET (10)	15.00	40.00
COMMON CARD (1-10)	2.00	5.00
STATED PRINT RUN 896 SETS		
1 The Mandalorian/Grogu	6.00	15.00
2 Darth Vader/Luke Skywalker	3.00	8.00

2013 Star Wars Jedi Legacy

COMPLETE SET (90)	6.00	15.00
UNOPENED BOX (24 PACKS)	60.00	70.00
UNOPENED PACK (8 CARDS)	2.50	3.00
COMMON CARD (1A-45L)	.20	.50
*BLUE: 1.2X TO 3X BASIC CARDS		
*MAGENTA: 4X TO 10X BASIC CARDS		
*GREEN: 5X TO 12X BASIC CARDS		
*GOLD/10: 50X TO 120X BASIC CARDS		
*P.P.BLACK/1: UNPRICED DUE TO SCARCITY		
*P.P.CYAN/1: UNPRICED DUE TO SCARCITY		
*P.P.MAGENTA/1: UNPRICED DUE TO SCARCITY		
*P.P.YELLOW/1: UNPRICED DUE TO SCARCITY		

2013 Star Wars Jedi Legacy Autographs

COMMON AUTO (UNNUMBERED)	8.00	20.00
STATED ODDS 1:72		
NNO Alan Harris	20.00	50.00
NNO Amy Allen	10.00	25.00
NNO Anthony Daniels	150.00	300.00
NNO Anthony Forrest	10.00	25.00
NNO Billy Dee Williams	100.00	200.00
NNO Carrie Fisher	500.00	1000.00
NNO Harrison Ford	1200.00	2000.00
NNO Ian McDiarmid	150.00	300.00
NNO James Earl Jones	250.00	400.00
NNO Jeremy Bulloch	60.00	120.00
NNO Kenny Baker	125.00	250.00
NNO Mark Hamill	500.00	800.00

2013 Star Wars Jedi Legacy Chewbacca Fur Relics

COMMON MEM (CR1-CR4)	125.00	250.00
STATED ODDS 1:720		

2013 Star Wars Jedi Legacy Connections

COMPLETE SET (15)	5.00	12.00
COMMON CARD (C1-C15)	.60	1.50
*P.P.BLACK/1: UNPRICED DUE TO SCARCITY		
*P.P.CYAN/1: UNPRICED DUE TO SCARCITY		
*P.P.MAGENTA/1: UNPRICED DUE TO SCARCITY		
*P.P.YELLOW/1: UNPRICED DUE TO SCARCITY		
STATED ODDS 1:2		

2013 Star Wars Jedi Legacy Ewok Fur Relics

COMMON CARD (ER1-ER4)	20.00	50.00
STATED ODDS 1:120		
ER1 Wicket W. Warrick	125.00	250.00
ER4 Widdle Warrick	100.00	200.00

2013 Star Wars Jedi Legacy Film Cels

COMMON CARD (FR1-FR30)	10.00	25.00
STATED ODDS 1:BOX		
FR6 Darth Vader	20.00	50.00

2013 Star Wars Jedi Legacy Dual Film Cels

COMPLETE SET (6)	120.00	250.00
COMMON CARD (DFR1-DFR6)	20.00	50.00
STATED ODDS 1:144		
DFR1 Darth Vader/Luke Skywalker	30.00	60.00

2013 Star Wars Jedi Legacy Triple Film Cels

COMPLETE SET (10)	250.00	500.00
COMMON CARD (TFR1-TFR10)	30.00	60.00
STATED ODDS 1:144		

2013 Star Wars Jedi Legacy Influencers

COMPLETE SET (18)	5.00	12.00
COMMON CARD (I1-I18)	.50	1.25
*P.P.BLACK/1: UNPRICED DUE TO SCARCITY		
*P.P.CYAN/1: UNPRICED DUE TO SCARCITY		
*P.P.MAGENTA/1: UNPRICED DUE TO SCARCITY		
*P.P.YELLOW/1: UNPRICED DUE TO SCARCITY		
STATED ODDS 1:2		

2013 Star Wars Jedi Legacy Jabba's Sail Barge Relics

COMPLETE SET (5)	300.00	600.00
COMMON CARD (JR1-JR5)	50.00	100.00
STATED ODDS 1:336		
JR1 Luke Skywalker	100.00	200.00
JR2 Leia Organa	100.00	200.00
JR3 Boba Fett	75.00	150.00

2013 Star Wars Jedi Legacy The Circle is Now Complete

COMPLETE SET (12)	35.00	70.00
COMMON CARD (CC1-CC12)	4.00	10.00
*P.P.BLACK/1: UNPRICED DUE TO SCARCITY		
*P.P.CYAN/1: UNPRICED DUE TO SCARCITY		
*P.P.MAGENTA/1: UNPRICED DUE TO SCARCITY		
*P.P.YELLOW/1: UNPRICED DUE TO SCARCITY		
STATED ODDS 1:12		
NNO1 Luke Skywalker PROMO		

2013 Star Wars Jedi Legacy Promos

COMMON CARD	3.00	8.00
P1 Battle Through Blood	8.00	20.00
(Darth Vader)		
P2 Battle Through Blood	8.00	20.00
(Luke Skywalker)		
P3 Challenge of a Fallen Jedi	8.00	20.00
(Anakin vs. Count Dooku)		
P4 Challenge of a Fallen Jedi	8.00	20.00
(Luke vs. Vader)		
P5 Death of a Mentor	3.00	8.00
(Qui Gon vs. Darth Maul)/(Philly Non-Sports Show Exclusive)		
NNO Darth Vader Disc	1.50	4.00
NNO Luke Skywalker Disc	1.50	4.00
NNO Two Paths. Two Journeys. One Destiny		
(5 X 7 Jumbo)		

2015 Star Wars Journey to The Force Awakens

COMPLETE SET (110)	10.00	25.00
COMMON CARD (1-110)	.20	.50
*JABBA SLIME GREEN: .5X TO 1.2X BASIC CARDS		
*BLACK: .6X TO 1.5X BASIC CARDS		
*DEATH STAR SILVER: .75X TO 2X BASIC CARDS		
*LTSBR. NEON PINK: 1.5X TO 4X BASIC CARDS		
*PURPLE: 4X TO 10X BASIC CARDS		
*HOTH ICE/150: 6X TO 15X BASIC CARDS		
*GOLD/50: 10X TO 25X BASIC CARDS		
*HOLOGRAM/25: 15X TO 40X BASIC CARDS		
*RED IMPERIAL/1: UNPRICED DUE TO SCARCITY		
*P.P. BLACK/1: UNPRICED DUE TO SCARCITY		
*P.P. CYAN/1: UNPRICED DUE TO SCARCITY		
*P.P. MAGENTA/1: UNPRICED DUE TO SCARCITY		
*P.P. YELLOW/1: UNPRICED DUE TO SCARCITY		

2015 Star Wars Journey to The Force Awakens Autographs

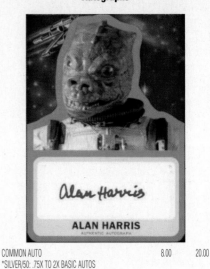

ALAN HARRIS

COMMON AUTO	8.00	20.00
*SILVER/50: .75X TO 2X BASIC AUTOS		
*GOLD/10: UNPRICED DUE TO SCARCITY		
*RED/1: UNPRICED DUE TO SCARCITY		
*P.P.BLACK/1: UNPRICED DUE TO SCARCITY		
*P.P.CYAN/1: UNPRICED DUE TO SCARCITY		
*P.P.MAGENTA/1: UNPRICED DUE TO SCARCITY		
*P.P.YELLOW/1: UNPRICED DUE TO SCARCITY		
NNO Alan Harris	10.00	25.00
NNO Amy Allen	12.00	30.00
NNO Angus MacInnes	8.00	20.00
NNO Anthony Daniels	200.00	400.00
NNO Ashley Eckstein	15.00	40.00
NNO Bai Ling	15.00	40.00
NNO Billy Dee Williams	50.00	100.00
NNO Caroline Blakiston	10.00	25.00
NNO Carrie Fisher	120.00	250.00
NNO David Prowse	80.00	150.00
NNO Dickey Beer	10.00	25.00
NNO Femi Taylor	12.00	30.00
NNO Hassani Shapi	12.00	30.00
NNO Jeremy Bulloch	25.00	60.00
NNO Jerome Blake	10.00	25.00
NNO John Ratzenberger	12.00	30.00
NNO Kenji Oates	10.00	25.00
NNO Kenneth Colley	10.00	25.00
NNO Kenny Baker	100.00	200.00
NNO Mark Hamill	225.00	350.00
NNO Michonne Bourriague	12.00	30.00
NNO Mike Quinn	25.00	60.00
NNO Nika Futterman	10.00	25.00
NNO Olivia d'Abo	80.00	150.00
NNO Orli Shoshan	10.00	25.00
NNO Pam Rose	10.00	25.00
NNO Peter Mayhew	50.00	100.00
NNO Ray Park	25.00	60.00
NNO Rohan Nichol	12.00	30.00
NNO Steven Blum	10.00	25.00
NNO Taylor Gray	12.00	30.00
NNO Tiya Sircar	25.00	60.00
NNO Vanessa Marshall	15.00	40.00
NNO Wayne Pygram	12.00	30.00

2015 Star Wars Journey to The Force Awakens Behind-the-Scenes

COMPLETE SET (9)	5.00	12.00
COMMON CARD (BTS1-BTS9)	1.00	2.50
*P.P.BLACK/1: UNPRICED DUE TO SCARCITY		
*P.P.CYAN/1: UNPRICED DUE TO SCARCITY		
*P.P.MAGENTA/1: UNPRICED DUE TO SCARCITY		
*P.P.YELLOW/1: UNPRICED DUE TO SCARCITY		

2015 Star Wars Journey to The Force Awakens Blueprints

COMPLETE SET (8)	15.00	40.00
COMMON CARD (BP1-BP8)	3.00	8.00
BP1 BB-8	6.00	15.00
BP3 Millennium Falcon	5.00	12.00
BP4 X-Wing Fighter	4.00	10.00

2015 Star Wars Journey to The Force Awakens
Character Stickers

COMPLETE SET (18)	15.00	40.00
COMMON CARD (S1-S18)	1.25	3.00
*P.P.BLACK/1: UNPRICED DUE TO SCARCITY		
*P.P.CYAN/1: UNPRICED DUE TO SCARCITY		
*P.P.MAGENTA/1: UNPRICED DUE TO SCARCITY		
*P.P.YELLOW/1: UNPRICED DUE TO SCARCITY		
S1 Luke Skywalker	1.50	4.00
S2 Han Solo	2.00	5.00
S9 BB-8	2.50	6.00
S10 Captain Phasma	1.50	4.00
S11 Kylo Ren	2.00	5.00
S14 Darth Vader	2.00	5.00
S15 Boba Fett	1.50	4.00
S17 Kylo Ren	2.00	5.00
S18 Yoda	1.50	4.00

2015 Star Wars Journey to The Force Awakens
Choose Your Destiny

COMPLETE SET (9)	12.00	30.00
COMMON CARD (CD1-CD9)	2.50	6.00

2015 Star Wars Journey to The Force Awakens
Classic Captions

COMPLETE SET (8)	15.00	40.00
COMMON CARD (CC1-CC8)	4.00	10.00

2015 Star Wars Journey to The Force Awakens
Cloth Stickers

COMPLETE SET (9)	8.00	20.00
COMMON CARD (CS1-CS9)	1.50	4.00
CS6 Kylo Ren	2.00	5.00
CS9 Kylo Ren (w/TIE Fighters)	2.00	5.00

2015 Star Wars Journey to The Force Awakens
Concept Art

COMPLETE SET (9)	5.00	12.00
COMMON CARD (CA1-CA9)	1.00	2.50
*P.P.BLACK/1: UNPRICED DUE TO SCARCITY		
*P.P.CYAN/1: UNPRICED DUE TO SCARCITY		
*P.P.MAGENTA/1: UNPRICED DUE TO SCARCITY		
*P.P.YELLOW/1: UNPRICED DUE TO SCARCITY		

2015 Star Wars Journey to The Force Awakens
Dual Autographs

STATED PRINT RUN 3 SER.#'d SETS
UNPRICED DUE TO SCARCITY

1 M.Hamill/K.Baker
2 I.McDiarmid/W.Pygram
3 P.Mayhew/A.Daniels
4 M.Hamill/D.Prowse

2015 Star Wars Journey to The Force Awakens
Family Legacy Matte Backs

COMPLETE SET (8)	10.00	25.00
COMMON CARD (FL1-FL8)	1.50	4.00
*GLOSSY: .5X TO 1.2X BASIC CARDS		
*P.P.BLACK/1: UNPRICED DUE TO SCARCITY		
*P.P.CYAN/1: UNPRICED DUE TO SCARCITY		
*P.P.MAGENTA/1: UNPRICED DUE TO SCARCITY		
*P.P.YELLOW/1: UNPRICED DUE TO SCARCITY		
FL1 Boba Fett and Jango Fett	2.00	5.00
FL2 Anakin Skywalker and Luke Skywalker	2.00	5.00
FL3 Padme Amidala and Leia Organa	2.00	5.00

2015 Star Wars Journey to The Force Awakens
Heroes of the Resistance

COMPLETE SET (9)	6.00	15.00
COMMON CARD (R1-R9)	1.25	3.00
*P.P.BLACK/1: UNPRICED DUE TO SCARCITY		
*P.P.CYAN/1: UNPRICED DUE TO SCARCITY		
*P.P.MAGENTA/1: UNPRICED DUE TO SCARCITY		
*P.P.YELLOW/1: UNPRICED DUE TO SCARCITY		
R4 BB-8	2.00	5.00
R8 The Millennium Falcon	1.50	4.00

2015 Star Wars Journey to The Force Awakens
Patches

COMPLETE SET (20)	150.00	300.00
COMMON CARD (P1-P20)	8.00	20.00
P1 Kylo Ren	12.00	30.00
P3 Captain Phasma	12.00	30.00
P9 BB-8	12.00	30.00
P18 BB-8	12.00	30.00

2015 Star Wars Journey to The Force Awakens
Power of the First Order

COMPLETE SET (8)	6.00	15.00
COMMON CARD (FD1-FD8)	1.25	3.00
*P.P.BLACK/1: UNPRICED DUE TO SCARCITY		
*P.P.CYAN/1: UNPRICED DUE TO SCARCITY		
*P.P.MAGENTA/1: UNPRICED DUE TO SCARCITY		
*P.P.YELLOW/1: UNPRICED DUE TO SCARCITY		
FD1 Kylo Ren	2.00	5.00
FD2 Captain Phasma	1.50	4.00

2015 Star Wars Journey to The Force Awakens
Silhouette Foil

COMPLETE SET (8)	4.00	10.00
COMMON CARD (1-8)	.75	2.00
*P.P.BLACK/1: UNPRICED DUE TO SCARCITY		
*P.P.CYAN/1: UNPRICED DUE TO SCARCITY		
*P.P.MAGENTA/1: UNPRICED DUE TO SCARCITY		
*P.P.YELLOW/1: UNPRICED DUE TO SCARCITY		
ERRONEOUSLY LISTED AS A 9-CARD SET		
ON THE CARD BACKS		
5 Kylo Ren	1.50	4.00
7 Captain Phasma	1.25	3.00

2015 Star Wars Journey to The Force Awakens
Sketches

NNO Achilleas Kokkinakis
NNO Adam Talley
NNO Adrian Rivera
NNO Alex Iniguez
NNO Andrew "Drone" Cosson
NNO Bien Flores
NNO Brian Reedy
NNO Bruce Gerlach
NNO Chris Henderson
NNO Chris Raimo
NNO Dan Gorman
NNO Dan Parsons
NNO Daniel Contois
NNO Danny Haas
NNO Darrin Pepe
NNO David Rabbitte
NNO Don Pedicini Jr.
NNO Eric Lehtonen
NNO Fer Galicia
NNO FLOSI
NNO Francois Chartier
NNO Greg Pedersen
NNO Ingrid Hardy
NNO Irma "Aimo" Ahmed
NNO J. Peltz
NNO Jan Duursema
NNO Jason Adams
NNO Jason Brower
NNO Jason Chalker
NNO Jason Crosby
NNO Jason Flowers
NNO Jason Martin
NNO Jeff Mallinson
NNO Jessica Hickman
NNO Joel Biske
NNO John Sloboda
NNO Josh Lyman
NNO Justin ...
NNO Karen Hallion
NNO Kimberly Dunaway
NNO Kiley Beecher
NNO Kris Penix
NNO Lord Mesa
NNO Marcia "MDYE" Dye
NNO Marco D. Carrillo
NNO Matt Hebb
NNO Matt Stewart
NNO Michael "Locoduck" Duron
NNO Michael Cohen
NNO Nicole Falk
NNO Omar Maya Velazquez
NNO Otis Frampton
NNO Pablo Diaz
NNO Rich Molinelli
NNO Robert Hendrickson
NNO Robert Jimenez
NNO Robert Teranishi
NNO Sarah Wilkinson
NNO Scott Blair
NNO Shane McCormack
NNO Solly Mohamed
NNO Stephanie Swanger
NNO Strephon Taylor
NNO Sue Thomas
NNO Tim Proctor
NNO Tina Berardi
NNO Todd Aaron Smith
NNO Ward Silverman
NNO Wilson Ramos Jr.

2015 Star Wars Journey to The Force Awakens
Triple Autographs

STATED PRINT RUN 5 SER.#'d SETS
UNPRICED DUE TO SCARCITY

1 McDiarmid/Park/Pygram
2 Prowse/Park/Pygram

2015 Star Wars Journey to The Force Awakens
Promos

COMPLETE SET (6)	10.00	25.00
COMMON CARD (P1-P6)	2.00	5.00
P1 Luke Skywalker	6.00	15.00
(SDCC Marvel Star Wars Lando exclusive)		
P6 Kanan Jarrus	5.00	12.00
(NYCC exclusive)		

2015 Star Wars Journey to The Force Awakens UK

COMPLETE SET (208)	30.00	80.00
COMMON CARD	.30	.75
LEY Yoda		
LEBF Boba Fett		
LECH Chewbacca		
LEHS Han Solo		
LELC Lando Calrissian		
LELS Luke Skywalker		
LEPL Princess Leia		
LER2 R2-D2		
LEST Stormtrooper		
LETE The Emperor		

2017 Star Wars Journey to The Last Jedi

COMPLETE SET (110)	12.00	30.00
UNOPENED BOX (24 PACKS)	85.00	100.00
UNOPENED PACK (8 CARDS)	3.00	4.00
COMMON CARD (1-110)	.20	.50
*GREEN STAR.: .5X TO 1.2X BASIC CARDS	.25	.60
*PINK STAR.: .6X TO 1.5X BASIC CARDS	.30	.75
*BLACK STAR.: .75X TO 2X BASIC CARDS	.40	1.00
*SILVER STAR.: 1.2X TO 3X BASIC CARDS	.60	1.50
*PURPLE STAR.: 2X TO 5X BASIC CARDS	1.00	2.50
*WHITE STAR./199: 12X TO 30X BASIC CARDS	6.00	15.00
*ORANGE STAR./50: 15X TO 40X BASIC CARDS	8.00	20.00
*GOLD STAR./25: 25X TO 60X BASIC CARDS	12.00	30.00
*IMP. RED/1: UNPRICED DUE TO SCARCITY		
*P.P.BLACK/1: UNPRICED DUE TO SCARCITY		
*P.P.CYAN/1: UNPRICED DUE TO SCARCITY		

*P.P.MAGENTA/1: UNPRICED DUE TO SCARCITY
*P.P.YELLOW/1: UNPRICED DUE TO SCARCITY

2017 Star Wars Journey to The Last Jedi Allies

COMPLETE SET (5)	50.00	100.00
COMMON CARD (1-5)	10.00	25.00

*P.P.BLACK/1: UNPRICED DUE TO SCARCITY
*P.P.CYAN/1: UNPRICED DUE TO SCARCITY
*P.P.MAGENTA/1: UNPRICED DUE TO SCARCITY
*P.P.YELLOW/1: UNPRICED DUE TO SCARCITY
GAMESTOP EXCLUSIVE

2017 Star Wars Journey to The Last Jedi Autographs

*GOLD/10: UNPRICED DUE TO SCARCITY
*IMP. RED/1: UNPRICED DUE TO SCARCITY
*P.P.BLACK/1: UNPRICED DUE TO SCARCITY
*P.P.CYAN/1: UNPRICED DUE TO SCARCITY
*P.P.MAGENTA/1: UNPRICED DUE TO SCARCITY
*P.P.YELLOW/1: UNPRICED DUE TO SCARCITY

AAD	Adam Driver		
AAE	Ashley Eckstein		
AAP	Alistair Petrie		
AAS	Andy Serkis		
AAT	Alan Tudyk		
ABD	Ben Daniels	20.00	50.00
ABH	Brian Herring	12.00	30.00
ABL	Billie Lourd		
ABW	Billy Dee Williams		
ACD	Cristina da Silva	12.00	30.00
ACF	Carrie Fisher		
ACR	Clive Revill		
ACT	Catherine Taber	15.00	40.00
ADB	Dee Bradley Baker	12.00	30.00
ADC	Dave Chapman	20.00	50.00
ADL	Daniel Logan	12.00	30.00
ADP	Duncan Pow	8.00	20.00
ADR	Daisy Ridley		
ADY	Donnie Yen		
AFJ	Felicity Jones		
AFP	Freddie Prinze Jr.		
AFW	Forest Whitaker		
AGC	Gwendoline Christie		
AGT	George Takei		
AHC	Hayden Christensen		
AHF	Harrison Ford		
AIU	Iko Uwais		
AIW	Ian Whyte	10.00	25.00
AJB	John Boyega		
AJC	Jim Cummings	10.00	25.00
AJD	Julie Dolan	10.00	25.00
AJI	Jason Isaacs		
AKB	Kenny Baker		
AKF	Kate Fleetwood		
AKY	Keone Young	15.00	40.00
AMH	Mark Hamill		
APB	Paul Blake	15.00	40.00
APM	Peter Mayhew		
APW	Paul Warren	10.00	25.00
ARA	Riz Ahmed		
ARC	Richard Cunningham	12.00	30.00
ARP	Ray Park		
ASG	Stefan Grube	12.00	30.00
ASR	Scott Richardson	15.00	40.00
ASW	Sam Witwer		
ATB	Thomas Brodie-Sangster		
ATC	Tosin Cole		
ATK	Tom Kane		
ATW	Tom Wilton	12.00	30.00
AWP	Wayne Pygram	10.00	25.00
AYR	Yayan Ruhian		
AZD	Zarene Dallas	12.00	30.00
AADA	Anthony Daniels		
AADX	Adam Driver Unmasked		
ACAR	Cecp Arif Rahman	15.00	40.00
ADAR	Derek Arnold		
ADBA	Dave Barclay	10.00	25.00
ADRX	Daisy Ridley Scavenger		
AGGA	Gloria Garcia	12.00	30.00
AGGA	Greg Grunberg		
AIMD	Ian McDiarmid		
AIME	Ian McElhinney	12.00	30.00
AJBL	Jerome Blake	10.00	25.00

AJBU	Jeremy Bulloch		
ASDB	Sharon Duncan-Brewster	15.00	40.00

2017 Star Wars Journey to The Last Jedi Blueprints

COMPLETE SET (7)	8.00	20.00
COMMON CARD (1-7)	2.00	5.00

*P.P.BLACK/1: UNPRICED DUE TO SCARCITY
*P.P.CYAN/1: UNPRICED DUE TO SCARCITY
*P.P.MAGENTA/1: UNPRICED DUE TO SCARCITY
*P.P.YELLOW/1: UNPRICED DUE TO SCARCITY

2017 Star Wars Journey to The Last Jedi Character Retro Stickers

COMPLETE SET (18)	100.00	200.00
COMMON CARD (1-18)	6.00	15.00

*P.P.BLACK/1: UNPRICED DUE TO SCARCITY
*P.P.CYAN/1: UNPRICED DUE TO SCARCITY
*P.P.MAGENTA/1: UNPRICED DUE TO SCARCITY
*P.P.YELLOW/1: UNPRICED DUE TO SCARCITY

2017 Star Wars Journey to The Last Jedi Characters

COMPLETE SET (16)	12.00	30.00
COMMON CARD (1-16)	1.25	3.00

*P.P.BLACK/1: UNPRICED DUE TO SCARCITY
*P.P.CYAN/1: UNPRICED DUE TO SCARCITY
*P.P.MAGENTA/1: UNPRICED DUE TO SCARCITY
*P.P.YELLOW/1: UNPRICED DUE TO SCARCITY

2017 Star Wars Journey to The Last Jedi Choose Your Destiny

COMPLETE SET (10)	8.00	20.00
COMMON CARD (1-10)	1.25	3.00

*P.P.BLACK/1: UNPRICED DUE TO SCARCITY
*P.P.CYAN/1: UNPRICED DUE TO SCARCITY
*P.P.MAGENTA/1: UNPRICED DUE TO SCARCITY
*P.P.YELLOW/1: UNPRICED DUE TO SCARCITY

2017 Star Wars Journey to The Last Jedi Darkness Rises

COMPLETE SET (6)	6.00	15.00
COMMON CARD (1-6)	1.50	4.00

2017 Star Wars Journey to The Last Jedi Dual Autographs

STATED PRINT RUN 5 SER.#'d SETS
UNPRICED DUE TO SCARCITY

NNO Serkis/Driver
NNO Ridley/Driver
NNO Ridley/Herring
NNO Grunberg/Lourd

2017 Star Wars Journey to The Last Jedi Family Legacy

COMPLETE SET (6)	5.00	12.00
COMMON CARD (1-6)	1.25	3.00

*P.P.BLACK/1: UNPRICED DUE TO SCARCITY
*P.P.CYAN/1: UNPRICED DUE TO SCARCITY
*P.P.MAGENTA/1: UNPRICED DUE TO SCARCITY
*P.P.YELLOW/1: UNPRICED DUE TO SCARCITY

2017 Star Wars Journey to The Last Jedi Illustrated Characters

PORGS

COMPLETE SET (14)	10.00	25.00
COMMON CARD (1-14)	1.00	2.50

*P.P.BLACK/1: UNPRICED DUE TO SCARCITY
*P.P.CYAN/1: UNPRICED DUE TO SCARCITY
*P.P.MAGENTA/1: UNPRICED DUE TO SCARCITY
*P.P.YELLOW/1: UNPRICED DUE TO SCARCITY

2017 Star Wars Journey to The Last Jedi Patches

COMMON CARD (UNNUMBERED)	5.00	12.00
*ORANGE/99: .75X TO 2X BASIC CARDS	10.00	25.00
*GOLD/25: 1.2X TO 3X BASIC CARDS	15.00	40.00

*IMP. RED/1: UNPRICED DUE TO SCARCITY

2017 Star Wars Journey to The Last Jedi Rey Continuity

COMPLETE SET (10)	12.00	30.00
COMMON CARD (1-5)	1.25	3.00
COMMON CARD (6-10)	2.00	5.00

*P.P.BLACK/1: UNPRICED DUE TO SCARCITY
*P.P.CYAN/1: UNPRICED DUE TO SCARCITY
*P.P.MAGENTA/1: UNPRICED DUE TO SCARCITY
*P.P.YELLOW/1: UNPRICED DUE TO SCARCITY
RANDOMLY INSERTED INTO PACKS
1-5 JOURNEY TO THE LAST JEDI EXCLUSIVE
6-10 THE LAST JEDI SER.1 EXCLUSIVE
11-15 THE LAST JEDI SER.2 EXCLUSIVE

2017 Star Wars Journey to The Last Jedi Six-Person Autographed Booklet

STATED PRINT RUN 1 SER.#'d SET
UNPRICED DUE TO SCARCITY

NNO Ford/Hamill/Fisher/Ridley/Boyega/Herring

2017 Star Wars Journey to The Last Jedi Sketches

UNPRICED DUE TO SCARCITY

NNO Jason Brower
NNO Jason Heil
NNO Jason Sobol
NNO Jay Manchand
NNO Jay Salce
NNO Jeff Mallinson
NNO Jerry Bennett
NNO Jessica Hickman
NNO Jim Mehsling
NNO Jim O'Riley
NNO JM Smith
NNO John Soukup
NNO Jonathan Caustrita
NNO Jordan Maison
NNO Joshua Bommer
NNO Kaela Croft
NNO Kallan Archer
NNO Kevin Liell
NNO Kris Penix
NNO Kyle Babbitt
NNO Kyle Newman
NNO Lawrence Reynolds
NNO Lee Lightfoot
NNO Louise Draper
NNO Marcia Dye
NNO Mark Mangum
NNO Marsha Parkins

NNO Matt Applegate
NNO Matt Langford
NNO Matt Maldonado
NNO Matt Steffens
NNO Matt Stewart
NNO Matthew Buttich
NNO Matthew Sutton
NNO Melike Acar
NNO Michael Brady
NNO Michael Duron
NNO Michael Mastermaker
NNO Michelle Rayner
NNO Mick and Matt Glebe
NNO Mike Barnard
NNO Mohamed Jilani
NNO Neil Camera
NNO Nicholas Baltra
NNO Nick Justus
NNO Nolan Dykstra
NNO Norvierto P. Basio
NNO Pablo Diaz
NNO Patrick Giles
NNO Phil Hassewer
NNO Phillip Trujillo
NNO Preston Asevedo
NNO Ray Richardson
NNO Rey Paez
NNO Rich Molinelli
NNO Richard Serrao
NNO Rob Teranishi
NNO Robert Hendrickson
NNO Rory McQueen
NNO Roy Cover
NNO Ryan Edwards
NNO Scott Jones
NNO Shane Molina
NNO Shaow Siong
NNO Solly Mohamed
NNO Stephanie Swanger
NNO Ted Dastick Jr.
NNO Tim Dowler
NNO Tim Proctor
NNO Tina Berardi
NNO Tod Smith
NNO Todd Rayner
NNO Trent Westbrook
NNO Vincenzo D'Ippolito
NNO Ward Silverman
NNO Achilleas Kokkinakis
NNO Adam Worton
NNO Alex Iniguez
NNO Alex Mines
NNO Andrew Fry
NNO Andrew Lopez
NNO Andy Duggan
NNO Angelina Benedetti
NNO Anil Sharma
NNO Anthony Skubis
NNO Ashleigh Popplewell
NNO Ben AbuSaada
NNO Ben Goddard
NNO Bobby Blakely
NNO Brad Hudson
NNO Brandon Pyle
NNO Brendan Purchase
NNO Brendan Shaw
NNO Brent Ragland
NNO Brent Scotchmer
NNO Brett Farr
NNO Bruce Gerlach
NNO Bryan Silverbax
NNO Bryan Snuffer
NNO Bryce King II
NNO Carlos Cabaleiro
NNO Cathy Razim
NNO Chad LaForce
NNO Chad Scheres
NNO Charlie Cody
NNO Chris Clark
NNO Chris Willdig
NNO Clinton Yeager
NNO Corey Galal

NNO D.J. Coffman
NNO Dan Curto
NNO Dan Gorman
NNO Daniel Cooney
NNO Danny Kidwell
NNO Darrin Pepe
NNO Dave Dabila
NNO Dave Fowler
NNO Dean Drummond
NNO Dennis Gortakowski
NNO Dylan Riley
NNO Eddie Price
NNO Eric Lehtonen
NNO Eric White
NNO Freddy Lopez
NNO Garrett Dix
NNO Gavin Williams
NNO George Joseph
NNO Gerald Garcia
NNO Ibrahim Ozkan
NNO Ingrid Hardy
NNO J Hammond
NNO J. P. Perez
NNO Jamie Cosley
NNO Jamie Richards

2017 Star Wars Journey to The Last Jedi Triple Autographs

UNPRICED DUE TO SCARCITY

NNO Serkis/Driver/Christie
NNO Ridley/Driver/Boyega

2019 Star Wars Journey to The Rise of Skywalker

COMPLETE SET (110)	10.00	25.00
COMMON CARD (1-110)	.20	.50

*GREEN: .75X TO 2X BASIC CARDS
*SILVER: 1.2X TO 3X BASIC CARDS
*BLACK/199: 3X TO 8X BASIC CARDS
*ORANGE/50: 6X TO 15X BASIC CARDS
*GOLD/25: 12X TO 30X BASIC CARDS
*RED/1: UNPRICED DUE TO SCARCITY
*P.P.BLACK/1: UNPRICED DUE TO SCARCITY
*P.P.CYAN/1: UNPRICED DUE TO SCARCITY
*P.P.MAGENTA/1: UNPRICED DUE TO SCARCITY
*P.P.YELLOW/1: UNPRICED DUE TO SCARCITY

2019 Star Wars Journey to The Rise of Skywalker Six-Person Autographs

UNPRICED DUE TO SCARCITY

NNO Ridley/Boyega/Tran/Serkis/Driver/Gleeson
SAGG Ford/Fisher/Ridley/Boyega/Baker/Daniels

2019 Star Wars Journey to The Rise of Skywalker Autographed Commemorative Patches

*RED/1: UNPRICED DUE TO SCARCITY
STATED PRINT RUN 10 SER.#'d SETS
UNPRICED DUE TO SCARCITY

NNO Adam Driver
NNO Andy Serkis
NNO Daisy Ridley
NNO Domhnall Gleeson
NNO Greg Grunberg
NNO John Boyega
NNO Joonas Suotamo
NNO Matthew Wood
NNO Mike Quinn
NNO Paul Kasey

2019 Star Wars Journey to The Rise of Skywalker Autographs

COMMON AUTO	5.00	12.00

*GOLD/25: UNPRICED DUE TO SCARCITY
*RED/1: UNPRICED DUE TO SCARCITY
*P.P.BLACK/1: UNPRICED DUE TO SCARCITY
*P.P.CYAN/1: UNPRICED DUE TO SCARCITY
*P.P.MAGENTA/1: UNPRICED DUE TO SCARCITY
*P.P.YELLOW/1: UNPRICED DUE TO SCARCITY
RANDOMLY INSERTED INTO PACKS

AAD Adam Driver		
AAD Anthony Daniels		
AAE Adrian Edmondson	5.00	12.00
AAJ Andrew Jack	5.00	12.00
AAL Amanda Lawrence	5.00	12.00
AAS Andy Serkis 1		

AAS Andy Serkis 2		
AAS Arti Shah	6.00	15.00
ABL Billie Lourd		
ABV Brian Vernel		
ACC Cavin Cornwall	8.00	20.00
ACC Crystal Clarke		
ACF Carrie Fisher		
ADA David Acord		
ADC Dave Chapman		
ADG Domhnall Gleeson		
ADR Daisy Ridley		
AEE Emun Elliott		
AGG Greg Grunberg		
AHC Hermione Corfield	12.00	30.00
AHF Harrison Ford		
AHS Hugh Skinner	6.00	15.00
AIU Iko Uwais	5.00	12.00
AIW Ian Whyte	6.00	15.00
AJB John Boyega 1		
AJB John Boyega 2		
AJS Joonas Suotamo		
AJV Jimmy Vee	8.00	20.00
AKB Kenny Baker		
AKS Kiran Shah	5.00	12.00
ALC Lily Cole	6.00	15.00
ALD Laura Dern		
AMQ Mike Quinn	6.00	15.00
ANC Nathalie Cuzner	5.00	12.00
APK Paul Kasey	5.00	12.00
APW Paul Warren	5.00	12.00
ARM Rocky Marshall		
ASA Sebastian Armesto		
ASG Stefan Grube	5.00	12.00
ATK Tom Kane	6.00	15.00
ATR Tim Rose		
ATW Tom Wilton	6.00	15.00
AWD Warwick Davis		
ACAR Cecep Arif Rahman		
ADAV Derek Arnold		
AGGJ Gloria Garcia	6.00	15.00
AKMT Kelly Marie Tran		
ATBS Thomas Brodie-Sangster		

2019 Star Wars Journey to The Rise of Skywalker Battle Lines

YODA vs. COUNT DOOKU — BATTLE LINES

COMPLETE SET (10)	25.00	60.00
COMMON CARD (BL1-BL10)	4.00	10.00

*P.P.BLACK/1: UNPRICED DUE TO SCARCITY
*P.P.CYAN/1: UNPRICED DUE TO SCARCITY
*P.P.MAGENTA/1: UNPRICED DUE TO SCARCITY
*P.P.YELLOW/1: UNPRICED DUE TO SCARCITY
RANDOMLY INSERTED IN PACKS

2019 Star Wars Journey to The Rise of Skywalker Character Foil

COMPLETE SET (8)	6.00	15.00
COMMON CARD (FC1-FC8)	1.00	2.50

*P.P.BLACK/1: UNPRICED DUE TO SCARCITY
*P.P.CYAN/1: UNPRICED DUE TO SCARCITY
*P.P.MAGENTA/1: UNPRICED DUE TO SCARCITY
*P.P.YELLOW/1: UNPRICED DUE TO SCARCITY
RANDOMLY INSERTED INTO PACKS

2019 Star Wars Journey to The Rise of Skywalker Character Stickers

COMPLETE SET (19)	10.00	25.00
COMMON CARD (CS1-CS19)	1.25	3.00

*P.P.BLACK/1: UNPRICED DUE TO SCARCITY
*P.P.CYAN/1: UNPRICED DUE TO SCARCITY
*P.P.MAGENTA/1: UNPRICED DUE TO SCARCITY

TRADING CARDS

*P.P.YELLOW/1: UNPRICED DUE TO SCARCITY
RANDOMLY INSERTED INTO PACKS

2019 Star Wars Journey to The Rise of Skywalker
Choose Your Destiny

COMPLETE SET (10)	12.00	30.00
COMMON CARD (CD1-CD10)	2.00	5.00

*P.P.BLACK/1: UNPRICED DUE TO SCARCITY
*P.P.CYAN/1: UNPRICED DUE TO SCARCITY
*P.P.MAGENTA/1: UNPRICED DUE TO SCARCITY
*P.P.YELLOW/1: UNPRICED DUE TO SCARCITY
RANDOMLY INSERTED INTO PACKS

2019 Star Wars Journey to The Rise of Skywalker
Commemorative Jumbo Patches

COMMON MEM	3.00	8.00

*BLACK/99: .5X TO 1.2X BASIC MEM
*ORANGE/50: .6X TO 1.5X BASIC MEM
*GOLD/25: UNPRICED DUE TO SCARCITY
*RED/1: UNPRICED DUE TO SCARCITY
RANDOMLY INSERTED INTO PACKS

JPF	Finn	5.00	12.00
JPR	Rey	6.00	15.00
JPAH	Vice Admiral Holdo	4.00	10.00
JPBB	BB-8	4.00	10.00
JPC3	C-3PO	4.00	10.00
JPCT	C'ai Threnalli	4.00	10.00
JPHS	Han Solo	6.00	15.00
JPKC	Lieutenant Connix	5.00	12.00
JPLC	Lando Calrissian	4.00	10.00
JPLO	General Leia Organa	5.00	12.00
JPLS	Luke Skywalker	5.00	12.00
JPPA	Padmé Amidala	5.00	12.00
JPPD	Poe Dameron	4.00	10.00
JPR2	R2-D2	4.00	10.00

2019 Star Wars Journey to The Rise of Skywalker
Commemorative Patches

COMMON MEM	3.00	8.00

*BLACK/99: .5X TO 1.2X BASIC MEM
*ORANGE/50: .6X TO 1.5X BASIC MEM
*GOLD/25: UNPRICED DUE TO SCARCITY
*RED/1: UNPRICED DUE TO SCARCITY
RANDOMLY INSERTED INTO PACKS

PCCR	Chewbacca	5.00	12.00
PCFR	Finn	4.00	10.00
PCRR	Rey	6.00	15.00
PCCPK	Captain Phasma	4.00	10.00
PCHSR	Han Solo	8.00	20.00
PCKFO	Kylo Ren	5.00	12.00
PCKRK	Kylo Ren	5.00	12.00
PCKRT	Kylo Ren	6.00	15.00
PCLOR	General Leia Organa	5.00	12.00
PCLSR	Luke Skywalker	5.00	12.00
PCPDX	Poe Dameron	5.00	12.00
PCPFO	Captain Phasma	4.00	10.00
PCPXP	Poe Dameron	5.00	12.00
PCSFO	Supreme Leader Snoke	4.00	10.00
PCSLK	Supreme Leader Snoke	4.00	10.00

2019 Star Wars Journey to The Rise of Skywalker
Dual Autographs

STATED PRINT RUN 5 SER.#'d SETS
UNPRICED DUE TO SCARCITY

DASD A.Serkis/A.Driver
DASG A.Serkis/D.Gleeson
DADB A.Daniels/K.Baker
DARD D.Ridley/A.Driver
DAGC G.Grunberg/H.Corfield
DATN K.Tran/V.Ngo

DADS L.Dern/Hugh Skinner
DAKR P.Kasey/T.Rose

2019 Star Wars Journey to The Rise of Skywalker
Illustrated Characters

COMPLETE SET (16)	12.00	30.00
COMMON CARD (IC1-IC16)	1.25	3.00

*P.P.BLACK/1: UNPRICED DUE TO SCARCITY
*P.P.CYAN/1: UNPRICED DUE TO SCARCITY
*P.P.MAGENTA/1: UNPRICED DUE TO SCARCITY
*P.P.YELLOW/1: UNPRICED DUE TO SCARCITY
RANDOMLY INSERTED INTO PACKS

2019 Star Wars Journey to The Rise of Skywalker
Schematics

COMPLETE SET (10)	5.00	12.00
COMMON CARD (S1-S10)	.75	2.00

*P.P.BLACK/1: UNPRICED DUE TO SCARCITY
*P.P.CYAN/1: UNPRICED DUE TO SCARCITY
*P.P.MAGENTA/1: UNPRICED DUE TO SCARCITY
*P.P.YELLOW/1: UNPRICED DUE TO SCARCITY
RANDOMLY INSERTED INTO PACKS

2019 Star Wars Journey to The Rise of Skywalker
Sketches

UNPRICED DUE TO SCARCITY

NNO Adam Milton
NNO Aleksandar Gigov
NNO Ashlee Brienzo
NNO Ashley Villers
NNO Aston Cover
NNO Basak Cetinkaya
NNO Ben AbuSaada
NNO Cameron Tobias
NNO Carlos Cabaleiro
NNO Chris Kay
NNO Dan Gorman
NNO David Storey
NNO Dean Drummond
NNO Eric Lehtonen
NNO Gregg Mitchell
NNO Ibrahim Ozkan
NNO Ingrid Hardy
NNO Jamison Murdock
NNO Jason Sobol
NNO John Bruce
NNO John Pleak
NNO Kelly Baber
NNO Kevin Cleveland
NNO Mai Irving
NNO Marcia Dye
NNO Marsha Parkins
NNO Matt Stewart
NNO Matthew Hirons
NNO Matthew Skillern
NNO Michael Sealie
NNO Michelle Rayner
NNO Neil Camera
NNO Nick Gribbon
NNO Patricio Carrasco
NNO Rich Henneman
NNO Rob Teranishi
NNO Sebastian Cortez
NNO Shaow Siong
NNO Stirling Ford
NNO Tim Shinn
NNO Trent Westbrook
NNO Vincenzo D'Ippolito
NNO Zach Woolsey

2019 Star Wars Journey to The Rise of Skywalker
Triple Autographs

UNPRICED DUE TO SCARCITY

TASRD Serkis/Ridley/Driver
TADBM Daniels/Baker/Mayhew
TADCS Davis/Cole/Shah
TADSL Dern/Skinner/Lawrence

2019 Star Wars Kylo Ren Continuity

1	Kylo Ren
2	Kylo Ren
3	Kylo Ren
4	Kylo Ren
5	Kylo Ren
6	Kylo Ren
7	Kylo Ren
8	Kylo Ren
9	Kylo Ren
10	Kylo Ren

1996 Star Wars Laser

0 Star Wars 20th Anniversary Commemorative Magazine	3.00	8.00

2016 Star Wars LEGO Droid Tales

COMPLETE SET (9)	15.00	40.00
UNOPENED PACK (3 CARDS)	6.00	8.00
COMMON CARD (DT1-DT9)		

ONE PACK INSERTED INTO
STAR WARS LEGO DROID TALES DVD

2019-21 Star Wars Living Set

COMMON CARD	4.00	10.00

TOPPS ONLINE EXCLUSIVE

1	Darth Vader/3,909*	20.00	50.00
2	Nien Nunb/2,888*	6.00	15.00
3	R2-D2/2,710*	8.00	20.00
4	Stormtrooper/2,601*	6.00	15.00
5	Bossk/2,205*	5.00	12.00
6	Val/2,161*	5.00	12.00
7	Queen Amidala/2,038*	15.00	40.00
8	Death Star Gunner/1,922*	5.00	12.00
9	Grand Admiral Thrawn/1,760*	30.00	75.00
10	Uncle Owen Lars/1,721*	6.00	15.00
11	Wedge Antilles/1,662*	12.00	30.00
12	Dengar/1,641*	8.00	20.00
13	Jar Jar Binks/1,692*	12.00	30.00
14	Moloch/1,565*	8.00	20.00
15	Orson Krennic/1,385*	20.00	50.00
16	Jawa/1,441*	15.00	40.00
17	Lando Calrissian/1,427*	15.00	40.00
18	Rancor/1,405*	12.00	30.00
19	Ezra Bridger/1,375*	15.00	40.00
20	Admiral Piett/1,378*	10.00	25.00
21	Han Solo/2,376*	25.00	60.00
22	Tasu Leech/1,501*	6.00	15.00
23	Mon Mothma/1,435*	12.00	30.00
24	Wampa/1,454*	8.00	20.00
25	Darth Maul/1,739*	50.00	100.00
26	Tallie Lintra/1,493*	6.00	15.00
27	Shaak Ti/1,311*	20.00	50.00
28	Quay Tolsite/1,307*	15.00	40.00
29	4-LOM/1,356*	20.00	50.00
30	BB-8/1,502*	15.00	40.00
31	Aurra Sing/1,343*	12.00	30.00
32	Tobias Beckett/1,395*	8.00	20.00
33	Wicket W. Warrick/1,390*	30.00	75.00
34	Scout Trooper/1,283*	15.00	40.00
35	General Hux/1,170*	25.00	60.00
36	Dak Ralter/1,164*	15.00	40.00
37	Bail Organa/1,124	12.00	30.00
38	Gamorrean Guard/1,161*	8.00	20.00
39	Sebulba/1,101*	12.00	30.00
40	Kanan Jarrus/1,086*	30.00	75.00
41	K-2SO/1,151*	50.00	100.00
42	Echo Base Trooper/1,136*	12.00	30.00
43	Maz Kanata/1,122*	15.00	40.00
44	Captain Needa/1,108*	5.00	12.00
45	Salacious B. Crumb/1,090*	15.00	40.00
46	Chirrut Imwe/1,102*	10.00	25.00
47	Rey/1,503*	60.00	120.00
48	Savage Opress/1,114*	75.00	150.00
49	Captain Phasma/1,011	50.00	100.00
50	Cliegg Lars/938*	60.00	120.00
51	L3-37/902*	50.00	100.00
52	Nute Gunray/985*	75.00	150.00
53	General Grievous/1,007*	100.00	200.00

54 Saw Gerrera/967*	100.00	200.00	
55 Finn/1,079*	25.00	60.00	
56 Imperial Pilots/1,021*	30.00	75.00	
57 Dorme/2,021*	12.00	30.00	
58 The Child/9,663*	30.00	75.00	
59 Supreme Leader Snoke/942*	50.00	100.00	
60 Plo Koon/887*	125.00	250.00	
61 Greedo/1,178*	30.00	75.00	
62 Young Anakin Skywalker/1,207*	15.00	40.00	
63 Poe Dameron/1,301	15.00	40.00	
64 Mother Talzin/1,203	30.00	75.00	
65 Watto/1,259*	20.00	50.00	
66 Darth Sidious/1,422*	10.00	25.00	
67 Jyn Erso/1,425*	20.00	50.00	
68 BB-9E/1,068*	15.00	40.00	
69 Max Rebo/956*	50.00	100.00	
70 Count Dooku/946*	50.00	100.00	
71 Admiral Ackbar/1,041*	60.00	120.00	
72 Young Boba Fett/1,158*	50.00	100.00	
73 C-3PO/1,156*	25.00	60.00	
74 Lady Proxima/959*	50.00	100.00	
75 Kylo Ren/1,187*	20.00	50.00	
76 Kit Fisto/960*	30.00	75.00	
77 Princess Leia/2,093*	15.00	40.00	
78 Lieutenant Connix/1,351*	12.00	30.00	
79 Emperor Palpatine/1,103*	50.00	100.00	
80 Porg/1,130*	20.00	50.00	
81 Ahsoka Tano/1,293*	100.00	200.00	
82 Bala Tik/992*	15.00	40.00	
83 Boba Fett/1,913*	60.00	120.00	
84 Tauntaun/1,190*	12.00	30.00	
85 Kuill/1,068*	30.00	75.00	
86 Elite Praetorian Guard/1,038*	15.00	40.00	
87 Dryden Vos/1,003*	25.00	60.00	
88 Bistan/996*	50.00	100.00	
89 Paige Tico/996*	30.00	75.00	
90 Rose Tico/901*	50.00	100.00	
91 Grand Moff Tarkin/1,042*	12.00	30.00	
92 Galen Erso/1,005*	20.00	50.00	
93 Vice Admiral Holdo/1,079*	15.00	40.00	
94 General Veers/979*	30.00	75.00	
95 Jango Fett/1,252*	20.00	50.00	
96 Jannah/1,074*	12.00	30.00	
97 Hera Syndulla/1,131*	12.00	30.00	
98 Jabba the Hutt/1,395*	10.00	25.00	
99 Obi-Wan Kenobi/2,656*	8.00	20.00	
100 Luke Skywalker/2,833*	10.00	25.00	
101 Royal Guard/1,255*	10.00	25.00	
102 Captain Rex/1,259*	12.00	30.00	
103 Babu Frik/1,279*	8.00	20.00	
104 Mas Amedda/1,105*	8.00	20.00	
105 Fennec Shand/1,217*	12.00	30.00	
106 Zorri Bliss/1,244*	6.00	15.00	
107 Cassian Andor/1,246*	8.00	20.00	
108 Clone Trooper/1,257*	5.00	12.00	
109 Kazuda "Kaz" Xiono/1,241*	6.00	15.00	
110 Aayla Secura/1,286*	10.00	25.00	
111 Peli Motto/1,305*	6.00	15.00	
112 Yaddle/1,328*	6.00	15.00	
113 Sabine Wren/1,480*	12.00	30.00	
114 Allegiant General Pryde/1,222*	6.00	15.00	
115 Baze Malbus/1,268*	10.00	25.00	
116 The Grand Inquisitor/1,228*	8.00	20.00	
117 Ben Solo/2,304*	12.00	30.00	
118 Rio Durant/1,325*	5.00	12.00	
119 Bodhi Rook/1,277*	6.00	15.00	
120 Mythrol/1,265*	5.00	12.00	
121 Logray/1,303*	6.00	15.00	
122 Chancellor Valorum/	5.00	12.00	
123 Qi'Ra/1,737*	8.00	20.00	
124 Battle Droid/1,376*	6.00	15.00	
125 Snap Wexley/1,191*	5.00	12.00	
126 Bendu/1,114*	8.00	20.00	
127 Cara Dune/2,316*	15.00	40.00	
128 Klaud/1,421*	6.00	15.00	
129 Rebolt/1,259*	6.00	15.00	
130 Zam Wesell/1,293*	5.00	12.00	
131 Moff Gideon/1,411*	6.00	15.00	
132 Torra Doza/1,184*	5.00	12.00	
133 Jan Dodonna/1,209*	5.00	12.00	
136 Pre Vizsla/1,317*	8.00	20.00	
137 Cal Kestis/1,278*	6.00	15.00	
139 Ello Asty/1,242*	6.00	15.00	
140 First Order TIE Fighter Pilot/1,319*	5.00	12.00	
141 D-0/1,283*	6.00	15.00	
142 Bazine Netal/1,023*	8.00	20.00	
144 Second Sister/1,215*	6.00	15.00	
145 The Mandalorian/4,283*	15.00	40.00	
146 Bo-Katan Kryze/1,352*	12.00	30.00	
147 WG-22/1,186*	6.00	15.00	
148 The Client/1,291*	8.00	20.00	
150 Master Codebreaker/1,215*	6.00	15.00	
151 Bo Keevil/1,139*	6.00	15.00	
152 Blurrg/1,250*	5.00	12.00	
153 Vulptex/1,142*	8.00	20.00	
154 IG-88/1,298*	6.00	15.00	
155 Stass Allie/1,192*	8.00	20.00	
156 Xi'an/1,296*	5.00	12.00	
157 General Leia Organa/1,740*	6.00	15.00	
159 Chopper/1,332*	10.00	25.00	
160 Toro Calican/1,269*	6.00	15.00	
162 2-1B Droid/1,148*	6.00	15.00	
163 Iden Versio/1,286*	6.00	15.00	
164 Ap'lek/1,251*	5.00	12.00	
165 Bo-Katan Kryze/2,171*	10.00	25.00	
166 Commander Cody/1,541*	6.00	15.00	
167 Yoda/5,157*	8.00	20.00	
168 Mace Windu/2,985*	5.00	12.00	
171 Han Solo/1,838*	5.00	12.00	
172 Dark Trooper/1,945*	5.00	12.00	
176 Tusken Raider/1,811*	6.00	15.00	
177 The Armorer/2,277*	10.00	25.00	
178 Slowen Lo/1,388*	5.00	12.00	
179 Loth-cat/1,544*	8.00	20.00	
180 Beru Lars/1,435*	5.00	12.00	
181 Therm Scissorpunch/1,519*	6.00	15.00	
182 Seventh Sister/1,586*	8.00	20.00	
185 Aurodia Ventafoli/1,731*	8.00	20.00	
186 Darth Bane/2,548*	6.00	15.00	
187 Alexsandr Kallus/1,504*	6.00	15.00	
188 Malakili/1,466*	6.00	15.00	
190 Neeku Vozo/1,416*	5.00	12.00	
191 Cobb Vanth/2,048*	5.00	12.00	
192 Sagwa/1,504*	5.00	12.00	
195 Axe Woves/2,155*	6.00	15.00	
197 Wes Janson/1,437*	5.00	12.00	
198 Emir Wat Tambor/1,376*	5.00	12.00	
202 Hunter/1,873*	8.00	20.00	
203 Caretakers/1,303*	5.00	12.00	
204 Sidon Ithano/1,363*	6.00	15.00	
205 Boolio/1,296*	5.00	12.00	
207 Barriss Offee/1,363*	8.00	20.00	
208 FN-2199/1,430*	8.00	20.00	
211 Pamich Nerro Goode/1,160*	8.00	20.00	
213 Chief Chirpa/1,505*	6.00	15.00	
214 Luminara Unduli/1,340*	6.00	15.00	
215 Koska Reeves/2,637*	12.00	30.00	
219 Dexster Jettster/1,102	6.00	15.00	
220 Sarlacc/1,146*	8.00	20.00	
223 Commander Pyre/1,345*	6.00	15.00	
224 Padme Amidala/3,356*	10.00	25.00	
225 Captain Panaka/1,246*	5.00	12.00	
226 Clone Commander Bly/1,343*	6.00	12.00	
227 Enfys Nest/1,514*	8.00	20.00	
228 Tank Trooper/1,443*	6.00	15.00	
229 Sy Snootles/1,299*	6.00	15.00	
231 Biggs Darklighter/1,266*	5.00	12.00	
233 Bib Fortuna/1,621*	5.00	12.00	
234 Boba Fett/3,700*	10.00	25.00	
235 Ponda Baba/1,374*			
236 Doctor Cornelius Evazan/1,382*			
237 Wrecker/1,680*			
238 Lieutenant Mitaka/1,258*			
239 Wuher/1,233*			
240 Taun We/1,314*			
243 Crosshair/2,137*			
244 Korkie Kryze/1,343*			
245 Bultar Swan/1,200*			
246 Derek "Hobbie" Klivia/1,173*			
247 Jabba the Hutt/			
248 Qui-Gonn Jinn/			
NNO Checklist 1-100/1,667*			
NNO Checklist 101-200/1,582*			

THE MANDALORIAN

2020 Star Wars The Mandalorian Journey of the Child

COMPLETE SET (25)	5.00	12.00
UNOPENED BOX (32 CARDS)	8.00	20.00
COMMON CARD (1-25)	.20	.50

*GREEN: .6X TO 1.5X BASIC CARDS
*RED/99: 1X TO 2.5X BASIC CARDS
*BLUE/50: 1.5X TO 4X BASIC CARDS
*ORANGE/10: UNPRICED DUE TO SCARCITY
*STEEL/1: UNPRICED DUE TO SCARCITY

2020 Star Wars The Mandalorian Journey of the Child Illustrated

COMPLETE SET (5)	2.50	6.00
COMMON CARD (1-5)	.75	2.00

*GREEN: .6X TO 1.5X BASIC CARDS
*RED/99: 1X TO 2.5X BASIC CARDS
*BLUE/50: 1.5X TO 4X BASIC CARDS
*ORANGE/10: UNPRICED DUE TO SCARCITY
*STEEL/1: UNPRICED DUE TO SCARCITY
STATED ODDS 1 SET PER BOX

2019 Star Wars The Mandalorian Season 1

COMPLETE SET (40)
COMMON EPISODE 1 (1-5)
COMMON EPISODE 2 (6-10)
COMMON EPISODE 3 (11-15)
COMMON EPISODE 4 (16-20)
COMMON EPISODE 5 (21-25)
COMMON EPISODE 6 (26-30)
COMMON EPISODE 7 (31-35)
COMMON EPISODE 8 (36-40)
TOPPS ONLINE EXCLUSIVE

1 The Mythrol Discovers He Is Wanted/714*
2 The Razor Crest Attacked/714*
3 The Mandalorian Draws His Weapon/714*
4 Kuiil Leads the Way/714*
5 IG-11 Is After the Bounty/714*
6 Fighting off Trandoshan Warriors/553*
7 The Mandalorian Repairs His Armor/553*
8 Scaling the Sandcrawler/553*
9 Fighting the Beast/553*
10 Recovering the Egg/553*
11 Returning to the Client/1,315*
12 The Child Looks On/1,315*
13 Delivering the Bounty/1,315*
14 Backup Arrives/1,315*
15 This Is the Way/1,315*
16 Landing on Sorgan/1,004*
17 Cara Dune and the Mandalorian Meet/1,004*
18 Ready for Battle/1,004*
19 Facing the AT-ST Raider/1,004*
20 Leaving the Village/1,004*
21 Meeting Mechanic Peli Motto/1,179*

22 The Mark - Assassin Fennec Shand/1,179*
23 Toro Calican and the Mandalorian Ride Off/1,179*
24 Showdown with Shand/1,179*
25 The Child Survives the Shootout/1,179*
26 Attacked by Security Droids/998*
27 The Mandalorian and Mercenaries Confronted/998*
28 Sneaking Up Behind Mayfeld/998*
29 Saved by the Mandalorian/998*
30 Tracked by the New Republic/998*
31 Discussing the Situation on Navarro/884*
32 Bringing the Mandalorian In/884*
33 The Client Hears from Moff Gideon/884*
34 Moff Gideon Demands the Child/884*
35 Imperial Troopers Assemble/2,219*
36 Taking out the Stormtroopers/2,219*
37 Receiving the Jetpack/2,219*
38 IG-11's Sacrifice/2,219*
39 TIE Fighter Trouble/2,219*
40 A Clan of Two/2,219*

2019 Star Wars The Mandalorian Season 1 Trailer Set

COMPLETE SET (10)	10.00	25.00
COMMON CARD (1-10)	2.00	5.00
STATED PRINT RUN 1,425 SER.#'d SETS		

2020 Star Wars The Mandalorian Season 1

COMPLETE SET (100)	15.00	40.00
UNOPENED BOX (7 PACKS)		
UNOPENED PACK (8 CARDS)		
COMMON CARD (1-100)	.40	1.00
*BLUE: .5X TO 1.2X BASIC CARDS		
*PURPLE: .75X TO 2X BASIC CARDS		
*BRONZE/50: 3X TO 8X BASIC CARDS		
*SILVER/25: 5X TO 12X BASIC CARDS		
*GOLD/10: UNPRICED DUE TO SCARCITY		
*BLACK/1: UNPRICED DUE TO SCARCITY		
*BESKAR/1: UNPRICED DUE TO SCARCITY		
*P.P.BLACK/1: UNPRICED DUE TO SCARCITY		
*P.P.CYAN/1: UNPRICED DUE TO SCARCITY		
*P.P.MAGENTA/1: UNPRICED DUE TO SCARCITY		
*P.P.YELLOW/1: UNPRICED DUE TO SCARCITY		

2020 Star Wars The Mandalorian Season 1 Aliens and Creatures

COMPLETE SET (10)	8.00	20.00
COMMON CARD (AC1-AC10)	1.25	3.00
*RED/99: .5X TO 1.2X BASIC CARDS		
*BRONZE/50: .75X TO 2X BASIC CARDS		
*SILVER/25: UNPRICED DUE TO SCARCITY		
*GOLD/10: UNPRICED DUE TO SCARCITY		
*BLACK/1: UNPRICED DUE TO SCARCITY		
*P.P.BLACK/1: UNPRICED DUE TO SCARCITY		
*P.P.CYAN/1: UNPRICED DUE TO SCARCITY		
*P.P.MAGENTA/1: UNPRICED DUE TO SCARCITY		
*P.P.YELLOW/1: UNPRICED DUE TO SCARCITY		
STATED ODDS 1:7		

2020 Star Wars The Mandalorian Season 1 Autographs

COMMON AUTO	8.00	20.00
*RED/99: .5X TO 1.2X BASIC AUTOS		
*BRONZE/50: .6X TO 1.5X BASIC AUTOS		
*SILVER/25: UNPRICED DUE TO SCARCITY		
*GOLD/10: UNPRICED DUE TO SCARCITY		
*BLACK/1: UNPRICED DUE TO SCARCITY		
*P.P.BLACK/1: UNPRICED DUE TO SCARCITY		
*P.P.CYAN/1: UNPRICED DUE TO SCARCITY		
*P.P.MAGENTA/1: UNPRICED DUE TO SCARCITY		
*P.P.YELLOW/1: UNPRICED DUE TO SCARCITY		
STATED ODDS 1:19 HOBBY		
STATED ODDS 1:372 RETAIL BLASTER		
ADB Dmitrious Bistrevsky	10.00	25.00
AGC Gina Carano	100.00	200.00
AGE Giancarlo Esposito	50.00	100.00
AML Matt Lanter	10.00	25.00
AMR Misty Rosas	15.00	40.00
AOA Omid Abtahi	12.00	30.00
ATF Tait Fletcher	12.00	30.00
ACBF Chris Bartlett as Ferryman	10.00	25.00
ACBZ Chris Bartlett as Zero	12.00	30.00

2020 Star Wars The Mandalorian Season 1 Autographs Bronze

STATED PRINT RUN 50 SER.#'d SETS		
ACW Carl Weathers EXCH	125.00	250.00

2020 Star Wars The Mandalorian Season 1 Autographs Red

AES Emily Swallow	100.00	200.00
AHS Horatio Sanz	25.00	60.00

2020 Star Wars The Mandalorian Season 1 Characters

COMPLETE SET (18)	10.00	25.00
COMMON CARD (C1-C18)	1.25	3.00
*RED/99: .75X TO 2X BASIC CARDS		
*BRONZE/50: 1X TO 2.5X BASIC CARDS		
*SILVER/25: UNPRICED DUE TO SCARCITY		
*GOLD/10: UNPRICED DUE TO SCARCITY		
*BLACK/1: UNPRICED DUE TO SCARCITY		
*P.P.BLACK/1: UNPRICED DUE TO SCARCITY		
*P.P.CYAN/1: UNPRICED DUE TO SCARCITY		
*P.P.MAGENTA/1: UNPRICED DUE TO SCARCITY		
*P.P.YELLOW/1: UNPRICED DUE TO SCARCITY		
STATED ODDS 1:2 HOBBY & RETAIL BLASTER		

2020 Star Wars The Mandalorian Season 1 Commemorative Medallions

COMMON MEM	6.00	15.00
*RED/99: .5X TO 1.2X BASIC MEM		
*BRONZE/50: .6X TO 1.5X BASIC MEM		
*SILVER/25: UNPRICED DUE TO SCARCITY		
*GOLD/10: UNPRICED DUE TO SCARCITY		
*BLACK/1: UNPRICED DUE TO SCARCITY		
STATED ODDS 1:98 HOBBY		
STATED ODDS 1:1 RET.BLASTER BOXES		
MAH The Armorer	12.00	30.00
MBM Blurrg	10.00	25.00
MCC The Child	15.00	40.00
MCH The Child	15.00	40.00
MCM The Child	15.00	40.00
MGC Greef Karga	8.00	20.00
MMC The Mandalorian	12.00	30.00
MMH The Mandalorian	12.00	30.00
MMM The Mandalorian	12.00	30.00
MOH Omera	8.00	20.00
MTC Toro Calican	10.00	25.00
MCDC Cara Dune	10.00	25.00
MCDH Cara Dune	10.00	25.00
MIGC IG-11	12.00	30.00
MMGC Moff Gideon	8.00	20.00

2020 Star Wars The Mandalorian Season 1 Concept Art

COMPLETE SET (10)	8.00	20.00
COMMON CARD (CA1-CA10)	1.25	3.00
*RED/99: .75X TO 2X BASIC CARDS		
*BRONZE/50: 1X TO 2.5X BASIC CARDS		
*SILVER/25: UNPRICED DUE TO SCARCITY		
*GOLD/10: UNPRICED DUE TO SCARCITY		
*BLACK/1: UNPRICED DUE TO SCARCITY		
*P.P.BLACK/1: UNPRICED DUE TO SCARCITY		
*P.P.CYAN/1: UNPRICED DUE TO SCARCITY		
*P.P.MAGENTA/1: UNPRICED DUE TO SCARCITY		
*P.P.YELLOW/1: UNPRICED DUE TO SCARCITY		
STATED ODDS 1:7 HOBBY & RETAIL BLASTER		

2020 Star Wars The Mandalorian Season 1 Dual Autographs

*GOLD/10: UNPRICED DUE TO SCARCITY		
*BLACK/1: UNPRICED DUE TO SCARCITY		
STATED ODDS 1:1,258 HOBBY		
STATED ODDS 1:25,176 RETAIL BLASTER		
STATED PRINT RUN 25 SER.#'d SETS		
UNPRICED DUE TO SCARCITY		
DACW G.Carano/C.Weathers		

DAFW T.Fletcher/R.Watson
DAHA W.Herzog/O.Abtahi
DAHC W.Herzog/G.Carano
DANC N.Nolte/G.Carano
DANW N.Nolte/T.Waititi
DAPC P.Pascal/G.Carano
DAPE P.Pascal/G.Esposito
DAPH P.Pascal/W.Herzog
DAPN P.Pascal/N.Nolte
DAPW P.Pascal/T.Waititi
DAPCW P.Pascal/C.Weathers

2020 Star Wars The Mandalorian Season 1 Silhouetted Sketches

STATED ODDS 1:278 HOBBY
STATED ODDS 1:5,513 RETAIL BLASTER
UNPRICED DUE TO SCARCITY

NNO Adam Beck
NNO Allen Grimes
NNO Andrew Fernandes
NNO Andrew Fry
NNO Andrew Sanchez
NNO Angel Aviles
NNO Anil Sharma
NNO Anthony Ellison
NNO Anthony Skubis
NNO Ashlee Brienzo
NNO Ashley Marsh
NNO Barry Renshaw
NNO Basak Cetinkaya
NNO Benjamin Lombart
NNO Bob Stevlic
NNO Bobby Blakey
NNO Brad Hudson
NNO Brandon Blevins
NNO Brett Farr
NNO Candice Dailey
NNO Carlos Cabaleiro
NNO Carolyn Craggs
NNO Chris Colyer
NNO Chris Kay
NNO Cyrus Sherkat
NNO Dan Gorman
NNO Daniel Riveron
NNO Danny Kidwell
NNO Darren James
NNO Darrin Pepe
NNO Dawn Murphy
NNO Dean Drummond
NNO Desiree Rodigue
NNO Don Pedicini Jr.
NNO Eli Hyder
NNO Eric Lehtonen
NNO Erik Maell
NNO Frank Sansone
NNO Gabe Farber
NNO Gavin Williams
NNO Gerard Garcia Jr.
NNO Gorkem Demir
NNO Guilherme Rocha
NNO Ingrid Hardy
NNO Jake Minor
NNO Jamie Cosley
NNO Jamie Richards
NNO Jason Adams
NNO Jason Davies
NNO Jason Montoya
NNO Jason Queen
NNO Jason Sobol
NNO Jay Manchand
NNO Jeff Abar
NNO Jennifer Allyn
NNO Jessica Hickman
NNO Jim Mehsling
NNO JM Smith
NNO Joe Corroney
NNO John Pleak
NNO Jonathan Beistline
NNO Josh Bommer
NNO Joshua Caleb King
NNO Jude Gallagher
NNO Karl Jones

NNO Keith Farnum
NNO Kelly Baber
NNO Kevin Cleveland
NNO Kevin Graham
NNO Kursat Cetiner
NNO Lindsey Greyling
NNO Logan Monette
NNO Luke Rushton
NNO Maggie Ransom
NNO Mai Irving
NNO Marcia Dye
NNO Mark Necchi
NNO Marlo Agunos
NNO Marsha Parkins
NNO Matt Langford
NNO Matt Maldonado
NNO Matt Stewart
NNO Matthew Sutton
NNO Melike Acar
NNO Michael Mastermaker
NNO Michael Sealie
NNO Michelle Rayner
NNO Mick and Matt Glebe
NNO Mike James
NNO Nick Allsopp
NNO Nick Gribbon
NNO Norviento Basio
NNO Oscar Chavez
NNO Patricio Carrasco
NNO Patrick Giles
NNO Phillip Trujillo
NNO Quinton Baker
NNO Rees Finlay
NNO Rey Paez
NNO Rich Hennemann
NNO Rich Molinelli
NNO Richard Serrao
NNO Rob Teranishi
NNO Robert Garcia
NNO Robert Hendrickson
NNO Rodney Roberts
NNO Ryan Finley
NNO Ryan Santos
NNO Sammy Gomez
NNO Seth Groves
NNO Shaow Siong
NNO Sheikh Islam
NNO Solly Mohamed
NNO Tim Shinn
NNO Tina Berardi
NNO Trent Westbrook
NNO Veronica Smith
NNO Vincenzo D'Ippolito
NNO Ward Silverman
NNO Wayne Tully
NNO Zach Woolsey

2020 Star Wars The Mandalorian Season 1 Sketches

STATED ODDS 1:27 HOBBY
STATED ODDS 1:543 RETAIL BLASTER
UNPRICED DUE TO SCARCITY

NNO Adam Beck
NNO Allen Grimes
NNO Andrew Fernandes
NNO Andrew Fry
NNO Andrew Sanchez
NNO Angel Aviles
NNO Anil Sharma
NNO Anthony Ellison
NNO Anthony Skubis
NNO Ashlee Brienzo
NNO Ashley Marsh
NNO Barry Renshaw
NNO Basak Cetinkaya
NNO Benjamin Lombart
NNO Bob Stevlic
NNO Bobby Blakey
NNO Brad Hudson
NNO Brandon Blevins
NNO Brett Farr
NNO Candice Dailey

NNO Carlos Cabaleiro
NNO Carolyn Craggs
NNO Chris Colyer
NNO Chris Kay
NNO Cyrus Sherkat
NNO Dan Gorman
NNO Daniel Riveron
NNO Danny Kidwell
NNO Darren James
NNO Darrin Pepe
NNO Dawn Murphy
NNO Dean Drummond
NNO Desiree Rodigue
NNO Don Pedicini Jr.
NNO Eli Hyder
NNO Eric Lehtonen
NNO Erik Maell
NNO Frank Sansone
NNO Gabe Farber
NNO Gavin Williams
NNO Gerard Garcia Jr.
NNO Gorkem Demir
NNO Guilherme Rocha
NNO Ingrid Hardy
NNO Jake Minor
NNO Jamie Cosley
NNO Jamie Richards
NNO Jason Adams
NNO Jason Davies
NNO Jason Montoya
NNO Jason Queen
NNO Jason Sobol
NNO Jay Manchand
NNO Jeff Abar
NNO Jennifer Allyn
NNO Jessica Hickman
NNO Jim Mehsling
NNO JM Smith
NNO Joe Corroney
NNO John Pleak
NNO Jonathan Beistline
NNO Josh Bommer
NNO Joshua Caleb King
NNO Jude Gallagher
NNO Karl Jones
NNO Keith Farnum
NNO Kelly Baber
NNO Kevin Cleveland
NNO Kevin Graham
NNO Kursat Cetiner
NNO Lindsey Greyling
NNO Logan Monette
NNO Luke Rushton
NNO Maggie Ransom
NNO Mai Irving
NNO Marcia Dye
NNO Mark Necchi
NNO Marlo Agunos
NNO Marsha Parkins
NNO Matt Langford
NNO Matt Maldonado
NNO Matt Stewart
NNO Matthew Sutton
NNO Melike Acar
NNO Michael Mastermaker
NNO Michael Sealie
NNO Michelle Rayner
NNO Mick and Matt Glebe
NNO Mike James
NNO Nick Allsopp
NNO Nick Gribbon
NNO Norviento Basio
NNO Oscar Chavez
NNO Patricio Carrasco
NNO Patrick Giles
NNO Phillip Trujillo
NNO Quinton Baker
NNO Rees Finlay
NNO Rey Paez
NNO Rich Hennemann
NNO Rich Molinelli
NNO Richard Serrao

NNO Rob Teranishi
NNO Robert Garcia
NNO Robert Hendrickson
NNO Rodney Roberts
NNO Ryan Finley
NNO Ryan Santos
NNO Sammy Gomez
NNO Seth Groves
NNO Shaow Siong
NNO Sheikh Islam
NNO Solly Mohamed
NNO Tim Shinn
NNO Tina Berardi
NNO Trent Westbrook
NNO Veronica Smith
NNO Vincenzo D'Ippolito
NNO Ward Silverman
NNO Wayne Tully
NNO Zach Woolsey

2020 Star Wars The Mandalorian Season 1 Sourced Fabric Relics

COMMON MEM	30.00	75.00

*BRONZE/50: .5X TO 1.2X BASIC MEM
*SILVER/25: UNPRICED DUE TO SCARCITY
*GOLD/10: UNPRICED DUE TO SCARCITY
*BLACK/1: UNPRICED DUE TO SCARCITY
STATED ODDS 1:175 HOBBY EXCLUSIVE

2020 Star Wars The Mandalorian Season 1 Tools of the Bounty Hunter

COMPLETE SET (10)	10.00	25.00
COMMON CARD (TB1-TB10)	1.50	4.00

*RED/99: .5X TO 1.2X BASIC CARDS
*BRONZE/50: .6X TO 1.5X BASIC CARDS
*SILVER/25: UNPRICED DUE TO SCARCITY
*GOLD/10: UNPRICED DUE TO SCARCITY
*BLACK/1: UNPRICED DUE TO SCARCITY
*P.P.BLACK/1: UNPRICED DUE TO SCARCITY
*P.P.CYAN/1: UNPRICED DUE TO SCARCITY
*P.P.MAGENTA/1: UNPRICED DUE TO SCARCITY
*P.P.YELLOW/1: UNPRICED DUE TO SCARCITY
STATED ODDS 1:7 HOBBY & RETAIL BLASTER

2020 Star Wars The Mandalorian Season 1 Triple Autographs

*BLACK/1: UNPRICED DUE TO SCARCITY
STATED ODDS 1:3,774 HOBBY
STATED ODDS 1:88,115 RETAIL BLASTER
STATED PRINT RUN 5 SER.#'d SETS
UNPRICED DUE TO SCARCITY

TACWN Carano/Weathers/Nolte
TAFWB Fletcher/Watson/Bistrevsky
TAHAC Herzog/Abtahi/Carano
TANCW Nolte/Carano/Waititi
TAPCN Pascal/Carano/Nolte
TAPCW Pascal/Carano/Waititi

2020 Star Wars The Mandalorian Season 2

COMPLETE SET (40)
COMPLETE CH.9 SET (5)
COMPLETE CH.10 SET (5)
COMPLETE CH.11 SET (5)
COMPLETE CH.12 SET (5)

COMPLETE CH.13 SET (5)
COMPLETE CH.14 SET (5)
COMPLETE CH.15 SET (5)
COMPLETE CH.16 SET (5)
COMMON CH.9 (1-5)
COMMON CH.10 (6-10)
COMMON CH.11 (11-15)
COMMON CH.12 (16-20)
COMMON CH.13 (21-25)
COMMON CH.14 (26-30)
COMMON CH.15 (31-35)
COMMON CH.16 (36-40)

1 Gamorreans Prepare to Fight/1,527*
2 What Brings You Here Stranger?/1,527*
3 The Child Looks On/1,527*
4 Plotting with Tusken Raiders/1,527*
5 The Krayt Dragon Fights Back/1,527*
6 Offering Safe Passage/1,540*
7 Forbidden Snack/1,540*
8 Flanked by X-Wings/1,540*
9 The Razor Crest Takes on Damage/1,540*
10 Ice Spiders Attack/1,540*
11 A Happy Reunion/1,459*
12 Meeting Bo-Katan/1,459*
13 Food Fight/1,459*
14 Planning the Raid/1,459*
15 Overtaking the Imperial Gozanti/1,459*
16 Return to Nevarro/1,468*
17 A New Student/1,468*
18 Paying Off Debts/1,468*
19 Speeder Bike in Pursuit/1,468*
20 A Familiar Foe Returns/1,468*
21 In Search of Information/1,982*
22 An Offer of Beskar/1,982*
23 A Strong Attachment/1,982*
24 Ahsoka vs. the Magistrate/1,982*
25 May the Force Be with You/1,982*
26 Connecting with the Force/1,844*
27 I Want My Armor Back/1,844*
28 Boba Fett Takes Out Stormtroopers/1,844*
29 Dark Troopers on a Mission/1,844*
30 Moff Gideon Confronts the Child/1,844*
31 Reunited with an Old Enemy/1,582*
32 Surveying the Rhydonium Facility/1,582*
33 Fighting off Pirates/1,582*
34 Behind Enemy Lines/1,582*
35 Snipers at the Ready/1,582*
36 Recruiting for the Rescue Mission/2,172*
37 Aboard the Imperial Cruiser/2,172*
38 Activating the Dark Troopers/2,172*
39 Confrontation on the Bridge/2,172*
40 A New Journey Awaits/2,172*

2021 Star Wars The Mandalorian Season 2

COMPLETE SET (100)	12.00	30.00
COMMON CARD (1-100)	.25	.60

*BLUE: 1.2X TO 3X BASIC CARDS
*PURPLE: 2.5X TO 6X BASIC CARDS
*BRONZE/50: 8X TO 20X BASIC CARDS
*SILVER/25: 15X TO 40X BASIC CARDS
*GOLD/10: UNPRICED DUE TO SCARCITY
*BLACK/1: UNPRICED DUE TO SCARCITY
*P.P.BLACK/1: UNPRICED DUE TO SCARCITY
*P.P.CYAN/1: UNPRICED DUE TO SCARCITY
*P.P.MAGENTA/1: UNPRICED DUE TO SCARCITY
*P.P.YELLOW/1: UNPRICED DUE TO SCARCITY

2021 Star Wars The Mandalorian Season 2 Autographed Commemorative Metal Buttons

*BLACK/1: UNPRICED DUE TO SCARCITY
RANDOMLY INSERTED INTO PACKS

AMCW Carl Weathers
AMPP Pedro Pascal
AMSK Simon Kassianides

2021 Star Wars The Mandalorian Season 2 Autographs

COMMON AUTO	10.00	25.00

*RED/99: SAME VALUE AS BASIC
*BRONZE/50: .5X TO 1.2X BASIC AUTOS
*SILVER/25: .6X TO 1.5X BASIC AUTOS
*GOLD/10: UNPRICED DUE TO SCARCITY
*BLACK/1: UNPRICED DUE TO SCARCITY

*P.P.BLACK/1: UNPRICED DUE TO SCARCITY
*P.P.CYAN/1: UNPRICED DUE TO SCARCITY
*P.P.MAGENTA/1: UNPRICED DUE TO SCARCITY
*P.P.YELLOW/1: UNPRICED DUE TO SCARCITY
RANDOMLY INSERTED INTO PACKS

ACB Chris Bartlett	12.00	30.00
ACW Carl Weathers	150.00	300.00
AGE Giancarlo Esposito	60.00	120.00
AHS Horatio Sanz	30.00	75.00
ALS Leilani Shiu	15.00	40.00
AMR Misty Rosas	20.00	50.00
APA Philip Alexander	12.00	30.00
APL Paul Sun-Hyung Lee	30.00	75.00
APP Pedro Pascal	600.00	1200.00
ASK Simon Kassianides	30.00	75.00
ATM Temuera Morrison	150.00	300.00
ADLI Diana Lee Inosanto	20.00	50.00

2021 Star Wars The Mandalorian Season 2 Characters

COMMON CARD (C1-C14)	.75	2.00

*BRONZE/50: 3X TO 8X BASIC CARDS
*SILVER/25: 2X TO 5X BASIC CARDS
*GOLD/10: UNPRICED DUE TO SCARCITY
*BLACK/1: UNPRICED DUE TO SCARCITY
*P.P.BLACK/1: UNPRICED DUE TO SCARCITY
*P.P.CYAN/1: UNPRICED DUE TO SCARCITY
*P.P.MAGENTA/1: UNPRICED DUE TO SCARCITY
*P.P.YELLOW/1: UNPRICED DUE TO SCARCITY
RANDOMLY INSERTED INTO PACKS

C1 The Mandalorian	1.50	4.00
C2 The Child	2.00	5.00
C4 Moff Gideon	1.25	3.00
C8 Cobb Vanth	1.50	4.00
C9 Dark Trooper	1.25	3.00
C11 Bo-Katan Kryze	1.50	4.00
C12 Koska Reeves	1.50	4.00
C13 Ahsoka Tano	3.00	8.00
C14 Boba Fett	1.50	4.00

2021 Star Wars The Mandalorian Season 2 Characters NYCC Promos

ANNCD PRINT RUN 250 COPIES

NYCC2 The Mandalorian
NYCC3 The Child

2021 Star Wars The Mandalorian Season 2 The Child

COMPLETE SET (12)	15.00	40.00
COMMON CARD (TC1-TC12)	2.00	5.00

*BRONZE/50: 2X TO 5X BASIC CARDS
*SILVER/25: 5X TO 12X BASIC CARDS
*GOLD/10: UNPRICED DUE TO SCARCITY
*DKSBR METAL/5: UNPRICED DUE TO SCARCITY
*BLACK/1: UNPRICED DUE TO SCARCITY
*P.P.BLACK/1: UNPRICED DUE TO SCARCITY
*P.P.CYAN/1: UNPRICED DUE TO SCARCITY
*P.P.MAGENTA/1: UNPRICED DUE TO SCARCITY
*P.P.YELLOW/1: UNPRICED DUE TO SCARCITY
RANDOMLY INSERTED INTO PACKS

2021 Star Wars The Mandalorian Season 2 Comic Covers

COMPLETE SET (7)	15.00	40.00
COMMON CARD (CC1-CC7)	3.00	8.00

*BRONZE/50: 2X TO 5X BASIC CARDS
*SILVER/25: 3X TO 8X BASIC CARDS
*GOLD/10: UNPRICED DUE TO SCARCITY
*DKSBR METAL./5: UNPRICED DUE TO SCARCITY
*BLACK/1: UNPRICED DUE TO SCARCITY
*P.P.BLACK/1: UNPRICED DUE TO SCARCITY
*P.P.CYAN/1: UNPRICED DUE TO SCARCITY
*P.P.MAGENTA/1: UNPRICED DUE TO SCARCITY
*P.P.YELLOW/1: UNPRICED DUE TO SCARCITY
RANDOMLY INSERTED INTO PACKS

2021 Star Wars The Mandalorian Season 2 Commemorative Metal Buttons

COMMON MEM	5.00	12.00

*RED/99: SAME VALUE AS BASIC
*BRONZE/50: .5X TO 1.2X BASIC CARDS
*SILVER/25: .6X TO 1.5X BASIC CARDS
*GOLD/10: UNPRICED DUE TO SCARCITY
*BLACK/1: UNPRICED DUE TO SCARCITY

RANDOMLY INSERTED INTO PACKS

MCCB The Child	10.00	25.00
MCCF The Child	10.00	25.00
MCMB The Mandalorian	12.00	30.00
MCMC The Mandalorian	12.00	30.00
MCMF The Mandalorian	12.00	30.00
MCBHW Bo-Katan Kryze	8.00	20.00
MCBMF Bo-Katan Kryze	8.00	20.00
MCBTW Bo-Katan Kryze	8.00	20.00
MCCCC The Child	10.00	25.00
MCCGC The Child	10.00	25.00
MCCMC The Child	10.00	25.00
MCCMF The Child	10.00	25.00
MCKHW Koska Reeves	10.00	25.00
MCKTW Koska Reeves	10.00	25.00
MCMGC The Mandalorian	12.00	30.00
MCMHW The Mandalorian	12.00	30.00
MCMMC The Mandalorian	12.00	30.00
MCMMF The Mandalorian	12.00	30.00
MCMTW The Mandalorian	12.00	30.00
MCPMF Ahsoka Tano	15.00	40.00

2021 Star Wars The Mandalorian Season 2 Concept Art

COMPLETE SET (16)	20.00	50.00
COMMON CARD (CA1-CA16)	2.50	6.00

*BRONZE/50: .6X TO 1.5X BASIC CARDS
*SILVER/25: 2X TO 5X BASIC CARDS
*GOLD/10: UNPRICED DUE TO SCARCITY
*BLACK/1: UNPRICED DUE TO SCARCITY
*P.P.BLACK/1: UNPRICED DUE TO SCARCITY
*P.P.CYAN/1: UNPRICED DUE TO SCARCITY
*P.P.MAGENTA/1: UNPRICED DUE TO SCARCITY
*P.P.YELLOW/1: UNPRICED DUE TO SCARCITY
RANDOMLY INSERTED INTO PACKS

2021 Star Wars The Mandalorian Season 2 Dual Autographs

*GOLD/10: UNPRICED DUE TO SCARCITY
*BLACK/1: UNPRICED DUE TO SCARCITY
RANDOMLY INSERTED INTO PACKS

DAPG G.Esposito/P.Pascal
DAPW C.Weathers/P.Pascal
DAWA P.Alexander/A.Wraith
DAWS H.Sanz/C.Weathers

2021 Star Wars The Mandalorian Season 2 Prop Relics

*SILVER/25: UNPRICED DUE TO SCARCITY
*GOLD/10: UNPRICED DUE TO SCARCITY
*BLACK/1: UNPRICED DUE TO SCARCITY
STATED PRINT RUN 50 SER.#'d SETS

PRAF The Armorer/Razor Crest	200.00	400.00
PRCR The Child/Razor Crest	350.00	700.00
PRKR Kuiil/Razor Crest		
PRMF The Mandalorian/Chimney	250.00	500.00
PRMR The Mandalorian/Chimney	250.00	500.00

2021 Star Wars The Mandalorian Season 2 Sourced Fabric Relics

COMMON MEM	50.00	100.00

*BRONZE/50: .5X TO 1.2X BASIC MEM
*SILVER/25: .6X TO 1.5 BASIC MEM
*GOLD/10: UNPRICED DUE TO SCARCITY
*BLACK/1: UNPRICED DUE TO SCARCITY
STATED PRINT RUN 99 SER.#'d SETS

FRM Mythrol/Jacket	50.00	100.00
FRAA Ahsoka Tano/Pants	100.00	200.00
FRAB Ahsoka Tano/Arm Wraps	125.00	250.00
FRAC Ahsoka Tano/Body Suit	125.00	250.00
FRGG Gamorrean Guard/Shirt	50.00	100.00
FRMG Magistrate Morgan Elsbeth/Body Suit	60.00	120.00

2021 Star Wars The Mandalorian Season 2 Triple Autographs

*BLACK/1: UNPRICED DUE TO SCARCITY

TAPWE Pascal/Esposito/Weathers
TAPWS Sanz/Pascal/Weathers

2020 Star Wars The Mandalorian Season 2 Trailer Set

COMPLETE SET (7)	15.00	40.00
COMMON CARD (1-7)	4.00	10.00

STATED PRINT RUN 1,482 SETS

1995 Star Wars Mastervisions

COMPLETE BOXED SET (36)	10.00	25.00
COMMON CARD (1-36)	.30	.75

1995 Star Wars Mastervisions Promos

COMMON CARD	.75	2.00
P2 Luke on Hoth	1.25	3.00
(Star Wars Galaxy Magazine Exclusive)		

2015 Star Wars Masterwork

COMPLETE SET W/O SP (50)	60.00	120.00
UNOPENED BOX (4 MINIBOXES)	300.00	350.00
UNOPENED MINIBOX (5 CARDS)	80.00	95.00
COMMON CARD (1-50)	2.00	5.00
COMMON CARD (51-75)	5.00	12.00
*BLUE/299: .5X TO 1.2X BASIC CARDS		
*BLUE SP/299: 2X TO .50X BASIC CARDS		
*SILVER/99: .75X TO 2X BASIC CARDS		
*SILVER SP/99: .3X TO .80X BASIC CARDS		
*GREEN/50: 1.2X TO 3X BASIC CARDS		
*GREEN SP/50: .5X TO 1.2X BASIC CARDS		
*P.P.BLACK/1: UNPRICED DUE TO SCARCITY		
*P.P.CYAN/1: UNPRICED DUE TO SCARCITY		
*P.P.MAGENTA/1: UNPRICED DUE TO SCARCITY		
*P.P.YELLOW/1: UNPRICED DUE TO SCARCITY		

2015 Star Wars Masterwork Autographs

COMMON AUTO	8.00	20.00
*FRAMED/28: UNPRICED DUE TO SCARCITY		
*FOIL/25: UNPRICED DUE TO SCARCITY		
*CANVAS/10: UNPRICED DUE TO SCARCITY		
*WOOD/1: UNPRICED DUE TO SCARCITY		
STATED ODDS 1:4		
NNO Alan Harris	10.00	25.00
NNO Amy Allen	12.00	30.00
NNO Angus MacInnes	10.00	25.00
NNO Anthony Daniels	120.00	250.00
NNO Ashley Eckstein	15.00	40.00
NNO Billy Dee Williams	100.00	200.00
NNO Carrie Fisher	600.00	1000.00
NNO Chris Parsons	10.00	25.00
NNO Dermot Crowley	10.00	25.00
NNO Dickey Beer	8.00	20.00
NNO Gerald Home	10.00	25.00
NNO Harrison Ford	1800.00	3000.00
NNO James Earl Jones	300.00	450.00
NNO Jeremy Bulloch	20.00	50.00
NNO Jesse Jensen	10.00	25.00
NNO John Morton	15.00	40.00
NNO John Ratzenberger	12.00	30.00
NNO Julian Glover	12.00	30.00
NNO Kenneth Colley	10.00	25.00
NNO Kenny Baker	150.00	300.00
NNO Mark Hamill	400.00	750.00
NNO Michonne Bourriague	10.00	25.00
NNO Mike Quinn	12.00	30.00
NNO Oliver Ford Davies	10.00	25.00
NNO Orli Shoshan	10.00	25.00
NNO Pam Rose	10.00	25.00
NNO Paul Brooke	12.00	30.00
NNO Peter Mayhew	75.00	150.00
NNO Phil Eason	10.00	25.00
NNO Rusty Goffe	12.00	30.00
NNO Tim Rose	15.00	40.00
NNO Wayne Pygram	10.00	25.00

2015 Star Wars Masterwork Companions

COMPLETE SET (10)	25.00	60.00
COMMON CARD (C1-C10)	10.00	10.00
*RAINBOW/299: .6X TO 1.5X BASIC CARDS		

---

*CANVAS/99: 1X TO 2.5X BASIC CARDS		
*WOOD/50: 1.2X TO 3X BASIC CARDS		
*CLEAR ACE./25: 1.5X TO 4X BASIC CARDS		
*METAL/10: UNPRICED DUE TO SCARCITY		
*GOLDEN METAL/1: UNPRICED DUE TO SCARCITY		
*P.P.BLACK/1: UNPRICED DUE TO SCARCITY		
*P.P.CYAN/1: UNPRICED DUE TO SCARCITY		
*P.P.MAGENTA/1: UNPRICED DUE TO SCARCITY		
*P.P.YELLOW/1: UNPRICED DUE TO SCARCITY		
C1 Han Solo and Chewbacca	6.00	15.00
C2 Luke and Leia	6.00	15.00
C3 Vader and Palpatine	5.00	12.00
C5 C-3PO and R2-D2	5.00	12.00
C8 R2-D2 and Luke Skywalker	5.00	12.00
C10 Boba Fett and Jango Fett	5.00	12.00

2015 Star Wars Masterwork Defining Moments

COMPLETE SET (10)	25.00	60.00
COMMON CARD (DM1-DM10)	4.00	10.00
*RAINBOW/299: .6X TO 1.5X BASIC CARDS		
*CANVAS/99: 1X TO 2.5X BASIC CARDS		
*WOOD/50: 1.2X TO 3X BASIC CARDS		
*CLEAR ACE./25: 1.5X TO 4X BASIC CARDS		
*METAL/10: UNPRICED DUE TO SCARCITY		
*GOLDEN METAL/1: UNPRICED DUE TO SCARCITY		
*P.P.BLACK/1: UNPRICED DUE TO SCARCITY		
*P.P.CYAN/1: UNPRICED DUE TO SCARCITY		
*P.P.MAGENTA/1: UNPRICED DUE TO SCARCITY		
*P.P.YELLOW/1: UNPRICED DUE TO SCARCITY		
DM1 Darth Vader	5.00	12.00
DM2 Luke Skywalker	5.00	12.00
DM3 Han Solo	8.00	20.00
DM4 Princess Leia Organa	5.00	12.00
DM7 Anakin Skywalker	5.00	12.00
DM8 Obi-Wan Kenobi	5.00	12.00
DM10 Chewbacca	5.00	12.00

2015 Star Wars Masterwork Dual Autograph Booklets

STATED PRINT RUN 5 SER. #'d SETS	
UNPRICED DUE TO SCARCITY	
1 A.Daniels/K.Baker	
2 B.Williams/M.Quinn	
3 J.Bulloch/C.Parsons	
4 M.Hamill/J.Jones	

2015 Star Wars Masterwork Gold-Stamped Sketches

NNO Adam Talley
NNO Adrian Rivera
NNO Bill Pulkovski
NNO Brandon Gallo
NNO Brent Ragland
NNO Brian DeGuire
NNO Brian Kong
NNO Chad "CWM" McCown
NNO Chris Henderson
NNO Christian N. St. Pierre
NNO Clay McCormack
NNO Dan Bergren
NNO Dan Cooney
NNO Dan Parsons
NNO Daniel Contois
NNO Darrin Pepe
NNO David J. Williams
NNO Davide Fabbri
NNO Denae Frazier
NNO Don Pedicini Jr
NNO Eric Kowalick
NNO Erik Hodson
NNO Francois Chartier
NNO Gavin Hunt
NNO Gyula Nemeth
NNO Irma "Aimo" Ahmed
NNO James Henry Smith
NNO Jamie Snell
NNO Jason Crosby
NNO Jason Davies
NNO Jason Durden
NNO Jeff Carlisle
NNO Jeff "GeckoArt" Chandler
NNO Jeff Confer
NNO Jeff Zapata

NNO Jeffrey Benitez
NNO John Haun
NNO Jon Morris
NNO Jorge Baeza
NNO Karen Hallion
NNO Karen Hinson
NNO Ken Branch
NNO Ken Knudtsen
NNO Kevin Doyle
NNO Kevin Graham
NNO Kimberly Dunaway
NNO Kris Penix
NNO Lawrence Reynolds
NNO Lee Kohse
NNO Lin Workman
NNO Lord Mesa
NNO Marck Labas
NNO Mark Hammermeister
NNO Mary Bellamy
NNO Michael "Locoduck" Duron
NNO Mick & Matt Glebe
NNO Mikey Babinsky
NNO Nick "NIK" Neocleus
NNO Omar Maya Velasquez
NNO Pablo Diaz
NNO Patrick Giles
NNO Rhiannon Owens
NNO Rich Molinelli
NNO Robert Hendrickson
NNO Robert Jimenez
NNO Robert Teranishi
NNO Russ Maheras
NNO Scott Houseman
NNO Scott Zambelli
NNO Stephanie Swanger
NNO Steven Black
NNO Steven Burch
NNO Strephon Taylor
NNO Ted Dastick Jr
NNO Terry Pavlet
NNO Tim Proctor
NNO Tod Allen Smith
NNO Tom Hodges
NNO Wilson Ramos, Jr.
NNO Zuno

2015 Star Wars Masterwork Puzzle Sketches

NNO Brian DeGuire
NNO Chris Raimo
NNO Jason Crosby
NNO Joe Hogan
NNO Lawrence Reynolds
NNO Lord Mesa
NNO Nik Neocleous
NNO Pablo Diaz
NNO Steve Burch
NNO Tomoko Taniguchi

2015 Star Wars Masterwork Return of the Jedi Bunker Relics Bronze

COMMON CARD	12.00	30.00
*SILVER/77: .75X TO 2X BASIC CARDS		
CARDS 1, 2, 3, 4, 10, 12 SER.#'d TO 155		
CARDS 5, 6, 7, 8, 9, 11 #'d TO 255		
1 Han Solo/155	20.00	50.00
2 Princess Leia Organa/155	20.00	50.00
3 Chewbacca/155	15.00	40.00
4 Luke Skywalker/155	25.00	60.00
10 Ewok (frame)/155	15.00	40.00
12 Han, Leia & Luke/155	20.00	50.00

2015 Star Wars Masterwork Scum and Villainy

COMPLETE SET (10)	25.00	60.00
COMMON CARD (SV1-SV10)	4.00	10.00
*RAINBOW/299: 1.5X TO 6X BASIC CARDS		
*CANVAS/99: 1X TO 2.5X BASIC CARDS		
*WOOD/50: 1.2X TO 3X BASIC CARDS		
*CLEAR ACE./25: 1.5X TO 4X BASIC CARDS		
*METAL/10: UNPRICED DUE TO SCARCITY		
*GOLDEN METAL/1: UNPRICED DUE TO SCARCITY		
*P.P.BLACK/1: UNPRICED DUE TO SCARCITY		
*P.P.CYAN/1: UNPRICED DUE TO SCARCITY		
*P.P.MAGENTA/1: UNPRICED DUE TO SCARCITY		

2015 Star Wars Masterwork Autographed Pen Relics

STATED PRINT RUN 1 SER.#'d SET
UNPRICED DUE TO SCARCITY

NNO Alan Harris
NNO Amy Allen
NNO Angus MacInnes
NNO Anthony Daniels
NNO Ashley Eckstein
NNO Billy Dee Williams
NNO Bonnie Piesse
NNO Bruce Spence
NNO Caroline Blakiston
NNO Carrie Fisher
NNO Chris Parsons
NNO Dermot Crowley
NNO Dickey Beer
NNO Gerald Home
NNO Harrison Ford
NNO Ian Liston
NNO James Earl Jones
NNO Jeremy Bulloch
NNO Jerome Blake
NNO Jesse Jensen
NNO John Morton
NNO John Ratzenberger
NNO Julian Glover
NNO Kenneth Colley
NNO Kenny Baker
NNO Mark Hamill
NNO Matt Sloan
NNO Michonne Bourriague
NNO Mike Quinn
NNO Oliver Ford Davies
NNO Orli Shoshan
NNO Pam Rose
NNO Paul Brooke
NNO Peter Mayhew
NNO Phil Eason
NNO Ralph Brown
NNO Rusty Goffe
NNO Tim Rose
NNO Wayne Pygram
NNO Zachariah Jensen

2015 Star Wars Masterwork Sketch Booklets

UNPRICED DUE TO SCARCITY

1 Chris Raimo
2 Darrin Pepe
3 Jeff Zapata
4 Patrick Giles
5 Steven Black

2015 Star Wars Masterwork Sketches

NNO Aaron Smith
NNO Adam Talley
NNO Adrian Rivera
NNO Adrianna Vanderstelt
NNO Alex Buechel
NNO Andrew "Drone" Cosson
NNO Anthony Pugh
NNO Bill Maus
NNO Bill Pulkovski
NNO Bob Stevlic
NNO Brandon Bracamonte
NNO Brandon Gallo
NNO Brent Ragland
NNO Brian DeGuire
NNO Brian Kong
NNO Chris Hamer
NNO Chris Henderson
NNO Chris Raimo
NNO Chris Ring
NNO Chris West

NNO Christian N. St. Pierre
NNO Clay McCormack
NNO Dan Bergren
NNO Dan Cooney
NNO Dan Gorman
NNO Dan Parsons
NNO Dan Smith
NNO Dana Black
NNO Daniel Contois
NNO Darin Radimaker
NNO Darrin Pepe
NNO David J. Williams
NNO David Rabbitte
NNO Davide Fabbri
NNO Denae Frazier
NNO Don Pedicini Jr.
NNO Doug Cowan
NNO Elfie Lebouleux
NNO Eric Kowalick
NNO Eric Lehtonen
NNO Erik Hodson
NNO Francois Chartier
NNO Gary Kezele
NNO Gavin Hunt
NNO GeckoArt
NNO Grant Gould
NNO Gyula Nemeth
NNO Ingrid Hardy
NNO Irma "Aimo" Ahmed
NNO James "Bukshot" Bukauskas
NNO James Henry Smith
NNO Jamie Snell
NNO Jason Adams
NNO Jason Chalker
NNO Jason Crosby
NNO Jason Davies
NNO Jason Durden
NNO Jason Flowers
NNO Jason Goad
NNO Jason M. Kincaid
NNO Jason Sobol
NNO Jason Walker
NNO Jay Kretzer
NNO Jeff "GeckoArt" Chandler
NNO Jeff Carlisle
NNO Jeff Confer
NNO Jeff Mallinson
NNO Jeff Parsons
NNO Jeff Zapata
NNO Jeffrey Benitez
NNO Jenn DePaola
NNO Joe Allard
NNO Joe Corroney
NNO Joe Hogan
NNO Joel Biske
NNO John Haun
NNO John Sloboda
NNO John Soukup
NNO Jon Morris
NNO Jorge Baeza
NNO Justin Chung
NNO Kaela Croft
NNO Karen Hallion
NNO Karen Hinson
NNO Ken Branch
NNO Ken Knudtsen
NNO Kent Archer
NNO Kevin Doyle
NNO Kevin Graham
NNO Kimberly Dunaway
NNO Kris Penix
NNO Kyle Babbitt
NNO Lak Lim
NNO Lark Sudol
NNO Lawrence Reynolds
NNO Lee Kohse
NNO Lee Lightfoot
NNO Lin Workman
NNO LinZy Zom
NNO Lizzy "ELC" Carr
NNO Lord Mesa
NNO Marcia Dye

NNO Marck Labas
NNO Mark Hammermeister
NNO Mark Pingitore
NNO Martheus Wade
NNO Mary Bellamy
NNO Mat Nastos
NNO Matt Minor
NNO Matthew Kirscht
NNO Melike Acar
NNO Michael "Locoduck" Duron
NNO Michael Leavitt
NNO Mick & Matt Glebe
NNO Mike Hampton
NNO Mike Mayhew
NNO Mike Vasquez
NNO Mikey Babinsky
NNO Monte Moore
NNO Nathan Hamill
NNO Nick Neocleus
NNO Nicole Falk
NNO Omar Maya Velazquez
NNO Pablo Diaz
NNO Patrick Giles
NNO Paul "Gutz" Gutierrez
NNO Puiz Calzada
NNO Rhiannon Owens
NNO Rich Molinelli
NNO Robert Hendrickson
NNO Robert Jimenez
NNO Robert Teranishi
NNO Ron Conley
NNO Roy Cover
NNO Russ Maheras
NNO Russell Walks
NNO Sarah Wilkinson
NNO Scott Houseman
NNO Scott Rorie
NNO Scott Zambelli
NNO Sean Pence
NNO Sol Mohamed
NNO Stephanie Swanger
NNO Steve Oatney
NNO Steven Black
NNO Steven Burch
NNO Strephon Taylor
NNO Ted Dastick Jr
NNO Terry Pavlet
NNO Tim Dowler
NNO Tim Proctor
NNO Tim Shay
NNO Tina Berardi
NNO Tod Allen Smith
NNO Tom Hodges
NNO Tomoko Taniguchi
NNO Tony Miello
NNO Tyler Scarlett
NNO Val Hochberg
NNO Wilson Ramos, Jr.
NNO Zuno

2015 Star Wars Masterwork Stamp Relics

COMMON CARD	20.00	50.00
STATED ODDS 1:CASE		
NNO Anakin vs. Obi-Wan	50.00	100.00
NNO Ben (Obi-Wan) Kenobi	30.00	80.00
NNO Boba Fett	60.00	120.00
NNO C-3PO	25.00	60.00
NNO Darth Maul	50.00	100.00
NNO Darth Vader	30.00	80.00
NNO Emperor Palpatine	30.00	80.00
NNO Han Solo and Chewbacca	50.00	100.00
NNO Luke Skywalker	30.00	80.00
NNO The Millennium Falcon	50.00	100.00
NNO X-Wing Fighter	30.00	80.00

2015 Star Wars Masterwork Triple Autograph

STATED PRINT RUN 2 SER. #'d SETS
UNPRICED DUE TO SCARCITY

1 Hamill/Ford/Fisher

2015 Star Wars Masterwork Weapons Lineage Medallions

COMPLETE SET (30)	250.00	500.00
COMMON CARD	8.00	20.00
*SILVER/50: 1.2X TO 3X BASIC CARDS		
*GOLD/10: UNPRICED DUE TO SCARCITY		
STATED ODDS 1:6		
NNO Anakin Skywalker	10.00	25.00
Mace Windu's Lightsaber		
NNO Anakin Skywalker	12.00	30.00
Anakin Skywalker's Lightsaber		
NNO B. Fett's Blaster	10.00	25.00
NNO B. Fett's Blaster	12.00	30.00
NNO Darth Maul's Lightsaber	10.00	25.00
NNO Vader	10.00	25.00
Vader's Lightsaber		
NNO Vader	10.00	25.00
Vader's Lightsaber		
NNO Vader	10.00	25.00
Vader's Lightsaber		
NNO Vader Solo's Blaster	12.00	30.00
NNO Darth Vader	15.00	40.00
Luke Skywalker's Lightsaber		
NNO Han Solo	12.00	30.00
Han Solo's Blaster		
NNO Han Solo	12.00	30.00
Han Solo's Blaster		
NNO Han Solo	15.00	40.00
Luke Skywalker's Lightsaber		
NNO Luke Skywalker	10.00	25.00
Luke Skywalker's Lightsaber		
NNO Luke Skywalker	10.00	25.00
Luke Skywalker's Lightsaber		
NNO Mace Windu	10.00	25.00
Mace Windu's Lightsaber		
NNO Princess Leia Organa	10.00	25.00
Stormtrooper Blaster Rifle		
NNO Leia	12.00	30.00
Leia's Blaster		
NNO R2-D2	10.00	25.00
Luke's Lightsaber		
NNO Stormtrooper	12.00	30.00
Stormtrooper Blaster Rifle		
NNO Yoda	15.00	40.00
Yoda's Lightsaber		

2015 Star Wars Masterwork Wood Sketches

UNPRICED DUE TO SCARCITY

NNO Adam Talley
NNO Alex Buechel
NNO Bill Pulkovski
NNO Brent Raglund
NNO Chris West
NNO Christian N. St. Pierre
NNO Dan Cooney
NNO Dan Parsons
NNO Darrin Pepe
NNO David J. Williams
NNO Davide Fabbri
NNO Denae Frazier
NNO Don Pedicini Jr.
NNO Elfie Lebouleux
NNO Eric Lehtonen
NNO Erik Hodson

NNO Francois Chartier
NNO Gavin Hunt
NNO Gyula Nemeth
NNO Jason Crosby
NNO Jason Davies
NNO Jason Flowers
NNO Jason Goad
NNO Jay Kretzer
NNO Jeff Carlisle
NNO Jeff Mallinson
NNO Jeff Zapata
NNO Jeffrey Benitez
NNO John Soukup
NNO Jon Morris
NNO Ken Branch
NNO Kent Archer
NNO Kevin Doyle
NNO Kevin Graham
NNO Kimberly Dunaway
NNO Lee Kohse
NNO Lee Lightfoot
NNO Lord Mesa
NNO Marck Labas
NNO Mary Bellamy
NNO Mat Nastos
NNO Matt Smith
NNO Melike Acar
NNO Mick & Matt Glebe
NNO Monte Moore
NNO Nick "NIK" Neocleus
NNO Pablo Diaz
NNO Rich Molinelli
NNO Robert Hendrickson
NNO Robert Jimenez
NNO Robert Teranishi
NNO Roy Cover
NNO Russ Maheras
NNO Scott Rorie
NNO Sol Mohamed
NNO Stephanie Swanger
NNO Steven Burch
NNO Strephon Taylor
NNO Ted Dastick Jr.
NNO Tim Dowler
NNO Tim Proctor
NNO Todd Aaron Smith
NNO Val Hochberg
NNO Zuno

2016 Star Wars Masterwork

GREEDO

COMPLETE SET W/SP (75)	200.00	400.00
COMPLETE SET W/O SP (50)	30.00	80.00
UNOPENED BOX (4 PACKS)	150.00	200.00
UNOPENED PACK (5 CARDS)	50.00	60.00
COMMON CARD (1-75)	2.00	5.00
COMMON SP (51-75)	4.00	10.00
*BLUE MET.: SAME VALUE	2.00	5.00
*BLUE MET.SP: SAME VALUE	4.00	10.00
*SILVER MET./99: .75X TO 1.5X BASIC CARDS	3.00	8.00
*SILVER MET.SP/99: .30X TO .75X BASIC CARDS	3.00	8.00
*GREEN MET./50: 1.2X TO 3X BASIC CARDS	6.00	15.00

*GREEN MET.SP/50: .6X TO 1.5X BASIC CARDS	6.00	15.00
*LTSBR PURP./25: 1.5X TO 4X BASIC CARDS	8.00	20.00
*LTSBR PURP.SP/25: .75X TO 2X BASIC CARDS	8.00	20.00
*GOLD/1: UNPRICED DUE TO SCARCITY		
*P.P.BLACK/1: UNPRICED DUE TO SCARCITY		
*P.P.CYAN/1: UNPRICED DUE TO SCARCITY		
*P.P.MAGENTA/1: UNPRICED DUE TO SCARCITY		
*P.P.YELLOW/1: UNPRICED DUE TO SCARCITY		
66 Han Solo SP	6.00	15.00
71 Rey SP	8.00	20.00

2016 Star Wars Masterwork Alien Identification Guide

COMPLETE SET (10)	20.00	50.00
COMMON CARD (AI1-AI10)	2.50	6.00
*FOIL/299: .6X TO 1.5X BASIC CARDS	3.00	8.00
*CANVAS/99: .75X TO 2X BASIC CARDS	5.00	12.00
*WOOD/50: 1X TO 2.5X BASIC CARDS	6.00	15.00
*SILVER/10: UNPRICED DUE TO SCARCITY		
*GOLD/1: UNPRICED DUE TO SCARCITY		
*P.P.BLACK/1: UNPRICED DUE TO SCARCITY		
*P.P.CYAN/1: UNPRICED DUE TO SCARCITY		
*P.P.MAGENTA/1: UNPRICED DUE TO SCARCITY		
*P.P.YELLOW/1: UNPRICED DUE TO SCARCITY		
STATED ODDS 1:4		

2016 Star Wars Masterwork Autographs

COMMON CARD	6.00	15.00
*FOIL/50: .6X TO 1.5X BASIC CARDS		
*CANVAS/25: .75X TO 2X BASIC CARDS		
*WOOD/10: UNPRICED DUE TO SCARCITY		
*SILVER/10: UNPRICED DUE TO SCARCITY		
*GOLD/1: UNPRICED DUE TO SCARCITY		
*P.P.BLACK/1: UNPRICED DUE TO SCARCITY		
*P.P.CYAN/1: UNPRICED DUE TO SCARCITY		
*P.P.MAGENTA/1: UNPRICED DUE TO SCARCITY		
*P.P.YELLOW/1: UNPRICED DUE TO SCARCITY		
5 Andy Serkis	80.00	150.00
8 Ashley Eckstein	12.00	30.00
11 Caroline Blakiston	8.00	20.00
14 Clive Revill	12.00	30.00
15 Corey Dee Williams	8.00	20.00
19 David Ankrum	8.00	20.00
20 David Barclay	8.00	20.00
24 Dickey Beer	10.00	25.00
34 Jeremy Bulloch	15.00	40.00
39 John Coppinger	8.00	20.00
47 Mark Dodson	10.00	25.00
50 Matthew Wood	8.00	20.00
55 Mike Edmonds	8.00	20.00
56 Mike Quinn	8.00	20.00
65 Sam Witwer	8.00	20.00
73 Tim Dry	8.00	20.00
74 Tim Rose	8.00	20.00
75 Tiya Sircar	8.00	20.00

2016 Star Wars Masterwork Autographs Canvas

*CANVAS/25: .75X TO 2X BASIC CARDS
STATED ODDS 1:25
STATED PRINT RUN 25 SER.#'d SETS

1 Adam Driver	400.00	800.00
5 Andy Serkis	150.00	300.00
7 Anthony Daniels	80.00	150.00
10 Billy Dee Williams		
12 Carrie Fisher	300.00	600.00
16 Daisy Ridley	1200.00	2000.00
23 Denis Lawson	25.00	60.00
26 Freddie Prinze Jr.	30.00	80.00
29 Greg Grunberg	12.00	30.00
31 Harrison Ford/1		
32 Hugh Quarshie		
38 John Boyega		
42 Julian Glover		
43 Keisha Castle-Hughes		
48 Mark Hamill	250.00	500.00
52 Michael Carter	12.00	30.00
60 Peter Mayhew		
61 Ray Park		
79 Warwick Davis	15.00	40.00

2016 Star Wars Masterwork Autographs Foil

*FOIL/50: .6X TO 1.5X BASIC CARDS
STATED ODDS 1:30
STATED PRINT RUN 50 SER.#'d SETS

3	Alan Harris		
7	Anthony Daniels	50.00	100.00
28	George Takei	15.00	40.00
29	Greg Grunberg	10.00	25.00
32	Hugh Quarshie	10.00	25.00
38	John Boyega	120.00	250.00
60	Peter Mayhew	30.00	80.00

2016 Star Wars Masterwork Dual Autographs

STATED ODDS 1:4,658

NNO	Fisher/Baker		
NNO	Barclay/Philpott	25.00	60.00
NNO	McDiarmid/Revill		
NNO	Blake/Bowers	20.00	50.00
NNO	Hamill/Ridley		
NNO	Hamill/Baker		
NNO	Pygram/Stanton	15.00	40.00

2016 Star Wars Masterwork Gold-Stamped Sketches

STATED ODDS 1:110
UNPRICED DUE TO SCARCITY

NNO Alex Iniguez/18*
NNO Brad Hudson/16*
NNO Brent Ragland/10*
NNO Brian Kong/24*
NNO Carlos Cabaleiro/27*
NNO Chris Meeks/15*
NNO Dan Bergren/9*
NNO Darrin Pepe/7*
NNO Eric Lehtonen/9*
NNO Gus Mauk/9*
NNO Ingrid Hardy/3*
NNO Jason Brower/5*
NNO Jason Sobol/11*
NNO Jessica Hickman/20*
NNO Kevin Liell/16*
NNO Kris Penix/10*
NNO Lee Lightfoot/8*
NNO Marcia Dye/9*
NNO Matthew Stewart/14*
NNO Melike Acar/8*
NNO Rob Teranishi/37*
NNO Roy Cover/9*
NNO Solly Mohamed/23*
NNO Stephanie Swanger/9*
NNO Tim Proctor/5*
NNO Tina Berardi/4*

2016 Star Wars Masterwork Great Rivalries

COMPLETE SET (10)	15.00	40.00
COMMON CARD (GR1-GR10)	2.50	6.00

*FOIL/299: .6X TO 1.5X BASIC CARDS
*CANVAS/99: .75X TO 2X BASIC CARDS
*WOOD/50: 1X TO 2.5X BASIC CARDS
*SILVER/10: UNPRICED DUE TO SCARCITY
*GOLD/1: UNPRICED DUE TO SCARCITY
*P.P.BLACK/1: UNPRICED DUE TO SCARCITY
*P.P.CYAN/1: UNPRICED DUE TO SCARCITY
*P.P.MAGENTA/1: UNPRICED DUE TO SCARCITY
*P.P.YELLOW/1: UNPRICED DUE TO SCARCITY
STATED ODDS 1:2

2016 Star Wars Masterwork Medallion Relics

COMMON CARD	5.00	12.00
*SILVER/99: .6X TO 1.5X BASIC CARDS	8.00	20.00
*GOLD/10: 1.5X TO 4X BASIC CARDS	20.00	50.00

*PLATINUM/1: UNPRICED DUE TO SCARCITY
STATED ODDS 1:7

NNO	Han Solo Hoth	6.00	15.00
NNO	Han Solo Starkiller Base	6.00	15.00
NNO	Han Solo Yavin	6.00	15.00
NNO	Kylo Ren Starkiller Base		
NNO	Rey Starkiller Base	6.00	15.00

2016 Star Wars Masterwork Quad Autographed Booklet

STATED ODDS 1:20,960
UNPRICED DUE TO SCARCITY

1 McDiarmid/Jones/Glover/Colley

2016 Star Wars Masterwork Show of Force

COMPLETE SET (10)	25.00	60.00
COMMON CARD (SF1-SF10)	3.00	8.00
*FOIL/299: .6X TO 1.5X BASIC CARDS	5.00	12.00
*CANVAS/99: .75X TO 2X BASIC CARDS	6.00	15.00
*WOOD/50: 1X TO 2.5X BASIC CARDS	8.00	20.00

*SILVER/10: UNPRICED DUE TO SCARCITY
*GOLD/1: UNPRICED DUE TO SCARCITY
*P.P.BLACK/1: UNPRICED DUE TO SCARCITY
*P.P.CYAN/1: UNPRICED DUE TO SCARCITY
*P.P.MAGENTA/1: UNPRICED DUE TO SCARCITY
*P.P.YELLOW/1: UNPRICED DUE TO SCARCITY
STATED ODDS 1:4

SF10 Rey	4.00	10.00

2016 Star Wars Masterwork Sketch Booklets

STATED ODDS 1:4,195
UNPRICED DUE TO SCARCITY

1 Brad Hudson/2*
2 Brent Ragland/1*
3 Brian Kong/1*
4 Carlos Cabaleiro/1*
5 Chris Meeks/1*
6 Dan Bergren/2*
7 Darrin Pepe/1*
8 Eric Lehtonen/2*
9 Gus Mauk/1*
10 Jason Brower/1*
11 Kris Penix/2*
12 Lee Lightfoot/1*
13 Marcia Dye/2*
14 Melike Acar/1*
15 Rob Teranishi/2*
16 Solly Mohamed/1*
17 Stephanie Swanger/2*
18 Tim Proctor/2*

2016 Star Wars Masterwork Sketches

STATED ODDS 1:30
UNPRICED DUE TO SCARCITY

NNO Alex Iniguez/53*
NNO Brad Hudson/54*
NNO Brent Ragland/27*
NNO Brian Kong/62*
NNO Carlos Cabaleiro/78*
NNO Dan Bergren/33*
NNO Dan Cooney/105*
NNO Darrin Pepe/32*
NNO Eric Lehtonen/27*
NNO Gus Mauk/36*
NNO Ingrid Hardy/12*
NNO Jamie Cosley/52*
NNO Jason Brower/25*
NNO Jason Sobol/47*
NNO Jessica Hickman/48*
NNO Jordan Maison/39*
NNO Joshua Bommer/6*
NNO Kevin Liell/45*
NNO Kris Penix/26*
NNO Kyle Babbit/5*
NNO Lee Lightfoot/50*

NNO Marcia Dye/22*
NNO Matthew Stewart/43*
NNO Melike Acar/20*
NNO Rob Teranishi/193*
NNO Roy Cover/25*
NNO Scott Houseman/25*
NNO Solly Mohamed/52*
NNO Stephanie Swanger/28*
NNO Tim Proctor/13*
NNO Tina Berardi/20*

2016 Star Wars Masterwork Stamp Relics

COMPLETE SET (12)	100.00	200.00
COMMON CARD	8.00	20.00
*BRONZE/99: .6X TO 1.5X BASIC CARDS	12.00	30.00
*SILVER/50: .75X TO 2X BASIC CARDS	15.00	40.00

*GOLD/10: UNPRICED DUE TO SCARCITY
*PLATINUM/1: UNPRICED DUE TO SCARCITY
STATED ODDS 1:13
STATED PRINT RUN 249 SER.#'d SETS

NNO	Han Solo	10.00	25.00
NNO	Rey	12.00	30.00

2016 Star Wars Masterwork Triple Autographs

STATED ODDS 1:4,658
UNPRICED DUE TO SCARCITY

1 McDiarmid/Colley/Glover
2 Hamill/Boyega/Ridley
3 Hamill/Fisher/Baker

2016 Star Wars Masterwork Wood Sketches

STATED ODDS 1:442
UNPRICED DUE TO SCARCITY

NNO Alex Iniguez/10*
NNO Brad Hudson/15*
NNO Brent Ragland/1*
NNO Carlos Cabaleiro/15*
NNO Chris Meeks/5*
NNO Dan Bergren/4*
NNO Darrin Pepe/3*
NNO Eric Lehtonen/10*
NNO Gus Mauk/10*
NNO Ingrid Hardy/2*
NNO Jason Brower/10*
NNO Jessica Hickman/11*
NNO Joshua Bommer/3*
NNO Kris Penix/4*
NNO Kyle Babbit/5*
NNO Lee Lightfoot/10*
NNO Marcia Dye/5*
NNO Melike Acar/7*
NNO Rob Teranishi/2*
NNO Roy Cover/14*
NNO Solly Mohamed/8*
NNO Stephanie Swanger/2*
NNO Tim Proctor/5*
NNO Tina Berardi/9*

2017 Star Wars Masterwork

COMMON CARD (1-75)	2.50	6.00
COMMON SP (76-100)	5.00	12.00
*BLUE: .5X TO 1.25X BASIC CARDS	3.00	8.00
*GREEN/99: .6X TO 1.5X BASIC CARDS	4.00	10.00
*PURPLE/50: .75X TO 2X BASIC CARDS	5.00	12.00
*GOLD/25: 1X TO 2.5X BASIC CARDS	6.00	15.00

*RED/1: UNPRICED DUE TO SCARCITY
*P.P.BLACK/1: UNPRICED DUE TO SCARCITY
*P.P.CYAN/1: UNPRICED DUE TO SCARCITY
*P.P.MAGENTA/1: UNPRICED DUE TO SCARCITY
*P.P.YELLOW/1: UNPRICED DUE TO SCARCITY

2017 Star Wars Masterwork Adventures of R2-D2

COMMON CARD (AR1-AR10)	2.50	6.00
*RAINBOW FOIL: .5X TO 1.25X BASIC CARDS	3.00	8.00
*CANVAS: .6X TO 1.5X BASIC CARDS	4.00	10.00
*WOOD/50: .75X TO 2X BASIC CARDS	5.00	12.00
*METAL/10: UNPRICED DUE TO SCARCITY		
*GOLD TINTED/1: UNPRICED DUE TO SCARCITY		
*P.P.BLACK/1: UNPRICED DUE TO SCARCITY		
*P.P.CYAN/1: UNPRICED DUE TO SCARCITY		
*P.P.MAGENTA/1: UNPRICED DUE TO SCARCITY		
*P.P.YELLOW/1: UNPRICED DUE TO SCARCITY		

2017 Star Wars Masterwork Autographed Pen Relics

STATED PRINT RUN 1 SER.#'d SET
UNPRICED DUE TO SCARCITY

NNO Adam Driver
NNO Alan Ruscoe
NNO Alan Tudyk
NNO Andy Serkis
NNO Ashley Eckstein
NNO Ben Daniels
NNO Billy Dee Williams
NNO Brian Herring
NNO Clive Revill
NNO Daisy Ridley
NNO Daniel Logan
NNO David Acord
NNO David Bowers
NNO Derek Arnold
NNO Donnie Yen
NNO Felicity Jones
NNO Forest Whitaker
NNO Freddie Prinze Jr.
NNO Garrick Hagon
NNO Genevieve O'Reilly
NNO Gwendoline Christie
NNO Hayden Christensen
NNO Ian McDiarmid
NNO Ian McElhinney
NNO Ian Whyte
NNO Jeremy Bulloch
NNO Jerome Blake
NNO John Boyega
NNO Julian Glover
NNO Julie Dolan
NNO Kath Soucie
NNO Lars Mikkelson
NNO Lloyd Sherr
NNO Marc Silk
NNO Mary Elizabeth McGlynn
NNO Matthew Wood
NNO Nick Kellington
NNO Paul Kasey/Admiral Raddus
NNO Paul Kasey/Edrio Two Tubes
NNO Philip Anthony-Rodriguez
NNO Ray Park
NNO Richard Oldfield
NNO Riz Ahmed
NNO Robbie Daymond
NNO Sam Witwer
NNO Sarah Michelle Gellar
NNO Shardon Duncan-Brewster
NNO Stephen Stanton
NNO Taylor Gray
NNO Temuera Morrison
NNO Tim Rose
NNO Tiya Sircar
NNO Tom Baker
NNO Valene Kane

NNO Warwick Davis
NNO Zarene Dallas

2017 Star Wars Masterwork Autographs

COMMON CARD	6.00	15.00
*WOOD/10: UNPRICED DUE TO SCARCITY		
SILVER FRAMED/10>: UNPRICED DUE TO SCARCITY		
*GOLD TINTED/1: UNPRICED DUE TO SCARCITY		

NNO Adam Driver (horizontal)		
NNO Adam Driver (vertical)		
NNO Alan Tudyk	50.00	100.00
NNO Andy Serkis		
NNO Ashley Eckstein	15.00	40.00
NNO Ben Daniels	8.00	20.00
NNO Billy Dee Williams		
NNO Brian Herring	15.00	40.00
NNO Clive Revill	8.00	20.00
NNO Daisy Ridley		
NNO Dee Bradley Baker	10.00	25.00
NNO Derek Arnold	8.00	20.00
NNO Donnie Yen	60.00	120.00
NNO Felicity Jones (horizontal)		
NNO Felicity Jones (vertical)		
NNO Forest Whitaker (horizontal)		
NNO Forest Whitaker (vertical)		
NNO Freddie Prinze Jr.		
NNO Gwendoline Christie		
NNO Harrison Ford		
NNO Hayden Christensen	150.00	300.00
NNO Ian McDiarmid		
NNO Ian Whyte	10.00	25.00
NNO Jeremy Bulloch	15.00	40.00
NNO John Boyega (horizontal)		
NNO John Boyega (vertical)	60.00	120.00
NNO Julian Glover	12.00	30.00
NNO Lars Mikkelsen	25.00	60.00
NNO Mark Hamill		
NNO Mary Elizabeth McGlynn	12.00	30.00
NNO Matt Lanter	15.00	40.00
NNO Matthew Wood		
NNO Phil LaMarr	8.00	20.00
NNO Ray Park		
NNO Riz Ahmed		
NNO Robbie Daymond	10.00	25.00
NNO Sam Witwer	10.00	25.00
NNO Sarah Michelle Gellar		
NNO Temuera Morrison	25.00	60.00
NNO Tiya Sircar	8.00	20.00
NNO Tom Baker		
NNO Valene Kane	25.00	60.00
NNO Warwick Davis	10.00	25.00
NNO Zarene Dallas	8.00	20.00

2017 Star Wars Masterwork Droid Medallion Relics

COMMON CARD	5.00	12.00
*SILVER/40: .5X TO 1.2X BASIC RELICS	6.00	15.00
*GOLD/25: .6X TO 1.5X BASIC RELICS	8.00	20.00
*BLACK/1: UNPRICED DUE TO SCARCITY		
STATED PRINT RUN 150 SER.#'d SETS		

2017 Star Wars Masterwork Dual Autographs

*PURPLE/10: UNPRICED DUE TO SCARCITY
*GOLD/5: UNPRICED DUE TO SCARCITY
*RED/1: UNPRICED DUE TO SCARCITY

NNO Graves/Taber	20.00	50.00
NNO Daniels/Baker		
NNO Herring/Baker		
NNO Fisher/Baker		
NNO Barclay/Taylor	15.00	40.00
NNO Jones/Tudyk		
NNO Whitaker/Ahmed		
NNO Prinze Jr./Gellar		
NNO Christie/Boyega		
NNO Christensen/Baker		
NNO Christensen/Wood		
NNO McDiarmid/Christensen		
NNO Uwais/Qin-Fee	12.00	30.00
NNO Isaccs/Gray	20.00	50.00
NNO Ratzenberger/MacInnes	12.00	30.00
NNO Hamill/Christensen		
NNO Hamill/Baker		
NNO Salenger/Futterman	12.00	30.00
NNO Kasey/Stanton	12.00	30.00
NNO Marshall/Fleetwood		
NNO Witwer/Wilkinson	15.00	40.00
NNO Morrison/Logan	20.00	50.00
NNO Cole/Grube		

2017 Star Wars Masterwork Evolution of the Rebel Alliance

COMMON CARD (LP1-LP10)	2.50	6.00
*RAINBOW FOIL/249: .5X TO 1.25X BASIC CARDS	3.00	8.00
*CANVAS/99: .6X TO 1.5X BASIC CARDS	4.00	10.00
*WOOD/50: .75X TO 2X BASIC CARDS	5.00	12.00
*METAL/10: UNPRICED DUE TO SCARCITY		
*GOLD TINTED/1: UNPRICED DUE TO SCARCITY		
*P.P.BLACK/1: UNPRICED DUE TO SCARCITY		
*P.P.CYAN/1: UNPRICED DUE TO SCARCITY		
*P.P.MAGENTA/1: UNPRICED DUE TO SCARCITY		
*P.P.YELLOW/1: UNPRICED DUE TO SCARCITY		

2017 Star Wars Masterwork Film Strips

COMMON CARD (FCR1-FCR40)	10.00	25.00

2017 Star Wars Masterwork Hall of Heroes

COMPLETE SET (10)	12.00	30.00
COMMON CARD (HH1-HH10)	3.00	8.00
*RAINBOW FOIL: .5X TO 1.2X BASIC CARDS	4.00	10.00
*CANVAS: .6X TO 1.5X BASIC CARDS	5.00	12.00
*WOOD: UNPRICED DUE TO SCARCITY		
*METAL: UNPRICED DUE TO SCARCITY		
*GOLD TINTED: UNPRICED DUE TO SCARCITY		
*P.P.BLACK/1: UNPRICED DUE TO SCARCITY		
*P.P.CYAN/1: UNPRICED DUE TO SCARCITY		
*P.P.MAGENTA/1: UNPRICED DUE TO SCARCITY		
*P.P.YELLOW/1: UNPRICED DUE TO SCARCITY		

2017 Star Wars Masterwork Quad Autographed Booklets

UNPRICED DUE TO SCARCITY

NNO McDiarmid/Christensen/Park/Wood
NNO Hamill/Fisher/Daniels/Baker

2017 Star Wars Masterwork Silver Bordered Sketches

UNPRICED DUE TO SCARCITY

NNO Achilleas Kokkinakis
NNO Adam Schickling
NNO Adam Worton
NNO Alex Iniguez
NNO Alex Mines
NNO Andrew Fry
NNO Andrew Lopez
NNO Angelina Benedetti
NNO Anil Sharma
NNO Anthony Skubis
NNO Ben AbuSaada
NNO Ben Goddard
NNO Bill Pulkovski
NNO Bob Stevlic
NNO Bobby Blakey
NNO Brad Hudson
NNO Brad Utterstrom
NNO Brandon Blevins
NNO Brandon Pyle
NNO Brendan Purchase
NNO Brendan Shaw
NNO Brent Ragland
NNO Brent Scotchmer
NNO Brett Farr
NNO Bruce Gerlach
NNO Bryan Silverbax
NNO Bryce King II
NNO Caleb King
NNO Carlos Cabaleiro
NNO Cathy Razim
NNO Chad LaForce
NNO Chad Scheres
NNO Charlie Cody
NNO Chris Quinn
NNO Chris Schweizer
NNO Chris Willdig
NNO Clinton Yeager
NNO Corey Galal
NNO Dan Bergren
NNO Dan Burn Webster
NNO Dan Curto
NNO Dan Gorman
NNO Daniel Cooney
NNO Daniel Haas
NNO Danny Hayman
NNO Danny Kidwell
NNO Darrin Pepe
NNO Dave Dabila
NNO Dave Fowler
NNO Dave Gaskin
NNO Dave Strong
NNO Dave Waldeck
NNO David Angelo Roman
NNO Dean Drummond
NNO Dennis Gortakowski
NNO Don Pedicini Jr.
NNO Doug Snodgrass
NNO Dylan Riley
NNO Eddie Price
NNO Edward Serdenia
NNO Eli Hyder
NNO Eric Lehtonen
NNO Eric White
NNO Frank Kadar
NNO Garrett Dix
NNO Gavin Williams
NNO Gerard Garcia Jr.
NNO Gus Mauk
NNO Humberto Fuentes Navarro
NNO Huy Truong
NNO Ibrahim Ozkan
NNO Ingrid Hardy
NNO J Hammond
NNO Jamie Cosley
NNO Jamie Richards
NNO Jamie Thomas
NNO Jason Brower
NNO Jason Heil
NNO Jason Sobol

NNO Jay Manchand
NNO Jeff Mallinson
NNO Jeff Meuth
NNO Jerry Bennett
NNO Jessica Hickman
NNO Jim Mehsling
NNO Jim O'Riley
NNO John Bruce
NNO John DiBiase
NNO John Still
NNO Jose Ventura
NNO Joshua Bommer
NNO Kaela Croft
NNO Kallan Archer
NNO Kate Carleton
NNO Keith Carter
NNO Kelly Greider
NNO Kevin Cleveland
NNO Kevin Graham
NNO Kevin Liell
NNO Kevin P. West
NNO Kiley Beecher
NNO Kris Penix
NNO Kyle Babbitt
NNO Kyle Hickman
NNO Kyle Newman
NNO Lawrence Reynolds
NNO Lee Brown
NNO Lee Lightfoot
NNO Louise Draper
NNO Marcia Dye
NNO Mark Mangum
NNO Mark Stroud
NNO Marlo Agunos
NNO Marsha Parkins
NNO Matt Applegate
NNO Matt Langford
NNO Matt Maldonado
NNO Matt Steffens
NNO Matt Stewart
NNO Matthew Buttich
NNO Matthew Sutton
NNO Melike Acar
NNO Michael Brady
NNO Michael Duron
NNO Michael Mastermaker
NNO Michael Spivey
NNO Michelle Rayner
NNO Mick and Matt Glebe
NNO Mike Barnard
NNO Mike James
NNO Mohammad Jilani
NNO Nathan Ohlendorf
NNO Neil Camera
NNO Nicholas Baltra
NNO Nick Justus
NNO Norvierto P. Basio
NNO Pablo Diaz
NNO Patricio Carrasco
NNO Patrick Giles
NNO Paul Andrews
NNO Phil Hassewer
NNO Phillip Trujillo
NNO Ray Richardson
NNO Rees Finlay
NNO Rey Paez
NNO Rich Molinelli
NNO Richard Serrao
NNO Rob Teranishi
NNO Robert Hendrickson
NNO Rory McQueen
NNO Ruvel Abril
NNO Ryan Edwards
NNO Shane Molina
NNO Shaow Siong
NNO Skip Charron
NNO Solly Mohamed
NNO Stephanie Rosales
NNO Stephanie Swanger
NNO Steve Fuchs
NNO Ted Dastick Jr.
NNO Tiffany Groves

NNO Tim Proctor
NNO Tim Smith
NNO Tina Berardi
NNO Todd Rayner
NNO Trent Westbrook
NNO Vincenzo D'Ippolito
NNO Ward Silverman
NNO Xinjix

2017 Star Wars Masterwork Sketch Booklets

UNPRICED DUE TO SCARCITY

NNO Andrew Fry
NNO Ben AbuSaada
NNO Brad Hudson
NNO Dan Bergren
NNO Eli Hyder
NNO Ibrahim Ozkan
NNO Marlo Agunos
NNO Matt Stewart
NNO Michael Mastermaker
NNO Robert Hendrickson

2017 Star Wars Masterwork Sketches

UNPRICED DUE TO SCARCITY

NNO Achilleas Kokkinakis
NNO Adam Schickling
NNO Adam Worton
NNO Alex Iniguez
NNO Alex Mines
NNO Andrew Fry
NNO Andrew Lopez
NNO Angelina Benedetti
NNO Anil Sharma
NNO Anthony Skubis
NNO Ben AbuSaada
NNO Ben Goddard
NNO Bill Pulkovski
NNO Bob Stevlic
NNO Bobby Blakey
NNO Brad Hudson
NNO Brad Utterstrom
NNO Brandon Blevins
NNO Brandon Pyle
NNO Brendan Purchase
NNO Brendan Shaw
NNO Brent Ragland
NNO Brent Scotchmer
NNO Brett Farr
NNO Bruce Gerlach
NNO Bryan Silverbax
NNO Bryce King II
NNO Caleb King
NNO Carlos Cabaleiro
NNO Cathy Razim
NNO Chad LaForce
NNO Chad Scheres
NNO Charlie Cody
NNO Chris Quinn
NNO Chris Schweizer
NNO Chris Willdig
NNO Clinton Yeager
NNO Corey Galal
NNO Dan Bergren
NNO Dan Burn Webster
NNO Dan Curto
NNO Dan Gorman
NNO Daniel Cooney
NNO Daniel Haas
NNO Danny Hayman
NNO Danny Kidwell
NNO Darrin Pepe
NNO Dave Dabila
NNO Dave Fowler
NNO Dave Gaskin
NNO Dave Strong
NNO Dave Waldeck
NNO David Angelo Roman
NNO Dean Drummond
NNO Dennis Gortakowski
NNO Don Pedicini Jr.
NNO Doug Snodgrass
NNO Dylan Riley
NNO Eddie Price

NNO Edward Serdenia
NNO Eli Hyder
NNO Eric Lehtonen
NNO Eric White
NNO Frank Kadar
NNO Garrett Dix
NNO Gavin Williams
NNO Gerard Garcia Jr.
NNO Gus Mauk
NNO Humberto Fuentes Navarro
NNO Huy Truong
NNO Ibrahim Ozkan
NNO Ingrid Hardy
NNO J Hammond
NNO Jamie Cosley
NNO Jamie Richards
NNO Jamie Thomas
NNO Jason Brower
NNO Jason Heil
NNO Jason Sobol
NNO Jay Manchand
NNO Jeff Mallinson
NNO Jeff Meuth
NNO Jerry Bennett
NNO Jessica Hickman
NNO Jim Mehsling
NNO Jim O'Riley
NNO John Bruce
NNO John DiBiase
NNO John Still
NNO Jose Ventura
NNO Joshua Bommer
NNO Kaela Croft
NNO Kallan Archer
NNO Kate Carleton
NNO Keith Carter
NNO Kelly Greider
NNO Kevin Cleveland
NNO Kevin Graham
NNO Kevin Liell
NNO Kevin P. West
NNO Kiley Beecher
NNO Kris Penix
NNO Kyle Babbitt
NNO Kyle Hickman
NNO Kyle Newman
NNO Lawrence Reynolds
NNO Lee Brown
NNO Lee Lightfoot
NNO Louise Draper
NNO Marcia Dye
NNO Mark Mangum
NNO Mark Stroud
NNO Marlo Agunos
NNO Marsha Parkins
NNO Matt Applegate
NNO Matt Langford
NNO Matt Maldonado
NNO Matt Steffens
NNO Matt Stewart
NNO Matthew Buttich
NNO Matthew Sutton
NNO Melike Acar
NNO Michael Brady
NNO Michael Duron
NNO Michael Mastermaker
NNO Michael Spivey
NNO Michelle Rayner
NNO Mick and Matt Glebe
NNO Mike Barnard
NNO Mike James
NNO Mohammad Jilani
NNO Nathan Ohlendorf
NNO Neil Camera
NNO Nicholas Baltra
NNO Nick Justus
NNO Norvierto P. Basio
NNO Pablo Diaz
NNO Patricio Carrasco
NNO Patrick Giles
NNO Paul Andrews
NNO Phil Hassewer

NNO Phillip Trujillo
NNO Ray Richardson
NNO Rees Finlay
NNO Rey Paez
NNO Rich Molinelli
NNO Richard Serrao
NNO Rob Teranishi
NNO Robert Hendrickson
NNO Rory McQueen
NNO Ruvel Abril
NNO Ryan Edwards
NNO Shane Molina
NNO Shaow Siong
NNO Skip Charron
NNO Solly Mohamed
NNO Stephanie Rosales
NNO Stephanie Swanger
NNO Steve Fuchs
NNO Ted Dastick Jr.
NNO Tiffany Groves
NNO Tim Proctor
NNO Tim Smith
NNO Tina Berardi
NNO Todd Rayner
NNO Trent Westbrook
NNO Vincenzo D'Ippolito
NNO Ward Silverman
NNO Xinjix

2017 Star Wars Masterwork Source Material Jumbo Swatch Relics

COMMON CARD		25.00	60.00
JRCAR	Admiral Ackbar Resistance Uniform	30.00	75.00
JRCGE	Galen Erso Farmer Disguise	60.00	120.00
JRCGF	General Hux First Order Uniform	50.00	100.00
JRCRD	Rey Desert Tunic	200.00	400.00
JRCRO	Rey Outer Garment	150.00	300.00

2017 Star Wars Masterwork Triple Autographs

NNO Daniels/Herring/Baker
NNO Williams/Mayhew/Baker
NNO Jones/Tudyk/Ahmed
NNO Prinze Jr./Gray/Isaacs
NNO Ford/Fisher/Driver
NNO McDiarmid/Christensen/Baker
NNO McDiarmid/Christensen/Wood
NNO Bulloch/Morrison/Logan
NNO Hamill/Fisher/Baker
NNO Mayhew/Daniels/Baker

2017 Star Wars Masterwork Wood Sketches

UNPRICED DUE TO SCARCITY

NNO Achilleas Kokkinakis
NNO Adam Schickling
NNO Adam Worton
NNO Alex Iñiguez
NNO Alex Mines
NNO Andrew Fry
NNO Andrew Lopez
NNO Angelina Benedetti
NNO Anil Sharma
NNO Anthony Skubis
NNO Ben AbuSaada
NNO Ben Goddard
NNO Bill Pulkovski
NNO Bob Stevlic
NNO Bobby Blakey
NNO Brad Hudson
NNO Brad Utterstrom
NNO Brandon Blevins
NNO Brandon Pyle
NNO Brendan Purchase
NNO Brendan Shaw
NNO Brent Ragland
NNO Brent Scotchmer
NNO Brett Farr
NNO Bruce Gerlach
NNO Bryan Silverbax
NNO Bryce King II
NNO Caleb King
NNO Carlos Cabaleiro
NNO Cathy Razim
NNO Chad LaForce

NNO Chad Scheres
NNO Charlie Cody
NNO Chris Quinn
NNO Chris Schweizer
NNO Chris Willdig
NNO Clinton Yeager
NNO Corey Galal
NNO Dan Bergren
NNO Dan Burn Webster
NNO Dan Curto
NNO Dan Gorman
NNO Daniel Cooney
NNO Daniel Haas
NNO Danny Hayman
NNO Danny Kidwell
NNO Darrin Pepe
NNO Dave Dabila
NNO Dave Fowler
NNO Dave Gaskin
NNO Dave Strong
NNO Dave Waldeck
NNO David Angelo Roman
NNO Dean Drummond
NNO Dennis Gortakowski
NNO Don Pedicini Jr.
NNO Doug Snodgrass
NNO Dylan Riley
NNO Eddie Price
NNO Edward Serdenia
NNO Eli Hyder
NNO Eric Lehtonen
NNO Eric White
NNO Frank Kadar
NNO Garrett Dix
NNO Gavin Williams
NNO Gerard Garcia Jr.
NNO Gus Mauk
NNO Humberto Fuentes Navarro
NNO Huy Truong
NNO Ibrahim Ozkan
NNO Ingrid Hardy
NNO J Hammond
NNO Jamie Cosley
NNO Jamie Richards
NNO Jamie Thomas
NNO Jason Brower
NNO Jason Heil
NNO Jason Sobol
NNO Jay Manchand
NNO Jeff Mallinson
NNO Jeff Meuth
NNO Jerry Bennett
NNO Jessica Hickman
NNO Jim Mehsling
NNO Jim O'Riley
NNO John Bruce
NNO John DiBiase
NNO John Still
NNO Jose Ventura
NNO Joshua Bommer
NNO Kaela Croft
NNO Kallan Archer
NNO Kate Carleton
NNO Keith Carter
NNO Kelly Greider
NNO Kevin Cleveland
NNO Kevin Graham
NNO Kevin Liell
NNO Kevin P. West
NNO Kiley Beecher
NNO Kris Penix
NNO Kyle Babbitt
NNO Kyle Hickman
NNO Kyle Newman
NNO Lawrence Reynolds
NNO Lee Brown
NNO Lee Lightfoot
NNO Louise Draper
NNO Marcia Dye
NNO Mark Mangum
NNO Mark Stroud
NNO Marlo Agunos

NNO Marsha Parkins
NNO Matt Applegate
NNO Matt Langford
NNO Matt Maldonado
NNO Matt Steffens
NNO Matt Stewart
NNO Matthew Buttich
NNO Matthew Sutton
NNO Melike Acar
NNO Michael Brady
NNO Michael Duron
NNO Michael Mastermaker
NNO Michael Spivey
NNO Michelle Rayner
NNO Mick and Matt Glebe
NNO Mike Barnard
NNO Mike James
NNO Mohammad Jilani
NNO Nathan Ohlendorf
NNO Neil Camera
NNO Nicholas Baltra
NNO Nick Justus
NNO Norvierto P. Basio
NNO Pablo Diaz
NNO Patricio Carrasco
NNO Patrick Giles
NNO Paul Andrews
NNO Phil Hassewer
NNO Phillip Trujillo
NNO Ray Richardson
NNO Rees Finlay
NNO Rey Paez
NNO Rich Molinelli
NNO Richard Serrao
NNO Rob Teranishi
NNO Robert Hendrickson
NNO Rory McQueen
NNO Ruvel Abril
NNO Ryan Edwards
NNO Shane Molina
NNO Shaow Siong
NNO Skip Charron
NNO Solly Mohamed
NNO Stephanie Rosales
NNO Stephanie Swanger
NNO Steve Fuchs
NNO Ted Dastick Jr.
NNO Tiffany Groves
NNO Tim Proctor
NNO Tim Smith
NNO Tina Berardi
NNO Todd Rayner
NNO Trent Westbrook
NNO Vincenzo D'Ippolito
NNO Ward Silverman
NNO Xinjix

2018 Star Wars Masterwork

UNOPENED BOX (4 PACKS)	150.00	200.00
UNOPENED PACK (5 CARDS)	40.00	50.00
COMMON CARD (1-100)	2.50	6.00
COMMON SP (101-125)	6.00	15.00
*BLUE: .5X TO 1.2X BASIC CARDS		
*GREEN/99: .6X TO 1.5X BASIC CARDS		

*PURPLE/50: .75X TO 2X BASIC CARDS
*ORANGE/10: UNPRICED DUE TO SCARCITY
*BLACK/5: UNPRICED DUE TO SCARCITY
*GOLD/1: UNPRICED DUE TO SCARCITY
*P.P.BLACK/1: UNPRICED DUE TO SCARCITY
*P.P.CYAN/1: UNPRICED DUE TO SCARCITY
*P.P.MAGENTA/1: UNPRICED DUE TO SCARCITY
*P.P.YELLOW/1: UNPRICED DUE TO SCARCITY

101	Luke Skywalker SP	8.00	20.00
102	Princess Leia Organa SP	12.00	30.00
103	Rey SP	15.00	40.00
104	Finn SP	10.00	25.00
105	Obi-Wan Kenobi SP	10.00	25.00
106	Anakin Skywalker SP	10.00	25.00
108	Darth Vader SP	8.00	20.00
109	Darth Maul SP	8.00	20.00
110	Boba Fett SP	12.00	30.00
111	Han Solo SP	12.00	30.00
113	Lando Calrissian SP	10.00	25.00
114	Saw Gerrera SP	10.00	25.00
115	Jyn Erso SP	12.00	30.00
116	Captain Cassian Andor SP	10.00	25.00
119	Kylo Ren SP	10.00	25.00
121	Ahsoka Tano SP	8.00	20.00
124	Bo-Katan Kryze SP	8.00	20.00

2018 Star Wars Masterwork Autographed Commemorative Vehicle Patches

*BLACK/5: UNPRICED DUE TO SCARCITY
*GOLD/1: UNPRICED DUE TO SCARCITY
STATED PRINT RUN SER.#'d SETS
UNPRICED DUE TO SCARCITY

MPAAD Anthony Daniels
MPABH Brian Herring
MPABM Ben Mendelsohn
MPAFJ Felicity Jones
MPAGO Genevieve O'Reilly
MPAHC Hayden Christensen
MPAHQ Hugh Quarshie
MPAIM Ian McDiarmid
MPAJB John Boyega
MPALM Lars Mikkelsen
MPAMQ Mike Quinn
MPARA Riz Ahmed
MPASB Steve Blum
MPATG Taylor Gray
MPATS Tiya Sircar
MPAVM Vanessa Marshall
MPADBB Dee Bradley Baker
MPAFPJ Freddie Prinze Jr.
MPAGMT Guy Henry
MPAMEM Mary Elizabeth McGlynn

2018 Star Wars Masterwork Autographed Pen Relics

PRAD Adam Driver
PRAE Ashley Eckstein
PRAJ Andrew Jack
PRAK Andrew Kishino
PRAS Andy Serkis
PRAT Alan Tudyk
PRBD Ben Daniels
PRBH Brian Herring
PRBM Ben Mendelsohn
PRCB Caroline Blakiston
PRCR Clive Revill
PRDB David Barclay
PRDC Dave Chapman
PRDL Denis Lawson
PRDR Daisy Ridley
PRFW Forest Whitaker
PRGH Guy Henry
PRHC Hayden Christensen
PRHF Harrison Ford
PRHW Howie Weed
PRIM Ian McDiarmid
PRJB Jeremy Bulloch
PRJV Jimmy Vee
PRKL Ken Leung
PRLD Laura Dern
PRLM Lars Mikkelsen
PRML Matt Lanter
PRMM Mads Mikkelsen

PRNC Nathalie Cuzner
PRPK Paul Kasey
PRRP Ray Park
PRSW Sam Witwer
PRSW Simon Williamson
PRTW Tom Wilton
PRBDW Billy Dee Williams
PRCCK Crystal Clarke
PRCCS Cavin Cornwall
PRJAT James Arnold Taylor
PRJSL Jason Spisak
PRSLJ Samuel L. Jackson

2018 Star Wars Masterwork Autographs

COMMON AUTO	6.00	15.00
*BLUE FOIL/99: .5X TO 1.2X BASIC AUTOS		
*WOOD/10: UNPRICED DUE TO SCARCITY		
*SILVER FR./5: UNPRICED DUE TO SCARCITY		
*GOLD FR./1: UNPRICED DUE TO SCARCITY		
*P.P.BLACK/1: UNPRICED DUE TO SCARCITY		
*P.P.CYAN/1: UNPRICED DUE TO SCARCITY		
*P.P.MAGENTA/1: UNPRICED DUE TO SCARCITY		
*P.P.YELLOW/1: UNPRICED DUE TO SCARCITY		

AAE	Ashley Eckstein	12.00	30.00
AAK	Andrew Kishino	8.00	20.00
ABS	Brent Spiner	12.00	30.00
ACC	Cavin Cornwall	12.00	30.00
ADB	David Barclay	10.00	25.00
ADL	Denis Lawson	8.00	20.00
ADM	Daniel Mays	8.00	20.00
AGH	Guy Henry	8.00	20.00
AHW	Howie Weed	12.00	30.00
AJB	Jeremy Bulloch	15.00	40.00
AJV	Jimmy Vee	10.00	25.00
ALD	Laura Dern	100.00	200.00
ALM	Lars Mikkelsen	10.00	25.00
AML	Matt Lanter	8.00	20.00
AMW	Matthew Wood	10.00	25.00
ANC	Nathalie Cuzner	8.00	20.00
ARN	Robert Nairne	8.00	20.00
ASW	Simon Williamson	12.00	30.00
ATW	Tom Wilton	8.00	20.00
AJAT	James Arnold Taylor	10.00	25.00
AJSP	Jason Spisak	8.00	20.00
ASWT	Sam Witwer	12.00	30.00

2018 Star Wars Masterwork Commemorative Vehicle Patches

COMMON PATCH	4.00	10.00
*PURPLE/50: .6X TO 1.5X BASIC PATCHES		
*BLACK/5: UNPRICED DUE TO SCARCITY		
*GOLD/1: UNPRICED DUE TO SCARCITY		
STATED PRINT RUN 175 SER.#'d SETS		

MPBHF	Boba Fett	8.00	20.00
MPGEA	Grand Admiral Thrawn	6.00	15.00
MPGEK	Kassius Konstantine	6.00	15.00
MPGEM	Grand Moff Tarkin	6.00	15.00
MPGEP	Governor Arihnda Pryce	5.00	12.00
MPGEV	Darth Vader	5.00	12.00
MPGRB	Bail Organa	6.00	15.00
MPGRP	Padmé Amidala	8.00	20.00
MPJOA	Anakin Skywalker	5.00	12.00

MPJOO	Obi-Wan Kenobi	6.00	15.00
MPJQQ	Qui-Gon Jinn	5.00	12.00
MPPSA	Ahsoka Tano	5.00	12.00
MPPSE	Ezra Bridger	5.00	12.00
MPPSH	Hera Syndulla	5.00	12.00
MPPSZ	Zeb Orrelios	6.00	15.00
MPRAB	Bodhi Rook	5.00	12.00
MPRAH	Han Solo	12.00	30.00
MPRAJ	Jyn Erso	5.00	12.00
MPRAK	K-2SO	5.00	12.00
MPRAM	Baze Malbus	6.00	15.00
MPRAP	Princess Leia Organa	8.00	20.00
MPRAR	R2-D2	5.00	12.00
MPRAS	Luke Skywalker	6.00	15.00
MPRMH	Han Solo	10.00	25.00
MPRML	Lando Calrissian	5.00	12.00
MPRMN	Nien Nunb	5.00	12.00
MPRMP	Princess Leia Organa	8.00	20.00
MPRMS	Luke Skywalker	6.00	15.00
MPTRF	Finn	6.00	15.00
MPTRL	General Leia Organa	8.00	20.00
MPTRR	Rey	8.00	20.00

2018 Star Wars Masterwork Dual Autographs

*WOOD/10: UNPRICED DUE TO SCARCITY
*BLACK/5: UNPRICED DUE TO SCARCITY
GOLD/1: UNPRICED DUE TO SCARCITY

DAAT	R.Ahmed/A.Tudyk		
DABB	K.Baker/D.Barclay		
DABH	J.Boyega/B.Herring	75.00	150.00
DABO	C.Blakiston/G.O'Reilly		
DABR	E.Bauersfeld/K.Rotich	20.00	50.00
DABS	J.Boyega/J.Suotamo	75.00	150.00
DACP	H.Christensen/R.Park		
DACW	A.Cook/I.Whyte		
DAGA	S.Gellar/P.Anthony-Rodriguez		
DAGM	G.Takei/M.Lanter		
DAJM	F.Jones/B.Mendelsohn		
DALG	K.Leung/G.Grunberg	15.00	40.00
DAMH	B.Mendelsohn/G.Henry		
DAMM	L.Mikkelsen/M.McGlynn	20.00	50.00
DAPW	R.Park/M.Wood		
DARB	D.Ridley/J.Boyega		
DASD	M.Salenger/O.D'Abo	30.00	75.00
DATF	J.Taylor/N.Futterman		
DAWQ	B.Williams/M.Quinn		
DAWS	S.Witwer/S.Stanton		

2018 Star Wars Masterwork History of the Jedi

OBI-WAN KENOBI

COMPLETE SET (10)		10.00	25.00
COMMON CARD (HJ1-HJ10)		1.50	4.00

*RAINBOW/299: SAME VALUE AS BASIC
*CANVAS/25: 1.2X TO 3X BASIC CARDS
*WOOD/10: UNPRICED DUE TO SCARCITY
*METAL/5: UNPRICED DUE TO SCARCITY
*GOLD METAL/1: UNPRICED DUE TO SCARCITY
*P.P.BLACK/1: UNPRICED DUE TO SCARCITY
*P.P.CYAN/1: UNPRICED DUE TO SCARCITY
*P.P.MAGENTA/1: UNPRICED DUE TO SCARCITY
*P.P.YELLOW/1: UNPRICED DUE TO SCARCITY

HJ1	Yoda	2.50	6.00
HJ2	Mace Windu	2.50	6.00
HJ4	Qui-Gon Jinn	2.00	5.00
HJ5	Obi-Wan Kenobi	2.00	5.00
HJ6	Anakin Skywalker	2.00	5.00
HJ9	Luke Skywalker	2.00	5.00
HJ10	Rey	3.00	8.00

2018 Star Wars Masterwork Powerful Partners

COMPLETE SET (8)		10.00	25.00
COMMON CARD (PP1-PP8)		1.50	4.00

*RAINBOW/299: SAME VALUE AS BASIC
*WOOD/10: UNPRICED DUE TO SCARCITY
*METAL/5: UNPRICED DUE TO SCARCITY
*GOLD METAL/1: UNPRICED DUE TO SCARCITY
*P.P.BLACK/1: UNPRICED DUE TO SCARCITY
*P.P.CYAN/1: UNPRICED DUE TO SCARCITY
*P.P.MAGENTA/1: UNPRICED DUE TO SCARCITY
*P.P.YELLOW/1: UNPRICED DUE TO SCARCITY

PP1	Han Solo & Chewbacca	2.50	6.00
PP3	Luke Skywalker & Princess Leia Organa	2.50	6.00
PP4	Darth Vader & Grand Moff Tarkin	2.50	6.00
PP6	Jyn Erso & Captain Cassian Andor	3.00	8.00
PP7	Rey & Finn	3.00	8.00
PP8	Finn & Rose Tico	2.00	5.00

2018 Star Wars Masterwork Quad Autographed Booklets

UNPRICED DUE TO SCARCITY

NNO Fisher/Jones/Ridley/Dern
NNO Ridley/Driver/Boyega/Christie
NNO Jones/Yen/Ahmed/Tudyk
NNO Ford/Fisher/Williams/Mayhew

2018 Star Wars Masterwork Sketches

RANDOMLY INSERTED INTO PACKS
UNPRICED DUE TO SCARCITY

NNO Aaron Laurich
NNO Adam Beck
NNO Adam Worton
NNO Alex Iniguez
NNO Alex Mines
NNO Allen Grimes
NNO Andrew Arensberg
NNO Andrew Fernandes
NNO Andrew Fry
NNO Andrew Joynes
NNO Angel Aviles
NNO Angelina Benedetti
NNO Anil Sharma
NNO Basak Cetinkaya
NNO Ben AbuSaada
NNO Brad Hudson
NNO Brendan Purchase
NNO Brendan Shaw
NNO Brent Ragland
NNO Brent Scotchmer
NNO Brett Farr
NNO Caleb King
NNO Carlos Cabaleiro
NNO Carolyn Craggs
NNO Chris Quinn
NNO Chris West
NNO Colin Arthurs
NNO Corey Galal
NNO Dan Bergren
NNO Dan Curto
NNO Dan Gorman
NNO Dan Tearle
NNO Darren James
NNO Darrin Pepe

NNO Dave Gaskin
NNO Dean Drummond
NNO Doug Snodgrass
NNO Eric Lehtonen
NNO Eric Muller
NNO Frank Kadar
NNO Gabe Farber
NNO Garrett Dix
NNO Gavin Williams
NNO George Joseph
NNO Gerard Garcia Jr.
NNO Glen Kertes
NNO Glenn Porzig
NNO Glenn Savage
NNO Greg Mitchell
NNO Huy Truong
NNO Ian MacDougall
NNO Ingrid Hardy
NNO Jamie Cosley
NNO Jamie Richards
NNO Jason Adams
NNO Jason Davies
NNO Jason Miller
NNO Jason Queen
NNO Jason Sobol
NNO Jay Manchand
NNO Jay Salce
NNO Jeff Abar
NNO Jeff Mallinson
NNO Jennifer Allyn
NNO Jessica Hickman
NNO Jim Mehsling
NNO Jim O'Riley
NNO John Bruce
NNO John DiBiase
NNO John Pleak
NNO Jon McKenzie
NNO Jose Ventura
NNO Josh Bommer
NNO Juan Rosales
NNO Jude Gallagher
NNO Justin Castaneda
NNO Kaela Croft
NNO Kallan Archer
NNO Keith Farnum
NNO Kevin Cleveland
NNO Kyle Hickman
NNO Laura Atkinson
NNO Laura Martin
NNO Lee Hunt
NNO Logan Monette
NNO Louise Draper
NNO Maggie Ransom
NNO Marcia Dye
NNO Marlo Agunos
NNO Marsha Parkins
NNO Matt Langford
NNO Matt Stewart
NNO Matthew Hirons
NNO Matthew Lopez
NNO Matthew Sutton
NNO Mayumi Seto
NNO Michael Mastermaker
NNO Michael Mettlen
NNO Michelle Rayner
NNO Mick and Matt Glebe
NNO Mike James
NNO Mohammad Jilani
NNO Nathan Kennett
NNO Neil Camera
NNO Nick Justus
NNO Nikki Valenzuela
NNO Omar Salinas
NNO Patricio Carrasco
NNO Phil Hassewer
NNO Phillip Trujillo
NNO Rebecca Sharp
NNO Rees Finlay
NNO Rich Henneman
NNO Rich Molinelli
NNO Richard Serrao
NNO Rob Teranishi

NNO Robert Hendrickson
NNO Rodney Roberts
NNO Ronnie Crowther
NNO Ryan Finley
NNO Ryan Olsen
NNO Sammy Gomez
NNO Sebastian Cortez
NNO Shaow Siong
NNO Solly Mohamed
NNO Stephanie Rosales
NNO Ted Dastick Jr.
NNO Thomas Amici
NNO Tina Berardi
NNO Todd Aaron Smith
NNO Tony Riley
NNO Trent Westbrook
NNO Victor Moreno
NNO Ward Silverman

2018 Star Wars Masterwork Source Material Fabric Swatches

JRGH General Hux Jacket Lining		
JRLP Luke Skywalker Pants		
JRLT Luke Skywalker Tunic	75.00	150.00
JRPD Poe Dameron Jacket Lining	100.00	200.00
JRRG Poe Dameron Shirt	50.00	100.00
JRRS Jyn Erso Poncho		
JRRT Rey Desert Tunic Sleeves	150.00	300.00
JRCRT Rose Tico Ground Crew Flightsuit Lining	100.00	200.00

2018 Star Wars Masterwork Stamp Relics

COMMON MEM	6.00	15.00
*BLACK/5: UNPRICED DUE TO SCARCITY		
*GOLD/1: UNPRICED DUE TO SCARCITY		
RANDOMLY INSERTED INTO PACKS		
SBF Finn	8.00	20.00
SBP Poe Dameron	8.00	20.00
SBR Rey	10.00	25.00
SCC Chewbacca	8.00	20.00
SCH Han Solo	8.00	20.00
SCL Lando Calrissian	6.00	15.00
SCP Princess Leia Organa	12.00	30.00
SCR R2-D2	6.00	15.00
SCS Luke Skywalker	6.00	15.00
SKC Captain Cassian Andor	6.00	15.00
SKJ Jyn Erso	10.00	25.00
SKK K-2SO	12.00	30.00
SMF Finn	6.00	15.00
SMH Han Solo	8.00	20.00
SMR Rey	8.00	20.00
SPC Chewbacca	6.00	15.00
SPL Luke Skywalker	6.00	15.00
SPR Rey	12.00	30.00
SRA Anakin Skywalker	6.00	15.00
SRO Obi-Wan Kenobi	8.00	20.00
SRP PadmÈ Amidala	8.00	20.00
SSH General Hux	6.00	15.00
SSK Kylo Ren	10.00	25.00
SSP Captain Phasma	6.00	15.00

2018 Star Wars Masterwork Super Weapons

COMPLETE SET (7)	8.00	20.00
COMMON CARD (SW1-SW7)	2.00	5.00
*RAINBOW/299: .5X TO 1.2X BASIC CARDS		
*CANVAS/25: 1.2X TO 3X BASIC CARDS		
*WOOD/10: UNPRICED DUE TO SCARCITY		
*METAL/5: UNPRICED DUE TO SCARCITY		
*GOLD METAL/1: UNPRICED DUE TO SCARCITY		
*P.P.BLACK/1: UNPRICED DUE TO SCARCITY		
*P.P.CYAN/1: UNPRICED DUE TO SCARCITY		

*P.P.MAGENTA/1: UNPRICED DUE TO SCARCITY
*P.P.YELLOW/1: UNPRICED DUE TO SCARCITY

2018 Star Wars Masterwork Triple Autographs

*WOOD/10: UNPRICED DUE TO SCARCITY
*BLACK/5: UNPRICED DUE TO SCARCITY
*GOLD/1: UNPRICED DUE TO SCARCITY

TABPG Baker/Prinze Jr./Gray
TACML Christensen/Morrison/Logan
TAIES Eckstein/Salenger/Futterman
TAJMW Jones/Mendelsohn/Whitaker
TALGR Leung/Grunberg/Rose
TARBD Ridley/Boyega/Dern
TASDR Serkis/Driver/Ridley
TATLE Taylor/Lanter/Eckstein
TAVDC Vee/Daniels/Chapman
TAWMD Williams/Mayhew/Daniels

2019 Star Wars Masterwork Promo

NYCC2019 Darth Maul	6.00	15.00

2019 Star Wars Masterwork

COMPLETE SET (100)	15.00	40.00
COMMON CARD (1-100)	.60	1.50
*BLUE: .75X TO 2X BASIC CARDS		
*GREEN/99: 1.5X TO 4X BASIC CARDS		
*PURPLE/50: 2.5X TO 6X BASIC CARDS		
*ORANGE/10: UNPRICED DUE TO SCARCITY		
*BLACK/5: UNPRICED DUE TO SCARCITY		
*GOLD/1: UNPRICED DUE TO SCARCITY		
*P.P.BLACK/1: UNPRICED DUE TO SCARCITY		
*P.P.CYAN/1: UNPRICED DUE TO SCARCITY		
*P.P.MAGENTA/1: UNPRICED DUE TO SCARCITY		
*P.P.YELLOW/1: UNPRICED DUE TO SCARCITY		

2019 Star Wars Masterwork Autographed Commemorative Artifact Medallions

*ORANGE/10: UNPRICED DUE TO SCARCITY
*BLACK/5: UNPRICED DUE TO SCARCITY
*GOLD/1: UNPRICED DUE TO SCARCITY
RANDOMLY INSERTED INTO PACKS

AMCDRC Daisy Ridley
Luke's Compass
AMCDRR Daisy Ridley
Snoke's Ring
AMCFJK Felicity Jones
Jyn's Kyber Pendant
AMCGHI Guy Henry
Imperial Rank Badge
AMCHCB Hayden Christensen
Amidala's Belt Buckle
AMCHFD Harrison Ford
Han Solo's Dice
AMCJBM John Boyega
Rose Tico's Medallion
AMCJGI Julian Glover
Imperial Rank Badge
AMCKBL Kenny Baker
Yoda's Necklace
AMCKCI Kenneth Colley
Imperial Rank Badge
AMCMMK Mads Mikkelsen
Jyn's Kyber Pendant
AMCMPI Michael Pennington
Imperial Rank Badge
AMCRPC Ray Park
Sith Chalice
AMCVKK Valene Kane
Jyn's Kyber Pendant
AMCADRR Adam Driver
Snoke's Ring
AMCKMTM Kelly Marie Tran
Rose Tico's Medallion

2019 Star Wars Masterwork Autographed Pen Relics

PRAB Ahmed Best
PRAE Ashley Eckstein
PRAS Andy Serkis
PRAT Alan Tudyk
PRCL Charlotte Louise
PRCS Christopher Sean
PRDG Domhnall Gleeson
PRDL Denis Lawson

PRDR Daisy Ridley
PRDT David Tennant
PRDY Donald Faison
PRDY Donnie Yen
PREM Ewan McGregor
PRFW Forest Whitaker.
PRGC Billie Lourd
PRHC Hayden Christensen
PRHF Harrison Ford
PRIM Ian McDiarmid
PRJB Jeremy Bulloch
PRJI Jason Isaacs
PRJS Joonas Suotamo
PRJV Gwendoline Christie
PRKK Katy Kartwheel
PRLD Laura Dern
PRLL Lex Lang
PRLM Lars Mikkelsen
PRMA Mark Austin
PRML Matt Lanter
PRMM Mads Mikkelsen
PRMP Michael Pennington
PRMV Myrna Velasco
PRMW Matthew Wood
PRPB Paul Bettany
PRPR Paul Reubens
PRRA Riz Ahmed
PRRP Ray Park
PRSL Scott Lawrence
PRSM Suzie McGrath
PRTC Tim Curry
PRTF Tovah Feldshuh
PRTM Temuera Morrison
PRADR Adam Driver
PRAEH Alden Ehrenreich
PRBDW Billy Dee Williams
PRBMR Bobby Moynihan
PRDBB Dee Bradley Baker
PRFPJ Freddie Prinze Jr.
PRJAT James Arnold Taylor
PRKMT Kelly Marie Tran
PRMEM Mary Elizabeth McGlynn
PRRPG Ron Perlman
PRSWM Sam Witwer

2019 Star Wars Masterwork Autographs

COMMON AUTO	6.00	15.00
*BLUE/99: .5X TO 1.2X BASIC AUTOS		
*RAINBOW/50: .6X TO 1.5X BASIC AUTOS		
*CANVAS/25: UNPRICED DUE TO SCARCITY		
*WOOD/10: UNPRICED DUE TO SCARCITY		
*SILVER/5: UNPRICED DUE TO SCARCITY		
*GOLD/1: UNPRICED DUE TO SCARCITY		
*P.P.BLACK/1: UNPRICED DUE TO SCARCITY		
*P.P.CYAN/1: UNPRICED DUE TO SCARCITY		
*P.P.MAGENTA/1: UNPRICED DUE TO SCARCITY		
*P.P.YELLOW/1: UNPRICED DUE TO SCARCITY		
RANDOMLY INSERTED INTO PACKS		
AAE Ashley Eckstein	15.00	40.00
ACR Clive Revill	8.00	20.00
ACS Christopher Sean	10.00	25.00
ADT David Tennant	20.00	50.00
AFT Fred Tatasciore	8.00	20.00
AKK Katy Kartwheel	10.00	25.00
AKS Katee Sackhoff	15.00	40.00
ALL Lex Lang	10.00	25.00
ALM Lars Mikkelsen	8.00	20.00
AMA Mark Austin	20.00	50.00
AMP Michael Pennington	10.00	25.00
AMV Myrna Velasco	10.00	25.00
ANC Nazneen Contractor	8.00	20.00
ASL Scott Lawrence	12.00	30.00
AJAT James Arnold Taylor	8.00	20.00
AJBR Josh Brener	8.00	20.00
AJVM Jimmy Vee	8.00	20.00
ASIL Stephanie Silva	8.00	20.00

2019 Star Wars Masterwork Commemorative Artifact Medallions

COMMON MEM	3.00	8.00
*PURPLE/50: .5X TO 1.2X BASIC MEM		
*ORANGE/10: UNPRICED DUE TO SCARCITY		
*BLACK/5: UNPRICED DUE TO SCARCITY		

*GOLD/1: UNPRICED DUE TO SCARCITY
RANDOMLY INSERTED INTO PACKS

MCFR	Finn	5.00	12.00
MCJK	Jyn Erso	6.00	15.00
MCPR	Paige Tico	4.00	10.00
MCRR	Rose Tico	4.00	10.00
MCSD	Han Solo	6.00	15.00
MCYN	Yoda	6.00	15.00
MCASB	Anakin Skywalker	5.00	12.00
MCGJK	Galen Erso	5.00	12.00
MCHBH	Han Solo	6.00	15.00
MCKSR	Kylo Ren	6.00	15.00
MCLBH	Luke Skywalker	8.00	20.00
MCLJK	Lyra Erso	4.00	10.00
MCLSC	Luke Skywalker	10.00	25.00
MCLSY	Luke Skywalker	8.00	20.00
MCMRB	Grand Moff Tarkin	4.00	10.00
MCMSC	Darth Maul	5.00	12.00
MCOBH	Obi-Wan Kenobi	5.00	12.00
MCPDN	Poe Dameron	4.00	10.00
MCQAB	Queen Amidala	6.00	15.00
MCR2C	R2-D2	5.00	12.00
MCR2Y	R2-D2	5.00	12.00
MCRLC	Rey	8.00	20.00
MCRSR	Rey	8.00	20.00
MCSSB	Sabe	5.00	12.00
MCVSC	Darth Vader	6.00	15.00

2019 Star Wars Masterwork The Dark Side

COMPLETE SET (10)	8.00	20.00
COMMON CARD (DS1-DS10)	1.25	3.00

*RAINBOW/299: .6X TO 1.5X BASIC CARDS
*CANVAS/25: 1X TO 2.5X BASIC CARDS
*WOOD/10: UNPRICED DUE TO SCARCITY
*METAL/5: UNPRICED DUE TO SCARCITY
*GOLD/1: UNPRICED DUE TO SCARCITY
*P.P.BLACK/1: UNPRICED DUE TO SCARCITY
*P.P.CYAN/1: UNPRICED DUE TO SCARCITY
*P.P.MAGENTA/1: UNPRICED DUE TO SCARCITY
*P.P.YELLOW/1: UNPRICED DUE TO SCARCITY
RANDOMLY INSERTED INTO PACKS

2019 Star Wars Masterwork Defining Moments

COMPLETE SET (25)	12.00	30.00
COMMON CARD (DM1-DM25))	1.00	2.50

*RAINBOW/299: 1X TO 2.5X BASIC CARDS
*CANVAS/25: 2.5X TO 6X BASIC CARDS
*WOOD/10: UNPRICED DUE TO SCARCITY
*METAL/5: UNPRICED DUE TO SCARCITY
*GOLD METAL/1: UNPRICED DUE TO SCARCITY
*P.P.BLACK/1: UNPRICED DUE TO SCARCITY
*P.P.CYAN/1: UNPRICED DUE TO SCARCITY
*P.P.MAGENTA/1: UNPRICED DUE TO SCARCITY
*P.P.YELLOW/1: UNPRICED DUE TO SCARCITY
RANDOMLY INSERTED INTO PACKS

2019 Star Wars Masterwork Dual Autographs

*WOOD/10: UNPRICED DUE TO SCARCITY
*BLACK/5: UNPRICED DUE TO SCARCITY
*GOLD/1: UNPRICED DUE TO SCARCITY
STATED PRINT RUN 50 SER.#'d SETS

DAAK D.Arnold/N.Kellington
DAAW R.Ahmed/F.Whitaker
DABT J.Boyega/K.Tran
DACJ H.Christensen/S. Jackson
DACS L.Cole/K.Shah
DACW T.Curry/S.Witwer
DADQ O.Davies/H.Quarshie
DAEB A.Ehrenreich/P.Bettany
DAES A.Ehrenreich/J.Suotamo
DAGW S.Gellar/S.Witwer
DAHF G.Hagon/A.Forrest
DAIG J.Isaacs/T.Gray
DAJK A.Jack/J.Kenny
DAJM F.Jones/B.Mendelsohn
DALM S.Lawrence/S.McGrath
DALS M.Lanter/L.Sherr
DAMC E.McGregor/H.Christensen
DAMM B.Mendelsohn/M.Mikkelsen
DAMS M.Glynn/S.Stanton
DAMY L.Mikkelsen/K.Young
DAPC G.Proops/S.Capurro
DAPG M.Pennington/J.Glover

DARD D.Ridley/A.Driver
DASC A.Shah/A.Cook
DASG A.Serkis/D.Gleeson
DASL C.Sean/L.Lang
DASM C.Sean/S.McGrath
DASS J.Spisak/K.Soucie
DAVF M.Velasco/D.Faison
DAWM B.Williams/P.Mayhew
DAWR S.Williamson/D.Roy

2019 Star Wars Masterwork Film Cel Relics

FCB6 Bib Fortuna
FCC4 Chewbacca
FCC5 Chewbacca
FCC6 Chewbacca
FCO6 Oola
FCY5 Yoda
FCAA6 Admiral Ackbar
FCAP5 Admiral Piett
FCBF5 Boba Fett
FCBF6 Boba Fett
FCCP5 C-3PO
FCCP6 C-3PO
FCDV5 Darth Vader
FCDV6 Darth Vader
FCEP5 Emperor Palpatine
FCEP6 Emperor Palpatine
FCHS4 Han Solo
FCHS5 Han Solo
FCHS6 Han Solo
FCJH6 Jabba The Hutt
FCLB6 Boushh
FCLC5 Lando Calrissian
FCLC6 Lando Calrissian
FCLS4 Luke Skywalker
FCLS5 Luke Skywalker
FCLS6 Luke Skywalker
FCMJ6 Moff Jerjerrod
FCMR6 Sy Snootles
FCNN6 Nien Nunb
FCOK4 Obi-Wan Kenobi
FCOK6 Obi-Wan Kenobi
FCPL4 Princess Leia Organa
FCPL5 Princess Leia Organa
FCPL6 Princess Leia Organa
FCR25 R2-D2
FCR26 R2-D2
FCRC4 R2-D2 & C-3PO
FCSC6 Salacious Crumb
FCTL6 Logray
FCWW6 Wicket

2019 Star Wars Masterwork Heroes of the Rebellion

COMPLETE SET (15)	8.00	20.00
COMMON CARD (HR1-HR15)	1.00	2.50

*RAINBOW/299: .75X TO 2X BASIC CARDS
*CANVAS/25: 1.5X TO 4X BASIC CARDS
*WOOD/10: UNPRICED DUE TO SCARCITY
*METAL/5: UNPRICED DUE TO SCARCITY
*GOLD/1: UNPRICED DUE TO SCARCITY
*P.P.BLACK/1: UNPRICED DUE TO SCARCITY
*P.P.CYAN/1: UNPRICED DUE TO SCARCITY
*P.P.MAGENTA/1: UNPRICED DUE TO SCARCITY
*P.P.YELLOW/1: UNPRICED DUE TO SCARCITY
RANDOMLY INSERTED INTO PACKS

2019 Star Wars Masterwork Jumbo Costume Relics

*ORANGE/10: UNPRICED DUE TO SCARCITY
*BLACK/5: UNPRICED DUE TO SCARCITY
*GOLD/1: UNPRICED DUE TO SCARCITY
RANDOMLY INSERTED INTO PACKS

CRAC Air Traffic Controller
CRBB Beckett
CRBC Beckett
CRBT Beckett
CREN Enfys Nest
CRKJ Korso
CRKO Korso
CRQB Qi'Ra
CRQD Qi'Ra
CRWW Rebolt

CRENC Enfys Nest
CRENL Enfys Nest
CRHSC Han Solo
CRHSJ Han Solo
CRHSL Han Solo

2019 Star Wars Masterwork Quad Autograph Booklets

STATED PRINT RUN 2 SER.#'d SETS
UNPRICED DUE TO SCARCITY

QAESKD Ehrenreich/Suotamo/Kellyman/Davis
QAFFRD Ford/Fisher/Ridley/Driver
QAJWYT Jones/Whitaker/Yen/Tudyk
QAPGIG Prinze/Taylor/Jason/Gellar

2019 Star Wars Masterwork Sketches

RANDOMLY INSERTED INTO MINI BOXES
UNPRICED DUE TO SCARCITY

NNO Alex Iniguez
NNO Andrew Arensberg
NNO Andrew Fry
NNO Andrew Joynes
NNO Angel Aviles
NNO Angelina Benedetti
NNO Anil Sharma
NNO Anthony Figaro
NNO Antni Ellison
NNO Ashlee Brienzo
NNO Ashley Marsh
NNO Basak Cetinkaya
NNO Ben AbuSaada
NNO Brad Hudson
NNO Bruce Gerlach
NNO Caleb King
NNO Cameron Tobias
NNO Can Baran
NNO Candice Dailey
NNO Carlos Cabaleiro
NNO Carolyn Craggs
NNO Chris Kay
NNO Chris Meeks
NNO Cisco Rivera
NNO Colin Arthurs
NNO Dan Gorman
NNO Dan Tearle
NNO Darren James
NNO Darrin Pepe
NNO Dean Drummond
NNO Doug Snodgrass
NNO Eric Lehtonen
NNO Erik Maell
NNO Frank Kadar
NNO Fredd Gorham
NNO Garrett Dix
NNO Gavin Williams
NNO Gerard Garcia Jr.
NNO Huy Truong
NNO Ian MacDougall
NNO Ingrid Hardy
NNO James Henry Smith
NNO Jamie Cosley

NNO Jamie Murdock
NNO Jamie Richards
NNO Jason Adams
NNO Jason Queen
NNO Jay Manchand
NNO Jeff Abar
NNO Jessica Hickman
NNO Jim Mehsling
NNO Jim O'Riley
NNO John Bruce
NNO John DiBiase
NNO Jonathan Beistline
NNO Jose Ventura
NNO Josh Church
NNO Jude Gallagher
NNO Kallan Archer
NNO Keith Farnum
NNO Kelly Baber
NNO Kevin Cleveland
NNO Kevin P. West
NNO Kyle Hickman
NNO Laura Atkinson
NNO Laura Martin
NNO Lee Hunt
NNO Lee Kohse
NNO Liam Shalloo
NNO Lindsey Greyling
NNO Lloyd Mills
NNO Logan Monette
NNO Louise Draper
NNO Marcia Dye
NNO Marlo Agunos
NNO Marsha Parkins
NNO Matt Langford
NNO Matthew Hirons
NNO Mayumi Seto
NNO Michael Mastermaker
NNO Michael Sealie
NNO Michelle Rayner
NNO Mick and Matt Glebe
NNO Mike James
NNO Mike Stephens
NNO Mohammad Jilani
NNO Neil Camera
NNO Nick Allsopp
NNO Omar Salinas
NNO Patricio Carrasco
NNO Paul Schiers
NNO Phil Hassewer
NNO Phillip Trujillo
NNO Rachel Brady
NNO Rebecca Sharp
NNO Rich Hennemann
NNO Rich Molinelli
NNO Richard Serrao
NNO Rob Teranishi
NNO Robert Hendrickson
NNO Rodney Roberts
NNO Ronnie Crowther
NNO Ryan Finley
NNO Ryan Olsen
NNO Ryan Santos
NNO Sammy Gomez
NNO Seth Groves
NNO Shaow Siong
NNO Sheikh Islam
NNO Solly Mohamed
NNO Steve Alce
NNO Steve Potter
NNO Ted Dastick Jr.
NNO Thomas Amici
NNO Tim Dowler
NNO Tim Shinn
NNO Todd Aaron Smith
NNO Tony Riley
NNO Trent Westbrook
NNO Veronica Smith
NNO Vincenzo D'Ippolito
NNO Zach Woolsey

2019 Star Wars Masterwork The Ultimate Autograph Booklet

NNO Ford/Fisher/Williams/Mayhew/Baker/Daniels Christensen/Jackson/McGregor/Best/McDiarmid/Park/Jones/Mikkelsen/Whitaker/Yen/Ahmed/Tudyk/Mendelsohn/O'Reilly/Prinze/Isaacs/Lanter/Taylor/Eckstein/Baker/Ridley/Driver/Boyega/Tran/Gleeson/Christie/Lourd/Dern

2019 Star Wars Masterwork Triple Autographs

*WOOD/10: UNPRICED DUE TO SCARCITY
*BLACK/5: UNPRICED DUE TO SCARCITY
*GOLD/1: UNPRICED DUE TO SCARCITY
STATED PRINT RUN 25 SER.#'d SETS

TADGS Driver/Gleeson/Serkis
TAEBS Ehrenreich/Bettany/Suotamo
TAFWM Ford/Williams/Mayhew
TAGSE Gray/Sircar/Eckstein
TAJMM Jones/Mendelsohn/Mikkelsen
TAJTA Jones/Tudyk/Ahmed
TAMDB Mayhew/Daniels/Baker
TAMJC McGregor/Jackson/Christensen
TARBD Ridley/Boyega/Dern
TASML Sean/McGrath/Lawrence

2020 Star Wars Masterwork

COMPLETE SET (100)	15.00	40.00
UNOPENED BOX (4 MINIBOXES)	225.00	300.00
UNOPENED MINIBOX (5 CARDS)	60.00	75.00
COMMON CARD (1-100)	.60	1.50

*BLUE: .75X TO 2X BASIC CARDS
*GREEN/99: 1.5X TO 4X BASIC CARDS
*PURPLE/50: 2.5X TO 6X BASIC CARDS
*ORANGE/10: UNPRICED DUE TO SCARCITY
*BLACK/5: UNPRICED DUE TO SCARCITY
*GOLD/1: UNPRICED DUE TO SCARCITY
*P.P.BLACK/1: UNPRICED DUE TO SCARCITY
*P.P.CYAN/1: UNPRICED DUE TO SCARCITY
*P.P.MAGENTA/1: UNPRICED DUE TO SCARCITY
*P.P.YELLOW/1: UNPRICED DUE TO SCARCITY

2020 Star Wars Masterwork Autographed Commemorative Dog Tag Medallions

*ORANGE/10: UNPRICED DUE TO SCARCITY
*BLACK/5: UNPRICED DUE TO SCARCITY
*GOLD/1: UNPRICED DUE TO SCARCITY

ADKBW Kenny Baker
ADBFS Barbara Frankland
NNO Carrie Fisher
ADDLW Denis Lawson
NNO Harrison Ford
ADAFS Anthony Forrest
ADAMS Angus MacInnes
ADDLF Denis Lawson
ADDLX Denis Lawson
ADGHF Garrick Hagon
ADGHR Garrick Hagon
ADJGI Julian Glover
ADJKF Jack Klaff
ADJKR Jack Klaff
ADKCI Kenneth Colley
ADPBS Paul Blake
ADPMW Peter Mayhew
ADRGS Rusty Goffe

2020 Star Wars Masterwork Autographed Pen Relics

NNO Adam Driver
NNO Ahmed Best
NNO Alden Ehrenreich
NNO Andy Serkis
NNO Annabelle Davis

NNO Ashley Eckstein
NNO Ben Daniels
NNO Billie Lourd
NNO Billy Dee Williams
NNO Cameron Monaghan
NNO Carl Weathers
NNO Daisy Ridley
NNO Debra Wilson
NNO Dee Bradley Baker
NNO Denis Lawson
NNO Dominic Monaghan
NNO Donnie Yen
NNO Emily Swallow
NNO Erin Kellyman
NNO Ewan McGregor
NNO Giancarlo Esposito
NNO Gina Carano
NNO Greg Grunberg
NNO Harrison Ford
NNO Hayden Christensen
NNO Hermione Corfield
NNO Ian McDiarmid
NNO Janina Gavankar
NNO John Tui
NNO Joonas Suotamo
NNO Leeanna Walsman
NNO Mads Mikkelsen
NNO Michael Pennington
NNO Naomi Ackie
NNO Nick Kellington
NNO Nick Nolte
NNO Omid Abtahi
NNO Paul Blake
NNO Pedro Pascal
NNO Sam Witwer
NNO Taika Waititi
NNO Valene Kane
NNO Werner Herzog

2020 Star Wars Masterwork Autographs

COMMON AUTO	6.00	15.00

*BLUE/99: .5X TO 1.2X BASIC AUTOS
*RAINBOW/50: .6X TO 1.5X BASIC AUTOS
*CANVAS/25: UNPRICED DUE TO SCARCITY
*WOOD/10: UNPRICED DUE TO SCARCITY
*SILVER FR/5: UNPRICED DUE TO SCARCITY
*GOLD FR/1: UNPRICED DUE TO SCARCITY
*P.P.BLACK/1: UNPRICED DUE TO SCARCITY
*P.P.CYAN/1: UNPRICED DUE TO SCARCITY
*P.P.MAGENTA/1: UNPRICED DUE TO SCARCITY
*P.P.YELLOW/1: UNPRICED DUE TO SCARCITY

AAB	Ahmed Best	20.00	50.00
AAH	Amanda Hale	8.00	20.00
ACM	Cameron Monaghan	20.00	50.00
ADL	Denis Lawson	10.00	25.00
ADW	Debra Wilson	8.00	20.00
AEK	Erin Kellyman	20.00	50.00
AES	Emily Swallow	50.00	100.00
AGE	Giancarlo Esposito	75.00	150.00
AGG	Greg Grunberg	10.00	25.00
AJG	Janina Gavankar	15.00	40.00
AJT	John Tui	8.00	20.00
ALW	Leeanna Walsman	12.00	30.00
AML	Misty Lee	10.00	25.00
AMW	Matthew Wood	20.00	50.00
ANA	Naomi Ackie	15.00	40.00
AOA	Omid Abtahi	12.00	30.00
APB	Paul Blake	10.00	25.00
AVK	Valene Kane	10.00	25.00

AADW Annabelle Davis EXCH	10.00	25.00
AAEA Ashley Eckstein	60.00	120.00
ADBB Dee Bradley Baker	12.00	30.00
AHCT Hermione Corfield	15.00	40.00
ALRB Lynn Robertson Bruce	10.00	25.00

2020 Star Wars Masterwork Autographs Blue Foil

STATED PRINT RUN 99 SER.#'d SETS

ADY Donnie Yen	60.00	120.00
ASW Sam Witwer	20.00	50.00
ADMB Dominic Monaghan	15.00	40.00

2020 Star Wars Masterwork Autographs Rainbow Foil

STATED PRINT RUN 50 SER.#'d SETS

AWH Werner Herzog	100.00	200.00

2020 Star Wars Masterwork Behind-the-Scenes Autographed Pen Relics

NNO Ben Burtt
NNO Jake Lunt Davies
NNO Neal Scanlan
NNO Lee Towersey

2020 Star Wars Masterwork Behind-the-Scenes Autographs

COMMON AUTO	15.00	40.00

*RAINBOW/50: .5X TO 1.2X BASIC AUTOS
*CANVAS/25: UNPRICED DUE TO SCARCITY
*WOOD/10: UNPRICED DUE TO SCARCITY
*SILVER FR/5: UNPRICED DUE TO SCARCITY
*GOLD FR/1: UNPRICED DUE TO SCARCITY
*P.P.BLACK/1: UNPRICED DUE TO SCARCITY
*P.P.CYAN/1: UNPRICED DUE TO SCARCITY
*P.P.MAGENTA/1: UNPRICED DUE TO SCARCITY
*P.P.YELLOW/1: UNPRICED DUE TO SCARCITY
STATED PRINT RUN 99 SER.#'d SETS

BSABB Ben Burtt	30.00	75.00
BSALT Lee Towersey	25.00	60.00
BSANS Neal Scanlan	25.00	60.00

2020 Star Wars Masterwork Commemorative Dog Tag Medallions

COMMON MEM	4.00	10.00

*PURPLE/50: .5X TO 1.2X BASIC MEM
*ORANGE/10: UNPRICED DUE TO SCARCITY
*BLACK/5: UNPRICED DUE TO SCARCITY
*GOLD/1: UNPRICED DUE TO SCARCITY
STATED PRINT RUN 99 SER.#'d SETS

DTEB Sandtrooper	5.00	12.00
DTED Commander Daine Jir	5.00	12.00
DTES Stormtrooper	6.00	15.00
DTET Grand Moff Tarkin	6.00	15.00
DTEV Darth Vader	10.00	25.00
DTEX Death Star Trooper	8.00	20.00
DTFB Biggs Darklighter	5.00	12.00
DTFD Biggs Darklighter	5.00	12.00
DTFW Wedge Antilles	8.00	20.00
DTJC Chewbacca	6.00	15.00
DTJH Han Solo		25.00
DTJL Luke Skywalker	12.00	30.00
DTJP Princess Leia Organa	10.00	25.00
DTJR R2-D2	6.00	15.00
DTRD Garven Dreis	6.00	15.00
DTRJ John D. Branon	5.00	12.00
DTRW Wedge Antilles	8.00	20.00
DTSD Darth Vader	10.00	25.00
DTSG Greedo	5.00	12.00

DTST Stormtrooper	6.00	15.00
DTSV Jon "Dutch" Vander	5.00	12.00
DTXL Luke Skywalker	12.00	30.00
DTXW Wedge Antilles	8.00	20.00

2020 Star Wars Masterwork Dual Autographs

*CANVAS/25: UNPRICED DUE TO SCARCITY
*WOOD/10: UNPRICED DUE TO SCARCITY
*BLACK/5: UNPRICED DUE TO SCARCITY
*GOLD/1: UNPRICED DUE TO SCARCITY
STATED PRINT RUN 50 SER.#'d SETS

DADA H.Durst/D.Arnold	15.00	40.00
DADK H.Durst/I.Kenny	15.00	40.00
DADM R.Downes/V.Marshall	30.00	75.00
DAHP A.Harris/C.Parsons	30.00	75.00
DAMW T.Morrison/L.Walsman	60.00	120.00
DASL S.Smart/C.Louise	12.00	30.00

2020 Star Wars Masterwork Empire Strikes Back 40th Anniversary

COMPLETE SET (25)	30.00	75.00
COMMON CARD (ESB1-ESB25)	2.00	5.00

*RAINBOW/299: .5X TO 1.2X BASIC CARDS
*CANVAS/25: UNPRICED DUE TO SCARCITY
*WOOD/10: UNPRICED DUE TO SCARCITY
*METAL/5: UNPRICED DUE TO SCARCITY
*GOLD METAL/1: UNPRICED DUE TO SCARCITY
*P.P.BLACK/1: UNPRICED DUE TO SCARCITY
*P.P.CYAN/1: UNPRICED DUE TO SCARCITY
*P.P.MAGENTA/1: UNPRICED DUE TO SCARCITY
*P.P.YELLOW/1: UNPRICED DUE TO SCARCITY

2020 Star Wars Masterwork Quad Autographs

STATED PRINT RUN 2 SER.#'d SETS
UNPRICED DUE TO SCARCITY

NNO Ford/Fisher/Baker/Mayhew
NNO Ridley/Williams/Driver/Boyega
NNO Pascal/Carano/Nolte/Waititi
QAMN Nolte/Carano/Herzog/Esposito

2020 Star Wars Masterwork Sketches

UNPRICED DUE TO SCARCITY

NNO Adam Beck
NNO Allen Grimes
NNO Andrew Fry
NNO Andrew Sanchez
NNO Angel Aviles
NNO Angelina Benedetti
NNO Anil Sharma
NNO Anthony Skubis
NNO Antni Ellison
NNO Ashlee Brienzo
NNO Ashley Marsh
NNO Aston Cover
NNO Barry Renshaw
NNO Basak Cetinkaya
NNO Benjamin Lombart
NNO Bobby Blakey
NNO Brad Hudson
NNO Brandon Blevins
NNO Brett Farr
NNO Candice Dailey
NNO Carlos Cabaleiro
NNO Chris Colyer
NNO Chris Kay
NNO Cyrus Sherkat
NNO Dan Gorman
NNO Dan Tearle
NNO Daniel Riveron
NNO Darrin Pepe
NNO Dave Fowler
NNO Dawn Murphy
NNO Dean Drummond
NNO Don Pedicini Jr.
NNO Dwayne Carpenter
NNO Eric Lehtonen
NNO Frank Sansone
NNO Fredd Gorham
NNO Gabe Farber
NNO Garrett Dix
NNO Gavin Williams
NNO Guilherme Rocha
NNO Huy Truong
NNO Ingrid Hardy

NNO Jamie Cosley
NNO Jamie Murdock
NNO Jamie Richards
NNO Jason Adams
NNO Jason Davies
NNO Jason Montoya
NNO Jason Queen
NNO Jay Manchand
NNO Jeff Abar
NNO Jerold Bahr
NNO Jessica Hickman
NNO Jim Mehsling
NNO John Bruce
NNO John Pleak
NNO Jonathan Beistline
NNO Jonty Gates
NNO Joshua Caleb King
NNO Jude Gallagher
NNO Karl Jones
NNO Keith Farnum
NNO Kelly Baber
NNO Kevin Cleveland
NNO Kevin P. West
NNO Lindsey Greyling
NNO Logan Monette
NNO Lucas Peverill
NNO Luke Rushton
NNO Mai Irving
NNO Marcia Dye
NNO Mark Necchi
NNO Marlo Agunos
NNO Marsha Parkins
NNO Matt Stewart
NNO Matthew Hirons
NNO Mayumi Seto
NNO Michael Mastermaker
NNO Michael Munshaw
NNO Michelle Rayner
NNO Mick and Matt Glebe
NNO Mohammad Jilani
NNO Neil Camera
NNO Nick Gribbon
NNO Norviento Basio
NNO Oscar Chavez
NNO Patricio Carrasco
NNO Paul Maitland
NNO Paul Shiers
NNO Phillip Trujillo
NNO Quinton Baker
NNO Rees Finlay
NNO Rich Hennemann
NNO Richard Serrao
NNO Rob Teranishi
NNO Robert Garcia
NNO Robert Hendrickson
NNO Rodney Roberts
NNO Ronnie Crowther
NNO Ryan Finley
NNO Ryan Santos
NNO Sammy Gomez
NNO Semra Bulut
NNO Shaow Siong
NNO Solly Mohamed
NNO Steve Alce
NNO Thomas Amici
NNO Tim Shinn
NNO Trent Westbrook
NNO Vincenzo Dilppolito
NNO Ward Silverman
NNO Wayne Tully
NNO Zach Woolsey

2020 Star Wars Masterwork Sourced Fabric Dual Relics

COMMON MEM	30.00	75.00

*PURPLE/25: UNPRICED DUE TO SCARCITY
*ORANGE/10: UNPRICED DUE TO SCARCITY
*BLACK/5: UNPRICED DUE TO SCARCITY
*GOLD/1: UNPRICED DUE TO SCARCITY

DCBD Beckett/Dryden Vos	100.00	200.00
DCBQ Beckett/Qiira	100.00	200.00
DCDQ Dryden Vos/Qiira	125.00	250.00

DCFR Finn/Rose Tico	50.00	100.00
DCJB Jyn Erso/Bodhi Rook	75.00	150.00
DCJG Jyn Erso/Galen Erso	100.00	200.00
DCJM Jyn Erso/General Merrick	75.00	150.00
DCLF Luke Skywalker/Finn	50.00	100.00
DCLP Luke Skywalker/Poe Dameron	100.00	200.00
DCPG Poe Dameron/General Hux	60.00	120.00
DCRP Rey/Poe Dameron	125.00	250.00
DCRPJ Rey/Poe Dameron	125.00	250.00
DCRPW Rey/Poe Dameron	125.00	250.00

2020 Star Wars Masterwork Stamps

COMMON MEM	6.00	15.00
*GREEN/99: .5X TO 1.2X BASIC MEM		
*PURPLE/50: .6X TO 1.5X BASIC MEM		
*ORANGE/10: UNPRICED DUE TO SCARCITY		
*BLACK/5: UNPRICED DUE TO SCARCITY		
*GOLD/1: UNPRICED DUE TO SCARCITY		
SCAA Anakin Skywalker/Queen Amidala	8.00	20.00
SCCD Count Dooku/Count Dooku	10.00	25.00
SCCJ Chewbacca/Jannah	8.00	20.00
SCDM Darth Maul/Darth Maul	10.00	25.00
SCFP Finn/Poe Dameron	8.00	20.00
SCKS Kylo Ren/Sith Trooper	8.00	20.00
SCLC Lando Calrissian/Lando Calrissian	10.00	25.00
SCLL Lobot/Lando Calrissian	8.00	20.00
SCLW Logray/Wicket W. Warrick	8.00	20.00
SCOM Obi-Wan Kenobi/Darth Maul	10.00	25.00
SCPZ Poe Dameron/Zorii Bliss	10.00	25.00
SCQA Queen Amidala/Queen Amidala	8.00	20.00
SCQM Qui-Gon Jinn/Darth Maul	10.00	25.00
SCSS Sith Trooper/Sith Trooper	8.00	20.00
SCVM Darth Vader/Grand Moff Tarkin	10.00	25.00
SCYD Yoda/Count Dooku	8.00	20.00
SCPLW Princess Leia Organa/Wicket W. Warrick	10.00	25.00

2020 Star Wars Masterwork Triple Autographs

*WOOD/10: UNPRICED DUE TO SCARCITY
*BLACK/5: UNPRICED DUE TO SCARCITY
*GOLD/1: UNPRICED DUE TO SCARCITY
STATED PRINT RUN 25 SER.#'d SETS
UNPRICED DUE TO SCARCITY
TABPG Baker/Prinze Jr./Gray
TABTL Boyega/Tran/Lourd
TACLE Curry/Lanter/Eckstein
TADGC Driver/Gleeson/Christie
TAFFM Ford/Fisher/Mayhew
TAFWB Ford/Williams/Bulloch
TAGFG Goodson/Futterman/Gati
TAJWY Jones/Whitaker/Yen
TAMJC McGregor/Jackson/Christensen
TAPNW Pascal/Nolte/Waititi
TASMF Sean/McGrath/Faison

2020 Star Wars Masterwork Troopers of the Galactic Empire

COMPLETE SET (15)	15.00	40.00
COMMON CARD (TE1-TE15)	2.00	5.00
*RAINBOW/299: .5X TO 1.2X BASIC CARDS		
*CANVAS/25: UNPRICED DUE TO SCARCITY		
*WOOD/10: UNPRICED DUE TO SCARCITY		
*METAL/5: UNPRICED DUE TO SCARCITY		
*GOLD METAL/1: UNPRICED DUE TO SCARCITY		
*P.P.BLACK/1: UNPRICED DUE TO SCARCITY		
*P.P.CYAN/1: UNPRICED DUE TO SCARCITY		
*P.P.MAGENTA/1: UNPRICED DUE TO SCARCITY		
*P.P.YELLOW/1: UNPRICED DUE TO SCARCITY		

2020 Star Wars Masterwork Ultra Autographs

NNO Ford/Fisher/Williams/Mayhew/Baker
McDiarmid/Blakiston/Bulloch/Lawson/Davis
NNO Ridley/Driver/Boyega/Tran/Williams
Suotamo/Gleeson/McDiarmid/Monaghan/Lourd
UARO Jones/Mendelsohn/Whitaker/Yen/Ahmed
Tudyk/OReilly/Mikkelsen/Henry/Daniels

2020 Star Wars Masterwork The Wisdom of Yoda

"Impossible to see, the future is."

COMPLETE SET (10)	20.00	50.00
COMMON CARD (WY1-WY10)	3.00	8.00
*RAINBOW/299: .5X TO 1.2X BASIC CARDS		
*CANVAS/25: UNPRICED DUE TO SCARCITY		
*WOOD/10: UNPRICED DUE TO SCARCITY		
*METAL/5: UNPRICED DUE TO SCARCITY		
*GOLD METAL/1: UNPRICED DUE TO SCARCITY		
*P.P.BLACK/1: UNPRICED DUE TO SCARCITY		
*P.P.CYAN/1: UNPRICED DUE TO SCARCITY		
*P.P.MAGENTA/1: UNPRICED DUE TO SCARCITY		
*P.P.YELLOW/1: UNPRICED DUE TO SCARCITY		

2017 Star Wars May the 4th Be with You

COMPLETE SET (20)	12.00	30.00
COMPLETE FACTORY SET (21)	40.00	80.00
COMMON CARD (1-20)	1.00	2.50
*SILVER/10: 6X TO 15X BASIC CARDS	15.00	40.00
*GOLD/1: UNPRICED DUE TO SCARCITY		
RELEASED 5/4/2017		

2017 Star Wars May the 4th Be with You Autographs

COMMON CARD	10.00	25.00
*SILVER/10: .6X TO 1.5X BASIC AUTOS		
*GOLD/1: UNPRICED DUE TO SCARCITY		
STATED ODDS 1:SET		
1A Harrison Ford		
2A Mark Hamill	400.00	600.00
3A Carrie Fisher		
4A Kenny Baker		
5A Anthony Daniels	175.00	300.00
7A Jeremy Bulloch	25.00	60.00
8A Ian McDiarmid	250.00	400.00
10A Billy Dee Williams		
14A Kenneth Colley	12.00	30.00
16A Erik Bauersfeld	25.00	60.00
16A Tim Rose	15.00	40.00
19A Paul Blake		

1997-98 Star Wars Men Behind the Masks

COMMON CARD (P1-P4)		
P1 Darth Vader & Boba Fett	10.00	25.00
(Given to Auction Seat Holders)		
P2 Darth Vader & Boba Fett	10.00	25.00
(Given as Admission Ticket)		
P3 Peter Mayhew as Chewbacca	8.00	20.00
(Given to Auction Reserve Seat Holders)/1000*		
P4 Maria de Aragon as Greedo	10.00	25.00
(Show Exclusive)/800*		

1997-98 Star Wars Men Behind the Masks Test Issue

COMPLETE SET (7)		
COMMON CARD		
NNO Chewbacca	125.00	250.00
(prismatic foil/triangles)		
NNO Chewbacca	125.00	250.00
(prismatic foil/vertical lines)		
NNO Chewbacca	125.00	250.00
(refractor foil)		
NNO Greedo	125.00	250.00
(prismatic foil/spotted)		
NNO Greedo	125.00	250.00
(prismatic foil/triangles)		
NNO Greedo	125.00	250.00
(prismatic foil/vertical lines)		
NNO Greedo	125.00	250.00
(refractor foil)		

1994-96 Star Wars Metal

COMPLETE SET (60)	30.00	75.00
COMMON CARD (1-60)	1.00	2.50

1994-96 Star Wars Metal Promos

COMPLETE SET (3)	12.00	30.00
COMMON CARD (P1-P3)	6.00	15.00
P1 Star Wars Episode IV	6.00	15.00
P2 The Empire Strikes Back	6.00	15.00
P3 Return of the Jedi	6.00	15.00

1996 Star Wars Metal Art of Ralph McQuarrie

COMPLETE SET (20)	10.00	25.00
COMMON CARD (1-20)	1.00	2.50
COA Certificate of Authenticity		

1998 Star Wars Metal Bounty Hunters

COMPLETE SET (5)	2.50	6.00
COMMON CARD (1-5)	1.00	2.50
HSJH Han Solo and Jabba the Hutt SE		

1995 Star Wars Metal Dark Empire I

COMPLETE SET (6)	3.00	8.00
COMMON CARD (1-6)	1.00	2.50

1996 Star Wars Metal Dark Empire II

COMPLETE SET (6)	3.00	8.00
COMMON CARD (1-6)	1.00	2.50

1998 Star Wars Metal Jedi Knights

COMPLETE SET (5)	3.00	8.00
COMMON CARD (1-5)	1.00	2.50
MES Mos Eisley Spaceport SE	1.50	4.00

1998 Star Wars Metal Jedi Knights Avon

COMPLETE SET (4)	3.00	8.00
COMMON CARD (1-4)	1.00	2.50
WIC Wampa Ice Creature SE	1.50	4.00

1997 Star Wars Metal Shadows of the Empire

COMPLETE SET (6)	4.00	10.00
COMMON CARD (1-6)	1.00	2.50

2015 Star Wars Micro Collector Packs

COMPLETE SET (36)	60.00	120.00
COMMON CARD (1-36)	1.50	4.00
NNO 3-D Glasses	.40	1.00

2015 Star Wars Micro Collector Packs 3-D Posters

COMPLETE SET (6)	3.00	8.00
COMMON CARD	.60	1.50
STATED ODDS 1:1		

2015 Star Wars Micro Collector Packs Micro-Comics

COMPLETE SET (6)	4.00	10.00
COMMON CARD	.75	2.00
STATED ODDS 1:1		

1996 Star Wars Multimotion

2M Star Wars 20th Anniversary Commemorative Magazine	2.50	6.00

1999 Star Wars The New Jedi Order

NNO SDCC Exclusive	2.00	5.00

2018 Star Wars Nickel City Con Promos

COMPLETE SET (3)	3.00	8.00
COMMON CARD (P1-P3)	1.25	3.00
NNO Darth Vader	2.00	5.00
NNO Luke Skywalker	1.50	4.00

2015 Star Wars NYCC Oversized Exclusives

COMPLETE SET (70)	75.00	150.00
COMMON CARD (1-70)	2.00	5.00

2020 Star Wars On-Demand 3-D Lenticular

3D1 Darth Vader
3D2 Luke Skywalker
3D3 Princess Leia Organa
3D4 Han Solo
3D5 R2-D2

3D6 C-3PO
3D7 Chewbacca
3D8 Yoda
3D9 Boba Fett
3D10 Obi-Wan Kenobi
3D11 Lando Calrissian
3D12 Wicket W. Warrick
3D13 Jabba the Hutt
3D14 Stormtrooper
3D15 Admiral Ackbar
3D16 Boushh
3D17 Grand Moff Tarkin
3D18 Greedo
3D19 Wedge Antilles
3D20 Imperial Guard
3D21 Scout Trooper
3D22 Tusken Raider
3D23 Qui-Gon Jinn
3D24 PadmÈ Amidala
3D25 Queen Amidala
3D26 Jar Jar Binks
3D27 Obi-Wan Kenobi
3D28 Mace Windu
3D29 Darth Maul
3D30 Anakin Skywalker
3D31 Jango Fett
3D32 Bail Organa
3D33 General Grievous
3D34 Darth Sidious
3D35 Zam Wesell
3D36 Jyn Erso
3D37 Galen Erso
3D38 Captain Cassian Andor
3D39 Director Krennic
3D40 Bodhi Rook
3D41 K-2SO
3D42 Chirrut Œmwe
3D43 Baze Malbus
3D44 Saw Gerrera
3D45 Mon Mothma
3D46 Han Solo
3D47 Lando Calrissian
3D48 Qi'ra
3D49 L3-37
3D50 Tobias Beckett
3D51 Dryden Vos
3D52 Enfys Nest
3D53 Range Trooper
3D54 Rey
3D55 General Leia Organa
3D56 Supreme Leader Snoke
3D57 Han Solo
3D58 Luke Skywalker
3D59 Maz Kanata
3D60 Poe Dameron
3D61 General Hux
3D62 Porg
3D63 First Order TIE Pilot
3D64 Kylo Ren
3D65 BB-8
3D66 Captain Phasma
3D67 Nien Nunb
3D68 Snap Wexley
3D69 Rey
3D70 Finn
3D71 Poe Dameron
3D72 Kylo Ren
3D73 Zorii Bliss
3D74 Rose Tico
3D75 Lando Calrissian
3D76 Jannah
3D77 Kaydel Ko Connix
3D78 Emperor Palpatine
3D79 Allegiant General Pryde
3D80 D-O
3D81 Babu Frik
3D82 The Mandalorian
3D83 The Child
3D84 Cara Dune

3D85 IG-11
3D86 Greef Karga
3D87 The Client
3D88 Kuiil
3D89 The Armorer
3D90 Moff Gideon
3D91 Ahsoka Tano
3D92 Anakin Skywalker
3D93 Obi-Wan Kenobi
3D94 Captain Rex
3D95 Asajj Ventress
3D96 Grand Admiral Thrawn
3D97 Sabine Wren
3D98 Kanan Jarrus
3D99 The Grand Inquisitor
3D100 Ezra Bridger

2021 Star Wars On-Demand The High Republic

*RED/10: UNPRICED DUE TO SCARCITY
*PLATINUM/1: UNPRICED DUE TO SCARCITY
ANNCD PRINT RUN 1,180 SETS

1 Avar Kriss
2 Loden Greatstorm
3 Sskeer
4 Keeve Trennis
5 Ram Jamoram
6 Vernestra Rwoh
7 Yoda
8 Orla Jareni
9 Bell Zettifar
10 Burryaga
11 Reath Silas
12 Lula Talisola
13 Chancellor Lina Soh
14 Affie Hollow
15 Leox Gyasi
16 Geode
17 The Nihil
18 Lourna Dee
19 Marchion Ro
20 Drengir

2021 Star Wars On-Demand The High Republic Cover Art

STATED ODDS 1:1 W/ PARALLELS

1 Light of Jedi
2 Into the Dark
3 A Test of Courage
4 Adventures #1
5 Marvel #1

2019 Star Wars On-Demand The Power of the Dark Side

COMPLETE SET W/EXCL. (26)	15.00	40.00
COMPLETE SET W/O EXCL. (25)	10.00	25.00
COMMON CARD (1-26)	1.25	3.00

*BLUE: 1X TO 2.5X BASIC CARDS
*PURPLE/10: UNPRICED DUE TO SCARCITY
*GREEN/5: UNPRICED DUE TO SCARCITY
*GOLD/1: UNPRICED DUE TO SCARCITY
STATED PRINT RUN 700 SETS
SDCC SITH TROOPER PRINT RUN 300 CARDS

26 Sith Trooper/300*	8.00	20.00

(SDCC Exclusive)

2019 Star Wars On-Demand The Power of the Dark Side Autographs

*PURPLE/10: UNPRICED DUE TO SCARCITY
*GREEN/5: UNPRICED DUE TO SCARCITY
*GOLD/1: UNPRICED DUE TO SCARCITY
STATED OVERALL ODDS 1:SET

2A Ian McDiarmid
3A Hayden Christensen
4A Guy Henry
5A Nika Futterman
7A Barbara Goodson
8A Matthew Wood
9A Ray Park
10A Sam Witwer

11A Adam Driver
12A Domhnall Gleeson
13A Andy Serkis
15A Jeremy Bulloch
17A Ben Mendelsohn
18A Paul Bettany
20A Lars Mikkelson
21A Jason Isaacs
22A Sarah Michelle Gellar
23A Philliph Anthony Rodriguez
24A Kathleen Gati

2019 Star Wars On-Demand The Power of the Dark Side Galactic Battles

COMPLETE SET (6)	15.00	40.00
COMMON CARD (G1-G6)	4.00	10.00
STATED ODDS 1:SET		

2019 Star Wars On-Demand The Power of the Light Side

COMPLETE SET W/EXCL. (26)	15.00	40.00
COMPLETE SET W/O EXCL.(25)	10.00	25.00
COMMON CARD (1-25)	1.25	3.00

*BLUE: 1X TO 2.5X BASIC CARDS
*PURPLE/10: UNPRICED DUE TO SCARCITY
*GREEN/5: UNPRICED DUE TO SCARCITY
*GOLD/1: UNPRICED DUE TO SCARCITY

26 Luke Skywalker	12.00	30.00

(NYCC Exclusive)

2019 Star Wars On-Demand The Power of the Light Side Autographs

*PURPLE/10: UNPRICED DUE TO SCARCITY
*GREEN/5: UNPRICED DUE TO SCARCITY
*GOLD/1: UNPRICED DUE TO SCARCITY
STATED ODDS 1:SET

2A Carrie Fisher
3A Harrison Ford
4A Peter Mayhew
5A Billy Dee Williams
6A Kenny Baker
7A Anthony Daniels
8A Caroline Blakiston
11A Tim Rose
12A Hayden Christensen
13A Samuel L. Jackson
14A Ewan McGregor
17A Daisy Ridley
19A John Boyega
20A Felicity Jones
21A Hermione Corfield
22A Matt Lanter
23A James Arnold Taylor
24A Ashley Eckstein
25A Taylor Gray

2019 Star Wars On-Demand The Power of the Light Side Galactic Battles

COMPLETE SET (6)	25.00	60.00
COMMON CARD (G1-G6)	4.00	10.00
STATED ODDS 1:SET		

2019 Star Wars On-Demand Women of Star Wars

COMPLETE SET (25)	12.00	30.00
COMMON CARD (1-25)	.75	2.00

*PURPLE: 2X TO 5X BASIC CARDS
*BLUE/10: UNPRICED DUE TO SCARCITY
*RED/5: UNPRICED DUE TO SCARCITY
*GOLD/1: UNPRICED DUE TO SCARCITY

2019 Star Wars On-Demand Women of Star Wars Autographs

Amy Allen as
Aayla Secura

COMMON AUTO	8.00	20.00

*BLUE/10: UNPRICED DUE TO SCARCITY
*RED/5: UNPRICED DUE TO SCARCITY
*GOLD/1: UNPRICED DUE TO SCARCITY
STATED OVERALL ODDS 1:SET

1 Carrie Fisher		
2 Daisy Ridley	300.00	500.00
3 Felicity Jones	125.00	250.00
4 Genevieve O'Reilly	10.00	25.00
5 Ashley Eckstein	15.00	40.00
6 Sarah Michelle Gellar	75.00	150.00
7 Vanessa Marshall	12.00	30.00
8 Tiya Sircar	10.00	25.00
9 Nika Futterman	10.00	25.00
10 Laura Dern		
12 Tovah Feldshuh	15.00	40.00
13 Orli Shoshan	12.00	30.00
15 Billie Lourd	60.00	120.00
16 Gwendoline Christie		

2019 Star Wars On-Demand Women of Star Wars Evolution of Leia

COMPLETE SET (8)	75.00	150.00
COMMON CARD (EL1-EL8)	12.00	30.00

2019 Star Wars On-Demand Women of Star Wars Women of the Galaxy

COMPLETE SET (10)	75.00	150.00
COMMON CARD (WG1-WG10)	10.00	25.00

RANDOMLY INSERTED INTO SETS

1995 Star Wars The Power of the Force

NNO Luke Skywalker	2.00	5.00

2011 Star Wars Power Plates

COMPLETE SET W/SP (30)	75.00	150.00
COMP.SET W/O SP (24)	50.00	100.00
UNOPENED BOX (48 PACKS)	120.00	150.00
UNOPENED PACK (1 PLATE)	2.50	3.00
COMMON PLATE	3.00	8.00
COMMON PLATE SP	5.00	12.00
SP STATED ODDS 1:8		

1999 Star Wars Preview Guide

NNO Pod Racers		5.00

(Orange County Register Exclusive)

1997 Star Wars Quality Bakers

COMPLETE SET (10)	12.00	30.00
COMMON CARD (1-10)	2.00	5.00

2016 Star Wars Rancho Obi-Wan Little Debbie

COMPLETE SET (12)	20.00	50.00
COMMON CARD (1-12)	2.50	6.00

STATED ODDS 1:1 BOXES OF STAR CRUNCH

2018 Star Wars On-Demand Rebels Series Finale

COMPLETE SET (20)	15.00	40.00
COMMON CARD (1-20)	1.25	3.00

*BLUE: 1X TO 2.5X BASIC CARDS
*PURPLE/10: UNPRICED DUE TO SCARCITY
*RED/5: UNPRICED DUE TO SCARCITY
*GOLD/1: UNPRICED DUE TO SCARCITY
STATED PRINT RUN 461 SETS

2018 Star Wars On-Demand Rebels Series Finale Autographs

*PURPLE/10: UNPRICED DUE TO SCARCITY
*RED/5: UNPRICED DUE TO SCARCITY
*GOLD/1: UNPRICED DUE TO SCARCITY
STATED OVERALL ODDS 1:SET

NNO Ashley Eckstein		
NNO Dee Bradley Baker	12.00	30.00
NNO Forest Whitaker		
NNO Freddie Prinze Jr.		
NNO Genevieve O'Reilly	10.00	25.00
NNO Ian McDiarmid	60.00	120.00
NNO Lars Mikkelsen	30.00	75.00
NNO Mary Elizabeth McGlynn	15.00	40.00
NNO Stephen Stanton	12.00	30.00
NNO Steve Blum	15.00	40.00
NNO Taylor Gray		
NNO Tom Baker		
NNO Vanessa Marshall		
NNO Warwick Davis		

2015 Star Wars Rebels

COMPLETE SET (100)	6.00	15.00
UNOPENED BOX (24 PACKS)	40.00	50.00
UNOPENED PACK (6 CARDS)	2.00	2.50
COMMON CARD (1-100)	.12	.30

*FOIL: 2X TO 5X BASIC CARDS

2015 Star Wars Rebels Stickers

COMPLETE SET (20)	5.00	12.00
COMMON CARD (1-20)	.40	1.00

2015 Star Wars Rebels Tattoos

COMPLETE SET (10)	6.00	15.00
COMMON CARD (1-10)	1.00	2.50

STATED ODDS 1:8

2017 Star Wars Rebels Season 4 Preview Set

COMPLETE SET (25)	30.00	80.00
UNOPENED BOXED SET (27 CARDS)		
COMMON CARD	2.00	5.00

*PURPLE/25: 1.2X TO 3X BASIC CARDS
*SILVER/10: UNPRICED DUE TO SCARCITY
*GOLD/5: UNPRICED DUE TO SCARCITY
*RED/1: UNPRICED DUE TO SCARCITY
RELEASED 10/17/2017

2017 Star Wars Rebels Season 4 Preview Set Autographs

FREDDIE PRINZE JR. AS
KANAN JARRUS

*GOLD/5: UNPRICED DUE TO SCARCITY
*RED/1: UNPRICED DUE TO SCARCITY
STATED ODDS 1:1 PER BOX SET

NNO Freddie Prinze Jr.		
NNO Taylor Gray		
NNO Vanessa Marshall		
NNO Tiya Sircar		
NNO Steve Blum		
NNO Ashley Eckstein		
NNO Sam Witwer		
NNO Jason Isaacs		
NNO Philip Anthony Rodriguez		
NNO Sarah Michelle Gellar		
NNO Stephen Stanton	12.00	30.00
NNO Billy Dee Williams		
NNO Forest Whitaker		
NNO Stephen Stanton		
NNO Genevieve OlReilly		
NNO Mary Elizabeth McGlynn	12.00	30.00
NNO Phil Lamarr		
NNO Tom Baker		
NNO Jim Cummings		

2014 Star Wars Rebels Subway Promos

COMPLETE SET (6)	6.00	15.00
COMMON CARD	1.50	4.00

2019 Star Wars Resistance Surprise Packs

COMPLETE SET (100)	12.00	30.00
UNOPENED BOX (PACKS)		
UNOPENED PACK (CARDS)		
COMMON CARD (1-100)	.25	.60

*BRONZE/50: 4X TO 10X BASIC CARDS
*SILVER/25: 6X TO 15X BASIC CARDS
*GOLD/10: UNPRICED DUE TO SCARCITY
*RED/1: UNPRICED DUE TO SCARCITY
*P.P.BLACK/1: UNPRICED DUE TO SCARCITY
*P.P.CYAN/1: UNPRICED DUE TO SCARCITY
*P.P.MAGENTA/1: UNPRICED DUE TO SCARCITY
*P.P.YELLOW/1: UNPRICED DUE TO SCARCITY

2019 Star Wars Resistance Surprise Packs Character Foil

COMPLETE SET (25)	12.00	30.00
COMMON CARD (1-25)	.75	2.00

2019 Star Wars Resistance Surprise Packs Danglers

COMPLETE SET (12)	12.00	30.00
COMMON CARD (1-12)	2.50	6.00

2019 Star Wars Resistance Surprise Packs Mini Albums

COMPLETE SET (4)	12.00	30.00
COMMON ALBUM	4.00	10.00

2019 Star Wars Resistance Surprise Packs Pop-Ups

COMPLETE SET (10)	6.00	15.00
COMMON CARD (1-10)	1.00	2.50

2019 Star Wars Resistance Surprise Packs Temporary Tattoos

COMPLETE SET (10)	8.00	20.00
COMMON CARD (1-10)	1.25	3.00

2016 Star Wars Rogue One Mission Briefing

COMPLETE SET (110)	8.00	20.00
UNOPENED BOX (24 PACKS)	85.00	100.00
UNOPENED PACK (8 CARDS)	4.00	5.00
COMMON CARD (1-110)	.20	.50

*BLACK: .75X TO 2X BASIC CARDS   .40   1.00
*GREEN: 1.2X TO 3X BASIC CARDS   .60   1.50
*BLUE: 1.5X TO 4X BASIC CARDS   .75   2.00
*GRAY/100: 8X TO 20X BASIC CARDS   4.00   10.00
*GOLD/50: 12X TO 30X BASIC CARDS   6.00   15.00
*ORANGE:/1: UNPRICED DUE TO SCARCITY
*P.P.BLACK/1: UNPRICED DUE TO SCARCITY
*P.P.CYAN/1: UNPRICED DUE TO SCARCITY
*P.P.MAGENTA/1: UNPRICED DUE TO SCARCITY
*P.P.YELLOW/1: UNPRICED DUE TO SCARCITY

2016 Star Wars Rogue One Mission Briefing Autographs

COMMON CARD	6.00	15.00

*BLACK/50: .6X TO 1.5X BASIC AUTOS
*BLUE/25: 1.2X TO 3X BASIC AUTOS

*GOLD/10: UNPRICED DUE TO SCARCITY
*ORANGE/1: UNPRICED DUE TO SCARCITY
*P.P.BLACK/1: UNPRICED DUE TO SCARCITY
*P.P.CYAN/1: UNPRICED DUE TO SCARCITY
*P.P.MAGENTA/1: UNPRICED DUE TO SCARCITY
*P.P.YELLOW/1: UNPRICED DUE TO SCARCITY
RANDOMLY INSERTED INTO PACKS

NNO Adrienne Wilkinson	12.00	30.00
NNO Al Lampert	10.00	25.00
NNO Anna Graves	15.00	40.00
NNO Barbara Frankland	10.00	25.00
NNO Brian Blessed	8.00	20.00
NNO Candice Orwell	12.00	30.00
NNO Catherine Taber		
NNO Clive Revill	12.00	30.00
NNO Corey Dee Williams	10.00	25.00
NNO Dave Barclay		
NNO David Ankrum	10.00	25.00
NNO Eric Lopez	10.00	25.00
NNO Femi Taylor	8.00	20.00
NNO Garrick Hagon	10.00	25.00
NNO George Roubicek	10.00	25.00
NNO Glyn Baker	10.00	25.00
NNO Ian Liston	10.00	25.00
NNO Jack Klaff	8.00	20.00
NNO Jim Cummings	12.00	30.00
NNO John Coppinger	15.00	40.00
NNO Kenneth Colley	8.00	20.00
NNO Lloyd Sherr	10.00	25.00
NNO Megan Udall	10.00	25.00
NNO Mercedes Ngoh	8.00	20.00
NNO Michaela Cottrell	8.00	20.00
NNO Mike Edmonds	12.00	30.00
NNO Oliver Walpole	10.00	25.00
NNO Paul Springer	12.00	30.00
NNO Rajia Baroudi	12.00	30.00
NNO Rich Oldfield	15.00	40.00
NNO Rusty Goffe	10.00	25.00
NNO Sam Witwer	15.00	40.00
NNO Scott Capurro	12.00	30.00
NNO Sean Crawford	10.00	25.00
NNO Stephen Stanton	8.00	20.00
NNO Tom Kane	8.00	20.00
NNO Wayne Pygram	10.00	25.00

2016 Star Wars Rogue One Mission Briefing Character Foil

COMPLETE SET (9)	12.00	20.00
COMMON CARD (1-9)	2.00	5.00

*P.P.BLACK/1: UNPRICED DUE TO SCARCITY
*P.P.CYAN/1: UNPRICED DUE TO SCARCITY
*P.P.MAGENTA/1: UNPRICED DUE TO SCARCITY
*P.P.YELLOW/1: UNPRICED DUE TO SCARCITY
STATED ODDS 1:8

2016 Star Wars Rogue One Mission Briefing Comic Strips Inserts

COMPLETE SET (12)	8.00	20.00
COMMON CARD (1-12)	1.25	3.00

---

*P.P.BLACK/1: UNPRICED DUE TO SCARCITY
*P.P.CYAN/1: UNPRICED DUE TO SCARCITY
*P.P.MAGENTA/1: UNPRICED DUE TO SCARCITY
*P.P.YELLOW/1: UNPRICED DUE TO SCARCITY

2016 Star Wars Rogue One Mission Briefing The Death Star

COMPLETE SET (9)	6.00	15.00
COMMON CARD (1-9)	.75	2.00

*P.P.BLACK/1: UNPRICED DUE TO SCARCITY
*P.P.CYAN/1: UNPRICED DUE TO SCARCITY
*P.P.MAGENTA/1: UNPRICED DUE TO SCARCITY
*P.P.YELLOW/1: UNPRICED DUE TO SCARCITY
STATED ODDS 1:4

2016 Star Wars Rogue One Mission Briefing Dual Autographs

STATED PRINT RUN 3 SER.#'d SETS
UNPRICED DUE TO SCARCITY

1 C.Fisher
  C.Blakiston
2 M.Hamill
  D.Lawson

2016 Star Wars Rogue One Mission Briefing Heroes of the Rebel Alliance

COMPLETE SET (9)	10.00	25.00
COMMON CARD (1-9)	1.50	3.00

*P.P.BLACK/1: UNPRICED DUE TO SCARCITY
*P.P.CYAN/1: UNPRICED DUE TO SCARCITY
*P.P.MAGENTA/1: UNPRICED DUE TO SCARCITY
*P.P.YELLOW/1: UNPRICED DUE TO SCARCITY
STATED ODDS 1:8

1 Luke Skywalker	2.00	5.00
2 Princess Leia	2.00	5.00
3 Han Solo	2.00	5.00
4 Chewbacca	1.50	4.00
6 Obi-Wan Kenobi	1.50	4.00
7 R2-D2	1.50	4.00

2016 Star Wars Rogue One Mission Briefing Mission Briefing Monday

COMPLETE SET (36)	150.00	300.00
COMMON CARD	6.00	15.00

NOV.7, 2016 (MBME1-MBME6)/206*
NOV.14, 2016 (MBM1-MBM5)/226*
NOV.21, 2016 (MBM6-MBM10)/218*
NOV.28, 2016 (MBM11-MBM15)/212*
DEC.5, 2016 (MBM16-MBM20)/224*
DEC.12, 2016 (MBM21-MBM25)/234*
DEC.19, 2016 (MBM26-MBM30)/252*

2016 Star Wars Rogue One Mission Briefing Montages

COMPLETE SET (9)	15.00	40.00
COMMON CARD (1-9)	3.00	8.00

*P.P.BLACK/1: UNPRICED DUE TO SCARCITY
*P.P.CYAN/1: UNPRICED DUE TO SCARCITY
*P.P.MAGENTA/1: UNPRICED DUE TO SCARCITY
*P.P.YELLOW/1: UNPRICED DUE TO SCARCITY
STATED ODDS 1:24

1 Storming the Beach	3.00	8.00
2 Imperial Assault	3.00	8.00
3 Jyn Erso	5.00	12.00
4 Within Rebel Base	3.00	8.00
5 Patrol of the Empire	3.00	8.00
6 Fearsome Death Trooper	3.00	8.00
7 Director Krennic	3.00	8.00
8 In Flames	3.00	8.00
9 Rebel Ensemble	3.00	8.00

2016 Star Wars Rogue One Mission Briefing NYCC Exclusives

COMPLETE SET (10)	12.00	30.00
COMMON CARD (E1-E10)	2.00	5.00
2016 NYCC EXCLUSIVE		

2016 Star Wars Rogue One Mission Briefing Patches

COMPLETE SET (12)	50.00	100.00
COMMON CARD (M1-M12)	3.00	8.00

*GRAY/100: .75X TO 2X BASIC CARDS
*GOLD/50: 1.5X TO 4X BASIC CARDS
*RED/10: 3X TO 8X BASIC CARDS
STATED ODDS 1:26

1 Jyn Erso	6.00	15.00
3 L-1 Droid	5.00	12.00
4 Admiral Raddus	4.00	10.00
6 TIE Fighter Pilot	4.00	10.00
7 Shoretrooper	4.00	10.00
10 Captain Cassian Andor	5.00	12.00
11 Bistan	4.00	10.00

2016 Star Wars Rogue One Mission Briefing Quad Autograph

STATED PRINT RUN 2 SER.#'d SETS
UNPRICED DUE TO SCARCITY

1 Hamill/Lawson/Klaff/Hagon

2016 Star Wars Rogue One Mission Briefing Sketches

COMPLETE ARTIST LIST (33)
UNPRICED DUE TO SCARCITY

NNO Alex Iniguez
NNO Angelina Benedetti
NNO Bill Pulkovski
NNO Brad Hudson
NNO Brent Ragland
NNO Brian Kong
NNO Carlos Cabaleiro
NNO Chris Meeks
NNO Dan Parsons
NNO Danny Haas
NNO Darrin Pepe
NNO Eric Lehtonen
NNO Francois Chartier
NNO Hayden Davis
NNO Ingrid Hardy
NNO James Henry Smith
NNO Jamie Cosley
NNO Jason Bommer
NNO Jason Sobol
NNO Jeff Mallinson
NNO Jessica Hickman
NNO Jonathan Caustrita
NNO Kevin Liell
NNO Kevin P. West
NNO Kyle Babbitt
NNO Marcia Dye
NNO Matt Stewart
NNO Rob Teranishi
NNO Robert Hendrickson
NNO Roy Cover
NNO Solly Mohamed
NNO Stephanie Swanger
NNO Tina Berardi

2016 Star Wars Rogue One Mission Briefing Stickers

COMPLETE SET (18)	10.00	25.00
COMMON CARD (1-18)	1.00	2.50

*P.P.BLACK/1: UNPRICED DUE TO SCARCITY
*P.P.CYAN/1: UNPRICED DUE TO SCARCITY
*P.P.MAGENTA/1: UNPRICED DUE TO SCARCITY
*P.P.YELLOW/1: UNPRICED DUE TO SCARCITY
STATED ODDS 1:12

1 Jyn Erso		1.50	4.00
13 Darth Vader		2.00	5.00

2016 Star Wars Rogue One Mission Briefing Triple Autographs

STATED PRINT RUN 3 SER.#'d SETS
UNPRICED DUE TO SCARCITY

1 Fisher/Blakiston/Crowley
2 Hamill/Lawson/Hagon

2016 Star Wars Rogue One Mission Briefing Villains of the Galactic Empire

COMPLETE SET (8)	8.00	20.00
COMMON CARD (1-8)	1.25	3.00

*P.P.BLACK/1: UNPRICED DUE TO SCARCITY
*P.P.CYAN/1: UNPRICED DUE TO SCARCITY
*P.P.MAGENTA/1: UNPRICED DUE TO SCARCITY
*P.P.YELLOW/1: UNPRICED DUE TO SCARCITY
STATED ODDS 1:8

1 Darth Vader	1.25	5.00

1999 Star Wars Sci-Fi Expo Celebrity Promos

P1 Garrick Hagon	8.00	20.00
(Biggs Darklighter)		
P2 Peter Mayhew	8.00	20.00
(Chewbacca)		

2015 Star Wars SDCC Oversized Exclusives

COMPLETE SET (100)	120.00	250.00
COMMON CARD (1-100)	2.00	5.00

1997 Star Wars SE Trilogy 3-D Doritos Discs

COMPLETE SET (20)	5.00	12.00
COMMON CARD	.40	1.00

1997 Star Wars SE Trilogy 3-D Doritos-Cheetos

COMPLETE SET (6)	3.00	8.00
COMMON CARD (1-6)	.75	2.00

1996 Star Wars Shadows of the Empire

COMPLETE SET (100)	15.00	40.00
COMMON CARD (1-72, 83-100)	.15	.40
COMMON ETCHED (73-78)	2.00	5.00
COMMON EMBOSSED (79-82)	3.00	8.00
73-78 STATED ODDS 1:9		
79-82 STATED ODDS 1:18		

1996 Star Wars Shadows of the Empire Promos

COMMON CARD	1.00	2.50
SOTE1 Xizor	2.00	5.00
SOTE2 Darth Vader	2.00	5.00
SOTE3 Luke Skywalker	2.00	5.00
SOTE4 Dash Rendar & Leebo	2.00	5.00
SOTE5 Boba Fett	8.00	15.00
(Convention Exclusive)		
SOTE6 Guri	2.00	5.00
SOTE7 C-3PO & R2-D2	2.00	5.00
NNO SOTE3-SOTE1 (Luke Skywalker/Darth Vader)		

2021 Star Wars Signature Series Autographs

*GREEN/25: UNPRICED DUE TO SCARCITY
*ORANGE/10: UNPRICED DUE TO SCARCITY
*BLACK/5: UNPRICED DUE TO SCARCITY
*RED/1: UNPRICED DUE TO SCARCITY

AA Annabelle Davis	10.00	25.00
AS Stephen Stanton		
AA2 Annabelle Davis	10.00	25.00
AAF Anthony Forrest	6.00	15.00
AAG Anna Graves	6.00	15.00
AAH Alden Ehrenreich		
AAS Andy Serkis		
ABB Ben Burtt		
ABL Billie Lourd		
ABM Ben Mendelsohn		
ABW Billy Dee Williams		
ACC Cavin Cornwall	6.00	15.00
ACF Carrie Fisher		
ACH Clint Howard		
ACM Cameron Monaghan	15.00	40.00
ACW Carl Weathers		
ADA Derek Arnold	6.00	15.00
ADB Dee Bradley Baker	15.00	40.00
ADC Dave Chapman	8.00	20.00
ADF Donald Faison		
ADG Domhnall Gleeson		
ADL Daniel Logan	8.00	20.00

ADM Dominic Monaghan		
ADR Daisy Ridley		
ADT Dee Tails		
ADW Debra Wilson	10.00	25.00
ADY Donnie Yen		
AES Emily Swallow		
AEW Ewan McGregor		
AFJ Felicity Jones		
AFP Freddie Prinze Jr.		
AFW Forest Whitaker		
AGC Gwendoline Christie		
AGE Giancarlo Esposito	50.00	100.00
AGG Greg Grunberg	12.00	30.00
AGO Genevieve O'Reilly		
AGP Greg Proops	6.00	15.00
AHC Hayden Christensen		
AHD Harley Durst	6.00	15.00
AHF Harrison Ford		
AHS Horatio Sanz	15.00	40.00
AIM Ian McDiarmid		
AIR Ian Ruskin	6.00	15.00
AIW Ian Whyte	10.00	25.00
AJB John Boyega	30.00	75.00
AJK Jaime King	10.00	25.00
AJR Jerome Blake	8.00	20.00
AJS Joonas Suotamo	60.00	120.00
AJT James Arnold Taylor	15.00	40.00
AKB Kenny Baker		
AKT Kelly Marie Tran		
ALT Lee Towersey	15.00	40.00
AMD Matt Doran	6.00	15.00
AMM Mads Mikkelsen		
ANF Nika Futterman	10.00	25.00
ANK Nick Kellington	6.00	15.00
ANN Nick Nolte		
APA Philip Anthony-Rodriguez	10.00	25.00
APB Paul Bettany		
APM Peter Mayhew		
APP Pedro Pascal		
ARA Riz Ahmed		
ARD Robin Atkin Downes	6.00	15.00
ARP Ray Park		
AS2 Stephen Stanton		
AS3 Stephen Stanton		
ASJ Samuel L. Jackson		
ASW Sam Witwer	15.00	40.00
ATD Tim Dry	6.00	15.00
ATF Tovah Feldshuh	6.00	15.00
ATG Taylor Gray		
ATK Tom Kenny	8.00	20.00
ATM Temuera Morrison	50.00	100.00
ATR Tim Rose		
ATW Taika Waititi		
AWA Denis Lawson	12.00	30.00
AWD Warwick Davis	30.00	75.00
AWH Werner Herzog		
AAB2 Ahmed Best		
AAB3 Ahmed Best		
AAD2 Adam Driver		
AAD3 Adam Driver		
AAE2 Ashley Eckstein		
AAE3 Ashley Eckstein		
AAF2 Anthony Forrest	6.00	15.00
AAG2 Anna Graves	6.00	15.00
AAH2 Alden Ehrenreich		
AAS2 Andy Serkis		
AASG Arti Shah	5.00	12.00
ABB2 Ben Burtt		
ABBE Blair Bess	8.00	20.00
ABL2 Billie Lourd		
ABL3 Billie Lourd		
ABMR Bobby Moynihan	6.00	15.00
ABW2 Billy Dee Williams		
ABW3 Billy Dee Williams		
ACC2 Cavin Cornwall	6.00	15.00
ACDW Corey Dee Williams	12.00	30.00
ACF2 Carrie Fisher		
ADA2 Derek Arnold		
ADA3 Derek Arnold		
ADB2 Dee Bradley Baker	5.00	12.00
ADB3 Dee Bradley Baker	6.00	15.00
ADC2 Dave Chapman	12.00	30.00

ADG2 Domhnall Gleeson		
ADG3 Domhnall Gleeson		
ADL2 Daniel Logan	8.00	20.00
ADR2 Daisy Ridley		
ADR3 Daisy Ridley		
ADT2 Dee Tails		
ADT3 Dee Tails		
AEW2 Ewan McGregor		
AEW3 Ewan McGregor		
AFJ2 Felicity Jones		
AFJ3 Felicity Jones		
AFP2 Freddie Prinze Jr.		
AGC2 Gwendoline Christie		
AGCM Gina Carano		
AGG2 Greg Grunberg	12.00	30.00
AHC2 Hayden Christensen		
AHC3 Hayden Christensen		
AHF2 Harrison Ford		
AHF3 Harrison Ford		
AIM2 Ian McDiarmid		
AIM3 Ian McDiarmid		
AIW2 Ian Whyte	8.00	20.00
AJB2 John Boyega	30.00	75.00
AJB3 John Boyega	30.00	75.00
AJR2 Jerome Blake		
AJS2 Joonas Suotamo	60.00	120.00
AJT2 James Arnold Taylor	15.00	40.00
AJT3 James Arnold Taylor	12.00	30.00
AJTS John Tui	8.00	20.00
AKB2 Kenny Baker		
AKB3 Kenny Baker		
AKT2 Kelly Marie Tran		
ANF2 Nika Futterman	10.00	25.00
ANF3 Nika Futterman	10.00	25.00
ANK2 Nick Kellington	8.00	20.00
APM2 Peter Mayhew		
APM3 Peter Mayhew		
ARD2 Robin Atkin Downes	8.00	20.00
ARP2 Ray Park		
ARP3 Ray Park		
ARPC Ron Perlman		
ASJ2 Samuel L. Jackson		
ASJ3 Samuel L. Jackson		
ASW2 Sam Witwer	25.00	60.00
ASW3 Sam Witwer		
ATBS Thomas Brodie-Sangster	5.00	12.00
ATG2 Taylor Gray		
ATK2 Tom Kenny	10.00	25.00
ATK3 Tom Kenny	10.00	25.00
ATM2 Temuera Morrison	75.00	150.00
ATR2 Tim Rose		
ATR3 Tim Rose		
AWA2 Denis Lawson	12.00	30.00
AWA3 Denis Lawson	12.00	30.00
AWD2 Warwick Davis		
AWD3 Warwick Davis		

2021 Star Wars Signature Series Dual Autographs

*RED/1: UNPRICED DUE TO SCARCITY
STATED PRINT RUN 5 SER.#'d SETS
UNPRICED DUE TO SCARCITY

DABC G.Christie/J.Boyega
DACM I.McDiarmid/H.Christensen
DAEB A.Ehrenreich/P.Bettany
DAJM B.Mendelsohn/F.Jones
DALE A.Eckstein/M.Lanter
DAPE G.Esposito/P.Pascal
DARD D.Ridley/A.Driver
DAWM P.Mayhew/B.Williams

2021 Star Wars Signature Series Triple Autographs

*RED/1: UNPRICED DUE TO SCARCITY
STATED PRINT RUN 5 SER.#'d SETS
UNPRICED DUE TO SCARCITY

TADCG Driver/Christie/Gleeson
TAEFS Futterman/Eckstein/Salenger
TAESK Ehrenreich/Suotamo/Kellyman
TAJWA Jones/Whitaker/Ahmed
TAPGM Prinze Jr./Gray/Marshall
TAPWN Pascal/Waititi/Nolte
TARDB Ridley/Driver/Boyega
TARTL Ridley/Tran/Lourd

2019 Star Wars Skywalker Saga

COMPLETE SET (100)	8.00	20.00
COMMON CARD (1-100)	.20	.50

*ORANGE: .6X TO 1.5X BASIC CARDS
*BLUE: .75X TO 2X BASIC CARDS
*GREEN/99: 2.5X TO 6X BASIC CARDS
*PURPLE/25: 6X TO 15X BASIC CARDS
*RED/1: UNPRICED DUE TO SCARCITY
*P.P.BLACK/1: UNPRICED DUE TO SCARCITY
*P.P.CYAN/1: UNPRICED DUE TO SCARCITY
*P.P.MAGENTA/1: UNPRICED DUE TO SCARCITY
*P.P.YELLOW/1: UNPRICED DUE TO SCARCITY

2019 Star Wars Skywalker Saga Allies

COMPLETE SET (10)	6.00	15.00
COMMON CARD (A1-A10)	.75	2.00

*GREEN/99: 1X TO 2.5X BASIC CARDS
*PURPLE/25: 3X TO 8X BASIC CARDS
*RED/1: UNPRICED DUE TO SCARCITY
*P.P.BLACK/1: UNPRICED DUE TO SCARCITY
*P.P.CYAN/1: UNPRICED DUE TO SCARCITY
*P.P.MAGENTA/1: UNPRICED DUE TO SCARCITY
*P.P.YELLOW/1: UNPRICED DUE TO SCARCITY
STATED ODDS 1:12 HOBBY & BLASTER

2019 Star Wars Skywalker Saga Autographs

ERIN KELLYMAN AS ENFYS NEST

*PURPLE/5: UNPRICED DUE TO SCARCITY
*RED/1: UNPRICED DUE TO SCARCITY
*P.P.BLACK/1: UNPRICED DUE TO SCARCITY
*P.P.CYAN/1: UNPRICED DUE TO SCARCITY
*P.P.MAGENTA/1: UNPRICED DUE TO SCARCITY
*P.P.YELLOW/1: UNPRICED DUE TO SCARCITY
STATED ODDS 1:39 HOBBY; 1:826 BLASTER

AAB Ahmed Best		
AAD Anthony Daniels		
AAS Andy Serkis		
AAT Alan Tudyk		
ABH Brian Herring	6.00	15.00
ABL Billie Lourd		
ABM Ben Mendelsohn		
ACF Carrie Fisher		
ADB David Barclay	6.00	15.00
ADG Domhnall Gleeson		
ADL Daniel Logan	5.00	12.00
ADR Daisy Ridley		
ADY Donnie Yen		
AEK Erin Kellyman	30.00	75.00
AEM Ewan McGregor		
AFJ Felicity Jones		
AFW Forest Whitaker		
AGH Garrick Hagon	6.00	15.00
AGO Genevieve O'Reilly		
AHC Hayden Christensen		
AHF Harrison Ford		
AIM Ian McDiarmid		
AJB Jerome Blake	5.00	12.00
AKB Kenny Baker		
AKK Katy Kartwheel	12.00	30.00
AML Matt Lanter		
AMM Mads Mikkelsen		
ANF Nika Futterman	5.00	12.00
APB Paul Bettany		
APL Phil LaMarr	6.00	15.00
APM Peter Mayhew		
ARA Riz Ahmed		
ARP Ray Park		
ASC Silas Carson	5.00	12.00
ATM Temuera Morrison		
AWD Warwick Davis		
AADK Adam Driver		
AAEH Alden Ehrenreich		
AASW Andy Secombe	5.00	12.00
ABDW Billy Dee Williams		
AHCV Hayden Christensen		
AIMS Ian McDiarmid		
AJAT James Arnold Taylor		
AJBF John Boyega		
AJSC Joonas Suotamo		
ASLJ Samuel L. Jackson		
ATKY Tom Kane	6.00	15.00

2019 Star Wars Skywalker Saga Commemorative Blueprint Relics

COMMON MEM	5.00	12.00

*ORANGE/99: SAME VALUE AS BASIC
*BLUE/50: .5X TO 1.2X BASIC MEM
*GREEN/25: .75X TO 2X BASIC MEM
*PURPLE/5: UNPRICED DUE TO SCARCITY
*RED/1: UNPRICED DUE TO SCARCITY
STATED ODDS 1:64 HOBBY; 1:218 BLASTER

BPIS Imperial Speeder Bike	6.00	15.00
BPMF Millennium Falcon	8.00	20.00
BPSI Slave I	6.00	15.00
BPST AT-ST	6.00	15.00
BPTI Tie Interceptor	6.00	15.00
BPXW X-wing Fighter	6.00	15.00

2019 Star Wars Skywalker Saga Commemorative Nameplate Patches

COMMON ANAKIN	3.00	8.00
COMMON KYLO	4.00	10.00
COMMON LEIA	4.00	10.00
COMMON LUKE	5.00	12.00

*ORANGE/99: SAME VALUE AS BASIC
*BLUE/50: .5X TO 1.2X BASIC MEM
*GREEN/25: .75X TO 2X BASIC MEM
*PURPLE/5: UNPRICED DUE TO SCARCITY
*RED/1: UNPRICED DUE TO SCARCITY
STATED ODDS 1:1 BLASTER

NPA General Leia Organa/A	4.00	10.00
NPE Princess Leia Organa/E	4.00	10.00
NPI General Leia Organa/I	4.00	10.00
NPL Princess Leia Organa/L	4.00	10.00
NPA2 Anakin Skywalker/A	3.00	8.00
NPAA Anakin Skywalker/A	3.00	8.00
NPAI Anakin Skywalker/I	3.00	8.00
NPAK Anakin Skywalker/K	3.00	8.00
NPAN Anakin Skywalker/N	3.00	8.00
NPKK Kylo Ren/K	4.00	10.00
NPKL Kylo Ren/L	4.00	10.00
NPKO Kylo Ren/O	4.00	10.00
NPKY Kylo Ren/Y	4.00	10.00
NPLE Luke Skywalker/E	5.00	12.00
NPLK Luke Skywalker/K	5.00	12.00
NPLL Luke Skywalker/L	5.00	12.00
NPLU Luke Skywalker/U	5.00	12.00
NPN2 Anakin Skywalker/N	3.00	8.00

2019 Star Wars Skywalker Saga Dual Autographs

STATED ODDS 1:7,572 HOBBY; 1:68,310 BLASTER
UNPRICED DUE TO SCARCITY
DAFD C.Fisher/A.Driver
DAJM S.L.Jackson/I.McDiarmid
DALD P.LeMarr/J.Dolan
DALE M.Lanter/A.Eckstein
DAPC K.Baker/R.Goffe
DAPM F.Prinze Jr./V.Marshall
DATG J.Taylor/A.Graves
DAWM B.Williams/P.Mayhew

2019 Star Wars Skywalker Saga Enemies

STAR WARS
ENEMIES
TUSKEN RAIDER

COMPLETE SET (10)	6.00	15.00
COMMON CARD (E1-E10)	.75	2.00

*GREEN/99: 1X TO 2.5X BASIC CARDS
*PURPLE/25: 3X TO 8X BASIC CARDS
*RED/1: UNPRICED DUE TO SCARCITY
*P.P.BLACK/1: UNPRICED DUE TO SCARCITY
*P.P.CYAN/1: UNPRICED DUE TO SCARCITY
*P.P.MAGENTA/1: UNPRICED DUE TO SCARCITY
*P.P.YELLOW/1: UNPRICED DUE TO SCARCITY
STATED ODDS 1:12 HOBBY; 1:12 BLASTER

2019 Star Wars Skywalker Saga Iconic Looks

COMPLETE SET (10)	6.00	15.00
COMMON CARD (IL1-IL10)	.75	2.00

*GREEN/99: 1X TO 2.5X BASIC CARDS
*PURPLE/25: 3X TO 8X BASIC CARDS
*RED/1: UNPRICED DUE TO SCARCITY
*P.P.BLACK/1: UNPRICED DUE TO SCARCITY
*P.P.CYAN/1: UNPRICED DUE TO SCARCITY
*P.P.MAGENTA/1: UNPRICED DUE TO SCARCITY
*P.P.YELLOW/1: UNPRICED DUE TO SCARCITY
STATED ODDS 1:4 HOBBY & BLASTER

2019 Star Wars Skywalker Saga Path of the Jedi

COMPLETE SET (10)	6.00	15.00
COMMON CARD (PJ1-PJ10)	.75	2.00

*GREEN/99: 1X TO 2.5X BASIC CARDS
*PURPLE/25: 3X TO 8X BASIC CARDS
*RED/1: UNPRICED DUE TO SCARCITY
*P.P.BLACK/1: UNPRICED DUE TO SCARCITY
*P.P.CYAN/1: UNPRICED DUE TO SCARCITY
*P.P.MAGENTA/1: UNPRICED DUE TO SCARCITY
*P.P.YELLOW/1: UNPRICED DUE TO SCARCITY
STATED ODDS 1:2 HOBBY & BLASTER

2019 Star Wars Skywalker Saga Sketches

STATED ODDS 1:85 HOBBY; 1:307 BLASTER
UNPRICED DUE TO SCARCITY
NNO Fredd Gorham
NNO Gerard Garcia Jr.
NNO Huy Truong
NNO Ian MacDougall
NNO Ingrid Hardy
NNO Jamie Richards
NNO Jay Manchand
NNO Jennifer Allyn
NNO Jim Mehsling
NNO John Bruce
NNO John DiBiase
NNO John Pleak
NNO Jose Ventura
NNO Josh Church
NNO Jude Gallagher
NNO Kelly Baber
NNO Kevin Cleveland
NNO Kevin P. West
NNO Lindsey Greyling
NNO Madison Emerick
NNO Marcia Dye
NNO Marsha Parkins
NNO Matthew Hirons

NNO Michael Mastermaker
NNO Mohammad Jilani
NNO Nathan Ohlendorf
NNO Neil Camera
NNO Paul Schiers
NNO Phil Hassewer
NNO Rachel Brady
NNO Rebecca Sharp
NNO Rees Finlay
NNO Rich Hennemann
NNO Rich Molinelli
NNO Richard Serrao
NNO Rob Teranishi
NNO Robert Garcia
NNO Rodney Roberts
NNO Ryan Finley
NNO Ryan Olsen
NNO Sammy Gomez
NNO Shaow Siong
NNO Solly Mohamed
NNO Thomas Amici
NNO Tim Shinn
NNO Tina Berardi
NNO Tod Smith
NNO Todd Aaron & Veronica Smith
NNO Trent Westbrook
NNO Vincent D'Ippolito
NNO Zach Woolsey
NNO Adam Beck
NNO Andrew Arensberg
NNO Andrew Fry
NNO Anil Sharma
NNO Anthony Ellison
NNO Ari Arnaldsson
NNO Ashlee Brienzo
NNO Ashley Marsh
NNO Ben AbuSaada
NNO Brad Hudson
NNO Brandon Blevins
NNO Brent Scotchmer
NNO Caleb King
NNO Carlos Cabaleiro
NNO Carolyn Craggs
NNO Chris Kay
NNO Cisco Rivera
NNO Colin Arthurs
NNO Dan Gorman
NNO Dan Tearle
NNO Darren James
NNO Eli Hyder
NNO Eric Lehtonen

2019 Star Wars Skywalker Saga Skywalker Legacy

COMPLETE SET (11)	6.00	15.00
COMMON CARD (FT1-FT11)	1.00	2.50

*GREEN/99: 1.5X TO 4X BASIC CARDS
*PURPLE/25: 2.5X TO 6X BASIC CARDS
*RED/1: UNPRICED DUE TO SCARCITY
*P.P.BLACK/1: UNPRICED DUE TO SCARCITY
*P.P.CYAN/1: UNPRICED DUE TO SCARCITY
*P.P.MAGENTA/1: UNPRICED DUE TO SCARCITY
*P.P.YELLOW/1: UNPRICED DUE TO SCARCITY
STATED ODDS 1:12 HOBBY & BLASTER

2019 Star Wars Skywalker Saga Triple Autographs

STATED ODDS 1:8,708 HOBBY; 1:168,310 BLASTER
STATED PRINT RUN SER.#'d SETS
UNPRICED DUE TO SCARCITY

TABCR Blakiston/Crowley/Rose
TABCT Taylor/Barclay/Carter
TAFFD Driver/Fisher/Ford
TAMBD Daniels/Baker/Mayhew
TAWCB Carson/Wood/Blake

1978 Star Wars Spaceship Hang Gliders

COMPLETE SET (4)	75.00	150.00
COMMON CARD	20.00	50.00

2017 Star Wars Stellar Signatures

COMMON AUTOS	25.00	60.00
*BLUE/25: .5X TO 1.2X BASIC AUTOS	30.00	75.00

*GREEN/20: UNPRICED DUE TO SCARCITY
*PURPLE/10: UNPRICED DUE TO SCARCITY

---

*GOLD/5: UNPRICED DUE TO SCARCITY
*GALACTIC BLACK/1: UNPRICED DUE TO SCARCITY
*IMPERIAL RED/1: UNPRICED DUE TO SCARCITY
*REB.ALL.ORANGE/1: UNPRICED DUE TO SCARCITY
STATED PRINT RUN 40 SER.#'d SETS
100 TOTAL BOXES PRODUCED

NNO Adam Driver	400.00	650.00
NNO Alan Tudyk	100.00	175.00
NNO Andy Serkis	75.00	150.00
NNO Ashley Eckstein	60.00	120.00
NNO Ben Mendelsohn EXCH		
NNO Billy Dee Williams	75.00	150.00
NNO Brian Herring	30.00	75.00
NNO Carrie Fisher	300.00	500.00
NNO Daisy Ridley	800.00	1200.00
NNO Donnie Yen	75.00	150.00
NNO Felicity Jones	300.00	500.00
NNO Forest Whitaker	75.00	150.00
NNO Freddie Prinze Jr.	50.00	100.00
NNO Genevieve O'Reilly	50.00	100.00
NNO Gwendoline Christie	250.00	400.00
NNO Harrison Ford	2500.00	4000.00
NNO Hayden Christensen	250.00	400.00
NNO Ian McDiarmid	250.00	400.00
NNO Jeremy Bulloch	30.00	75.00
NNO John Boyega	120.00	250.00
NNO Joonas Suotamo	30.00	75.00
NNO Kenny Baker	75.00	150.00
NNO Lars Mikkelsen	75.00	150.00
NNO Mark Hamill EXCH		
NNO Matthew Wood	30.00	75.00
NNO Peter Mayhew	75.00	150.00
NNO Ray Park	60.00	120.00
NNO Riz Ahmed	50.00	100.00
NNO Sarah Michelle Gellar	120.00	250.00
NNO Stephen Stanton EXCH		
NNO Temuera Morrison	30.00	75.00
NNO Tim Curry	100.00	175.00
NNO Tom Baker	100.00	200.00
NNO Warwick Davis	50.00	100.00

2018 Star Wars Stellar Signatures

COMMON AUTO	20.00	50.00

*BLUE/25: SAME VALUE AS BASIC AUTOS
*GREEN/20: UNPRICED DUE TO SCARCITY
*PURPLE/10: UNPRICED DUE TO SCARCITY
*GOLD/5: UNPRICED DUE TO SCARCITY
*BLACK/1: UNPRICED DUE TO SCARCITY
*ORANGE/1: UNPRICED DUE TO SCARCITY
*RED/1: UNPRICED DUE TO SCARCITY

AAD Anthony Daniels	125.00	250.00
AAE Ashley Eckstein	30.00	75.00
AAS Andy Serkis	50.00	100.00
AAT Alan Tudyk	50.00	100.00
ABH Brian Herring	25.00	60.00
ACB Caroline Blakiston	25.00	60.00
ADG Domhnall Gleeson	125.00	250.00
ADR Daisy Ridley	400.00	600.00
AEB Erik Bauersfeld	50.00	100.00
AEK Erin Kellyman	125.00	250.00
AFW Forest Whitaker	60.00	120.00
AGG Greg Grunberg	25.00	60.00
AHC Hayden Christensen	125.00	250.00
AHF Harrison Ford	800.00	1400.00
AIM Ian McDiarmid	100.00	200.00
AJB Jeremy Bulloch	30.00	75.00
AJI Jason Isaacs	30.00	75.00
AJS Joonas Suotamo	50.00	100.00
AKB Kenny Baker	100.00	200.00
ALD Laura Dern	60.00	120.00
AMM Mads Mikkelsen	125.00	250.00
APR Paul Reubens	75.00	150.00
ARA Riz Ahmed	30.00	75.00
ARP Ray Park	50.00	100.00
ATC Tim Curry	50.00	100.00
AADR Adam Driver	200.00	350.00
ABDW Billy Dee Williams	75.00	150.00
ASLJ Samuel L. Jackson	600.00	800.00

2018 Star Wars Stellar Signatures Autographed Relics

COMMON AUTO	60.00	120.00

*BLUE/25: SAME VALUE AS BASIC AUTOS

---

*GREEN/20: UNPRICED DUE TO SCARCITY
*PURPLE/10: UNPRICED DUE TO SCARCITY
*GOLD/5: UNPRICED DUE TO SCARCITY
*BLACK/1: UNPRICED DUE TO SCARCITY
*ORANGE/1: UNPRICED DUE TO SCARCITY
*RED/1: UNPRICED DUE TO SCARCITY

ARD Paul Bettany	150.00	300.00
ARJ Felicity Jones	200.00	350.00

2018 Star Wars Stellar Signatures Dual Autographs

*GREEN/20: UNPRICED DUE TO SCARCITY
*PURPLE/10: UNPRICED DUE TO SCARCITY
*GOLD/5: UNPRICED DUE TO SCARCITY
*BLACK/1: UNPRICED DUE TO SCARCITY
*ORANGE/1: UNPRICED DUE TO SCARCITY
*RED/1: UNPRICED DUE TO SCARCITY

DABB J.Bulloch/D.Barclay
DABM J.Bulloch/T.Morrison
DABO C.Blakiston/G.O'Reilly
DACW H.Christensen/M.Wood
DAFB C.Fisher/K.Baker
DAMM L.Mikkelsen/M.McGlynn
DAMP I.McDiarmid/R.Park
DAOM G.O'Reilly/I.McElhinney
DARD D.Ridley/A.Driver
DASV J.Suotamo/J.Vee
DASW S.Stanton/S.Witwer
DATL J.Taylor/M.Lanter
DAWA F.Whitaker/R.Ahmed
DAWQ B.Williams/M.Quinn

2018 Star Wars Stellar Signatures Sketches

STATED ODDS 1:BOX
UNPRICED DUE TO SCARCITY

NNO Carlos Cabaleiro
NNO Kris Penix

2019 Star Wars Stellar Signatures

COMMON AUTO	15.00	40.00

*GREEN/20: UNPRICED DUE TO SCARCITY
*PURPLE/10: UNPRICED DUE TO SCARCITY
*GOLD/5: UNPRICED DUE TO SCARCITY
*BLACK/1: UNPRICED DUE TO SCARCITY

AADR	Adam Driver	125.00	250.00
AAB	Ahmed Best	50.00	100.00
AAT	Alan Tudyk	30.00	75.00
AAE	Alden Ehrenreich	200.00	400.00
AAS	Andy Serkis	30.00	75.00
ABL	Billie Lourd	60.00	120.00
ABDW	Billy Dee Williams	60.00	120.00
ABMY	Bobby Moynihan	25.00	60.00
ADR	Daisy Ridley	300.00	500.00
ADB	David Barclay		
ADT	David Tennant EXCH		
ADGL	Domhnall Gleeson	100.00	200.00
ADFA	Donald Faison	25.00	60.00
ADY	Donnie Yen	50.00	100.00
AEK	Erin Kellyman	50.00	100.00
AEM	Ewan McGregor	500.00	1000.00
AFW	Forest Whitaker	30.00	75.00
AFPJ	Freddie Prinze Jr.	25.00	60.00
AHF	Harrison Ford	600.00	1200.00
AHC	Hayden Christensen	125.00	250.00
AHCO	Hermione Corfield	25.00	60.00
AIM	Ian McDiarmid	100.00	200.00
AJB	Jeremy Bulloch	30.00	75.00
AKMT	Kelly Marie Tran	75.00	150.00
AKB	Kenny Baker	60.00	120.00
ALM	Lars Mikkelsen	50.00	100.00
ALD	Laura Dern	30.00	75.00
AMM	Mads Mikkelsen	75.00	150.00
APB	Paul Bettany	75.00	150.00
APR	Paul Reubens	50.00	100.00
ARP	Ray Park	25.00	60.00
ARA	Riz Ahmed	20.00	50.00
ATC	Tim Curry	20.00	50.00
AWD	Warwick Davis	20.00	50.00

2019 Star Wars Stellar Signatures Dual Autographs

*PURPLE/10: UNPRICED DUE TO SCARCITY
*GOLD/5: UNPRICED DUE TO SCARCITY
*BLACK/1: UNPRICED DUE TO SCARCITY
*ORANGE/1: UNPRICED DUE TO SCARCITY
*RED/1: UNPRICED DUE TO SCARCITY
STATED ODDS 4:BOXED SET
STATED PRINT RUN 25 SER.#'d SETS

DALC	A.Lawrence/H.Corfield		
DAES	A.Eckstein/T.Sircar	30.00	75.00
DABW	B.Williams/J.Bulloch		
DAMW	B.Williams/P.Mayhew		
DARD	D.Ridley/A.Driver		
DAKD	E.Kellyman/W.Davis	60.00	120.00
DAMC	E.McGregor/H.Christensen		
DAFD	H.Ford/A.Driver		
DAMC	I.McDiarmid/H.Christensen		
DATL	J.Taylor/M.Lanter	25.00	60.00
DAIG	J.Isaacs/T.Gray	25.00	60.00
DAMD	L.Mikkelsen/W.Davis	50.00	100.00
DAFT	N.Futterman/J.Taylor	25.00	60.00
DAPB	R.Park/P.Bettany		
DAPW	R.Park/S.Witwer	50.00	100.00
DAWB	S.Witwer/P.Bettany		

2019 Star Wars Stellar Signatures Oversized Sketches

STATED ODDS 1:BOXED SET
UNPRICED DUE TO SCARCITY

NNO Dan Bergren

2019 Star Wars Stellar Signatures Stellar Art Reproduction

COMPLETE SET (100)	750.00	1500.00
COMMON CARD (1-100)	10.00	25.00
STATED ODDS 1:SET PER BOXED SET		

2020 Star Wars Stellar Signatures

COMMON AUTO	25.00	60.00

*BLUE/25: UNPRICED DUE TO SCARCITY
*GREEN/20: UNPRICE DUE TO SCARCITY
*PURPLE/10: UNPRICED DUE TO SCARCITY
*GOLD/5: UNPRICED DUE TO SCARCITY
*GALACTIC BLACK/1: UNPRICED DUE TO SCARCITY
*IMPERIAL RED/1: UNPRICED DUE TO SCARCITY
*REBEL ALLIANCE ORANGE/1: UNPRICED DUE TO SCARCITY
100 TOTAL BOXES WERE PRODUCED

AAB	Ahmed Best	25.00	60.00
AAD	Adam Driver	200.00	400.00
ABB	Ben Burtt	60.00	120.00
ABL	Billie Lourd	60.00	120.00
ACM	Cameron Monaghan	25.00	60.00
ACW	Carl Weathers	200.00	400.00
ADL	Denis Lawson	50.00	100.00
ADM	Dominic Monaghan	25.00	60.00
ADR	Daisy Ridley	500.00	1000.00
ADW	Debra Wilson	25.00	60.00
ADY	Donnie Yen	75.00	150.00
AEM	Ewan McGregor	500.00	1000.00
AES	Emily Swallow	125.00	250.00
AGC	Gina Carano	250.00	500.00
AGE	Giancarlo Esposito	75.00	150.00
AGG	Greg Grunberg	25.00	60.00
AHC	Hayden Christensen	100.00	200.00
AHF	Harrison Ford	1000.00	2000.00
AIM	Ian McDiarmid	100.00	200.00
AJG	Janina Gavankar	500.00	1000.00
AKB	Kenny Baker	75.00	150.00
ALD	Laura Dern EXCH	30.00	75.00
ANA	Naomi Ackie	50.00	100.00
ANN	Nick Nolte	200.00	350.00
AOA	Omid Abtahi	50.00	100.00
APP	Pedro Pascal	750.00	1500.00
ASW	Sam Witwer	50.00	100.00
ATM	Temuera Morrison EXCH	25.00	60.00
ATW	Taika Waititi	200.00	400.00
AWH	Werner Herzog	100.00	200.00
AAE1	Alden Ehrenreich	150.00	300.00
AAE2	Ashley Eckstein	100.00	200.00
AASL	Andy Serkis	50.00	100.00
ABDW	Billy Dee Williams	75.00	150.00
AJBF	Jeremy Bulloch	100.00	200.00
AJSC	Joonas Suotamo	60.00	120.00

2020 Star Wars Stellar Signatures 5x7 Oversized Sketches

UNPRICED DUE TO SCARCITY

NNO Carlos Cabaleiro
NNO Louise Draper

2020 Star Wars Stellar Signatures Dual Autographs

DABP	B.Burtt/M.Pennington
DAFW	H.Ford/B.Williams
DAGM	G.Grunberg/D.Monaghan
DAGT	A.Graves/C.Taber
DAHA	W.Herzog/O.Abtahi
DALE	M.Lanter/A.Eckstein
DAMC	I.McDiarmid/H.Christensen
DAMC	E.McGregor/H.Christensen
DAMM	L.Mikkelsen/M.McGlynn
DAMW	C.Monaghan/D.Wilson
DANC	N.Nolte/G.Carano
DARD	D.Ridley/A.Driver

2020 Star Wars Stellar Signatures Stellar Art Reproduction

COMPLETE SET (100)	500.00	750.00
COMMON CARD (1-100)	6.00	15.00
STATED ODDS 1 SET PER BOX		

2020 Star Wars Stellar Signatures Triple Autographs

TAFET Bulloch/Morrison/Logan
TALMG Lourd/Monaghan/Grunberg
TAOAA Taylor/Lanter/Eckstein

1997 Star Wars Stickers US

COMPLETE SET (66)	7.50	20.00
COMMON CARD (1-66)	.20	.50
PRODUCED BY PANINI		

1997 Star Wars Trilogy The Complete Story

COMPLETE SET (72)	6.00	15.00
COMMON CARD (1-72)	.25	.60
0 Promo	1.00	2.00

1997 Star Wars Trilogy The Complete Story Laser

COMPLETE SET (6)	6.00	15.00
COMMON CARD (LC1-LC6)	1.25	3.00
STATED ODDS 1:9		

1997 Star Wars Trilogy Merlin

COMPLETE SET (125)	10.00	25.00
UNOPENED BOX (48 PACKS)	25.00	40.00
UNOPENED PACK (5 CARDS)	1.00	1.25
COMMON CARD (1-125)	.15	.40

1997 Star Wars Trilogy Merlin Case-Toppers

COMPLETE SET (3)	20.00	50.00
COMMON CARD (P1-P3)	8.00	20.00
STATED ODDS 1:CASE		

1997 Star Wars Trilogy Special Edition

COMPLETE SET (72)	6.00	15.00
UNOPENED BOX (36 PACKS)	80.00	100.00
UNOPENED PACK (9 CARDS)	2.50	3.00
COMMON CARD (1-72)	.15	.40
13D ISSUED AS BOX TOPPER		
13D X-Wings Departing	6.00	15.00

1997 Star Wars Trilogy Special Edition Holograms

COMPLETE SET (2)	10.00	25.00
COMMON CARD (1-2)	6.00	15.00
STATED ODDS 1:18		

1997 Star Wars Trilogy Special Edition Laser

COMPLETE SET (6)	6.00	15.00
COMMON CARD (LC1-LC6)	1.25	3.00
STATED ODDS 1:9		

1997 Star Wars Trilogy Special Edition Promos

COMPLETE SET (8)	10.00	25.00
COMMON CARD (P1-P8)	1.25	3.00
P1 Three Stormtroopers	4.00	10.00
P4 Sandcrawler	3.00	8.00
P5 Jawa and Landspeeder	3.00	8.00
P6 Millennium Falcon	3.00	8.00

1997 Star Wars Trilogy Special Edition Kenner Promos

COMPLETE SET (4)	10.00	25.00
COMMON CARD (H1-H4)	4.00	10.00

1997 Star Wars Trilogy Special Edition Micro Machine Promos

COMPLETE SET (5)	12.00	30.00
COMMON CARD (G1-G5)	4.00	10.00

1997 Star Wars Vehicles

COMPLETE SET (72)	5.00	12.00
UNOPENED BOX (36 PACKS)	40.00	50.00
UNOPENED PACK (5 CARDS)	1.25	1.50
COMMON CARD (1-72)	.15	.40

1997 Star Wars Vehicles 3-D

COMPLETE SET (3)	25.00	60.00
COMMON CARD	8.00	20.00
STATED ODDS 1:36		
3 Princess Leia	15.00	40.00
Luke Skywalker		

1997 Star Wars Vehicles Cut-Away

COMPLETE SET (4)	7.50	20.00
COMMON CARD (C1-C4)	2.50	6.00
STATED ODDS 1:18		

1997 Star Wars Vehicles Promos

P1A Darth Vader & Stormtroopers on Speeder Bikes (chromium)/3200*	12.00	30.00
P1B Darth Vader & Stormtroopers on Speeder Bikes (refractor)/320*	30.00	75.00
P2A Stormtroopers on Speeder Bikes (chromium)/1600*	20.00	50.00
P2B Stormtroopers on Speeder Bikes (refractor)/160*	50.00	100.00
NNO 2-Card Sheet		

2021 Star Wars Visions Episode 1 The Duel

1 The Ronin/665*
2 Prepared for Battle/665*
3 The Ronin, B5-56 & Sullustan Shopkeeper/665*
4 Sith Bandit Leader/665*
5 The Village/665*

2021 Star Wars Visions Episode 2 Tatooine Rhapsody

1 Jay Is a Big Dreamer/501*
2 Jabba the Hutt/501*
3 The Band Prepares to Play/501*
4 Jay, Kurti & Lan/501*
5 Boba Fett in Pursuit/501*

2021 Star Wars Visions Episode 3 The Twins

1 Am Enters the Room/461*
2 Am Is a True Believer in the Dark Side/461*
3 Karre Pushes Against the Dark Purpose/461*
4 The Star Destroyer/461*
5 R-DUO Is a Trusty Companion/461*

2021 Star Wars Visions Episode 4 The Elder

1 Dan & Tajin/539*
2 The Elder/539*
3 Dan & His Lightsaber/539*
4 Showdown/539*
5 The Elder Is Stronger Than He Looks/539*

2021 Star Wars Visions Episode 5 The Village Bride

1 F & Valco/463*
2 F: A Young Jedi/463*
3 Saku & the Villagers/463*
4 Izuma/463*
5 Haru & Asu/463*

2021 Star Wars Visions Episode 6 Akakiri

1 Tsubaki & Masago Battle/484*
2 Tsubaki & Misa/484*
3 Masago & His Army/484*
4 Tsubaki: A Jedi with a Dark Destiny/484*
5 Senshuu & Kamahachi/484*

2021 Star Wars Visions Episode 7 T0-B1

1 The Inquisitor Arrives/517*
2 T0-B1: A Cybernetic Boy/517*
3 Mitaka: A Loving, Protective Scientist/517*
4 Mitaka & T0-B1/517*
5 T0-B1 Dreams of Becoming a Jedi/517*

2021 Star Wars Visions Episode 8 The Ninth Jedi

1 Ethan Summoned by Mysterious Jedi Master/474*
2 Zhima/474*

3 The Warriors Assemble/474*
4 Juro & Roden Clash/474*
5 Juro & Kara/474*

2021 Star Wars Visions Episode 9 Lop and Ocho

1 A Happy Family/466*
2 Lop Training/466*
3 Lop, TD-4 & Yasaburo/466*
4 Lop & TD-4/466*
5 The Encroaching Empire/466*

2017 Star Wars Widevision Bonus Abrams

COMPLETE SET (4)	
COMMON CARD (1-4)	

1 Display Box, 1995
2 Foil Wrapper, 1995
3 Card No.1, 1995
Art By John Berkey
4 Topps Finest Card No. C-1, 1995
Art By Ralph McQuarrie

2015 Star Wars Wrapper Metal Card Set

1 Star Wars Series 1 C-3PO
2 Star Wars Series 2 Darth Vader
3 Star Wars Series 3 R2-D2
4 Star Wars Series 4 Luke and Obi-Wan
5 Star Wars Series 5 X-Wing Fighter
6 Empire Strikes Back Series 1 Darth Vader Red
7 Empire Strikes Back Series 2 Darth Vader Blue
8 Empire Strikes Back Series 3 Darth Vader Yellow
9 Return of the Jedi Series 1 Darth Vader
10 Return of the Jedi Series 1 Jabba the Hutt
11 Return of the Jedi Series 1 Luke Skywalker
12 Return of the Jedi Series 1 Wicket
13 Return of the Jedi Series 2 C-3PO
14 Return of the Jedi Series 2 Lando Calrissian
15 Return of the Jedi Series 2 Princess Leia

1999 Star Wars X-Wing Rogue Squadron

COMMON CARD	2.50	6.00

2020 Women of Star Wars

COMPLETE SET (100)	8.00	20.00
COMMON CARD (1-100)	.20	.50
*ORANGE: .5X TO 1.2X BASIC CARDS		
*BLUE: .6X TO 1.5X BASIC CARDS		
*GREEN/99: 4X TO 10X BASIC CARDS		
*PURPLE/25: 8X TO 20X BASIC CARDS		
*BLACK/5: UNPRICED DUE TO SCARCITY		
*RED/1: UNPRICED DUE TO SCARCITY		
*P.P.BLACK/1: UNPRICED DUE TO SCARCITY		
*P.P.CYAN/1: UNPRICED DUE TO SCARCITY		
*P.P.MAGENTA/1: UNPRICED DUE TO SCARCITY		
*P.P.YELLOW/1: UNPRICED DUE TO SCARCITY		

2020 Women of Star Wars Autographs

COMMON AUTO	4.00	10.00
*ORANGE/99: .5X TO 1.2X BASIC AUTOS		
*BLUE/50: .6X TO 1.5X BASIC AUTOS		
*PURPLE/25: .75X TO 2X BASIC AUTOS		
*BLACK/5: UNPRICED DUE TO SCARCITY		
*RED/1: UNPRICED DUE TO SCARCITY		
*P.P.BLACK/1: UNPRICED DUE TO SCARCITY		
*P.P.CYAN/1: UNPRICED DUE TO SCARCITY		

*P.P.MAGENTA/1: UNPRICED DUE TO SCARCITY
*P.P.YELLOW/1: UNPRICED DUE TO SCARCITY
STATED ODDS 1:14

AAA Amy Allen	10.00	25.00
AAF Anna Francolini	5.00	12.00
AAG Anna Graves	5.00	12.00
AAP Angelique Perrin	6.00	15.00
ACC Crystal Clarke	5.00	12.00
ACL Charlotte Louise	5.00	12.00
ACT Catherine Taber	5.00	12.00
AJD Julie Dolan	5.00	12.00
AJK Jaime King	8.00	20.00
ALC Lily Cole	5.00	12.00
ALW Leeanna Walsman	8.00	20.00
AML Misty Lee	6.00	15.00
AMV Myrna Velasco	6.00	15.00
ANC Nazneen Contractor	5.00	12.00
AOS Orli Shoshan	8.00	20.00
ATS Tiya Sircar	10.00	25.00

2020 Women of Star Wars Autographs Blue

STATED PRINT RUN 50 SER.#'d SETS

AAH Amanda Hale	8.00	20.00
AJH Jessica Henwick	12.00	30.00
AMB Michonne Bourriague	12.00	30.00
ANF Nika Futterman	15.00	40.00
ASM Suzie McGrath	6.00	15.00
AVR Vinette Robinson	10.00	25.00

2020 Women of Star Wars Autographs Orange

STATED PRINT RUN 99 SER.#'d SETS

AAB Anna Brewster	6.00	15.00
ADW Debra Wilson	10.00	25.00
AEK Erin Kellyman	15.00	40.00
AHC Hermione Corfield	12.00	30.00
AJG Janina Gavankar	15.00	40.00
AVM Vanessa Marshall	10.00	25.00

2020 Women of Star Wars Autographs Purple

STATED PRINT RUN 25 SER.#'d SETS

AAE Ashley Eckstein	50.00	100.00
ACB Caroline Blakiston	20.00	50.00
ANA Naomi Ackie	60.00	120.00
AGCM Gina Carano	200.00	400.00
AKCH Keisha Castle-Hughes	25.00	60.00

2020 Women of Star Wars Dual Autographs

*PURPLE/25: UNPRICED DUE TO SCARCITY
*BLACK/5 UNPRICED DUE TO SCARCITY
*RED/1: UNPRICED DUE TO SCARCITY

DAAS A.Allen/O.Shoshan
DADL L.Dern/A.Lawrence
DADS O.d'Abo/M.Salenger
DAEF A.Eckstein/N.Futterman
DAHC J.Henwick/H.Corfield
DAJK F.Jones/V.Kane
DALA B.Lourd/N.Ackie
DAMS V.Marshall/T.Sircar
DART D.Ridley/K.Tran
DASL S.Smart/C.Louise
DATN K.Tran/V.Ngo
DAVM M.Velasco/S.McGrath

2020 Women of Star Wars Iconic Moments

COMPLETE SET (22)	12.00	30.00
COMMON CARD (IM1-IM22)	1.25	3.00
*GREEN/99: .6X TO 1.5X BASIC CARDS		
*PURPLE/25: 1.2X TO 3X BASIC CARDS		
*BLACK/5: UNPRICED DUE TO SCARCITY		
*RED/1: UNPRICED DUE TO SCARCITY		

*P.P.BLACK/1: UNPRICED DUE TO SCARCITY
*P.P.CYAN/1: UNPRICED DUE TO SCARCITY
*P.P.MAGENTA/1: UNPRICED DUE TO SCARCITY
*P.P.YELLOW/1: UNPRICED DUE TO SCARCITY

2020 Women of Star Wars Journey of Leia Organa

COMPLETE SET (8)	10.00	25.00
COMMON CARD (JL1-JL8)	1.50	4.00

*P.P.BLACK/1: UNPRICED DUE TO SCARCITY
*P.P.CYAN/1: UNPRICED DUE TO SCARCITY
*P.P.MAGENTA/1: UNPRICED DUE TO SCARCITY
*P.P.YELLOW/1: UNPRICED DUE TO SCARCITY
STATED ODDS 1:7

2020 Women of Star Wars Panoramic Sketches

NNO Alex Mines
NNO Andrew Fry
NNO Anil Sharma
NNO Anthony Skubis
NNO Ashlee Brienzo Lentini
NNO Ashleigh Popplewell
NNO Ashley Marsh
NNO Ashley Villers
NNO Brad Hudson
NNO Caleb King
NNO Can Baran
NNO Candice Dailey
NNO Carlos Cabaleiro
NNO Chris Kay
NNO Chris Meeks
NNO Clara Bujtor
NNO Cyrus Sherkat
NNO Dan Gorman
NNO Dan Tearle
NNO Darrin Pepe
NNO Dawn Murphy
NNO Elfie Lebouleux
NNO Eric Lehtonen
NNO Frank Kadar
NNO Huy Truong
NNO Ingrid Hardy
NNO Jake Minor
NNO Jamie Murdock
NNO Jason Davies
NNO Jason Sobol
NNO Jay Manchand
NNO Jessica Hickman
NNO Jim Mehsling
NNO Joe Corroney
NNO Kaela Croft
NNO Kayla Wright
NNO Laura Martin
NNO Lee Lightfoot
NNO Lindsey Greyling
NNO Maggie Ransom
NNO Mai Irving
NNO Marcia Dye
NNO Marsha Parkins
NNO Matt Stewart
NNO Matthew Hirons
NNO Matthew Sutton
NNO Mayumi Seto
NNO Michael Mastermaker
NNO Michelle Rayner
NNO Miranda Gainey

NNO Mohammad Jilani
NNO Patricio Carrasco
NNO Phillip Trujillo
NNO Rebecca Sharp
NNO Rich Molinelli
NNO Rob Teranishi
NNO Robert Hendrickson
NNO Ryan Finley
NNO Stephanie Swanger
NNO Thomas Amici
NNO Tim Shinn
NNO Trent Westbrook
NNO Veronica Smith
NNO Zach Woolsey

2020 Women of Star Wars Powerful Pairs

COMPLETE SET (28)	15.00	40.00
COMMON CARD (PP1-PP28)	.75	2.00

*GREEN/99: .6X TO 1.5X BASIC CARDS
*PURPLE/25: 1.2X TO 3X BASIC CARDS
*BLACK/5: UNPRICED DUE TO SCARCITY
*RED/1: UNPRICED DUE TO SCARCITY
*P.P.BLACK/1: UNPRICED DUE TO SCARCITY
*P.P.CYAN/1: UNPRICED DUE TO SCARCITY
*P.P.MAGENTA/1: UNPRICED DUE TO SCARCITY
*P.P.YELLOW/1: UNPRICED DUE TO SCARCITY
STATED ODDS 1:3

2020 Women of Star Wars Sketches

NNO Alex Mines
NNO Andrew Fry
NNO Anil Sharma
NNO Anthony Skubis
NNO Ashlee Brienzo Lentini
NNO Ashleigh Popplewell
NNO Ashley Marsh
NNO Ashley Villers
NNO Brad Hudson
NNO Caleb King
NNO Can Baran
NNO Candice Dailey
NNO Carlos Cabaleiro
NNO Chris Kay
NNO Chris Meeks
NNO Clara Bujtor
NNO Cyrus Sherkat
NNO Dan Gorman
NNO Dan Tearle
NNO Darrin Pepe
NNO Dawn Murphy

NNO Elfie Lebouleux
NNO Eric Lehtonen
NNO Frank Kadar
NNO Huy Truong
NNO Ingrid Hardy
NNO Jake Minor
NNO Jamie Murdock
NNO Jason Davies
NNO Jason Sobol
NNO Jay Manchand
NNO Jessica Hickman
NNO Jim Mehsling
NNO Joe Corroney
NNO Kaela Croft
NNO Kayla Wright
NNO Laura Martin
NNO Lee Lightfoot
NNO Lindsey Greyling
NNO Maggie Ransom
NNO Mai Irving
NNO Marcia Dye
NNO Marsha Parkins
NNO Matt Stewart
NNO Matthew Hirons
NNO Matthew Sutton
NNO Mayumi Seto
NNO Michael Mastermaker
NNO Michelle Rayner
NNO Miranda Gainey
NNO Mohammad Jilani
NNO Patricio Carrasco
NNO Phillip Trujillo
NNO Rebecca Sharp
NNO Rich Molinelli
NNO Rob Teranishi
NNO Robert Hendrickson
NNO Ryan Finley
NNO Stephanie Swanger
NNO Thomas Amici
NNO Tim Shinn
NNO Trent Westbrook
NNO Veronica Smith
NNO Zach Woolsey

2020 Women of Star Wars Triple Autographs

*RED/1: UNPRICED DUE TO SCARCITY

NNO Allen/d'Abo/Futterman
NNO Fisher/Jones/Ridley
NNO Ridley/Tran/Lourd
NNO Dern/Lawrence/Lourd
NNO Velasco/McGrath/McGlynn
NNO Gellar/Eckstein/Sircar

2020 Women of Star Wars Weapon of Choice

COMPLETE SET (24)	12.00	30.00
COMMON CARD (WC1-WC24)	1.00	2.50

*GREEN/99: .6X TO 1.5X BASIC CARDS
*PURPLE/25: 1.5X TO 4X BASIC CARDS
*BLACK/5: UNPRICED DUE TO SCARCITY
*RED/1: UNPRICED DUE TO SCARCITY
*P.P.BLACK/1: UNPRICED DUE TO SCARCITY
*P.P.CYAN/1: UNPRICED DUE TO SCARCITY
*P.P.MAGENTA/1: UNPRICED DUE TO SCARCITY
*P.P.YELLOW/1: UNPRICED DUE TO SCARCITY

TCG

1995 Star Wars Premiere

COMPLETE SET (324)	75.00	150.00
BOOSTER BOX (36 PACKS)	75.00	150.00
BOOSTER PACK (15 CARDS)	3.00	6.00
RELEASED IN DECEMBER 1995		
1 5D6-RA-7 (Fivedesix) R1	2.00	4.00
2 Admiral Motti R2	1.25	2.50
3 Chief Bast U1	.50	1.00
4 Colonel Wullf Yularen U1	.50	1.00
5 Commander Praji U2	.50	1.00
6 Darth Vader R1	.50	1.00
7 Dathcha U1	5.00	10.00
8 Death Star Trooper C2	15.00	30.00
9 Djas Puhr R2	.50	1.00
10 Dr. Evazan R2	.20	.40
11 DS-61-2 U1	1.25	2.50
12 DS-61-3 R1	1.25	2.50
13 EG-6 (Eegee-Six) U2	.50	1.00
14 Feltipern Trevagg U1	.50	1.00
15 Garindan R2	1.25	2.50
16 General Tagge R2	1.25	2.50
17 Grand Moff Tarkin R1	5.00	10.00
18 Imperial Pilot C2	.20	.40
19 Imperial Trooper Guard C2	.20	.40
20 Jawa DARK C2	.20	.40
21 Kitik Keedlkak R1	2.00	4.00
22 Labria R2	.20	.40
23 Lieutenant Tanbris U2	1.25	2.50
24 LIN-V8M (Elleyein-Veeateemm) C1	.50	1.00
25 Miiiyoom Onith U2	.50	1.00
26 MSE-6 ëMousei Droid U1	.50	1.00
27 Myo R2	1.25	2.50
28 Ponda Baba U1	.50	1.00
29 Prophetess U1	.50	1.00
30 R1-G4 (Arone-Geefour) C2	.20	.40

31 R4-M9 (Arfour-Emmnine) C2	.20	.40
32 Stormtrooper C3	.20	.40
33 Tonnika Sisters R1	2.00	4.00
34 Tusken Raider C2	.20	.40
35 WED-9-M1 ëBanthaí Droid R2	1.25	2.50
36 Wuher U2	.50	1.00
37 Blaster Scope U1	.50	1.00
38 Caller DARK U2	.50	1.00
39 Comlink C1	.20	.40
40 Droid Detector C2	.20	.40
41 Fusion Generator Supply Tanks DARK C2	.20	.40
42 Observation Holocam U2	.50	1.00
43 Restraining Bolt DARK C2	.20	.40
44 Stormtrooper Backpack C2	.20	.40
45 Stormtrooper Utility Belt C2	.20	.40
46 A Disturbance In The Force U1	.50	1.00
47 Baniss Keeg C2	.20	.40
48 Blast Door Controls U2	.50	1.00
49 Blaster Rack U1	.50	1.00
50 Dark Hours U2	.50	1.00
51 Death Star Sentry U1	.50	1.00
52 Disarmed DARK R1	2.00	4.00
53 Expand The Empire R1	2.00	4.00
54 Fear Will Keep Them In Line R2	1.25	2.50
55 I Find Your Lack Of Faith Disturbing R1	2.00	4.00
56 live Lost Artoo! U1	.50	1.00
57 Jawa Pack U1	.50	1.00
58 Juri Juice R2	1.25	2.50
59 Ket Maliss C2	.20	.40
60 Lateral Damage R2	1.25	2.50
61 Luke? Luuuuke! U1	.50	1.00
62 Macroscan C2	.20	.40
63 Molator R1	2.00	4.00
64 Organaís Ceremonial Necklace R1	2.00	4.00
65 Presence Of The Force R1	2.00	4.00
66 Reactor Terminal U2	.50	1.00
67 Send A Detachment Down R1	2.00	4.00
68 Sunsdown U1	.50	1.00
69 Tactical Re-Call R2	1.25	2.50
70 Wrong Turn U1	.50	1.00
71 Your Eyes Can Deceive You U1	2.00	4.00
72 Alter DARK U1	.50	1.00
73 Boring Conversation Anyway R1	2.00	4.00
74 Charming To The Last R2	1.25	2.50
75 Collateral Damage C2	.20	.40
76 Counter Assault C1	.20	.40
77 Dark Collaboration R1	2.00	4.00
78 Dark Jedi Presence R1	6.00	12.00
79 Dark Maneuvers C2	.20	.40
80 Dead Jawa C2	.20	.40
81 Elis Helrot U2	.50	1.00
82 Emergency Deployment U1	.50	1.00
83 Evacuate? U2	.50	1.00
84 Full Scale Alert U2	.50	1.00
85 Gravel Storm U2	.50	1.00

86 I Have You Now R2	1.25	2.50
87 I've Got A Problem Here C2	.20	.40
88 Imperial Reinforcements C1	.20	.40
89 Imperial Code Cylinder C2	.20	.40
90 It's Worse C2	.20	.40
91 Imperial Barrier DARK C2	.20	.40
92 Kintan Strider C1	.20	.40
93 Limited Resources U2	.50	1.00
94 Local Trouble R1	2.00	4.00
95 Lone Pilot R2	1.25	2.50
96 Lone Warrior R2	1.25	2.50
97 Look Sir, Droids R1	2.00	4.00
98 Moment Of Triumph R2	1.25	2.50
99 Nevar Yalnal R2	1.25	2.50
100 Ommni Box C2	.20	.40
101 Overload C2	.20	.40
102 Physical Choke R1	2.00	4.00
103 Precise Attack C2	.20	.40
104 Scanning Crew C2	.20	.40
105 Sense DARK U1	.50	1.00
106 Set For Stun C2	.20	.40
107 Takeel C2	.20	.40
108 Tallon Roll C2	.20	.40
109 The Circle Is Now Complete R1	2.00	4.00
110 The Empireís Back U1	.50	1.00
111 Trinto Duaba U1	.50	1.00
112 Trooper Charge U2	.50	1.00
113 Tusken Scavengers C2	.20	.40
114 Utinni! DARK R1	2.00	4.00
115 Vaderís Eye R1	2.00	4.00
116 Weíre All Gonna Be A Lot Thinner! R1	2.00	4.00
117 You Overestimate Their Chances C1	.50	1.00
118 Your Powers Are Weak, Old Man R1	.20	.40
119 Alderaan DARK R1	2.00	4.00
120 Dantooine DARK U1	.50	1.00
121 Death Star: Central Core U2	.50	1.00
122 Death Star: Detention Block Corridor C1	.20	.40
123 Death Star: Docking Bay 327 DARK C2	.20	.40
124 Death Star: Level 4 Military Corridor U1	.50	1.00
125 Death Star: War Room U2	.50	1.00
126 Kessel U2	1.25	2.50
127 Tatooine DARK C2	.20	.40
128 Tatooine: Cantina DARK R2	1.25	2.50
129 Tatooine: Docking Bay 94 DARK C2	.20	.40
130 Tatooine: Jawa Camp DARK C1	.20	.40
131 Tatooine: Jundland Wastes C1	.20	.40
132 Tatooine: Larsi Moisture Farm DARK C1	.20	.40
133 Tatooine: Mos Eisley DARK C1	.20	.40
134 Yavin 4 DARK C2	.20	.40
135 Yavin 4: Docking Bay DARK C2	.20	.40
136 Yavin 4: Jungle DARK U2	.50	1.00
137 Black 2 R1	4.00	8.00
138 Black 3 U1	.50	1.00
139 Devastator R1	4.00	8.00
140 Imperial-Class Star Destroyer U1	1.25	2.50

141	TIE Advanced x1 U2	.50	1.00
142	TIE Fighter C2	.20	.40
143	TIE Scout C2	.20	.40
144	Vader's Custom TIE R1	6.00	12.00
145	Bantha U2	.50	1.00
146	Lift Tube DARK C2	.20	.40
147	Sandcrawler DARK R2	1.25	2.50
148	Ubrikkian 9000 Z001 C2	.20	.40
149	Assault Rifle R2	1.25	2.50
150	Blaster Rifle DARK C1	.20	.40
151	Boosted TIE Cannon U1	.50	1.00
152	Dark Jedi Lightsaber U1	.60	1.25
153	Gaderffii Stick C2	.20	.40
154	Han Seeker R2	1.25	2.50
155	Imperial Blaster DARK C2	.20	.40
156	Ion Cannon U1	.50	1.00
157	Laser Projector U2	.50	1.00
158	Light Repeating Blaster Rifle R1	2.00	4.00
159	Luke Seeker R2	1.25	2.50
160	Timer Mine DARK C2	.20	.40
161	Turbolaser Battery R2	1.25	2.50
162	Vader's Lightsaber R1	5.00	10.00
163	2X-3KPR (Tooex) U1	.50	1.00
164	Beru Lars U2	.50	1.00
165	Biggs Darklighter R2	1.25	2.50
166	BoShek U1	.50	1.00
167	C-3PO (See-Threepio) R1	5.00	10.00
168	CZ-3 (Seezee-Three) C1	.20	.40
169	Dice Ibegon R2	1.25	2.50
170	Dutch R1	4.00	8.00
171	Figrin D'an U2	.50	1.00
172	General Dodonna U1	.50	1.00
173	Han Solo R1	7.50	15.00
174	Jawa LIGHT C2	.20	.40
175	Jek Porkins U1	.50	1.00
176	Kabe U1	.50	1.00
177	Kal'Falnl C'ndros R1	2.00	4.00
178	Leesub Sirln R2	.20	.40
179	Leia Organa R1	1.25	2.50
180	LIN-V8K (Elleyein-Veeatekay) C1	6.00	12.00
181	Luke Skywalker R1	10.00	20.00
182	Momaw Nadon U2	.50	1.00
183	Obi-Wan Kenobi R1	6.00	12.00
184	Owen Lars U1	.50	1.00
185	Pops U1	.50	1.00
186	R2-X2 (Artoo-Extoo) C2	.20	.40
187	R4-E1 (Arfour-Eeone) C2	.20	.40
188	Rebel Guard C2	.20	.40
189	Rebel Pilot C2	.20	.40
190	Rebel Trooper C3	.20	.40
191	Red Leader R1	4.00	8.00
192	Shistavanen Wolfman C2	.20	.40
193	Talz C2	.20	.40
194	WED-9-M1 'Bantha' Droid R2	1.25	2.50
195	Wioslea U1	.50	1.00
196	Caller LIGHT U2	.50	1.00
197	Electrobinoculars C2	.20	.40
198	Fusion Generator Supply Tanks LIGHT C2	.20	.40
199	Hydroponics Station U2	.50	1.00
200	Restraining Bolt LIGHT C2	.20	.40
201	Targeting Computer U1	.50	1.00
202	Tatooine Utility Belt C2	.20	.40
203	Vaporator C2	.20	.40
204	A Tremor In The Force U1	.50	1.00
205	Affect Mind R1	2.00	4.00
206	Beggar R1	2.00	4.00
207	Crash Site Memorial U1	.50	1.00
208	Death Star Plans R1	2.00	4.00
209	Demotion R2	1.25	2.50
210	Disarmed Light R1	2.00	4.00
211	Ellorrs Madak C2	.20	.40
212	Eyes In The Dark U1	.50	1.00
213	Jawa Siesta U1	.50	1.00
214	Kessel LIGHT U2	2.00	4.00
215	K'lor'slug R1	.50	1.00
216	Lightsaber Proficiency R1	2.00	4.00
217	Mantellian Savrip R2	1.25	2.50
218	Nightfall U1	.50	1.00
219	Obi-Wan's Cape R1	2.00	4.00
220	Our Most Desperate Hour R1	2.00	4.00
221	Plastoid Armor U2	.20	.40
222	Rebel Planners R2	1.25	2.50
223	Restricted Deployment U1	.50	1.00
224	Revolution R1	2.00	4.00
225	Rycar Ryjerd U1	.50	1.00
226	Saiitorr Kal Fas C2	.20	.40
227	Special Modifications U1	.50	1.00
228	Traffic Control U2	.50	1.00
229	Tusken Breath Mask U1	.50	1.00
230	Yavin Sentry U2	.50	1.00
231	Yerka Mig U1	.20	.40
232	A Few Maneuvers C2	.20	.40
233	Alter LIGHT U1	.50	1.00
234	Beru Stew U2	.50	1.00
235	Cantina Brawl R1	2.00	4.00
236	Collision! C2	.20	.40
237	Combined Attack C2	.20	.40
238	Don't Get Cocky R1	2.00	4.00
239	Don't Underestimate Our Chances C1	.20	.40
240	Droid Shutdown C2	.20	.40
241	Escape Pod U2	.50	1.00
242	Friendly Fire C2	.20	.40
243	Full Throttle R2	1.25	2.50
244	Gift Of The Mentor R1	2.00	4.00
245	Han's Back U2	.50	1.00
246	Han's Dice C2	.20	.40
247	Hear Me Baby, Hold Together C2	.20	.40
248	Help Me Obi-Wan Kenobi R1	2.00	4.00
249	How Did We Get Into This Mess? U2	.50	1.00
250	Hyper Escape C2	.20	.40
251	I've Got A Bad Feeling About This C2	.20	.40
252	It Could Be Worse C2	1.25	2.50
253	Into The Garbage Chute, Flyboy R2	.20	.40
254	Jedi Presence R1	2.00	4.00
255	Krayt Dragon Howl R1	2.00	4.00
256	Leia's Back U2	.50	1.00
257	Luke's Back U2	.50	1.00
258	Move Along... R1	2.00	4.00
259	Nabrun Leids U2	.50	1.00
260	Narrow Escape C2	.20	.40
261	Noble Sacrifice R2	1.25	2.50
262	Old Ben C2	.20	.40
263	On The Edge R2	1.25	2.50
264	Out Of Nowhere U2	.50	1.00
265	Panic U1	.50	1.00
266	Radar Scanner C2	.20	.40
267	Rebel Barrier C2	.20	.40
268	Rebel Reinforcements C1	.20	.40
269	Return Of A Jedi U2	.50	1.00
270	Scomp Link Access C2	.20	.40
271	Sense LIGHT U1	.50	1.00
272	Skywalkers R1	2.00	4.00
273	Solo Han R2	1.25	2.50
274	Spaceport Speeders U2	.50	1.00
275	Surprise Assault C1	.20	.40
276	Thank The Maker R2	1.25	2.50
277	The Bith Shuffle C2	.20	.40
278	The Force Is Strong With This One R2	1.25	2.50
279	This Is All Your Fault U1	.50	1.00
280	Utinni! LIGHT R1	2.00	4.00
281	Warrior's Courage R2	1.25	2.50
282	We're Doomed C2	.20	.40
283	Alderaan LIGHT U2	1.25	2.50
284	Dantooine LIGHT U1	.50	1.00
285	Death Star: Detention Block Control Room U2	.50	1.00
286	Death Star: Docking Bay 327 LIGHT C2	.20	.40
287	Death Star: Trash Compactor U1	.50	1.00
288	Kessel LIGHT U2	.50	1.00
289	Tatooine LIGHT C2	.20	.40
290	Tatooine: Cantina LIGHT R2	1.25	2.50
291	Tatooine: Docking Bay 94 LIGHT C2	.20	.40
292	Tatooine: Dune Sea C1	.20	.40
293	Tatooine: Jawa Camp LIGHTC1	.20	.40
294	Tatooine: Larsi Moisture Farm LIGHT U2	.50	1.00
295	Tatooine: Mos Eisley LIGHT C1	.20	.40
296	Tatooine: Obi-Wan's Hut R1	2.00	4.00
297	Yavin 4: LIGHT C2	.20	.40
298	Yavin 4: Docking Bay LIGHT C1	.20	.40
299	Yavin 4: Jungle LIGHT C2	2.00	4.00
300	Yavin 4: Massassi Throne Room R1	.50	1.00
301	Yavin 4: Massassi War Room U2	.50	1.00
302	Corellian Corvette U2	.60	1.25
303	Gold 1 R2	1.25	2.50
304	Gold 5 R2	1.25	2.50
305	Millenium Falcon R1	5.00	10.00
306	Red 1 U1	.50	1.00
307	Red 3 R2	1.25	2.50
308	X-wing C2	.20	.40
309	Y-wing C2	.20	.40
310	Lift Tube LIGHT C2	.20	.40
311	Luke's X-34 Landspeeder U2	.50	1.00
312	Sandcrawler LIGHT R2	1.25	2.50
313	SoroSuub V-35 Landspeeder C2	.20	.40
314	Blaster C2	.20	.40
315	Blaster Rifle LIGHT C2	.20	.40
316	Han's Heavy Blaster Pistol R2	1.25	2.50
317	Jedi Lightsaber U1	.50	1.00
318	Leia's Sporting Blaster U1	.50	1.00
319	Obi-Wan's Lightsaber R1	4.00	8.00
320	Proton Torpedoes C2	.20	.40
321	Quad Laser Cannon U1	.50	1.00
322	Tagge Seeker R2	1.25	2.50
323	Tarkin Seeker R2	1.25	2.50
324	Timer Mine LIGHT C2	.20	.40

1996 Star Wars Hoth

	COMPLETE SET (163)	50.00	100.00
	BOOSTER BOX (36 PACKS)	50.00	100.00
	BOOSTER PACK (15 CARDS)	2.00	4.00
	RELEASED IN NOVEMBER 1996		
1	AT-AT Driver C2	.20	.40

2 Admiral Ozzel R1	2.00	4.00
3 Captain Lennox U1	.60	1.25
4 Captain Piett R2	2.00	4.00
5 FX-10 (Effex-ten) C2	.20	.40
6 General Veers R1	5.00	10.00
7 Imperial Gunner C2	.20	.40
8 Lieutenant Cabbel U2	.60	1.25
9 Probe Droid C2	.20	.40
10 Snowtrooper C3	.20	.40
11 Snowtrooper Officer C1	.20	.40
12 Wampa R2	2.00	4.00
13 Deflector Shield Generators U2	.60	1.25
14 Evacuation Control U1	.60	1.25
15 Portable Fusion Generator C2	.20	.40
16 Probe Antennae U2	.60	1.25
17 Breached Defenses U2	.60	1.25
18 Death Mark R1	2.00	4.00
19 Death Squadron U1	.60	1.25
20 Frostbite LIGHT C2	.20	.40
21 Frozen Dinner R1	2.00	4.00
22 High Anxiety R1	2.00	4.00
23 Ice Storm LIGHT U1	.60	1.25
24 Image Of The Dark Lord R2	2.00	4.00
25 Imperial Domination U1	.60	1.25
26 Meteor Impact? R1	2.00	4.00
27 Mournful Roar R1	2.00	4.00
28 Responsibility Of Command R1	2.00	4.00
29 Silence Is Golden U2	.60	1.25
30 The Shield Doors Must Be Closed U1	.60	1.25
31 This Is Just Wrong R1	2.00	4.00
32 Too Cold For Speeders U1	.60	1.25
33 Weapon Malfunction R1	2.00	4.00
34 Target The Main Generator R2	2.00	4.00
35 A Dark Time For The Rebellion C1	.20	.40
36 Cold Feet C2	.20	.40
37 Collapsing Corridor R2	2.00	4.00
38 ComScan Detection C2	.20	.40
39 Crash Landing U1	.60	1.25
40 Debris Zone R2	2.00	4.00
41 Direct Hit U1	.60	1.25
42 Exhaustion U2	.60	1.25
43 Exposure U1	.60	1.25
44 Furry Fury R2	2.00	4.00
45 He Hasn't Come Back Yet C2	.20	.40
46 I'd Just As Soon Kiss A Wookiee C2	.20	.40
47 Imperial Supply C1	.20	.40
48 Lightsaber Deficiency U1	.60	1.25
49 Oh, Switch Off C2	.20	.40
50 Our First Catch Of The Day C2	.20	.40
51 Probe Telemetry C2	.20	.40
52 Scruffy-Looking Nerf Herder R2	2.00	4.00
53 Self-Destruct Mechanism U1	.60	1.25
54 Stop Motion C2	.20	.40
55 Tactical Support R2	2.00	4.00
56 That's It, The Rebels Are There! U2	.60	1.25
57 Trample R1	2.00	4.00
58 Turn It Off! Turn It Off! C1	.20	.40
59 Walker Barrage U1	.60	1.25
60 Wall Of Fire U1	.60	1.25
61 Yaggle Gakkle R2	2.00	4.00
62 Hoth DARK U2	.60	1.25
63 Hoth: Defensive Perimeter LIGHT C2	.20	.40
64 Hoth: Echo Command Center U1	.60	1.25
65 Hoth: Echo Corridor DARK U2	.60	1.25
66 Hoth: Echo Docking Bay LIGHT C2	.20	.40
67 Hoth: Ice Plains C2	.20	.40
68 Hoth: North Ridge LIGHT U2	.20	.40
69 Hoth: Wampa Cave R2	2.00	4.00
70 Ord Mantell LIGHT U2	.60	1.25
71 Stalker R1	6.00	12.00

72 Tyrant R1	5.00	10.00
73 Blizzard 1 R1	4.00	8.00
74 Blizzard 2 R2	2.00	4.00
75 Blizzard Scout 1 R1	4.00	8.00
76 Blizzard Walker U2	.60	1.25
77 AT-AT Cannon U1	.60	1.25
78 Echo Base Operations R2	2.00	4.00
79 Infantry Mine LIGHT C2	.20	.40
80 Probe Droid Laser U2	.60	1.25
81 Vehicle Mine LIGHT C2	.20	.40
82 2-1B (Too-Onebee) R1	2.00	4.00
83 Cal Alder U2	.60	1.25
84 Commander Luke Skywalker R1	10.00	20.00
85 Dack Ralter R2	2.00	4.00
86 Derek 'Hobbie' Klivian U1	.60	1.25
87 Electro-Rangefinder U1	.60	1.25
88 Echo Base Trooper Officer C1	.20	.40
89 Echo Trooper Backpack C2	.20	.40
90 FX-7 (Effex-Seven) C2	.20	.40
91 General Carlist Rieekan R2	2.00	4.00
92 Jeroen Webb U1	.60	1.25
93 K-3PO (Kay-Threepio) R1	2.00	4.00
94 Major Bren Derlin R2	2.00	4.00
95 R2 Sensor Array C2	.20	.40
96 R5-M2 (Arfive-Emmtoo) C2	.20	.40
97 Rebel Scout C1	.20	.40
98 Rogue Gunner C2	.20	.40
99 Romas Lock Navander U2	.60	1.25
100 Shawn Valdez U1	.60	1.25
101 Tamizander Rey U2	.60	1.25
102 Tauntaun Handler C2	.20	.40
103 Tigran Jamiro U1	.60	1.25
104 Toryn Farr U1	.60	1.25
105 WED-1016 'Techie' Droid C1	.20	.40
106 Wes Janson R2	2.00	4.00
107 Wyron Serper U2	.60	1.25
108 Zev Senesca R2	2.00	4.00
109 Artillery Remote R2	2.00	4.00
110 EG-4 (Eegee-Four) C1	.20	.40
111 Hoth LIGHT U2	.60	1.25
112 R-3PO (Ar-Threepio) DARK R2	2.00	4.00
112 R-3PO (Ar-Threepio) LIGHT R2	2.00	4.00
113 Bacta Tank R2	3.00	6.00
114 Disarming Creature R1	2.00	4.00
115 Echo Base Trooper C3	.20	.40
116 E-web Blaster C1	.20	.40
117 Frostbite DARK C2	.20	.40
118 Ice Storm DARK U1	.60	1.25
119 Tauntaun Bones U1	.60	1.25
120 The First Transport Is Away! R1	2.00	4.00
121 Attack Pattern Delta U1	.60	1.25
122 Dark Dissension R1	2.00	4.00
123 Fall Back! C2	.20	.40
124 I Thought They Smelled Bad C2	2.00	4.00
125 It Can Wait C2	.20	.40
126 Lucky Shot U1	.60	1.25
127 Nice Of You Guys To Drop By C2	.20	.40
128 One More Pass U1	.60	1.25
129 Perimeter Scan C2	.20	.40
130 Rug Hug R1	2.00	4.00
131 Under Attack U1	.60	1.25
132 Walker Sighting U2	.60	1.25
133 Who's Scruffy-Looking? R1	2.00	4.00
134 You Have Failed Me	2.00	4.00
135 You Will Go To The Dagobah System R1	2.00	4.00
136 Hoth Survival Gear C2	.20	.40
137 Hoth: Defensive Perimeter DARK C2	.20	.40
138 Hoth: Echo Command Center	.60	1.25
139 Hoth: Echo Corridor LIGHT C2	.20	.40
140 Hoth: Echo Docking Bay DARK C2	.20	.40

141 Hoth: Echo Med Lab C2	.20	.40
142 Hoth: Main Power Generators U2	.60	1.25
143 Hoth: North Ridge DARK C2	.20	.40
144 Hoth: Snow Trench C2	.20	.40
145 Ord Mantell DARK C2	.20	.40
146 Medium Transport U2	.60	1.25
147 Rogue 1 R1	4.00	8.00
148 Rogue 2 R2	2.00	4.00
149 Rogue 3 R1	4.00	8.00
150 Snowspeeder U2	.60	1.25
151 Tauntaun C2	.20	.40
152 Anakin's Lightsaber R1	10.00	20.00
153 Atgar Laser Cannon U2	.60	1.25
154 Concussion Grenade R1	2.00	4.00
155 Dual Laser Cannon U1	.60	1.25
156 Golan Laser Battery U1	.60	1.25
157 Infantry Mine DARK C2	.20	.40
158 Medium Repeating Blaster Cannon C1	.20	.40
159 Planet Defender Ion Cannon R2	2.00	4.00
160 Power Harpoon U1	.60	1.25
161 Surface Defense Cannon R2	2.00	4.00
162 Vehicle Mine DARK C2	.20	.40

1996 Star Wars Jedi Pack

COMPLETE SET (11)	3.00	8.00
RELEASED IN 1996		
1 Hyperoute Navigation Chart PM	.60	1.25
2 Dark Forces PM	.60	1.25
3 Eriadu PM	.60	1.25
4 For Luck PM	.60	1.25
5 Gravity Shadow PM	.60	1.25
6 Han PM	.60	1.25
7 Leia PM	.60	1.25
8 Luke's T-16 Skyhopper PM	.60	1.25
9 Motti PM	.60	1.25
10 Tarkin PM	.60	1.25
11 Tedn Dahai PM	.60	1.25

1996 Star Wars A New Hope

COMPLETE SET (162)	50.00	100.00
BOOSTER BOX (36 PACKS)	50.00	100.00
BOOSTER PACK (15 CARDS)	2.00	4.00
RELEASED IN JULY 1996		
1 Advosze C2	.20	.40
2 Captain Khurgee U1	.60	1.25
3 DS-61-4 R2	2.00	4.00
4 Dannik Jerriko R1	2.00	4.00
5 Danz Borin U2	.60	1.25
6 Death Star R2	6.00	12.00
7 Defel C2	.20	.40
8 Greedo R1	5.00	10.00

9 Hem Dazon R1	2.00	4.00	79 Leia Seeker R2	2.00	4.00	149 Youíre All Clear Kid! R1	2.00	4.00
10 IT-O (Eyetee-Oh) R1	2.00	4.00	80 Superlaser R2	3.00	6.00	150 Gold 2 R1	.60	1.25
11 Imperial Commander C2	.20	.40	81 URoRRuRiRiRís Hunting Rifle U1	.60	1.25	151 Red 2 R1	2.00	4.00
12 Imperial Squad Leader C3	.20	.40	82 Arcona C2	.20	.40	152 Red 5 R1	5.00	10.00
13 Lirin Carín U2	.60	1.25	83 Brainiac R1	4.00	8.00	153 Red 6 U1	.60	1.25
14 Lt. Pol Treidum C1	.20	.40	84 Chewbacca R2	10.00	20.00	154 Tantive IV R1	6.00	12.00
15 Lt. Shann Childsen U1	.60	1.25	85 Commander Evram Lajaie C1	.20	.40	155 Yavin 4: Briefing Room U1	.60	1.25
16 Mosep U2	.60	1.25	86 Commander Vanden Willard U2	.60	1.25	156 Incom T-16 Skyhopper C2	.20	.40
17 Officer Evax C1	.20	.40	87 Corellian C2	.20	.40	157 Rogue Bantha U1	.60	1.25
18 R2-Q2 (Artoo-Kyootoo) C2	.20	.40	88 Doikk Naíts U2	.60	1.25	158 Bowcaster R2	2.00	4.00
19 R3-T6 (Arthree-Teesix) R1	2.00	4.00	89 Garouf Lafoe U2	.60	1.25	159 Jawa Ion Gun C2	.20	.40
20 R5-A2 (Arfive-Aytoo) C2	.20	.40	90 Het Nkik U2	.60	1.25	160 Lukeís Hunting Rifle U1	.60	1.25
21 Reegesk U2	.60	1.25	91 Hunchback R1	2.00	4.00	161 Motti Seeker R2	2.00	4.00
22 Reserve Pilot U1	.60	1.25	92 Ickabel Giont U2	.60	1.25	162 SW-4 Ion Cannon R2	2.00	4.00
23 Rodian C2	.20	.40	93 Magnetic Suction Tube DARK R2	2.00	4.00			
24 Tech Moír U2	.60	1.25	94 Nalan Cheel U2	.60	1.25			
25 Trooper Davin Felth R2	2.00	4.00	95 R2-D2 (Artoo-Detoo) R2	10.00	20.00			
26 U-3PO (Yoo-Threepio) R1	2.00	4.00	96 R5-D4 (Arfive-Defour) C2	.20	.40			
27 URoRRuRiRiR U2	.60	1.25	97 RA-7 (Aray-Seven) C2	.20	.40			
28 WED15-I7 éSeptoidí Droid U2	.60	1.25	98 Rebel Commander C2	.20	.40			
29 Dianoga R2	2.00	4.00	99 Rebel Squad Leader C3	.20	.40			
30 Death Star Tractor Beam R2	2.00	4.00	100 Rebel Tech C1	.20	.40			
31 Hypo R1	2.00	4.00	101 Saurin C2	.20	.40			
32 Laser Gate U2	.60	1.25	102 Tiree U2	.60	1.25			
33 Maneuver Check R2	2.00	4.00	103 Tzizvvt R2	2.00	4.00			
34 Tractor Beam U1	.60	1.25	104 Wedge Antilles R1	10.00	20.00			
35 Astromech Shortage U2	.60	1.25	105 Zutton C1	.20	.40			
36 Besieged R2	2.00	4.00	106 Fire Extinguisher U2	.60	1.25			
37 Come With Me C2	.20	.40	107 Magnetic Suction Tube LIGHT R2	2.00	4.00			
38 Dark Waters R2	2.00	4.00	108 Rectenna C2	.20	.40			
39 Hyperwave Scan U1	.60	1.25	109 Remote C2	.20	.40			
40 Imperial Justice C2	.20	.40	110 Sensor Panel U1	.60	1.25			
41 Krayt Dragon Bones U1	.60	1.25	111 Cell 2187 R1	2.00	4.00			
42 Merc Sunlet C2	.20	.40	112 Commence Recharging R2	2.00	4.00			
43 Program Trap U1	.60	1.25	113 Eject! Eject! C2	.20	.40			
44 Spice Mines Of Kessel R1	2.00	4.00	114 Grappling Hook C2	.20	.40			
45 Swilla Corey C2	.20	.40	115 Logistical Delay U2	.60	1.25			
46 Tentacle C2	.20	.40	116 Lukeís Cape R1	2.00	4.00			
47 Thereíll Be Hell To Pay U2	.60	1.25	117 M-HYD èBinaryí Droid U1	.60	1.25			
48 Undercover LIGHT U2	.60	1.25	118 Scanner Techs U1	.60	1.25			
49 Commence Primary Ignition R2	2.00	4.00	119 Solomahal C2	.20	.40			
50 Evader U1	.60	1.25	120 Theyíre On Dantooine R1	2.00	4.00			
51 Ghhhk C2	.20	.40	121 Undercover DARK U2	.60	1.25			
52 Iím On The Leader R1	2.00	4.00	122 Whatíre You Tryiní To Push On Us? U2	.60	1.25			
53 Informant U1	.60	1.25	123 Attack Run R2	2.00	4.00			
54 Monnok C2	.20	.40	124 Advance Preparation U1	.60	1.25			
55 Ngíok C2	.20	.40	125 Alternatives To Fighting U1	.60	1.25			
56 Oo-ta Goo-ta, Solo? C2	.20	.40	126 Blast The Door, Kid! C2	.20	.40			
57 Retract the Bridge R1	2.00	4.00	127 Blue Milk C2	.20	.40			
58 Sniper U1	.60	1.25	128 Corellian Slip C2	.20	.40			
59 Stunning Leader C2	.20	.40	129 Double Agent R2	2.00	4.00			
60 This Is Some Rescue! U1	.60	1.25	130 Grimtaash C2	.20	.40			
61 We Have A Prisoner C2	.20	.40	131 Houjix C2	.20	.40			
62 Death Star Gunner C1	.20	.40	132 I Have A Very Bad Feeling About This C2	.20	.40			
63 Death Star: Conference Room U1	.60	1.25	133 Iím Here To Rescue You U1	.60	1.25			
64 Imperial Holotable R1	2.00	4.00	134 Let The Wookiee Win R1	7.50	15.00			
65 Kashyyyk LIGHTC1	.20	.40	135 Out Of Commission U2	.60	1.25			
66 Kiffex R1	2.00	4.00	136 Quite A Mercenary C2	.20	.40			
67 Ralltiir LIGHT C1	.20	.40	137 Sabotage U1	.60	1.25			
68 Sandcrawler: Droid Junkheap R1	2.00	4.00	138 Sorry About The Mess U1	.60	1.25			
69 Tatooine: Bluffs R1	2.00	4.00	139 Wookiee Roar R1	2.00	4.00			
70 Black 4 U2	.60	1.25	140 Y-wing Assault Squadron U1	.60	1.25			
71 Conquest R1	6.00	12.00	141 Clakídor VII R2	2.00	4.00			
72 TIE Assault Squadron U1	.60	1.25	142 Corellia R1	2.00	4.00			
73 TIE Vanguard C2	.20	.40	143 Death Star: Trench R2	2.00	4.00			
74 Victory-Class Star Destroyer U1	.60	1.25	144 Dejarik Hologameboard R1	2.00	4.00			
75 Bespin Motors Void Spider THX 1138 C2	.20	.40	145 Kashyyyk DARK C1	.20	.40			
76 Mobquet A-1 Deluxe Floater C2	.20	.40	146 Ralltiir DARK C1	.20	.40			
77 Enhanced TIE Laser Cannon C2	.20	.40	147 Sandcrawler: Loading Bay R1	2.00	4.00			
78 Jawa Blaster C2	.20	.40	148 Yavin 4: Massasi Ruins U1	.60	1.25			

1997 Star Wars Cloud City

COMPLETE SET (180)	50.00	100.00
BOOSTER BOX (60 PACKS)	50.00	100.00
BOOSTER PACK (9 CARDS)	2.00	4.00
RELEASED IN NOVEMBER 1997		

1 Ability, Ability, Ability C	.20	.40
2 Abyss U	.60	1.25
3 Access Denied C	.20	.40
4 Advantage R	2.00	4.00
5 Aiiii! Aaa! Aggggggggggg! R	2.00	4.00
6 All My Urchins R	2.00	4.00
7 All Too Easy R	2.00	4.00
8 Ambush R	2.00	4.00
9 Armed And Dangerous U	.60	1.25
10 Artoo, Come Back At Once! R	2.00	4.00
11 As Good As Gone C	.20	.40
12 Atmospheric Assault R	2.00	4.00
13 Beldonís Eye R	2.00	4.00
14 Bespin DARK U	.60	1.25
15 Bespin LIGHT U	.60	1.25
16 Bespin: Cloud City DARK U	.60	1.25
17 Bespin: Cloud City LIGHT U	.60	1.25
18 Binders C	.20	.40
19 Bionic Hand R	2.00	4.00
20 Blasted Droid C	.20	.40
21 Blaster Proficiency C	.20	.40
22 Boba Fett R	12.00	25.00
23 Boba Fettís Blaster Rifle R	5.00	10.00
24 Bounty C	.20	.40
25 Brief Loss Of Control R	2.00	4.00
26 Bright Hope R	2.00	4.00
27 Captain Bewil R	2.00	4.00
28 Captain Han Solo R	12.00	25.00
29 Captive Fury U	.60	1.25
30 Captive Pursuit C	.20	.40
31 Carbon-Freezing U	.60	1.25

TRADING CARD GAMES AND MINIATURES

#	Card	Lo	Hi
32	Carbonite Chamber Console U	.60	1.25
33	Chasm U	.60	1.25
34	Chief Retwin R	2.00	4.00
35	Civil Disorder C	.20	.40
36	Clash Of Sabers U	.60	1.25
37	Cloud Car DARK C	.20	.40
38	Cloud Car LIGHT C	.20	.40
39	Cloud City Blaster DARK C	.20	.40
40	Cloud City Blaster LIGHT C	.20	.40
41	Cloud City Engineer C	.20	.40
42	Cloud City Sabacc DARK U	.60	1.25
43	Cloud City Sabacc LIGHT U	.60	1.25
44	Cloud City Technician C	.20	.40
45	Cloud City Trooper DARK C	.20	.40
46	Cloud City Trooper LIGHT C	.20	.40
47	Cloud City: Carbonite Chamber DARK U	.60	1.25
48	Cloud City: Carbonite Chamber LIGHT U	.60	1.25
49	Cloud City: Chasm Walkway DARK C	.20	.40
50	Cloud City: Chasm Walkway LIGHT C	.20	.40
51	Cloud City: Dining Room R	2.00	4.00
52	Cloud City: East Platform	.20	.40
53	Cloud City: Guest Quarters R	2.00	4.00
54	Cloud City: Incinerator DARK C	.20	.40
55	Cloud City: Incinerator LIGHT C	.20	.40
56	Cloud City: Lower Corridor DARK U	.60	1.25
57	Cloud City: Lower Corridor LIGHT U	.60	1.25
58	Cloud City: Platform 327	.20	.40
59	Cloud City: Security Tower C	.20	.40
60	Cloud City: Upper Plaza	.20	.40
61	Cloud City: Upper Plaza	.60	1.25
62	Clouds DARK C	.20	.40
63	Clouds LIGHT C	.20	.40
64	Commander Desanne U	.60	1.25
65	Computer Interface C	.20	.40
66	Courage Of A Skywalker R	2.00	4.00
67	Crack Shot U	.60	1.25
68	Cyborg Construct U	.60	1.25
69	Dark Approach R	2.00	4.00
70	Dark Deal R	2.00	4.00
71	Dark Strike C	.20	.40
72	Dash C	.20	.40
73	Despair R	2.00	4.00
74	Desperate Reach U	.60	1.25
75	Dismantle On Sight R	2.00	4.00
76	Dodge C	.20	.40
77	Double Back U	.60	1.25
78	Double-Crossing, No-Good Swindler C	.20	.40
79	E Chu Ta C	.20	.40
80	E-3PO R	2.00	4.00
81	End This Destructive Conflict R	2.00	4.00
82	Epic Duel R	3.00	6.00
83	Fall Of The Empire U	.60	1.25
84	Fall Of The Legend U	.60	1.25
85	Flight Escort R	2.00	4.00
86	Focused Attack R	2.00	4.00
87	Force Field R	2.00	4.00
88	Forced Landing R	2.00	4.00
89	Frozen Assets R	2.00	4.00
90	Gambler's Luck R	2.00	4.00
91	Glancing Blow R	2.00	4.00
92	Haven R	2.00	4.00
93	He's All Yours, Bounty Hunter R	2.00	4.00
94	Heart Of The Chasm U	.60	1.25
95	Hero Of A Thousand Devices U	.60	1.25
96	Higher Ground R	2.00	4.00
97	Hindsight R	2.00	4.00
98	Hopping Mad R	2.00	4.00
99	Human Shield C	.20	.40
100	I Am Your Father R	2.00	4.00
101	I Don't Need Your Scum, Either R	2.00	4.00
102	I Had No Choice R	2.00	4.00
103	Imperial Decree U	.60	1.25
104	Imperial Trooper Guard Dainsom U	.60	1.25
105	Impressive, Most Impressive R	2.00	4.00
106	Innocent Scoundrel U	.60	1.25
107	Interrogation Array R	2.00	4.00
108	Into The Ventilation Shaft, Lefty R	2.00	4.00
109	It's A Trap! U	.60	1.25
110	Kebyc U	.60	1.25
111	Keep Your Eyes Open C	.20	.40
112	Lando Calrissian DARK R	7.50	15.00
113	Lando Calrissian LIGHT R	7.50	15.00
114	Lando's Wrist Comlink U	.60	1.25
115	Leia Of Alderaan R	3.00	6.00
116	Levitation Attack U	.60	1.25
117	Lieutenant Cecius U	.60	1.25
118	Lieutenant Sheckil R	2.00	4.00
119	Lift Tube Escape C	.20	.40
120	Lobot R	4.00	8.00
121	Luke's Blaster Pistol R	2.00	4.00
122	Mandalorian Armor R	3.00	6.00
123	Mostly Armless R	2.00	4.00
124	NOOOOOOOOOOOO! R	2.00	4.00
125	Obsidian 7 R	3.00	6.00
126	Obsidian 8 R	3.00	6.00
127	Off The Edge R	2.00	4.00
128	Old Pirates R	2.00	4.00
129	Out Of Somewhere U	.60	1.25
130	Path Of Least Resistance C	.20	.40
131	Point Man R	2.00	4.00
132	Prepare The Chamber U	.60	1.25
133	Princess Leia R	6.00	12.00
134	Projective Telepathy U	.60	1.25
135	Protector R	2.00	4.00
136	Punch It! R	2.00	4.00
137	Put That Down C	.20	.40
138	Redemption R	4.00	8.00
139	Release Your Anger R	2.00	4.00
140	Rendezvous Point On Tatooine R	2.00	4.00
141	Rescue In The Clouds C	.20	.40
142	Restricted Access C	.20	.40
143	Rite Of Passage C	.20	.40
144	Shattered Hope U	.60	1.25
145	Shocking Information C	.20	.40
146	Shocking Revelation C	.20	.40
147	Slave I R	6.00	12.00
148	Slip Sliding Away R	2.00	4.00
149	Smoke Screen R	2.00	4.00
150	Somersault C	.20	.40
151	Sonic Bombardment U	.60	1.25
152	Special Delivery C	.20	.40
153	Surprise R	2.00	4.00
154	Surreptitious Glance R	2.00	4.00
155	Swing-And-A-Miss U	.60	1.25
156	The Emperor's Prize R	2.00	4.00
157	This Is Even Better R	2.00	4.00
158	This Is Still Wrong R	2.00	4.00
159	Tibanna Gas Miner DARK C	.20	.40
160	Tibanna Gas Miner LIGHT C	.20	.40
161	TIE Sentry Ships C	.20	.40
162	Treva Horme U	.60	1.25
163	Trooper Assault C	.20	.40
164	Trooper Jerrol Blendin U	.60	1.25
165	Trooper Utris M'toc U	.60	1.25
166	Ugloste R	2.00	4.00
167	Ugnaught C	.20	.40
168	Uncontrollable Fury R	2.00	4.00
169	Vader's Bounty R	2.00	4.00
170	Vader's Cape R	2.00	4.00
171	We'll Find Han R	2.00	4.00
172	We're The Bait R	2.00	4.00
173	Weapon Levitation U	.60	1.25
174	Weapon Of An Ungrateful Son U	.60	1.25
175	Weather Vane DARK U	.60	1.25
176	Weather Vane LIGHT U	.60	1.25
177	Why Didn't You Tell Me? R	2.00	4.00
178	Wiorkettle U	.60	1.25
179	Wookiee Strangle R	2.00	4.00
180	You Are Beaten U	.60	1.25

1997 Star Wars Dagobah

• Son Of Skywalker

	Lo	Hi
COMPLETE SET (181)	50.00	100.00
BOOSTER BOX (60 PACKS)	50.00	100.00
BOOSTER PACK (9 CARDS)	1.50	3.00
RELEASED ON APRIL 23, 1997		

#	Card	Lo	Hi
1	3,720 To 1 C	.20	.40
2	4-LOM R	4.00	8.00
3	4-LOM's Concussion Rifle R	3.00	6.00
4	A Dangerous Time C	.20	.40
5	A Jedi's Strength U	.60	1.25
6	Anger, Fear, Aggression C	.20	.40
7	Anoat DARK U	.60	1.25
8	Anoat LIGHT U	.60	1.25
9	Apology Accepted C	.20	.40
10	Asteroid Field DARK C	.20	.40
11	Asteroid Field LIGHT C	.20	.40
12	Asteroid Sanctuary C	.20	.40
13	Asteroids Do Not Concern Me R	2.00	4.00
14	Astroid Sanctuary C	.20	.40
15	Astromech Translator C	.20	.40
16	At Peace R	2.00	4.00
17	Avenger R	6.00	12.00
18	Away Put Your Weapon U	.60	1.25
19	Awwww, Cannot Get Your Ship Out C	.20	.40
20	Bad Feeling Have I R	2.00	4.00
21	Big One DARK U	.60	1.25
22	Big One LIGHT U	.60	1.25
23	Big One: Asteroid Cave	.60	1.25
24	Big One: Asteroid Cave	.60	1.25
25	Blasted Varmints C	.20	.40
26	Bog-wing DARK C	.20	.40
27	Bog-wing LIGHT C	.20	.40
28	Bombing Run R	2.00	4.00
29	Bossk R	5.00	10.00
30	Bossk's Mortar Gun R	3.00	6.00
31	Broken Concentration R	2.00	4.00
32	Captain Needa R	3.00	6.00
33	Close Call C	.20	.40
34	Closer?! U	.60	1.25
35	Comm Chief C	.20	.40
36	Commander Brandei U	.60	1.25

37	Commander Gherant U	.60	1.25
38	Commander Nemet U	.60	1.25
39	Control DARK U	.60	1.25
40	Control LIGHT U	.60	1.25
41	Corporal Derdram U	.60	1.25
42	Corporal Vandolay U	.60	1.25
43	Corrosive Damage R	2.00	4.00
44	Dagobah U	.60	1.25
45	Dagobah: Bog Clearing R	2.00	4.00
46	Dagobah: Cave R	2.00	4.00
47	Dagobah: Jungle U	.60	1.25
48	Dagobah: Swamp U	.60	1.25
49	Dagobah: Training Area C	.20	.40
50	Dagobah: Yodaís Hut R	3.00	6.00
51	Defensive Fire C	.20	.40
52	Dengar R	2.00	4.00
53	Dengarís Blaster Carbine R	2.00	4.00
54	Descent Into The Dark R	2.00	4.00
55	Do, Or Do Not C	.20	.40
56	Domain Of Evil U	.60	1.25
57	Dragonsnake R	2.00	4.00
58	Droid Sensorscope C	.20	.40
59	Effective Repairs R	2.00	4.00
60	Egregious Pilot Error R	2.00	4.00
61	Encampment C	.20	.40
62	Executor R	12.00	25.00
63	Executor: Comm Station U	.60	1.25
64	Executor: Control Station U	.60	1.25
65	Executor: Holotheatre R	2.00	4.00
66	Executor: Main Corridor C	.20	.40
67	Executor: Meditation Chamber R	2.00	4.00
68	Failure At The Cave R	2.00	4.00
69	Fear C	.20	.40
70	Field Promotion R	2.00	4.00
71	Flagship R	2.00	4.00
72	Flash Of Insight U	.60	1.25
73	Found Someone You Have U	.60	1.25
74	Frustration R	2.00	4.00
75	Great Warrior C	.20	.40
76	Grounded Starfighter U	.60	1.25
77	Hanís Toolkit R	2.00	4.00
78	He Is Not Ready C	.20	.40
79	Hiding In The Garbage R	2.00	4.00
80	HoloNet Transmission U	.60	1.25
81	Houndís Tooth R	4.00	8.00
82	I Have A Bad Feeling About This R	2.00	4.00
83	I Want That Ship R	2.00	4.00
84	IG-2000 R	3.00	6.00
85	IG-88 R	6.00	12.00
86	IG-88ís Neural Inhibitor R	3.00	6.00
87	IG-88ís Pulse Cannon R	3.00	6.00
88	Imbalance U	.60	1.25
89	Imperial Helmsman C	.20	.40
90	Ineffective Maneuver U	.60	1.25
91	It Is The Future You See R	2.00	4.00
92	Jedi Levitation R	2.00	4.00
93	Knowledge And Defense C	.20	.40
94	Landing Claw R	2.00	4.00
95	Lando System? R	2.00	4.00
96	Levitation U	.60	1.25
97	Lieutenant Commander Ardan U	.60	1.25
98	Lieutenant Suba R	2.00	4.00
99	Lieutenant Venka U	.60	1.25
100	Light Maneuvers R	2.00	4.00
101	Location, Location, Location R	2.00	4.00
102	Lost In Space R	2.00	4.00
103	Lost Relay C	.20	.40
104	Lukeís Backpack R	2.00	4.00
105	Mist Hunter R	3.00	6.00
106	Moving To Attack Position C	.20	.40

107	Much Anger In Him R	2.00	4.00
108	Mynock DARK C	.20	.40
109	Mynock LIGHT C	.20	.40
110	Never Tell Me The Odds C	.20	.40
111	No Disintegrations! R	2.00	4.00
112	Nudj C	.20	.40
113	Obi-Wanís Apparition R	2.00	4.00
114	Order To Engage R	2.00	4.00
115	Polarized Negative Power Coupling R	2.00	4.00
116	Portable Fusion Generator C	.20	.40
117	Precision Targeting U	.60	1.25
118	Proton Bombs U	.60	1.25
119	Punishing One R	3.00	6.00
120	Quick Draw C	.20	.40
121	Raithal DARK R	2.00	4.00
122	Raithal LIGHT U	.60	1.25
123	Rebel Flight Suit C	.20	.40
124	Recoil In Fear C	.20	.40
125	Reflection R	2.00	4.00
126	Report To Lord Vader R	2.00	4.00
127	Res Luk Raíauf R	2.00	4.00
128	Retractable Arm C	.20	.40
129	Rogue Asteroid DARK C	.20	.40
130	Rogue Asteroid LIGHT C	.20	.40
131	Rycarís Run R	2.00	4.00
132	Scramble U	.60	1.25
133	Shoo! Shoo! U	.60	1.25
134	Shot In The Dark U	.60	1.25
135	Shut Him Up Or Shut Him Down U	.60	1.25
136	Size Matters Not R	2.00	4.00
137	Sleen C	.20	.40
138	Smugglerís Blues R	2.00	4.00
139	Something Hit Us! U	.60	1.25
140	Son of Skywalker R	12.00	25.00
141	Space Slug DARK R	2.00	4.00
142	Space Slug LIGHT U	.60	1.25
143	Star Destroyer: Launch Bay C	.20	.40
144	Starship Levitation U	.60	1.25
145	Stone Pile R	2.00	4.00
146	Sudden Impact U	.60	1.25
147	Take Evasive Action C	.20	.40
148	The Dark Path R	2.00	4.00
149	The Professor R	2.00	4.00
150	There Is No Try C	.20	.40
151	Theyíd Be Crazy To Follow Us C	.20	.40
152	This Is More Like It R	2.00	4.00
153	This Is No Cave R	2.00	4.00
154	Those Rebels Wonít Escape Us C	.20	.40
155	Through The Force Things	2.00	4.00
156	TIE Avenger C	.20	.40
157	TIE Bomber U	.60	1.25
158	Tight Squeeze R	2.00	4.00
159	Transmission Terminated U	.60	1.25
160	Tunnel Vision U	.60	1.25
161	Uncertain Is The Future C	.20	.40
162	Unexpected Interruption R	2.00	4.00
163	Vine Snake DARK C	.20	.40
164	Vine Snake LIGHT C	.20	.40
165	Visage Of The Emperor R	2.00	4.00
166	Visored Vision C	.20	.40
167	Voyeur C	.20	.40
168	Warrant Officer MíKae U	.60	1.25
169	Wars Not Make One Great U	.60	1.25
170	We Can Still Outmaneuver Them R	2.00	4.00
171	We Donít Need Their Scum R	2.00	4.00
172	WHAAAAAAAAOOOOW! R	2.00	4.00
173	What Is Thy Bidding, My Master? R	2.00	4.00
174	Yoda R	12.00	25.00
175	Yoda Stew U	.60	1.25
176	Yoda, You Seek Yoda R	2.00	4.00

177	Yodaís Gimer Stick R	2.00	4.00
178	Yodaís Hope U	.60	1.25
179	You Do Have Your Moments U	.60	1.25
180	Zuckuss R	3.00	6.00
181	Zuckussí Snare Rifle R	2.00	4.00

1997 Star Wars First Anthology

COMPLETE SET (6)	3.00	8.00
RELEASED IN 1997		
1 Boba Fett PV	1.25	2.50
2 Commander Wedge Antilles PV	1.25	2.50
3 Death Star Assault Squadron PV	1.25	2.50
4 Hit And Run PV	1.25	2.50
5 Jabbaís Influence PV	1.25	2.50
6 X-wing Assault Squadron PV	1.25	2.50

1997 Star Wars Rebel Leaders

COMPLETE SET (2)	1.25	3.00
RELEASED IN 1997		
1 Gold Leader In Gold 1 PM	1.50	3.00
2 Red Leader In Red 1 PM	1.50	3.00

1998 Star Wars Enhanced Premiere

COMPLETE SET (6)	3.00	8.00
RELEASED IN 1998		
1 Boba Fett With Blaster Rifle PM	1.25	2.50
2 Darth Vader With Lightsaber PM	1.25	2.50
3 Han With Heavy Blaster Pistol PM	1.25	2.50
4 Leia With Blaster Rifle PM	1.25	2.50
5 Luke With Lightsaber PM	1.25	2.50
6 Obi-Wan With Lightsaber PM	1.25	2.50

1998 Star Wars Jabba's Palace

COMPLETE SET (180)	40.00	80.00
BOOSTER BOX (60 PACKS)	40.00	80.00
BOOSTER PACK (9 CARDS)	1.00	2.00
RELEASED IN MAY 1998		
1 8D8 R	2.00	4.00
2 A Gift U	.60	1.25
3 Abyssin C	.20	.40
4 Abyssin Ornament U	.60	1.25
5 All Wrapped Up U	.60	1.25
6 Amanaman R	2.00	4.00
7 Amanin C	.20	.40
8 Antipersonnel Laser Cannon U	.60	1.25
9 Aqualish C	.20	.40
10 Arc Welder U	.60	1.25
11 Ardon Vapor Crell R	2.00	4.00
12 Artoo R	5.00	10.00
13 Artoo, I Have A Bad	.60	1.25
14 Attark R	2.00	4.00
15 Aved Luun R	2.00	4.00
16 Biomarr Monk C	.20	.40
17 Bane Malar R	2.00	4.00
18 Bantha Fodder C	.20	.40
19 Barada R	2.00	4.00
20 Baragwin C	.20	.40
21 Bargaining Table U	.60	1.25
22 Beedo R	2.00	4.00
23 BG-J38 R	2.00	4.00
24 Bib Fortuna R	2.00	4.00
25 Blaster Deflection R	2.00	4.00
26 Bo Shuda U	.60	1.25
27 Bubo U	.60	1.25
28 Cane Adiss U	.60	1.25
29 Chadra-Fan C	.20	.40
30 Chevin C	.20	.40
31 Choke C	.20	.40
32 Corellian Retort U	.60	1.25
33 CZ-4 C	.20	.40
34 Den Of Thieves U	.60	1.25
35 Dengar's Modified Riot Gun R	2.00	4.00
36 Devaronian C	.20	.40
37 Don't Forget The Droids C	.20	.40
38 Double Laser Cannon R	2.00	4.00
39 Droopy McCool R	2.00	4.00
40 Dune Sea Sabacc DARK U	.60	1.25
41 Dune Sea Sabacc LIGHT U	.60	1.25
42 Elom C	.20	.40
43 Ephant Mon R	2.00	4.00
44 EV-9D9 R	2.00	4.00
45 Fallen Portal U	.60	1.25
46 Florn Lamproid C	.20	.40
47 Fozec R	2.00	4.00
48 Gailid R	2.00	4.00
49 Gamorrean Ax C	.20	.40
50 Gamorrean Guard C	.20	.40
51 Garon Nas Tal R	2.00	4.00
52 Geezum R	2.00	4.00
53 Ghoel R	2.00	4.00
54 Giran R	2.00	4.00
55 Gran C	.20	.40
56 Hinemthe C	.20	.40
57 Herat R	2.00	4.00
58 Hermi Odle R	2.00	4.00
59 Hidden Compartment U	.60	1.25
60 Hidden Weapons U	.60	1.25
61 Holoprojector U	.60	1.25
62 Hutt Bounty R	2.00	4.00
63 Hutt Smooch U	.60	1.25
64 I Must Be Allowed To Speak R	2.00	4.00
65 Information Exchange U	.60	1.25
66 Ishi Tib C	.20	.40
67 Ithorian C	.20	.40
68 JiQuille R	2.00	4.00
69 Jabba the Hutt R	6.00	12.00
70 Jabba's Palace Sabacc DARK U	.60	1.25
71 Jabba's Palace Sabacc LIGHT U	.60	1.25
72 Jabba's Palace:	.60	1.25
73 Jabba's Palace:	.60	1.25
74 Jabba's Palace: Droid Workshop U	.60	1.25
75 Jabba's Palace: Dungeon U	.60	1.25
76 Jabba's Palace:	.60	1.25
77 Jabba's Palace:	.60	1.25
78 Jabba's Palace: Rancor Pit U	.60	1.25
79 Jabba's Sail Barge R	4.00	8.00
80 Jabba's Sail Barge: Passenger Deck R	2.00	4.00
81 Jedi Mind Trick R	2.00	4.00
82 Jess R	2.00	4.00
83 Jet Pack U	.60	1.25
84 Kalit R	2.00	4.00
85 Ke Chu Ke Kakuta? C	.20	.40
86 Kiffex R	2.00	4.00
87 Kirdo III R	2.00	4.00
88 Kithaba R	2.00	4.00
89 Kitonak C	.20	.40
90 Klaatu R	2.00	4.00
91 Klatooinian Revolutionary C	.20	.40
92 Laudica R	2.00	4.00
93 Leslomy Tacema R	2.00	4.00
94 Life Debt R	2.00	4.00
95 Loje Nella R	2.00	4.00
96 Malakili R	2.00	4.00
97 Mandalorian Mishap U	.60	1.25
98 Max Rebo R	2.00	4.00
99 Mos Eisley Blaster DARK C	.20	.40
100 Mos Eisley Blaster LIGHT C	.20	.40
101 Murttoc Yine R	2.00	4.00
102 Nal Hutta R	2.00	4.00
103 Nar Shaddaa Wind Chimes U	.60	1.25
104 Nikto C	.20	.40
105 Nizuc Bek R	2.00	4.00
106 None Shall Pass C	.20	.40
107 Nysad R	2.00	4.00
108 Oola R	2.00	4.00
109 Ortolan C	.20	.40
110 Ortugg R	2.00	4.00
111 Palejo Reshad R	2.00	4.00
112 Pote Snitkin R	2.00	4.00
113 Princess Leia Organa R	5.00	10.00
114 Projection Of A Skywalker U	.60	1.25
115 Pucumir Thryss R	2.00	4.00
116 Quarren C	.20	.40
117 Quick Reflexes C	.20	.40
118 Rikik Dínec, Hero Of The Dune Sea R	2.00	4.00
119 Rancor R	4.00	8.00
120 Rayc Ryjerd R	2.00	4.00
121 Ree-Yees R	2.00	4.00
122 Rennek R	2.00	4.00
123 Resistance U	.60	1.25
124 Revealed U	.60	1.25
125 Saelt-Marae R	2.00	4.00
126 Salacious Crumb R	2.00	4.00
127 Sandwhirl DARK U	.60	1.25
128 Sandwhirl LIGHT U	.60	1.25
129 Scum And Villainy R	2.00	4.00
130 Sergeant Doallyn R	2.00	4.00
131 Shasa Tiel R	2.00	4.00
132 Sic-Six C	.20	.40
133 Skiff DARK C	.20	.40
134 Skiff LIGHT C	.20	.40
135 Skrilling C	.20	.40
136 Skull U	.60	1.25
137 Snivvian C	.20	.40
138 Someone Who Loves You U	.60	1.25
139 Strangle R	2.00	4.00
140 Tamtel Skreej R	4.00	8.00
141 Tanus Spijek R	2.00	4.00
142 Tatooine: Desert DARK C	.20	.40
143 Tatooine: Desert LIGHT C	.20	.40
144 Tatooine: Great Pit Of Carkoon U	.60	1.25
145 Tatooine: Hutt Canyon U	.60	1.25
146 Tatooine: Jabba's Palace U	.60	1.25
147 Taym Dren-garen R	2.00	4.00
148 Tessek R	2.00	4.00
149 The Signal C	.20	.40
150 Thermal Detonator R	3.00	6.00
151 Thul Fain R	2.00	4.00
152 Tibrin R	2.00	4.00
153 Torture C	.20	.40
154 Trandoshan C	.20	.40
155 Trap Door U	.60	1.25
156 Twi'lek Advisor C	.20	.40
157 Ultimatum U	.60	1.25
158 Unfriendly Fire R	2.00	4.00
159 Vedain R	2.00	4.00
160 Velken Tezeri R	2.00	4.00
161 Vibro-Ax DARK C	.20	.40
162 Vibro-Ax LIGHT C	.20	.40
163 Vizam R	2.00	4.00
164 Vul Tazaene R	2.00	4.00
165 Weapon Levitation U	.60	1.25
166 Weequay Guard C	.20	.40
167 Weequay Hunter C	.20	.40
168 Weequay Marksman U	.60	1.25
169 Weequay Skiff Master C	.20	.40
170 Well Guarded U	.60	1.25
171 Whiphid C	.20	.40
172 Wittin R	2.00	4.00
173 Wooof R	2.00	4.00
174 Worrt U	.60	1.25
175 Wounded Wookiee U	.60	1.25
176 Yarkora C	.20	.40
177 Yarna d'al' Gargan U	.60	1.25
178 You Will Take Me To Jabba Now C	.20	.40
179 Yoxgit R	2.00	4.00
180 Yuzzum C	.20	.40

1998 Star Wars Official Tournament Sealed Deck

COMPLETE SET (18)	4.00	10.00
RELEASED IN 1998		
1 Arleil Schous PM	.60	1.25

2 Black Squadron TIE PM	.60	1.25
3 Chall Bekan PM	.60	1.25
4 Corulag DARK PM	.60	1.25
5 Corulag LIGHT PM	.60	1.25
6 Dreadnaught-Class Heavy Cruiser PM	.60	1.25
7 Faithful Service PM	.60	1.25
8 Forced Servitude PM	.60	1.25
9 Gold Squadron Y-wing PM	.60	1.25
10 It's a Hit! PM	.60	1.25
11 Obsidian Squadron TIE PM	.60	1.25
12 Rebel Trooper Recruit PM	.60	1.25
13 Red Squadron X-wing PM	.60	1.25
14 Stormtrooper Cadet PM	.60	1.25
15 Tarkin's Orders PM	.60	1.25
16 Tatooine: Jundland Wastes PM	.60	1.25
17 Tatooine: Tusken Canyon PM	.60	1.25
18 Z-95 Headhunter PM	.60	1.25

1998 Star Wars Second Anthology

COMPLETE SET (6)	4.00	10.00
RELEASED IN 1998		
1 Flagship Operations PV	1.50	3.00
2 Mon Calamari Star Cruiser PV	1.50	3.00
3 Mon Mothma PV	1.50	3.00
4 Rapid Deployment PV	1.50	3.00
5 Sarlacc PV	1.50	3.00
6 Thunderflare PV	1.50	3.00

1998 Star Wars Special Edition

COMPLETE SET (324)	75.00	150.00
BOOSTER BOX (30 PACKS)	60.00	120.00
BOOSTER PACK (9 CARDS)	3.00	6.00

RELEASED IN NOVEMBER 1998		
1 ISB Operations / Empire's Sinister Agents R	1.50	3.00
2 2X-7KPR (Tooex) C	.20	.40
3 A Bright Center To The Universe U	.60	1.25
4 A Day Long Remembered U	.60	1.25
5 A Real Hero R	1.50	3.00
6 Air-2 Racing Swoop C	.20	.40
7 Ak-rev U	.60	1.25
8 Alderaan Operative C	.20	.40
9 Alert My Star Destroyer! C	.20	.40
10 All Power To Weapons C	.20	.40
11 All Wings Report In R	1.50	3.00
12 Anoat Operative DARK C	.20	.40
13 Anoat Operative LIGHT C	.20	.40
14 Antilles Maneuver C	.20	.40
15 ASP-707 (Ayesspee) F	1.00	2.00
16 Balanced Attack U	.60	1.25
17 Bantha Herd R	1.25	2.50
18 Barquin D'an U	.60	1.25
19 Ben Kenobi R	3.00	6.00
20 Blast Points C	.20	.40
21 Blown Clear U	.60	1.25
22 Boba Fett R	2.50	5.00
23 Boelo R	1.50	3.00
24 Bossk In Hound's Tooth R	1.50	3.00
25 Bothan Spy C	.20	.40
26 Bothawui F	1.00	2.00
27 Bothawui Operative C	.20	.40
28 Brangus Glee R	1.25	2.50
29 Bren Quersey U	.60	1.25
30 Bron Burs R	1.25	2.50
31 B-wing Attack Fighter F	1.00	2.00
32 Camie R	1.50	3.00
33 Carbon Chamber Testing	1.50	3.00
34 Chyler U	.60	1.25
35 Clakdor VII Operative U	.60	1.25
36 Cloud City Celebration R	1.50	3.00
37 Cloud City Occupation R	2.00	4.00
38 Cloud City: Casino DARK U	.60	1.25
39 Cloud City: Casino LIGHT U	.60	1.25
40 Cloud City: Core Tunnel U	.60	1.25
41 Cloud City: Downtown Plaza DARK R	1.50	3.00
42 Cloud City: Downtown Plaza LIGHT R	1.50	3.00
43 Cloud City: Interrogation Room C	.20	.40
44 Cloud City: North Corridor C	.20	.40
45 Cloud City: Port Town District U	.60	1.25
46 Cloud City: Upper Walkway C	.20	.40
47 Cloud City: West Gallery DARK C	.20	.40
48 Cloud City: West Gallery LIGHT C	.20	.40
49 Colonel Feyn Gospic R	1.50	3.00
50 Combat Cloud Car F	1.00	2.00
51 Come Here You Big Coward! C	.20	.40
52 Commander Wedge Antilles R	1.50	3.00
53 Coordinated Attack C	.20	.40
54 Corellia Operative U	.60	1.25
55 Corellian Engineering Corporation R	1.50	3.00
56 Corporal Grenwick R	1.25	2.50
57 Corporal Prescott U	.60	1.25
58 Corulag Operative C	.20	.40
59 Coruscant Celebration R	1.25	2.50
60 Coruscant DARK R	4.00	8.00
61 Coruscant LIGHT R	1.50	3.00
62 Coruscant: Docking Bay C	.20	.40
63 Coruscant: Imperial City U	.60	1.25
64 Coruscant: Imperial Square R	2.00	4.00
65 Counter Surprise Assault R	1.50	3.00
66 Dagobah U	.60	1.25
67 Dantooine Base Operations	1.25	2.50
68 Dantooine Operative C	.20	.40
69 Darklighter Spin C	.20	.40

70 Darth Vader, Dark Lord Of The Sith R	10.00	20.00
71 Death Squadron Star Destroyer R	1.50	3.00
72 Death Star Assault Squadron R	1.50	3.00
73 Death Star R	2.00	4.00
74 Death Star: Detention Block Control Room C	.20	.40
75 Death Star: Detention Block Corridor C	.20	.40
76 Debnoli R	1.50	3.00
77 Desert DARK F	1.00	2.00
78 Desert LIGHT F	1.00	2.00
79 Desilijic Tattoo U	.60	1.25
80 Desperate Tactics C	.20	.40
81 Destroyed Homestead R	1.50	3.00
82 Dewback C	.20	.40
83 Direct Assault C	.20	.40
84 Disruptor Pistol DARK F	1.00	2.00
85 Disruptor Pistol LIGHT F	1.00	2.00
86 Docking And Repair Facilities R	1.50	3.00
87 Dodo Bodonawieedo U	.60	1.25
88 Don't Tread On Me R	1.50	3.00
89 Down With The Emperor! U	.60	1.25
90 Dr. Evazan's Sawed-off Blaster U	.60	1.25
91 Draw Their Fire U	.60	1.25
92 Dreaded Imperial Starfleet R	2.00	4.00
93 Droid Merchant C	.20	.40
94 Dune Walker R	2.00	4.00
95 Echo Base Trooper Rifle C	.20	.40
96 Elyhek Rue U	.60	1.25
97 Entrenchment R	1.25	2.50
98 Eriadu Operative C	.20	.40
99 Executor: Docking Bay U	.60	1.25
100 Farm F	1.00	2.00
101 Feltipern Trevagg's Stun Rifle U	.60	1.25
102 Firepower C	.20	.40
103 Firin Morett U	.60	1.25
104 First Aid F	1.00	2.00
105 First Strike U	.60	1.25
106 Flare-S Racing Swoop C	.20	.40
107 Flawless Marksmanship C	.20	.40
108 Floating Refinery C	.20	.40
109 Fondor U	.60	1.25
110 Forest DARK F	1.00	2.00
111 Forest LIGHT F	1.00	2.00
112 Gela Yeens U	.60	1.25
113 General McQuarrie R	1.25	2.50
114 Gold 3 U	.60	1.25
115 Gold 4 U	.60	1.25
116 Gold 6 U	.60	1.25
117 Goo Nee Tay R	1.50	3.00
118 Greeata U	.60	1.25
119 Grondorn Muse R	1.25	2.50
120 Harc Seff U	.60	1.25
121 Harvest R	2.00	4.00
122 Heavy Fire Zone C	.20	.40
123 Heroes Of Yavin R	1.25	2.50
124 Heroic Sacrifice U	.60	1.25
125 Hidden Base	2.50	5.00
126 Hit And Run R	1.25	2.50
127 Hol Okand U	.60	1.25
128 Homing Beacon R	1.50	3.00
129 Hoth Sentry U	.60	1.25
130 Hunt Down And Destroy The Jedi	2.50	5.00
131 Hunting Party R	1.50	3.00
132 I Can't Shake Him! C	.20	.40
133 Iasa, The Traitor Of Jawa Canyon R	1.25	2.50
134 IM4-099 F	1.00	2.00
135 Imperial Atrocity R	5.00	10.00
136 Imperial Occupation / Imperial Control R	1.50	3.00
137 Imperial Propaganda R	5.00	10.00
138 In Range C	.20	.40
139 Incom Corporation R	1.25	2.50

#	Card		
140	InCom Engineer C	.20	.40
141	Intruder Missile DARK F	1.00	2.00
142	Intruder Missile LIGHT F	1.00	2.00
143	Itís Not My Fault! F	1.00	2.00
144	Jabba R	1.50	3.00
145	Jabbaís Influence R	1.25	2.50
146	Jabbaís Space Cruiser R	2.00	4.00
147	Jabbaís Through With You U	.60	1.25
148	Jabbaís Twerps U	.60	1.25
149	Joh Yowza R	1.25	2.50
150	Jungle DARK F	1.00	2.00
151	Jungle LIGHT F	1.00	2.00
152	Kalitís Sandcrawler R	1.50	3.00
153	Kashyyyk Operative DARK U	.60	1.25
154	Kashyyyk Operative LIGHT U	.60	1.25
155	Kessel Operative U	.60	1.25
156	Ketwol R	1.25	2.50
157	Kiffex Operative DARK U	.60	1.25
158	Kiffex Operative LIGHT U	.60	1.25
159	Kirdo III Operative C	.20	.40
160	Koensayr Manufacturing R	1.50	3.00
161	Krayt Dragon R	1.50	3.00
162	Kuat Drive Yards R	2.00	4.00
163	Kuat U	.60	1.25
164	Landoís Blaster Rifle R	1.50	3.00
165	Legendary Starfighter C	.20	.40
166	Leiaís Blaster Rifle R	1.50	3.00
167	Lieutenant Lepira U	.60	1.25
168	Lieutenant Naytaan U	.60	1.25
169	Lieutenant Tarn Mison R	1.50	3.00
170	Lobel C	.20	.40
171	Lobot R	1.50	3.00
172	Local Defense U	.60	1.25
173	Local Uprising / Liberation R	1.50	3.00
174	Lyn Me U	.60	1.25
175	Major Palo Torshan R	1.50	3.00
176	Makurth F	1.00	2.00
177	Maneuvering Flaps C	.20	.40
178	Masterful Move C	.20	.40
179	Mechanical Failure R	1.25	2.50
180	Meditation R	2.00	4.00
181	Medium Bulk Freighter U	.60	1.25
182	Melas R	1.50	3.00
183	Mind What You Have Learned	2.00	4.00
184	Moisture Farmer C	.20	.40
185	Nal Hutta Operative C	.20	.40
186	Neb Dulo U	.60	1.25
187	Nebit R	1.50	3.00
188	Niado Duegad U	.60	1.25
189	Nick Of Time U	.60	1.25
190	No Bargain U	.60	1.25
191	Old Times R	1.25	2.50
192	On Target C	.20	.40
193	One-Arm R	1.50	3.00
194	Oppressive Enforcement U	.60	1.25
195	Ord Mantell Operative C	.20	.40
196	Organized Attack C	.20	.40
197	OS-72-1 In Obsidian 1 R	1.50	3.00
198	OS-72-10 R	1.50	3.00
199	OS-72-2 In Obsidian 2 R	1.50	3.00
200	Outer Rim Scout R	2.50	5.00
201	Overwhelmed C	.20	.40
202	Patrol Craft DARK C	.20	.40
203	Patrol Craft LIGHT C	.20	.40
204	Planetary Subjugation U	.60	1.25
205	Ponda Babaís Hold-out Blaster U	.60	1.25
206	Portable Scanner C	.20	.40
207	Power Pivot C	.20	.40
208	Precise Hit C	.20	.40
209	Pride Of The Empire C	.20	.40
210	Princess Organa R	2.00	4.00
211	Put All Sections On Alert C	.20	.40
212	R2-A5 (Artoo-Ayfive) U	.60	1.25
213	R3-A2 (Arthree-Aytoo) U	.60	1.25
214	R3-T2 (Arthree-Teetoo) R	1.50	3.00
215	Raithal Operative C	.20	.40
216	Ralltiir Freighter Captain F	1.00	2.00
217	Ralltiir Operations	2.50	5.00
218	Ralltiir Operative C	.20	.40
219	Rapid Fire C	.20	.40
220	Rappertunie U	.60	1.25
221	Rebel Ambush C	.20	.40
222	Rebel Base Occupation R	1.25	2.50
223	Rebel Fleet R	1.50	3.00
224	Red 10 U	.60	1.25
225	Red 7 U	.60	1.25
226	Red 8 U	.60	1.25
227	Red 9 U	.60	1.25
228	Relentless Pursuit C	.20	.40
229	Rendezvous Point R	1.50	3.00
230	Rendili F	1.00	2.00
231	Rendili StarDrive R	1.25	2.50
232	Rescue The Princess R	1.50	3.00
233	Return To Base R	1.50	3.00
234	Roche U	.60	1.25
235	Rock Wart F	1.00	2.00
236	Rogue 4 R	2.50	5.00
237	Ronto DARK C	.20	.40
238	Ronto LIGHT C	.20	.40
239	RRíuruurrr R	1.50	3.00
240	Ryle Torsyn U	.60	1.25
241	Rystall R	2.50	5.00
242	Sacrifice F	1.00	2.00
243	Sandspeeder F	1.00	2.00
244	Sandtrooper F	1.00	2.00
245	Sarlacc R	1.50	3.00
246	Scrambled Transmission U	.60	1.25
247	Scurrier F	1.00	2.00
248	Secret Plans U	.60	1.25
249	Sentinel-Class Landing Craft F	1.00	2.00
250	Sergeant Edian U	.60	1.25
251	Sergeant Hollis R	1.50	3.00
252	Sergeant Major Bursk U	.60	1.25
253	Sergeant Major Enfield R	1.25	2.50
254	Sergeant Merril U	.60	1.25
255	Sergeant Narthax R	1.50	3.00
256	Sergeant Torent R	1.50	3.00
257	S-Foils C	.20	.40
258	SFS L-s9.3 Laser Cannons C	.20	.40
259	Short-Range Fighters R	1.50	3.00
260	Sienar Fleet Systems R	1.50	3.00
261	Slayn and Korpil Facilities R	1.25	2.50
262	Slight Weapons Malfunction C	.20	.40
263	Soth Petikkin R	1.25	2.50
264	Spaceport City DARK F	1.00	2.00
265	Spaceport City LIGHT F	1.00	2.00
266	Spaceport Docking Bay DARK F	1.00	2.00
267	Spaceport Docking Bay LIGHT F	1.00	2.00
268	Spaceport Prefectís Office F	1.00	2.00
269	Spaceport Street DARK F	1.00	2.00
270	Spaceport Street LIGHT F	1.00	2.00
271	Spiral R	2.00	4.00
272	Star Destroyer! R	1.50	3.00
273	Stay Sharp! U	.60	1.25
274	Steady Aim C	.20	.40
275	Strategic Reserves R	1.50	3.00
276	Suppressive Fire C	.20	.40
277	Surface Defense R	1.50	3.00
278	Swamp DARK F	1.00	2.00
279	Swamp LIGHT F	1.00	2.00
280	Swoop Mercenary F	1.00	2.00
281	Sy Snootles R	1.50	3.00
282	T-47 Battle Formation R	1.50	3.00
283	Tarkinís Bounty U	.60	1.25
284	Tatooine Celebration R	2.00	4.00
285	Tatooine Occupation R	2.50	5.00
286	Tatooine: Anchorhead F	1.00	2.00
287	Tatooine: Beggaris Canyon R	1.25	2.50
288	Tatooine: Jabbaís Palace C	.20	.40
289	Tatooine: Jawa Canyon DARK U	.60	1.25
290	Tatooine: Jawa Canyon LIGHT U	.60	1.25
291	Tatooine: Krayt Dragon Pass F	1.00	2.00
292	Tatooine: Tosche Station C	.20	.40
293	Tauntaun Skull C	.20	.40
294	Tawss Khaa R	1.25	2.50
295	The Planet That Itís Farthest From U	.60	1.25
296	Thedit R	1.50	3.00
297	Theron Nett U	.60	.1.25
298	Theyíre Coming In Too Fast! C	.20	.40
299	Theyíre Tracking Us C	.20	.40
300	Theyíve Shut Down The Main Reactor C	.20	.40
301	Tibrin Operative C	.20	.40
302	TIE Defender Mark I F	1.00	2.00
303	TK-422 R	1.50	3.00
304	Trooper Sabacc DARK F	1.00	2.00
305	Trooper Sabacc LIGHT F	1.00	2.00
306	Uh-oh! U	.60	1.25
307	Umpass-stay R	1.25	2.50
308	UriRuír R	1.50	3.00
309	URoRRuRíRiRis Bantha R	1.50	3.00
310	Uutkik R	1.50	3.00
311	Vaderís Personal Shuttle R	1.50	3.00
312	Vengeance R	1.50	3.00
313	Wakeelmui U	.60	1.25
314	Watch Your Back! C	.20	.40
315	Weapons Display C	.20	.40
316	Wise Advice U	.60	1.25
317	Wittinís Sandcrawler R	1.50	3.00
318	Womp Rat C	.20	.40
319	Wookiee F	1.00	2.00
320	Wrist Comlink C	.20	.40
321	X-wing Assault Squadron R	1.50	3.00
322	X-wing Laser Cannon C	.20	.40
323	Yavin 4 Trooper F	1.00	2.00
324	Yavin 4: Massassi Headquarters R	1.50	3.00

1999 Star Wars Endor

COMPLETE SET (180)	75.00	150.00
BOOSTER BOX (30 PACKS)	75.00	150.00
BOOSTER PACK (9 CARDS)	3.50	7.00
RELEASED IN JUNE 1999		

1 AT-ST Pilot C	.20	.40
2 Biker Scout Trooper C	.20	.40
3 Colonel Dyer R	2.00	4.00
4 Commander Igar R	2.00	4.00
5 Corporal Avarik U	.60	1.25
6 Corporal Drazin U	.60	1.25
7 Corporal Drelosyn R	2.00	4.00
8 Corporal Misik R	1.50	3.00
9 Corporal Oberk R	2.00	4.00
10 Elite Squadron Stormtrooper C	.20	.40
11 Lieutenant Arnet U	.60	1.25
12 Lieutenant Grond U	.60	1.25
13 Lieutenant Renz R	1.25	2.50
14 Lieutenant Watts R	2.00	4.00
15 Major Hewex R	1.25	2.50
16 Major Marquand R	2.50	5.00
17 Navy Trooper C	.20	.40
18 Navy Trooper Fenson R	1.50	3.00
19 Navy Trooper Shield Technician C	.20	.40
20 Navy Trooper Vesden U	.60	1.25
21 Sergeant Barich R	3.00	6.00
22 Sergeant Elsek U	.60	1.25
23 Sergeant Irol R	2.50	5.00
24 Sergeant Tarl U	.60	1.25
25 Sergeant Wallen R	2.50	5.00
26 An Entire Legion Of My Best Troops U	.60	1.25
27 Aratech Corporation R	1.50	3.00
28 Battle Order U	.30	.80
29 Biker Scout Gear U	.60	1.25
30 Closed Door R	1.25	2.50
31 Crossfire R	5.00	10.00
32 Early Warning Network R	1.25	2.50
33 Empireís New Order R	1.25	2.50
34 Establish Secret Base R	2.50	5.00
35 Imperial Academy Training C	.20	.40
36 Imperial Arrest Order U	.60	1.25
37 Ominous Rumors R	1.25	2.50
38 Perimeter Patrol R	1.50	3.00
39 Pinned Down U	.60	1.25
40 Relentless Tracking R	1.25	2.50
41 Search And Destroy U	.60	1.25
42 Security Precautions R	4.00	8.00
43 Well-earned Command R	1.25	2.50
44 Accelerate C	.20	.40
45 Always Thinking With Your Stomach R	4.00	8.00
46 Combat Readiness C	.20	.40
47 Compact Firepower C	.20	.40
48 Counterattack R	1.25	2.50
49 Dead Ewok C	.20	.40
50 Donit Move! C	.20	.40
51 Eee Chu Wawa! C	.20	.40
52 Endor Scout Trooper C	.20	.40
53 Freeze! U	.60	1.25
54 Go For Help! C	.20	.40
55 High-speed Tactics U	.60	1.25
56 Hot Pursuit C	.20	.40
57 Imperial Tyranny C	.20	.40
58 Itís An Older Code R	1.25	2.50
59 Main Course U	.60	1.25
60 Outflank C	.20	.40
61 Pitiful Little Band C	.20	.40
62 Scout Recon C	.20	.40
63 Sneak Attack C	.20	.40
64 Wounded Warrior R	2.50	5.00
65 You Rebel Scum R	1.50	3.00
66 Carida U	.60	1.25
67 Endor Occupation R	1.25	2.50
68 Endor: Ancient Forest U	.60	1.25
69 Endor: Back Door LIGHT U	.60	1.25
70 Endor: Bunker LIGHT U	.60	1.25

71 Endor: Dark Forest R	4.00	8.00
72 Endor: Dense Forest LIGHT C	.20	.40
73 Endor: Ewok Village LIGHT U	.60	1.25
74 Endor: Forest Clearing U	.60	1.25
75 Endor: Great Forest LIGHT C	.20	.40
76 Endor: Landing Platform	.20	.40
77 Endor DARK U	.60	1.25
78 Lambda-class Shuttle C	.20	.40
79 Speeder Bike LIGHT C	.20	.40
80 Tempest 1 R	1.25	2.50
81 Tempest Scout 1 R	1.50	3.00
82 Tempest Scout 2 R	3.00	6.00
83 Tempest Scout 3 R	1.25	2.50
84 Tempest Scout 4 R	4.00	8.00
85 Tempest Scout 5 R	3.00	6.00
86 Tempest Scout 6 R	4.00	8.00
87 Tempest Scout U	.60	1.25
88 AT-ST Dual Cannon R	10.00	20.00
89 Scout Blaster C	.20	.40
90 Speeder Bike Cannon U	.60	1.25
91 Captain Yutani U	.60	1.25
92 Chewbacca of Kashyyyk R	1.25	2.50
93 Chief Chirpa R	1.50	3.00
94 Corporal Beezer U	.60	1.25
95 Corporal Delevar U	.60	1.25
96 Corporal Janse U	.60	1.25
97 Corporal Kensaric R	2.00	4.00
98 Daughter of Skywalker R	12.00	25.00
99 Dresselian Commando C	.20	.40
100 Endor LIGHT U	.60	1.25
101 Ewok Sentry C	.20	.40
102 Ewok Spearman C	.20	.40
103 Ewok Tribesman C	.20	.40
104 General Crix Madine R	1.50	3.00
105 General Solo R	1.25	2.50
106 Graak R	1.25	2.50
107 Kazak R	1.50	3.00
108 Lieutenant Greeve R	1.25	2.50
109 Lieutenant Page R	2.50	5.00
110 Logray R	1.25	2.50
111 Lumat U	.60	1.25
112 Mon Mothma R	2.00	4.00
113 Orrimaarko R	1.25	2.50
114 Paploo U	.60	1.25
115 Rabin U	.60	1.25
116 Romba R	1.25	2.50
117 Sergeant Brooks Carlson R	1.25	2.50
118 Sergeant Bruckman R	1.25	2.50
119 Sergeant Junkin U	.60	1.25
120 Teebo R	1.25	2.50
121 Threepio R	2.00	4.00
122 Wicket R	1.25	2.50
123 Wuta U	.60	1.25
124 Aim High R	1.50	3.00
125 Battle Plan U	.60	1.25
126 Commando Training C	.20	.40
127 Count Me In R	1.25	2.50
128 I Hope Sheís All Right U	.60	1.25
129 I Wonder Who They Found U	.60	1.25
130 Insurrection U	.60	1.25
131 Thatís One R	1.25	2.50
132 Wokling R	10.00	20.00
133 Deactivate The Shield Generator R	2.00	4.00
134 Careful Planning C	.20	.40
135 Covert Landing U	.60	1.25
136 Endor Operations / Imperial Outpost R	4.00	8.00
137 Ewok And Roll C	.20	.40
138 Ewok Log Jam C	.20	.40
139 Ewok Rescue C	.20	.40
140 Firefight C	.20	.40

141 Fly Casual R	1.25	2.50
142 Free Ride U	.60	1.25
143 Get Alongside That One U	.60	1.25
144 Here We Go Again R	1.25	2.50
145 I Have A Really Bad	.20	.40
146 I Know R	2.00	4.00
147 Lost In The Wilderness R	1.25	2.50
148 Rapid Deployment R	1.25	2.50
149 Sound The Attack C	.20	.40
150 Surprise Counter Assault R	1.25	2.50
151 Take The Initiative C	.20	.40
152 This Is Absolutely Right R	1.25	2.50
153 Throw Me Another Charge U	.60	1.25
154 Were You Looking For Me? R	6.00	12.00
155 Wookiee Guide C	.20	.40
156 Yub Yub! C	.20	.40
157 Chandrila U	.60	1.25
158 Endor Celebration R	1.25	2.50
159 Endor: Back Door DARK U	.60	1.25
160 Endor: Bunker DARK U	.60	1.25
161 Endor: Chief Chirpaís Hut R	5.00	10.00
162 Endor: Dense Forest DARK C	.20	.40
163 Endor: Ewok Village DARK U	.60	1.25
164 Endor: Great Forest DARK C	.20	.40
165 Endor: Hidden Forest Trail U	.60	1.25
166 Endor: Landing Platform	.20	.40
167 Endor: Rebel Landing Site (Forest) R	4.00	8.00
168 Rebel Strike Team	2.00	4.00
169 Tydirium R	2.00	4.00
170 YT-1300 Transport C	.20	.40
171 Chewieís AT-ST R	5.00	10.00
172 Ewok Glider C	.20	.40
173 Speeder Bike DARK C	.20	.40
174 A280 Sharpshooter Rifle R	4.00	8.00
175 BlasTech E-11B Blaster Rifle C	.20	.40
176 Chewbaccaís Bowcaster R	4.00	8.00
177 Ewok Bow C	.20	.40
178 Ewok Catapult U	.60	1.25
179 Ewok Spear C	.20	.40
180 Explosive Charge U	.60	1.25

1999 Star Wars Enhanced Cloud City

COMPLETE SET (12)	12.00	25.00
RELEASED IN 1999		
1 4-LOM With Concussion Rifle PM	2.50	5.00
2 Any Methods Necessary PM	3.00	6.00
3 Boba Fett in Slave I PM	1.50	3.00
4 Chewie With Blaster Rifle PM	1.50	3.00
5 Crush The Rebellion PM	2.00	4.00
6 Dengar In Punishing One PM	1.50	3.00
7 IG-88 With Riot Gun PM	5.00	10.00
8 Lando In Millennium Falcon PM	1.50	3.00
9 Lando With Blaster Pistol PM	1.50	3.00
10 Quiet Mining Colony PM	1.50	3.00
11 This Deal Is Getting Worse All The Time	1.50	3.00
12 Z-95 Bespin Defense Fighter PM	1.50	3.00

1999 Star Wars Enhanced Jabba's Palace

COMPLETE SET (12)	20.00	40.00
RELEASE IN 1999		
1 Bossk With Mortar Gun PM	1.50	3.00
2 Boushh PM	2.00	4.00
3 Court Of The Vile Gangster	1.50	3.00
4 Dengar With Blaster Carbine PM	1.50	3.00
5 IG-88 In IG-2000 PM	1.50	3.00
6 Jodo Kast PM	2.50	5.00
7 Mara Jade, The Emperorís Hand PM	12.00	25.00
8 Mara Jadeís Lightsaber PM	2.50	5.00
9 Master Luke PM	4.00	8.00

10 See-Threepio PM	1.50	3.00
11 You Can Either Profit By This...	1.50	3.00
12 Zuckuss In Mist Hunter PM	2.00	4.00

2000 Star Wars Death Star II

COMPLETE SET (182)	200.00	300.00
BOOSTER BOX (30 PACKS)	150.00	250.00
BOOSTER PACK (11 CARDS)	5.00	9.00
RELEASED IN JULY 2000		
1 Accuser R	1.50	3.00
2 Admiral Ackbar XR	1.50	3.00
3 Admiral Chiraneau R	2.00	4.00
4 Admiral Piett XR	1.25	2.50
5 Anakin Skywalker R	1.25	2.50
6 Aquaris C	.15	.30
7 A-wing C	.15	.30
8 A-wing Cannon C	.15	.30
9 Baron Soontir Fel R	2.00	4.00
10 Battle Deployment R	1.50	3.00
11 Black 11 R	1.25	2.50
12 Blue Squadron 5 U	.50	1.00
13 Blue Squadron B-wing R	2.00	4.00
14 Bring Him Before Me	1.25	2.50
Take Your Fatherís Place R		
15 B-wing Attack Squadron R	1.25	2.50
16 B-wing Bomber C	.15	.30
17 Capital Support R	1.25	2.50
18 Captain Godherdt U	.50	1.00
19 Captain Jonus U	.50	1.00
20 Captain Sarkli R	1.25	2.50
21 Captain Verrack U	.50	1.00
22 Captain Yorr U	.50	1.00
23 Chimaera R	3.00	6.00
24 Close Air Support C	.15	.30
25 Colonel Cracken R	1.25	2.50
26 Colonel Davod Jon U	.50	1.00
27 Colonel Jendon R	1.25	2.50
28 Colonel Salm U	.50	1.00
29 Combat Response C	.15	.30
30 Combined Fleet Action R	1.25	2.50
31 Commander Merrejk R	1.50	3.00
32 Concentrate All Fire R	1.25	2.50
33 Concussion Missiles DARK C	.15	.30
34 Concussion Missiles LIGHT C	.15	.30
35 Corporal Marmor U	.50	1.00
36 Corporal Midge U	.50	1.00
37 Critical Error Revealed C	.15	.30
38 Darth Vaderís Lightsaber R	1.25	2.50
39 Death Star II R	1.50	3.00
40 Death Star II: Capacitors C	.15	.30
41 Death Star II: Coolant Shaft C	.15	.30

42 Death Star II: Docking Bay C	.15	.30
43 Death Star II: Reactor Core C	.15	.30
44 Death Star II: Throne Room R	1.25	2.50
45 Defiance R	1.50	3.00
46 Desperate Counter C	.15	.30
47 Dominator R	1.25	2.50
48 DS-181-3 U	.50	1.00
49 DS-181-4 U	.50	1.00
50 Emperor Palpatine UR	30.00	60.00
51 Emperorís Personal Shuttle R	1.25	2.50
52 Emperorís Power U	.50	1.00
53 Endor Shield U	.50	1.00
54 Enhanced Proton Torpedoes C	.15	.30
55 Fighter Cover R	2.50	5.00
56 Fighters Coming In R	1.25	2.50
57 First Officer Thaneespi R	1.25	2.50
58 Flagship Executor R	1.50	3.00
59 Flagship Operations R	1.25	2.50
60 Force Lightning R	2.50	5.00
61 Force Pike C	.15	.30
62 Gall C	.15	.30
63 General Calrissian R	1.25	2.50
64 General Walex Blissex U	.50	1.00
65 Gold Squadron 1 R	1.25	2.50
66 Gray Squadron 1 U	.50	1.00
67 Gray Squadron 2 U	.50	1.00
68 Gray Squadron Y-wing Pilot C	.15	.30
69 Green Leader R	1.25	2.50
70 Green Squadron 1 R	1.25	2.50
71 Green Squadron 3 R	1.25	2.50
72 Green Squadron A-wing R	1.50	3.00
73 Green Squadron Pilot C	.15	.30
74 Head Back To The Surface C	.15	.30
75 Heading For The Medical Frigate C	.15	.30
76 Heavy Turbolaser Battery DARK C	.15	.30
77 Heavy Turbolaser Battery LIGHT C	.15	.30
78 Home One R	5.00	10.00
79 Home One: Docking Bay C	.15	.30
80 Home One: War Room R	1.50	3.00
81 Honor Of The Jedi U	.50	1.00
82 I Feel The Conflict U	.50	1.00
83 Iíll Take The Leader R	3.00	6.00
84 Iím With You Too R	2.00	4.00
85 Imperial Command R	5.00	10.00
86 Inconsequential Losses C	.15	.30
87 Independence R	1.50	3.00
88 Insertion Planning C	.15	.30
89 Insignificant Rebellion U	.50	1.00
90 Intensify The Forward Batteries R	1.25	2.50
91 Janus Greejatus R	1.25	2.50
92 Judicator R	2.00	4.00
93 Karie Neth U	.50	1.00
94 Keir Santage U	.50	1.00
95 Kin Kian U	.50	1.00
96 Launching The Assault R	1.25	2.50
97 Leave Them To Me C	.15	.30
98 Letís Keep A Little Optimism Here C	.15	.30
99 Liberty R	1.50	3.00
100 Lieutenant Blount R	1.25	2.50
101 Lieutenant Endicott U	.50	1.00
102 Lieutenant Hebsly U	.50	1.00
103 Lieutenant síToo Vees U	.50	1.00
104 Lieutenant Telsij U	.50	1.00
105 Lord Vader R	10.00	20.00
106 Luke Skywalker, Jedi Knight UR	30.00	60.00
107 Lukeís Lightsaber R	2.00	4.00
108 Luminous U	.50	1.00
109 Major Haashin U	.50	1.00
110 Major Mianda U	.50	1.00
111 Major Olander Brit U	.50	1.00

112 Major Panno U	.50	1.00
113 Major Rhymer U	.50	1.00
114 Major Turr Phennir U	.50	1.00
115 Masanya R	2.00	4.00
116 Menace Fades U	.15	.30
117 Mobilization Points C	.15	.30
118 Moff Jerjerrod R	1.25	2.50
119 Mon Calamari DARK C	.15	.30
120 Mon Calamari LIGHT C	.15	.30
121 Mon Calamari Star Cruiser R	1.50	3.00
122 Myn Kyneugh R	1.25	2.50
123 Nebulon-B Frigate U	.50	1.00
124 Nien Nunb R	1.50	3.00
125 Obsidian 10 U	.50	1.00
126 Onyx 1 R	1.50	3.00
127 Onyx 2 U	.50	1.00
128 Operational As Planned C	.15	.30
129 Orbital Mine C	.15	.30
130 Our Only Hope U	.50	1.00
131 Overseeing It Personally R	1.25	2.50
132 Prepared Defenses C	.15	.30
133 Rebel Leadership R	4.00	8.00
134 Red Squadron 1 R	1.25	2.50
135 Red Squadron 4 U	.50	1.00
136 Red Squadron 7 U	.50	1.00
137 Rise, My Friend R	1.25	2.50
138 Royal Escort C	.15	.30
139 Royal Guard C	.15	.30
140 Saber 1 R	7.50	15.00
141 Saber 2 U	.50	1.00
142 Saber 3 U	.50	1.00
143 Saber 4 U	.50	1.00
144 Scimitar 1 U	.50	1.00
145 Scimitar 2 U	.50	1.00
146 Scimitar Squadron TIE C	.15	.30
147 Scythe 1 U	.50	1.00
148 Scythe 3 U	.50	1.00
149 Scythe Squadron TIE C	.15	.30
150 SFS L-s7.2 TIE Cannon C	.15	.30
151 Sim Aloo R	1.25	2.50
152 Something Special Planned For Them C	.15	.30
153 Squadron Assignments C	.15	.30
154 Staging Areas C	.15	.30
155 Strike Planning R	1.25	2.50
156 Strikeforce C	.15	.30
157 Sullust DARK C	.15	.30
158 Sullust LIGHT C	.15	.30
159 Superficial Damage C	.15	.30
160 Superlaser Mark II U	.50	1.00
161 Taking Them With Us R	1.50	3.00
162 Tala 1 R	1.25	2.50
163 Tala 2 R	1.25	2.50
164 Ten Numb R	1.25	2.50
165 That Thingís Operational R	1.25	2.50
166 The Emperorís Shield R	1.25	2.50
167 The Emperorís Sword R	1.25	2.50
168 The Time For Our Attack Has Come C	.15	.30
169 The Way Of Things U	.50	1.00
170 There Is Good In Him	1.25	2.50
I Can Save Him R		
171 Thunderflare R	1.25	2.50
172 TIE Interceptor C	.15	.30
173 Twilight Is Upon Me R	1.25	2.50
174 Tycho Celchu R	1.50	3.00
175 Visage R	1.25	2.50
176 Weíre In Attack Position Now R	3.00	6.00
177 Wedge Antilles, Red Squadron Leader R	2.00	4.00
178 You Cannot Hide Forever U	.50	1.00
179 You Must Confront Vader R	2.00	4.00

180	Young Fool R	1.25	2.50
181	Your Destiny C	.15	.30
182	Your Insight Serves You Well U	.50	1.00

2000 Star Wars Jabba's Palace Sealed Deck

COMPLETE SET (20)		5.00	12.00
RELEASE DATE FALL, 2000			
1	Agents In The Court	.50	1.00
	No Love For The Empire PM		
2	Hutt Influence PM	.50	1.00
3	Jabba's Palace: Antechamber PM	.50	1.00
4	Jabba's Palace: Lower Passages PM	.50	1.00
5	Lando With Vibro-Ax PM	.50	1.00
6	Let Them Make The First Move / My Kind Of Scum	.50	1.00
	Fearless And Inventive PM		
7	Mercenary Pilot PM	.50	1.00
8	Mighty Jabba PM	.50	1.00
9	No Escape PM	.50	1.00
10	Ounee Ta PM	.50	1.00
11	Palace Raider PM	.50	1.00
12	Power Of The Hutt PM	.50	1.00
13	Racing Skiff DARK PM	.50	1.00
14	Racing Skiff LIGHT PM	.50	1.00
15	Seeking An Audience PM	.50	1.00
16	Stun Blaster DARK PM	.50	1.00
17	Stun Blaster LIGHT PM	.50	1.00
18	Tatooine: Desert Heart PM	.50	1.00
19	Tatooine: Hutt Trade Route (Desert) PM	.50	1.00
20	Underworld Contacts PM	.50	1.00

2000 Star Wars Reflections II

COMPLETE SET (54)		20.00	50.00
BOOSTER BOX (30 PACKS)		150.00	250.00
BOOSTER PACK (11 CARDS)		5.00	10.00
RELEASED IN DECEMBER 2000			
1	There Is No Try and	.75	1.50
	Oppressive Enforcement PM		
2	Abyssin Ornament and	.50	1.00
	Wounded Wookiee PM		
3	Agents Of Black Sun	.50	1.00
	Vengence Of The Dark Prince PM		
4	Alter and Collateral Damage PM	.75	1.50
5	Alter and Friendly Fire PM	.75	1.50
6	Arica PM	2.50	5.00
7	Artoo and Threepio PM	.75	1.50
8	Black Sun Fleet PM	.50	1.00
9	Captain Gilad Pellaeon PM	.75	1.50
10	Chewbacca, Protector PM	.75	1.50
11	Control and Set For Stun PM	.75	1.50
12	Control and Tunnel Vision PM	1.25	2.50
13	Corran Horn PM	2.00	4.00

14	Dark Maneuvers and Tallon Roll PM	1.25	2.50
15	Dash Rendar PM	1.50	3.00
16	Defensive Fire and Hutt Smooch PM	.50	1.00
17	Do, Or Do Not and Wise Advice PM	.50	1.00
18	Dr Evazan and Ponda Baba PM	.50	1.00
19	Evader and Monnok PM	.75	1.50
20	Ghhhk and Those Rebels	.50	1.00
	Won't Escape Us PM		
21	Grand Admiral Thrawn PM	3.00	6.00
22	Guri PM	1.50	3.00
23	Houjix and Out Of Nowhere PM	.75	1.50
24	Jabba's Prize PM	.50	1.00
25	Kir Kanos PM	.50	1.00
26	LE-BO2D9 [Leebo] PM	.50	1.00
27	Luke Skywalker, Rebel Scout PM	1.25	2.50
28	Mercenary Armor PM	.50	1.00
29	Mirax Terrik PM	.75	1.50
30	Nar Shaddaa Wind Chimes	.50	1.00
	and Out Of Somewhere PM		
31	No Questions Asked PM	.50	1.00
32	Obi-Wan's Journal PM	.50	1.00
33	Ommni Box and It's Worse PM	.50	1.00
34	Out of Commission and	1.25	2.50
	Transmission Terminated PM		
35	Outrider PM	.75	1.50
36	Owen Lars and Beru Lars PM	.50	1.00
37	Path Of Least	.50	1.00
	Resistance and Revealed PM		
38	Prince Xizor PM	2.00	4.00
39	Pulsar Skate PM	.50	1.00
40	Sense and Recoil In Fear PM	.75	1.50
41	Sense and Uncertain Is The Future PM	.75	1.50
42	Shocking Information and Grimtaash PM	.50	1.00
43	Sniper and Dark Strike PM	.50	1.00
44	Snoova PM	1.25	2.50
45	Sorry About The Mess	.75	1.50
	and Blaster Proficiency PM		
46	Stinger PM	.50	1.00
47	Sunsdown and	.50	1.00
	Too Cold For Speeders PM		
48	Talon Karrde PM	.75	1.50
49	The Bith Shuffle and	.50	1.00
	Desperate Reach PM		
50	The Emperor PM	2.00	4.00
51	Vigo PM	2.00	4.00
52	Virago PM	.50	1.00
53	Watch Your Step	.50	1.00
	This Place Can Be A Little Rough PM		
54	Yoda Stew and You Do Have Your Moments PM	.50	1.00

2000 Star Wars Third Anthology

COMPLETE SET (6)		4.00	10.00
RELEASED IN 2000			
1	A New Secret Base PM	1.25	2.50
2	Artoo-Detoo In Red 5 PM	1.25	2.50
3	Echo Base Garrison PM	1.25	2.50
4	Massassi Base Operations	1.25	2.50
	One In A Million PM		
5	Prisoner 2187 PM	1.25	2.50
6	Set Your Course For Alderaan	1.25	2.50
	The Ultimate Power In The Universe PM		

2001 Star Wars Coruscant

COMPLETE SET (188)		120.00	250.00
BOOSTER BOX (30 PACKS)		300.00	400.00
BOOSTER PACK (11 CARDS)		12.00	15.00
RELEASED IN AUGUST 2001			
1	A Tragedy Has Occurred U	.50	1.00
2	A Vergence In The Force U	.50	1.00
3	Accepting Trade Federation Control U	.50	1.00
4	Aks Moe R	1.50	3.00
5	All Wings Report In and Darklighter Spin R	7.50	15.00
6	Allegations Of Corruption U	.50	1.00
7	Alter DARK U	.50	1.00
8	Alter LIGHT U	.50	1.00
9	Another Pathetic Lifeform U	.50	1.00
10	Are You Brain Dead?! R	2.00	4.00
11	Ascertaining The Truth U	.50	1.00
12	Baseless Accusations C	.15	.30
13	Baskol Yeesrim U	.50	1.00
14	Battle Droid Blaster Rifle C	.15	.30
15	Battle Order and First Strike R	1.25	2.50
16	Battle Plan and Draw Their Fire R	2.00	4.00
17	Begin Landing Your Troops U	.50	1.00
18	Blockade Flagship: Bridge R	4.00	8.00
19	Captain Madakor R	1.25	2.50
20	Captain Panaka R	1.25	2.50
21	Chokk U	.50	1.00
22	Control DARK U	.50	1.00
23	Control LIGHT U	.50	1.00
24	Coruscant DARK C	.15	.30
25	Coruscant LIGHT C	.15	.30
26	Coruscant Guard DARK C	.15	.30
27	Coruscant Guard LIGHT C	.15	.30
28	Coruscant: Docking Bay DARK C	.15	.30
29	Coruscant: Docking Bay LIGHT C	.15	.30
30	Coruscant: Galactic Senate DARK C	.15	.30
31	Coruscant: Galactic Senate LIGHT C	.15	.30
32	Coruscant: Jedi Council Chamber R	4.00	8.00
33	Credits Will Do Fine C	.15	.30
34	Darth Maul, Young Apprentice R	15.00	30.00
35	Daultay Dofine R	1.50	3.00

36 Depa Billaba R	1.50	3.00	
37 Destroyer Droid R	12.00	25.00	
38 Dioxis R	1.25	2.50	
39 Do They Have A Code Clearance? R	1.25	2.50	
40 Droid Starfighter C	.15	.30	
41 Drop! U	.50	1.00	
42 Edcel Bar Gane C	.15	.30	
43 Enter The Bureaucrat U	.50	1.00	
44 Establish Control U	.50	1.00	
45 Free Ride and Endor Celebration R	2.00	4.00	
46 Freon Drevan U	.50	1.00	
47 Gardulla The Hutt U	.50	1.00	
48 Graxol Kelvyyn U	.50	1.00	
49 Grotto Werribee R	1.50	3.00	
50 Gungan Warrior C	.15	.30	
51 Horox Ryyder C	.15	.30	
52 I Will Not Defer U	.50	1.00	
53 Iíve Decided To Go Back C	.15	.30	
54 Imperial Arrest Order and Secret Plans R	4.00	8.00	
55 Imperial Artillery R	4.00	8.00	
56 Inconsequential Barriers C	.15	.30	
57 Insurrection and Aim High R	3.00	6.00	
58 Jawa DARK C	.15	.30	
59 Jawa LIGHT C	.15	.30	
60 Keder The Black R	1.25	2.50	
61 Ki-Adi-Mundi U	.50	1.00	
62 Kill Them Immediately C	.15	.30	
63 Lana Dobreed U	.50	1.00	
64 Laser Cannon Battery U	.50	1.00	
65 Liana Merian U	.50	1.00	
66 Lieutenant Williams U	.50	1.00	
67 Little Real Power C	.15	.30	
68 Lott Dod R	1.50	3.00	
69 Mace Windu R	10.00	20.00	
70 Malastare DARK U	.50	1.00	
71 Malastare LIGHT U	.50	1.00	
72 Mas Amedda U	.50	1.00	
73 Master Qui-Gon R	4.00	8.00	
74 Masterful Move and Endor Occupation R	2.50	5.00	
75 Maul Strikes R	2.50	5.00	
76 Maulís Sith Infiltrator R	4.00	8.00	
77 Might Of The Republic R	3.00	6.00	
78 Mind Tricks Donít Work On Me U	.50	1.00	
79 Mindful Of The Future C	.15	.30	
80 Motion Supported U	.50	1.00	
81 Murr Danod R	1.25	2.50	
82 My Lord, Is That Legal?	.50	1.00	
I Will Make It Legal U			
83 My Loyal Bodyguard U	.50	1.00	
84 Naboo Blaster C	.15	.30	
85 Naboo Blaster Rifle DARK C	.15	.30	
86 Naboo Blaster Rifle LIGHT C	.15	.30	
87 Naboo Defense Fighter C	.15	.30	
88 Naboo Fighter Pilot C	.15	.30	
89 Naboo Security Officer Blaster C	.15	.30	
90 Naboo DARK U	.50	1.00	
91 Naboo LIGHT U	.50	1.00	
92 Naboo: Battle Plains DARK C	.15	.30	
93 Naboo: Battle Plains LIGHT C	.15	.30	
94 Naboo: Swamp DARK C	.15	.30	
95 Naboo: Swamp LIGHT C	.15	.30	
96 Naboo: Theed Palace	.15	.30	
Courtyard DARK C			
97 Naboo: Theed Palace	.15	.30	
Courtyard LIGHT C			
98 Naboo: Theed Palace	.15	.30	
Docking Bay DARK C			
99 Naboo: Theed Palace	.15	.30	
Docking Bay LIGHT C			
100 Naboo: Theed Palace	.15	.30	

Throne Room DARK C			
101 Naboo: Theed Palace	.15	.30	
Throne Room LIGHT C			
102 Neimoidian Advisor U	.50	1.00	
103 Neimoidian Pilot C	.15	.30	
104 New Leadership Is Needed C	.15	.30	
105 No Civility, Only Politics C	.15	.30	
106 No Money, No Parts, No Deal!	.50	1.00	
Youíre A Slave? U			
107 Nute Gunray R	1.25	2.50	
108 Odin Nesloor U	.50	1.00	
109 On The Payroll Of The Trade Federation C	.15	.30	
110 Orn Free Taa C	.15	.30	
111 Our Blockade Is Perfectly Legal U	.50	1.00	
112 P-59 R	4.00	8.00	
113 P-60 R	2.00	4.00	
114 Panakaís Blaster R	1.50	3.00	
115 Passel Argente C	.15	.30	
116 Phylo Gandish R	2.00	4.00	
117 Plea To The Court U	.50	1.00	
118 Plead My Case To The Senate	.50	1.00	
Sanity And Compassion U			
119 Plo Koon R	4.00	8.00	
120 Queen Amidala, Ruler Of Naboo R	5.00	10.00	
121 Queenís Royal Starship R	1.50	3.00	
122 Radiant VII R	2.00	4.00	
123 Rebel Artillery R	4.00	8.00	
124 Republic Cruiser C	.15	.30	
125 Reveal Ourselves To The Jedi C	.15	.30	
126 Ric Olie R	1.25	2.50	
127 Rune Haako R	1.25	2.50	
128 Sabe R	1.50	3.00	
129 Sache U	.50	1.00	
130 Secure Route U	.50	1.00	
131 Security Battle Droid C	.15	.30	
132 Security Control U	.50	1.00	
133 Sei Taria U	.50	1.00	
134 Senator Palpatine	4.00	8.00	
(head and shoulders) R			
135 Senator Palpatine (head shot) R	15.00	30.00	
136 Sense DARK U	.50	1.00	
137 Sense LIGHT U	.50	1.00	
138 Short Range Fighters and	3.00	6.00	
Watch Your Back! R			
139 Speak With The Jedi Council R	4.00	8.00	
140 Squabbling Delegates R	1.50	3.00	
141 Stay Here, Where Itís Safe C	.15	.30	
142 Supreme Chancellor Valorum R	1.25	2.50	
143 Tatooine DARK U	.50	1.00	
144 Tatooine LIGHT U	.50	1.00	
145 Tatooine: Marketplace DARK C	.15	.30	
146 Tatooine: Marketplace LIGHT C	.15	.30	
147 Tatooine: Mos Espa Docking Bay DARK C	.15	.30	
148 Tatooine: Mos Espa Docking Bay LIGHT C	.15	.30	
149 Tatooine: Wattoís Junkyard DARK C	.15	.30	
150 Tatooine: Wattoís Junkyard LIGHT C	.15	.30	
151 TC-14 R	1.25	2.50	
152 Televan Koreyy R	1.25	2.50	
153 Tendau Bendon U	.50	1.00	
154 Tey How U	.50	1.00	
155 The Gravest Of Circumstances U	.50	1.00	
156 The Hyperdrive Generatorís Gone	.50	1.00	
Weíll Need A New One U			
157 The Phantom Menace R	5.00	10.00	
158 The Point Is Conceded C	.15	.30	
159 They Will Be No Match For You R	1.25	2.50	
160 Theyíre Still Coming Through! U	.50	1.00	
161 This Is Outrageous! U	.50	1.00	
162 Thrown Back C	.15	.30	
163 Tikkes C	.15	.30	

164 Toonbuck Toora U	.50	1.00	
165 Trade Federation Battleship U	.50	1.00	
166 Trade Federation Droid Control Ship R	1.50	3.00	
167 Tusken Raider C	.15	.30	
168 Vote Now! DARK R	1.25	2.50	
169 Vote Now! LIGHT R	1.50	3.00	
170 We Must Accelerate Our Plans R	10.00	20.00	
171 We Wish To Board At Once R	2.50	5.00	
172 Weíre Leaving C	.15	.30	
173 Wipe Them Out, All Of Them U	.50	1.00	
174 Yade Mírak U	.50	1.00	
175 YanÈ U	.50	1.00	
176 Yarua U	.50	1.00	
177 Yeb Yeb Ademithorn C	.15	.30	
178 Yoda, Senior Council Member R	3.00	6.00	
179 You Cannot Hide Forever	3.00	6.00	
and Mobilization Points R			
180 You've Got A Lot Of	1.50	3.00	
Guts Coming Here R			
181 Your Insight Serves You Well	1.25	2.50	
and Staging Areas R			
182 Coruscant Dark Side List 1	.15	.30	
183 Coruscant Dark Side List 2	.15	.30	
184 Coruscant Light Side List 1	.15	.30	
185 Coruscant Light Side List 2	.15	.30	
186 Coruscant Rule Card 1	.15	.30	
187 Coruscant Rule Card 2	.15	.30	
188 Coruscant Rule Card 3	.15	.30	

2001 Star Wars Reflections III

COMPLETE SET (96)	80.00	150.00
BOOSTER BOX (30 PACKS)	250.00	350.00
BOOSTER PACK (11 CARDS)	7.50	15.00
RELEASED IN 2001		
1 A Close Race PM	1.25	2.50
2 A Remote Planet PM	1.25	2.50
3 A Tragedy Has Occured PM	1.50	3.00
4 A Useless Gesture PM	1.25	2.50
5 Aim High PM	1.50	3.00
6 Allegations of Corruption PM	1.25	2.50
7 An Unusual Amount Of Fear PM	1.25	2.50
8 Another Pathetic Lifeform PM	1.25	2.50
9 Armament Dismantled PM	1.25	2.50
10 Battle Order PM	1.25	2.50
11 Battle Plan PM	1.50	3.00
12 Bib Fortuna PM	1.25	2.50
13 Blizzard 4 PM	2.50	5.00
14 Blockade Flagship: Hallway PM	1.25	2.50
15 Blow Parried PM	1.25	2.50
16 Boba Fett, Bounty Hunter PM	6.00	12.00
17 Chewie, Enraged PM	2.00	4.00

18 Clinging To The Edge PM	1.25	2.50
19 Colo Claw Fish DARK PM	1.25	2.50
20 Colo Claw Fish LIGHT PM	1.25	2.50
21 Come Here You Big Coward PM	1.50	3.00
22 Conduct Your Search PM	1.50	3.00
23 Crossfire PM	1.25	2.50
24 Dark Rage PM	1.25	2.50
25 Darth Maulís Demise PM	1.25	2.50
26 Deep Hatred PM	1.25	2.50
27 Desperate Times PM	1.25	2.50
28 Diversionary Tactics PM	1.25	2.50
29 Do They Have A Code Clearance? PM	1.50	3.00
30 Do, Or Do Not PM	1.25	2.50
31 Donít Do That Again PM	1.25	2.50
32 Echo Base Sensors PM	1.50	3.00
33 Energy Walls DARK PM	1.25	2.50
34 Energy Walls LIGHT PM	1.25	2.50
35 Ewok Celebration PM	1.25	2.50
36 Fall Of A Jedi PM	1.25	2.50
37 Fanfare PM	1.25	2.50
38 Fear Is My Ally PM	1.25	2.50
39 Force Push PM	1.50	3.00
40 Han, Chewie, and The Falcon PM	6.00	12.00
41 He Can Go About His Business PM	1.25	2.50
42 Horace Vancil PM	1.25	2.50
43 Inner Strength PM	1.25	2.50
44 Jabba Desilijic Tiure PM	1.25	2.50
45 Jar Jarís Electropole PM	1.25	2.50
46 Jedi Leap PM	1.25	2.50
47 Lando Calrissian, Scoundrel PM	2.50	5.00
48 Landoís Not A System, Heís A Man PM	1.25	2.50
49 Leave them to Me PM	1.25	2.50
50 Leia, Rebel Princess PM	3.00	6.00
51 Letís Keep A Little Optimism Here PM	1.25	2.50
52 Lord Maul PM	7.50	15.00
53 Maulís Double-Bladed Lightsaber PM	2.50	5.00
54 Naboo: Theed Palace	1.25	2.50
Generator Core DARK PM		
55 Naboo: Theed Palace	1.25	2.50
Generator Core LIGHT PM		
56 Naboo: Theed Palace	1.25	2.50
Generator DARK PM		
57 Naboo: Theed Palace	1.25	2.50
Generator LIGHT PM		
58 No Escape PM	1.25	2.50
59 No Match For A Sith PM	1.25	2.50
60 Obi-Wan Kenobi, Jedi Knight PM	2.00	4.00
61 Obi-Wanís Lightsaber PM	1.25	2.50
62 Only Jedi Carry That Weapon PM	1.25	2.50
63 Opee Sea Killer DARK PM	1.25	2.50
64 Opee Sea Killer LIGHT PM	1.25	2.50
65 Oppressive Enforcement PM	1.25	2.50
66 Ounee Ta PM	1.25	2.50
67 Planetary Defenses PM	1.25	2.50
68 Prepare For A Surface Attack PM	1.25	2.50
69 Qui-Gon Jinn, Jedi Master PM	3.00	6.00
70 Qui-Gonís End PM	1.50	3.00
71 Reistance PM	1.25	2.50
72 Sando Aqua Monster DARK PM	1.25	2.50
73 Sando Aqua Monster LIGHT PM	1.25	2.50
74 Secret Plans PM	1.25	2.50
75 Sio Bibble PM	1.25	2.50
76 Stormtrooper Garrison PM	5.00	10.00
77 Strike Blockaded PM	1.25	2.50
78 The Ebb Of Battle PM	1.25	2.50
79 The Hutts Are Gangsters PM	1.25	2.50
80 There Is No Try PM	1.50	3.00

81 They Must Never Again	1.25	2.50
Leave This City PM		
82 Thok and Thug PM	1.25	2.50
83 Through The Corridor PM	1.25	2.50
84 Ultimatum PM	1.25	2.50
85 Unsalvageable PM	1.25	2.50
86 Weíll Let Fate-a Decide, Huh? PM	1.25	2.50
87 Weapon Of A Fallen Mentor PM	1.25	2.50
88 Weapon Of A Sith PM	1.25	2.50
89 Where Are Those Droidekas?! PM	1.25	2.50
90 Wipe Them Out, All Of Them PM	1.25	2.50
91 Wise Advice PM	1.25	2.50
92 Yoda, Master Of The Force PM	5.00	10.00
93 You Cannot Hide Forever PM	1.25	2.50
94 Youíve Never Won A Race? PM	1.25	2.50
95 Your Insight Serves You Well PM	1.25	2.50
96 Your Ship? PM	1.50	3.00

2001 Star Wars Tatooine

COMPLETE SET (95)	25.00	60.00
BOOSTER BOX (30 PACKS)	50.00	100.00
BOOSTER PACK (11 CARDS)	2.50	5.00
RELEASED IN MAY 2001		
1 A Jediís Concentration C	.15	.30
2 A Jediís Focus C	.15	.30
3 A Jediís Patience C	.15	.30
4 A Jediís Resilience U	.50	1.00
5 A Million Voices Crying Out R	1.00	2.00
6 A Step Backward U	.50	1.00
7 Anakinís Podracer R	1.00	2.00
8 Aurra Sing R	2.00	4.00
9 Ben Quadinarosí Podracer C	.15	.30
10 Boonta Eve Podrace DARK R	1.25	2.50
11 Boonta Eve Podrace LIGHT R	1.00	2.00
12 Brisky Morning Munchen R	1.00	2.00
13 Caldera Righim C	.15	.30
14 Changing The Odds C	.15	.30
15 Daroe R	1.00	2.00
16 Darth Maul R	2.00	4.00
17 Deneb Both U	.50	1.00
18 Donít Do That Again C	.15	.30
19 Dud Boltís Podracer C	.15	.30
20 Either Way, You Win U	.50	1.00
21 End Of A Reign R	1.00	2.00
22 Entering The Arena U	.50	1.00
23 Eopie C	.15	.30
24 Eventually Youíll Lose U	.50	1.00
25 Fanfare C	.15	.30

.26 Gamall Wironicc U	.50	1.00
27 Ghana Gleemort U	.50	1.00
28 Gragra U	.50	1.00
29 Great Shot, Kid! R	1.00	2.00
30 Grugnak U	.50	1.00
31 His Name Is Anakin C	.15	.30
32 Hit Racer U	.50	1.00
33 I Canít Believe Heís Gone C	.15	.30
34 I Did It! R	1.00	2.00
35 I Will Find Them Quickly, Master R	1.00	2.00
36 Iím Sorry R	1.00	2.00
37 If The Trace Was Correct U	.50	1.00
38 Jar Jar Binks R	1.00	2.00
39 Jedi Escape C	.15	.30
40 Join Me! U	.50	1.00
41 Keeping The Empire Out Forever R	1.00	2.00
42 Lathe U	.50	1.00
43 Lightsaber Parry C	.15	.30
44 Loci Rosen U	.50	1.00
45 Losing Track C	.15	.30
46 Maulís Electrobinoculars C	.15	.30
47 Maulís Lightsaber R	1.00	2.00
48 Neck And Neck U	.50	1.00
49 Ni Chuba Na?? C	.15	.30
50 Obi-wan Kenobi, Padawan Learner R	1.25	2.50
51 Padme Naberrie R	2.50	5.00
52 Pit Crews U	.50	1.00
53 Pit Droid C	.15	.30
54 Podrace Prep U	.50	1.00
55 Podracer Collision U	.50	1.00
56 Quietly Observing U	.50	1.00
57 Qui-Gon Jinn R	2.00	4.00
58 Qui-Gon Jinnís Lightsaber R	1.25	2.50
59 Rachalt Hyst U	.50	1.00
60 Sebulba R	1.00	2.00
61 Sebulbaís Podracer R	1.00	2.00
62 Shmi Skywalker R	1.00	2.00
63 Sith Fury C	.15	.30
64 Sith Probe Droid R	1.25	2.50
65 Start Your Engines! U	.50	1.00
66 Tatooine: City Outskirts U	.50	1.00
67 Tatooine: Desert Landing Site R	1.00	2.00
68 Tatooine: Mos Espa DARK C	.15	.30
69 Tatooine: Mos Espa LIGHT C	.15	.30
70 Tatooine: Podrace Arena DARK C	.15	.30
71 Tatooine: Podrace Arena LIGHT C	.15	.30
72 Tatooine: Podracer Bay C	.15	.30
73 Tatooine: Slave Quarters U	.50	1.00
74 Teemto Pagaliesí Podracer C	.15	.30
75 The Camp C	.15	.30
76 The Shield Is Down! R	1.00	2.00
77 There Is No Conflict C	.15	.30
78 Threepio With His Parts Showing R	1.50	3.00
79 Too Close For Comfort U	.50	1.00
80 Vaderís Anger C	.15	.30
81 Watto R	1.50	3.00
82 Wattoís Box C	.15	.30
83 Wattoís Chance Cube U	.50	1.00
84 We Shall Double Our Efforts! R	1.00	2.00
85 What Was It U	.50	1.00
86 Yotts Orren U	.50	1.00
87 You May Start Your Landing R	1.00	2.00
88 You Swindled Me! U	.50	1.00
89 You Want This, Donít You? C	.15	.30
90 Youíll Find Iím Full Of Surprises U	.50	1.00
91 Tatooine Dark Side List	.15	.30
92 Tatooine Light Side List	.15	.30
93 Tatooine Rule Card 1	.15	.30
94 Tatooine Rule Card 2	.15	.30
95 Tatooine Rule Card 3	.15	.30

2001 Star Wars Theed Palace

- Mace Windu, Jedi Master 1

Jedi Council member who is known to be one of the strongest members of the Council. Has come to Naboo to investigate the death of the mysterious "dark warrior."

POWER 6 ABILITY 7 JEDI MASTER

Deploys -2 on Naboo. While on Naboo, once during your control phase may use 1 Force to cancel Maul's immunity to attrition for remainder of turn. Immune to attrition < 3 (< 5 while on Naboo).

COMPLETE SET (121)	80.00	150.00
BOOSTER BOX (30 PACKS)	400.00	500.00
BOOSTER PACK (11 CARDS)	15.00	20.00
RELEASED IN DECEMBER 2001		
FINAL EXPANSION PRODUCT BY DECIPHER		
1 3B3-10 U	.30	.75
2 3B3-1204 U	.30	.75
3 3B3-21 U	.30	.75
4 3B3-888 U	.30	.75
5 AAT Assault Leader R	1.25	2.50
6 AAT Laser Cannon U	.30	.75
7 Activate The Droids C	.15	.30
8 After Her! R	1.00	2.00
9 Amidala's Blaster R	1.00	2.00
10 Armored Attack Tank U	.30	.75
11 Artoo, Brave Little Droid R	2.00	4.00
12 Ascension Guns U	.30	.75
13 At Last We Are Getting Results C	.15	.30
14 Battle Droid Officer C	.15	.30
15 Battle Droid Pilot C	.15	.30
16 Big Boomers! C	.15	.30
17 Blockade Flaghip R	2.00	4.00
18 Blockade Flagship: Docking Bay DARK U	.30	.75
19 Blockade Flagship: Docking Bay LIGHT U	.30	.75
20 Bok Askol U	.30	.75
21 Booma C	.15	.30
22 Boss Nass R	1.50	3.00
23 Bravo 1 R	1.00	2.00
24 Bravo 2 U	.30	.75
25 Bravo 3 U	.30	.75
26 Bravo 4 U	.30	.75
27 Bravo 5 U	.30	.75
28 Bravo Fighter R	1.00	2.00
29 Captain Tarpals R	1.00	2.00
30 Captain Tarpals' Electropole C	.15	.30
31 Captian Daultay Dofine R	1.00	2.00
32 Cease Fire! C	.15	.30
33 Corporal Rushing U	.30	.75
34 Dams Denna U	.30	.75
35 Darth Maul With Lightsaber R	12.00	25.00
36 Darth Sidious R	25.00	50.00
37 DFS Squadron Starfighter C	.15	.30
38 DFS-1015 U	.30	.75
39 DFS-1308 R	1.00	2.00
40 DFS-327 C	.15	.30
41 Droid Racks R	1.50	3.00
42 Droid Starfighter Laser Cannons C	.15	.30
43 Drop Your Weapons C	.15	.30

44 Electropole C	.15	.30
45 Energy Shell Launchers C	.15	.30
46 Fambaa C	.15	.30
47 Fighters Straight Ahead U	.30	.75
48 General Jar Jar R	1.50	3.00
49 Get To Your Ships! C	.15	.30
50 Gian Speeder C	.15	.30
51 Gimme A Lift! R	1.00	2.00
52 Gungan Energy Shield C	.15	.30
53 Gungan General C	.15	.30
54 Gungan Guard C	.15	.30
55 Halt! C	.15	.30
56 I'll Try Spinning R	1.00	2.00
57 Infantry Battle Droid C	.15	.30
58 Invasion / In Complete Control U	.30	.75
59 It's On Automatic Pilot C	.15	.30
60 Jerus Jannick U	.30	.75
61 Kaadu C	.15	.30
62 Let's Go Left R	1.00	2.00
63 Lieutenant Arven Wendik U	.30	.75
64 Lieutenant Chamberlyn U	.30	.75
65 Lieutenant Rya Kirsch U	.30	.75
66 Mace Windu, Jedi Master R	7.50	15.00
67 Master, Destroyers! R	1.25	2.50
68 Multi Troop Transport U	.30	.75
69 Naboo Celebration R	1.00	2.00
70 Naboo Occupation R	1.25	2.50
71 Naboo: Boss Nass's Chambers U	.30	.75
72 Naboo: Otoh Gunga Entrance U	.30	.75
73 Naboo: Theed Palace Hall U	.30	.75
74 Naboo: Theed Palace Hallway U	.30	.75
75 No Giben Up, General Jar Jar! R	1.00	2.00
76 Nothing Can Get Through Are Shield R	1.25	2.50
77 Nute Gunray, Neimoidian Viceroy R	2.50	5.00
78 Officer Dolphe U	.30	.75
79 Officer Ellberger U	.30	.75
80 Officer Perosei U	.30	.75
81 OOM-9 U	.30	.75
82 Open Fire! C	.15	.30
83 OWO-1 With Backup R	1.50	3.00
84 Panaka, Protector Of The Queen R	3.00	6.00
85 Proton Torpedoes C	.15	.30
86 Queen Amidala R	10.00	20.00
87 Qui-Gon Jinn With Lightsaber R	7.50	15.00
88 Rayno Vaca U	.30	.75
89 Rep Been U	.30	.75
90 Ric Olie, Bravo Leader R	1.00	2.00
91 Rolling, Rolling, Rolling R	1.25	2.50
92 Royal Naboo Security Officer C	.15	.30
93 Rune Haako, Legal Counsel R	1.50	3.00
94 Senate Hovercam DARK R	1.25	2.50
95 Senate Hovercam LIGHT R	1.25	2.50
96 Sil Unch U	.30	.75
97 Single Trooper Aerial Platform C	.15	.30
98 SSA-1015 U	.30	.75
99 SSA-306 U	.30	.75
100 SSA-719 R	1.50	3.00
101 STAP Blaster Cannons C	.15	.30
102 Steady, Steady C	.15	.30
103 Take Them Away C	.15	.30
104 Take This! C	.15	.30
105 Tank Commander C	.15	.30
106 The Deflector Shield Is Too Strong R	1.00	2.00
107 There They Are! U	.30	.75
108 They Win This Round R	1.00	2.00
109 This Is Not Good C	.15	.30
110 Trade Federation Landing Craft C	.15	.30
111 TT-6 R	1.25	2.50
112 TT-9 R	1.00	2.00
113 We Didnt Hit It C	.15	.30

114 We Donit Have Time For This R	1.25	2.50
115 We Have A Plan	.15	.30
They Will Be Lost And Confused C		
116 Weire Hit Artoo C	.15	.30
117 Wesa Gotta Grand Army C	.15	.30
118 Wesa Ready To Do Our-sa Part C	.15	.30
119 Whoooo! C	.15	.30
120 Theed Palace Dark Side List	.15	.30
121 Theed Palace Light Side List	.15	.30

2002 Star Wars Attack of the Clones

9 Darth Tyranus
CHARACTER - DARK JEDI MASTER

50 G
$
7 P
5 H

Pay 1 Force → Tyranus gets +2 power for this attack.
Pay 3 Force → Evade 3 (Prevent up to 3 damage to Tyranus.)
Pay 2 Force → Deflect 1 (Prevent 1 damage to Tyranus, and Tyranus may do that much damage to a unit of your choice in the Character arena.)
"The battle is far from over."

© 2002 LUCASFILM LTD. & ® ® TM. GAME DESIGN: WIZARDS. 14/180 ★

COMPLETE SET (180)	30.00	80.00
BOOSTER BOX (36 PACKS)	20.00	40.00
BOOSTER PACK (11 CARDS)	1.00	1.50
*FOIL: .75X TO 2X BASIC CARDS		
RELEASED IN APRIL 2002		
1 Anakin Skywalker (A) R	.75	1.50
2 Anakin Skywalker (B) R	.75	1.50
3 Assassin Droid ASN-121 (A) R	.75	1.50
4 Bail Organa (A) R	.75	1.50
5 Battle Fatigue R	.75	1.50
6 Boba Fett (A) R	.75	1.50
7 Captain Typho (A) R	.75	1.50
8 Clear the Skies R	.75	1.50
9 Clone Officer R	.75	1.50
10 Dark Rendezvous R	.75	1.50
11 Dark Side's Command R	.75	1.50
12 Dark Side's Compulsion R	.75	1.50
13 Darth Sidious (A) R	.75	1.50
14 Darth Tyranus (A) R	.75	1.50
15 Destruction of Hope R	.75	1.50
16 Dexter Jettster (A) R	.75	1.50
17 Geonosian Sentry R	.75	1.50
18 Hero's Duty R	.75	1.50
19 Hero's Flaw R	.75	1.50
20 Interference in the Senate R	.75	1.50
21 Jango Fett (A) R	.75	1.50
22 Jango Fett (B) R	.75	1.50
23 Jar Jar Binks (A) R	.75	1.50
24 Jedi Call for Help R	.75	1.50
25 Jedi Council Summons R	.75	1.50
26 Jedi Knight's Deflection R	.75	1.50
27 Lama Su (A) R	.75	1.50
28 Luxury Airspeeder U	.25	.50
29 A Moment's Rest R	.75	1.50
30 Naboo Defense Station R	.75	1.50
31 Obi-Wan Kenobi (A) R	.75	1.50
32 Obi-Wan's Starfighter (A) R	.75	1.50
33 Order Here R	.75	1.50
34 Padmè Amidala (A) R	.75	1.50
35 Padmè Amidala (B) R	.75	1.50

#	Card		
36	PadmÈ's Yacht (A) R	.75	1.50
37	Plo Koon (A) R	.75	1.50
38	Plot the Secession R	.75	1.50
39	Power Dive R	.75	1.50
40	Queen Jamillia (A) R	.75	1.50
41	R2-D2 (A) R	.75	1.50
42	San Hill (A) U	.25	.50
43	Second Effort R	.75	1.50
44	Seek the Council's Wisdom R	.75	1.50
45	Shu Mai (A) U	.25	.50
46	Slave I (A) R	.75	1.50
47	Spirit of the Fallen R	.75	1.50
48	Target the Senator R	.75	1.50
49	Taun We (A) R	.75	1.50
50	Trade Federation Battleship Core R	.75	1.50
51	Tyranus's Edict R	.75	1.50
52	Tyranus's Geonosian Speeder (A) R	.75	1.50
53	Tyranus's Solar Sailer (A) R	.75	1.50
54	Tyranus's Wrath R	.75	1.50
55	War Will Follow R	.75	1.50
56	Ward of the Jedi R	.75	1.50
57	Windu's Solution R	.75	1.50
58	Yoda (A) R	.75	1.50
59	Yoda's Intervention R	.75	1.50
60	Zam Wesell (A) R	.75	1.50
61	Acklay U	.25	.50
62	Anakin Skywalker (C) U	.25	.50
63	Anakin's Inspiration U	.25	.50
64	AT-TE Walker 23X U	.25	.50
65	AT-TE Walker 71E R	.75	1.50
66	Attract Enemy Fire U	.25	.50
67	C-3PO U	.25	.50
68	Capture Obi-Wan U	.25	.50
69	Chancellor Palpatine (A) R	.75	1.50
70	Chase the Villain U	.25	.50
71	Cheat the Game U	.25	.50
72	Cliegg Lars (A) U	.25	.50
73	Clone Warrior 4/163 U	.25	.50
74	Clone Warrior 5/373 U	.25	.50
75	Commerce Guild Droid Platoon U	.25	.50
76	CordÈ (A) U	.25	.50
77	Coruscant Freighter AA-9 (A) U	.25	.50
78	Dark Speed U	.25	.50
79	Darth Tyranus (B) U	.25	.50
80	Departure Time U	.25	.50
81	Destroyer Droid, P Series U	.25	.50
82	Down in Flames U	.25	.50
83	Droid Control Ship U	.25	.50
84	Elan Sleazebaggano (A) R	.75	1.50
85	Geonosian Guard U	.25	.50
86	Geonosian Warrior U	.25	.50
87	Go to the Temple U	.25	.50
88	Infantry Battle Droid, B1 Series U	.25	.50
89	Jango Fett (C) U	.25	.50
90	Jawa Sandcrawler U	.25	.50
91	Jedi Patrol U	.25	.50
92	Kaminoan Guard U	.25	.50
93	Kit Fisto (A) U	.25	.50
94	Master and Apprentice U	.25	.50
95	Naboo Security Guard U	.25	.50
96	Naboo Spaceport U	.25	.50
97	Nexu U	.25	.50
98	Nute Gunray (A) U	.25	.50
99	Obi-Wan Kenobi (B) U	.25	.50
100	PadmÈ Amidala (C) U	.25	.50
101	Poggle the Lesser (A) R	.25	.50
102	Reek U	.25	.50
103	Republic Assault Ship U	.25	.50
104	Republic Cruiser C	.12	.25
105	Shaak Ti (A) U	.25	.50
106	Ship Arrival U	.25	.50
107	Splinter the Republic U	.25	.50
108	Strength of Hate U	.25	.50
109	Subtle Assassination U	.25	.50
110	Super Battle Droid 8EX U	.25	.50
111	Trade Federation Battleship U	.25	.50
112	Trade Federation C-9979 U	.25	.50
113	Tyranus's Gift U	.25	.50
114	Underworld Connections U	.25	.50
115	Wat Tambor (A) U	.25	.50
116	Watto (A) U	.25	.50
117	Weapon Response U	.25	.50
118	Wedding of Destiny U	.25	.50
119	Yoda (B) U	.25	.50
120	Zam's Airspeeder (A) U	.25	.50
121	Anakin Skywalker (D) C	.12	.25
122	Battle Droid Squad C	.12	.25
123	Bravo N-1 Starfighter C	.12	.25
124	Chancellor's Guard Squad C	.12	.25
125	Clone Platoon C	.12	.25
126	Clone Squad C	.12	.25
127	Commerce Guild Droid 81 C	.12	.25
128	Commerce Guild Starship C	.12	.25
129	Corellian Star Shuttle C	.12	.25
130	Darth Tyranus (C) C	.12	.25
131	Destroyer Droid Squad C	.12	.25
132	Droid Starfighter DFS-4CT C	.12	.25
133	Droid Starfighter Squadron C	.12	.25
134	Droid Starfighter Wing C	.12	.25
135	Elite Jedi Squad C	.12	.25
136	Flying Geonosian Squad C	.12	.25
137	Geonosian Defense Platform C	.12	.25
138	Geonosian Fighter C	.12	.25
139	Geonosian Squad C	.12	.25
140	Gozanti Cruiser C	.12	.25
141	Hatch a Clone C	.12	.25
142	Hero's Dodge C	.12	.25
143	High-Force Dodge C	.12	.25
144	Hyperdrive Ring C	.12	.25
145	InterGalactic Banking Clan Starship C	.12	.25
146	Jango Fett (D) C	.12	.25
147	Jedi Starfighter 3R3 C	.12	.25
148	Knockdown C	.12	.25
149	Lost in the Asteroids C	.12	.25
150	Lull in the Fighting C	.12	.25
151	Mending C	.12	.25
152	N-1 Starfighter C	.12	.25
153	Naboo Cruiser C	.12	.25
154	Naboo Royal Starship C	.12	.25
155	Naboo Senatorial Escort C	.12	.25
156	Naboo Starfighter Squadron C	.12	.25
157	Obi-Wan Kenobi (C) C	.12	.25
158	Padawan's Deflection C	.12	.25
159	PadmÈ Amidala (D) C	.12	.25
160	Patrol Speeder C	.12	.25
161	Peace on Naboo C	.12	.25
162	Pilot's Dodge C	.12	.25
163	Recon Speeder C	.12	.25
164	Republic Attack Gunship UH-478 C	.12	.25
165	Repulsorlift Malfunction C	.12	.25
166	Return to Spaceport C	.12	.25
167	Rickshaw C	.12	.25
168	Slumming on Coruscant C	.12	.25
169	Sonic Shockwave C	.12	.25
170	Speeder Bike Squadron C	.12	.25
171	Starship Refit C	.12	.25
172	Surge of Power C	.12	.25
173	Swoop Bike C	.12	.25
174	Take the Initiative C	.12	.25
175	Target Locked C	.12	.25
176	Taylander Shuttle C	.12	.25
177	Techno Union Starship C	.12	.25
178	Trade Federation War Freighter C	.12	.25
179	Walking Droid Fighter C	.12	.25
180	Zam Wesell (B) C	.12	.25

2002 Star Wars A New Hope

COMPLETE SET (180)		30.00	80.00
BOOSTER BOX (36 PACKS)		25.00	50.00
BOOSTER PACK (11 CARDS)		1.50	3.00
*FOIL: .75X TO 2X BASIC CARDS			
RELEASED IN OCTOBER 2002			
1	Admiral Motti (A) R	.75	1.50
2	Beru Lars (A) R	.75	1.50
3	Blaster Barrage R	.75	1.50
4	Capture the Falcon R	.75	1.50
5	Contingency Plan R	.75	1.50
6	Dannik Jerriko (A) R	.75	1.50
7	Darth Vader (A) R	1.50	3.00
8	Desperate Confrontation R	1.00	2.00
9	Destroy Alderaan R	.75	1.50
10	Dianoga (A) R	.75	1.50
11	Disturbance in the Force R	.75	1.50
12	It's Not Over Yet R	.75	1.50
13	EG-6 Power Droid R	.75	1.50
14	Elite Stormtrooper Squad R	.75	1.50
15	Figrin D'an (A) R	1.00	2.00
16	Greedo (A) R	.75	1.50
17	Hold 'Em Off R	.75	1.50
18	Imperial Blockade R	.75	1.50
19	Imperial Navy Helmsman R	.75	1.50
20	Imperial Sentry Droid R	.75	1.50
21	IT-0 Interrogator Droid R	1.00	2.00
22	Jawa Leader R	.75	1.50
23	Krayt Dragon R	.75	1.50
24	Leia's Kiss R	.75	1.50
25	Luke Skywalker (B) R	.75	1.50
26	Luke Skywalker (A) R	.75	1.50
27	Luke's Speeder (A) R	.75	1.50
28	Luke's X-Wing (A) R	.75	1.50
29	Momaw Nadon (A) R	1.25	2.50
30	Most Desperate Hour R	.75	1.50
31	No Escape R	.75	1.50
32	Obi-Wan Kenobi (E) R	.75	1.50
33	Obi-Wan's Prowess R	.75	1.50
34	Obi-Wan's Task R	.75	1.50
35	Our Only Hope R	.75	1.50
36	Owen Lars (A) R	.75	1.50
37	Plan of Attack R	.75	1.50
38	Princess Leia (A) R	.75	1.50
39	Protection of the Master R	.75	1.50
40	R5-D4 (A) R	.75	1.50
41	Rebel Crew Chief R	.75	1.50
42	Rebel Lieutenant R	.75	1.50
43	Regroup on Yavin R	.75	1.50
44	Sandtrooper R	.75	1.50
45	Starfighter's End R	.75	1.50
46	Stormtrooper TK-421 R	.75	1.50
47	Strategy Session R	.75	1.50
48	Strike Me Down R	.75	1.50
49	Surprise Attack R	.75	1.50

50 Tantive IV (A) R	.75	1.50
51 Tarkin's Stench R	.75	1.50
52 TIE Fighter Elite Pilot U	.25	.50
53 Tiree (A) R	.75	1.50
54 Tractor Beam R	.75	1.50
55 URoRRuR'R'R (A) R	.75	1.50
56 Imperial Manipulation R	.75	1.50
57 Vader's Leadership R	.75	1.50
58 Vader's TIE Fighter (A) R	.75	1.50
59 Wedge Antilles (A) R	.75	1.50
60 Yavin 4 Hangar Base R	.75	1.50
61 Astromech Assistance U	.25	.50
62 Benefits of Training U	.25	.50
63 Biggs Darklighter (A) U	.25	.50
64 C-3PO (C) U	.25	.50
65 Commander Praji (A) U	.25	.50
66 Tatooine Sandcrawler U	.25	.50
67 Darth Vader (B) U	.25	.50
68 Death Star Hangar Bay U	.25	.50
69 Death Star Plans U	.25	.50
70 Death Star Scanning Technician U	.25	.50
71 Death Star Superlaser Gunner U	.25	.50
72 Death Star Turbolaser Gunner U	.25	.50
73 Demonstration of Power U	.25	.50
74 Devastator (A) U	.25	.50
75 Dissolve the Senate U	.25	.50
76 Error in Judgment U	.25	.50
77 Fate of the Dragon U	.25	.50
78 General Dodonna (A) U	.25	.50
79 General Tagge (A) U	.25	.50
80 Han's Courage U	.25	.50
81 Imperial Control Station U	.25	.50
82 Imperial Navy Lieutenant U	.25	.50
83 Insignificant Power U	.25	.50
84 Into the Garbage Chute C	.12	.25
85 Jawa U	.25	.50
86 Jawa Collection Team U	.25	.50
87 Jedi Extinction U	.25	.50
88 Jon Dutch Vander (A) U	.25	.50
89 Learning the Force U	.25	.50
90 Lieutenant Tanbris (A) U	.25	.50
91 LIN Demolitionmech U	.25	.50
92 Luke Skywalker (C) U	.25	.50
93 Luke's Warning U	.25	.50
94 Mounted Stormtrooper U	.25	.50
95 Mouse Droid U	.25	.50
96 Obi-Wan Kenobi (F) U	.25	.50
97 Oil Bath U	.25	.50
98 Princess Leia (B) U	.25	.50
99 R2-D2 (C) U	.25	.50
100 Rebel Blockade Runner U	.25	.50
101 Rebel Control Officer U	.25	.50
102 Rebel Control Post U	.25	.50
103 Rebel Marine U	.25	.50
104 Rebel Surrender U	.25	.50
105 Rebel Trooper U	.25	.50
106 Remote Seeker Droid U	.25	.50
107 Press the Advantage U	.25	.50
108 Stabilize Deflectors U	.25	.50
109 Star Destroyer Commander U	.25	.50
110 Stormtrooper Charge U	.25	.50
111 Stormtrooper DV-692 U	.25	.50
112 Stormtrooper Squad Leader U	.25	.50
113 Stormtrooper TK-119 U	.25	.50
114 Support in the Senate U	.25	.50
115 Disrupt the Power System U	.25	.50
116 Tatooine Speeder U	.25	.50

117 Tusken Sharpshooter U	.25	.50
118 Vader's Interference U	.25	.50
119 Vader's TIE Fighter (B) U	.75	1.50
120 Wuher (A) U	.25	.50
121 Air Cover C	.12	.25
122 Precise Blast C	.12	.25
123 Stay Sharp C	.12	.25
124 Carrack Cruiser C	.12	.25
125 Darth Vader (C) C	.12	.25
126 Death Star Cannon Tower C	.12	.25
127 Death Star Guard Squad C	.12	.25
128 Domesticated Bantha C	.12	.25
129 Flare-S Swoop C	.12	.25
130 Ground Support C	.12	.25
131 Imperial Detention Block C	.12	.25
132 Imperial Star Destroyer C	.12	.25
133 Incom T-16 Skyhopper C	.12	.25
134 Into Hiding C	.12	.25
135 Jawa Squad C	.12	.25
136 Jawa Supply Trip C	.12	.25
137 Jump to Lightspeed C	.12	.25
138 Luke Skywalker (D) C	.12	.25
139 Luke's Repairs C	.12	.25
140 Moisture Farm C	.12	.25
141 Planetary Defense Turret C	.12	.25
142 Nowhere to Run C	.12	.25
143 Obi-Wan Kenobi (G) C	.12	.25
144 Jedi Intervention C	.12	.25
145 Obi-Wan's Plan C	.12	.25
146 Penetrate the Shields C	.12	.25
147 Preemptive Shot C	.12	.25
148 Princess Leia (C) C	.12	.25
149 Rebel Fighter Wing C	.12	.25
150 Rebel Honor Company C	.12	.25
151 Rebel Marine Squad C	.12	.25
152 Rebel Pilot C	.12	.25
153 Rebel Squad C	.12	.25
154 Rescue C	.12	.25
155 Slipping Through C	.12	.25
156 SoruSuub V-35 Courier C	.12	.25
157 Synchronized Assault C	.12	.25
158 Stormtrooper Assault Team C	.12	.25
159 Stormtrooper DV-523 C	.12	.25
160 Stormtrooper Patrol C	.12	.25
161 Stormtrooper Squad C	.12	.25
162 TIE Fighter DS-3-12 C	.12	.25
163 TIE Fighter DS-73-3 C	.12	.25
164 TIE Fighter DS-55-6 C	.12	.25
165 TIE Fighter DS-61-9 C	.12	.25
166 TIE Fighter Pilot C	.12	.25
167 TIE Fighter Squad C	.12	.25
168 Tusken Squad C	.12	.25
169 Vader's Grip U	.12	.25
170 Victory-Class Star Destroyer C	.12	.25
171 Well-Aimed Shot C	.12	.25
172 X-wing Red One C	.12	.25
173 X-wing Red Three C	.12	.25
174 X-wing Red Two C	.12	.25
175 X-wing Attack Formation C	.12	.25
176 Y-wing Gold One C	.12	.25
177 Y-wing Gold Squadron C	.12	.25
178 YT-1300 Transport C	.12	.25
179 YV-664 Light Freighter C	.12	.25
180 Z-95 Headhunter C	.12	.25

2002 Star Wars Sith Rising

COMPLETE SET (90)	15.00	40.00
BOOSTER BOX (36 PACKS)	25.00	50.00
BOOSTER PACK (11 CARDS)	1.00	2.00

*FOIL: .75X TO 2X BASIC CARDS
RELEASED IN JULY 2002

1 Aayla Secura (A) R	.75	1.50
2 Anakin Skywalker (E) R	.75	1.50
3 Aurra Sing (A) R	.75	1.50
4 Chancellor Palpatine (B) R	.75	1.50
5 Clone Captain R	.75	1.50
6 Clone Facility R	.75	1.50
7 Darth Maul (A) R	.75	1.50
8 Darth Maul (C) R	.75	1.50
9 Darth Sidious (B) R	.75	1.50
10 Darth Tyranus (D) R	.75	1.50
11 Geonosian Picadors R	.75	1.50
12 Impossible Victory R	.75	1.50
13 Jango Fett (E) R	.75	1.50
14 Jedi Bravery R	.75	1.50
15 Jedi Starfighter Wing R	.75	1.50
16 Jocasta Nu (A) R	.75	1.50
17 Mace Windu (A) R	.75	1.50
18 Mace Windu (C) R	.75	1.50
19 Massiff R	.75	1.50
20 Nute Gunray (B) R	.75	1.50
21 Republic Drop Ship R	.75	1.50
22 Sio Bibble (A) R	.75	1.50
23 Sith Infiltrator (A) R	.75	1.50
24 Slave I (B) R	.75	1.50
25 Super Battle Droid 5TE R	.75	1.50
26 Trade Federation Control Core R	.75	1.50
27 Tusken Camp R	.75	1.50
28 Twilight of the Republic R	.75	1.50
29 Unfriendly Fire R	.75	1.50
30 Yoda (C) R	.75	1.50
31 Aiwha Rider U	.25	.50
32 C-3PO (B) U	.25	.50
33 Careful Targeting U	.25	.50
34 Clever Escape U	.25	.50
35 Clone Trooper 6/298 U	.25	.50
36 Darth Maul (B) U	.25	.50
37 Darth Tyranus (E) U	.25	.50
38 Destroyer Droid, W Series U	.25	.50
39 Female Tusken Raider U	.25	.50
40 Fog of War U	.25	.50
41 Geonosian Scout U	.25	.50
42 Hailfire Droid U	.25	.50
43 Homing Spider Droid U	.25	.50
44 Infantry Battle Droid U	.25	.50
45 Jedi Heroes U	.25	.50

46 Jedi Starfighter Scout U		.25	.50
47 Mace Windu (B) U		.25	.50
48 Moment of Truth U		.25	.50
49 Obi_Wan Kenobi (D) U		.25	.50
50 Out of His Misery U		.25	.50
51 PadmÈ Amidala (E) U		.25	.50
52 Passel Argente (A) U		.25	.50
53 Price of Failure U		.25	.50
54 R2-D2 (B) U		.25	.50
55 Recognition of Valor U		.25	.50
56 Sun Fac (A) U		.25	.50
57 Techno Union Warship U		.25	.50
58 Trade Federation Offensive U		.25	.50
59 Tusken Raider U		.25	.50
60 Visit the Lake Retreat U		.25	.50
61 Acclamator-Class Assault Ship C		.12	.25
62 Aggressive Negotiations C		.12	.25
63 Anakin Skywalker (F) C		.12	.25
64 AT-TE Troop Transport C		.12	.25
65 Battle Droid Assault Squad C		.12	.25
66 Brutal Assault C		.12	.25
67 Clone Trooper Legion C		.12	.25
68 Commerce Guild Cruiser C		.12	.25
69 Commerce Guild Spider Droid C		.12	.25
70 Concentrated Fire C		.12	.25
71 Corsucant Speeder C		.12	.25
72 Darth Maul (D) C		.12	.25
73 Diplomatic Cruiser C		.12	.25
74 Droid Starfighter DFS-1VR C		.12	.25
75 Geonosian Artillery Battery C		.12	.25
76 Geonosian Defense Fighter C		.12	.25
77 Maul's Strategy C		.12	.25
78 Mobile Assault Cannon C		.12	.25
79 Naboo Starfighter Wing C		.12	.25
80 Nubian Yacht C		.12	.25
81 Padawan and Senator C		.12	.25
82 Reassemble C-3PO C		.12	.25
83 Republic LAAT/i Gunship C		.12	.25
84 Retreat Underground R		.12	.25
85 Run the Gauntlet C		.12	.25
86 Senatorial Cruiser C		.12®	.25
87 Shoot Her or Something C		.12	.25
88 Super Battle Droid Squad C		.12	.25
89 Suppressing Fire C		.12	.25
90 Trade Federation Warship C		.12	.25

2003 Star Wars Battle of Yavin

COMPLETE SET (105)	60.00	120.00
BOOSTER BOX (36 PACKS)	30.00	50.00
BOOSTER PACK (11 CARDS)	2.50	5.00
*FOIL: .75X TO 2X BASIC CARDS		

RELEASED IN MARCH 2003

1 Artoo's Repairs R		2.50	5.00
2 Blow This Thing R		2.00	4.00
3 Celebrate the Victory R		1.00	2.00
4 Chariot Light Assault Vehicle R		1.00	2.00
5 Chewbacca (B) R		5.00	10.00
6 Chewbacca (A) R		5.00	10.00
7 Chief Bast (A) R		2.50	5.00
8 Colonel Wullf Yularen (A) R		2.50	5.00
9 Darth Vader (D) R		5.00	10.00
10 Death Star (A) R		4.00	8.00
11 Death Star (C) R		4.00	8.00
12 Garven Dreis (A) R		1.50	3.00
13 Grand Moff Tarkin (A) R		4.00	8.00
14 Han Solo (B) R		6.00	12.00
15 Han Solo (A) R		5.00	10.00
16 Hero's Potential R		.25	.50
17 Jek Porkins (A) R		.75	1.50
18 Lieutenant Shann Childsen (A) R		1.50	3.00
19 Luke Skywalker (E) R		5.00	10.00
20 Luke's Skyhopper (A) R		.25	.50
21 Luke's X-wing (B) R		2.50	5.00
22 Millennium Falcon (A) R		2.50	5.00
23 Millennium Falcon (B) R		2.50	5.00
24 Millennium Falcon (C) R		2.50	5.00
25 Obi-Wan Kenobi (H) R		5.00	10.00
26 Obi-Wan's Guidance R		1.00	2.00
27 Princess Leia (D) R		1.50	3.00
28 R2-X2 (A) R		1.50	3.00
29 R2-Q5 (A) R		1.50	3.00
30 Rebel Ground Crew Chief R		1.00	2.00
31 Second Wave R		1.50	3.00
32 Stormtrooper Commander R		5.00	10.00
33 Vader's Fury R		2.50	5.00
34 X-wing Squadron R		2.50	5.00
35 Your Powers Are Weak R		1.50	3.00
36 Alien Rage U		.50	1.00
37 C-3PO (D) U		.50	1.00
38 Chewbacca (C) U		.50	1.00
39 Commander Willard (A) U		.50	1.00
40 Countermeasures U		.50	1.00
41 Darth Vader (E) U		.50	1.00
42 Death Star (B) U		.50	1.00
43 Death Star Trooper U		.50	1.00
44 Deflectors Activated U		.50	1.00
45 Grand Moff Tarkin (B) U		.50	1.00
46 Grand Moff Tarkin (C) U		.50	1.00
47 Han Solo (C) U		.50	1.00
48 Heavy Fire Zone U		.50	1.00
49 Imperial Dewback U		.50	1.00
50 Interrogation Droid U		.50	1.00
51 Jawa Crawler U		.50	1.00
52 Jawa Scavenger U		.50	1.00
53 Labria (A) U		.50	1.00
54 Let the Wookiee Win U		.50	1.00
55 Luke Skywalker (F) U		.50	1.00
56 Luke's Speeder (B) U		.50	1.00
57 Mobile Command Base U		.50	1.00
58 Obi-Wan's Handiwork U		.50	1.00
59 Princess Leia (E) U		.50	1.00
60 R2-D2 (D) U		.50	1.00
61 Rebel Armored Freerunner U		.50	1.00
62 Refit on Yavin U		.50	1.00
63 Sabers Locked U		.50	1.00
64 Stormtrooper KE-829 U		.50	1.00
65 Tatooine Hangar U		.50	1.00
66 Tusken Raider Squad U		.50	1.00
67 Tusken War Party U		.50	1.00
68 Untamed Ronto U		.50	1.00
69 WED Treadwell U		.50	1.00
70 Womp Rat U		.50	1.00
71 Accelerate C		.25	.50
72 Blast It! C		.25	.50
73 Chewbacca (D) C		.25	.50
74 Corellian Corvette C		.25	.50
75 Creature Attack C		.25	.50
76 Luke Skywalker (G) C		.25	.50
77 Darth Vader (F) C		.25	.50
78 Death Star Turbolaser Tower C		.25	.50
79 Dewback Patrol C		.25	.50
80 Escape Pod C		.25	.50
81 Greedo's Marksmanship C		.25	.50
82 Han Solo (D) C		.25	.50
83 Han's Evasion C		.25	.50
84 Imperial Landing Craft C		.25	.50
85 Jawa Salvage Team C		.25	.50
86 Juggernaut U		.25	.50
87 Star Destroyer C		.25	.50
88 Malfunction C		.25	.50
89 Outrun C		.25	.50
90 Pilot's Speed C		.25	.50
91 Rebel Defense Team C		.25	.50
92 Sandtrooper Squad C		.25	.50
93 Stormtrooper Assault C		.25	.50
94 Stormtrooper TK-875 C		.25	.50
95 Stormtrooper Platoon C		.25	.50
96 Stormtrooper Regiment C		.25	.50
97 TIE Defense Squadron C		.25	.50
98 TIE Fighter DS-73-5 C		.25	.50
99 TIE Fighter DS-29-4 C		.25	.50
100 TIE Fighter DS-55-2 C		.25	.50
101 Trust Your Feelings C		.25	.50
102 Visit to Mos Eisley C		.25	.50
103 X-wing Red Squadron C		.25	.50
104 X-wing Red Ten C		.25	.50
105 Y-wing Gold Two C		.25	.50

2003 Star Wars The Empire Strikes Back

COMPLETE SET (210)	100.00	200.00
BOOSTER BOX (36 PACKS)	400.00	550.00
BOOSTER PACK (11 CARDS)	1.25	2.50
*FOIL: .75X TO 2X BASIC CARDS		

RELEASED IN NOVEMBER 2003

1 2-1B Medical Droid (A) R		1.50	3.00
2 Admiral Firmus Piett (B) R		1.50	3.00
3 AT-AT Assault Group R		1.50	3.00
4 Avenger (A) R		5.00	10.00
5 Blizzard Force Snowtrooper R		1.50	3.00
6 Blizzard One (A) R		1.50	3.00
7 C-3PO (E) R		1.50	3.00
8 Captain Lorth Needa (A) R		1.50	3.00

#	Card		
9	Carbon Freezing Chamber R	6.00	12.00
10	Chewbacca (E) U	1.50	3.00
11	Chewbacca (G) R	1.50	3.00
12	Dack Ralter (A) R	1.50	3.00
13	Dangerous Gamble R	1.50	3.00
14	Dark Cave R	1.50	3.00
15	Darth Vader (H) R	2.50	5.00
16	Darth Vader (I) R	4.00	8.00
17	Decoy Tactics R	1.50	3.00
18	Desperate Times R	1.50	3.00
19	Echo Base R	4.00	8.00
20	Emperor's Bidding R	1.50	3.00
21	Emperor's Prize R	1.50	3.00
22	Executor (A) R	1.50	3.00
23	Failed for the Last Time R	1.50	3.00
24	Future Sight R	1.50	3.00
25	FX-7 Medical Droid (A) R	1.50	3.00
26	General Carlist Rieekan (A) R	1.50	3.00
27	General Maximilian Veers (B) R	1.50	3.00
28	Go for the Legs R	1.50	3.00
29	Han Solo (G) R	2.50	5.00
30	Jedi Test R	1.50	3.00
31	Jedi's Failure R	1.50	3.00
32	K-3PO (A) R	1.50	3.00
33	Kiss From Your Sister R	1.50	3.00
34	Lando Calrissian (A) R	3.00	6.00
35	Lando Calrissian (D) R	3.00	6.00
36	Lieutenant Wes Janson (A) R	2.50	5.00
37	Lobot (A) R	1.50	3.00
38	Luke Skywalker (J) R	7.50	15.00
39	Luke Skywalker (K) R	6.00	12.00
40	Luke's Snowspeeder (A) R	5.00	10.00
41	Luke's Wrath R	1.50	3.00
42	Luke's X-wing (c) R	2.50	5.00
43	Major Bren Derlin (A) R	1.50	3.00
44	Mara Jade (A) R	1.50	3.00
45	Millennium Falcon (E) R	2.50	5.00
46	Millennium Falcon (F) R	2.50	5.00
47	Millennium Falcon (G) R	2.50	5.00
48	Obi-Wan's Spirit (A) R	1.50	3.00
49	Occupation R	1.50	3.00
50	Parting of Heroes R	1.50	3.00
51	Planetary Ion Cannon R	1.50	3.00
52	Princess Leia (G) R	2.50	5.00
53	Quest for Truth R	1.50	3.00
54	R2-D2 (G) R	1.50	3.00
55	R2-D2's Heroism R	1.50	3.00
56	Rally the Defenders R	1.50	3.00
57	Sacrifice R	1.50	3.00
58	Search for the Rebels R	1.50	3.00
59	Stormtrooper Swarm R	1.50	3.00
60	Streets of Cloud City R	1.50	3.00
61	Toryn Farr (A) R	1.50	3.00
62	Vader's Imperial Shuttle (A) R	2.50	5.00
63	Wampa Cave R	1.50	3.00
64	Wedge Antilles (B) R	5.00	10.00
65	Wedge's Snowspeeder (A) R	5.00	10.00
66	Yoda (F) R	1.50	3.00
67	Yoda (G) R	1.50	3.00
68	Yoda (H) R	1.50	3.00
69	Yoda's Training R	1.50	3.00
70	Zev Senesca (A) R	1.50	3.00
71	3,720 to 1 U	.50	1.00
72	Admiral Firmus Piett (A) U	.50	1.00
73	Admiral Kendal Ozzel (A) U	.50	1.00
74	Outmaneuver Them U	.50	1.00
75	All Terrain Troop Transport U	.50	1.00
76	Anti-Infantry Laser Battery U	.50	1.00
77	Asteroid Field U	.50	1.00
78	AT-AT Driver U	.50	1.00
79	Blizzard Force AT-ST U	.50	1.00
80	Battle the Wampa U	.50	1.00
81	Cloud City Penthouse U	.50	1.00
82	Cloud City Prison U	.50	1.00
83	Bespin Twin-Pod Cloud Car U	.50	1.00
84	Blockade U	.50	1.00
85	Bright Hope (A) U	.50	1.00
86	C-3PO (F) U	.50	1.00
87	Change in Destiny U	.50	1.00
88	Chewbacca (F) R	.50	1.00
89	Darth Vader (G) R	.50	1.00
90	Darth Vader (K) U	.50	1.00
91	Death Mark U	.50	1.00
92	Derek Hobbie Klivian (A) U	.50	1.00
93	Don't Get All Mushy U	.50	1.00
94	Dragonsnake U	.50	1.00
95	Emergency Repairs U	.50	1.00
96	Carbon Freeze U	.50	1.00
97	Executor Bridge U	.50	1.00
98	Executor Hangar U	.50	1.00
99	Quicker Easier More Seductive U	.50	1.00
100	General Maximilian Veers (A) U	.50	1.00
101	Han Enchained U	.50	1.00
102	Han Solo (F) U	.50	1.00
103	Hoth Icefields U	.50	1.00
104	Imperial Fleet U	.50	1.00
105	Imperial Misdirection U	.50	1.00
106	Jungles of Dagobah U	.50	1.00
107	Lambda-Class Shuttle U	.50	1.00
108	Lando Calrissian (C) U	.50	1.00
109	Leia's Warning U	.50	1.00
110	Luke Skywalker (I) U	.50	1.00
111	Medical Center U	.50	1.00
112	Millennium Falcon (D) U	.50	1.00
113	Mynock U	.50	1.00
114	Painful Reckoning U	.50	1.00
115	Princess Leia (H) U	.50	1.00
116	Probe Droid U	.50	1.00
117	Probot U	.50	1.00
118	R2-D2 (F) U	.50	1.00
119	Rebel Fleet U	.50	1.00
120	Rebel Hoth Army U	.50	1.00
121	Rebel Trenches U	.50	1.00
122	Rebel Troop Cart U	.50	1.00
123	Redemption (A) U	.50	1.00
124	See You In Hell U	.50	1.00
125	Self Destruct U	.50	1.00
126	Shield Generator U	.50	1.00
127	Snowspeeder Rogue Ten U	.50	1.00
128	Snowspeeder Squad U	.50	1.00
129	Snowtrooper Elite Squad U	.50	1.00
130	Stormtrooper Sentry U	.50	1.00
131	Surprise Reinforcements U	.50	1.00
132	TIE Bomber Pilot U	.50	1.00
133	TIE Bomber Squad U	.50	1.00
134	TIE Pursuit Pilot U	.50	1.00
135	Torture Room U	.50	1.00
136	Vader's Call U	.50	1.00
137	Vicious Attack U	.50	1.00
138	Wampa U	.50	1.00
139	Yoda's Hut U	.50	1.00
140	725 to 1 C	.25	.50
141	All Terrain Armored Transport C	.25	.50
142	All Terrain Scout Transport C	.25	.50
143	Alter the Deal C	.25	.50
144	Antivehicle Laser Cannon C	.25	.50
145	Armor Plating C	.25	.50
146	Space Slug C	.25	.50
147	Blizzard Force AT-AT C	.25	.50
148	Precise Attack C	.25	.50
149	Belly of the Beast C	.25	.50
150	Cloud City Battleground C	.25	.50
151	Cloud City Dining Hall C	.25	.50
152	Cloud City Landing Platform C	.25	.50
153	Bespin System C	.25	.50
154	Blizzard C	.25	.50
155	Bogwing C	.25	.50
156	Close the Shield Doors C	.25	.50
157	Darth Vader (J) C	.25	.50
158	Vader's Vengeance C	.25	.50
159	Dagobah System C	.25	.50
160	Explore the Swamps C	.25	.50
161	Float Away C	.25	.50
162	Force Throw C	.25	.50
163	Gallofree Medium Transport C	.25	.50
164	Ground Assault C	.25	.50
165	Han Solo (E) C	.25	.50
166	Han's Attack U	.25	.50
167	Han's Promise C	.25	.50
168	Hanging Around C	.25	.50
169	Hope of Another C	.25	.50
170	Hoth Battle Plains C	.25	.50
171	Hoth System C	.25	.50
172	Imperial II-Class Star Destroyer C	.25	.50
173	Jedi Master's Meditation C	.25	.50
174	Jedi Trap C	.25	.50
175	Kuat Lancer-Class Frigate C	.25	.50
176	Kuat Nebulon-B Frigate C	.25	.50
177	Lando Calrissian (B) C	.25	.50
178	Lando's Repairs C	.25	.50
179	Leap into the Chasm C	.25	.50
180	Luke Skywalker (H) C	.25	.50
181	Meditation Chamber C	.25	.50
182	Navy Trooper C	.25	.50
183	Princess Leia (F) C	.25	.50
184	Probe the Galaxy C	.25	.50
185	Rebel Command Center C	.25	.50
186	Rebel Escape Squad C	.25	.50
187	Rebel Hangar C	.25	.50
188	Rebel Trench Defenders C	.25	.50
189	Rebel Assault Frigate C	.25	.50
190	Dreadnaught Heavy Cruiser C	.25	.50
191	Snowspeeder Rogue Two C	.25	.50
192	Snowstorm C	.25	.50
193	Snowtrooper Heavy Weapons Team C	.25	.50
194	Snowtrooper Squad C	.25	.50
195	Snowtrooper Guard C	.25	.50
196	Imperial II Star Destroyer C	.25	.50
197	Strange Lodgings C	.25	.50
198	Swamps of Dagobah C	.25	.50
199	Tauntaun C	.25	.50
200	Tauntaun Mount C	.25	.50
201	TIE Bomber EX-1-2 C	.25	.50
202	TIE Bomber EX-1-8 C	.25	.50
203	TIE Fighter EX-4-9 C	.25	.50
204	TIE Fighter OS-72-8 C	.25	.50
205	TIE Pursuit Squad C	.25	.50
206	Trust Her Instincts C	.25	.50
207	Visions of the Future C	.25	.50
208	Well-Earned Meal C	.25	.50
209	X-wing Rogue Seven C	.25	.50
210	Y-wing Gold Six C	.25	.50

2003 Star Wars Jedi Guardians

COMPLETE SET (105) 60.00 120.00
BOOSTER BOX (36 PACKS) 120.00 250.00
BOOSTER PACK (11 CARDS) 5.00 7.00
*FOIL: .75X TO 2X BASIC CARDS
RELEASED IN JULY 2003

1	Adi Gallia (A) R	1.50	3.00
2	Anakin Skywalker (H) R	1.50	3.00
3	Aurra Sing (B) R	1.50	3.00
4	Boba Fett (B) R	1.50	3.00
5	Coup de Grace U	1.50	3.00
6	Dark Dreams R	1.50	3.00
7	Darth Maul (E) R	4.00	8.00
8	Darth Sidious (C) R	1.50	3.00
9	Darth Tyranus (F) R	2.50	5.00
10	Eeth Koth (A) R	1.50	3.00
11	Even Piell (A) R	1.50	3.00
12	Furious Charge C	1.50	3.00
13	Gather the Council R	1.50	3.00
14	Guidance of the Chancellor C	1.50	3.00
15	Homing Missile R	1.50	3.00
16	Jango Fett (G) R	1.50	3.00
17	Jedi Council Quorum R	1.50	3.00
18	Jedi Youngling R	1.50	3.00
19	Ki-Adi-Mundi (A) R	1.50	3.00
20	Kouhun R	1.50	3.00
21	Mace Windu (D) R	3.00	6.00
22	Trade Federation Battle Freighter C	1.50	3.00
23	Obi-Wan Kenobi (I) R	1.50	3.00
24	Obi-Wan's Starfighter (B) R	2.50	5.00
25	Oppo Rancisis (A) R	1.50	3.00
26	Padme Amidala (F) R	2.50	5.00
27	Plo Koon (B) R	1.50	3.00
28	R2-D2 (E) R	1.50	3.00
29	Remember the Prophecy R	1.50	3.00
30	Saesee Tiin (A) R	2.50	5.00
31	Senator Tikkes (A) R	1.50	3.00
32	Shaak Ti (B) R	2.50	5.00
33	Shmi Skywalker (A) R	2.50	5.00
34	Slave I (C) R	1.50	3.00
35	Trade Federation Blockade Ship C	1.50	3.00
36	Rapid Recovery R	1.50	3.00
37	Tipoca Training Ground R	1.50	3.00
38	Trade Federation Core Ship C	1.50	3.00
39	Tyranus's Geonosis Speeder (B) C	1.50	3.00
40	Unified Attack U	1.50	3.00
41	Yoda (D) R	6.00	12.00
42	Zam Wesell (D) R	1.50	3.00

43	Zam's Airspeeder (B) R	1.50	3.00
44	Battle Droid Division U	.50	1.00
45	Battle Protocol Droid (A) U	.50	1.00
46	Call for Reinforcements U	.50	1.00
47	Tyranus's Power C	.50	1.00
48	Clone Cadet U	.50	1.00
49	Coleman Trebor (A) U	.50	1.00
50	Corporate Alliance Tank Droid U	.50	1.00
51	Coruscant Air Bus U	.50	1.00
52	Depa Billaba (A) U	.50	1.00
53	Executioner Cart U	.50	1.00
54	FA-4 (A) U	.50	1.00
55	Jango Fett (F) U	.50	1.00
56	Jedi Arrogance U	.50	1.00
57	Jedi Training Exercise U	.50	1.00
58	Jedi Knight's Survival U	.50	1.00
59	Jedi Superiority U	.50	1.00
60	Lightsaber Gift U	.50	1.00
61	Lightsaber Loss U	.50	1.00
62	Neimoidian Shuttle (A) U	.50	1.00
63	Obi-Wan Kenobi (J) U	.50	1.00
64	Orray U	.50	1.00
65	Padme's Yacht (B) U	.50	1.00
66	Underworld Investigations C	.50	1.00
67	Protocol Battle Droid (A) U	.50	1.00
68	Qui-Gon Jinn (B) U	.50	1.00
69	Republic Communications Tower U	.50	1.00
70	RIC-920 U	.50	1.00
71	Sun-Fac (B) U	.50	1.00
72	Tactical leadership U	.50	1.00
73	Tame the Beast U	.50	1.00
74	Train For War U	.50	1.00
75	Tyranus's Return U	.50	1.00
76	Tyranus's Solar Sailer (B) U	.50	1.00
77	Yoda (E) U	.50	1.00
78	Zam Wesell (C) U	.50	1.00
79	Anakin Skywalker (I) C	.25	.50
80	Mobile Artillery Division C	.25	.50
81	Captured Reek C	.25	.50
82	Clone Fire Team C	.25	.50
83	Close Pursuit C	.25	.50
84	Darth Tyranus (G) C	.25	.50
85	Destroyer Droid Team U	.25	.50
86	Diplomatic Barge C	.25	.50
87	Droid Deactivation C	.25	.50
88	Droid Starfighter Assault Wing C	.25	.50
89	Trade Federation Droid Bomber C	.25	.50
90	Forward Command Center C	.25	.50
91	Geonosian Fighter Escort C	.25	.50
92	Gondola Speeder C	.25	.50
93	Gunship Offensive C	.25	.50
94	Jedi Starfighter Squadron C	.25	.50
95	Obi-Wan's Maneuver C	.25	.50
96	Plan for the Future C	.25	.50
97	Republic Assault Transport C	.25	.50
98	Republic Attack Gunship C	.25	.50
99	Republic Light Assault Cruiser C	.25	.50
100	Republic Hyperdrive Ring C	.25	.50
101	Saboath Starfighter C	.25	.50
102	Scurrier C	.25	.50
103	Separatist Battle Droid C	.25	.50
104	Shaak C	.25	.50
105	Synchronized Systems C	.25	.50

2004 Star Wars The Phantom Menace

COMPLETE SET (90) 50.00 100.00
BOOSTER BOX (36 PACKS) 200.00 250.00
BOOSTER PACK (11 CARDS) 1.50 3.00
*FOIL: .75X TO 2X BASIC CARDS
RELEASED IN JULY 2004

1	Ann and Tann Gella (A) R	2.50	5.00
2	Aurra Sing (C) R	1.50	3.00
3	Bongo Sub R	1.50	3.00
4	Boss Nass (A) R	1.50	3.00
5	C-9979 R	1.50	3.00
6	Corridors of Power R	1.50	3.00
7	Dark Woman (A) R	2.50	5.00
8	Darth Maul (F) R	2.50	5.00
9	Duel of the Fates R	1.50	3.00
10	Fambaa Shield Beast R	1.50	3.00
11	Fight on All Fronts R	1.50	3.00
12	Gardulla the Hutt (A) R	1.50	3.00
13	Gas Attack R	1.50	3.00
14	Gungan Grand Army R	2.00	4.00
15	Guardian Mantis (A) R	1.50	3.00
16	In Disguise R	1.50	3.00
17	Jar Jar Binks (B) R	1.50	3.00
18	Jedi Temple R	1.50	3.00
19	Ki-Adi-Mundi (B) R	2.50	5.00
20	Marauder-Class Corvette R	1.50	3.00
21	Negotiate the Peace R	1.50	3.00
22	Nute Gunray (C) R	1.50	3.00
23	Orn Free Taa (A) R	1.50	3.00
24	Otoh Gunga R	1.50	3.00
25	Podracing Course R	1.50	3.00
26	Quinlan Vos (A) R	1.50	3.00
27	Sando Aqua Monster R	1.50	3.00
28	Sith Infiltrator (B) R	1.50	3.00
29	Walking Droid Starfighter R	1.50	3.00
30	Watto's Shop R	1.50	3.00
31	A'Sharad Hett (A) U	1.50	3.00
32	Anakin Skywalker (J) U	4.00	8.00
33	Anakin's Podracer (A) U	2.50	5.00
34	Bravo Starfighter U	.50	1.00
35	Captain Panaka (A) U	.50	1.00
36	Captain Tarpals (A) U	.50	1.00
37	Citadel Cruiser U	.50	1.00
38	Colo Claw Fish U	.50	1.00
39	Discuss It in Committee U	.50	1.00
40	Durge (A) U	.50	1.00
41	Falumpaset U	.50	1.00
42	Gungan Battle Wagon U	.50	1.00
43	Gungan Catapult U	.50	1.00
44	Inferno (A) U	.50	1.00
45	Kaadu Scout U	.50	1.00

46 Let the Cube Decide U		.50	1.00
47 Modified YV-330 (A) U		.50	1.00
48 Naboo System U		.50	1.00
49 Qui-Gon Jinn (D) U		.50	1.00
50 Ric Olié (A) U		.50	1.00
51 Royal Cruiser U		.50	1.00
52 Rune Haako (A) U		.50	1.00
53 Sebulba (A) U		.50	1.00
54 Sebulba's Podracer (A) U		.50	1.00
55 Streets of Theed U		.50	1.00
56 Trade Federation Hangar U		.50	1.00
57 Trade Federation MTT U		.50	1.00
58 Vilmarh Grahrk (A) U		.50	1.00
59 Watto (B) U		.50	1.00
60 Yaddle (A) U		.50	1.00
61 A Bigger Fish C		.25	.50
62 Aayla Secura (B) C		.25	.50
63 Blockade (TPM) C		.25	.50
64 Blockade Battleship C		.25	.50
65 CloakShape Fighter C		.25	.50
66 Darth Sidious (D) C		.25	.50
67 Delta Six Jedi Starfighter C		.25	.50
68 Eopie C		.25	.50
69 Finis Valorum (B) C		.25	.50
70 Flash Speeder C		.25	.50
71 Gian Speeder C		.25	.50
72 Gungan Kaadu Squad C		.25	.50
73 Jedi Transport C		.25	.50
74 Melt Your Way In C		.25	.50
75 Mos Espa C		.25	.50
76 Naboo Pilot C		.25	.50
77 Obi-Wan Kenobi (K) C		.25	.50
78 Opee Sea Killer C		.25	.50
79 Podrace C		.25	.50
80 Qui-Gon Jinn (C) C		.25	.50
81 Sith Probe Droid C		.25	.50
82 Sneak Attack C		.25	.50
83 Swamps of Naboo C		.25	.50
84 TC-14 (A) C		.25	.50
85 Theed Power Generator C		.25	.50
86 Theed Royal Palace C		.25	.50
87 Trade Federation AAT C		.25	.50
88 Trade Federation STAP C		.25	.50
89 Unconventional Maneuvers C		.25	.50
90 Yinchorri Fighter C		.25	.50

2004 Star Wars Return of the Jedi

COMPLETE SET (109)		50.00	100.00
BOOSTER BOX (36 PACKS)		100.00	200.00
BOOSTER PACK (11 CARDS)		3.00	5.00
*FOIL: .75X TO 2X BASIC CARDS			

RELEASED IN OCTOBER 2004			
1 Admiral Ackbar (A) R		1.50	3.00
2 Anakin Skywalker (K) R		1.50	3.00
3 Anakin's Spirit (A) R		1.50	3.00
4 Bargain with Jabba R		1.50	3.00
5 Bib Fortuna (A) R		1.50	3.00
6 Chewbacca (J) R		1.50	3.00
7 Darth Vader (P) R		1.50	3.00
8 Death Star II (B) R		1.50	3.00
9 Emperor Palpatine (E) R		1.50	3.00
10 Endor Imperial Fleet R		1.50	3.00
11 Endor Rebel Fleet R		1.50	3.00
12 Endor Shield Generator R		1.50	3.00
13 Ephant Mon (A) R		1.50	3.00
14 Endor Regiment R		1.50	3.00
15 Free Tatooine R		1.50	3.00
16 Han Solo (K) R		1.50	3.00
17 Home One (A) R		1.50	3.00
18 Honor the Fallen R		1.50	3.00
19 Jabba the Hutt (A) R		1.50	3.00
20 Jabba's Dancers R		1.50	3.00
21 Jabba's Palace R		1.50	3.00
22 Jabba's Spies R		1.50	3.00
23 Lando Calrissian (H) R		1.50	3.00
24 Luke Skywalker (N) R		1.50	3.00
25 Malakili (A) R		1.50	3.00
26 Max Rebo Band (A) R		1.50	3.00
27 Mixed Battlegroup R		1.50	3.00
28 Mon Mothma (A) R		1.50	3.00
29 Nien Nunb (A) R		1.50	3.00
30 Occupied Tatooine R		1.50	3.00
31 Progress Report R		1.50	3.00
32 Rancor R		1.50	3.00
33 Reactor Core R		1.50	3.00
34 Salacious B. Crumb (A) R		1.50	3.00
35 Sarlacc (A) R		1.50	3.00
36 Scythe Squadron (A) R		1.50	3.00
37 Throne Room R		1.50	3.00
38 Trap Door! R		1.50	3.00
39 Vader's Guile R		1.50	3.00
40 Yoda's Spirit (A) R		1.50	3.00
41 Baited Trap U		.50	1.00
42 Boba Fett (H) U		.50	1.00
43 C-3PO (H) U		.50	1.00
44 Captain Lennox (A) U		.50	1.00
45 Chief Chirpa (A) U		.50	1.00
46 Darth Vader (N) U		.50	1.00
47 Desperate Bluff U		.50	1.00
48 Emperor Palpatine (D) U		.50	1.00
49 Ewok Village U		.50	1.00
50 Free Bespin U		.50	1.00
51 Free Endor U		.50	1.00
52 Han Solo (J) U		.50	1.00
53 Ionization Weapons U		.50	1.00
55 Jabba the Hutt (C) U		.50	1.00
56 Jabba's Sail Barge (A) U		.50	1.00
57 Lando Calrissian (I) U		.50	1.00
58 Luke Skywalker (O) U		.50	1.00
59 Millennium Falcon (J) U		.50	1.00
60 Occupied Bespin U		.50	1.00
61 Occupied Endor U		.50	1.00
62 Princess Leia (J) U		.50	1.00
63 R2-D2 (I) U		.50	1.00
64 Rancor Pit U		.50	1.00
65 Red Squadron X-wing U		.50	1.00
66 Skiff U		.50	1.00
67 Vader's Summons U		.50	1.00
68 Wicket W. Warrick (A) U		.50	1.00
69 Wookiee Hug U		.50	1.00
70 Worrt U		.50	1.00

71 A-wing C		.25	.50
72 B-wing C		.25	.50
73 Cantina Bar Mob C		.25	.50
74 Chewbacca (K) C		.25	.50
75 Close Quarters C		.25	.50
76 Elite Royal Guard C		.25	.50
77 Darth Vader (O) C		.25	.50
78 Death Star Battalion C		.25	.50
79 Death Star II (A) C		.25	.50
80 Decoy C		.25	.50
81 Dune Sea C		.25	.50
82 Elite Squad C		.25	.50
83 Emperor Palpatine (C) C		.25	.50
84 Ewok Artillery C		.25	.50
85 Ewok Glider C		.25	.50
86 Fly Casual C		.25	.50
87 Force Lightning C		.25	.50
88 Forest AT-AT C		.25	.50
89 Forest AT-ST C		.25	.50
90 Endor Attack Squad C		.25	.50
91 Forests of Endor C		.25	.50
92 Free Coruscant C		.25	.50
93 Gray Squadron Y-wing C		.25	.50
94 High-Speed Dodge C		.25	.50
95 Imperial Speeder Bike C		.25	.50
96 Imperial-Class Star Destroyer C		.25	.50
97 Jabba's Guards C		.25	.50
98 Lightsaber Throw C		.25	.50
99 Log Trap C		.25	.50
100 Luke Skywalker (M) C		.25	.50
101 Mon Calamari Cruiser C		.25	.50
102 Occupied Coruscant C		.25	.50
103 Oola (A) C		.25	.50
104 Princess Leia (K) C		.25	.50
105 Rebel Scouts C		.25	.50
106 Royal Guards C		.25	.50
107 Scout Trooper C		.25	.50
108 Surprising Strength C		.25	.50
109 TIE Interceptor C		.25	.50
110 Savage Attack C		.25	.50

2004 Star Wars Rogues and Scoundrels

COMPLETE SET (105)		50.00	100.00
BOOSTER BOX (36 PACKS)		40.00	80.00
BOOSTER PACK (11 CARDS)		1.50	3.00
*FOIL: .75X TO 2X BASIC CARDS			
RELEASED IN APRIL 2004			
1 Admiral Firmus Piett (C) R		1.50	3.00
2 Boba Fett (G) R		1.50	3.00
3 Bossk (A) R		1.50	3.00
4 Call For Hunters R		1.50	3.00

#	Name		
5	Chewbacca (I) R	1.50	3.00
6	Commander Nemet (A) R	1.50	3.00
7	Dantooine System R	1.50	3.00
8	Dark Sacrifice R	1.50	3.00
9	Dengar (A) R	1.50	3.00
10	Doctor Evazan (A) R	1.50	3.00
11	Guri (A) R	1.50	3.00
12	Han Solo (I) R	1.50	3.00
13	Het Nkik (A) R	1.50	3.00
14	Hounds Tooth (A) R	1.50	3.00
15	IG-2000 (A) R	1.50	3.00
16	IG-88 (A) R	1.50	3.00
17	Dune Sea Krayt Dragon R	1.50	3.00
18	Lando Calrissian (F) R	1.50	3.00
19	Lando Calrissian (G) R	1.50	3.00
20	Lando's Influence R	1.50	3.00
21	Lobot (B) R	1.50	3.00
22	Mara Jade (B) R	1.50	3.00
23	Millennium Falcon (I) R	1.50	3.00
24	Mist Hunter (A) R	1.50	3.00
25	Modal Nodes (A) R	1.50	3.00
26	Prince Xizor (A) R	1.50	3.00
27	Princess Leia (I) R	1.50	3.00
28	Slave 1 (F) R	1.50	3.00
29	Stinger (A) R	1.50	3.00
30	Take A Prisoner R	1.50	3.00
31	Trash Compactor R	1.50	3.00
32	Virago (A) R	1.50	3.00
33	Yoda (I) R	1.50	3.00
34	Yoda's Lesson R	1.50	3.00
35	Zuckuss (A) R	1.50	3.00
36	4 Lom (A) U	.50	1.00
37	AT-AT U	.50	1.00
38	Bespin Cloud Car Squad U	.50	1.00
39	Big Asteroid U	.50	1.00
40	Boba Fett (F) U	.50	1.00
41	C 3PO (G) U	.50	1.00
42	Chewbacca (H) U	.50	1.00
43	Cloud City Wing Guard U	.50	1.00
44	Darth Vader (M) U	.50	1.00
45	Death Star Control Room U	.50	1.00
46	Garindan (A) U	.50	1.00
47	Greedo (B) U	.50	1.00
48	Han Solo (H) U	.50	1.00
49	Han's Sacrifice U	.50	1.00
50	Holoprojection Chamber U	.50	1.00
51	Human Shield U	.50	1.00
52	Kessel System U	.50	1.00
53	Lando Calrissian (E) U	.50	1.00
54	Lando's Trickery U	.50	1.00
55	Luke Skywalker (L) U	.50	1.00
56	Luke's X-wing (D) U	.50	1.00
57	Millennium Falcon (H) U	.50	1.00
58	Ponda Baba (A) U	.50	1.00
59	Punishing One (A) U	.50	1.00
60	R2-D2 (H) U	.50	1.00
61	Redoubled Effort U	.50	1.00
62	E-3PO (A) U	.50	1.00
63	Slave 1 (E) U	.50	1.00
64	Slave 1 (D) U	.50	1.00
65	Space Slug {RaS} U	.50	1.00
66	Outrider (A) U	.50	1.00
67	Ugnaught U	.50	1.00
68	Vendetta U	.50	1.00
69	Enraged Wampa U	.50	1.00
70	Lars Homestead U	.50	1.00
71	2-1B's Touch C	.25	.50
72	Bantha Herd C	.25	.50
73	Base Guards C	.25	.50
74	Bespin Patrol Cloud Car C	.25	.50

#	Name		
75	Boba Fett (C) C	.25	.50
76	Boba Fett (D) C	.25	.50
77	Boba Fett (E) C	.25	.50
78	Darth Vader (L) C	.25	.50
79	Dash Rendar (A) C	.25	.50
80	Disrupting Strike C	.25	.50
81	Falcon's Needs C	.25	.50
82	Jabba's Death Mark C	.25	.50
83	Kabe (A) C	.25	.50
84	Kyle Katarn (A) C	.25	.50
85	Lando System? C	.25	.50
86	Leebo (A) C	.25	.50
87	Luke's Garage C	.25	.50
88	Luke's Vow C	.25	.50
89	Medium Asteroid C	.25	.50
90	Mos Eisley C	.25	.50
91	Mos Eisley Cantina C	.25	.50
92	Muftak C	.25	.50
93	No Good To Me Dead C	.25	.50
94	Ord Mantell System C	.25	.50
95	Sleen C	.25	.50
96	Small Asteroid C	.25	.50
97	Zutton (A) C	.25	.50
98	Star Destroyer (RaS) C	.25	.50
99	Stormtrooper Detachment C	.25	.50
100	Streets Of Tatooine C	.25	.50
101	Tatooine Desert C	.25	.50
102	Tie Fighter C	.25	.50
103	Tusken Warrior C	.25	.50
104	Unmodified Snowspeeder C	.25	.50
105	X Wing Escort C	.25	.50

2005 Star Wars Revenge of the Sith

COMPLETE SET (110)		50.00	100.00
BOOSTER BOX (36 PACKS)		30.00	60.00
BOOSTER PACK (11 CARDS)		1.25	2.50
*FOIL: .75X TO 2X BASIC CARDS			
RELEASED IN MAY 2005			

#	Name		
1	Anakin Skywalker (M) R	1.50	3.00
2	Bail Organa (B) R	1.50	3.00
3	Chewbacca (M) R	1.50	3.00
4	Commerce Guild Droid 81-X R	1.50	3.00
5	Commerce Guild Starship (ROTS) R	1.50	3.00
6	Coruscant Shuttle R	1.50	3.00
7	Darth Sidious (G) R	1.50	3.00
8	Darth Tyranus (I) R	1.50	3.00
9	Darth Vader (R) R	1.50	3.00
10	Darth Vader (S) R	1.50	3.00
11	Dismiss R	1.50	3.00
12	Droid Security Escort R	1.50	3.00
13	Engine Upgrade R	1.50	3.00

#	Name		
14	Foil R	1.50	3.00
15	Palpatine's Sanctum R	1.50	3.00
16	Grand Moff Tarkin (D) R	1.50	3.00
17	It Just Might Work R	1.50	3.00
18	Jar Jar Binks (C) R	1.50	3.00
19	Lightsaber Quick Draw R	1.50	3.00
20	Mace Windu (F) R	1.50	3.00
21	Mas Amedda (A) R	1.50	3.00
22	Mustafar Battle Grounds R	1.50	3.00
23	Mustafar System R	1.50	3.00
24	Nos Monster R	1.50	3.00
25	Obi-Wan Kenobi (N) R	1.50	3.00
26	PadmÈ Amidala (G) R	1.50	3.00
27	R4-P17 (A) R	1.50	3.00
28	Rage of Victory R	1.50	3.00
29	Recusant-Class Light Destroyer R	1.50	3.00
30	Republic Fighter Wing R	1.50	3.00
31	Sacrifice the Expendable R	1.50	3.00
32	Separatist Fleet R	1.50	3.00
33	Spinning Slash R	1.50	3.00
34	Strike with Impunity R	1.50	3.00
35	Stubborn Personality R	1.50	3.00
36	Super Battle Droid 7EX R	1.50	3.00
37	Theta-Class Shuttle R	1.50	3.00
38	Unexpected Attack R	1.50	3.00
39	Venator-Class Destroyer R	1.50	3.00
40	Yoda (K) R	1.50	3.00
41	Acclamator II-Class Assault Ship U	.50	1.00
42	AT-AP U	.50	1.00
43	C-3PO (I) U	.50	1.00
44	Chancellor's Office U	.50	1.00
45	Combined Squadron Tactics U	.50	1.00
46	Confusion U	.50	1.00
47	Darth Sidious (F) U	.50	1.00
48	Darth Vader (Q) U	.50	1.00
49	Destroyer Droid, Q Series U	.50	1.00
50	Droid Missiles U	.50	1.00
51	Elite Guardian U	.50	1.00
52	Hardcell-Class Transport U	.50	1.00
53	Jedi Concentration U	.50	1.00
54	Jedi Master's Deflection U	.50	1.00
55	Kashyyyk System U	.50	1.00
56	Naboo Star Skiff U	.50	1.00
57	Nute Gunray (D) U	.50	1.00
58	Obi-Wan Kenobi (L) U	.50	1.00
59	PadmÈ Amidala (H) U	.50	1.00
60	Patrol Mode Vulture Droid U	.50	1.00
61	GH-7 Medical Droid U	.50	1.00
62	R2-D2 (J) U	.50	1.00
63	Thread The Needle U	.50	1.00
64	Thwart U	.50	1.00
65	Treachery U	.50	1.00
66	Techno Union Interceptor U	.50	1.00
67	Utapau System U	.50	1.00
68	Vehicle Shields Package U	.50	1.00
69	Vehicle Weapons Package U	.50	1.00
70	Yoda (J) U	.50	1.00
71	Anakin Skywalker (L) C	.25	.50
72	Anakin's Starfighter (A) C	.25	.50
73	ARC-170 Starfighter C	.25	.50
74	AT-RT C	.25	.50
75	BARC Speeder C	.25	.50
76	Blaster Pistol C	.25	.50
77	Blaster Rifle C	.25	.50
78	Buzz Droid C	.25	.50
79	Chewbacca (L) C	.25	.50
80	Coruscant Emergency Ship C	.25	.50
81	Darth Sidious (E) C	.25	.50
82	Darth Tyranus (H) C	.25	.50
83	DC0052 Intergalactic Airspeeder C	.25	.50

84	Diving Attack C	.25	.50
85	Droid Battlestaff C	.25	.50
86	Droid Tri-Fighter C	.25	.50
87	Force Dodge C	.25	.50
88	HAVw A6 Juggernaut C	.25	.50
89	Homing Missiles Salvo C	.25	.50
90	IBC Hailfire Droid C	.25	.50
91	Instill Doubt C	.25	.50
92	InterGalactic Banking Clan Cruiser C	.25	.50
93	Jedi Lightsaber C	.25	.50
94	Jedi Piloting C	.25	.50
95	Meditate C	.25	.50
96	Obi-Wan Kenobi (M) C	.25	.50
97	Plo Koon's Starfighter (A) C	.25	.50
98	Power Attack C	.25	.50
99	Republic Assault Gunboat C	.25	.50
100	Security Droid C	.25	.50
101	Sith Lightsaber C	.25	.50
102	STAP Squad C	.25	.50
103	Surge of Strength C	.25	.50
104	Tank Droid C	.25	.50
105	TF Battle Droid Army C	.25	.50
106	Trade Federation Cruiser C	.25	.50
107	Unity of the Jedi C	.25	.50
108	Utapau Sinkhole C	.25	.50
109	Vulture Droid Starfighter C	.25	.50
110	V-wing Clone Starfighter C	.25	.50

2015 Star Wars Between the Shadows

12710633	A Hero's Trial	1.00	2.00
12720634	Luke Skywalker	1.00	2.00
12730635	Speeder Bike	1.00	2.00
12740636	Luke's Lightsaber	1.00	2.00
12750637	I Am a Jedi	1.00	2.00
12760065	Heat of Battle	1.00	2.00
12810638	The Master's Domain	1.00	2.00
12820639	Yoda	1.00	2.00
12830640	Bogwing	1.00	2.00
12840641	Yoda's Hut	1.00	2.00
12850089	Lightsaber Deflection	1.00	2.00
12860642	The Jedi's Resolve	1.00	2.00
12910643	Following Fate	1.00	2.00
12920644	Obi-Wan Kenobi	1.00	2.00
12930106	R2-D2	1.00	2.00
12940645	Obi-Wan's Lightsaber	1.00	2.00
12950646	Noble Sacrifice	1.00	2.00
12960133	Target of Opportunity	1.00	2.00
13010647	Journey Through the Swamp	1.00	2.00

13020648	Jubba Bird	1.00	2.00
13030648	Jubba Bird	1.00	2.00
13040649	Knobby White Spider	1.00	2.00
13050650	Life Creates It	1.00	2.00
13060651	Size Matters Not	1.00	2.00
13110652	Sacrifice at Endor	1.00	2.00
13120653	Ewok Hunter	1.00	2.00
13130653	Ewok Hunter	1.00	2.00
13140654	Funeral Pyre	1.00	2.00
13150655	Unexpected Assistance	1.00	2.00
13160656	Retreat to the Forest	1.00	2.00
13210657	Commando Raid	1.00	2.00
13220658	Lieutenant Judder Page	1.00	2.00
13230659	Page's Commandos	1.00	2.00
13240659	Page's Commandos	1.00	2.00
13250065	Heat of Battle	1.00	2.00
13260133	Target of Opportunity	1.00	2.00
13310660	Calling In Favors	1.00	2.00
13320661	Talon Karrde	1.00	2.00
13330662	Skipray Blastboat	1.00	2.00
13340662	Skipray Blastboat	1.00	2.00
13350663	Dirty Secrets	1.00	2.00
13360664	Clever Ruse	1.00	2.00
13410665	No Disintegrations	1.00	2.00
13420666	Boba Fett	1.00	2.00
13430667	Freelance Hunter	1.00	2.00
13440668	Flamethrower	1.00	2.00
13450378	Prized Possession	1.00	2.00
13460669	Entangled	1.00	2.00
13510670	Masterful Manipulation	1.00	2.00
13520671	Prince Xizor	1.00	2.00
13530672	Black Sun Headhunter	1.00	2.00
13540673	Debt Collector	1.00	2.00
13550674	Shadows of the Empire	1.00	2.00
13560675	The Prince's Scheme	1.00	2.00
13610676	All Out Brawl	1.00	2.00
13620677	Zekka Thyne	1.00	2.00
13630673	Debt Collector	1.00	2.00
13640678	Armed to the Teeth	1.00	2.00
13650669	Entangled	1.00	2.00
13660169	Heat of Battle	1.00	2.00
13710679	The Best That Credits Can Buy	1.00	2.00
13720680	Virago	1.00	2.00
13730672	Black Sun Headhunter	1.00	2.00
13740681	Rise of the Black Sun	1.00	2.00
13750682	Warning Shot	1.00	2.00
13760170	Target of Opportunity	1.00	2.00
13810683	The Hunters	1.00	2.00
13820684	Boushh	1.00	2.00
13830685	Snoova	1.00	2.00
13840686	A Better Offer	1.00	2.00
13850542	Pay Out	1.00	2.00
13860687	Show of Force	1.00	2.00
13910688	The Investigation	1.00	2.00
13920689	Ysanne Isard	1.00	2.00
13930690	Imperial Intelligence Officer	1.00	2.00
13940690	Imperial Intelligence Officer	1.00	2.00
13950691	Confiscation	1.00	2.00
13960692	Official Inquiry	1.00	2.00
14010693	Family Connections	1.00	2.00
14020694	General Tagge	1.00	2.00
14030695	Security Task Force	1.00	2.00
14040695	Security Task Force	1.00	2.00
14050696	Imperial Discipline	1.00	2.00
14060697	Precision Fire	1.00	2.00

2015 Star Wars Chain of Command

1611	A Hero's Beginning	1.00	2.00
1612	Luke's X-34 Landspeeder	1.00	2.00
1613	Owen Lars	1.00	2.00
1614	Moisture Vaporator	1.00	2.00
1615	Unfinished Business	1.00	2.00
1616	Supporting Fire	1.00	2.00
1621	Breaking the Blockade	1.00	2.00
1622	Smuggling Freighter	1.00	2.00
1623	Smuggling Freighter	1.00	2.00
1624	Duros Smuggler	1.00	2.00
1625	Duros Smuggler	1.00	2.00
1626	Surprising Maneuver	1.00	2.00
1631	The Imperial Bureaucracy	1.00	2.00
1632	Sate Pestage	1.00	2.00
1633	Advisor to the Emperor	1.00	2.00
1634	Quarren Bureaucrat	1.00	2.00
1635	Endless Bureaucracy	1.00	2.00
1636	Supporting Fire	1.00	2.00
1641	The Last Grand Admiral	1.00	2.00
1642	Grand Admiral Thrawn	1.00	2.00
1643	Noghri Bodyguard	1.00	2.00
1644	Noghri Bodyguard	1.00	2.00
1645	Chain of Command	2.50	5.00
1646	Supporting Fire	1.00	2.00
1651	Nar Shaddaa Drift	1.00	2.00
1652	Race Circuit Champion	1.00	2.00
1653	Racing Swoop	1.00	2.00
1654	Racing Swoop	1.00	2.00
1655	Black Market Exchange	1.00	2.00
1656	Cut Off	1.00	2.00

2015 Star Wars Draw Their Fire

14610722	The Survivors	1.00	2.00
14620723	Qu Rahn	1.00	2.00
14630724	Sulon Sympathizer	1.00	2.00
14640725	Shien Training	1.00	2.00
14650061	Force Rejuvenation	1.00	2.00
14660256	Protection	1.00	2.00
14710726	Called to Arms	1.00	2.00
14720727	Gray Squadron Gunner	1.00	2.00
14730728	Gray Squadron Y-Wing	1.00	2.00
14740729	Advanced Proton Torpedoes	1.00	2.00
14750730	Desperation	1.00	2.00
14760133	Target of Opportunity	1.00	2.00
14810731	The Daring Escape	1.00	2.00
14820732	LE-B02D9	1.00	2.00
14830733	Outrider	1.00	2.00
14840734	Spacer Cantina	1.00	2.00
14850735	Punch It	1.00	2.00
14860702	Stay on Target	1.00	2.00
14910736	The Emperor's Sword	1.00	2.00
14920737	Maarek Stele	1.00	2.00
14930738	Delta One	1.00	2.00
14940739	Advanced Concussion Missiles	1.00	2.00
14950740	Hand of the Emperor	1.00	2.00
14960169	Heat of Battle	1.00	2.00
15010741	Guarding the Wing	1.00	2.00
15020742	DS-61-3	1.00	2.00
15030743	Black Squadron Fighter	1.00	2.00
15040743	Black Squadron Fighter	1.00	2.00
15050744	Elite Pilot Training	1.00	2.00
15060170	Target of Opportunity	1.00	2.00

2015 Star Wars Imperial Entanglement

17110838	House Edge	1.00	2.00
17120839	Lando Calrissian	1.00	2.00
17130840	Herglic Sabacc Addict	1.00	2.00
17140022	Cloud City Casino	1.00	2.00
17150841	Sabacc Shift	1.00	2.00
17160842	The Gambler's Trick	1.00	2.00
17210843	Debt of Honor	1.00	2.00
17220844	Chewbacca	1.00	2.00
17230845	Wookiee Defender	1.00	2.00
17240846	Kashyyyk Resistance Hideout	1.00	2.00
17250847	Wookiee Rage	1.00	2.00
17260256	Protection	1.00	2.00
17310848	Fortune and Fate	1.00	2.00
17320849	Lady Luck	1.00	2.00
17330850	Cloud City Technician	1.00	2.00
17340850	Cloud City Technician	1.00	2.00

17350851	Central Computer	1.00	2.00
17360133	Target of Opportunity	1.00	2.00
17410852	Honor Among Thieves	1.00	2.00
17420853	Mirax Terrik	1.00	2.00
17430854	Fringer Captain	1.00	2.00
17440854	Fringer Captain	1.00	2.00
17450855	Special Discount	1.00	2.00
17460856	One Last Trick	1.00	2.00
17510857	Renegade Reinforcements	1.00	2.00
17520858	Corporal Dansra Beezer	1.00	2.00
17530210	Renegade Squadron Operative	1.00	2.00
17540859	Hidden Backup	1.00	2.00
17550860	Directed Fire	1.00	2.00
17560861	Last Minute Reinforcements	1.00	2.00
17610862	Mysteries of the Rim	1.00	2.00
17620863	Outer Rim Mystic	1.00	2.00
17630863	Outer Rim Mystic	1.00	2.00
17640864	Niman Training	1.00	2.00
17650864	Niman Training	1.00	2.00
17660865	Force Illusion	1.00	2.00
17710866	Planning the Rescue	1.00	2.00
17720867	General Airen Cracken	1.00	2.00
17730868	Alliance Infiltrator	1.00	2.00
17740869	Superior Intelligence	1.00	2.00
17750870	Undercover	1.00	2.00
17760117	Rescue Mission	1.00	2.00
17810871	The Tarkin Doctrine	1.00	2.00
17820872	Grand Moff Tarkin	1.00	2.00
17830873	Stormtrooper Assault Team	1.00	2.00
17840874	Rule by Fear	1.00	2.00
17850875	Moment of Triumph	1.00	2.00
17860171	Twist of Fate	1.00	2.00
17910876	Might of the Empire	1.00	2.00
17920877	Chimaera	1.00	2.00
17930878	DP20 Corellian Gunship	1.00	2.00
17940879	Fleet Staging Area	1.00	2.00
17950392	Tractor Beam	1.00	2.00
17960880	The Empire Strikes Back	1.00	2.00
18010881	Enforced Loyalty	1.00	2.00
18020882	Colonel Yularen	1.00	2.00
18030883	Lieutenant Mithel	1.00	2.00
18040884	MSE-6 'Mouse' Droid	1.00	2.00
18050024	Control Room	1.00	2.00
18060885	The Imperial Fist	1.00	2.00
18110886	Imperial Entanglements	1.00	2.00
18120887	Imperial Raider	1.00	2.00
18130888	VT-49 Decimator	1.00	2.00
18140888	VT-49 Decimator	1.00	2.00
18150889	Customs Blockade	1.00	2.00
18160890	Ion Cannon	1.00	2.00
18210891	Phantoms of Imdaar	1.00	2.00
18220892	TIE Phantom	1.00	2.00
18230892	TIE Phantom	1.00	2.00
18240893	Enhanced Laser Cannon	1.00	2.00
18250894	Fighters Coming In!	1.00	2.00
18260169	Heat of Battle	1.00	2.00
18310895	Brothers of the Sith	1.00	2.00
18320896	Gorc	1.00	2.00
18330897	Pic	1.00	2.00
18340898	Telepathic Connection	1.00	2.00
18350062	Force Stasis	1.00	2.00
18360899	Force Invisibility	1.00	2.00
18410900	The Hutt's Menagerie	1.00	2.00
18420901	Malakili	1.00	2.00
18430902	Jabba's Rancor	1.00	2.00
18440903	Bubo	1.00	2.00
18450904	Underground Entertainment	1.00	2.00
18460905	Jabba's Summons	1.00	2.00

2015 Star Wars Jump to Lightspeed

1661	The Forgotten Masters	1.00	2.00
1662	Tira Saa	1.00	2.00
1663	Lost Master	1.00	2.00
1664	Lost Master	1.00	2.00
1665	A Gift from the Past	1.00	2.00
1666	Echoes of the Force	1.00	2.00
1671	Heroes of the Rebellion	1.00	2.00
1672	Tycho Celchu	1.00	2.00
1673	Wes Janson	1.00	2.00
1674	Rogue Six	1.00	2.00
1675	Rogue Nine	1.00	2.00
1676	Ready for Takeoff	1.00	2.00
1681	That Bucket of Bolts	1.00	2.00
1682	Han Solo	1.00	2.00
1683	Millennium Falcon	1.00	2.00
1684	Well Paid	1.00	2.00
1685	Well Paid	1.00	2.00
1686	Heat of Battle	1.00	2.00
1691	The Reawakening	1.00	2.00
1692	Arden Lyn	1.00	2.00
1693	Dark Side Apprentice	1.00	2.00
1694	Return to Darkness	1.00	2.00
1695	Give in to Your Anger	1.00	2.00
1696	Give in to Your Anger	1.00	2.00
1701	Behind the Black Sun	1.00	2.00
1702	Guri	1.00	2.00
1703	Freelance Assassin	1.00	2.00
1704	Hidden Vibroknife	1.00	2.00
1705	Threat Removal	1.00	2.00
1706	Heat of Battle	1.00	2.00

2015 Star Wars Ready for Takeoff

14110698	Rogue Squadron Assault	1.00	2.00
14120699	Derek 'Hobbie' Klivian	1.00	2.00
14130700	Rogue Squadron X-Wing	1.00	2.00
14140700	Rogue Squadron X-Wing	1.00	2.00
14150701	Pilot Ready Room	1.00	2.00
14160702	Stay on Target	1.00	2.00

14210703	Memories of Taanab	1.00	2.00
14220704	Lando Calrissian	1.00	2.00
14230705	System Patrol Craft	1.00	2.00
14240705	System Patrol Craft	1.00	2.00
14250706	Conner Net	1.00	2.00
14260707	A Little Maneuver	1.00	2.00
14310708	Black Squadron Formation	1.00	2.00
14320709	IMauleri Mithel	1.00	2.00
14330710	Black Two	1.00	2.00
14340146	TIE Advanced	1.00	2.00
14350711	Death Star Ready Room	1.00	2.00
14360712	Stay on Target	1.00	2.00
14410713	The Empireis Elite	1.00	2.00
14420714	Baron Fel	1.00	2.00
14430715	181st TIE Interceptor	1.00	2.00
14440715	181st TIE Interceptor	1.00	2.00
14450716	Flight Academy	1.00	2.00
14460712	Stay on Target	1.00	2.00
14510717	The Grand Heist	1.00	2.00
14520718	Niles Ferrier	1.00	2.00
14530719	Novice Starship Thief	1.00	2.00
14540719	Novice Starship Thief	1.00	2.00
14550720	Pirate Hideout	1.00	2.00
14560721	Salvage Operation	1.00	2.00

2016 Star Wars Destiny Awakening

COMPLETE SET (174)		450.00	650.00
BOOSTER BOX (36 PACKS)		80.00	120.00
BOOSTER PACK (5 CARDS+1 DIE)		4.00	6.00
RELEASED IN DECEMBER 2016			
1	Captain Phasma L	7.50	15.00
2	First Order Stormtrooper R	2.50	5.00
3	General Grievous R	2.50	5.00
4	General Veers R	2.50	5.00
5	AT ST L	6.00	12.00
6	First Order TIE Fighter R	2.50	5.00
7	Commanding Presence L	7.50	15.00
8	F 11D Rifle S	2.00	4.00
9	Count Dooku R	2.50	5.00
10	Darth Vader L	15.00	30.00
11	Kylo Ren S	1.25	2.50
12	Nightsister R	2.50	5.00
13	Force Choke L	10.00	20.00
14	Immobilize R	2.50	5.00
15	Kylo Rens Lightsaber L	10.00	20.00
16	Sith Holocron R	7.50	13.00
17	Infantry Grenades R	2.50	5.00
18	Speeder Bike Scout R	2.50	5.00
19	Bala Tik R	2.50	5.00
20	Jabba the Hutt L	12.00	25.00
21	Jango Fett R	2.50	5.00
22	Tusken Raider R	2.50	5.00
23	Crime Lord L	7.50	15.00
24	Flame Thrower R	2.50	5.00
25	Gaffi Stick R	2.50	5.00
26	On the Hunt R	2.50	5.00
27	Admiral Ackbar R	2.50	5.00
28	Leia Organa R	2.50	5.00
29	Poe Dameron L	12.00	25.00
30	Rebel Trooper R	2.50	5.00
31	Launch Bay L	5.00	10.00
32	Black One L	4.00	8.00
33	Scout R	2.50	5.00
34	Survival Gear R	2.50	5.00
35	Luke Skywalker L	12.00	25.00
36	Padawan R	2.50	5.00
37	Qui Gon Jinn R	2.50	5.00
38	Rey S	2.00	4.00
39	Force Protection R	2.50	5.00
40	Jedi Robes R	2.50	5.00
41	Luke Skywalkers Lightsaber L	7.50	15.00
42	One With the Force L	12.00	25.00
43	BB 8 R	2.50	5.00
44	Reys Staff R	2.50	5.00
45	Finn S	2.00	4.00
46	Han Solo L	10.00	20.00
47	Hired Gun R	2.50	5.00
48	Padme Amidala R	2.50	5.00
49	Millennium Falcon L	7.50	15.00
50	Diplomatic Immunity R	2.50	5.00
51	DL 44 Heavy Blaster Pistol R	2.50	5.00
52	Infiltrate R	2.50	5.00
53	Outpost R	2.50	5.00
54	DH 17 Blaster Pistol R	2.50	5.00
55	IQA 11 Blaster Rifle R	2.50	5.00
56	Promotion R	2.50	5.00
57	Force Throw S	5.00	10.00
58	Force Training R	2.50	5.00
59	Lightsaber S	2.00	4.00
60	Mind Probe S	4.00	8.00
61	Comlink R	2.50	5.00
62	Datapad R	2.50	5.00
63	Holdout Blaster R	10.00	20.00
64	Black Market R	2.50	5.00
65	Cunning R	2.50	5.00
66	Jetpack R	2.50	5.00
67	Thermal Detonator L	12.00	25.00
68	Cannon Fodder C	.10	.20
69	Closing the Net C	.10	.20
70	Endless Ranks U	1.00	2.00
71	Occupation C	.10	.20
72	Probe C	.10	.20
73	Sweep the Area C	.10	.20
74	Tactical Mastery U	2.00	4.00
75	The Best Defense U	.20	.40
76	Drudge Work C	.10	.20
77	Local Garrison U	.20	.40
78	Personal Escort C	.10	.20
79	Abandon All Hope U	.20	.40
80	Boundless Ambition C	.10	.20
81	Enrage C	.10	.20
82	Feel Your Anger C	.10	.20
83	Force Strike U	.60	1.25
84	Intimidate C	.10	.20
85	Isolation C	.10	.20
86	No Mercy U	2.00	4.00
87	Pulling the Strings C	.10	.20
88	Emperors Favor U	.20	.40
89	Power of the Dark Side S	.30	.60
90	Hidden in Shadow U	.20	.40
91	Nowhere to Run U	.20	.40
92	Ace in the Hole U	.60	1.25
93	Armed to the Teeth C	.10	.20
94	Confiscation U	.20	.40
95	Fight Dirty U	.20	.40
96	Go for the Kill C	.10	.20
97	He Doesnt Like You C	.10	.20
98	Lying in Wait C	.10	.20
99	Backup Muscle C	.10	.20
100	My Kind of Scum C	.10	.20
101	Underworld Connections U	.75	1.50
102	Prized Possession U	.20	.40
103	Commando Raid U	.20	.40
104	Defensive Position C	.10	.20
105	Field Medic C	.10	.20
106	Hit and Run C	.10	.20
107	Its a Trap U	.60	1.25
108	Natural Talent C	.10	.20
109	Rearm U	.20	.40
110	Retreat U	.20	.40
111	Strategic Planning C	.10	.20
112	Surgical Strike C	.10	.20
113	Resistance HQ U	.20	.40
114	Anticipate U	.20	.40
115	Defensive Stance C	.10	.20
116	Force Misdirection C	.10	.20
117	Heroism C	.10	.20
118	Noble Sacrifice C	.10	.20
119	Patience C	.10	.20
120	Return of the Jedi U	.20	.40
121	Riposte C	.10	.20
122	Willpower U	.30	.60
123	Jedi Council U	.20	.40
124	Awakening S	.50	1.00
125	The Force is Strong C	.10	.20
126	Daring Escape U	.20	.40
127	Dont Get Cocky C	.10	.20
128	Draw Attention C	.10	.20
129	Hyperspace Jump U	.20	.40
130	Let the Wookiee Win U	.20	.40
131	Negotiate C	.10	.20
132	Scavenge C	.10	.20
133	Shoot First U	.20	.40
134	Smuggling C	.10	.20
135	Play the Odds U	.20	.40
136	Street Informants C	.10	.20
137	Second Chance U	1.25	2.50
138	Award Ceremony C	.10	.20
139	Dug In U	2.00	4.00
140	Firepower C	.10	.20
141	Leadership U	.30	.60
142	Logistics C	.10	.20
143	Squad Tactics C	.10	.20
144	Supporting Fire U	.20	.40
145	Deflect C	.10	.20
146	Disturbance in the Force C	.10	.20
147	Mind Trick U	.30	.60
148	The Power of the Force C	.10	.20
149	Use the Force S	.60	1.25
150	It Binds All Things U	1.00	2.00
151	Aim S	.30	.75
152	All In U	1.00	2.00
153	Block C	.10	.20
154	Close Quarters Assault S	.75	1.50
155	Dodge C	.10	.20
156	Flank U	.20	.40
157	Take Cover C	.10	.20
158	Disarm C	.10	.20
159	Electroshock U	3.00	6.00
160	Reversal U	.75	1.50
161	Scramble C	.10	.20
162	Unpredictable C	.10	.20

163 Infamous U	1.25	2.50	
164 Hunker Down C	.10	.20	
165 Command Center U	.20	.40	
166 Echo Base U	.20	.40	
167 Emperors Throne Room U	.20	.40	
168 Frozen Wastes S	.50	1.00	
169 Imperial Armory C	.10	.20	
170 Jedi Temple C	.10	.20	
171 Rebel War Room C	.10	.20	
172 Mos Eisley Spaceport C	.10	.20	
173 Separatist Base C	.10	.20	
174 Starship Graveyard S	1.25	2.50	

2017 Star Wars Destiny Spirit of Rebellion

COMPLETE SET (160)	400.00	550.00
BOOSTER BOX (36 PACKS)	100.00	130.00
BOOSTER PACK (5 CARDS+1 DIE)	4.00	6.00
UNLISTED C	.10	.20
UNLISTED U	.25	.40
UNLISTED R	3.00	5.00
RELEASED ON MAY 4, 2017		
1 Death Trooper R	3.00	6.00
2 FN 2199 R	2.00	4.00
3 Director Krennic L	6.00	12.00
4 TIE Pilot R	2.00	4.00
5 E Web Emplacement R	5.00	10.00
6 Imperial Discipline R	2.00	4.00
7 DT 29 Heavy Blaster Pistol R	2.00	4.00
8 Z6 Riot Control Baton L	12.00	25.00
9 Asajj Ventress R	2.00	4.00
10 Darth Vader R	2.00	4.00
11 Palpatine L	12.00	25.00
12 Royal Guard R	2.00	4.00
13 Commando Shuttle R	2.00	4.00
14 Force Lightning L	10.00	20.00
15 Lightsaber Pike R	5.00	10.00
16 Lure of Power R	2.00	4.00
17 Interrogation Droid R	2.00	4.00
18 Aurra Sing R	2.00	4.00
19 Guavian Enforcer R	2.00	4.00
20 IG 88 L	6.00	12.00
21 Unkar Plutt R	2.00	4.00
22 Slave I L	6.00	12.00
23 Blackmail L	6.00	12.00
24 Personal Shield R	2.00	4.00
25 Vibroknucklers R	2.00	4.00
26 Baze Malbus L	6.00	12.00
27 Mon Mothma R	2.00	4.00
28 Rebel Commando R	2.00	4.00
29 Temmin "Snap" Wexley R	2.00	4.00
30 C 3PO R	2.00	4.00
31 U Wing L	6.00	12.00

32 A180 Blaster R	2.00	4.00
33 Overkill R	2.00	4.00
34 Jedi Acolyte R	2.00	4.00
35 Chirrut Œmwe R	2.00	4.00
36 Luminara Unduli R	2.00	4.00
37 Obi Wan Kenobi L	6.00	12.00
38 Delta 7 Interceptor R	2.00	4.00
39 Handcrafted Light Bow L	6.00	12.00
40 Force Heal R	2.00	4.00
41 Journals of Ben Kenobi R	2.00	4.00
42 R2 D2 R	2.00	4.00
43 Chewbacca L	6.00	12.00
44 Jyn Erso R	2.00	4.00
45 Maz Kanata R	2.00	4.00
46 Outer Rim Smuggler R	2.00	4.00
47 Smuggling Freighter R	2.00	4.00
48 Bowcaster L	6.00	12.00
49 Lone Operative R	2.00	4.00
50 Mazs Goggles L	6.00	12.00
51 Supply Line R	2.00	4.00
52 Astromech R	2.00	4.00
53 Rocket Launcher L	20.00	35.00
54 Force Push R	2.00	4.00
55 Force Speed L	50.00	100.00
56 Makashi Training R	2.00	4.00
57 Vibroknife R	10.00	20.00
58 Quadjumper L	6.00	12.00
59 Ascension Gun R	5.00	10.00
60 Con Artist R	2.00	4.00
61 Battle Formation C	.10	.20
62 Imperial War Machine U	.20	.40
63 Lockdown C	.10	.20
64 Sustained Fire U	.20	.40
65 Traitor U	.20	.40
66 Trench Warfare C	.10	.20
67 Undying Loyalty C	.10	.20
68 We Have Them Now U	.30	.60
69 Attrition C	.10	.20
70 Imperial Inspection U	.30	.60
71 Anger U	.60	1.25
72 Lightsaber Throw U	.50	1.00
73 Manipulate C	.10	.20
74 No Disintegreations C	.10	.20
75 Now You Will Die U	.10	.20
76 Rise Again U	.75	1.50
77 The Price of Failure C	.10	.20
78 Dark Presence U	.75	1.50
79 Now I Am The Master C	.10	.20
80 Doubt C	.10	.20
81 Arms Deal C	.10	.20
82 Bait and Switch C	.10	.20
83 Friends in High Places U	.20	.40
84 Loose Ends U	.20	.40
85 One Quarter Portion C	.10	.20
86 Relentless Pursuit C	.10	.20
87 Scrap Buy U	.20	.40
88 Salvage Stand C	.10	.20
89 Armor Plating U	.50	1.00
90 Emergency Evacuation U	.20	.40
91 Friendly Fire U	.20	.40
92 Guerrilla Warfare C	.10	.20
93 Our Only Hope U	.20	.40
94 Rebel Assault C	.10	.20
95 Sensor Placement U	.20	.40
96 Spirit of Rebellion C	.10	.20
97 Planetary Uprising U	.50	1.00
98 Spy Net C	.10	.20
99 Tactical Aptitude C	.10	.20
100 Caution U	.60	1.25
101 Destiny C	.10	.20

102 Determination C	.10	.20
103 Guard U	.20	.40
104 Krayt Dragon Howl C	.10	.20
105 My Ally Is The Force U	.50	1.00
106 Synchronicity C	.10	.20
107 Your Eyes Can Decive You U	.20	.40
108 Protective Mentor C	.10	.20
109 Confidence C	.10	.20
110 Garbagell Do C	.10	.20
111 Hold On C	.10	.20
112 Rebel U	.20	.40
113 Long Con C	.10	.20
114 Loth Cat and Mouse C	.10	.20
115 Never Tell Me the Odds U	.20	.40
116 Planned Explosion U	.20	.40
117 Double Dealing C	.10	.20
118 Life Debt U	.20	.40
119 Bombing Run U	.20	.40
120 Collateral Damage C	.10	.20
121 Salvo U	.30	.60
122 Suppression C	.10	.20
123 Aftermath C	.10	.20
124 Air Superiority C	.10	.20
125 Training U	2.00	4.00
126 Wingman C	.10	.20
127 Decisive Blow C	.10	.20
128 High Ground C	.10	.20
129 Momentum Shift U	.20	.40
130 Overconfidence C	.10	.20
131 Premonitions U	.20	.40
132 Rejuvenate C	.10	.20
133 Trust Your Instincts U	1.00	2.00
134 Meditate C	.10	.20
135 Force Illusion U	2.00	4.00
136 Evade C	.10	.20
137 New Orders U	.50	1.00
138 Parry C	.10	.20
139 Swiftness C	.10	.20
140 Resolve U	.20	.40
141 Ammo Belt C	.10	.20
142 Bolt Hole C	.10	.20
143 Cheat U	.60	1.25
144 Diversion C	.10	.20
145 Fair Trade U	.20	.40
146 Friends in Low Places C	.10	.20
147 Sabotage U	.20	.40
148 Improvisation C	.10	.20
149 Outmaneuver C	.10	.20
150 Fast Hands U	4.00	7.00
151 Carbon Freezing Chamber U	.20	.40
152 Cargo Hold C	.10	.20
153 Docking Bay C	.10	.20
154 Ewok Village C	.10	.20
155 Mazs Castle U	.20	.40
156 Moisture Farm U	.20	.40
157 Otoh Gunga C	.10	.20
158 Secluded Beach C	.10	.20
159 Secret Facility U	.20	.40
160 War Torn Streets C	.10	.20

2018 Star Wars Destiny Empire at War

COMPLETE SET (160)	300.00	550.00
BOOSTER BOX (36 PACKS)	85.00	120.00
BOOSTER PACK (5 CARDS+1 DIE)	3.00	5.00
UNLISTED C	.10	.20
UNLISTED U	.40	.60
UNLISTED R	2.00	5.00
RELEASED ON DECEMBER 10, 2018		
1 †Ciena Reet† Adept Pilot R	2.50	5.00
2 General Huxt- Aspiring Commander R	2.50	5.00

#	Card	Lo	Hi
3	MagnaGuard R	2.50	5.00
4	Thrawn -†Master Strategist L	10.00	20.00
5	AT-DP R	2.50	5.00
6	Probe Droid R	2.50	5.00
7	T-7 Ion Disruptor Rifle L	7.50	15.00
8	Quinlan Vos†- Dark Disciple R	2.50	5.00
9	Servant of the Dark Side R	2.50	5.00
10	Seventh Sister†- Agile Inquisitor L	7.50	15.00
11	Grand Inquisitor†- Sith Loyalist L	7.50	15.00
12	Darth Vader's TIE Advanced R	2.50	5.00
13	ID9 Seeker Droid R	2.50	5.00
14	Temptation R	2.50	5.00
15	Grand Inquisitor's Lightsaber L	7.50	15.00
16	Bazine Netal†- Master Manipulator R	2.50	5.00
17	†Bosskt† Wookiee Slayer R	2.50	5.00
18	Cad Bane†- Vicious Mercenary L	10.00	20.00
19	Gamorrean Guard R	2.50	5.00
20	Hound's Tooth L	7.50	15.00
21	Cable Launcher R	2.50	5.00
22	LL-30 Blaster Pistol R	2.50	5.00
23	Relby-V10 Mortar Gun R	2.50	5.00
24	General Rieekan†- Defensive Mastermind R	2.50	5.00
25	Hera Syndulla - Phoenix Leader R	2.50	5.00
26	K-2SO†Reprogrammed Droid L	7.50	15.00
27	Rookie Pilot R	2.50	5.00
28	Ghost L	7.50	15.00
29	Y-Wing R	2.50	5.00
30	A280 Blaster Rifle R	2.50	5.00
31	Ahsoka Tano†- Force Operative L	12.00	25.00
32	Jedi Instructor R	2.50	5.00
33	Kanan Jarrus†- Rebel Jedi R	2.50	5.00
34	Mace Windu†- Jedi Champion L	7.50	15.00
35	Training Remote R	2.50	5.00
36	Master of the Council L	7.50	15.00
37	Coordination R	2.50	5.00
38	Ezra Bridger†- Force-sensitive Thief R	2.50	5.00
39	Lando Calrissian†- Galactic Entrepreneur R	2.50	5.00
40	Sabine Wren†- Explosives Expert L	7.50	15.00
41	Wookiee Warrior R	2.50	5.00
42	Chopper L	7.50	15.00
43	Energy Slingshot R	2.50	5.00
44	Tough Haggler R	2.50	5.00
45	T-47 Airspeeder R	2.50	5.00
46	LR1K Sonic Cannon L	7.50	15.00
47	Electrostaff R	2.50	5.00
48	Natural Pilot R	2.50	5.00
49	Ancient Lightsaber L	25.00	45.00
50	Psychometry R	2.50	5.00
51	Shoto Lightsaber R	2.50	5.00
52	Weapons Cache R	2.50	5.00
53	BD-1 Cutter Vibro AX R	2.50	5.00
54	Extortion R	2.50	5.00
55	X-8 Night Sniper L	7.50	15.00
56	Z-95 Headhunter R	2.50	5.00
57	Chance Cube R	2.50	5.00
58	EMP Grenades R	2.50	5.00
59	Lead by Example R	2.50	5.00
60	Scatterblaster R	2.50	5.00
61	Commandeer U	.30	.60
62	Crossfire C	.10	.20
63	Drop Your Weapon! U	.30	.60
64	Imperial Backing U	.30	.60
65	Prepare for War C	.10	.20
66	Red Alert C	.10	.20
67	Ruthless Tactics C	.10	.20
68	Take Prisoner U	.30	.60
69	Imperial HQ C	.10	.20
70	As You Command C	.10	.20
71	Cornered Prey C	.10	.20
72	Indomitable C	.10	.20
73	It Will All Be Mine U	.30	.60
74	Kill Them All C	.10	.20
75	Unyielding U	.30	.60
76	Insidious C	.10	.20
77	Hate U	.30	.60
78	Anarchy U	.30	.60
79	Bounty Postings C	.10	.20
80	Buy Out U	.30	.60
81	Coercion U	.30	.60
82	Only Business Matters C	.10	.20
83	Pilfered Goods U	.30	.60
84	Twin Shadows U	.30	.60
85	Hutt Ties C	.10	.20
86	Deadly U	.30	.60
87	No Survivors C	.10	.20
88	Detention Center U	.30	.60
89	All Quiet On The Front U	.30	.60
90	Entrenched U	.30	.60
91	Fortuitous Strike C	.10	.20
92	Rearguard C	.10	.20
93	Reckless Reentry U	.30	.60
94	Strike Briefing C	.10	.20
95	Swift Strike C	.10	.20
96	Rally Aid U	.30	.60
97	Shield Generator C	.10	.20
98	At Peace C	.10	.20
99	Bestow C	.10	.20
100	Bring Balance U	.30	.60
101	Reaping The Crystal U	.30	.60
102	Secret Mission C	.10	.20
103	Trust The Force C	.10	.20
104	Funeral Pyre C	.10	.20
105	Yoda's Quarters U	.30	.60
106	Fearless U	.30	.60
107	Against The Odds C	.10	.20
108	Appraise C	.10	.20
109	Bad Feeling C	.10	.20
110	Double Cross U	.30	.60
111	Impersonate U	.30	.60
112	Local Patrol C	.10	.20
113	Quick Escape U	.30	.60
114	Tenacity C	.10	.20
115	Running Interference U	.30	.60
116	Thermal Paint C	.10	.20
117	Defiance C	.10	.20
118	Covering Fire C	.10	.20
119	Deploy Squadron C	.10	.20
120	Fall Back U	.30	.60
121	Feint U	.30	.60
122	Flanking Maneuver U	.30	.60
123	Heat Of Battle C	.10	.20
124	Pinned Down C	.10	.20
125	The Day is Ours C	.10	.20
126	Drop Zone U	.30	.60
127	Tech Team C	.10	.20
128	Battle of Wills U	.30	.60
129	Force Vision C	.10	.20
130	Lightsaber Pull C	.10	.20
131	Lightsaber Training C	.10	.20
132	No Surrender C	.10	.20
133	Something familiar U	.30	.60
134	Voices Cry Out C	.10	.20
135	Keen Instincts U	.30	.60
136	Battle Rage C	.10	.20
137	Disable C	.10	.20
138	Persuade C	.10	.20
139	Pickpocket C	.10	.20
140	Threaten U	.30	.60
141	Trickery U	.30	.60
142	Truce C	.10	.20
143	Stolen Cache C	.10	.20
144	Hidden Agenda U	.30	.60
145	Mandalorian Armor C	.10	.20
146	Dangerous Mission C	.10	.20
147	Endurance U	.30	.60
148	Partnership C	.10	.20
149	Recycle C	.10	.20
150	Rend C	.10	.20
151	Roll On C	.10	.20
152	Plastoid Armor C	.10	.20
153	B'Omarr Monastery†- Teth C	.10	.20
154	Fort Anaxes†- Anaxes U	.30	.60
155	Garel Spaceport†- Garel U	.30	.60
156	Imperial Academy†- Lothal U	.30	.60
157	Main Plaza†- Vashka C	.10	.20
158	Medical Center†- Kaliida Shoals U	.30	.60
159	Port District†- Bespin U	.30	.60
160	Weapons Factory Alpha†- Cymoon 1 U	.30	.60

2018 Star Wars Destiny Rivals Starter Deck

COMPLETE SET (20)
DRAFT SET BOX (20 CARDS+9 DICE)
RELEASED ON FEBRUARY 15, 2018

1 Anakin Skywalker - Conflicted Apprentice
2 Lobot - Cyborg Aide
3 Ketsu Onyo - Black Sun Operative
4 Jawa Scavenger
5 Hidden Motive
6 Crafted Lightsaber
7 Targeting Computer
8 Fang Fighter
9 Tinker
10 Verpine Sniper Rifle
11 Emulate
12 Fight Back
13 Resourceful
14 Surprise Attack
15 Supply Pack
16 T-21 Repeating Blaster
17 Vibrosword
18 Bespin Wing Guard
19 Dry Fields - Atollon
20 Sith Temple - Malachor

2018 Star Wars Destiny Legacies

COMPLETE SET (180)
BOOSTER BOX (36 PACKS)
BOOSTER PACK (5 CARDS+1 DIE)
RELEASED ON FEBRUARY 1, 2018

#	Card	Lo	Hi
1	Dark Advisor R	.50	1.00
2	Maul - Vengeful One L	7.50	15.00
3	Mother Talzin - Nightsister Matriarch R	.50	1.00
4	Palpatine - Darth Sidious R	.50	1.00
5	Kylo Ren's Starfighter L	2.00	4.00
6	Crystal Ball R	.50	1.00
7	Force Rend R	.50	1.00
8	Maul's Lightsaber L	10.00	20.00
9	Battle Droid R	.50	1.00
10	Kallus - Agent of the Empire R	.50	1.00
11	Nute Gunray - Separatist Viceroy R	.50	1.00
12	Tarkin - Grand Moff L	2.50	5.00
13	Veteran Stormtrooper ST		
14	Separatist Landing Craft R	.50	1.00
15	Fragmentation Grenade R	.50	1.00
16	Grand Moff L	3.00	6.00
17	Kallus' Bo-Rifle L	1.00	2.00
18	Bib Fortuna - Majordomo R	.50	1.00
19	Boba Fett - Deadly Mercenary ST		
20	Doctor Aphra - Artifact Hunter L	7.50	15.00

#	Card	Lo	Hi
21	Greedo - Unlucky Mercenary L	1.50	3.00
22	Rebel Traitor R	.50	1.00
23	Ark Angel R	.50	1.00
24	BT-1 R	.50	1.00
25	Slave I ST		
26	Hunter Instinct ST		
27	Wrist Rockets ST		
28	BB-9E R	.50	1.00
29	Aayla Secura - Jedi General R	.50	1.00
30	Jedi Temple Guard R	.50	1.00
31	Luke Skywalker - Unlikely Hero ST		
32	Obi-Wan Kenobi - Jedi Master R	.50	1.00
33	Yoda - Wizened Master L	12.00	25.00
34	ETA-2 Interceptor R	.50	1.00
35	R2-D2 ST		
36	Force Meditation R	.50	1.00
37	Obi-Wan Kenobi's Lightsaber L	6.00	12.00
38	Clone Trooper R	.50	1.00
39	Finn - Soldier of Necessity L	1.50	3.00
40	Rose - Skilled Mechanic R	.50	1.00
41	Wedge Antilles - Squad Leader R	.50	1.00
42	Mortar Team R	.50	1.00
43	Resistance Bomber R	.50	1.00
44	Camouflaged Rifle R	.50	1.00
45	Rebellion Leader L	1.00	2.00
46	Han Solo - Savvy Smuggler ST		
47	Jar Jar Binks - Clumsy Outcast R	.50	1.00
48	Jedha Partisan R	.50	1.00
49	Saw Gerrera - Extremist Leader L	3.00	6.00
50	Zeb Orrelios - The Last Lasat L	7.50	15.00
51	Runaway Boomas R	.50	1.00
52	Millennium Falcon ST		
53	Roguish Charm R	.50	1.00
54	Zeb Orrelios' Bo-Rifle L	1.50	3.00
55	Republic Cruiser R	.50	1.00
56	Force Focus ST		
57	Force Wave L	7.50	15.00
58	Heirloom Lightsaber ST		
59	Hush-98 Comlink R	.50	1.00
60	Ground Battalion R	.50	1.00
61	Lookout Post R	.50	1.00
62	Auto Cannon R	.50	1.00
63	E-11 Blaster R	.50	1.00
64	74-Z Speeder Bike ST		
65	Hondo Ohnaka - Respected Businessman R	.50	1.00
66	Pirate Speeder Tank L		
67	Bartering R	.50	1.00
68	Gang Up R	.50	1.00
69	Vibrocutlass R	.50	1.00
70	Modified HWK-290 R	.50	1.00
71	Canto Bight Pistol R	.50	1.00
72	Hidden Blaster ST		
73	Hunting Rifle ST		
74	Stun Baton R	.50	1.00
75	Consumed By The Dark Side C	.15	.30
76	Dark Scheme C	.15	.30
77	Double Strike U	.20	.40
78	Frighten C	.15	.30
79	I Am Your Father U	.20	.40
80	Snare U	.20	.40
81	Spell of Removal C	.15	.30
82	Witch Magick C	.15	.30
83	Nightsister Coven U	.20	.40
84	Battle Fatigue C	.15	.30
85	Crush the Rebellion U	.20	.40
86	Imperial Might C	.15	.30
87	Scorched Earth U	.20	.40
88	Shrapnel Blast C	.15	.30
89	Target Practice C	.15	.30
90	Three Steps Ahead U	.20	.40

#	Card	Lo	Hi
91	Command Bridge U	.20	.40
92	Delve U	.20	.40
93	Free-For-All U	.20	.40
94	In Pursuit U	.20	.40
95	No Good To Me Dead C	.15	.30
96	Rumors C	.15	.30
97	Subdue C	.15	.30
98	Take Flight C	.15	.30
99	Outnumber C	.15	.30
100	Adapt C	.15	.30
101	Ataru Strike U	.20	.40
102	Heightened Awareness ST		
103	Investigate C	.15	.30
104	Strength Through Weakness U	.20	.40
105	Unbreakable C	.15	.30
106	Defensive Teaching U	.20	.40
107	Yoda's Hut U	.20	.40
108	Attack Run C	.15	.30
109	Equip C	.15	.30
110	Final Moment U	.20	.40
111	Light 'Em Up C	.15	.30
112	Mend U	.20	.40
113	Refit C	.15	.30
114	Special Modification U	.20	.40
115	Suppression Field U	.20	.40
116	Bravado C	.15	.30
117	Easy Pickings U	.20	.40
118	Explosive Tactics U	.20	.40
119	Impulsive C	.15	.30
120	Scruffy Looking Nerf-Herder C	.15	.30
121	Smuggler's Run C	.15	.30
122	Maz's Vault U	.20	.40
123	Diplomatic Protection U	.20	.40
124	Into The Garbage Chute U	.20	.40
125	Alter C	.15	.30
126	Ancient Wisdom C	.15	.30
127	Feel The Force C	.15	.30
128	Invigorate ST		
129	Legacies U	.20	.40
130	Mislead C	.15	.30
131	Respite C	.15	.30
132	Stronger You Have Become U	.20	.40
133	The Force Is With Me C	.15	.30
134	Perseverance C	.15	.30
135	Resilient U	.20	.40
136	Crackdown C	.15	.30
137	Crash Landing ST		
138	Law and Order C	.15	.30
139	Locked and Loaded C	.15	.30
140	Reinforce U	.20	.40
141	Strength in Numbers C	.15	.30
142	Sudden Impact U	.20	.40
143	Superior Position C	.15	.30
144	Target Intel C	.15	.30
145	Bubble Shield U	.20	.40
146	Cover Team C	.15	.30
147	Bamboozle C	.15	.30
148	Cantina Brawl U	.20	.40
149	Counter Strike C	.15	.30
150	Dangerous Maneuver C	.15	.30
151	Entangle ST		
152	Face-Off C	.15	.30
153	Hasty Exit C	.15	.30
154	Lure U	.20	.40
155	Quick Draw C	.15	.30
156	Vandalize U	.20	.40
157	Well-Connected C	.15	.30
158	Defend C	.15	.30
159	Dive C	.15	.30
160	Ice Storm C	.15	.30

#	Card	Lo	Hi
161	No Cheating U	.20	.40
162	Shelter C	.15	.30
163	Backup Specialist C	.15	.30
164	Remote Stockpile C	.15	.30
165	Scrap Heap U	.20	.40
166	Bodyguard U	.20	.40
167	Quickdraw Holster C	.15	.30
168	Espionage U	.20	.40
169	Fortify U	.20	.40
170	Preemptive Strike U	.20	.40
171	Profitable Connection U	.20	.40
172	Stolen Intel C	.15	.30
173	Taking Ground C	.15	.30
174	Arid Wasteland - Geonosis ST		
175	Citadel Landing Zone - Scarif C	.15	.30
176	Imperial Palace - Coruscant U	.20	.40
177	Launch Deck - Home One U	.20	.40
178	Outer Rim Outpost - Nal Hutta ST		
179	Petranaki Arena - Geonosis C	.15	.30
180	Power Generator Trench - Death Star I U	.20	.40

2018 Star Wars Destiny Way of the Force

COMPLETE SET (160)
BOOSTER BOX (36 PACKS)
BOOSTER PACK (5 CARDS+1 DIE)
RELEASED ON JULY 5, 2018

1	Count Dooku - Darth Tyranus R
2	Fifth Brother - Intimidating Enforcer R
3	Force Sensitive Outcast R
4	Snoke - Supreme Leader L
5	Crush Hope U
6	Dark Ritual U
7	Lack of Faith U
8	No Escape C
9	Power From Pain U
10	Triple Threat C
11	Undermine U
12	Dark Empowerment C
13	Count Dooku's Solar Sailer R
14	Bardottan Sphere R
15	Fifth Brother's Lightsaber L
16	Force Fear R
17	Torment C
18	Arihnda Pryce - Unscrupulous Governor R
19	Executioner R
20	Firmus Piett - Ambitious Admiral R
21	General Grievous - Fearsome Cyborg L
22	Art of War U
23	Furious Assault U
24	Machine Replacement C
25	Opening Volley C
26	Overrun U
27	Testing Procedure C
28	Well-armed C
29	Blockade U
30	Climate Disruption Array U
31	General Grievous' Wheel Bike L
32	Imperial Troop Transport R
33	Planetary Bombardment L
34	Executioner's Axe R
35	DJ - Treacherous Rogue L
36	Jabba The Hutt - Renowned Gangster R
37	Mandalorian Super Commando R
38	Sebulba - Cutthroat Podracer R
39	By Any Means C
40	Cocky C
41	Extreme Hubris U
42	Nefarious Deed C
43	Paid Off U
44	Partners in Crime C

45 Quarrel C
46 Rancorous U
47 Sebulba Always Wins U
48 Sticky Situation C
49 0-0-0 R
50 Sebulba's Podracer R
51 Formidable L
52 Underhanded Tactics R
53 Way of the Dark C
54 Ezra Bridger - Aspiring Jedi R
55 Jedi Sentinel R
56 Luke Skywalker - Reluctant Instructor L
57 Plo Koon - Jedi Protector R
58 Fond Memories C
59 Loth-Wolf Bond C
60 Luke's Training U
61 Pacify U
62 Propel C
63 Renewed Purpose C
64 Steadfast C
65 Plo Koon's Starfighter R
66 A99 Aquata Breather U
67 Ezra Bridger's Lightsaber L
68 Guardian of the Whills U
69 Luke Skywalker's Lightning Rod R
70 There Is No Try R
71 Boss Nass - Bombastic Ruler R
72 Gungan Warrior R
73 Leia Organa - Heart of the Resistance L
74 Rex - Clone Captain L
75 Blaze of Glory C
76 Desperate Hour C
77 First Aid C
78 Gungan Offensive U
79 Motivate U
80 Reposition C
81 Long-Term Plan U
82 Gungan Catapult R
83 Resistance Crait Speeder R
84 Suppressive Fire U
85 Electropole R
86 Inspiring Presence U
87 Rex's Blaster Pistol L
88 Anakin Skywalker - Podracing Prodigy R
89 Bo-Katan Kryze - Deathwatch Lieutenant R
90 Cassian Andor - Rebellion Operative L
91 Trusted Informant R
92 Clandestine Operation U
93 Closing the Deal C
94 Defensive Racing U
95 Dumb Luck U
96 Mechanical Insight C
97 Narrow Escape C
98 Rigged Detonation C
99 Righteous Cause C
100 Scoping the Target U
101 Shootout C
102 Anakin Skywalker's Podracer R
103 N-1 Starfighter R
104 CR-2 Heavy Blaster R
105 Stealthy L
106 Way of the Light C
107 Dex's Diner U
108 Become One C
109 Beguile C
110 Control U
111 Division in the Force C
112 Flames of the Past U
113 Peace and Quiet C
114 Turn the Tide C
115 Built to Last U
116 Honed Skills C
117 Dagger of Mortis L
118 Force Jump R
119 Way of the Force U
120 Change of Fate C
121 Glancing Shot C
122 Grand Entrance C
123 Hostile Takeover U
124 Overload C
125 Reconstruct C
126 Take the Fight to Them C
127 Home Turf Advantage U
128 Ammo Reserves C
129 ARC-170 Starfighter R
130 Hailfire Droid Tank L
131 Weapon Master C
132 Friend or Foe C
133 In The Crosshairs C
134 Podracer Betting U
135 Reprogram U
136 Risky Move U
137 Start Your Engines! U
138 Calling in Favors U
139 Prized Goods C
140 Streetwise C
141 XS Stock Light Freighter R
142 Darksaber L
143 Mandalorian Vambraces R
144 Respected Businessman C
145 V-1 Thermal Detonator R
146 Extract C
147 Free Fall C
148 Made to Suffer U
149 Nature's Charm C
150 Quell C
151 Under Attack C
152 Lotho Minor Junkers R
153 Podracer R
154 Macrobinoculars R
155 Boonta Eve Classic U
156 Arena of Death - Nar Shaddaa U
157 Bendu's Lair - Atollon R
158 Comm Tower - Scarif C
159 Mos Espa Arena - Tatooine U
160 Rift Valley - Dathomir U

2018 Star Wars Destiny Across the Galaxy

COMPLETE SET (160)
BOOSTER BOX (36 PACKS)
BOOSTER PACK (5 CARDS+1 DIE)
RELEASED ON NOVEMBER 9, 2018

1 Darth Vader - Terror To Behold L	25.00	50.00
2 Luce - Callous Nightsister R	.50	1.00
3 Nightbrother R	.50	1.00
4 Savage Opress - Reckless Warrior R	.50	1.00
5 Burst Of Lightning C	.15	.30
6 Endow U	.20	.40
7 Fear and Dead Men U	.20	.40
8 I Am The Senate U	.20	.40
9 Let The Hate Flow C	.15	.30
10 Darth Vader's Meditation Chamber U	.20	.40
11 Galactic Deception C	.15	.30
12 Stifle U	.20	.40
13 Vader's Fist L		
14 Bloodlust C	.15	.30
15 Chain Sickle R	.50	1.00
16 Darth Vader's Lightsaber L	15.00	30.00
17 Energy Bow R	.50	1.00
18 Iden Versio - Inferno Squad Commander L		
19 Mauler Mithel - Vader's Wingman R	.50	1.00
20 Super Battle Droid R	.50	1.00
21 Wulff Yularen - ISB Colonel R	.50	1.00
22 Browbeat C	.15	.30
23 Commence Primary Ignition U	.20	.40
24 Drop 'Em U	.20	.40
25 Hatching A Plan C	.15	.30
26 Imposing Presence C	.15	.30
27 In Tandem C	.15	.30
28 Questioned Loyalty U	.20	.40
29 Reach The Stars C	.15	.30
30 Black Two R	.50	1.00
31 TIE Fighter R	.50	1.00
32 Umbaran Hover Tank L		
33 Vigilance C	.15	.30
34 Inferno Squad ID10 Seeker Droid R	.50	1.00
35 Dryden Voss - Ruthless Crime Lord L	6.00	12.00
36 Tobias Beckett - Thief For Hire L		
37 Val - Headstrong Renegade R	.50	1.00
38 Act Of Cruelty C	.15	.30
39 Cunning Ruse C	.15	.30
40 Exploit C	.15	.30
41 First Claim C	.15	.30
42 Heated Confrontation C	.15	.30
43 In a Bind U	.20	.40
44 Shakedown C	.15	.30
45 Sidestep U	.20	.40
46 Wanton Destruction U	.20	.40
47 DÈj‡ Vu U	.20	.40
48 Firespray-31 R	.50	1.00
49 Relentless C	.15	.30
50 Donderbus Blaster Pistol R	.50	1.00
51 Grappling Boa R	.50	1.00
52 Tobias Beckett's Rifle R	.50	1.00
53 Vow Of Vengeance U	.20	.40
54 Retribution U	.20	.40
55 Barriss Offee - Studious Padawan R	.50	1.00
56 Force Mystic R	.50	1.00
57 Kit Fisto - Shii-cho Master R	.50	1.00
58 Qui-Gon Jinn - Defiant Jedi Master L		
59 Bewilder C	.15	.30
60 Finishing Strike U	.20	.40
61 Gathering Intelligence C	.15	.30
62 Hold Off C	.15	.30
63 Insight C	.15	.30
64 Into Exile U	.20	.40
65 Repulse C	.15	.30
66 Safeguard C	.15	.30
67 Immutability C	.15	.30
68 Counterstroke R	.50	1.00
69 Lightsaber Training Staff R	.50	1.00
70 Pillio Star Compass R	.50	1.00
71 Qui-Gon Jinn's Lightsaber L		
72 Biggs Darklighter - Rebellion Ace R	.50	1.00
73 Clone Commander Cody - Loyal Strategist R	.50	1.00
74 Jyn Erso - Daring Infiltrator L		
75 Rebel Engineer R	.50	1.00
76 Aerial Advantage C	.15	.30
77 Attack of The Clones U	.20	.40
78 Dogfight U	.20	.40
79 Evacuate U	.20	.40
80 Inflame C	.15	.30
81 Outgun C	.15	.30
82 Turn The Tables U	.20	.40
83 Armed Escort C	.15	.30
84 BB-8 L	2.50	5.00
85 Black One R	.50	1.00
86 X-Wing R	.50	1.00
87 Jyn Erso's Blaster L		
88 R2 Astromech C	.15	.30

89 Lando Calrissian - Smooth and Sophisticated L		
90 Leia Organa - Boushh L	.50	1.00
91 L3-37 - Droid Revolutionary R	.50	1.00
92 A Good Investment C	.15	.30
93 Aid From Above U	.20	.40
94 Daring Gambit U	.20	.40
95 Drop In C	.15	.30
96 Hijack U	.20	.40
97 Karabast! C	.15	.30
98 Leverage C	.15	.30
99 Reluctance U	.20	.40
100 Slice And Dice U	.20	.40
101 Through The Pass C	.15	.30
102 Escape Craft R	.50	1.00
103 Millennium Falcon L		
104 On The Mark C	.15	.30
105 Decoy U	.20	.40
106 Energy Pike R	.50	1.00
107 Token Of Affection R	.50	1.00
108 At Odds C	.15	.30
109 Common Cause U	.20	.40
110 Conflicted C	.15	.30
111 Deadly Advance C	.15	.30
112 No Questions Asked U	.20	.40
113 Relinquish C	.15	.30
114 You Were My Friend C	.15	.30
115 Bitter Rivalry U	.20	.40
116 Foresight C	.15	.30
117 Nexus Of Power R	.50	1.00
118 Force Lift R	.50	1.00
119 Shatterpoint R	.50	1.00
120 Treasured Lightsaber R	.50	1.00
121 Attack Formation C	.15	.30
122 Barrel Roll C	.15	.30
123 Deployment C	.15	.30
124 Fleet Command C	.15	.30
125 Intense Fire C	.15	.30
126 Revised Order C	.15	.30
127 Snuff Out U	.20	.40
128 Transfer U	.20	.40
129 Armored Reinforcement U	.20	.40
130 Senate Chamber R	.50	1.00
131 Dorsal Turret R	.50	1.00
132 Handheld L-S1 Cannon L		
133 Triple Laser Turret R	.50	1.00
134 Han Solo - Independent Hotshot L	5.00	10.00
135 Qi'Ra - Street Savvy R	.50	1.00
136 Across The Galaxy C	.15	.30
137 Cash Out C	.15	.30
138 Dismantle U	.20	.40
139 Fight Fire With Fire C	.15	.30
140 Indifferent C	.15	.30
141 Quick Thinking C	.15	.30
142 Shock Tactic U	.20	.40
143 Double Down U	.20	.40
144 Improvised Defense C	.15	.30
145 Shadow Caster L		
146 Arc Caster R	.50	1.00
147 Black Sun Blaster Pistol R	.50	1.00
148 Flame Projector R	.50	1.00
149 Shriek C	.15	.30
150 T-16 Skyhopper C	.15	.30
151 X-34 Landspeeder C	.15	.30
152 Laser Cannon C	.15	.30
153 Systems Gauge U	.20	.40
154 Targeting Astromech U	.20	.40
155 No Allegiance U	.20	.40

156 Solidarity U	.20	.40
157 Landing Dock - Scipio U	.20	.40
158 Occupied City - Lothal U	.20	.40
159 Theed Royal Palace - Naboo U	.20	.40
160 Training Room - Kamino U	.20	.40

2019 Star Wars Destiny Convergence

COMPLETE SET (180)
BOOSTER BOX (36 PACKS)
BOOSTER PACK (5 CARDS+1 DIE)
RELEASED ON MARCH 28, 2019

1 Asajj Ventress - Swift And Cunning R
2 Palpatine - Unlimited Power L
3 Sentinel Messenger R
4 Sly Moore - Aide to the Emperor R
5 Mind Extraction U
6 A Tale of Tragedy C
7 Breaking Bonds C
8 Fit of Rage C
9 Forsaken U
10 Isolation C
11 No Mercy U
12 Forbidden Lore U
13 Imperialis R
14 Force Storm L
15 Malice R
16 Palpatine's Lightsaber L
17 Sith Teachings R
18 Captain Phasma - Stormtrooper Commander L
19 Commando Droid ST
20 First Order Stormtrooper R
21 General Grievous - Droid Armies Commander ST
22 Wat Tambor - Techno Union Foreman R
23 A Sinister Peace C
24 Make Demands C
25 Probe C
26 Pulverize C
27 Roger, Roger ST
28 The Best Defense... C
29 Defoliator Tank ST
30 Imperial Officer R
31 Megablaster Troopers L
32 Stap Droid ST
33 E-5 Blaster Carbine ST
34 Modular Frame ST
35 Dengar - Ruthless Tracker R
36 Jabba The Hutt - Influential Kingpin L
37 Quarren Tracker C
38 Watto - Stubborn Gambler R
39 Death Mark C
40 Enticing Reward U
41 Barter With Blood U
42 Conveyex Robbery U
43 Exterminate U
44 Fight Dirty U
45 Hard Bargain U
46 Hunt Them Down C
47 Bounty Board U
48 Punishing One R
49 Crime Lord L
50 Dengar's Fire Blade R
51 Skilled Tracker R
52 Separatist Conspiracy U
53 Assassin Droid ST
54 Ahsoka Tano - Brash Prodigy R
55 Lor San Tekka - True Believer R
56 Mace Windu - Inspiring Master R
57 Obi-Wan Kenobi - Ardent Avenger ST
58 Vigilant Jedi R
59 A Friend Lost C

60 Channel The Force C		
61 Defensive Stance C		
62 Disciplined Mind C		
63 Strong Intuition C		
64 Upper Hand ST		
65 Obi-Wan Kenobi's Interceptor ST		
66 Uneti Force Tree U		
67 Yoda's Spirit L		
68 Jedi Holocron R		
69 Lore Hunter C		
70 Mace Windu's Lightsaber L		
71 Republic Jedi Armor ST		
72 K-2SO - Incognito R		
73 Kes Dameron - Courageous Sergeant R		
74 Naboo Palace Guard R		
75 PadmÈ Amidala - Resolute Senator L		
76 Target Acquired U		
77 Aggressive Negotiations U		
78 Field Medic C		
79 Honorable Sacrifice U		
80 Power Surge U		
81 Unfetter C		
82 A-Wing R		
83 Concerted Effort U		
84 LAAT Gunship L		
85 PadmÈ Amidala's Royal Starship R		
86 Overkill R		
87 Resistance Ring R		
88 Chewbacca - The Beast L		
89 Ezra Bridger - Resourceful Cutpurse R		
90 Maz Kanata - Canny Negotiator R		
91 Satine Kryze - Hope of Mandalore ST		
92 Calculated Risk C		
93 Convergence U		
94 Draw Attention C		
95 Flee the Scene U		
96 Instigate C		
97 Reap the Reward U		
98 Sure Shot C		
99 We're Home U		
100 Laser Tripwire U		
101 Rebel Cache R		
102 Chewbacca's Blaster Rifle L		
103 Custom Bandolier C		
104 Moxie R		
105 Secrets Laid Bare C		
106 Attunement C		
107 Circle of Shelter U		
108 Deflecting Slash U		
109 Fatal Blow C		
110 Overqualified C		
111 Twin Strike C		
112 Use The Force C		
113 Force Flow ST		
114 Lightsaber Mastery U		
115 Diatium Power Cell U		
116 It Binds All Things U		
117 Force Pull R		
118 Lightsaber ST		
119 Soresu Mastery L		
120 Soresu Training R		
121 Hampered U		
122 Automated Defense C		
123 Domination U		
124 Energize C		
125 Forced Compliance C		
126 Fresh Supplies C		
127 Measure for Measure C		
128 No Answer C		
129 Rout U		

130 Seize the Day C
131 Squad Tactics C
132 Strike Back C
133 Advanced Training U
134 Conscript Squad R
135 Press the Advantage C
136 Tech Team C
137 V-Wing R
138 A300 Blaster R
139 Quicksilver Baton L
140 Riot Shield U
141 Enfys Nest - Fearsome Outlaw L
142 Enfys Nest's Marauder R
143 Wanted C
144 Electroshock U
145 For a Price C
146 Prey Upon C
147 Rendezvous C
148 Skullduggery C
149 Truce C
150 Unpredictable C
151 Profiteering U
152 Entourage L
153 Seeking The Truth C
154 Smuggling Ring C
155 Starviper R
156 Enfys Nest's Electroripper R
157 Mandalorian Jetpack ST
158 Ordnance Launcher R
159 Unscrupulous R
160 Shock Collar C
161 Wounded C
162 Bacta Therapy U
163 Block C
164 Dodge C
165 Electromagnetic Pulse C
166 Near Miss C
167 Unshackle C
168 Fickle Mercenaries R
169 Grievance Striker ST
170 Protective Suit U
171 Punch Dagger ST
172 Sonic Detonators R
173 Command Center - Lothal U
174 Deathwatch Hideout - Concordia ST
175 Fighting Pit - Mimban U
176 Lair of General Grievous - Vassek 3 ST
177 Mean Streets - Corellia U
178 Military Camp - Kaller U
179 Salt Flats - Crait U
180 Watto's Shop - Tatooine U

2019 Star Wars Destiny Allies of Necessity Starter Deck

COMPLETE SET (20)
DRAFT SET BOX (20 CARDS+9 DICE)
RELEASED ON APRIL 25, 2019

1 Count Dooku - Corrupted Politician		2.50	5.00
2 Count Dooku's Lightsaber		4.00	8.00
3 Sniper Team		1.00	2.00
4 Astrogation		.50	1.00
5 Knighthood		1.50	3.00
6 Fenn Rau - Mandalorian Protector		.50	1.00
7 Test of Character		.50	1.00
8 Grand Design		.50	1.00
9 Outer Rim Outlaw		.50	1.00
10 Shadowed		.50	1.00
11 Perilous Escapade		.50	1.00
12 Hired Muscle		.50	1.00
13 Clawdite Shapeshifter		.50	1.00
14 Chance Encounter		.50	1.00
15 Flank		.50	1.00
16 Allies of Necessity		.50	1.00
17 LR-57 Combat Droid		.50	1.00
18 Electro Sword		.50	1.00
19 Chalmun's Cantina - Tatooine		.50	1.00
20 Wheeta Palace - Nal Hutta		.50	1.00

2019 Star Wars Destiny Spark of Hope

COMPLETE SET (160)
BOOSTER BOX (36 PACKS)
BOOSTER PACK (5 CARDS+1 DIE)
RELEASED ON JULY 5, 2019

1 Dark Mystic R
2 Kylo Ren - Bound By The Force R
3 Maul - Skilled Duelist L
4 Nightsister Zombie C
5 Old Daka - Nightsister Necromancer R
6 Chancellor's Edict C
7 Hex C
8 Possessed U
9 Uncontrollable Rage C
10 Act of Betrayal C
11 Dark Magick C
12 Sinister Ruse C
13 Tantrum C
14 Weave The Ichor C
15 Order 66 U
16 Scimitar R
17 Ancient Magicks R
18 Recovered Sith Lightsaber R
19 Talisman of Resurrection L
20 Conan Motti - Overconfident Officer R
21 Gideon Hask - Inferno Squad Commando R
22 Mudtrooper R
23 Thrawn - Grand Admiral L
24 Priority Target C
25 Counterintelligence C
26 Crushing Advantage C
27 Execute Order 66 U
28 Rally the Troops C
29 To Victory C
30 Warning Siren C
31 Cultural Records R
32 Hostile Territory U
33 Separatist Embargo U
34 Superlaser Siege Cannon L
35 Crimson Star U
36 Mastermind R
37 TL-50 Heavy Repeater R
38 4-LOM - Calculating Criminal R
39 IG-88 - Single-Minded R
40 Jango Fett - Armed To The Teeth L
41 Zuckuss - The Uncanny One R
42 Armed To The Teeth C
43 Desperate Measures C
44 Misinformation C
45 Tireless Pursuit C
46 Bounty Hunters' Guild U
47 IG-2000 R
48 Impound U
49 Mist Hunter R
50 Predatory Banker U
51 0-0-0 Protocol Matrix R
52 Armor Plating C
53 Gauntlet Rockets R
54 Pulse Cannon L
55 Acceptable Losses C
56 R2-D2 - Loyal Companion L
57 Rey - Bound By The Force R
58 Yoda - Mystical Mentor R
59 Youngling U
60 Refusal U
61 Destiny Fulfilled U
62 Exchange Of Information C
63 Heroic Stand U
64 Humble Service C
65 Jedi Mind Trick U
66 Moving Rocks U
67 Yoda's Protection C
68 Caretaker Village U
69 Professor Huyang R
70 Qui-Gon Jinn's Spirit L
71 Three Lessons U
72 Jedi Lightsaber R
73 Sacred Jedi Texts R
74 Yoda's Lightsaber L
75 Amilyn Holdo - Vice Admiral L
76 Bail Organa - Alderaanian Senator R
77 C-3PO - Perfect Gentleman L
78 Hoth Trooper U
79 Droids' Day Out U
80 Happy Beeps C
81 Lightspeed Assault U
82 Our Situation is Desperate C
83 Rebel Assault C
84 Spark of Hope C
85 Take Control U
86 B-Wing R
87 Firm Resolve U
88 GH-7 Droid R
89 Resistance Trench Fighters R
90 EL-16 Heavy Field Blaster R
91 Salvaged Arm U
92 Tico Pendant C
93 Chief Chirpa - Bright Tree Village Elder R
94 Chopper - Metal Menace R
95 Ewok Warrior C
96 Han Solo - Old Swindler L
97 Wicket - Crafty Scout R
98 Ensnare U
99 Net Trap C
100 Rolling Logs C
101 Ewok Ambush C
102 Glider Attack U
103 Jump To Lightspeed U
104 Reassemble U
105 Chief Chirpa's Hut R
106 Mr. Bones L
107 Ewok Bow R
108 Han Solo's Blaster L
109 Han Solo's Dice R
110 Support of the Tribe C
111 Fateful Companions U
112 Alter Fate C
113 Clever Distraction C
114 Dark Reflections C
115 Decisive Blow C
116 Draw Closer U
117 Polarity C
118 Pushing Slash C
119 Temporary Truce U
120 Force Connection U
121 Mysteries Of The Force U
122 Niman Mastery L
123 Niman Training R
124 Untamed Power R
125 Chain Lightning C
126 Focused Fire C
127 Hull Breach C

#	Card		
128	Off The Sensors C		
129	Seizing Territory C		
130	Shields Are Down C		
131	Shortcut U		
132	You Are In Command Now U		
133	Aftermath C		
134	AT-RT R		
135	Coruscant Police R		
136	Admiral L		
137	Communication Module U		
138	Dead Or Alive C		
139	Bad Credit C		
140	Disassemble C		
141	Encircle U		
142	I Performed Violence C		
143	Kinship U		
144	Outpace C		
145	Practice Makes Perfect C		
146	Reversal C		
147	Simple Mistake U		
148	Unify C		
149	Any Means Necessary U		
150	Canto Bight Security L		
151	Mining Guild TIE Fighter R		
152	Bounty Hunter Mask C		
153	DX-2 Disruptor Blaster Pistol R		
154	Inflict Pain U		
155	Grappling Arm R		
156	Rocket Booster R		
157	Canto Casino - Canto Bight U		
158	Jabba's Palace - Tatooine U		
159	Nightsister Lair - Dathomir C		
160	Snoke's Throne Room - Supremacy U		

2020 Star Wars Destiny Covert Missions

COMPLETE SET (159)
BOOSTER BOX (36 PACKS)
BOOSTER PACK (5 CARDS+1 DIE)
RELEASED ON MARCH 6, 2020

#	Card		
1	Darth Bane - Ancient Master L		
2	Darth Vader - Victor Leader R	.50	1.00
4	Snoke's Praetorian Guard R	.50	1.00
5	Recurring Nightmare R	.50	1.00
6	Entropic Blast C	.15	.30
7	Legacy of the Sith U	.30	.75
8	Pincer Movement U	.30	.75
9	Quad Slam U	.30	.75
10	Trap the Blade C	.15	.30
11	Treason U	.30	.75
12	Rule of Two U	.30	.75
13	Bloodletting C	.15	.30
14	Darth Vader's Tie Advanced R	.50	1.00
15	Ancient Sith Armor U	.30	.75
16	Death Field L		
17	Pong Krell's Lightsaber R	.50	1.00
18	Sith Lord L		
19	Vibro-Arbir Blades R	.50	1.00
20	Commander Pyre - Harsh Negotiator R	.50	1.00
21	Director Krennic - Death Star Mastermind L		
22	Elrik Vonreg - Major Baron R	.50	1.00
23	Imperial Death Trooper R	.50	1.00
24	Imperial Pilot U	.30	.75
25	Cruel Methods C	.15	.30
26	Call to Action C	.15	.30
27	Face the Enemy U	.30	.75
28	I'll Handle This Myself C	.15	.30
29	Taking Charge C	.15	.30
30	Construct the Death Star U	.30	.75
31	Elrik Vonreg's TIE Interceptor R	.50	1.00
32	The "Duchess" L		
33	TIE Bomber R	.50	1.00
34	Viper Probe Droid U	.30	.75
35	Commander Pyre's Blaster R	.50	1.00
36	Director U	.30	.75
37	E-11D Blaster Rifle R	.50	1.00
38	Boba Fett - Infamous and Ruthless L		
39	Kragan Gorr - Pirate Captain R	.50	1.00
40	Pyke Sentinel U	.30	.75
41	Synara San - Opportunistic Infiltrator R	.50	1.00
42	Trandoshan Hunter R	.50	1.00
43	Forced Labor C	.15	.30
44	Pestering R	.50	1.00
45	Change of Fortune C	.15	.30
46	Opportune Strike C	.15	.30
47	Plunder U	.30	.75
48	Warning Shot C	.15	.30
49	Pirate Ship R	.50	1.00
50	Slave I L		
51	Boba Fett's Wrist Laser R	.50	1.00
52	Pyke Blaster R	.50	1.00
53	Anakin Skywalker - Dedicated Mentor L		
54	Jedi Knight R	.50	1.00
55	Kanan Jarrus - Jedi Exile R	.50	1.00
56	Luke Skywalker - Red Five R	.50	1.00
57	Forestall C	.15	.30
58	Fresh Start C	.15	.30
59	Luminous Beings Are We U	.30	.75
60	Nullify C	.15	.30
61	Skillful Deterrence U	.30	.75
62	Stand Firm C	.15	.30
63	Trust Your Feelings C	.15	.30
64	Valiant Deed C	.15	.30
65	Jedi Trails U	.30	.75
66	Luke Skywalker's X-Wing R	.50	1.00
67	Anakin Skywalker's Lightsaber L		
68	Kanan Jarrus' Lightsaber R	.50	1.00
69	Padawan Braid C	.15	.30
70	Hera Syndulla - Seasoned Captain L		
71	Kashyyyk Warrior R	.50	1.00
72	Kazuda Xiono - Naive Hotshot R	.50	1.00
73	Poe Dameron - Reckless Aviator L		
74	Tarfful - Chieftain of Kachirho R	.50	1.00
75	Feat of Strength C	.15	.30
76	Imposing Force C	.15	.30
77	Plan of Attack C	.15	.30
78	Run To Safety C	.15	.30
79	Swing In C	.15	.30
80	Trench Run U	.30	.75
81	Destroy the Death Star U	.30	.75
82	Fireball R	.50	1.00
83	Ghost L		
83	Rebel Hangar L		
84	Phantom R	.50	1.00
86	Wookiee Protection U	.30	.75
87	Fortitude C	.15	.30
88	Master Smuggler R	.50	1.00
89	Sabine Wren - Artistic and Resourceful R	.50	1.00
90	Sinjir Rath Velus - Ex-Loyalty Officer L		
91	Torra Doza - Energetic Thrill-Seeker R	.50	1.00
92	Vengeful Wookiee U	.30	.75
93	As One C	.15	.30
94	Lead From the Front U	.30	.75
95	Loth-Cat and Mouse C	.15	.30
96	Pride and Joy U	.30	.75
97	Reciprocate C	.15	.30
98	Blue Ace R	.50	1.00
99	Bucket R	.50	1.00
100	Sabine Wren's TIE Fighter R	.50	1.00
101	Custom Paint Job U	.30	.75
102	Fling U	.30	.75
103	Wookiee Rage U	.30	.75
104	Spectre Cell U	.30	.75
105	Valorous Tribe U	.30	.75
106	Acute Awareness C	.15	.30
107	Bestow Wisdom U	.30	.75
108	Falling Avalanche U	.30	.75
109	Fluid Riposte U	.15	.30
110	Infuse the Force C	.15	.30
111	On Guard C	.15	.30
112	Side By Side C	.15	.30
113	Seeking Knowledge C	.15	.30
114	Shien Mastery L		
115	Shien Training R	.50	1.00
116	Systems Malfunction R	.50	1.00
117	Assail C	.15	.30
118	Command and Conquer C	.15	.30
119	Covert Mission C	.15	.30
120	Embark C	.15	.30
121	Flanked by Wingmen C	.15	.30
122	Joint Maneuver U	.30	.75
123	Sneak Attack U	.30	.75
124	Under Fire C	.15	.30
125	Tactical Delay C	.15	.30
126	Death Star Plans U	.30	.75
127	Experimental Booster R	.50	1.00
128	Licensed to Fly C	.15	.30
129	Nar Shaddaa Thief U	.30	.75
130	Controlled Chaos U	.30	.75
131	Dangerous Escape C	.15	.30
132	Deadlock C	.15	.30
133	Monopolize C	.15	.30
134	Reap C	.15	.30
135	Rogue Tendencies C	.15	.30
136	Survival Instinct C	.15	.30
137	Taken by Surprise C	.15	.30
138	Think on Your Feet C	.15	.30
139	Coaxium Heist U	.30	.75
140	Cloud Car R	.50	1.00
141	Double Agent U	.30	.75
142	Improvised Explosive C	.15	.30
143	Raiding Party R	.50	1.00
144	Repurposing U	.30	.75
145	Magna-Glove L		
146	Z-6 Jetpack L		
147	Jawa Junk Dealer C	.15	.30
148	Outdated Tech U	.30	.75
149	Eject U	.30	.75
150	Harmless Trick C	.15	.30
151	Salvaged Parts C	.15	.30
152	Standoff C	.15	.30
153	Utinni! C	.15	.30
154	Merchant Freighter C	.15	.30
155	Sandcrawler R	.50	1.00
156	Wretched Hive U	.30	.75
157	Abandoned Refinery - Saveren U	.30	.75
158	Colossus - Castilon U	.30	.75
159	Pyke Syndicate Mine - Kessel U	.30	.75
160	Valley of the Dark Lords - Moraband C	.15	.30

1999 Young Jedi Menace of Darth Maul

COMPLETE SET (140)	10.00	25.00
BOOSTER BOX (30 PACKS)	30.00	50.00
BOOSTER PACK (11 CARDS)	1.00	2.00
RELEASED ON MAY 12, 1999		
1 Obi-Wan Kenobi, Young Jedi R	3.00	6.00
2 Qui-Gon Jinn, Jedi Master R	2.50	5.00
3 Jar Jar Binks, Gungan Chuba Thief R	1.50	3.00
4 Anakin Skywalker, Podracer Pilot R	1.25	2.50
5 Padme Naberrie, Handmaiden R	2.00	4.00
6 Captain Panaka, Protector of the Queen R	1.25	2.50
7 Mace Windu, Jedi Master R	1.50	3.00
8 Queen Amidala, Ruler of Naboo R	2.00	4.00
9 Queen Amidala, Royal Leader R	2.00	4.00
10 Yoda, Jedi Master R	2.00	4.00
11 R2-D2, Astromech Droid R	1.50	3.00
12 C-3PO, Anakin's Creation R	1.50	3.00
13 Boss Nass, Leader of the Gungans U	.50	1.00
14 Ric Olie, Ace Pilot U	.50	1.00
15 Captain Tarpals, Gungan Guard U	.50	1.00
16 Rabe, Handmaiden U	.50	1.00
17 Rep Been, Gungan U	.50	1.00
18 Mas Amedda, Vice Chancellor U	.50	1.00
19 Naboo Officer, Battle Planner U	.50	1.00
20 Naboo Security, Guard C	.15	.30
21 Bravo Pilot, Veteran Flyer C	.15	.30
22 Gungan Official, Bureaucrat C	.15	.30
23 Gungan Soldier, Scout C	.15	.30
24 Gungan Guard C	.15	.30
25 Gungan Warrior, Infantry C	.15	.30
26 Gungan Soldier, Veteran C	.15	.30
27 Ishi Tib, Warrior C	.15	.30
28 Ithorian, Merchant C	.15	.30
29 Jawa, Thief C	.15	.30
30 Jawa, Bargainer S	.15	.30
31 Royal Guard, Leader C	.15	.30
32 Royal Guard, Veteran C	.15	.30
33 Obi-Wan Kenobi, Jedi Padawan S	.15	.30
34 Obi-Wan Kenobi's Lightsaber R	1.50	3.00
35 Jedi Lightsaber	.50	1.00
36 Anakin Skywalker's Podracer R	1.25	2.50
37 Captain Panaka's Blaster C	.15	.30
38 Jar Jar Binks' Electropole U	.50	1.00
39 Electropole C	.15	.30
40 Eopie C	.15	.30
41 Kaadu C	.15	.30
42 Flash Speeder C	.15	.30
43 Jawa Ion Blaster C	.15	.30
44 Naboo Blaster C	.15	.30
45 Blaster C	.15	.30
46 Blaster Rifle C	.15	.30

47 Anakin Skywalker	.50	1.00
48 Are You An Angel? U	.50	1.00
49 Cha Skrunee Da Pat, Sleemo C	.15	.30
50 Counterparts U	.50	1.00
51 Da Beings Hereabouts Cawazy C	.15	.30
52 Enough Of This Pretense U	.50	1.00
53 Fear Attracts The Fearful U	.50	1.00
54 Gungan Curiosity C	.15	.30
55 He Was Meant To Help You U	.50	1.00
56 I Have A Bad Feeling About This U	.50	1.00
57 I've Been Trained In Defense U	.50	1.00
58 Security Volunteers C	.15	.30
59 Shmi's Pride U	.50	1.00
60 The Federation Has Gone Too Far C	.15	.30
61 The Negotiations Were Short C	.15	.30
62 The Queen's Plan C	.15	.30
63 We're Not In Trouble Yet U	.50	1.00
64 Yousa Guys Bombad! R	1.00	2.00
65 Tatooine Podrace Arena S	.15	.30
66 Coruscant Capital City S	.15	.30
67 Naboo Theed Palace S	.15	.30
68 Bravo 1, Naboo Starfighter U	.50	1.00
69 Naboo Starfighter C	.15	.30
70 Republic Cruiser, Transport C	.15	.30
71 Darth Maul, Sith Apprentice R	4.00	8.00
72 Darth Sidious, Sith Master R	2.50	5.00
73 Sebulba, Bad-Tempered Dug R	1.50	3.00
74 Watto, Slave Owner R	1.25	2.50
75 Aurra Sing, Bounty Hunter R	2.00	4.00
76 Jabba the Hutt, Vile Crime Lord R	1.50	3.00
77 Gardulla the Hutt, Crime Lord U	.50	1.00
78 Destroyer Droid Squad	1.00	2.00
79 Battle Droid Squad, Assault Unit R	1.25	2.50
80 Ben Quadinaros, Podracer Pilot U	.50	1.00
81 Gasgano, Podracer Pilot U	.50	1.00
82 Mawhonic, Podracer Pilot U	.50	1.00
83 Teemto Pagalies, Podracer Pilot U	.50	1.00
84 Bib Fortuna, Twi'lek Advisor U	.50	1.00
85 Ann and Tann Gella	.50	1.00
86 Gragra, Chuba Peddler C	.15	.30
87 Passel Argente, Senator C	.15	.30
88 Trade Federation Tank	1.25	2.50
89 Destroyer Droid, Wheel Droid C	.15	.30
90 Destroyer Droid, Defense Droid C	.15	.30
91 Sith Probe Droid, Spy Drone C	.15	.30
92 Pit Droid, Engineer C	.15	.30
93 Pit Droid, Heavy Lifter C	.15	.30
94 Pit Droid, Mechanic C	.15	.30
95 Tusken Raider, Nomad C	.15	.30
96 Tusken Raider, Marksman C	.15	.30
97 Battle Droid: Pilot, MTT Division C	.15	.30
98 Battle Droid: Security, MTT Division C	.15	.30
99 Battle Droid: Infantry, MTT Division C	.15	.30
100 Battle Droid: Officer, MTT Division C	.15	.30
101 Battle Droid: Pilot, AAT Division C	.15	.30
102 Battle Droid: Security, AAT Division C	.15	.30
103 Battle Droid: Infantry, AAT Division C	.15	.30
104 Battle Droid: Officer, AAT Division C	.15	.30
105 Neimoidian, Trade Federation Pilot S	.15	.30
106 Darth Maul, Sith Lord S	.60	1.25
107 Sith Lightsaber R	1.25	2.50
108 Aurra Sing's Blaster Rifle R	1.00	2.00
109 Sebulba's Podracer R	1.00	2.00
110 Ben Quadinaros' Podracer U	.50	1.00
111 Gasgano's Podracer U	.50	1.00
112 Mawhonic's Podracer U	.50	1.00
113 Teemto Pagalies' Podracer U	.50	1.00

114 Trade Federation Tank Laser Cannon U	.50	1.00
115 Multi Troop Transport U	.50	1.00
116 STAP U	.50	1.00
117 Tatooine Thunder Rifle C	.15	.30
118 Battle Droid Blaster Rifle C	.15	.30
119 Blaster C	.15	.30
120 Blaster Rifle C	.15	.30
121 At Last We Will Have Revenge R	1.00	2.00
122 Begin Landing Your Troops C	.15	.30
123 Boonta Eve Podrace U	.50	1.00
124 Grueling Contest U	.50	1.00
125 In Complete Control C	.15	.30
126 Kaa Bazza Kundee Hodrudda! U	.50	1.00
127 Opee Sea Killer C	.15	.30
128 Podrace Preparation U	.50	1.00
129 Sandstorm C	.15	.30
130 Sniper C	.15	.30
131 The Invasion Is On Schedule C	.15	.30
132 Vile Gangsters U	.50	1.00
133 Watto's Wager U	.50	1.00
134 You Have Been Well Trained R	1.00	2.00
135 Tatooine Desert Landing Site S	.15	.30
136 Coruscant Jedi Council Chamber S	.15	.30
137 Naboo Gungan Swamp S	.15	.30
138 Darth Maul's Starfighter	1.50	3.00
139 Droid Starfighter C	.15	.30
140 Battleship	.15	.30

1999 Young Jedi Menace of Darth Maul Foil

COMPLETE SET (18)	6.00	15.00
RELEASED ON MAY 12, 1999		
F1 Obi-Wan Kenobi, Young Jedi R	4.00	8.00
F2 Jar-Jar Binks, Gungan Chuba Thief R	2.00	4.00
F3 Mace Windu, Jedi Master U	2.00	4.00
F4 Queen Amidala, Ruler of Naboo U	3.00	6.00
F5 C-3PO, Anakin's Creation U	2.00	4.00
F6 Obi-Wan Kenobi's Lightsaber C	1.50	3.00
F7 Anakin Skywalker's Podracer C	1.25	2.50
F8 Bravo 1, Naboo Starfighter C	.60	1.25
F9 Republic Cruiser, Transport C	.60	1.25
F10 Darth Maul, Sith Apprentice R	5.00	10.00
F11 Darth Sidious, Sith Master R	3.00	6.00
F12 Destroyer Droid Squad	1.00	2.00
F13 Battle Droid Squad, Assault Unit U	1.00	2.00
F14 Sebulba's Podracer U	1.00	2.00
F15 Ben Quadinaros' Podracer C	.60	1.25
F16 Gasgano's Podracer C	.60	1.25
F17 Mawhonic's Podracer C	.60	1.25
F18 Teemto Pagalies' Podracer C	.60	1.25

1999 Young Jedi The Jedi Council

COMPLETE SET (140)	8.00	20.00
BOOSTER BOX (30 PACKS)	20.00	30.00
BOOSTER BOX (11 CARDS)	.75	1.25
RELEASED ON OCTOBER 27, 1999		
1 Obi-Wan Kenobi, Jedi Apprentice R	2.50	5.00
2 Qui-Gon Jinn, Jedi Protector R	2.00	4.00
3 Jar Jar Binks, Gungan Outcast R	1.25	2.50
4 Anakin Skywalker, Child of Prophecy R	1.25	2.50
5 Padme Naberrie, Queen's Handmaiden R	1.50	3.00
6 Captain Panaka, Amidala's Bodyguard R	1.00	2.00
7 Mace Windu	1.25	2.50
8 Queen Amidala, Representative of Naboo R	1.50	3.00
9 Queen Amidala, Voice of Her People R	1.50	3.00
10 Yoda, Jedi Council Member R	1.50	3.00
11 R2-D2, Loyal Droid R	1.25	2.50
12 Ki-Adi-Mundi, Cerean Jedi Knight R	1.25	2.50
13 Adi Gallia, Corellian Jedi Master U	.50	1.00
14 Depa Billaba, Jedi Master U	.50	1.00
15 Eeth Koth, Zabrak Jedi Master U	.50	1.00
16 Even Piell, Lannik Jedi Master U	.50	1.00
17 Oppo Rancisis, Jedi Master U	.50	1.00
18 Plo Koon, Jedi Master U	.50	1.00
19 Saesee Tiin, Iktotchi Jedi Master U	.50	1.00
20 Yaddle, Jedi Master U	.50	1.00
21 Yarael Poof, Quermian Jedi Master U	.50	1.00
22 Boss Nass, Gungan Leader U	.50	1.00
23 Ric Olié, Chief Pilot U	.50	1.00
24 Captain Tarpals, Gungan Battle Leader U	.50	1.00
25 Eirtae, Handmaiden U	.50	1.00
26 Valorum, Supreme Chancellor C	.15	.30
27 Sci Taria, Chancellor's Aide C	.15	.30
28 Naboo Officer, Liberator C	.15	.30
29 Bravo Pilot, Naboo Volunteer C	.15	.30
30 Naboo Security, Amidala's Guard C	.15	.30
31 Republic Captain, Officer C	.15	.30
32 Republic Pilot, Veteran C	.15	.30
33 Coruscant Guard	.15	.30
34 Coruscant Guard, Peacekeeper C	.15	.30
35 Coruscant Guard, Officer C	.15	.30
36 Coruscant Guard, Chancellor's Guard C	.15	.30
37 Wookiee Senator, Representative C	.15	.30
38 Galactic Senator, Delegate S	.15	.30
39 Obi-Wan Kenobi, Jedi Warrior S	.15	.30
40 Qui-Gon Jinn's Lightsaber R	1.00	2.00
41 Amidala's Blaster R	1.00	2.00
42 Adi Gallia's Lightsaber U	.50	1.00
43 Coruscant Guard Blaster Rifle U	.50	1.00
44 Ascension Gun C	.15	.30
45 Electropole C	.15	.30
46 Kaadu C	.15	.30
47 Flash Speeder C	.15	.30
48 Gian Speeder C	.15	.30
49 Naboo Blaster C	.15	.30
50 Blaster C	.15	.30
51 Blaster Rifle C	.15	.30
52 Balance To The Force U	.50	1.00
53 Brave Little Droid U	.50	1.00
54 Dos Mackineeks No Comen Here! C	.15	.30
55 Galactic Chancellor C	.15	.30
56 Hate Leads To Suffering U	.50	1.00
57 I Will Not Cooperate U	.50	1.00
58 Invasion! C	.15	.30
59 May The Force Be With You C	.15	.30
60 Senator Palpatine C	.15	.30
61 The Might Of The Republic C	.15	.30
62 We Don't Have Time For This C	.15	.30
63 We Wish To Board At Once C	.15	.30
64 Wisdom Of The Council R	1.00	2.00
65 Tatooine Mos Espa S	.15	.30
66 Coruscant Jedi Council Chamber S	.15	.30

67 Naboo Gungan Swamp S	.15	.30
68 Bravo 2, Naboo Starfighter U	.50	1.00
69 Naboo Starfighter C	.15	.30
70 Radiant VII, Republic Cruiser Transport C	.15	.30
71 Darth Maul, Master of Evil R	3.00	6.00
72 Darth Sidious, Lord of the Sith R	2.00	4.00
73 Sebulba, Podracer Pilot R	1.25	2.50
74 Watto, Junk Merchant R	1.00	2.00
75 Jabba the Hutt, Gangster R	1.25	2.50
76 Nute Gunray, Neimoidian Viceroy R	1.00	2.00
77 Rune Haako, Neimoidian Advisor R	1.00	2.00
78 Destroyer Droid Squad, Defense Division R	1.00	2.00
79 Battle Droid Squad, Escort Unit R	1.00	2.00
80 Trade Federation Tank, Assault Division R	1.00	2.00
81 Lott Dod, Neimoidian Senator R	1.00	2.00
82 Fode and Beed, Podrace Announcer R	1.00	2.00
83 Clegg Holdfast, Podracer Pilot U	.50	1.00
84 Dud Bolt, Podracer Pilot U	.50	1.00
85 Mars Guo, Podracer Pilot U	.50	1.00
86 Ody Mandrell, Podracer Pilot U	.50	1.00
87 Ratts Tyerell, Podracer Pilot U	.50	1.00
88 Aks Moe, Senator C	.15	.30
89 Horox Ryyder, Senator C	.15	.30
90 Edcel Bar Gane, Roona Senator C	.15	.30
91 Galactic Delegate, Representative C	.15	.30
92 Destroyer Droid, Assault Droid C	.15	.30
93 Destroyer Droid, Battleship Security C	.15	.30
94 Sith Probe Droid, Hunter Droid C	.15	.30
95 Rodian, Mercenary C	.15	.30
96 Battle Droid: Pilot, Assault Division C	.15	.30
97 Battle Droid: Security, Assault Division C	.15	.30
98 Battle Droid: Infantry, Assault Division C	.15	.30
99 Battle Droid: Officer, Assault Division C	.15	.30
100 Battle Droid: Pilot, Guard Division C	.15	.30
101 Battle Droid: Security, Guard Division C	.15	.30
102 Battle Droid: Infantry, Guard Division C	.15	.30
103 Battle Droid: Officer, Guard Division C	.15	.30
104 Neimoidian Aide	.15	.30
105 Darth Maul, Sith Warrior S	.15	.30
106 Darth Maul's Lightsaber R	1.00	2.00
107 Darth Maul's Sith Speeder R	1.00	2.00
108 Clegg Holdfast's Podracer U	.50	1.00
109 Dud Bolt's Podracer U	.50	1.00
110 Mars Guo's Podracer U	.50	1.00
111 Ody Mandrell's Podracer U	.50	1.00
112 Ratts Tyerell's Podracer U	.50	1.00
113 Trade Federation Tank Laser Cannon U	.50	1.00
114 Multi Troop Transport U	.50	1.00
115 STAP U	.50	1.00
116 Thermal Detonator U	.50	1.00
117 Battle Droid Blaster Rifle C	.15	.30
118 Blaster C	.15	.30
119 Blaster Rifle C	.15	.30
120 I Object! C	.15	.30
121 I Will Deal With Them Myself C	.15	.30
122 Let Them Make The First Move R	1.00	2.00
123 Move Against The Jedi First C	.15	.30
124 Open Fire! U	.50	1.00
125 Seal Off The Bridge U	.50	1.00
126 Start Your Engines! U	.50	1.00
127 Switch To Bio C	.15	.30
128 Take Them To Camp Four C	.15	.30
129 Very Unusual C	.15	.30
130 Vote Of No Confidence C	.15	.30
131 We Are Meeting No Resistance C	.15	.30
132 We Have Them On The Run U	.50	1.00
133 Yoka To Bantha Poodoo C	.15	.30
134 Your Little Insurrection Is At An End U	.50	1.00
135 Tatooine Podrace Arena S	.15	.30
136 Coruscant Galactic Senate S	.15	.30

137 Naboo Battle Plains S	.15	.30
138 Sith Infiltrator, Starfighter U	.50	1.00
139 Droid Starfighter C	.15	.30
140 Battleship, Trade Federation Transport C	.15	.30

1999 Young Jedi The Jedi Council Foil

COMPLETE SET (18)	4.00	10.00
RELEASED ON OCTOBER 27, 1999		
F1 Obi-Wan Kenobi, Jedi Apprentice UR	3.00	6.00
F2 Qui-Gon Jinn, Jedi Protector SR	1.25	2.50
F3 Padmè Naberrie	1.25	2.50
F4 Captain Panaka	1.00	2.00
F5 Mace Windu	1.50	3.00
F6 Queen Amidala	2.00	4.00
F7 R2-D2, Loyal Droid VR	2.00	4.00
F8 Qui-Gon Jinn's Lightsaber VR	.60	1.25
F9 Amidala's Blaster VR	.60	1.25
F10 Darth Maul, Master of Evil UR	3.00	6.00
F11 Darth Sidious, Lord of the Sith UR	2.00	4.00
F12 Watto, Junk Merchant SR	1.00	2.00
F13 Jabba the Hutt, Gangster SR	1.00	2.00
F14 Nute Gunray, Neimoidian Viceroy SR	1.00	2.00
F15 Rune Haako, Neimoidian Advisor VR	.60	1.25
F16 Lott Dod, Neimoidian Senator VR	.60	1.25
F17 Darth Maul's Lightsaber VR	.60	1.25
F18 Darth Maul's Sith Speeder VR	.60	1.25

2000 Young Jedi Battle of Naboo

COMPLETE SET (140)	8.00	20.00
BOOSTER BOX (30 PACKS)	15.00	30.00
BOOSTER PACK (11 CARDS)	.75	1.25
RELEASED ON APRIL 5, 2000		
1 Obi-Wan Kenobi, Jedi Knight R	2.00	4.00
2 Qui-Gon Jinn, Jedi Ambassador R	1.50	3.00
3 Jar Jar Binks, Bombad Gungan General R	1.00	2.00
4 Anakin Skywalker, Padawan R	1.00	2.00
5 Padme Naberrie, Amidala's Handmaiden R	1.25	2.50
6 Captain Panaka, Veteran Leader R	.75	1.50
7 Mace Windu, Jedi Speaker R	1.00	2.00
8 Queen Amidala, Resolute Negotiator R	1.25	2.50
9 Queen Amidala, Keeper of the Peace R	1.25	2.50
10 Yoda, Jedi Elder R	1.25	2.50
11 R2-D2, The Queen's Hero R	1.00	2.00
12 Boss Nass, Gungan Chief U	.30	.75
13 Ric Olie, Bravo Leader U	.30	.75
14 Captain Tarpals, Gungan Officer U	.30	.75
15 Sio Bibble, Governor of Naboo U	.30	.75
16 Sabe, Handmaiden Decoy Queen U	.30	.75
17 Sache, Handmaiden U	.30	.75
18 Yane, Handmaiden U	.30	.75
19 Naboo Officer, Squad Leader U	.30	.75

20	Naboo Officer, Commander C	.12	.25
21	Naboo Bureaucrat, Official C	.12	.25
22	Naboo Security, Trooper C	.12	.25
23	Naboo Security, Defender C	.12	.25
24	Bravo Pilot, Ace Flyer C	.12	.25
25	Coruscant Guard, Chancellor's Escort C	.12	.25
26	Alderaan Diplomat, Senator C	.12	.25
27	Council Member, Naboo Governor C	.12	.25
28	Gungan Warrior, Veteran C	.12	.25
29	Gungan Guard, Lookout C	.12	.25
30	Gungan General, Army Leader C	.12	.25
31	Gungan Soldier, Infantry C	.12	.25
32	Rep Officer, Gungan Diplomat S	.12	.25
33	Obi-Wan Kenobi, Jedi Negotiator S	.12	.25
34	Mace Windu's Lightsaber R	.75	1.50
35	Eeth Koth's Lightsaber U	.30	.75
36	Captain Tarpals' Electropole U	.30	.75
37	Planetary Shuttle C	.12	.25
38	Fambaa C	.12	.25
39	Electropole C	.12	.25
40	Kaadu C	.12	.25
41	Flash Speeder C	.12	.25
42	Blaster C	.12	.25
43	Heavy Blaster C	.12	.25
44	Capture The Viceroy C	.12	.25
45	Celebration C	.12	.25
46	Guardians Of The Queen U	.30	.75
47	Gunga City C	.12	.25
48	Gungan Battle Cry U	.30	.75
49	How Wude! U	.30	.75
50	I Will Take Back What Is Ours C	.12	.25
51	Jedi Force Push U	.30	.75
52	Meeeesa Lika Dis! C	.12	.25
53	NOOOOOOOOOOO! R	.75	1.50
54	Thanks, Artoo! U	.30	.75
55	The Chancellor's Ambassador U	.30	.75
56	The Will Of The Force R	.75	1.50
57	Young Skywalker U	.30	.75
58	Your Occupation Here Has Ended C	.12	.25
59	Bombad General U	.30	.75
60	Kiss Your Trade Franchise Goodbye U	.30	.75
61	There's Always A Bigger Fish C	.12	.25
62	Uh-Oh! C	.12	.25
63	We Wish To Form An Alliance C	.12	.25
64	Tatooine Desert Landing Site S	.12	.25
65	Coruscant Galactic Senate S	.12	.25
66	Naboo Battle Plains S	.12	.25
67	Amidala's Starship, Royal Transport R	.75	1.50
68	Bravo 3, Naboo Starfighter U	.30	.75
69	Naboo Starfighter C	.12	.25
70	Republic Cruiser, Transport C	.12	.25
71	Darth Maul, Dark Lord of the Sith R	2.50	5.00
72	Darth Sidious, Sith Manipulator R	1.50	3.00
73	Sebulba, Dangerous Podracer Pilot R	.75	1.50
74	Watto, Toydarian Gambler R	.75	1.50
75	Aurra Sing, Mercenary R	1.00	2.00
76	Jabba The Hutt, Crime Lord R	.75	1.50
77	Nute Gunray, Neimoidian Despot R	.75	1.50
78	Rune Haako, Neimoidian Deputy R	.75	1.50
79	Destroyer Droid Squad, Guard Division R	.75	1.50
80	Battle Droid Squad, Guard Unit R	.75	1.50
81	Trade Federation Tank, Guard Division R	.75	1.50
82	Trade Federation Tank, Patrol Division R	.75	1.50
83	P-59, Destroyer Droid Commander U	.30	.75
84	OOM-9, Battle Droid Commander U	.30	.75
85	Daultay Dofine, Neimoidian Attendant U	.30	.75
86	Diva Shaliqua, Singer U	.30	.75
87	Diva Funquita, Dancer U	.30	.75
88	Bith, Musician U	.30	.75
89	Quarren, Smuggler U	.30	.75

90	Toonbuck Toora, Senator U	.30	.75
91	Aqualish, Galactic Senator C	.12	.25
92	Twi'lek Diplomat, Senator C	.12	.25
93	Weequay, Enforcer C	.12	.25
94	Nikto, Slave C	.12	.25
95	Pacithhip, Prospector C	.12	.25
96	Destroyer Droid, Vanguard Droid C	.12	.25
97	Destroyer Droid, MTT Infantry C	.12	.25
98	Sith Probe Droid, Remote Tracker C	.12	.25
99	Battle Droid: Pilot, Patrol Division C	.12	.25
100	Battle Droid: Security, Patrol Division C	.12	.25
101	Battle Droid: Infantry, Patrol Division C	.12	.25
102	Battle Droid: Officer, Patrol Division C	.12	.25
103	Battle Droid: Pilot, Defense Division C	.12	.25
104	Battle Droid: Security, Defense Division C	.12	.25
105	Battle Droid: Infantry, Defense Division C	.12	.25
106	Battle Droid: Officer, Defense Division C	.12	.25
107	Neimoidian Advisor, Bureaucrat S	.12	.25
108	Darth Maul, Evil Sith Lord S	.12	.25
109	Darth Maul's Lightsaber R	1.00	2.00
110	Sith Lightsaber R	.75	1.50
111	Darth Maul's Electrobinoculars U	.30	.75
112	Trade Federation Tank Laser Cannon U	.30	.75
113	Multi Troop Transport U	.30	.75
114	STAP U	.30	.75
115	Battle Droid Blaster Rifle C	.12	.25
116	Blaster C	.12	.25
117	Blaster Rifle C	.12	.25
118	A Thousand Terrible Things C	.12	.25
119	Armored Assault C	.12	.25
120	Death From Above C	.12	.25
121	Don't Spect A Werm Welcome C	.12	.25
122	I Will Make It Legal C	.12	.25
123	Not For A Sith R	.75	1.50
124	Now There Are Two Of Them U	.30	.75
125	Sith Force Push U	.30	.75
126	The Phantom Menace U	.30	.75
127	They Win This Round C	.12	.25
128	We Are Sending All Troops C	.12	.25
129	After Her! C	.12	.25
130	Da Dug Chaaa! U	.30	.75
131	Sando Aqua Monster C	.12	.25
132	They Will Not Stay Hidden For Long C	.12	.25
133	This Is Too Close! U	.30	.75
134	Tatooine Mos Espa S	.12	.25
135	Coruscant Capital City S	.12	.25
136	Naboo Theed Palace S	.12	.25
137	Droid Control Ship	.30	.75
	Trade Federation Transport U		
138	Sith Infiltrator, Starfighter U	.30	.75
139	Droid Starfighter C	.12	.25
140	Battleship, Trade Federation Transport C	.12	.25

2000 Young Jedi Battle of Naboo Foil

	COMPLETE SET (18)	4.00	10.00
F1	Obi-Wan Kenobi, Jedi Knight UR	2.00	4.00
F2	Qui-Gon Jinn, Jedi Ambassador UR	1.00	2.00
F3	Queen Amidala, Keeper of the Peace SR	1.00	2.00
F4	Yoda, Jedi Elder SR	1.00	2.00
F5	R2-D2, The Queen's Hero SR	1.00	2.00
F6	Queen Amidala, Resolute Negotiator VR	.75	1.50
F7	Mace Windu's Lightsaber VR	.50	1.00
F8	The Will Of The Force VR	.50	1.00
F9	Amidala's Starship, Royal Transport VR	.50	1.00
F10	Darth Maul, Dark Lord of the Sith UR	2.00	4.00
F11	Aurra Sing, Mercenary UR	1.00	2.00
F12	Nute Gunray	.75	1.50
	Neimoidian Despot SR		
F13	Destroyer Droid Squad	.75	1.50
	Guard Division SR		

F14	Trade Federation Tank	.75	1.50
	Guard Division SR		
F15	Battle Droid Squad, Guard Unit VR	.50	1.00
F16	Trade Federation Tank	.50	1.00
	Patrol Division VR		
F17	Darth Maul's Lightsaber VR	.50	1.00
F18	Not For A Sith VR	.50	1.00

2000 Young Jedi Duel of the Fates

	COMPLETE SET (60)	5.00	12.00
	BOOSTER BOX (30 PACKS)	30.00	40.00
	BOOSTER PACK (11 CARDS)	1.00	1.50
	RELEASED ON NOVEMBER 8, 2000		
1	Obi-Wan Kenobi, Jedi Student R	2.00	4.00
2	Qui-Gon Jinn, Jedi Mentor UR	1.50	3.00
3	Anakin Skywalker, Rookie Pilot R	1.00	2.00
4	Captain Panaka, Security Commander R	.75	1.50
5	Mace Windu, Jedi Councilor R	1.00	2.00
6	Queen Amidala, Young Leader R	1.25	2.50
7	Yoda, Jedi Philosopher R	1.25	2.50
8	R2-D2, Repair Droid R	1.00	2.00
9	Ric Olie, Starship Pilot R	.75	1.50
10	Bravo Pilot, Flyer C	.12	.25
11	Valorum, Leader of the Senate C	.12	.25
12	Qui-Gon Jinn's Lightsaber	.75	1.50
	Wielded by Obi-Wan Kenobi R		
13	Booma U	.30	.75
14	A Powerful Opponent C	.12	.25
15	Come On, Move! U	.30	.75
16	Critical Confrontation C	.12	.25
17	Gungan Mounted Troops U	.30	.75
18	Naboo Fighter Attack C	.12	.25
19	Qui-Gon's Final Stand C	.12	.25
20	Run The Blockade C	.12	.25
21	Twist Of Fate C	.12	.25
22	You Are Strong With The Force U	.30	.75
23	Gungan Energy Shield U	.30	.75
24	He Can See Things Before They Happen U	.30	.75
25	Jedi Meditation U	.30	.75
26	Jedi Training U	.30	.75
27	Naboo Royal Security Forces U	.30	.75
28	Pounded Unto Death C	.12	.25
29	Senate Guard C	.12	.25
30	Naboo Starfighter C	.12	.25
31	Darth Maul, Student of the Dark Side UR	2.00	4.00
32	Darth Sidious, Master of the Dark Side R	1.25	2.50
33	Aurra Sing, Trophy Collector R	1.00	2.00
34	Tey How, Neimoidian Command Officer R	.75	1.50
35	OWO-1, Battle Droid Command Officer R	.75	1.50
36	Rayno Vaca, Taxi Driver R	.75	1.50
37	Baskol Yeesrim, Gran Senator R	.75	1.50
38	Starfighter Droid, DFS-327 R	.75	1.50
39	Starfighter Droid, DFS-1104 R	.75	1.50
40	Starfighter Droid, DFS-1138 R	.75	1.50
41	Jedi Lightsaber, Stolen by Aurra Sing U	.30	.75
42	Coruscant Taxi U	.30	.75
43	Neimoidian Viewscreen C	.12	.25
44	Battle Droid Patrol U	.30	.75
45	Change In Tactics C	.12	.25
46	Dangerous Encounter C	.12	.25
47	Darth Maul Defiant C	.12	.25
48	Impossible! C	.12	.25
49	It's A Standoff! U	.30	.75
50	Mobile Assassin U	.30	.75
51	Power Of The Sith C	.12	.25
52	Starfighter Screen C	.12	.25
53	To The Death C	.12	.25
54	Use Caution U	.30	.75
55	Blockade U	.30	.75
56	End This Pointless Debate U	.30	.75

#		Lo	Hi
57	The Duel Begins U	.30	.75
58	The Jedi Are Involved U	.30	.75
59	Where Are Those Droidekas? U	.30	.75
60	Droid Starfighter C	.12	.25

2000 Young Jedi Enhanced Menace of Darth Maul

#		Lo	Hi
P1	Qui-Gon Jinn, Jedi Protector	2.50	5.00
P2	Mace Windu, Jedi Warrior	1.50	3.00
P3	Queen Amidala, Cunning Warrior	5.00	10.00
P4	Darth Maul, Sith Assassin	2.50	5.00
P5	Sebulba, Champion Podracer Pilot	5.00	10.00
P6	Trade Federation Tank, Assault Leader	3.00	6.00

2001 Young Jedi Boonta Eve Podrace

		Lo	Hi
COMPLETE SET (63)		4.00	10.00
BOOSTER BOX (30 PACKS)		30.00	40.00
BOOSTER PACK (11 CARDS)		1.00	1.50
RELEASED ON SEPTEMBER 5, 2001			

#		Lo	Hi
1	Anakin Skywalker, Boonta Eve Podracer Pilot UR	1.00	2.00
2	Yoda, Jedi Instructor R	1.25	2.50
3	C-3PO, Human-Cyborg Relations Droid R	1.00	2.00
4	Jira, Pallie Vendor R	.75	1.50
5	Kitster, Anakin's Friend R	.75	1.50
6	Wald, Anakin's Friend R	.75	1.50
7	Seek, Anakin's Friend U	.30	.75
8	Amee, Anakin's Friend U	.30	.75
9	Melee, Anakin's Friend U	.30	.75
10	Captain Tarpals, Gungan Leader R	.75	1.50
11	Boles Roor, Podracer Pilot U	.30	.75
12	Elan Mak, Podracer Pilot U	.30	.75
13	Neva Kee, Podracer Pilot U	.30	.75
14	Wan Sandage, Podracer Pilot U	.30	.75
15	Shmi Skywalker, Anakin's Mother R	.75	1.50
16	Boles Roor's Podracer U	.30	.75
17	Elan Mak's Podracer U	.30	.75
18	Neva Kee's Podracer U	.30	.75
19	Wan Sandage's Podracer U	.30	.75
20	Comlink C	.12	.25
21	Hold-Out Blaster C	.12	.25
22	Dis Is Nutsen C	.12	.25
23	Masquerade C	.12	.25
24	No Giben Up, General Jar Jar C	.12	.25
25	What Does Your Heart Tell You? C	.12	.25
26	All-Out Defense U	.30	.75
27	Bravo Squadron C	.12	.25
28	Hologram Projector C	.12	.25
29	Boonta Eve Classic R	.75	1.50
30	Amidala's Starship R	.75	1.50
31	Sebulba, Dug Podracer Pilot UR	.75	1.50
32	Watto, Podrace Sponsor R	.75	1.50

#		Lo	Hi
33	Aurra Sing, Formidable Adversary R	1.00	2.00
34	Jabba The Hutt, O Grandio Lust R	.75	1.50
35	TC-14, Protocol Droid R	.75	1.50
36	Orr'UrRuuR'R, Tusken Raider Leader Rare R	.75	1.50
37	UrrOr'RuuR, Tusken Raider Warrior U	.30	.75
38	RuuR'Ur, Tusken Raider Sniper C	.12	.25
39	Sil Unch, Neimoidian Comm Officer U	.30	.75
40	Graxol Kelvyyn and Shakka U	.30	.75
41	Corix Venne, Bith Musician C	.12	.25
42	Reike Th'san, Arms Smuggler R	.75	1.50
43	Meddun, Nikto Mercenary U	.30	.75
44	Rum Sleg, Bounty Hunter R	.75	1.50
45	Aehrrley Rue, Freelance Pilot U	.30	.75
46	Jedwar Seelah, Explorer Scout U	.30	.75
47	Chokk, Klatooinian Explosives Expert C	.12	.25
48	Tatooine Backpack C	.12	.25
49	Gaderffii Stick C	.12	.25
50	Hold-Out Blaster C	.12	.25
51	Watto's Datapad U	.30	.75
52	Colo Claw Fish C	.12	.25
53	He Always Wins! C	.12	.25
54	Bounty Hunter C	.12	.25
55	Two-Pronged Attack C	.12	.25
56	All-Out Attack U	.30	.75
57	Eventually You'll Lose U	.30	.75
58	Gangster's Paradise U	.30	.75
59	Boonta Eve Classic R	.75	1.50
60	Viceroy's Battleship R	.75	1.50
R1	Rule Card 1	.10	.20
R2	Rule Card 2	.10	.20
R3	Rule Card 3	.12	.25

2001 Young Jedi Enhanced Battle of Naboo

		Lo	Hi
COMPLETE SET (12)		30.00	80.00
RELEASED IN 2001			

#		Lo	Hi
P8	Obi-Wan Kenobi, Jedi Avenger	5.00	10.00
P9	Anakin Skywalker, Tested By The Jedi Council	12.00	25.00
P10	PadmÈ Naberrie, Loyal Handmaiden	15.00	30.00
P11	Captain Panaka, Royal Defender	2.50	5.00
P12	Yoda, Wise Jedi	5.00	10.00
P13	R2-D2, Starship Maintenance Droid	6.00	12.00
P14	Darth Sidious, The Phantom Menace	2.50	5.00
P15	Watto, Risk Taker	5.00	10.00
P16	Aurra Sing, Scoundrel	5.00	10.00
P17	Jabba The Hutt	5.00	10.00
P18	Nute Gunray, Neimoidean Bureaucrat	3.00	6.00
P19	Rune Haako, Neimoidean Lieutenant	6.00	12.00

2001 Young Jedi Reflections

		Lo	Hi
COMPLETE SET (106)		200.00	350.00
RELEASED ON JULY 18, 2001			

#		Lo	Hi
A1	Jar Jar Binks, Bombad Gungan General	1.50	3.00
	Jar Jar Binks' Electropole		
A2	Boss Nass, Gungan Chief	2.50	5.00
	Fambaa		
A3	Adi Gallia, Corellian Jedi Master	2.00	4.00
	Adi Gallia's Lightsaber		
A4	Eeth Koth, Zabrak Jedi Master	2.50	5.00
	Eeth Koth's Lightsaber		
A5	Ki-Adi-Mundi, Cerean Jedi Knight	2.50	5.00
	Jedi Lightsaber, Constructed by Ki-Adi-Mundi		
A6	Valorum, Supreme Chancellor	1.50	3.00
	Planetary Shuttle		
A7	Aurra Sing, Trophy Collector	2.50	5.00
	Jedi Lightsaber, Stolen by Aurra Sing		
A8	Nute Gunray, Neimoidian Viceroy	2.00	4.00
	Neimoidian Viewscreen		
A9	OOM-9, Battle Droid Commander	2.00	4.00
	Battle Droid Blaster Rifle		
A10	OWO-1, Battle Droid Command Officer	2.50	5.00
	STAP		
A11	P-59, Destroyer Droid Commander	2.00	4.00
	Multi Troop Transport		
A12	Toonbuck Toora, Senator	2.50	5.00
	Coruscant Taxi		
C1	Are You An Angel?	1.00	2.00
	I've Been Trained In Defense		
C2	Brave Little Droid	.75	1.50
	Counterparts		
C3	Celebration	1.00	2.00
	Gungan Mounted Trooops		
C4	Enough Of This Pretense	.75	1.50
	I Will Not Cooperate		
C5	Fear Attracts The Fearful	1.00	2.00
	How Wude!		
C6	I Have A Bad Feeling About This	1.00	2.00
	NOOOOOOOOOOO!		
C7	Jedi Force Push	1.00	2.00
	We're Not In Trouble Yet		
C8	Dos Mackineeks No Comen Here!	1.00	2.00
	Bombad General		
C9	At last we will have revenge	.50	1.00
	Sith force push		
C10	The Queen's Plan	1.00	2.00
	Naboo Royal Security Forces		
C11	The Might Of The Republic	1.00	2.00
	Senate Guard		
C12	The Negotiations Were Short	1.00	2.00
	Qui-Gon's Final Stand		
C13	Wisdom Of The Council	1.00	2.00
	Jedi Training		
C14	Yousa Guys Bombad!	1.00	2.00
	Uh-Oh!		
C15	A Thousand Terrible Things & We Are Sending All Troops	.75	1.50
C16	Battle Droid Patrol & In Complete Control	.75	1.50
C17	Boonta Eve Podrace & Kaa Bazza Kundee Hodrudda!	.75	1.50
C18	Podrace Preparation & Yoka To Bantha Poodoo	1.00	2.00
C19	Switch To Bio & Your Little Insurrection Is At An End	.50	1.00
C20	The Phantom Menace & Use Caution	1.00	2.00
D1	Dos Mackineeks No Comen Here!	1.00	2.00
	Bombad General		
D2	Gunga City	1.00	2.00
	Gungan Energy Shield		
D3	The Queen's Plan	1.00	2.00
	Naboo Royal Security Forces		
D4	The Might Of The Republic	1.00	2.00
	Senate Guard		

D5 The Negotiations Were Short / Qui-Gon's Final Stand	1.00	2.00
D6 Wisdom Of The Council / Jedi Training	1.00	2.00
D7 Yousa Guys Bombad! / Uh-Oh!	1.00	2.00
D8 Grueling Contest / Da Dug Chaaa!	1.00	2.00
D9 Let Them Make The First Move / Very Unusual	.50	1.00
D10 Now There Are Two Of Them / The Duel Begins	.75	1.50
D11 Opee Sea Killer / To The Death	1.00	2.00
D12 Starfighter Screen / Blockade	1.00	2.00
D13 We Have Them On The Run / Where Are Those Droidekas?	1.00	2.00
D14 You Have Been Well Trained / After Her!	.50	1.00
2BEP Yoda, Jedi Instructor (foil)	3.00	6.00
2MDM Qui-Gon Jinn, Jedi Master (foil)	12.00	25.00
3BEP C-3PO, Human-Cyborg Relations Droid (foil)	3.00	6.00
4BEP Jira, Pallie Vendor (foil)	1.50	3.00
4BON Anakin Skywalker, Padawan (foil)	4.00	8.00
4TJC Anakin Skywalker, Child of Prophecy (foil)	7.50	15.00
5BEP Kitster, Anakin's Friend (foil)	2.50	5.00
6BEP Wald, Anakin's Friend (foil)	2.00	4.00
7BON Mace Windu, Jedi Speaker (foil)	12.00	25.00
9MDM Queen Amidala, Royal Leader (foil)	4.00	8.00
9TJC Queen Amidala, Voice of Her People (foil)	5.00	10.00
10MDM Yoda, Jedi Master (foil)	2.50	5.00
1DOTF Obi-Wan Kenobi, Jedi Student (foil)	7.50	15.00
2DOTF Qui-Gon Jinn, Jedi Mentor (foil)	4.00	8.00
30BEP Amidala's Starship, Queen's Transport (foil)	2.50	5.00
32BEP Watto, Podrace Sponsor (foil)	2.50	5.00
33BEP Aurra Sing, Formidable Adversary (foil)	5.00	10.00
34BEP Jabba The Hutt, O Grandio Lust (foil)	2.50	5.00
35BEP TC-14, Protocol Droid (foil)	2.50	5.00
36BEP Orr'UrRuuR'R, Tusken Raider Leader (foil)	2.50	5.00
3DOTF Anakin Skywalker, Rookie Pilot (foil)	4.00	8.00
4DOTF Captain Panaka, Security Commander (foil)	2.50	5.00
5DOTF Mace Windu, Jedi Councilor (foil)	3.00	6.00
60BEP Viceroy's Battleship, Trade Federation Transport (foil)	2.00	4.00
6DOTF Queen Amidala, Young Leader (foil)	4.00	8.00
72BON Darth Sidious, Sith Manipulator (foil)	4.00	8.00
73BON Sebulba, Dangerous Podracer Pilot (foil)	10.00	20.00
73TJC Sebulba, Podracer Pilot (foil)	2.00	4.00
74BON Watto, Toydarian Gambler (foil)	1.25	2.50
74MDM Watto, Slave Owner (foil)	2.50	5.00
75MDM Aurra Sing, Bounty Hunter (foil)	5.00	10.00
76BON Jabba The Hutt, Crime Lord (foil)	2.50	5.00
78BON Rune Haako, Neimoidian Deputy (foil)	2.50	5.00
78TJC Destroyer Droid Squad, Defense Division (foil)	4.00	8.00
79TJC Battle Droid Squad, Escort Unit (foil)	2.50	5.00
7DOTF Yoda, Jedi Philosopher (foil)	5.00	10.00
80TJC Trade Federation Tank, Assault Division (foil)	7.50	15.00
88MDM Trade Federation Tank, Armored Division (foil)	2.50	5.00
31DOTF Darth Maul, Student of the Dark Side (foil)	4.00	8.00
32DOTF Darth Sidious, Master of the Dark Side (foil)	12.00	25.00
33DOTF Aurra Sing, Trophy Collector (foil)	2.00	4.00
P1EMDM Qui-Gon Jinn, Jedi Protector (foil)	5.00	10.00
P2EMDM Mace Windu, Jedi Warrior (foil)	5.00	10.00
P3EMDM Queen Amidala, Cunning Warrior (foil)	10.00	20.00
P4EMDM Darth Maul, Sith Assassin (foil)	10.00	20.00
P5EMDM Sebulba, Champion Podracer Pilot (foil)	2.50	5.00
P6EMDM Trade Federation Tank, Assault Leader (foil)	2.00	4.00
P7PREM Shmi Skywalker, Anakin's Mother (foil)	2.00	4.00
P8EBON Obi-Wan Kenobi, Jedi Avenger (foil)	4.00	8.00
P9EBON Anakin Skywalker, Tested by the Jedi Council (foil)	4.00	8.00
P10EBON PadmÈ Naberrie, Loyal Handmaiden (foil)	2.50	5.00
P11EBON Captain Panaka, Royal Defender (foil)	2.50	5.00
P12EBON Yoda, Wise Jedi (foil)	5.00	10.00
P13EBON R2-D2, Starship Maintenance Droid (foil)	4.00	8.00
P14EBON Darth Sidious, The Phantom Menace (foil)	4.00	8.00
P15EBON Watto, Risk Taker (foil)	2.50	5.00
P16EBON Aurra Sing, Scoundrel (foil)	2.00	4.00
P17EBON Jabba The Hutt, Tatooine Tyrant (foil)	2.50	5.00
P18EBON Nute Gunray, Neimoidian Bureaucrat (foil)	2.00	4.00
P19EBON Rune Haako, Neimoidian Lieutenant (foil)	2.50	5.00

MINIATURES

2004 Star Wars Rebel Storm Miniatures

RELEASED ON SEPTEMBER 3, 2004

1 4-LOM R	5.00	10.00
2 Bespin Guard C	.30	.75
3 Boba Fett VR	25.00	50.00
4 Bossk R	5.00	10.00
5 Bothan Spy U	.75	1.50
6 C-3PO R	5.00	10.00
7 Chewbacca R	6.00	12.00
8 Commando on Speeder Bike VR	12.00	25.00
9 Darth Vader, Dark Jedi R	6.00	12.00
10 Darth Vader, Sith Lord VR	12.00	25.00
11 Dengar R	5.00	10.00
12 Duros Mercenary U	.75	1.50
13 Elite Hoth Trooper U	.75	1.50
14 Elite Rebel Trooper C	.30	.75
15 Elite Snowtrooper U	.75	1.50
16 Elite Stormtrooper U	.75	1.50
17 Emperor Palpatine VR	15.00	30.00
18 Ewok C	.30	.75
19 Gamorrean Guard U	.75	1.50
20 General Veers R	5.00	10.00
21 Grand Moff Tarkin R	5.00	10.00
22 Greedo R	5.00	10.00
23 Han Solo R	5.00	10.00
24 Heavy Stormtrooper U	.75	1.50
25 Hoth Trooper C	.30	.75
26 IG-88 R	5.00	10.00
27 Imperial Officer U	.75	1.50
28 Ithorian Scout U	.75	1.50
29 Jabba the Hutt VR	12.00	25.00
30 Jawa C	.30	.75
31 Lando Calrissian R	5.00	10.00
32 Luke Skywalker, Jedi Knight VR	15.00	30.00
33 Luke Skywalker, Rebel R	6.00	12.00
34 Mara Jade Emperor's Hand R	5.00	10.00
35 Mon Calamari Mercenary C	.30	.75
36 Obi-Wan Kenobi VR	12.00	25.00
37 Princess Leia, Captive VR	12.00	25.00
38 Princess Leia, Senator R	6.00	12.00
39 Probe Droid VR	10.00	20.00
40 Quarren Assassin U	.75	1.50
41 R2-D2 R	6.00	12.00
42 Rebel Commando U	.75	1.50
43 Rebel Officer U	.75	1.50
44 Rebel Pilot C	.30	.75
45 Rebel Trooper C	.30	.75
46 Rebel Trooper C	.30	.75
47 Royal Guard U	.75	1.50
48 Sandtrooper on Dewback VR	10.00	20.00
49 Scout Trooper on Bike VR	10.00	20.00
50 Scout Trooper U	.75	1.50
51 Snowtrooper C	.30	.75
52 Stormtrooper C	.30	.75
53 Stormtrooper C	.30	.75
54 Stormtrooper C	.30	.75
55 Stormtrooper Officer U	.75	1.50
56 Tusken Raider C	.30	.75
57 Twi'lek Bodyguard U	.75	1.50
58 Twi'lek Scoundrel C	.30	.75
59 Wampa VR	10.00	20.00
60 Wookiee Soldier C	.30	.75

2004 Star Wars Clone Strike Miniatures

COMPLETE SET (60)	150.00	300.00

RELEASED ON DECEMBER 13, 2004

1 48 Super Battle Droid U	.75	1.50
2 Aayla Secura VR	10.00	20.00
3 Aerial Clone Trooper Captain R	6.00	12.00
4 Agen Kolar R	6.00	12.00
5 Anakin Skywalker VR	12.00	25.00
6 Aqualish Spy C	.30	.75
7 ARC Trooper U	.75	1.50
8 Asajj Ventress R	6.00	12.00
9 Aurra Sing VR	15.00	30.00
10 Battle Droid C	.30	.75
11 Battle Droid C	.30	.75
12 Battle Droid C	.30	.75
13 Battle Droid Officer U	.75	1.50
14 Battle Droid on STAP R	6.00	12.00
15 Captain Typho R	6.00	12.00
16 Clone Trooper C	.30	.75
17 Clone Trooper C	.30	.75
18 Clone Trooper Commander U	.75	1.50
19 Clone Trooper Grenadier C	.30	.75
20 Clone Trooper Sergeant C	.30	.75
21 Count Dooku VR	12.00	25.00
22 Dark Side Acolyte U	.75	1.50
23 Darth Maul VR	15.00	30.00
24 Darth Sidious VR	12.00	25.00
25 Destroyer Droid R	6.00	12.00
26 Devaronian Bounty Hunter C	.30	.75
27 Durge R	6.00	12.00
28 Dwarf Spider Droid R	6.00	12.00
29 General Grievous VR	15.00	30.00

#			
30	General Kenobi R	6.00	12.00
31	Geonosian Drone C	.30	.75
32	Geonosian Overseer U	.75	1.50
33	Geonosian Picador on Orray R	6.00	12.00
34	Geonosian Soldier U	.75	1.50
35	Gran Raider C	.30	.75
36	Gungan Cavalry on Kaadu R	6.00	12.00
37	Gungan Infantry C	.30	.75
38	Ishi Tib Scout U	.75	1.50
39	Jango Fett R	6.00	12.00
40	Jedi Guardian U	.75	1.50
41	Ki-Adi-Mundi R	6.00	12.00
42	Kit Fisto R	6.00	12.00
43	Klatooinian Enforcer C	.30	.75
44	Luminara Unduli R	6.00	12.00
45	Mace Windu VR	12.00	25.00
46	Naboo Soldier U	.75	1.50
47	Nikto Soldier C	.30	.75
48	Padme Amidala VR	10.00	20.00
49	Plo Koon R	6.00	12.00
50	Quarren Raider U	.75	1.50
51	Qui-Gon Jinn VR	10.00	20.00
52	Quinlan Vos VR	10.00	20.00
53	Rodian Mercenary U	.75	1.50
54	Saesee Tiin R	6.00	12.00
55	Security Battle Droid C	.30	.75
56	Super Battle Droid U	.75	1.50
57	Weequay Mercenary C	.30	.75
58	Wookiee Commando U	.75	1.50
59	Yoda VR	15.00	30.00
60	Zam Wesell R	6.00	12.00

2005 Star Wars Revenge of the Sith Miniatures

COMPLETE SET (61)		120.00	250.00
RELEASED ON APRIL 2, 2005			
1	Agen Kolar, Jedi Master R	6.00	12.00
2	Alderaan Trooper U	.75	1.50
3	Anakin Skywalker, Jedi Knight R	6.00	12.00
4	AT-RT VR	12.00	25.00
5	Bail Organa VR	10.00	20.00
6	Captain Antilles R	6.00	12.00
7	Chewbacca of Kashyyk VR	12.00	25.00
8	Clone Trooper C	.30	.75
9	Clone Trooper C	.30	.75
10	Clone Trooper Commander U	.75	1.50
11	Clone Trooper Gunner C	.30	.75
12	Jedi Knight U	.75	1.50
13	Mace Windu, Jedi Master VR	15.00	30.00
14	Mon Mothma VR	10.00	20.00
15	Obi-Wan Kenobi, Jedi Master R	6.00	12.00
16	Polis Massa Medic C	.30	.75
17	R2-D2, Astromech Droid VR	12.00	25.00
18	Senate Guard U	.75	1.50
19	Shaak Ti R	6.00	12.00
20	Stass Allie R	6.00	12.00
21	Tarfful R	6.00	12.00
22	Wookiee Berserker C	.30	.75
23	Wookiee Scout U	.75	1.50
24	Yoda, Jedi Master R	7.50	15.00
25	Battle Droid C	.30	.75
26	Battle Droid C	.30	.75
27	Bodyguard Droid U	.75	1.50
28	Bodyguard Droid U	.75	1.50
29	Darth Tyranus R	6.00	12.00
30	Destroyer Droid R	6.00	12.00
31	General Grievous, Jedi Hunter VR	15.00	30.00
32	General Grievous, Supreme Commander R	6.00	12.00
33	Grievous's Wheel Bike VR	12.00	25.00
34	Muun Guard U	.75	1.50
35	Neimoidian Soldier U	.75	1.50
36	Neimoidian Soldier U	.75	1.50
37	San Hill R	6.00	12.00
38	Separatist Commando C	.30	.75
39	Super Battle Droid C	.30	.75
40	Super Battle Droid C	.30	.75
41	Wat Tambor R	6.00	12.00
42	Boba Fett, Young Mercenary R	6.00	12.00
43	Chagrian Mercenary Commander U	.75	1.50
44	Devaronian Soldier C	.30	.75
45	Gotal Fringer U	.75	1.50
46	Human Mercenary U	.75	1.50
47	Iktotchi Tech Specialist U	.75	1.50
48	Medical Droid R	6.00	12.00
49	Nautolan Soldier C	.30	.75
50	Sly Moore R	6.00	12.00
51	Tion Medon R	6.00	12.00
52	Utapaun Soldier C	.30	.75
53	Utapaun Soldier C	.30	.75
54	Yuzzem C	.30	.75
55	Zabrak Fringer C	.30	.75
56	Anakin Skywalker Sith Apprentice VR	12.00	25.00
57	Dark Side Adept U	.75	1.50
58	Darth Vader VR	15.00	30.00
59	Emperor Palpatine, Sith Lord VR	15.00	30.00
60	Royal Guard U	.75	1.50

2005 Star Wars Universe Miniatures

COMPLETE SET (61)		150.00	300.00
RELEASED ON AUGUST 19, 2005			
1	Abyssin Black Sun Thug C	.30	.75
2	Acklay U	.75	1.50
3	Admiral Ackbar VR	10.00	20.00
4	ASP-7 U	.75	1.50
5	AT-ST R	7.50	15.00
6	B'omarr Monk R	7.50	15.00
7	Baron Fel VR	15.00	30.00
8	Battle Droid U	.75	1.50
9	Battle Droid U	.75	1.50
10	Bith Rebel C	.30	.75
11	Chewbacca, Rebel Hero R	7.50	15.00
12	Clone Trooper C	.30	.75
13	Clone Trooper on BARC Speeder R	10.00	20.00
14	Dark Side Marauder U	.75	1.50
15	Dark Trooper Phase III U	.75	1.50
16	Darth Maul on Speeder VR	12.00	25.00
17	Darth Vader, Jedi Hunter R	7.50	15.00
18	Dash Rendar R	7.50	15.00
19	Dr. Evazan VR	10.00	20.00
20	Dressellian Commando C	.30	.75
21	Elite Clone Trooper U	.75	1.50
22	Flash Speeder U	.75	1.50
23	Gonk Power Droid C	.30	.75
24	Grand Admiral Thrawn VR	15.00	30.00
25	Guri R	7.50	15.00
26	Hailfire Droid U	.75	1.50
27	Han Solo, Rebel Hero R	7.50	15.00
28	Kaminoan Ascetic C	.30	.75
29	Kyle Katarn VR	10.00	20.00
30	Lando Calrissian, Hero of Taanab R	7.50	15.00
31	Lobot R	6.00	12.00
32	Luke Skywalker on Tauntaun R	10.00	20.00
33	Luke Skywalker, Jedi Master VR	15.00	30.00
34	New Republic Commander U	.75	1.50
35	New Republic Trooper C	.30	.75
36	Nexu U	.75	1.50
37	Nien Nunb R	6.00	12.00
38	Nightsister Sith Witch U	.75	1.50
39	Noghri U	.75	1.50
40	Nom Anor R	7.50	15.00
41	Nute Gunray R	6.00	12.00
42	Obi-Wan on Boga VR	12.00	25.00
43	Ponda Baba R	6.00	12.00
44	Prince Xizor VR	10.00	20.00
45	Princess Leia, Rebel Hero VR	10.00	20.00
46	Rancor VR	15.00	30.00
47	Reek U	.75	1.50
48	Rodian Black Sun Vigo U	.75	1.50
49	Shistavanen Pilot U	.75	1.50
50	Stormtrooper C	.30	.75
51	Stormtrooper Commander U	.75	1.50
52	Super Battle Droid C	.30	.75
53	Super Battle Droid Commander U	.75	1.50
54	Tusken Raider on Bantha U	.75	1.50
55	Vornskr C	.30	.75
56	Warmaster Tsavong Lah VR	12.00	25.00
57	Wedge Antilles R	7.50	15.00
58	X-1 Viper Droid U	.75	1.50
59	Young Jedi Knight C	.30	.75
60	Yuuzhan Vong Subaltern U	.75	1.50
61	Yuuzhan Vong Warrior C	.30	.75

2006 Star Wars Champions of the Force Miniatures

COMPLETE SET (61)		120.00	250.00
RELEASED ON JUNE 6, 2006			
1	Arcona Smuggler C	.30	.75

2	Barriss Offee R	6.00	12.00
3	Bastila Shan VR	10.00	20.00
5	Clone Commander Bacara R	6.00	12.00
6	Clone Commander Cody R	7.50	15.00
7	Clone Commander Gree R	6.00	12.00
8	Corran Horn R	6.00	12.00
9	Coruscant Guard C	.30	.75
10	Crab Droid U	.75	1.50
11	Dark Jedi U	.75	1.50
12	Dark Jedi Master U	.75	1.50
13	Dark Side Enforcer U	.75	1.50
14	Dark Trooper Phase I C	.30	.75
15	Dark Trooper Phase II U	.75	1.50
16	Dark Trooper Phase II VR	10.00	20.00
17	Darth Bane VR	12.00	25.00
18	Darth Malak VR	12.00	25.00
19	Darth Maul, Champion of the Sith R	7.50	15.00
20	Darth Nihilus VR	10.00	20.00
21	Darth Sidious, Dark Lord of the Sith R	6.00	12.00
22	Depa Billaba R	6.00	12.00
23	Even Piell R	6.00	12.00
24	Exar Kun VR	12.00	25.00
25	General Windu R	6.00	12.00
26	Gundark Fringe U	.75	1.50
27	HK-47 VR	10.00	20.00
28	Hoth Trooper with Atgar Cannon R	6.00	12.00
29	Jacen Solo VR	10.00	20.00
30	Jaina Solo VR	10.00	20.00
31	Jedi Consular U	.75	1.50
32	Jedi Guardian U	.75	1.50
33	Jedi Padawan U	.75	1.50
34	Jedi Sentinel U	.75	1.50
35	Jedi Weapon Master C	.30	.75
36	Kashyyyk Trooper C	.30	.75
37	Luke Skywalker, Young Jedi VR	12.00	25.00
38	Mas Amedda R	7.50	15.00
39	Massassi Sith Mutant U	.75	1.50
41	Octuparra Droid R	6.00	12.00
42	Old Republic Commander U	.75	1.50
43	Old Republic Trooper U	.75	1.50
44	Old Republic Trooper C	.30	.75
45	Queen Amidala R	6.00	12.00
46	Qui-Gon Jinn, Jedi Master R	7.50	15.00
47	R5 Astromech Droid C	.30	.75
48	Republic Commando Boss U	.75	1.50
49	Republic Commando Fixer C	.30	.75
50	Republic Commando Scorch C	.30	.75
51	Republic Commando Sev C	.30	.75
52	Saleucami Trooper C	.30	.75
53	Sandtrooper C	.30	.75
54	Sith Assault Droid U	.75	1.50
55	Sith Trooper C	.30	.75
56	Sith Trooper C	.30	.75
57	Sith Trooper Commander U	.75	1.50
58	Snowtrooper with E-Web Blaster R	6.00	12.00
59	Ugnaught Demolitionist C	.30	.75
60	Ulic Qel-Droma VR	7.50	15.00
61	Utapau Trooper C	.30	.75
62	Varactyl Wrangler C	.30	.75
63	Yoda of Dagobah VR	12.00	25.00

2006 Star Wars Bounty Hunters Miniatures

COMPLETE SET (60)		150.00	300.00
RELEASED ON SEPTEMBER 23, 2006			
1	4-LOM, Bounty Hunter R	6.00	12.00
2	Aqualish Assassin C	.30	.75
3	Ayy Vida R	6.00	12.00
4	Basilisk War Droid U	.75	1.50
5	Bib Fortuna R	6.00	12.00
6	Bith Black Sun Vigo U	.75	1.50
7	Boba Fett, Bounty Hunter VR	20.00	40.00
8	BoShek R	6.00	12.00
9	Bossk, Bounty Hunter R	7.50	15.00
10	Boushh R	6.00	12.00
11	Calo Nord●R	6.00	12.00
12	Chewbacca w/C-3PO VR	10.00	20.00
13	Commerce Guild Homing Spider Droid U	.75	1.50
14	Corellian Pirate U	.75	1.50
15	Corporate Alliance Tank Droid U	.75	1.50
16	Dannik Jerriko VR	7.50	15.00
17	Dark Hellion Marauder on Swoop Bike U	.75	1.50
18	Dark Hellion Swoop Gang Member C	.30	.75
19	Defel Spy C	.30	.75
20	Dengar, Bounty Hunter R	7.50	15.00
21	Djas Puhr R	6.00	12.00
22	Droid Starfighter in Walking Mode R	7.50	15.00
23	E522 Assassin Droid U	.75	1.50
24	Gamorrean Thug C	.30	.75
25	Garindan R	6.00	12.00
26	Han Solo, Scoundrel VR	7.50	15.00
27	Huge Crab Droid U	.75	1.50
28	Human Blaster-for-Hire C	.30	.75
29	IG-88, Bounty Hunter VR	12.00	25.00
30	ISP Speeder R	6.00	12.00
31	Jango Fett, Bounty Hunter VR	15.00	30.00
32	Klatooinian Hunter C	.30	.75
33	Komari Vosa R	7.50	15.00
34	Lord Vader VR	10.00	20.00
35	Luke Skywalker of Dagobah R	7.50	15.00
36	Mandalore the Indomitable VR	12.00	25.00
37	Mandalorian Blademaster U	.75	1.50
38	Mandalorian Commander U	.75	1.50
39	Mandalorian Soldier C	.30	.75
40	Mandalorian Supercommando C	.30	.75
41	Mandalorian Warrior C	.30	.75
42	Mistryl Shadow Guard U	.75	1.50
43	Mustafarian Flea Rider R	6.00	12.00
44	Mustafarian Soldier C	.30	.75
45	Nikto Gunner on Desert Skiff VR	10.00	20.00
46	Nym VR	7.50	15.00
47	Princess Leia, Hoth Commander R	7.50	15.00
48	Quarren Bounty Hunter C	.30	.75
49	Rebel Captain U	.75	1.50
50	Rebel Heavy Trooper U	.75	1.50
51	Rebel Snowspeeder U	.75	1.50
52	Rodian Hunt Master U	.75	1.50
53	Talon Karrde VR	7.50	15.00
54	Tamtel Skreej VR	7.50	15.00
55	Tusken Raider Sniper C	.30	.75
56	Utapaun on Dactillion VR	7.50	15.00
57	Weequay Leader U	.75	1.50
58	Weequay Thug C	.30	.75
59	Young Krayt Dragon VR	10.00	20.00
60	Zuckuss R	7.50	15.00

2007 Star Wars Alliance and Empire Miniatures

COMPLETE SET (60)		100.00	200.00
RELEASED IN MAY 2007			
1	Admiral Piett R	5.00	10.00
2	Advance Agent, Officer U	.75	1.50
3	Advance Scout C	.30	.75
4	Aurra Sing, Jedi Hunter VR	10.00	20.00
5	Biggs Darklighter VR	7.50	15.00
6	Boba Fett, Enforcer VR	12.00	25.00
7	C-3PO and R2-D2 R	5.00	10.00
8	Chadra-Fan Pickpocket U	.75	1.50
9	Chewbacca, Enraged Wookiee R	5.00	10.00
10	Darth Vader, Imperial Commander VR	12.00	25.00
11	Death Star Gunner U	.75	1.50
12	Death Star Trooper C	.30	.75
13	Duros Explorer C	.30	.75
14	Elite Hoth Trooper C	.30	.75
15	Ephant Mon VR	7.50	15.00
16	Ewok Hang Glider R	5.00	10.00
17	Ewok Warrior C	.30	.75
18	Gamorrean Guard C	.30	.75
19	Han Solo in Stormtrooper Armor R	5.00	10.00
20	Han Solo on Tauntaun VR	10.00	20.00
21	Han Solo Rogue R	5.00	10.00
22	Heavy Stormtrooper U	.75	1.50
23	Human Force Adept C	.30	.75
24	Imperial Governor Tarkin R	5.00	10.00
25	Imperial Officer U	.75	1.50
26	Ithorian Commander U	.75	1.50
27	Jabba, Crime Lord VR	7.50	15.00
28	Jawa on Ronto VR	7.50	15.00
29	Jawa Trader U	.75	1.50
30	Lando Calrissian, Dashing Scoundrel R	5.00	10.00
31	Luke Skywalker, Champion of the Force VR	12.00	25.00
32	Luke Skywalker, Hero of Yavin R	5.00	10.00
33	Luke's Landspeeder VR	7.50	15.00
34	Mara Jade, Jedi R	5.00	10.00
35	Mon Calamari Tech Specialist C	.30	.75
36	Nikto Soldier C	.30	.75
37	Obi-Wan Kenobi, Force Spirit VR	7.50	15.00
38	Princess Leia R	5.00	10.00
39	Quinlan Vos, Infiltrator VR	10.00	20.00

40 Rampaging Wampa VR	7.50	15.00
41 Rebel Commando C	.30	.75
42 Rebel Commando Strike Leader U	.75	1.50
43 Rebel Leader U	.75	1.50
44 Rebel Pilot C	.30	.75
45 Rebel Trooper U	.75	1.50
46 Rodian Scoundrel U	.75	1.50
47 Scout Trooper U	.75	1.50
48 Snivvian Fringer C	.30	.75
49 Snowtrooper C	.30	.75
50 Storm Commando R	5.00	10.00
51 Stormtrooper C	.30	.75
52 Stormtrooper Officer U	.75	1.50
53 Stormtrooper on Repulsor Sled VR	10.00	20.00
54 Talz Spy Fringe U	.75	1.50
55 Trandoshan Mercenary U	.75	1.50
56 Tusken Raider C	.30	.75
57 Twi'lek Rebel Agent U	.75	1.50
58 Wicket R	5.00	10.00
59 Wookiee Freedom Fighter C	.30	.75
60 Yomin Carr R	6.00	12.00

2007 Star Wars The Force Unleashed Miniatures

COMPLETE SET (60)	350.00	800.00
RELEASED IN 2007		
1 Darth Revan VR	50.00	100.00
2 Kazdan Paratus R	5.00	10.00
3 Shaak Ti, Jedi Master VR	10.00	20.00
4 Chewbacca of Hoth VR	5.00	10.00
5 Elite Hoth Trooper C	5.00	10.00
6 Golan Arms DF.9 Anti-Infantry Battery UC	5.00	10.00
7 Han Solo in Carbonite VR	5.00	10.00
8 Han Solo of Hoth VR	5.00	10.00
9 Hoth Trooper Officer UC	5.00	10.00
10 Hoth Trooper with Repeating Blaster Cannon UC	5.00	10.00
11 Juno Eclipse R	5.00	10.00
12 K-3PO R	5.00	10.00
13 Luke Skywalker, Hoth Pilot Unleashed R	5.00	10.00
14 Luke Skywalker and Yoda VR	7.50	15.00
15 Luke's Snowspeeder VR	7.50	15.00
16 Master Kota R	7.50	15.00
17 Mon Calamari Medic C	5.00	10.00
18 Obi-Wan Kenobi, Unleashed R	5.00	10.00
19 Princess Leia of Cloud City R	5.00	10.00
20 Rebel Marksman UC	5.00	10.00
21 Rebel Troop Cart UC	5.00	10.00
22 Rebel Trooper on Tauntaun R	5.00	10.00
23 Rebel Vanguard UC	5.00	10.00
24 2-1B R	5.00	10.00
25 Vader's Secret Apprentice, Redeemed R	10.00	20.00
26 Verpine Tech Rebel C	5.00	10.00
27 Wedge Antilles, Red Two Rebel R	5.00	10.00
28 Wookiee Warrior Rebel C	5.00	10.00
29 Admiral Ozzel R	5.00	10.00
30 AT-AT Driver UC	5.00	10.00
31 Dark trooper UC	5.00	10.00
32 Darth Vader, Unleashed VR	5.00	10.00
33 Emperor's Shadow Guard UC	5.00	10.00
34 Evo Trooper UC	5.00	10.00
35 Felucian Stormtrooper Officer UC	5.00	10.00
36 Gotal Imperial Assassin C	5.00	10.00
37 Imperial Navy trooper C	5.00	10.00
38 Raxus Prime Trooper C	5.00	10.00
39 Snowtrooper C	5.00	10.00
40 Star Destroyer Officer UC	5.00	10.00
41 Stormtrooper UC	5.00	10.00
42 TIE Crawler UC	5.00	10.00
43 Vader's Apprentice, Unleashed VR	5.00	10.00
44 Wookiee Hunter AT-ST R	7.50	15.00
45 Garm Bel Iblis R	5.00	10.00

46 Amanin Scout UC	5.00	10.00
47 Boba Fett, Mercenary VR	25.00	50.00
48 Caamasi Noble C	5.00	10.00
49 Cloud Car Pilot C	5.00	10.00
50 Felucian Warrior on Rancor VR	20.00	40.00
51 Junk golem UC	5.00	10.00
52 Knobby white spider UC	5.00	10.00
53 Maris Brood VR	7.50	15.00
54 Muun Tactics Broker C	5.00	10.00
55 Mynock UC	5.00	10.00
56 PROXY R	5.00	10.00
57 Telosian Tank Droid UC	5.00	10.00
58 Uggernaught R	5.00	10.00
59 Ugnaught Boss UC	5.00	10.00
60 Ugnaught Tech UC	5.00	10.00

2008 Star Wars Knights of the Old Republic Miniatures

COMPLETE SET (60)	330.00	800.00
RELEASED ON AUGUST 7, 2008		
1 Atton Rand VR	5.00	10.00
2 Bao-Dur R	5.00	10.00
3 Carth Onasi VR	10.00	20.00
4 Juggernaut War Droid C	5.00	10.00
5 Master Lucien Draay VR	5.00	10.00
6 Mira VR	15.00	30.00
7 Old Republic Captain UC	5.00	10.00
8 Old Republic Guard C	5.00	10.00
9 Squint VR	5.00	10.00
10 Visas Marr R	5.00	10.00
11 Wookiee Elite Warrior C	5.00	10.00
12 Wookiee Trooper C	5.00	10.00
13 Darth Malak, Dark Lord of the Sith VR	5.00	10.00
14 Darth Sion VR	30.00	60.00
15 Elite Sith Trooper UC	5.00	10.00
16 Sith Assassin UC	5.00	10.00
17 Sith Guard C	12.00	25.00
18 Sith Heavy Assault Droid UC	5.00	10.00
19 Sith Marauder UC	5.00	10.00
20 Sith Operative C	5.00	10.00
21 Sith Trooper Captain UC	5.00	10.00
22 Captain Panaka R	5.00	10.00
23 Captain Tarpals R	5.00	10.00
24 Gungan Artillerist C	5.00	10.00
25 Gungan Shieldbearer UC	5.00	10.00
26 Gungan Soldier C	5.00	10.00
27 Jar Jar Binks VR	15.00	30.00
28 Obi-Wan Kenobi, Padawan VR	5.00	10.00
29 Supreme Chancellor Palpatine R	5.00	10.00
30 Han Solo, Smuggler R	5.00	10.00
31 Leia Organa, Senator VR	5.00	10.00
32 Luke Skywalker, Jedi R	5.00	10.00
33 Darth Vader, Scourge of the Jedi R	5.00	10.00
34 RA-7 Death Star Protocol Droid UC	5.00	10.00
35 General Wedge Antilles R	5.00	10.00
36 ASN Assassin Droid UC	5.00	10.00
37 Boma UC	5.00	10.00
38 Czerka Scientist C	5.00	10.00

39 Echani Handmaiden C	5.00	10.00
40 GenoHaradan Assassin C	5.00	10.00
41 Jarael C	5.00	10.00
42 Jawa Scout C	5.00	10.00
43 Jolee Bindo VR	5.00	10.00
44 Juhani VR	12.00	25.00
45 Kreia VR	5.00	10.00
46 Massiff UC	5.00	10.00
47 Mission Vao R	10.00	20.00
48 Rakghoul UC	5.00	10.00
49 Shyrack UC	5.00	10.00
50 T1 Series Bulk Loader Droid UC	5.00	10.00
51 T3-M4 R	7.50	15.00
52 Tusken Raider Scout C	5.00	10.00
53 Zaalbar R	5.00	10.00
54 Zayne Carrick R	5.00	10.00
55 Mandalore the Ultimate VR	25.00	50.00
56 Mandalorian Captain UC	5.00	10.00
57 Mandalorian Commando C	5.00	10.00
58 Mandalorian Marauder C	5.00	10.00
59 Mandalorian Quartermaster UC	5.00	10.00
60 Mandalorian Scout C	5.00	10.00

2008 Star Wars Legacy of the Force Miniatures

COMPLETE SET (60)	300.00	700.00
RELEASED ON MARCH 28, 2008		
1 Nomi Sunrider VR	7.50	15.00
2 Old Republic Recruit C	5.00	10.00
3 Old Republic Scout C	5.00	10.00
4 Darth Caedus VR	15.00	30.00
5 Darth Krayt VR	15.00	30.00
6 Darth Nihl VR	5.00	10.00
7 Darth Talon VR	25.00	50.00
8 Lumiya, the Dark Lady R	5.00	10.00
9 Republic Commando Training Sergeant U	5.00	10.00
10 Darth Tyranus, Legacy of the dark side R	5.00	10.00
11 Bothan Noble U	5.00	10.00
12 Deena Shan R	5.00	10.00
13 Elite Rebel Commando U	5.00	10.00
14 General Dodonna R	5.00	10.00
15 Luke Skywalker, Legacy of the Light Side R	5.00	10.00
16 Rebel Honor Guard C	5.00	10.00
17 Twi'lek Scout C	5.00	10.00
18 Antares Draco R	6.00	12.00
19 Emperor Roan Fel VR	5.00	10.00
20 Imperial Knight U	5.00	10.00
21 Imperial Knight U	5.00	10.00
22 Imperial Pilot C	5.00	10.00
23 Imperial Security Officer U	5.00	10.00
24 Jagged Fel R	5.00	10.00
25 Marasiah Fel R	5.00	10.00
26 Moff Morlish Veed VR	5.00	10.00
27 Moff Nyna Calixte R	5.00	10.00
28 Noghri Commando U	5.00	10.00
29 Shadow Stormtrooper U	5.00	10.00
30 Corellian Security Officer U	5.00	10.00

31	Galactic Alliance Scout C	5.00	10.00
32	Galactic Alliance Trooper C	5.00	10.00
33	Han Solo, Galactic Hero R	5.00	10.00
34	Kyle Katarn, Jedi Battlemaster VR	5.00	10.00
35	Leia Organa Solo, Jedi Knight VR	5.00	10.00
36	Luke Skywalker, Force Spirit VR	5.00	10.00
37	Mara Jade Skywalker VR	7.50	15.00
38	Shado Vao R	5.00	10.00
39	Wolf Sazen VR	5.00	10.00
40	Cade Skywalker, Bounty Hunter VR	5.00	10.00
41	Deliah Blue R	5.00	10.00
42	Dug Fringer U	5.00	10.00
43	Duros Scoundrel C	5.00	10.00
44	Gotal Mercenary C	5.00	10.00
45	Guard Droid C	5.00	10.00
46	Human Bodyguard C	5.00	10.00
47	Human Scoundrel C	5.00	10.00
48	Human Scout C	5.00	10.00
49	Jariah Syn R	5.00	10.00
50	Kel Dor Bounty Hunter C	5.00	10.00
51	Rodian Blaster for Hire U	5.00	10.00
52	Trandoshan Mercenary C	5.00	10.00
53	Boba Fett, Mercenary Commander VR	5.00	10.00
54	Canderous Ordo R	5.00	10.00
55	Mandalorian Gunslinger U	5.00	10.00
56	Mandalorian Trooper U	5.00	10.00
57	Yuuzhan Vong Elite Warrior U	5.00	10.00
58	Yuuzhan Vong Jedi Hunter U	5.00	10.00
59	Yuuzhan Vong Shaper U	5.00	10.00
60	Yuuzhan Vong Warrior C	5.00	10.00

2008 Star Wars The Clone Wars Miniatures

COMPLETE SET (40)		200.00	400.00
RELEASED ON NOVEMBER 4, 2008			
1	Darth Sidious Hologram VR	5.00	10.00
2	Ahsoka Tano VR	12.00	25.00
3	Anakin Skywalker Champion of Nelvaan R	5.00	10.00
4	Anakin Skywalker on STAP VR	5.00	10.00
5	ARC Trooper Sniper U	5.00	10.00
6	Barriss Offee, Jedi Knight R	5.00	10.00
7	Captain Rex VR	5.00	10.00
8	Clone Trooper on Gelagrub R	5.00	10.00
9	Commander Gree R	5.00	10.00
10	Elite Clone Trooper Commander U	5.00	10.00
11	Elite Clone Trooper Grenadier C	5.00	10.00
12	Galactic Marine U	5.00	10.00
13	General Aayla Secura R	7.50	15.00
14	Heavy Clone Trooper C	5.00	10.00
15	Mon Calamari Knight U	5.00	10.00
16	Odd Ball R	5.00	10.00
17	Padmé Amidala Senator VR	6.00	12.00
18	Star Corps Trooper U	5.00	10.00
19	Wookiee Scoundrel C	5.00	10.00
20	Yoda on Kybuck VR	5.00	10.00
21	Battle Droid C	5.00	10.00
22	Battle Droid C	5.00	10.00
23	Battle Droid Sniper U	5.00	10.00

24	Chameleon Droid R	5.00	10.00
25	Durge, Jedi Hunter VR	12.00	25.00
26	General Grievous, Droid Army Commander VR	5.00	10.00
27	Heavy Super Battle Droid C	5.00	10.00
28	IG-100 MagnaGuard U	5.00	10.00
29	Neimoidian Warrior C	5.00	10.00
30	Quarren Isolationist U	5.00	10.00
31	Rocket Battle Droid U	5.00	10.00
32	Super Battle Droid C	5.00	10.00
33	Techno Union Warrior C	5.00	10.00
34	Aqualish Warrior C	5.00	10.00
35	Gha Nachkt R	5.00	10.00
36	Human Soldier of Fortune C	5.00	10.00
37	IG-86 Assassin Droid U	5.00	10.00
38	Nelvaanian Warrior U	5.00	10.00
39	Trandoshan Scavenger U	5.00	10.00
40	Utapaun Warrior C	5.00	10.00

2008 Star Wars The Clone Wars Miniatures Starter

COMPLETE SET (6)		20.00	50.00
RELEASED ON NOVEMBER 4, 2008			
1	General Obi-Wan Kenobi	4.00	8.00
2	Clone Trooper	4.00	8.00
3	Clone Trooper Commander	4.00	8.00
4	Count Dooku of Serenno	4.00	8.00
5	Security Battle Droid	4.00	8.00
6	Super Battle Droid Commander	4.00	8.00

2009 Star Wars Galaxy at War Miniatures

COMPLETE SET (40)		60.00	160.00
RELEASED ON OCTOBER 27, 2009			
1	501st Clone Trooper C	2.00	4.00
2	A4-Series Lab Droid U	2.00	4.00
3	Admiral Yularen VR	2.00	4.00
4	Aqualish Technician C	2.00	4.00
5	ARF Trooper C	2.00	4.00
6	Asajj Ventress, Strike Leader R	2.00	4.00

7	AT-TE Driver C	2.00	4.00
8	B3 Ultra Battle Droid U	2.00	4.00
9	Battle Droid C	2.00	4.00
10	Battle Droid Sergeant U	2.00	4.00
11	Cad Bane VR	2.00	4.00
12	Captain Argyus VR	2.00	4.00
13	Captain Mar Tuuk VR	2.00	4.00
14	Captain Rex, 501st Commander R	2.00	4.00
15	Clone Trooper Pilot C	2.00	4.00
16	Clone Trooper Sergeant U	2.00	4.00
17	Clone Trooper with Night Vision C	2.00	4.00
18	Clone Trooper with Repeating Blaster U	2.00	4.00
19	Commander Ahsoka R	2.00	4.00
20	Commander Cody R	2.00	4.00
21	Commando Droid C	2.00	4.00
22	Commando Droid C	2.00	4.00
23	Commando Droid Captain U	2.00	4.00
24	Elite Senate Guard U	2.00	4.00
25	General Grievous, Scourge of the Jedi R	2.00	4.00
26	General Skywalker R	2.00	4.00
27	General Whorm Loathsom VR	2.00	4.00
28	Hondo Ohnaka VR	2.00	4.00
29	IG-100 MagnaGuard Artillerist U	2.00	4.00
30	IG-100 MagnaGuard U	2.00	4.00
31	Jedi Master Kit Fisto R	2.00	4.00
32	LR-57 Combat Droid U	2.00	4.00
33	Nahdar Vebb VR	2.00	4.00
34	Obi-Wan Kenobi, Jedi General R	2.00	4.00
35	R7 Astromech Droid U	2.00	4.00
36	Rodian Trader C	2.00	4.00
37	Senate Commando C	2.00	4.00
38	Treadwell Droid U	2.00	4.00
39	Wat Tambor, Techno Union Foreman VR	2.00	4.00
40	Weequay Pirate C	2.00	4.00

2009 Star Wars Imperial Entanglements Miniatures

COMPLETE SET (40)		180.00	450.00
RELEASED ON MARCH 17, 2009			
1	Bothan Commando C	5.00	10.00
2	C-3PO, Ewok Deity VR	5.00	10.00
3	General Crix Madine R	5.00	10.00
4	General Rieekan VR	6.00	12.00
5	Leia, Bounty Hunter VR	5.00	10.00
6	Luke Skywalker, Rebel Commando VR	10.00	20.00
7	Rebel Commando Pathfinder U	5.00	10.00
8	Rebel Trooper C	5.00	10.00
9	R2-D2 with Extended Sensor R	5.00	10.00
10	Veteran Rebel Commando C	5.00	10.00
11	Arica R	5.00	10.00
12	Darth Vader, Legacy of the Force VR	10.00	20.00
13	Emperor Palpatine on Throne VR	12.00	25.00
14	Imperial Dignitary U	5.00	10.00
15	Moff Tiaan Jerjerrod R	5.00	10.00
16	181st Imperial Pilot U	5.00	10.00
17	Sandtrooper C	5.00	10.00
18	Sandtrooper Officer U	5.00	10.00

#	Name		
19	Scout Trooper C	5.00	10.00
20	Shock Trooper U	5.00	10.00
21	Snowtrooper C	5.00	10.00
22	Snowtrooper Commander U	5.00	10.00
23	Stormtrooper C	5.00	10.00
24	Thrawn Mitth'raw'nuruodo R	5.00	10.00
25	Kyp Durron R	5.00	10.00
26	Bacta Tank U	5.00	10.00
27	Bespin Guard C	5.00	10.00
28	Chiss Mercenary C	5.00	10.00
29	Dash Rendar, Renegade Smuggler VR	7.50	15.00
30	Duros Scout C	5.00	10.00
31	Ewok Scout C	5.00	10.00
32	Jawa Scavenger C	5.00	10.00
33	Lobot, Computer Liaison Officer R	5.00	10.00
34	Logray, Ewok Shaman R	5.00	10.00
35	Mercenary Commander U - resembling Airen Cracken	5.00	10.00
36	Mouse Droid U	5.00	10.00
37	Twi'lek Black Sun Vigo U	5.00	10.00
38	Ugnaught Droid Destroyer U	5.00	10.00
39	Whiphid Tracker U	5.00	10.00
40	Xizor VR	10.00	20.00

2009 Star Wars Jedi Academy Miniatures

COMPLETE SET (40)		200.00	450.00
RELEASED ON JUNE 30, 2009			
1	Anakin Solo R	5.00	10.00
2	Antarian Ranger C	5.00	10.00
3	Cade Skywalker, Padawan R	5.00	10.00
4	Crimson Nova Bounty Hunter UC	5.00	10.00
5	Darth Maul, Sith apprentice VR	12.00	25.00
6	Darth Plagueis VR	12.00	25.00
7	Darth Sidious, Sith Master R	5.00	10.00
8	Death Watch Raider C	5.00	10.00
9	Disciples of Ragnos C	5.00	10.00
10	Exceptional Jedi Apprentice UC	5.00	10.00
11	Felucian UC	5.00	10.00
12	Grand Master Luke Skywalker R	7.50	15.00
13	Grand Master Yoda R	6.00	12.00
14	Heavy Clone Trooper C	5.00	10.00
15	HK-50 Series Assassin Droid UC	5.00	10.00
16	Imperial Sentinel U	5.00	10.00
17	Jedi Battlemaster UC	5.00	10.00
18	Jedi Crusader UC	5.00	10.00
19	Jensaarai Defender UC	5.00	10.00
20	Kol Skywalker VR	5.00	10.00
21	Krath War Droid C	5.00	10.00
22	Kyle Katarn, Combat Instructor R	5.00	10.00
23	Leia Skywalker, Jedi Knight R	5.00	10.00

24	Master K'Kruhk VR	5.00	10.00
25	Naga Sadow VR	7.50	15.00
26	Peace Brigade Thug C	5.00	10.00
27	Praetorite Vong Priest UC	5.00	10.00
28	Praetorite Vong Warrior C	5.00	10.00
29	Qui-Gon Jinn, Jedi Trainer R	5.00	10.00
30	R4 Astromech Droid C	5.00	10.00
31	Reborn C	5.00	10.00
32	Rocket Battle Droid C	5.00	10.00
33	Sith apprentice UC - resembling Darth Bandon	5.00	10.00
34	Sith Lord U	5.00	10.00
35	Stormtrooper C	5.00	10.00
36	The Dark Woman VR	10.00	20.00
37	The Jedi Exile VR	12.00	25.00
38	Vodo-Siosk Baas VR	7.50	15.00
39	Youngling C	5.00	10.00
40	Yuuzhan Vong Ossus Guardian UC	5.00	10.00

2010 Star Wars Dark Times Miniatures

COMPLETE SET (40)		75.00	200.00
RELEASED ON JANUARY 26, 2010			
1	4-LOM, Droid Mercenary R	2.00	4.00
2	501st Legion Clone Commander UC	2.00	4.00
3	501st Legion Clone Trooper C	2.00	4.00
4	501st Legion Stormtrooper C	2.00	4.00
5	ARF Trooper UC	2.00	4.00
6	A'Sharad Hett VR	7.50	15.00
7	Bomo Greenbark VR	2.00	4.00
8	Bossk, Trandoshan Hunter R	2.00	4.00
9	Boushh, Ubese Hunter R	2.00	4.00
10	Chewbacca, Fearless Scout VR	2.00	4.00
11	Dass Jennir VR	5.00	10.00
12	Dengar, Hired Killer R	2.00	4.00
13	EG-5 Jedi Hunter Droid UC	4.00	8.00
14	Elite Sith Assassin UC	2.00	4.00
15	Emperor's Hand UC	2.00	4.00
16	Ferus Olin VR	2.00	4.00
17	Gungan Bounty Hunter C	2.00	4.00
18	Human Engineer C	2.00	4.00
19	IG-88, Assassin Droid	4.00	8.00
20	Imperial Engineer C	2.00	4.00
21	Imperial Inquisitor UC	2.00	4.00
22	Imperial Sovereign Protector UC	2.00	4.00
23	Jax Pavan VR	2.00	4.00
24	Jedi Watchman C	2.00	4.00
25	Kir Kanos VR	5.00	10.00
26	K'Kruhk VR	2.00	4.00
27	Kota's Elite Militia UC	2.00	4.00
28	Kota's Militia C	2.00	4.00
29	Major Maximilian Veers R	2.00	4.00
30	Mandalorian Jedi Hunter UC	2.00	4.00
31	Merumeru R	2.00	4.00

32	Rodian Brute C	2.00	4.00
33	Rodian Raider C	2.00	4.00
34	Talz Chieftain UC	2.00	4.00
35	Talz Warrior C	2.00	4.00
36	Togorian Soldier UC	2.00	4.00
37	Trandoshan Elite Mercenary UC	5.00	10.00
38	Trianii Scout UC	2.00	4.00
39	T'Surr C	2.00	4.00
40	Zuckuss, Bounty Hunter C	6.00	12.00

2010 Star Wars Masters of the Force Miniatures

COMPLETE SET (40)		115.00	280.00
RELEASED APRIL 6, 2010			
1	Cay Qel-Droma VR	7.50	15.00
2	Jedi Healer UC	3.00	6.00
3	Jedi Instructor - resembling Coleman Trebor UC	3.00	6.00
4	Jedi Sith Hunter UC	3.00	6.00
5	Lord Hoth VR	3.00	6.00
6	Freedon Nadd VR	3.00	6.00
7	Kit Fisto, Jedi Master R	3.00	6.00
8	Master Windu R	3.00	6.00
9	Plo Koon, Jedi Master R	5.00	10.00
10	Rodian Diplomat UC	3.00	6.00
11	Saesee Tiin, Jedi Master R	7.50	15.00
12	Voolvif Monn VR	12.00	25.00
13	Battle Droid Officer C	3.00	6.00
14	Anakin Skywalker, Force Spirit R	3.00	6.00
15	General Han Solo R	3.00	6.00
16	Lando Calrissian, Rebel Leader R	3.00	6.00
17	Rebel Soldier C	3.00	6.00
18	Red Hand Trooper UC	3.00	6.00
19	Yoda, Force Spirit VR	3.00	6.00
20	Arden Lyn VR	3.00	6.00
21	Darth Vader, Sith apprentice R	3.00	6.00
22	Ganner Rhysode VR	3.00	6.00
23	Blood Carver Assassin C	3.00	6.00
24	Chiss Trooper UC	3.00	6.00
25	Ewok Warrior C	3.00	6.00
26	Gamorrean Bodyguard C	3.00	6.00
27	Ghhhk UC	4.00	8.00
28	Grievous, Kaleesh Warlord VR	3.00	6.00
29	Houjix C	3.00	6.00
30	K'lor'slug UC	4.00	8.00
31	Kaminoan Medic UC	3.00	6.00
32	Kintan Strider C	3.00	6.00
33	Mantellian Savrip C	3.00	6.00
34	Molator UC	3.00	6.00
35	Monnok UC	3.00	6.00
36	Ng'ok UC	4.00	8.00
37	Sullustan Scout C	3.00	6.00
38	Toydarian Soldier C	3.00	6.00
39	Far-Outsider C	3.00	6.00
40	Taung Warrior C	3.00	6.00

Miscellaneous

PRICE GUIDE

HOT WHEELS

2014 Hot Wheels Star Wars Character Cars Black Cards 1:64

1	Darth Vader	10.00	20.00
2	R2-D2	5.00	10.00
3	Luke Skywalker	5.00	10.00
4	Chewbacca	4.00	8.00
5	Yoda	4.00	8.00
6	Tusken Raider	5.00	10.00
7	501st Clone Trooper	8.00	15.00
8	Stormtrooper	4.00	8.00
9	Darth Maul	4.00	8.00
10	Boba Fett	6.00	12.00
11	Chopper (Star Wars Rebels)	5.00	10.00
12	The Inquisitor (Star Wars Rebels)	4.00	8.00
13	C-3PO	8.00	15.00
14	Wicket the Ewok	5.00	10.00
15	Kanan Jarrus (Star Wars Rebels)	4.00	8.00
16	Zeb (Star Wars Rebels)	4.00	8.00
17	Kylo Ren	5.00	10.00
18	BB-8	8.00	15.00
19	General Grievous	6.00	12.00
20	Han Solo (The Force Awakens)	8.00	15.00
21	First Order Stormtrooper	6.00	12.00
22	Obi-Wan Kenobi	12.00	25.00
23	Rey	8.00	15.00
24	Jabba the Hutt	5.00	10.00
25	Admiral Ackbar	5.00	10.00
26	First Order Flametrooper	6.00	12.00
27	Battle Droid	6.00	12.00
28	Sabine Wren (Star Wars Rebels)	12.50	25.00
29	Clone Shock Trooper (UER #27)		
30	C-3PO (The Force Awakens)	8.00	15.00
31	Sidon Ithano (The Force Awakens)	8.00	15.00
32	Jango Fett	6.00	12.00

2014 Hot Wheels Star Wars Character Cars Blue Cards 1:64

1	Darth Vader	4.00	8.00
2	R2-D2	4.00	8.00
3	Luke Skywalker	4.00	8.00
4	Chewbacca	6.00	12.00
5	Yoda	7.50	15.00
6	Tusken Raider	4.00	8.00
7	501st Clone Trooper	4.00	8.00
8	Stormtrooper	4.00	8.00
9	Darth Maul	5.00	10.00
10	Boba Fett	4.00	8.00
11	Chopper (Star Wars Rebels)	4.00	8.00
12	The Inquisitor (Star Wars Rebels)	3.00	6.00
13	C-3PO	6.00	12.00
14	Wicket the Ewok	4.00	8.00
15	Kanan Jarrus (Star Wars Rebels)	5.00	10.00
16	Zeb (Star Wars Rebels)		
17	Kylo Ren		
18	BB-8		
19	General Grievous		
20	Han Solo (The Force Awakens)		
21	First Order Stormtrooper	6.00	12.00
22	Obi-Wan Kenobi		
23	Rey		
24	Jabba the Hutt		
25	Admiral Ackbar		
26	First Order Flametrooper		
27	Battle Droid		
28	Sabine Wren (Star Wars Rebels)		
29	Clone Shock Trooper (UER #27)		
30	C-3PO (The Force Awakens)		
31	Sidon Ithano (The Force Awakens)		
32	Jango Fett		

2014 Hot Wheels Star Wars Saga Walmart Exclusives 1:64

1	Gearonimo (The Phantom Menace)	5.00	10.00
2	Nitro Scorcher (Attack of the Clones)	6.00	12.00
3	Duel Fueler (Revenge of the Sith)	8.00	15.00
4	Motoblade (A New Hope)		
5	Spectyte (Empire Strikes Back)	10.00	20.00
6	Ballistik (Return of the Jedi)	4.00	8.00
7	Brutalistic (The Clone Wars)	4.00	8.00
8	Jet Threat 3.0 (Star Wars Rebels)	12.00	25.00

2014-16 Hot Wheels Star Wars Exclusives 1:64

1	Darth Vader (w/lightsaber box) (2014 SDCC Exclusive)	80.00	150.00
2	R2-KT (2015 Star Wars Celebration Make-a-Wish Foundation Exclusive)	40.00	80.00
3	First Order Stormtrooper (2015 SDCC Exclusive)	25.00	50.00
4	Carships Trench Run Set (2016 SDCC Exclusive)	50.00	100.00
5	Boba Fett Prototype Armor (2016 Star Wars Celebration Exclusive)	25.00	50.00

2014-16 Hot Wheels Star Wars Target Exclusive 5-Packs 1:64

1 Character Cars (Battle-Damaged Stormtrooper
   Luke Skywalker/Darth Vader/Yoda/Chewbacca) 25.00 50.00
2 Light Side vs. Dark Side (Luke Skywalker
   Obi-Wan Kenobi/Anakin Skywalker/Emperor Palpatine/Kylo Ren) 15.00 30.00
3 Heroes of the Resistance (Chewbacca/Han Solo/Rey
   Poe Dameron/Maz Kanata) 20.00 40.00

2015 Hot Wheels Star Wars Walmart Exclusives 1:64

1 Obi-Wan Kenobi
   (Jedi Order Scorcher) 4.00 8.00
2 Darth Maul
   (Sith Scoopa di Fuego) 5.00 10.00
3 Clone Trooper
   (Galactic Republic Impavido 1) 4.00 8.00
4 General Grievous
   (Separatists Sinistra) 4.00 8.00
5 Luke Skywalker
   (Rebel Alliance Enforcer) 4.00 8.00
6 Darth Vader
   (Galactic Empire Prototype H-24) 5.00 10.00
7 Poe Dameron
   (Resistance Fast Felion) 4.00 8.00
8 Kylo Ren
   (First Order Ettorium) 4.00 8.00

2015-16 Hot Wheels Star Wars Character Cars Black Carded 2-Packs 1:64

1 Chewbacca & Han Solo 5.00 10.00
2 R2-D2 & C-3PO (weathered) 4.00 8.00
3 Obi-Wan Kenobi & Darth Vader 20.00 40.00
4 501st Clone Trooper & Battle Droid 4.00 8.00
5 Emperor Palpatine vs. Yoda 8.00 15.00
6 Darth Vader & Princess Leia 10.00 20.00
7 Captain Phasma & First Order Stormtrooper 5.00 10.00
8 Rey vs. First Order Flametrooper 8.00 15.00
9 BB-8 & Poe Dameron 10.00 20.00
10 Han Solo vs. Greedo 12.00 25.00
11 Boba Fett & Bossk
12 Luke Skywalker vs. Rancor
13 Stormtrooper & Death Trooper (Rogue One) 8.00 15.00

2015-16 Hot Wheels Star Wars Character Cars Blue Carded 2-Packs 1:64

1 Chewbacca & Han Solo 6.00 12.00
2 R2-D2 & C-3PO (weathered) 6.00 12.00
3 Obi-Wan Kenobi & Darth Vader 6.00 12.00
4 501st Clone Trooper & Battle Droid 8.00 15.00
5 Emperor Palpatine vs. Yoda
6 Darth Vader & Princess Leia 6.00 12.00
7 Captain Phasma & First Order Stormtrooper
8 Rey vs. First Order Flametrooper
9 BB-8 & Poe Dameron
10 Han Solo vs. Greedo 8.00 15.00
11 Boba Fett & Bossk
12 Luke Skywalker vs. Rancor
13 Stormtrooper & Death Trooper (Rogue One) 10.00 20.00

2015-16 Hot Wheels Star Wars Tracksets 1:64

1 TIE Factory Takedown (w/Ezra Bridger car) 12.00 25.00
2 Throne Room Raceway (w/Luke Skywalker car) 12.00 25.00
3 Death Star Battle Blast (w/X-Wing inspired vehicle) 10.00 20.00
4 Blast & Battle Lightsaber Launcher (w/Darth Vader car) 8.00 15.00
5 Starkiller Base Battle (w/Finn car)
6 Rancor Rumble set (w/Gamorrean Guard car) 15.00 30.00

2017 Hot Wheels Star Wars 40th Anniversary Carships 1:64

NNO Millennium Falcon 6.00 12.00
NNO TIE Advanced XI Prototype 6.00 12.00
NNO TIE Fighter 5.00 10.00
NNO X-Wing Fighter 5.00 10.00
NNO Y-Wing Fighter 8.00 15.00

2017 Hot Wheels Star Wars 40th Anniversary Character Cars 1:64

NNO Biggs Darklighter
   (Celebration Exclusive) 12.00 25.00
NNO Chewbacca 5.00 10.00
NNO Darth Vader 6.00 12.00
NNO Luke Skywalker 4.00 8.00

NNO Princess Leia 5.00 10.00
NNO R2-D2 4.00 8.00
NNO Stormtrooper 4.00 8.00

2017 Hot Wheels Star Wars 40th Anniversary Starships 1:64

NNO Millennium Falcon 8.00 15.00
NNO Star Destroyer 10.00 20.00
NNO TIE Advanced X1 Prototype 6.00 12.00
NNO TIE Fighter 6.00 12.00
NNO X-Wing Fighter 6.00 12.00
NNO Y-Wing Fighter 8.00 15.00

2017 Hot Wheels Star Wars The Last Jedi 2-Packs 1:64

NNO BB-8 & Poe Dameron 8.00 15.00
NNO Boba Fett & Bossk 6.00 12.00
NNO Jabba the Hutt & Han Solo in Carbonite 12.00 25.00
NNO Kylo Ren & Snoke 15.00 30.00
NNO R2-D2 & C-3PO 8.00 15.00
NNO Rey (Jedi Training) & Luke Skywalker 15.00 30.00

2017 Hot Wheels Star Wars The Last Jedi Carships 1:64

NNO First Order TIE Fighter 6.00 12.00
NNO Kylo Ren's TIE Silencer
NNO Millennium Falcon
NNO Poe's X-Wing Fighter
NNO Resistance Ski Speeder
NNO Y-Wing Fighter

2017 Hot Wheels Star Wars The Last Jedi Character Cars 1:64

NNO	BB-8	7.50	15.00
NNO	BB-9E	6.00	12.00

NNO	C-3PO	4.00	8.00
NNO	Captain Phasma	4.00	8.00
NNO	Chewbacca	4.00	8.00
NNO	Darth Vader	5.00	10.00
NNO	Elite Praetorian Guard	10.00	20.00
NNO	Finn	7.50	15.00
NNO	First Order Executioner	5.00	10.00
NNO	First Order Stormtrooper		
NNO	Kylo Ren	6.00	12.00
NNO	Luke Skywalker	5.00	10.00
NNO	R2-D2	4.00	8.00
NNO	Rey (Jedi Training)	6.00	12.00

2017 Hot Wheels Star Wars The Last Jedi Character Cars All-Terrain 1:64

NNO	BB-8	10.00	20.00
NNO	Darth Vader		

NNO	Luke Skywalker		
NNO	Stormtrooper		

2017 Hot Wheels Star Wars The Last Jedi Starships 1:64

NNO	First Order Heavy Assault Walker
NNO	First Order Special Forces TIE Fighter
NNO	First Order Star Destroyer
NNO	Kylo Ren's TIE Silencer
NNO	Kylo Ren's TIE Silencer (boxed)
	(SDCC Exclusive)
NNO	Millennium Falcon
NNO	Poe's Ski Speeder
NNO	Resistance Bomber
NNO	Resistance X-Wing Fighter

LEGO

1999 LEGO Star Wars Episode I

7101	Lightsaber Duel	30.00	60.00
7111	Droid Fighter	30.00	60.00
7121	Naboo Swamp	35.00	70.00
7131	Anakin's Podracer	50.00	100.00
7141	Naboo Fighter	60.00	120.00
7151	Sith Infiltrator	60.00	120.00
7161	Gungan Sub	75.00	150.00
7171	Mos Espa Podrace	125.00	200.00

1999 LEGO Star Wars Episode IV

7110	Landspeeder	40.00	80.00
7140	X-Wing Fighter	150.00	300.00
7150	TIE Fighter & Y-Wing	100.00	200.00

1999 LEGO Star Wars Episode V

7130	Snowspeeder	50.00	100.00

1999 LEGO Star Wars Episode VI

7128	Speeder Bikes	35.00	70.00

2000 LEGO Star Wars Episode I

7115	Gungan Patrol	30.00	60.00
7124	Flash Speeder	20.00	40.00
7155	Trade Federation AAT	50.00	100.00
7159	Star Wars Bucket	60.00	120.00
7184	Trade Federation MTT	125.00	250.00

2000 LEGO Star Wars Episode IV

7190	Millennium Falcon	200.00	350.00

2000 LEGO Star Wars Episode V

7144	Slave I	60.00	120.00

2000 LEGO Star Wars Episode VI

7104	Desert Skiff	25.00	50.00
7134	A-Wing Fighter	35.00	70.00
7180	B-Wing at Rebel Control Center	50.00	100.00

2000 LEGO Star Wars Minifigure Pack

3340	Emperor Palpatine, Darth Maul and Darth Vader Minifig Pack - Star Wars #1	50.00	100.00
3341	Luke Skywalker, Han Solo and Boba Fett Minifig Pack - Star Wars #2	40.00	80.00
3342	Chewbacca and 2 Biker Scouts Minifig Pack - Star Wars #3	25.00	50.00
3343	2 Battle Droids and Command Officer Minifig Pack - Star Wars #4	25.00	50.00

2000 LEGO Star Wars Technic

8000	Pit Droid	30.00	60.00
8001	Battle Droid	50.00	100.00
8002	Destroyer Droid	150.00	250.00

2000 LEGO Star Wars Ultimate Collector Series

7181	TIE Interceptor	300.00	600.00
7191	X-Wing Fighter	450.00	900.00

2001 LEGO Star Wars Episode I

7126	Battle Droid Carrier	35.00	70.00
7186	Watto's Junkyard	100.00	200.00

2001 LEGO Star Wars Episode IV

7106	Droid Escape	25.00	50.00
7146	TIE Fighter	60.00	120.00

2001 LEGO Star Wars Episode VI

7127	Imperial AT-ST	30.00	60.00
7166	Imperial Shuttle	100.00	200.00

2001 LEGO Star Wars Technic

8007	C-3PO	50.00	100.00
8008	Stormtrooper	30.00	60.00

2001 LEGO Star Wars Ultimate Collector Series

10018	Darth Maul	500.00	1,000.00
10019	Rebel Blockade Runner	1,500.00	3,000.00

2002 LEGO Star Wars Episode I

7203	Jedi Defense I	35.00	70.00
7204	Jedi Defense II	25.00	50.00

2002 LEGO Star Wars Episode II

7103	Jedi Duel	50.00	100.00
7113	Tusken Raider Encounter	35.00	70.00
7133	Bounty Hunter Pursuit	150.00	300.00
7143	Jedi Starfighter	50.00	100.00
7153	Jango Fett's Slave I	200.00	400.00
7163	Republic Gunship	350.00	700.00

2002 LEGO Star Wars Episode IV

7142	X-Wing Fighter	100.00	200.00
7152	TIE Fighter & Y-Wing	50.00	100.00

2002 LEGO Star Wars Episode V

7119	Twin-Pod Cloud Car	25.00	50.00

2002 LEGO Star Wars Episode VI

7139	Ewok Attack	40.00	80.00
7200	Final Duel I	35.00	70.00
7201	Final Duel II	20.00	40.00

2002 LEGO Star Wars Miniature Building Set

3219	Mini TIE Fighter	12.50	25.00

2002 LEGO Star Wars Product Collection

65081	R2-D2 & C-3PO Droid Collectors Set	50.00	100.00
65145	X-Wing Fighter TIE Fighter & Y-Wing Fighter Collectors Set		
65153	Jango Fett's Slave I with Bonus Cargo Case	200.00	350.00

2002 LEGO Star Wars Technic

8009	R2-D2	30.00	60.00
8010	Darth Vader	60.00	120.00
8011	Jango Fett	40.00	80.00
8012	Super Battle Droid	30.00	60.00

2002 LEGO Star Wars Ultimate Collector Series

7194	Yoda	300.00	600.00
10026	Naboo Starfighter Special Edition	300.00	600.00
10030	Imperial Star Destroyer	600.00	1,200.00

2003 LEGO Star Wars Episode II

4482	AT-TE	250.00	450.00
4478	Geonosian Fighter	75.00	150.00
4481	Hailfire Droid	100.00	200.00

2003 LEGO Star Wars Episode IV

4477	T-16 Skyhopper	25.00	50.00

2003 LEGO Star Wars Episode V

4483	AT-AT	250.00	500.00
4479	TIE Bomber	100.00	200.00
10123	Cloud City	600.00	1,200.00

2003 LEGO Star Wars Episode VI

4475	Jabba's Message	30.00	60.00
4476	Jabba's Prize	50.00	100.00
4480	Jabba's Palace	150.00	300.00

2003 LEGO Star Wars Miniature Building Set

4484	X-Wing Fighter & TIE Advanced	15.00	30.00
4485	Sebulba's Podracer & Anakin's Podracer	15.00	30.00
4486	AT-ST & Snowspeeder	20.00	40.00
4487	Jedi Starfighter & Slave I	12.00	25.00
4488	Millennium Falcon	25.00	50.00
4489	AT-AT	25.00	50.00
4490	Republic Gunship	20.00	40.00
4491	MTT	12.50	25.00

2003 LEGO Star Wars Product Collection

4207901	Star Wars MINI Bonus Pack		

2003 LEGO Star Wars Ultimate Collector Series

10129	Rebel Snowspeeder	250.00	500.00

2004 LEGO Star Wars Episode IV

4501	Mos Eisley Cantina	100.00	200.00
7262	TIE Fighter and Y-Wing	100.00	200.00

2004 LEGO Star Wars Episode V

4500	Rebel Snowspeeder	50.00	100.00
4502	X-Wing Fighter	200.00	350.00
4504	Millennium Falcon	150.00	300.00

2004 LEGO Star Wars Legends

10131	TIE Fighter Collection	150.00	300.00

2004 LEGO Star Wars Miniature Building Set

4492	Star Destroyer	20.00	40.00
4493	Sith Infiltrator	20.00	40.00
4494	Imperial Shuttle	25.00	50.00
4495	AT-TE	12.00	25.00
6963	X-Wing Fighter	15.00	30.00
6964	Boba Fett's Slave I	12.00	25.00
6965	TIE Interceptor	12.00	25.00

2004 LEGO Star Wars Product Collection

65707	Bonus/Value Pack		

2004 LEGO Star Wars Ultimate Collector Series

10134	Y-Wing Attack Starfighter	300.00	600.00

2005 LEGO Star Wars Episode III

6966	Jedi Starfighter	8.00	15.00
6967	ARC Fighter	8.00	15.00
6968	Wookiee Attack		
7250	Clone Scout Walker	30.00	60.00
7251	Darth Vader Transformation	50.00	100.00
7252	Droid Tri-Fighter	25.00	50.00
7255	General Grievous Chase	75.00	150.00
7256	Jedi Starfighter and Vulture Droid	60.00	120.00
7257	Ultimate Lightsaber Duel	100.00	200.00
7258	Wookiee Attack	75.00	150.00
7259	ARC-170 Fighter	100.00	200.00
7260	Wookiee Catamaran	100.00	200.00
7261	Clone Turbo Tank	150.00	300.00
7283	Ultimate Space Battle	200.00	350.00

2005 LEGO Star Wars Episode IV

7263	TIE Fighter	60.00	120.00
10144	Sandcrawler	200.00	400.00

2005 LEGO Star Wars Episode VI

7264 Imperial Inspection	150.00	300.00

2005 LEGO Star Wars Product Collection

65771 Episode III Collectors' Set	100.00	200.00
65828 Bonus/Value Pack		
65844 Bonus/Value Pack		
65845 Bonus/Value Pack		

2005 LEGO Star Wars Exclusives

PROMOSW002 Anakin Skywalker
   (2005 International Toy Fair Exclusive)
PROMOSW003 Luminara Unduli (2005 International Toy Fair Exclusive)
SW117PROMO Darth Vader (2005 Nurnberg Toy Fair Exclusive)
TF05 Star Wars V.I.P. Gala Set
   (2005 International Toy Fair Exclusive)

2005 LEGO Star Wars Ultimate Collector Series

10143 Death Star II	1,000.00	2,000.00

2006 LEGO Star Wars Episode III

6205 V-wing Fighter	30.00	60.00
72612 Clone Turbo Tank (non-light-up edition)	150.00	300.00

2006 LEGO Star Wars Episode IV

6211 Imperial Star Destroyer	300.00	600.00

2006 LEGO Star Wars Episode V

6209 Slave I	125.00	250.00
6212 X-Wing Fighter	80.00	150.00

2006 LEGO Star Wars Episode VI

6206 TIE Interceptor	60.00	120.00
6207 A-Wing Fighter	30.00	60.00
6208 B-Wing Fighter	100.00	200.00
6210 Jabba's Sail Barge	300.00	600.00

2006 LEGO Star Wars Product Collection

66142 Bonus/Value Pack		
66150 Bonus/Value Pack		
66221 Bonus/Value Pack		

2006 LEGO Star Wars Ultimate Collector Series

10174 Imperial AT-ST	350.00	600.00
10175 Vader's TIE Advanced	600.00	1,000.00

2007 LEGO Star Wars Episode I

7660 Naboo N-1 Starfighter with Vulture Droid	35.00	70.00
7662 Trade Federation MTT	350.00	700.00
7663 Sith Infiltrator	50.00	100.00
7665 Republic Cruiser	200.00	350.00

2007 LEGO Star Wars Episode III

7654 Droids Battle Pack	40.00	80.00
7655 Clone Troopers Battle Pack	35.00	70.00
7656 General Grievous Starfighter	40.00	80.00
7661 Jedi Starfighter with Hyperdrive Booster Ring	125.00	250.00

2007 LEGO Star Wars Episode IV

7658 Y-Wing Fighter	50.00	100.00
7659 Imperial Landing Craft	60.00	120.00

2007 LEGO Star Wars Episode V

7666 Hoth Rebel Base	100.00	200.00
10178 Motorised Walking AT-AT	300.00	600.00

2007 LEGO Star Wars Episode VI

7657 AT-ST	80.00	150.00

2007 LEGO Star Wars Legends

7664 TIE Crawler	75.00	150.00

2007 LEGO Star Wars Minifigure Pack

4521221 Gold Chrome Plated C-3PO/10,000*	550.00	1,000.00
PROMOSW004 Star Wars Celebration IV Exclusive/500*	600.00	1,000.00

2007 LEGO Star Wars Ultimate Collector Series

10179 Ultimate Collector's Millennium Falcon	4,000.00	7,500.00

2008 LEGO Star Wars The Clone Wars

7669 Anakin's Jedi Starfighter	40.00	80.00
7670 Hailfire Droid & Spider Droid	40.00	80.00
7673 MagnaGuard Starfighter	60.00	120.00
7674 V-19 Torrent	100.00	200.00
7675 AT-TE Walker	300.00	450.00
7676 Republic Attack Gunship	300.00	600.00

7678 Droid Gunship	50.00	100.00
7679 Republic Fighter Tank	120.00	200.00
7680 The Twilight	125.00	250.00
7681 Separatist Spider Droid	75.00	150.00
8031 V-19 Torrent	10.00	20.00
20006 Clone Turbo Tank	20.00	40.00

2008 LEGO Star Wars Episode III

7671 AT-AP Walker	60.00	120.00

2008 LEGO Star Wars Episode V

8029 Mini Snowspeeder	6.00	12.00

2008 LEGO Star Wars Legends

7667 Imperial Dropship	25.00	50.00
7668 Rebel Scout Speeder	30.00	60.00
7672 Rogue Shadow	150.00	300.00

2008 LEGO Star Wars Miniature Building Set

8028 TIE Fighter	6.00	15.00

2008 LEGO Star Wars Miscellaneous

COMCON001 Clone Wars
   (2008 SDCC Exclusive)

2008 LEGO Star Wars Ultimate Collector Series

10186 General Grievous	125.00	250.00
10188 Death Star	350.00	700.00

2009 LEGO Star Wars The Clone Wars

7748 Corporate Alliance Tank Droid	40.00	75.00
7751 Ahsoka's Starfighter and Droids	125.00	250.00
7752 Count Dooku's Solar Sailer	100.00	200.00
7753 Pirate Tank	60.00	120.00
8014 Clone Walker Battle Pack	50.00	100.00
8015 Assassin Droids Battle Pack	20.00	40.00
8016 Hyena Droid Bomber	50.00	100.00
8018 Armored Assault Tank (AAT)	125.00	250.00
8019 Republic Attack Shuttle	125.00	250.00
8033 General Grievous' Starfighter	8.00	15.00
8036 Separatist Shuttle	40.00	75.00
8037 Anakin's Y-Wing Starfighter	150.00	300.00
8039 Venator-Class Republic Attack Cruiser	450.00	750.00
10195 Republic Dropship with AT-OT Walker	1,000.00	1,500.00
20007 Republic Attack Cruiser	12.00	25.00
20009 AT-TE Walker	15.00	30.00
20010 Republic Gunship	12.50	25.00
30004 Battle Droid on STAP	10.00	20.00
30006 Clone Walker	10.00	20.00
COMCON010 Mini Republic Dropship Mini AT-TE Brickmaster Pack		
(SDCC 2009 Exclusive)		

2009 LEGO Star Wars Episode IV

7778	Midi-Scale Millennium Falcon	75.00	150.00
8017	Darth Vader's TIE Fighter	150.00	300.00
10198	Tantive IV	150.00	300.00

2009 LEGO Star Wars Episode V

7749	Echo Base	40.00	80.00

2009 LEGO Star Wars Episode VI

7754	Home One Mon Calamari Star Cruiser	100.00	200.00
8038	The Battle of Endor	150.00	300.00
30005	Imperial Speeder Bike	12.00	25.00

2009 LEGO Star Wars Minifigure Pack

4547551	Chrome Darth Vader	120.00	250.00

2009 LEGO Star Wars SDCC Exclusives

COMCON004	Collectible Display Set 1
COMCON005	Collectible Display Set 2
COMCON006	Collectible Display Set 4
COMCON007	Collectible Display Set 5
COMCON008	Collectible Display Set 3
COMCON009	Collectible Display Set 6
COMCON011	Holo-Brick Archives

2009 LEGO Star Wars Product Collection

66308	3 in 1 Superpack

2010 LEGO Star Wars The Clone Wars

8085	Freeco Speeder	25.00	50.00
8086	Droid Tri-Fighter	40.00	75.00
8093	Plo Koon's Jedi Starfighter	60.00	120.00
8095	General Grievous' Starfighter	60.00	120.00
8098	Clone Turbo Tank	200.00	400.00
8128	Cad Bane's Speeder	50.00	100.00
30050	Republic Attack Shuttle	10.00	20.00

2010 LEGO Star Wars Episode III

8088	ARC-170 Starfighter	200.00	350.00
8091	Republic Swamp Speeder	30.00	60.00
8096	Emperor Palpatine's Shuttle	75.00	150.00

2010 LEGO Star Wars Episode IV

8092	Luke's Landspeeder	30.00	60.00
8099	Midi-Scale Imperial Star Destroyer	60.00	120.00

2010 LEGO Star Wars Episode V

8083	Rebel Trooper Battle Pack	12.50	25.00
8084	Snowtrooper Battle Pack	12.50	25.00
8089	Hoth Wampa Cave	50.00	100.00
8097	Slave I	100.00	200.00
8129	AT-AT Walker	250.00	450.00
20018	AT-AT Walker	15.00	30.00

2010 LEGO Star Wars Legends

8087	TIE Defender	80.00	150.00

2010 LEGO Star Wars Miniature Building Set

20016	Imperial Shuttle	10.00	20.00

2010 LEGO Star Wars Minifigure Pack

2853590	Chrome Stormtrooper	60.00	120.00
2853835	White Boba Fett Figure	60.00	120.00

2010 LEGO Star Wars Miscellaneous

BOBAFETT1	White Boba Fett minifig and Star Wars Book	400.00	600.00

2010 LEGO Star Wars Product Collection

66341	Star Wars Super Pack 3 in 1
66364	Star Wars Super Pack 3 in 1
66366	Star Wars Super Pack 3 in 1
66368	Star Wars Super Pack 3 in 1

2010 LEGO Star Wars Ultimate Collector Series

10212	Imperial Shuttle	600.00	1,000.00
10215	Obi-Wan's Jedi Starfighter	200.00	350.00

2011 LEGO Star Wars The Clone Wars

7868	Mace Windu's Jedi Starfighter	125.00	250.00
7869	Battle for Geonosis	100.00	200.00
7913	Clone Trooper Battle Pack	40.00	75.00
7914	Mandalorian Battle Pack	40.00	75.00
7930	Bounty Hunter Assault Gunship	60.00	120.00
7931	T-6 Jedi Shuttle	100.00	200.00
7957	Sith Nightspeeder	35.00	70.00
7959	Geonosian Starfighter	50.00	100.00
7964	Republic Frigate	250.00	500.00
20021	Bounty Hunter Assault Gunship	10.00	20.00
30053	Republic Attack Cruiser	8.00	15.00

2011 LEGO Star Wars Episode I

7877	Naboo Starfighter	50.00	100.00
7929	The Battle of Naboo	75.00	150.00
7961	Darth Maul's Sith Infiltrator	75.00	150.00
7962	Anakin Skywalker and Sebulba's Podracers	100.00	200.00
30052	AAT	8.00	15.00

2011 LEGO Star Wars Episode IV

7965	Millennium Falcon	200.00	400.00

2011 LEGO Star Wars Episode V

7879	Hoth Echo Base	125.00	250.00
20019	Slave I	15.00	30.00

2011 LEGO Star Wars Episode VI

7956	Ewok Attack	40.00	75.00
30054	AT-ST	12.50	25.00

2011 LEGO Star Wars Legends

7915	Imperial V-wing Starfighter	20.00	50.00

2011 LEGO Star Wars Miniature Building Set

30051	Mini X-Wing	8.00	15.00
30055	Vulture Droid	8.00	15.00

2011 LEGO Star Wars Minifigure Pack

2856197	Shadow ARF Trooper	50.00	100.00

2011 LEGO Star Wars Exclusive

PROMOSW007	Star Wars Miniland Figures
	(2011 Toy Fair Collector's Party Exclusive)

2011 LEGO Star Wars Product Collection

66377	Star Wars Super Pack 3 in 1	60.00	120.00

66378	Star Wars Super Pack 3 in 1		
66395	Star Wars Super Pack 3 in 1	60.00	120.00
66396	Star Wars Super Pack 3 in 1		

2011 LEGO Star Wars Seasonal Set

COMCON015	Advent calendar		
	(2011 SDCC Exclusive)	60.00	120.00
7958	Star Wars Advent Calendar	30.00	60.00

2011 LEGO Star Wars Ultimate Collector Series

10221	Super Star Destroyer	800.00	1,500.00

2012 LEGO Star Wars The Clone Wars

9488	Elite Clone Trooper & Commando Droid Battle Pack	50.00	100.00
9491	Geonosian Cannon	50.00	100.00
9498	Saesee Tiin's Jedi Starfighter	40.00	75.00
9515	Malevolence	250.00	500.00
9525	Pre Vizsla's Mandalorian Fighter	150.00	300.00
30059	MTT	8.00	15.00

2012 LEGO Star Wars Episode I

9499	Gungan Sub	100.00	200.00
30057	Anakin's Pod Racer	7.50	15.00
30058	STAP	8.00	15.00
5000063	Chrome TC-14	25.00	50.00
COMCON019	Sith Infiltrator		
	(2012 SDCC Exclusive)	80.00	150.00

2012 LEGO Star Wars Episode III

9494	Anakin's Jedi Interceptor	75.00	150.00
9526	Palpatine's Arrest	200.00	350.00

2012 LEGO Star Wars Episode IV

9490	Droid Escape	30.00	60.00
9492	TIE Fighter	75.00	150.00
9493	X-Wing Starfighter	75.00	150.00
9495	Gold Leader's Y-Wing Starfighter	60.00	120.00
COMCON024	Luke Skywalker's Landspeeder Mini		
	(2012 NYCC Exclusive)	120.00	250.00

2012 LEGO Star Wars Episode V

CELEBVI	Mini Slave I		
	(2012 Star Wars Celebration VI Exclusive)	150.00	300.00

2012 LEGO Star Wars Episode VI

9489	Endor Rebel Trooper & Imperial Trooper Battle Pack	25.00	50.00
9496	Desert Skiff	40.00	80.00
9516	Jabba's Palace	200.00	400.00

2012 LEGO Star Wars Miniature Building Set

30056	Star Destroyer	8.00	15.00

2012 LEGO Star Wars Minifigure Pack

5000062	Darth Maul	25.00	50.00

2012 LEGO Star Wars The Old Republic

9497	Republic Striker-class Starfighter	75.00	150.00
9500	Sith Fury-class Interceptor	200.00	350.00

2012 LEGO Star Wars Planet Set

9674	Naboo Starfighter & Naboo	40.00	80.00
9675	Sebulba's Podracer & Tatooine	8.00	15.00
9676	TIE Interceptor & Death Star	15.00	30.00
9677	X-Wing Starfighter & Yavin 4	10.00	20.00
9678	Twin-Pod Cloud Car & Bespin	10.00	20.00
9679	AT-ST & Endor	8.00	15.00

2012 LEGO Star Wars Product Collection

66411	Super Pack 3-in-1		
66431	Super Pack 3-in-1		
66432	Super Pack 3-in-1		

2012 LEGO Star Wars Seasonal Set

9509	Star Wars Advent Calendar	30.00	60.00

2012 LEGO Star Wars Ultimate Collector Series

10225	R2-D2	350.00	600.00
10227	B-Wing Starfighter	300.00	500.00

2013 LEGO Star Wars The Clone Wars

11905	Brickmaster Star Wars: Battle for the Stolen Crystals parts	15.00	30.00
30240	Z-95 Headhunter	8.00	15.00
30241	Mandalorian Fighter	8.00	15.00
30242	Republic Frigate	8.00	15.00
30243	Umbaran MHC	8.00	15.00
75002	AT-RT	40.00	80.00
75004	Z-95 Headhunter	100.00	200.00
75012	BARC Speeder with Sidecar	125.00	250.00
75013	Umbaran MHC (Mobile Heavy Cannon)	100.00	200.00
75022	Mandalorian Speeder	60.00	120.00
75024	HH-87 Starhopper	50.00	100.00

2013 LEGO Star Wars Episode II

75000	Clone Troopers vs. Droidekas	40.00	75.00
75015	Corporate Alliance Tank Droid	60.00	120.00
75016	Homing Spider Droid	75.00	150.00
75017	Duel on Geonosis	60.00	120.00
75019	AT-TE	250.00	500.00
75021	Republic Gunship	300.00	600.00
5001709	Clone Trooper Lieutenant	8.00	15.00

2013 LEGO Star Wars Episode V

75014	Battle of Hoth	80.00	150.00
5001621	Han Solo (Hoth)	8.00	15.00

2013 LEGO Star Wars Episode VI

75003	A-Wing Starfighter	40.00	75.00
75005	Rancor Pit	100.00	200.00
75020	Jabba's Sail Barge	200.00	350.00

2013 LEGO Star Wars The Old Republic

75001	Republic Troopers vs. Sith Troopers	30.00	60.00
75025	Jedi Defender-class Cruiser	125.00	250.00

2013 LEGO Star Wars Originals

75018	JEK-14's Stealth Starfighter	80.00	150.00
COMCON032	Jek-14 Mini Stealth Starfighter		
	(2013 SDCC Exclusive)	120.00	250.00
MAY2013	Holocron Droid	12.00	25.00
TRU03	Mini Jek-14 Stealth Fighter		
	(2013 Toys R Us Exclusive)	12.00	25.00
YODACHRON	Yoda Chronicles Promotional Set	1,500.00	2,000.00

2013 LEGO Star Wars Planet Set

75006	Jedi Starfighter & Planet Kamino	15.00	30.00
75007	Republic Assault Ship & Planet Coruscant	20.00	40.00
75008	TIE Bomber & Asteroid Field	17.50	35.00
75009	Snowspeeder & Hoth	25.00	50.00
75010	B-Wing Starfighter & Planet Endor	25.00	50.00
75011	Tantive IV & Planet Alderaan	25.00	50.00

2013 LEGO Star Wars Product Collection

66449	Super Pack 3-in-1	80.00	150.00
66456	Star Wars Value Pack	100.00	200.00
66473	LEGO Star Wars Super Pack	120.00	250.00

2013 LEGO Star Wars Promotional Set

NYCC2013	Yoda display box		
	(2013 NYCC Exclusive)		
YODA	Yoda minifig, NY I Heart Torso	120.00	250.00

2013 LEGO Star Wars Seasonal Set

75023	Star Wars Advent Calendar	40.00	75.00

2013 LEGO Star Wars Ultimate Collector Series

10236	Ewok Village	300.00	500.00
10240	Red Five X-Wing Starfighter	250.00	400.00

2014 LEGO Star Wars The Clone Wars

75045	Republic AV-7 Anti-Vehicle Cannon	125.00	200.00
75046	Coruscant Police Gunship	150.00	300.00

2014 LEGO Star Wars Episode I

75058	MTT	200.00	350.00

2014 LEGO Star Wars Episode III

30244	Anakin's Jedi Interceptor	8.00	15.00
30247	ARC-170 Starfighter	8.00	15.00
75035	Kashyyyk Troopers	40.00	75.00
75036	Utapau Troopers	50.00	100.00
75037	Battle on Saleucami	50.00	100.00
75038	Jedi Interceptor	50.00	100.00
75039	V-Wing Starfighter	75.00	150.00
75040	General Grievous' Wheel Bike	60.00	120.00
75041	Vulture Droid	60.00	120.00
75042	Droid Gunship	60.00	120.00
75043	AT-AP	75.00	150.00
75044	Droid Tri-Fighter	50.00	100.00

2014 LEGO Star Wars Episode IV

75034	Death Star Troopers	25.00	50.00
75052	Mos Eisley Cantina	75.00	150.00
75055	Imperial Star Destroyer	250.00	450.00

2014 LEGO Star Wars Episode V

75049	Snowspeeder	40.00	75.00
75054	AT-AT	200.00	400.00

2014 LEGO Star Wars Episode VI

30246	Imperial Shuttle	12.00	25.00
75050	B-Wing	75.00	150.00

2014 LEGO Star Wars MicroFighters

75028	Clone Turbo Tank	25.00	50.00
75029	AAT	15.00	30.00
75030	Millennium Falcon	25.00	50.00
75031	TIE Interceptor	15.00	30.00
75032	X-Wing Fighter	20.00	40.00
75033	Star Destroyer	12.00	25.00

2014 LEGO Star Wars Minifigure Pack

5002122	TC-4	15.00	30.00

2014 LEGO Star Wars The Old Republic

5002123	Darth Revan	50.00	100.00

2014 LEGO Star Wars Original Content

75051	Jedi Scout Fighter	100.00	200.00

2014 LEGO Star Wars Product Collection

66479	Value Pack		
66495	Star Wars Value Pack		
66512	Rebels Co-Pack		
66514	Microfighter Super Pack 3 in 1		
66515	Microfighter Super Pack 3 in 1		

2014 LEGO Star Wars Toys R Us Exclusives

TRUGHOST	The Ghost Micro-Model	10.00	20.00
TRUTIE	TIE Fighter		
TRUXWING	X-Wing		

2014 LEGO Star Wars Rebels

75048	The Phantom	80.00	150.00
75053	The Ghost	350.00	600.00
COMCON039	The Ghost Starship/1000*		
	(2014 SDCC Exclusive)	125.00	250.00
FANEXPO001	The Ghost Starship		
	(2014 Fan Expo Exclusive)	60.00	120.00

2014 LEGO Star Wars Seasonal Set

75056	Star Wars Advent Calendar	75.00	150.00

2014 LEGO Star Wars Ultimate Collector Series

75059	Sandcrawler	300.00	500.00

2015 LEGO Star Wars Buildable Figures

75107	Jango Fett	25.00	50.00
75108	Clone Commander Cody	20.00	40.00
75109	Obi-Wan Kenobi	20.00	40.00
75110	Luke Skywalker	25.00	50.00
75111	Darth Vader	25.00	50.00
75112	General Grievous	50.00	100.00

2015 LEGO Star Wars The Clone Wars

75087	Anakin's Custom Jedi Starfighter	75.00	150.00

2015 LEGO Star Wars Episode I

75080	AAT	50.00	100.00
75086	Battle Droid Troop Carrier	125.00	250.00
75091	Flash Speeder	25.00	50.00
75092	Naboo Starfighter	60.00	120.00
75096	Sith Infiltrator	100.00	175.00

2015 LEGO Star Wars Episode II

75085	Hailfire Droid	50.00	100.00

2015 LEGO Star Wars Episode IV

75081	T-16 Skyhopper	25.00	50.00
5002947	Admiral Yularen	10.00	20.00

2015 LEGO Star Wars Episode VI

30272	A-Wing Starfighter	10.00	20.00
75093	Death Star Final Duel	75.00	150.00
75094	Imperial Shuttle Tydirium	100.00	200.00

2015 LEGO Star Wars The Force Awakens

30276	First Order Special Forces TIE Fighter	10.00	20.00
75099	Rey's Speeder	12.00	30.00
75100	First Order Snowspeeder	25.00	50.00
75101	First Order Special Forces TIE Fighter	75.00	150.00
75102	Poe's X-Wing Fighter	75.00	150.00
75103	First Order Transporter	125.00	200.00
75104	Kylo Ren's Command Shuttle	60.00	120.00
75105	Millennium Falcon	125.00	250.00
5002948	C-3PO	10.00	20.00
30UNIQUE15	Force Friday Commemorative Brick	7.50	15.00

2015 LEGO Star Wars Legends

75079	Shadow Troopers	20.00	40.00
75088	Senate Commando Troopers	30.00	60.00
75089	Geonosis Troopers	30.00	60.00

2015 LEGO Star Wars Magazine Gift

SW911506	Snowspeeder	8.00	15.00
SW911508	Mini Slave I	12.50	25.00
SW911509	Imperial Shooter	8.00	15.00
SW911510	Micro Star Destroyer and TIE Fighter		
SW911511	Jedi Weapon Stand		
SWCOMIC1	Mini X-Wing Starfighter	15.00	30.00

2015 LEGO Star Wars MicroFighters

75072	ARC-170 Starfighter	20.00	40.00
75073	Vulture Droid	12.00	25.00
75074	Snowspeeder	12.00	25.00

75075 AT-AT	20.00	40.00
75076 Republic Gunship	12.00	25.00
75077 Homing Spider Droid	15.00	30.00

2015 LEGO Star Wars Product Collection

66533 Microfighter 3 in 1 Super Pack	25.00	50.00
66534 Microfighter 3 in 1 Super Pack	15.00	30.00
66535 Battle Pack 2 in 1	60.00	120.00
66536 Luke Skywalker and Darth Vader	60.00	120.00

2015 LEGO Star Wars Exclusives

CELEB2015 Tatooine Mini-Build/1000*		
(2015 Star Wars Celebration Exclusive)	125.00	200.00
FANEXPO2015 Tatooine Mini Build		
(2015 Fan Expo Exclusive)	125.00	200.00
SDCC2015 Dagobah Mini Build		
(2015 SDCC Exclusive)	100.00	200.00
TRUWOOKIEE Wookiee Gunship		
(2015 Toys R Us Exclusive)	8.00	15.00
TRUXWING Poe's X-Wing Fighter		
(2015 Toys R Us Exclusive)	10.00	20.00

2015 LEGO Star Wars Rebels

30274 AT-DP	8.00	15.00
30275 TIE Advanced Prototype	8.00	15.00
75078 Imperial Troop Transport	12.00	25.00
75082 TIE Advanced Prototype	20.00	40.00
75083 AT-DP	50.00	100.00
75084 Wookiee Gunship	50.00	100.00
75090 Ezra's Speeder Bike	15.00	30.00
75106 Imperial Assault Carrier	80.00	150.00
5002938 Stormtrooper Sergeant	8.00	15.00
5002939 The Phantom	8.00	15.00

2015 LEGO Star Wars Seasonal Set

75097 Star Wars Advent Calendar	20.00	40.00

2015 LEGO Star Wars Ultimate Collector Series

75060 Slave I	200.00	400.00
75095 TIE Fighter	150.00	300.00

2016 LEGO Star Wars Battlefront

75133 Rebel Alliance Battle Pack	20.00	40.00
75134 Galactic Empire Battle Pack	20.00	40.00

2016 LEGO Star Wars Buildable Figures

75113 Rey	12.00	25.00
75114 First Order Stormtrooper	20.00	40.00

75115 Poe Dameron	12.00	25.00
75116 Finn	10.00	20.00
75117 Kylo Ren	20.00	40.00
75118 Captain Phasma	20.00	40.00
75119 Sergeant Jyn Erso	12.50	25.00
75120 K-2SO	15.00	30.00
75121 Imperial Death Trooper	17.50	35.00

2016 LEGO Star Wars Episode III

75135 Obi-Wan's Jedi Interceptor	50.00	100.00
75142 Homing Spider Droid	60.00	120.00
75151 Clone Turbo Tank	150.00	300.00

2016 LEGO Star Wars Episode IV

75136 Droid Escape Pod	20.00	40.00

2016 LEGO Star Wars Episode V

75137 Carbon-Freezing Chamber	40.00	75.00
75138 Hoth Attack	25.00	50.00

2016 LEGO Star Wars The Force Awakens

30277 First Order Star Destroyer	8.00	15.00
30278 Poe's X-Wing Fighter	6.00	12.00
30279 Kylo Ren's Command Shuttle	6.00	12.00
30602 First Order Stormtrooper	10.00	20.00
30605 Finn (FN-2187)	6.00	12.00
75131 Resistance Trooper Battle Pack	15.00	30.00
75132 First Order Battle Pack	12.50	25.00
75139 Battle on Takodana	20.00	40.00
75140 Resistance Troop Transporter	60.00	120.00
75148 Encounter on Jakku	30.00	60.00
75149 Resistance X-Wing Fighter	75.00	150.00
5004406 First Order General	8.00	15.00

2016 LEGO Star Wars Magazine Gift

SW911607 Millennium Falcon	6.00	12.00
SW911608 Landspeeder	6.00	12.00

SW911609 Naboo Starfighter	6.00	12.00
SW911610 Probe Droid	6.00	12.00
SW911611 AAT	6.00	12.00
SW911612 Acklay	6.00	12.00
SW911613 TIE Bomber	6.00	12.00
SW911614 Yoda's Hut	6.00	12.00
SW911615 AT-AT	6.00	12.00
SW911616 MTT	6.00	12.00
SW911617 Palpatine's Shuttle	7.50	15.00

2016 LEGO Star Wars MicroFighters

75125 Resistance X-Wing Fighter	12.00	25.00
75126 First Order Snowspeeder	10.00	20.00
75127 The Ghost	12.00	25.00
75128 TIE Advanced Prototype	12.00	25.00
75129 Wookiee Gunship	8.00	15.00
75130 AT-DP	12.00	25.00

2016 LEGO Star Wars Miscellaneous

11912 Star Wars: Build Your Own Adventure Parts		

2016 LEGO Star Wars Originals

75145 Eclipse Fighter	40.00	75.00
75147 StarScavenger	50.00	100.00

2016 LEGO Star Wars Product Collection

66542 Microfighters Super Pack 3 in 1	12.00	25.00
66543 Microfighters Super Pack 3 in 1	15.00	30.00
5005217 Death Star Ultimate Kit		

2016 LEGO Star Wars Promotional Set

6176782 Escape the Space Slug	125.00	250.00
TRUFALCON Millennium Falcon		
(2016 Toys R Us Exclusive)	12.50	25.00

2016 LEGO Star Wars Rebels

75141 Kanan's Speeder Bike	30.00	60.00
75150 Vader's TIE Advanced vs. A-Wing Starfighter	100.00	200.00
75157 Captain Rex's AT-TE	125.00	250.00
75158 Rebel Combat Frigate	200.00	400.00
5004408 Rebel A-Wing Pilot	6.00	12.00

2016 LEGO Star Wars Rogue One

75152 Imperial Assault Hovertank	50.00	100.00
75153 AT-ST Walker	75.00	150.00
75154 TIE Striker	40.00	75.00
75155 Rebel U-Wing Fighter	100.00	200.00
75156 Krennic's Imperial Shuttle	100.00	200.00

2016 LEGO Star Wars Seasonal Set

75146	Star Wars Advent Calendar	30.00	60.00

2016 LEGO Star Wars Ultimate Collector Series

75098	Assault on Hoth	300.00	550.00
75159	Death Star	400.00	750.00

2017 LEGO Star Wars BrickHeadz

41498	Boba Fett & Han Solo in Carbonite		
	NYCC Exclusive	150.00	300.00

2017 LEGO Star Wars Buildable Figures

75523	Scarif Stormtrooper	15.00	30.00
75524	Chirrut Imwe	10.00	20.00
75525	Baze Malbus	10.00	20.00
75526	Elite TIE Fighter Pilot	20.00	40.00
75528	Rey	12.50	25.00
75529	Elite Praetorian Guard	20.00	40.00
75530	Chewbacca	25.00	50.00
75531	Stormtrooper Commander	20.00	40.00
75532	Scout Trooper & Speeder Bike	40.00	75.00

2017 LEGO Star Wars The Clone Wars

75168	Yoda's Jedi Starfighter	40.00	75.00

2017 LEGO Star Wars Episode I

75169	Duel on Naboo	50.00	100.00

2017 LEGO Star Wars Episode II

75191	Jedi Starfighter (w/hyperdrive)	125.00	250.00

2017 LEGO Star Wars Episode III

75183	Darth Vader Transformation	30.00	60.00

2017 LEGO Star Wars Episode IV

75173	Luke's Landspeeder	25.00	50.00

2017 LEGO Star Wars Episode VI

75174	Desert Skiff Escape	35.00	70.00
75175	A-Wing Starfighter	50.00	100.00

2017 LEGO Star Wars The Force Awakens

75166	First Order Transport Speeder Battle Pack	15.00	30.00
75178	Jakku Quadjumper	25.00	50.00
75180	Rathtar Escape	50.00	100.00

2017 LEGO Star Wars The Last Jedi

30497	First Order Heavy Assault Walker	8.00	15.00
75176	Resistance Transport Pod	20.00	40.00
75177	First Order Heavy Scout Walker	30.00	75.00
75179	Kylo Ren's TIE Fighter	50.00	100.00
75187	BB-8	100.00	200.00
75188	Resistance Bomber	75.00	150.00
75189	First Order Heavy Assault Walker	150.00	300.00
75190	First Order Star Destroyer	150.00	300.00

2017 LEGO Star Wars Legends

75182	Republic Fighter Tank	15.00	30.00

2017 LEGO Star Wars Magazine Gift

SW911618	Flash Speeder	7.50	15.00
SW911719	Kanan Jarrus	6.00	12.00
SW911720	The Ghost	7.50	15.00
SW911721	Imperial Combat Driver	10.00	20.00
SW911722	TIE Advanced	10.00	20.00
SW911723	Vulture Droid	7.50	15.00
SW911724	A-Wing	7.50	15.00
SW911725	Sandcrawler	10.00	20.00
SW911726	Imperial Snowtrooper	7.50	15.00
SW911727	Rey's Speeder	10.00	20.00
SW911728	First Order Snowspeeder	7.50	15.00
SW911729	Droid Gunship	7.50	15.00
SW911730	Y-Wing	6.00	12.00

2017 LEGO Star Wars MicroFighters

75160	U-Wing	12.50	25.00
75161	TIE Striker	12.50	25.00
75162	Y-Wing	12.50	25.00
75163	Krennic's Imperial Shuttle	10.00	20.00

2017 LEGO Star Wars Originals

75167	Bounty Hunter Speeder Bike Battle Pack	30.00	60.00
75185	Tracker I	50.00	100.00
75186	The Arrowhead	75.00	150.00

2017 LEGO Star Wars Promotional

30611	R2-D2	17.50	35.00
CELEB2017	Detention Block Rescue	150.00	300.00
SWMF	Millennium Falcon	7.50	15.00
TRUBB8	BB-8	6.00	12.00
TRULEIA	Princess Leia	7.50	15.00

2017 LEGO Star Wars Rebels

75170	The Phantom	50.00	100.00

2017 LEGO Star Wars Rogue One

30496	U-Wing Fighter	7.50	15.00
40176	Scarif Stormtrooper	12.00	25.00
40268	R3-M2	7.50	15.00
75164	Rebel Trooper Battle Pack	20.00	40.00
75165	Imperial Trooper Battle Pack	17.50	35.00
75171	Battle on Scarif	50.00	100.00
75172	Y-Wing Starfighter	75.00	150.00

2017 LEGO Star Wars Seasonal

75184	Star Wars Advent Calendar	20.00	40.00

2017 LEGO Star Wars Ultimate Collector Series

75144	Snowspeeder	250.00	500.00
75192	Millennium Falcon	750.00	1,500.00

2018 LEGO Star Wars Buildable Figures

75533	Boba Fett	40.00	75.00
75534	Darth Vader	30.00	60.00
75535	Han Solo	12.50	25.00
75536	Range Trooper	30.00	60.00
75537	Darth Maul	25.00	50.00
75538	Super Battle Droid		
75539	501st Legion Clone Trooper & AT-RT Walker		

2018 LEGO Star Wars The Clone Wars

75199	General Grievous' Combat Speeder	40.00	80.00
75214	Anakin's Jedi Starfighter	25.00	50.00

2018 LEGO Star Wars Episode II

75206	Jedi and Clone Troopers Battle Pack	25.00	50.00

MISCELLANEOUS

2018 LEGO Star Wars Episode IV

75198	Tatooine Battle Pack	20.00	40.00
75205	Mos Eisley Cantina	40.00	80.00
75218	X-Wing Starfighter	100.00	200.00
75220	Sandcrawler	150.00	300.00
75221	Imperial Landing Craft	75.00	150.00

2018 LEGO Star Wars Episode V

75203	Hoth Medical Chamber	40.00	75.00
75208	Yoda's Hut	40.00	75.00

2018 LEGO Star Wars The Last Jedi

30380	Kylo Ren's Shuttle	10.00	20.00
40298	DJ	10.00	20.00
75188	Resistance Bomber (Finch Dallow)	150.00	300.00
75197	First Order Specialists Battle Pack	15.00	30.00
75200	Ahch-To Island Training	20.00	40.00
75201	First Order AT-ST	30.00	60.00
75202	Defense of Crait	50.00	100.00
75216	Snoke's Throne Room	40.00	75.00
75230	Porg	75.00	150.00

2018 LEGO Star Wars Legends

75204	Sandspeeder	15.00	30.00

2018 LEGO Star Wars Magazine Gift

SW911831	Kylo Ren's Shuttle	7.50	15.00
SW911832	Imperial Shuttle Pilot	12.50	25.00
SW911833	Imperial Shuttle	6.00	12.00
SW911834	Finn	10.00	20.00
SW911835	Dwarf Spider Droid	10.00	20.00
SW911836	Quadjumper	7.50	15.00
SW911837	AT-ST	12.50	25.00
SW911838	Probe Droid	10.00	20.00
SW911839	Obi-Wan Kenobi	10.00	20.00
SW911840	Droideka	7.50	15.00

SW911841	Poe Dameron's X-Wing Fighter		
SW911842	Star Destroyer	10.00	20.00
SW911843	Luke Skywalker		

2018 LEGO Star Wars Master Builder

75222	Betrayal at Cloud City	500.00	1,000.00

2018 LEGO Star Wars Microfighters

75193	Millennium Falcon	12.50	25.00
75194	First Order TIE Fighter	10.00	20.00
75195	Ski Speeder vs. First Order Walker	15.00	30.00
75196	A-Wing vs. TIE Silencer	15.00	30.00

2018 LEGO Star Wars Promotional

40288	BB-8	12.50	25.00
75512	Millennium Falcon Cockpit (SDCC Exclusive)	100.00	200.00
5005376	Star Wars Anniversary Pod	15.00	30.00
5005747	Black Card Display Stand	60.00	120.00
6252770	Leia Organa	12.50	25.00
6252808	Chewbacca	12.50	25.00
6252810	Han Solo		
6252811	Obi-Wan Kenobi	7.50	15.00
6252812	Luke Skywalker	12.50	25.00
PORG	Porg		

2018 LEGO Star Wars Seasonal

75213	Star Wars Advent Calendar	12.50	25.00

2018 LEGO Star Wars Solo

30381	Imperial TIE Fighter	7.50	15.00
30498	Imperial AT-Hauler	10.00	20.00
40299	Kessel Mine Worker	12.50	25.00
40300	Han Solo Mudtrooper	25.00	50.00
75207	Imperial Patrol Battle Pack	10.00	20.00
75209	Han Solo's Landspeeder	20.00	40.00
75210	Moloch's Landspeeder	30.00	60.00
75211	Imperial TIE Fighter	125.00	250.00
75212	Kessel Run Millennium Falcon	150.00	300.00
75215	Cloud-Rider Swoop Bikes	25.00	50.00
75217	Imperial Conveyex Transport	45.00	90.00
75219	Imperial AT-Hauler	60.00	120.00

2018 LEGO Star Wars Ultimate Collector Series

75181	Y-Wing Starfighter	250.00	500.00

2019 LEGO Star Wars

11920	Parts for Star Wars: Build Your Own Adventure Galactic Missions

2019 LEGO Star Wars 4-Plus

75235	X-Wing Starfighter Trench Run	20.00	40.00
75237	TIE Fighter Attack	12.50	25.00
75247	Rebel A-Wing Starfighter	10.00	20.00

2019 LEGO Star Wars Battlefront

75226	Inferno Squad Battle Pack	12.50	25.00

2019 LEGO Star Wars Boost

75253	Droid Commander	150.00	300.00

2019 LEGO Star Wars Episode I

30383	Naboo Starfighter	5.00	10.00
30461	Podracer	7.50	15.00
75258	Anakin's Podracer ñ 20th Anniversary Edition	25.00	50.00

2019 LEGO Star Wars Episode III

75233	Droid Gunship	30.00	60.00
75234	AT-AP Walker	25.00	50.00
75261	Clone Scout Walker ñ 20th Anniversary Edition	20.00	40.00

2019 LEGO Star Wars Episode IV

30624	Obi-Wan Kenobi Mini-Figure	15.00	30.00
75229	Death Star Escape	15.00	30.00
75244	Tantive IV	200.00	400.00
75246	Death Star Cannon	25.00	50.00

2019 LEGO Star Wars Episode V

30384	Snowspeeder	5.00	10.00
75239	Hoth Generator Attack	12.50	25.00
75241	Action Battle Echo Base Defence	20.00	40.00
75243	Slave I ñ 20th Anniversary Edition	75.00	150.00
75259	Snowspeeder ñ 20th Anniversary Edition	50.00	100.00

2019 LEGO Star Wars Episode VI

75238	Action Battle Endor Assault	15.00	30.00

2019 LEGO Star Wars The Force Awakens

75236	Duel on Starkiller Base	15.00	30.00

2019 LEGO Star Wars The Last Jedi

75225	Elite Praetorian Guard Battle Pack	10.00	20.00

2019 Star Wars Legends

75262	Imperial Dropship ñ 20th Anniversary Edition	20.00	40.00

MISCELLANEOUS

2019 Star Wars Magazine Gift

911943	Luke Skywalker		
911944	Resistance Bomber	4.00	8.00
911945	Slave I	3.00	6.00
911946	U-Wing	4.00	8.00
911947	IG-88	3.00	6.00
911948	AT-M6	3.00	6.00
911949	Millennium Falcon	4.00	8.00
911950	B-Wing	3.00	6.00
911951	First Order Stormtrooper	3.00	6.00
911952	Jedi Interceptor	6.00	12.00
911953	First Order SF TIE Fighter		
911954	Kylo Ren's TIE Silencer		

2019 LEGO Star Wars The Mandalorian

75254	AT-ST Raider	50.00	100.00

2019 LEGO Star Wars Microfighters

75223	Naboo Starfighter	7.50	15.00
75224	Sith Infiltrator	6.00	12.00
75228	Escape Pod vs. Dewback	10.00	20.00

2018 LEGO Star Wars Miscellaneous

75251	Darth Vader's Castle	75.00	150.00
75255	Yoda	60.00	120.00

2019 LEGO Star Wars Promotional

40333	Battle of Hoth - 20th Anniversary Edition	25.00	50.00
40362	Battle of Endor	30.00	60.00
75227	Darth Vader Bust	50.00	100.00
75522	Mini Boost Droid Commander	30.00	75.00
LUKE1	Luke Skywalker		
TANTIVEIV	Tantive IV		
XWING1	Mini X-Wing Fighter		
XWING2	X-Wing		

2019 LEGO Star Wars Resistance

75240	Major Vonreg's TIE Fighter	40.00	75.00
75242	Black Ace TIE Interceptor	50.00	100.00

2019 LEGO Star Wars The Rise of Skywalker

75248	Resistance A-Wing Starfighter	25.00	50.00
75249	Resistance Y-Wing Starfighter	40.00	80.00
75250	Pasaana Speeder Chase	25.00	50.00
75256	Kylo Ren's Shuttle	75.00	150.00
75257	Millennium Falcon	100.00	200.00
77901	Sith Trooper Bust SDCC	100.00	200.00

2019 LEGO Star Wars Seasonal

75245	Star Wars Advent Calendar	30.00	60.00

2019 LEGO Star Wars Ultimate Collector Series

75252	Imperial Star Destroyer	400.00	800.00

2020 LEGO Star Wars 4-Plus

75268	Snowspeeder	20.00	40.00

2020 LEGO The Clone Wars

75280	501st Legion Clone Troopers	30.00	75.00
75283	Armored Assault Tank (AAT)	30.00	75.00

2020 LEGO Star Wars Episode III

75269	Duel on Mustafar	20.00	40.00
75281	Anakin's Jedi Interceptor	30.00	75.00
75286	General Grievous's Starfighter	50.00	100.00

2020 LEGO Star Wars Episode IV

75270	Obi-Wan's Hut	30.00	60.00
75271	Luke Skywalker's Landspeeder	20.00	40.00

2020 LEGO Star Wars Episode V

75288	AT-AT	150.00	300.00

2020 LEGO Star Wars Episode VI

75291	Death Star Final Duel		

2020 LEGO Star Wars Galaxy's Edge

75293	Resistance I-TS Transport	75.00	150.00

2020 LEGO Star Wars Helmet Collection

75274	TIE Fighter Pilot	40.00	80.00
75276	Stormtrooper	40.00	80.00
75277	Boba Fett	50.00	100.00

2020 LEGO Star Wars Magazine Gift

912055	Snowspeeder	3.00	6.00
912056	TIE Striker	4.00	8.00
912057	R2-D2 and MSE-6	4.00	8.00
912058	Sith Infiltrator	3.00	6.00
912059	Elite Praetorian Guard	4.00	8.00
912060	A-Wing	3.00	5.00
912061	AT-AT	4.00	8.00
912062	Stormtrooper	5.00	10.00
912063	Resistance X-Wing		
912064	TIE Dagger		
912065	Luke Skywalker		
912066	Jedi Interceptor		
912067	TIE Interceptor		

2020 LEGO Star Wars The Mandalorian

75267	Mandalorian Battle Pack	12.50	25.00
75292	The Razor Crest	100.00	200.00
75318	The Child		

2020 LEGO Star Wars Master Builder

75290	Mos Eisley Cantina	400.00	600.00

2020 LEGO Star Wars Microfighters

75263	Resistance Y-Wing Microfighter	6.00	12.00
75264	Kylo Ren's Shuttle Microfighter	6.00	12.00
75265	T-16 Skyhopper vs Bantha Microfighters	12.50	25.00

2020 LEGO Star Wars Promotional

40407	Death Star II Battle	60.00	120.00
75294	Bespin Duel	15.00	30.00
77904	Nebulon-B Frigate		
6346097	Yoda's Lightsaber		
6346098	Yoda's Lightsaber	75.00	150.00

2020 LEGO Star Wars The Rise of Skywalker

30386	Poe Dameron's X-Wing Fighter	6.00	12.00
75266	Sith Troopers Battle Pack	10.00	20.00

75272	Sith TIE Fighter	40.00	80.00
75273	Poe Dameron's X-Wing Fighter	40.00	80.00
75278	D-O	30.00	60.00
75284	Knights of Ren Transport Ship	50.00	100.00

2020 LEGO Star Wars Seasonal

| 75279 | Star Wars Advent Calendar | 25.00 | 50.00 |

2020 LEGO Star Wars Ultimate Collector Series

| 75275 | A-Wing Starfighter | 200.00 | 400.00 |

2021 LEGO Star Wars The Bad Batch

| 75314 | The Bad Batch Attack Shuttle | 60.00 | 120.00 |

2021 LEGO Star Wars The Clone Wars

| 75310 | Duel on Mandalore | 15.00 | 30.00 |
| 75316 | Mandalorian Starfighter | 40.00 | 80.00 |

2021 LEGO Star Wars Episode IV

| 75300 | Imperial TIE Fighter | 30.00 | 75.00 |
| 75301 | Luke Skywalker's X-Wing Fighter | 40.00 | 80.00 |

2021 LEGO Star Wars Episode V

| 75296 | Darth Vader Meditation Chamber | 50.00 | 100.00 |
| 75306 | Imperial Probe Droid | 30.00 | 75.00 |

2021 LEGO Star Wars Episode VI

| 30388 | Imperial Shuttle | 12.50 | 25.00 |
| 75302 | Imperial Shuttle | 50.00 | 100.00 |

2021 LEGO Star Wars The Force Awakens

| 75297 | Resistance X-Wing Starfighter | 20.00 | 40.00 |

2021 LEGO Star Wars Helmet Collection

| 75304 | Darth Vader | 30.00 | 75.00 |
| 75305 | Scout Trooper | 30.00 | 60.00 |

2021 LEGO Star Wars Magazine Gift

912168	The Mandalorian	10.00	20.00
912169	Emperor Palpatine	10.00	20.00
912170	V-Wing	7.50	15.00
912171	TIE Bomber	7.50	15.00
912172	Jedi Starfighter	5.00	10.00
912173	Rey and BB-8	12.50	25.00
912174	Sith Trooper	6.00	12.00
912175	AT-ST Raider	5.00	10.00
912176	Clone Turbo Tank	7.50	15.00

2021 LEGO Star Wars The Mandalorian

| 75299 | Trouble on Tatooine | 25.00 | 50.00 |
| 75311 | Imperial Armoured Marauder | 30.00 | 60.00 |

75312	Boba Fett's Starship	30.00	60.00
75315	Imperial Light Cruiser	100.00	200.00
75319	The Armorer's Mandalorian Forge	30.00	60.00

2021 LEGO Star Wars Microfighters

| 75295 | Millennium Falcon Microfighter | 12.50 | 25.00 |
| 75298 | AT-AT vs. Tauntaun Microfighters | 10.00 | 20.00 |

2021 LEGO Star Wars Miscellaneous

| 75308 | R2-D2 | 100.00 | 200.00 |

2021 LEGO Star Wars Product Collection

| 66674 | Skywalker Adventure Pack | | |

2021 LEGO Star Wars Promotional

| 40451 | Tatooine Homestead | 15.00 | 30.00 |

2021 LEGO Star Wars Seasonal

| 75307 | Star Wars Advent Calendar | 20.00 | 40.00 |

2021 LEGO Star Wars Ultimate Collector Series

| 75309 | Republic Gunship | 300.00 | 600.00 |

1993-97 Micro Machines Star Wars Planet Playsets

65872 Ice Planet Hoth	15.00	40.00
65995 Cloud City (w/Twin-Pod Cloud Car)	8.00	20.00
65858A Planet Tatooine (1994)	10.00	25.00
65858B Planet Tatooine (1996)	8.00	20.00
65859A Planet Dagobah (1994)	10.00	25.00
65859B Planet Dagobah (1996)		
65871A Death Star from A New Hope (1994)	10.00	25.00
65871B Death Star from A New Hope (1996)	5.00	12.00
65873A Planet Endor (w/Imperial AT-ST)(1993)	8.00	20.00
65873B Planet Endor (w/Imperial AT-ST)(1997)	6.00	15.00

1993-98 Micro Machines Star Wars Vehicle 3-Packs

65123 Imperial Landing Craft/Death Star/S-Swoop	8.00	20.00
65124 Outrider Tibanna/Gas Refinery/V-35 Landspeeder	6.00	15.00
65886 Star Wars A New Hope #1	6.00	15.00
65886 Star Wars A New Hope (silver)		
65887 Star Wars Empire Strikes Back (silver)	5.00	12.00
65887 Star Wars Empire Strikes Back #2		
65888 Star Wars Return of the Jedi #3		
65888 Star Wars Return of the Jedi (silver)		
65897 Star Wars A New Hope #4		
65898 Star Wars Empire Strikes Back #5	5.00	12.00
65899 Star Wars Return of the Jedi #6		
66111 TIE Interceptor/Imperial Star Destroyer/Rebel Blockade Runner	5.00	12.00
66112 Landspeeder/Millennium Falcon/Jawa Sandcrawler	8.00	20.00
66113 Darth Vader's TIE Fighter/Y-Wing Starfighter/X-Wing Starfighter	5.00	12.00
66114 Snowspeeder/Imperial AT-AT/Imperial Probot	15.00	40.00
66115 Rebel Transport/TIE Bomber/Imperial AT-ST	6.00	15.00
66116 Escort Frigate/Slave I/Twin-Pod Cloud Car	5.00	12.00
66117 Desert Sail Barge/Mon Calamari Star Cruiser/Speeder Bike and Rebel Pilot		
66118 Speeder Bike and Imperial Pilot/Imperial Shuttle Tydirium/TIE Starfighter		
66119 Super Star Destroyer Executor		
A-Wing Starfighter/B-Wing Starfighter	10.00	25.00
66137 Lars Family Landspeeder/Death Star II/T-16 Skyhopper	8.00	20.00
66138 Bespin Cloud City/Mon Calamari Rebel Cruiser/Escape Pod	6.00	15.00
66139 A-Wing Starfighter/Y-Wing Starfighter/TIE Starfighter	10.00	25.00
66155 2 Red Squad X-Wings/Green Squad X-Wing		

1994 Micro Machines Star Wars Fan Club Pieces

18279 Han Solo and the Millennium Falcon	6.00	15.00
28450 Darth Vader and Imperial Star Destroyer	6.00	15.00

1994-96 Micro Machines Star Wars Gift Sets

64624 Bronze Finish Collector's Gift Set	12.00	30.00
65836 Rebel Force Gift Set	6.00	15.00
65837 Imperial Force Gift Set	5.00	12.00
65847 11-Piece Collector's Gift Set	10.00	25.00
65851 A New Hope	5.00	12.00
65852 Empire Strikes Back		
65853 Return of the Jedi	8.00	20.00
65856 Rebel Force Gift Set 2nd Edition	6.00	15.00
65857 Imperial Force Gift Set 2nd Edition		
67079 Star Wars Trilogy Gift Set	15.00	40.00
68042 Rebel vs. Imperial Forces		

1994-97 Micro Machines Star Wars Collector's Sets

64598 Galaxy Battle Collector's Set 2nd Edition	8.00	20.00
64601 Master Collector's Edition (19 Items)	15.00	40.00
64602 Galaxy Battle Collector's Set	10.00	25.00
66090 Droids	10.00	25.00
68048 Master Collector's Edition (40 Items)	8.00	20.00

1994-99 Micro Machines Star Wars Transforming Action Sets

65694 TIE Fighter Pilot/Academy	10.00	25.00
65695 Royal Guard/Death Star II	15.00	40.00

65811 C-3PO/Cantina	10.00	25.00
65812 Darth Vader/Bespin	10.00	25.00
65813 R2-D2/Jabba's Palace	12.00	30.00
65814 Stormtrooper/Death Star	12.00	30.00
65815 Chewbacca/Endor	10.00	25.00
65816 Boba Fett/Cloud City	15.00	40.00
65817 Luke Skywalker/Hoth	10.00	25.00
66551 Jar Jar Binks/Naboo	6.00	15.00
66552 Battle Droid/Trade Federation Droid Control Ship		
66553 Darth Maul/Theed Generator	30.00	80.00
66554 Gungan Sub/Otoh Gunga		
67094 Star Destroyer/Space Fortress	15.00	40.00
67095 Slave I/Tatooine	10.00	25.00
68063 Yoda/Dagobah	12.00	30.00
68064 Jabba/Mos Eisley Spaceport	15.00	40.00

1995 Micro Machines Star Wars Action Fleet Playsets

67091 Ice Planet Hoth (w/Battle-Damaged Snow Speeder		
Luke Skywalker on Tauntaun	10.00	25.00
Wampa Ice Creature/Rebel Pilot/Princess Leia/2-1B Droid)		
67092 The Death Star (w/Darth Vader's Battle-Damaged TIE Fighter		
Imperial Pilot	10.00	25.00
Imperial Gunner/Darth Vader/Stormtrooper		
Imperial Royal Guard/Emperor Palpatine)		
67093 Yavin Rebel Base (w/Battle-Damaged X-Wing/Wedge Antilles		
R2 Unit	12.00	30.00
Luke Skywalker/Han Solo/Princess Leia/Rebel Sentry)		
68177 Naboo Hangar Final Combat (w/Obi-Wan Kenobi		
Darth Maul/Qui-Gon Jinn)	20.00	50.00

1995 Micro Machines Star Wars Gold Classic

67085 X-Wing Fighter and Slave I	12.00	30.00
67086 Imperial Shuttle		
67088 Millennium Falcon and TIE Fighter	30.00	80.00

1995-03 Micro Machines Star Wars Action Fleet Vehicles

46846 AT-TE		
46848 Solar Sailer		
46849 Millennium Falcon	12.00	30.00
46850 X-Wingfighter		
47045 Luke Skywalker's Snowspeeder		
47224 Imperial AT-AT	8.00	20.00
47287 Republic Gunship		
47305 Slave I	5.00	12.00
47356 TIE Advance X1		
47414 Naboo N-1 Starfighter		
47425 Republic Assault Ship	30.00	80.00
47766 Anakin's Speeder		

47767	Zam Wessel Speeder		
47768	Homing Spider Droid	4.00	10.00
47994	Jedi Starfighter	8.00	20.00
47995	Star Destroyer		
47997	Mon Calamari Cruiser	8.00	20.00
66989	Rancor (w/Gamorrean Guard and Luke Skywalker)	10.00	25.00
66990	Virago (w/Prince Xizor and Guri)	10.00	25.00
66991	X-Wing Starfighter (w/Wedge and R2 Unit)		
66992	Y-Wing Starfighter (red)(w/Gold Leader and R2 Unit)		
66993	A-Wing Starfighter (green)(w/Rebel pilot and Mon Mothma)	8.00	20.00
66994	B-Wing Starfighter (w/Rebel pilot and Admiral Ackbar)	10.00	25.00
66995	TIE Fighter (w/Imperial pilot and Grand Moff Tarkin)		
66996	Bespin Twin-Pod Cloud Car (w/Cloud Car pilot and Lobot)		
66997	Y-Wing Starfighter (blue)(w/Blue Leader and R2 Unit)	10.00	25.00
66998	X-Wing Starfighter (w/Jek Porkins and R2 Unit)		
67014	Jabba's Sail Barge (w/Jabba the Hutt/Saelt Marae and R2-D2)	12.00	30.00
67031	Luke's X-Wing Starfighter (w/Luke and R2-D2)	15.00	40.00
67032	Darth Vader's TIE Fighter (w/Darth Vader and Imperial pilot)		
67033	Imperial AT-AT (w/Imperial drive and snowtrooper)	10.00	25.00
67034	A-Wing Starfighter (w/C-3PO and Rebel pilot)	6.00	15.00
67035	Imperial Shuttle Tydirium (w/Han Solo and Chewbacca)		
67036	Rebel Snowspeeder (w/Luke Skywalker and Rebel gunner)		
67039	Jawa Sandcrawler (w/Jawa and scavenger droid)	8.00	20.00
67040	Y-Wing Starfighter (w/Gold Leader and R2 Unit)	8.00	20.00
67041	Slave I (w/Boba Fett and Han Solo)	12.00	30.00
67058	TIE Interceptor (w/2 Imperial pilots)	8.00	
67059	TIE Bomber (w/Imperial pilot and Imperial Naval pilot)	10.00	25.00
67077	Landspeeder and Imperial AT-ST 2-Pack	10.00	25.00
	(w/Luke Skywalker/Obi-Wan Kenobi/Imperial Driver/Stormtrooper)		
67098	Luke's X-Wing from Dagobah (w/Luke Skywalker and R2-D2)	8.00	20.00
	(1998 Toy Fair Magazine Exclusive)		
67100	Millennium Falcon (w/Han Solo and Chewbacca)		
67101	Rebel Blockade Runner (w/Princess Leia and Rebel trooper)	8.00	20.00
67102	Incom T-16 Skyhopper (w/Luke Skywalker and Biggs Darklighter)	6.00	15.00
67103	Imperial Landing Craft (w/Sandtrooper and Imperial Officer)	15.00	40.00
67105	TIE Defender (w/Imperial pilot and Moff Jerjerrod)	30.00	80.00
67106	E-Wing Starfighter (w/Rebel pilot and R7 Unit)		
68131	Naboo Starfighter (w/Anakin)		
68132	Trade Federation MTT (w/Battle Droid)	25.00	60.00
68133	Sebulba's Pod Racer (w/Sebulba)		
68134	Republic Cruiser (w/Qui-Gon Jinn)	12.00	30.00
68135	Droid Fighter (w/Daultry Dofine)		
68136	Gungan Sub (w/Qui-Gon Jinn)	4.00	10.00
68137	Flash Speeder (w/Naboo Royal Guard)		
68138	Trade Federation Landing Ship (w/Battle Droid)		
68140	Mars Guo's Pod Racer (w/Mars Guo)		
68180	Gian Speeder and Theed Palace		
	(w/Captain Panaka/Naboo Foot Soldier/2 Battle Droids)		
79050	Anakin's Pod Racer (w/Anakin)		
79967	Royal Starship (w/Rick Olie)	25.00	60.00
79968	Droid Control Ship (w/Neimoidian Commander)		
79971	Trade Federation Tank (w/Battle Droid)	12.00	30.00
79972	Sith Infiltrator (w/Darth Maul)	30.00	80.00
1327CM6	Darth Vader's TIE Fighter (w/Darth Vader and Imperial pilot)		

1996 Micro Machines Star Wars Adventure Gear

68031	Vader's Lightsaber (w/Death Star Trench/X-Wing Imperial Gunner/Grand Moff Tarkin/Darth Vader)	8.00	20.00
68032	Luke's Binoculars (w/Yavin Rebel Base/Y-Wing Luke Skywalker/R5 Droid/Wedge Antilles)	8.00	20.00

1996 Micro Machines Star Wars Epic Collections

66281	Heir to the Empire	8.00	20.00
66282	Jedi Search	6.00	15.00
66283	The Truce at Bakura	8.00	20.00

1996 Micro Machines Star Wars Exclusives

66091	Balance of Power (Special Offer)		
68060	Star Wars Trilogy (Special Giveaway)	20.00	50.00

1996 Micro Machines Star Wars Shadows of the Empire

66194	Stinger/IG-2000/Guri/Darth Vader/Asp	5.00	12.00
66195	Virago/Swoop with Rider/Prince Xizor/Emperor Palpatine	6.00	15.00
66196	Outrider/Hound's Tooth/Dash Rendar/LE-B02D9	10.00	25.00

1996 Micro Machines Star Wars X-Ray Fleet

67071	Darth Vader's TIE Fighter/A-Wing Starfighter		
67072	X-Wing Starfighter/Imperial AT-AT		
67073	Millennium Falcon/Jawa Sandcrawler	6.00	15.00
67074	Boba Fett's Slave I/Y-Wing Starfighter		

1996-97 Micro Machines Star Wars Action Sets

65878	Millennium Falcon (w/Y-Wing/Mynock/Han Solo/Chewbacca Lando Calrissian/Nien Nunb/Leia	20.00	50.00
65996	Rebel Transport (w/X-Wing/Rebel mechanic/General Rieekan/Major Derlin)		

1996-98 Micro Machines Star Wars Character Sets

66081	Imperial Stormtroopers	10.00	25.00
66082	Ewoks	10.00	25.00
66083	Rebel Pilots	6.00	15.00
66084	Imperial Pilots	6.00	15.00
66096	Jawas	5.00	12.00
66097	Imperial Officers	6.00	15.00
66098	Echo Base Troops	5.00	12.00
66099	Imperial Naval Troops	8.00	20.00
66108	Rebel Fleet Troops	8.00	20.00
66109	Tusken Raiders	6.00	15.00
66158	Classic Characters	8.00	20.00
67112	Endor Rebel Strike Force	10.00	25.00
67113	Imperial Scout Troopers	5.00	12.00
67114	Bounty Hunters	10.00	25.00

1996-98 Micro Machines Star Wars Mini Heads

68021	Boba Fett/Admiral Ackbar/Gamorrean Guard	5.00	12.00
68022	Greedo/Nien Nunb/Tusken Raider	5.00	12.00
68023	Jawa/Yoda/Leia	5.00	12.00
68024	Bib Fortuna/Figrin D'an/Scout Trooper	4.00	10.00
68038	Darth Vader Set	5.00	10.00
68046	C-3PO Set		
NNO	Pizza Hut Set		

1996-99 Micro Machines Star Wars Battle Packs

68011	Rebel Alliance	6.00	15.00
68012	Galactic Empire	6.00	15.00
68013	Aliens and Creatures	6.00	15.00
68014	Galactic Hunters	6.00	15.00
68015	Shadow of the Empire	6.00	15.00
68016	Dune Sea	6.00	15.00
68017	Droid Escape	6.00	15.00
68018	Desert Palace	6.00	15.00
68035	Endor Adventure	8.00	20.00
68036	Mos Eisley Spaceport	12.00	30.00
68037	Cantina Encounter	6.00	15.00
68090	Cantina Smugglers and Spies	8.00	20.00
68091	Hoth Attack	10.00	25.00
68092	Death Star Escape	6.00	15.00
68093	Endor Victory	12.00	30.00
68094	Lars Family Homestead	8.00	20.00
68095	Imperial Troops	15.00	40.00
68096	Rebel Troops	10.00	25.00

1996-99 Micro Machines Star Wars Die-Cast Vehicles

66267	Death Star	10.00	25.00
66268	A-Wing Starfighter		
66269	Snowspeeder		
66270	TIE Bomber	8.00	20.00
66271	Landspeeder		
66272	Executor (w/Star Destroyer)	6.00	15.00
66273	Slave I		
66520	Royal Starship	5.00	12.00
66523	Gian Speeder		
66524	Trade Federation Battleship	6.00	15.00
66525	Sith Infiltrator	4.00	10.00
66526	Republic Cruiser		
66527	Trade Federation Tank	6.00	15.00
66528	Sebulba's Pod Racer		
79021	Trade Federation Droid Starfighter		
66261A	X-Wing Starfighter (bubble)		
66261B	X-Wing Starfighter (stripe)		
66262A	Millennium Falcon (bubble)	5.00	12.00
66262B	Millennium Falcon (stripe)	8.00	20.00
66263A	Imperial Star Destroyer (bubble)	4.00	10.00
66263B	Imperial Star Destroyer (stripe)	4.00	10.00

66264A	TIE Fighter (bubble)		
66264B	TIE Fighter (stripe)		
66265A	Y-Wing Starfighter (bubble)		
66265B	Y-Wing Starfighter (stripe)		
66266A	Jawa Sandcrawler (bubble)	6.00	15.00
66266B	Jawa Sandcrawler (stripe)	4.00	10.00

1996-99 Micro Machines Star Wars Electronic Action Fleet Vehicles

73419	AT-AT (w/Snowtrooper and Imperial Driver)	15.00	40.00
79072	FAMBAA		
79073	Trade Federation Tank		

1996-99 Micro Machines Star Wars Series Alpha

73421	X-Wing Starfighter	8.00	20.00
73422	Imperial Shuttle	10.00	25.00
73423	Rebel Snowspeeder	6.00	15.00
73424	Imperial AT-AT	8.00	20.00
73430	Twin-Pod Cloud Car		
73431	Y-Wing Starfighter		
73432	B-Wing Starfighter		
97033	Naboo Fighter		
97034	Droid Fighter		
97035	Sith Infiltrator	25.00	60.00
97036	Royal Starship		

1997 Micro Machines Star Wars Classic Duels

68301	TIE Fighter vs. X-Wing Starfighter	
68302	TIE Interceptor vs. Millennium Falcon	

1997 Micro Machines Star Wars Double Takes

75118	Death Star (w/Millennium Falcon/Obi-Wan Kenobi/Owen Lars	30.00	80.00
	Ronto and Jawas/Beru Lars/2 Scurriers		

1997-98 Micro Machines Star Wars Flight Controllers

73417	Luke Skywalker's X-Wing Starfighter		
73418	Darth Vader's TIE Fighter	10.00	25.00
73440	Y-Wing Starfighter	8.00	20.00
73441	TIE Interceptor	8.00	20.00

1998-99 Micro Machines Star Wars Action Fleet Mini Scenes

68121	STAP Invasion (w/STAP/Jar Jar Binks/Battle Droid)	5.00	12.00
68122	Destroyer Droid Ambush		

	(w/Destroyer Droid/Obi-Wan Kenobi/TC-14)	4.00	10.00
68123	Gungan Assault (w/Gungan/Kaadu/Battle Droid)	4.00	10.00
68124	Sith Pursuit (w/Sith speeder/Darth Maul/Qui-Gon Jinn)		
79025	Trade Federation Raid		
	(w/Trade Federation MTT/Ikopi/Jar Jar Binks/Qui-Gon Jinn)	5.00	12.00
79026	Throne Room Reception		
	(w/Throne Room/Sio Bibble/Nute Gunray)	6.00	15.00
79027	Watto's Deal (w/Watto's Shop/Anakin/Pit droid)		
79028	Generator Core Duel		
	(w/generator core/Darth Maul/Obi-Wan Kenobi)	8.00	20.00

1998-99 Micro Machines Star Wars Platform Action Sets

66541	Pod Race Arena	8.00	20.00
66542	Naboo Temple Ruins	6.00	15.00
66543	Galactic Senate	6.00	15.00
66544	Galactic Dogfight	10.00	25.00
66545	Theed Palace		
66546	Tatooine Desert		

1999 Micro Machines Star Wars Deluxe Platform Action Sets

66561	Royal Starship Repair	30.00	80.00
66562	Theed Palace Assault	100.00	200.00

1999 Micro Machines Star Wars Deluxe Action Sets

68156	Pod Racer Hangar Bay (w/pit droid and pit mechanic)		
68157	Mos Espa Market (w/Anakin Skywalker and C-3PO)	8.00	20.00
68158	Otoh Gunga (w/Obi-Wan Kenobi and Jar Jar Binks)		
68159	Theed Palace		

1999 Micro Machines Star Wars Mega Platform Set

66566	Trade Federation MTT/Naboo Battlefield	25.00	60.00

1999 Micro Machines Star Wars Pod Racer

66531	Pack 1 (w/Anakin and Ratts Tyerl)	5.00	12.00
66532	Pack 2 (w/Sebulba and Clegg Holdfast)	5.00	12.00
66533	Pack 3 (w/Dud Bolt and Mars Guo)	5.00	12.00
66534	Pack 4 (w/Boles Roor and Neva Kee)	5.00	12.00
66548A	Build Your Own Pod Racer Green (Galoob)	5.00	12.00

66548B	Build Your Own Pod Racer Yellow (Galoob)	5.00	12.00
97023A	Build Your Own Pod Racer Black (Hasbro)	5.00	12.00
97023B	Build Your Own Pod Racer Blue (Hasbro)	5.00	12.00

1999 Micro Machines Star Wars Pod Racing Gravity Track

66566	Beggar's Canyon Challenge		
66570	Boonta Eve Challenge	15.00	40.00
66577	Arch Canyon Adventure		

1999 Micro Machines Star Wars Turbo Pod Racers

68148	Gasgano	
68149	Ody Mandrell	

2002 Micro Machines Star Wars Action Fleet Movie Scenes

32549	Dune Sea Ambush (w/Tusken Raider		
	Bantha/Luke's Landspeeder)	5.00	12.00
32553	Tatooine Droid Hunter (w/Dewback		
	Sandtrooper/Escape Pod)	6.00	15.00
32554	Imperial Endor Pursuit (w/Luke Skywalker		
	Scout Trooper/2 speeder bikes/AT-ST)	6.00	15.00
32557	Mos Eisley Encounter (w/Ranto/Jawa/Black Landspeeder)	5.00	12.00

2005-09 Star Wars Titanium Series 3-Inch Die-Cast

1	A-Wing Fighter
2	A-Wing Fighter (blue)
3	A-Wing Fighter (green)
4	Aayla Secura's Jedi Starfighter
5	Amidala's Star Skiff
6	Anakin Skywalker's Pod Racer
7	Anakin's Jedi Starfighter (Coruscant)
8	Anakin's Jedi Starfighter (Mustafar)
9	Anakin's Jedi Starfighter with Hyperspace Ring
10	Anakin Skywalker's Jedi Starfighter (The Clone Wars)
11	Anakin's Modified Jedi Starfighter (Clone Wars)
12	ARC-170 Fighter
13	ARC-170 Fighter (green)
14	ARC-170 Fighter (Clone Wars deco)
15	ARC-170 Starfighter (The Clone Wars)
16	ARC-170 Fighter (Flaming Wampa)
17	ARC-170 Starfighter (Lucky Lekku)
18	AT-AP
19	AT-AP (The Clone Wars)
20	AT-AT Walker
21	AT-AT Walker (Endor)
22	AT-AT Walker (Shadow)
23	AT-OT
24	AT-OT (The Clone Wars)
25	AT-RT
26	AT-RT (Kashyyyk)
27	AT-RT (Utapau)
28	AT-ST
29	AT-ST (Hoth deco)
30	AT-ST (dirty)
31	AT-TE
32	AT-TE (The Clone Wars)
33	Jedi Starfighter with Hyperdrive Ring (green/black)
34	Jedi Starfighter with Hyperdrive Ring (green/blue)

35 B-Wing Starfighter
36 B-Wing Starfighter (orange)
37 B-Wing Starfighter (Dagger Squadron)
38 BARC Speeder
39 Clone Turbo Tank
40 Clone Turbo Tank (Snow deco)
41 Cloud Car
42 Darth Maul's Sith Speeder
43 Darth Vader's Sith Starfighter
44 Darth Vader's TIE Advanced x1 Starfighter
45 Darth Vader's TIE Advanced x1 Starfighter (white)
46 Death Star
47 Dewback with Stormtrooper
48 Droid Gunship
49 Droid Tri-Fighter
50 Droid Tri-Fighter (Battle Damage)
51 Executor
52 Firespray Interceptor
53 General Grievous' Starfighter
54 Hailfire Droid
55 Hound's Tooth
56 Hyena Droid Bomber
57 IG-2000
58 Imperial Attack Cruiser
59 Imperial Landing Craft
60 Imperial Shuttle
61 Imperial Shuttle (Emperor's Hand)
62 Invisible Hand
63 Jabba's Desert Skiff
64 Jabba's Sail Barge
65 Jedi Starfighter (Hot Rod)
66 Kit Fisto's Jedi Starfighter
67 Landspeeder
68 Mace Windu's Jedi Starfighter
69 Mace Windu's Jedi Starfighter (repaint)
70 Mace Windu's Jedi Starfighter with Hyperdrive Ring
71 Malevolence
72 Millennium Falcon
73 Millennium Falcon (Battle Ravaged)
74 Millennium Falcon (Episode III)
75 Mist Hunter
76 Mon Calamari Star Cruiser
77 Naboo Fighter
78 Naboo Patrol Fighter
79 Naboo Royal Cruiser
80 Naboo Royal Starship
81 Nebulon-B Escort Frigate
82 Neimoidian Shuttle
83 Obi-Wan's Jedi Starfighter (Coruscant)
84 Obi-Wan's Jedi Starfighter (Utapau)
85 Obi-Wan's Jedi Starfighter with Hyperspace Ring
86 Obi-Wan's Jedi Starfighter (The Clone Wars)
87 Outrider
88 P-38 Starfighter / Magnaguard Starfighter
89 Plo Koon's Jedi Starfighter with Hyperspace Ring
90 Punishing One
91 Rebel Blockade Runner
92 Rebel Transport
93 Republic Attack Cruiser
94 Republic Attack Cruiser (The Clone Wars)
95 Republic Attack Shuttle
96 Republic Cruiser
97 Republic Fighter Tank
98 Republic Gunship
99 Republic Gunship – Clone Wars (Titanium Limited)

100 Republic Gunship (Closed Doors)
101 Republic Gunship (Command Gunship deco)
102 Republic Gunship (The Clone Wars)
103 Republic Gunship (Lucky Lekku)
104 Republic V-Wing Fighter
105 Rogue Shadow
106 Saesee Tiin's Jedi Starfighter with Hyperspace Ring
107 Sandcrawler
108 Sandspeeder
109 Sebulba's Pod Racer
110 Shadow Scout on Speeder Bike
111 Shadow Trooper Gunship
112 Sith Infiltrator
113 Slave 1 - Boba Fett
114 Slave 1 – Jango Fett
115 Slave 1 – Jango Fett (Battle Damage)
116 Slave 1 - Silver (Titanium Limited)
117 Snowspeeder
118 Snowspeeder (Luke's)
119 Snowspeeder (Vintage deco)
120 Speeder Bike - Blizzard Force
121 Speeder Bike - Kashyyyk
122 Speeder Bike - Leia
123 Speeder Bike - Luke Skywalker
124 Speeder Bike - Paploo
125 Speeder Bike - Scout Trooper
126 Star Destroyer
127 Star Destroyer (repaint)
128 Swamp Speeder
129 Swamp Speeder (Dirty deco)
130 T-16 Skyhopper
131 TIE Bomber
132 TIE Bomber (Battle Damage)
133 TIE Defender
134 TIE Fighter
135 TIE Fighter (Battle Damage)
136 TIE Fighter – White (Titanium Limited)
137 TIE Fighter (Ecliptic Evader)
138 TIE Interceptor
139 TIE Interceptor (Royal Guard)
140 TIE Interceptor (Baron Fel)
141 Tantive IV
142 Trade Federation AAT
143 Trade Federation AAT (Clone Wars deco)
144 Trade Federation AAT (The Clone Wars)
145 Trade Federation Battleship
146 Trade Federation Landing Craft
147 Trade Federation MTT
148 The Twilight
149 V-19 Torrent Starfighter
150 V-Wing Starfighter
151 V-Wing Starfighter (Imperial)
152 Virago
153 Vulture Droid
154 Vulture Droid (The Clone Wars)
155 Wookiee Flyer
156 X-Wing Fighter
157 X-Wing Starfighter (Biggs Darklighter's Red 3)
158 X-Wing Fighter (Dagobah)
159 X-Wing Starfighter (John Branon's Red 4)
160 X-Wing Fighter (Luke Skywalker's Red 5)
161 X-Wing Starfighter (Red Leader's Red 1)
162 X-Wing Fighter (Wedge Antilles)
163 X-Wing Starfighter (Wedge Antilles' Red 2)

164 Xanadu Blood
165 XP-34 Landspeeder
166 Y-Wing Bomber
167 Y-Wing Bomber (Anakin's)
168 Y-Wing Fighter
169 Y-Wing Fighter (Davish Krail's Gold 5)
170 Y-Wing Fighter (Gold Leader)
171 Y-Wing Starfighter (green deco)
172 Y-Wing Fighter (Red deco)
173 Z-95 Headhunter

2015 Micro Machines Star Wars The Force Awakens Playsets

1 First Order Stormtrooper (w/Poe Dameron and transport)	6.00	15.00
2 Millennium Falcon (w/smaller Millennium Falcon and stormtrooper)	8.00	20.00
3 R2-D2 (w/Chewbacca/2 snowtroopers and transport)	5.00	12.00
4 Star Destroyer (w/Kylo Ren/Finn/X-Wing/TIE Fighter)	12.00	30.00

2015 Micro Machines Star Wars The Force Awakens Vehicles

1 Battle of Hoth (ESB)	5.00	12.00
2 Clone Army Raid (AOTC)	4.00	10.00
3 Desert Invasion	4.00	10.00
4 Droid Army (ROTS)	5.00	12.00
5 Endor Forest Battle (ROTJ)	6.00	15.00
6 First Order Attacks	4.00	10.00
7 First Order TIE Fighter Attack	4.00	10.00
8 Galactic Showdown	5.00	12.00
9 Imperial Pursuit (ANH)	4.00	10.00
10 Inquisitor's Hunt (Rebels)	4.00	10.00
11 Speeder Chase	5.00	12.00
12 Trench Run (ANH)	6.00	15.00

Marvel STAR WARS (1977-1986)

1 July 1977 / "Star Wars: A New Hope" adaptation Part 1	75.00	200.00
1 July 1977 / Star Wars 35-cent price variant	3,000.00	6,000.00
2 August 1977 / "Star Wars: A New Hope" adaptation Part 2	25.00	60.00
2 August 1977 / Star Wars 35-cent price variant	1,000.00	3,000.00
3 September 1977 / "Star Wars: A New Hope" adaptation Part 3	15.00	40.00
3 September 1977 / Star Wars 35-cent price variant	500.00	1,000.00
4 October 1977 / "Star Wars: A New Hope" adaptation Part 4	15.00	40.00
4 October 1977 / Star Wars 35-cent price variant	500.00	1,000.00
5 November 1977 / "Star Wars: A New Hope" adaptation Part 5	15.00	40.00
6 December 1977 / "Star Wars: A New Hope" adaptation Part 6	15.00	40.00
7 January 1978	8.00	20.00
8 February 1978	10.00	25.00
9 March 1978	8.00	20.00
10 April 1978	8.00	20.00
11 May 1978	8.00	20.00
12 June 1978 / 1st appearance of Governor Quarg	8.00	20.00
13 July 1978 / John Byrne & Terry Austin cover	10.00	25.00
14 August 1978	8.00	20.00
15 September 1978	8.00	20.00
16 October 1978 / 1st appearance of Valance	8.00	20.00
17 November 1978	6.00	15.00
18 December 1978	6.00	15.00
19 January 1979	6.00	15.00
20 February 1979	6.00	15.00
21 March 1979	6.00	15.00
22 April 1979	6.00	15.00
23 May 1979 / Darth Vader appearance	6.00	15.00
24 June 1979	6.00	15.00
25 July 1979	6.00	15.00
26 August 1979	6.00	15.00
27 September 1979	6.00	15.00
28 October 1979	6.00	15.00
29 November 1979 / 1st appearance of Tyler Lucian	6.00	15.00
30 December 1979	5.00	12.00
31 January 1980	5.00	12.00
32 February 1980	5.00	12.00
33 March 1980	5.00	12.00
34 April 1980	5.00	12.00
35 May 1980 / Darth Vader cover	6.00	15.00
36 June 1980	5.00	12.00
37 July 1980	5.00	12.00
38 August 1980	5.00	12.00
39 September 1980 / "The Empire Strikes Back" adaptation - Part 1	8.00	20.00
40 October 1980 / "The Empire Strikes Back" adaptation - Part 2	8.00	20.00
41 November 1980 / "The Empire Strikes Back" adaptation - Part 3	8.00	20.00
42 December 1980 / "The Empire Strikes Back" adaptation - Part 4, "Bounty Hunters" cover w/Boba Fett	100.00	250.00
43 January 1981 / "The Empire Strikes Back" adaptation - Part 5	12.00	30.00
44 February 1981 / "The Empire Strikes Back" adaptation - Part 6	8.00	20.00
45 March 1981	5.00	12.00
46 April 1981	5.00	12.00
47 May 1981 / 1st appearance Captain Kligson	5.00	12.00
48 June 1981 / Princess Leia vs. Darth Vader	8.00	20.00
49 July 1981 / "The Last Jedi" story title on cover	6.00	15.00
50 August 1981 / Giant-Size issue	6.00	15.00
51 September 1981	5.00	12.00
52 October 1981 / Darth Vader cover	6.00	15.00
53 November 1981	5.00	12.00
54 December 1981	5.00	12.00
55 January 1982 / 1st appearance Plif	5.00	12.00
56 February 1982	5.00	12.00
57 March 1982	5.00	12.00
58 April 1982	5.00	12.00
59 May 1982	5.00	12.00
60 June 1982	5.00	12.00
61 July 1982	5.00	12.00
62 August 1982	5.00	12.00
63 September 1982	5.00	12.00
64 October 1982	5.00	12.00
65 November 1982	5.00	12.00
66 December 1982	5.00	12.00
67 January 1983	5.00	12.00
68 February 1983 / Boba Fett cover	60.00	150.00
69 March 1983	5.00	12.00
70 April 1983	5.00	12.00
71 May 1983	5.00	12.00
72 June 1983	5.00	12.00
73 July 1983	5.00	12.00
74 August 1983	5.00	12.00
75 September 1983	5.00	12.00
76 October 1983	5.00	12.00
77 November 1983	5.00	12.00
78 December 1983	5.00	12.00
79 January 1984	5.00	12.00
80 February 1984	5.00	12.00
81 March 1984 / Boba Fett appearance	40.00	100.00
82 April 1984	5.00	12.00
83 May 1984	5.00	12.00
84 June 1984	5.00	12.00
85 July 1984	5.00	12.00
86 August 1984	5.00	12.00
87 September 1984	5.00	12.00
88 October 1984 / 1st appearance of Lumiya	6.00	15.00
89 November 1984	5.00	12.00
90 December 1984	5.00	12.00
91 January 1985	6.00	15.00
92 February 1985 / Giant-Size issue	8.00	20.00
93 March 1985	6.00	15.00
94 April 1985	6.00	15.00
95 May 1985	6.00	15.00
96 June 1985	6.00	15.00
97 July 1985	6.00	15.00
98 August 1985	6.00	15.00
99 September 1985	6.00	15.00
100 October 1985 / Giant-Size issue	10.00	25.00
101 November 1985	8.00	20.00
102 December 1985	8.00	20.00
103 January 1986	8.00	20.00
104 March 1986	8.00	20.00
105 May 1986	8.00	20.00
106 July 1986	10.00	25.00
107 September 1986 / Final issue	30.00	80.00

Marvel STAR WARS Annual

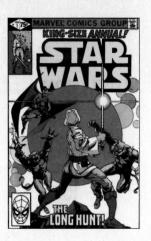

1	Star Wars Annual 1979	6.00	15.00
2	Star Wars Annual 1982	6.00	15.00
3	Star Wars Annual 1983	6.00	15.00

STAR WARS: RETURN OF THE JEDI MINI-SERIES (1983-1984)

1	October 1983 / "Return of the Jedi" adaptation Part 1	4.00	10.00
2	November 1983 / "Return of the Jedi" adaptation Part 2	3.00	8.00
3	December 1983 / "Return of the Jedi" adaptation Part 3	3.00	8.00
4	January 1984 / "Return of the Jedi" adaptation Part 4	3.00	8.00

JOURNEY TO STAR WARS: THE FORCE AWAKENS - SHATTERED EMPIRE (2015)

1	November 2015	1.50	4.00
1	November 2015 / Blank Cover Variant	3.00	8.00
1	November 2015 / 1:20 Hyperspace Variant	3.00	8.00
1	November 2015 / 1:25 Movie Photo Variant	3.00	8.00
1	November 2015 / 1:25 Marco Checchetto Variant	5.00	12.00
2	December 2015	1.50	4.00
2	December 2015 / 1:25 Movie Photo Variant	4.00	10.00
2	December 2015 / 1:25 Kris Anka Variant	4.00	10.00
3	December 2015	1.50	4.00
3	December 2015 / 1:25 Movie Photo Variant	4.00	10.00
3	December 2015 / 1:25 Mike Deodato Jr. Variant	4.00	10.00
4	December 2015	1.50	4.00
4	December 2015 / 1:25 Movie Photo Variant	4.00	10.00
4	December 2015 / 1:25 Sara Pichelli Variant	4.00	10.00

Marvel STAR WARS (2015-)

1	March 2015	3.00	8.00
1	March 2015 / Blank Cover Variant	12.00	30.00
1	March 2015 / Skottie Young "Baby" Variant	3.00	8.00
1	March 2015 / Luke Skywalker Action Figure Variant	10.00	25.00
1	March 2015 / 1:15 Movie Photo Variant	4.00	10.00
1	March 2015 / 1:20 Sara Pichelli Variant	4.00	10.00
1	March 2015 / 1:25 "Two Suns" Variant	3.00	8.00
1	March 2015 / 1:25 Bob McLeod Variant	4.00	10.00
1	March 2015 / 1:50 Alex Ross Variant	20.00	50.00
1	March 2015 / 1:50 J. Scott Campbell Variant	15.00	40.00
1	March 2015 / 1:100 Joe Quesada Variant	15.00	40.00
1	March 2015 / 1:200 Alex Ross Sketch Variant	30.00	80.00
1	March 2015 / 1:500 Joe Quesada Sketch Variant	75.00	200.00
1	April 2015 / 2nd printing	4.00	10.00
1	April 2015 / 3rd printing	4.00	10.00
1	June 2015 / 4th printing	4.00	10.00
1	July 2015 / 5th printing	4.00	10.00
1	September 2015 / 6th printing (double cover)	6.00	15.00
1	7th printing	4.00	10.00
2	April 2015	4.00	10.00
2	April 2015 / Han Solo Action Figure Variant	15.00	40.00
2	April 2015 / Sergio Aragones Variant	3.00	8.00
2	April 2015 / 1:25 Leinil Francis Yu Variant	6.00	15.00
2	April 2015 / 1:25 Howard Chaykin Variant	6.00	15.00
2	April 2015 / 1:100 John Cassaday Sketch Variant	20.00	50.00
2	May 2015 / 2nd printing	4.00	10.00
2	June 2015 / 3rd printing	3.00	8.00
2	July 2015 / 4th printing	3.00	8.00
2	August 2015 / 5th printing	3.00	8.00
2	6th printing	3.00	8.00
3	May 2015	2.50	6.00
3	May 2015 / Obi-Wan Kenobi Action Figure Variant	2.50	6.00
3	May 2015 / 1:25 Leinil Francis Yu Variant	6.00	15.00
3	May 2015 / 1:100 John Cassaday Sketch Variant	15.00	40.00
3	July 2015 / 2nd printing	2.00	5.00
3	July 2015 / 3rd printing	2.00	5.00
3	4th printing	2.00	5.00

4	June 2015	2.50	6.00
4	June 2015 / Chewbacca Action Figure Variant	2.50	6.00
4	June 2015 / 1:25 Giuseppe Camuncoli Variant	5.00	12.00
4	June 2015 / 1:100 John Cassaday Sketch Variant	25.00	60.00
4	2nd printing	2.00	5.00
5	July 2015	2.00	5.00
5	July 2015 / C-3PO Action Figure Variant	2.50	6.00
5	July 2015 / 1:100 John Cassaday Sketch Variant	15.00	40.00
5	2nd printing	2.00	5.00
6	August 2015	2.00	5.00
6	August 2015 / R2-D2 Action Figure Variant	3.00	8.00
6	2nd printing	2.00	5.00
6	3rd printing	2.00	5.00
7	September 2015	2.00	5.00
7	September 2015 / Stormtrooper Action Figure Variant	2.50	6.00
7	September 2015 / 1:25 Simone Bianchi Variant Cover	3.00	8.00
7	September 2015 / 1:25 Tony Moore Variant Cover	3.00	8.00
7	September 2015 / 1:100 John Cassaday Sketch Variant	15.00	40.00
8	October 2015	2.00	5.00
8	October 2015 / Tusken Raider Action Figure Variant	2.50	6.00
8	October 2015 / 1:50 John Cassaday Variant	6.00	15.00
8	October 2015 / 1:100 Stuart Immonen Sketch Variant	15.00	40.00
9	November 2015	2.00	5.00
9	November 2015 / Star Destroyer Commander Action Figure Variant	2.50	6.00
9	November 2015 / 1:100 Stuart Immonen Sketch Variant	15.00	40.00
10	December 2015	2.00	5.00
10	December 2015 / Jawa Action Figure Variant	2.50	6.00
10	December 2015 / 1:100 Stuart Immonen Sketch Variant	25.00	60.00
11	January 2016	2.00	5.00
11	January 2016 / Luke Skywalker: X-Wing Pilot Action Figure Variant	2.50	6.00
11	January 2016 / 1:100 Stuart Immonen Sketch Variant	15.00	40.00
12	January 2016	2.00	5.00
12	January 2016 / Greedo Action Figure Variant	2.50	6.00
12	January 2016 / 1:100 Stuart Immonen Sketch Variant	15.00	40.00
13	February 2016	2.00	5.00
13	February 2016 / R5-D4 Action Figure Variant	2.50	6.00
13	February 2016 / Clay Mann Variant	2.50	6.00
13	March 2016 / 2nd printing	2.00	5.00
14	March 2016	2.00	5.00
14	March 2016 / Hammerhead Action Figure Variant	2.50	6.00
14	March 2016 / Clay Mann Variant	2.50	6.00
14	April 2016 / 2nd printing	2.00	5.00
15	March 2016	2.00	5.00
15	March 2016 / Snaggletooth Action Figure Variant	2.50	6.00
15	March 2016 / 1:100 Mike Mayhew Sketch Variant	15.00	40.00
15	May 2016 / 2nd printing	2.00	5.00
16	April 2016	2.00	5.00
16	April 2016 / Death Star Droid Action Figure Variant	2.50	6.00
16	April 2016 / 1:25 Stuart Immonen Variant	4.00	10.00
16	April 2016 / 1:25 Leinil Francis Yu Variant	4.00	10.00

il 2016 / 1:100 Terry Dodson Sketch Variant	15.00	40.00
ay 2016	2.00	5.00
17 May 2016 / Walrus Man Action Figure Variant	2.50	6.00
17 May 2016 / 1:25 Leinil Francis Yu Variant	4.00	10.00
17 May 2016 / 1:100 Terry Dodson Sketch Variant	15.00	40.00
18 June 2016	2.00	5.00
18 June 2016 / Power Droid Action Figure Variant	2.50	6.00
18 June 2016 / 1:100 Leinil Francis Yu Sketch Variant	20.00	50.00
19 July 2016	2.00	5.00
19 July 2016 / Leia Organa: Bespin Gown Action Figure Variant	3.00	8.00
19 July 2016 / 1:100 Leinil Francis Yu Sketch Variant	15.00	40.00
20 August 2016	2.00	5.00
20 August 2016 / Yoda Action Figure Variant	4.00	10.00
20 August 2016 / 1:100 Mike Mayhew Sketch Variant	15.00	40.00
21 September 2016	2.00	5.00
21 September 2016 / Stormtrooper: Hoth Battle Gear Action Figure Variant	3.00	8.00
21 September 2016 / 1:100 David Aja Sketch Variant	60.00	150.00
22 October 2016	2.00	5.00
22 October 2016 / Dengar Action Figure Variant	2.50	6.00
22 October 2016 / 1:100 Mike Deodato Sketch Variant	20.00	50.00
23 November 2016	2.00	5.00
23 November 2016 / Rebel Soldier: Hoth Battle Gear Action Figure Variant	2.50	6.00
23 November 2016 / 1:25 Jorge Molina Variant	5.00	12.00
23 November 2016 / 1:100 Mike Deodato Sketch Variant	20.00	50.00
24 December 2016'	2.00	5.00
24 December 2016 / Lobot Action Figure Variant	2.50	6.00
24 December 2016 / 1:100 Mike Deodato Sketch Variant	20.00	50.00
25 January 2017	2.00	5.00
25 January 2017 / IG-88 Action Figure Variant	2.50	6.00
25 January 2017 / 1:100 Mike Deodato Sketch Variant	20.00	50.00
26 February 2017'	2.00	5.00
26 February 2017 / 2-1B Action Figure Variant	2.50	6.00
26 February 2017 / Qui-Gon Jinn Action Figure Variant	20.00	50.00
26 February 2017' / 1:100 Mike Deodato Sketch Variant	20.00	50.00
27 March 2017'	2.00	5.00
27 March 2017 / R2-D2 with Sensorscope Action Figure Variant	2.50	6.00
27 March 2017 / Star Wars 40th Anniversary Variant	4.00	10.00
28 April 2017'	2.00	5.00
28 April 2017 / C-3PO Removable Limbs Action Figure Variant	2.50	6.00
28 April 2017 / Star Wars 40th Anniversary Variant	4.00	10.00
29 May 2017'	2.00	5.00
29 May 2017 / Luke Skywalker: Hoth Battle Gear Action Figure Variant	2.50	6.00
29 May 2017 / Star Wars 40th Anniversary Variant	3.00	8.00
30 June 2017'	2.00	5.00
30 June 2017 / AT-AT Commander Action Figure Variant	2.50	6.00
30 June 2017 / Star Wars 40th Anniversary Variant	3.00	8.00
31 July 2017'	2.00	5.00
31 July 2017 / Luke Skywalker: Bespin Fatigues Action Figure Variant	2.50	6.00
31 July 2017 / Star Wars 40th Anniversary Variant	3.00	8.00
32 August 2017'	2.00	5.00
32 August 2017 / FX-7 Medical Droid Action Figure Variant	2.50	6.00
32 August 2017 / Star Wars 40th Anniversary Variant	3.00	8.00
33 September 2017'	2.00	5.00
33 September 2017 / Bespin Security Guard Action Figure Variant	2.50	6.00
33 September 2017 / Star Wars 40th Anniversary Variant	3.00	8.00
34 October 2017'	2.00	5.00
34 October 2017 / Han Solo: Hoth Outfit Action Figure Variant	2.50	6.00
34 October 2017 / Star Wars 40th Anniversary Variant	3.00	8.00
35 October 2017'	2.00	5.00
35 October 2017 / Ugnaught Action Figure Variant	2.50	6.00
35 October 2017 / Star Wars 40th Anniversary Variant	3.00	8.00
36 November 2017'	2.00	5.00
36 November 2017 / Leia Organa: Hoth Outfit Action Figure Variant	3.00	8.00
36 November 2017 / Star Wars 40th Anniversary Variant	3.00	8.00
37 December 2017'	2.00	5.00
37 December 2017 / Rebel Commander Action Figure Variant	2.50	6.00
37 December 2017 / Star Wars 40th Anniversary Variant	3.00	8.00
38 January 2018'	2.00	5.00
38 January 2018 / Michael Walsh Variant	2.00	5.00
38 January 2018 / AT-AT Driver Action Figure Variant	3.00	8.00
38 January 2018 / 1:25 Pepe Larraz Variant	5.00	12.00
38 January 2018 / 1:50 Terry Dodson Variant	12.00	30.00
38 January 2018 / Star Wars 40th Anniversary Variant	3.00	8.00
39 January 2018'	2.00	5.00
39 January 2018 / Imperial Commander Action Figure Variant	3.00	8.00
40 February 2018'	2.00	5.00
40 February 2018 / Star Wars 40th Anniversary Variant	3.00	8.00
40 February 2018 / Luke Skywalker: Yavin Fatigues Action Figure Variant	20.00	50.00
41 March 2018'	2.00	5.00
41 March 2018 / Zuckuss Action Figure Variant	3.00	8.00
41 March 2018 / Rey Galactic Icons Variant	6.00	15.00
42 March 2018'	2.00	5.00
42 March 2018 / 4-LOM Action Figure Variant	3.00	8.00
43 April 2018'	2.00	5.00
43 April 2018 / Imperial TIE Fighter Pilot Action Figure Variant	3.00	8.00
43 April 2018 / Poe Dameron Galactic Icons Variant	2.50	6.00
44 May 2018'	2.00	5.00
44 May 2018 / (Twin Pod) Cloud Car Pilot Action Figure Variant	3.00	8.00
44 May 2018 / Captain Phasma Galactic Icons Variant	2.50	6.00
45 May 2018'	2.00	5.00
45 May 2018 / Bib Fortune Action Figure Variant	3.00	8.00
46 June 2018'	2.00	5.00
46 June 2018 / Ree-Yees Action Figure Variant	3.00	8.00
46 June 2018 / Han Solo Galactic Icons Variant	2.50	6.00
47 July 2018'	2.00	5.00
47 July 2018 / Weequay Action Figure Variant	3.00	8.00
47 July 2018 / Qi'ra Galactic Icons Variant	2.50	6.00
48 July 2018'	2.00	5.00
48 July 2018 / Bespin Security Guard Action Figure Variant	3.00	8.00
49 August 2018'	2.00	5.00
49 August 2018 / Emperor's Royal Guard Action Figure Variant	3.00	8.00
49 August 2018 / Sheev Palpatine Galactic Icons Variant	2.50	6.00
50 September 2018'	2.50	6.00
50 September 2018 / David Marquez Variant	2.50	6.00
50 September 2018 / The Emperor Action Figure Variant	4.00	10.00
50 September 2018 / Thrawn Galactic Icons Variant	4.00	10.00
50 September 2018 / 1:25 Phil Noto Variant	5.00	12.00
50 September 2018 / 1:50 Terry Dodson Variant	12.00	30.00
50 September 2018 / 1:100 Terry Dodson Virgin Variant	30.00	80.00
50 October 2018 / 2nd printing	2.50	6.00
51 September 2018'	2.00	5.00
51 September 2018 / Chief Chirpa Action Figure Variant	3.00	8.00
51 September 2018 / Jabba the Hutt Action Figure Variant	20.00	50.00
52 October 2018'	2.00	5.00
52 October 2018 / Lando Calrissian: Skiff Guard Disguise Action Figure Variant	3.00	8.00
52 October 2018 / Ben Kenobi Galactic Icons Variant	2.50	6.00
53 November 2018'	2.00	5.00
53 November 2018 / Logray (Ewok Shaman) Action Figure Variant	3.00	8.00
54 November 2018'	2.00	5.00
54 November 2018 / Squid Head Action Figure Variant	3.00	8.00
55 December 2018'	2.00	5.00
55 December 2018 / Klaatu Action Figure Variant	3.00	8.00
55 December 2018 / Cad Bane Galactic Icons Variant	2.50	6.00

Marvel STAR WARS ANNUAL (2015-)

1 February 2016	2.00	5.00
1 February 2016 / Blank Cover Variant	3.00	8.00
2 January 2017'	2.00	5.00
2 January 2017 / Elsa Charretier Variant	2.00	5.00
3 November 2017'	2.00	5.00
3 November 2017 / Rod Reis Variant	2.00	5.00
4 July 2018'	2.50	6.00
4 July 2018 / 1:25 John Tyler Christopher Variant	200.00	500.00

COMICS

Marvel DARTH VADER (2015-2016)

1 April 2015	5.00	12.00
1 April 2015 / Blank Cover Variant	8.00	20.00
1 April 2015 / Skottie Young "Baby" Variant	6.00	15.00
1 April 2015 / Darth Vader Action Figure Variant	8.00	20.00
1 April 2015 / 1:15 Movie Photo Variant	8.00	20.00
1 April 2015 / 1:25 John Cassaday Variant	20.00	50.00
1 April 2015 / 1:25 Whilce Portacio Variant	20.00	50.00
1 April 2015 / 1:25 Mike Del Mundo Variant	25.00	60.00
1 April 2015 / 1:50 J. Scott Campbell Variant	30.00	80.00
1 April 2015 / 1:50 Alex Ross Variant	20.00	50.00
1 April 2015 / 1:200 Alex Ross Sketch Variant	75.00	200.00
1 2nd printing	10.00	25.00
1 3rd printing	20.00	50.00
1 4th printing	25.00	60.00
1 5th printing	30.00	80.00
2 April 2015	5.00	12.00
2 April 2015 / 1:25 Dave Dorman Variant	12.00	30.00
2 April 2015 / 1:25 Salvador Larroca Variant	12.00	30.00
2 2nd printing	8.00	20.00
2 3rd printing	10.00	25.00
2 4th printing	12.00	30.00
2 5th printing	12.00	30.00
3 May 2015 / 1st appearance of Dr. Aphra, 0-0-0 & BT-1	60.00	150.00
3 May 2015 / 1:25 Salvador Larroca Variant	300.00	600.00
3 2nd printing	50.00	120.00
3 3rd printing	75.00	200.00
3 4th printing	125.00	300.00
4 June 2015	4.00	10.00
4 June 2015 / 1:25 Salvador Larroca Variant	12.00	30.00
4 2nd printing	8.00	20.00
4 3rd printing	12.00	30.00
4 4th printing	15.00	40.00
5 July 2015	2.50	6.00
5 July 2015 / 1:25 Salvador Larroca Variant	10.00	25.00
5 2nd printing	5.00	12.00
6 August 2015	2.50	6.00
6 2nd printing	5.00	12.00
7 September 2015	2.50	6.00
8 October 2015	2.50	6.00
9 November 2015	2.50	6.00
9 November 2015 / 1:25 Adi Granov Variant	10.00	25.00
10 December 2015	2.50	6.00
11 December 2015	2.50	6.00
12 January 2016	2.50	6.00
13 January 2016	2.50	6.00
13 January 2016 / Clay Mann Variant	2.50	6.00
13 2nd printing	5.00	12.00

14 February 2016	2.50	6.00
14 February 2016 / Clay Mann Variant	2.50	6.00
14 2nd printing	5.00	12.00
15 March 2016	2.50	6.00
15 April 2016 / Clay Mann Variant	2.50	6.00
15 May 2016 / 1:25 Francesco Francavilla Variant	12.00	30.00
15 June 2016 / 1:100 Mark Brooks Sketch Variant	40.00	100.00
15 2nd printing	5.00	12.00
16 April 2016	2.50	6.00
16 2nd printing	5.00	12.00
17 May 2016	2.50	6.00
18 May 2016	2.50	6.00
19 June 2016	2.50	6.00
20 July 2016	2.50	6.00
20 July 2016 / Inspector Thanoth Action Figure Variant	2.50	6.00
20 July 2016 / "The Story Thus Far" Reilly Brown Variant	2.50	6.00
20 2nd printing	5.00	12.00
21 August 2016	2.50	6.00
21 August 2016 / Tulon Action Figure Variant	2.50	6.00
21 2nd printing	5.00	12.00
22 August 2016	2.50	6.00
22 August 2016 / Cylo Action Figure Variant	2.50	6.00
22 2nd printing	5.00	12.00
23 September 2016	2.50	6.00
23 September 2016 / BT-1 Action Figure Variant	2.50	6.00
23 2nd printing	5.00	12.00
24 October 2016	2.50	6.00
24 0-0-0 (Triple-Zero) Action Figure Variant	2.50	6.00
25 December 2016 / final issue	2.50	6.00
25 December 2016 / Doctor Aphra Action Figure Variant	4.00	10.00
25 December 2016 / Adi Granov Variant	2.50	6.00
25 December 2016 / Jamie McKelvie Variant	3.00	8.00
25 December 2016 / Karmome Shirahama Variant	3.00	8.00
25 December 2016 / Salvador Larroca Variant	2.50	6.00
25 December 2016 / 1:25 Chris Samnee Variant	10.00	25.00
25 December 2016 / 1:25 Sara Pichelli Variant	10.00	25.00
25 December 2016 / 1:25 Cliff Chiang Variant	20.00	50.00
25 December 2016 / 1:50 Michael Cho Variant	25.00	60.00
25 December 2016 / 1:100 Joe Quesada Variant	60.00	150.00
25 December 2016 / 1:200 Joe Quesada Sketch Variant	125.00	300.00

Marvel DARTH VADER ANNUAL (2015-2016)

1 February 2015	3.00	
1 February 2015 / Blank Cover Variant	6.00	

Marvel STAR WARS: THE FORCE AWAKENS (2016-2017)

1 August 2016 / "Star Wars: The Force Awakens " adaptation Part 1	4.00	10.00
1 August 2016 / Blank Cover Variant	12.00	30.00
1 August 2016 / 1:15 Movie Photo Variant	20.00	50.00
1 August 2016 / 1:25 Phil Noto Variant	10.00	25.00
1 August 2016 / 1:50 John Cassaday Variant	12.00	30.00
1 August 2016 / 1:75 Esad Ribic Sketch Variant	20.00	50.00
1 August 2016 / 1:100 Joe Quesada Variant	150.00	400.00
1 August 2016 / 1:200 John Cassaday Sketch Variant	25.00	60.00
1 August 2016 / 1:300 Joe Quesada Sketch Variant	400.00	800.00
2 September 2016 / "Star Wars: The Force Awakens " adaptation Part 2	1.50	4.00
2 September 2016 / 1:15 Movie Photo Variant	4.00	10.00
2 September 2016 / 1:25 Chris Samnee Variant	6.00	15.00
2 September 2016 / 1:75 Mike Mayhew Sketch Variant	30.00	80.00
3 October 2016 / "Star Wars: The Force Awakens" adaptation Part 3	1.50	4.00
3 October 2016 / 1:15 Movie Photo Variant	4.00	10.00
3 October 2016 / 1:75 Mike Deodato Jr. Sketch Variant	30.00	80.00
4 November 2016 / "Star Wars: The Force Awakens" adaptation Part 4	1.50	4.00
4 November 2016 / 1:15 Movie Photo Variant	4.00	10.00
4 November 2016 / 1:75 Mike Del Mundo Sketch Variant	30.00	80.00
5 December 2016 / "Star Wars: The Force Awakens" adaptation Part 5	1.50	4.00
5 December 2016 / 1:15 Movie Photo Variant	6.00	15.00
5 December 2016 / 1:75 Rafael Albuquerque Sketch Variant	50.00	120.00
6 January 2017 / "Star Wars: The Force Awakens" adaptation Part 6	1.50	4.00
6 January 2017 / 1:15 Movie Photo Variant	8.00	20.00
6 January 2017 / 1:25 Esad Ribic Variant	10.00	25.00
6 January 2017 / 1:75 Paolo Rivera Variant	30.00	80.00

COMICS